Professional Cooking

FIFTH EDITION

Photography by
J. GERARD SMITH

Professional Cooking

Wayne Gisslen

With a foreword by
ANDRÈ J. COINTREAU
President, Le Cordon Bleu

Featuring recipes from

Le Cordon Bleu
L'Art Culinaire
Paris—1895

JOHN WILEY & SONS, INC.

Library of Congress Cataloging-in-Publication Data:
Gisslen, Wayne, 1946-
  Professional cooking / Wayne Gisslen ; with a foreword by André J. Cointreau ;
  photography by Gerard Smith.—5th ed.
      p. cm.
   ISBN 0-471-39711-3 (cloth: college)—ISBN 0-471-43625-9 (cloth: trade)
   1. Quantity cookery. 2. Food service.   I. Title.
  TX820 .G54 2001
  641.57—dc21
                                                                    2001046853

Printed in the United States of America.

10 9 8 7 6 5 4 3 2 1

To Mary Ellen

Contents

Recipe Contents

Chapter 13
Cooking Poultry and Game

Chapter 15
Cooking Fish and Shellfish

About Le Cordon Bleu

With schools on five continents, in France, Great Britain, Japan, Australia, and the Americas, and a student body made up of fifty nationalities, Le Cordon Bleu is well known and highly regarded around the gastronomic world. Le Cordon Bleu and its master chefs have a tradition of excellence in the culinary arts and are committed to furthering the appreciation of fine food and fine living. Already involved in consulting and the promotion of a variety of culinary products, Le Cordon Bleu has successfully developed partnerships with major hospitality institutions and with the cruise industry through a relationship with Radisson Seven Seas Cruises.

Le Cordon Bleu Addresses

Le Cordon Bleu Paris
8 Rue Léon Delhomme
Paris 75015
France
Phone: 33-1-53-68-22-50
Fax: 33-1-48-56-03-96
paris@cordonbleu.net

Le Cordon Bleu London
114 Marylebone Lane
London, W1U 2HH
England
Phone: 44-20-7935-3503
Fax: 44-20-7935-7621
london@cordonbleu.net

Le Cordon Bleu Mexico
Universidad Anahuac
Av. Lomas Anahuac s/n
Lomas Anahuac
Mexico CP 52760
Mexico
Phone: 52-555-627-0210
Fax: 52-555-627-0210, ext 8724

Le Cordon Bleu Paris
Ottawa Culinary Arts Institute
School and Restaurant
453 Laurier Avenue East
Ottawa
Ontario, K1N 6R4
Canada
Phone: 1-613-236-4459
1-613-236-CHEF (2433)
Fax: 1-613-236-2460
ottawa@cordonbleu.net

Le Cordon Bleu U.S.A.
40 Enterprise Avenue
Secaucus, NJ 07094-2517
Toll-free number: 1-800-457-CHEF (2433)
Phone: 1-201-617-5221
Fax: 1-201-617-1914
info@cordonbleu.net

Le Cordon Bleu Adelaide
Management Courses and Corporate Office
Days Road
Regency Park
South Australia 5010
Australia
Phone: 618-8346-3700
Fax: 618-8346-3755
australia@cordonbleu.net

Le Cordon Bleu Sydney
250 Blaxland Road
Ryde
Sydney, NSW 2112
Australia 5008
Phone: 618-8348-4659
Fax: 618-8348-4661
australia@cordonbleu.net

Le Cordon Bleu Korea
53-12 Chungpa-Dong, 2Ka
Yongsan-Ku
Seoul
140 742
Korea
Phone: 82-2-710-9385
Fax: 82-2-710-9285

Le Cordon Bleu Peru
Av Nunez de Balboa 530
Miraflores, Lima 18
Peru
Phone: 51-1-447-0437
Fax: 51-1-242-9209

Le Cordon Bleu Tokyo
Roob-1, 28-13 Sarugaku-Cho,
Daikanyama
Shibuya-Ku
Tokyo 150-0033
Japan
Phone: 81-3-5489-0141
Fax: 81-3-5489-0145
tokyo@cordonbleu.net

Le Cordon Bleu Yokohama
2-18-1, Takashima
Nishi-Ku
Yokohama-Shi
Kanagawa
Japan
Phone: 81-4-5440-4720
Fax: 81-4-5440-4722

http: www.cordonbleu.net
e-mail: info@cordonbleu.net

Foreword

Le Cordon Bleu–*L'Art Culinaire* is delighted once again to work with author Wayne Gisslen on the fifth edition of *Professional Cooking.* This collaboration underlines the importance of French culinary technique at the service of the global gastronomic world. It has always been the philosophy of Le Cordon Bleu that, through mastering and understanding of French culinary techniques, processes, and methods, students gain the tools and confidence with which to create their own masterpieces. Le Cordon Bleu envisions the fifth edition of *Professional Cooking* as being one of those culinary tools by balancing tradition with cutting-edge innovation.

Founded in Paris in 1895, today Le Cordon Bleu has over twenty Institutes and programs in twelve countries on five continents and has more students worldwide than any other culinary education provider. Le Cordon Bleu maintains close relations with the culinary industry and benefits from its international recognition as the standard of excellence. Known for classical French cuisine, Le Cordon Bleu continues to teach long-celebrated culinary traditions while creating a balanced, harmonious, and flavorsome repertoire of contemporary and international cuisines.

Le Cordon Bleu's authority on culinary techniques, training, and development are recognized and supported by noted establishments such as the Ministry of Tourism of Shanghai, China, and the government of Australia. Le Cordon Bleu has also provided training in the French culinary arts to many organizations, including the Chefs of the Club Managers Association of America and Radisson Seven Seas Cruises.

Each year Le Cordon Bleu master chefs pass on their knowledge to a student body of over fifty nationalities and share their expertise and craft at a variety of annual festivals and culinary events around the world. Our chefs hail from Michelin-starred restaurants and top hotel kitchens and are winners of world-renowned international competitions.

Through its schools around the globe, Le Cordon Bleu has proven that French culinary techniques can be applied to a variety of world cuisines. Each campus reflects the local influences of its host country. Students and master chefs alike are encouraged to explore and experiment using ethnic ingredients to "fuse" new flavors and encourage new trends in cuisine and fine dining. Therefore, it seemed natural that Le Cordon Bleu should once again join forces with author Wayne Gisslen in preparing this edition of *Professional Cooking.*

Professional Cooking has been a mainstay in North American universities, community colleges, and culinary schools specializing in hospitality management and the culinary arts. It has been used to train hundreds of thousands of chefs and cooks. Created by the talented Wayne Gisslen, the text teaches, through its clear writing style, precise photography, and recipes, first to understand and then to perform—presenting a no-nonsense view of the workings of a professional kitchen.

Wayne Gisslen has balanced his practical knowledge with a clean, methodical, and pedagogical approach to make this a reference for a lifetime. *Professional Cooking's* flexible format is the reason why we consider it to be the best textbook for promoting good theory and practice, and it has the adaptability to be used all over the world. For Le Cordon Bleu this is a necessary tool for any kitchen, at work or at home. In the fifth edition of *Professional Cooking,* Le Cordon Bleu chefs and Wayne Gisslen combine their knowledge and experience to create a definitive text and reference book.

The collaboration with Wayne Gisslen once again results in a strong partnership and friendship that has strengthened this edition and will continue with other projects.

André J. Cointreau
President and CEO
Le Cordon Bleu–*L'Art Culinaire*

Preface

Readers of earlier editions of *Professional Cooking* will quickly recognize that the most prominent change in the fifth edition of this classic text is its totally new design. Not only is this modern look more appealing to the eye, but also the redesigned layout makes it easier to use and easier to read than ever before. *Professional Cooking*, which for nearly twenty years has been the standard reference and learning tool in its field and has trained hundreds of thousands of chefs and cooks, enters its third decade as a fresh and vital text.

But the new design is only one of the changes that make this edition more useful. Input from instructors, students, and other readers have always been valuable in helping the text meet the needs of its users. In response to this input, new material and new recipes on garde manger, charcuterie, game cookery, and other topics, as detailed below, have been added.

WHAT'S NEW

Many important additions have been made to *Professional Cooking* to make it even more useful and versatile. Among the most important additions and changes are the following:

- A new chapter devoted to cured and smoked foods and to the production of fresh, cured, and smoked sausages.
- A new chapter introducing the art of garde manger, with procedures and recipes for a variety of pâtés and terrines.
- New information on game and game cookery, including both furred and feathered game products. Also new in this edition is material on specialty products such as ostrich and emu.
- Approximately 100 new recipes, bringing the book's total to about 1100.
- Many new photographs in all sections of the book, illustrating even more clearly the variety of techniques and procedures necessary in the modern kitchen.
- Reformulation of some of the popular classic recipes to give smaller yields, in response to requests from instructors.
- This red logo indicates recipes that I have developed and tested.
- This blue logo indicates recipes that were developed and tested by Le Cordon Bleu.

THE RECIPES

The recipes in this book are planned and organized to reinforce the basic skills that the student is learning. In each case, specific recipes follow a discussion of theories, guidelines, and general procedures applicable to a defined category of foods and/or cooking methods. Students are encouraged, by means of recipe variations, to see how they can apply these procedures to other ingredients, and to see the similarities and differences among various preparations.

Attention to the basics has always been the hallmark of the text. Because the purpose of the text is to teach fundamental cooking techniques, it is important to illustrate these techniques—and to allow the student to experience them—with fundamental, straightforward recipes that reveal the connection between general theory and specific application in the most direct way. Retaining most of the recipes of earlier editions, while modernizing where appropriate, serves this purpose.

While basic preparations illustrating fundamental principles are the core of the recipe collection, the book builds on these primary techniques to include more advanced styles of preparation. More challenging recipes, including many new to this edition, enable readers to refine their techniques and to prepare dishes of increasing sophistication. The more than 100 recipes developed and tested by the chefs of Le Cordon Bleu, which first appeared here in the previous edition, help immeasurably to enrich the learning experience of students. These recipes are regularly used by Le Cordon Bleu chefs on five continents to train students for work in the kitchens of the finest restaurants in the world.

What makes a dish feel modern is as much a matter of presentation as it is of ingredients or recipe instructions. How an item, along with its garnish and sauce, is plated can make it look rustic or elegant, simple or elaborate, traditional or modern. Photographs accompanying the recipes illustrate a variety of preparations and plating styles. As the photographs show, a simple item such as a sautéed chicken breast can be as stylish as a complicated dish requiring exotic or expensive ingredients.

Readers are urged to study Chapter 5, "The Recipe: Its Structure and Its Use," before actually proceeding with any of the recipes. This will help them to know how to use the recipes in this book as well as to understand the structure and limitations of the many kinds of recipes they will be using in their careers.

While every culinary program has different requirements, the recipes in this book should be adaptable to any purpose. Most major recipes are written for 24 or 25 portions, a quantity that can be converted easily to higher or lower yields if necessary. Those recipes requiring more costly ingredients, those that are generally made to order, or those that are more complex are written for smaller yields, such as 10, 12, or 16 portions. In addition, variations often indicate ingredient substitutions so that the recipes will fit different budgetary requirements and different local or regional tastes.

NUTRITIONAL INFORMATION

Cooks and chefs are increasingly aware of the importance of learning to prepare healthful foods. To support this effort, nutritional analyses have been included for each main recipe. These analyses were done using the software program Genesis R & D 6.00, which calculates nutrients based on ingredients. It is important to realize that the actual nutrients in a prepared dish will vary depending on many factors, just as the taste, texture, and appearance of a dish will vary depending on the skill of the cook and the quality of the ingredients. The following factors should also be taken into account when reading the nutritional analyses:

- Where a portion size is indicated in the recipe, the analysis is per portion. Where there is no portion size, such as for stock and sauce recipes as well as most of the recipes in the baking chapters, the analysis is usually per ounce; for most hors d'oeuvre recipes, analysis is per piece.
- The following ingredients are not included in the analyses: ingredients listed "to taste" or "as needed"; ingredients in sachets and bouquets garnis; optional ingredients; garnishes such as parsley sprigs.
- Stocks are adjusted for removal of bones, mirepoix, and other ingredients that are strained out.
- Ingredients in mirepoix are not included except for a small amount of sodium.
- If there is a range for an ingredient quantity, the smaller number was used for analysis.
- Adjustments are made for recipes in which the food is degreased or the fat is skimmed off. The amount of fat remaining will vary depending on how thoroughly the item is degreased.
- Fat has been added for pan-fried and deep-fried foods based on a percentage of the total weight. The amount of fat actually absorbed will vary depending on the temperature of the fat, the cooking time, and the surface area of the food.
- For marinated foods, 10 percent of the marinade is included in the analysis, unless the marinade is used to make a sauce, in which case all the marinade is, of course, included.
- The amount of fat used for sautéing has been estimated for the analysis.
- The numbers for each nutrient are rounded off according to FDA rounding rules for food labeling.

- The "(% cal.)" information following the fat content in each analysis refers to percentage of calories from fat, and is required to determine whether or not a recipe can be labeled as low in fat. It can't be used to determine percentage of fat in the total diet.

To help you become more aware of the fat content of various dishes, those dishes that are especially low in fat are designated by a special heart symbol to the right of the recipe title. *Low in fat* means, according to FDA labeling laws, that the food contains 3 grams of fat or less per reference amount (or serving size indicated in the analysis) if the reference amount is greater than 30 grams (about 1 ounce). If the reference amount is 30 grams or less, the fat content must also be 3 grams of fat or less per 50 grams of the food. This is to prevent making foods sound low in fat just by making the portion size smaller. Main dish items and meals must contain 3 grams of fat or less per 100 grams, and not more than 30 percent of calories from fat.

GOALS AND ORGANIZATION OF THIS BOOK

This book has a dual goal: understanding—that is, an *understanding* of cooking theory, of how to cook—and *performing*—that is, the mastery of a set of manual skills and the ability to apply them to a wide range of cooking styles and products.

The current revision retains the fourth edition's basic structure and organization, which created the flexibility that has made *Professional Cooking* adaptable to nearly any course of study. The basic cooking methods (dry-heat methods, moist-heat methods, and so on) are introduced early on. Then, within each of the main cooking chapters, the material is arranged by cooking method.

Thus, for those curricula that are organized by cooking method, it is a simple matter to select the appropriate sections—for example, moist-heat methods—from the meat, poultry, fish, and vegetable chapters. At the same time, the arrangement of the chapters by product type enables the instructor to emphasize how the basic cooking methods differ as they are applied to different products.

The new *Professional Cooking* focuses, as did the earlier editions, on the development of flexible skills, which are essential for success in a cooking career. Modern food service is evolving rapidly. There is a tremendous variety of establishments on the scene today, from the executive dining room to the school cafeteria, from the simplest short-order coffee shop to the most exclusive restaurant or club, from kitchens that make extensive use of convenience foods to those that use only fresh produce. The graduate who understands the workings of foods and the interplay among ingredients, cooking methods, cost factors, and other elements can function successfully in any type of food service operation.

THE ROLE OF THE CHEF-INSTRUCTOR

No textbook, of course, can serve as a substitute for practical kitchen experience. Furthermore, a book can not replace an experienced chef-instructor, who can give practical demonstrations, supervise students' work, answer questions, and give advice and assistance as the need arises. Every instructor has had unique experience and has developed special techniques and procedures. Many chefs, in fact, disagree with one another on a number of points. Although this book presents methods and recipes that are widely used and accepted, many instructors will prefer procedures that differ from some of those explained in this text, and they may wish to supplement the recipes in this book with some of their own. Throughout the book, the instructor's input is encouraged. Exposure to a variety of recipes and techniques can only enrich the students' education and enhance the depth of their experience.

FEATURES

Pronunciation Guides and Glossaries

Much kitchen terminology is taken from French. Phonetic guides are included for difficult words, giving the approximate pronunciation using English sounds. (Exact rendering is impossible in many cases, because French has a number of sounds that don't exist in English.) Because food workers must be able to communicate with each other, definitions of terms introduced in the text are summarized in the glossaries at the end of the book. Additionally, vocabularies from Le Cordon Bleu enable readers to move smoothly between North American, British, and French terminology.

Illustrations

Hundreds of clear, concise, full-color photographs illustrate basic manual techniques, shown from the point of view of the person performing them. Additional photographs illustrate hundreds of ingredients and finished dishes.

Format

This book is designed to be readable and useful. The format emphasizes and highlights key points in colored type, italics, and numbered sequences, so that basic information can be located and reviewed at a glance.

Realistic Procedures

Although supported by discussions of cooking theory, procedures given here are based on actual practices in the industry. Attention is given not just to quantity production but also to the special problems of cooking to order. Presentation and service of the finished product are considered in detail as is pre-preparation or *mise en place*—so essential to the organization of a working restaurant. At the same time, the major emphasis is on quality, too often neglected in the quest for convenience.

Even a book as large as this one cannot possibly contain all a cook needs to know. Other information is included if it has a direct bearing on kitchen and bakeshop work. More specialized information, such as stewarding and managerial skills, has to be omitted. Finally, although much of what we talk about is strongly influenced by the cooking of other nations, especially France, the practices discussed are those of North American food service.

CD-ROM

The CD-ROM, designed to complement the book, accompanies the academic edition of this book and utilizes *ChefTec Tutor*™ software, a professional-level software program used in the food service industry. The CD-ROM contains nearly 600 recipes from this book, plus a range of useful features that make them easy to adapt and manipulate to suit individual needs:

- Add, edit, modify, and print recipes, portion sizes, or yield and create shopping lists.
- Preloaded ingredient prices allow for costing of a recipe.
- Search recipes by main ingredient, meal, and cuisine type.
- Resize recipes in U.S. or metric measurements.
- Perform metric conversions instantly.
- Calculate nutritional analyses of recipes in FDA format, and update nutritional analysis if an ingredient is changed.

Supplements

To enhance mastery of the material in *Professional Cooking*, the following student and instructor supplements are available:

The *Study Guide* (ISBN 0-471-21953-3) contains review materials, practice problems, and exercises. (Answers to questions are included in the Instructor's Manual.)

The *Instructor's Manual with Study Guide Solutions* (ISBN 0-471-20776-4) includes teaching suggestions and test questions. The test questions are also available in electronic form on a CD-ROM and on our Web Site, available to course instructors upon request.

The *Student Workbook* (ISBN 0-471-20881-7) has been developed by the National Restaurant Association Educational Foundation in consultation with the author, for its ProMgmt. certificate program. The workbook contains exercises and a study outline for each chapter, and an 80-question practice test. The practice test assists students in preparing for the certificate examination. In addition, an *Instructor's Guide* (ISBN 0-471-20880-9) is available to course instructors to complement and highlight information in the textbook and *Student Workbook.*

The newly updated and revised Web Site contains information for the student and instructor, and is available at www.wiley.com/procooking.

Acknowledgments

Photographer Jim Smith has been my partner in these texts for more than twenty years. His hundreds of photographs are an indispensable part of *Professional Cooking* and valuable teaching tools. I can never thank him enough. Thanks also to Anne Smith for all her support and assistance through the years, and to Ryan Basten for his work in Jim's studio.

The fourth edition of *Professional Cooking* saw the beginning of Le Cordon Bleu's participation in the development of this text, a participation that continued with the third edition of *Professional Baking* and now with the fifth of *Professional Cooking*. My deepest gratitude goes to André J. Cointreau, president of Le Cordon Bleu, and to Chefs Patrick Lebouc, Patrick Terrien, Michel Cliché, MOF, Jean-Claude Boucheret, Gregory Steneck, and Andrew Males.

Christin Loudon, who calculated nutritional analyses in the fourth edition, has again contributed her expertise and culinary understanding to provide analyses for the new recipes in this edition, for which I thank her most warmly. I would also like to thank Drew Appleby, whose expertly written test questions form an important part of the support materials for this text.

The staff at Goodfellow's Restaurant in Minneapolis, Minnesota, truly understand the meaning of hospitality. For two day-long sessions of photography in Goodfellow's kitchen, we received welcome, assistance, and cooperation beyond all expectations. I would like to express my warmest and most enthusiastic thanks to Executive Chef Kevin Cullen, Executive Sous Chef Jack Riebel, General Manager John Day, Manager Martina Priadka, and Assistant Manager Tim Berg, as well as to everyone in the kitchen and dining room. They all made us feel like family.

I would also like to thank The New York Restaurant School for the use of their kitchens for the cover photography shoot. I would especially like to acknowledge Michael Iannacone, Kenneth Goldberg, Midge Elias, and Alfred Parcells. In addition, the following students from The New York Restaurant School generously gave of their time to act as models for the cover: Randie Anderson, Lisa Llanos, Ga-Hee Loncaric, Jude Michel, Johan Mestanza, Juliet T. Nuamah, Theresa L. Oxley, Patricia Parkes, and William Popov.

Because the best ingredients are essential to good cooking, I would like to extend a special thanks to Jay and Jane Bunting of Wayzata Bay Spice Company and Blue River Gourmet for helping me obtain high-quality seasonings for recipe testing, and to Jay Flattum, owner of Lofton Ridge Deer and Bison Farm, for supplying specialty meats at a moment's notice. In addition, a warm thank-you goes to Larry DeVries, Chef-Instructor at Crocus Plains Regional Secondary School, Brandon, Manitoba, for his continuing support, counsel, and friendship.

The list of culinary and hospitality professionals who have provided support, guidance, advice, and constructive criticism for all five editions of this book has grown so long that it isn't possible to mention everyone in these paragraphs. I can only hope that I have not omitted many of them in the list of reviewers that follows. I would also like to thank all those unnamed individuals who have corresponded with me over the years to point out errors and to offer suggestions.

This project would not have been possible without the critical judgment and support of my wife, Mary Ellen Griffin, to whom I owe my deepest thanks.

Finally, I would like to thank everyone at John Wiley and Sons who worked so hard on this project: Fred Bernardi, Diana Cisek, Tzviya Siegman, Julie Kerr, Lynne Marsala, Lee Goldstein (of LeeGDesign), and especially my editor and friend, JoAnna Turtletaub.

REVIEWERS

I would like to acknowledge the following instructors who have contributed to this book over five editions by suggesting revisions and additions, and answering survey questions.

George Akau
Clark College
Vancouver, WA

Erik Anderson
Camosun College
Victoria, British Columbia

Angela M. Anderson
Miami Dade Community College
Miami, FL

Robert Anderson
Des Moines Area Community College
Ankeny, IA

Alan Argulski
Genesee Community College
Batavia, NY

Moses Ball
Atlantic Vocational-Technical Center
Coconut Creek, FL

Carl A. Behnke
Purdue University
West Lafayette, IN

Joseph L. Belvedere Jr.
Paul Smith's College
Paul Smiths, NY

Perry Bentley
Okanagan University College
Kelowna, British Columbia

Claire A. Berg
Brookdale Community College
Howell, NJ

Nancy Berkoff
Los Angeles Trade Technical College
Los Angeles, CA

Leslie Bilderback
California School of Culinary Arts
South Pasadena, CA

George Bissonette
Pikes Peak Community College
Colorado Springs, CO

Peter Blakeman
George Brown College
Toronto, Ontario

LeRoy Blanchard
Los Angeles Trade Technical College
Los Angeles, CA

Roy Blundell
College Lasalle
Montrèal, Quebec

Pete Bordi
Penn State University
University Park, PA

Roy Butterworth
New Brunswick Community College
Moncton, New Brunswick

Alfredo Cabaccingan
Kapiolani Community College
Honolulu, HI

Harska Chacko
University of New Orleans
New Orleans, LA

Daniel Charna
Ashland College
Ashland, OH

Albert D. Cipryk
Niagara College
Niagara Falls, Ontario

Jesse Clemons
State Technical Institute at Memphis
Memphis, TN

Alec O. Cline
American Culinary Federation, Inc.
Redwood City, CA

Michael M. Collins
San Jacinto College
Pasadena, TX

Randall Colman
Sullivan County Community College
Loch Sheldrake, NY

Mike Costello
St. Cloud Area Vocational-Technical
   Institute
St. Cloud, MN

Chris Cutler
Georgian College
Barrie, Ontario

William J. Daly
State University of New York at
   Cobleskill
Cobleskill, NY

Juanita M. Decker
Waukesha County Technical Institute
Pewaukee, WI

Bob Demers
Niagara College
Niagara Falls, Ontario

Larry DeVries
Brandon School District
Brandon, Manitoba

Marian Dobbins
Tucson, AZ

Bob Dowden
Nova Scotia Community College
Kentville, Nova Scotia

Dominique and Cindy Duby
DC Duby School
Richmond, British Columbia

Dale Dunham
Oklahoma State University
Okmulgee, OK

Michael Durrer
Algonquin College
Nepean, Ontario

Michael A. Elliott
Liason College
Toronto, Ontario

Evan Enowitz
Grossmont College
El Cajon, CA

Daniel Esposito
Canadore College
North Bay, Ontario

Guy Ethier
Canadian Federation of Chefs &
   Cooks
Surrey, British Columbia

Mark Facklam
The Cooking and Hospitality Institute
   of Chicago
Chicago, IL

Fred T. Faria
Johnson & Wales University
Providence, RI

Alan Fleming
Algonquin College
Ottawa, Ontario

Robyn L. Flipse
Brooksdale Community College
Lincroft, NJ

Sandra Flowerday
Educational Consultant
Charlotte, MI

Sandra Foley
Gogebic Community College
Ironwood, MI

Willard L. Geach
Long Beach City College
Long Beach, CA

Joan W. Geerken
State University of New York at
Cobleskill
Cobleskill, NY

Dave Gibson
Niagara College
Niagara Falls, Ontario

Gilles Godin
Nova Scotia Community College
Stellarton, Nova Scotia

James Goering
El Centro College
Dallas, TX

Jeff Graves
Purdue University
West Lafayette, IN

Juliet Groux
West Liberty State College
West Liberty, WV

Robert S. Haynes
Lambton College
Sarnia, Ontario

John D. Hedley
Los Angeles Trade-Technical College
Los Angeles, CA

Rosemary L. Hedlund
Des Moines Area Community College
Ankeny, IA

Iris Helveston
State of Florida
Department of Education
Tampa, FL

Maynard G. Hemmah
Moorhead Area Vocational-Technical
Institute
Moorhead, MN

Margaret A. Howard
Sheridan Vocational-Technical Center
Hollywood, FL

Russ Hudson
North Island College
Courtenay, British Columbia

Lynn Huffman
Texas Tech University
Lubbock, TX

Anne L. Jachim
Moraine Valley Community College
Palos Hills, IL

Daniel K. Jeatran
Milwaukee Area Technical College
Milwaukee, WI

Frank F. Johnson, Jr.
University of South Florida
Tampa, FL

Roosevelt Johnson
Sidney North Colver Vocational-
Technical Institute
New Orleans, LA

Todd Jones
Mattatuck Community College
Waterbury, CT

Mike Jung
Hennepin Technical Center
Brooklyn Park, MN

Tom King
Cabrillo College
Aptos, CA

Suzanne Little, M. S., R. D.
San Jacinto College
Pasadena, TX

Shirley Lotze
Western Wisconsin Technical Institute
LaCrosse, WI

Robert M. Lyna
Southern Maine Vocational-Technical
Institute
South Portland, ME

George Macht
College of DuPage
Glen Ellyn, IL

Merle Maerz
Selkirk College
Nelson, British Columbia

Sylvia Marple
University of New Hampshire
Durham, NH

Valeria S. Mason
State Department of Education
Gainesville, FL

John McDonald
St. Augustine Technical Center
St. Augustine, FL

Terence F. McDonough
Erie Community College
Buffalo, NY

Marcia W. McDowell
Monroe Community College
Rochester, NY

Linda McDuffie
North Seattle Community College
Seattle, WA

Robert McLean
The Fay School
Southboro, MA

Ann Miglio
Williamsport Area Community
College
Williamsport, PA

Harold O. Mishoe
Southern Maine Vocational-Technical
Institute
South Portland, ME

Ken W. Myers
University of Minnesota-Crookston
Crookston, MN

Kathy Niemann
Portland State University
Portland, OR

William T. Norvell
William Rainey Harper College
Palatine, IL

Andrew Ormiston
Brandon, Manitoba

Gary Page
Grand Valley State College
Allendale, MI

Michael Palmer
Western Culinary Institute
Portland, OR

Philip Panzarino
New York City Technical College
Brooklyn, NY

Jayne Pearson
Manchester Community College
Manchester, CT

Richard Petrello
Withlacoochee Vocational-Technical
Center
Inverness, FL

William F. Petsch
Pinellas Vocational Technical Institute
Clearwater, FL

Michael Piccinino
Shasta College
Redding, CA

Tony Rechsteiner
Northern Lights College
Dawson Creek, British Columbia

John Reimers
Red River College
Winnipeg, Manitoba

Larry Richardson
Hinds Junior College-Jackson Branch
Jackson, MI

Neil Rittenaur
North Dakota State College of Science
Wahpeton, ND

Hubert E. Robert
Holyoke Community College
Holyoke, PA

Richard Roberts
Wake Technical Community College
Raleigh, NC

Ricardo G. Saenz
Renton Vocational-Technical Institute
Renton, WA

Robert R. Santos
Maui Community College
Kahului, HI

Frank Schellings
Diablo Valley College
Pleasant Hill, CA

David Schneider
Macomb Community College
Mt. Clemens, MI

Charlotte Schwyn
Delta College
Stockton, CA

Roy John Sharp
Portland Community College
Portland, OR

Settimio Sicoli
Vancouver Community College
Vancouver, British Columbia

Diane Sinkinson
Cape Fear Community College
Wilmington, NC

Norman C. Smith
Sir Sanford Fleming College
Peterborough, Ontario

Reuel J. Smith
Truckee Meadows Community College
Reno, NV

William Sprowl
Mt. San Jacinto College
San Jacinto, CA

Nancy S. Steryous
St. Petersburg Vocational-Technical
Institute
St. Petersburg, FL

Siegfried Stober
Joliet Junior College
Joliet, IL

Peter Sugameli
Wayne Community College
Detroit, MI

Julia Sullivan
Copiah-Lincoln Jr. College
Wesson, MI

William Thornton
St. Phillips College
San Antonio, TX

Sheila A. Tillman
Asheville-Buncombe Tech Community
College
Asheville, NC

S. W. (Stan) Townsend
Northern Alberta Institute of
Technology
Edmonton, Alberta

Robin W. Turner
State University of New York at Delhi
Delhi, NY

Jerry L. Vincent
Johnson County Community College
Overland Park, KS

Barbara Vredeveld
Iowa Western Community College
Council Bluffs, IA

D. Michael Wallace
North Island College
Courtenay, British Columbia

R. G. Werth
Asheville-Buncombe Technical College
Asheville, NC

J. William White
Pinellas County School System
St. Petersburg, FL

Doris Wilkes
Florida Hospitality Education Program
The Florida State University
Tallahassee, FL

Wes J. Wilkinson
Lambton College
Sarnia, Ontario

Ronald S. Wolf
Florida Community College
Jacksonville, FL

Ron Wong
Northern Alberta Institute of
Technology
Edmonton, Alberta

Tony Wood
Hospitality Industry Education
Advisory Committee
Surrey, British Columbia

Ronald Zabkiewicz
South Technical Education Center
Boynton Beach, FL

Mike Zema
Elgin Community College
Elgin, IL

Ronald Zwerger
Elgin Community College
Elgin, IL

Professional Cooking

chapter 1

The Food Service Industry

This is an exciting time to begin a career in food service. Interest in dining and curiosity about new foods are greater than ever. More new restaurants open every year. Many restaurants are busy every night, and restaurant chains number among the nation's largest corporations. The chef, once considered a domestic servant, has become respected as an artist and skilled craftsperson.

The growth of the food service industry creates a demand for thousands of skilled people every year. Many people are attracted by a career that is challenging and exciting and, above all, provides the chance to find real satisfaction in doing a job well.

Unfortunately, many people see only the glamorous side of food service and fail to understand that this is a tiny part of the picture. The public does not often see the years of training, the long hours, and the tremendous pressures that lie behind every success.

Before you start your practical studies, covered in later chapters, it is good to know a little about the profession you are entering. This chapter gives you a brief overview of modern food service, including how it got to where it is today and where it is headed.

A Short History of Modern Food Service

The value of history is that it helps us understand the present and the future. In food service, knowledge of our professional heritage helps us see why we do things as we do, how our cooking techniques have been developed and refined, and how we can continue to develop and innovate in the years ahead.

After reading this chapter, you should be able to

1. Name and describe four major developments that have significantly changed the food service industry in the twentieth century.

2. Identify seven major stations in a classical kitchen.

3. Explain how the size and type of an operation influence the organization of the modern kitchen.

4. Identify and describe three skill levels of food production personnel.

5. Identify eight behavioral characteristics that food service workers should develop and maintain to achieve the highest standards of professionalism.

THE ORIGINS OF CLASSICAL AND MODERN CUISINE

Quantity cookery has existed for thousands of years, as long as there have been large groups of people to feed, such as armies. But modern food service is said to have begun shortly after the middle of the eighteenth century, when a Parisian named Boulanger began selling dishes that he referred to as "restoratives." (The word *restaurant* comes from the French verb *restaurer*, "to restore.") Before this time, food production in France was controlled by guilds. Caterers, pastry makers, roasters, and pork butchers held licenses to prepare specific items. An innkeeper, in order to serve a meal to guests, had to get the various menu items from those operations that were licensed to provide them. Guests had little or no choice and simply ate what was available for that meal. Boulanger's establishment, on the other hand, provided choices for customers. In challenging the rules of the guilds, Boulanger unwittingly changed the course of food service history.

The changes that had already begun received a great stimulus as a result of the French Revolution in 1793. Before this time, the great chefs were employed in the houses of the French nobility. With the revolution and the end of the monarchy, many chefs, suddenly out of work, opened restaurants in and around Paris to support themselves.

The great chef of this time was *Marie-Antoine Carême* (1784–1833), whose career spanned the first 30 years of the nineteenth century. Carême is credited as the founder of classical cuisine. As a young man, he learned all the branches of cooking, and he dedicated his career to refining and organizing culinary techniques. His many books contain the first really systematic account of cooking principles, recipes, and menu making.

As a chef to kings, heads of state, and wealthy patrons, Carême became famous as the creator of elaborate, elegant display pieces, the ancestors of our modern wedding cakes, sugar sculptures, and ice and tallow carvings. But it was Carême's practical and theoretical work as an author and chef that was responsible, to a large extent, for bringing cooking out of the Middle Ages and into the modern period.

ESCOFFIER

Georges-Auguste Escoffier (1847–1935) was the greatest chef of his time and is revered by chefs and gourmets as the father of twentieth-century cookery. His two main contributions were the simplification of classical cuisine and the classical menu and the reorganization of the kitchen.

It is hard to believe that Escoffier's elaborate multicourse banquets are a simplification of anything. But in the typical banquet menu of the eighteenth century, each course consisted of as many as 20 separate dishes—or more!—mostly a variety of meats and poultry, all placed on the table at once. Guests helped themselves to the few dishes they could reach. Carême began the reform, but Escoffier brought the menu into the twentieth century.

Escoffier rejected what he called the "general confusion" of the old menus, in which sheer quantity seemed to be the most important factor. Instead, he called for order and diversity and emphasized the careful selection of one or two dishes per course, dishes that would follow one another harmoniously and that would delight the taste with their delicacy and simplicity.

Escoffier's books and recipes are still important reference works for professional chefs. The basic cooking methods and preparations we study today are based on Escoffier's work.

Escoffier's second major achievement, the reorganization of the kitchen, resulted in a streamlined workplace that was better suited to turning out the simplified dishes and menus that he instituted. The system he established is still in use today, especially in large hotels and full-service restaurants, as we discuss later in this chapter.

MODERN DEVELOPMENTS

Today's kitchens look much different from those of Escoffier's day, even though our basic cooking principles are the same. Also, the dishes we eat have gradually changed due to the innovations and creativity of modern chefs. The process of simplification and refinement, to which Carême and Escoffier made monumental contributions, is still going on, adapting classical cooking to modern conditions and tastes.

Many developments in the twentieth century have led to changes in the food service industry.

Development of New Equipment

We take for granted such basic equipment as gas and electric ranges and ovens and electric refrigerators. But even these essential tools did not exist until fairly recently. The easily controlled heat of modern cooking equipment, as well as motorized food cutters, mixers, and other processing equipment, has greatly simplified food production.

Research and technology continue to produce sophisticated tools for the kitchen. Some of these products, such as tilting skillets and steam-jacketed kettles, can do many jobs and are popular in many kitchens. Others can perform specialized tasks rapidly and efficiently, but their usefulness depends on volume because they are designed to do only a few jobs.

Modern equipment has enabled many food service operations to change their production methods. With sophisticated cooling, freezing, and heating equipment, it is possible to prepare some foods further in advance and in larger quantities. Some large multiunit operations prepare food for all their units in a large central commissary. The food is prepared in quantity, packaged, chilled or frozen, then heated or cooked to order in the individual units.

Development and Availability of New Food Products

Modern refrigeration and rapid transportation caused revolutionary changes in eating habits. For the first time, fresh foods of all kinds—meats, fish, vegetables, and fruits—became available all year. Exotic delicacies can now be shipped from anywhere in the world and arrive fresh and in peak condition.

The development of preservation techniques—not just refrigeration but also freezing, canning, freeze-drying, vacuum-packing, and irradiation—increased the availability of most foods and made affordable some foods that were once rare and expensive.

Techniques of food preservation have had another effect. It is now possible to do some or most of the preparation and processing of foods before shipping rather than in the food service operation itself. Thus, convenience foods have come into being. Convenience foods continue to account for an increasing share of the total food market.

Some professional cooks think of new convenience food products and new equipment as a threat to their position. They fear that these products will eliminate the need for skilled chefs because everything will be prepared or done by machine. However, handling convenience products properly still requires skill and knowledge. The quality of the product as served depends on how well the cook handles it. Furthermore, many new food products and new types of equipment are intended to do work that takes little or no skill, such as peeling potatoes and puréeing vegetables. Convenience foods and advanced equipment free cooks from drudgery so that they have more time to spend on those jobs that do require skill and experience.

Sanitary and Nutritional Awareness

The development of the sciences of microbiology and nutrition had a great impact on food service. One hundred years ago, there was little understanding of the causes of food poisoning and food spoilage. Food handling practices have come a long way since Escoffier's day.

Also, little knowledge of nutritional principles was available until fairly recently. Today, nutrition is an important part of a cook's training. Customers are also more knowledgeable and therefore more likely to demand healthful, well-balanced menus.

Modern Cooking Styles

All these developments have helped change cooking styles, menus, and eating habits. The evolution of cuisine that has been going on for hundreds of years continues. Changes occur not only because of technological developments, such as those just described, but also because of our reactions to culinary traditions.

Two opposing forces can be seen at work throughout the history of cooking. One is the urge to simplify, to eliminate complexity and ornamentation, and instead to emphasize the plain, natural tastes of basic, fresh ingredients. The other is the urge to invent, to highlight the creativity of the chef, with an accent on fancier, more complicated presentations and procedures. Both these forces are valid and healthy; they continually refresh and renew the art of cooking.

Recent history provides an example of these trends. Reacting to what they saw as a heavy, stodgy, overly complicated classical cuisine, a number of French chefs in the late 1960s and early 1970s became famous for a style called *nouvelle cuisine* ("new cooking"). They rejected many traditional principles, such as a dependence on flour to thicken sauces, and instead urged simpler, more natural flavors and preparations, with lighter sauces and seasonings and shorter cooking times. Very quickly, however, this "simpler" style became extravagant and complicated, famous for strange combinations of foods and fussy, ornate arrangements and designs. By the 1980s, many people were saying that nouvelle cuisine was dead.

It isn't dead, of course, any more than the cuisine of Escoffier is dead. The best achievements of nouvelle cuisine have taken a permanent place in the classical tradition. Meanwhile, many of the excesses have been forgotten. It is probably fair to say that most of the best new ideas and the lasting accomplishments were those of classically trained chefs with a solid grounding in the basics.

North American traditional dishes and regional specialties represent the combination of cooking traditions brought by immigrant settlers with the indigenous ingredients of a bountiful land. For many years, critics often argued that menus in most North American restaurants offered the same monotonous, mediocre food. Within the past 20 years, by contrast, North American cooking has become fashionable, and almost any local specialty is declared "classic." The fact is, however, that in any country, one finds both good and bad food. It takes a skilled cook with a knowledge of the basics to prepare exceptional food, whether it is American, Canadian, classical French, or any other.

The growth of food service holds great promise for new cooks and chefs. Technology will continue to make rapid changes in our industry, and men and women are needed who can adapt to these changes and respond to new challenges. Although automation and convenience foods will no doubt grow in importance, imaginative chefs who can create new dishes and develop new techniques and styles will always be needed, as will skilled cooks who can apply both old and new techniques to produce high-quality foods in all kinds of facilities, from restaurants and hotels to schools and hospitals.

The Organization of Modern Kitchens

THE BASIS OF KITCHEN ORGANIZATION

The purpose of kitchen organization is to assign or allocate tasks so that they can be done efficiently and properly and so that all workers know what their responsibilities are.

The way a kitchen is organized depends on several factors.

1. The menu.

   The kinds of dishes to be produced obviously determine the jobs that need to be done. The menu is, in fact, the basis for the entire operation. Because of its importance, we devote a whole chapter to a study of the menu (Chapter 6).

2. **The type of establishment.**
   The major types of food service establishments are listed as follows:
   - Hotels
   - Institutional kitchens
        Schools
        Hospitals
        Employee lunchrooms
        Airline catering
        Military food service
        Correctional institutions
   - Catering and banquet services
   - Fast-food restaurants
   - Carry-out or take-out food facilities
   - Full-service restaurants

3. **The size of the operation (the number of customers and the volume of food served).**

4. **The physical facilities, including the equipment in use.**

THE CLASSICAL BRIGADE

As you learned earlier in this chapter, one of Escoffier's important achievements was the reorganization of the kitchen. He divided the kitchen into departments, or stations, based on the kinds of foods they produced. A station chef was placed in charge of each department. In a small operation, the station chef may be the only worker in the department. But in a large kitchen, each station chef might have several assistants.

This system, with many variations, is still used today, especially in large hotels with traditional kinds of food service. The major positions are as follows:

1. The *chef* is the person in charge of the kitchen. In large establishments, this person has the title of *executive chef*. The executive chef is a manager who is responsible for all aspects of food production, including menu planning, purchasing, costing, and planning work schedules.

2. The *sous chef* (**soo** shef) is directly in charge of production. Because the executive chef's responsibilities require a great deal of time in the office, the sous chef takes command of the actual production and the minute-by-minute supervision of the staff.

3. The *station chefs*, or *chefs de partie*, are in charge of particular areas of production. The following are the most important station chefs:
   - The *sauce chef*, or *saucier* (so-see-**ay**), prepares sauces, stews, and hot hors d'oeuvres, and sautés foods to order. This is usually the highest position of all the stations.
   - The *fish cook*, or *poissonier* (pwah-so-**nyay**), prepares fish dishes. (This station may be handled by the saucier in some kitchens.)
   - The *vegetable cook*, or *entremetier* (awn-truh-met-**yay**), prepares vegetables, soups, starches, and eggs. Large kitchens may divide these duties among the *vegetable cook*, the *fry cook*, and the *soup cook*.
   - The *roast cook*, or *rotisseur* (ro-tee-**sur**), prepares roasted and braised meats and their gravies and broils meats and other items to order. A large kitchen may have a separate *broiler cook*, or *grillardin* (gree-ar-**dan**), to handle the broiled items. The broiler cook may also prepare deep-fried meats and fish.
   - The *pantry chef*, or *garde manger* (gard-mawn-**zhay**), is responsible for cold foods, including salads and dressings, pâtés, cold hors d'oeuvres, and buffet items.
   - The *pastry chef*, or *pâtissier* (pa-tees-**syay**), prepares pastries and desserts.
   - The *relief cook*, *swing cook*, or *tournant* (toor-**nawn**) replaces other station heads.

4. *Cooks* and *assistants* in each station or department help with the particular duties that are assigned to them. For example, the assistant vegetable cook may wash, peel, and trim vegetables. With experience, assistants may be promoted to station cooks and then to station chefs.

MODERN KITCHEN ORGANIZATION

As you can see, only a large establishment needs a staff like the classical brigade just described. In fact, some large hotels have even larger staffs, with other positions such as separate day and night sous chefs, assistant chef, banquet chef, butcher, baker, and so on.

Most modern operations, on the other hand, are smaller than this. The size of the classical brigade may be reduced simply by combining two or more positions where the workload allows it. For example, the *second cook* may combine the duties of the sauce cook, fish cook, soup cook, and vegetable cook.

A typical medium-size operation may employ a chef, a second cook, a broiler cook, a pantry cook, and a few cooks' helpers.

A *working chef* is in charge of operations that are not large enough to have an executive chef. In addition to being in charge of the kitchen, the working chef also handles one of the production stations. For example, he or she may handle the sauté station, plate foods during service, and help on other stations when needed.

Small kitchens may have only a chef, one or two cooks, and perhaps one or two assistants to handle simple jobs, such as washing and peeling vegetables.

In many small operations, the *short-order cook* is the backbone of the kitchen during service time. This cook may handle the broiler, deep fryer, griddle, sandwich production, and even some sautéed items. In other words, the short-order cook's responsibility is preparation of foods that can be quickly prepared to order.

By contrast, establishments such as school cafeterias may do no cooking to order at all. Stations and assignments are based on the requirements of quantity preparation rather than cooking to order.

SKILL LEVELS

The preceding discussion is necessarily very general because there are so many kinds of kitchen organizations. Titles vary also. The responsibilities of the worker called the *second cook*, for example, are not necessarily the same in every establishment. Escoffier's standardized system has evolved in many directions.

One title that is often misunderstood and much abused is *chef*. The general public tends to refer to anyone with a white hat as a chef, and people who like to cook for guests in their homes refer to themselves as amateur chefs.

Strictly speaking, the name *chef* should be reserved for one who is *in charge of a kitchen* or a part of a kitchen. The word *chef* is French for "chief" or "head." Studying this book will not make you a chef. That title must be earned by experience not only in preparing food but also in managing a staff and in planning production. Use the word *chef* with respect, because when you become a chef, you will want the same respect.

Skills required of food production personnel vary not only with the job level but also with the establishment and the kind of food prepared. The director of a hospital kitchen and the head chef in a French restaurant need different skills. The skills needed by a short-order cook in a coffee shop are not exactly the same as those needed by a production worker in a school cafeteria. Nevertheless, we can group skills into three general categories.

1. Supervisory.
   The head of a food service kitchen, whether called executive chef, head chef, working chef, or kitchen director, must have management and supervisory skills as well as a thorough knowledge of food production. Leadership positions require an individual who understands organizing and motivating people, planning menus and production procedures, controlling costs and managing budgets, and purchasing food supplies and equipment. Even if he or she does no cooking at all, the chef must be an experienced cook in order to schedule production, instruct workers, and control quality. Above all, the chef must be able to work well with people, even under extreme pressure.

2. **Skilled and technical.**

   While the chef is the head of an establishment, the cooks are the backbone. These workers carry out the actual food production. Thus, they must have knowledge of and experience in cooking techniques, at least for all the dishes made in their own department. In addition, they must be able to function well with their fellow workers and to coordinate with other departments. Food production is a team activity.

3. **Entry level.**

   Entry-level jobs in food service usually require no particular skills or experience. Workers in these jobs are assigned such work as washing vegetables and preparing salad greens. As their knowledge and experience increase, they may be given more complex tasks and eventually become skilled cooks. Many executive chefs began their careers as pot washers who got a chance to peel potatoes when the pot sink was empty.

Beginning in an entry-level position and working one's way up with experience has been the traditional method of advancing in a food service career. Today, however, many cooks are graduates of one- or two-year cooking schools. But even with such an education, many new graduates begin at entry-level positions. This is as it should be and certainly should not be seen as a discouragement. Schools teach general cooking knowledge, while every food service establishment requires specific skills, according to its own menu and its own procedures. Experience as well as theoretical knowledge is needed to be able to adapt to real-life working situations. However, students who have studied and learned well should be able to work their way up much more rapidly than the beginners with no knowledge at all.

Standards of Professionalism

What does it take to be a good food service worker?

The emphasis of a food service education is on learning a set of skills. But in many ways, *attitudes* are more important than skills because a good attitude will help you not only learn skills but also persevere and overcome the many difficulties you will face in your career.

The successful food service worker follows an unwritten code of behavior and set of attitudes we call *professionalism*. Let's look at some of the qualities that a professional must have.

POSITIVE ATTITUDE TOWARD THE JOB

In order to be a good professional cook, you have to like cooking and want to do it well. Being serious about your work doesn't mean you can't enjoy it. But the enjoyment comes from the satisfaction of doing your job well and making everything run smoothly.

Every experienced chef knows the stimulation of the rush. When it's the busiest time of the evening, the orders are coming in so fast you can hardly keep track of them, and every split second counts—then, when everyone digs in and works together and everything clicks, there's real excitement in the air. But this excitement comes only when you work for it.

A cook with a positive attitude works quickly, efficiently, neatly, and safely. Professionals have pride in their work and want to make sure that the work is something to be proud of.

STAYING POWER

Food service requires physical and mental stamina, good health, and a willingness to work hard. It is hard work. The pressures can be intense and the hours long and grueling. You may be working evenings and weekends when everyone else is playing. And the work can be monotonous. You might think it's drudgery to hand-shape two or three dozen dinner rolls for your baking class, but wait until you get that great job in the big hotel and are told to make 3000 canapés for a party.

ABILITY TO WORK WITH PEOPLE

Few of you will work in an establishment so small that you are the only person on the staff. Food service work is teamwork, and it's essential to be able to work well on a team and to cooperate with your fellow workers. You can't afford to let ego problems, petty jealousy, departmental rivalries, or feelings about other people get in the way of doing the job well. In the old days, many chefs were famous for their temper tantrums. Fortunately, self-control is more valued today.

EAGERNESS TO LEARN

There is more to learn about cooking than you will learn in a lifetime. But isn't it great to try? The greatest chefs in the world are the first to admit that they have more to learn, and they keep working, experimenting, and studying.

The food service industry is changing so rapidly that it is vital to be open to new ideas. No matter how good your techniques are, you might learn an even better way.

A FULL RANGE OF SKILLS

Most people who become professional cooks do so because they like to cook. This is an important motivation, but it is also important to develop and maintain other skills that are necessary for the profession. To be successful, a cook must understand and manage food cost and other financial matters, manage and maintain proper inventories, deal with purveyors, and understand personnel management.

EXPERIENCE

One of our most respected chefs has said, "You don't really know how to cook a dish until you have done it a thousand times."

There is no substitute for years of experience. Studying cooking principles in books and in schools can get your career off to a running start. You may learn more about basic cooking theories from your chef instructors than you could in several years of working your way up from washing vegetables. But if you want to become an accomplished cook, you need practice, practice, and more practice. A diploma will not make you a chef.

DEDICATION TO QUALITY

Many people think that only a special category of food can be called *gourmet food*. It's hard to say exactly what that is. Apparently, the only thing so-called gourmet foods have in common is high price.

The only distinction worth making is between well-prepared food and poorly prepared food. There is good roast duckling à l'orange and there is bad roast duckling à l'orange. There are good hamburgers and French fries, and there are bad hamburgers and French fries.

Whether you work in a fancy French restaurant, a fast-food restaurant, a college cafeteria, or a catering house, you can do your job well, or not. The choice is yours.

High quality doesn't necessarily mean high price. It costs no more to cook green beans properly than to overcook them. But in order to produce high-quality food, you must want to. It is not enough to know how.

GOOD UNDERSTANDING OF THE BASICS

Experimentation and innovation in cooking are the order of the day. Brilliant chefs are breaking old boundaries, inventing dishes that would have been unthinkable years ago. There seems to be no limit to what can be tried.

However, the very chefs who seem to be most revolutionary are the first to insist on the importance of solid grounding in basic techniques and in the classic methods practiced since Escoffier's day. In order to innovate, you have to know where to begin.

For the beginner, knowing the basics will help you take better advantage of your experience. When you watch a practiced cook at work, you will understand better what you are seeing and will know what questions to ask. In order to play great music on the piano, you first have to learn to play scales and exercises.

That's what this book is about. It's not a course in French cooking or American cooking or gourmet cooking or coffee shop cooking. It's a course in the basics. When you finish the book, you will not know everything. But you should be ready to take good advantage of the many rewarding years of food service experience ahead of you.

Terms for Review

Carême	sous chef	rotisseur	working chef
Escoffier	station chef	grillardin	short-order cook
nouvelle cuisine	saucier	garde manger	professionalism
chef	poissonier	pâtissier	
executive chef	entremetier	tournant	

Questions for Discussion

1. Escoffier is sometimes called the father of modern food service. What were his most important accomplishments?
2. Discuss several ways in which modern technology has changed the food service industry.
3. What is the purpose of kitchen organization? Is the classical system of organization developed by Escoffier the best one for all types of kitchens? Why or why not?
4. True or false: A cook in charge of the sauce and sauté station in a large hotel needs to have supervisory skills as well as cooking skills. Explain your answer.
5. True or false: If a culinary arts student in a professional school studies hard, works diligently, gets top grades, and shows real dedication, he or she will be qualified to be a chef upon graduation. Explain your answer.

chapter 2

Sanitation and Safety

In the last chapter, we talked about professionalism in food service. Professionalism is an attitude that reflects pride in the quality of your work. One of the most important ways of demonstrating professional pride is in the area of sanitation and safety. Pride in quality is reflected in your appearance and work habits. Poor hygiene, poor grooming and personal care, and sloppy work habits are nothing to be proud of.

Even more important, poor sanitation and safety can cost a lot of money. Poor food handling procedures and unclean kitchens cause illness, unhappy customers, and even fines, summonses, and lawsuits. Increased food spoilage raises food costs. Poor kitchen safety results in injuries, medical bills, and workdays lost. Finally, poor sanitation and safety habits show lack of respect for your customers, for your fellow workers, and for yourself.

In this chapter you will study the causes of food-borne diseases and kitchen injuries, and you will learn ways of preventing them. Prevention, of course, is the most important thing to learn. It is not as important to be able to recite the names of disease-causing bacteria as it is to be able to prevent their growth in food.

Sanitation

Rules of personal hygiene and sanitary food handling were not just invented to make your life difficult. There are good reasons for all of them. Instead of starting this chapter with lists of rules, we will first talk about the causes of food-borne diseases. Then, when we get to the rules, you will know why they are important. This will make them easier to remember and to practice.

The rules presented in this chapter are only basic guidelines. Local health departments have more detailed regulations. *All food service operators are responsible for knowing the health department regulations in their own city and state.*

The information presented here is practical as well as theoretical. It should not merely be learned but should be put to use systematically. One effective system that food service establishments can use to ensure food safety is called the Hazard Analysis Critical Control Point (HACCP) system. This practical program identifies possible danger points and sets up procedures for corrective action. HACCP is introduced later in this chapter.

Introduction to Microbiology

Microbiology is the study of tiny, usually single-celled organisms that can be seen only with a microscope. Although these organisms sometimes occur in clusters large enough to be seen with the naked eye, they are not usually visible. This is one reason why they can be so dangerous. Just because food looks good doesn't mean that it is safe.

Four kinds of microorganisms can contaminate food and cause illness: *bacteria, viruses, parasites,* and *fungi.* Most food-borne diseases are caused by bacteria, so most of our attention in this chapter is focused on them, but the other types can be dangerous as well.

Studying this chapter will not make you a microbiologist. In fact, some of the information in the next several pages you may forget very quickly—names like *Clostridium perfringens*, for instance. The importance of these first sections is not simply to exercise your memory of difficult facts, it is to help you understand how and why disease-causing microorganisms such as bacteria grow and spread so that you are better able to prevent food-borne disease.

KINDS OF BACTERIA

Bacteria are everywhere—in the air, in the water, in the ground, on our food, on our skin, inside our bodies. Scientists have various ways of classifying and describing these bacteria. As food workers, we are interested in a way of classifying them that may be less scientific but is more practical to our work.

1. **Harmless bacteria.**
    Most bacteria fall into this category. They are neither helpful nor harmful to us. We are not concerned with them in food sanitation.

2. **Beneficial bacteria.**
    These bacteria are helpful to us. For example, many live in the intestinal tract, where they fight harmful bacteria, aid the digestion of food, and produce certain nutrients. In food production, bacteria make possible the manufacture of many foods, including cheese, yogurt, and sauerkraut.

3. **Undesirable bacteria.**
    These are the bacteria that are responsible for food spoilage. They cause souring, putrefying, and decomposition. These bacteria may or may not cause disease, but they offer a built-in safety factor: They announce their presence by means of sour odors, sticky or slimy surfaces, and discoloration. As long as we use common sense and follow the rule that says, "when in doubt, throw it out," we are relatively safe from these bacteria.
    We are concerned with these bacteria for two reasons:

    *   Food spoilage costs money.
    *   Food spoilage is a sign of improper food handling and storage. This means that the next kind of bacteria is probably present.

After reading this chapter, you should be able to

1. Describe steps to prevent food poisoning and food-borne diseases in the following areas: personal hygiene; food handling and storage techniques; cleaning and sanitizing procedures; and pest control.

2. Identify safe workplace habits that prevent injuries from the following: cuts, burns, operation of machinery and equipment, and lifting.

3. Identify safe workplace habits that minimize the likelihood of fires and falls.

4. **Disease-causing bacteria, or pathogens.**

These are the bacteria that cause most food-borne illness, the bacteria that we are most concerned with.

Pathogens do not necessarily leave detectable odors or tastes in food. In other words, you can't tell if food is contaminated by smelling, tasting, or looking at it. The only way to protect food against pathogenic bacteria is by proper hygiene and sanitary food handling and storage techniques.

BACTERIAL GROWTH

Bacteria multiply by splitting in half. Under ideal conditions for growth, they can double in number every 15 to 30 minutes. This means that one single bacterium could multiply to a million in less than 6 hours!

Conditions for Growth

1. **Food.**

Bacteria require some kind of food in order to grow. They like many of the foods we do. Foods with sufficient amounts of proteins are best for bacterial growth. These include meats, poultry, fish, dairy products, and eggs, as well as some grains and vegetables.

2. **Moisture.**

Bacteria require water in order to absorb food. Dry foods will not support bacterial growth. Foods with a very high salt or sugar content are also relatively safe, because these ingredients make the bacteria unable to use the moisture present.

3. **Temperature.**

Bacteria grow best at warm temperatures. *Temperatures between 41°F and 140°F (5°C and 60°C) will promote the growth of disease-causing bacteria.* This temperature range is called the *Food Danger Zone*.

Note: In the past, 45°F (7°C) was considered the lower limit of the Food Danger Zone. Health experts now recommend a lower temperature to provide an extra measure of safety.

4. **Acidity or alkalinity.**

In general, disease-producing bacteria like a neutral environment, neither too acidic nor too alkaline. The acidity or alkalinity of a substance is indicated by a measurement called *pH*. The scale ranges from 0 (strongly acidic) to 14 (strongly alkaline). A pH of 7 is neutral. Pure water has a pH of 7.

5. **Air.**

Most bacteria require oxygen to grow. These are called *aerobic*. Some bacteria are *anaerobic*, which means they can grow only if there is no air present, such as in metal cans. Botulism, one of the most dangerous forms of food poisoning, is caused by anaerobic bacteria.

6. **Time.**

When bacteria are introduced to a new environment, they need time to adjust to their surroundings before they start growing. This time is called the *lag phase*. If other conditions are good, the lag phase may last about 1 hour or somewhat longer.

If it weren't for the lag phase, there would be much more food-borne disease than there is. This time delay makes it possible to have foods at room temperature *for very short periods* in order to work on them.

Foods that provide a good environment for the growth of disease-causing microorganisms are called *potentially hazardous foods*. Looking back at our list of conditions for growth of bacteria, we can see that protein foods with sufficient moisture and neutral pH are the most likely to host bacteria that cause disease. Of the conditions in the list, the one over which we have the most control is *temperature*.

Potentially hazardous foods fall into three general categories, plus two specific items that do not fit into these categories:

1. Any food that is derived from animals, or any food containing animal products, including meat, poultry, fish, shellfish, and dairy products.

2. Any food that is derived from plants and has been cooked, partially cooked, or otherwise heat-treated. This category includes not only cooked vegetables but also such items as cooked pasta, cooked rice, and tofu (soybean curd).

3. Raw seed sprouts.

4. Sliced melons (because the edible flesh can be contaminated by organisms on the rind exterior, which has been in contact with soil).

5. Garlic and oil mixtures (because the oil seals the garlic from the air, fostering the growth of anaerobic bacteria, as explained on p. 15).

Foods that are not potentially hazardous include dried or dehydrated foods, foods that are strongly acidic, and commercially processed foods that are still in their original unopened, sealed containers.

LOCOMOTION

Bacteria do not have feet. They can move from place to place in only one way: They must be carried.

Foods can become contaminated by any of the following means:

Hands	Air
Coughs and sneezes	Water
Other foods	Insects
Equipment and utensils	Rats and mice

PROTECTION AGAINST BACTERIA

Because we know how and why bacteria grow, we should now be able to keep them from growing. Because we know how bacteria get from place to place, we should now know how to keep them from getting into our food.

There are three basic principles of food protection against bacteria. These principles are the reasons behind nearly all the sanitation techniques that we discuss in the rest of this chapter.

1. **Keep bacteria from spreading.**
   Don't let food touch anything that may contain disease-producing bacteria, and protect food from bacteria in the air.

2. **Stop bacteria from growing.**
   Take away the conditions that encourage bacteria to grow. In the kitchen, our best weapon is temperature. *The most effective way to prevent bacterial growth is to keep foods below 41°F (5°C) or above 140°F (60°C).* These temperatures won't necessarily kill bacteria; they'll just slow down their growth greatly.

3. **Kill bacteria.**
   Most disease-causing bacteria are killed if they are subjected to a temperature of 170°F (77°C) for 30 seconds or higher temperatures for shorter times. This enables us to make food safe by cooking and to sanitize dishes and equipment with heat. The term *sanitize* means to kill disease-causing bacteria.
   Certain chemicals also kill bacteria. These may be used for sanitizing equipment.

Food-Borne Diseases

As you know, most food-borne illnesses are caused by bacteria. But there are other causes, too. This section summarizes the main food-borne diseases in the United States. For each disease, pay particular attention to the way it is spread, the foods involved, and the means of prevention.

Please note that this is not a complete list of all food-borne diseases. Rather, these are the most common ones.

BACTERIAL DISEASES

Two kinds of diseases are caused by bacteria: intoxications and infections.

1. *Intoxications* are caused by poisons (toxins) that the bacteria produce while they are growing in the food. It is these poisons, not the bacteria themselves, that cause the diseases.
2. *Infections* are caused by bacteria (or other organisms) that get into the intestinal system and attack the body.

The first two bacterial diseases we discuss, botulism and staphylococcus food poisoning, are intoxications. The third, *Escherichia coli,* can be either an intoxication or an infection. The rest are infections.

Botulism

Caused by toxins produced by the bacterium *Clostridium botulinum,* botulism attacks the nervous system and is usually *fatal,* even if only a small amount of poisoned food is eaten. The bacteria are anaerobic (do not grow in air) and do not grow in high-acid foods. Most outbreaks are caused by improper canning techniques. The toxin (although not the bacteria) is destroyed by boiling (212°F/100°C) for 20 minutes.

> *Source of bacteria:* soil on vegetables and other foods.
> *Foods usually involved:* home-canned, low-acid vegetables (very rare in commercially canned foods).
> *Prevention:* Use only commercially canned foods. Discard *without tasting* any bulged or damaged cans or foods with off odors.

Staphylococcus Food Poisoning (Staph)

Caused by toxins produced in foods by the bacterium *Staphylococcus aureus,* staph is probably the most common food poisoning, characterized by nausea, vomiting, stomach cramps, diarrhea, and prostration.

> *Source of bacteria:* usually food workers.
> *Foods usually involved:* custards and desserts made with dairy products, potato salad, protein salads, ham, hollandaise sauce, many other high-protein foods.
> *Prevention:* Practice good hygiene and work habits. Do not handle foods if you have an illness or infection. Clean and sanitize all equipment. Keep foods below 41°F (5°C) or above 140°F (60°C).

Escherichia coli

This bacterium causes severe illness, either as an intoxication or an infection. Severe abdominal pain, nausea, vomiting, diarrhea, and other symptoms result from *E. coli* intoxication. As an infection, *E. coli* causes intestinal inflammation and bloody diarrhea. While the illness normally lasts from one to three days, it can lead to long-term illness in some cases.

> *Source of bacteria:* intestinal tracts of humans and some animals, especially cattle; contaminated water.
> *Foods usually involved:* raw or undercooked red meats, unpasteurized dairy products, sometimes fish from contaminated water, prepared foods such as mashed potatoes and cream pies.
> *Prevention:* Cook foods, including red meats, thoroughly; avoid cross-contamination. Practice good hygiene.

Salmonella

The food infection caused by salmonella bacteria exhibits symptoms that are similar to those of staph poisoning, though the disease may last longer. Most poultry carry this bacteria.

> *Source of bacteria:* contaminated meats and poultry; fecal contamination by food workers.
> *Foods usually involved:* poultry, meats, eggs, poultry stuffings, gravies, raw foods, shellfish from polluted waters.
> *Prevention:* Practice good personal hygiene, proper food storage and handling, and insect and rodent control. Wash hands and sanitize all equipment and cutting surfaces after handling raw poultry. Use certified shellfish.

Clostridium perfringens

This is another infection characterized by nausea, cramps, stomach pain, and diarrhea. The bacteria are hard to destroy because they are not always killed by cooking.

Source of bacteria: soil, fresh meats, human carriers.
Foods usually involved: meats and poultry, reheated or unrefrigerated gravies and sauces.
Prevention: Keep foods hot (above 140°F/60°C) or cold (below 41°F/5°C).

Streptococcal (Strep) Infections

The symptoms of this disease are fever and sore throat.

Sources of bacteria: coughs, sneezes, infected food workers.
Foods usually involved: any food contaminated by coughs, sneezes, or infected food workers, then served without further cooking.
Prevention: Do not handle food if you are infected. Protect displayed food (salad bars, pastry carts, etc.) from customers' sneezes and coughs.

OTHER FOOD INFECTIONS

Hepatitis A (Virus)

This is a severe disease that can last for many months.

Source of contamination: contaminated water or ice, shellfish from polluted waters, raw fruits and vegetables, milk and milk products, infected food workers.
Foods usually involved: shellfish eaten raw, any food contaminated by an infected person.
Prevention: Practice good health and hygiene. Use only certified shellfish from safe waters.

Norwalk Virus Gastroenteritis (Virus)

This disease affects the digestive tract, causing nausea, vomiting, stomach cramps, diarrhea, fever.

Source of contamination: human intestinal tract, contaminated water.
Foods usually involved: water, shellfish from polluted waters, raw vegetables and fruits.
Prevention: Practice good health and hygiene. Use only certified shellfish from safe waters. Use sanitary, chlorinated water. Cook foods to safe internal temperatures.

Trichinosis (Parasite)

This disease is often mistaken for the flu at first, but it can last for a year or more. It is caused by a tiny worm that becomes embedded in the muscles.

Source of contamination: infected pork from hogs that ate unprocessed garbage. Modern farming practices have eliminated most, but not all, of this problem.
Foods usually involved: pork products.
Prevention: Trichinosis organisms are killed if held at a temperature of 137°F (58°C) for 10 seconds. To be safe, cook all pork products to an internal temperature of at least 150°F (65°C). Some authorities recommend a higher temperature (165°F/74°C). Canadian pork is considered to be free of trichinosis and does not need to be cooked to these temperatures.

Anisakiasis (Parasite)

Like trichinosis, this disease is caused by a tiny roundworm. Symptoms are tingling sensation in the throat, vomiting up worms, abdominal pain, nausea.

Source of contamination: ocean fish, especially bottom-feeding fish.
Foods usually involved: raw or undercooked fish, such as cod, haddock, fluke, herring, flounder, monkfish, salmon.
Prevention: Cook fish properly. Fish to be eaten raw should be frozen at −4°F (−20°C) or lower for 7 days or 31°F (−1°C) or lower for 15 hours in a blast freezer.

CHEMICAL POISONING AND OTHER PROBLEMS OF FOOD SAFETY

Some kinds of chemical poisoning are caused by the use of defective or improper equipment or equipment that has been handled improperly. The following toxins (except lead) create symptoms that show themselves very quickly, usually within 30 minutes of eating poisoned food. To prevent these diseases, do not use the materials that cause them.

1. **Antimony.**
   Caused by storing or cooking acid foods in chipped gray enamelware.

2. **Cadmium.**
   Caused by cadmium-plated ice cube trays or containers.

3. **Cyanide.**
   Caused by silver polish containing cyanide.

4. **Lead.**
   Caused by lead water pipes, solder containing lead, or utensils containing lead.

5. **Copper.**
   Caused by unclean or corroded copper utensils, acid foods cooked in unlined copper utensils, or carbonated beverages in contact with copper tubing.

6. **Zinc.**
   Caused by cooking foods in zinc-plated (galvanized) utensils.

Other chemical contamination can result from exposure of foods to various chemicals used in commercial food service establishments. Examples include cleaning compounds, polishing compounds, and insecticides. Prevent contamination by keeping these items physically separated from foods. Do not use them around food. Label all containers properly. Rinse cleaned equipment thoroughly.

Physical contamination is contamination of food with objects that may not be toxic but that may cause injury or discomfort. Examples include pieces of glass from a broken container, metal shavings from an improperly opened can, stones from poorly sorted dried beans, soil from poorly washed vegetables, insects or insect parts, and hair. Proper food handling is necessary to avoid physical contamination.

Personal Hygiene

Earlier in this chapter, we said that most food-borne disease is caused by bacteria. Now we change that statement slightly to say that *most food-borne disease is caused by bacteria spread by food workers.*

The first step in preventing food-borne disease is good personal hygiene. Even when we are healthy, we have bacteria all over our skin and in our nose and mouth. Some of these bacteria, if given the chance to grow in food, will make people ill.

1. Do not work with food if you have any communicable disease or infection.
2. Bathe or shower daily.
3. Wear clean uniforms and aprons.
4. Keep hair neat and clean. Always wear a hat or hairnet.
5. Keep mustaches and beards trimmed and clean. Better yet, be clean-shaven.
6. Wash hands and exposed parts of arms before work and as often as necessary during work, including:
   - After eating, drinking, or smoking.
   - After using the toilet.
   - After touching or handling anything that may be contaminated with bacteria.
7. Cover coughs and sneezes, then wash hands.
8. Keep your hands away from your face, eyes, hair, and arms.
9. Keep fingernails clean and short. Do not wear nail polish.
10. Do not smoke or chew gum while on duty.
11. Cover cuts or sores with clean bandages.
12. Do not sit on worktables.

Food Storage

The following rules of safe food storage have two purposes:

1. To prevent contamination of foods.
2. To prevent growth of bacteria that may already be in foods.

Temperature control is an important part of food storage. Perishable foods must be kept out of the Food Danger Zone—41°F to 140°F (5°C to 60°C)—as much as possible, because these temperatures support bacterial growth. See Figure 2.1 for a chart of important temperatures.

DRY FOOD STORAGE

Dry food storage pertains to those foods not likely to support bacterial growth in their normal state. These foods include

Flour
Sugar and salt
Cereals, rice, and other grains
Dried beans and peas

Ready-prepared cereals
Breads and crackers
Oils and shortenings
Canned and bottled foods (unopened)

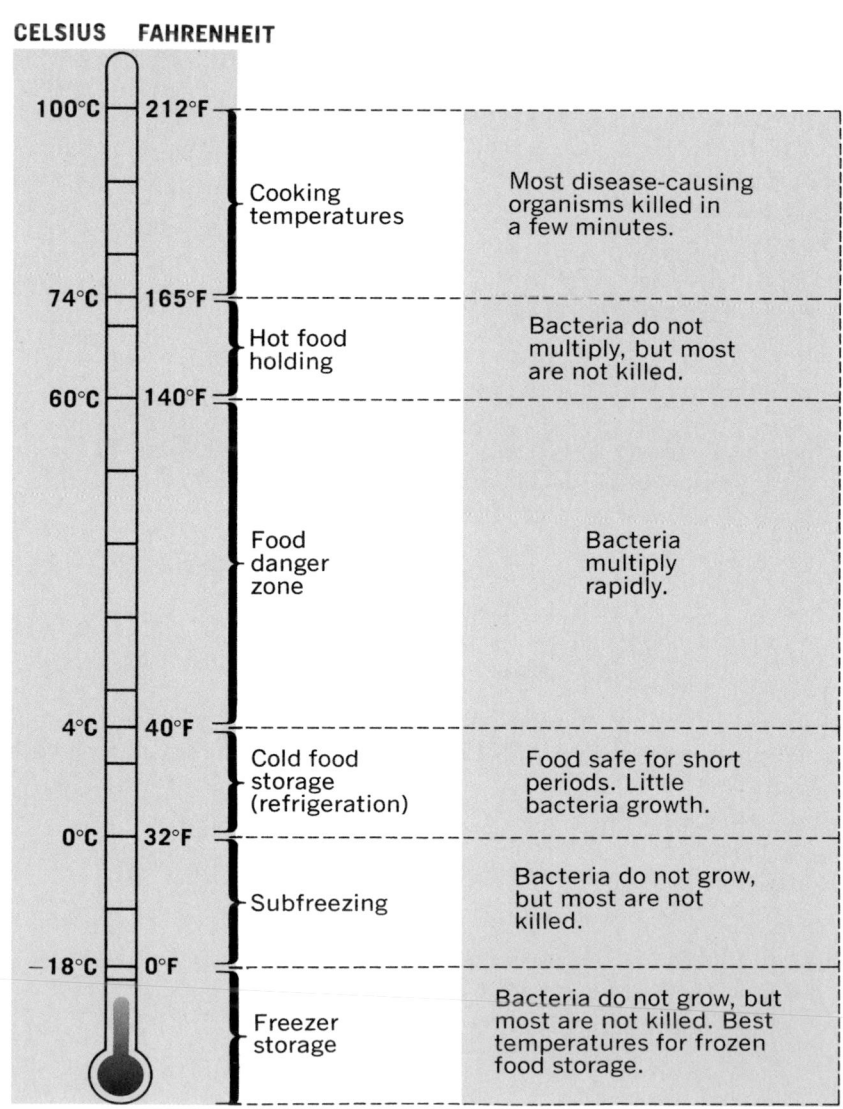

Figure 2.1 Important temperatures in sanitation and food protection.

1. Store dry foods in a cool, dry place, off the floor, away from the wall, and not under a sewer line.
2. Keep all containers tightly closed to protect from insects, rodents, and dust. Dry foods can be contaminated, even if they don't need refrigeration.

FREEZER STORAGE

1. Keep frozen foods at 0°F (−18°C) or lower.
2. Keep all frozen foods tightly wrapped or packaged to prevent freezer burn.
3. Label and date all items.
4. Thaw frozen foods properly. Do not thaw at room temperature, because the surface temperature will go above 41°F (5°C) before the inside is thawed, resulting in bacterial growth. These methods may be used:
   - In refrigerator.
   - Under cold running water.
   - In a microwave oven, if the item is to be cooked or served immediately.

REFRIGERATOR STORAGE

1. Keep all perishable foods properly refrigerated. Note that the lower limit of the Food Danger Zone (41°F/5°C) is only the upper limit for refrigerator storage. Most foods keep even better at lower temperatures. The major exception is fresh fruits and vegetables, which are not considered potentially hazardous foods. See Table 2.1 for preferred storage temperatures for various foods.
2. Do not overcrowd refrigerators. Leave space between items so that cold air can circulate.
3. Keep refrigerator doors shut except when removing or putting in foods.
4. Keep shelves and interiors of refrigerators clean.
5. Store raw and cooked items separately if possible.
6. If raw and cooked foods must be kept in the same refrigerator, keep cooked foods above raw foods. If cooked foods are kept below raw foods, they can become contaminated by drips and spills. Then, if they are not to be cooked again before serving, they may be hazardous.
7. Keep refrigerated foods wrapped or covered and in sanitary containers.
8. Do not let any unsanitary surface, such as the bottoms of other containers, touch any food.
9. Chill foods as quickly as possible over ice or in a cold-water bath before placing in refrigerator. A gallon of stock placed in a refrigerator hot off the stove may take 10 hours to go below 41°F (5°C), giving bacteria plenty of time to grow.
10. When holding foods such as protein salads in a cold bain-marie or refrigerated table for service, do not heap the food above the level of the container. The food above this level will not stay cold enough.

HOT FOOD HOLDING

1. To keep foods hot for service, use steam tables or other equipment that will keep all parts of all foods above 140°F (60°C) at all times.
2. Keep foods covered.
3. Bring foods to holding temperature as quickly as possible by using ovens, steamers, rangetop pots and pans, or other cooking equipment. Do not warm cold foods by placing them directly in the steam table. They will take too long to heat, and bacteria will have time to grow.
4. Do not let ready-to-eat foods come in contact with any contaminated surface.

TABLE 2.1

Food Storage Temperatures

Raw vegetables and fruits (see note)	40°–45°F	4°–7°C
Eggs	38°–40°F	3°–4°C
Milk and cream	36°–40°F	2°–4°C
Poultry and meat	32°–36°F	0°–2°C
Fish and seafood	30°–34°F	−1°–1°C

Note: Potatoes, onions, and winter squash are best held at cool temperatures (50°–65°F or 10°–18°C).

Food Handling and Preparation

We face two major sanitation problems when handling and preparing food. The first is *cross-contamination*, which is the transfer of bacteria to food from another food or from equipment or work surfaces.

The second problem is that, while we are working on it, food is usually at a temperature between 41°F and 140°F (5°C to 60°C), or in the Food Danger Zone. The lag phase of bacteria growth (p. 15) helps us a little but, to be safe, we must keep foods out of the danger zone whenever possible.

1. Start with clean, wholesome foods from reputable purveyors. Whenever applicable, buy government-inspected meats, poultry, fish, dairy, and egg products.
2. Handle foods as little as possible. Use tongs, spatulas, or other utensils instead of hands when practicable.
3. Use clean, sanitized equipment and worktables.
4. Clean and sanitize cutting surfaces and equipment after handling raw poultry, meat, fish, or eggs and before working on another food.
5. Clean as you go. Don't wait until the end of the workday.
6. Wash raw fruits and vegetables thoroughly.
7. When bringing foods out of refrigeration, do not bring out more than you can process in 1 hour.
8. Keep foods covered unless in immediate use.
9. Do not let any perishable foods remain in the Food Danger Zone for more than 1 hour.
10. Boil leftover gravies, sauces, soups, and vegetables before serving.
11. Don't mix leftovers with freshly prepared foods.
12. Chill all ingredients for protein salads and potato salads *before* combining.
13. Chill custards, cream fillings, and other hazardous foods as quickly as possible by pouring them into shallow, sanitized pans, covering them, and refrigerating. Do not stack the pans.
14. In countries where trichinosis is considered to be a problem, cook all pork products to an internal temperature of at least 150°F (65°C).

Cleaning and Sanitizing Equipment

Cleaning means removing visible soil. *Sanitizing* means killing disease-causing bacteria. Two ways of killing bacteria are by *heat* and by *chemicals*.

MANUAL DISHWASHING

Figure 2.2 shows the setup of a three-compartment sink for washing dishes, glassware, and eating utensils by hand.

Procedure for Manual Dishwashing

1. **Scrape and rinse.**
The purpose of this step is to keep the wash water cleaner longer.

2. **Wash.**
Use warm water at 110°F to 120°F (43°C to 49°C) and a good detergent. Scrub well with a brush to remove all traces of soil and grease.

3. **Rinse.**
Use clean, warm water to rinse off detergent. Change the water frequently, or use running water with an overflow, as in Figure 2.2.

4. **Sanitize.**
Place utensils in a rack and immerse in hot water at 170°F (77°C) for 30 seconds. (A gas or electric heating element is needed to hold water at this temperature.)

5. **Drain and air dry.**
Do not towel dry. This may recontaminate utensils. Do not touch food contact surfaces of sanitized dishes, glasses, and silverware.

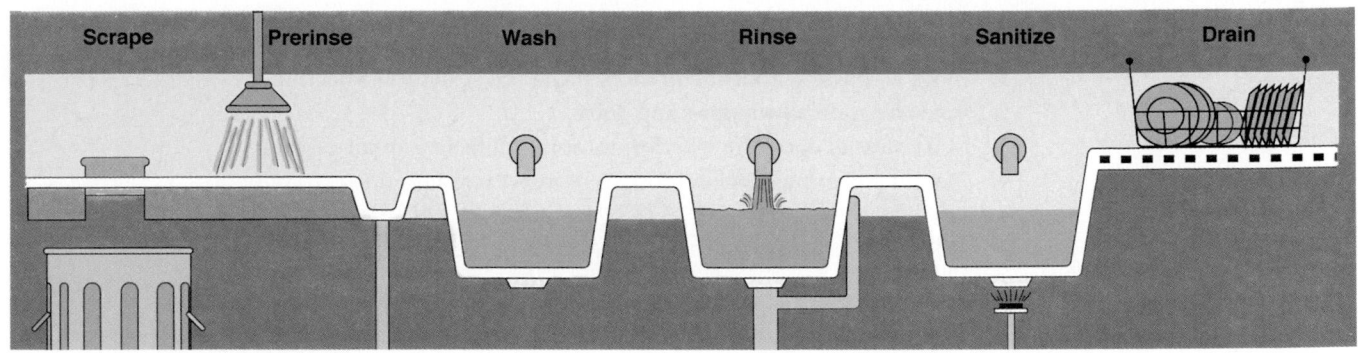

Figure 2.2 Setup of three-compartment sink for manual dishwashing.

MECHANICAL DISHWASHING

The steps in washing dishes by machine are the same as in the hand method, except that the machine does the washing, rinsing, and sanitizing.

Procedure for Mechanical Dishwashing

1. Scrape and rinse.

2. Rack dishes so that dishwasher spray will strike all surfaces.

3. Run machine for a full cycle.

4. Sanitizing temperatures:
180°F (82°C) for machines that sanitize by heat
140°F (60°C) for machines that sanitize by chemical disinfectant

5. Air dry and inspect dishes. Do not touch food contact surfaces.

WASHING KITCHEN UTENSILS AND EQUIPMENT

1. Use the same three-compartment sink setup and procedure as for manual dishwashing.

2. Do not use scouring powder or steel wool. These may make scratches where bacteria can hide. Also, pieces of steel wool break off and can remain in the pan and thus get into food.

3. Utensils with baked-on foods should be scraped and rinsed, soaked in the first compartment to loosen the baked-on food, then scraped and rinsed again.

4. Kitchen equipment may be sanitized with *chemical disinfectants* instead of heat. Use an approved disinfectant, and follow the instructions on the label.

CLEANING AND SANITIZING STATIONARY EQUIPMENT AND WORK SURFACES

1. Unplug electric equipment before cleaning. You could seriously injure yourself if you accidentally hit the power switch while you are cleaning a piece of equipment.

2. Disassemble equipment when possible. (This obviously doesn't apply to such equipment as worktables.) All immersible parts should be cleaned and sanitized like kitchen utensils.

3. Wash all food contact surfaces, using a detergent solution and clean cloths.

4. Sanitize all surfaces with a double-strength sanitizing solution and with clean cloths used only for this purpose.

5. Allow to air dry.

6. Reassemble equipment.

Rodent and Insect Control

Rats, mice, flies, and cockroaches can spread disease by contaminating food and food contact surfaces. Any sign of rodent or insect infestation is usually considered a serious violation of health codes.

There are four basic methods of pest control. We start with the most important and most effective.

BUILD THEM OUT

1. Block all possible rodent entrances, including structural defects in the building.
2. Put screens on all windows and doors.
3. Make sure all doors are self-closing, or install fly fans or air curtains.
4. Inspect incoming supplies for signs of insect infestation.

ELIMINATE HARBORAGE AND BREEDING PLACES

1. Repair holes in walls and floors, and any other structural defects.
2. Eliminate narrow spaces between and behind equipment, counters, or other fixtures, and hollow spaces made by false bottoms in counters, cabinets, etc.
3. Store food and supplies off the floor.
4. Seal all cracks and crevices. Repair loose tiles, wall coverings, and so on.
5. Remove all fly-breeding places inside and out: garbage, manure, general filth.

ELIMINATE FOOD SUPPLIES

1. Keep all foods tightly covered or wrapped.
2. Keep garbage containers tightly covered, and use metal (ratproof) garbage cans.
3. Clean up all spilled food.
4. General sanitation: Keep floors, walls, and equipment clean.

EXTERMINATE

Hire a qualified, licensed exterminator who knows how to use poisons, insecticides, and traps. Most poisons should not be used in a food production operation, so it's better not to do the job yourself.

Extermination is a temporary solution only. For permanent freedom from rodents and insects, you must rely on the other methods of control.

Setting Up a System for Food Safety

Once you have learned the information in the first part of this chapter, you must apply it in the kitchen.

Many food service operations have designed food safety systems that enable food workers to keep a close check on food items whenever there is a risk of contamination or of the growth of pathogens. In the most effective systems, nothing is left to chance. At each stage of food production and storage, workers refer to written guidelines that explain what to look for and what action to take if the standards are not met. Having a written set of guidelines helps everyone avoid costly mistakes.

THE HACCP SYSTEM

One effective food safety system is called the *Hazard Analysis Critical Control Point* system, or *HACCP*. Versions of this system are being widely adopted throughout the food service industry.

The following discussion is a brief introduction to the basic concepts of HACCP. For a more detailed explanation, you may refer to other published material listed in the Bibliography (pp. 899–900). The discussion below is based on information presented in those books.

The Steps of the HACCP System

The purpose of HACCP is to identify, monitor, and control dangers of food contamination. It is a system of seven steps:

1. Assess hazards.
2. Identify critical control points (CCPs).
3. Set up procedures for critical control points.
4. Monitor critical control points.
5. Take corrective actions.

6. Set up a record-keeping system.
7. Verify that the system is working.

These steps are the basis of the following discussion.

The Flow of Food

HACCP begins with a concept called the *flow of food*. This term refers to the movement of food through a food service operation, from receiving through various stages of storage, preparation, and service, until it gets to the final consumer.

The flow of food is different for each item being prepared. Some menu items involve many steps. For example, a luncheon dish of creamed chicken and vegetables over rice might have the following steps:

Receiving raw ingredients (chicken, vegetables, cream, rice, etc.)
Storing raw ingredients
Preparing ingredients (washing, cutting, trimming, etc.)
Cooking
Holding and serving
Cooling and storing leftovers
Reheating, holding, and storing leftovers

Even the simplest items undergo several steps. For example, a cake that is bought already prepared from a commercial baker and served as dessert will go through at least the following steps on its way to the customer:

Receiving   Storing   Serving

Hazards and Critical Control Points

At each of these steps, as foods flow through the operation, risks can lead to dangerous conditions, which are called *hazards*. These hazards can be divided into three categories:

1. *Contamination,* such as cross-contamination from a soiled cutting surface; torn packaging that permits insect infestation; working on food without washing hands; spilling cleaning chemicals on food.
2. *Growth of bacteria and other pathogens* due to such conditions as inadequate refrigeration or storage, and holding hot foods below 140°F (60°C).
3. *Survival of pathogens or the continued presence of toxins,* usually because of inadequate cooking or heating or inadequate sanitizing of equipment and surfaces.

Note that these hazards correspond to the sanitation techniques discussed on page 16 (keep bacteria from spreading, stop bacteria from growing, kill bacteria). The important difference is that the hazards addressed by HACCP include chemical and other hazards in addition to disease-causing organisms. Naturally, however, most of the hazards we are concerned with are those that affect *potentially hazardous foods* (see p. 15).

At each step where there is a risk of one of these hazards, it is possible to take action that eliminates the hazard or reduces it to a minimum. Such actions are called *critical control points* or CCPs. In simple language, setting up an HACCP system starts with reviewing the flow of food to figure out where something might go wrong, then deciding what can be done about it. In the language of HACCP, these steps are called "assessing the hazards" and "identifying critical control points."

Setting Standards and Following Procedures

The next step in designing an HACCP food safety system is setting up procedures for critical control points. At each critical control point, food workers need to know what standards have to be met, what procedures to follow to meet the standards, and what to do if they aren't met. To reduce the chances for making mistakes, these standards and procedures are written out. Whenever possible, they should be included in the operation's recipes. In Chapter 5, you will see how CCPs are incorporated into a standardized recipe.

Some procedures are general and include the sanitation rules discussed earlier in this chapter. For example: Wash hands before handling food and after handling raw foods; hold foods above 140°F (60°C) or below 41°F (5°C). Others apply to specific items. For example: Roast a particular meat to an internal temperature of at least 165°F (74°C).

Careful observation is needed to know when standards are met. This often involves measuring. The only way to know, for example, that a roast has reached the required internal temperature is to measure it, using a clean, sanitized thermometer.

Managers must ensure that all employees are trained to follow procedures and have the equipment needed to do the job.

Once these procedures are developed, additional steps in setting up an HACCP system are important to ensure that the system is effective: monitoring critical control points, taking corrective action if procedures are not followed, keeping records of all aspects of the system, and verifying that the system is working.

As this brief introduction to HACCP implies, establishing such a system to control all aspects of food production requires more information than this chapter has space for. Refer to the Bibliography for more detailed information.

LEARNING MORE ABOUT FOOD SAFETY

It is important for you to understand that food safety and sanitation is a large and complex topic. The first half of this chapter is only an introduction to the study of food safety. To advance in a food service career, you will be required to demonstrate a detailed knowledge of the subject well beyond what can be presented in such a short space. Entire textbooks are devoted to kitchen sanitation and safety. Many organizations, including local and regional health departments and organizations such as the National Restaurant Association Educational Foundation (in the United States), sponsor training programs leading to certificates of competency in food safety. Cooks in supervisory positions may be required to hold such a certificate. The health and safety of your clientele depends on your diligent study.

Safety

Kitchen work is usually considered a relatively safe occupation, at least in comparison with many industrial jobs. Nevertheless, the kitchen has many hazards. Minor injuries from cuts and burns are very common, and more serious injuries are all too possible. The quantity of very hot equipment and of powerful machinery, combined with the busy, sometimes frantic pace, make it important for everyone to work carefully and with constant attention to rules of safety.

The Safe Workplace

Most of this section is concerned with ways that workers can prevent certain kinds of accidents, such as cuts, burns, and falls. However, it is much easier to develop and practice habits that prevent accidents if safety is built into the workplace.

The management of a food service operation must see to it that the structure and equipment have necessary safety features.

1. Structure, equipment, and electric wiring in good repair.
2. Adequate lighting on work surfaces and in corridors.
3. Nonslip floors.
4. Clearly marked exits.
5. Equipment supplied with necessary safety devices.
6. Heat-activated fire extinguishers over cooking equipment, especially deep fryers.
7. Conveniently located emergency equipment, such as fire extinguishers, fire blankets, and first-aid kits.
8. Clearly posted emergency telephone numbers.
9. Smooth traffic patterns to avoid collisions between workers.

Preventing Cuts

1. Keep knives sharp. A sharp knife is safer than a dull one because it requires less pressure and is less likely to slip.
2. Use a cutting board. Do not cut against a metal surface. Place a damp towel under the board to keep it from slipping.
3. Pay attention to your work when using a knife or cutting equipment.
4. Cut away from yourself and other workers.
5. Use knives only for cutting, not for such jobs as opening bottles.
6. Don't try to catch a falling knife. Step back and let it fall.
7. Don't put knives in a sink, under water, or any place where they can't be seen.
8. Clean knives carefully, with the sharp edge away from you.
9. Store knives in a safe place, such as in a rack, when not in use.
10. Carry knives properly. Hold the knife beside you, point down, with the sharp edge back and away from you. Don't swing your arm. Whenever possible, carry knives in a sheath. Warn people when you are walking past them with a knife in hand.
11. Keep breakable items, such as dishes and glassware, out of the food production area.
12. Don't put breakable items in the pot sink.
13. Sweep up, don't pick up, broken glass.
14. Discard chipped or cracked dishes and glasses.
15. Use special containers for broken dishes and glasses. Don't throw them in with other garbage.
16. If there is broken glass in the sink, drain the sink before trying to take out the glass.
17. Remove all nails and staples when opening crates and cartons, and dispose of them.

Preventing Burns

1. Always assume a pot handle is hot. Don't just grab it with your bare hand.
2. Use dry pads or towels to handle hot pans. Wet ones will create steam, which can burn you.
3. Keep pan handles out of the aisle so people won't bump into them. Also, keep handles away from open flames of gas burners.
4. Don't fill pans so full that they are likely to spill hot foods.
5. Get help when moving heavy containers of hot food.
6. Open lids away from you to let steam escape safely.
7. Use care when opening compartment steamers.
8. Make sure gas is well vented before trying to light ovens or pilot lights. Strike matches before turning on the gas. Also, strike matches away from yourself.
9. Wear long sleeves and a double-breasted jacket to protect yourself from spilled or spattered hot foods or fat. Also, wear sturdy leather shoes with closed toes.
10. Dry foods before putting them in frying fat, or hot fat may splatter on you.
11. When placing foods in hot fat, let them fall away from you so that fat will not splash on you.
12. Keep liquids away from the deep fryer. If a liquid were spilled into the fryer, the suddenly created steam could spray hot fat on anyone nearby.
13. Always warn people when you are walking behind them with hot pans or when you are walking behind someone who is working with hot items.
14. Warn service people about hot plates.

Preventing Fires

1. Know where fire extinguishers are located and how to use them.
2. Use the right kind of fire extinguisher. There are three classes of fires, and fire extinguishers should be labeled according to the kind of fire for which they can be used.
   • Class A fires: wood, paper, cloth, ordinary combustibles.
   • Class B fires: burning liquids, such as grease, oil, gasoline, solvents.
   • Class C fires: switches, motors, electrical equipment, and so forth.

Never use water or a Class A fire extinguisher on a grease fire or electrical fire. You will only spread the fire.

3. Keep a supply of salt or baking soda handy to put out fires on rangetops.
4. Keep hoods and other equipment free from grease buildup.
5. Don't leave hot fat unattended on the range.
6. Smoke only in designated areas. Do not leave burning cigarettes unattended.
7. If a fire alarm sounds and if you have time, turn off all gas and electric appliances before leaving the building.
8. Keep fire doors closed.
9. Keep exits free from obstacles.

Preventing Injuries from Machines and Equipment

1. Do not use any equipment unless you understand its operation.
2. Use all guards and safety devices on equipment. Set slicing machines at zero (blade closed) when not in use.
3. Don't touch or remove food from any kind of equipment while it is running, not even with a spoon or spatula.
4. Unplug electric equipment before disassembling or cleaning.
5. Make sure the switch is off before plugging in equipment.
6. Do not touch or handle electric equipment, including switches, if your hands are wet or if you are standing in water.
7. Wear properly fitting clothing and tuck in apron strings to avoid getting them caught in machinery.
8. Use equipment only for the purpose intended.
9. Stack pots and other equipment properly on pot racks so that they are stable and not likely to fall.

Preventing Falls

1. Clean up spills immediately.
2. Throw salt on a slippery spot to make it less slippery while a mop is being fetched.
3. Keep aisles and stairs clear and unobstructed.
4. Don't carry objects too big to see over.
5. Walk, don't run.
6. Use a safe ladder, not chairs or piles of boxes, to reach high shelves or to clean high equipment.

Preventing Strains and Injuries from Lifting

1. Lift with the leg muscles, not the back. Figure 2.3 shows proper lifting technique.
2. Don't turn or twist the back while lifting, and make sure your footing is secure.
3. Use a cart to move heavy objects long distances, or get help.

Figure 2.3 Proper lifting technique. (a) Squat on one knee, then lift with the leg muscles. (b) Do not bend over and lift with the back.

(a)   (b)

Terms for Review

bacteria	sanitation	trichinosis	flow of food
pathogen	intoxication	Food Danger Zone	hazard
aerobic	infection	cross-contamination	critical control
anaerobic	botulism	sanitize	point
lag phase	staph	physical contamination	Class A, B, and C
potentially hazardous food	salmonella	HACCP	fires

Questions for Discussion

1. True or false: Holding food in a steam table above 140°F (60°C) kills disease-causing bacteria and eliminates the problem of food poisoning. Explain your answer.

2. True or false: Canning foods eliminates air so disease-causing bacteria can't grow. Explain your answer.

3. Which of the following foods can become contaminated by disease-causing organisms?

Chocolate éclairs	Dinner rolls
Potato salad	Shrimp cocktail
Roast beef	After-dinner mints
Lettuce	Saltine crackers
Turkey sandwich	Rice pudding

4. How often should you wash your hands when working on food?

5. Why is temperature control one of the most effective weapons against bacterial growth? What are some important temperatures to remember?

6. What is the importance of cleaning and sanitizing equipment and cutting boards immediately after working on raw poultry?

7. You are making egg salad, and you have just cooked the eggs. What step do you take before chopping the eggs and mixing them with the other ingredients? Why?

8. Is it possible for a dish to be clean but not sanitized? Sanitized but not clean?

9. Explain the concepts of *hazards* and *critical control points*. Give at least three examples of each.

10. What are the three general categories of potentially hazardous foods? Give examples of each category. Give examples of foods that are not potentially hazardous.

11. True or false: The lower limit of the Food Danger Zone is the proper refrigeration temperature for perishable foods. Discuss.

12. What are the seven steps of HACCP?

chapter 3

Tools and Equipment

Thorough knowledge of equipment is essential for success in the kitchen. Few food service operations depend on nothing more than a range and an oven, an assortment of pots and pans, and knives and other hand tools. Modern technology continues to develop more and more specialized and technically advanced tools to reduce kitchen labor.

Much of this equipment is so complex or so sophisticated that only firsthand instruction and practice will teach you how to operate it effectively and safely. Other items, especially hand tools, are simple and need no explanation but require much practice to develop good manual skills.

A vast array of specialized equipment is available for today's kitchens. It would take a large book, not just a short chapter, to explain all of the many items you will come in contact with in your career—items such as pasta machines, crêpe machines, burger formers, breading machines, cookie droppers, beverage machines, Greek gyro broilers, doughnut glazers, conveyor fryers, and so on. In this technological age, nearly every year brings new tools to simplify various tasks.

This chapter introduces you to the most commonly used equipment in food service kitchens. It cannot, in this short space, serve as an operating manual for every model of every machine you will use. It cannot take the place of demonstration by your instructor and of actual experience.

Introduction to Quantity Food Equipment

Before we look at specific items, we must first consider some points relating to the use of equipment in general.

After reading this chapter, you should be able to identify the do's and don'ts associated with the safe and efficient use of standard cooking equipment; processing equipment; holding and storage equipment; measuring devices; and knives, hand tools, and small equipment.

FOOD EQUIPMENT CAN BE DANGEROUS

Modern cooking and food processing equipment has an extraordinary capacity to burn, cut, smash, mangle, and amputate various parts of the tender human body. This may sound like a harsh way to begin a chapter, but the intent is not to intimidate you or scare you but to inspire a healthy respect for the importance of proper safety and operating procedures.

Never use a piece of equipment until you are thoroughly familiar with its operation and all its features. You must also learn how to know when a machine is not operating correctly. When this happens, shut it down immediately and report the malfunction to a supervisor.

NOT ALL MODELS ARE ALIKE

Each manufacturer introduces slight variations on the basic equipment. While all convection ovens operate on the same basic principles, each model is slightly different, if only in the location of the switches. It is important to study the operating manual supplied with each item or to be broken in by someone who already knows that item well and has operated it.

CLEANING IS PART OF THE OPERATING PROCEDURE

Thorough, regular cleaning of all equipment is essential. Most large equipment can be partially disassembled for cleaning. Again, every model is slightly different. Operating manuals should describe these procedures in detail. If a manual is not available, you must get the information from someone who knows the equipment.

CONSERVE ENERGY

At one time, it was standard procedure for the chef to turn on the ovens and ranges first thing in the day and keep them on all day. Today, high energy costs have made such practices very expensive. Fortunately, modern equipment takes less time to heat.

Know the preheating time for all your cooking equipment so you don't need to turn it on before it's necessary. Plan production so that equipment that requires a lot of energy is not on for long periods when not in use.

YOUR HANDS ARE YOUR BEST TOOLS

Machines are intended to be laborsaving devices. However, the usefulness of specialized processing equipment often depends on the volume of food it handles. It takes less time for a cook to slice a few pounds of onions by hand than to set up a slicing attachment, pass the onions through it, and break down and clean the equipment. This is why it is so important to develop good manual skills.

Cooking Equipment

RANGETOPS

The range is still the most important piece of cooking equipment in the kitchen, even though many of its functions have been taken over by other tools, such as steamers, steam kettles, tilting skillets, and ovens.

Types of Cooktops

1. *Open elements* (burners), either electric coils or gas flames. These tops are the fastest to heat and can be turned off after short use. However, cooktop space is limited to one pot per burner.

2. *Flattop* or *hot top* (lightweight). Burners covered with steel plate. More cook space is available. Top will support moderately heavy weights.

3. *Heavy-duty flattop.* Burners covered with heavy cast steel. The top will support many heavy pots. A thick top requires longer preheating. Set burners for different levels, and adjust cooking heat by moving pots to different spots on the top.

4. *Induction cooktops.* A fairly new type of rangetop, the induction cooktop is slowly making its way into commercial kitchens. This equipment does not become hot itself. Rather, it works by magnetically agitating the molecules in steel or iron cookware so that the cookware becomes hot. As a result, much less energy is used and the kitchen stays cooler, because only the pots and pans and their contents become hot. There are no hot surfaces or open flames. Also, no warm-up is required. The top can be turned instantly on or off.

   The disadvantage of this cooktop is that only iron or steel pots can be used. Traditional aluminum or copper cookware will not work. Some manufacturers of cookware have responded to the new demand by producing pots and pans made of aluminum sandwiched between layers of stainless steel. In this way, the good heat-conducting qualities of aluminum are preserved as well as adapted to this new technology.

Do's and Don'ts

1. Make sure gas pilots are lit before turning on burners. If burners do not light, turn off gas and allow the gas to ventilate before trying again to light pilots or burners.

2. Adjust air intake so that gas flames are blue with a white tip for maximum heat.

3. Do not keep flattop ranges on high heat unless items are being cooked over them. Damage to tops could result.

Open burner-gas range with griddle
Courtesy of Vulcan Hart Company.

Flattop range
Courtesy of Vulcan Hart Company.

OVENS

The oven and the rangetop are the two workhorses of the traditional kitchen, which is why the two are so often found in the same unit. Ovens are enclosed spaces in which food is heated, usually by hot air or, in some newer kinds of ovens, by microwaves or infrared radiation.

In addition to roasting and baking, ovens can do many of the jobs normally done on the rangetop. Many foods can be simmered, stewed, braised, or poached in the oven, freeing the rangetop and the chef's attention for other tasks.

There are many kinds of ovens beyond those discussed here, but they are often for specialty or high-volume uses. These include *conveyor ovens*, which carry foods through the oven on a steel conveyor belt; *holding ovens* or *warmers*, which are designed to hold many types of foods at serving temperatures for extended periods without drying out or overcooking (this category includes ovens that also cook the food, then automatically switch to holding temperature); and high-volume *roll-in ovens*, with large doors into which one can roll carts loaded with trays of food.

Conventional Ovens

Conventional ovens operate simply by heating air in an enclosed space. The most common ovens are part of the range unit, although separate oven units or ovens as part of a broiler unit are also available. *Stack ovens* are units that consist of individual shelves or decks arranged one above the other. Pans are placed directly on the oven deck rather than on wire shelves. Temperatures are adjustable for each deck.

Stack or deck ovens
Courtesy of Blodgett.

Do's and Don'ts

Many of these points apply to other types of ovens as well.

1. Preheat ovens thoroughly, but no longer than necessary, to avoid excess energy use.

2. To avoid high energy loss and interruption of cooking, do not open the door any more often than necessary.

3. Space items well to allow for heat circulation.

4. Be sure the pilot light is on before turning on gas ovens.

Convection Ovens

Convection ovens contain fans that circulate the air and distribute the heat rapidly throughout the interior. Because of the forced air, foods cook more quickly at lower temperatures. Also, shelves can be placed closer together than in conventional ovens without blocking the heat flow.

Do's and Don'ts

1. For most products, set the temperature 25°F to 50°F (15°C to 30°C) lower than for conventional ovens. Check manufacturer's recommendations.

2. Watch cooking times closely. The forced heat cooks more quickly and tends to dry out some foods excessively if they are overcooked. Roasts shrink more than they do in conventional ovens.

3. Many convection oven models should not be operated with the blower switch off, as the motor may burn out.

4. The forced air of a convection oven may deform some soft items. Cake batters, for example, develop ripples. Check manufacturer's recommendations.

Convection oven
Courtesy of Vulcan Hart Company.

Revolving Ovens

Revolving ovens, also called *reel ovens*, are large chambers containing many shelves or trays on an attachment like a Ferris wheel. This oven eliminates the problem of hot spots or uneven baking because the mechanism rotates the foods throughout the oven.

Revolving ovens are used in bakeshops and in high-volume operations.

Slow-Cook-and-Hold Ovens

While the traditional oven is nothing more than a heated box equipped with a thermostat, some modern ovens have more sophisticated features, such as computerized electronic controls and special probes that sense when a roast is done and tell the oven to switch from cooking temperature to holding temperature.

Many of these ovens are designed to be especially useful for low-temperature roasting (see p. 240). The sensitive controls make it possible to cook at steady, reliable temperatures of 200°F (95°C) or lower and to hold foods at 140°F (60°C) for long periods. Large cuts of meat take many hours to roast at a low temperature like 200°F (95°C). By setting the controls in advance, the operator can even let meats roast overnight, unattended.

These ovens are available as convection ovens and as regular stationary-air ovens.

Combination Steamer Ovens

The combination steamer oven, also called a *combi oven*, is a relatively new kind that can be operated in three modes: as a convection oven, as a convection steamer (see p. 38), and, with both functions on at once, as a high-humidity oven. Injecting moisture into an oven while roasting meats can help to reduce shrinkage and drying.

Combination steamer oven
Courtesy of Vulcan Hart Company.

Barbecue Ovens or Smoke Ovens

Barbecue ovens are like conventional ovens, but with one important difference: They are able to produce wood smoke, which surrounds the food and adds flavor while it bakes or roasts. Special woods, such as hickory, mesquite, or fruit woods such as apple or cherry, must be added to the smoke-producing part of the oven according to the manufacturer's instructions. This device is usually nothing more complicated than an electric heating element that heats small blocks or chips of the wood so that they are hot enough to smoke but not hot enough to burst into flame.

Depending on the model, various cooking features are available. Thus, ovens may have smokeless roast/bake cycles, cold-smoke cycles (with the smoke element on but the oven off), holding cycles, and broiling capabilities.

Microwave oven
Photo courtesy of Hobart Corporation.

Infrared or Reconstituting Ovens

Infrared units contain quartz tubes or plates that generate intense infrared heat. These ovens are used primarily for reconstituting frozen foods. They bring large quantities of foods to serving temperature in a short time. The heat is even and controllable.

Microwave Ovens

In these ovens, special tubes generate microwave radiation, which creates heat inside the food. Microwave cooking is discussed in detail in Chapter 4.

BROILERS AND SALAMANDERS

Broilers are sometimes called *overhead broilers* to avoid confusing them with grills. Overhead broilers generate heat from above, and food items are placed on a grate

Heavy-duty broiler
Courtesy of Vulcan Hart Company.

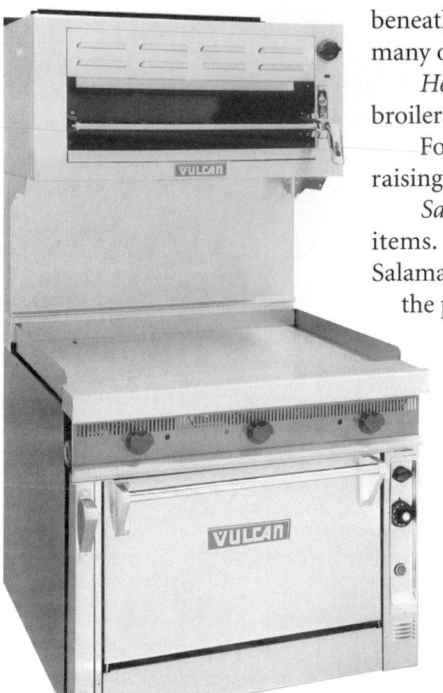

Salamander (above range)
Courtesy of Vulcan Hart Company.

Gas grill
Courtesy of Vulcan Hart Company.

beneath the heat source. Broiling is a favorite way of preparing steaks, chops, chicken, and many other items.

Heavy-duty broilers produce very high heat and consume vast quantities of energy. Some broilers are said to go as high as 2000°F (1100°C) at the burner.

Foods must be watched closely to avoid burning. Cooking temperature is adjusted by raising or lowering the grate that holds the food.

Salamanders are small broilers used primarily for browning or glazing the tops of some items. They may also be used for broiling small quantities during off-peak hours. Salamanders are usually mounted above the range, as illustrated in the photo. In addition, the photo of an open-burner gas range on page 33 shows a salamander under the griddle.

GRILLS

Grills are used for the same cooking operations as broilers except the heat source is below the grid that holds the food rather than above it. Many people like grilled foods because of their charcoal taste, which is created by smoke from meat fats that drip into the heat source.

Although smoke from meat fats creates the taste that people associate with grilled foods, actual wood smoke flavors, such as hickory or mesquite, can be added to foods if those woods are burned in the grill under the food. In order to do this, you must use a grill designed to burn such fuels.

Types

Many grill models are in use. The major differences in operation among them are due to the difference in heat source—gas, electricity, or charcoal.

To operate, set areas of the grill to different temperatures and place foods in the areas with the appropriate cooking temperature. Keep grills clean, as the high temperatures can easily start grease fires.

GRIDDLES

Griddles are flat, smooth, heated surfaces on which food is cooked directly. Pancakes, French toast, hamburgers and other meats, eggs, and potato items are the foods most frequently cooked on a griddle. Griddles are available as separate units or as part of a rangetop (p. 33).

Clean griddle surfaces after every use so that they will cook at peak efficiency. Polish with a griddle stone or griddle cloth until the surface shines. Follow the grain of the metal to avoid scratching.

Condition griddles after each cleaning or before each use to create a nonstick surface and to prevent rusting. Procedure: Spread a thin film of oil over the surface and heat to 400°F (200°C). Wipe clean and repeat until griddle has a smooth, nonstick finish.

ROTISSERIES

Rotisserie broilers cook meats and other foods by turning them slowly in front of electric- or gas-powered heating elements. Even though classical cooking theory categorizes spit-cooking as roasting, these cookers are more closely related to broilers in that the foods are cooked by the infrared heat of the elements.

Although they are especially suitable for chicken and other poultry, rotisseries can be used to cook any meat that can be fastened to a spit.

Both enclosed (ovenlike) rotisseries and open or unclosed units are available. Small units hold about 8 chickens, and sizes range all the way to very large models that can hold as many as 70 chickens.

Because the heating elements are on the side (or sometimes above), the fats and juices don't drip into the flames as they do with grills. Drip pans catch juices, which can be used for basting or gravy making.

DEEP FRYERS

A deep fryer has only one use—to cook foods in hot fat. Yet because of the popularity of fried foods, this function is an important one.

Standard deep fryers are powered by either gas or electricity and have thermostatic controls that maintain fat at preset temperatures.

Automatic fryers remove food from the fat automatically after a preset time.

Pressure fryers are covered fry kettles that fry foods under pressure. Foods cook faster, even at a lower fat temperature.

Do's and Don'ts

Frying procedures and the care of frying fat are discussed in detail in Chapter 4. The following points relate to the operation of the equipment.

1. When filling kettles with solid fats, set the thermostat at 250°F (120°C) until the fat has melted enough to cover the heating elements.
2. Keep kettles filled to the fill line.
3. Make sure the drain valve is shut before adding fat to the empty kettle.
4. Check the accuracy of the thermostat regularly by reading the fat temperature with a thermometer.

Deep fryers
Courtesy of Vulcan Hart Company.

Cleaning

Cleaning procedures differ greatly depending on the model. Here is a general procedure.

1. Shut off the power.
2. Drain the fat through a filter into a dry container (unless you are discarding it). Be sure the container is large enough to hold all the fat before you start.
3. Flush food particles from sides and bottom of kettle with some of the hot fat.
4. Wash the kettle with a mild detergent solution. If the kettle is not removable, turn on fryer and bring the detergent solution almost to a boil (beware of foaming over). Scrub with a stiff brush.
5. Drain and rinse thoroughly with clean water.
6. Dry the kettle, heating elements, and baskets thoroughly.
7. Refill with strained or fresh fat.

TILTING SKILLET

The tilting skillet, also known as the *tilting brazier* and *tilting fry pan*, is a versatile and efficient piece of equipment. It can be used as a griddle, fry pan, brazier, stewpot, stockpot, steamer, and bain-marie or steam table.

The tilting skillet is a large, shallow, flat-bottomed pot. Or, to look at it another way, it is a griddle with 6-inch-high sides and a cover. It has a tilting mechanism that enables liquids to be poured out of it. Power may be gas or electric.

Clean the skillet immediately after each use, before food has time to dry on. Add water, turn on the skillet to heat it, and scrub thoroughly.

Tilting skillet
Courtesy of Vulcan Hart Company.

STEAM-JACKETED KETTLES

Steam-jacketed kettles, or steam kettles, are sometimes thought of as stockpots that are heated not just on the bottom but on the sides as well. This comparison is only partly accurate. Steam kettles heat much more quickly and have more uniform and controllable heat than pots on the range.

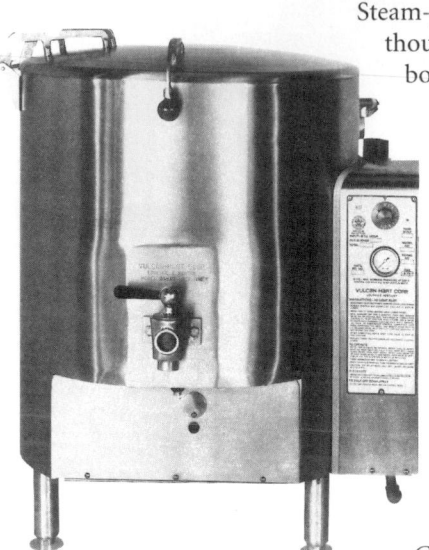

Types

Steam kettles range in capacity from 2 gallons to over 100 gallons. Some large institutional kettles hold 4000 gallons. *Tilt* or *trunnion kettles* can be tilted for emptying, either by turning a wheel or by pulling a lever. *Nontilt* kettles are emptied by a spigot and drain on the bottom. Heat is controlled by regulating the steam flow or by adjusting the thermostat. Steam may be from an outside source or self-generated.

Exercise caution when operating all steam equipment. Steam can cause serious burns.

Clean immediately after use to avoid drying on food, as for tilting skillets. Disassemble spigot and drain, and clean with a bottle brush.

Small tilt (trunnion) kettle
Courtesy of Vulcan Hart Company.

Large floor-model steam kettle
Courtesy of Vulcan Hart Company.

STEAM COOKERS

Steam cookers are ideal for cooking vegetables and many other foods rapidly and with minimum loss of nutrients and flavor. For this reason, they are becoming more common in both large and small kitchens.

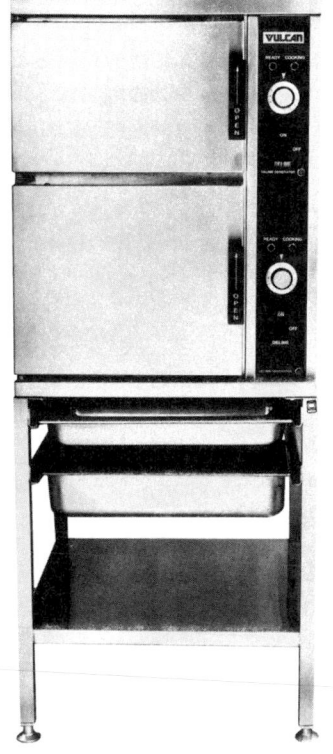

Types

Pressure steamers cook foods under a pressure of 15 pounds per square inch (high-pressure steamers) or 4 to 6 pounds per square inch (low-pressure steamers). They are operated by a timer, which shuts the equipment off after a preset time. The door cannot be opened until the pressure returns to zero.

Pressureless or *convection steamers* do not operate under pressure. Jets of steam are directed at the food to speed the heat transfer, just as the fan in a convection oven speeds cooking. The door can be opened any time during cooking.

All steamers hold standard-size counter pans (12 × 20 inches) or fractions thereof. Their capacity varies from one to many pans.

Operation of steamers varies greatly, depending on the model. Check operating manuals and be sure you understand a particular model well before attempting to operate it.

Caution is important with all steam equipment because of the danger of severe burns.

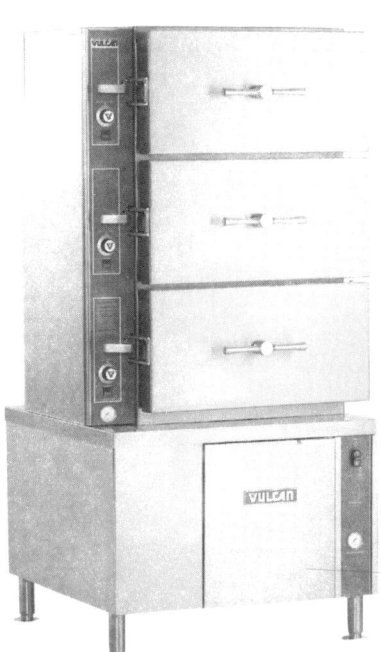

Pressure steamer
Courtesy of Vulcan Hart Company.

Convection steamer
Courtesy of Vulcan Hart Company.

Processing Equipment

MIXERS

Vertical mixers are important and versatile tools for many kinds of food mixing and processing jobs, both in the bakeshop and in the kitchen.

Types

Bench-model mixers range in capacity from 5 to 20 quarts. Floor models are available as large as 140 quarts. Adaptor rings enable several sizes of bowls to be used on one machine. Most mixers have three operating speeds.

Agitator Attachments

There are three main mixing attachments, plus some specialized ones. The *paddle* is a flat blade used for general mixing. The *wire whip* is used for such tasks as beating cream and eggs and making mayonnaise. The *dough arm* is used for mixing and kneading yeast doughs.

Small table-model mixer
Photo courtesy of Hobart Corporation.

Large floor-model mixer
Photo courtesy of Hobart Corporation.

 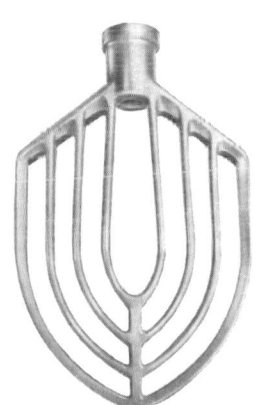 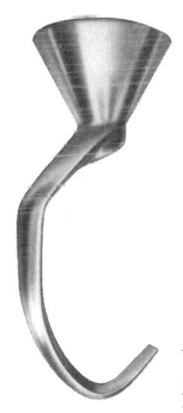

*Mixer attachments:
(left) whip, (center) paddle, (right) dough arm*
Photos courtesy of Hobart Corporation.

Do's and Don'ts

1. Make sure bowl and mixing attachment are firmly in place before turning on machine.
2. Make sure you are using the right size attachment for the bowl. Using a 40-quart paddle with a 30-quart bowl could cause serious damage. Sizes in quarts are marked on the sides of large bowls and on the tops of attachments.
3. Turn off machine before scraping down the bowl or inserting a spoon, scraper, or hand into the bowl. Mixer motors are powerful and can cause serious injury.
4. Turn off machine before changing speeds.

FOOD CUTTER

Food chopper
Photo courtesy of Hobart
Corporation.

The food cutter or food chopper, familiarly known as the *buffalo chopper*, is a common piece of equipment used for general food chopping. A variety of attachments (described in the next section) makes it a versatile tool.

General Operation

Food is placed in a rotating bowl, which carries the food to a pair of knives that are spinning rapidly under a cover. The fineness of the cut depends on how long the food is left in the machine.

Do's and Don'ts

1. Always make sure the machine is completely assembled before use.
2. The cover lock knob must be closed before the machine can be turned on.
3. Never try to reach under the bowl cover while the machine is running.
4. For uniform chopping, place the food in the bowl all at one time.
5. Keep the knives sharp. Dull knives will bruise food rather than cut it cleanly.

ATTACHMENTS FOR MIXERS AND FOOD CHOPPERS

The following are the most common of the many attachments designed to fit both the food chopper and the vertical mixer.

*Grinder attachment
(on separate motor)*
Photo courtesy of Hobart
Corporation.

1. The *food grinder* is used mostly for grinding meats, although other moist foods may be ground also. Food is forced through a feed tube into a screw, which pushes the food through holes in a plate, where it is cut by a rotating blade. The size of the holes regulates the fineness of the grind.

   Make sure the rotating blade is attached properly, cutting edge out, when assembling the grinder.

2. The *slicer/shredder* consists of a hopper and a lever that feeds the food onto a rotating disk or plate. The plate cuts or shreds the food and drops it into a receiving container. The slicing plate may be adjusted to cut various thicknesses.

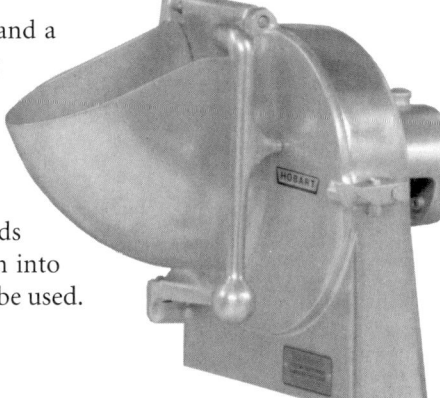

3. The *dicer* attachment forces foods through a grid-type blade that cuts them into perfect dice. Blades of different sizes may be used.

SLICER

The slicer is a valuable machine because it slices foods more evenly and uniformly than can be done by hand. Thus it is valuable for portion control and for reducing cutting loss.

Slicer/shredder attachment
Photo courtesy of Hobart Corporation.

Types

Most modern slicers have blades set at an angle. Slices fall away from these blades with less breaking and folding than from vertical blades.

With manual machines, the operator must move the carriage back and forth to slice the food. Automatic machines move the carriage with an electric motor.

Slicer
Photo courtesy of Hobart
Corporation.

Do's and Don'ts

1. Be sure the machine is properly assembled before using.
2. Always use the end weight to press the food against the blade. This protects the hand from serious cuts and provides a more even pressure on the food, resulting in more uniform slices.
3. Set the thickness control knob at zero when the machine is not in use or is being cleaned.
4. Always unplug the machine before dismantling and cleaning.
5. Keep the blade sharp with the sharpening stones provided with the slicer.

VERTICAL CUTTER/MIXER AND FOOD PROCESSOR

The vertical cutter/mixer (VCM) is like a large, powerful, high-speed blender. It is used to chop and mix large quantities of foods very rapidly. It can also be used for puréeing (soups, for example) and for mixing liquids.

Types

VCMs range in size from 15 to 80 quarts. The small models have a hand-operated mixing baffle, which moves the foods into the blades. Larger machines have automatic baffles.

Food processors, like the ones popular today in home kitchens, actually were used in commercial kitchens, especially in Europe, years before the home models were introduced. The professional models are 2 to 4 times larger than the home models. Because they are much smaller than VCMs, they are not well suited to high-volume work. Instead, they are mostly used for specialized tasks, such as puréeing raw meats and fish for delicate pâtés and mousses.

Do's and Don'ts

1. Watch processing times closely. Chopping times are very short, so an extra second can make cabbage soup out of coleslaw.
2. Make sure the machine is properly assembled before use.
3. After turning the machine off, allow the blades to come to a full stop before opening the cover.
4. Keep the blades sharp. Dull blades bruise food.

Food processor
Photo courtesy of Hobart Corporation.

Holding and Storage Equipment

HOT FOOD HOLDING EQUIPMENT

Several types of equipment are used to keep food hot for service. This equipment is designed to hold foods above 140°F (60°C) in order to prevent the growth of bacteria that can cause disease. Because food continues to cook at these temperatures, it should be held for as short a time as possible.

1. *Steam tables* are standard holding equipment for serving lines. Standard-size counter pans or hotel pans are used as inserts to hold the foods. Flat or domed covers may be used to cover the foods.

    Check water levels in steam tables periodically to make sure they don't go dry. (Electrically heated counters that operate dry—without steam—are also available.)

2. A *bain-marie* is a hot-water bath. Containers of foods are set on a rack in a shallow container of water, which is heated by electricity, gas, or steam. The bain-marie is used more in the production area, while the steam table is used in the service area.

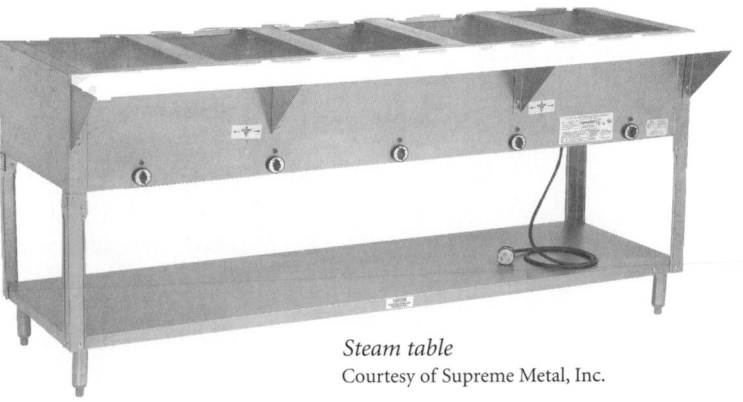

Steam table
Courtesy of Supreme Metal, Inc.

3. *Overhead infrared lamps* are used in service areas to keep plated food warm before it is picked up by the service staff. They are also used for keeping large roasts warm.

    Foods dry out quickly under holding lamps. This is a disadvantage for almost all foods except for French fries and other deep-fried foods, which lose their crispness if they are kept moist.

COLD FOOD STORAGE EQUIPMENT

The quality of the food you serve depends to a great degree on refrigeration equipment. By keeping foods cold, usually below 41°F (5°C), the refrigerator (known in the trade as the "cooler" or the "box") guards against spoilage and bacterial growth.

Freezers are used to hold foods for longer times, or to store foods purchased in frozen form.

There are so many sizes, models, and designs of refrigeration equipment that it would be futile to try to describe them all here.

To enable refrigerators and freezers to work at top efficiency, observe the following rules:

1. Place items far enough apart and away from the inside walls of refrigerators so that cold air can circulate. Freezers, on the other hand, work most efficiently when they are full.

2. Keep the door closed as much as possible. When storing or removing an item, do it quickly and shut the door.

3. Keep stored foods well wrapped or covered to prevent drying and transfer of odors. (Meats are an exception to this rule; see p. 236.)

4. Keep refrigerators spotlessly clean.

Pots, Pans, and Containers

METALS AND CONDUCTIVITY

A good cooking utensil distributes heat evenly and uniformly. If it does not, it will develop hot spots that are likely to burn or scorch the food being cooked. Two factors affect a pan's ability to cook evenly:

1. *Thickness of the metal.* A heavy-gauge pot cooks more evenly than one made of thin metal. Thickness is most important on the bottom.

2. *Kind of metal.* Different metals have different conductivity, which means the speed at which they transfer heat. The following materials are used for cooking equipment:

    • *Aluminum* is used for most cooking utensils in food service kitchens. It is a very good conductor, and its light weight makes pots and pans easy to handle. Because it is a relatively soft metal, it should not be banged around or abused.

       Do not use aluminum for storage or for long cooking of strong acids because it reacts chemically with many foods. Also, it tends to discolor light-colored foods such as sauces, especially if they are stirred or beaten with a metal spoon or whip.

       Pans made of *anodized aluminum*, sold under such brand names as Calphalon, have surfaces that are harder and more corrosion-resistant than regular aluminum pans do. Although this is not, strictly speaking, a nonstick finish, it is less porous than untreated aluminum, so foods are less likely to stick. Also, it is more resistant to acids than regular aluminum, and it will not discolor light-colored foods. Its disadvantages are that it is more expensive and not quite as durable as standard aluminum.

    • *Copper* is the best heat conductor of all and was once widely used for cooking utensils. However, it is extremely expensive and requires a great deal of care. Also it is very heavy. Today it is used mostly for show.

       Copper reacts chemically with many foods to create poisonous compounds, so copper pans must be lined with another metal, such as tin or stainless steel.

- *Stainless steel* is a poor heat conductor. Cooking pots and pans made of it tend to scorch foods easily. Stainless steel is ideal for storage containers because it will not react with foods as aluminum does. It is also used for low-temperature cooking or holding equipment, such as steamer pans and counter pans, where scorching or hot spots are not a problem.

  Stainless-steel pots and pans are also available with a heavy layer of copper or aluminum bonded to the bottom. Heavy aluminum pans may also be lined with stainless steel on the inside, or on both the inside and outside. This feature gives the advantages of stainless steel (its hardness, durability, nonreactivity with acid foods, and nondiscoloration of light sauces) with the heat-conducting qualities of copper or aluminum. These pans are usually expensive.

- *Cast iron* is a favorite material with many chefs because of its ability to distribute heat evenly and to maintain high temperatures for long periods. It is used in griddles and heavy skillets. Cast-iron cracks easily if dropped. It rusts quickly unless kept properly conditioned and dry (see p. 619 for conditioning pans).

- *Porcelain enamel-lined pans* should not be used. In fact, they are forbidden by some health departments. They scratch and chip easily, providing good hiding places for bacteria. Also, certain kinds of gray enamel can cause food poisoning if chipped.

- *Nonstick plastic-type coatings*, known by brand names including Teflon and Silverstone, provide a slippery finish, but one that requires a lot of care because it is easily scratched. Do not use metal spoons or spatulas with this equipment. Many chefs keep a set of nonstick egg pans and use them for no other purpose.

  Because more customers are requesting low-fat foods, nonstick coatings are increasing in popularity. They enable cooks to sauté foods with little or no fat.

- *Glass* and *earthenware* have limited use in commercial kitchens because they are very breakable. They are poor conductors of heat but are resistant to corrosion and food acids.

POTS AND PANS AND THEIR USES

1. **Stockpot.**
   A large, deep, straight-sided pot for preparing stocks and simmering large quantities of liquids. Stockpots with spigots allow liquid to be drained off without disturbing the solid contents or lifting the pot. Sizes: 8 to 200 quarts (or liters).

2. **Saucepot.**
   Round pot of medium depth. Similar to a stockpot but shallower, making stirring or mixing easier. Used for soups, sauces, and other liquids. Sizes: 6 to 60 quarts (or liters).

3. **Brazier.**
   Round, broad, shallow, heavy-duty pot with straight sides. Used for browning, braising, and stewing meats. Sizes: 11 to 30 quarts (or liters).

4. **Saucepan.**
   Similar to a small, shallow, light saucepot, but with one long handle instead of two loop handles. May have straight or slanted sides. Used for general range-top cooking. Sizes: 1½ to 15 quarts (or liters).

5. **Sauté pan, straight-sided.**
   Similar to a shallow, straight-sided saucepan, but heavier. Used for browning, sautéing, and frying. Because of its broad surface area, the sauté pan is used for cooking sauces and other liquids when rapid reduction is required. Sizes: 2½ to 5 inches (65 to 130 mm) deep; 6 to 16 inches (160 to 400 mm) in diameter.

6. **Sauté pan, slope-sided.**
   Also called *fry pan*. Used for general sautéing and frying of meats, fish, vegetables, and eggs. The sloping sides allow the cook to flip and toss items without using a spatula, and they make it easier to get at the food when a spatula is used. Sizes: 6 to 14 inches (160 to 360 mm) top diameter.

Stockpot

Stockpot with spigot

Saucepot

Brazier

Saucepan

Straight-sided sauté pan

Slope-sided sauté pan

Cast-iron skillet

Sheet pan

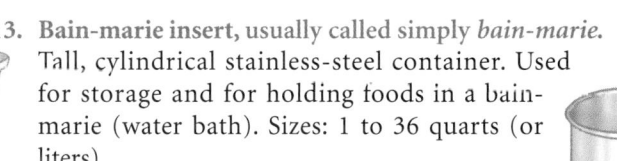

Bake pan

Roasting pan

Hotel pan

7. **Cast-iron skillet.**
Very heavy, thick-bottomed fry pan. Used for pan frying when very steady, even heat is desired.

8. **Double boiler.**
Lower section, similar to a stockpot, holds boiling water. Upper section holds foods that must be cooked at low temperatures and cannot be cooked over direct heat. Size of top section: 4 to 36 quarts (or liters).

9. **Sheet pan or bun pan.**
Shallow rectangular pan (1 inch/25 mm deep) for baking cakes, rolls, and cookies, and for baking or broiling certain meats and fish. Sizes: full pan, 18 × 26 inches (46 × 66 cm); half pan, 18 ×13 inches (46 × 33 cm)

10. **Bake pan.**
Rectangular pan about 2 inches (50 mm) deep. Used for general baking. Comes in a variety of sizes.

11. **Roasting pan.**
Large rectangular pan, deeper and heavier than bake pan. Used for roasting meats and poultry.

12. **Hotel pan,** also called **counter pan, steam table pan,** or **service pan.**
Rectangular pans, usually made of stainless steel. Designed to hold foods in service counters. Also used for baking and steaming, and foods can then be served from same pan. Also used for storage. Standard size: 12 × 20 inches. Fractions of this size (½, ⅓, etc.) are also available. Standard depth: 2½ inches (65 mm). Deeper sizes are also available. (Standard metric pan is 325 × 530 mm.)

13. **Bain-marie insert,** usually called simply *bain-marie.*
Tall, cylindrical stainless-steel container. Used for storage and for holding foods in a bain-marie (water bath). Sizes: 1 to 36 quarts (or liters).

14. **Stainless-steel bowl.**
Round-bottomed bowl. Used for mixing and whipping and for production of hollandaise, mayonnaise, whipped cream, and egg white foams. Round construction enables whip to reach all areas. Comes in many sizes.

Double boiler

Bain-marie inserts

Measuring Devices

The following equipment is discussed in terms of U.S. measurements. Comparable items in metric units are also available.

1. *Scales.* Most recipe ingredients are measured by weight, so accurate scales are very important. *Portion scales* are used for measuring ingredients as well as for portioning products for service. The baker's *balance scale* is discussed in Chapter 26.

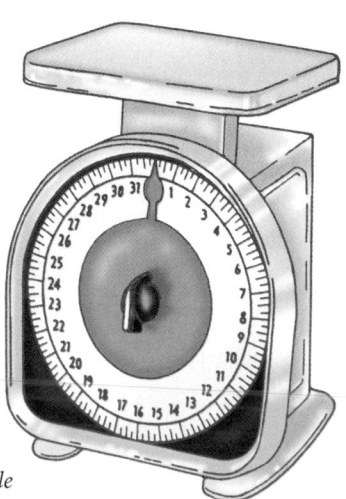

Portion scale

TABLE 3.1

Scoop Sizes

Scoop Number	U.S. Measure		Metric Measure	
	Volume	Approximate Weight	Volume	Approximate Weight
6	⅔ cup	5 oz	160 mL	140 g
8	½ cup	4 oz	120 mL	110 g
10	3 fl. oz	3–3½ oz	90 mL	85–100 g
12	⅓ cup	2½–3 oz	80 mL	70–85 g
16	¼ cup	2–2½ oz	60 mL	60–70 g
20	1½ fl. oz	1¾ oz	45 mL	50 g
24	1⅓ fl. oz	1⅓ oz	40 mL	40 g
30	1 fl. oz	1 oz	30 mL	30 g
40	0.8 fl. oz	0.8 oz	24 mL	23 g
60	½ fl. oz	½ oz	15 mL	15 g

Note: Weights vary greatly with different foods, depending on how compact they are. Best practice is to weigh a spoonful of an item before proceeding with portioning.

Liquid volume measure

2. *Volume measures* used for liquids have lips for easy pouring. Sizes are pints, quarts, half gallons, and gallons. Each size is marked off into fourths by ridges on the sides.

3. *Measuring cups* are available in 1-, ½-, ⅓-, and ¼-cup sizes. They can be used for both liquid and dry measures.

4. *Measuring spoons* are used for measuring very small volumes: 1 tablespoon, 1 teaspoon, ½ teaspoon, and ¼ teaspoon. They are used most often for spices and seasonings.

5. *Ladles* are used for measuring and portioning liquids. The size, in ounces, is stamped on the handle.

6. *Scoops* come in standard sizes and have a lever for mechanical release. They are used for portioning soft solid foods. Scoop sizes are listed in Table 3.1. The number of the scoop indicates the number of level scoopfuls per quart (or liter). In actual use, a rounded scoopful is often more practical, so exact weights will vary.

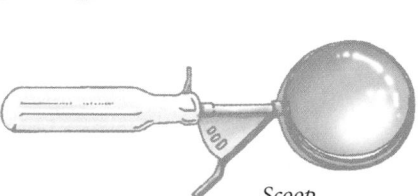

Ladles

7. *Thermometers* measure temperatures. There are many kinds for many purposes.

- A *meat thermometer* indicates internal temperature of meats. It is inserted before cooking and left in the product during cooking.

- An *instant-read thermometer* gives readings within a few seconds of being inserted in a food product. It reads from 0°F to 220°F. Many chefs carry these in their jacket pockets like a pen, ready whenever needed. Instant-read thermometers must not be left in meats during roasting or they will be damaged.

- *Fat thermometers* and *candy thermometers* test temperatures of frying fats and sugar syrups. They read up to 400°F.

- Special thermometers are used to test the accuracy of oven, refrigerator, and freezer thermostats.

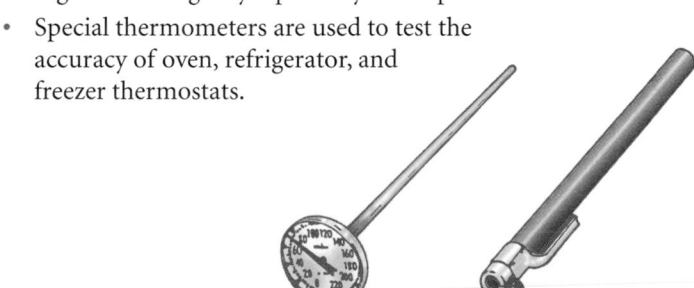

Instant-read thermometers

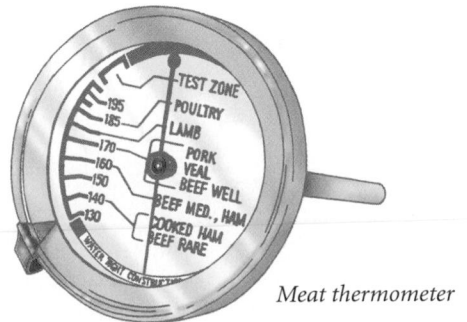

Scoop

Meat thermometer

Knives, Hand Tools, and Small Equipment

KNIFE MATERIALS

The metal that a knife blade is made of is an important consideration, as the metal must be able to take and hold a very fine edge.

1. *Carbon steel* was for many years the traditional favorite because it can be honed to an extremely sharp edge. Its disadvantages are that it corrodes and discolors easily, especially when used with acid foods and onions. Also, it discolors some foods (such as hard-cooked eggs) and may leave a metallic taste. Because of these disadvantages, it has given way to another material, high-carbon stainless steel (described in item 3 below), which is now the preferred material for the best knives.

2. *Traditional stainless-steel alloys* will not rust or corrode, but they are much harder to sharpen than carbon steel. Stainless steel is used mostly for low-cost, lightweight knives.

3. *High-carbon stainless steel* is a relatively new alloy that combines the best aspects of carbon steel and stainless steel. It takes an edge almost as well as carbon steel, and it will not rust, corrode, or discolor. Knives made of this material are highly prized and relatively expensive.

KNIFE HANDLES

The *tang* is the portion of the metal blade that is inside the handle. The highest-quality, most durable knives have a *full tang*, which means that the tang runs the *full length* of the handle.

KNIVES AND THEIR USES

French knife or chef's knife

1. **French knife or chef's knife.**
   Most frequently used knife in the kitchen, for general-purpose chopping, slicing, dicing, and so on. Blade is wide at the heel and tapers to a point. Blade length of 10 inches (260 mm) is most popular for general work. Larger knives are for heavy cutting and chopping. Smaller blades are for more delicate work.
   This is your most important tool, so you must learn to handle it and care for it well. Chapter 7 explains its use in detail.

Utility knife

2. **Utility knife or salad knife.**
   Narrow, pointed knife 6 to 8 inches (160 to 200 mm) long. Used mostly for pantry work, cutting and preparing lettuce, fruits, and so on. Also useful for carving roast chicken and duck.

Paring knife

3. **Paring knife.**
   Small pointed blade 2 to 4 inches (50 to 100 mm) long. Used for trimming and paring vegetables and fruits.

Boning knife

4. **Boning knife.**
   Thin, pointed blade about 6 inches (160 mm) long. Used for boning raw meats and poultry. Stiff blades are used for heavier work. Flexible blades are used for lighter work and for filleting fish.

Slicer

5. **Slicer.**
   Long, slender, flexible blade up to 14 inches (360 mm) long. Used for carving and slicing cooked meats.

6. **Serrated slicer.**
   Like a slicer, but with serrated edge. Used for cutting breads, cakes, and similar items.

Serrated slicer

7. **Butcher knife.**
   Heavy, broad, slightly curved blade. Used for cutting, sectioning, and trimming raw meats in the butcher shop.

Butcher knife

8. **Scimitar** or **steak knife.**
   Curved, pointed blade. Used for accurate cutting of steaks.

Scimitar

9. **Cleaver.**
   Very heavy, broad blade. Used for cutting through bones.

10. **Oyster knife.**
    Short, rigid, blunt knife with dull edge. Used for opening oysters.

11. **Clam knife.**
    Short, rigid, broad-bladed knife with a slight edge. Used for opening clams.

Cleaver

12. **Vegetable peeler.**
    Short tool with a slotted, swiveling blade. Used for peeling vegetables and fruits.

13. **Steel.**
    Not a knife, but an essential part of the knife kit. Used for truing and maintaining knife edges. (See Chapter 7.)

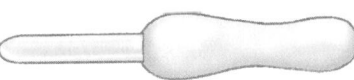
Oyster knife

14. **Cutting board.**
    This is an important partner to the knife. Hardwood boards are favored by many chefs. Hard rubber or plastic boards are thought to be more sanitary, but there is some evidence that bacteria survive longer on plastic and rubber than on wood. Cutting boards must be kept very clean.
    Note: In some communities, wooden boards are prohibited by health regulations.

Clam knife

Vegetable peeler

HAND TOOLS AND SMALL EQUIPMENT

1. **Ball cutter, melon ball scoop,** or **parisienne knife.**
   Blade is a small, cup-shaped half-sphere. Used for cutting fruits and vegetables into small balls.

Steel

2. **Cook's fork.**
   Heavy, two-pronged fork with a long handle. Used for lifting and turning meats and other items. Must be strong enough to hold heavy loads.

Ball cutter

3. **Straight spatula** or **palette knife.**
   A long, flexible blade with a rounded end. Used mostly for spreading icing on cakes and for mixing and bowl scraping.

4. **Sandwich spreader.**
   A short, stubby spatula. Used for spreading fillings and spreads on sandwiches.

Cook's fork

Straight spatula

5. **Offset spatula.**
   Broad blade, bent to keep hand off hot surfaces. Used for turning and lifting eggs, pancakes, and meats on griddles, grills, sheet pans, and so on. Also used as a scraper to clean bench or griddle.

Sandwich spreader

6. **Rubber spatula** or **scraper.**
   Broad, flexible rubber or plastic tip on long handle. Used to scrape bowls and pans. Also used for folding in egg foams or whipped cream.

Offset spatula

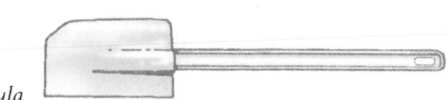
Rubber spatula

Pie server

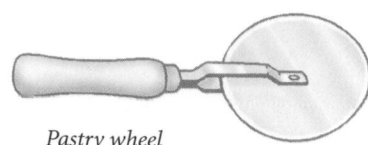

Pastry wheel

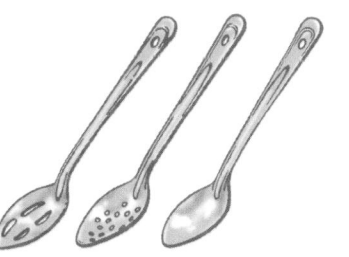

Spoons: slotted, perforated, solid

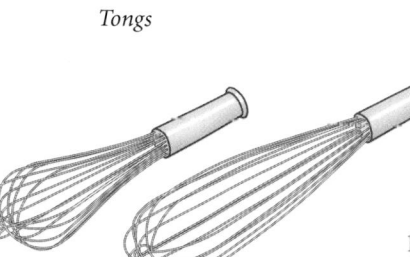

Wire whips

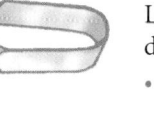

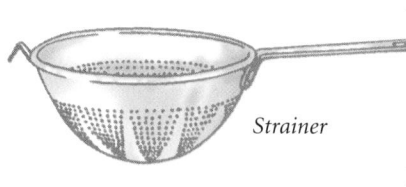

Strainer

7. **Pie server.**
   A wedge-shaped offset spatula. Used for lifting pie wedges from pan.

8. **Bench scraper or dough knife.**
   A broad, stiff piece of metal with a wooden handle on one edge. Used to cut pieces of dough and to scrape workbenches.

Bench scraper

9. **Pastry wheel or wheel knife.**
   A round, rotating blade on a handle. Used for cutting rolled-out doughs and pastry and baked pizza.

10. **Spoons: solid, slotted, and perforated.**
    Large stainless-steel spoons that hold about 3 ounces (90 mL). Used for stirring, mixing, and serving. Slotted and perforated spoons are used when liquid must be drained from solids.

11. **Skimmer.**
    Perforated disk, slightly cupped, on a long handle. Used for skimming froth from liquids and for removing solid pieces from soups, stocks, and other liquids.

12. **Tongs.**
    Spring-type or scissors-type tools used to pick up and handle foods.

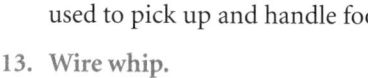

Skimmer

13. **Wire whip.**
    Loops of stainless-steel wire fastened to a handle. There are two kinds of whips:
    - Heavy whips are straight, stiff, and have relatively few wires. Used for general mixing, stirring, and beating, especially heavy liquids.
    - Balloon whips or piano-wire whips have many flexible wires. Used for whipping eggs, cream, and hollandaise, and for mixing thinner liquids.

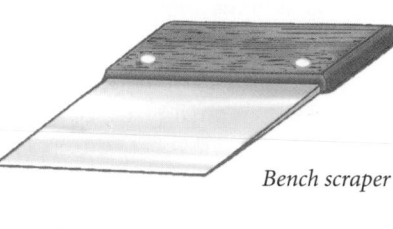

China cap

14. **China cap.**
    Cone-shaped strainer. Used for straining stocks, soups, sauces, and other liquids. Pointed shape allows the cook to drain liquids through a relatively small opening.

15. **Fine china cap or chinois (shee-nwah).**
    China cap with very fine mesh. Used when great clarity or smoothness is required in a liquid.

Chinois

16. **Strainer.**
    Round-bottomed, cup-shaped strainer made of screen-type mesh or perforated metal. Used for straining pasta, vegetables, and so on.

17. **Sieve.**
    Screen-type mesh supported in a round metal frame. Used for sifting flour and other dry ingredients.

Sieve

Tongs

18. **Colander.**
Large perforated bowl made of stainless steel or aluminum. Used to drain washed or cooked vegetables, salad greens, pasta, and other foods.

Colander

19. **Food mill.**
A tool with a hand-turned blade that forces foods through a perforated disk. Interchangeable disks have different coarseness or fineness. Used for puréeing foods.

Food mill

20. **Grater.**
A four-sided metal box with grids of varying sizes. Used for shredding and grating vegetables, cheese, citrus rinds, and other foods.

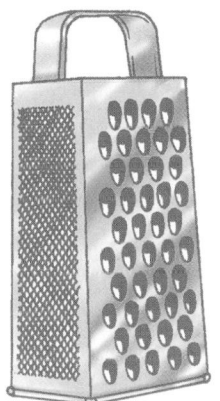

Box grater

21. **Zester.**
Small hand tool used for removing the colored part of citrus peels in thin strips.

Zester

22. **Channel knife.**
Small hand tool used mostly in decorative work. (See Chapter 24.)

Channel knife

23. **Pastry bag and tubes.**
Cone-shaped cloth or plastic bag with open end that can be fitted with metal tubes or tips of various shapes and sizes. Used for shaping and decorating with items such as cake icing, whipped cream, duchesse potatoes, and soft dough.

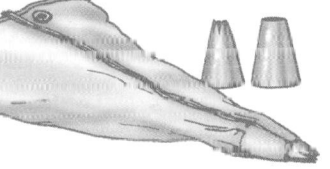

24. **Pastry brush.**
Used to brush items with egg wash, glaze, etc.

Pastry brush

Pastry bag and tubes

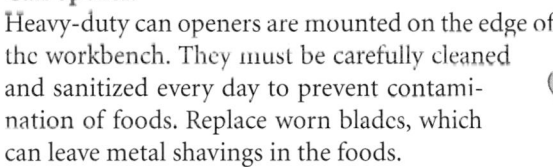

25. **Can opener.**
Heavy-duty can openers are mounted on the edge of the workbench. They must be carefully cleaned and sanitized every day to prevent contamination of foods. Replace worn blades, which can leave metal shavings in the foods.

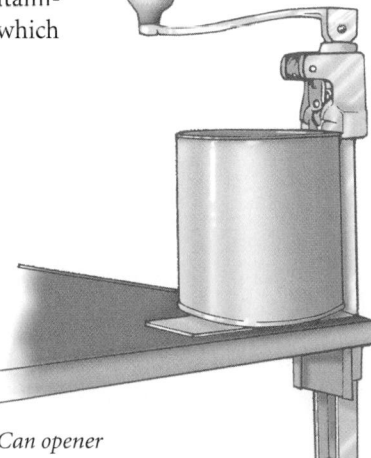

Can opener

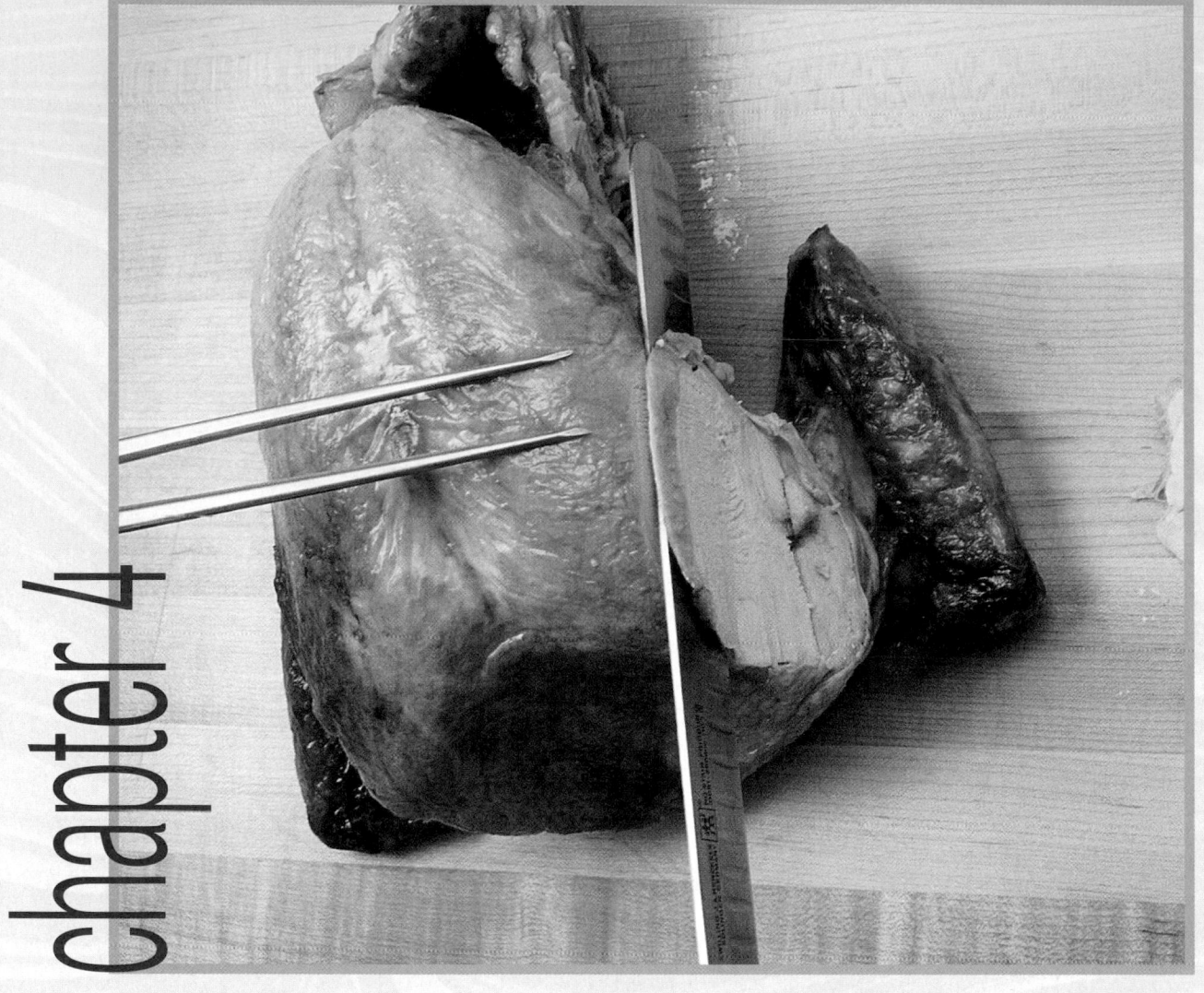

chapter 4

Basic Cooking Principles

No written recipe can be 100 percent accurate. No matter how carefully a recipe is written, the judgment of the cook is still the most important factor in making a preparation turn out well. A cook's judgment is based on experience, on an understanding of the raw materials available, and on knowledge of basic cooking principles.

This chapter deals with basic principles. You will learn about what happens to food when it is heated, about how food is cooked by different cooking methods, and about rules of seasoning and flavoring. It is important to understand the theories so that you can then put them into practice successfully in the kitchen.

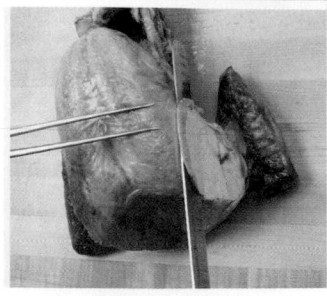

Heat and Food

To cook food means to heat it in order to make certain changes in it. Skillful cooks know exactly what changes they want to make and what they have to do to get them right. To learn these cooking skills, it is important for you to know why foods behave as they do when heated. For this, you have to study a little theory to support your practice in the kitchen.

Perhaps not all the parts in this section will make sense to you at first. But they should become clearer to you after you have thought about them in relation to specific techniques, as demonstrated by your instructor. Later in your studies, when you are learning about cooking meats, fish, vegetables, and other foods, review this section from time to time. Not only will you understand it better, but also it should help you make more sense of the procedures you are learning and practicing.

Effects of Heat on Foods

Foods are composed of proteins, fats, carbohydrates, and water, plus small amounts of other compounds such as minerals (including salt), vitamins, pigments (coloring agents), and flavor elements. It is important to understand how these components react when heated or mixed with other foods. You will then be better equipped to correct cooking faults when they occur and to anticipate the effects of changing cooking methods, cooking temperatures, or ingredient proportions.

In other words, when you know why foods behave as they do, you can then understand how to get them to behave as you want them to.

PROTEINS

1. Protein is a major component of meats, poultry, fish, eggs, milk, and milk products. It is present in smaller amounts in nuts, beans, and grains.

2. *Coagulation.* As proteins are heated, they become firm, or *coagulate.* As the temperature increases, they shrink, become firmer, and lose more moisture. Exposure of proteins to excessive heat toughens them and makes them dry. Most proteins complete coagulation or are cooked at 160°F to 185°F (71°C to 85°C).

3. *Connective tissues* are special proteins that are present in meats. Meats with a great deal of connective tissue are tough, but some connective tissues are dissolved when cooked slowly with moisture. By cooking tough meats properly, therefore, they can be made more tender. These techniques are explained in Chapter 10.

4. *Acids,* such as lemon juice, vinegar, and tomato products, do two things to proteins:
   • They speed coagulation.
   • They help dissolve some connective tissues.

CARBOHYDRATES

1. Starches and sugars are both carbohydrates. Both compounds are present in foods in many forms. They are found in fruits, vegetables, grains, beans, and nuts. Meats and fish also contain a small amount of carbohydrate.

2. For the cook, the two most important changes in carbohydrates caused by heat are caramelization and gelatinization.
   • *Caramelization* is the browning of sugars. The browning of sautéed vegetables and the golden color of bread crust are forms of caramelization.
   • *Gelatinization* occurs when starches absorb water and swell. This is a major principle in the thickening of sauces and in the production of breads and pastries.
     Acids inhibit gelatinization. A sauce thickened with flour or starch will be thinner if it contains acid.

After reading this chapter, you should be able to

1. Name the most important components of foods and describe what happens to them when they are cooked.

2. Name and describe the three ways in which heat is transferred to food in order to cook it.

3. List three factors that affect cooking times.

4. Explain the differences between moist-heat cooking methods, dry-heat cooking methods, and dry-heat cooking methods using fat.

5. Describe each basic cooking method used in the commercial kitchen.

6. Identify five properties that determine the quality of a deep-fried product.

7. Explain the difference between a seasoning and a flavoring ingredient and give examples of each.

8. Identify appropriate times for adding seasoning ingredients to the cooking process in order to achieve optimal results.

9. Identify appropriate times for adding flavoring ingredients to the cooking process in order to achieve optimal results.

10. List eleven guidelines for using herbs and spices in cooking.

FRUIT AND VEGETABLE FIBER

1. *Fiber* is the name for a group of complex substances that give structure and firmness to plants. This fiber cannot be digested.
2. The softening of fruits and vegetables in cooking is, in part, the breaking down of fiber.
3. Sugar makes fiber firmer. Fruit cooked with sugar keeps its shape better than fruit cooked without sugar.
4. Baking soda (and other alkalis) makes fiber softer. Vegetables should not be cooked with baking soda because they become mushy and lose vitamins.

FATS

1. Fats are present in meats, poultry, fish, eggs, milk products, nuts and whole grains, and, to a lesser extent, vegetables and fruits. Fats are also important as cooking mediums, as for frying.
2. Fats can be either solid or liquid at room temperature. Liquid fats are called oils. The melting point of solid fats varies.
3. When fats are heated, they begin to break down. When hot enough, they deteriorate rapidly and begin to smoke. The temperature at which this happens is called the *smoke point*, and it varies by type of fat. A stable fat—one with a high smoke point—is an important consideration in deep-fat frying.

MINERALS, VITAMINS, PIGMENTS, AND FLAVOR COMPONENTS

1. Minerals and vitamins are important to the nutritional quality of the food. Pigments and flavor components are important to a food's appearance and taste and may determine whether the food is appetizing enough to eat. So it is important to preserve all these elements.
2. All of these components may be leached out, or dissolved away, from foods during cooking.
3. Vitamins and pigments may also be destroyed by heat, by long cooking, and by other elements present during cooking.
4. It is important, then, to select cooking methods that preserve, as much as possible, a food's nutrients and appearance. This is addressed whenever cooking techniques are explained in the remainder of this book.

Heat Transfer

In order for food to be cooked, heat must be transferred from the heat source (such as a gas flame or an electric element) to and through the food. Understanding the ways in which heat is transferred and the speed at which it is transferred helps the cook control the cooking process.

Heat is transferred in three ways: conduction, convection, and radiation.

CONDUCTION

Conduction occurs in two ways:

1. When heat moves directly from one item to something touching it. For example: from the top of the range to a soup pot placed on it, from the pot to the broth inside, and from the broth to the solid food items in it.
2. When heat moves from one part of something to an adjacent part of the same item. For example: from the exterior of a roast to the interior, or from a sauté pan to its handle.

Different materials conduct heat at different speeds. Heat moves rapidly through copper and aluminum, more slowly in stainless steel, more slowly yet in glass and porcelain. Air is a very poor conductor of heat.

CONVECTION

Convection occurs when heat is spread by the movement of air, steam, or liquid (including hot fat). There are two kinds of convection:

1. **Natural.**
   Hot liquids and gases rise while cooler ones sink. Thus, in any oven, kettle of liquid, or deep-fat fryer a constant, natural circulation distributes heat.

2. **Mechanical.**
   In convection ovens and convection steamers, fans speed the circulation of heat. Thus, heat is transferred more quickly to the food, and the food cooks faster.

Stirring is a form of mechanical convection. Thick liquids cannot circulate as quickly as thin ones, so the rate of natural convection is slower. This explains, in part, why it is so easy to scorch thick soups and sauces. The heat is not carried away from the bottom of the pan quickly enough, so it stays concentrated on the bottom and scorches the food. Stirring redistributes the heat and helps prevent this. (Using heavy pots made of a material that conducts heat well also helps prevent scorching because the pot conducts the heat more quickly and evenly all across the bottom and up the sides.)

RADIATION

Radiation occurs when energy is transferred by waves from the source to the food. The waves themselves are not actually heat energy but are changed into heat energy when they strike the food being cooked. (Light waves, radio waves, and X rays are examples of radiation not used for cooking.)

Two kinds of radiation are used in the kitchen:

1. **Infrared.**
   Broiling is the most familiar example of infrared cooking. In a broiler, an electric element or a ceramic element heated by a gas flame becomes so hot that it gives off infrared radiation, which cooks the food. High-intensity infrared ovens are designed to heat food rapidly.

2. **Microwave.**
   In microwave cooking, the radiation generated by the oven penetrates partway into the food, where it agitates the molecules of water. The friction this agitation causes creates heat, which cooks the food.
   - Because microwave radiation affects only water molecules, a completely waterless material will not heat in a microwave oven. Plates become hot only when heat is *conducted* to them by hot foods.
   - Because most microwaves penetrate no more than about 2 inches (50 mm) into foods, heat is transferred to the center of large pieces of food by *conduction*, just as in roasting.

   Cooking with microwaves is discussed in more detail later in this chapter.

Cooking Times

It takes time to heat a food to a desired temperature, the temperature at which a food is "done" (meaning that the desired changes have taken place). This time is affected by three factors:

1. **Cooking temperature.**
   This means the temperature of the air in the oven, the fat in the fryer, the surface of a griddle, or the liquid in which a food is cooking.

2. **The speed of heat transfer.**
   Different cooking methods transfer heat at different rates, as shown by these examples:
   Air is a poor conductor of heat, while steam is much more efficient. A jet of steam (212°F/100°C) will easily burn your hand, but you can safely reach into an oven at 500°F (260°C). This is why it takes longer to bake potatoes than to steam them.
   A convection oven cooks faster than a conventional oven, even if both are set at the same temperature. The forced air movement transfers heat more rapidly.

3. **Size, temperature, and individual characteristics of the food.**
   For example:

   A small beef roast cooks faster than a large one.
   A chilled steak takes longer to broil than one at room temperature.
   Fish items generally cook more quickly than meats.

Because there are so many variables, it is difficult or even impossible to determine exact cooking times in most recipes. Different ovens, fryers, and steamers, for example, may transfer heat more or less efficiently or have different recovery times. Roasting charts that give cooking times for various cuts of meat can be used only as guidelines, and the cook must use his or her judgment to make the final determination of doneness. This matter of cooking times is discussed again in the next chapter.

Cooking Methods

Cooking methods are classified as moist heat or dry heat.

> *Moist-heat methods* are those in which the heat is conducted to the food product by water or water-based liquids such as stock and sauces, or by steam.
>
> *Dry-heat methods* are those in which the heat is conducted without moisture, that is, by hot air, hot metal, radiation, or hot fat. We usually divide dry-heat methods into two categories: without fat and with fat.

Different cooking methods are suited to different kinds of foods. For example, some meats are high in connective tissue and will be tough unless this tissue is broken down slowly by moist heat. Other meats are low in connective tissue and are naturally tender. They are at their best and juiciest when cooked with dry heat to a rare or medium-done stage.

Many other factors must be considered when choosing cooking methods for meats, fish, and vegetables, such as the flavor and appearance imparted by browning, the flavor imparted by fats, and the firmness or delicacy of the product. These factors are taken up as individual foods are discussed in later chapters.

The basic cooking methods are summarized here. Their practical application to foods is discussed in detail in the remainder of the book and reinforced by your instructors' demonstrations and your own experience and practice.

Moist-Heat Methods

POACH, SIMMER, AND BOIL

Poaching, simmering, and boiling all mean cooking a food in water or a seasoned and flavored liquid. The temperature of the liquid determines the method.

1. To *boil* means to cook in a liquid that is bubbling rapidly and is greatly agitated. Water boils at 212°F (100°C) at sea level. No matter how high the burner is turned, the temperature of the liquid will go no higher.

   Boiling is generally reserved for certain vegetables and starches. The high temperature toughens the proteins of meats, fish, and eggs, and the rapid bubbling breaks up delicate foods.

2. To *simmer* means to cook in a liquid that is bubbling very gently. Temperature is about 185°F to 205°F (85°C to 96°C).

   Most foods cooked in a liquid are simmered. The higher temperatures and intense agitation of boiling are detrimental to most foods. The word *boiled* is sometimes used as a menu term, as when simmered fresh beef is called "boiled beef."

3. To *poach* means to cook in a liquid, usually a small amount, that is hot but not actually bubbling. Temperature is about 160°F to 180°F (71°C to 82°C).

   Poaching is used to cook delicate foods such as fish and eggs out of the shell. It is also used to partially cook foods such as variety meats in order to eliminate undesirable flavors and to firm the product before final cooking.

4. A rule of thumb: Whether a food is to be simmered or boiled, the liquid is often brought to a full boil at first. This compensates for the lowering of the temperature when the food items are added. The heat is then adjusted to maintain a steady temperature.

5. To *blanch* means to cook an item partially and very briefly, usually in water but sometimes by other methods (as when French fries are blanched in deep fat).

   There are two ways of blanching in water:

   • Place the item in cold water, bring to a boil, and simmer briefly. Cool the item by plunging it into cold water.

      Purpose: to dissolve out blood, salt, or impurities from certain meats and bones.

   • Place the item in rapidly boiling water and return the water to the boil. Remove the item and cool in cold water.

      Purpose: to set the color and destroy harmful enzymes in vegetables, or to loosen the skins of tomatoes, peaches, and similar items for easier peeling.

6. Altitude note: The boiling point of water decreases as altitude above sea level is increased. At 5000 feet (1500 meters) above sea level, water boils at about 203°F (95°C). Thus, it takes longer to boil foods to doneness at high altitudes because the temperature is lower.

STEAM

To *steam* means to cook foods by exposing them directly to steam.

1. In quantity cooking, steaming is usually done in special steam cookers, which are designed to accept standard-size pans. Steaming can also be done on a rack above boiling water. This method is more cumbersome, however, and is used only occasionally in food service. Cooking in a steam-jacketed kettle is not steaming because the steam does not actually touch the food.

2. Steaming also refers to cooking an item tightly wrapped or in a covered pan so that it cooks in the steam formed by its own moisture. This method is used in cooking items *en papillote*, wrapped in parchment paper (or foil). "Baked" potatoes wrapped in foil are actually steamed.

3. Steam at normal pressure is 212°F (100°C), the same as boiling water. However, it carries much more heat than boiling water and cooks foods very rapidly. Cooking times must be carefully controlled to avoid overcooking.

4. A *pressure steamer* is a steam cooker that holds in steam under pressure. The temperature of the steam then goes higher than 212°F (100°C), as the following chart shows:

Pressure	Steam Temperature
5 psi (pounds per square inch)	227°F (106°C)
10 psi	240°F (116°C)
15 psi	250°F (121°C)

   Because of these temperatures, pressure steaming is an extremely rapid method of cooking and must be carefully controlled and timed.

5. Steaming is widely used for vegetables. It cooks them rapidly, without agitation, and minimizes the dissolving away of nutrients that occurs when vegetables are boiled.

BRAISE

To *braise* means to cook covered in a small amount of liquid, usually after preliminary browning. In almost all cases, the liquid is served with the product as a sauce.

Braising is sometimes referred to as a *combination cooking method* because the product is first browned, using dry heat, before it is cooked with a liquid. Nevertheless, in most cases, moist heat is responsible for most of the cooking process, and the browning may be thought of as a preliminary technique. The purpose of the browning step is not so much to cook the item as to develop color and flavor.

1. Braised meats are usually browned first using a dry-heat method such as pan-frying. This gives a desirable appearance and flavor to the product and to the sauce.

2. Braising also refers to cooking some vegetables, such as lettuce or cabbage, at low temperature in a small amount of liquid without first browning in fat, or with only a light preliminary sautéing.

3. Foods being braised are usually not completely covered by the cooking liquid. The top of the product is actually cooked by the steam held in the covered pot. Pot roasts, for example, are cooked in liquid that covers the item by one-third to two-thirds. The exact amount depends on how much sauce is needed for service. This method yields a flavorful, concentrated sauce.

4. In some preparations, especially of poultry and fish, no liquid is added. This is still considered braising because steam is trapped by the cover and the item cooks in its own moisture and in the moisture of other ingredients, such as vegetables.

5. Braising may be done on the range or in the oven. Oven-braising has three major advantages:
    *   Uniform cooking. The heat strikes the braising pot on all sides, not just the bottom.
    *   Less attention required. Foods braise at a low, steady temperature without having to be checked constantly.
    *   Range space is free for other purposes.

Dry-Heat Methods

ROAST AND BAKE

To *roast* and to *bake* both mean to cook foods by surrounding them with hot, dry air, usually in an oven. Cooking on a spit in front of an open fire may also be considered roasting.

The term *roasting* usually applies to meats and poultry. The term *baking* usually applies to breads, pastries, vegetables, and fish. It is a more general term than roasting, although, in practice, there is little or no difference in the actual technique, and the terms are often interchangeable (except for breads and pastries).

Please note, however, that it has recently become fashionable on menus to apply the term *roasted* to a wide variety of foods, including meats, poultry, fish, and vegetables that are not actually baked or roasted but are sautéed, fried, or braised. One restaurant even labeled steamed vegetables as "roasted baby vegetables."

1. Cooking *uncovered* is essential to roasting. Covering holds in steam, changing the process from dry-heat to moist-heat cooking, such as braising or steaming.

2. Meat is usually roasted on a rack (or, if it is a rib roast, on its own natural rack of bones). The rack prevents the meat from simmering in its own juices and fat. It also allows hot air to circulate all around the product.

3. When roasting in a conventional oven, the cook should allow for uneven temperatures by occasionally changing the position of the product. The back of the oven is often hotter because heat is lost at the door.

4. To *barbecue* means to cook with dry heat created by the burning of hardwood or by the hot coals of this wood. In other words, barbecuing is a roasting or grilling technique requiring a wood fire.

    Authentic, traditional barbecue is done in wood-burning ovens or pits, but these are not really practical for the average restaurant that wants to add barbecued items to the menu. So today, most barbecuing is done in specially designed smoke ovens or cookers. In principle,

Figure 4.1 Rangetop smoke-roasting.

Place hardwood chips or sawdust in a disposable hotel pan. Place over moderately high heat and heat until the wood begins to smoke.

Place the items to be cooked on a rack and set the rack over the chips so that the food is not touching the chips. Cover tightly with another pan and cook for desired time.

these units work like regular ovens, except that they also have a device that heats small pieces of hardwood to produce smoke. Foods should be suspended in the ovens or placed on racks so that the smoke can contact all surfaces.

Technically, the foods cooked in these units cannot be said to be barbecued, as the heat is created by electric or gas burners. But because of the wood smoke, the results can be nearly identical.

5. *Smoke-roasting* is a procedure done on top of the stove in a closed container, using wood chips to make smoke. Use this procedure for small, tender, quick-cooking items such as fish fillets, tender meat and poultry pieces, and some vegetables.

   To smoke-roast, place a layer of fine hardwood chips or shavings on the bottom of a hotel pan (see Figure 4.1). Disposable pans may be used for light smoking. Place a rack in the pan over the chips and lay the seasoned food items on the rack. Cover tightly with a second hotel pan or with aluminum foil. Place on the cooktop (making sure that the ventilating hood is on!) over moderate heat. Smoke will begin rising from the wood chips. After about five minutes, remove the food items from the smoke-roaster and, if necessary, complete the cooking in the oven. Leaving the food in the smoke too long will result in a strong, bitter taste.

BROIL

To *broil* means to cook with radiant heat from above.

Note: The terms *broiling*, *grilling*, and *griddling* are sometimes confused. Grilling (see below) is often called *broiling*, and griddling is called *grilling*. This book uses the terms that refer to the equipment used. Thus, broiling is done in a broiler, grilling on a grill, and griddling on a griddle.

1. Broiling is a rapid, high-heat cooking method that is usually used only for tender meats, poultry, fish, and a few vegetable items.
2. Note the following rules of broiling:
   • Turn heat on full. Cooking temperature is regulated by moving the rack nearer to or farther from the heat source.
   • Use lower heat for larger, thicker items, and for items to be cooked well done. Use higher heat for thinner pieces and for items to be cooked rare. This is done so that the inside and outside are cooked to the desired degree at the same time. It takes practice and experience to cook foods of different thickness to the right degree of doneness inside with the desired amount of surface browning.
   • Preheat the broiler. This helps to sear the product quickly, and the hot broiler will make the desired grill marks on the food.
   • Foods may be dipped in oil to prevent sticking and to minimize drying. (This may not be necessary if the food is high in fat.) Care should be taken, as too much oil on a hot broiler grate may cause a fire.
   • Turn foods over only once, to cook from both sides but to avoid unnecessary handling.
3. A low-intensity broiler called a *salamander* is used for browning or melting the top of some items before service.

GRILL, GRIDDLE, AND PAN-BROIL

Grilling, griddling, and pan-broiling are all dry-heat cooking methods that use heat from below.

1. *Grilling* is done on an open grid over a heat source, which may be charcoal, an electric element, or a gas-heated element. Cooking temperature is regulated by moving the items to hotter or cooler places on the grill. Grilled meats should be turned to achieve desired grill markings, just as in broiling.

2. *Griddling* is done on a solid cooking surface called a griddle, with or without small amounts of fat to prevent sticking. The temperature is adjustable and is much lower (around 350°F/177°C) than on a grill. In addition to meats, items such as eggs and pancakes are cooked on a griddle.

   Grooved griddles have a solid top with raised ridges. They are designed to cook like grills but to create less smoke. Meats cooked on a grooved griddle do not have the charcoal-grilled flavor imparted by smoke from burning fats.

3. *Pan-broiling* is like griddling except that it is done in a sauté pan or skillet instead of on a griddle surface. Fat must be poured off as it accumulates, or the process becomes pan-frying. No liquid is added, and the pan is not covered, or else the item would steam.

Dry-Heat Methods Using Fat

SAUTÉ

To *sauté* means to cook quickly in a small amount of fat.

1. The French word *sauter* means "to jump," referring to the action of tossing small pieces of food in a sauté pan (see Figure 17.1). However, larger foods, such as slices of meat and pieces of chicken, are sautéed without actually being tossed in the pan.

2. Note these two important principles:
   * Preheat the pan before adding the food to be sautéed. The food must start cooking at high heat, or it will begin to simmer in its own juices.
   * Do not overcrowd the pan. Doing so lowers the temperature too much, and again the food begins to simmer in its own juices.

3. Meats to be sautéed are often dusted with flour to prevent sticking and to help achieve uniform browning.

4. After a food is sautéed, a liquid such as wine or stock is often swirled in the pan to dissolve browned bits of food sticking to the bottom. This is called *deglazing*. This liquid becomes part of a sauce served with the sautéed items.

PAN-FRY

To *pan-fry* means to cook in a moderate amount of fat in a pan over moderate heat.

1. Pan-frying is similar to sautéing except that more fat is generally used and the cooking time is longer. The method is used for larger pieces of food, such as chops and chicken pieces, and the items are not tossed by flipping the pan, as they often are in sautéing.

2. Pan-frying is usually done over lower heat than sautéing because of the larger pieces being cooked.

3. The amount of fat depends on the food being cooked. Only a small amount is used for eggs, for example, while as much as 1 inch (2.5 cm) or more may be used for pan-fried chicken.

4. Most foods must be turned at least once for even cooking. Some larger foods may be removed from the pan and finished in the oven to prevent excessive surface browning. This method of finishing in the oven is also used to simplify production when large quantities of foods must be pan-fried.

DEEP-FRY

To *deep-fry* means to cook a food submerged in hot fat. Quality in a deep-fried product is characterized by the following properties:

Minimum fat absorption	Attractive golden color
Minimum moisture loss	Crisp surface or coating
(that is, not overcooked)	No off flavors imparted by the frying fat

Many foods are dipped in a breading or batter before frying. This forms a protective coating between food and fat and helps to give the product crispness, color, and flavor. Obviously, the quality of the breading or batter affects the quality of the finished product (see Chapter 7, pp. 120–122).

Guidelines for Deep-Frying

1. **Fry at proper temperatures.**
Most foods are fried at 350°F to 375°F (175°C to 190°C). Excessive greasiness in fried foods is usually caused by frying at too low a temperature.

2. **Don't overload the baskets.**
Doing so greatly lowers the fat temperature.

3. **Use good-quality fat.**
The best fat for frying has a high smoke point (the temperature at which the fat begins to smoke and to break down rapidly).

4. **Replace about 15 to 20 percent of the fat with fresh fat after use each day.**
This extends frying life.

5. **Discard spent fat.**
Old fat loses frying ability, browns excessively, and imparts off flavors.

6. **Avoid frying strong and mild-flavored foods in the same fat, if possible.**
French fries should not taste like fried fish.

7. **Fry as close to service as possible.**
Do not leave foods in the basket above the fry kettle, and do not hold under heat lamps for more than a few minutes. The foods' moisture quickly makes the breading or coating soggy.

8. **Protect fat from its enemies:**
Heat. Turn fryer off or to a lower holding temperature (200°F to 250°F/95°C to 120°C) when not in use.
Oxygen. Keep fat covered between services, and try to aerate the fat as little as possible when filtering.
Water. Remove excess moisture from foods before frying. Dry baskets and kettle thoroughly after cleaning. Keep liquids away from the fryer to prevent accidental spills.
Salt. Never salt foods over the fat.
Food particles. Shake loose crumbs off breaded items before placing over fat. Skim and strain fat frequently.
Detergent. Rinse baskets and kettle well after cleaning.

Pressure Frying

Pressure frying means deep-frying in a special covered fryer that traps steam given off by the foods being cooked and increases the pressure inside the kettle.

In a standard fryer, even though the fat may be at 350°F (175°C), the temperature inside the food will not rise above 212°F (100°C), the boiling point of water. Just as in a pressure steamer, a pressure fryer raises this temperature and cooks the food more quickly without excessive surface browning. At the same time, the fat temperature can be lower, 325°F (165°C) or less.

Pressure frying requires accurate timing because the product cannot be seen while it is cooking.

Microwave Cooking

Microwave cooking refers to the use of a specific tool rather than to a basic dry-heat or moist-heat cooking method. This equipment is used mostly for heating prepared foods and for thawing raw or cooked items. However, it can be used for primary cooking as well.

Different models of microwave ovens range in power from about 500 watts up to about 2000 watts. The higher the wattage, the more intense the energy the oven puts out and the faster it heats foods. Most models have switches or buttons that allow you to cook at different power levels.

One of the most important advantages of the microwave oven in à la carte cooking is that it enables you to heat individual portions of many foods to order quickly and evenly. Instead of keeping such foods as stews hot in the steam table, where they gradually become overcooked, you can keep them refrigerated (either in bulk or in individual portions) and reheat each order as needed. This is perhaps the main reason why most restaurants have one or more microwave ovens, even though they may not use them for primary cooking.

Because the microwave oven is a unique tool in food service, the cook should observe the following special points regarding its use:

1. Small items will not brown in a standard microwave. Large roasts may brown somewhat from the heat generated in the item itself. Some models of microwave ovens have added browning elements that use conventional heat.

2. Watch timing carefully. Overcooking is the most common error in microwave use. High energy levels cook small items very rapidly.

3. Large items should be turned once or twice for even cooking.

4. An on/off cycle is often used for large items to allow time for heat to be conducted to the interior.

5. If your equipment has a defrost cycle (which switches the oven to lower power), use this cycle rather than full power to thaw frozen foods. Lower power enables the item to thaw more evenly, with less danger of partially cooking it. If your oven does not have this feature, use an on/off cycle.

6. Sliced, cooked meats and other items that are likely to dry out in the microwave should be protected either by wrapping them loosely in plastic or wax paper or by covering them with a sauce or gravy.

7. Because microwaves act only on water molecules, foods with a high water content, such as vegetables, heat faster than denser, drier foods, such as cooked meats.

8. Foods at the edge of a dish or plate heat faster than foods in the center. This is because they are hit by rays bouncing off the walls of the oven as well as by rays directly from the energy source. Therefore:
   - Depress the center of casseroles so that the food is not as thick there as at the edges. This will help it heat more evenly.
   - When you are heating several foods at once on a plate, put the moist, quick-heating items like vegetables in the center and the denser, slower-heating items at the edges.

9. Because microwaves do not penetrate metal, aluminum foil and other metals shield foods from the radiant energy. For example, a potato wrapped in foil will not cook in a microwave oven.

   With older machines, it was a general rule not to put any metal in the oven, as the radiation could bounce off the metal and damage the magnetron (the oven's generator). With newer machines, it is possible to heat foods in foil pans and to shield certain parts of the food by covering them with pieces of foil so that they do not overheat. Follow the procedures recommended by the manufacturer.

Because microwaves cook so rapidly, they will not break down the connective tissues of less tender meats. Slow, moist cooking is necessary for dissolving these connective tissues.

The more food that is placed in a microwave at once, the longer the cooking time. Thus, the primary advantage of microwave cooking—speed—is lost with large roasts and other large quantities.

Summary of Cooking Terms

The following is an alphabetical list of terms that describe ways of applying heat to foods. Basic cooking methods described earlier are included, as well as more specific applications of these basic methods.

bake. To cook foods by surrounding them with hot, dry air. Similar to **roast**, but the term *bake* usually applies to breads, pastries, vegetables, and fish.

barbecue. (1) To cook with dry heat created by the burning of hardwood or by the hot coals of this wood. (2) Loosely, to cook over hot coals, such as on a grill or spit, often with a seasoned marinade or basting sauce.

blanch. To cook an item partially and very briefly in boiling water or in hot fat. Usually a pre-preparation technique, as to loosen peels of vegetables, fruits, and nuts, to partially cook French fries or other foods before service, to prepare for freezing, or to remove undesirable flavors.

boil. To cook in water or other liquid that is bubbling rapidly, about 212°F (100°C) at sea level and at normal pressure.

braise. (1) To cook covered in a small amount of liquid, usually after preliminary browning. (2) To cook (certain vegetables) slowly in a small amount of liquid without preliminary browning.

broil. To cook with radiant heat from above.

deep-fry. To cook submerged in hot fat.

deglaze. To swirl a liquid in a sauté pan, roast pan, or other pan to dissolve cooked particles of food remaining on the bottom.

dry-heat cooking methods. Methods in which heat is conducted to foods without the use of moisture.

fry. To cook in hot fat.

glaze. To give shine to the surface of a food by applying a sauce, aspic, sugar, or icing, and/or by browning or melting under a broiler or salamander or in an oven.

griddle. To cook on a flat, solid cooking surface called a griddle.

grill. To cook on an open grid over a heat source.

moist-heat cooking methods. Methods in which heat is conducted to foods by water or other liquid (except fat) or by steam.

pan-broil. To cook uncovered in a skillet or sauté pan without fat.

pan-fry. To cook in a moderate amount of fat in an uncovered pan.

(en) papillote. Wrapped in paper (or sometimes foil) for cooking so that the food is steamed in its own moisture.

parboil. To cook partially in a boiling or simmering liquid.

parcook. To cook partially by any method.

poach. To cook gently in water or other liquid that is hot but not actually bubbling, about 160°F to 180°F (71°C to 82°C).

reduce. To cook by simmering or boiling until the quantity of liquid is decreased, often to concentrate flavors.

roast. To cook foods by surrounding them with hot, dry air in an oven or on a spit in front of an open fire.

sauté. To cook quickly in a small amount of fat.

sear. To brown the surface of a food quickly at a high temperature.

simmer. To cook in water or other liquid that is bubbling gently, about 185°F to 205°F (85°C to 96°C).

smoke-roasting. To cook with dry heat in the presence of smoke, as on a rack over wood chips in a covered pan.

steam. To cook by direct contact with steam.

stew. To simmer a food or foods in a small amount of liquid, which is usually served with the food as a sauce.

sweat. To cook slowly in fat without browning, sometimes under a cover.

The Art of Seasoning and Flavoring

People eat because they enjoy the flavors of good food, not just because they must fill their stomachs to stay alive. Appearance, texture, and nutrition are important, too, but good taste is the first mark of good cooking.

Enhancement and adjustment of flavors is one of a cook's most critical tasks, a task requiring experience and judgment. Unfortunately, the fine art of seasoning and flavoring is too often abused.

The most important flavors of a particular preparation are the flavors of its main ingredients. Roast beef should taste like roast beef, green beans like green beans, sole stuffed with crabmeat like sole and crabmeat. It's a fact of life, however, that plain foods generally are a little bland to most palates, so the cook's job is to perk up the taste buds with a few added ingredients, so that the beef tastes more like beef, the green beans more like green beans.

Seasoning and Flavoring Defined

Strictly speaking, there is a difference between seasoning and flavoring.

Seasoning means enhancing the natural flavor of the food without significantly changing its flavor. Salt is the most important seasoning ingredient.

Flavoring means adding a new flavor to a food, thus changing or modifying the original flavor.

The difference between seasoning and flavoring is often one of degree. For example, salt is usually used only to season, not to flavor. But in the case of potato chips or pretzels, the salt is so predominant that it can be considered an added flavoring. On the other hand, nutmeg is normally used for its distinctive flavor, but just a dash can perk up the flavor of a cream sauce without actually being detectable to most people.

BASIC RULE OF SEASONING AND FLAVORING

Your main ingredients are your main sources of flavor. Use good-quality main ingredients, handle all foods with care, and employ correct cooking procedures.

Badly prepared foods cannot be rescued by a last-minute addition of spices. The function of spices, herbs, and seasonings is to heighten and to give extra interest to the natural flavors of foods, not to serve as main ingredients or to cover natural flavors.

When to Season and Flavor

SEASONING

1. The most important time for seasoning liquid foods is at the end of the cooking process.

   The last step in most recipes, whether written or not, is "adjust the seasoning." This means that you have to first taste and evaluate the product. Then you must decide what should be done, if anything, to improve the taste. Often, a little salt in a stew or a dash of fresh lemon juice in a sauce is enough.

   The ability to evaluate and correct flavors takes experience, and it is one of the most important skills a cook can develop.

2. Salt and other seasonings are also added at the beginning of cooking, particularly for larger pieces of food, when seasonings added at the end would not be absorbed or blended in but would just sit on the surface.

3. Adding some of the seasoning during the cooking process also aids in evaluating the flavor along the way.

4. Do not add much seasoning if it will be concentrated during cooking, as when a liquid is reduced.

FLAVORING

Flavoring ingredients can be added at the beginning, middle, or end, depending on the cooking time, the cooking process, and the flavoring ingredient.

1. Only a few flavorings can be added successfully at the end of cooking. These include fresh (not dried) herbs, sherry or flamed brandy, and condiments like prepared mustard and Worcestershire sauce.

2. Most flavorings need heat to release their flavors and time for the flavors to blend. Whole spices take longest. Ground spices release flavors more quickly and thus don't require as long a cooking time.

3. Too much cooking results in loss of flavor. Most flavors, whether in spices or in main ingredients, are volatile, which means they evaporate when heated. That is why you can smell food cooking.

Chives

Chervil

Basil

Garlic chives

Cilantro

Dill

Epazote

We can conclude that herbs and spices should cook with the foods long enough to release their flavors but not so long that their flavors are lost. If cooking times are short, you can generally add spices and herbs at the beginning or middle of cooking time. On the other hand, if cooking times are long, it is usually better to add them in the middle or toward the end of cooking time.

Note: Food safety experts recommend adding dried spices and herbs at least 30 minutes before the end of cooking so that any microorganisms they might carry will be destroyed.

Common Seasoning and Flavoring Ingredients

Any food product can be used as a flavoring ingredient, even meat (as when crumbled bacon is added to sautéed potatoes or diced ham is included in a mirepoix). Sauces, which are compound preparations containing many flavoring ingredients, are themselves used as flavorings for meat, fish, vegetables, and desserts.

We obviously cannot treat all possible flavoring ingredients here, but we discuss some of the most important as follows. A survey of herbs and spices is provided in Table 4.1 on pages 67–69. Ingredients used primarily in the bakeshop are discussed in Chapter 26.

1. *Salt* is the most important seasoning ingredient. Don't use too much. You can always add more, but you can't take it out.

2. *Pepper* comes in three forms: white, black, and green. They are actually the same berry but processed differently. (Black pepper is picked unripe; white is ripened and the hull is removed; green peppercorns are picked unripe and preserved before their color darkens.)

   • Whole and crushed *black pepper* is used primarily in seasoning and flavoring stocks and sauces and, sometimes, red meats. Ground black pepper is used in the dining room by the customer.

   • Ground *white pepper* is more important as a seasoning in the food service kitchen. Its flavor is slightly different from that of black pepper, and it blends well (in small quantities) with many foods. Its white color makes it visually undetectable in light-colored foods.

   • *Green peppercorns* are fairly expensive and are used in special recipes, primarily in luxury restaurants. The types packed in water, brine, or vinegar (those in water and in brine have better flavor) are soft. Wet-pack peppercorns are perishable. Water-packed peppercorns will keep only a few days in the refrigerator after they are opened, while the others will keep longer. Dried green peppercorns are also available.

Regular ginger and green ginger

Marjoram

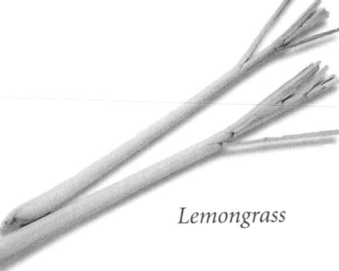

Lemongrass

Mint

Oregano

Parsley, flat

3. *Red pepper* or *cayenne* is completely unrelated to black and white pepper. It belongs to the same family as paprika and fresh sweet bell peppers. Used in tiny amounts, it gives a spicy hotness to sauces and soups without actually altering the flavor. In larger amounts, it gives both heat and flavor to many spicy foods, such as those of Mexico and India.

4. *Lemon juice* is an important seasoning, particularly for enlivening the flavor of sauces and soups.

5. *Fresh herbs* are almost always superior to dried herbs. They should be used whenever cost and availability permit. Not long ago, the only fresh herbs generally available in many areas were parsley, chives, and, sometimes, mint and dill. Now, however, most herbs are available fresh. The accompanying photos illustrate the most commonly used fresh herbs as well as some unusual fresh flavoring ingredients.

Parsley, curly

6. *Onion, garlic, shallots,* and other members of the onion family, as well as carrots and celery, are used as flavorings in virtually all stations of the kitchen except the bakeshop. Try to avoid the use of dried onion and garlic products. They have less flavor, and the fresh product is always available.

7. *Wine, brandy,* and other alcoholic beverages are used to flavor sauces, soups, and many entrées. Brandy should be boiled or flamed to eliminate the high percentage of alcohol, which would be unpleasant in the finished dish. Table wines usually need some cooking or reduction (either separately or with other ingredients) to produce the desired flavors. Fortified wines like sherry and Madeira, on the other hand, may be added as flavorings at the end of cooking.

Rosemary

8. *Prepared mustard* is a blend of ground mustard seed, vinegar, and other spices. It is used to flavor meats, sauces, and salad dressings and as a table condiment. For most cooking purposes, European styles such as Dijon (French) or Dusseldorf (German) work best, while the bright-yellow American ballpark style is more appropriate as a table condiment than as a cooking ingredient. A coarse, grainy style is sometimes called for in specialty recipes.

9. *Grated lemon* and *orange rind* is used in sauces, meats, and poultry (as in duckling à l'orange) as well as in the bakeshop. Only the colored outer portion, called the *zest*, which contains the flavorful oils, is used. The white pith is bitter.

10. *MSG*, or *monosodium glutamate*, is a flavor enhancer widely used in Asian cooking. MSG doesn't actually change the flavor of foods but acts on the taste buds. It has a bad reputation for causing chest pains and headaches in some individuals.

Sage

Using Herbs and Spices

DEFINITIONS

Herbs are the leaves of certain plants that usually grow in temperate climates. *Spices* are the buds, fruits, flowers, bark, seeds, and roots of plants and trees, many of which grow in tropical climates.

The distinction is often confusing, but it is not as important to know which flavorings are spices and which are herbs as it is to use them skillfully.

Tarragon

Thyme

Table 4.1 is not a substitute for familiarity with the actual products. Eventually, you should be able to identify by aroma, taste, and appearance any spice on your shelf without looking at the label. The accompanying photos illustrate a number of whole spices.

Guidelines for Using Herbs and Spices

1. Be familiar with each spice's aroma, flavor, and effect on food. Looking at a spice chart, including the one in this book, is no substitute for familiarity with the actual product.

2. Store dried herbs and spices in a cool place, tightly covered, in opaque containers. Heat, light, and moisture deteriorate herbs and spices rapidly.

3. Don't use stale spices and herbs, and don't buy more than you can use in about six months. Whole spices keep longer than ground, but both lose much flavor after six months.

4. Be cautious after you have replaced old spices. The fresher products are more potent, so the amount you used before might now be too much.

5. Use good-quality spices and herbs. It doesn't pay to economize here. The difference in cost is only a fraction of a cent per portion.

6. Whole spices take longer to release flavors than ground spices, so allow for adequate cooking time.

Top row, left to right: black peppercorns, green peppercorns, pink peppercorns.
Bottom row, left to right: white peppercorns, Sichuan peppercorns.

Top row, left to right: cloves, nutmeg, allspice, cinnamon sticks.
Bottom row, left to right: juniper berries, cardamom, saffron, star anise.

Top row, left to right: celery seed, dill seed, coriander seed, caraway seed.
Bottom row, left to right: fennel seed, cumin seed, anise seed.

7. Whole herbs and spices for flavoring a liquid are tied loosely in a piece of cheesecloth (called a *sachet*) for easy removal.

8. When in doubt, add less than you think you need. You can always add more, but it's hard to remove what you've already added.

9. Except in dishes like curry or chili, spices should not dominate. Often, they should not even be evident. If you can taste the nutmeg in the creamed spinach, there's probably too much nutmeg.

10. Herbs and spices added to uncooked foods, such as salads and dressings, need several hours for flavors to be released and blended.

11. Taste foods before serving, whenever possible. How else can you "adjust the seasoning"?

T A B L E 4.1

Herbs and Spices

Product	Market Forms	Description	Examples of Use
Allspice	Whole, ground	Small brown berry; flavor resembles blend of cinnamon, cloves, and nutmeg	Sausages and braised meats, poached fish, stewed fruits, pies, puddings
Anise seed	Whole, ground	Small seed; licorice flavor	Cookies, pastries, breads
Basil	Crushed leaves	Aromatic leaf; member of mint family	Tomatoes and tomato dishes, pesto (Italian basil sauce), egg dishes, lamb chops, eggplant, peas, squash
Bay leaf	Whole	Stiff, dark-green, oblong leaves; pungent aroma	One of the most important herbs; used in stocks, sauces, stews, braised meats
Caraway seed	Whole	Dark-brown, curved seeds; familiar rye bread seasoning	Rye bread, cabbage, sauerkraut, pork, cheese spreads, Eastern European dishes
Cardamom	Whole pod, ground seed	Tiny brown seeds inside white or green pod; sweet and aromatic; expensive	Pickling, Danish pastries, curries
Cayenne (red pepper)	Ground	Ground form of hot red pepper; looks like paprika, but is extremely hot	In small amounts in many sauces, soups, meat, fish, egg, and cheese dishes (see p. 65)
Celery seed	Whole, ground, ground mixed with salt (celery salt)	Tiny brown seeds with strong celery flavor	Salads, coleslaw, salad dressings, tomato products
Chervil	Crushed leaves	Herb with mild flavor of parsley and tarragon	Soups, salads, sauces, egg and cheese dishes
Chili powder	Ground blend	Blend of spices including cumin, chili peppers, oregano, garlic	Chili and Mexican dishes, egg dishes, appetizers, ground meat
Chive	Fresh, dried, frozen	Grasslike herb with onion flavor	Salads, egg and cheese dishes, fish, soups
Cilantro (fresh coriander, Chinese parsley)	Fresh leaves	The plant that produces coriander seeds; delicate texture; assertive, herbaceous aroma and flavor. Leaves resemble flat parsley	Widely used in Asian and Southwestern cooking and in dishes with various ethnic influences
Cinnamon	Sticks, ground	Aromatic bark of cinnamon or cassia tree	Pastries, breads, desserts, cooked fruits, ham, sweet potatoes, hot beverages
Clove	Whole, ground	Dried flower buds of a tropical tree; pungent, sweet flavor	Whole: marinades, stocks, sauces, braised meats, ham, pickling Ground: cakes, pastries, fruits
Coriander	Whole, ground	Round, light-brown, hollow seed, slightly sweet, musty flavor	Pickling, sausage, pork, curried dishes, gingerbread
Cumin seed	Whole, ground	Small seed resembling caraway, but lighter in color	Ingredient of curry and chili powders; sausages and meats; egg and cheese dishes
Curry powder	Ground blend	A mixture of 16 to 20 spices, including red pepper, turmeric, cumin, coriander, ginger, cloves, cinnamon, black pepper; different brands vary greatly in flavor and hotness	Curried dishes, eggs, vegetables, fish, soups, rice
Dill	Crushed leaves (called dill weed), whole seed	Herb and seed with familiar dill pickle flavor; seed is more pungent than the herb	Seed: pickling, sauerkraut, soups Herb: salads, cheese dishes, fish and shellfish, some vegetables
Epazote	Fresh and dried leaves	A pungent herb with coarse-textured leaves	Used in Mexican cooking; often cooked with beans
Fennel	Whole seed	Greenish-brown seeds similar in flavor to anise, but larger in size	Italian sausage, tomato sauce, fish
Garlic	Fresh: whole bulbs; dried: granulated, powder, and mixed with salt	Strong, aromatic member of onion family; fresh bulbs composed of many small cloves	Wide variety of foods
Ginger	Whole, ground (also fresh and candied or crystallized)	Light-brown, knobby root of ginger plant	Baked goods and desserts, fruits, curried dishes, braised meats; fresh: in Chinese and other Asian dishes

(Continued)

T A B L E 4.1

Herbs and Spices (Continued)

Product	Market Forms	Description	Examples of Use
Juniper berry	Whole	Slightly soft, purple berries with piney flavor; principal flavoring of gin	Marinades, game dishes, sauerkraut
Lemongrass	Fresh stalks	A tropical grass with a slightly bulbous base and an aroma of lemon	Used in Southeast Asian dishes and in dishes influenced by Asian cuisine
Mace	Whole ("blade"), ground	Orange outer covering of nutmeg; similar flavor, but milder	Baked goods, desserts, fruits, sausages, pork, fish, spinach, squash, other vegetables
Marjoram	Crushed leaves	Gray-green herb with pleasant aroma and slightly minty flavor, similar to oregano, but much milder	Pâtés and ground meats, braised meats, sauces, roast lamb, poultry and poultry stuffings
Mint	Leaves	Aromatic herb with familiar cool flavor; two varieties: spearmint and peppermint	Lamb, fruits, tea and fruit beverages, peas, carrots, potatoes
Mustard seed	Whole, ground (also prepared mustard; see p. 65)	Very pungent seed in two varieties: white or yellow, and brown—brown is stronger	Cheese and egg dishes, pickling, meats, sauces and gravies
Nutmeg	Whole, ground	Sweet, aromatic kernel of nutmeg fruit	Soups, cream sauces, chicken, veal, many vegetables (spinach, mushrooms, squash, potatoes), desserts, custards, breads, pastries
Oregano	Leaves, ground	Pungent herb, known as the "pizza herb"	Italian and Mexican dishes, tomato products
Paprika	Ground	Ground form of a dried, sweet red pepper. Spanish variety is brighter in color, mild in flavor; Hungarian is darker and more pungent	Spanish: used (or overused) primarily as garnish on light-colored foods Hungarian: goulash, braised meats and poultry, sauces
Parsley	Fresh: whole sprigs, in bunches; dried: in flakes	Most widely used herb. Dark-green curly or flat leaves with delicate, sweet flavor	Almost all foods
Pepper, black and white	Whole (peppercorns); ground fine, medium, or coarse	Small black or creamy white, hard berry. Pungent flavor and aroma	Most widely used spice (see p. 64)
Pepper, red	(see Cayenne)		
Peppercorn, pink	Whole	Bright-pink, dried seed or berry; pungent, floral taste; unrelated to black pepper	Limited uses in meat, poultry, and fish dishes; sauce garnish; used in peppercorn mixtures
Poppy seed	Whole	Tiny blue-black seeds with faint but distinctive flavor	Garnish for breads and rolls, buttered noodles; ground: in pastry fillings
Rosemary	Whole	Light-green leaves resembling pine needles	Lamb, braised meats and poultry, soups, tomato and meat sauces
Saffron	Whole (thread)	Red stigma of saffron crocus. Gives bright-yellow color to foods. Mild, distinctive flavor. Very expensive	Should be steeped in hot liquid before use. Rice dishes, poultry, seafood, bouillabaisse, baked goods
Sage	Whole, rubbed (finer consistency than whole leaves), ground	Pungent gray-green herb with fuzzy leaves	Pork, poultry, stuffings, sausage, beans, tomatoes
Savory	Crushed leaves	Fragrant herb of mint family; summer savory is preferred to winter	Many meat, poultry, fish, egg, and vegetable dishes
Sesame seed	Whole (hulled or unhulled)	Small yellowish seed with nutlike taste. Familiar hamburger bun garnish. High oil content	Bread and roll garnish
Sichuan peppercorn	Whole	Brown seed pod, usually partially opened; spicy, peppery flavor, but unrelated to black peppercorns	Chinese and other Asian dishes; spicy meat and poultry dishes

TABLE 4.1

Herbs and Spices *(Continued)*

Product	Market Forms	Description	Examples of Use
Star anise	Whole or broken	Dried, star-shaped seed pod, with an aniselike flavor (but unrelated to anise) but more aromatic	Used primarily to flavor stewed or braised Chinese dishes
Tarragon	Crushed leaves	Delicate green herb with flavor that is both minty and licoricelike	Béarnaise sauce, tarragon vinegar, chicken, fish, salads and dressings, eggs
Thyme	Crushed leaves, ground	Tiny brownish-green leaves; very aromatic	One of the most important and versatile of herbs; stocks, soups, sauces, meats poultry, tomatoes
Turmeric	Ground	Intense yellow root of ginger family; mild but distinctive peppery flavor	A basic ingredient of curry powder; pickles, relishes, salads, eggs, rice

Terms for Review

coagulation	infrared	roast	pan-fry
connective tissues	microwave	bake	deep-fry
caramelization	poach	barbecue	seasoning
gelatinization	simmer	smoke-roast	flavoring
fiber	boil	broil	volatile
smoke point	blanch	grill	herb
conduction	steam	griddle	spice
convection	en papillote	pan-broil	
radiation	braise	sauté	

Questions for Discussion

1. Your broiler cook has just broiled a codfish fillet that turned out dry, rubbery, and shrunken. Explain what happened to it.

2. Why might adding some tomato product to a beef stew help to make the meat more tender?

3. You are roasting a large quantity of ducklings and must use both your conventional ovens and your convection oven. You set all the ovens at the same temperature, but find the ducklings in the convection oven are done first. Why did this happen?

4. Arrange the following cooking methods in three groups, depending on whether they are moist-heat methods, dry-heat methods without fat, and dry-heat methods with fat: braising, roasting, deep-frying, sautéing, poaching, steaming, broiling, pressure frying, grilling, simmering.

5. What are some advantages of braising a pan of Swiss steaks in the oven instead of on the range?

6. A cook in your restaurant is roasting several pans of chickens. He thinks they are browning too fast and he covers the pans with foil to keep the chickens from browning too much more. What is wrong with this?

7. You are sautéing beef tenderloin tips for stroganoff, and you suddenly find that the meat is simmering in liquid rather than sautéing. What did you do wrong?

8. Your customers complain that your French fries are too greasy and soggy. How can you correct the problem?

9. What is meant by the phrase "adjust the seasoning"?

10. What is wrong with adding whole caraway seed to a portion of goulash just before serving

Chilled Melon and Mint Soup

Yield: 3 qt (3 L)   **Portions:** 12   **Portion size:** 8 oz (250 mL)

U.S.	Metric	Ingredients
3 lb	1.4 kg	Galia melon (see note)
3 lb 8 oz	1.6 kg	Charentais melon (see note)
4 lb	1.9 kg	Honeydew melon
1 lb 4 oz	600 g	Watermelon
to taste	to taste	Lemon juice
to taste	to taste	Sugar
2 oz	60 g	Mint leaves, finely chopped
		Garnish:
as needed	as needed	Mint sprigs

PROCEDURE

1. Quarter the melons. Scrape the seeds from the galia, Charentais, and honeydew melons. Remove as many seeds as possible from the watermelon. Cut the flesh of each type of melon into balls with a ball cutter and place in a bowl. Cover and refrigerate.

2. Scoop the remaining flesh from the melons. Place in a food processor and purée. (Do not use a blender unless you remove all the watermelon seeds first, as it will chop the seeds into fine bits.) Strain to remove watermelon seeds.

3. Taste and, if required, add lemon juice and sugar to taste.

4. Stir in the chopped mint. Pour over the melon balls and chill for at least 2 hours.

5. At service time, ladle into chilled bowls and garnish with sprigs of mint.

Per serving:
Calories, 60; Protein, 1 g; Fat, 0 g (0% cal.); Cholesterol, 0 mg; Carbohydrates, 15 g; Fiber, 1 g; Sodium, 15 mg.

Note: If galia melon is not available, use yellow-fleshed honeydew. If Charentais melon is not available, use cantaloupe.

Chilled Melon and Mint Soup

See these soup recipes in other chapters:

Clear Soup with Shrimp (Japanese) and variations (p. 719)
Miso Soup (p. 719)
Zuppa di Ceci e Riso (Italian Chick Pea and Rice Soup) (p. 739)
Caldo Verde (p. 749)

chapter 5

The Recipe: Its Structure and Its Use

Recipes are important tools for the cook because they are a means of recording and passing along essential information. Learning to cook without being able to consult recipes would be like learning to play the piano without using written music.

In spite of their importance, written recipes have many limitations, as we discuss in this chapter. No matter how detailed a recipe may be, it assumes that you already have certain knowledge—that you understand the terminology it uses, for example, and that you know how to measure ingredients.

In this chapter, we discuss various kinds of recipes and their structure, and we learn how recipes are used in a commercial kitchen. In particular, we examine techniques for measuring ingredients and portions, for converting recipes, and for calculating food cost with the aid of written recipes.

The Written Recipe

THE USES AND LIMITATIONS OF RECIPES

A recipe is a set of instructions for producing a certain dish. In order to duplicate a desired preparation, it is necessary to have a precise record of the ingredients, their amounts, and the way in which they are combined and cooked. This is the purpose of a recipe.

Many people believe that learning to cook means simply learning recipes. Knowledgeable cooks, on the other hand, are able to prepare food without written recipes, if they have to, because they have a good understanding of basic principles and techniques. A recipe is a way of applying basic techniques to specific ingredients.

If you have read the preceding chapter, or have even casually leafed through this book, you know that it is not just a book of recipes. Although there are hundreds of recipes in this book, they take up a relatively small part of it. Your main concern is learning techniques and procedures that you can apply to any recipe.

The main purpose of learning basic cooking principles is not to be able to cook without recipes, however, but to understand the recipes you use. As we said in the beginning of this chapter, every recipe assumes that you have certain knowledge, so that you can understand the instructions and follow them correctly.

Some recipes supply very little information and some supply a great deal. But no matter how detailed it is, a written recipe can't tell you everything, and some judgment by the cook is always required. There are several reasons for this:

1. **Food products are not uniform.**
    Food ingredients are natural products, so they are not uniform like machine bolts, ballpoint pens, and typing paper. One tomato may be riper than another, one carrot more tender or sweeter than another, one oyster saltier than another. Such variations may affect how the ingredients are handled, how long they are cooked, what proportions are needed, and how much seasoning is required.

2. **Kitchens do not have the same equipment.**
    Different pans distribute heat at different rates. Different broilers heat to different temperatures. Liquid evaporates from wide pots faster than from tall, narrow ones, and so on.

3. **It is impossible to give exact instructions for many processes.**
    How do you set the burner if the instructions say "Cook over medium heat"? How thick is a "thick" sauce? How long do you broil a rare steak?

The difference between an experienced cook and a beginning cook is the ability to make judgments about these variables.

STANDARDIZED RECIPES

1. **Definition.**
    A *standardized recipe* is a set of instructions describing the way a particular establishment prepares a particular dish. In other words, it is a customized recipe developed by an operation for the use of its own cooks, using its own equipment, to be served to its own patrons.

2. **The structure of a standardized recipe.**
    Recipe formats differ from operation to operation, but nearly all of them try to include as much precise information as possible. The following details may be listed:
    *   Name of the recipe.
    *   Yield, including total yield, number of portions, and exact portion size.
    *   Ingredients and exact amounts, listed in order of use.
    *   Equipment needed, including measuring equipment, pan sizes, portioning equipment, and so on.
    *   Directions for preparing the dish. Directions are kept as simple as possible.
    *   Preparation and cooking times.

After reading this chapter, you should be able to

1. List three basic limitations of written recipes.

2. Identify three reasons for using judgment when following a recipe.

3. State the two functions of a standardized recipe and list eight types of information it is likely to include.

4. Define the purpose of an instructional recipe and describe how it differs from a standardized recipe.

5. Identify the three methods used to measure ingredients and provide an example of the types of ingredients commonly measured by each method.

6. Name the five techniques used for portion control in plating and service.

7. Name the four basic units of measurement in the metric system and what each measures.

8. Apply the two-part formula required to convert recipes to a higher or lower yield and identify factors that can negatively impact results when cooking with a converted recipe.

9. Define yield-cost analysis and explain the distinction between as purchased and edible portion quantities of food.

10. Perform yield-cost analysis.

11. Calculate raw food costs.

- Directions for portioning, plating, and garnishing.
- Directions for breaking down the station, cleaning up, and storing leftovers.

3. **The function of standardized recipes.**
   An operation's own recipes are used to control production. They do this in two ways:
   - **They control quality.** Standardized recipes are detailed and specific. This is to ensure that the product is the same every time it is made and served, no matter who cooks it.
   - **They control quantity.** First, they indicate precise quantities for every ingredient and how they are to be measured. Second, they indicate exact yields and portion sizes, and how the portions are to be measured and served.

4. **The limitations of standardized recipes.**
   Standardized recipes have the same problems as all recipes—the problems that we discussed earlier regarding variations in foods, equipment, and vagueness of instructions. These problems can be reduced by writing the recipe carefully, but they cannot be eliminated. Even if an operation uses good standardized recipes, a new employee making a dish for the first time will usually require some supervision to make sure he or she interprets the instructions the same way as the rest of the staff. These limitations don't invalidate standardized recipes. If anything, they make exact directions even more important. But they do mean that experience and knowledge are still very important.

Table 5.1 gives an example of a standardized recipe based on a recipe in this book. Compare and note the differences between this recipe and the recipe on page 336, an instructional recipe (explained in the following section). In particular, note the following differences:

- There are no metric units. Because this recipe is designed for a single kitchen in the United States, only one set of measurements is needed.
- The procedure appears below the ingredients rather than in a column to the right. An operation can choose any recipe format, but the operation using this recipe wants to emphasize collecting and measuring all ingredients before beginning to cook.
- The recipe includes Critical Control Points. The operation using this recipe has established a HACCP system. Food safety instructions are included as part of the standardized recipe. (Read or review the section on HACCP, pp. 24–26, if necessary.)

INSTRUCTIONAL RECIPES

The recipes in this book are *not* standardized recipes. Remember that a standardized recipe is custom-made for a particular operation. The recipes in this book are obviously not.

The purpose of a standardized recipe is to direct and control the production of a particular food item. Directions must be as complete and exact as possible.

The purpose of the instructional recipes in this book is to teach basic cooking techniques. They provide an opportunity for you to practice, with specific ingredients, the general procedures you have learned.

If you glance at any of the recipes in this book, you will see that they do not contain all the features of a standardized recipe, as described in the previous section. In particular, you will see the following differences:

1. **Instructions for preparation.**
   In most cases, recipes in this book follow a discussion of a basic procedure. The recipes are examples of the general procedure, and they give you experience in applying what you have learned. The information you are given in the recipe instructions is intended primarily to encourage you to think and to learn a technique, not just to turn out a product. You should consult your instructor when you have a question about a procedure.

2. **Variations and optional ingredients.**
   Many recipes are followed by variations. These are actually whole recipes given in abbreviated terms. It is possible to write them out as separate, full-length recipes. (You are encouraged to do this before preparing a variation, as a learning experience.)

   Giving recipes as variations rather than as separate recipes encourages you to see the patterns behind each. Again, you are learning techniques, not just recipes. You develop a lot more understanding of what you are doing if you see Spanish rice and Turkish pilaf, for

TABLE 5.1

Chicken Breasts Parmesan

Portion size: 1 chicken breast, 4 oz   **Total yield:** 12 portions

Quantity	Ingredients	Equipment
4 oz	Flour	2 half-size hotel pans
1¼ tsp	Salt	1 2-qt stainless-steel bowl
½ tsp	Ground white pepper	1 wire whip
5	Whole eggs, size large	1 meat mallet
3½ oz	Grated parmesan cheese	4 12-in. sauté pans
1½ oz	Whole milk	1-oz ladle
12	Boneless, skinless chicken breasts, 4 oz each	tongs
		plastic wrap
4 oz	Clarified butter	instant-read thermometer, sanitized

PROCEDURE

Advance Prep:

CCP 1. Collect and measure all ingredients. *Refrigerate eggs, cheese, milk, and chicken at 40°F or lower until needed.*

2. Collect all equipment.

3. Place the flour in a hotel pan. Season with the salt and white pepper.

4. Break the eggs into the stainless-steel bowl and discard the shells. Beat with the wire whip until foamy. Add the grated cheese and milk. Mix in with the whip.

CCP 5. *Cover the bowl with plastic wrap and refrigerate at below 40°F until needed.*

6. Flatten the chicken breasts lightly with the meat mallet until ½ inch thick. Place the breasts in a hotel pan.

CCP *Cover with plastic wrap. Refrigerate at below 40°F until ready to cook.*

CCP 7. *Clean and sanitize the mallet and the work surface. Wash hands thoroughly.*

Cooking:

8. Place one of the sauté pans over moderate heat. Allow to heat 2 minutes.

9. Measure 1 oz clarified butter into the pan.

10. One at a time, dip 3 chicken breasts in the seasoned flour until completely coated on both sides. Shake off excess. Dip in the

CCP egg mixture. Coat both sides completely. *Return remaining chicken and egg mixture to refrigerator.*

CCP 11. Place the 3 breasts in the sauté pan. *Wash hands after handling the raw chicken and before handling cooked food.*

12. Cook the chicken over moderate heat until golden brown on the bottom. Using the tongs, turn over and continue to

CCP cook *until the chicken reaches an internal temperature of 165°–170°F. Test internal temperature with sanitized instant-read thermometer.*

CCP 13. Repeat with the remaining chicken breasts, using clean sauté pans. *If your work is interrupted before completion, cover and refrigerate chicken and egg mixture.*

CCP 14. *If the chicken is not served immediately, hold in a heated holding cabinet to maintain internal temperature of 145°F.*

CCP 15. *Discard leftover egg mixture and seasoned flour. Do not use for any other products. Clean and sanitize all equipment.*

example, or coconut cream pie and chocolate pudding as variations of the same basic techniques rather than as separate, unrelated recipes.

Your instructors may have their own variations, or they may wish to make changes in the basic recipes in order to teach you certain points. Unlike standardized recipes, instructional recipes are not engraved in stone.

COOKING WITH JUDGMENT

When you make a recipe for the first time, you should apply your knowledge and thinking about the recipe in relation to the skills you have. In particular, you should determine the following points:

1. **What are the basic cooking methods?**
   When you read the recipe for Sauerbraten (p. 292), you will quickly figure out that the cooking method used is braising (even if the word "braise" is never used in the recipe). Then you should review in your mind everything you know about basic braising procedures.

2. **What are the characteristics of the ingredients?**

   If the sauerbraten recipe calls for bottom round of beef, for example, you should ask yourself, "What do I know about bottom round? Is it lean or fatty? Tough or tender? How do these traits affect cooking?"

3. **What are the functions of the ingredients?**

   What does the vinegar do in the sauerbraten recipe? What about the vegetables? The gingersnaps?

   When you have gained more experience, you will be able to easily answer these questions. You will know what ingredients contribute to flavor, to texture, or to body, and how they do it.

4. **What are the cooking times?**

   Most of the recipes in this book do not give cooking times, except as general guidelines to help you plan production. This is because cooking times are too variable to be stated exactly.

   Instead, you will learn how to test for doneness by observing changes in the product. You must be able to judge when a product has reached the right temperature, the proper texture or consistency, or the desired taste.

   When you learn to cook with judgment, you will be able to cook with most recipes, even poorly written ones. You will be able to see what might be wrong with a new recipe before you try it and to make adjustments in it. You will know how to substitute ingredients or use different equipment. You will even be able to create new recipes.

   Remember we said that some recipes supply very little information and depend largely on the cook's knowledge. With enough experience, you will even be able to cook from recipes like the following, a complete recipe for Fillets of Sole Bercy, quoted in its entirety from *Le Répertoire de la Cuisine*, a favorite book used by chefs in classical French cooking: "Poached with shallots and chopped parsley, white wine and fish stock. Reduce the stock, add butter, and coat the fish, glaze."

Measurement

Many restaurants budget a profit of 10 percent or less. This means that a sandwich selling for $3.00 makes a profit of only 30 cents. If the cook happens to put a half-ounce too much meat in the sandwich, the operation is probably losing money on it. No wonder so many restaurants go out of business.

Careful measurement is one of the most important parts of food production. It is important for consistent quality each time a recipe is prepared and served. And it is important for cost controls.

There are two important kinds of measurement in the kitchen:

1. Ingredient measurement
2. Portion measurement, or portion control

INGREDIENT MEASUREMENT

Weight

Weighing is the most accurate method of measuring ingredients. It is the method used for most solid ingredients.

Accurate scales are necessary for weighing. Small portion scales are often used in the kitchen because of their convenience. Balance scales are used in the bakeshop (see p. 759 for procedure).

Procedure for Weighing Ingredients on a Portion Scale

1. Place receiving container, if any, on the scale.

2. Set the scale so that it reads zero.

3. Add the item being weighed to the container (or place on scale, if no container is used) until the scale reads desired weight.

To be able to weigh ingredients, you must observe the difference between AP (as purchased) weight and EP (edible portion) weight.

AP weight is the weight of the item as purchased, before any trimming is done.
EP weight is the weight after all inedible or nonservable parts are trimmed off.

Recipes sometimes specify which weight they are referring to. When they don't, you must judge from the instructions.

1. If a recipe calls for "2 lb potatoes" and the first instruction is "scrub, peel, and eye the potatoes," then you know that AP weight is called for.
2. If the recipe calls for "2 lb peeled, diced potatoes," then you know that the EP weight is called for. You will need more than 2 lb AP.

Volume

Volume measures are used for liquids. Measuring a liquid by volume is usually faster than weighing it, and accuracy is good.

Solid ingredients are usually not measured by volume because they cannot usually be measured accurately by this method. One pint of chopped onions will vary considerably in weight, depending on how large or small the onions are cut and whether the volume measure is filled loosely or packed.

Dry ingredients such as flour or sugar are usually weighed in the bakeshop. However, they are sometimes measured by volume in the kitchen, when speed is more important than accuracy. To measure dry ingredients by volume, fill a dry-volume measure until the ingredient is mounded over the top. Then level it off with a spatula or other straight edge.

Very small quantities, such as ¼ teaspoon salt, are measured by volume when the amount is too small to weigh.

Count

Measuring ingredients by count is done in these circumstances:

1. When units are in fairly standard sizes. *Examples:* 6 large eggs for a pancake batter; 8 parsley stems for a stock.
2. When serving portions are determined by numbers of units. *Examples:* 1 baked apple per portion; 6 fried shrimp per portion.

PORTION CONTROL

Portion control is the measurement of portions to ensure that the correct amount of an item is served. In order for portion control to be carried out, cooks and service personnel must be aware of proper portion sizes. These facts are usually indicated on the house recipes and on the working menu used in the kitchen and service area.

Portion Control in Preparation

Portion control actually begins with the measuring of ingredients. If this is not done correctly, then the yield of the recipe will be thrown off.

When portions are determined by count—1 hamburger patty, 2 tomato slices, 1 wedge of pie—then the units must be measured or cut according to instructions: 4 ounces of meat per patty; ¼-inch slices of "5 × 6" tomatoes; 8 equal wedges per pie.

Portion Control in Plating and Service

Portioning for service may be done by the cook, as in a short-order restaurant, or by the service personnel, as in a cafeteria. The following tools and techniques are used.

1. Count.
   Examples: 1 slice of ham per order; 5 shrimp per order. This is accurate if cutting and other prep work have been done correctly.

2. **Weight.**

   Example: 4 ounces of sliced ham per order. A portion scale must be at the serving station for this method of portion control.

3. **Volume.**

   Ladles, scoops, and kitchen spoons come in standard sizes and are used for portioning. The exact size of the ladle or scoop must be determined in advance and indicated on service instructions.

   Kitchen spoons, either solid or perforated, are not as accurate for portioning but are often used for convenience and speed. You must be able to judge by eye how full to fill the spoon (rounded, heaped, etc.). Check a spoonful on a portion scale from time to time to make sure you are being consistent.

4. **Even division.**

   Examples: cutting a pie into 8 equal wedges; cutting a pan of lasagne 4 by 6 to make 24 equal portions.

5. **Standard fill.**

   Standard-size dishes, cups, or glasses are filled to a given level, as judged by eye. *Example:* a glass of orange juice. This is actually a form of volume measure.

UNITS OF MEASURE

The system of measurement used in the United States is complicated. Even when people have used the system all their lives, they still sometimes have trouble remembering things like how many fluid ounces are in a quart or how many feet are in a mile.

Table 5.2 lists abbreviations used in this book. Table 5.3 lists equivalents among the units of measure used in the kitchen. You should memorize these thoroughly so you don't have to lose time making simple calculations.

THE METRIC SYSTEM

The United States is the only major country that uses the complex system of measurement we have just described. Other countries use a much simpler system called the *metric system*. It is possible that some day the metric system may be used in U.S. kitchens. Even if this never happens, it is useful, in this age of international influences on cooking, to be able to read and use recipes from around the world. So it is a good idea to become familiar with the metric system.

Basic Units

In the metric system, there is one basic unit for each type of measurement:

The *gram* is the basic unit of weight.
The *liter* is the basic unit of volume.
The *meter* is the basic unit of length.
The *degree Celsius* is the basic unit of temperature.

Larger or smaller units are made simply by multiplying or dividing by 10, 100, 1000, and so on. These divisions are expressed by *prefixes*. The ones you will need to know are:

kilo- (kill-o) = 1000
deci- (dess-i) = 1/10
centi- (sent-i) = 1/100
milli- (mill-i) = 1/1000

Once you know these basic units, there is no longer any need for complicated tables like Table 5.3. Table 5.4 summarizes the metric units you will need to know in the kitchen.

TABLE 5.2

Abbreviations of U.S. Units in This Book

Pound	lb
Ounce	oz
Gallon	gal
Quart	qt
Pint	pt
Cup	cup (abbreviation not used)
Fluid ounce	fl. oz or oz
Tablespoon	tbsp
Teaspoon	tsp
Inch	in.

TABLE 5.3

Units of Measure— U.S. System

Weight	
1 pound	= 16 ounces
Volume	
1 gallon	= 4 quarts
1 quart	= 2 pints
	or
	4 cups
	or
	32 (fluid) ounces
1 pint	= 2 cups
	or
	16 (fluid) ounces
1 cup	= 8 (fluid) ounces
1 (fluid) ounce	= 2 tablespoons
1 tablespoon	= 3 teaspoons
Length	
1 foot	= 12 inches

Note: One fluid ounce (usually called simply "ounce") of water weighs 1 ounce. One pint of water weighs 1 pound.

TABLE 5.4

Metric Units

Basic Units

Quantity	Unit	Abbreviation
Weight	gram	g
Volume	liter	L
Length	meter	m
Temperature	degree Celsius	°C

Divisions and Multiples

Prefix/ Example	Meaning	Abbreviation
kilo-	1000	k
kilogram	1000 grams	kg
deci-	$\frac{1}{10}$	d
deciliter	0.1 liter	dL
centi-	$\frac{1}{100}$	c
centimeter	0.01 meter	cm
milli-	$\frac{1}{1000}$	m
millimeter	0.001 meter	mm

Converting to Metric

Most people think that the metric system is much harder to learn than it really is. This is because they think about metric units in terms of U.S. units. They read that there are 28.35 grams in an ounce, and they are immediately convinced that they will never be able to learn metrics.

Do not worry about being able to convert between U.S. and metric units. This is a very important point to remember, especially if you think that the metric system might be hard to learn.

The reason for this is simple. You will usually be working in either one system or the other. You will rarely, if ever, have to convert from one to the other. (An exception might be if you have equipment based on one system but want to use a recipe written in the other.) If U.S. kitchens change to the metric system, everyone will use scales that measure in grams and kilograms, volume measures that measure in liters and deciliters, and thermometers that indicate degrees Celsius. And everyone will use recipes that indicate these units. No one will have to worry about how many grams are in an ounce. All one will have to remember is the information in Table 5.4.

To become accustomed to working in metric units, it is helpful to have a feel for how large the units are. The following equivalents may be used to help you visualize metric units. They are not exact conversion factors. (When you need exact conversion factors, see Appendix 1.)

A *kilogram* is slightly more than 2 pounds.
A *gram* is about $\frac{1}{30}$ ounce. (A half-teaspoon of flour weighs a little less than a gram.)
A *liter* is slightly more than a quart.
A *deciliter* (100 milliliters) is slightly less than a half-cup.
A *centiliter* (10 milliliters) is about 2 teaspoons.
A *meter* is slightly more than 3 feet.
A *centimeter* is about $\frac{3}{8}$ inch.
0°C is the freezing point of water (32°F).
100°C is the boiling point of water (212°F).
An increase or decrease of *1 degree Celsius* is equivalent to about 2 degrees Fahrenheit.

Metric Recipes

Many recipe writers in the United States print exact metric equivalents in their recipes. As a result, you will see recipes calling for 454 grams of potatoes, 28.35 grams of butter, or a baking temperature of 191°C. No wonder people are afraid of the metric system!

Kitchens in countries that use the metric system do not work with such impractical numbers, any more than we normally use figures like 1 lb 1¼ oz potatoes, 2.19 oz butter, or a baking temperature of 348°F. That would defeat the purpose of the metric system, which is to be simple and practical. If you have a chance to look at a French cookbook, you will see nice, even numbers like 1 kg, 200 g, and 4 dl. (Note that the metric abbreviations used in this book are consistent with common usage in Canada. Abbreviations used in Europe are somewhat different, such as lowercase "l" instead of uppercase "L" for liter.)

The metric equivalents in the recipes in this book are rounded off. What's more, they are not always rounded off in the same way. In some places, you may see 1 pound rounded off to 500 grams, in other places to 450 grams. The object is to keep the proportions and the total yield as close as possible while arriving at practical measurements. Unfortunately, it is not always possible to keep the proportions exactly the same because the U.S. system is not decimal-based like the metric system. In some cases, the metric quantities may produce slightly different results due to these varying proportions, but these differences are small. If you have U.S. equipment, use the U.S. units, and if you have metric equipment, use the metric units. You should rarely have to worry about converting between the two.

Converting Recipes

Unless you are working in an operation that uses only its own standardized recipes, you will frequently be required to convert recipes to different quantities. For example, you may have a recipe for 50 portions of Swiss steak but need only 25 portions.

Converting recipes is an important technique. It is a skill you will probably need to use many times in this book. There is no "best" yield to write recipes for, as every operation, every school, and every individual has different needs.

Nearly everyone instinctively can double a recipe or cut it in half. It seems more complicated, though, to change a recipe from 10 to 18 portions, say, or from 50 to 35. Actually, the principle is exactly the same: You multiply each ingredient by a number called a conversion factor, as follows:

Procedure for Converting Total Yield

1. Divide the desired yield by the recipe yield:

$$\frac{\text{new yield}}{\text{old yield}} = \text{conversion factor}$$

2. Multiply each ingredient quantity by the conversion factor:

$$\text{conversion factor} \times \text{old quantity} = \text{new quantity}$$

In order to do this in the U.S. system, you usually have to convert all weights to ounces and all volumes to fluid ounces. (This is not necessary in the metric system.)

Example 1: You have a recipe for 10 portions of Broccoli Mornay requiring 3 lb AP broccoli and 2½ cups Mornay Sauce. Convert to 15 portions.

$$\frac{\text{new yield}}{\text{old yield}} = \frac{15}{10} = 1.5$$

Broccoli: 3 lb = 48 oz
48 oz × 1.5 = 72 oz = 4 lb 8 oz

Sauce: 2 ½ cups = 20 oz
20 oz × 1.5 = 30 oz = 3¾ cups

Example 2: You have a recipe for 10 portions of Broccoli Mornay requiring 1500 grams AP broccoli and 600 mL Mornay Sauce. Convert to 15 portions.

$$\frac{\text{new yield}}{\text{old yield}} = \frac{15}{10} = 1.5$$

Broccoli: 1500 g × 1.5 = 2250 g
Sauce: 600 mL × 1.5 = 900 mL

Procedure for Changing Portion Sizes

If your recipe yields, let's say, 20 portions, 4 ounces each, and you need 30 portions, 5 ounces each, you must add a few extra steps to the conversion process.

1. Determine total yield of the recipe by multiplying the number of portions by the portion size:

$$\text{portions} \times \text{portion size} = \text{total yield (old)}$$

2. Determine the total yield you desire by multiplying the desired number of portions by the desired portion size:

$$\text{desired portions} \times \text{desired portion size} = \text{total yield (new)}$$

3. Divide desired yield by recipe yield to get the conversion factor:

$$\frac{\text{total yield (new)}}{\text{total yield (old)}} = \text{conversion factor}$$

4. Multiply each ingredient by the conversion factor:

$$\text{conversion factor} \times \text{old quantity} = \text{new quantity}$$

Note: The conversion factor may sometimes turn out to be 1. In these cases, the total yield is obviously the same, and the recipe does not need to be changed.

In order to make these procedures clearer, let's work through the conversion of a full recipe to give you practice with the equations. The following examples are in the U.S. system of measures. For metric examples, see Appendix 4, page 894.

In the first column that follows is a list of ingredients for a sautéed beef dish. As you can see, the quantities given in the second column are enough to make eight portions at 8 ounces each.

Beef tenderloin tips and mushrooms à la crème
Portions: 8
Portion size: 8 oz

Butter	2 oz
Onions	4 oz
Flour	1 tbsp
Mushrooms	½ lb
Beef tenderloin	2½ lb
White wine	½ cup
Prepared mustard	2 tsp
Brown sauce	1½ pt
Heavy cream	1 cup
Salt	to taste
Pepper	to taste

Let's say we need 18 portions instead of 8. To find the conversion factor, we divide the new yield by the old yield:

$$\frac{\text{new yield}}{\text{old yield}} = \frac{18}{8} = 2.25$$

To convert the recipe to 18 portions, we simply multiply each ingredient quantity by this conversion factor of 2.25.

First, to make this easier, we should change pounds to ounces and cups, pints, and quarts to fluid ounces, using the figures in Table 5.3. For example, to change the measurement for beef tenderloin to ounces, multiply 2½ (the weight in pounds) by 16 (the number of ounces in a pound) to get 40 ounces.

The equivalents we need for this recipe are as follows:

½ lb equals 8 ounces
2½ pounds equals 40 ounces
½ cup equals 4 fluid ounces
1½ pints equals 24 fluid ounces

In Example 1 below, we have substituted these equivalent quantities. Then we have multiplied all the ingredient quantities by the conversion factor to get the quantities that we need for 18 portions. Check through all the calculations to make sure you follow them. The quantities for salt and pepper will still, of course, be indicated as "to taste."

Now let's suppose we want to find the quantities needed to give us 40 portions, 6 ounces each. Because the portion size changes, we must use the second procedure explained previously.

Example 1

Ingredient	Quantity	Times	Conversion Factor	Equals	New Quantity
Butter	2 oz	×	2.25	=	4.5 oz
Onions	4 oz	×	2.25	=	9 oz
Flour	1 tbsp	×	2.25	=	2.25 tbsp *or* 2 tbsp plus ¾ tsp
Mushrooms	8 oz	×	2.25	=	18 oz *or* 1 lb 2 oz
Beef tenderloin	40 oz	×	2.25	=	90 oz *or* 5 lb 10 oz
White wine	4 fl. oz	×	2.25	=	9 fl. oz
Prepared mustard	2 tsp	×	2.25	=	4½ tsp *or* 1½ tbsp
Brown sauce	24 fl. oz	×	2.25	=	54 fl. oz *or* 3 pt plus 6 fl. oz
Heavy cream	8 fl. oz	×	2.25	=	18 fl. oz *or* 2¼ cups

Example 2

Ingredient	Quantity	Times	Conversion Factor	Equals	New Quantity
Butter	2 oz	×	3.75	=	7.5 oz
Onions	4 oz	×	3.75	=	15 oz
Flour	1 tbsp	×	3.75	=	3.75 tbsp *or* 3 tbsp plus 2¼ tsp
Mushrooms	8 oz	×	3.75	=	30 oz *or* 1 lb 14 oz
Beef tenderloin	40 oz	×	3.75	=	150 oz *or* 9 lb 6 oz
White wine	4 fl. oz	×	3.75	=	15 fl. oz
Prepared mustard	2 tsp	×	3.75	=	7.5 tsp *or* 2½ tbsp
Brown sauce	24 fl. oz	×	3.75	=	90 fl. oz *or* 5 pt plus 10 fl. oz
Heavy cream	8 fl. oz	×	3.75	=	30 fl. oz *or* 3¾ cups

First, to find the total yield of the old recipe, we multiply the number of portions by the portion size:

$$8 \text{ (portions)} \times 8 \text{ oz} = 64 \text{ oz}$$

Do the same calculation for the desired yield:

$$40 \text{ (portions)} \times 6 \text{ oz} = 240 \text{ oz}$$

When we divide the new yield by the old yield (240 divided by 64), we arrive at a conversion factor of 3.75. In Example 2, we have done the conversions using the new factor of 3.75.

PROBLEMS IN CONVERTING RECIPES

For the most part, these conversion procedures work well. But when you make some very large conversions—from 10 to 400 portions, for example, or from 500 to 6—you may encounter problems.

For example, you may have to make major equipment changes, like from a 2-quart saucepot to a large steam kettle. Consequently, you have to adjust your techniques and, sometimes, even ingredients. Evaporation rates may be different, thickening agents may need increasing or decreasing, seasonings and spices may have to be cut back. Or sometimes quantities may be too large or too small to mix properly.

This is one more example of the importance of cooking with judgment. Experienced chefs develop a feel for these problems over the years. When you make such adjustments on converted recipes, be sure to make a note of them for future reference.

Although there are no fixed rules you can learn for these adjustments, it is possible to list the most common types of problems encountered so that you can be on the alert for them when making recipe conversions. In general, most of the pitfalls fall into one of the following categories.

Measuring

This is most often a problem when you are expanding small recipes, such as when you want to take a consumer recipe for four portions and adapt it to a high-volume operation such as a large cafeteria. Many such recipes use volume measures for both solids and liquids. As we explained earlier, volume measurement of solids is inaccurate. Of course, small inaccuracies can become large ones when a recipe is multiplied. Therefore, it is important to be cautious and to test carefully when you are converting a recipe that uses volume measures for solid ingredients.

This problem is largely avoided when all solids are measured by weight. But such items as spices and seasonings may be too small to be measured accurately by weight. For this reason, it is usually a good idea to cut back on spices and salt in a converted recipe. You can always add more if you taste the product and decide it needs more seasoning.

Surface and Volume

If you have studied geometry, you may remember that a cube with a volume of 1 cubic foot has a top surface area of 1 square foot. But if you double the volume of the cube, the top surface area is not doubled but is in fact only about 1½ times as large.

What in the world, you ask, does this have to do with cooking? Consider the following example.

Suppose you have a good recipe for a half-gallon of cream soup, which you normally make in a small soup pot. You want to make 16 gallons of the soup, so you multiply all ingredients by a conversion factor of 32 and make the soup in a steam kettle. To your surprise, not only do you end up with more soup than you expected, but it turns out rather thin and watery. What happened?

Your converted recipe has 32 times as much volume to start, but the amount of surface area has not increased nearly as much. Because the ratio of surface area to volume is less, there is less evaporation. This means that there is less reduction and less thickening, and the flavors are not as concentrated. To correct this problem, you would have to use less stock, and preferably a stock that is more concentrated.

Suppose instead that you made the expanded recipe in a tilting skillet. In this case, there is so much surface area that the liquid would evaporate very quickly, resulting in an overly thickened and overly seasoned soup.

Differences in surface area and volume can cause other problems as well. Food service operations have to be more careful than home cooks do about food spoilage and the Food Danger Zone (Chapter 2), because large volumes of food cool down and heat up much more slowly than small volumes do.

For the same reason, a home baker worries about keeping a bread dough warm so that it will ferment, but a commercial baker worries about keeping a dough cool enough so that it doesn't ferment too fast. This is because a large batch of dough has so much volume in comparison with its surface area that it tends to retain heat rather than cool down quickly to room temperature.

Equipment

When you change the size of a recipe, you must often change the equipment, too. This change often means that the recipe does not work in the same way. Cooks must be able to use their judgment to anticipate these problems and to modify their procedures to avoid them. The example just given, of cooking a large batch of soup in a steam kettle or in a tilting skillet, is among the kinds of problems that can arise when you change cooking utensils.

Other problems can arise because of mixers or other processing equipment. For example, if you break down a salad dressing recipe to make only a small quantity, you might find that there is so little liquid in the mixing machine that the beaters don't blend the ingredients properly.

Or you might have a recipe for a muffin batter that you usually make in small quantities and mix the batter by hand. When you increase the recipe greatly, you find you have too much to do by hand. Therefore, you use a mixer but keep the mixing time the same. Because the mixer does the job so efficiently, you overmix the batter and end up with poor-quality muffins.

Many mixing and stirring jobs can be done only by hand. This is easy with small quantities but difficult with large batches. The result is often an inferior product. On the other hand, some handmade products are better if they are done in large batches. It is hard, for example, to make a very small batch of puff pastry because the dough cannot be rolled and folded properly.

Time

Some people make the mistake of thinking that if you double a recipe, you must also double the cooking time. That this is an error can be shown by a simple example. Assume that it takes 15 minutes to cook a steak in a broiler. If you put two steaks in the broiler, it still takes 15 minutes to cook them, not 30 minutes.

If all other things are equal, cooking times stay the same when a recipe is converted. Problems arise, however, because all other things are not always equal. For example, a large pot of liquid takes longer to bring to a boil than a small pot. Therefore, the total cooking time is longer.

On the other hand, a big kettle of vegetable soup that you are making ahead for tomorrow's lunch takes longer to cool than a small pot. Meanwhile, the vegetables continue to cook in the retained heat during the cooling. In order to avoid overcooking, you may need to undercook the large batch slightly.

In cases where the cooking time must be increased, you sometimes might find that you have to increase the amount of herbs and spices. This is because the flavors are volatile (see p. 63), and more flavor is lost because of the increased cooking time. (Another answer to this problem is to add the spices later.)

Changing recipe sizes can affect not only cooking times but also mixing times. The best way to avoid this problem is to rely not on printed cooking and mixing times but on your own judgment and skills to tell you when a product is properly cooked or properly blended.

Recipe Problems

Many recipes have flaws, either in the quantities or types of ingredients or in the cooking procedures. When the item is made in small quantities, these flaws may not be noticeable, or the cook may almost unconsciously or automatically make adjustments during production. When the recipe is multiplied, however, the flaws may suddenly become apparent and the product quality lower. The only solution here is to carefully test recipes and to have a good understanding of basic cooking principles.

Food Cost

Food service operations are businesses. This means that someone in the operation has to worry about budgets, cost accounting, bills, and profits. Usually this is the job of the manager, while the cook takes care of food production.

The cooks have a great deal of responsibility for food cost controls, however. They must always be conscious of accurate measurement, portion control, and careful processing, cooking, and handling of foods to avoid excess trimming loss, shrinkage, and waste.

The manager, on the other hand, is concerned with determining budgets, calculating profits and expenses, and so on. We cannot deal with these subjects here, as this is a book about food preparation. But you may encounter them later in your studies or in your career.

Every cook should understand three areas of cost accounting, however—doing yield analyses, calculating raw food cost or portion cost, and using food cost percentages.

FOOD COST PERCENTAGES

An individual operation's food cost percentage is usually determined by the budget. The chef is interested in this figure because it tells him or her whether the menu prices and the costs for each item are in line.

The food cost percentage of a menu item equals the raw food cost or portion cost divided by the menu price:

$$\text{percentage} = \frac{\text{food cost}}{\text{menu price}}$$

You can use this figure in two ways:

1. If you know the menu price and want to see what your food cost should be in order to be within the budget, multiply the menu price by the percentage:

    $$\text{food cost} = \text{menu price} \times \text{percentage}$$

    Example: Menu price is $6.75 and food cost percentage is 35%.

    $$35\% = 0.35$$

    $$6.75 \times 0.35 = \$2.36$$

2. If you know the food cost and want to determine what the menu price should be at a particular percentage, divide the cost by the percentage:

    $$\text{menu price} = \frac{\text{food cost}}{\text{percentage}}$$

    Example: Food cost is $1.60 and food cost percentage is 40%.

    $$\frac{\$1.60}{40\%} = \frac{\$1.60}{0.40} = \$4.00$$

YIELD COST ANALYSIS

In order to calculate portion costs of recipes, you must first determine the costs of your ingredients. For many ingredients, this is relatively easy. You just look at your invoices or at price lists from your purveyors.

Many recipes, however, specify trimmed weight rather than the weight you actually pay for. For example, a stew might call for 2 pounds of sliced onions. Let's say that you pay 24 cents a pound for onions, and, to get 2 pounds of sliced onions, you need 2¼ pounds of untrimmed onions. In order to calculate the cost of the recipe correctly, you have to figure out what you actually paid for the onions. In this case, the true cost is 54 cents (2¼ lb × $.24 per lb), not 48 cents (2 lb × $.24 per lb).

The following are two frequently used abbreviations that you must understand:

- AP stands for *as purchased*. This means the untrimmed quantity, in the same form in which it is purchased. This is the amount that you pay for.
- EP stands for *edible portion*. This means the raw, uncooked quantity after all trimming is done. This is the quantity that you actually cook.

In the case of fruits and vegetables, the best way to determine AP quantities for use in costing recipes is to make a note of them when you are preparing the item. Tables of vegetable and fruit trimming yields in Chapters 16 and 19 will also help you. (Chapter 16 explains how to use these figures.)

In the case of ingredients such as meats and fish, figuring the cost can be a little more complicated. If you buy precut portion-controlled steaks or fish fillets and use them just as you receive them, your AP and EP costs are the same. But if you buy whole loins of beef or whole fish and cut them yourself, you have to do a yield cost analysis in order to determine your actual costs.

TABLE 5.5

Raw Yield Test Form

Item _____ Test number _____ Date _____

Purveyor _____ Price per pound _____ Total cost _____

AP weight (1) _____ Lb price (2) _____ Total cost (3) _____

Trim, salvage, and waste:

Item	Weight	Value/lb	Total Value (lb × value)
(4)			
(5)			
(6)			
(7)			
(8)			
(9)			
(10)			
	Total Weight (4 thru 10) (11) _____	Total Value (4 thru 10) (12) _____	

Total yield of item (13) _____

Net cost (3 minus 12) (14) _____

Cost per lb (14 divided by 13) (15) _____

Percentage of increase (15 divided by 2) (16) _____

The examples discussed in the remainder of this chapter use U.S. measures. For metric examples, see Appendix 4, pages 895-896.

Raw Yield Test

Suppose you work in a restaurant that serves veal scaloppine. The restaurant buys whole legs of veal. It is your job to bone out the veal, trim off all fat and connective tissue, separate the muscles at the seams, and cut the large pieces into scaloppine.

A typical whole leg of veal might weigh 30 pounds and cost $5.00 a pound for a total cost of $150.00. After finishing your trimming and cutting, you find you have 18 pounds of veal scaloppine. How do you figure the cost per pound of this meat?

The simplest example would be if you threw away all the trimmings, bones, and scrap meat. Then you would know that your 18 pounds of veal cost you $150.00. Dividing $150 by 18 pounds gives you a cost per pound of $8.33.

But in your restaurant, you don't throw away the trimmings. You make stock with the bones, grind up the small trimmings for meatballs, use the larger trimmings for veal stew, and sell the fat to the fat collector who picks up all your waste fat once a week. Now you must do a yield test to figure your costs.

Table 5.5 shows a typical form that you might use for a yield test. For simplification, the blanks in the form are of two types. The dotted lines are to be filled in by reading your invoices and by taking the weights from your actual yield test. The solid lines are to be filled in by doing calculations.

Note that in Table 5.6, the form has been filled in with the results of a yield test on a leg of veal. We go through the form step by step.

The executive chef in this restaurant fills out the first two lines based on the invoice, gives you the form, and requests you to do the test. You fill out the rest of the form, beginning with blank 1 on the third line. You proceed as follows:

TABLE 5.6

Completed Raw Yield Test Form

Item	veal leg to scaloppine	Test number	3	Date	6/5/02
Purveyor	ABC Meats	Price per pound	$5.00	Total cost	$150
AP weight (1)	30 lb	Lb price (2)	$5.00	Total cost (3)	$150

Trim, salvage, and waste:

	Item	Weight	Value/lb	Total Value (lb × value)
(4)	fat	2½ lb	$ .12	$ .30
(5)	bone	3 lb 5 oz	$ .38	$1.26
(6)	ground veal	2 lb 2 oz	$4.89	$10.39
(7)	stew meat	3 lb	$5.29	$15.87
(8)	unusable trim	14 oz	0	0
(9)	cutting loss	3 oz	0	0
(10)				
Total Weight (4 thru 10) (11)	12 lb		Total Value (4 thru 10) (12)	$27.82

Total yield of item (13)	18 lb
Net cost (3 minus 12) (14)	$122.18
Cost per lb (14 divided by 13) (15)	$6.79
Percentage of increase (15 divided by 2) (16)	1.36 (136%)

1. Weigh the whole leg of veal and enter the weight in blank 1. Copy the price per pound and total cost from line 2 to blanks 2 and 3.

    Note that blank 3 can also be arrived at by multiplying the weight by the price per pound. However, suppose the veal were left in the cooler for several more days and dried out a bit. The weight then might be 29½ pounds. By multiplying 29.5 by $5.00, you would get a total cost of $147.50. But because the price you paid was actually $150, it is important to use that figure and not fill in the blank by multiplying.

2. Break down the veal into all its component parts and record the weights of the trim and waste, starting in blank 4. In this case, there are only six items: fat, bones, small meat scraps for grinding, meat for stew, unusable waste, and cutting loss.

    Record the weight of the finished scaloppine in blank 13.

    (What is *cutting loss*? This is not something you can actually weigh. However, there is always some loss of weight due to particles of meat and fat sticking to the cutting board, to drying, and to other factors. So when you add up all your weights, you find that they total less than 30 lb. To determine cutting loss, add up blanks 4 through 8 and blank 13. Subtract this total from line 1.)

3. Enter the values per pound of the trim, salvage, and waste on lines 4 through 10. In this case, these numbers are given to you by the executive chef from the invoices.

    *   The fat collector pays 12 cents a pound for waste fat.
    *   When you have to buy extra bones for your stockpot, you have to pay 38 cents a pound for them, so this is their value to you. This is also the figure you use when you cost out your stock recipe. If you didn't make stock and threw out the bones, you'd enter zero in this blank.
    *   Similarly, the values entered for ground veal and stew meat are the prices you'd have to pay if you bought them.
    *   Unusable trim and cutting loss have no value, so you enter zero.

4. Calculate the total values of each item on lines 4 through 10 by multiplying the weight by the value per pound. Note that this particular form tells you how to do all the calculations.

5. Add the weights in lines 4 through 10 and enter the total in blank 11. Add the total values in lines 4 through 10 and enter this figure in blank 12.

6. Subtract the total value of all the trim (blank 12) from the price you paid for the veal (blank 3). This gives you the net cost of your 18 pounds of scaloppine.

7. To find the cost per pound of the scaloppine, divide the net cost (blank 14) by the weight (blank 13). This is the figure you will use in costing recipes for veal scaloppine.

8. The percentage of increase in the last line is determined by dividing the net cost per pound (blank 15) by the price per pound of the whole leg (blank 2). This figure can be used as follows:

    Suppose next week you buy another leg of veal from the same purveyor, but the price has gone up to $5.29. Instead of doing another yield test, you can simply multiply this new price by the percentage of increase ($5.29 times 1.36), to get a new cost per pound of $7.19.

Cooked Yield Test

Earlier we introduced two important abbreviations, AP (as purchased) and EP (edible portion). A third expression sometimes used is *AS*, meaning *as served*. When foods such as fruits are served raw, AS may be the same as EP. But if the food is cooked, these weights are different.

In the case of the veal scaloppine, your recipe portions, and therefore your portion costs, are based on raw weight. For example, your scaloppine recipe might call for 5½ ounces of raw meat per portion.

In some cases, on the other hand, your portions may be based on cooked weight. This is most often true of roasts. For example, let's say you buy whole fresh hams, bone and trim them, and serve them as roasts, allowing 6 ounces of sliced, cooked meat per portion. To arrive at your cost, you will have to do a cooked yield test, as illustrated by Tables 5.7 and 5.8. (This form may

TABLE 5.7

Cooked Yield Test Form

Item _____ Test number _____ Date _____

AP price per lb _____

Cooking temperature _____

Net raw weight (1) _____   Net cost per lb (2) _____

                                        Total net cost (3) _____

Weight as served (4) _____

Cooked cost per lb (3 divided by 4) (5) _____

Shrinkage (1 minus 4) (6) _____

Percentage of shrinkage (6 divided by 1) (7) _____

Total percentage of cost increase (5 divided by AP price per lb) (8) _____

TABLE 5.8

Completed Cooked Yield Test Form

Item   roast fresh ham   Test number   2   Date   6/5/02

AP price per lb $3.49

Cooking temperature   325°

Net raw weight (1)   12 lb   Net cost per lb (2) $3.93

                                 Total net cost (3) $47.16

Weight as served (4)   8 lb 4 oz

Cooked cost per lb (3 divided by 4) (5) $5.72

Shrinkage (1 minus 4) (6)   3¾ lb

Percentage of shrinkage (6 divided by 1) (7)   31%

Total percentage of cost increase (5 divided by AP price per lb) (8)   164%

be printed on the same sheet of paper as the raw yield test form so that an operation can have a complete cost analysis on one form.)

This form has been filled in with the results of a cooked yield test done on a roast, boneless fresh ham. Let's assume that this same ham has already had a raw yield test done on it.

The first half of the form, through blank 3, is filled in before the test starts. The numbers for blanks 1, 2, and 3 are taken from the raw yield test form, but you should double-check the net raw weight by weighing the item again before roasting.

Enter the total weight of cooked ham served in blank 4. You arrive at this figure by recording the total number of portions served and multiplying this number by the portion size. Let's say that 22 portions are served at 6 ounces each. This gives us a total of 132 ounces (22 × 6), or 8¼ pounds.

You might be tempted to simply weigh the whole roast after cooking and trimming. Remember, though, that there will be some waste—crumbs on the slicer or cutting board, spillage of juices, and so on. It is more accurate to record the weight that you actually sell.

If this had been a bone-in roast, you would have another reason to carve the meat before weighing, because you could not include the weight of the bone in your as-served figure.

The remaining blanks on the form are determined by doing the calculations, just as you would do the calculations for the raw yield test.

Example: Costing a Recipe
Item: Baked Rice

Ingredient Amount	Recipe Quantity	AP Quantity	Price	Total
Rice, long grain	4 lb	4 lb	$0.62/lb	$2.48
Butter	12 oz	0.75 lb	1.97/lb	1.48
Onions	1 lb	1.2 lb	0.36/lb	0.43
Chicken stock	4 qt	4 qt	0.25/qt	1.00
Salt	1 oz	$\frac{1}{16}$ lb	0.15/lb	0.01
			Total cost	$5.40
			Number of portions	50
			Cost per portion	$0.11

Note: Cost of chicken stock is determined by costing out the operation's recipe for chicken stock.

PORTION COSTS

Portion cost or *raw food cost* is the total cost of all the ingredients in a recipe divided by the number of portions served:

$$\text{portion cost} = \frac{\text{cost of ingredients}}{\text{number of portions}}$$

Here we cost out a sample recipe to show you how the procedure works. First, note the following points and keep them in mind when you are calculating portion costs. Many errors in costing are caused by forgetting one of these points.

1. Costs must be based on AP (as purchased) amounts, even though recipes often give EP (edible portion) quantities. These terms are explained in the preceding section.

2. Include *everything*. That means the lemon wedge and parsley garnish for the fish fillet, the cream and sugar that go with the coffee, and the oil that was used for pan-frying the eggplant. These are sometimes called *hidden costs*.

    Seasonings and spices are a typical example of hidden costs that are difficult to calculate. Some operations add up the cost of all seasonings used in a year and divide that by the total food cost to get a percentage. This percentage is added to each item. For example, if the cost of an item is $2.00 and the seasoning cost percentage is 5%, the total cost is $2.00 plus 5% of $2.00, or $2.10.

    Other hidden costs can be calculated in the same way. For example, you could figure out your cost percentage for frying fat and add the percentage to all deep-fried foods.

    Some restaurants take an arbitrary figure for all hidden costs, usually from 8 to 12 percent, and add this to all menu items.

3. Record the number of portions *actually served*, not just the number the recipe is intended to serve. If the roast shrank more than you expected during cooking, or if you dropped a piece of cake on the floor, those costs still have to be covered.

Procedure for Calculating Portion Cost

1. List ingredients and quantities of recipe as prepared.

2. Convert the recipe quantities to AP (as purchased) quantities.

3. Determine the price of each ingredient (from invoices, price lists, etc.). The units in this step and in step 2 must be the same in order for you to do the calculation.

4. Calculate the total cost of each ingredient by multiplying the price per unit by the number of units needed.

5. Add the ingredient costs to get the total recipe cost.

6. Divide the total cost by the number of portions served to get the cost per portion.

Terms for Review

recipe	meter	milli-	EP weight
standardized recipe	degree Celsius	raw food cost	AS weight
portion control	kilo-	portion cost	yield test
gram	deci-	food cost percentage	hidden cost
liter	centi-	AP weight	

Questions for Discussion

1. What are some reasons written recipes can't be 100 percent exact and must depend on the cook's judgment? Select two or three recipes (from this book or any other) and try to determine where they depend on the cook's judgment.

2. What is the purpose of a standardized recipe?

3. What are the three basic ways of measuring ingredients? Which method is used for most solid ingredients, and why?

4. What is the first step in portion control? List four other techniques in portion control.

5. Make the following conversions in the U.S. system of measurement:

   3½ pounds = _____ ounces

   6 cups = _____ pints

   8½ quarts = _____ fluid ounces

   ¾ cup = _____ tablespoons

   46 ounces = _____ pounds

   2½ gallons = _____ fluid ounces

   5 pounds 5 ounces divided by 2 = _____

   10 teaspoons = _____ fluid ounces

6. Make the following conversions in the metric system:

   1.4 kilograms = _____ grams

   53 deciliters = _____ liters

   15 centimeters = _____ millimeters

   2590 grams = _____ kilograms

   4.6 liters = _____ deciliters

   220 centiliters = _____ deciliters

7. Turn to the recipe for Swedish Meatballs on page 293. Convert it to yield 35 portions.

8. Discuss the main types of problems you may face when converting recipe yields.

9. What is the difference between AP weight and EP weight? Explain how these terms are related to calculating costs per portion of menu items.

10. The following problems are calculations with food cost percentages, portion cost, and menu price. For each problem, two of these figures are given. Find the third.

Food cost percentage	Portion cost	Menu price
a. ____	$1.24	$4.95
b. 40%	____	$2.50
c. 30%	$2.85	____

VEGETABLE TASTING MENU

Artichoke Barigoule with Roasted Pepper Tapenade
and Herb Salad

White Bean Purée with Escarole, Roasted Tomato
and Lemon Confit

Roasted Root Vegetables with Soubise
and Truffle Vinaigrette

Polenta Cake with Figs and Wilted Greens

Mushroom Tart Tatin

Dessert Amuse

Tasting Dessert

Petits Fours

75

Tasting Menus Require the Participation of the Entire Table

AUTUMN TASTING MENU

Torchon of Foie Gras with Figs, Pistachio
and Mint

Sea Scallop with Salsify, Sauternes and Vanilla

Turbot with Lentils, Savoy Cabbage,
Root Vegetables and Red Wine

Braised Fresh Bacon with Mostarda
and Chestnut-Honey Glazed Turnips

Rack of Lamb with Artichokes, Tomato
and Olive Gratin

Dessert Amuse

Tasting Dessert

Petits Fours

90

Tasting Menus Require the Participation of the Entire Table

The Menu

A menu is a list of dishes served or available to be served at a meal. To the customer in a restaurant, it is a list of dishes from which to make selections for a meal. To the cook, it is a list of dishes to be prepared. But our familiarity with the menu simply as a list of foods tends to hide its importance as a management tool.

Nearly every aspect of the operation of a food service business depends on the menu. In fact, it is fair to say that the menu is the single most important document in the business. Purchasing, production, sales, cost accounting, labor management, even the kitchen layout and equipment selection of a new facility—all are based on the menu.

You can see why it is essential to pay careful attention to the writing of the menu and why so many factors are considered. In this chapter, we discuss these factors from the point of view of kitchen production. How does one construct a menu that builds sales by offering the best choices to the customer and that also promotes efficiency and productivity?

After reading this chapter, you should be able to

1. **Name and explain the factors that influence the make-up of a menu.**

2. **Describe the differences between static and cycle menus, and between *à la carte* and *table d'hôte* menus.**

3. **List in order of their usual service the various courses that might appear in modern menus.**

4. **Devise balanced menus that contain an adequate variety of foods and that can be efficiently and economically prepared.**

5. **Describe how to incorporate the total utilization of foods concept into menu planning.**

6. **Describe ways that cooks can incorporate nutrition principles into their cooking.**

Menu Forms and Functions

Menus must be planned for the people eating the food. This sounds like a simple rule, but it is frequently forgotten. You must never forget that the customer is the main reason for being in business.

This rule means that, in most operations, the taste and preferences of the cooks or chefs are of little importance when planning the menu. True, some of the most famous restaurants exist primarily as showcases for the chef's own artistry, but these are only a small percentage of all food service establishments. Instead, the taste and preferences of the clientele must be given top priority if the business is to succeed. The kind of clientele the business serves influences the form the menu takes.

THE CLIENTELE

Type of Institution

Each kind of operation has a different menu because each serves the needs of different clientele.

Hotels must provide a variety of services for their guests, from budget-minded tourists to businesspeople on expense accounts, from quick breakfast and sandwich counters to elegant dining rooms and banquet halls.

Hospitals must satisfy the dietary needs of the patients.

Schools must consider the ages of the students and their tastes and nutritional needs.

Employee food services need menus that offer substantial but quickly served food for working customers.

Catering and banquet operations depend on menus that are easily prepared for large numbers but that are lavish enough for parties and special occasions.

Fast-food and take-out operations require limited menus featuring inexpensive, easily prepared, easily served foods for people in a hurry.

Full-service restaurants range from simple neighborhood diners to expensive, elegant restaurants. Menus, of course, must be planned according to the customers' needs. Trying to institute a menu of high-priced, luxurious foods in a café situated in a working-class neighborhood will probably not succeed.

Customer Preferences

Even facilities with captive audiences, such as school cafeterias and hospital kitchens, must produce food that is appealing to their customers and in sufficient variety to keep them from getting bored with the same old things. Grumbling about the food is a favorite sport among students, but at least it can be kept to a minimum.

Restaurants have an even harder job because their customers don't just grumble if they don't like the selections. They don't come back. People are becoming more and more interested in trying unfamiliar foods, especially ethnic foods. Nevertheless, tastes vary in different regions of the country, in different neighborhoods, in different age groups, and in different social and ethnic backgrounds. Foods that are enjoyed by some people are completely rejected by others.

Prices must be kept in line with the customers' ability and willingness to pay. Prices, of course, place limits on what foods can be offered.

KIND OF MEAL

Menus vary not only for different kinds of operations but for different meals as well.

Breakfast

Breakfast menus are fairly standard within any one country. A restaurant has to offer the usual selection of fruits, juices, eggs, cereals, pancakes, waffles, breakfast meats, and regional specialties because this is what customers want and expect. In addition, featuring one or two unusual items on the menu—such as an English muffin topped with creamed crabmeat and a poached egg, a special kind of country ham, or an assortment of freshly made fruit sauces or syrups for the pancakes and waffles—often attracts additional customers. Breakfast menus must feature foods that can be prepared quickly and can be eaten in a hurry.

Lunch

The following factors are important to consider when planning lunch menus.

1. **Speed.**
   Like breakfast customers, luncheon diners are usually in a hurry. They are generally working people who have a limited time to eat. Foods must be prepared quickly and be easy to serve and eat. Sandwiches, soups, and salads are important items on many lunch menus.

2. **Simplicity.**
   Menu selections are fewer, and fewer courses are served. In many cases, customers select only one course. Luncheon specials—combinations of two or three items, such as soup and a sandwich or omelet and salad, offered at a single price—satisfy the need for simplicity and speed.

3. **Variety.**
   In spite of the shortness of the menu and the simplicity of the selections, luncheon menus must have variety. This is because many customers eat at the same restaurant several times a week, or even every day. In order to keep the menu short, many operations offer several luncheon specials every day, so there is always something new on the menu.

Dinner

Dinner is usually the main meal and is eaten in a more leisurely fashion than either breakfast or lunch. Of course, some people are in a hurry in the evening, too, but, in general, people come to a restaurant to relax over a substantial meal. Dinner menus offer more selections and more courses. Not surprisingly, prices and check averages are also higher than at lunch.

TYPES OF MENUS

Static and Cycle Menus

A *static menu* is one that offers the same dishes every day. These menus are used in restaurants and other establishments where the clientele changes daily or where enough items are listed on the menu to offer sufficient variety. A static menu may be in place indefinitely, or it may change at regular intervals, such as every season, every month, or even every week.

Some restaurants use a menu that is part static and part variable. This means that they have a basic menu of foods prepared every day, plus daily specials to offer more variety without putting too much strain on the kitchen. The daily specials may take advantage of seasonal produce and other occasionally available foods that the chef or purchaser finds in the wholesale market.

A *cycle menu* is one that changes every day for a certain period; after this period, the daily menus repeat in the same order. For example, a seven-day cycle menu has a different menu every day for a week and repeats each week. This kind of menu is used in such operations as schools and hospitals, where the number of choices must be kept small. The cycle menu is a way of offering variety.

À la Carte and Table d'Hôte

An *à la carte* menu is one in which each individual item is listed separately, with its own price. The customer makes selections from the various courses and side dishes to make up a meal. (*Note:* The term *à la carte* is also used to refer to cooking to order, as opposed to cooking ahead in large batches.)

Table d'hôte (tobble dote) originally meant a fixed menu with no choices—like a meal you would be served if you were invited to someone's home for dinner. Banquet menus are familiar examples of this kind of menu. The term has also come to mean a menu that offers a selection of complete meals at set prices. In other words, a customer may choose from among several selections, each of which includes an entrée and side dishes plus other courses, such as appetizer, salad, and dessert. Each full meal selection has a single package price.

Many restaurants use a combination of à la carte and table d'hôte selections. For example, a steak house may include salad, potato, vegetable, and beverage with the entrée choice, while additional dishes like appetizers and desserts may be offered at extra cost.

Closely related to the table d'hôte menu is the *prix fixe* (pree fix), meaning "fixed price," menu. On a pure prix fixe menu, only one price is given. Each guest may choose one selection from each course offered, and the total meal costs the single price indicated. Often, on such menus, a few items featuring costly ingredients carry an extra charge, called a *supplement* (see Figure 6.1). The supplement is usually indicated in parentheses after the listing. It is best to limit

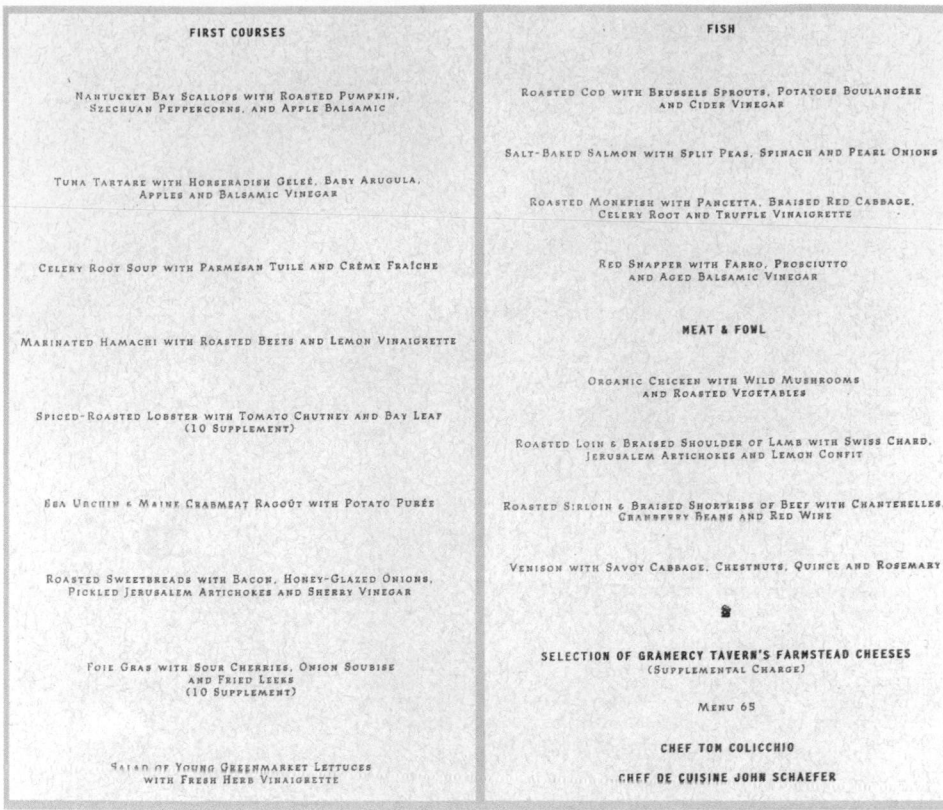

the number of supplements as much as possible. Too many extra charges on a prix fixe menu can leave customers frustrated and angry.

A special variety of the prix fixe menu sometimes used in fine restaurants is the *tasting menu*, also known by its French name, *menu dégustation*. A tasting menu (Figure 6.2) is offered in addition to the regular menu and gives patrons a chance to try a larger number of the chef's creations. The menu may feature 5 or 6 or even as many as 10 or 12 individual courses served in small portions. Because of the complexity of service, a restaurant may require that the tasting menu can be served only if everyone at the table orders it. Tasting menus may change daily, depending on the chef's choices and the availability of ingredients.

Figure 6.1 An example of a prix fixe menu from a fine dining restaurant (Gramercy Tavern, New York, NY).

Building the Menu

A *course* is a food or group of foods served at one time or intended to be eaten at the same time. In a restaurant, the courses are normally served in sequence, allowing enough time for each to be eaten before the next is served. In a cafeteria, the customers may select all their courses at once—appetizer, salad, main dish and vegetables, and dessert, for example—but eat them in a particular order.

In the following pages, we discuss the various principles that apply to planning the courses that make up a menu. The main purpose of these principles is to lend variety and interest to a meal. They are not merely arbitrary rules that you must follow for no reason.

THE CLASSICAL MENU

Today's menus are descendants of elaborate banquet menus served in the nineteenth and early twentieth centuries. These menus had 12 or more courses, and the sequence in which they were served was well established by tradition.

The following sequence of courses is typical of one that may have been served at a great banquet early in the twentieth century.

1. **Cold hors d'oeuvre**
   small, savory appetizers

2. **Soup**
   clear soup, thick soup, or broth

3. **Hot hors d'oeuvre**
   small, hot appetizers

4. **Fish**
   any seafood item

5. **Main course or pièce de resistance**
   a large cut of roasted or braised meat, usually beef, lamb, or venison, with elaborate vegetable garnishes

6. **Hot entrée**
   individual portions of meat or poultry, broiled, braised, or pan-fried, etc.

7. **Cold entrée**
   cold meats, poultry, fish, pâté, and so on

8. **Sorbet**
   a light ice or sherbet, sometimes made of wine, to refresh the appetite before the next course

9. **Roast**
   usually roasted poultry, accompanied by or followed by a salad

10. **Vegetable**

    usually a special vegetable preparation, such as artichokes or asparagus, or a more unusual vegetable such as cardoons

11. **Sweet**

    what we call dessert—cakes and tarts, pudding, soufflés, etc.

12. **Dessert**

    fruit and cheese and, sometimes, small cookies or petits fours

MODERN MENUS: COURSES AND ARRANGEMENT

Such extensive classical menus are rarely served today. Even grand, elegant banquets comprising many courses are usually shorter than the menu we just described. However, if you study that menu, you will be able to see the basic pattern of modern menus hiding amid all those courses.

The main dish is the centerpiece of the modern meal. If the meal consists of only one dish, it is considered the main course, even if it is a salad or a bowl of soup. There is usually only one main course, although large banquets may still have more than one, such as a poultry dish followed by a meat dish.

One or more dishes may be served before the main dish. These are usually light in character so that the customer is not satiated before the main course.

Study the following outline of the modern menu and compare it to the classical menu. The notes that follow explain several aspects that may be puzzling. Then, in the next sections, we discuss how to select specific dishes for each course to arrive at a balanced menu.

The Modern Menu

First courses	Appetizer
	Soup
	(Fish)
	Salad
Main dish	Meat, poultry, or fish
	Vegetable accompaniment
Dessert dishes	Salad
	Fruits and cheeses
	Sweets

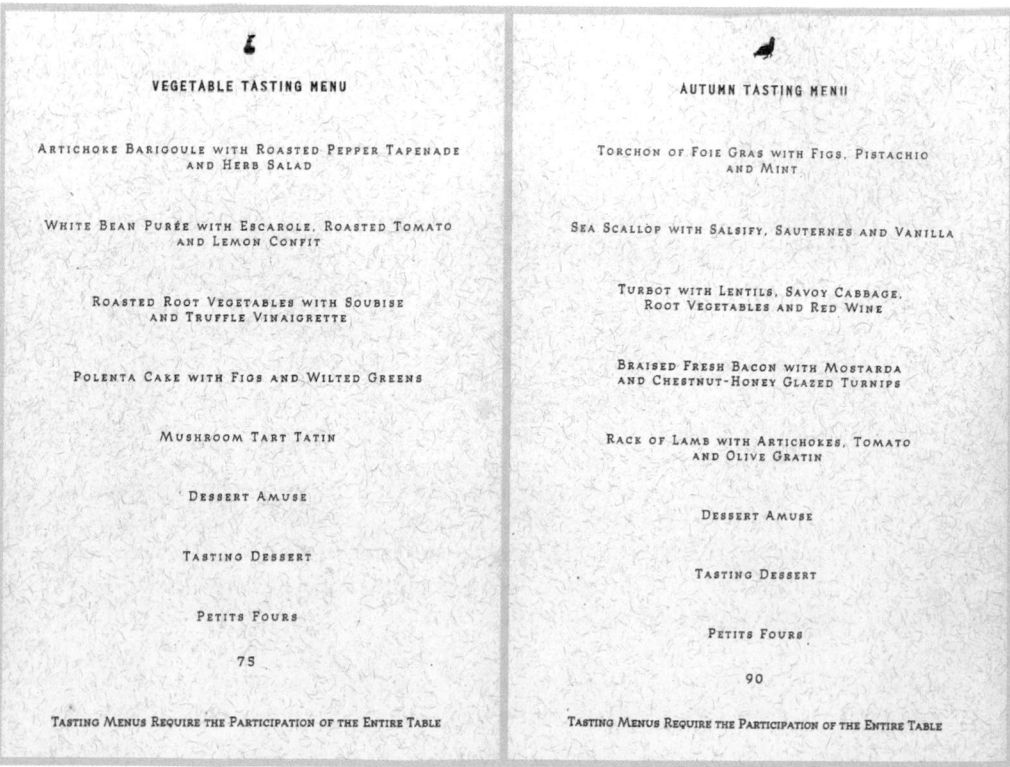

Figure 6.2 An example of two tasting menus from a fine dining restaurant (Gramercy Tavern, New York, NY).

Notes

- Appetizer, soup, and salad are the three courses usually served before the main course. One, two, or all three of them may be served, and they are usually served in this order. Thus, meals may have the following courses:

Appetizer	Soup	Salad
Main dish	Main dish	Main dish
Appetizer	Soup	Appetizer
Soup	Salad	Salad
Main dish	Main dish	Main dish

Appetizer
Soup
Salad
Main dish

- A fish course is sometimes included in more formal dinners, after appetizer and soup courses. It should be a relatively small portion, and the main dish should not also be fish.
- Salads may be served either before or after the main course (but not both). In more traditional meals, they are served after the main course to refresh the appetite before the cheese and sweet courses. Serving the salad before the main course is a comparatively recent development.
- Sometimes, one or more of the first courses is served at the same time as the main dish, possibly on the same plate. This is especially popular on luncheon menus, where quick service is desired. Thus, you will find soup and sandwich combinations, salad and omelet combinations, and so on.
- If both cheese and sweets are served for dessert, they may come in either order. English menus have cheese after the sweets, while French menus generally place the sweets last.

VARIETY AND BALANCE

Balancing a menu means providing enough variety and contrast so that the meal holds interest from the first course to the last. To balance a menu, you must develop a feeling for which foods complement each other or provide pleasing contrasts. And you must avoid repeating flavors and textures as much as possible.

These principles apply whether you are planning a banquet menu, where the diners have no choices; a school cafeteria menu, where students have only a few choices; or a large à la carte menu, where customers have many choices.

Of course, with an à la carte menu, the customers' own choices determine how balanced their own meals are. There's nothing wrong with listing a creamed dish among the appetizers and another creamed dish among the main dishes. But you should offer enough choices so that the customers can easily select balanced meals if they desire. In other words, if half the appetizers and half the entrée selections are served in a cream sauce, you're not offering enough variety.

The following factors must be considered in balancing a menu.

1. **Flavors.**
   Don't repeat foods with the same or similar tastes. This applies to any predominant flavor, whether of the main ingredient, of the spices, of the sauce, and so on. For example:
   - Don't serve broiled tomato halves with the main dish if the appetizer has a tomato sauce.
   - Don't serve both a spicy, garlicky appetizer and a spicy, garlicky main dish. On the other hand, don't make everything too bland.
   - Unless you operate a specialty restaurant like a steak house or a seafood restaurant, balance the menu among meats (beef, pork, lamb, veal), poultry, and fish.
   - Acid or tart foods are often served as accompaniments to fatty foods because they help cut the fatty taste. This is why applesauce and pork, mint sauce and lamb, and orange sauce and duckling are such classic combinations.

2. **Textures.**
   Texture applies to the softness or firmness of foods, their feel in the mouth, whether or not they are served with sauces, and so on. Don't repeat foods with the same or similar texture. For example:

- Serve a clear soup instead of a thick soup if the main course is served with a cream sauce. On the other hand, a cream soup goes well before a simple sautéed or broiled item.
- Don't serve too many mashed or puréed foods unless you are running a baby-food restaurant.
- Don't serve too many heavy, starchy items.

3. **Appearance.**
   Serve foods with a variety of colors and shapes. Colorful vegetables are especially valuable for livening up the appearance of meats, poultry, fish, and starches, which tend to be mostly white or brown. (Creating attractive food is discussed in Chapter 24.)

There are so many possible combinations of foods that it is impossible to give rules that cover all of them. Besides, creative chefs are continually experimenting with new combinations, breaking old rules, and coming up with exciting menus. Years of experience, however, are required to develop this kind of creativity and a feel for what makes certain combinations work. In the meantime, pay close attention to the principles discussed.

KITCHEN CAPABILITIES AND AVAILABILITY OF FOODS

Physical conditions place limitations on your menu. Depending on your equipment, your labor force, and the foods available to you, certain items will be inconvenient, difficult, or even impossible to serve.

Equipment Limitations
Know the capacities of your equipment and plan menus accordingly. If your broiler capacity is 200 steaks an hour and you plan a banquet menu for 400 people that features broiled shrimp as an appetizer and broiled steaks as a main course, you're in big trouble.

Spread the workload evenly among your equipment. If you have ovens, a broiler, and a fryer, balance the roasted and braised items, the broiled items, and the fried items. Don't let the broiler stand idle while orders are backed up at the deep fryer. Also, using a variety of cooking methods adds variety of taste and texture to the menu.

Personnel Limitations
Spread the workload evenly among the workers. As with equipment, you don't want the fry cook to have more than he or she can handle, while the broiler cook has little to do.

Spread the workload throughout the day. Balance the cooked-to-order items against the cooked-ahead items so that you don't have to do everything at the last minute.

Offer items that the cooks are able to prepare. Don't put items on the menu that are above the skill level of the staff.

Availability of Foods
Use foods in season. Foods out of season are expensive and often low in quality, and their supply is undependable. Don't put asparagus on the menu if you can't get good asparagus.

Use foods locally available. Fresh seafood is the most obvious example of a food that is hard to get in some regions unless you—and your customers—are willing to pay premium prices.

COMPLETE UTILIZATION OF FOODS

You can't afford to throw food away any more than you can afford to throw money away. Total utilization of foods must be planned into menus. Whether or not this is done can make or break a food service operation.

1. **Use all edible trim.**
   Unless you use only portion-controlled meats, poultry, and fish and only frozen and canned vegetables, you will have edible trim. You can either throw it away and call it a loss, or you can use it and make money on it.
   Plan recipes that utilize these trimmings and put them on the menu. For example:
- Use small meat scraps for soups, chopped meat, pâtés, creamed dishes, croquettes.
- Use larger meat trimmings for soups, stews, braised items.
- Use bones for stocks and soups.
- Use vegetable trimmings for purées, soups, stews, stocks, fillings for omelets and crêpes.
- Use day-old breads for stuffings, breading, French toast, croutons, meat extender.

2. **Don't add an item to the menu unless you can use the trimmings.**
   This is really the same as the preceding item, looking from the opposite angle. In other words, don't put rissolé potatoes on your menu unless you also plan to serve an item that uses the trimmings, such as whipped potatoes or croquettes.

3. **Plan production to avoid leftovers.**
   The best way to use leftovers is not to create them in the first place. Handling food twice—once as a fresh item and once as a leftover—is more expensive and time-consuming than handling it once, and it almost always results in loss of quality. Limited menus—that is, with fewer selections—decrease the likelihood of leftovers.

4. **Plan ahead for use of leftovers.**
   Careful planning of production can keep leftovers to a minimum. But some leftovers are almost inevitable, and it's better for your costs to use them than to throw them out.
   Whenever you put an item on the menu that could become a leftover, you should have a recipe ready that will use it. This is better than being surprised with leftovers that you don't know what to do with.
   For example, if you served roast chicken for dinner one day, you might plan on chicken salad for a luncheon special the next day.
   Remember to handle all leftovers according to proper sanitary procedures.

5. **Avoid minimum-use perishable ingredients.**
   Minimum-use ingredients are those that are used in one or two items on your menu. For example, an operation might serve chicken breast topped with sautéed mushrooms but not use mushrooms in any other item. When the ingredient is perishable, the result is a high percentage of spoilage or waste.
   This situation can be remedied in any of three ways.
   - Change the recipe to eliminate the minimum-use ingredient.
   - Eliminate the item from the menu.
   - Add other items to the menu using the ingredient.
     Be careful not to unbalance the menu, however, by using an ingredient in too many dishes. Try to avoid both extremes.

MENU ACCURACY

When you have selected the items you want to include on your menu, be sure to label them accurately. Giving misleading names to menu items is not only dishonest and unfair to the customer, it is actually illegal in some localities that have adopted truth-in-menu laws, and you can be prosecuted for fraud. Furthermore, customers who feel confused or cheated may not come back.

Calling something chicken salad if it is made with turkey, veal cutlet if it is made with pork, or whipped cream if it is actually artificial whipped topping is such obvious mislabeling that it can hardly be accidental. However, some kinds of menu inaccuracies result not from intentional deception but from simple misunderstanding. In particular, look out for these types of labeling problems:

1. **Point of origin.**
   If your menu lists "Maine lobsters," they must be from Maine. Roquefort dressing must be made with Roquefort cheese from Roquefort, France. Idaho potatoes must be from Idaho. On the other hand, generally accepted names or names that indicate type rather than origin can be used. For example: Swiss cheese, French bread, Swedish meatballs.

2. **Grade or quality.**
   U.S. Choice and Canada A are names of grades, and you'd better be using those grades if you say you are. Incidentally, the word prime in "prime rib" indicates a cut, not a grade. But if you say "U.S. Prime Rib," you are now talking about a grade.

3. **Cooking method.**
   A menu item described as "grilled" or "roasted" should be cooked by the method indicated. Billing a pan-fried item as "roasted" because it sounds better on the menu misrepresents the item and risks disappointing the customer.

4. **"Fresh."**
   If you call something fresh, it must be fresh, not frozen, canned, or dried. There is no such thing as "fresh frozen."

5. **"Imported."**
   An item labeled "imported" must come from outside the country.

6. **"Homemade."**
   The word homemade means that the item was made on the premises. Adding a few fresh carrots to canned vegetable soup does not make it homemade.

7. **Size or portion.**
   If you indicate a portion size on the menu, be sure you serve that size (within allowable tolerances). A "10-ounce steak" must weigh at least 10 ounces before cooking (9½ ounces would be within allowable tolerance). "Jumbo shrimp" are not just big shrimp. They are a specific size.

Some other common violations are the following:

Listing "maple syrup" and serving maple-flavored syrup.
Listing "Coke" (a brand name) and serving another brand of cola.
Listing "butter" and serving margarine.
Listing coffee or breakfast cereal "with cream" and serving milk.
Listing "ground round" and serving other ground beef.

Nutritional Considerations

Menu planners must have a basic understanding of nutrition because the human body requires a variety of foods in order to function and to be healthy.

The food service worker's responsibility to provide nutritious food and well-balanced menus depends, in part, on the operation. School and hospital food services must, of course, plan menus carefully to meet basic nutritional needs. A qualified dietitian is usually required in such establishments.

The obligations of restaurateurs are more subtle. Because they are in business to sell food, they must offer foods that will attract customers. Those who plan menus are as concerned with presenting attractive, flavorful foods as they are with serving nutritious foods. Also, if the menu is à la carte, there is no way to ensure that a customer will order items that make up a nutritionally balanced meal.

But restaurateurs do have an obligation to offer a choice. That is, menus should be planned so that customers can order well-balanced meals if they desire. People are becoming more concerned with fitness and health, so a nutritiously balanced menu may even help attract customers.

NUTRIENTS

1. Nutrients are certain chemical compounds that are present in foods and that fulfill one or more of the following functions:
   - Supply energy for body functions.
   - Build and replace cells that make up body tissues.
   - Regulate body processes.

2. There are six categories of nutrients:

   - Carbohydrates
   - Fats
   - Proteins
   - Vitamins
   - Minerals
   - Water

   In addition, there is a substance in foods that is not, strictly speaking, a nutrient, but that is necessary for healthful body functioning:

   - Fiber

CALORIES

The *calorie* is a unit of measurement used to measure energy. It is defined as the amount of heat needed to raise the temperature of 1 kilogram of water by 1°C.

Remember that one of the functions of nutrients is to supply energy to the body. The calorie is used to measure how much energy certain foods supply for these functions. In our overfed society, calories have come to be viewed as something to be avoided. Nevertheless, without sufficient food energy, we could not live.

Carbohydrates, proteins, and fats can be used by the body to supply energy.

1 gram of carbohydrate supplies 4 calories
1 gram of protein supplies 4 calories
1 gram of fat supplies 9 calories

KINDS OF NUTRIENTS AND THEIR IMPORTANCE

Each of the nutrients listed has certain characteristics and functions in the body. These are discussed below in general terms. For a summary of individual nutrients and the foods in which they are found, see Table 6.1.

Carbohydrates

Carbohydrates are the most important source of food energy. *Starches* are complex carbohydrates. They are found in such foods as grains, bread, peas and beans, and many vegetables and fruits. *Sugars* are simple carbohydrates. They are found in sweets and, to a lesser extent, in fruits and vegetables.

Most authorities believe that complex carbohydrates are better for you than simple carbohydrates. This is partly because starchy foods also have many other nutrients, while sweets have few other nutrients. Also, there is some evidence that a lot of sugar in the diet may contribute to heart and circulatory diseases.

The term *fiber* refers to a group of carbohydrates that cannot be used by the body. Therefore, fiber supplies no food energy. However, it is important for the proper functioning of the intestinal tract and the elimination of body waste. In addition, there is evidence that sufficient dietary fiber helps prevent some kinds of cancers. Fruits and vegetables, especially if raw, and whole grains supply dietary fiber.

Fats

Fats supply energy to the body in highly concentrated form. Also, some fatty acids are necessary for regulating certain body functions. Third, fats act as carriers of fat-soluble vitamins (vitamins A, D, E, and K).

Fats may be classified as *saturated, monounsaturated,* or *polyunsaturated.* These terms reflect chemical differences in the composition of fats. Cooks do not need to know the chemical structure of fats, but they should understand their nutritional characteristics and the foods in which they are found. Many foods contain a combination of these three types, with one type predominating.

Saturated fats are solid at room temperature. Animal products—meats, poultry, fish, eggs, dairy products—and solid shortenings are the major source of saturated fats. Tropical oils such as coconut oil and palm kernel oil are also rich in saturated fats. Health authorities believe that these fats contribute significantly to heart disease and other health problems.

Polyunsaturated fats and monounsaturated fats are liquid at room temperature. Although too much of any kind of fat is bad for the health, these fats are considered to be more healthful than saturated fats. Polyunsaturated fats are found in vegetable oil such as corn oil, safflower oil, sunflower oil, and cottonseed oil. High levels of monounsaturated fats are found in olive oil and canola oil. Both kinds of unsaturated fats are also found in other plant products as well, including whole grains, nuts, and some fruits and vegetables.

Cholesterol is a fatty substance that has been closely linked with heart disease because it collects on the walls of arteries and blocks the flow of blood to the heart and other vital organs. It is found only in animal products and is especially high in egg yolks, butterfat, and organ meats such as liver and brains. In addition, the human body can manufacture its own cholesterol, so not all the cholesterol in the blood is necessarily from foods. Nevertheless, experts generally agree that it is best to keep the cholesterol in the diet as low as possible.

Recent research has suggested that monounsaturated fat may actually lower the levels of the most harmful kinds of cholesterol in the body. This may explain the relatively low incidence of

TABLE 6.1

Major Nutrients

Nutrient	Major Dietary Sources	Functions in the Body
Carbohydrates	Grains (including breads and pasta) Dried beans Potatoes Corn Sugar	Major source of energy (calories) for all body functions. Necessary for proper utilization of fats. Unrefined carbohydrates supply fiber, important for proper waste elimination.
Fats	Meats, poultry, and fish Dairy products Eggs Cooking fats and shortening Salad dressings	Supply food energy (calories). Supply essential fatty acids. Carry fat-soluble vitamins.
Proteins	Meats, poultry, and fish Milk and cheese Eggs Dried beans and peas Nuts	Major building material of all body tissues. Supply energy (calories). Help make up enzymes and hormones, which regulate body functions.
Vitamin A	Liver Butter and cream Green and yellow vegetables and fruits Egg yolks	Helps skin and mucous membranes resist infection. Promotes healthy eyes and makes night vision possible.
Thiamin (Vitamin B_1)	Pork Whole grains and fortified grains Nuts Legumes Green vegetables	Needed for utilization of carbohydrates for energy. Promotes normal appetite and healthy nervous system. Prevents beriberi.
Riboflavin (Vitamin B_2)	Organ meats Milk products Whole grains and fortified grains	Needed for utilization of carbohydrates and other nutrients. Promotes healthy skin and eyes.
Niacin (a B vitamin)	Liver Meat, poultry, and fish Legumes	Needed for utilization of energy foods. Promotes healthy nervous system, skin, and digestion. Prevents pellagra.
Vitamin B_{12}	Most animal and dairy products	Promotes healthy blood and nervous system.
Vitamin C (Ascorbic Acid)	Citrus fruits Tomatoes Potatoes Dark-green, leafy vegetables Peppers, cabbage, and broccoli Cantaloupe Berries	Strengthens body tissues. Promotes healing and resistance to infection. Prevents scurvy.
Vitamin D	Fortified milk products Formed in skin when exposed to sunlight	Necessary for utilization of calcium and phosphorus to promote healthy bones, teeth, and muscle tissue.
Vitamin E	Unsaturated fats (vegetable oils, nuts, whole grains, etc.)	Protects other nutrients.
Calcium	Milk products Leafy vegetables Canned fish with bones	Forms bones and teeth. Necessary for healthy muscles and nerves.
Iron	Liver and red meat Raisins and prunes Egg yolks Leafy vegetables Dried beans Whole grains	Needed for formation of red blood cells.

heart disease in Mediterranean regions where olive oil is the most widely used fat. This research has helped to popularize the use of olive oil in other parts of the world, especially in North America.

Remember, however, that *too much fat of any kind is bad for the health.* Do not make the mistake of thinking that monounsaturated fats are good for you and can be used in excess.

Proteins

Proteins are known as the building blocks of the body. They are essential for growth, for building body tissues, and for basic body functions. They can also be used for energy if the diet does not contain enough carbohydrates and fats.

Proteins consist of substances called *amino acids.* The body is able to manufacture many of them, but there are eight amino acids that it cannot manufacture and must get from foods. A food protein that contains all eight essential amino acids is called a *complete protein.* Meats, poultry, fish, eggs, and dairy products contain complete proteins.

Proteins that lack one or more of these essential amino acids are called *incomplete proteins.* Foods high in incomplete proteins include nuts, grains, and dried beans and other legumes. Foods that, *if eaten together,* supply all the amino acids are called *complementary proteins.* For example, cornmeal tortillas topped with chili beans supply complete protein because the corn supplies the amino acids lacking in the beans. Beans and rice are another example of complementary proteins.

Vitamins

Vitamins are present in foods in extremely small quantities, but they are essential for regulating body functions. Unlike proteins, fats, and carbohydrates, they supply no energy, but some of them must be present in order for energy to be utilized in the body. Also, lack of certain vitamins causes *deficiency diseases.*

Vitamins are classified as *water soluble* and *fat soluble.* The water-soluble vitamins (the B vitamins and vitamin C) are not stored in the body and must be eaten every day. Foods containing these vitamins should be handled so that vitamins are not dissolved into the cooking water and lost (as discussed in Chapter 16).

Fat-soluble vitamins (A, D, E, and K) can be stored in the body, so they do not need to be eaten every day, as long as the total amount eaten over a period of time is sufficient.

Minerals

Minerals, like vitamins, are also consumed in very small quantities and are essential for regulating certain body processes. The most important minerals in the diet are calcium, phosphorus, iron, copper, iodine, sodium, and potassium.

Sodium, a component of table salt, is somewhat of a health problem—not because we don't get enough of it but because many people get too much. Too much sodium is thought to contribute to high blood pressure. Health authorities are trying to convince people to reduce the sodium in their diets, primarily by salting foods less.

THE BALANCED DIET

In order to stay healthy, we must consume a varied diet that contains all the essential nutrients. In addition, we must limit our intake of foods that can be harmful in large quantities. Although researchers still have much to learn about nutrition and our knowledge is constantly changing, there is strong evidence about what good eating patterns are. According to government health agencies, the following guidelines are suggested for maintaining a healthful diet. It should be noted that these are only general recommendations for people who are already healthy and want to stay that way. They are not necessarily for those who need special diets because of disease or other abnormal conditions.

1. **Eat a variety of foods.**
   The greater variety of foods we eat, the more likely we are to get all the nutrients we require. Daily intake from each of the food groups helps to ensure a balanced diet. In the United States, these food groups form what is known as the food guide pyramid. Figure 6.3(a) shows the standard pyramid developed by the U.S.D.A. Canadian nutrition experts have

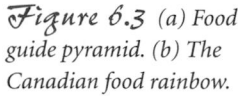

Figure 6.3 (a) Food guide pyramid. (b) The Canadian food rainbow.

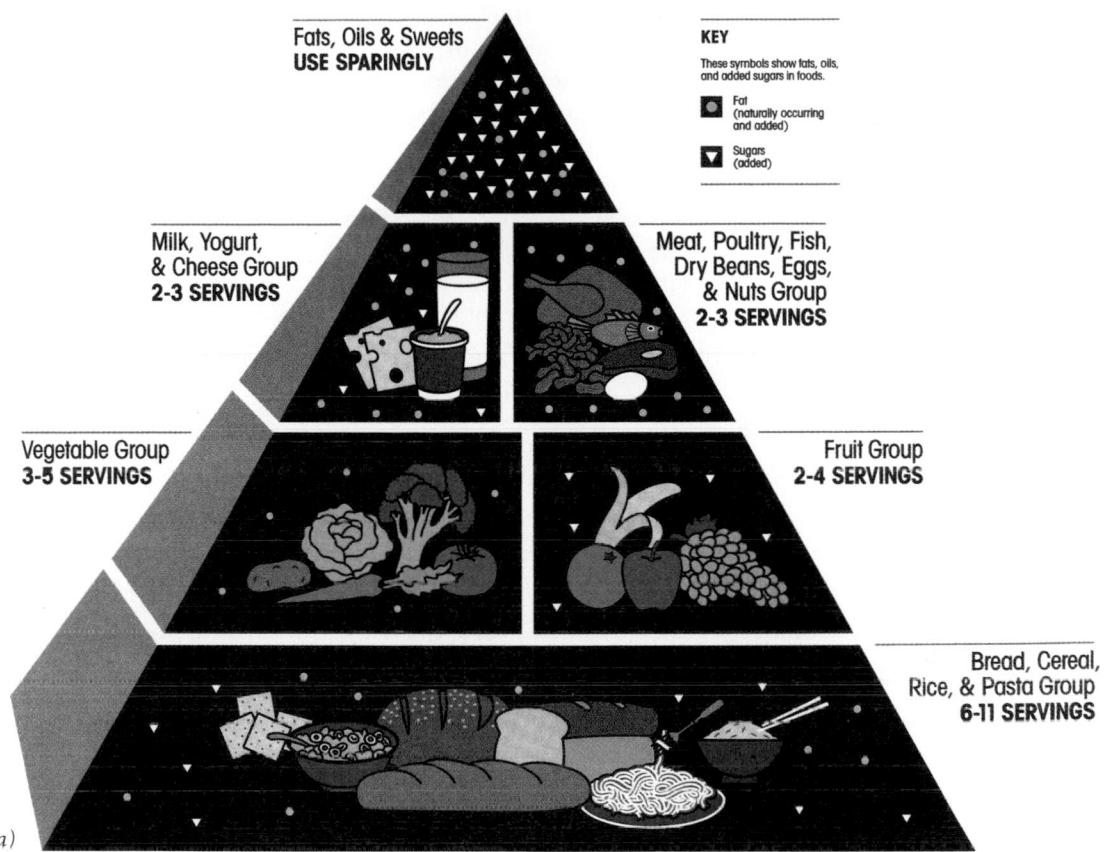

Fats, Oils & Sweets
USE SPARINGLY

KEY

These symbols show fats, oils, and added sugars in foods.

● Fat (naturally occurring and added)

▼ Sugars (added)

Milk, Yogurt, & Cheese Group
2-3 SERVINGS

Meat, Poultry, Fish, Dry Beans, Eggs, & Nuts Group
2-3 SERVINGS

Vegetable Group
3-5 SERVINGS

Fruit Group
2-4 SERVINGS

Bread, Cereal, Rice, & Pasta Group
6-11 SERVINGS

(a)

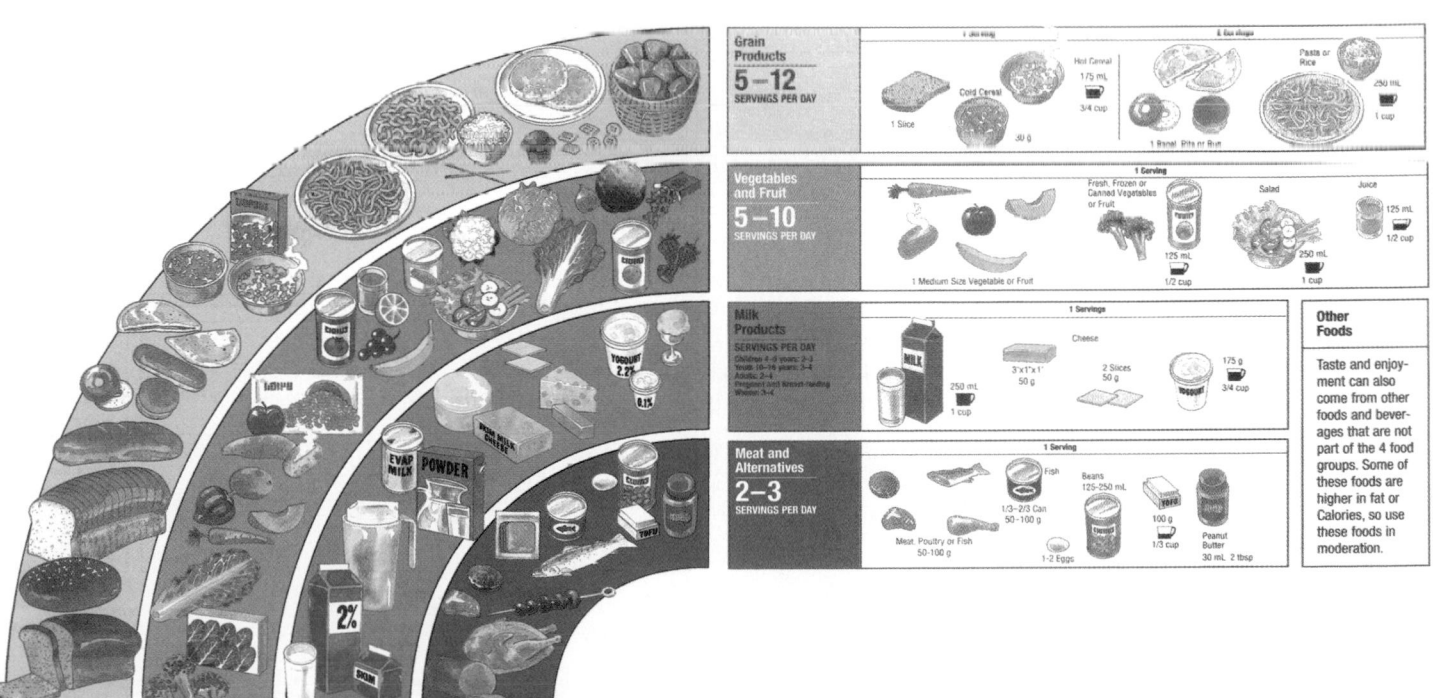

Grain Products
Choose whole grain and enriched products more often.

Vegetables and Fruit
Choose dark green and orange vegetables and orange fruit more often.

Milk Products
Choose lower-fat milk products more often.

Meat and Alternatives
Choose leaner meats, poultry and fish, as well as dried peas, beans and lentils more often.

(b)

devised a "Food Guide to Healthy Eating," usually referred to as the food rainbow because of its format [Figure 6.3(b)]. In the Canadian rainbow as well as in the U.S. pyramid, the number of daily servings of each group is indicated in the diagram. In addition, the Canadian guide gives information about standard portion sizes as well as number of servings.

2. **Maintain healthy weight.**
People who are greatly overweight are more likely to develop certain chronic diseases, such as high blood pressure, heart disease, and stroke. Anyone who consumes more calories than he or she burns off will gain weight. The only way to lose weight is to take in fewer calories than you burn.

   Rather than depending on crash diets, it is usually better to lose weight slowly and gradually, to develop better habits of eating, and to increase physical activity. To get all the nutrients you need while cutting down on calories, cut down on foods that are high in calories but low in nutrients, especially fat and fatty foods, sugar and sweets, and alcohol.

3. **Choose a diet that is low in fat, saturated fat, and cholesterol.**
As mentioned above, high fat intake, especially of saturated fats and cholesterol, is associated with such conditions as heart disease and high blood pressure. Although other factors contribute to these diseases, such as heredity and smoking, following this recommendation should increase the chances of staying healthy.

   In a recommended diet, no more than about 30 percent of the calories are in the form of fat. In the average diets in some Western countries, about 40 percent of the calories are from fat.

4. **Choose a diet with plenty of vegetables, fruits, and grain products.**
If you decrease your fat intake, as recommended in point 3, you will need a larger proportion of carbohydrates in your diet to supply energy. The nutritional advantages of complex carbohydrates over refined ones and of fiber in the diet are discussed in the preceding section on nutrients. Vegetables, fruits, and grains are dietary sources of starch and fiber as well as vitamins and minerals.

5. **Use sugars only in moderation.**
Many Western diets include excessive amounts of sugar. For example, the average American consumes well over 100 pounds of sweeteners a year, not only as table sugar but also in candies, sweets, jams, jellies, soft drinks, ice cream, breakfast cereals, flavored milks, catsup, and so on. Too much sugar contributes to tooth decay and provides empty calories, adding to overweight and obesity problems without supplying significant amounts of important nutrients.

6. **Use salt and sodium only in moderation.**
Sodium, as noted earlier, appears to contribute to high blood pressure. For people who already have high blood pressure, it is especially important to cut down on sodium in the diet. The best ways to do this are to decrease the use of salt in the kitchen and at the table and to limit the intake of prepared foods that are high in salt, such as potato chips, salted nuts, pretzels, pickled foods, cured meats, and salty condiments like soy sauce.

7. **If you drink alcoholic beverages, do so in moderation.**
Alcoholic beverages are high in calories while providing few other nutrients. Heavy drinking may cause a variety of serious diseases. Moderate drinking—one or two drinks a day— appears to do little harm and may, in fact, be of some benefit.

THE VEGETARIAN DIET

More and more people are following some form of vegetarian diet. It is important that cooks and chefs who want to please their customers learn something about various vegetarian diets so that they can meet the needs of the dining public.

The *vegan* diet is the most restrictive form of vegetarianism. Vegans eat plant products only. All animal products, including dairy products and eggs, are off limits.

- *Stainless steel* is a poor heat conductor. Cooking pots and pans made of it tend to scorch foods easily. Stainless steel is ideal for storage containers because it will not react with foods as aluminum does. It is also used for low-temperature cooking or holding equipment, such as steamer pans and counter pans, where scorching or hot spots are not a problem.

  Stainless-steel pots and pans are also available with a heavy layer of copper or aluminum bonded to the bottom. Heavy aluminum pans may also be lined with stainless steel on the inside, or on both the inside and outside. This feature gives the advantages of stainless steel (its hardness, durability, nonreactivity with acid foods, and nondiscoloration of light sauces) with the heat-conducting qualities of copper or aluminum. These pans are usually expensive.

- *Cast iron* is a favorite material with many chefs because of its ability to distribute heat evenly and to maintain high temperatures for long periods. It is used in griddles and heavy skillets. Cast-iron cracks easily if dropped. It rusts quickly unless kept properly conditioned and dry (see p. 619 for conditioning pans).

- *Porcelain enamel-lined pans* should not be used. In fact, they are forbidden by some health departments. They scratch and chip easily, providing good hiding places for bacteria. Also, certain kinds of gray enamel can cause food poisoning if chipped.

- *Nonstick plastic-type coatings*, known by brand names including Teflon and Silverstone, provide a slippery finish, but one that requires a lot of care because it is easily scratched. Do not use metal spoons or spatulas with this equipment. Many chefs keep a set of nonstick egg pans and use them for no other purpose.

  Because more customers are requesting low-fat foods, nonstick coatings are increasing in popularity. They enable cooks to sauté foods with little or no fat.

- *Glass* and *earthenware* have limited use in commercial kitchens because they are very breakable. They are poor conductors of heat but are resistant to corrosion and food acids.

POTS AND PANS AND THEIR USES

1. **Stockpot.**
   A large, deep, straight-sided pot for preparing stocks and simmering large quantities of liquids. Stockpots with spigots allow liquid to be drained off without disturbing the solid contents or lifting the pot. Sizes: 8 to 200 quarts (or liters).

2. **Saucepot.**
   Round pot of medium depth. Similar to a stockpot but shallower, making stirring or mixing easier. Used for soups, sauces, and other liquids. Sizes: 6 to 60 quarts (or liters).

3. **Brazier.**
   Round, broad, shallow, heavy-duty pot with straight sides. Used for browning, braising, and stewing meats. Sizes: 11 to 30 quarts (or liters).

4. **Saucepan.**
   Similar to a small, shallow, light saucepot, but with one long handle instead of two loop handles. May have straight or slanted sides. Used for general range-top cooking. Sizes: 1½ to 15 quarts (or liters).

5. **Sauté pan, straight-sided.**
   Similar to a shallow, straight-sided saucepan, but heavier. Used for browning, sautéing, and frying. Because of its broad surface area, the sauté pan is used for cooking sauces and other liquids when rapid reduction is required. Sizes: 2½ to 5 inches (65 to 130 mm) deep; 6 to 16 inches (160 to 400 mm) in diameter.

6. **Sauté pan, slope-sided.**
   Also called *fry pan*. Used for general sautéing and frying of meats, fish, vegetables, and eggs. The sloping sides allow the cook to flip and toss items without using a spatula, and they make it easier to get at the food when a spatula is used. Sizes: 6 to 14 inches (160 to 360 mm) top diameter.

Stockpot

Stockpot with spigot

Saucepot

Brazier

Saucepan

Straight-sided sauté pan

*Slope-sided
sauté pan*

Cast-iron skillet

Sheet pan

Bake pan

Roasting pan

Hotel pan

7. **Cast-iron skillet.**
Very heavy, thick-bottomed fry pan. Used for pan frying when very steady, even heat is desired.

8. **Double boiler.**
Lower section, similar to a stockpot, holds boiling water. Upper section holds foods that must be cooked at low temperatures and cannot be cooked over direct heat. Size of top section: 4 to 36 quarts (or liters).

9. **Sheet pan or bun pan.**
Shallow rectangular pan (1 inch/25 mm deep) for baking cakes, rolls, and cookies, and for baking or broiling certain meats and fish. Sizes: full pan, 18 × 26 inches (46 × 66 cm); half pan, 18 ×13 inches (46 × 33 cm)

10. **Bake pan.**
Rectangular pan about 2 inches (50 mm) deep. Used for general baking. Comes in a variety of sizes.

11. **Roasting pan.**
Large rectangular pan, deeper and heavier than bake pan. Used for roasting meats and poultry.

12. **Hotel pan,** also called **counter pan, steam table pan,** or **service pan.**
Rectangular pans, usually made of stainless steel. Designed to hold foods in service counters. Also used for baking and steaming, and foods can then be served from same pan. Also used for storage. Standard size: 12 × 20 inches. Fractions of this size (½, ⅓, etc.) are also available. Standard depth: 2½ inches (65 mm). Deeper sizes are also available. (Standard metric pan is 325 × 530 mm.)

13. **Bain-marie insert,** usually called simply *bain-marie.*
Tall, cylindrical stainless-steel container. Used for storage and for holding foods in a bain-marie (water bath). Sizes: 1 to 36 quarts (or liters).

14. **Stainless-steel bowl.**
Round-bottomed bowl. Used for mixing and whipping and for production of hollandaise, mayonnaise, whipped cream, and egg white foams. Round construction enables whip to reach all areas. Comes in many sizes.

Double boiler

Bain-marie inserts

Measuring Devices

The following equipment is discussed in terms of U.S. measurements. Comparable items in metric units are also available.

1. *Scales.* Most recipe ingredients are measured by weight, so accurate scales are very important. *Portion scales* are used for measuring ingredients as well as for portioning products for service. The baker's *balance scale* is discussed in Chapter 26.

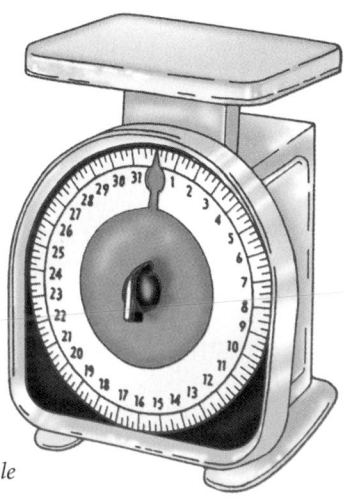

Portion scale

Lacto-vegetarians eat dairy products in addition to plant products but will not eat other animal products.

Lacto-ovo-vegetarians eat dairy and egg products as well as plant products.

Pesco-vegetarians eat fish and plant products but not meat or poultry. They may or may not eat dairy and egg products.

The major nutritional concern of a vegetarian diet is getting enough protein. Dairy products, eggs, and fish supply good-quality protein, but vegans must plan their diets carefully in order to get adequate protein. Some plant products, such as grains, nuts, and dried beans, contain proteins, but, with the exception of soy beans and soy products such as tofu, these are incomplete proteins (see p. 102). Vegans must eat a variety of these foods in order to get complete proteins in their diet.

Vegetarianism may be based on strong ethical or moral beliefs or on health concerns. Naturally, the chef who cares for his or her customers is eager to respect their beliefs and concerns. But in addition to people who have a strong commitment to vegetarianism, many others eat meat on other occasions but choose vegetarian items simply because the choices are so appealing. Chefs who create satisfying, innovative choices for vegetarians often find that a good vegetarian menu selection helps stimulate repeat business among a wide variety of customers.

COOKING HEALTHFUL MEALS

Restaurateurs and chefs are becoming more and more attentive to people's health and diet concerns. Many of them are reexamining their menus, modifying some of their cooking practices, and adding new, healthful items to their menus. Some have developed new menus that are specially planned to follow as closely as possible the seven recommendations listed previously.

An increased health consciousness has affected the way we think about food and the way we cook. Professional cooks are making their foods more healthful in several ways:

1. **Using less fat in cooking.**
    Cooking methods that require no added fat, such as simmering, poaching, baking, steaming, and grilling, can be considered the most healthful.

    For sautéing, nonstick pans are becoming more widely used because little or no fat is needed. With regular pans, one can be careful to use as little fat as possible.

    Grilling is popular because it can be done without first coating the food with fat. If this is done, however, one must be careful not to let the food dry out.

    Using less fat in cooking also means using ingredients with less fat. Excess external fat can be trimmed from meats and poultry. Low-fat sauces, such as salsas and vegetable purées, can often be used instead of high-fat sauces. Recipes can often be modified so that quantities of high-fat ingredients, such as butter, cheese, and bacon, are reduced.

2. **Using unsaturated fats.**
    When you do use fats, try to substitute monounsaturated fats, such as olive oil or canola oil, for saturated fats when appropriate.

3. **Emphasizing flavor.**
    Taste is the most important factor in preparing nutritious food. The most vitamin-packed dish does no one any good if it is uneaten because it doesn't taste good. Preparing flavorful foods requires knowledge of the principles of cooking. You can't rely simply on nutritional information.

4. **Using the freshest, highest-quality foods possible.**
    In order to prepare delicious foods with little or no added salt and with less reliance on high-fat, high-sodium sauces and condiments, it is important to use high-quality natural ingredients at their peak of flavor. Healthful cooking means letting the true flavors of foods dominate.

    To enhance natural flavors without added salt, cooks are using more fresh herbs, hot seasonings such as chilies, ginger, and pepper, and flavorful ingredients like garlic, browned onions, and flavored vinegars.

5. **Storing foods properly.**
   Foods in storage lose nutrients as they get older. The loss of nutrients can be slowed, however, by proper storage. This applies particularly to proper refrigeration. For each category of perishable food discussed in this book, pay close attention to how the foods should be stored.

6. **Modifying portion sizes.**
   It is not necessary to feature huge slabs of meat to serve satisfying meals. Smaller portions of well-trimmed meat, poultry, or fish, nicely balanced on the plate with an assortment of attractive, fresh vegetables and complex carbohydrates are likely to be more healthful.

   Sauces often get the blame for adding calories to a meal, but if a sauce is flavorful, you don't need much. Make a better sauce and serve less of it. Also, if a sauce isn't too thick, it won't cling as heavily to the food, and a little will go a longer way.

7. **Giving customers a choice.**
   Offer a menu with a variety of foods so that customers can choose a well-balanced meal suited to their needs and desires. It's not necessary to cook only "diet food," but a menu that offers French fries as the only available starch is not well balanced.

   Be flexible in the kitchen. A good chef should be willing to modify menu items to meet dietary requirements and to satisfy special requests from his or her customers.

8. **Training the dining room staff.**
   Some restaurants offer special "spa menus" in addition to their regular menus, or they highlight "healthy" items with a special symbol. Unfortunately, this approach may suggest to some people that the highlighted menu items are boring "health food," while the other menu items are unhealthful because they aren't flagged. Consequently, many chefs prefer to train their dining room personnel to answer customers' questions about the menu and to offer suggestions when asked.

9. **Using nutritional information.**
   Studying the nutritional content of foods aids in planning healthful menus. Many publications are available that list nutritional contents of most common food items. Some restaurants have even hired the part-time services of registered dietitians to analyze their menus and give advice on how to make their food more healthful.

   Hiring a dietitian is, of course, not practical for every operation. On the other hand, a basic awareness of nutrition helps every professional minimize the fat, cholesterol, and sodium in and maximize the nutritional content and balance of the foods they serve.

Terms for Review

static menu	fresh	polyunsaturated fat	vitamin
cycle menu	imported	monounsaturated	vegan
à la carte	homemade	fat	lacto-vegetarian
table d'hôte	calorie	cholesterol	lacto-ovo-
prix fixe	carbohydrate	complete protein	vegetarian
course	fiber	complementary	pesco-vegetarian
minimum-use ingredient	saturated fat	protein	

Questions for Discussion

1. What role is played by the chef's favorite dishes when a menu is written?

2. What are the main differences among breakfast, lunch, and dinner menus?

3. Which of the following are most likely to have static menus?

   Fast-food restaurant
   High school cafeteria
   Employee lunchroom
   Army mess
   French restaurant

4. The following menus are made up of dishes prepared from recipes in this book. Evaluate each one for variety and balance.

   Clear vegetable soup
   Green salad with French dressing
   Chicken fricassée
       Cauliflower au gratin

   Scotch broth
   Cucumber and tomato salad
   Roast rack of lamb with spring vegetables

   Oysters casino
   Vichyssoise
   Broiled steak
       Baked potato
       Buttered green beans

   Cream of mushroom soup
   Waldorf salad
   Veal scaloppine à la crème
       Broccoli mornay
       Rice pilaf

   Oxtail soup
   Coleslaw
   Beef pot roast
       Braised green cabbage
       Bouillon potatoes

   Gazpacho
   Tomato and avocado salad
   Chicken Pojarski
       Baked acorn squash
       Duchesse potatoes

5. What is the best solution to the problem of using up leftovers? What is the next best solution?

6. What are the U.S. government's seven dietary guidelines for Americans? Discuss.

7. As a cook, what are some ways that you can reduce the fat and sodium content of your menu offerings?

8. How can you ensure a nutritionally balanced menu without actually calculating the nutrient content of every item?

9. Discuss and compare the healthful or unhealthful qualities of saturated fats, polyunsaturated fats, and monounsaturated fats. Give examples of each type.

chapter 7

Mise en Place

To be successful in the food service industry, cooks need more than the ability to prepare delicious, attractive, and nutritious foods. They must have a talent for organization and efficiency. In any kitchen, a great many tasks must be completed over a given time and by a limited number of workers. No matter when these tasks are done, they all must come together at one crucial point: service time. Only if advance preparation has been done thoroughly and systematically will service go smoothly.

Good chefs take pride in the thoroughness and quality of their advance preparation, or *mise en place* (meez-on-plahss). This French term, meaning "everything put in place," has become almost a professional password in American kitchens because food service professionals understand its importance to the success of the establishment.

This chapter deals with the basic concepts of mise en place as well as a number of specific operations that are normally part of the mise en place.

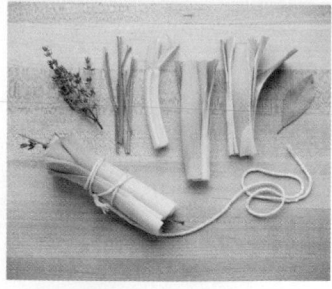

Planning and Organizing Production

Even on the simplest level, pre-preparation is necessary. If you prepare only one short recipe, you must first:

- Assemble your tools.
- Assemble your ingredients.
- Wash, trim, cut, prepare, and measure your raw materials.
- Prepare your equipment (preheat oven, line baking sheets, etc.).

Only then can you begin the actual preparation.

When many items are to be prepared in a commercial kitchen, the situation is much more complex. Dealing with this complexity is the basis of kitchen organization.

After reading this chapter, you should be able to:

1. Define *mise en place* and explain why care must be taken in its planning.

2. Describe five general steps used in planning mise en place.

3. Explain the difference in preparation requirements for set meal service and extended meal service.

4. List five guidelines to observe when sharpening a chef's knife.

5. Demonstrate major cutting techniques required in food preparation.

6. Describe basic precooking and marinating procedures.

7. Set up and use a standard breading station.

8. Define *convenience foods* in the context of mise en place and list eight guidelines for their use.

THE PROBLEM

Every food service operation faces a basic conflict between two unavoidable facts:

1. There is far too much work to do in a kitchen to leave until the last minute, so some work must be done ahead.

2. Most foods are at their best quality immediately after preparation, and they deteriorate as they are held.

THE SOLUTION

To solve this problem, the chef must plan the pre-preparation carefully. Planning generally follows these steps:

1. **Break each menu item down into its stages of production.**
   Turn to any recipe in this book. Note that the procedures are divided into a sequence of steps that must be done in a certain order to make a finished product.

2. **Determine which stages may be done in advance.**
   - The first step of any recipe, whether written or not, is always part of advance preparation: *assembling and preparing the ingredients.* This includes cleaning and cutting produce, cutting and trimming meats, and preparing breadings and batters for frying.
   - Succeeding steps of a recipe may be done in advance *if the foods can then be held without loss of quality.*
   - Final cooking should be done as close as possible to service for maximum freshness.

   Frequently, separate parts of a recipe, such as a sauce or a stuffing, are prepared in advance, and the dish is assembled at the last minute.

   In general, items cooked by dry-heat methods, such as broiled steaks, sautéed fish, and French-fried potatoes, do not hold well. Large roasts are an important exception to this rule. Items cooked by moist heat, such as braised beef, soups, and stews, are usually better suited to reheating or holding in a steam table. Very delicate items should always be freshly cooked.

3. **Determine the best way to hold the item at its final stage of pre-preparation.**
   - Sauces and soups are frequently kept hot, above 140°F (60°C), for service in steam tables or other holding equipment. Many foods such as vegetables, however, should be kept hot for only short periods because they quickly become overcooked.
   - Refrigerator temperatures, below 41°F (5°C), are best for preserving the quality of most foods, especially perishable meats, fish, and vegetables, before final cooking or reheating.

4. **Determine how long it takes to prepare each stage of each recipe. Plan a production schedule beginning with the preparations that take the longest.**
   Many operations can be carried on at once because they don't all require your complete attention the full time. It may take 6 to 8 hours to make a stock, but you don't have to stand and watch it all that time.

5. **Examine recipes to see if they might be revised for better efficiency and quality as served.**
   For example:
   - Instead of preparing a full batch of green peas and holding for service in the steam table, you might blanch and chill them, then heat portions to order in a sauté pan, steamer, or microwave oven.

- Instead of holding a large batch of veal scaloppine in mushroom sauce in the steam table, you might prepare and hold the sauce, sauté the veal to order, combine with a portion of the sauce, and serve fresh from the pan.

Caution: Unless you are in charge of the kitchen, do not change a recipe without authorization from your supervisor.

THE GOAL

The goal of pre-preparation is to do as much work in advance as possible *without loss of quality*.

At service time, all energy can then be used for finishing each item immediately before serving, with the utmost attention to quality and freshness.

Many preparation techniques in common use are designed for the convenience of the cooks at the expense of quality. Remember, quality should always take highest priority.

ADAPTING PREPARATION TO STYLE OF SERVICE

The way you plan production and do your mise en place depends in large part on the style of meal service. The following discussion of *set meal service* and *extended meal service* illustrates the basic differences.

Set Meal Service

- All customers eat at one time.
- Often called "quantity cooking" because large batches are prepared in advance.
- Examples: school cafeterias, banquets, employee dining rooms.

The traditional method of set meal preparation, still widely used, is to prepare the entire quantity of each item in a single large batch and to keep it hot for the duration of the meal service. This method has two major disadvantages:

- Deterioration of quality due to long holding.
- Large quantities of leftovers.

Modern high speed equipment, such as pressure steamers, convection ovens, infrared ovens, and microwave ovens, make possible a system called *small-batch cooking*. Quantities needed are divided in smaller batches, placed in pans ready for final cooking or heating, then cooked only as needed. The advantages of this system are as follows:

- Fresher food, because it is not held as long.
- Fewer leftovers, because pans not needed are not cooked.

Small-batch cooking also accommodates items prepared in advance and frozen or chilled for storage.

Extended Meal Service

- Customers eat at different times.
- Often called "à la carte cooking" because customers usually select items from a written menu (*carte* in French).
- Examples: restaurants, short-order counters.

Individual items are cooked to order rather than cooked ahead, but pre-preparation is extensive, down to the final cooking stage.

The short-order cook, for example, must have everything ready to go: cold meats, tomatoes and other sandwich ingredients sliced and arranged, spreads prepared and ready, hamburger patties shaped, garnishes prepared, and so on. If the cook has to stop during service to do any of these things, orders will back up and service will get behind.

A steak that takes 10 minutes to broil may be cut and trimmed in advance, but broiling should be started 10 minutes before it is to be served.

Obviously, if the last step in a recipe is to braise the item for 1½ hours, one cannot wait until an order comes in before beginning to braise. An experienced cook can estimate closely how many orders will be needed during the meal period and prepare a batch that, ideally, will be finished braising just when service begins.

Note the differences in these two methods for Chicken Chasseur. In both cases, the final product is chicken in a brown sauce with mushrooms, shallots, white wine, and tomatoes.

1. **Quantity method—Chicken Chasseur:**
   Brown chicken in fat; remove.
   Sauté shallots and mushrooms in same fat.
   Add flour to make a roux.
   Add white wine, tomatoes, brown stock, seasonings; simmer until thickened.
   Add chicken; braise until done.

2. **À la carte method—Chicken Chasseur:**
   Prepare Sauce Chasseur in advance; hold in bain-marie.
   For each order:
   Brown chicken in sauté pan; finish cooking in oven.
   Deglaze pan with white wine; reduce.
   Add one portion of sauce; add chicken and simmer briefly; serve.

MISE EN PLACE: THE REQUIRED TASKS

Up to this point, we have discussed planning the production schedule. Our planning helps us determine what tasks we must do before beginning the final cooking during the meal service period. Chefs refer to performing these preliminary tasks as "doing the mise en place." In many restaurants, especially large ones, the mise en place is extensive. It includes the preparation of stocks, sauces, breadings, and batters as well as the cutting and trimming of all the meat, poultry, fish, and vegetables that the chef expects will be needed during the meal service. A large part of a cook's workday is spent doing mise en place. This means that a large part of learning how to cook is learning how to do mise en place.

The remainder of this chapter discusses the most basic and general skills required for a mise en place. The most basic of these are knife skills. More specific techniques required for individual food products are explained in appropriate chapters later in the book. For example, vegetable trimming techniques are discussed in the first vegetable chapter, methods for cutting chicken in the first poultry chapter.

Using the Knife

Many kinds of laborsaving tools are available for cutting, chopping, and slicing fresh foods. Chapter 3 lists the basic kinds.

The chef's knife or French knife, however, is still the cook's most important and versatile cutting tool. The knife is more precise than a machine. Unless you are cutting a large quantity, the knife can even be faster. Cleaning a large machine takes time.

To get the best use out of your knife, *you must learn to keep it sharp and to handle it properly.*

KEEPING A SHARP EDGE

The Sharpening Stone

A stone is the best tool for sharpening a chef's knife. The best electric sharpeners do an excellent job of sharpening chef's knives, but many models wear away too much of your expensive knife without making a good edge. You may not be lucky enough to have ready use of a good electric sharpener, so it is important to know how to sharpen a knife on a stone.

Follow these guidelines:

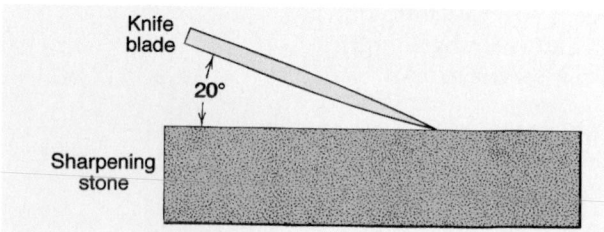

Figure 7.1 When sharpening a knife, hold the blade at a 20-degree angle to the stone.

1. Hold the blade at a constant 20-degree angle to the stone, as shown in Figure 7.1.
2. Make light, even strokes, the same number on each side of the blade.
3. Sharpen in one direction only to get a regular, uniform edge.
4. Do not oversharpen.
5. Finish with a few strokes on the steel (see next section), then wipe the blade clean.

Figure 7.2 illustrates one of several sharpening methods. There are other good ones, too, and your instructor may prefer a method not illustrated here.

Figure 7.2 Using a sharpening stone.

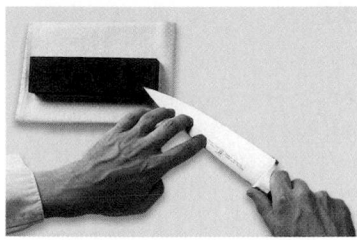 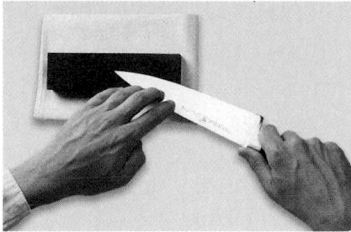  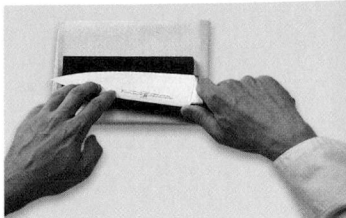

(a) Hold the knife firmly. Start with the tip of the knife against the stone as shown, and hold the edge against the stone at a 20-degree angle. Use the guiding hand to keep an even pressure on the blade.

(b) Start to draw the knife over the stone. Press very gently on the blade.

(c) Keep the motion smooth, using even, light pressure.

(d) Draw the knife across the stone all the way to the heel of the blade.

The Steel

This tool is used not to sharpen the edge but to *true the edge* (to perfect it, or to smooth out irregularities) and to *maintain the edge* (to keep it sharp as it is used).

Observe these guidelines for using the steel:

1. Hold the blade at a constant 20-degree angle to the steel, just as when using the stone (Figure 7.2). A smaller angle will be ineffective. A larger one will dull the edge.
2. Make light strokes. Do not grind the knife against the steel.
3. Make even, regular strokes. Alternate each stroke, first on one side of the blade, then on the other.
4. Use no more than five or six strokes on each side of the blade. Too much steeling can actually dull the blade.
5. Use the steel often. Then you will rarely have to sharpen the knife on the stone.

Figure 7.3 illustrates one of several steeling methods. This one is popular, but several others are equally correct. Carefully observe your instructors' demonstrations of their preferred methods.

Figure 7.3 Using a steel.

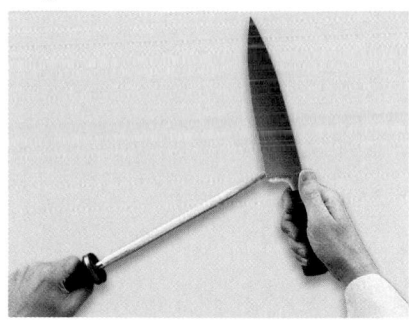 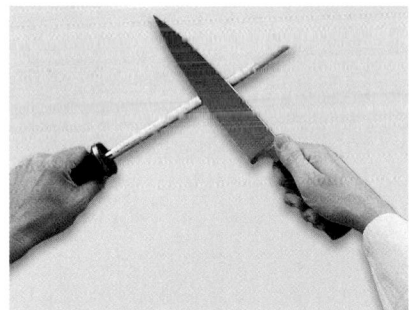 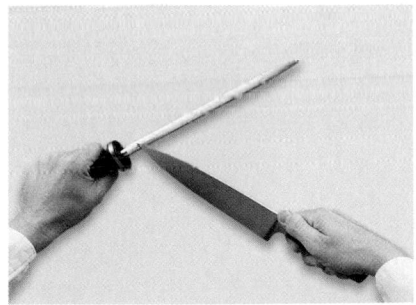

(a) Hold the steel and the knife away from your body. With the knife in a vertical position and at a 20-degree angle to the steel, touch the steel with the heel of the blade.

(b) Pass the knife lightly along the steel, bringing the blade down in a smooth arc.

(c) Complete the movement. Do not strike the guard of the steel with the tip of the blade.

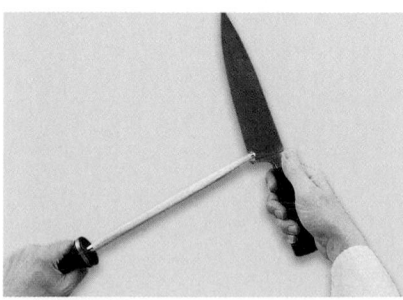  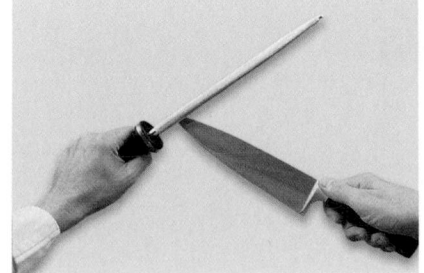

(d, e, f) Repeat the motion on the other side of the steel.

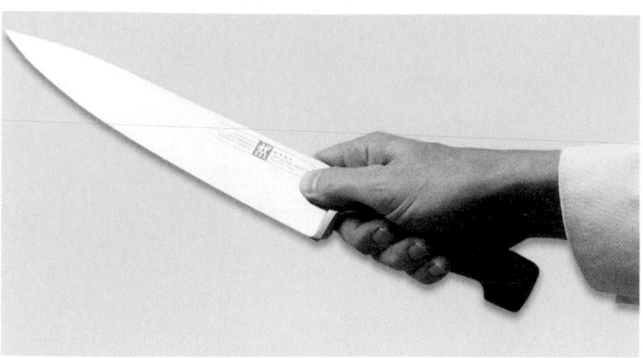

Figure 7.4 Grasping the blade of the knife between the thumb and forefinger gives the worker good control over the blade.

HANDLING THE KNIFE

The Grip

A proper grip gives you maximum control over the knife. The proper grip increases your cutting accuracy and speed, prevents slipping, and lessens the chance of an accident. The type of grip you use depends, in part, on the job you are doing and the size of the knife.

The grip illustrated in Figure 7.4 is one of the most frequently used for general cutting and slicing. Many chefs feel that actually grasping the blade with the thumb and forefinger in this manner gives them greatest control.

Holding the knife may feel awkward at first, but practice will make it seem natural. Watch your instructors demonstrate the grips they use, then practice under their supervision.

The Guiding Hand

While one hand controls the knife, the other hand controls the product being cut. Proper positioning of the hand achieves three goals:

1. **Hold the item being cut.**
   In Figure 7.5, the item is held firmly so that it will not slip.

2. **Guide the knife.**
   Note that the knife blade slides against the fingers. The position of the hand controls the cut.

3. **Protect the hand from cuts.**
   Fingertips are curled under, out of the way of the blade.

BASIC CUTS AND SHAPES

Cutting food products into uniform shapes and sizes is important for two reasons:

1. It ensures even cooking.
2. It enhances the appearance of the product.

Figure 7.6 shows some common shapes, with their names and dimensions.
The following terms describe other cutting techniques:

Chop: to cut into irregularly shaped pieces.
Concasser (con-cass-say): to chop coarsely.
Mince: to chop into very fine pieces.
Emincer (em-man-say): to cut into very thin slices (does not mean "to mince").
Shred: to cut into thin strips, either with the coarse blade of a grater (manual or power) or with a chef's knife.

Figure 7.5 The position of the guiding hand, which holds the item being cut or sliced and also guides the blade, from two points of view.

CUTTING TECHNIQUES

Different parts of the blade are appropriate for different purposes, as shown in Figure 7.7. (*Note:* Prying off bottle caps is not a function of any part of the knife.)

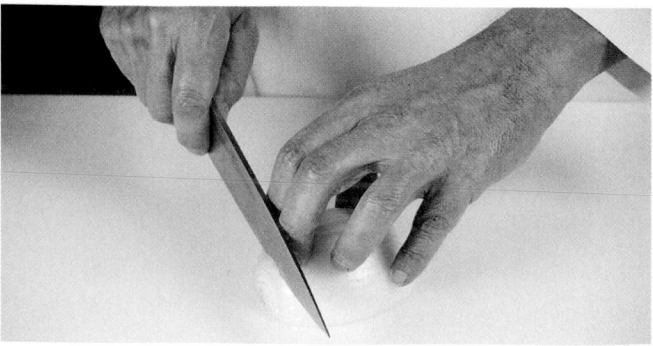

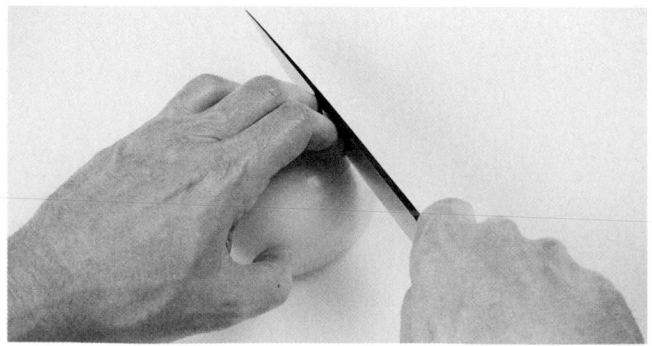

1. **Slicing.**
   Two basic slicing techniques are illustrated in Figures 7.8 and 7.9.

2. **Dicing.**
   Figure 7.10 shows the steps in dicing a product, here using a potato to illustrate.

3. **Dicing an onion.**
   Dicing an onion presents a special problem for cutting because its form is in layers, not a solid piece. This technique is illustrated in Figure 7.11.

4. **Peeling grapefruit.**
   This technique, as shown in Figure 7.12, can also be used for peeling yellow turnips or other round vegetables and fruits with heavy peels.

Figure 7.6 Basic cuts and shapes.

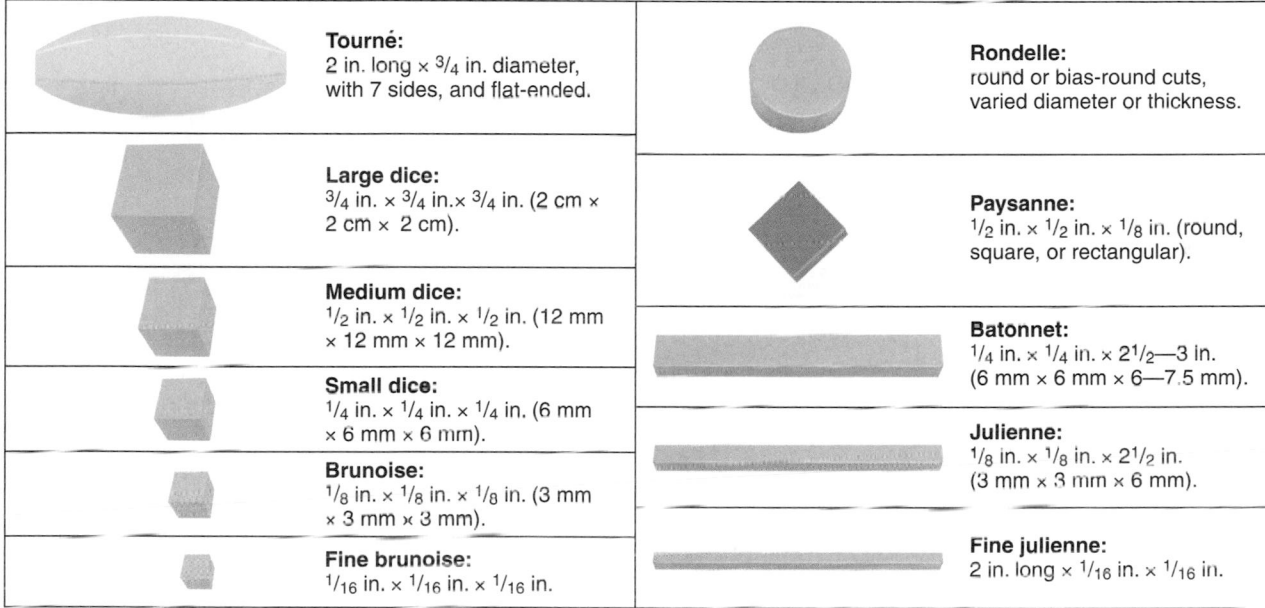

Tourné: 2 in. long × ³/₄ in. diameter, with 7 sides, and flat-ended.

Large dice: ³/₄ in. × ³/₄ in. × ³/₄ in. (2 cm × 2 cm × 2 cm).

Medium dice: ¹/₂ in. × ¹/₂ in. × ¹/₂ in. (12 mm × 12 mm × 12 mm).

Small dice: ¹/₄ in. × ¹/₄ in. × ¹/₄ in. (6 mm × 6 mm × 6 mm).

Brunoise: ¹/₈ in. × ¹/₈ in. × ¹/₈ in. (3 mm × 3 mm × 3 mm).

Fine brunoise: ¹/₁₆ in. × ¹/₁₆ in. × ¹/₁₆ in.

Rondelle: round or bias-round cuts, varied diameter or thickness.

Paysanne: ¹/₂ in. × ¹/₂ in. × ¹/₈ in. (round, square, or rectangular).

Batonnet: ¹/₄ in. × ¹/₄ in. × 2¹/₂—3 in. (6 mm × 6 mm × 6—7.5 mm).

Julienne: ¹/₈ in. × ¹/₈ in. × 2¹/₂ in. (3 mm × 3 mm × 6 mm).

Fine julienne: 2 in. long × ¹/₁₆ in. × ¹/₁₆ in.

Tourné: 2 in. long × ¾ in. diameter, with 7 sides, and flat-ended (see p. 488).
Large dice: ¾ in. × ¾ in. × ¾ in. (2 cm × 2 cm × 2 cm).
Medium dice: ½ in. × ½ in. × ½ in. (12 mm × 12 mm × 12 mm).
Small dice: ¼ in. × ¼ in. × ¼ in. (6 mm × 6 mm × 6 mm).
Brunoise (broon-wahz): ⅛ in. × ⅛ in. × ⅛ in.
   (3 mm × 3 mm × 3 mm).

Fine brunoise: ¹/₁₆ in. × ¹/₁₆ in. × ¹/₁₆ in. (1.5 mm × 1.5 mm × 1.5 mm).
Rondelle: round or bias-round cuts, varied diameter or thickness.
Paysanne: ½ in. × ½ in. × ⅛ in. (round, square, or rectangular).
Batonnet: ¼ in. × ¼ in. × 2½–3 in. (6 mm × 6 mm × 6–7.5 cm).
Julienne (or allumette potatoes): ⅛ in. × ⅛ in. × 2½ in.
   (3 mm × 3 mm × 6 cm).
Fine julienne: ¹/₁₆ in. × ¹/₁₆ in. × 2 in. (1.5 mm × 1.5 mm × 5 cm).

Figure 7.7 Using different parts of the knife blade.

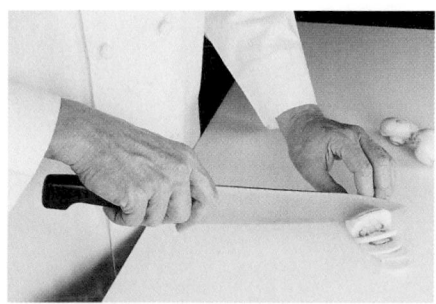 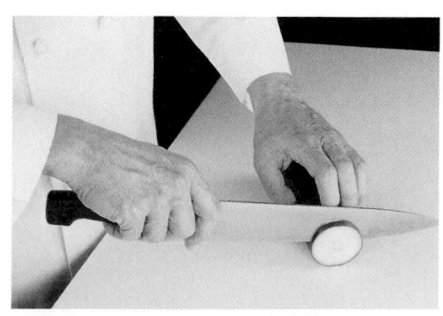 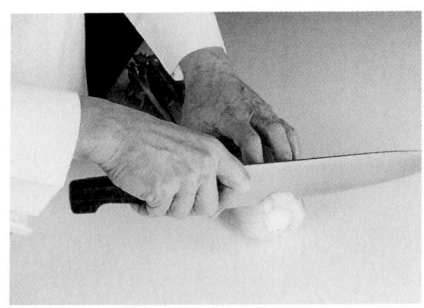

(a) The tip of the knife, where the blade is thinnest and narrowest, is used for delicate work and small items.

(b) The center of the blade is used for most general work.

(c) The heel of the knife is used for heavy or coarse work, especially when greater force is required.

Figure 7.8 Slicing technique 1.

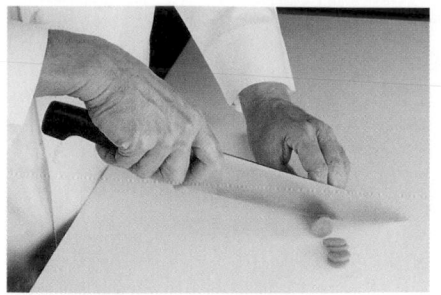 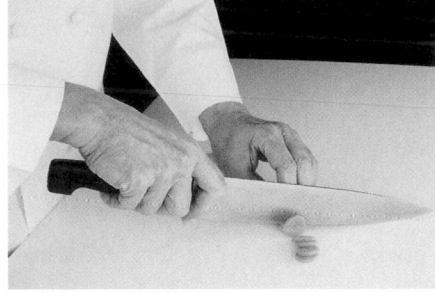 

(a) Start the knife at a sharp angle, with the tip of the knife on the cutting board.

(b) Move the knife forward and down to slice through the carrot.

(c) Finish the cut with the knife against the board. For the second slice, raise the heel of the knife and pull it backward, but be sure the tip always stays on the board.

Figure 7.9 Slicing technique 2.

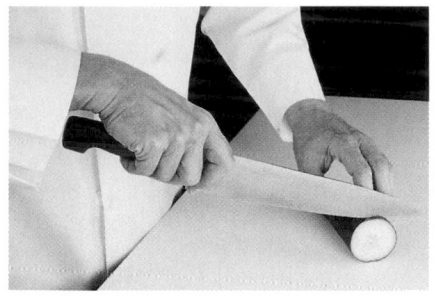 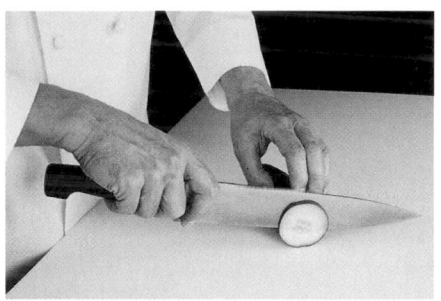 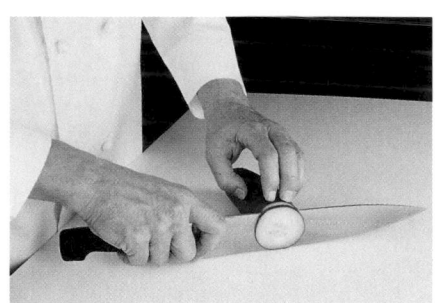

(a) Start the blade at a 45-degree angle, with the tip on the cucumber against the fingers of the guiding hand.

(b, c) Slice downward and forward through the item.

Figure 7.10 Dicing a potato.

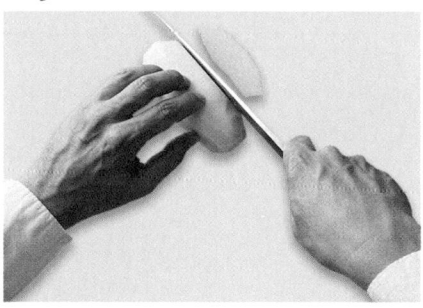 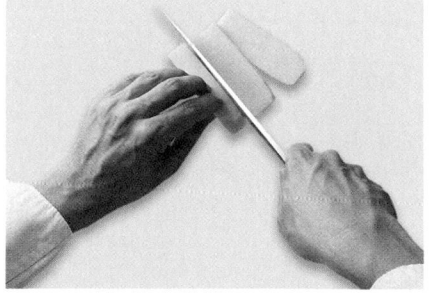

(a) Square off the peeled, eyed potato by cutting a slice from all sides. Use the trimmings for mashed potatoes or soup.

(b) Cut the potato into even slices of the desired thickness. Here we are making a ¼-inch dice, so the slices are ¼ inch thick.

 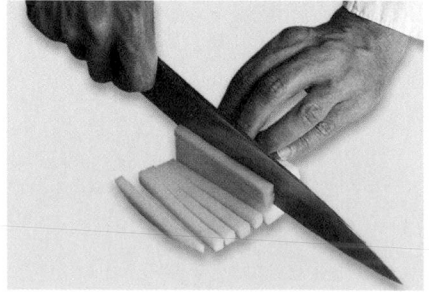 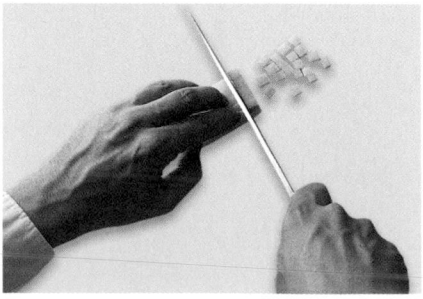

(c) Stack the slices and again slice across the stack in even ¼-inch slices. You now have batonnet potatoes, slightly smaller than regular French fries. Slices ⅛ inch thick would give you allumette potatoes.

(d) Looking from this angle shows how the slices have been stacked up.

(e) Pile the batonnets together and cut across in slices ¼ inch apart. You now have perfect ¼-inch dice.

Figure 7.11 Dicing an onion.

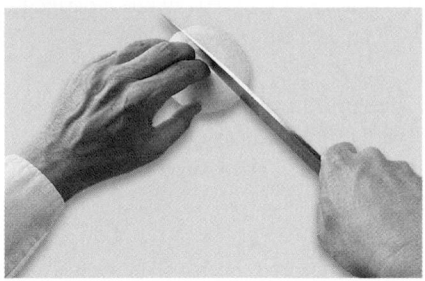
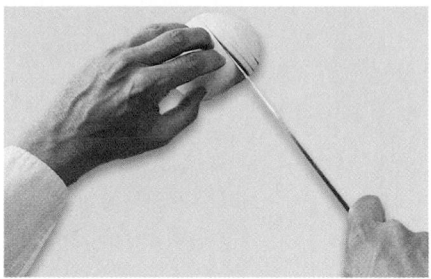
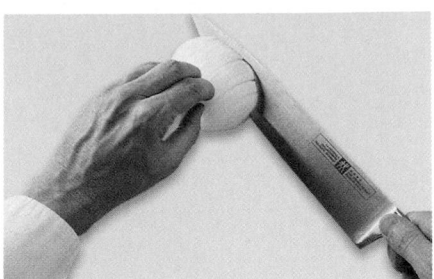

(a) Cut the peeled onion in half lengthwise, through the root end. Place one half on the cutting board, cut side down.

(b) With the root end away from you, make a series of vertical lengthwise cuts. Do not cut through the root end. The closer together you make the cuts, the smaller the dice will be.

(c) Holding the onion carefully at the top, make a few horizontal cuts toward but not through the root end, which is holding the onion together.

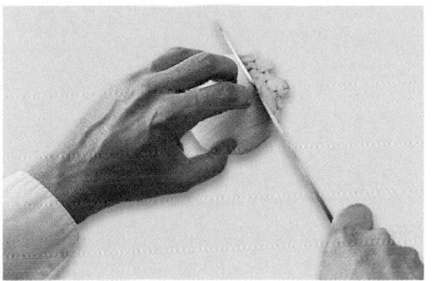
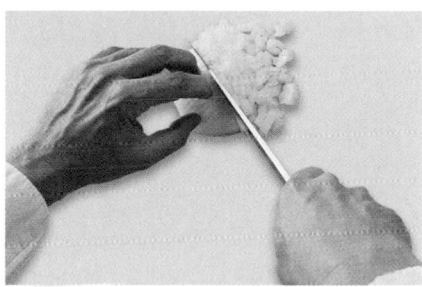

(d) Finally, slice across the onion to separate it into dice. Again, the closer together the cuts, the smaller the dice.

(e) Continue making slices almost to the root end. The root end may be rough cut for mirepoix, to be used for stocks, sauces, and roasts.

Figure 7.12 Peeling a grapefruit.

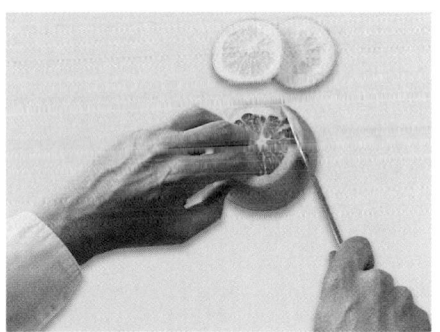
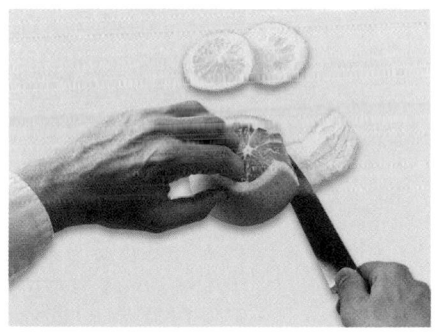

(a) Cut off the ends of the grapefruit and turn it on a flat end so that it is stable. Slice off a section of the peel, following the contour of the grapefruit.

(b) Make sure that the cut is deep enough to remove the peel but not so deep as to waste the product.

(c) Continue making slices around the grapefruit until all the peel is removed.

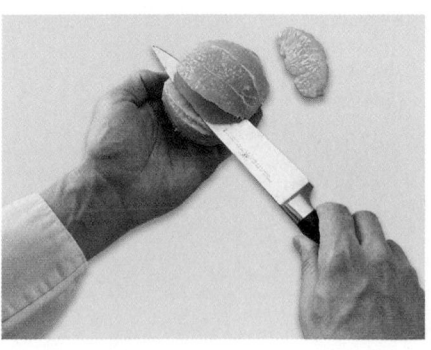

(d) Slice or section the fruit. (Squeeze the remaining pulp for juice.)

Figure 7.13 *Chopping with a French knife.*

Holding the tip of the knife against the cutting board, rock the knife rapidly up and down. At the same time, gradually move the knife sideways across the product on the board so that the cuts pass through all parts of the pile of food. After several cuts, redistribute the pile and begin again. Continue until the product is chopped as fine as you want.

5. **Chopping.**
   This chopping technique is used to cut a product when no specific shape is needed. Figure 7.13 illustrates chopping parsley.
6. **Chiffonade.**
   This term refers to cutting leaves into fine shreds. It is applied most often to lettuce and sorrel. To cut chiffonade, remove the heavy leaf ribs, roll the leaves into a tight cylinder, then slice crosswise into thin shreds, as shown in Figure 7.14.
7. **Cutting citrus zest.**
   With a paring knife, cut strips from the citrus peel, removing only the colored part, not the white part below it. Then, with a chef's knife, cut into thin strips or julienne, as shown in Figures 7.15a–b. An alternative method is to use a citrus zester, as shown in Figure 7.15c.

Preliminary Cooking and Flavoring

Advance preparation often requires certain precooking and flavoring of ingredients to make them ready for use in the finished recipe.

On the most obvious level, if a recipe for chicken salad calls for cooked, diced chicken, you must first cook the chicken before you can proceed with the recipe. A complete cooking procedure, in such a case, is part of the mise en place or pre-preparation.

BLANCHING AND PARCOOKING

Partial cooking is a significant part of advance preparation. It requires a degree of culinary skill and judgment to determine when and how much cooking is necessary or desirable.

Partial cooking may be done by any moist-heat or dry-heat method. Those commonly used are simmering or boiling (parboiling), steaming, and deep-frying (especially for potatoes). The term *blanching* may mean any of these methods, but it usually implies *very brief* cooking.

There are four main reasons for blanching or parcooking:

1. **To increase holding qualities.**
   Heating helps preserve foods by:
   • Destroying bacteria that cause spoilage.
   • Destroying enzymes that discolor foods (as when potatoes turn brown) and help them deteriorate.

Figure 7.14
Cutting a chiffonade of sorrel.

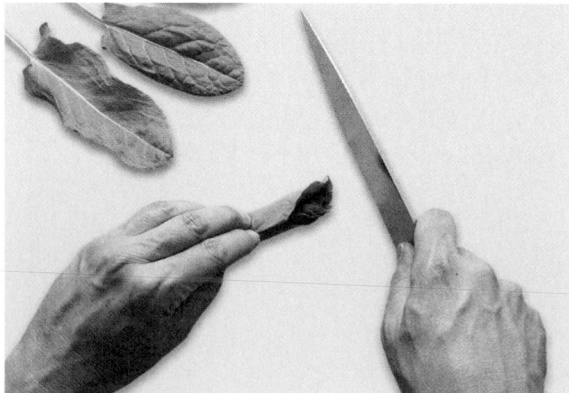

(a) Roll the leaves into a cylinder.

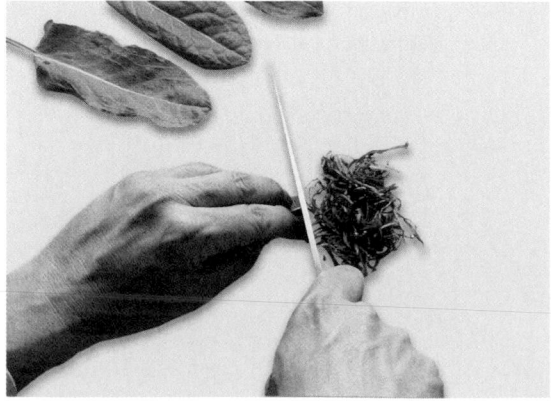

(b) Cut crosswise into thin strips or shreds.

Figure 7.15 *Cutting citrus zest.*

  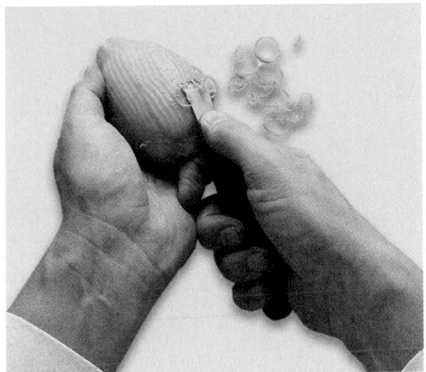

(a) Use a paring knife to cut thin strips from the peel, being careful to cut only the outer colored part, not the inner white pith.

(b) Cut the strips of peel into julienne.

(c) Alternatively, draw a zesting tool over the fruit to cut thin strips of zest.

2. **To save time.**
    It takes less time to finish parboiled vegetables for service than it does raw vegetables. Large batches of foods may be blanched and chilled, and individual portions then finished to order.

    Items such as roast duck, which would take too long to cook completely to order, are often roasted half to three-quarters done, then finished as the orders are received.

3. **To remove undesirable flavors.**
    Some variety meats and certain strong-flavored vegetables such as rutabaga are sometimes blanched to make them milder and more acceptable to the customer.

4. **To enable the product to be processed further.**
    For example, vegetables and fruits such as tomatoes and peaches, as well as some nuts, are blanched to loosen the skins for peeling.

    Sweetbreads are blanched so that they are firm enough for slicing and breading or other kinds of handling.

MARINATING

To marinate means to soak a food product in a seasoned liquid in order to:

1. Flavor the product.
2. Tenderize the product.

The tenderizing effect of the acids in the marinade is relatively small. It is still essential to match the proper cut of meat with the proper cooking techniques for greatest tenderness.

The marinade can also serve as the cooking medium and become part of the sauce. Vegetable marinades, called *vinaigrettes*, are served cold with the vegetables as salads or hors d'oeuvres, without further cooking or processing.

Marinades have three categories of ingredients:

1. **Oil.**
    Oil helps preserve the meat's moisture. Sometimes it is omitted, especially for long marinations, when the oil would only float on top, out of contact with the product being marinated.

    Tasteless vegetable oils are used when a neutral flavor is required. Specialty oils, such as olive oil, are used to add flavor to the item being marinated.

2. **Acid from vinegar, lemon juice, wine.**
    Acid helps tenderize protein foods.

    It carries flavors (its own and dissolved flavors from spices and herbs).

    Use caution when employing strong acids, such as vinegar and lemon juice. A marinade that is too acidic will partially coagulate the protein of the meat, making it seem partially cooked. When the meat is then cooked, its texture will not be as desirable. Strong acids can be used in marinades if they are used in small quantities or if the meat is marinated for only a few hours.

3. **Flavorings—spices, herbs, vegetables.**
   A wide choice is available, depending on the purpose.
       Whole spices release flavors more slowly, so they are more suitable for long marinations.

Kinds of Marinades

1. **Cooked.**
   Used when long keeping quality is important. Modern refrigeration has made cooked marinades less widely used. An advantage of cooked marinades is that spices release more flavor into the marinade when it is cooked.

2. **Raw.**
   Most widely used for long marination under refrigeration. For example, see the recipe for Sauerbraten, page 292.

3. **Instant.**
   The range of flavors and purposes is wide. Used for marinating a few minutes up to several hours or overnight. For example, see the recipe for London Broil, page 259.

4. **Dry.**
   A dry marinade, also called a *dry rub* or a *spice rub,* is a mixture of salt, spices, and herbs that is rubbed or patted onto the surface of a meat, poultry, or fish item. In some cases, a little oil or a moist ingredient such as crushed garlic is mixed with the spices to make a paste. The item is then refrigerated to allow it time to absorb the flavors. The rub may be left on the item or scraped off before cooking. This technique is widely used for barbecued meats. For an example of a dry marinade, see page 322.
       Dry marinades are an effective way to flavor meats. Naturally, because a dry marinade usually doesn't contain an acid, you can't expect it to produce the slight tenderizing effects of liquid marinades containing acids.

Guidelines for Marinating

1. Marinate under refrigeration (unless product is to be cooked for only a few minutes).

2. The thicker the product, the longer it takes for the marinade to penetrate. Some foods are marinated a week or longer.

3. Use an acid-resistant container, such as stainless steel, glass, crockery, or some plastics.

4. Tie spices in a cheesecloth bag (sachet) if easy removal is important.

5. Cover product completely with marinade. When marinating small items for a short time, you may use less liquid, but you must then turn the product frequently for even penetration.

Preparation for Frying

Most foods to be deep-fried, with the major exception of potatoes, are first given a protective coating of breading or batter. This coating serves four purposes:

1. It helps retain moisture and flavor in the product.
2. It protects the fat against the moisture and salt in the food, which speed deterioration of frying fat.
3. It protects the food from absorbing too much fat.
4. It gives crispness, flavor, and good appearance to the product.

BREADING

Breading means coating a product with bread crumbs or other crumbs or meal before deep-frying, pan-frying, or sautéing. The most widely used method for applying these coatings is called the *Standard Breading Procedure.*

The Three Stages of the Standard Breading Procedure

1. **Flour.**
   Helps the breading stick to the product.

2. **Egg wash.**
   A mixture of eggs and liquid, usually milk or water. More eggs give greater binding power but increase the cost. A small quantity of oil is occasionally added to the egg wash.

3. **Crumbs.**
   Combine with the egg wash to create a crisp, golden coating when fried. Fine, dry bread crumbs are most often used and give good results. Other products used are fresh bread crumbs, crushed corn flakes or other cereal, cracker meal, and cornmeal.

Procedure for Proper Breading

Figure 7.16 illustrates a station setup for the Standard Breading Procedure.

1. Dry the product to get a thin, even coating of flour.

2. Season the product—or, for greater efficiency, season the flour (step 3). Do not season the crumbs. The presence of salt in contact with the frying fat helps break down the fat and shorten its life.

3. Dip the product in flour to coat evenly. Shake off excess.

4. Dip in egg wash to coat completely. Remove. Let excess drain off so that crumb coating will be even.

5. Dip in bread crumbs. Cover with crumbs and press gently on product. Make sure it is coated completely. Remove. Carefully shake off excess.

6. Fry immediately or hold for service.

7. To hold for later service, place in a single layer on a pan or rack and refrigerate. Do not hold very moist items, such as raw clams or oysters. The breading will quickly become soggy.

8. Strain egg wash and sift flour and crumbs as often as necessary to remove lumps.

Figure 7.16 Setup of station for Standard Breading Procedure.

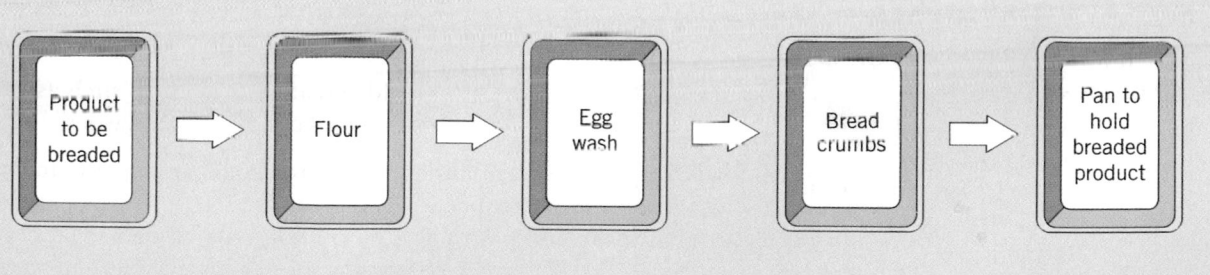

Right-handed cooks work from left to right. Left-handed cooks work from right to left.

For small items like scallops and oysters, breading may be done with the aid of a series of wire baskets placed in the flour, wash, and crumbs, instead of by hand. The procedure is the same except that the baskets are used to lift and shake small quantities of the product and to transfer them to the next basket.

To keep one hand dry during breading, use your right hand (if you are right-handed; left-handed persons reverse the procedure) only for handling the flour and crumbs. Use your other hand for handling the product when it is wet.

DREDGING WITH FLOUR

Purpose

The purpose of dredging is to give a thin, even coating of flour to a product.

Meats to be sautéed or pan-fried are often dredged with flour to give them an even, brown color and to prevent sticking.

Vegetables such as sticks of zucchini are sometimes coated only in flour before deep-frying to give them a light golden color and very thin coating.

Procedure
Follow steps 1 to 3 of the Standard Breading Procedure (p. 121).

BATTERS

Batters are semiliquid mixtures containing flour or other starch. They are used in deep-frying to give a crisp, flavorful coating. There are many formulas and variations for batters.

1. Many liquids are used, including milk, water, and beer.
2. Eggs may or may not be used.
3. Thicker batters make thicker coatings. Too thick a batter will make a heavy, unpalatable coating.
4. Leavenings are frequently used to give a lighter product. These may be:
    *   Baking powder
    *   Beaten egg whites
    *   Carbonation from the beer or seltzer used in the batter

Three recipes for basic, typical batters are given in the recipe for Deep-Fried Onion Rings, page 481. These batters may be used on a wide variety of products.

Handling Convenience Foods

Convenience foods are playing an increasingly prominent role in the food service industry. Their use has become so important that no student of professional cooking can afford to be without knowledge of them.

A convenience food may be defined as *any product that has been partially or completely prepared or processed by the manufacturer.* In other words, when you buy a convenience product, you are having the manufacturer do some or all of your preparation for you.

Of course, you must pay for this service, as reflected in the price of the product. Although buying the convenience product will likely cost you more than buying the raw materials, you save in increased kitchen efficiency. As you remember from Chapter 5, labor costs as well as food costs must be figured into your menu prices.

Processed foods for restaurants and institutions range from partially prepared items that can be used as components in your recipes, such as frozen fish fillets, peeled potatoes, concentrated stock bases, and frozen puff pastry dough, to fully prepared items that need only be reconstituted or served as is, such as frozen prepared entrées and frozen pies and pastries. Some items, like frozen French fries, have wide acceptance, while other more fully prepared foods continue to be resisted by both customer and operator.

In general, the more completely a product has been prepared by the manufacturer, the less it will reflect the individuality of the food service operator—the less opportunity the cooks have to give it their own character and quality.

Is a stock made from scratch better than a product made from a convenience base? Most quality-conscious chefs would probably answer "Yes!" But the correct answer is, "Not if the homemade stock is poorly made." No matter what products you use, there is no substitute for quality and care. The fresh product is potentially the best, but not if it is badly stored or handled. Convenience foods also need proper handling to maintain their quality.

The key to understanding and handling convenience foods is considering them as normal products with part of the pre-prep completed rather than as totally different kinds of products unlike your normal raw materials. *Convenience products are not a substitute for culinary knowledge and skill.* They should be a tool for the good cook rather than a crutch for the bad cook. It takes as much understanding of basic cooking principles to handle convenience products as it does fresh, raw ingredients, particularly if you want the convenience product to taste as much like the fresh as possible.

Guidelines for Handling Convenience Foods

1. **Handle with the same care you give fresh, raw ingredients.**
   Most loss of quality in convenience foods comes from assuming that they are damage-proof and can be treated haphazardly.

2. **Examine as soon as received.**
   Particularly, check frozen foods—with a thermometer—to make sure they have not thawed in transit. Put away at once.

3. **Store properly.**
   Frozen foods must be held at 0°F (-18°C) or lower. Check your freezer with a thermometer regularly. Refrigerated foods must stay chilled, below 41°F (5°C), to slow spoilage. Shelf-stable foods (dry products, canned goods, etc.) are shelf-stable only when stored properly, in a cool, dry place, tightly sealed.

4. **Know the shelf life of each product.**
   Nothing will keep forever, not even convenience foods. (Some, like peeled potatoes, are even more perishable than unprocessed ingredients.) Rotate stock according to the first in, first out principle. And don't stock more than necessary.

5. **Defrost frozen foods properly.**
   Ideally, defrost in a tempering box set at 28°F to 30°F (-2°C to -1°C) or, lacking that, in the refrigerator. This takes advance planning and timing, because large items take several days to thaw.
   If you are short of time, the second-best way to defrost foods is under cold, running water, in the original wrapper.
   Never defrost at room temperature or in warm water. The high temperatures encourage bacterial growth and spoilage.
   Do not refreeze thawed foods. Quality will greatly deteriorate.
   Certain foods, like frozen French fries and some individual-portion prepared entrées, are designed to be cooked without thawing.

6. **Know how and to what extent the product has been prepared.**
   Partially cooked foods need less heating in final preparation than do raw foods. Some cooks prepare frozen, cooked crab legs, for example, as though they were raw, but by the time the customer receives them, they are overcooked, dry, and tasteless. Frozen vegetables, for a second example, have been blanched and often need only to be heated briefly.
   Manufacturers are happy to give full directions and serving suggestions for their products. At least you should read the package directions.

7. **Use proper cooking methods.**
   Be flexible. Much modern equipment has been designed especially for convenience foods. Don't restrict yourself to conventional ranges and ovens if compartment steamers, convection ovens, or microwave ovens might do a better job more efficiently.

8. **Treat convenience foods as though you, not the manufacturer, did the pre-preparation.**
   Make the most of your opportunity to use creativity and to serve the best quality you can. Your final preparation, plating, and garnish should be as careful as though you made it from scratch.

Terms for Review

mise en place	brunoise	allumette	emincer	Standard Breading
holding temperatures	small dice	batonnet	shred	Procedure
set meal service	medium dice	chop	chiffonade	batter
extended meal service	large dice	concasser	blanch	convenience food
rough prep	julienne	mince	marinate	portion control

Questions for Discussion

1. How does preparation differ for set meal service and extended meal service?
2. It has been said that à la carte cooking, or cooking to order, is nothing more than small-batch cooking carried to its extreme. Based on what you know about pre-preparation, what do you think this statement means?
3. Why is it important to learn to cut foods accurately and uniformly?
4. Name six basic vegetable cuts and give their dimensions.
5. Give six examples of foods that might be blanched or parcooked during pre-preparation, and give a reason for each.
6. Describe in detail how to set up a breading station and how to use it to bread veal cutlets.
7. The manager of the restaurant in which you are a cook has decided to try using frozen, breaded shrimp instead of having you bread shrimp by hand, but she is worried about customer acceptance and asks for your help. How will you handle the new product?

chapter 8

Stocks and Sauces

The importance of stocks in the kitchen is indicated by the French word for stock: *fond*, meaning "foundation" or "base." In classical cuisine, the ability to prepare good stocks is the most basic of all skills because so much of the work of the entire kitchen depends on them. A good stock is the foundation of soups, sauces, and most braised foods and stews.

In modern kitchens, stocks have lost much of the importance they once had. In the first place, increased reliance on portion-controlled meats has made bones for stock a rarity in most establishments. Second, making stocks requires extra labor, which most restaurants today aren't able to provide. Finally, more food today is served without sauces, so stocks aren't seen to be quite as necessary.

Nevertheless, the finest cuisine still depends on soups and sauces based on high-quality stocks. So stock making remains an essential skill that you should learn early in your training. Stocks and sauces are almost never served by themselves but are components of many other preparations. You will need to refer to this chapter in connection with many other subjects.

The preparation of stocks has been simplified in many ways since the days of Escoffier, although this does not mean that it demands less care or skill. Few chefs today bother to tie vegetables for a stock into a bundle, for example. They're going to be strained out anyway. The number and variety of ingredients is usually not as great as it once was. Nor is it common to cook stocks for as many hours as were once thought necessary. All these details are taken up one by one in this section.

A stock may be defined as a clear, thin (that is, unthickened) liquid flavored by soluble substances extracted from meat, poultry, and fish, and their bones, and from vegetables and seasonings. Our objective in preparing stocks is to select the proper ingredients and then to extract the flavors we want—in other words, to combine the correct ingredients with the correct procedure.

Ingredients

BONES

Bones are the major ingredient of stocks (except water, of course). Most of the flavor and body of stocks are derived from the bones of beef, veal, chicken, fish, and, occasionally, lamb, pork, ham, and game. (Vegetable stocks, an exception, draw their flavor entirely from vegetables; see p. 128.)

The kinds of bones used determine the kind of stock.

Chicken stock, of course, is made from chicken bones.

White stock is made from beef or veal bones or a combination of the two. Chicken bones or even pork bones are sometimes added in small quantity.

Brown stock is made from beef or veal bones that have been browned in an oven.

Fish stock is made from fish bones and trimmings left over after filleting. Bones from lean white fish give the best stock. Fat fish are not normally used. The term f*umet* is often used for a flavorful fish stock, especially one made with wine. See the note at the beginning of the recipe for fish stock (p. 132).

Lamb, game, turkey, and *other stocks* have specialized uses.

In Chapter 4, we discussed a group of proteins called connective tissue. Remember that some of these proteins are dissolved when cooked with slow, moist heat. Chapter 10, "Understanding Meats," offers more information about these substances. There are two basic facts that you should learn and understand:

1. When certain connective tissues (called *collagen*) break down, they form *gelatin*. This gives body to a stock, an important feature of its quality. A well-made stock thickens or even solidifies when chilled.

2. *Cartilage* is the best source of gelatin in bones. Younger animals have more cartilage in their skeletons. As they become older, this hardens into solid bone, which is harder to dissolve into stocks. *Knuckle bones*, on the joints of major bones, have a lot of cartilage and are valued in stock making. Neck bones and shank bones are also used a great deal.

Cut large bones into pieces about 3 inches (8 centimeters) long. This exposes more surface area and aids extraction. Also, the bones are easier to handle.

MEAT

Because of its cost, meat is rarely used in stock making any more. (Exception: Chicken hearts and gizzards are often used in chicken stock.)

Occasionally, a broth is produced as a result of simmering meat or poultry, as when fowl is cooked for dishes like creamed chicken. This broth can then be used like a stock. However, the chicken is considered the object of the game in this case. The broth is just a byproduct.

In this book, we use the word *broth* to mean a flavorful liquid obtained from the simmering of meats and/or vegetables.

MIREPOIX

Aromatic vegetables are the second most important contributors of flavor to stocks. (In the case of vegetable stocks, they are the most important.)

Mirepoix (meer-pwah) is a combination of onions, carrots, and celery. It is a basic flavoring preparation that is used in all areas of cooking, not only for flavoring stocks but also for sauces, soups, meats, poultry, fish, and vegetables. (The classical mirepoix of decades ago contained a wider variety of ingredients, sometimes including ham or bacon, leeks and other vegetables, and one or more fresh herbs. The modern version is considerably simplified.)

Learn the proportions in Table 8.1 well. Mirepoix is a basic preparation that you will need throughout your career.

A *white mirepoix*, made without carrots, is used when it is necessary to keep the stock as colorless as possible. Mushroom trimmings may be added to white mirepoix. When cost permits, it is a good idea to include leeks in the mirepoix in place of part of the onions. They give an excellent flavor.

In vegetable stocks, a variety of vegetables is used in addition to or in place of the traditional mirepoix; see page 128 for a brief discussion.

Cutting Mirepoix

Chop the vegetables coarsely into pieces of relatively uniform size. As mirepoix is rarely served, it is not usually necessary to cut it neatly.

The size depends on how long the mirepoix will cook. If it will cook a long time, as for beef stock, cut the vegetables into large pieces (1 to 2 inches [3 to 5 cm]). Cutting into small pieces is necessary for releasing flavors in a short time, as when used for fish stock.

ACID PRODUCTS

Acids, as noted in Chapter 4 (p. 52), help dissolve connective tissues. Thus, they are sometimes used in stock making to extract flavor and body from bones.

Tomato products contribute flavor and some acid to brown stocks. They are not used for white stocks because they would give an undesirable color. Similarly, when making brown stocks, be careful not to add too much tomato, because this may make the stock cloudy.

Wine is occasionally used, especially for fish stocks. Its flavor contribution is probably more important than its acidity.

SCRAPS AND LEFTOVERS

In some kitchens, a stockpot is kept going all day, and various scraps are constantly being thrown in. This may or may not be a good idea.

Scraps may be used in stocks if they are *clean, wholesome, and appropriate to the stock being made.* If done correctly, stock making is a good way of utilizing trimmings that would otherwise be thrown out. It is better to save trimmings and use them in a planned way rather than to throw them into the stock randomly.

A *stockpot is not a garbage disposal*, and the final product is only as good as the ingredients and the care that go into it.

SEASONINGS AND SPICES

1. *Salt* is usually not added when making stocks. Stocks are never used as is but are reduced, concentrated, and combined with other ingredients. If salt were added, it might become too concentrated. Some chefs salt stocks very lightly because they feel it aids in extracting flavor.

2. *Herbs and spices* should be used only lightly. They should never dominate a stock or have a pronounced flavor.

   Herbs and spices are usually tied in a cheesecloth bag called a *sachet* (sa-shay; French for "bag"). The sachet (Figure 8.1) is tied by a string to the handle of the stockpot so it can be removed easily at any time.

   A *bouquet garni* is an assortment of fresh herbs and other aromatic ingredients tied in a bundle with string. A basic bouquet garni contains pieces of leek and celery, thyme sprigs, bay leaf, and parsley stems (see Figure 8.2). The ingredients can be changed to suit different recipes.

TABLE 8.1

Mirepoix

To Make:	1 Pound	400 Grams
Onions	8 oz	200 g
Celery	4 oz	100 g
Carrots	4 oz	100 g

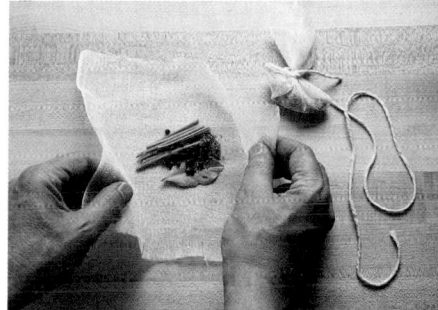

Figure 8.1 To make a sachet, place the spices and herbs in the center of a square of clean cheesecloth. Draw the corners together and tie with a length of twine. For making stock, use a piece of twine long enough so that it can be tied to the handle of the stockpot for easy removal.

Figure 8.2 Tie the herbs and aromatic vegetables for a bouquet garni in a bundle. To tie small herbs securely, enclose them between the two halves of leek.

TABLE 8.2

White Stock (Including Chicken Stock)

To Make:	1 Gallon	4 Liters
Bones	5–6 lb	2.5–3 kg
Mirepoix	1 lb	500 g
Water	5–6 qt	5–6 L
Sachet	1	1

TABLE 8.3

Brown Stock

To Make:	1 Gallon	4 Liters
Bones	5–6 lb	2.5–3 kg
Mirepoix	1 lb	500 g
Tomato product	8 oz	250 g
Water	5–6 qt	5–6 L
Sachet	1	1

TABLE 8.4

Fish Stock

To Make:	1 Gallon	4 Liters
Bones	4–6 lb	2–3 kg
Mirepoix	8 oz	250 g
Water	1 gal	4 L
White wine	8 oz	250 mL
Sachet	1	1

The following seasonings, in varying quantities, are commonly used for stocks:

Thyme	Parsley stems
Bay leaves	Cloves, whole
Peppercorns	Garlic (optional)

INGREDIENT PROPORTIONS

The proportions in Tables 8.2, 8.3, and 8.4 are basic, effective, and widely used, but they are not an ironclad rule. Nearly every chef will have some variations.

Many cooks use ratios to help them remember the basic proportions, as follows:

Bones—50 percent
Mirepoix—10 percent
Water—100 percent

INGREDIENTS FOR VEGETABLE STOCKS

Vegetable stocks, made without any animal products, play an important role in vegetarian cooking and are also used in more traditional kitchens in response to customers' requests for light, healthful dishes. The basic ingredients for vegetable stocks are vegetables, herbs and spices, water, and, sometimes, wine.

Ingredients and proportions can vary greatly. If you want a particular flavor to predominate, use a larger quantity of that vegetable. For example, if you want a broth tasting primarily of asparagus, use a large quantity of asparagus to make it, with smaller quantities of more neutral vegetables (like onion and celery) to round out the flavor. For a more neutral, all-purpose vegetable stock, avoid strong-flavored vegetables and use more balanced proportions of the various ingredients.

Here are a few additional guidelines for making vegetable stocks or broths:

1. Starchy vegetables such as potatoes, sweet potatoes, and winter squash make a stock cloudy. Use them only if clarity is not important.
2. Some vegetables, especially strong-flavored ones, are best avoided. Brussels sprouts, cauliflower, and artichokes can overwhelm a stock with a strong flavor or odor. Dark-green, leafy vegetables, especially spinach, develop an unpleasant flavor when cooked for a long time. Beets turn a stock red.
3. Cook long enough to extract flavors, but not so long that flavors are lost. Best cooking times are 30 to 45 minutes.
4. Sweating the vegetables in a small amount of oil before adding water gives them a mellower flavor, but this step can be omitted. Butter can be used if it is not necessary to avoid all animal products.

Procedures

Making stock may seem, at first glance, to be a simple procedure. However, many steps are involved, each with a rather complicated set of reasons. If you are to be successful at making consistently good stocks, you must understand not only what to do but why you are doing it.

The following outlines give procedures for making basic stocks as well as the reasons for every step. After learning these procedures and checking with your instructors for any modifications or variations they may have, you will be able to turn to the individual recipes, where the steps are given again, but without explanations.

BLANCHING BONES

In Chapter 4, we discussed proteins coagulating when heated. Many proteins dissolve in cold water but solidify into small particles or into froth or scum when heated. It is these particles that make a stock cloudy. Much of the technique of stock making involves avoiding cloudiness to produce a clear stock.

The purpose of blanching bones is to rid them of some of the impurities that cause cloudiness. The bones of *young animals*, especially veal and chicken, are highest in blood and other impurities that cloud and discolor stocks.

Chefs disagree on the importance of blanching. Many feel that it is needed to produce clear white stocks. Others feel that blanching causes valuable flavors to be lost. Fish bones, at any rate, are not blanched because of their short cooking time.

Procedure for Blanching Bones

1. **Rinse bones in cold water.**
This washes off blood and other impurities from the surface. It is especially important if the bones are not strictly fresh.

2. **Place bones in stockpot or steam-jacketed kettle and cover with cold water.**
Impurities dissolve more readily in cold water. Adding hot water would retard extraction.

3. **Bring the water to a boil.**
As the water heats, impurities solidify (coagulate) and rise to the surface as scum.

4. **Drain the bones and rinse them well.**
The bones are now ready for the stock pot.

PREPARING WHITE STOCKS

A good white stock has rich, full flavor, good body, clarity, and little or no color. Chicken stocks may have a light yellow color.

Procedure for Preparing White Stocks

1. **Cut the bones into pieces, 3 to 4 inches (8 to 10 cm) long.**
This exposes more surface area and helps extraction. A meat saw is used to cut heavy veal and beef bones. Fish and chicken bones don't need to be cut, but whole carcasses should be chopped for more convenient handling.

2. **Rinse the bones in cold water. (If desired, chicken, veal, or beef bones may be blanched.)**
This removes some impurities that cloud the stock or, if the bones are old, give an off taste.

3. **Place bones in a stockpot or steam-jacketed kettle and add cold water to cover.**
Starting in cold water speeds extraction. Starting in hot water delays it because many proteins are soluble in cold water but not in hot.

4. **Bring water to a boil, then reduce to a simmer. Skim the scum that comes to the surface.**
Skimming is important for a clear stock because the scum (which is fat and coagulated protein) will cloud the stock if it is broken up and mixed back into the liquid.

5. **Add the chopped mirepoix and the herbs and spices.**
Remember, the size to which you cut mirepoix depends on how long it is to be cooked.

6. **Do not let the stock boil. Keep it at a low simmer.**
Boiling makes the stock cloudy because it breaks up solids into tiny particles that get mixed into the stock.

7. **Skim the surface as often as necessary during cooking.**

8. **Keep the water level above the bones. Add more water if the stock reduces below this level.**
Cooking bones exposed to air will turn dark and thus darken or discolor the stock. Also, they do not release flavor into the water if the water doesn't touch them.

9. **Simmer for recommended length of time:**

Beef and veal bones	6 to 8 hours
Chicken bones	3 to 4 hours
Fish bones	30 to 45 minutes

Most modern chefs do not simmer stocks as long as earlier generations of chefs did. It is true that longer cooking extracts more gelatin, but gelatin isn't the only factor in a good stock. Flavors begin to break down or degenerate over time. The above times are felt to be the best for obtaining full flavor while still getting a good portion of gelatin into the stock.

10. **Skim the surface and strain off the stock through a china cap lined with several layers of cheesecloth.**
Adding a little cold water to the stock before skimming stops the cooking and brings more fat and impurities to the surface.

11. **Cool the stock as quickly as possible, as follows:**
   • Set the pot in a sink with blocks, a rack, or some other object under it. This is called *venting*. It allows cold water to flow under the pot as well as around it.

- Run cold water into the sink, but not higher than the level of the stock or the pot will become unsteady. An overflow pipe keeps the water level right and allows for constant circulation of cold water (see Figure 8.3).
- Stir the pot occasionally so that all the stock cools evenly. Hang a ladle in the pot so that you can give it a quick stir whenever you pass the sink without actually taking extra time to do it.

Cooling stock quickly and properly is important. Improperly cooled stock can spoil in 6 to 8 hours because it is a good breeding ground for bacteria.

Do not set the hot stock in the walk-in or, worse yet, the reach-in. All that heat and steam will overload the refrigerator and may damage other perishables as well as the equipment.

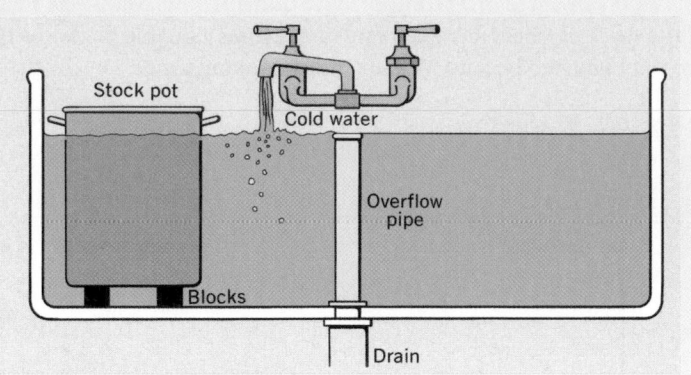

Figure 8.3 Setup for cooling stocks in a cold-water bath.

12. **When cool, refrigerate the stock in covered containers. Stock will keep 2 to 3 days if properly refrigerated.**

Basic White Stock

Yield: 2 gal (8 L)

U.S.	Metric	Ingredients	PROCEDURE
10–12 lb	5–6 kg	Bones: chicken, veal, or beef	
10–12 qt	10–12 L	Cold water	
		Mirepoix:	
1 lb	500 g	Onion, chopped	
8 oz	250 g	Carrot, chopped (optional)	
8 oz	250 g	Celery, chopped	
		Sachet:	
1	1	Bay leaf	
¼ tsp	1 mL	Thyme	
¼ tsp	1 mL	Peppercorns	
6–8	6–8	Parsley stems	
2	2	Whole cloves	

PROCEDURE
1. Review instructions for stock preparation (pp. 129–130).
2. If beef or veal bones are whole, cut them into pieces, 3–4 inches (8–10 cm) long, with a meat saw. Rinse the bones in cold water.
3. Blanch the bones: Place them in a stockpot, cover with cold water, and bring to a boil. Drain and rinse.
4. Place the bones in the stockpot and cover with cold water. Bring to a boil, reduce heat to simmer, and skim the scum carefully.
5. Add the mirepoix and sachet ingredients (tied in cheesecloth).
6. Simmer for required length of time, skimming the surface as often as necessary.
   Beef and veal: 6–8 hours
   Chicken: 3–4 hours
   Add water if necessary to keep bones covered.
7. Strain through a china cap lined with several layers of cheesecloth.
8. Cool the stock, vented, in a cold-water bath, and refrigerate.

Per 1 ounce:
Calories, 1; Protein, .1 g; Fat, 0 g (0% cal.); Cholesterol, 1 mg; Carbohydrates, 0 g; Fiber, 0 g; Sodium, 2 mg.

VARIATIONS

Prepare *White Lamb Stock, Turkey Stock,* and *Ham Stock* according to the basic procedure, substituting the appropriate bones.

Vegetable Stock

Omit the bones. Reduce the water to 9 qt (9 L). Use half the quantity of onions and celery in the basic recipe. Add the following ingredients: ½ oz (15 g) garlic, chopped; 4 oz (125 g) leeks; 8 oz (250 g) mushrooms, sliced; 2 oz (60 g) fennel, sliced. Sweat the onion, garlic, and leek in ½ oz (15 mL) olive oil before adding the remaining ingredients. Cook the stock 30–45 minutes.

PREPARING BROWN STOCKS

The difference between brown stocks and white stocks is that the bones and mirepoix are browned for the brown stock. This causes a few complications, as you will see. Otherwise, the procedure is essentially the same.

Two methods for browning are given on page 131.

Procedure for Preparing Brown Stocks

1. Cut the bones into pieces, 3 to 4 inches (8 to 10 cm) long, as for white stock. Veal and/or beef bones are used for brown stock.

2. Do not wash or blanch the bones. The moisture would hinder browning.

3. Place the bones in a roasting pan in one layer and brown in a hot oven at 375°F (190°C) or higher (see Figure 8.4). The bones must be well browned to color the stock sufficiently. This takes over an hour. Some chefs prefer to oil the bones lightly before browning.

4. When the bones are well browned, remove them from the pan and place them in a stockpot. Cover with cold water and bring to a simmer.

5. Drain and reserve the fat from the roasting pan. Deglaze the pan by adding water and stirring over heat until all the brown drippings are dissolved or loosened. Add to stockpot.

6. While the stock is getting started, place the mirepoix in the roasting pan with some of the reserved fat and brown the vegetables well in the oven. (See alternative procedure below.)

7. When the water in the stockpot comes to a simmer, skim and continue as for white stock.

8. Add the browned vegetables and the tomato product to the stockpot. If desired, they may be held out until 3 to 4 hours before the end of the cooking time.

9. Continue as for white stock.

Figure 8.4 *Preparing brown stock.*

(a) *Roast the bones in a hot oven until well browned.*

(b) *Place the bones in a stockpot and add the appropriate amount of water.*

(c) *While the bones are beginning to simmer, brown the mirepoix, using the same roasting pan set on top of the stove or in the oven. Add the browned mirepoix to the stockpot.*

(d) *Deglaze the roasting pan with water. Add the liquid to the stockpot.*

(e) *This stock has simmered slowly for 8 hours. Note that the sachet is tied to the handle of the pot with twine for easy removal.*

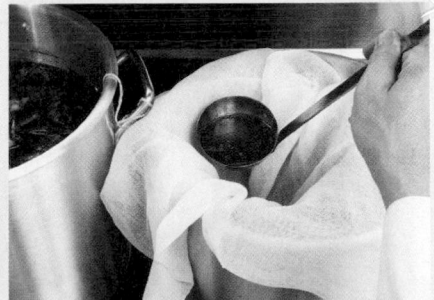

(f) *Strain the stock through a china cap lined with cheesecloth.*

Alternative Procedure

The mirepoix may be browned with the bones. When the bones are half browned, add the mirepoix to the pan and continue roasting until bones and vegetables are browned. Tomato may be added toward the end of browning time, but exercise caution—tomato purée burns easily.

Some chefs use this method because it eliminates some steps. Others prefer to brown the mirepoix separately so that it can be added to the stock later in the cooking time.

Basic Brown Stock

Yield: 2 gal (8 L)

U.S.	Metric	Ingredients	PROCEDURE
10–12 lb	5–6 kg	Bones: veal or beef	1. Review instructions for stock preparation (p. 131).
10–12 qt	10–12 L	Cold water	2. If bones are whole, cut into pieces, 3–4 inches (8–10 cm) long, with a meat saw.
			3. Place the bones in a roasting pan in a hot oven (400°F/200°C) and brown them well.
			4. Remove bones from pan and place in a stockpot. Cover with water and bring to a simmer. Skim and let stock continue to simmer.
			5. Drain and reserve the fat in the roasting pan. Deglaze the pan with water and add to stockpot.
		Mirepoix:	6. Toss the mirepoix with some of the reserved fat and brown well in the oven.
1 lb	500 g	Onion, chopped	
8 oz	250 g	Carrot, chopped	7. Add the browned mirepoix, the tomato product, and the sachet to the stockpot.
8 oz	250 g	Celery, chopped	
1 lb	500 g	Tomatoes or tomato purée	8. Continue to simmer for a total cooking time of 6–8 hours, skimming the surface as necessary. Add water as needed to keep bones covered.
		Sachet:	
1	1	Bay leaf	
¼ tsp	1 mL	Thyme	9. Strain through a china cap lined with several layers of cheese-cloth.
¼ tsp	1 mL	Peppercorns	
6–8	6–8	Parsley stems	10. Cool the stock, vented, in a cold-water bath, and refrigerate.
2	2	Whole cloves	

Per 1 ounce:
Calories, 2; Protein, .20 g; Fat, .1 g (43% cal.); Cholesterol, 1 mg; Carbohydrates, .1 g; Fiber, 0 g; Sodium, 2 mg.

VARIATIONS

Prepare *Brown Lamb Stock* and *Game Stock* according to the basic procedure, substituting the appropriate bones.

 ## Fish Stock or Fumet

Fish stock may be made according to the same recipe as white stock. The following method yields a slightly more flavorful stock due to the preliminary sweating of mirepoix and bones in the butter and to the addition of wine.

Yield: 1 gal (4 L)

U.S.	Metric	Ingredients	PROCEDURE
1 oz	30 g	Butter	1. Butter the bottom of a heavy stockpot or saucepot. Place the mirepoix in the bottom of the pot and the bones over the top of it. Cover the bones loosely with a round of brown paper or parchment.
		Mirepoix:	
4 oz	125 g	Onion, chopped fine	
2 oz	60 g	Celery, chopped fine	
2 oz	60 g	Carrot, chopped fine (optional)	2. Set the pot over low heat and cook slowly for about 5 minutes, until the bones are opaque and begin to exude juices.
2 oz	60 g	Mushroom trimmings (optional)	3. Add the wine, bring to a simmer, then add the sachet and water to cover.
4–6 lb	2–3 kg	Bones from lean fish	
8 oz	250 mL	White wine (dry)	4. Bring to a simmer again, skim, and let simmer for 30–45 minutes.
1 gal	4 L	Cold water	
		Sachet:	5. Strain through a china cap lined with several layers of cheese-cloth.
½	½	Bay leaf	
¼ tsp	1 mL	Peppercorns	6. Cool, vented, in a cold-water bath, and refrigerate.
6–8	6–8	Parsley stems	
1	1	Whole clove	

Per 1 ounce:
Calories, 4; Protein, .4 g; Fat, .2 g (36% cal.); Cholesterol, .5 mg; Carbohydrates, .1 g; Fiber, 0 g; Sodium, 3 mg.

Reductions and Glazes

Stocks are concentrated by boiling or simmering them to evaporate part of the water. This is called *making a reduction* or *reducing*.

Reduction is an important technique in sauce making and in many other areas of cooking because it produces a more flavorful product by concentrating it. A reduced stock also has more body because the gelatin is concentrated.

WHAT ARE GLAZES?

A *glaze*—or, in French, *glace* (glahss)—is a stock that is reduced until it coats the back of a spoon. It is so concentrated—reduced by three-fourths or more—that it is solid and rubbery when refrigerated.

Glazes are used as flavorings in sauce making and in some meat, poultry, fish, and vegetable preparations. Only small amounts are needed because they are so concentrated.

Glazes diluted to original strength do not taste like the stocks they were made from. The long cooking changes the flavors somewhat.

KINDS OF GLAZES

1. Meat glaze, or *glace de viande* (glahss duh vee awnd)—made from brown stock.
2. Chicken glaze, or *glace de volaille* (voh lye)—made from chicken stock.
3. Fish glaze, or *glace de poisson* (pwah sohn)—made from fish stock.

Procedure for Preparing Glazes

1. Reduce the stock over moderate heat.
2. Skim the surface frequently.
3. When reduced by half to two-thirds, strain into a smaller, heavy saucepan and continue to reduce over lower heat until it is syrupy and coats a spoon.
4. Pour into containers, cool, cover, and refrigerate.
5. Glazes will keep for several weeks or longer if properly stored. They may also be frozen.

Convenience Bases

The cost, both in time and materials, of making stocks in modern kitchens has led to the widespread use of concentrated convenience products known as *bases*. These are diluted with water to make flavored liquids similar to stocks.

Glazes can be considered bases and, in fact, they are the original bases, used long before today's manufacturers started producing convenience products.

JUDGING QUALITY

Bases vary greatly in quality. The best ones are composed mainly of meat extracts. These are perishable products and need to be refrigerated.

Many bases are made primarily from salt, however—an expensive way to buy salt, we might add. *Read the list of ingredients.* Avoid products that list salt first. The best way to judge the quality of a base is to dilute it and compare its flavor to that of a well-made stock.

USING BASES

Bases can be improved with little labor by simmering the diluted or made-up product for a short time with some mirepoix, a sachet, and a few bones or meat trimmings if possible. This helps to give a fresher, more natural taste to a highly processed product.

Bases are also added to stocks to supplement them when only a small quantity of stock is on hand.

In addition, bases are sometimes added to weak stocks to give them more flavor, but this is not as good a practice as making the stock properly in the first place.

Using bases requires taste and judgment, just as other areas of cookery do. If used without care and restraint, bases can detract from the quality of your cooking. But, used carefully, they can be a valuable tool in some situations. Always taste and evaluate as you cook.

There is no substitute for a well-made stock. But it is also true that a good base may be better than a poorly made stock. It all depends on the skills you are learning now.

Sauces

Like stocks, sauces have lost some of the importance they once had in commercial kitchens—except, of course, in the best restaurants serving what may be considered luxury cuisine. Some of this decline is due to changes in eating habits and to increased labor costs.

However, much of the change is due to misunderstanding. How many times have you heard someone say, "I don't go for all those sauces all over everything; I like good, simple food." No doubt this person puts catsup—a sweetened tomato sauce—on hamburgers, gravy on mashed potatoes, and tartar sauce on fried fish.

The misunderstandings arise from poorly made sauces. No one likes thick, pasty cream sauces on vegetables or oversalted but otherwise flavorless brown sauces gumming up their meat. But just because some cooks made bad sauces is no reason to reject all sauce cookery.

In fact, many chefs feel that good sauces are the pinnacle of all cooking, both in the skill they require and in the interest and excitement they can give to food. Very often, the most memorable part of a really fine meal is the sauce that enhances the meat or fish.

A sauce works like a seasoning. It enhances and accents the flavor of the food; it should not dominate or hide the food.

A good cook knows that sauces are as valuable as salt and pepper. Even a simple grilled steak is made even better when it has an added touch, something as simple as a slice of seasoned butter melting on it, or as refined as a spoonful of béarnaise sauce.

No matter where you work, sauce-making techniques are basic skills you will need in all your cooking. Croquettes, soufflés, and mousses have sauces as their base, nearly all braised foods are served with sauces made of their cooking liquids, and basic pan gravies, certainly favorites everywhere, are made with the same techniques as the classic sauces.

Understanding Sauces

THE FUNCTIONS OF SAUCES

A sauce may be defined as a flavorful liquid, usually thickened, that is used to season, flavor, and enhance other foods.

A sauce adds the following qualities to foods:

Moistness	Appearance (color and shine)
Flavor	Interest and appetite appeal
Richness	

THE STRUCTURE OF SAUCES

The major sauces we consider here are made of three kinds of ingredients.

1. A liquid, the body of the sauce
2. A thickening agent
3. Additional seasoning and flavoring ingredients

To understand sauce making, you must first learn how to prepare these components and then how to combine them into finished sauces.

Liquid

A liquid ingredient provides the body or base of most sauces. Most classic sauces are built on five liquids or bases. The resulting sauces are called *leading sauces* or *mother sauces*.

> White stock (chicken, veal, or fish)—for velouté sauces
> Brown stock—for brown sauce or espagnole (ess pahn yohl)
> Milk—for béchamel
> Tomato plus stock—for tomato sauce
> Clarified butter—for hollandaise

The most frequently used sauces are based on stock. The quality of these sauces depends on the stock-making skills you learned in the previous section.

Thickening Agents

A sauce must be thick enough to cling lightly to the food. Otherwise, it will just run off and lie in a puddle in the plate. This doesn't mean that it has to be heavy and pasty.

Starches are still the most commonly used thickening agents, although they are used less often than in the past. We discuss starches and other thickening agents in detail below.

Other Flavoring Ingredients

Although the liquid that makes up the bulk of the sauce provides the basic flavor, other ingredients are added to make variations on the basic themes and to give a finished character to the sauces.

Adding specified flavoring ingredients to basic sauces is the key to the whole catalog of classic sauces. Most of the hundreds of sauces listed in the standard repertoires are made by adding one or more flavoring ingredients to one of the five basic sauces or leading sauces.

As in all of cooking, sauce making is largely a matter of learning a few building blocks and then building with them.

STARCHES AS THICKENERS

1. Starches are the most common and most useful thickeners for sauce making. Flour is the principal starch used. Others available to the chef include cornstarch, arrowroot, waxy maize, instant or pregelatinized starch, bread crumbs, and other vegetable and grain products like potato starch and rice flour. These are discussed later.

2. Starches thicken by *gelatinization*, which, as discussed in Chapter 4, is the process by which starch granules absorb water and swell to many times their original size.

    Another important point made in Chapter 4 is that acids inhibit gelatinization. Whenever possible, do not add acid ingredients to sauces until the starch has fully gelatinized.

3. Starch granules must be separated before heating in liquid to avoid lumping. If granules are not separated, lumping occurs because the starch on the outside of the lump quickly gelatinizes into a coating that prevents the liquid from reaching the starch inside.

    Starch granules are separated in two ways:

    - **Mixing the starch with fat.** This is the principle of the *roux*, which we discuss now, and of *beurre manié*, which is discussed in the next section.
    - **Mixing the starch with a cold liquid.** This is the principle used for starches such as cornstarch. It can also be used with flour, but as we note later, the result is an inferior sauce. A mixture of raw starch and cold liquid is called *slurry*.

ROUX INGREDIENTS

Roux (roo) is a *cooked* mixture of *equal parts by weight* of fat and flour.

Fat

The cooking fats employed for making roux are as follows:

Clarified butter is preferred for the finest sauces because of its flavor. The butter is clarified (p. 152) because the moisture content of whole butter tends to gelatinize some of the starch and makes the roux hard to work.

Margarine is widely used in place of butter because of its lower cost. However, its flavor is inferior to butter, so it does not make as fine a sauce. The quality of margarine varies from brand to brand.

Animal fats, such as chicken fat, beef drippings, and lard, are used when their flavor is appropriate to the sauce. Thus, chicken fat can be used for chicken velouté, and beef drippings can be used for beef gravy. When properly used, animal fats can enhance the flavor of a sauce.

Vegetable oil and *shortening* can be used for roux but, because they add no flavor, they are not preferred. Solid shortening also has the disadvantage of having a high melting point, which gives it an unpleasant fuzzy feeling in the mouth. It is best reserved for the bakeshop and the fry kettle.

Today, roux-thickened sauces are often condemned for health reasons because of the fat content of the roux. It should be remembered, however, that when a roux-bound velouté or brown sauce is properly made, most of the fat is released and skimmed off before the sauce is served.

Flour

The thickening power of flour depends, in part, on its starch content. Bread flour has less starch and more protein than cake flour. Eight parts (such as ounces or grams) of cake flour has the same thickening power as 10 parts of bread flour.

Bread flour frequently is used for general cooking purposes in commercial kitchens even though it has less thickening power than cake flour or pastry flour. Most sauce recipes in this book, as well as in other books, are based on bread flour or on all-purpose flour, which has similar thickening power. Proportions of roux to liquid must be adjusted if another flour is used.

Flour is sometimes browned dry in the oven for use in brown roux. A heavily browned flour has only one-third the thickening power of unbrowned flour.

In addition to starch, wheat flour also contains proteins and other components. As a roux-thickened sauce is simmered, these components rise to the surface as scum. They then can be skimmed off. Sauces are generally simmered for a time even after the starch is completely gelatinized so that these "impurities" can be cooked off. This improves the texture, gloss, and clarity of a sauce.

Ingredient Proportions

Correct amounts of fat and flour—*equal parts by weight*—are important to a good roux. There must be enough fat to coat all the starch granules, but not too much. In fact, Escoffier called for even less fat than our standard proportions (8 parts fat to 9 parts flour).

A good roux is stiff, not runny or pourable. A roux with too much fat is called a slack roux. Using excess fat not only increases the cost of the roux unnecessarily, but the excess fat rises to the top of the sauce, where it either is skimmed off or makes the sauce look greasy.

PREPARING ROUX

Figure 8.5 Cooking white roux.

A roux must be cooked so that the finished sauce does not have the raw, starchy taste of flour. The three kinds of roux differ in how much they are cooked.

White roux is cooked for just a few minutes, just enough to cook out the raw taste. Cooking is stopped as soon as the roux has a frothy, chalky, slightly gritty appearance, before it has begun to color. White roux is used for béchamel and other white sauces based on milk. In spite of its name, white roux is actually a pale yellow, because it is made from butter and (usually) unbleached flour. Figure 8.5 illustrates the production of white roux.

Blond roux, or pale roux, is cooked a little longer, just until the roux begins to change to a slightly darker color. Cooking must then be stopped. Blond roux is used for veloutés, sauces based on white stocks. The sauces have a pale ivory color.

Brown roux is cooked until it takes on a light-brown color and a nutty aroma. Cooking must take place over low heat so that the roux browns evenly without scorching. For a deeper brown roux, the flour may be browned in an oven before adding to the fat. A heavily browned roux has only about one-third the thickening power of white roux, but it contributes flavor and color to brown sauces.

Basic Procedure for Making All Roux

1. Melt fat.

2. Add correct amount of flour and stir until fat and flour are thoroughly mixed.

3. Cook to required degree for white, blond, or brown roux.

Cooking is done in a saucepan on top of the stove, and the roux is stirred for even cooking. Use low heat for brown roux, moderate heat for white or blond roux. Large quantities may be baked in an oven. Some restaurants make up batches large enough to last for several days or a week.

INCORPORATING THE ROUX

Combining the roux and liquid to obtain a smooth, lump-free sauce is a skill that takes practice to master. It's a good idea to practice the various techniques with water, under the guidance of your instructor, so that you understand what you are doing before you start working with valuable stocks.

General Principles

Liquid may be added to roux, or roux may be added to liquid.

The liquid may be hot or cooled, but not ice cold. A very cold liquid will solidify the fat in the roux.

The roux may be warm or cold, but not sizzling hot. Adding a hot liquid to a very hot roux causes spattering and, possibly, lumps.

Within these general guidelines, there is room for a number of variations. Two of them are described here. Because successful use of roux is largely a matter of experience, you are advised to profit from your instructors' experience when they demonstrate these techniques or whichever methods they prefer.

Equipment note: Stainless-steel pans are best for white sauces. Whipping in an aluminum pan makes the sauce gray.

Procedures for Incorporating Roux

Method 1: Adding Liquid to Roux

This method is used when a roux is made up specifically for the one sauce, gravy, or soup being prepared.

1. Use a heavy saucepot to prevent scorching either the roux or the sauce.

2. When the roux is made, remove the pan from the fire for a few minutes to cool slightly.

3. Slowly pour in the liquid, all the while beating vigorously with a wire whip to prevent lumps from forming.

If the liquid is hot (such as simmering milk for béchamel sauce), you will have to beat especially well, because the starch will gelatinize quickly.

If the liquid is cool, you can add a quantity of it, beat to dissolve the roux, then add the remainder of the liquid, hot or cool.

4. Bring the liquid to a boil, continuing to beat well. The roux does not reach its full thickening power until near the boiling point.

5. Simmer the sauce, stirring from time to time, until all the starchy taste of the flour has been cooked out.

This will take at least 10 minutes, but the flavor and consistency of the sauce will improve if it is cooked longer. Many chefs feel that 20 minutes of simmering is a bare minimum. Others cook some sauces for an hour or longer.

6. When the sauce is finished, it may be kept hot in a bain-marie or cooled for later use. Either way, it should be covered or should have a thin film of butter melted onto the top to prevent a skin from forming.

Method 2: Adding the Roux to the Liquid

Many restaurants make up large batches of roux to last all day or even all week. This method may be used in these situations.

1. Bring the liquid to a simmer in a heavy pot.

2. Add a small quantity of roux and beat vigorously with a whip to break up all lumps.

3. Continue to beat small quantities into the simmering liquid until the desired consistency is reached. Remember that roux must simmer for a time to thicken completely, so do not add roux too quickly or you risk overthickening the sauce.

4. Continue to simmer until the roux is cooked out and no starchy taste remains.

5. If the sauce is to simmer a long time, underthicken it because it will thicken as it reduces.

TABLE 8.5

Roux Proportions in Sauces

Sauce	Butter	Flour	Roux	Liquid
Thin or light	6 oz/190 g	6 oz/190 g	12 oz/375 g	1 gal/4 L
Medium	8 oz/250 g	8 oz/250 g	1 lb/500 g	1 gal/4 L
Thick or heavy	12 oz/375 g	12 oz/375 g	1½ lb/750 g	1 gal/4 L

PROPORTIONS OF ROUX TO LIQUID

Table 8.5 indicates the quantities of roux needed to thicken 1 gallon or 4 liters of liquid to thin, medium, and thick consistencies.

How thick is a thick sauce? Obviously, these are not precise, scientific terms that can be defined easily. Experience can be the only teacher in this case. This is another good reason to practice with roux and water, so that you can, with experience, produce the exact consistency you want.

You also have available the techniques of dilution and reduction to adjust the consistency of a sauce (see p. 140), and you will learn how to use beurre manié and other thickening agents.

Other Thickening Agents

STARCHES

1. *Beurre manié* (burr mahnyay) is a mixture of equal parts soft, raw butter and flour worked together to form a smooth paste. It is used for quick thickening at the end of cooking, to finish a sauce. The raw butter adds flavor and gives a sheen to the sauce when it melts.

    To use, drop very small pieces into a simmering sauce and stir with a whip until smooth. Repeat until desired consistency is reached. Simmer just a few minutes more to cook the flour, then remove from the fire.

2. *Whitewash* is a thin mixture of flour and cold water. Sauces made with whitewash have neither as good a flavor nor as fine a texture as those made with roux. *Whitewash is not recommended for use.*

3. *Cornstarch* produces a sauce that is almost clear, with a glossy texture.

    To use, mix with cold water or other cold liquid until smooth. Stir into the hot liquid. Bring to a boil and simmer until the liquid turns clear and there is no starchy taste. Do not boil for a long period or the starch may break down and the liquid become thin. Sauces thickened with cornstarch may thin out if held on the steam table for long periods. Cornstarch is used extensively in sweet sauces to accompany certain meats as well as in desserts and dessert sauces. It has roughly twice the thickening power of flour.

4. *Arrowroot* is used like cornstarch, but it gives an even clearer sauce. Its use is limited by its high cost.

5. *Waxy maize* is used for sauces that are to be frozen. Flour and other starches break down and lose their thickening power when frozen. Waxy maize does not. It is handled like cornstarch.

6. *Pregelatinized* or *instant starches* have been cooked, or gelatinized, then redried. Thus, they can thicken a cold liquid without heating. These starches are rarely used in sauce making but are frequently used in the bakeshop.

7. *Bread crumbs* and other crumbs will thicken a liquid quickly because they have already been cooked, like instant starches. Bread crumbs may be used when smoothness of texture is not desired. A common example is the use of gingersnap crumbs to thicken sauerbraten gravy.

8. *Vegetable purées, ground nuts, and other solids.* A simple tomato sauce is basically a seasoned vegetable purée. The sauce gets its texture from the thickness of the main ingredient. No additional thickener is needed.

    Using this same principle, we can add body or texture to sauces by adding a smooth vegetable purée, or by puréeing mirepoix or other vegetables with the sauce. Other puréed or finely ground ingredients, such as ground nuts, add texture as well as flavor to a sauce.

EGG YOLK AND CREAM LIAISON

Egg yolks have the power to thicken a sauce slightly due to coagulation of egg proteins when heated.

Caution must be used when thickening with egg yolks because of the danger of curdling. This happens when the proteins coagulate too much and separate from the liquid.

Pure egg yolks coagulate at about 140°F to 158°F (60°C to 70°C). For this reason, they are beaten with heavy cream before use. This raises their curdling temperature to 180°F to 185°F (82°C to 85°C). (Note that this is still well below the boiling point.) The heavy cream also adds thickness and flavor to the sauce.

Egg yolks have only a slight thickening power. The *liaison*, which is a binding agent made of cream and egg yolks, is used primarily to give richness of flavor and smoothness of texture to a sauce and only secondarily to give a slight thickening. Also, because of the instability of the egg yolks, it is used only as a finishing technique. Incorporating a liaison is illustrated in Figure 8.6.

Procedure for Using a Liaison

1. Beat together the egg yolks and cream in a stainless-steel bowl. Normal proportions are 2 to 3 parts cream to 1 part egg yolks.

2. Very slowly add a little of the hot liquid to the liaison, beating constantly. This is known as *tempering*.

3. Off the heat, add the warmed, diluted liaison to the rest of the sauce, stirring well as you pour it in.

4. Return the sauce to low heat to warm it gently, but do not heat it higher than 180°F (82°C) or it will curdle. In no circumstances should it boil.

5. Hold for service above 140°F (69°C) for sanitation reasons, but lower than 180°F (82°C).

EGG YOLK EMULSIFICATION

Egg yolks are also used as the thickening agent for hollandaise and related sauces, but in this case the principle is entirely different. The entire procedure will be discussed in detail when we get to the hollandaise family of sauces, page 155.

REDUCTION

Simmering a sauce to evaporate some of the water thickens the sauce because only the water evaporates, not the solids. As the solids become more concentrated, the sauce becomes thicker. This technique has always been important for finishing sauces (see the next section). It has become more important as a basic thickening technique as modern chefs use less starch for thickening.

Use caution when reducing stock-based sauces. If such a sauce is reduced too much, the concentration of gelatin may give it a gluey or sticky texture, and it will congeal quickly on plates. Also, the sauce may have a heavily cooked taste that is not as appealing as the fresher, livelier taste of a stock that has not been cooked as much.

Figure 8.6 Adding a liaison to a sauce.

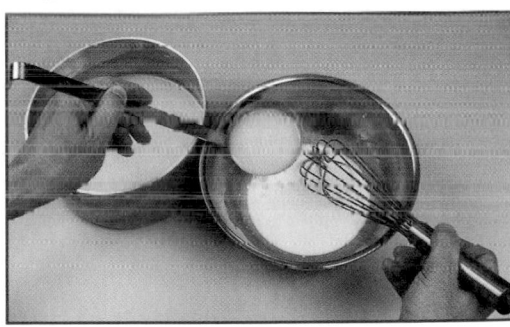

(a) Slowly stir a little of the hot sauce (chicken velouté, in this picture) into the mixture of cream and egg yolks to warm it and dilute it.

Finishing Techniques

Remember that the three basic elements of a finished sauce are a liquid, a thickening agent, and additional seasoning and flavoring ingredients. We have discussed in detail how liquids are combined with thickening agents to make the basic sauces. In the next section, we look at the way families of sauces are built upon these bases by the addition of flavoring ingredients.

Sauces may be modified or added to in a great many ways. Among these methods are a number of basic techniques that are used over and over again for making sauces. Before we study the structure of the sauce families, it will be helpful to look at these basic finishing techniques.

(b) Stir the tempered liaison back into the remaining sauce.

REDUCTION

1. **Using reduction to concentrate basic flavors.**
   If we simmer a sauce for a long time, some of the water evaporates. The sauce becomes more concentrated, and the resulting product is more flavorful. This is the same technique used when making glazes from stocks. Some reduction takes place in nearly all sauces, depending on how long they are simmered.

2. **Using reduction to adjust textures.**
   Concentrating a sauce by reduction also thickens it because only the water evaporates, not the roux or other solids. A skilled sauce chef uses both reduction and dilution to give a sauce the precise texture sought. If a sauce is too thin, it may be simmered until it reaches desired thickness. Or the chef may add a large quantity of stock or other liquid to a thickened sauce to thin it out greatly, then simmer it again until it is reduced to just the right consistency. By doing this, the chef also gives more flavor to the sauce.

3. **Using reduction to add new flavors.**
   If we can add a liquid to a sauce, then reduce it to concentrate it, why can't we reduce a liquid first and then add it to a sauce?
   In fact, this is one of the most important techniques in sauce making. We have already mentioned that glazes—reduced stocks—are used to flavor sauces. Reductions of other liquids, especially red and white wines, are used a great deal in this way.
   Skip ahead to the recipe for Bordelaise Sauce, page 160. Note how the red wine is cooked down with shallots, pepper, and herbs to one-fourth its original volume. Not only is the flavor of the wine concentrated but also the flavor from the other spices is extracted. This reduction is a powerful flavoring agent that gives Bordelaise Sauce its distinctive taste. Reduction allows you to add a great deal of flavor to a sauce without adding much liquid.

Terminology

To reduce by one-half means to cook away one-half of the volume, so that half is left.
To reduce by three-fourths means to cook away three-fourths of the volume, so that only one-fourth is left.
To reduce au sec (oh seck) means to reduce until dry or nearly dry.

STRAINING

If you have learned how to use a roux properly, you should be able to make a smooth, lump-free sauce. However, to bring a sauce's texture to perfection, to create the velvety smoothness that is important to a good sauce, straining is necessary. Even a slight graininess that you can't see, you can still feel on your tongue.
Straining through a china cap lined with several layers of cheesecloth is effective. Very fine sieves are also available for straining sauces. Straining is usually done before final seasoning.

DEGLAZING

To *deglaze* means to swirl a liquid in a sauté pan or other pan to dissolve cooked particles of food remaining on the bottom.
This term was discussed in relation to the basic technique of sautéing in Chapter 4 and again in connection with the production of brown stock. It is also an important technique for finishing sauces that accompany sautéed items.
A liquid such as wine or stock is used to deglaze a sauté pan and then is reduced by one-half or three-fourths. This reduction, with the added flavor of the pan drippings, is then added to the sauce that is served with the item.

ENRICHING WITH BUTTER AND CREAM

1. **Liaison.**
   In addition to being a thickening agent, the liaison of egg yolks and cream is used to finish a sauce by giving it extra richness and smoothness.

2. **Heavy cream.**

   Heavy cream has long been used to give flavor and richness to sauces. The most obvious example is adding cream to basic Béchamel Sauce to make Cream Sauce.

3. **Butter.**

   A useful enriching technique, both in classical and in modern cooking, is called *finishing with butter*, or *monter au beurre* (mohn tay oh burr).

   To finish a sauce with butter, simply add a few pieces of softened butter to the hot sauce and swirl it in until it melts. The sauce should then be served immediately; if it is allowed to stand, the butter may separate.

   Finishing a sauce with butter gives it a little extra shine and smoothness as well as adding to it the rich, fresh taste of raw butter.

SEASONING

Whether or not a sauce is to be given a final enrichment of liaison, cream, or butter, it must be checked carefully for seasonings before serving. Remember that the last step in any recipe, whether written or not, is "adjust the seasonings."

1. *Salt* is the most important seasoning for sauces. *Lemon juice* is also important. These two seasonings emphasize the flavors that are already there by stimulating the taste buds. *Cayenne* and *white pepper* are perhaps third and fourth in importance.

2. *Sherry* and *Madeira* are frequently used as final flavorings. These wines are added at the end of cooking (unlike red and white table wines, which must be cooked in a sauce) because their flavors are easily evaporated by heat.

Sauce Families

LEADING SAUCES

One more time, let's look at the three basic building blocks of sauce cookery, this time from a slightly different angle.

liquid + thickening agent = leading sauce

leading sauce + additional flavorings = small sauce

We have talked about five basic liquids for sauces: milk, white stock, brown stock, tomato purée (plus stock), and clarified butter. From these we get our five leading sauces, also known as *mother sauces*, as shown in Chart 8.1.

To these five sauces, we add one more: *fond lié* (fone lee ay), meaning "thickened stock." It is sometimes used in place of espagnole.

brown stock + cornstarch = fond lié

You should understand that these charts are a bit oversimplified. Most of these sauces have a few other ingredients for flavoring. Yet knowing this basic structure is the key to making sauces.

CHART 8.1

The Leading Sauces

Liquid	Thickening Agent	Leading Sauce
Milk	+ White roux	= Béchamel sauce
White stock (veal chicken, fish)	+ White or blond roux	= Velouté (veal velouté, chicken velouté, fish velouté)
Brown stock	+ Brown roux	= Brown sauce or espagnole
Tomato plus stock	+ (Optional roux)	= Tomato sauce
Butter	+ Egg yolks	= Hollandaise

Note: Roux is not used in all tomato sauces, as tomato purée is naturally thick.

SMALL SAUCES

The major leading sauces—béchamel; veal, chicken, and fish veloutés; and espagnole—are rarely used by themselves as sauces. They are more important as the bases for other sauces, called *small sauces*. Tomato sauce and hollandaise are used as they are, but they, too, are important as bases for small sauces.

Let's expand our sauce family chart one more generation to include examples of the small sauces in order to show the relationships (see Chart 8.2).

CHART 8.2

The Small Sauces

Basic Ingredient	Leading Sauce	Secondary Leading Sauce	Small Sauce
White Sauces			
Milk ⟶	Béchamel ⟶		Cream, Mornay, Cheddar Cheese, Nantua, Soubise, Mustard
White Veal Stock ⟶	Veal Velouté ⟶	Allemande ⟶	Poulette, Aurora, Hungarian, Curry
Chicken Stock ⟶	Chicken Velouté ⟶	Suprême ⟶	Mushroom, Albufera or Ivory, Hungarian, Curry
Fish Stock ⟶	Fish Velouté ⟶	White Wine Sauce ⟶	Normandy, Bercy, Mushroom, Herb
Brown Sauces			
Brown Stock ⟶	Espagnole ⟶ / Fond Lié ⟶	Demiglaze / Demiglaze ⟶ / Demiglaze	Bordelaise, Robert, Charcutière, Chasseur, Deviled (Diable), Lyonnaise, Madeira, Perigueux, Piquante, Mushroom, Bercy
Red Sauces			
Tomato plus stock ⟶	Tomato Sauce ⟶		Creole, Portuguese, Spanish
Butter Sauces			
Butter ⟶	Hollandaise ⟶		Maltaise, Mousseline
	Béarnaise ⟶		Choron, Foyot

Chart 8.2 is probably a little more complicated than you had expected because of the extra arrows and the extra category of secondary leading sauces. These are relatively easy to explain.

1. **Secondary Leading White Sauces.**
   These three sauces—allemande, suprême, and white wine—are really finished sauces, like other small sauces. But they are used so often to build other small sauces that they rate a special category.

   For example, to make suprême sauce, you add cream to chicken velouté.

   To make albufera sauce, you can add meat glaze (glace de viande) to your suprême sauce. Or, if you don't have suprême sauce, you can make it by adding both cream and meat glaze to chicken velouté. This is why there are two sets of arrows in the chart.

   Allemande, suprême, and white wine sauces are also known as the *main small sauces*. If the concept of secondary leading white sauces seems too confusing at first, you may simply think of them as small sauces. The important thing is to understand how the sauces are derived.

2. **Demiglaze.**
   - Demiglaze is defined as half brown sauce plus half brown stock, reduced by half. In French, it is known as *demi-glace* (dem me glahss.) Most chefs prefer demiglaze to espagnole as a base for small sauces because of its more concentrated, more fully developed flavor.

     Note: It is possible to make small sauces directly from espagnole, but they will not be as fine.

   - Some modern chefs feel that espagnole is too heavy for modern tastes and that lighter sauces are required. These chefs prepare demiglaze from fond lié by reducing it with mirepoix, white wine, and seasonings, or by simply reducing by half a flavorful brown stock.

     In other words, demiglaze may be considered a well-flavored brown stock, reduced by half (*demi* means "half"), thickened with roux or cornstarch or left unthickened (except by natural gelatin).

3. **Small sauces listed twice.**
   Notice, for example, that mushroom sauce is listed under both chicken velouté and fish velouté. This means that you should use the stock of the product you are serving with the sauce. Mushroom sauce for chicken should be made out of chicken velouté, for fish, out of fish velouté. To be even more confusing, mushroom sauce is also made with brown sauce. Bercy sauce is also made as both a white and a brown sauce. These are considered unrelated sauces that happen to have the same name.

4. **Hollandaise and béarnaise.**
   These are essentially two variations of the same kind of sauce, with different flavorings. Each has its own small family of small sauces.

STANDARDS OF QUALITY FOR SAUCES

1. **Consistency and body.**
   Smooth, with no lumps.
   Not too thick or pasty, but thick enough to coat the food lightly.

2. **Flavor.**
   Distinctive but well-balanced flavor.
   Proper degree of seasoning.
   No starchy taste.
   The flavor should be selected to enhance or complement the food (such as suprême sauce with chicken or white wine sauce with fish) or to provide a pleasing contrast (such as a béarnaise sauce with grilled beef or raisin sauce with ham).

3. **Appearance.**
   Smooth, with a good shine.
   Good color for its type (rich, deep brown for brown sauce, pale ivory for velouté, white—not gray—for cream sauce).

OTHER SAUCES

As usual, not everything fits into one package. Beyond the five major sauce families, a number of other preparations don't follow these basic patterns. We encounter these later in the chapter.

These other preparations include these groups:

Simple and compound butters, including simple browned butter as well as butter combined with different flavorings.

Pan gravies, or sauces made with the pan drippings of the meat or poultry they are served with.

Miscellaneous hot sauces, which are not made like any of the five basic sauces. These include such items as raisin sauce (for ham) and sour cream sauce.

Miscellaneous cold sauces include not only sauces for meats, like Cumberland sauce and horseradish sauce, but also vinaigrettes, mayonnaise, and their variations, covered in Chapter 19.

MODERN SAUCES

Most of the emphasis in this chapter is on techniques for producing classic sauces. It is a mistake to argue that these sauces are not important and that modern sauce making is entirely different. Modern sauces still depend on the basic classical techniques, even though the emphasis may have changed. For example, a chef in a modern kitchen may prepare a sauce for a sautéed meat item at the last minute by deglazing a sauté pan with a little wine, adding some reduced brown stock, and finishing the sauce by swirling in a little butter. As you can see, these are all techniques used in the production of classical sauces. Learning to make classical sauces is an important foundation for learning modern cooking.

While many of the recipes in this book, especially the traditional ones, incorporate sauces prepared in advance, many of the others, especially the more modern ones, incorporate sauces made at the last minute.

Production

BÉCHAMEL

The classic version of the standard white sauce, béchamel, was made with lean veal and herbs and spices simmered with the sauce for an hour or with white veal stock added to the sauce and then reduced. This is rarely done today.

Nevertheless, the plain béchamel used today—simply milk and roux—can be improved by simmering the sauce with onion and spices. These may be omitted, of course, but the sauce will have less flavor.

Béchamel Sauce

Yield: 1 gal (4 L)

U.S.	Metric	Ingredients	PROCEDURE
		Roux:	1. Review instructions for making and incorporating roux (p. 137).
8 oz	250 g	Clarified butter	2. Heat the butter in a heavy saucepot over low heat. Add the flour and make a white roux. Cool the roux slightly.
8 oz	250 g	Bread flour	
1 gal	4 L	Milk	3. In another saucepan, scald the milk. Gradually add it to the roux, beating constantly.
1	1	Small whole onion, peeled	4. Bring the sauce to a boil, stirring constantly. Reduce heat to a simmer.
1	1	Whole clove	5. Stick the bay leaf to the onion with the clove and add to the sauce. Simmer at least 15 minutes or, if possible, for 30 minutes or more. Stir occasionally while cooking.
1	1	Bay leaf, small	
to taste	to taste	Salt	6. Adjust the consistency with more hot milk, if necessary.
to taste	to taste	Nutmeg	7. Season *very lightly* with salt, nutmeg, and white pepper. Spice flavors should not dominate.
to taste	to taste	White pepper	8. Strain the sauce through a china cap lined with cheesecloth. Cover or spread melted butter on surface to prevent skin formation. Keep hot in a bain-marie, or cool in a cold-water bath for later use.

Per 1 ounce:
Calories, 40; Protein, 1 g; Fat, 3 g (63% cal.); Cholesterol, 10 mg;
Carbohydrates, 3 g; Fiber, 0 g; Sodium, 30 mg.

VARIATIONS

Light Béchamel
Use 12 oz (375 g) roux.

Heavy Béchamel
Use 1½ lb (750 g) roux.

Small Sauces

For each of the following sauces, add the ingredients indicated to *1 qt (1 L) béchamel sauce.* Season to taste

Cream Sauce
4–8 oz (125–250 mL) heavy cream, heated or tempered.

Mornay Sauce
4 oz (125 g) grated Gruyère cheese and 2 oz (60 g) parmesan, stirred in until just melted. Finish, off heat, with 2 oz (60 g) raw butter. Thin out with a little hot milk, if necessary, or use a stock or broth appropriate for the dish being prepared.

Mornay Sauce for Glazing or Gratinéeing
Finish Mornay sauce with liaison of 2 egg yolks and 2 oz (60 mL) heavy cream.

Cheddar Cheese Sauce
8 oz (250 g) cheddar cheese, ½ tsp (2 mL) dry mustard, 2 tsp (10 mL) Worcestershire sauce.

Mustard Sauce
4 oz (125 g) prepared mustard.

Soubise Sauce
1 lb (500 g) onions, finely diced, cooked slowly in 2 oz (60 g) butter without browning. Simmer with sauce 15 minutes and force through a fine sieve.

Tomatoed Soubise Sauce
Add 1 pt (500 mL) thick tomato purée to 1 qt (1 L) soubise sauce.

Nantua Sauce
6 oz (175 g) Shrimp Butter (p. 154), 4 oz (125 mL) heavy cream.
(*Note:* Classic Nantua sauce is made with crayfish, not readily available in many regions.)

VELOUTÉ

The three velouté sauces are the bases of many variations. Instructions for the small sauces indicate which of the three to use. If more than one are given, the choice depends on what you are serving it with.

Note: In North America, chicken velouté is used much more often than veal velouté. Many of the sauces at one time made with veal stock are now made with chicken stock.

Velouté Sauce (Veal, Chicken, or Fish)

Yield: 2 qt (2 L)

U.S.	Metric	Ingredients	PROCEDURE
		Roux:	1. Review instructions for making and incorporating roux (p. 137).
4 oz	125 g	Clarified butter	2. Heat the butter in a heavy saucepot over low heat. Add the flour and make a blond roux. Cool the roux slightly.
4 oz	125 g	Bread flour	
2½ qt	2.5 L	White stock, hot (veal, chicken, or fish)	3. Gradually add the hot stock to the roux, beating constantly. Bring to a boil, stirring constantly. Reduce heat to a simmer.
			4. Simmer the sauce very slowly for 1 hour. Stir occasionally, and skim the surface when necessary. Add more stock if needed to adjust consistency.
			5. Do not season velouté, as it is not used as is but as an ingredient in other preparations.
			6. Strain through a china cap lined with cheesecloth. Cover or spread melted butter on surface to prevent skin formation. Keep hot in a bain-marie, or cool in a cold-water bath for later use.

Per 1 ounce:
Calories, 25; Protein, 0 g; Fat, 2 g (82% cal.); Cholesterol, 5 mg;
Carbohydrates, 1 g; Fiber, 0 g; Sodium, 20 mg.

White Wine Sauce

Yield: 2 qt (2 L)

U.S.	Metric	Ingredients	PROCEDURE
8 oz	250 mL	White wine (dry)	1. Reduce the wine by half in a saucepan.
2 qt	2 L	Fish velouté	2. Add the velouté and simmer until reduced to desired consistency.
8 oz	250 mL	Heavy cream, hot	3. Slowly stir in the hot (or tempered) cream.
2 oz	60 g	Butter	4. Remove from heat and swirl in the raw butter, cut into pieces.
to taste	to taste	Salt	5. Season to taste with salt, white pepper, and a few drops of lemon juice.
to taste	to taste	White pepper	
to taste	to taste	Lemon juice	6. Strain through cheesecloth.

Per 1 ounce:
Calories, 45; Protein, 0 g; Fat, 4 g (85% cal.); Cholesterol, 10 mg;
Carbohydrates, 1 g; Fiber, 0 g; Sodium, 30 mg.

VARIATION

Instead of adding the hot or tempered heavy cream, make a liaison with 5 egg yolks and 8 oz (250 mL) cold heavy cream. Incorporate the liaison using the procedure on p. 139. Then continue with step 4 in the recipe.

Suprême Sauce

Yield: 2 qt (2 L)

U.S.	Metric	Ingredients	PROCEDURE
2 qt	2 L	Chicken velouté	1. Place the velouté in a saucepan and simmer over moderate heat until reduced by about one-fourth. Stir occasionally.
1 pt	500 mL	Heavy cream	
2 oz	60 g	Butter	2. Pour the cream into a stainless-steel bowl and temper it by slowly stirring in a little of the hot sauce. Stir this mixture slowly back into the sauce in the pan and return the sauce just to a simmer.
to taste	to taste	Salt	
to taste	to taste	White pepper	
to taste	to taste	Lemon juice	3. Swirl in the raw butter, cut into pieces. Season to taste with salt, white pepper, and a few drops of lemon juice.

Per 1 ounce:
Calories, 50; Protein, 1 g; Fat, 5 g (79% cal.); Cholesterol, 20 mg;
Carbohydrates, 2 g; Fiber, 0 g; Sodium, 30 mg.

4. Strain through cheesecloth.

Allemande Sauce

Yield: 2 qt (2 L)

U.S.	Metric	Ingredients	PROCEDURE
2 qt	2 L	Veal velouté (see note)	1. Review instructions for incorporating a liaison (p. 139).
		Liaison:	2. Place the velouté in a saucepan and simmer a few minutes over moderate heat until slightly reduced.
4	4	Egg yolks	
8 oz	250 mL	Heavy cream	3. Beat the egg yolks and cream together in a stainless-steel bowl.
½ oz	15 mL	Lemon juice	4. Temper the liaison by *slowly* beating in about one-third of the hot sauce. Then slowly stir this mixture back into the sauce in the pan.
to taste	to taste	Salt	5. Reheat to just below simmering. Do not boil.
to taste	to taste	White pepper	6. Add lemon juice, salt, and white pepper to taste and strain through cheesecloth.

Per 1 ounce:
Calories, 40; Protein, 1 g; Fat, 3.5 g (72% cal.); Cholesterol, 25 mg; Carbohydrates, 2 g; Fiber, 0 g; Sodium, 20 mg.

Note: Allemande sauce, strictly speaking, should be made with veal velouté. However, as chicken velouté is much more common in North America, allemande sauce and the small sauces derived from it are often made with chicken velouté.

Small Sauces

For each of the following sauces, add the listed ingredients to 1 qt (1 L) *veal, chicken,* or *fish velouté, suprême sauce, allemande sauce,* or *white wine sauce* as indicated. Season the sauce to taste.

Poulette

Simmer 8 oz (250 g) white mushrooms or mushroom trimmings with velouté when making *allemande.* Make allemande, strain. Finish with 2 tbsp (30 mL) chopped parsley and lemon juice to taste.

Aurora

Add 6 oz (175 g) tomato purée to 1 qt (1 L) *veal* or *chicken velouté, suprême sauce,* or *allemande sauce.*

Hungarian

Sweat 2 oz (60 g) minced onion and 1 tbsp (15 mL) paprika in 1 oz (25 g) butter until soft. Add ½ cup (100 mL) white wine and reduce by half. Add 1 qt (1 L) *veal* or *chicken velouté,* simmer 10 minutes, and strain.

Ivory or Albufera

Add 2 oz (60 g) meat glaze (glace de viande) to 1 qt (1 L) *suprême sauce.*

Curry

Cook 4 oz (125 g) mirepoix, cut brunoise, in 1 oz (25 g) butter until tender but not brown. Add 1 tbsp (15 mL) curry powder, 1 crushed garlic clove, pinch thyme, ½ bay leaf, and 2–4 parsley stems and cook another minute. Add 1 qt (1 L) *veal, chicken,* or *fish velouté.* Simmer 20 minutes, add ½ cup (125 mL) cream, strain, and season with salt and lemon juice.

Mushroom

Sauté 4 oz (125 g) sliced mushrooms in 1 oz (25 g) butter, adding 1 tbsp (15 mL) lemon juice to keep them white. Add to *suprême, allemande,* or *white wine* sauce or to appropriate velouté.

Bercy

Reduce by two-thirds: 2 oz (60 g) chopped shallots and ½ cup (125 mL) white wine. Add 1 qt (1 L) *fish velouté,* reduce slightly, and finish with 2 oz (60 g) raw butter, 2 tbsp (30 mL) chopped parsley, and lemon juice to taste.

Herb

To *white wine sauce* add chopped parsley, chives, and tarragon to taste.

Normandy

To 1 qt (1 L) *fish velouté* add 4 oz (125 mL) mushroom cooking liquid (or 4 oz/125 g mushroom trimmings) and 4 oz (125 mL) oyster liquid or fish fumet. Reduce by one-third. Finish with a liaison of 4 egg yolks and 1 cup (250 mL) cream. Strain and swirl in 3 oz (75 g) raw butter.

Anchovy

Follow the instructions for Normandy sauce but, in place of the raw butter used to finish the sauce, substitute 6 oz (175 g) anchovy butter.

Shrimp

To 1 qt (1 L) *white wine sauce,* add 4 oz (125 g) shrimp butter and a dash of cayenne. If desired, garnish with 4 oz (125 g) diced, cooked shrimp.

Venetian

Combine ½ cup (125 mL) each white wine and tarragon vinegar, ½ oz (15 g) chopped shallots, and 2 tsp (10 mL) chervil. Reduce by two-thirds. Add 1 qt (1 L) *white wine sauce* and simmer 2–3 minutes. Strain. Add tarragon to taste.

Horseradish

Add 2 oz (60 g) drained horseradish, ½ cup (125 mL) heavy cream, and 2 tsp (10 mL) dry mustard dissolved in 1 oz (30 mL) vinegar to 1 qt (1 L) *velouté* made with beef or veal stock or broth from Boiled Beef (p. 280).

ESPAGNOLE OR BROWN SAUCE

As one glance at the procedure for making espagnole will tell you, this sauce is more complicated than béchamel or velouté. Because it is the starting point for the hearty, flavorful sauces that accompany red meats, it is necessary to give it extra flavor and richness with mirepoix. Some chefs even add more browned bones and cook the sauce as long as a stock.

Note how the roux is made in the espagnole recipe. Though mirepoix is also cooked in the fat, the basic principle is the same as when you make a simple roux in a separate pot.

Brown Sauce or Espagnole

Yield: 1 gal (4 L)

U.S.	Metric	Ingredients	PROCEDURE
		Mirepoix:	1. Sauté the mirepoix in the butter until well browned.
1 lb	500 g	Onions, medium dice	2. Add the flour and stir to make the roux. Continue to cook until the
8 oz	250 g	Carrots, medium dice	roux is browned.
8 oz	250 g	Celery, medium dice	3. Gradually stir in the brown stock and tomato purée, stirring con-
8 oz	250 g	Butter	stantly until the mixture comes to a boil.
8 oz	250 g	Bread flour	4. Reduce heat to simmer and skim the surface. Add the sachet and let
6 qt	6 L	Brown stock	simmer for about 2 hours, until the sauce is reduced to 1 gal (4 L).
8 oz	250 g	Tomato purée	Skim as often as necessary.
		Sachet:	5. Strain through a china cap lined with several layers of cheesecloth.
½	½	Bay leaf	Press on the mirepoix gently to extract their juices.
¼ tsp	1 mL	Thyme	6. Cover or spread melted butter on surface to prevent skin formation.
6–8	6–8	Parsley stems	Keep hot in a bain-marie, or cool in a cold-water bath for later use.

Per 1 ounce:
Calories, 25; Protein, 1 g; Fat, 1.5 g (53% cal.); Cholesterol, 5 mg;
Carbohydrates, 2 g; Fiber, 0 g; Sodium, 20 mg.

Fond Lié

In its simplest form, *fond lié*, or *jus lié*, is a brown stock thickened lightly with cornstarch. Its quality can be improved, however, by applying the technique used for making espagnole. That is, reduce brown stock with browned mirepoix and tomato purée or tomato paste. Then thicken with cornstarch and strain. You can use the same ratio of stock to mirepoix as for espagnole.

Fond Lié or Jus Lié

Yield: 1 qt (1 L)

U.S.	Metric	Ingredients	PROCEDURE
1 qt	1 L	Brown stock	1. Bring the stock to a boil in a saucepan. Reduce heat to a simmer.
1 oz	30 g	Cornstarch	2. Dissolve the starch in a small amount of cold stock or water. Stir
		or arrowroot	it into the simmering stock.
			3. Simmer until thickened and clear.

Per 1 ounce:
Calories, 5; Protein, 0 g; Fat, 0 g (0% cal.); Cholesterol, 0 mg;
Carbohydrates, 1 g; Fiber, 0 g; Sodium, 0 mg.

VARIATION

For added flavor, the stock can be reduced with browned mirepoix and tomato (as for espagnole) before being thickened. Browned bones may also be added.

 ## Demiglaze

Yield: 1 gal (4 L)

U.S.	Metric	Ingredients	PROCEDURE
1 gal	4 L	Brown sauce	1. Combine the sauce and stock in a saucepan and simmer until reduced by half.
1 gal	4 L	Brown stock	2. Strain through a chinois (fine china cap) or a regular china cap lined with cheesecloth. Cover to prevent a skin from forming. Keep hot in a bain marie, or cool in a cold-water bath for later use.

Per 1 ounce:
Calories, 25; Protein, 1 g; Fat, 1.5 g (53% cal.); Cholesterol, 5 mg; Carbohydrates, 2 g; Fiber, 0 g; Sodium, 20 mg.

Small Sauces

For each of the following sauces, add the listed ingredients to 1 qt (1 L) demiglaze, as indicated.

Bordelaise
Reduce by three-fourths: 1 cup (250 mL) dry red wine, 2 oz (60 g) chopped shallots, ¼ tsp (1 mL) crushed peppercorns, a pinch of thyme, and ½ bay leaf. Add 1 qt (1 L) demiglaze, simmer 15 to 20 minutes, and strain. Swirl in 2 oz (60 g) raw butter, cut in pieces. Garnish with diced or sliced beef marrow, poached in salted water.

Marchand de Vin (Wine Merchant)
Reduce 6 oz (200 mL) red wine and 2 oz (60 g) chopped shallots by three-fourths. Add 1 qt (1 L) demiglaze, simmer, and strain.

Robert
Cook 4 oz (125 g) chopped onion in butter without browning. Add 1 cup (250 mL) white wine and reduce by two-thirds. Add 1 qt (1 L) demiglaze and simmer 10 minutes. Strain and add 2 tsp (10 mL) dry mustard and a pinch of sugar dissolved in a little lemon juice.

Charcutière
Garnish Robert sauce with sour pickles, cut julienne.

Chasseur
Sauté 6 oz (175 g) sliced mushrooms and 2 oz (60 g) minced shallots in 2 oz (60 g) butter. Add 1 cup (250 mL) white wine and reduce by three-fourths. Add 1 qt (1 L) demiglaze and 8 oz (250 g) diced tomato. Simmer 5 minutes and add 2 tsp (10 mL) chopped parsley.

Diable (Deviled)
Reduce by two-thirds: 8 oz (250 mL) white wine, 4 oz (125 g) chopped shallots, ½ tsp (2 mL) crushed peppercorns. Add 1 qt (1 L) demiglaze and simmer 20 minutes. Season with cayenne to taste and strain.

Madeira
Reduce 1 qt (1 L) demiglaze by about ½ cup (100 mL). Add 3 to 4 oz (100 mL) Madeira wine.

Périgueux
Garnish Madeira sauce with finely diced truffle.

Poîvrade
Brown 1 lb (500 g) mirepoix in butter. Add 4 oz (125 mL) red wine and 1½ pt (750 mL) Red Wine Marinade for Game (p. 255) and reduce by one-half. Add 1 qt (1 L) demiglaze and reduce by one-third over low heat. Add ½ tsp (2 mL) crushed peppercorns and simmer 10 minutes. Strain.

Port Wine
Follow instructions for Madeira sauce, but use port wine instead of Madeira.

Italian Sauce
Sauté 1 lb (500 g) finely chopped mushrooms and ½ oz (15 g) minced shallots in 2 oz (60 g) butter until all moisture is evaporated. Add 1 cup (250 mL) white wine and reduce by half. Add 1 oz (30 g) tomato paste and 1 qt (1 L) demiglaze and simmer 10 minutes. Add 2 tbsp (30 mL) chopped parsley.

Mushroom
Sauté 8 oz (250 g) sliced mushrooms and 1 oz (30 g) minced shallots in 2 oz (60 g) butter until browned. Add 1 qt (1 L) demiglaze and simmer about 10 minutes. Add 2 oz (60 mL) sherry and a few drops of lemon juice.

Bercy
Reduce by three-fourths: 1 cup (250 mL) dry white wine and 4 oz (125 g) chopped shallots. Add 1 qt (1 L) demiglaze and simmer 10 minutes.

Piquante
Reduce by two-thirds: 4 oz (125 g) minced shallots, 4 oz (125 mL) wine vinegar, and 4 oz (125 mL) white wine. Add 1 qt (1 L) demiglaze and simmer until slightly reduced. Add 2 oz (60 g) capers, 2 oz (60 g) sour pickles, cut brunoise, 1 tbsp (15 mL) chopped parsley, and ½ tsp (2 mL) tarragon.

Lyonnaise
Sauté 4 oz (125 g) onions in 2 oz (60 g) butter until slightly browned. Add ½ cup (125 mL) white wine vinegar and reduce by half. Add 1 qt (1 L) demiglaze and simmer 10 minutes.

TOMATO SAUCE

Classical tomato sauce, as explained by Escoffier, is made with a roux, but this is rarely done in modern kitchens. The texture of the puréed tomatoes is sufficient to give the sauce the proper texture, even when no starch thickener is used.

This type of sauce may be referred to as a *coulis* (koo-lee). This French term means, in modern kitchens, a purée of vegetables or fruits, used as a sauce. A recipe for another coulis, of sweet peppers, is found on page 161.

Three main techniques are used to purée vegetables and other ingredients for coulis:

1. Puréeing the product in a food processor or blender
2. Passing the product through a food mill
3. Forcing the product through a fine sieve

Of these three methods, the third, forcing through a fine sieve, usually makes the smoothest purée, but it is also the most time-consuming. If you want a smooth purée but the product is difficult to force through a sieve, you can use one of the other methods first, then pass the purée through the sieve to make it smoother.

Tomato Sauce I

Yield: 1 gal (4 L)

U.S.	Metric	Ingredients	PROCEDURE
4 oz	125 g	Salt pork	1. Render the salt pork in a heavy saucepot, but do not brown it.
8 oz	250 g	Onion, medium dice	
8 oz	250 g	Carrots, medium dice	2. Add the onion and carrots and sauté until slightly softened, but do not brown.
4 qt	4 L	Tomatoes, canned or fresh, coarsely chopped	3. Add the tomatoes and their juice, the tomato purée, bones, and sachet. Bring to a boil, reduce heat, and simmer over
2 qt	2 L	Tomato purée, canned	very low heat (see note) for 1½–2 hours, until reduced to
1 lb	500 g	Ham bones or browned pork bones	desired consistency.
		Sachet:	4. Remove sachet and bones. Strain sauce or pass it through a food mill.
2 cloves	2 cloves	Garlic, crushed	5. Adjust the seasoning with salt and a little sugar.
1	1	Bay leaf	
¼ tsp	1 mL	Thyme	
¼ tsp	1 mL	Rosemary	
¼ tsp	1 mL	Peppercorns, crushed	
to taste	to taste	Salt	
to taste	to taste	Sugar	

Per 1 ounce:
Calories, 20; Protein, 1 g; Fat, 1 g (36% cal.); Cholesterol, 0 mg;
Carbohydrates, 3 g; Fiber, 1 g; Sodium, 120 mg.

Note: Tomato sauce scorches easily, so heat must be very low. The sauce may be cooked in a slow oven (300°F/150°C), loosely covered, to reduce the danger of scorching.

VARIATION

Tomato Sauce II (Vegetarian)
Omit the salt pork. Sweat the vegetables in 2 oz (60 mL) olive oil. Omit the bones.

Tomato Sauce III

See Tomato Sauce for Pasta, page 516.

Small Sauces

For each of the following sauces, add the listed ingredients to 1 qt (1 L) tomato sauce, as indicated.

Portugaise (Portuguese)

Sauté 4 oz (125 g) onions, cut brunoise, in 1 oz (30 mL) oil. Add 1 lb (500 g) tomato concassé (see p. 445) and 1 tsp (5 mL) crushed garlic. Simmer until reduced by about one-third. Add 1 qt (1 L) tomato sauce, adjust seasonings, and add 2–4 tbsp (30–60 mL) chopped parsley.

Spanish

Lightly sauté in oil without browning: 6 oz (175 g) onion, small dice; 4 oz (125 g) green pepper, small dice; and 1 clove garlic, chopped fine. Add 4 oz (125 g) sliced mushrooms and sauté. Add 1 qt (1 L) tomato sauce and season to taste with salt, pepper, and hot red pepper sauce.

Creole

Sauté in oil: 4 oz (125 g) onion, small dice; 4 oz (125 g) celery, sliced; 2 oz (60 g) green pepper, small dice; 1 tsp (5 mL) chopped garlic. Add 1 qt (1 L) tomato sauce, 1 bay leaf, pinch thyme, and ½ tsp (2 mL) grated lemon rind. Simmer 15 minutes. Remove bay leaf and season to taste with salt, pepper, and cayenne.

Fresh Tomato Coulis with Garlic

Yield: 1 pt (500 mL)

U.S.	Metric	Ingredients	PROCEDURE
3 oz	90 g	Shallots, chopped fine	1. Sweat the shallots and garlic in olive oil until soft.
6 cloves	6 cloves	Garlic, chopped fine	2. Add the tomatoes and cook until excess liquid has cooked out and the sauce is thick.
2 oz	60 mL	Olive oil	
1 lb 8 oz	750 g	Tomatoes, peeled, seeded, and chopped	3. Season to taste.
to taste	to taste	Salt	
to taste	to taste	White pepper	

Per 1 ounce:
Calories, 45; Protein, 1 g; Fat, 3.5 g (66% cal.); Cholesterol, 0 mg;
Carbohydrates, 3 g; Fiber, 1 g; Sodium, 5 mg.

BUTTER SAUCES

The fifth leading sauce is hollandaise. Hollandaise and its cousin béarnaise are unlike the sauces we have been studying because their major ingredient is not stock or milk but butter.

Before tackling the complexities of hollandaise, we first look at simpler butter preparations used as sauces.

1. **Melted butter.**

   This is the simplest butter preparation of all, and one of the most widely used, especially as a dressing for vegetables.

   Unsalted or *sweet butter* has the freshest taste and is ideal for all sauce making.

2. **Clarified butter.**

   Butter consists of butterfat, water, and milk solids. *Clarified butter* is purified butterfat, with water and milk solids removed (see page 152). It is necessary for many cooking operations. Clarified butter is used in sautéing, because the milk solids of unclarified butter would burn at such high temperatures. It is used in making hollandaise because the water of unclarified butter would change the consistency of the sauce.

3. **Brown Butter.**

Known as *beurre noisette* (burr nwah zett) in French, this is whole melted butter that has been heated until it turns light brown and gives off a nutty aroma. It is usually prepared at the last minute and served over fish, white meats, eggs, and vegetables.

Care must be taken not to burn the butter, as the heat of the pan will continue to brown it even after it is removed from the fire.

4. **Black Butter.**

Black butter, or *beurre noir* (burr nwahr), is made like brown butter but heated until it is a little darker, and it is flavored with a few drops of vinegar. Capers, chopped parsley, or both are sometimes added.

To avoid dangerous spattering of the vinegar in the hot butter, many chefs pour the butter over the food item, then deglaze the pan with the vinegar and pour that over the item.

5. **Meunière Butter.**

This is served with fish cooked à la Meunière (see p. 401). Brown butter is seasoned with lemon juice and poured over the fish, which has been sprinkled with chopped parsley.

As in the case of black butter, dangerous spattering can result when moisture is added to hot butter. To avoid this, cooks often sprinkle the lemon juice directly on the fish before pouring on the brown butter.

Procedures for Clarifying Butter

Method 1 (Figure 8.7)

1. Melt the butter in a heavy saucepan over moderate heat.
2. Skim the froth from the surface.
3. Carefully pour off the clear melted butter into another container, leaving the milky liquid at the bottom of the saucepan.

Method 2

1. Melt the butter in a heavy saucepan over moderate heat.
2. Skim the froth from the surface.
3. Leave the pan on the heat and continue to skim the froth from the surface at intervals. The water in the bottom will boil and gradually evaporate.
4. When the butter looks clear and no longer forms a scum on top, strain off the butter through cheesecloth into another container.

    You will need 1¼ lb (625 g) raw butter to make 1 lb (500 g) clarified butter; 1 lb (500 g) raw butter yields 12 to 13 oz (about 400 g) clarified butter.

Figure 8.7 Clarifying butter.

(a) Skim the foam from the top of the melted butter. *(b) Ladle off the clear, melted fat.* *(c) Continue until only the milky liquid remains in the bottom of the pan.*

6. **Compound butters.**

   Compound butters are made by softening raw butter and mixing it with various flavoring ingredients. The mixture is then rolled into a cylinder in waxed paper.

   Compound butters have two main uses:

   - Slices of the firm butter are placed on hot grilled items at service time. The butter melts over the item and sauces it.
   - Small portions are swirled into sauces to finish them and give them a desired flavor.

   Easy as they are to make, compound butters can transform a plain broiled steak into a truly special dish.

   The favorite compound butter for steaks is maître d'hôtel butter (may truh doh tel). Variations are given after the recipe.

7. **Beurre Blanc.**

   Beurre blanc (burr blon) is a sauce made by whipping a large quantity of raw butter into a small quantity of a flavorful reduction of white wine and vinegar, so that the butter melts and forms an emulsion with the reduction. The technique is basically the same as *monter au beurre* (p. 141) except that the proportion of butter to liquid is much greater.

   Beurre blanc can be made quickly and easily by adding cold butter all at once and whipping vigorously over moderately high heat. The temperature of the butter keeps the sauce cool enough to prevent it from separating. Be sure to remove it from the heat before all the butter is melted, and continue whipping. It is better to remove the sauce from the heat too soon rather than too late because it can always be rewarmed slightly if necessary. Figure 8.8 illustrates this procedure.

   Some chefs prefer to use low heat and add the butter a little at a time in order to reduce the chance of overheating and breaking the sauce. The process takes a little longer, but the result is the same.

   Beurre blanc should be held at a warm, not a hot, temperature and stirred or whipped from time to time so that the fat and water do not separate. For more stable mixtures of fat and water—called *emulsions*—see the discussion of hollandaise beginning on page 155.

Figure 8.8 Preparing beurre blanc

(a) Reduce the liquids (usually wine and vinegar) with chopped shallots.

(b) Whip in the raw butter just until the butter is melted and forms a smooth sauce.

(c) Leave in the shallots or strain them out. Strained beurre blanc has a light, smooth, creamy texture.

Maître d'Hôtel Butter

Yield: about 1 lb (500 g)

U.S.	Metric	Ingredients	PROCEDURE
1 lb	500 g	Butter	1. Using a mixer with the paddle attachment, beat the butter at low speed until it is smooth and creamy.
¼ cup	60 mL	Chopped parsley	2. Add the remaining ingredients and beat slowly until completely mixed.
1½ oz	50 mL	Lemon juice	3. Roll the butter into a cylinder about 1 inch (2½ cm) thick in a sheet of parchment or waxed paper. Chill until firm.
pinch	pinch	White pepper	4. To serve, cut slices ¼ inch (½ cm) thick and place on broiled or grilled items just before service.

Per 1 ounce:
Calories, 200; Protein, 0 g; Fat, 23 g (100% cal.); Cholesterol, 60 mg; Carbohydrates, 0 g; Fiber, 0 g; Sodium, 230 mg.

VARIATIONS

For each kind of seasoned butter, add to 1 lb (500 g) butter the listed ingredients instead of the parsley, lemon juice, and pepper.

Anchovy Butter

2 oz (60 g) anchovy fillets, mashed to a paste.

Garlic Butter

1 oz (30 g) garlic, mashed to a paste (see p. 441).

Escargot (Snail) Butter

Garlic butter plus ½ cup (125 mL) chopped parsley, salt, white pepper.

Shrimp Butter

½ lb (250 g) cooked shrimp and shells, ground very fine. Force shrimp butter through a fine sieve to remove pieces of shell.

Mustard Butter

3–4 oz (100 g) Dijon-style mustard.

Herb Butter

Chopped fresh herbs to taste.

Scallion or Shallot Butter

2 oz (60 g) minced scallions or shallots.

Curry Butter

4–6 tsp (20–30 mL) curry powder heated gently with 1 oz (30 g) butter, then cooled.

Beurre Blanc

Yield: 1 pt (500 mL)

U.S.	Metric	Ingredients	PROCEDURE
8 oz	250 mL	Dry white wine	1. Combine the wine, vinegar, and shallots in a saucepan. Reduce until about 1 oz (30 mL) liquid remains.
1½ oz	50 mL	White wine vinegar	
1 oz	30 g	Shallots, chopped	
1 lb	500 g	Cold butter	2. Cut the butter into small pieces.
to taste	to taste	Salt	3. Add the butter to the hot reduction. Set the pan over moderately high heat and whip vigorously. When the butter is nearly all melted and incorporated, remove from the heat and continue to whip until smooth.
			4. Season to taste. The shallots may be left in the sauce or strained out.
			5. Hold the sauce in a warm, not hot, place until served. Stir or whip it from time to time.

Per 1 ounce:
Calories, 210; Protein, 0 g; Fat, 23 g (94% cal.); Cholesterol, 60 mg; Carbohydrates, 1 g; Fiber, 0 g; Sodium, 240 mg.

VARIATIONS

Herbed Butter Sauce

Add your choice of chopped fresh herbs to the finished beurre blanc, or use an herbed compound butter instead of the plain raw butter to make beurre blanc.

Beurre Rouge (Red Butter Sauce)

Use dry red wine instead of white wine to make the reduction. For good color, use a young, bright red wine.

Red Wine Butter Sauce for Fish

Yield: 1 pt 4 oz (600 mL)

U.S.	Metric	Ingredients	PROCEDURE
1 qt	1 L	Red wine	1. Combine the red wine and shallots in a saucepan. Reduce until almost completely evaporated.
3½ oz	100 g	Shallots, chopped fine	
7 oz	200 mL	Fish stock	2. Add the fish stock. Reduce by two-thirds.
1 lb	500 g	Cold butter	3. Cut the butter into small pieces.
to taste	to taste	Salt	4. Add the butter to the hot reduction. Set the pan over moderately high heat and whip vigorously. When the butter is nearly all incorporated, remove from the heat and continue to whip until smooth.
to taste	to taste	White pepper	
			5. Season to taste. The shallots may be left in the sauce or strained out.

Per 1 ounce:
Calories, 200; Protein, 0 g; Fat, 18 g (81% cal.); Cholesterol, 50 mg;
Carbohydrates, 2 g; Fiber, 0 g; Sodium, 190 mg.

HOLLANDAISE AND BÉARNAISE

Hollandaise is considered an egg-thickened sauce, but the egg doesn't thicken by coagulation as it does in a liaison or in a custard sauce. Instead, it works by emulsification.

An *emulsion* is a uniform mixture of two unmixable liquids. In the case of hollandaise, the two liquids are melted butter and water (including the water in the lemon juice or the vinegar reduction). The two stay mixed and thick because the butter is beaten into tiny droplets and the egg yolks hold the droplets apart. You will encounter emulsion again when you prepare mayonnaise and other salad dressings in Chapter 14.

Two recipes for hollandaise are given. The first is the classic version, flavored with lemon and a vinegar reduction (see Figure 8.9). The second, flavored with just lemon juice, is used more often today because it is quicker and easier.

Figure 8.9 Making hollandaise sauce.

(a) Combine the egg yolks and reduction in a stainless-steel bowl.

(b) Whip over a hot-water bath.

(c) Continue to whip over hot water until thick and light.

(d) Very slowly whip in the butter. (Set the bowl in a saucepan lined with a kitchen towel to hold it steady.)

(e) The finished sauce should be thick but pourable.

Guidelines for Preparing Hollandaise and Béarnaise

Students tend to be afraid of hollandaise because it has a reputation for being difficult to make. True, precautions are necessary to avoid overcooking the eggs and for getting the right consistency. But if you follow the instructions in the recipe carefully and keep in mind these guidelines, you should have no trouble.

Many of these rules have one object in common: Don't overcook the egg yolks, or they will lose their ability to emulsify.

1. **Cool the reduction before adding the yolks, or they will overcook.**

2. **Use the freshest eggs possible for the best emulsification.**
   For safety, pasteurized eggs are recommended (see pp. 614 and 897).

3. **Beat the yolks over hot water.**
   An experienced cook is able to beat them over direct heat, if care is taken, without making scrambled eggs. Until you have gained some confidence, it is safer to use a hot-water bain-marie.

4. **Use a round-bottomed stainless-steel bowl.**
   The whip must be able to reach all the eggs to beat them evenly. Also, stainless steel will not discolor the sauce or give it a metallic flavor.

5. **Have the butter warm but not hot, or it may overcook the eggs. If it is too cool, it might solidify.**

6. **Add the butter slowly at first.**
   The yolks can only absorb a little at a time. Add a few drops at first and beat in thoroughly before adding more. If you add butter faster than it can be absorbed, the emulsion may break.

7. **Don't add more butter than the egg yolks can hold.**
   Remember this standard proportion:
   6 egg yolks per pound (450 g) clarified butter

8. **Broken or curdled hollandaise can be rescued.**
   First, try adding a teaspoon of cold water and beating vigorously. If this doesn't work, start over with a couple of egg yolks and repeat the procedure from step 6 in the recipe, adding the broken sauce as you would the butter.

Holding Hollandaise Sauce

Hollandaise sauce, as well as other sauces in this family, poses a special safety problem. It must be kept warm for service, but it needs to be held below 140°F (60°C) so that the eggs don't curdle. Unfortunately, bacteria grow quickly in this temperature range. Therefore, extra care must be taken to avoid food-borne diseases.

The following sanitation procedures must be observed to avoid the danger of food poisoning:

1. Make sure all equipment is perfectly clean.

2. Hold sauce no longer than 1½ hours. Make only enough to serve in this time, and discard any that is left over.

3. Never mix an old batch of sauce with a new batch.

4. Never hold hollandaise or béarnaise—or any other acid product—in aluminum. Use stainless-steel containers.

Recipes for hollandaise and béarnaise sauces begin on page 159.

FLAVORED OILS

Flavored oils make a light, interesting alternative to vinaigrettes and other sauces when used to dress a wide variety of dishes. They are especially suitable for simple steamed, sautéed, or grilled items, but they can be used with various cold foods as well. When used as a sauce, the oil is usually drizzled around or, sometimes, over the item on the plate. A tablespoon or so (15 mL) per portion is often enough.

The simplest way to flavor an oil is simply to put some of the flavoring ingredient in the oil and let it stand until the oil has taken on enough of the flavor. For most flavorings, however, this is not the best way to extract the most flavor. The flavoring ingredient may need some kind of preparation before adding it to the oil. For example, dry spices develop more flavor if they are first heated gently with a little bit of the oil.

Refrigerating flavored oils is recommended. As you will recall from Chapter 2, botulism is caused by a kind of bacteria that grows in the absence of air. Because the oil prevents air from reaching the flavoring ingredients, if any botulism bacteria are present in the flavorings (especially possible with fresh, raw roots), those bacteria could grow while covered with oil if not refrigerated.

The following procedure outlines the basic method for making flavored oils, depending on the type of ingredients. Unless otherwise indicated, use a mild or flavorless oil, such as safflower, canola, corn, or grapeseed. In some cases, as with garlic, the flavoring goes well with olive oil, but usually the goal is to have the pure taste of the flavoring ingredient unmasked by the flavor of the oil.

Procedure for Making Flavored Oils

1. Prepare the flavoring ingredient in one of the following ways:

Chop fresh roots (such as horseradish, garlic, shallots, ginger) or strong herbs (fresh rosemary, sage, thyme, oregano) by hand or in a food processor.

Grate citrus zests.

Blanch tender herbs (parsley, basil, tarragon, chervil, cilantro) in boiling water for 10 seconds. Drain immediately and refresh under cold water. Dry well.

Gently heat dried, ground spices (cinnamon, cumin, curry powder, ginger, mustard, paprika) in a small amount of oil just until it starts to give off an aroma.

2. Place the flavoring ingredient in a jar or other closable container. Add oil.

3. Close the jar and shake it well. Let stand 30 minutes at room temperature, then refrigerate.

4. The oil is ready to use as soon as it has taken on the desired flavor, which may be as soon as 1 hour, depending on the ingredient. After 2 days, strain the oil through a chinois lined with a paper coffee filter. Store in the refrigerator.

PAN GRAVIES

Pan gravy is a sauce made with juices or drippings of the meat or poultry with which it is being served. Standard pan gravies are similar to brown sauces. Instead of being made with espagnole or demiglaze as a base, however, they are made from pan drippings plus roux plus stock or water and sometimes milk or cream.

Jus (zhoo) refers to unthickened juices from a roast. When the roast is served with these clear, natural juices, it is said to be served *au jus* (oh zhoo), meaning "with juice." Stock is usually added to the pan juices so that there is enough quantity to serve.

The preparation of both gravy and jus are properly part of meat cookery, and recipes and detailed procedures are included in the meat and poultry chapters.

The principle recipes are on page 243 (Roast Beef Gravy) and page 317 (Roast Turkey with Giblet Gravy). Gravy making is also incorporated in the recipes for Roast Stuffed Shoulder of Lamb (p. 244), Roast Loin of Pork with Sage and Apples (p. 249), and Roast Chicken with Natural Gravy (p. 314).

Now that you have studied sauce making in detail, however, it will be helpful to give a general procedure for making pan gravies so that you can see how similar it is to making brown sauce and how the same techniques you have just learned are applied to a different product.

Basic Procedures for Making Pan Gravy

Method 2 has fewer steps, but Method 1 is actually quicker for large quantities and gives greater control over final consistency.

Method 1

1. **Remove the roast from the roasting pan.**
   If you have not added mirepoix to the pan during roasting, you can do so now.

2. **Clarify the fat.**
   Set the roasting pan over high heat and cook until all the moisture has evaporated, leaving only the fat, mirepoix, and the brown (caramelized) drippings. Pour off and save the fat.

3. **Deglaze the pan.**
   Pour stock or other liquid into the roasting pan. Stir over heat until caramelized drippings are dissolved.

4. **Combine with stock and simmer.**
   Pour the deglazing liquid, plus mirepoix, into a large pot with desired amount of stock. Simmer until mirepoix is well cooked. Skim the surface well to remove fat and scum.

5. **Make a roux or, alternatively, a slurry of arrowroot or cornstarch and water.**
   For roux, measure enough of the fat from step 2 to make the correct amount of roux for the volume of gravy. Make a blond or brown roux, as desired. For starch slurry, see page 138.

6. **Thicken the gravy with the roux or starch slurry.**

7. **Strain.**

8. **Adjust seasonings.**

Method 2

1. Remove the roast from the roasting pan.

2. Clarify the fat.

3. Add flour to the roasting pan and make a roux.

4. Add stock. Stir until thickened and the pan is deglazed.

5. Strain. Skim excess fat.

6. Adjust consistency, if necessary, with more stock or more roux.

7. Season.

In addition to the sauce recipes in this chapter, others are included elsewhere in this book, often as components of other recipes. Among the more important of these are vinaigrette and mayonnaise variations. These are traditionally used as salad dressings but are also used as sauces for meat, seafood, and vegetable items.

The following recipes appear on the pages indicated:

Hollandaise Sauce I

Yield: 1 qt (1 L)

U.S.	Metric	Ingredients
2½ lb	1125 g	Butter
¼ tsp	1 mL	Peppercorns, crushed
¼ tsp	1 mL	Salt
3 oz	100 mL	White vinegar or wine vinegar
2 oz	60 mL	Cold water
12	12	Egg yolks (see note after Hollandaise II)
2–4 tbsp	30–60 mL	Lemon juice
to taste	to taste	Salt
to taste	to taste	Cayenne

PROCEDURE

1. Review the guidelines for preparing hollandaise and béarnaise (p. 156).
2. Clarify the butter (see p. 152). You should have about *2 lb (900 g) clarified butter*. Keep the butter warm but not hot.
3. Combine the peppercorns, salt, and vinegar in a saucepan and reduce until nearly dry (*au sec*). Remove from heat and add the cold water.
4. To make it easier to beat with a wire whip, it is best now to transfer this diluted, cooled reduction to a stainless-steel bowl. Use a clean rubber spatula to make sure you transfer all the flavoring material to the bowl.
5. Add the egg yolks to the bowl and beat well.
6. Hold the bowl over a hot-water bath and continue to beat the yolks until they are thickened and creamy.
7. Remove the bowl from the heat. Using a ladle, slowly and gradually beat in the warm clarified butter. Add the butter drop by drop at first. If the sauce becomes too thick to beat before all the butter is added, beat in a little of the lemon juice.
8. When all the butter has been added, beat in lemon juice to taste and adjust seasoning with salt and cayenne. If necessary, thin the sauce with a few drops of warm water.
9. Strain through cheesecloth and keep warm (not hot) for service. Hold no longer than 1½ hours (see p. 156).

Per 1 ounce:
Calories, 280; Protein, 1 g; Fat, 31 g (99% cal.); Cholesterol, 155 mg; Carbohydrates, 0 g; Fiber, 0 g; Sodium, 310 mg.

Hollandaise Sauce II

Yield: 1 qt (1 L)

U.S.	Metric	Ingredients
2½ lb	1125 g	Butter
12	12	Egg yolks (see note)
2 oz	60 mL	Cold water
3 oz	100 mL	Lemon juice
to taste	to taste	Salt
to taste	to taste	Cayenne

PROCEDURE

1. Review the guidelines for preparing hollandaise and béarnaise (p. 156).
2. Clarify the butter (see p. 152). You should have about *2 lb (900 g) clarified butter*. Keep the butter warm but not hot.
3. Place the egg yolks and cold water in a stainless-steel bowl and beat well. Beat in a few drops of lemon juice.
4. Hold the bowl over a hot-water bath and continue to beat until the yolks are thickened and creamy.
5. Remove the bowl from the heat. Using a ladle, slowly and gradually beat in the warm butter. Add the butter drop by drop at first. If the sauce becomes too thick to beat before all the butter is added, beat in a little of the lemon juice.
6. When all the butter has been added, beat in lemon juice to taste and adjust seasoning with salt and cayenne. If necessary, thin the sauce with a few drops of warm water.
7. Keep warm (not hot) for service. Hold no longer than 1½ hours (see p. 156).

Per 1 ounce:
Calories, 280; Protein, 1 g; Fat, 31 g (99% cal.); Cholesterol, 155 mg; Carbohydrates, 0 g; Fiber, 0 g; Sodium, 300 mg.

Note: For safety, pasteurized eggs are recommended.

Small Sauces

Maltaise

To 1 qt (1 L) hollandaise add 2–4 oz (60–125 mL) orange juice (from blood oranges, if possible) and 2 tsp (10 mL) grated orange rind. Serve with asparagus.

Mousseline

Whip 1 cup (250 mL) heavy cream until stiff and fold into 1 qt (1 L) hollandaise.

Béarnaise Sauce

Yield: 1 qt (1 L)

U.S.	Metric	Ingredients	PROCEDURE
2½ lb	1125 kg	Butter	1. Review the guidelines for preparing hollandaise and béarnaise (p. 156). 2. Clarify the butter (see p. 152). You should have about *2 lb (900 g) clarified butter*. Keep the butter warm but not hot.
2 oz 1 cup 2 tsp 1 tsp 12	60 g 250 mL 10 mL 5 mL 12	Shallots, chopped White wine vinegar Tarragon Peppercorns, crushed Egg yolks (see note)	3. Combine the shallots, vinegar, tarragon, and peppercorns in a saucepan and reduce by three-fourths. Remove from the heat and cool slightly. 4. To make it easier to beat with a wire whip, it is best now to transfer this reduction to a stainless-steel bowl. Use a clean rubber spatula to make sure you get it all. Let the reduction cool a little. 5. Add the egg yolks to the bowl and beat well. 6. Hold the bowl over a hot-water bath and continue to beat the yolks until they are thickened and creamy. 7. Remove the bowl from the heat. Using a ladle, slowly and gradually beat in the warm, clarified butter. Add the butter drop by drop at first. If the sauce becomes too thick to beat before all the butter is added, beat in a little lemon juice or warm water. 8. Strain the sauce through cheesecloth.
to taste to taste to taste 2 tbsp 1 tsp	to taste to taste to taste 30 mL 5 mL	Salt Cayenne Lemon juice Chopped parsley Tarragon	9. Season to taste with salt, cayenne, and a few drops of lemon juice. Mix in the parsley and tarragon. 10. Keep warm (not hot) for service. Hold no longer than 1½ hours (see p. 156).

Per 1 ounce:
Calories, 280; Protein, 1 g; Fat, 31 g (97% cal.); Cholesterol, 155 mg;
Carbohydrates, 1 g; Fiber, 0 g; Sodium, 300 mg.

Note: For safety, pasteurized eggs are recommended.

Small Sauces

Foyot
Add 2 oz (60 g) melted meat glaze (glace de viande) to 1 qt (1 L) béarnaise.

Choron
Add 2 oz (60 g) tomato paste to 1 qt (1 L) béarnaise.

Shallot Oil

Yield: 1 pt (500 mL)

U.S.	Metric	Ingredients	PROCEDURE
2–3 tbsp 1 pt	30 g 500 mL	Shallots, chopped Flavorless oil, such as canola, corn, safflower, grapeseed	1. Combine the chopped shallots and the oil in a jar. Shake well. 2. Let stand for 30 minutes. Refrigerate. 3. The oil is ready to use as soon as it has taken on the desired flavor, which may be in 1–2 hours. After 2 days, strain the oil through a paper coffee filter. Store in the refrigerator.

Per 1 ounce:
Calories, 240; Protein, 0 g; Fat, 27 g (100% cal.);
Cholesterol, 0 g; Carbohydrates, 0 g; Fiber, 0 g; Sodium, 0 mg.

VARIATIONS

Ginger Oil, Horseradish Oil, or Garlic Oil
Substitute ginger root, horseradish, or garlic for the shallots in the basic recipe. For best results, chop the ginger or horseradish very fine in a food processor or grate with a fine-holed grater. For garlic oil, substitute olive oil for the flavorless oil if desired.

Lemon or Orange Oil
Substitute 3–4 tbsp (30 g) grated lemon or orange zest for the shallots in the basic recipe.

Shallot Oil *(Continued)*

Rosemary Oil, Sage Oil, Thyme Oil, or Oregano Oil

Substitute 3½ oz (100 g) chopped fresh rosemary, sage, thyme, or oregano for the shallots in the basic recipe.

Cinnamon Oil, Cumin Oil, Curry Oil, Ginger Oil, or Paprika Oil

Substitute 3 tbsp (45 mL) of one of the above ground, dried spices for the shallots in the basic recipe. In a small pan, combine the spice with just enough of the oil to make a thin paste. Heat gently just until the spice starts to give off an aroma. Be careful not to burn the spice. Paprika, especially, darkens quickly. Add the spice mixture to the remaining oil. Let stand, refrigerate, and filter as in the basic recipe.

Basil Oil, Parsley Oil, Chervil Oil, or Cilantro Oil

Select the desired quantity of one of the above fresh herbs. Drop into boiling water. Blanch for 10 seconds. Drain and refresh under cold water. Drain again and pat dry with towels. Put the herbs in a blender and add a small amount of olive oil. Blend to make a paste. Measure the volume of the paste and add 4 times that volume of olive oil. Shake and let stand. Refrigerate and strain as in the basic recipe.

MISCELLANEOUS WARM OR HOT SAUCES

Bell Pepper Coulis

Yield: 2½ pt (1.25 L)

U.S.	Metric	Ingredients	PROCEDURE
4 lb	4 lb	Red or yellow bell peppers	1. Split the peppers in half lengthwise. Remove the cores, seeds, and membranes. Chop the peppers coarsely.
2 oz	60 mL	Olive oil	2. Heat the olive oil in a saucepot over low heat.
2 oz	60 g	Shallots, chopped	3. Add the shallots and peppers. Cover and sweat over low heat until the vegetables are soft, about 20 minutes.
4 oz	125 mL	Chicken stock, vegetable stock, or water	4. Add the stock or water. Simmer 2–3 minutes.
			5. Purée the vegetables and liquid in a blender, then pass through a strainer.
1–4 oz	30–125 mL	Additional stock or water	6. Adjust the texture by adding water or stock to thin it.
to taste	to taste	Salt	7. Add salt and white pepper to taste.
to taste	to taste	White pepper	

Per 1 ounce:
Calories, 25; Protein, 0 g; Fat, 1.5 g (53% cal.); Cholesterol, 0 mg;
Carbohydrates, 3 g; Fiber, 1 g; Sodium, 0 mg.

VARIATION

Bell Pepper and Tomato Couli

Combine bell pepper coulis with an equal volume of tomato purée.

White Wine Cream Sauce for Fish

Yield: 1½ pt (750 mL)

U.S.	Metric	Ingredients	PROCEDURE
2 oz	60 g	Shallots, chopped	1. Combine the shallots and white wine in a saucepan. Reduce until almost dry.
14 oz	400 mL	Dry white wine	2. Add the fish stock and reduce by two-thirds.
1 pt 12 oz	800 mL	Fish stock	3. Add the cream and reduce slightly.
14 oz	400 mL	Heavy cream	4. Swirl in the butter (monter au beurre).
4 oz	125 g	Butter	5. Add the chopped parsley. Season to taste.
1½ oz	45 g	Chopped parsley	
to taste	to taste	Salt	
to taste	to taste	Pepper	

Per 1 ounce:
Calories, 105; Protein, 1 g; Fat, 10 g (83% cal.); Cholesterol, 35 mg;
Carbohydrates, 1 g; Fiber, 0 g; Sodium, 50 mg.

Yogurt Sour Cream Sauce

Yield: 1 pt 4 oz (600 mL)

U.S.	Metric	Ingredients	PROCEDURE
1 tbsp	15 g	Butter	1. Melt the butter in a pan and sweat the shallots until soft.
3½ oz	100 g	Shallots, chopped fine	2. Add the wine and reduce by half, then add the chicken stock and reduce again until syrupy. Strain into a clean pan.
5 oz	150 mL	White wine	
1½ pt	700 mL	Chicken stock	3. Allow to cool slightly before adding the sour cream and the yogurt. Reheat gently and season.
8 oz	250 g	Sour cream	
8 oz	250 g	Yogurt, plain	

Per 1 ounce:
Calories, 45; Protein, 1 g; Fat, 3.5 g (65% cal.); Cholesterol, 10 mg;
Carbohydrates, 2 g; Fiber, 0 g; Sodium, 20 mg.

Sauce Vierge

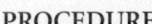

Yield: 1 pt (500 mL)

U.S.	Metric	Ingredients	PROCEDURE
7 oz	200 mL	Olive oil	1. Warm the olive oil.
4 oz	110 mL	Lemon juice	2. Add the lemon juice, garlic, basil, tomatoes, and olives.
2 tsp	7 g	Garlic, chopped	3. Season to taste with salt, pepper, and hot pepper sauce.
1 tbsp	7 g	Basil, chopped	4. Serve warm.
5½ oz	160 g	Tomatoes, peeled, seeded, diced	
2 oz	50 g	Black olives, diced	
to taste	to taste	Salt	
to taste	to taste	Pepper	
to taste	to taste	Hot pepper sauce	

Per 1 ounce:
Calories, 120; Protein, 0 g; Fat, 13 g (94% cal.); Cholesterol, 0 mg;
Carbohydrates, 2 g; Fiber, 0 g; Sodium, 30 mg.

Port Wine Sauce

Yield: 1 pt (500 mL)

U.S.	Metric	Ingredients	PROCEDURE
1 qt 4 oz	1.25 L	Ruby port wine	1. Using a stainless-steel saucepot, reduce the port wine over moderate heat by three-fourths.
4 oz	125 mL	Glace de viande	2. Add the glace de viande.
to taste	to taste	Salt	3. If desired, thicken lightly with a slurry of cornstarch or arrowroot mixed with cold water.
to taste	to taste	White pepper	
as needed	as needed	Cornstarch or arrowroot	4. Season to taste with salt and white pepper.
2 oz	60 g	Butter	5. Just before serving, swirl in the raw butter (monter au beurre).

Per 1 ounce:
Calories, 60; Protein, 1 g; Fat, 3 g (40% cal.); Cholesterol, 10 mg;
Carbohydrates, 4 g; Fiber, 0 g; Sodium, 55 mg.

Applesauce

Yield: about 1 qt (1 L)

U.S.	Metric	Ingredients	PROCEDURE
4 lb	2 kg	Apples (see note)	1. Cut the apples into quarters and remove the cores. Skins may be left on because they will be strained out later. (Red peels will color the sauce pink.) Dice the apples coarsely.
to taste	to taste	Sugar (see step 4)	2. Place the apples in a heavy saucepan with about 2 oz (60 mL) water. Cover.
to taste	to taste	Lemon juice	3. Set the pan over low heat and cook the apples slowly until very soft. Stir occasionally.
			4. Add sugar to taste. The amount needed depends on the sweetness of the apples, but the sauce should be tart, not too sweet.
			5. Add a little lemon juice to taste.
			6. Pass the sauce through a food mill.
			7. If the sauce is too thin or watery, let simmer, uncovered, until thickened.
			8. Serve warm or cold with roast pork or duck.

Per 1 ounce:
Calories, 25; Protein, 0 g; Fat, 0 g (0% cal.); Cholesterol, 0 mg; Carbohydrates, 6 g; Fiber, 1 g; Sodium, 0 mg.

Note: Use tart cooking apples such as Rome. Do not use Red Delicious.

Barbecue Sauce

Yield: ½ gal (2 L)

U.S.	Metric	Ingredients	PROCEDURE
1 qt	1 L	Tomato purée	1. Place all ingredients in a heavy saucepan and bring to a boil. Reduce heat and simmer about 20 minutes, until slightly reduced and flavors are well blended. Stir occasionally during cooking so the sauce does not scorch on the bottom.
1 pt	500 mL	Water	2. Adjust seasoning.
⅔ cup	150 mL	Worcestershire sauce	
½ cup	125 mL	Cider vinegar	
½ cup	125 mL	Vegetable oil	
8 oz	250 g	Onion, chopped fine	
4 tsp	20 mL	Garlic, chopped fine	
2 oz	60 g	Sugar	
1 tbsp	15 mL	Dry mustard	
2 tsp	10 mL	Chili powder	
1 tsp	5 mL	Black pepper	
to taste	to taste	Salt	

Per 1 ounce:
Calories, 25; Protein, 0 g; Fat, 2 g (60% cal.); Cholesterol, 0 mg; Carbohydrates, 3 g; Fiber, 0 g; Sodium, 30 mg.

Note: This sauce is not intended to be eaten as is but to be cooked with other foods. See recipe for Barbecued Spareribs (p. 249) and for Barbecued Pork Sandwich (p. 591).

Chile Barbecue Sauce

Yield: 2½ pt (1.25 L)

U.S.	Metric	Ingredients	PROCEDURE
1½ pt	750 mL	Bottled chili sauce	1. Combine all ingredients in a heavy saucepot. Bring to a boil.
8 oz	250 mL	Soy sauce	2. Simmer 15 minutes.
2 oz	60 g	Dark brown sugar	3. Strain.
1½ oz	45 mL	Worcestershire sauce	4. Adjust the seasoning with salt if necessary. (It is not likely additional salt will be needed; the soy sauce is salty.)
1 pt	500 mL	Water	
6 oz	175 mL	Lemon juice	
1 tbsp	15 mL	Hot red pepper sauce	
2	2	Whole chipotle chiles	
3 tbsp	45 mL	Chile powder	

Per 1 ounce:
Calories, 35; Protein, 1 g; Fat, 0 g (0% cal.); Cholesterol, 0 mg;
Carbohydrates, 8 g; Fiber, 1 g; Sodium, 620 mg.

Soy Barbecue Sauce

Yield: 1 qt (1 L)

U.S.	Metric	Ingredients	PROCEDURE
12 oz	375 mL	Japanese-style soy sauce	1. In a saucepot, combine all ingredients except the oil.
4 oz	125 mL	Brown sugar	2. Bring to a simmer. Reduce by one-third.
8 oz	250 mL	Sake (Japanese rice wine) or dry sherry	3. Strain.
8 oz	250 mL	Water	
6 oz	175 mL	Lemon juice	
2 tbsp	30 mL	Chopped fresh ginger	
1 tbsp	15 mL	Chopped garlic	
8 oz	250 mL	Vegetable oil	4. Add the oil. Before using, mix well to emulsify; this is easily done in a blender.

Per 1 ounce:
Calories, 90; Protein, 1 g; Fat, 7 g (66% cal.); Cholesterol, 0 mg;
Carbohydrates, 5 g; Fiber, 0 g; Sodium, 610 mg.

MISCELLANEOUS COLD SAUCES

Fruit Salsa

Yield: 2 lb (1 kg)

U.S.	Metric	Ingredients	PROCEDURE
8 oz	250 g	Honeydew melon, seeded, rind removed	1. Chop the melon, papaya, mango, bell pepper, and jalapeño pepper into fine dice. Be careful to save the juices that are released.
8 oz	250 g	Papaya, peeled and seeded	2. Combine the chopped fruit, peppers, onion, lime juice, and cilantro in a bowl.
8 oz	250 g	Mango, peeled and pitted	3. Season to taste with salt.
4 oz	125 g	Red bell pepper, cored and seeded	4. Refrigerate until served.
1 oz	30 g	Jalapeño pepper, stemmed and seeded	
3 oz	90 g	Red onion, cut brunoise	
4 oz	125 mL	Lime juice	
2 tbsp	30 mL	Cilantro, chopped	
to taste	to taste	Salt	

Per 1 ounce:
Calories, 15; Protein, 0 g; Fat, 0 g (0% cal.); Cholesterol, 0 mg;
Carbohydrates, 3 g; Fiber, 0 g; Sodium, 0 mg.

Tartar Sauce

Yield: about 1 qt (1 L)

U.S.	Metric	Ingredients	PROCEDURE
4 oz	125 g	Dill pickles or sour gherkins	1. Chop the pickles and onions very fine. Chop the capers if they are large, or leave whole if small.
2 oz	60 g	Onions	
2 oz	60 g	Capers	2. Press the pickles and capers in a fine sieve or squeeze out in a piece of cheesecloth so that they don't make the sauce too liquid.
1 qt	1 L	Mayonnaise	
2 tbsp	30 mL	Chopped parsley	3. Combine all ingredients in a stainless-steel bowl and mix well.

Per 1 ounce:
Calories, 200; Protein, 0 g; Fat, 22 g (98% cal.); Cholesterol, 15 mg;
Carbohydrates, 1 g; Fiber, 0 g; Sodium, 240 mg.

VARIATION

Rémoulade Sauce

Add 1 tbsp (15 mL) anchovy paste or mashed anchovies to tartar sauce.

Aioli I

Yield: about 1 pt 4 oz (600 mL)

U.S.	Metric	Ingredients	PROCEDURE
10 cloves	10 cloves	Garlic	1. Crush the garlic to a fine paste with the salt.
⅛ tsp	0.5 mL	Salt	2. Add the egg yolks and beat until thoroughly combined.
3	3	Egg yolks	3. A few drops at a time, begin adding the olive oil, beating constantly. Do not add the oil any faster than it can be absorbed.
1 pt	500 mL	Olive oil	
1–2 tbsp	15–30 mL	Lemon juice	4. After about half the oil is added, the mixture will be very stiff. Add a few drops of the lemon juice at this point.

5. Continue adding the remaining oil gradually. From time to time, add a few more drops of the lemon juice. The finished aioli should be like a stiff mayonnaise. Adjust the seasoning with additional salt if necessary.

Per 1 ounce:
Calories, 200; Protein, 1 g; Fat, 22 g (99% cal.); Cholesterol, 30 mg;
Carbohydrates, 1 g; Fiber, 0 g; Sodium, 15 mg.

Horseradish Sauce (Sauce Raifort)

Yield: about 1 pt (500 mL)

U.S.	Metric	Ingredients	PROCEDURE
1 cup	250 mL	Heavy cream	1. Whip the cream until stiff, but do not overwhip.
¼ cup	60 mL	Prepared horseradish, drained	2. Mix the horseradish with a little of the whipped cream, then fold into the rest of the cream.
to taste	to taste	Salt	3. Season to taste with salt.

Per 1 ounce:
Calories, 50; Protein, 0 g; Fat, 6 g (93% cal.); Cholesterol, 20 mg;
Carbohydrates, 1 g; Fiber, 0 g; Sodium, 10 mg.

Note: This sauce should be made just before service.

Cocktail Sauce

Yield: 2 qt (2 L)

U.S.	Metric	Ingredients	PROCEDURE
1 qt	1 L	Catsup	1. Combine all ingredients and mix.
2½ cups	600 mL	Chili sauce	2. Chill.
1 cup	250 mL	Prepared horseradish	3. Serve as a dip with shrimp, crab, lobster, raw clams, or raw oysters.
4 oz	125 mL	Lemon juice	
2 tbsp	30 mL	Worcestershire sauce	
dash	dash	Hot red pepper sauce	

Per 1 ounce:
Calories, 30; Protein, 1 g; Fat, 0 g (0% cal.); Cholesterol, 0 mg;
Carbohydrates, 7 g; Fiber, 0 g; Sodium, 330 mg.

Mignonette Sauce

Yield: 1 qt (1 L)

U.S.	Metric	Ingredients	PROCEDURE
1 qt	1 L	Wine vinegar	1. Combine all ingredients.
8 oz	250 g	Shallots, cut brunoise	2. Chill.
1 tsp	5 mL	Salt	3. Serve 1 oz (30 mL) per portion as a cocktail sauce for oysters or clams on the half shell.
1 tsp	5 mL	White pepper	
2 tsp	5 mL	Tarragon	

Per 1 ounce:
Calories, 5; Protein, 0 g; Fat, 0 g (0% cal.); Cholesterol, 0 mg;
Carbohydrates, 1 g; Fiber, 0 g; Sodium, 75 mg.

Lime and Ginger Chutney

Yield: 14 oz (400 g)

U.S.	Metric	Ingredients	PROCEDURE
4	4	Limes	1. Grate the zest of the limes, then peel and segment the limes. Cut each segment into 4 or 5 pieces.
1¾ oz	50 g	Raisins	2. Soak the raisins in the brandy.
1 oz	30 mL	Brandy	3. In a stainless-steel saucepan, combine the grated lime zest, soaked raisins, onions, garlic, ginger, saffron, bay leaf, cloves, white wine vinegar, lemon juice, orange juice, brown sugar, and tomato paste. Simmer until almost dry. Cool.
3½ oz	100 g	Onions, chopped fine	
1 clove	1 clove	Garlic, chopped fine	
1 oz	25 g	Ginger root, grated	4. Add the lime segments and stir in.
small pinch	small pinch	Saffron	5. Serve at once or keep 2–3 weeks in a sterilized jar.
1	1	Bay leaf	
2	2	Cloves	
3½ oz	100 mL	White wine vinegar	
2 oz	60 mL	Lemon juice	
6 oz	175 mL	Orange juice	
2½ oz	75 g	Brown sugar	
1 tsp	5 mL	Tomato paste	

Per 1 ounce:
Calories, 50; Protein, 1 g; Fat, 0 g (0% cal.); Cholesterol, 0 mg;
Carbohydrates, 13 g; Fiber, 1 g; Sodium, 5 mg.

Fig Compote

Yield: 1 lb 4 oz (625 g)

U.S.	Metric	Ingredients	PROCEDURE
1 lb	500 g	Dried figs, preferably light rather than black figs	1. Trim the figs by cutting off the hard stem ends.
4 oz	125 mL	Lemon juice	2. Cut the figs into medium dice.
8 oz	250 mL	Water	3. Combine all ingredients in a saucepan.
2 tbsp	30 mL	Sugar	4. Bring to a boil. Reduce heat and simmer until the liquid has evaporated.
¼ tsp	1 mL	Ground cumin	5. Serve warm or cooled.
¼ tsp	1 mL	Cinnamon	
⅛ tsp	0.5 mL	Ground cloves	
⅛ tsp	0.5 mL	Cayenne	

Per 1 ounce:
Calories, 60; Protein, 1 g; Fat, 0 g (0% cal.); Cholesterol, 0 mg;
Carbohydrates, 17 g; Fiber, 2 g; Sodium, 0 mg.

Terms for Review

stock	glaze	whitewash	small sauce	compound
broth	glace de viande	demiglaze	béchamel	butter
mirepoix	sauce	liaison	velouté	emulsion
sachet	slurry	au sec	espagnole	pan gravy
bouquet garni	roux	deglaze	fond lié	jus
venting	white roux	monter au beurre	clarified butter	au jus
reduction	beurre manié	leading sauce	brown butter	

Questions for Discussion

1. Which bones make a more gelatinous stock, beef or veal?
2. The stockpot is often considered a good way to use trimmings from meats and vegetables. Do you agree? Explain.
3. How should vegetables for mirepoix be cut?
4. Explain the importance of blanching bones before making stocks.
5. Why should stock not be boiled? What about covering the stockpot?
6. Explain the procedure for cooling stock. Why is it important?
7. Why is an understanding of stocks important even if you work in an establishment that uses only bases?
8. You have just prepared a suprême sauce, but your supervisor says it's too thin. It must be served in 5 minutes. What can you do to correct it?
9. What are the two methods for preparing starches so that they can be incorporated into hot liquids? Why are they necessary, and how do they work?
10. Why is it necessary to be able to thicken a sauce with a roux without making lumps, if the sauce is going to be strained anyway?
11. You are preparing a gravy for a batch of Swiss steaks that are to be frozen for later use. What thickening agent will you use?
12. Name the five leading sauces and their major ingredients. List at least two small sauces made from each.
13. What precautions must be taken when finishing and holding allemande sauce?
14. What are the similarities between espagnole and pan gravy? The differences?
15. What precautions are necessary when making hollandaise to avoid overcooking the eggs or curdling the sauce?

chapter 9

Soups

The popularity of soups today may be due to increased nutrition consciousness, to a desire for simpler or lighter meals, or to an increased appreciation of how appetizing and satisfying soups can be. Whatever the reasons, they emphasize the importance of soup-making skills.

If you have already studied the preparation of stocks and sauces in Chapter 8, you now have at your disposal the major techniques for the preparation of soups. You know how to make stocks and how to use thickening agents such as roux and liaison.

In addition, a few other techniques are necessary for you to master before you are able to prepare all the different types of soups that are popular today. As in sauce making, a few basic techniques are the building blocks that you can use to create a wide variety of appetizing soups.

Understanding Soups

Soup, according to the dictionary, is a liquid food derived from meat, poultry, fish, or vegetables. This definition is all right as far as it goes, but there's a lot it doesn't tell us. Is a stock, straight from the stockpot, a soup? Is beef stew liquid enough to be called soup?

We're interested more in production techniques than in definitions. However, a few more definitions are necessary before we can go into the kitchen, so that we can talk to each other in the same language. Definitions aren't rules, so don't be alarmed if you hear other books or chefs use these terms differently. What matters is that you learn the techniques and are able to adapt them to many uses.

Classifications of Soups

Soups can be divided into three basic categories: clear or unthickened soups, thick soups, and special soups that don't fit the first two categories.

Most of these soups, no matter what their final ingredients may be, are based on stock. Thus, the quality of the soup depends on the stock-making skills discussed in Chapter 8.

CLEAR SOUPS

These soups are all based on a clear, unthickened broth or stock. They may be served plain or garnished with a variety of vegetables and meats.

1. *Broth* and *bouillon* are two terms used in many ways but, in general, they both refer to simple, clear soups without solid ingredients. We have already defined broth (Chapter 8) as a flavorful liquid obtained from the simmering of meats and/or vegetables.

   Broth is usually a byproduct of simmering meat or poultry. The recipes for Simmered Fresh Beef Brisket (p. 280) and for "Boiled" Fowl (p. 338) produce not only the cooked meat or poultry but also flavorful broths that can be served as soups when properly seasoned and garnished.

   To prepare a brown meat broth, follow the procedure in the recipe for Simmered Fresh Beef Brisket, but first brown the meat and mirepoix well before adding water. Flavorful cuts such as beef shank, chuck, or neck are good for making broths.

2. *Vegetable soup* is a clear, seasoned stock or broth with the addition of one or more vegetables and, sometimes, meat or poultry products and starches.

3. *Consommé* is a rich, flavorful stock or broth that has been clarified to make it perfectly clear and transparent. The process of clarification is a technique that we study in detail.

   Far from being just a plain old cup of broth, a well-made consommé is one of the greatest of all soups. Its sparkling clarity is a delight to the eye, and its rich, full flavor, strength, and body make it a perfect starter for an elegant dinner.

THICK SOUPS

Unlike clear soups, thick soups are opaque rather than transparent. They are thickened either by adding a thickening agent such as a roux, or by puréeing one or more of their ingredients to provide a heavier consistency.

1. *Cream soups* are soups that are thickened with roux, beurre manié, liaison, or other added thickening agents, plus milk and/or cream. They are similar to velouté and béchamel sauces—in fact, they may be made by diluting and flavoring either of these two leading sauces.

   Cream soups are usually named after their major ingredient, such as cream of chicken or cream of asparagus.

2. *Purées* are soups that are naturally thickened by puréeing one or more of their ingredients. They are not as smooth and creamy as cream soups.

After reading this chapter, you should be able to

1. Describe three basic categories of soups.

2. Identify standard appetizer and main course portion sizes for soups.

3. State the procedures for holding soups for service and for serving soups at the proper temperatures.

4. List three groups of soup garnishes.

5. Prepare clarified consommé.

6. Prepare vegetable soups and other clear soups.

7. Prepare cream soups.

8. Prepare purée soups.

9. Prepare bisques, chowders, specialty soups, and national soups.

Purées are normally based on starchy ingredients. They may be made from dried legumes (such as split pea soup) or from fresh vegetables with a starchy ingredient such as potatoes or rice added. Purées may or may not contain milk or cream.

3. *Bisques* are thickened soups made from shellfish. They are usually prepared like cream soups and are almost always finished with cream.

The term *bisque* is sometimes used on menus for a variety of vegetable soups. In these cases, it is really a marketing term rather than a technical term, so it is impossible to give a definition that covers all uses.

4. *Chowders* are hearty soups made from fish, shellfish, and/or vegetables. Although they are made in many ways, they usually contain milk and potatoes.

5. *Potage* is a term sometimes associated with certain thick, hearty soups, but it is actually a general term for soup. A clear soup is called a *potage clair* in French.

SPECIALTY AND NATIONAL SOUPS

This is a catch-all category that includes soups that don't fit well into the main categories and soups that are native to particular countries or regions.

Specialty soups are distinguished by unusual ingredients or methods, such as turtle soup, gumbo, peanut soup, and cold fruit soup.

Cold soups are sometimes considered specialty soups and, in fact, some of them are. But many other popular cold soups, such as jellied consommé, cold cream of cucumber soup, and vichyssoise (vee shee swahz) are simply cold versions of basic clear and thick soups.

VEGETARIAN SOUPS AND LOW-FAT SOUPS

A great variety of vegetable-based soups are suitable for vegetarian menus. To plan vegetarian menus, review the categories of vegetarianism discussed on pages 104-105. Vegetable soups for vegans must contain no meat or any other animal product and must be made with water or vegetable stock. To bind thick soups, use a starch slurry or a roux made with oil rather than butter. Lacto-vegetarians, on the other hand, accept soups containing butter, milk, or cream.

Because the appeal of vegetarian vegetable soups depends entirely on the freshness and the quality of the vegetables and not on the richness of meat stocks, be especially careful to use high-quality ingredients and to avoid overcooking.

Clear soups are especially suitable for people seeking low-fat foods. Consommés and clear vegetable soups are virtually fat-free, especially if the vegetables have not been sweated in fat before being simmered.

Thick soups can be kept low in fat by thickening them with a slurry of starch (such as arrowroot, potato starch, or cornstarch) and cold water rather than with a roux. For cream soups, reduce or omit the cream and instead use evaporated skim milk. Purée soups are usually more adaptable than cream soups to low-fat diets because the vegetable purée adds body and richness to the soup without requiring added fat. A little yogurt or evaporated skim milk can be used to give creaminess to a purée soup. Even garnishing a serving of soup with a teaspoonful of whipped cream gives a feeling of richness while adding only a gram or two of fat.

Service of Soups

STANDARD PORTION SIZES

Appetizer portion: 6 to 8 oz (200 to 250 mL)
Main course portion: 10 to 12 oz (300 to 350 mL)

TEMPERATURE

Serve hot soups hot, in hot cups or bowls.
Serve cold soups cold, in chilled bowls, or even nested in a larger bowl of crushed ice.

HOLDING FOR SERVICE

Strangely enough, some chefs who take the greatest care not to overcook meats or vegetables nevertheless keep a large kettle of soup on the steam table all day. You can imagine what a vegetable soup is like after 4 or 5 hours at these temperatures.

1. Small-batch cooking applies to soups as well as to other foods. Heat small batches frequently to replenish the steam table with fresh soup.

2. Consommés and some other clear soups can be kept hot for longer periods if the vegetable garnish is heated separately and added at service time.

GARNISH

Soup garnishes may be divided into three groups.

1. **Garnishes in the soup.**
    Major ingredients, such as the vegetables in clear vegetable soup, are often considered as garnishes. This group of garnishes also includes meats, poultry, seafood, pasta products, and grains such as barley or rice. They are treated as part of the preparation or recipe itself, not as something added on.

    Consommés are generally named after their garnish, such as consommé brunoise, which contains vegetables cut into brunoise shape (⅛-inch dice).

    Vegetable cream soups are usually garnished with carefully cut pieces of the vegetable from which they are made.

    An elegant way to serve soup with a solid garnish is to arrange the garnish attractively in the bottom of a heated soup plate. This plate is set before the diner, then the soup is ladled from a tureen by the dining room staff.

2. **Toppings.**
    Clear soups are generally served without toppings, to let the attractiveness of the clear broth and the carefully cut vegetables speak for themselves. Occasional exceptions are toppings of chopped parsley or chives.

    Thick soups, especially those that are all one color, are often decorated with a topping. Toppings should be placed on just before service so that they won't sink or lose their fresh appearance. Their flavors must be appropriate to the soup.

    Do not overdo soup toppings. The food should be attractive in itself.

    Topping suggestions for thick soups:

    > Fresh herbs (parsley, chives), chopped
    > Sliced almonds, toasted
    > Grated cheese
    > Sieved egg yolks
    > Chopped or riced egg whites
    > Croutons
    > Grated parmesan cheese
    > Crumbled bacon
    > Paprika
    > Sour cream or whipped cream

3. **Accompaniments.**
    In North America, soups are traditionally served with crackers. In addition to the usual saltines, other suggestions for crisp accompaniments are:

    > Melba toast
    > Corn chips
    > Breadsticks
    > Cheese straws
    > Profiteroles (tiny unsweetened cream puff shells)
    > Whole-grain wafers

Clear Soups

Consommé

When we define consommé as a clarified stock or broth, we are forgetting the most important part of the definition. The word *consommé* means, literally, "completed" or "concentrated." In other words, a consommé is a strong, concentrated stock or broth. In classical cuisine, this was all that was necessary for a stock to be called a consommé. In fact, two kinds were recognized: ordinary (or unclarified) consommé and clarified consommé.

Rule number one for preparing consommé is that the stock or broth must be strong, rich, and full-flavored. Clarification is second in importance to strength. A good consommé, with a mellow but full aroma and plenty of body (from the natural gelatin) that you can feel in your mouth, is one of the great pleasures of fine cuisine. But clarification is an expensive and time-consuming procedure, and, quite frankly, it's not worth the trouble if the soup is thin and watery.

HOW CLARIFICATION WORKS

Coagulation of proteins was an important subject in our discussion of stock making because one of our major concerns was how to keep coagulated proteins from making the stock cloudy. Strangely enough, this same process of coagulation enables us to clarify stocks to perfect transparency.

Remember that some proteins, especially those called albumins, dissolve in cold water. When the water is heated, they gradually solidify or coagulate and rise to the surface. If we control this process carefully, these proteins collect all the tiny particles that cloud a stock and carry them to the surface. The stock is then left perfectly clear.

If, on the other hand, we are not careful, these proteins break up as they coagulate and cloud the liquid even more, just as they can do when we make stock.

BASIC INGREDIENTS

The mixture of ingredients we use to clarify a stock is called the *clearmeat* or the *clarification*.

1. *Lean ground meat* is one of the major sources of protein that enables the clearmeat to do its job. It also contributes flavor to the consommé. The meat must be lean because fat is undesirable in a consommé. Beef shank, also called shin beef, is the most desirable meat because it is high in albumin proteins as well as in flavor and in gelatin, and it is very lean.

   Beef and/or chicken meat are used to clarify chicken consommé. Meat is not used, obviously, to make fish consommé. Ground lean fish may be used, but it is normal to omit flesh altogether and use only egg whites.

2. *Egg whites* are included in the clearmeat because, being mostly albumin, they greatly strengthen its clarifying power.

3. *Mirepoix* and other seasoning and flavoring ingredients are usually included because they add flavor to the finished consommé. They do not actually help in the clarification, except possibly to give solidity to the raft. The *raft* is the coagulated clearmeat, floating in a solid mass on top of the consommé.

   The mirepoix must be cut into fine pieces so that it will float with the raft.

   A large amount of a particular vegetable may be added if a special flavor is desired, as in, for example, essence of celery consommé.

4. *Acid ingredients* (tomato products for beef or chicken consommé, lemon juice or white wine for fish consommé) are often added because the acidity helps coagulate the protein. They are not absolutely necessary—the heat will coagulate the protein anyway—but many chefs like to use them.

Procedure for Preparing Consommé

1. Start with a well-flavored, cold, strong stock or broth.

   If your stock is weak, reduce it until it is concentrated enough, then cool it before proceeding, or plan on simmering the consommé longer to reduce while clarifying.

2. Select a heavy stockpot or soup pot, preferably one with a spigot at the bottom. The spigot enables you to drain off the finished consommé without disturbing the raft.

3. Combine the clearmeat ingredients in the soup pot and mix them vigorously.

4. Optional step: Mix in a small amount of cold water or stock—about 4 to 8 oz per pound (250 to 500 mL per kg) of meat—and let stand 30 to 60 minutes. This allows more opportunity for the proteins that do the clarifying to dissolve out of the meat.

   Note: Chefs disagree on the importance of this step. Some let the mixture stand overnight in the refrigerator. Others skip this step altogether. Check with your instructor.

5. Gradually add the cold, degreased stock and mix well with the clearmeat.

   The stock must be cold so that it doesn't cook the proteins on contact.

   Mixing distributes the dissolved proteins throughout the stock so that they can collect all the impurities more easily.

6. Set the pot over a moderately low fire and let it come to a simmer very slowly.

7. Stir the contents occasionally so that the clearmeat circulates throughout the stock and doesn't burn to the bottom.

8. When the simmering point is approaching, stop stirring. The clearmeat will rise to the surface and form a raft.

9. Move to lower heat so that the liquid maintains a slow simmer. Do not cover. Boiling would break up the raft and cloud the consommé. The same principle operates in stock making.

10. Let simmer 1½ hours without disturbing the raft.

11. Strain the consommé through a china cap lined with several layers of cheesecloth.

    If you are not using a stockpot with a spigot, ladle the consommé out carefully without breaking up the raft.

    Let the liquid drain through the cheesecloth by gravity. Do not force it, or fine particles will pass through and cloud the consommé.

12. Degrease.

    Remove all traces of fat from the surface. Strips of clean brown paper passed across the surface are effective in absorbing every last speck of fat without absorbing much consommé.

13. Adjust the seasonings.

    Kosher salt is preferred to regular table salt because it has no impurities or additives that could cloud the stock.

Emergency Procedures

1. **Clarifying hot stock.**

   If you do not have time to cool the stock properly before clarifying, at least cool it as much as you can. Even 10 minutes in a cold-water bath helps. Then, mix ice cubes or crushed ice with the clearmeat. This will help keep it from coagulating when the hot stock hits it. Proceed as in the basic method.

   Finally, review your production planning so that you can avoid this emergency in the future.

2. **Clarifying without meat.**

   In a pinch, you can clarify a stock with egg whites alone. Use at least 3 or 4 egg whites per gallon (4 liters) of stock, plus mirepoix if possible. Great care is necessary because the raft will be fragile and easily broken up.

   Egg whites and mirepoix alone are often used for clarifying fish stocks.

3. **Failed clarification.**

   If the clarification fails because you let it boil, or for some other reason, it can still be rescued, even if there is no time for another complete clarification.

   Strain the consommé, cool it as much as you can, then slowly add it to a mixture of ice cubes and egg whites. Carefully return to a simmer as in the basic method and proceed with the clarification.

   This should be done in emergencies only. The ice cubes dilute the consommé, and the egg white clarification is risky.

4. **Poor color.**

   Beef or veal consommé, made from brown stock, should have an amber color. It is not dark brown like canned consommé. Chicken consommé is a very pale amber.

   It is possible to correct a pale consommé by adding a few drops of caramel color to the finished soup. But for best results, check the color of the stock before clarification. If it is too pale, cut an onion in half and place it cut side down on a flattop range until it is black, or char it under a broiler. Add this to the clearmeat. The caramelized sugar of the onion will color the stock.

Consommé

Yield: 1 gal (4 L) **Portions:** 16 **Portion size:** 8 oz (250 mL)
  20 6 oz (200 mL)

U.S.	Metric	Ingredients	PROCEDURE
1 lb	500 g	Lean beef, preferably shin, ground	1. Review the information on preparing consommé, page 174.
		Mirepoix, chopped into small pieces:	2. Combine the beef, mirepoix, egg whites, tomatoes, herbs, and spices in a tall, heavy stockpot. Mix the ingredients vigorously with a wooden paddle or a heavy whip.
8 oz	250 g	Onion	
4 oz	125 g	Celery	
4 oz	125 g	Carrot	
8 oz	250 g	Egg whites	
8 oz	250 g	Canned tomatoes, crushed	
6–8	6–8	Parsley stems, chopped	
pinch	pinch	Thyme	
1	1	Bay leaf	
2	2	Whole cloves	
½ tsp	2 mL	Peppercorns, crushed	
5 qt	5 L	Cold beef or veal stock (brown or white)	3. Add about 1 pint (500 mL) cold stock and stir well. Let stand about 30 minutes. (Optional step: see p. 174 for explanation.)
			4. Gradually stir in the remaining stock. Be sure the stock is well mixed with the other ingredients.
			5. Set the pot on moderately low heat and let it come to a simmer very slowly. Stir occasionally.
			6. When the simmering point is approaching, stop stirring.
			7. Move the pot to lower heat and simmer very slowly for about 1½ hours. Do not stir or disturb the raft that forms on top.
			8. Very carefully strain the consommé through a china cap lined with several layers of cheesecloth.
			9. Degrease thoroughly.
			10. Season to taste.

Per serving:
Calories, 30; Protein, 3 g; Fat, 1 g (31% cal.); Cholesterol, 15 mg; Carbohydrates, 2 g; Fiber, 0 g; Sodium, 75 mg.

VARIATIONS

Double Consommé
Use twice the quantity of beef in the basic recipe. Add 8 oz (250 g) leeks to the mirepoix.

Chicken Consommé
Use chicken stock instead of beef or veal stock. Add to the clearmeat 8 oz (250 g) chicken trimmings (such as wing tips and necks) that have been chopped and browned in a hot oven. Omit tomato and add 1 oz (30 mL) lemon juice.

Cold Jellied Consommé
Unflavored gelatin must often be added to consommé to make jellied consommé. The amount needed depends on the strength of the stock and on the amount of jelling desired. Classically, a chilled consommé is only half jelled, more like a thick syrup. Some people, however, prefer a gelatin content high enough to solidify the consommé. In the following guidelines, use the lower quantity of gelatin for a partially jelled soup, the higher quantity for a fully jelled soup. Also, for tomatoed consommé (madrilène), increase the gelatin slightly because the acidity of the tomatoes weakens the gelatin.

1. If the stock is thin when cold, add 1–2 oz (30–60 g) gelatin per gallon (4 L).
2. If the stock is slightly jelled and syrupy when cold, add ½–1 oz (15–30 g) gelatin per gallon (4 L).
3. If the stock is jelled when cold, no gelatin is needed. Add up to ½ oz (15 g) per gallon (4 L) if a firmer texture is desired.

Gelatin may be added to the clearmeat (in step 2 of the recipe). This is the best method because there is no danger of clouding the consommé. It may also be added to the finished consommé after softening it in cold water. See page 566 for instructions on the use of gelatin.

Consommé Madrilène
Increase the tomatoes in the basic recipe to 24 oz (750 g). Use beef, veal, or chicken stock. Serve hot or jellied.

Essence of Celery Consommé
Increase the celery in the basic recipe to 1 lb (500 g).

Consommé au Porto
Flavor the finished consommé with 6–8 oz (200–250 mL) port wine per gallon (4 L).

Consommé au Sherry
Flavor the finished consommé with 6–8 oz (200–250 mL) sherry wine per gallon (4 L).

Garnished Consommés

For the following consommés, prepare and cook the garnish separately. At service time, add 1–2 tablespoons (15–30 mL) of the garnish to each portion. See page 115 for description of cuts.

Consommé Brunoise

Onion or leek, carrot, celery, and turnip (optional), cut brunoise. Sweat lightly in butter and simmer in a little consommé until tender.

Consommé Julienne

Onion or leek, carrot, and celery, cut julienne. Prepare like brunoise garnish.

Consommé Printanière

Small dice of spring vegetables: carrot, turnip, celery, green beans. Prepare like brunoise garnish.

Consommé Paysanne

Thin slices of leeks, carrots, celery, turnip, and cabbage. Prepare like brunoise garnish.

Consommé with Pearl Tapioca

Cooked pearl tapioca.

Consommé Vermicelli

Cooked broken vermicelli (very thin spaghetti).

Chicken and Celery Consommé

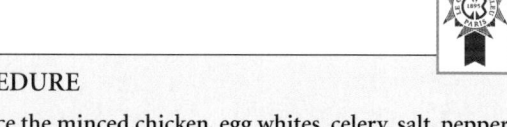

Yield: 1 gal (4 L)   **Portions:** 16   **Portion size:** 8 oz (250 mL)

U.S.	Metric	Ingredients	PROCEDURE
2 lb 12 oz	1.2 kg	Chicken leg meat, minced	1. Place the minced chicken, egg whites, celery, salt, pepper, and herbs in a saucepot.
12	12	Egg whites	
1 lb 6 oz	600 g	Celery, cut as for mirepoix	2. Stir in the stock and bring to simmering point over a moderate heat. Stir occasionally, paying particular attention to possible sticking or scorching of the ingredients on the base of the pot.
½ oz	15 g	Salt	
½ oz	15 g	Black peppercorns, crushed	
3	3	Thyme sprigs	3. Stop stirring as simmering point is approaching and simmer very gently without disturbing for 30 minutes.
2	2	Bay leaves	
20	20	Parsley stems	4. Strain the consommé through a china cap lined with several layers of cheesecloth. Skim and degrease thoroughly. Transfer to a clean pot.
5½ qt	5.5 L	Chicken stock	
10 oz	300 g	Chicken breast	5. Poach the chicken breast in chicken stock for 10 minutes. Cool in the stock to retain juiciness, then cut into cubes.
as needed	as needed	Chicken stock	
6 oz	180 g	Celery, cut julienne	6. At service time, reheat the soup and ladle into warm bowls. Sprinkle each portion with cubed chicken and the julienne of celery.

Per serving:
Calories, 35; Protein, 4 g; Fat, 1 g (27% cal.); Cholesterol, 15 mg;
Carbohydrates, 2 g; Fiber, 0 g; Sodium, 460 mg.

Vegetable Soups

Clear vegetable soups are made from a clear stock or broth, not necessarily clarified, with the addition of one or more vegetables and, sometimes, meat or poultry and/or pasta or grains. Most vegetable soups are made from meat or poultry stock or broth. Meatless or vegetarian soups are made from vegetable broth or water.

Guidelines for Preparing Vegetable Soups

Procedures for making these soups are not complicated. Most of them are made simply by simmering vegetables in stock until done. But care and attention to details are still necessary for producing a high-quality soup.

1. **Start with a clear, flavorful stock or broth.**
   This is one reason it's important to be able to make stocks that are clear, not cloudy.

2. **Select vegetables and other ingredients whose flavors go well together.**
   Don't just throw in everything you've got. Judgment, combined with experience, must be used to create a pleasing combination. Five or six vegetables are usually enough. More than that often makes a jumble.

3. **Cut vegetables uniformly.**
   Neat, careful cutting means uniform cooking and attractive appearance. Sizes of cuts are important, too. Pieces should be large enough to be identifiable but small enough to eat conveniently with a spoon.

4. **Cooking vegetables slowly in a little butter before combining with liquid improves their flavor and gives the soup a mellower, richer taste.**

5. **Cook starches such as grains and pasta separately and add to the soup later.**
   Cooking them in the soup makes it cloudy. Potatoes are sometimes cooked directly in the soup, but they should be rinsed of excess starch after cutting if you want to keep the soup as clear as possible.

6. **Observe differences in cooking times.**
   Add long-cooking vegetables first, short-cooking vegetables near the end. Some vegetables, like tomatoes, need be added to the hot soup only after it is removed from the fire.

7. **Don't overcook.**
   Some cooks feel that soups must be simmered a long time to extract flavors into the liquid. But you should already have done this when you made the stock! Vegetables in soup should be no more overcooked than vegetable side dishes, especially as the soup will probably spend a longer time in the steam table.

Clear Vegetable Soup

Yield: 6 qt (6 L)   Portions: 24   Portion size: 8 oz (250 mL)

U.S.	Metric	Ingredients	PROCEDURE
4 oz	125 g	Butter or chicken fat	1. Heat the butter in a heavy saucepot over medium-low heat.
1½ lb	750 g	Onions, small dice	2. Add the onions, carrots, celery, and turnip. Sweat the vegetables in the butter over low heat until they are about half cooked. Do not let them brown.
1 lb	500 g	Carrots, small dice	
1 lb	500 g	Celery, small dice	
12 oz	375 g	Turnip, small dice	
6 qt	6 L	Chicken stock	3. Add the stock. Bring to a boil and skim carefully. Simmer until vegetables are just barely tender.
1 lb	500 g	Drained canned tomatoes, coarsely chopped	4. Add the tomatoes and simmer another 5 minutes.
to taste	to taste	Salt	5. Degrease the soup and season with salt and white pepper.
to taste	to taste	White pepper	
12 oz	375 g	Frozen peas, thawed	6. Just before serving, add the peas.

Per serving:
Calories, 80; Protein, 3 g; Fat, 4.5 g (46% cal.); Cholesterol, 15 mg;
Carbohydrates, 9 g; Fiber, 2 g; Sodium, 125 mg.

VARIATIONS

Other vegetables may be used in addition to or in place of one or more of the vegetables in the basic recipe.

Add with the vegetables sweated in butter:

Leeks   Green cabbage
Rutabagas   Parsnips

Add to the simmering soup, timing the addition so that all the vegetables are done at the same time:

Potatoes   Lima beans
Green beans   Corn

Other cuts may be used for the vegetables instead of small dice, such as batonnet, julienne, or paysanne (see p. 115).

Vegetable Rice Soup

Add 1½–2 cups (350–500 mL) cooked rice to the finished soup.

Chicken Vegetable Rice Soup

Add 12 oz (375 g) cooked, diced chicken to vegetable rice soup.

Vegetable Beef Soup

Use beef stock instead of chicken stock. Add 12 oz (375 g) cooked, diced beef when the tomatoes are added. Also, add the juice from the tomatoes.

Vegetable Beef Barley Soup

Add 1½–2 cups (350–500 mL) cooked barley to vegetable beef soup.

Clear Vegetable Soup with Cranberry Beans

Piquant Vegetable Soup with Chickpeas

Yield: 6 qt (6 L)   Portions: 24   Portion size: 8 oz (250 mL)

U.S.	Metric	Ingredients	PROCEDURE
2 oz	60 mL	Vegetable oil	1. Heat the oil in a soup pot over moderate heat.
1¼ lb	625 g	Red onion, small dice	2. Add the onion, garlic, bell pepper, and green chile.
1 tbsp	15 mL	Garlic, chopped	Sweat the vegetables in the oil over low heat until they
1 lb	500 g	Green bell pepper, small dice	are about half cooked. Do not let them brown.
2–4 oz	60–125 g	Jalapeño or other green chile, cut brunoise	
5 qt	5 L	Chicken stock or vegetable stock	3. Add the stock. Bring to a boil and skim carefully. Simmer until the vegetables are just barely tender.
1¼ lb	625 g	Tomatoes, peeled, seeded, and chopped	4. Add the tomatoes, chickpeas, and corn. Simmer another 5 minutes.
1¼ lb	625 g	Cooked chickpeas	5. Shortly before serving, add the cooked green beans.
8 oz	250 g	Corn kernels, frozen or fresh	(The beans should be cooked separately and added at
8 oz	250 g	Green beans, cooked until just tender and cut into ½-inch (1-cm) pieces	the end so that their color won't be destroyed by the acidity of the tomatoes.)
to taste	to taste	Salt	6. Add salt and white pepper to taste.
to taste	to taste	White pepper	
to taste	to taste	Hot red pepper sauce (optional)	
		Garnish:	7. To serve, ladle a portion into soup plates and sprinkle with grated cheese and a little chopped cilantro.
12 oz	375 g	Grated cheddar cheese	
⅓ cup	75 mL	Chopped cilantro or whole cilantro leaves	

Per serving:
Calories, 160; Protein, 8 g; Fat, 8 g (45% cal.); Cholesterol, 20 mg;
Carbohydrates, 14 g; Fiber, 3 g; Sodium, 105 mg.

VARIATION

Piquant Vegetable Soup with Roasted Garlic

Roast 1 head of garlic, as explained on page 474. Separate and peel the cloves. Add them to the soup in step 4.

 ## Mushroom Barley Soup

Yield: 6 qt (6 L)   Portions: 24   Portion size: 8 oz (250 mL)

U.S.	Metric	Ingredients	PROCEDURE
8 oz	250 g	Barley	1. Cook the barley in boiling water until tender. Drain.
10 oz	300 g	Onion, cut brunoise	2. In a heavy saucepot or stockpot, sweat the vegetables
5 oz	150 g	Carrot, cut brunoise	in the fat until they are about half cooked. Do not let
5 oz	150 g	White turnip, cut brunoise	them brown.
2 oz	60 g	Butter or chicken fat	3. Add the chicken stock. Bring to a boil. Reduce heat
5 qt	5 L	Chicken stock	and simmer until the vegetables are just tender.
2 lb	1 kg	Mushrooms, diced	4. While the soup is simmering, sauté the mushrooms briefly in fat without letting them brown.
4 oz	125 g	Butter or chicken fat	5. Add the mushrooms and the drained, cooked barley
to taste	to taste	Salt	to the soup. Simmer another 5 minutes.
to taste	to taste	White pepper	6. Degrease the soup. Season to taste with salt and pepper.

Per serving:
Calories, 60; Protein, 3 g; Fat, 1 g (15% cal.); Cholesterol, 20 mg;
Carbohydrates, 10 g; Fiber, 3 g; Sodium, 75 mg.

Other Clear Soups

In addition to vegetable soups, many other clear or unthickened soups are known to various cuisines. They range from simple broths to elaborate concoctions of meats, vegetables, starches, and other ingredients. Although many contain vegetables, we don't classify them as vegetable soups because other ingredients are generally more prominent.

Chicken Noodle Soup

Yield: 6 qt (6 L)   **Portions:** 24   **Portion size:** 8 oz (250 mL)

U.S.	Metric	Ingredients	PROCEDURE
10 oz	300 g	Egg noodles	1. Cook the noodles in boiling, salted water. (See procedure for cooking pasta, p. 515.) Drain and rinse in cold water.
10 oz	300 g	Cooked chicken meat	2. Cut the chicken into small dice.
6 qt	6 L	Chicken stock	3. Bring the stock to a simmer. Season to taste with salt and white pepper. If stock doesn't have enough flavor, add more stock and reduce to concentrate the flavor.
to taste	to taste	Salt	
to taste	to taste	White pepper	4. Just before service, add the chicken and noodles to the stock. Let them heat through before serving.
as desired	as desired	Chopped parsley	5. Garnish each portion with a little chopped parsley.

Per serving:
Calories, 70; Protein, 6 g; Fat, 1.5 g (21% cal.); Cholesterol, 25 mg; Carbohydrates, 7 g; Fiber, 0 g; Sodium, 20 mg.

Note: See poultry chapter (p. 338) for preparing "boiled" chicken and broth for use in soups. Other leftover cooked chicken may also be used.

VARIATIONS

Beef Noodle Soup
Prepare as in basic recipe, using beef and beef stock.

Chicken or Beef Noodle Soup with Vegetables
Before adding the chicken and noodles, simmer 10 oz (300 g) diced carrots and 5 oz (150 g) diced celery in the stock until tender.

Chicken Tomato Bouillon with Pesto

Yield: 6 qt (6 L)   **Portions:** 24   **Portion size:** 8 oz (250 mL)

U.S.	Metric	Ingredients	PROCEDURE
6 qt	6 L	Chicken stock	1. Place the stock, juice, celery, onion, basil, and thyme in a saucepot. Bring to a boil.
2 qt	2 L	Tomato juice	
8 oz	250 g	Celery, chopped	2. Simmer about 45 minutes, until vegetables are soft and flavors are well blended.
8 oz	250 g	Onion, chopped	
1½ tsp	7 mL	Basil	3. Strain and season with salt, pepper, and a pinch of sugar.
½ tsp	2 mL	Thyme	
to taste	to taste	Salt	
to taste	to taste	Pepper	
pinch	pinch	Sugar	
12 oz	375 mL	Pesto (p. 520) thinned with olive oil	4. Garnish each portion with 1 tablespoon (15 mL) pesto lightly swirled into the soup.

Per serving:
Calories, 210; Protein, 3 g; Fat, 21 g (87% cal.); Cholesterol, 10 mg; Carbohydrates, 4 g; Fiber, 1 g; Sodium, 410 mg.

VARIATIONS

Chicken Tomato Bouillon with Rice
Add 2 cups (500 mL) cooked rice at service time.

Cold Chicken Tomato Bouillon
Chill the soup and add a few drops of lemon juice to taste. Serve each portion with a spoonful of sour cream.

Chicken Tomato Bouillon with Pesto

Brunswick Soup

Yield: 6 qt (6 L)   **Portions:** 24   **Portion size:** 8 oz (250 mL)

U.S.	Metric	Ingredients	PROCEDURE
10 oz	300 g	Onions, small dice	1. In a heavy pot, sweat the onions in the butter until about half cooked. Do not brown.
1 oz	30 g	Butter or oil	
5 qt	5 L	Chicken stock	2. Add the chicken stock and bring to a boil. Simmer about 10 minutes.
1¼ lb	600 g	Tomato concassé	3. Add the remaining vegetables and the chicken. Simmer until the vegetables are tender, about 10–15 minutes.
1¼ lb	600 g	Lima beans, frozen	
1¼ lb	600 g	Okra, fresh or frozen, cut in ¼-in. (½-cm) pieces	4. Season to taste with salt and white pepper.
1 lb	475 g	Corn, frozen	
1¼ lb	600 g	Cooked chicken meat and giblets, small dice	

Per serving:
Calories, 120; Protein, 10 g; Fat, 3 g (23% cal.); Cholesterol, 40 mg; Carbohydrates, 13 g; Fiber, 3 g; Sodium, 45 mg.

Oxtail Soup

Yield: 6 qt (6 L)   **Portions:** 24   **Portion size:** 8 oz (250 mL)

U.S.	Metric	Ingredients	PROCEDURE
6 lb	2.7 kg	Oxtails	1. Using a heavy chef's knife, cut the oxtails into sections at the joints.
		Mirepoix:	2. Place the oxtails in a bake pan and brown in a 450°F (230°C) oven. When they are partially browned, add the mirepoix to the pan and brown it along with the oxtails.
10 oz	300 g	Onion, medium dice	
5 oz	150 g	Carrot, medium dice	
5 oz	150 g	Celery, medium dice	3. Place the oxtails and mirepoix in a stockpot with the stock.
6 qt	6 L	Brown stock (see note)	4. Pour off the fat from the pan in which the meat was browned. Deglaze the pan with a little of the stock and add this to the stockpot.
		Sachet:	
1	1	Bay leaf	5. Bring to a boil. Reduce heat to a simmer and skim well. Add the sachet.
pinch	pinch	Thyme	
6	6	Peppercorns	6. Simmer until the meat is tender, about 3 hours. Add a little water if necessary during cooking to keep the meat completely covered.
2	2	Whole cloves	
1 clove	1 clove	Garlic	7. Remove the pieces of oxtail from the broth. Trim the meat off the bones and dice it. Place it in a small pan with a little of the broth. Keep warm if the soup is to be finished immediately, or chill for later use.
1¼ lb	600 g	Carrots, small dice	8. Strain the broth. Degrease carefully.
1¼ lb	600 g	White turnip, small dice	9. Sweat the carrots, turnips, and leeks in the butter until about half cooked.
10 oz	300 g	Leeks, white part only, cut julienne	
4 oz	125 g	Butter	10. Add the broth. Simmer until vegetables are tender.
10 oz	300 g	Tomatoes (canned), drained, coarsely chopped	11. Add the tomatoes and the reserved oxtail meat. Simmer another minute.
2 oz	60 mL	Sherry (optional)	12. Add the sherry, if desired. Season to taste with salt and pepper.
to taste	to taste	Salt	
to taste	to taste	Pepper	

Per serving:
Calories, 240; Protein, 24 g; Fat, 11 g (45% cal.); Cholesterol, 90 mg; Carbohydrates, 6 g; Fiber, 2 g; Sodium, 220 mg.

Note: Water is sometimes used instead of stock. If this is done, brown 4–5 lb (about 2 kg) beef or veal bones with the oxtails and simmer in the soup with them. Double the quantity of mirepoix.

VARIATION

Oxtail soup is often clarified. Chill the broth after step 7 and clarify like consommé. See page 174 for procedure.

Asian-Style Shrimp Soup with Egg Flowers

Yield: 3 qt (3 L)   Portions: 12   Portion size: 8 oz (250 mL)

U.S.	Metric	Ingredients	PROCEDURE
3 lb 4 oz	1.5 kg	Small shrimp	1. Using a pestle and mortar, crush the whole shrimp and crab shells.
3 lb 4 oz	1.5 kg	Crab shells (see note)	
1 lb	450 g	Onion, peeled and chopped	2. Heat the sesame oil in a brazier over medium heat. Add the shrimp, crab shells, onion, celery, garlic, and red pepper. Fry until golden, stirring.
10 oz	300 g	Celery stalks, medium dice	
1	1	Garlic head, cut in half horizontally	
7 oz	190 g	Red bell pepper, seeded, medium dice	3. Add the peppercorns, sea salt, ginger root, and lemongrass to the pot and mix well. Pour in the chicken stock, stir, and bring to a boil. Cook at a low simmer, uncovered, for 1 hour. Cool and refrigerate overnight if you want to develop a stronger flavor.
2 oz	60 mL	Oriental sesame oil	
1 oz	30 g	Black peppercorns, coarsely crushed	
1 oz	30 g	Sea salt	
2½ oz	75 g	Fresh ginger root, peeled, fine dice	4. Strain the stock into a clean saucepot. Heat the stock until warm, not hot.
6	6	Lemongrass stalks, roughly chopped	
4½ qt	4.5 L	Chicken stock	
7 oz	190 g	Red bell pepper, small dice	5. In a food processor or blender, blend together the red pepper, chicken meat, lemongrass, dill stems, kaffir lime leaf, star anise, tomato paste, and saffron threads. Add the egg whites and mix in well.
10 oz	300 g	Lean chicken meat, minced	
1	1	Lemongrass stalk, chopped	
2 oz	30 g	Dill stems	
1	1	Kaffir lime leaf (optional; see note)	6. Add this mixture to the warm stock. Whisk continuously over medium heat. When just about to boil, a frothy crust will form. Stop whisking.
2 pieces	2 pieces	Star anise	
1 tbsp	15 mL	Tomato paste	
2 tsp	2 g	Saffron threads	7. Make a small hole in the center of the crust with a spoon, taste the soup beneath, and season through the hole. Cook at low simmer for 20 minutes, then strain through a china cap lined with cheesecloth.
3	3	Egg whites	
		Garnish:	8. At service time, reheat the soup. Whisk the egg whites to break them up, but do not whip to a froth. Pour into the soup in a thin steady stream, stirring slowly with a fork to create a fine thread effect.
3	3	Egg whites	
4 oz	125 g	Small shrimp, peeled and cooked	
8 tsp	18 g	Chives, chopped	9. Serve the soup in warm bowls and garnish with the shrimp, chives, dill sprigs, and Japanese pickled ginger.
8 tsp	18 g	Dill sprigs	
4 tsp	18 g	Japanese pickled ginger	

Per serving:
Calories, 120; Protein, 13 g; Fat, 7 g (50% cal.); Cholesterol, 120 mg;
Carbohydrates, 3 g; Fiber, 0 g; Sodium, 1250 mg.

Note: If crab shells are not available, substitute half their weight of whole small shrimp or shrimp shells. Kaffir lime leaves are available in markets that sell Asian or Indian spices.

Thick Soups

Cream Soups

Learning to cook professionally, as you have already heard, is not learning recipes but learning basic techniques that you can apply to specific needs.

The basic techniques of sauce making were discussed in Chapter 8. If we tell you that cream soups are simply diluted velouté or béchamel sauces, flavored with the ingredient for which they are named, you should almost be able to make a cream of celery soup without any further instructions.

It's not quite that simple. There are some complications, but they are mostly a matter of detail. You already know the basic techniques.

THE CLASSIC CREAM SOUPS

In the great kitchens of several decades ago, cream soups were exactly as we have just described: diluted, flavored sauces. In fact, what we now call cream soups were divided into two groups, veloutés and creams.

1. Velouté soups consisted of
   Velouté sauce
   Puréed flavoring ingredient
   White stock, to dilute
   Liaison, to finish

2. Cream soups consisted of
   Béchamel sauce
   Puréed flavoring ingredient
   Milk (or white stock), to dilute
   Cream, to finish

These methods were natural to large kitchens that always had quantities of velouté and béchamel sauces on hand. Making a soup was simply a matter of finishing off a sauce.

Modern cooks view these methods as complicated and have devised other methods that seem simpler. But most of the sauce steps are involved—you still have to thicken a liquid with roux (or other starch), cook and purée the ingredients, and add the milk or cream.

The classical method is still important to learn. It will give you versatility, it makes excellent soup, and besides, it really isn't any harder or longer, in the final analysis. In addition, we explain two other methods much in use today.

But first, we consider a problem frequently encountered with cream soups.

CURDLING

Because cream soups contain milk or cream or both, curdling is a common problem. The heat of cooking and the acidity of many of the other soup ingredients are the causes of this curdling.

Fortunately, we can use one fact to avoid curdling: *roux and other starch thickeners stabilize milk and cream.* Caution is still necessary because soups are relatively thin and do not contain enough starch to be completely curdle proof.

Observe the following guidelines to help prevent curdling:

1. Do not combine milk and simmering soup stock without the presence of roux or other starch. Do one of the following:
   • Thicken the stock before adding milk.
   • Thicken the milk before adding it to the soup.

2. Do not add cold milk or cream to simmering soup. Do one of the following:
   • Heat the milk in a separate saucepan.
   • Temper the milk by gradually adding some of the hot soup to it. Then add it to the rest of the soup.

3. Do not boil soups after milk or cream has been added.

STANDARDS OF QUALITY FOR CREAM SOUPS

1. Thickness.
   About the consistency of heavy cream. Not too thick.

2. Texture.
   Smooth; no graininess or lumps (except garnish, of course).

3. Taste.
   Distinct flavor of the main ingredient (asparagus in cream of asparagus, etc.). No starchy taste from uncooked roux.

Basic Procedures for Making Cream Soups

The following methods apply to most cream soups. Individual ingredients may require variations.

Method 1

1. Prepare Velouté Sauce (p. 146) or Béchamel Sauce (p. 145), using roux.

2. Prepare the main flavoring ingredients. Cut vegetables into thin slices. Sweat them in butter about 5 minutes to develop flavor. *Do not brown.* Green, leafy vegetables must be blanched before stewing in butter. Cut poultry and seafood into small pieces for simmering.

3. Add flavoring ingredients from step 2 to the velouté or béchamel and simmer until tender. *Exception:* Finished tomato purée is added for cream of tomato; further cooking is not necessary.

4. Skim any fat or scum carefully from the surface of the soup.

5. Purée the soup using a food mill (Figure 9.1) or an immersion blender (Figure 9.2), then strain it through a fine china cap. Alternatively, just strain it through a fine china cap, pressing down hard on the solid ingredients to force out the liquid and some of the pulp. The soup should be very smooth.

    Poultry and seafood ingredients may be puréed or reserved for garnish.

6. Add hot white stock or milk to thin the soup to proper consistency.

7. Adjust seasonings.

8. At service time, finish with liaison (p. 139) or heavy cream.

Method 2

1. Sweat vegetable ingredients (except tomatoes) in butter; do not let them color.

2. Add flour. Stir well to make a roux. Cook the roux for a few minutes, but do not let it start to brown.

3. Add white stock, beating with a whip as you slowly pour it in.

4. Add any vegetables, other solid ingredients, or flavorings that were not sautéed in step 1.

5. Simmer until all ingredients are tender.

6. Skim any fat that has risen to the surface.

7. Purée and/or strain (as in Method 1).

8. Add hot white stock or milk to thin soup to proper consistency.

9. Adjust seasonings.

10. At service time, finish with heavy cream or liaison.

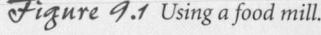
Figure 9.1 *Using a food mill.*

(a) *Purée soft foods by turning the crank of the mill to force them through small holes.*

(b) *Scrape the solids from the bottom of the mill after all the food has been forced through the plate.*

Method 3

1. Bring white stock to a boil.

2. Add vegetables and other flavoring ingredients. If desired, some or all of the vegetables may first be cooked slowly in butter for a few minutes to develop flavors.

3. Simmer until all ingredients are tender.

4. Thicken with roux, beurre manié, or other starch.

5. Simmer until no starch taste remains.

6. Skim fat from surface.

7. Purée and/or strain (as in Method 1).

8. Add hot or tempered milk and/or cream. A light cream sauce may be used, if desired, to avoid thinning the soup or curdling the milk.

9. Adjust seasonings.

Figure 9.2 *Using an immersion blender to purée a soup.*

Cream of Celery Soup (Cream Soup Method 1)

Yield: 6 qt (6 L)   **Portions:** 24   **Portion size:** 8 oz (250 mL)

U.S.	Metric	Ingredients	PROCEDURE
3 lb	1.5 kg	Celery, small dice	1. Review cream soup guidelines and Method 1 (p. 184).
12 oz	375 g	Onion, small dice	2. Sweat the celery and onions in the butter in a heavy sauce-
3 oz	90 g	Butter	pot until they are almost tender. Do not let them brown.
4½ qt	4.5 L	Velouté sauce, made with chicken or veal stock (see note)	3. Add the velouté to the pot. Simmer until the vegetables are very tender. 4. Skim any fat or scum from the soup. 5. Pass the soup through a food mill to purée it. 6. Pass the puréed soup through a fine china cap or through cheesecloth.
3 pt approximately	1.5 L approximately	Hot milk or white stock	7. Add enough hot milk or stock to bring the soup to the proper consistency.
to taste	to taste	Salt	8. Heat the soup again, but do not let it boil.
to taste	to taste	White pepper	9. Season to taste.
3 cups	750 mL	Heavy cream, hot Optional garnish:	10. At service time, add the cream. Add the garnish if desired.
6 oz	175 g	Celery, cut julienne, cooked	

Per serving:
Calories, 320; Protein, 5 g; Fat, 27 g (75% cal.); Cholesterol, 90 mg;
Carbohydrates, 15 g; Fiber, 1 g; Sodium, 240 mg.

Note: Béchamel may be used in place of velouté if desired. This is often done for vegetarian menus.

VARIATIONS, METHOD 1

For the following cream soups, make the substitutions in the basic recipe as indicated. Frozen and canned vegetables may be used, where appropriate, in place of fresh. Also, trimmings may be used if they are clean and of good quality, such as the bottom ends of asparagus and broccoli stalks.

Cream of Asparagus
Use 3 lb (1.5 kg) asparagus stalks in place of celery. Optional garnish: cooked asparagus tips.

Cream of Broccoli
Use 3 lb (1.5 kg) broccoli in place of celery. Optional garnish: small cooked broccoli florets.

Cream of Carrot
Use 3 lb (1.5 kg) carrots in place of celery. Garnish: chopped parsley.

Cream of Cauliflower
Use 3 lb (1.5 kg) cauliflower in place of celery. Optional garnish: tiny cooked cauliflower florets.

Cream of Corn
Use 3 lb (1.5 kg) whole kernel corn (fresh, frozen, or canned) in place of celery. Do not sweat the corn with the onions. Instead, sweat the onions alone, add the velouté, then add the corn. Garnish: corn kernels.

Cream of Cucumber
Use 3 lb (1.5 kg) peeled, seeded cucumber in place of celery. Optional garnish: small, diced, cooked cucumber.

Cream of Mushroom
Use 1½ lb (750 g) mushrooms in place of celery. Optional garnish: julienne, brunoise, or sliced cooked mushrooms.

Cream of Pea
Use 3 lb (1.5 kg) frozen green peas in place of celery. Do not sweat the peas with the onions. Add them after the velouté has been added.

Cream of Spinach
Use 3 lb (1.5 kg) fresh spinach or 2 lb (900 g) frozen spinach in place of celery. Do not sweat the spinach with the onion. Blanch it, drain it well, and add it to the velouté in step 3.

Cream of Watercress
Use 1½ lb (750 g) watercress in place of celery.

Cream of Chicken
Reduce celery to 6 oz (175 g) and add 6 oz (175 g) carrot (note that, together with the onion, this makes 1½ lb (750 g) mirepoix). Use a velouté sauce made with a strong, flavorful chicken stock. After the soup is strained, add 6 oz (175 g) cooked chicken meat, cut into julienne or fine dice.

Cold Cream Soups
Most cream soups are delicious cold as well as hot. For example, cold cream of cucumber soup is a special favorite in summer. Procedure:

1. Chill soup after step 9 in recipe.
2. Add cold cream after soup is well chilled.
3. Dilute with extra milk, cream, or stock if soup becomes too thick.
4. Season carefully. Cold foods require more seasonings.

Cream of Mushroom Soup (Cream Soup Method 2)

Yield: 6 qt (6 L)   Portions: 24   Portion size: 8 oz (250 mL)

U.S.	Metric	Ingredients	PROCEDURE
12 oz	375 g	Butter	1. Review cream soup guidelines and Method 2 (p. 184).
12 oz	375 g	Onion, chopped fine	2. Heat the butter in a heavy saucepot over moderate heat.
1½ lb	750 g	Mushrooms, chopped	
9 oz	275 g	Flour	3. Add the onions and mushrooms. Sweat the vegetables without letting them brown.
			4. Add the flour and stir to make a roux. Cook the roux for a few minutes, but do not let it start to brown.
4½ qt	4.5 L	White stock, chicken or veal, hot	5. Gradually beat in the stock. Bring to a boil, stirring with a whip as it thickens.
			6. Simmer until vegetables are very tender.
			7. Skim the soup carefully.
			8. Pass the soup through a food mill to purée it.
			9. Pass the puréed soup through a fine china cap or through cheesecloth.
3 pt approximately	1.5 L approximately	Hot milk	10. Add enough hot milk to the soup to bring it to the proper consistency.
to taste	to taste	Salt	11. Heat the soup again, but do not let it boil.
to taste	to taste	White pepper	12. Season to taste.
3 cups	750 mL	Heavy cream, hot Optional garnish:	13. At service time, add the cream. Add the garnish, if desired.
6 oz	175 g	Mushrooms, cut brunoise, sautéed in butter	

Per serving:
Calories, 300; Protein, 5 g; Fat, 25 g (75% cal.); Cholesterol, 85 mg;
Carbohydrates, 14 g; Fiber, 1 g; Sodium, 170 mg.

VARIATIONS, METHOD 2

For each variation, replace the mushrooms with the vegetable and quantity indicated. See the note to the variations for Cream of Celery Soup, page 185.

Cream of Asparagus
3 lb (1.5 kg) asparagus.

Cream of Broccoli
3 lb (1.5 kg) broccoli.

Cream of Carrot
3 lb (1.5 kg) carrots.

Cream of Cauliflower
3 lb (1.5 kg) cauliflower.

Cream of Celery
3 lb (1.5 kg) celery.

Cream of Corn
3 lb (1.5 kg) whole kernel corn.

Cream of Cucumber
3 lb (1.5 kg) peeled, seeded cucumber.

Cream of Green Pea
3 lb (1.5 kg) frozen peas. Add after step 5.

Cream of Spinach
3 lb (1.5 kg) fresh or 2 lb (900 g) frozen spinach. Blanch, drain, and add after step 5.

Cream of Watercress
1½ lb (750 g) watercress.

Cream of Chicken
6 oz (175 g) celery and 6 oz (175 g) carrot. Use strong chicken stock. Add 6 oz (175 g) cooked chicken meat, cut into julienne or fine dice, to the finished soup after straining.

Cream of Broccoli Soup (Cream Soup Method 3)

Yield: 6 qt (6 L)   Portions: 24   Portion size: 8 oz (250 mL)

U.S.	Metric	Ingredients	PROCEDURE
4½ qt	4.5 L	White stock, chicken or veal	1. Bring the stock to a boil in a heavy saucepot.
3 lb	1.5 kg	Broccoli (fresh or frozen), chopped	2. Add the broccoli and onion. (Optional: Vegetables may be sweated in butter first to develop flavors.)
12 oz	375 g	Onion, chopped fine	3. Simmer until the vegetables are tender. Do not overcook or the broccoli will lose its fresh, green color.
9 oz	275 g	Butter, clarified	4. Combine the butter and flour in a saucepan to make a roux. Cook the roux a few minutes, but do not let it color. Cool the roux slightly. (Note: Beurre manié may be used instead of roux.)
9 oz	275 g	Flour	5. Beat the roux into the soup. Simmer until no starch taste remains.
			6. Pass the soup through a food mill, then through a fine china cap or cheesecloth.
3 pt approximately	1.5 L approximately	Hot milk	7. Add enough hot milk to bring the soup to proper consistency.
to taste	to taste	Salt	8. Heat the soup again, but do not let it boil.
to taste	to taste	White pepper	9. Season to taste.
3 cups	750 mL	Heavy cream, hot Optional garnish:	10. At service time, add the heavy cream. If desired, add the garnish.
6 oz	175 g	Small broccoli florets, cooked	

Per serving:
Calories, 200; Protein, 6 g; Fat, 22 g (69% cal.); Cholesterol, 75 mg;
Carbohydrates, 16 g; Fiber, 2 g; Sodium, 150 mg.

VARIATIONS, METHOD 3

For other cream soups, replace the broccoli with 3 lb (1.5 kg) of any of the following:

Asparagus
Carrots
Cauliflower
Celery
Corn
Green peas
Spinach

Cream of Tomato Soup

Yield: 6 qt (6 L)   Portions: 24   Portion size: 8 oz (250 mL)

U.S.	Metric	Ingredients	PROCEDURE
4 oz	125 g	Salt pork, diced	1. In a heavy saucepot, cook the salt pork over medium heat to render the fat.
4 oz	125 g	Onion, medium dice	
2 oz	60 g	Carrots, medium dice	2. Add the onion, carrot, and celery. Sweat until they are slightly softened.
2 oz	60 g	Celery, medium dice	3. Add the flour and stir to make a roux. Cook the roux a few minutes.
2 oz	60 g	Flour	4. Slowly beat in the stock. Bring to a boil, stirring while the liquid thickens slightly.
3 qt	3 L	White stock	
2 lb	1 kg	Canned tomatoes	5. Add the tomatoes, tomato purée, and sachet. Simmer about 1 hour.
2 lb	1 kg	Tomato purée	6. Strain through a china cap. Press down on the solids with a ladle to force out all the juices and some of the pulp. (Alternative method: pass through a food mill, then strain.)
		Sachet:	
1	1	Bay leaf	
pinch	pinch	Thyme	7. If the soup is being made ahead, chill the tomato base and proceed to the next step just before service.
1	1	Whole clove	
2	2	Peppercorns, crushed	
2 qt	2 L	Cream sauce, hot	8. Return the tomato base to the saucepot and bring back to a simmer.
to taste	to taste	Salt	9. Stir in the hot cream sauce.
to taste	to taste	White pepper	10. If the soup is too thick, thin with a little stock.
			11. Season to taste with salt and pepper.

Per serving:
Calories, 210; Protein, 5 g; Fat, 15 g (64% cal.); Cholesterol, 45 mg;
Carbohydrates, 14 g; Fiber, 1 g; Sodium, 230 mg.

VARIATIONS

If you study this recipe, you will see that the first part (through step 6) is essentially a tomato sauce.

The recipe can be broken down as follows:

1 part	Tomato sauce
1 part	Stock
1 part	Cream sauce

Using this formula, you can also make cream of tomato soup from Tomato Sauce I (p. 150) or from canned tomato sauce. You can also make it from canned tomato purée if you simmer it with extra herbs, seasonings, and mirepoix. Check all seasonings and flavors carefully when using canned, prepared products.

Purée Soups

TECHNIQUES

Purée soups are made by simmering dried or fresh vegetables, especially high-starch vegetables, in stock or water, then puréeing the soup. Thus, they are relatively easy to prepare. Purée soups are not as smooth and refined as cream soups but are heartier and coarser in texture and character. Techniques vary greatly depending on the ingredients and the desired result.

Basic Procedure for Making Purée Soups

1. Sweat mirepoix or other fresh vegetables in fat.
2. Add liquid.
3. Add dried or starchy vegetables.
4. Simmer until vegetables are tender. Fresh vegetables should be completely cooked but not overcooked or falling apart.
5. Purée soup in a food mill or with an immersion blender.
    Variation: Some soups made from dried legumes, such as bean soup, are not puréed but are served as is or slightly mashed.
6. Purée soups are generally not bound with an added starch but rely on the starches present in the vegetables. Some fresh vegetable purées, however, settle out. These may be thickened with a little starch if desired.
7. Add cream if required.
8. Adjust seasonings.

Purée of Carrot Soup (Potage Crecy)

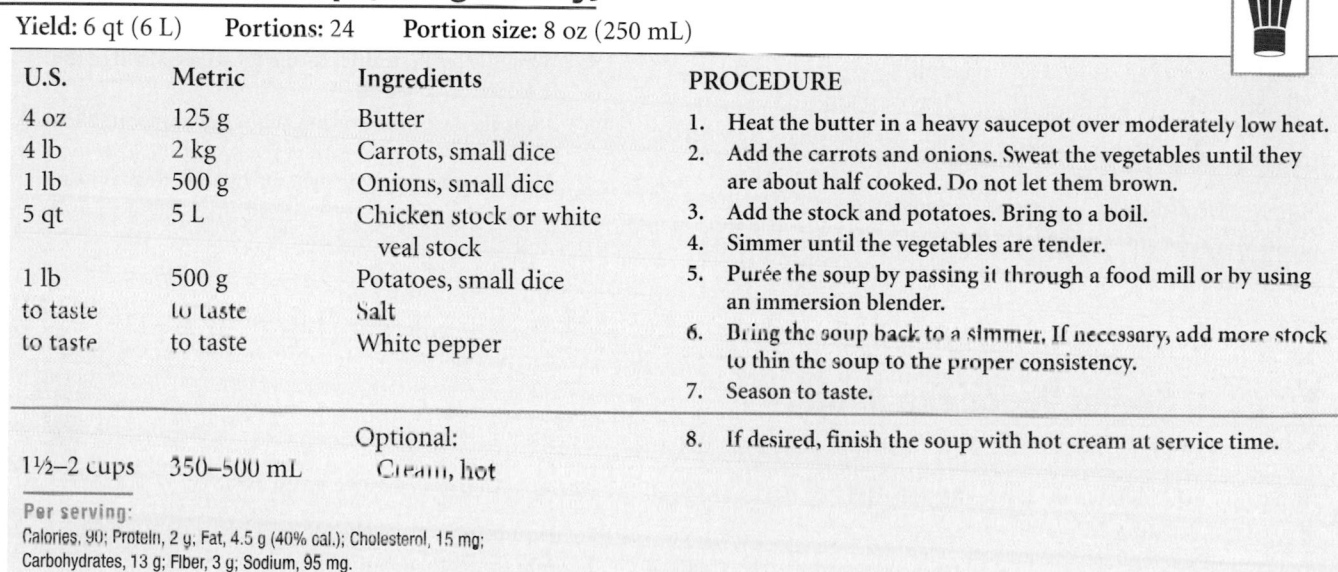

Yield: 6 qt (6 L)   **Portions:** 24   **Portion size:** 8 oz (250 mL)

U.S.	Metric	Ingredients	PROCEDURE
4 oz	125 g	Butter	1. Heat the butter in a heavy saucepot over moderately low heat.
4 lb	2 kg	Carrots, small dice	2. Add the carrots and onions. Sweat the vegetables until they
1 lb	500 g	Onions, small dice	are about half cooked. Do not let them brown.
5 qt	5 L	Chicken stock or white veal stock	3. Add the stock and potatoes. Bring to a boil.
			4. Simmer until the vegetables are tender.
1 lb	500 g	Potatoes, small dice	5. Purée the soup by passing it through a food mill or by using
to taste	to taste	Salt	an immersion blender.
to taste	to taste	White pepper	6. Bring the soup back to a simmer. If necessary, add more stock to thin the soup to the proper consistency.
			7. Season to taste.
		Optional:	8. If desired, finish the soup with hot cream at service time.
1½–2 cups	350–500 mL	Cream, hot	

Per serving:
Calories, 90; Protein, 2 g; Fat, 4.5 g (40% cal.); Cholesterol, 15 mg; Carbohydrates, 13 g; Fiber, 3 g; Sodium, 95 mg.

VARIATIONS

Rice may be used in place of potatoes as the binding agent in the above recipe or in any of the variations below *except* purée of potato, purée of potato and leek, and purée of watercress. Use 8 oz (250 g) raw rice in place of 1 lb (500 g) potatoes. The soup must be simmered until the rice is very soft.

Purée of Cauliflower Soup (Purée Dubarry)
Use 4 lb (2 kg) cauliflower in place of carrots.

Purée of Celery or Celery Root Soup
Use 4 lb (2 kg) celery or celery root in place of carrots.

Purée of Jerusalem Artichoke Soup
Use 4 lb (2 kg) Jerusalem artichoke in place of carrots.

Purée of Potato Soup (Potage Parmentier)
Omit carrots from basic recipe, add 10 oz (300 g) leeks to the onion and increase the potatoes to 5 lb (2.5 kg).

Purée of Potato and Leek Soup
Use 2 lb (1 kg) leeks in place of the carrots. Increase the potatoes to 2½ lb (1.25 kg).

Purée of Turnip Soup
Use 4 lb (2 kg) white turnips in place of carrots.

Purée of Watercress Soup
Prepare like purée of potato soup, but add 5 bunches watercress, chopped, when the potatoes are almost tender.

Purée of Mixed Vegetable Soup
Decrease carrots to 1¼ lb (600 g). Add 10 oz (300 g) each celery, turnips, leeks, and cabbage.

Potage Solferino
Combine equal parts purée of potato and leek soup and cream of tomato soup.

Purée of Green Pea Soup with Mint Cream

Yield: 6 qt (6 L)   **Portions:** 24   **Portion size:** 8 oz (250 mL)

U.S.	Metric	Ingredients	PROCEDURE
2 oz	60 g	Butter	1. Heat the butter in a heavy saucepot over moderately low heat.
6 oz	175 g	Onions, small dice	2. Add the onions and sweat them without letting them brown.
4 qt	4 L	Chicken stock	3. Add the stock and bring to a boil.
6 lb	3 kg	Peas, fresh or frozen	4. Add the peas. Simmer until the peas are soft, about 5 minutes.
to taste	to taste	Salt	5. Pass the soup through a food mill or purée with an immersion blender.
to taste	to taste	White pepper	6. Return the stock to a simmer. Add additional stock if necessary to bring to a proper consistency.
			7. Adjust the seasoning.
8 oz	250 mL	Heavy cream	8. At service time, heat the heavy cream and stir into the soup.
		Garnish:	9. Whip the cream until it forms soft peaks. Fold in the shredded mint leaves.
12 oz	375 mL	Heavy cream	10. Immediately before serving, place 1 tablespoon (15 mL) mint cream on top of each portion. (Within a few minutes, the whipped cream will melt into a mint-flecked foam.)
¼ cup	60 mL	Mint leaves, finely shredded	

Per serving:
Calories, 200; Protein, 7 g; Fat, 11 g (50% cal.); Cholesterol, 40 mg;
Carbohydrates, 18 g; Fiber, 6 g; Sodium, 40 mg.

Purée of Spring Vegetable Soup

Yield: 6 qt (6 L)   **Portions:** 24   **Portion size:** 8 oz (250 mL)

U.S.	Metric	Ingredients	PROCEDURE
2 oz	60 g	Butter	1. Heat the butter in a heavy soup pot over low heat.
2 lb	1 kg	Leeks, white part only, small dice	2. Add the leeks, potatoes, and celery. Sweat over low heat until fairly tender, about 10–15 minutes.
2 lb	1 kg	New potatoes, peeled, small dice	3. Add the peas, parsley, and tarragon. Sweat another 5 minutes.
1 lb	500 g	Celery, small dice	4. Add the stock. Simmer 10 minutes or more, until the vegetables are tender but not overcooked.
1 lb	500 g	Peas, fresh or frozen	5. Purée the soup with a food mill. If you use an immersion blender, pass the soup through a food mill or sieve after puréeing it in order to remove fibers from the celery.
¼ cup	60 mL	Chopped parsley	
1 tbsp	15 mL	Chopped fresh tarragon	
6 qt	6 L	Light vegetable stock or chicken stock	
8 oz	250 mL	Heavy cream	6. Heat the cream and stir it into the soup.
to taste	to taste	Salt	7. Adjust the seasonings with salt and white pepper.
to taste	to taste	White pepper	
		Garnish:	8. Whip the cream until it forms soft peaks. Fold in the chives.
8 oz	250 mL	Heavy cream	9. At service time, garnish each portion of soup with a spoonful of the chive cream. (Within a few minutes, the whipped cream will melt into a chive-flecked foam.)
2 tbsp	30 mL	Chopped chives	

Per serving:
Calories, 160; Protein, 4 g; Fat, 10 g (53% cal.); Cholesterol, 35 mg;
Carbohydrates, 16 g; Fiber, 3 g; Sodium, 65 mg.

Butternut Squash Soup with Caramelized Apples

Yield: 6 qt (6 L)   **Portions:** 24   **Portion size:** 8 oz (250 mL)

U.S.	Metric	Ingredients	PROCEDURE
8 oz	250 g	French bread	1. Cut the bread into slices ½ inch (1 cm) thick.
2 oz	60 g	Butter	2. Fry the bread in the butter until golden brown. (If desired, prepare additional croutons for garnish at the same time; see step 8.)
2 oz	60 g	Butter	3. Heat the butter in a heavy saucepot over moderately low heat.
8 oz	250 g	Onions, small dice	4. Add the onions, leeks, and carrots. Sweat them until they are about half cooked. Do not let them brown.
8 oz	250 g	Leeks, small dice	5. Add the squash, the stock, and the browned bread from step 2. Simmer until the vegetables are tender.
12 oz	375 g	Carrots, small dice	6. Purée the soup with a food mill or an immersion blender.
4 lb	2 kg	Butternut squash, medium dice	7. Bring the soup back to a simmer. Taste and adjust the seasonings.
5 qt	5 L	Chicken stock	
1½ tsp	7 mL	Salt	
½ tsp	2 mL	White pepper	
½ tsp	2 mL	Ground allspice	
½ tsp	2 mL	Ground ginger	
24	24	Croutons (see procedure)	8. Prepare croutons by browning slices of French bread in butter as in steps 1 and 2. For best appearance, use a slender loaf so that croutons aren't too big.
1½ lb	750 g	Tart, firm cooking apples	9. Peel and core apples. Cut into small dice.
1 oz	30 g	Butter	10. Heat the butter in a sauté pan and add the apples and sugar. Cook over moderate heat until the apples are brown and caramelized.
2 oz	60 g	Brown sugar	
12 oz	375 mL	Heavy cream (optional)	11. At service, heat the heavy cream (if using) and add to the soup.
as needed	as needed	Additional heavy cream or crème fraîche for garnish, if desired	12. For each portion, ladle the soup into a broad soup plate. Decorate the top of the soup with a swirl of cream, if desired. Heap a generous tablespoon (15 mL) of apple onto a crouton and carefully place in the soup.

Per serving:
Calories, 150; Protein, 3 g; Fat, 6 g (34% cal.); Cholesterol, 20 mg; Carbohydrates, 23 g; Fiber, 4 g; Sodium, 280 mg.

Potage Cressonière (Watercress Soup)

Yield: 4 qt (4 L)   **Portions:** 16   **Portion size:** 8 oz (250 mL)

U.S.	Metric	Ingredients	PROCEDURE
3 bunches	3 bunches	Watercress	1. Wash the watercress and separate the leaves from the stems. Set some of the nicer leaves aside for the garnish. Coarsely chop the stems and set aside. Quickly blanch the leaves in boiling salted water and refresh. Once completely cooled, drain. Squeeze out any excess water and finely chop.
1 lb	500 g	Leeks, white part only	2. Thinly slice the leeks and sweat in butter with the watercress stems. Gently cook until tender and all the liquid has evaporated.
3½ oz	100 g	Butter	3. Add the chicken stock or water and the potatoes, cut into large pieces. Bring to a boil.
3 qt	3 L	Chicken stock or water	4. Reduce the heat to a simmer and cook for 30 minutes or until the potatoes are tender. Add the cream, then add the blanched watercress. Blend in a blender until smooth, then strain. Season to taste.
2 lb 8 oz	1.2 kg	Potatoes, peeled and cut into large pieces	5. Serve in a shallow soup bowl and garnish with fresh watercress leaves.
7 oz	200 g	Crème fraîche	6. This soup can also be served cold.
to taste	to taste	Salt	
to taste	to taste	White pepper	

Per serving:
Calories, 170; Protein, 4 g; Fat, 10 g (51% cal.); Cholesterol, 30 mg; Carbohydrates, 18 g; Fiber, 2 g; Sodium, 90 mg.

Purée of Split Pea Soup

Yield: 6 qt (6 L)   Portions: 24   Portion size: 8 oz (250 mL)

U.S.	Metric	Ingredients	PROCEDURE
6 oz	175 g	Salt pork	1. Cut the salt pork into fine dice or pass through a grinder.
		Mirepoix:	2. Cook the salt pork slowly in a heavy saucepot to render the fat. Do not brown the pork.
10 oz	300 g	Onion, small dice	
5 oz	150 g	Celery, small dice	3. Add the mirepoix and sweat in the fat until the vegetables are slightly softened.
5 oz	150 g	Carrot, small dice	
6 qt	6 L	Ham stock (see note)	4. Add the ham stock and ham bone. Bring to a boil.
1	1	Ham bone or ham hock (optional)	5. Rinse the split peas under cold water. Drain in a strainer and add to the stock. Also add the sachet.
3 lb	1.5 kg	Green split peas	6. Cover and simmer until the peas are tender, about 1 hour.
		Sachet:	7. Remove the ham bone and sachet.
1	1	Bay leaf	8. Pass the soup through a food mill.
2	2	Whole cloves	9. Bring the soup back to a simmer. If it is too thick, bring it to proper consistency with a little stock or water.
6	6	Peppercorns	
to taste	to taste	Salt	10. Season to taste.
to taste	to taste	Pepper	11. If a ham hock was used, trim off the meat. Dice it and add it to the soup.

Per serving:
Calories, 230; Protein, 13 g; Fat, 7 g (26% cal.); Cholesterol, 5 mg;
Carbohydrates, 32 g; Fiber, 12 g; Sodium, 590 mg.

Note: Water may be used if ham stock is not available. In this case, the optional ham bone or ham hock should be used to provide flavor. Simmer the water and bone together for 1 hour or more before making the soup to extract more flavor.

VARIATIONS

Other dried vegetables are made into soups using the same procedure. Most dried beans should be soaked in cold water overnight to reduce cooking time. (Split peas may be soaked, but they cook quickly enough without soaking.)

Purée of White Bean Soup

Use 3 lb (1.5 kg) navy beans. Soak the beans overnight. Use chicken or veal stock in place of ham stock.

Purée of Yellow Split Pea Soup

Use yellow split peas instead of green.

Purée of Lentil Soup

Use 3 lb (1.5 kg) lentils. Soak overnight. Use either ham stock or white stock. Garnish with diced cooked bacon or ham or sliced frankfurters.

Purée of Kidney Bean Soup

Use 3 lb (1.5 kg) red kidney beans. Soak them overnight. Use white stock and add 2½ cups (600 mL) red wine to the soup when the beans are almost tender. Garnish with croutons sautéed in butter.

Purée of Black Bean Soup

Use 3 lb (1.5 kg) black turtle beans. Soak them overnight. Use white stock and the optional ham bone. Add 8 oz (250 mL) Madeira or sherry to the finished soup. Garnish with lemon slices and chopped hard-cooked egg.

Purée Mongole

Combine 3 qt (3 L) purée of green split pea soup and 2 qt (2 L) tomato purée. Dilute to proper consistency with about 1–2 qt (1–2 L) white stock. Garnish with cooked peas and with cooked julienne of carrots and leeks.

Nonpuréed Bean Soups

Prepare any of the above soups as directed, but purée only about one-fourth of the beans. Add this purée to the soup as a thickening agent.

Navy Bean Soup

Yield: 6 qt (6 L) **Portions:** 24 **Portion size:** 8 oz (250 mL)

U.S.	Metric	Ingredients	PROCEDURE
2 lb	1 kg	Dried navy beans	1. Soak the beans overnight in cold water.
4 oz	125 g	Bacon, diced	2. Place the bacon in a heavy saucepot over medium heat. Render the fat from the bacon, but do not cook until crisp.
4 oz	125 g	Onions, small dice	
8 oz	250 g	Carrots, small dice	3. Add the vegetables and cook over low heat until almost tender.
8 oz	250 g	Celery, small dice	
4 oz	125 g	Leeks, sliced	
3 cloves	3 cloves	Garlic, chopped	
5 qt	5 L	Stock or water	4. Add the stock or water and the ham hock. Bring to a boil.
1	1	Ham hock	5. Drain the beans and add them to the liquid. Also add the bay leaf, thyme, and pepper.
1	1	Bay leaf	
½ tsp	2 mL	Thyme	6. Cover and simmer until the beans are tender.
½ tsp	2 mL	Pepper	
1 qt	1 L	Canned tomatoes, with juice, crushed	7. Add the tomatoes to the soup and simmer another 15 minutes. Remove the bay leaf.
			8. Remove the ham hock from the soup. Cut off and dice the meat and add it to the soup. Discard the bones.
			9. Mash the beans lightly with a paddle or pass about one-fourth of the beans through a food mill. Add this purée back to the soup to thicken it.
			10. If the soup is too thick, thin it with a little stock.
			11. Adjust the seasoning.

Per serving:
Calories, 180; Protein, 10 g; Fat, 4 g (19% cal.); Cholesterol, 5 mg; Carbohydrates, 28 g; Fiber, 7 g; Sodium, 510 mg.

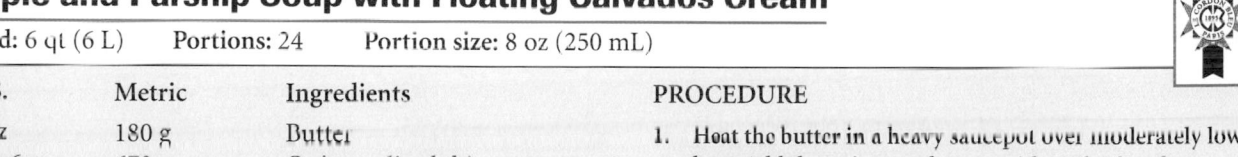

Apple and Parsnip Soup with Floating Calvados Cream

Yield: 6 qt (6 L) **Portions:** 24 **Portion size:** 8 oz (250 mL)

U.S.	Metric	Ingredients	PROCEDURE
6 oz	180 g	Butter	1. Heat the butter in a heavy saucepot over moderately low heat. Add the onions and sweat without letting them brown.
1 lb 6 oz	670 g	Onions, sliced thin	
2 lb	1 kg	Parsnips, peeled, large dice	2. Add the parsnips and apples, stirring to mix.
2 lb	1 kg	Cooking apples, peeled, cored, large dice	3. Add the stock and bring to a boil. Simmer until the parsnips and apples are tender, about 30 minutes.
6 qt	6 L	Chicken stock	4. Pass the soup through a food mill or purée in a blender. Then pass through a china cap.
to taste	to taste	Salt	5. Pour into a clean saucepot and bring to a boil.
to taste	to taste	White pepper	6. If the soup is too thick, thin with a little stock. Season to taste with salt and white pepper.
2½ pt	1.2 L	Heavy cream	7. Whip the cream until lightly thickened but not stiff. Do not overwhip. Mix the Calvados into the cream. This further mixing should thicken the cream so that it holds peaks.
12 oz	360 mL	Calvados	8. At service time, garnish each portion of the soup with a spoonful of the cream. Pass under the salamander or broiler very briefly to lightly brown the cream. Serve immediately.

Per serving:
Calories, 160; Protein, 1.5 g; Fat, 12 g (68% cal.); Cholesterol, 45 mg; Carbohydrates, 7 g; Fiber, 1 g; Sodium, 46 mg.

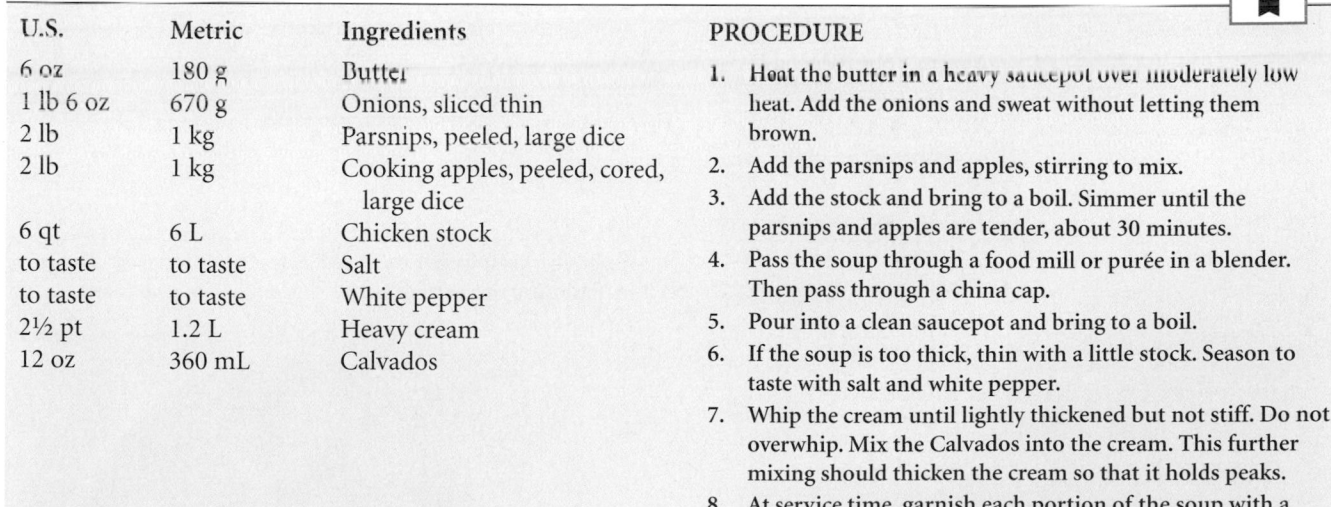

Potato and Leek Soup with Sorrel

Yield: 6 qt (6 L) Portions: 24 Portion size: 8 oz (250 mL)

U.S.	Metric	Ingredients	PROCEDURE
5 oz	140 g	Butter	1. Heat the butter in a large saucepot over moderately low heat. Add the onions and leeks. Sweat them without letting them brown.
1 lb 4 oz	600 g	Onions, sliced thin	2. Add the potatoes to the saucepot and stir.
1 lb 4 oz	600 g	Leeks, white part only, sliced thin	3. Add the stock, season, and bring to a boil. Simmer until the vegetables are very tender.
5 lb	2.4 kg	Potatoes, peeled, large dice	4. Purée the soup with a blender or food processor or use an immersion blender, then pass through a china cap if necessary.
5 qt	4.8 L	Chicken stock	5. Pour into a clean saucepot and bring to a boil.
to taste	to taste	Salt	6. If the soup is too thick, thin with a little stock.
to taste	to taste	White pepper	7. Wash and pick over the sorrel, removing thick stalks. Coarsely shred and add to the soup to serve.
12 oz	360 g	Fresh sorrel leaves	

Per serving:
Calories, 150; Protein, 3 g; Fat, 5 g (30% cal.); Cholesterol, 20 mg; Carbohydrates, 23 g; Fiber, 3 g; Sodium, 70 mg.

Spicy Black Bean Soup

Yield: 6 qt (6 L) Portions: 24 Portion size: 8 oz (250 mL)

U.S.	Metric	Ingredients	PROCEDURE
2 lb	1 kg	Black turtle beans	1. Soak the beans overnight in cold water.
1½ oz	50 mL	Olive oil	2. Heat the olive oil in a heavy soup pot over moderate heat.
8 oz	250 g	Onions, small dice	3. Add the onions, garlic, and jalapeño. Cook over low heat until almost tender.
4 cloves	4 cloves	Garlic, chopped	4. Add the chili powder, cumin, coriander, and bay leaf. Stir to mix in with the oil and vegetables.
2 oz	60 g	Jalapeño or other fresh green chile, chopped	5. Add the stock or water. Drain the soaked beans and add them to the pot.
4 tbsp	60 mL	Chili powder	6. Cover and simmer until the beans are just tender.
1½ tsp	7 mL	Cumin, ground	7. Add the tomatoes. Continue to simmer another 15–30 minutes, until the beans are completely tender and the flavors are well blended.
1½ tsp	7 mL	Coriander, ground	8. Add salt and hot pepper sauce to taste.
1	1	Bay leaf	
5 qt	5 L	White stock, vegetable stock, or water	
1 lb	500 g	Tomatoes (canned), drained and chopped	
to taste	to taste	Salt	
to taste	to taste	Hot pepper sauce	
		Garnish:	9. Carefully mix together the diced avocado and tomato. Garnish each portion of the soup with a spoonful of this mixture.
8 oz	250 g	Avocado, medium dice	
8 oz	250 g	Tomato, medium dice	

Per serving:
Calories, 170; Protein, 10 g; Fat, 4.5 g (22% cal.); Cholesterol, 5 mg; Carbohydrates, 25 g; Fiber, 9 g; Sodium, 55 mg.

Spicy Black Bean Soup

Chilled Leek and Potato Soup with Shrimp and Fennel Salad

Yield: 3 qt (3 L) plus garnish   **Portions:** 12   **Portion size:** 8 oz (250 mL) plus garnish

U.S.	Metric	Ingredients	PROCEDURE
1½ lb	750 g	Leeks, white part only	1. Cut the leeks and potatoes into thin slices.
1½ lb	750 g	Potatoes, peeled	2. Sweat the leeks in olive oil without letting them brown.
2 oz	60 mL	Olive oil	3. Add the stock and potatoes and bring to a boil. Simmer
4½ pt	2.25 L	Chicken stock	until the vegetables are tender.
to taste	to taste	Salt	4. Pass the soup through a food mill.
to taste	to taste	White pepper	5. If the soup is too thick, add a little stock to bring to
			proper consistency.
			6. Chill the soup thoroughly.
			7. Add salt and white pepper to taste.
12 oz	375 g	Tender fennel bulbs, trimmed (see note)	8. While the soup is chilling, prepare the garnish. Cut the fennel in half lengthwise through the base, then cut lengthwise into paper-thin slices (a slicing machine may be used). Cut these slices lengthwise into rough julienne.
4 tsp	20 mL	Lemon juice	
1 oz	30 mL	Olive oil	9. Toss with the lemon juice, then with half the olive oil.
to taste	to taste	Salt	Add salt and pepper to taste.
to taste	to taste	Pepper	10. Toss the shrimp with the remaining olive oil.
36	36	Small cooked shrimp (see note)	
8 oz	250 mL	Heavy cream	11. Stir the heavy cream and buttermilk into the chilled soup.
8 oz	250 mL	Buttermilk	12. Arrange the fennel salad in the center of broad soup plates. Arrange 3 shrimp on top of each mound of fennel.
			13. Place the soup plate in front of the diner, then ladle in a portion of soup from a tureen.

Per serving:
Calories, 240; Protein, 6 g; Fat, 15 g (55% cal.); Cholesterol, 55 mg; Carbohydrates, 22 g; Fiber, 3 g; Sodium, 90 mg.

Note: The fennel must be young and tender, as it is eaten raw. If only large bulbs are available, use the interior part and save the outer layers for another purpose.

Grilled shrimp are especially good for this soup.

VARIATIONS

The fennel and shrimp garnish may be omitted for a simpler presentation.
Water may be substituted for the stock. Leeks are flavorful enough to make a delicious soup even without stock.

Vichyssoise

Substitute butter for the olive oil. Omit the buttermilk and increase the heavy cream to 16–20 oz (500–600 mL). Omit the fennel and shrimp salad garnish. Garnish with chopped chives.

Chilled Leek and Potato Soup with Shrimp and Fennel Salad

Bisques

A bisque is a cream soup made with shellfish. At one time, bisques were thickened with rice, but today they are more frequently thickened with roux. Bisques are made basically like other cream soups, but they seem more complex because of the handling of the shellfish and the variety of flavoring ingredients often used. Expensive to prepare and rich in taste, they are considered luxury soups.

The term bisque has come to be used for a great variety of other soups, primarily because the word sounds nice. In this book, we reserve the term for shellfish cream soups.

Shrimp Bisque

Yield: 2 qt (2 L)   **Portions:** 10   **Portion size:** 6 oz (200 mL)

U.S.	Metric	Ingredients	PROCEDURE
1 oz	30 g	Butter	1. Heat the butter in a saucepan over medium heat.
2 oz	60 g	Onions, cut brunoise	2. Add the onions and carrots. Sauté until they are lightly browned.
2 oz	60 g	Carrots, cut brunoise	
1 lb	500 g	Small shrimp, shells on	3. Add the shrimp, bay leaf, thyme, and parsley stems. Sauté until the shrimp turn red.
small piece	small piece	Bay leaf	
pinch	pinch	Thyme	4. Add the tomato paste and stir well.
4	4	Parsley stems	5. Add the brandy and wine. Simmer until reduced by half.
1 oz	30 g	Tomato paste	6. Remove the shrimp. Peel and devein them. Return the shells to the saucepan.
2 oz	60 mL	Burnt brandy (see note)	
6 oz	200 mL	White wine	7. Cut the shrimp into small dice and reserve for garnish.
1 qt	1 L	Fish velouté	8. Add the fish velouté and stock to the saucepan. Simmer 10–15 minutes.
1 pt	500 mL	Fish stock	
1 cup	250 mL	Heavy cream, hot	9. Strain. Return the soup to the saucepan and bring back to a simmer.
to taste	to taste	Salt	
to taste	to taste	White pepper	10. At service time, add the hot cream and the diced shrimp. Season to taste.

Per serving:
Calories, 220; Protein, 8 g; Fat, 17 g (70% cal.); Cholesterol, 110 mg;
Carbohydrates, 6 g; Fiber, 0 g; Sodium, 180 mg.

Note: Burnt brandy is brandy that has been heated in a saucepan and flamed (carefully) to burn off the alcohol.

VARIATIONS

This recipe is based on Method 1 for making cream soups (p. 184), because it uses velouté as a base. You can also use fish stock instead of velouté and thicken the soup in other ways:

1. Beat in a beurre manié (p. 184), a little at a time, after step 8, until properly thickened.
2. Stir in a cornstarch slurry (cornstarch in cold water), a little at a time.
3. Simmer 2 oz (60 g) rice in 1 pt (500 mL) of the stock, until the rice is completely cooked. Liquefy in a blender or force through a fine sieve to purée the rice, and add to the soup. (This is the classical method.)

To *reduce food cost*, you may reduce the quantity of shrimp and add extra shrimp shells for flavor. Or, instead of using all the cooked shrimp for garnish, save most of them for another use.

Paprika is often used instead of tomato paste to color and flavor bisques. Substitute 1 tbsp (15 mL) Spanish paprika for the 1 oz (30 g) tomato paste.

Lobster Bisque

In place of shrimp, use live lobster, cut as shown in Figure 14.12. (Alternatively, to reduce food costs, use crushed lobster shells or rock lobster tails.)

Chowders

Chowders are chunky, hearty soups that are so full of good things that they sometimes are more like stews than soups. Many chowders are simply cream soups or purée soups that are not puréed but left chunky. Like other specialty regional soups, chowders resist categorization. However, most of them are based on fish or shellfish or vegetables, and most contain potatoes and milk or cream.

Potato Chowder

Yield: 6 qt (6 L)   Portions: 24   Portion size: 8 oz (250 mL)

U.S.	Metric	Ingredients	PROCEDURE
8 oz	250 g	Salt pork	1. Grind the salt pork or cut into very fine dice.
12 oz	375 g	Onions, medium dice	2. Render the pork fat in a heavy saucepot.
3 oz	90 g	Celery, medium dice	3. Add the onions and celery. Cook in the fat over moderate heat until nearly tender. Do not brown.
4 oz	125 g	Flour	4. Add the flour. Stir into the fat to make a roux. Cook the roux slowly for 4–5 minutes, but do not let it brown.
3½ qt	3.5 L	Chicken stock	5. Using a wire whip, slowly stir in the stock. Bring to a boil, stirring to make sure the liquid is smooth.
3 lb	1.5 kg	Potatoes, medium dice	6. Add the potatoes. Simmer until all the vegetables are tender.
3 pt	1.5 L	Milk, hot	7. Stir in the hot milk and cream.
1 cup	250 mL	Heavy cream, hot	8. Season to taste with salt and white pepper.
to taste	to taste	Salt	
to taste	to taste	White pepper	
as needed	as needed	Chopped parsley	9. Sprinkle each portion with a little chopped parsley for garnish.

Per serving:
Calories, 210; Protein, 5 g; Fat, 14 g (58% cal.); Cholesterol, 35 mg;
Carbohydrates, 18 g; Fiber, 1 g; Sodium, 180 mg.

VARIATION

Corn Chowder

Version 1. Prepare as in basic recipe, but reduce potatoes to 2¼ lb (1.1 kg). When vegetables are tender, add 3 lb (1.5 kg) frozen or drained canned whole kernel corn. (If using canned corn, replace part of the chicken stock with the corn liquid.)

Version 2. Prepare as in basic recipe, but reduce potatoes to 1½ lb (750 g). Add 3 lb (1.5 kg) canned cream-style corn when vegetables are tender.

Corn and Crab Chowder with Basil

Yield: 6 qt (6 L)   Portions: 24   Portion size: 8 oz (250 mL)

U.S.	Metric	Ingredients	PROCEDURE
3 oz	90 mL	Vegetable oil	1. Heat the oil in a heavy soup pot over moderate heat.
12 oz	375 g	Onions, medium dice	2. Add the onions and garlic.
2 cloves	2 cloves	Garlic, chopped	3. Cook over moderate heat until nearly tender. Do not brown.
3 oz	90 g	Flour	4. Add the flour. Stir into the fat to make a roux. Cook the roux slowly for 4–5 minutes, but do not let it brown.
3½ qt	3.5 L	Mild fish stock or chicken stock	5. Using a wire whip, slowly stir in the stock. Bring to a boil, stirring to make sure the liquid is smooth. Add the wine.
8 oz	250 mL	Dry white wine	6. Add the potatoes and bay leaves. Simmer until the potatoes are tender.
2 lb	1 kg	Potatoes, medium dice (see note)	
2	2	Bay leaves	
2 lb	1 kg	Corn kernels, fresh or frozen	7. Add the corn kernels and shredded basil. Return the soup to a simmer.
½ cup	125 mL	Fresh basil leaves, shredded	
2 lb	1 kg	Crabmeat	8. Add the crabmeat.
1 pt	500 mL	Milk, hot	9. Stir in the hot milk and cream.
8 oz	250 mL	Heavy cream, hot	10. Season to taste with salt and pepper.
to taste	to taste	Salt	
to taste	to taste	White pepper	

Per serving:
Calories, 220; Protein, 12 g; Fat, 9 g (36% cal.); Cholesterol, 45 mg;
Carbohydrates, 22 g; Fiber, 2 g; Sodium, 160 mg.

Note: For attractive color, use small red-skinned potatoes and do not peel them.

VARIATION

If a thicker soup is desired, increase the flour to 4 oz (125 g) and the oil to 4 oz (125 mL).

Corn and Crab Chowder with Basil

New England Clam Chowder

Yield: 6 qt (6 L)   **Portions:** 24   **Portion size:** 8 oz (250 mL)

U.S.	Metric	Ingredients	PROCEDURE
2 qt	2 L	Canned, minced clams, with their juice, or fresh shucked clams, with their juice (see note)	1. Drain the clams. If you are using fresh clams, chop them, being sure to save all the juice.
1½ qt	1.5 L	Water	2. Combine the juice and water in a saucepan. Bring to a boil.
			3. Remove from the heat and keep the liquid hot for step 7.
10 oz	300 g	Salt pork, ground or cut into fine dice	4. In a heavy saucepot or stockpot, render the salt pork over medium heat.
1 lb	500 g	Onions, small dice	5. Add the onions and cook slowly until they are soft, but do not brown.
4 oz	125 g	Flour	6. Add the flour and stir to make a roux. Cook the roux slowly for 3–4 minutes, but do not let it brown.
2 lb	1 kg	Potatoes, small dice	7. Using a wire whip, slowly stir the clam liquid and water into the roux. Bring to a boil, stirring constantly to make sure the liquid is smooth.
			8. Add the potatoes. Simmer until tender. (If you are using large, tough chowder clams, pass them once through a grinder and add them with the potatoes.)
2½ qt	2.5 L	Milk, hot	9. Stir in the clams and the hot milk and cream. Heat gently, but do not boil.
1 cup	250 mL	Heavy cream, hot	10. Season to taste with salt and white pepper.
to taste	to taste	Salt	
to taste	to taste	White pepper	

Per serving:
Calories, 300; Protein, 16 g; Fat, 17 g (52% cal.); Cholesterol, 65 mg;
Carbohydrates, 19 g; Fiber, 1 g; Sodium, 350 mg.

Note: If whole clams in the shell are used, you will need about 8–10 qt (8–10 L). Scrub them well. Combine with the 1½ qt (1½ L) water in a stockpot and simmer until the shells are open. Remove the clams from the shells and chop. Strain the liquid.

VARIATIONS

Manhattan Clam Chowder

Substitute 4 oz (125 mL) oil or 4 oz (125 g) butter for the salt pork. Add 10 oz (300 g) celery, small dice; 10 oz (300 g) carrots, small dice; and 1 tsp (5 mL) chopped garlic to the onions in step 5. Omit flour. Instead of milk, use 2½ qt (2½ L) chopped canned tomatoes and their juices. Omit cream.

New England Fish Chowder

Follow the procedure for New England clam chowder, but omit clams and water. Use 3 qt (3 L) fish stock instead of the clam juice and water mixture in step 7. Remove all skin and bones from 1¼ lb (625 g) haddock fillets. Cut into ¾ inch (2 cm) chunks. Add to the finished soup and *keep hot* (do not boil) until the fish is cooked, about 5 minutes.

Specialty Soups and National Soups

French Onion Soup Gratinée

Yield: 7½ qt (7.5 L)   Portions: 24   Portion size: 10 oz (300 mL)

U.S.	Metric	Ingredients	PROCEDURE
4 oz	125 g	Butter	1. Heat the butter in a stockpot over moderate heat. Add the onions and cook until they are golden. Stir occasionally.
5 lb	2.5 kg	Onions, sliced thin	*Note:* The onions must cook slowly and become evenly browned. This is a slow process and will take about 30 minutes. Do not brown too fast or use high heat.
6½ qt	6.5 L	Beef stock, or half beef and half chicken stock	2. Add the stock and bring to a boil. Simmer until the onions are very tender and the flavors are well blended, about 20 minutes.
to taste	to taste	Salt	3. Season to taste with salt and pepper. Add the sherry, if desired.
to taste	to taste	Pepper	
4–6 oz	125–175 mL	Sherry (optional)	4. Keep the soup hot for service.
as needed	as needed	French bread (see procedure)	5. Cut the bread into slices about ⅜ inch (1 cm) thick. You will need 1 or 2 slices per portion, or just enough to cover the top of the soup in its serving crock.
1½ lb	750 g	Gruyère or Swiss cheese, or a mixture, coarsely grated	6. Toast the slices in the oven or under the broiler.
			7. For each portion, fill an individual service soup crock with hot soup. Place one or two slices of the toast on top and cover with cheese. Pass under the broiler until the cheese is bubbling and lightly browned. Serve immediately.

Per serving:
Calories, 320; Protein, 15 g; Fat, 15 g (42% cal.); Cholesterol, 50 mg;
Carbohydrates, 31 g; Fiber, 3 g; Sodium, 410 mg.

VARIATION

Onion soup may be served without gratinéeing and with cheese croutons prepared separately. Toast the bread as in basic recipe. Place on a sheet pan. Brush lightly with butter and sprinkle each piece with grated cheese. (Parmesan may be mixed with the other cheese.) Brown under the broiler. Garnish each portion with one cheese crouton. (This method is less expensive because it uses much less cheese.)

Viennese-Style Vegetable Broth

Yield: 6 qt (6 L)   **Portions:** 24   **Portion size:** 8 oz (250 mL)

U.S.	Metric	Ingredients	PROCEDURE
3½ oz	100 g	Butter	1. Heat the butter in a saucepot over medium heat. Add the onion, turnip, and carrot brunoise to the pot and sweat without coloring.
7 oz	200 g	Onions, cut brunoise	
7 oz	200 g	Turnip, cut brunoise	
7 oz	200 g	Carrot, cut brunoise	2. Add the stock to the pot and quickly bring to a boil. Add the beans, leeks, and zucchini. Simmer for 5 minutes.
4½ qt	4.5 L	Chicken stock	
7 oz	200 g	Tender young green beans, cut brunoise or sliced thin	3. Add the herbs to the soup. Season to taste.
7 oz	200 g	Leeks, cut brunoise	4. At service time, mix together the cream and egg yolks to make a liaison. Slowly stir a little hot soup into the liaison, then add the tempered liaison to the soup. Carefully reheat the soup, but do not let it boil. Serve immediately.
7 oz	200 g	Zucchini, cut brunoise	
1½ oz	45 g	Chopped parsley	
1 tbsp	10 g	Fresh marjoram leaves, chopped fine (see note)	
1½ tsp	5 g	Fresh thyme (see note)	
1 pt	400 mL	Heavy cream	
4	4	Egg yolks	

Per serving:
Calories, 130; Protein, 2 g; Fat, 12 g (79% cal.); Cholesterol, 75 mg;
Carbohydrates, 5 g; Fiber, 1 g; Sodium, 65 mg.

Note: If fresh marjoram and thyme are not available, use one-third their quantity of dried herbs.

Roasted Garlic Soup with Black Olive Crostini

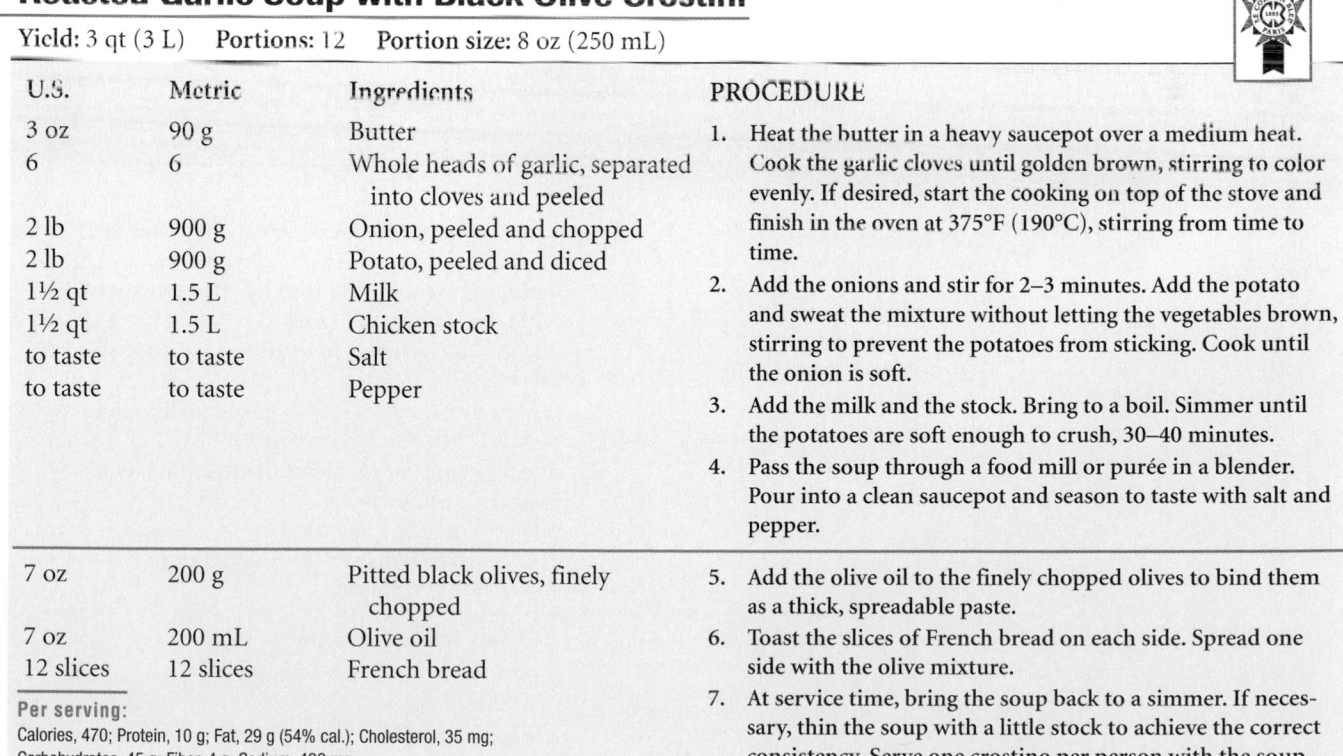

Yield: 3 qt (3 L)   **Portions:** 12   **Portion size:** 8 oz (250 mL)

U.S.	Metric	Ingredients	PROCEDURE
3 oz	90 g	Butter	1. Heat the butter in a heavy saucepot over a medium heat. Cook the garlic cloves until golden brown, stirring to color evenly. If desired, start the cooking on top of the stove and finish in the oven at 375°F (190°C), stirring from time to time.
6	6	Whole heads of garlic, separated into cloves and peeled	
2 lb	900 g	Onion, peeled and chopped	
2 lb	900 g	Potato, peeled and diced	
1½ qt	1.5 L	Milk	2. Add the onions and stir for 2–3 minutes. Add the potato and sweat the mixture without letting the vegetables brown, stirring to prevent the potatoes from sticking. Cook until the onion is soft.
1½ qt	1.5 L	Chicken stock	
to taste	to taste	Salt	
to taste	to taste	Pepper	
			3. Add the milk and the stock. Bring to a boil. Simmer until the potatoes are soft enough to crush, 30–40 minutes.
			4. Pass the soup through a food mill or purée in a blender. Pour into a clean saucepot and season to taste with salt and pepper.
7 oz	200 g	Pitted black olives, finely chopped	5. Add the olive oil to the finely chopped olives to bind them as a thick, spreadable paste.
7 oz	200 mL	Olive oil	6. Toast the slices of French bread on each side. Spread one side with the olive mixture.
12 slices	12 slices	French bread	7. At service time, bring the soup back to a simmer. If necessary, thin the soup with a little stock to achieve the correct consistency. Serve one crostino per person with the soup.

Per serving:
Calories, 470; Protein, 10 g; Fat, 29 g (54% cal.); Cholesterol, 35 mg;
Carbohydrates, 45 g; Fiber, 4 g; Sodium, 430 mg.

Minestrone

Yield: 6 qt (6 L)   **Portions:** 24   **Portion size:** 8 oz (250 mL)

U.S.	Metric	Ingredients	PROCEDURE
4 oz	125 mL	Olive oil	1. Heat the oil in a heavy pot over medium heat.
1 lb	500 g	Onions, sliced thin	2. Add the onions, celery, carrots, and garlic. Sweat them in the oil until they are almost tender. Do not brown.
8 oz	250 g	Celery, small dice	3. Add the cabbage and zucchini. Stir to mix the vegetables. Continue to sweat them for another 5 minutes.
8 oz	250 g	Carrots, small dice	
2 tsp	10 mL	Garlic, chopped	
8 oz	250 g	Green cabbage, shredded (see p. 440 for technique)	
8 oz	250 g	Zucchini, medium dice	
1 lb	500 g	Canned tomatoes, crushed	4. Add the tomatoes, stock, and basil. Bring to a boil, reduce heat, and simmer until the vegetables are almost cooked. (Do not overcook. The soup will continue to cook when the pasta is added.)
5 qt	5 L	White stock	
1 tsp	5 mL	Basil	
6 oz	175 g	Small macaroni, such as ditalini	5. Add the pasta and continue to simmer the soup until the pasta is cooked.
1½ lb	750 g	Drained, canned cannellini or other white beans (2 No. 2 cans)	6. Add the beans and bring the soup back to a boil.
¼ cup	60 mL	Chopped parsley	7. Add the parsley. Season to taste with salt and pepper.
to taste	to taste	Salt	
to taste	to taste	Pepper	
as needed	as needed	Parmesan cheese, grated	8. Just before service, stir in the parmesan cheese, or serve the cheese separately.

Per serving:
Calories, 150; Protein, 7 g; Fat, 7 g (40% cal.); Cholesterol, 10 mg;
Carbohydrates, 17 g; Fiber, 3 g; Sodium, 200 mg.

Gulyas

Yield: 3 qt (3 L)   **Portions:** 12   **Portion size:** 8 oz (250 mL)

U.S.	Metric	Ingredients	PROCEDURE
2 oz	60 g	Pork fatback or bacon	1. Grind the fatback or bacon or cut it into fine dice. Render the fat in a heavy pot. After the fat has rendered, remove the solids with a slotted spoon and discard or save for another use.
8 oz	250 g	Onions, medium dice	2. Add the onions to the fat in the pot and sweat. Do not brown.
1 lb 8 oz	750 g	Beef chuck or shank	
2 cloves	2 cloves	Garlic, chopped fine	3. Cut the beef into medium dice. Add to the onions and cook over low heat for 10 minutes.
½ tsp	2 mL	Caraway seeds	4. Add the garlic, caraway seeds, paprika, and tomato paste. Stir them in well.
2 tbsp	12 g	Hungarian paprika	
1 tbsp	15 mL	Tomato paste	5. Add the liquid. Simmer until the beef is almost tender. This may take 1 hour or more, depending on the type and quality of the meat.
2½ qt	2.5 L	Water or brown stock, hot	
1 lb	500 g	Potatoes, peeled, medium dice	6. Add the potatoes and simmer until done.
to taste	to taste	Salt	7. Season to taste with salt and pepper.
to taste	to taste	Pepper	

Per serving:
Calories, 210; Protein, 12 g; Fat, 14 g (60% cal.); Cholesterol, 40 mg;
Carbohydrates, 9 g; Fiber, 1 g; Sodium, 45 mg.

Borscht

Yield: 6 qt (6 L)   Portions: 24   Portion size: 8 oz (250 mL)

U.S.	Metric	Ingredients	PROCEDURE
2 lb	1 kg	Beef brisket or shank (see note)	1. Simmer the beef in the water or stock until tender.
3½ qt	3½ L	Water or beef stock	2. Remove the cooked beef from the broth and cut it into small dice.
			3. Measure the broth and, if necessary, add water to bring it back up to 3 qt (3 L).
			4. Return the meat to the broth.
4 oz	125 g	Butter	5. Heat the butter in a heavy pot. Add the onion, leeks, and the cabbage. Cook slowly in the butter for about 5 minutes.
8 oz	250 g	Onion, sliced thin	
8 oz	250 g	Leeks, white part and about ½ inch (1 cm) of green, cut julienne	
8 oz	250 g	Cabbage, shredded	
2 No. 2½ cans	2 No. 2½ cans	Beets (about 60 oz/1.7 kg) (see note)	6. Drain the beets and save the juice. Grate the beets on a coarse grater or chop them fine.
4 oz	125 g	Tomato purée	7. Add the mixture of onions, leeks, and cabbage, the beets, beet juice, tomato purée, vinegar, and sugar to the meat and broth.
4 oz	125 mL	Vinegar	
2 tbsp	30 g	Sugar	8. Bring to a boil and simmer until the vegetables are tender.
to taste	to taste	Salt	9. Season to taste with salt, white pepper, and more vinegar if desired.
to taste	to taste	White pepper	
as needed	as needed	Sour cream	10. Serve each portion topped with a spoonful of sour cream.

Per serving:
Calories, 150; Protein, 9 g; Fat, 9 g (53% cal.); Cholesterol, 40 mg;
Carbohydrates, 9 g; Fiber, 1 g; Sodium, 250 mg.

Note: Leftover cooked beef may be used. In this case, use 16–20 oz (500–625 g) cooked beef and use stock, not water.

If fresh raw beets are used, shred or grate them and sweat them with the onions.

VARIATION

Cold Borscht

Omit beef. Strain soup through a china cap, pressing down on the vegetables to force out all juices. Chill the soup and add lemon juice to taste. Serve with sour cream.

Velouté Agnes Sorel (Chicken and Leek Soup)

Yield: 3–3½ qt (3–3.5 L) plus garnish   Portions: 12   Portion size: 8 oz, plus 2½ oz garnish
(250 mL, plus 75 g garnish)

U.S.	Metric	Ingredients	PROCEDURE
2	2	Chickens, 3 lb (1.5 kg) each	1. Trim the chickens. Trim the vegetables as necessary. Place the chickens in water with the whole vegetables and bouquet garni. Simmer for 30 minutes. Remove the chickens from the broth. Strain the broth.
2	2	Carrots, whole, medium size	
2	2	Onions, whole, medium size	
2 stalks	2 stalks	Celery	
1	1	Leek	
5 qt	5 L	Water	
1	1	Bouquet garni	
13 oz	400 g	Leeks, white part only	2. Thinly slice the leeks.
1 lb	500 g	White button mushrooms	3. Wash the mushrooms. Cut the white part of the caps into julienne until you have 7 oz (200 g) julienne. Set the mushroom julienne aside for the garnish. Slice the remainder of the mushrooms.
3 oz	100 g	Butter	
3 oz	100 g	Rice powder (see note)	4. Sweat the sliced mushrooms and the leeks in butter.
5 oz	150 g	Crème fraîche	5. Add 3 qt (3 L) of the poaching liquid. Simmer about 30 minutes.
			6. Dissolve the rice powder in a little of the hot liquid, then gradually stir into the broth. Simmer a few minutes until thickened.
			7. Transfer to a blender or food processor and process until smooth. Mix in half the crème fraîche, then strain through a fine sieve.
5 oz	150 g	Crème fraîche	8. Mix the remaining crème fraîche and the egg yolks together in a small bowl. Add some of the hot liquid to temper, and mix well. Then incorporate the liaison into the soup over very low heat. Do not allow the soup to boil or the egg yolks will curdle.
4	4	Egg yolks	
5 oz	150 g	Cooked cured beef tongue	9. Remove the breast meat from the chickens. Save the legs for another use. Cut the breast meat into julienne. Similarly, cut the cured tongue into julienne.
			10. Gently sauté the reserved mushroom julienne in just enough butter to coat the bottom of a sauté pan.
			11. To serve, place the julienned garnish in the bottom of a serving bowl, then pour the hot soup over the garnish.

Per serving:
Calories, 300; Protein, 15 g; Fat, 21 g (63% cal.); Cholesterol, 145 mg;
Carbohydrates, 13 g; Fiber, 1 g; Sodium, 230 mg.

Note: If rice powder (also called cream of rice) is not available, substitute an equal weight of potato starch.

Scotch Broth

Yield: 6 qt (6 L)   Portions: 24   Portion size: 8 oz (250 mL)

U.S.	Metric	Ingredients	PROCEDURE
6 qt	6 L	White lamb stock	1. Bring 1 qt (1 L) of the stock to a boil in a saucepan.
4 oz	125 g	Barley	2. Add the barley and cover the pan. Simmer until tender.
1½ lb	750 g	Lean, boneless lamb shoulder or shank, cut in small dice	3. Bring the remaining 5 qt (5 L) of stock to a boil in another pot.
			4. Add the lamb and cover the pot. Simmer until the meat is almost tender.
4 oz	125 g	Butter	5. Heat the butter in a heavy pot over medium heat. Add the vegetables and sweat them in the butter until nearly tender.
12 oz	375 g	Onions, cut brunoise	
8 oz	250 g	Carrots, cut brunoise	6. Add the lamb and stock from step 4. Simmer until the meat and vegetables are tender.
8 oz	250 g	Celery, cut brunoise	
4 oz	125 g	Leeks, cut brunoise	7. Add the cooked barley and stock from step 2. Simmer about 5 minutes, until the flavors are well blended.
4 oz	125 g	Turnips, cut brunoise	
to taste	to taste	Salt	8. Season to taste with salt and pepper.
to taste	to taste	White pepper	
as needed	as needed	Chopped parsley	9. At serving time, sprinkle each portion with a little chopped parsley.

Per serving:
Calories, 120; Protein, 8 g; Fat, 7 g (51% cal.); Cholesterol, 35 mg; Carbohydrates, 7 g; Fiber, 2 g; Sodium, 80 mg.

Gazpacho

Yield: 2½ qt (2.5 L)   Portions: 12   Portion size: 6 oz (200 mL)

U.S.	Metric	Ingredients	PROCEDURE
2½ lb	1.2 kg	Tomatoes, peeled and chopped fine	1. If a blender is available, combine all ingredients in the blender and process until liquefied.
1 lb	500 g	Cucumbers, peeled and chopped fine	2. If a blender is not available, combine all ingredients except the olive oil. Pass through a food mill. If a smoother soup is desired, then pass through a fine sieve. Rub the solids through the sieve to purée them. Place the mixture in a stainless-steel bowl. Using the wire whip, slowly beat in the olive oil.
8 oz	250 g	Onions, peeled and chopped fine	
4 oz	125 g	Green peppers, seeded and chopped fine	
½ tsp	2 mL	Crushed garlic	
2 oz	60 g	Fresh white bread crumbs	
1 pt	500 mL	Cold water or tomato juice	
3 oz	90 mL	Red wine vinegar	
4 oz	125 mL	Olive oil	
to taste	to taste	Salt	3. Add salt, pepper, and cayenne or pepper sauce to taste.
to taste	to taste	Pepper	4. If necessary, adjust the tartness by adding a little lemon juice or vinegar.
to taste	to taste	Cayenne or hot red pepper sauce	
to taste	to taste	Lemon juice or vinegar	5. Chill the soup thoroughly.
		Garnish:	6. Combine garnish ingredients in a small bowl or bain-marie.
2 oz	60 g	Onion, small dice	
2 oz	60 g	Cucumber, small dice	7. At service time, ladle 6 oz (200 mL) gazpacho into chilled soup cups. Top with 1–2 tbsp (15–30 g) diced vegetable garnish. If desired, gazpacho may be served with ice cubes.
2 oz	60 g	Green pepper, small dice	

Per serving:
Calories, 130; Protein, 2 g; Fat, 10 g (63% cal.); Cholesterol, 0 mg; Carbohydrates, 11 g; Fiber, 2 g; Sodium, 35 mg.

Lightly Saffroned Mussel Soup

Yield: about 3¼–3½ qt (3.25–3.5 L)   **Portions:** 12   **Portion size:** 10 oz (300 mL)

U.S.	Metric	Ingredients	PROCEDURE
4 qt	4 L	Mussels	1. Clean the mussels thoroughly.
2½ oz	80 g	Shallots, minced	2. Place the mussels, shallots, garlic, celery, bouquet garni, and white wine in a covered pot. Cook until the mussels are open.
3 cloves	3 cloves	Garlic, crushed	
2 oz	70 g	Celery	3. Remove the mussels with a slotted spoon. Remove the mussels from their shells and, if necessary, remove any remaining beards from the mussels. Discard the shells.
1	1	Bouquet garni (see p. 127)	
1½ pt	800 mL	White wine	
			4. Carefully strain the cooking liquid through cheesecloth, pouring carefully so that any sand is left in the cooking pot.
3½ oz	100 g	Carrot, cut julienne	5. Sweat the julienned vegetables in the butter until just tender. Reserve for garnishing the soup.
3½ oz	100 g	Leek, cut julienne	
3 oz	80 g	Celery, cut julienne	
1½ oz	50 g	Butter	
1 pt 3 oz	600 mL	Crème fraîche	6. Measure the cooking liquid and add enough fish stock to bring the volume to 3 qt (3 L). Bring to a boil. Allow to reduce by 30–50%, depending on the saltiness of the liquid.
4 knife tips (see note)	4 knife tips (see note)	Powdered saffron (see note)	
18	18	Egg yolks	7. Place one half of the crème fraîche in a small bowl. Stir a little of the hot broth into the cream, then stir into the broth. Add the saffron and bring back to a boil.
to taste	to taste	Pepper	
3 tbsp	20 g	Minced chives	8. Mix the egg yolks with the remaining crème fraîche. Temper with a little of the hot soup, then add the mixture to the soup. Place on low heat and heat gently without letting it boil.
			9. Taste and season with a little pepper and, if necessary, salt. (Because mussels are salty, you will probably not need to add salt. Taste carefully.)
			10. To serve, place the julienned vegetables and the mussel meats in the bottoms of warmed broad soup plates, using about 1 oz (25 g) vegetables and 2½ oz (70 g) mussels per portion. Ladle the hot soup into the plates. Sprinkle with chives.

Per serving:
Calories, 510; Protein, 30 g; Fat, 32 g (58% cal.); Cholesterol, 420 mg; Carbohydrates, 13 g; Fiber, 1 g; Sodium, 660 mg.

Note: To measure something as precious as saffron powder, use the tip of a clean, dry knife to measure out the amount needed. If using saffron threads instead of powder, use a generous pinch of the threads.

Terms for Review

clear soup	purée soup	potage	clearmeat
vegetable soup	bisque	national soup	coagulation
consommé	chowder	clarification	raft
cream soup			

Chilled Melon and Mint Soup

Yield: 3 qt (3 L)   **Portions:** 12   **Portion size:** 8 oz (250 mL)

U.S.	Metric	Ingredients
3 lb	1.4 kg	Galia melon (see note)
3 lb 8 oz	1.6 kg	Charentais melon (see note)
4 lb	1.9 kg	Honeydew melon
1 lb 4 oz	600 g	Watermelon
to taste	to taste	Lemon juice
to taste	to taste	Sugar
2 oz	60 g	Mint leaves, finely chopped
		Garnish:
as needed	as needed	Mint sprigs

PROCEDURE

1. Quarter the melons. Scrape the seeds from the galia, Charentais, and honeydew melons. Remove as many seeds as possible from the watermelon. Cut the flesh of each type of melon into balls with a ball cutter and place in a bowl. Cover and refrigerate.
2. Scoop the remaining flesh from the melons. Place in a food processor and purée. (Do not use a blender unless you remove all the watermelon seeds first, as it will chop the seeds into fine bits.) Strain to remove watermelon seeds.
3. Taste and, if required, add lemon juice and sugar to taste.
4. Stir in the chopped mint. Pour over the melon balls and chill for at least 2 hours.
5. At service time, ladle into chilled bowls and garnish with sprigs of mint.

Per serving:
Calories, 60; Protein, 1 g; Fat, 0 g (0% cal.); Cholesterol, 0 mg; Carbohydrates, 15 g; Fiber, 1 g; Sodium, 15 mg.

Note: If galia melon is not available, use yellow-fleshed honeydew. If Charentais melon is not available, use cantaloupe.

Chilled Melon and Mint Soup

See these soup recipes in other chapters:

Clear Soup with Shrimp (Japanese) and variations (p. 719)
Miso Soup (p. 719)
Zuppa di Ceci e Riso (Italian Chick Pea and Rice Soup) (p. 739)
Caldo Verde (p. 749)

Questions for Discussion

1. You have 3 gallons (12 liters) of vegetable soup in the walk-in, prepared by a cook on the morning shift. You are going to serve the soup this evening, and your dinner service lasts from 6 until 10 P.M. How should you prepare the soup for service?
2. What are the most important characteristics of a good consommé?
3. Why is it important not to boil consommé during clarification?
4. What is the function of egg whites in clearmeat? Mirepoix? Tomato product?
5. In what order would you add the following items to a vegetable soup during cooking?
   Carrots   Shredded cabbage   Tomatoes   Barley   Diced cooked beef
6. Using Method 1 or 2, describe how you would prepare cream of watercress soup

Understanding Meats and Game

Meat is muscle tissue. It is the flesh of domestic animals (cattle, hogs, and lambs) and of wild game animals (such as deer). As a cook, chef, or food service operator, you will be spending more of your time and money on meats than on any other food.

It is important, then, to understand meats thoroughly in order to cook them well and profitably. Why are some meats tender and some tough? How can you tell one cut from another when there are so many? How do you determine the best way to cook each cut?

In order to answer questions like these, it is helpful to start at the most basic level of composition and structure. We then proceed to discuss grading and inspection, basic cuts, and appropriate cooking and storage methods. In addition, we discuss the characteristics of variety meats and of popular game meats. Only then can we best approach the individual cooking methods and recipes presented in the following chapters.

Composition, Structure, and Basic Quality Factors

Composition

Muscle tissue consists of three major components: water, protein, and fat.

WATER

Water is about 75 percent of muscle tissue. With such a high percentage of water, you can see why *shrinkage* can be a big problem in cooking meat. Too much moisture loss means dry meat, loss of weight, and loss of profit.

PROTEIN

Protein is an important nutrient and the most abundant solid material in meat. About 20 percent of muscle tissue is protein.

As we learned in Chapter 4, protein *coagulates* when it is heated. This means it becomes firmer and loses moisture. Coagulation is related to doneness. When protein has coagulated to the desired degree, the meat is said to be "done." Doneness is discussed later in this chapter.

Too high heat *toughens* protein.

FAT

Fat accounts for up to 5 percent of muscle tissue. Of course, there can be more fat surrounding the muscles. A beef carcass can be as much as 30 percent fat.

Because of health and dietary concerns, many meat animals are being bred and raised with a lower fat content than in past years. Nevertheless, a certain amount of fat is desirable for three reasons:

1. Juiciness.
   Marbling is fat that is deposited within the muscle tissue. The juiciness we enjoy in well-marbled beef is due more to fat than to moisture.
   Surface fat protects the meat—especially roasts—from drying out during cooking as well as in storage. Adding surface fats where they are lacking is called *barding*.

2. Tenderness.
   Marbling separates muscle fibers, making them easier to chew.

3. Flavor.
   Fat is perhaps the main source of flavor in meat. A well-marbled Prime (top grade) steak tastes "beefier" than the same cut of a lower grade.

CARBOHYDRATE

Meat contains a very small amount of carbohydrate. From the standpoint of nutrition, its quantity is so small that it is insignificant. It is important, however, because it plays a necessary part in the complex reactions that take place when meats are browned by roasting, broiling, or sautéing. Without this carbohydrate, the desirable flavor and appearance of browned meats would not be achieved.

Structure

MUSCLE FIBERS

Lean meat is composed of long, thin muscle fibers bound together in bundles. These determine the *texture* or *grain* of a piece of meat. Fine-grained meat is composed of small fibers bound in small bundles. Coarse-textured meat has large fibers.

Feel the cut surface of a tenderloin steak, and compare its smooth texture to the rough cut surface of brisket or bottom round.

CONNECTIVE TISSUE

Muscle fibers are bound together in a network of proteins called *connective tissues*. Also, each muscle fiber is covered in a sheath of connective tissue.

It is important for the cook to understand connective tissue for one basic reason: *connective tissue is tough*. To cook meats successfully, you should know

- Which meats are high in connective tissue and which are low.
- What are the best ways to make tough meats tender.

1. **Meats are highest in connective tissue if**
   - They come from muscles that are more exercised. Muscles in the legs, for example, have more connective tissue than muscles in the back.
   - They come from older animals. Veal is more tender than meat from a young steer, which, in turn, is more tender than meat from an old bull or cow. (Young animals have connective tissue, too, but it becomes harder to break down as the animal ages.)

2. **Meats high in connective tissue can be made more tender by using proper cooking techniques.** There are two kinds of connective tissue: *collagen*, which is white in color, and *elastin*, which is yellow.
   - **Collagen.**
     Long, slow cooking in the presence of moisture breaks down or dissolves collagen by turning it into gelatin and water. Of course, muscle tissue is about 75 percent water, so moisture is always present when meats are cooked. Except for very large roasts, however, long cooking by a dry-heat method has the danger of evaporating too much moisture and drying out the meat. Therefore, *moist-heat cooking methods at low temperatures are most effective for turning a meat high in connective tissue into a tender, juicy finished product.*
     Other factors also help tenderize collagen:

     Acid helps dissolve collagen. Marinating meat in an acid mixture, or adding an acid such as tomato or wine to the cooking liquid, helps tenderize.
     Enzymes are naturally present in meats. They break down some connective tissue and other proteins as meat ages (see "Aging," p. 213). These enzymes are inactive at freezing temperatures, slow acting under refrigeration, active at room temperature, and destroyed by heat above 140°F (60°C).
     Tenderizers are enzymes such as papain (extracted from papaya) that are added to meats by the cook or injected into the animal before slaughter. Exercise care when using enzyme tenderizers. Too long an exposure at room temperature can make the meat undesirably mushy.

   - **Elastin.**
     Older animals have a higher proportion of elastin than younger animals.
     Elastin is not broken down in cooking. Tenderizing can be accomplished only by *removing the elastin* (cutting away any tendons) and by mechanically *breaking up the fibers*, as in

     Pounding and cubing (cubed steaks)
     Grinding (hamburger)
     Slicing the cooked meat very thin against the grain (as in London broil)

Inspection and Grading

Cooks and food service operators in the United States are assisted in their evaluation of meats by a federal inspection and grading system.

Figure 10.1 USDA inspection stamp for meat.

INSPECTION

1. Inspection is a *guarantee of wholesomeness*, not of quality or tenderness. It means that the animal was not diseased and the meat is clean and fit for human consumption.
2. That the meat passed inspection is indicated by a round stamp (Figure 10.1).
3. Inspection is required by U.S. federal law—all meat must be inspected.

QUALITY GRADING

1. Grading is a *quality* designation.
2. The grade is indicated by a shield stamp (Figure 10.2).
3. Grading is *not required by U.S. law.* (Some packers use a *private grading system* and give different brand names to different grades. Reliability of private grades depends on the integrity of the packer.)

Figure 10.2 USDA grade stamp for meat.

Quality grading is based on the texture, firmness, and color of the lean meat, the age or maturity of the animal, and the marbling (the fat within the lean).

All these factors must be considered together. For example, old, tough meat can still have marbling, but it would rate a low grade because of the other factors. Table 10.1 summarizes USDA meat grades.

YIELD GRADING

In addition to quality grading, beef and lamb are graded according to how much usable meat in proportion to fat they have. The meatiest grade is Yield Grade 1. Poorest yield (much exterior fat) is Yield Grade 5.

Pork is yield graded from 1 to 4, but most pork is sold already cut and trimmed.

Veal, which has little fat, is not yield graded.

TABLE 10.1

USDA Meat Grades

Characteristics	Beef	Veal	Lamb	Pork
Highest quality, highest price, limited supply.	Prime	Prime	Prime	Pork used in food service is very consistent in quality and is not quality graded. It is inspected for wholesomeness and graded for yield.
High in quality, generally tender and juicy. Abundant supply. Widely used in food service as well as in retail.	Choice	Choice	Choice	
Lean meat, not as fine or tender. Economical. Can be tender and flavorful if cooked carefully. Used in many institutional food service operations.	Select	Good	Good	
Least frequently used in food service. Highest of these grades are sometimes used in institutional food service. Lowest of these grades are used by canners and processors.	Standard Commercial Utility Cutter Canner	Standard Utility Cull	Utility Cull	

Note: Quality varies within grades. For example, the best Choice beef is close to Prime, while the lowest Choice beef is close to Select.

GREEN MEAT

Soon after slaughter, an animal's muscles stiffen due to chemical changes in the flesh. This stiffness, called *rigor mortis*, gradually disappears. Softening takes three to four days for beef, less time for smaller carcasses like veal, lamb, and pork. This softening is caused by enzymes in the flesh.

Green meat is meat that has not had enough time to soften. It is tough and relatively flavorless. Because it takes several days for meats to reach the kitchen from the slaughterhouse, green meat is seldom a problem, except when meat is frozen while still green.

AGED MEAT

Enzyme action continues in muscle tissue even after meat is no longer green. This tenderizes the flesh even more and develops more flavor. Holding meats in coolers under controlled conditions to provide time for this natural tenderizing is called *aging*.

Beef and lamb can be aged because high-quality carcasses have enough fat cover to protect them from bacteria and from drying. Veal has no fat cover, so it is not aged. Pork does not require aging.

Aging does not mean just storing meat in the refrigerator. *There is a difference between aged meat and old meat.* Conditions must be carefully controlled so that the meat becomes naturally tender without spoiling. There are two primary methods used for aging.

1. **Wet aging.**
   Today, most wholesale meat carcasses are broken down into smaller cuts and enclosed in plastic vacuum packs. These packs are usually known by the trade name *Cryovac®*. The air- and moisture-proof packaging protects the meat from bacteria and mold, and it prevents weight loss due to drying. (However, Cryovac-aged meats often lose more weight in cooking than do dry-aged meats.) Vacuum-pack meats must be refrigerated.

2. **Dry aging.**
   Dry aging is the process of storing meats, usually large cuts, under carefully controlled conditions. The meat is not packaged or wrapped, and it is exposed to air on all sides. Temperature, humidity, and air circulation are precisely controlled to prevent spoilage. Ultraviolet lights are sometimes used in aging coolers to kill bacteria.

   Dry-aged meat can lose up to 20 percent of its weight through moisture loss, depending on the size of the cut and how long it is aged. Consequently, dry aging is a more expensive process than wet aging. Dry-aged meats are usually available from specialty purveyors only and at a higher price than wet-aged meats. Many customers are willing to pay a premium for fine dry-aged steaks because they are considered the best for flavor and texture.

Aging increases tenderness and flavor. An off taste is not characteristic of aged meat. *If a meat smells or tastes spoiled, it probably is.* Sometimes meats in vacuum packs have a musty aroma when first opened, but this disappears quickly.

Aging costs money. Storage costs, weight losses due to drying, and heavier trimming due to dried and discolored surfaces all add to the price of aged meat (although wet aging costs less than dry aging). As a meat purchaser, you will have to decide how much quality is worth how much cost for your particular establishment.

Understanding the Basic Cuts

The following discussion of meat cuts focuses on the four primary meat categories in the wholesale and retail markets: beef, lamb, veal, and pork. Keep in mind, however, that game animals, discussed later in the chapter, have the same bone and muscle structure and are generally divided into the same or similar cuts as nongame animals.

Meat cuts are based on two factors:

1. The muscle and bone structure of the meat.
2. Uses and appropriate cooking methods of various parts of the animal.

Food service suppliers in the United States may follow a set of specifications called Institution Meat Purchase Specifications (IMPS). (IMPS, including numbers and names of cuts, are the same as the National Association of Meat Purveyors Specifications, or NAMPS.) All cuts are described in detail and listed by number. This simplifies purchasing, as you can order by number for exactly the cut you want.

Available Forms: Carcasses, Partial Carcasses, Primals, and Fabricated Cuts

Beef, lamb, veal, and pork may be purchased in some or all of these forms.

CARCASSES

The carcass is the whole animal, minus entrails, head, feet, and hide (except pork, from which only the entrails and head are removed). Whole carcasses are rarely purchased by food service operators because of the skill and labor required in cutting and because of the problem of total utilization.

SIDES, QUARTERS, FORESADDLES, HINDSADDLES

These represent the first step in breaking down a carcass.

Again, these larger cuts are no longer frequently used in food service. Fewer establishments are cutting their own meats.

1. Beef is split first through the backbone into sides. Sides are divided between the 12th and 13th ribs into forequarter and hindquarter.
2. Veal and lamb are not split into sides but are divided between ribs 12 and 13 into foresaddle and hindsaddle.

    Note: A new cutting style has been developed for lamb. In this method, the foresaddle and hindsaddle are divided after the 13th rib. For more information, see the chart of lamb cuts on page 222. Both the new and the traditional styles are available according to the customers' needs.

3. Pork carcasses are not divided in this way. They are cut directly into primal cuts (below).

PRIMAL OR WHOLESALE CUTS

These are the primary divisions of quarters, foresaddles, hindsaddles, and carcasses. These cuts are still used, to some extent, in food service, because they

1. Are small enough to be manageable in many food service kitchens.
2. Are still large enough to allow a variety of cuts for different uses or needs.
3. Are easier to utilize completely than quarters or halves.

Each primal may be *fabricated*, or cut up and trimmed, in several ways. Primal cuts are always the starting point for smaller cuts. For this reason, it will benefit you to be able to identify each one. Study the charts and photos in Figures 10.3 through 10.6. (Please note that the lamb chart in Figure 10.5 shows the traditional cuts, not the new cuts mentioned previously.) Learn the names of the primals, their location on the carcass, and the most important cuts that come from each. Then, whenever you work with a piece of meat, try to identify it exactly and match it with its primal cut.

FABRICATED CUTS

Primal cuts are fabricated into smaller cuts for roasts, steaks, chops, cutlets, stewing meat, ground meat, and so forth, according to individual customer requirements and, if applicable, IMPS/NAMPS specifications.

The amount of trim and exact specifications can have many variations. For example, a beef primal rib can be trimmed and prepared for roasting at least nine ways.

Portion-controlled cuts are ready-to-cook meats cut according to customer's specifications. Steaks and chops are ordered either by weight per steak or by thickness. Portion-controlled cuts require the least work for the cook of all meat cuts. They are also the most expensive per pound of all categories of cuts.

Bone Structure

Knowing the bone structure of meat animals is essential for:

1. **Identification of meat cuts.**
   The distinctive shapes of the bones are often the best clue to the identification of a cut. Note how the shapes of the bones in the photographs in Figures 10.3 through 10.6 help your recognition.

2. **Boning and cutting meats.**
   Bones are often surrounded by flesh. You will need to know where they are even if you can't see them.

3. **Carving cooked meats.**
   Same reason as for number 2.

Study the chart of the beef skeleton in Figure 10.7 and learn the names of the major bones. Then compare the charts in Figures 10.3 through 10.6. You will see that the bone structures for all the animals are identical (except for pork, which has more than 13 ribs). Even the names are the same.

The photographs in Figures 10.3 through 10.6 depict typical primal and fabricated cuts of beef, lamb, veal, and pork.

Figure 10.3 Beef.

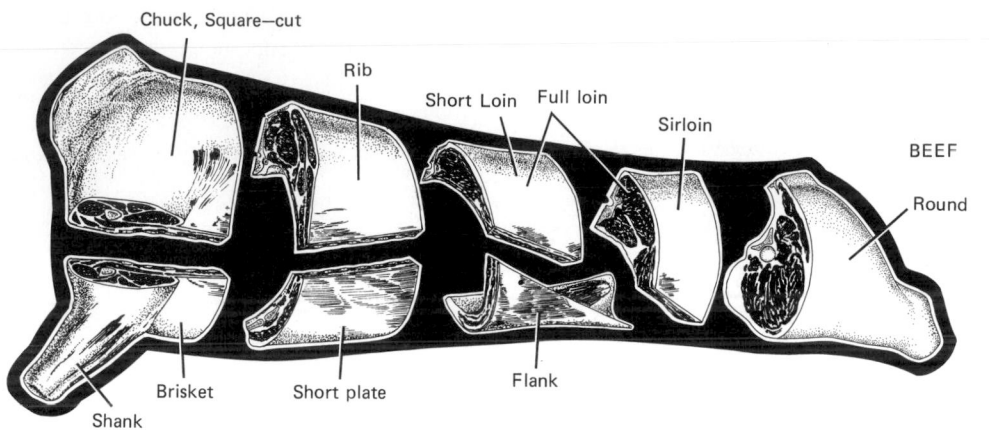

Figure 10.3a Primal (wholesale) beef meat cuts. (Courtesy National Live Stock and Meat Board.)

Beef chuck, boneless, separated into blade, clod, and arm

Beef rib, roast ready

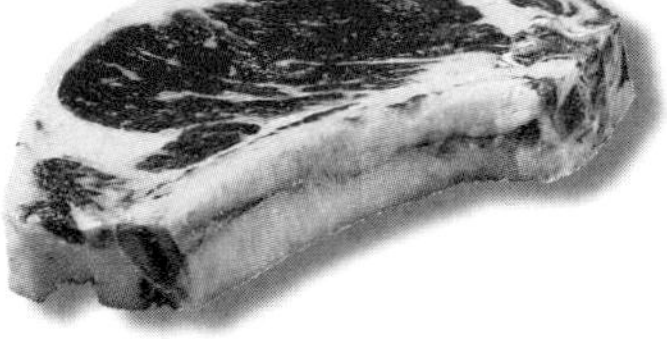

Beef rib steak

Beef short loin

Beef porterhouse steak

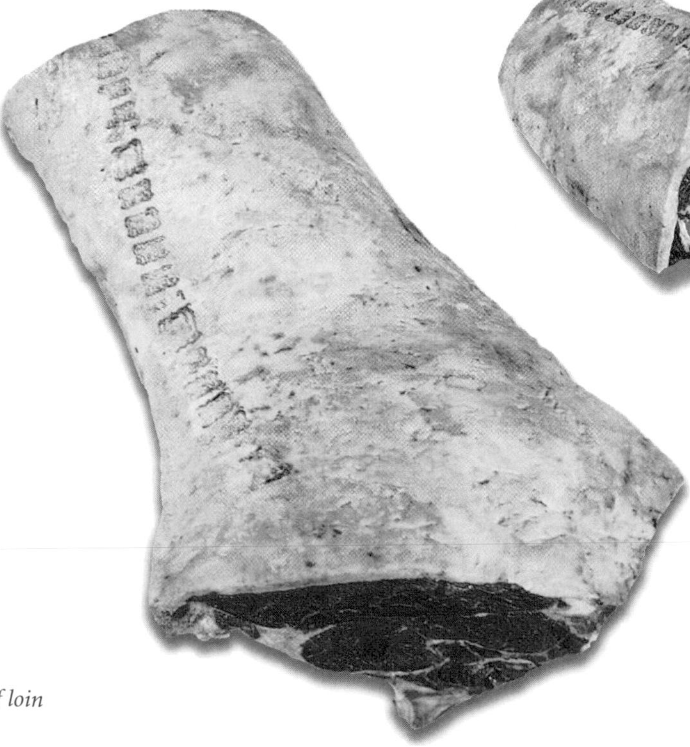

Beef loin

Beef T-bone steak

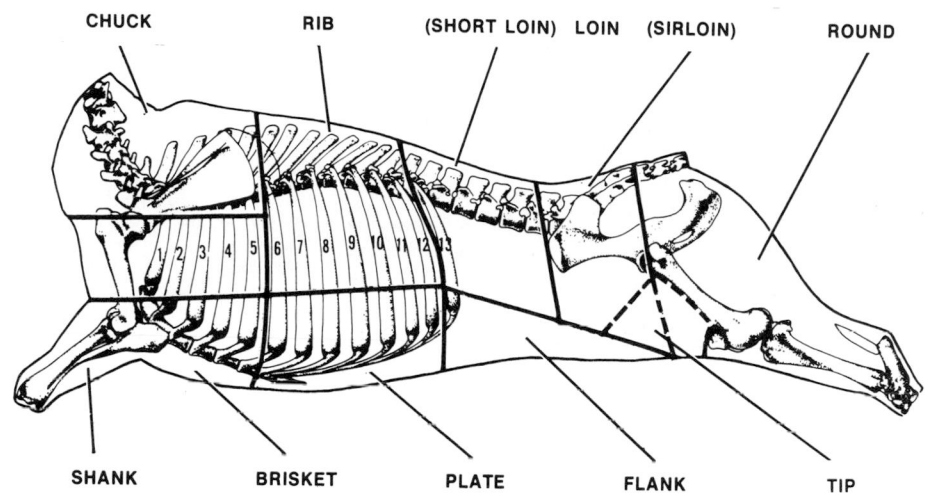

CHUCK
RIB
(SHORT LOIN) LOIN (SIRLOIN)
ROUND
1 2 3 4 5 6 7 8 9 10 11 12 13
SHANK
BRISKET
PLATE
FLANK
TIP

Figure 10.3b *Primal (wholesale) beef cuts and their bone structure.*
(Courtesy National Live Stock and Meat Board.)

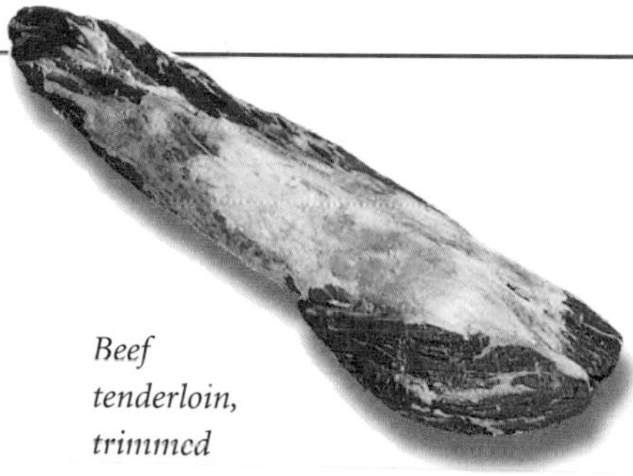

Beef tenderloin, trimmed

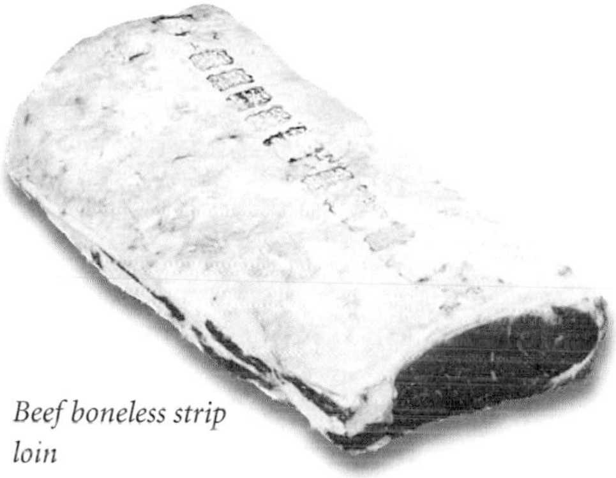

Beef boneless strip loin

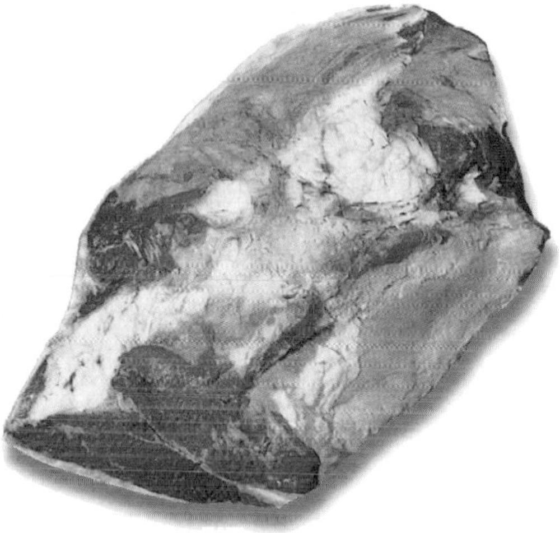

Beef outside (bottom) round

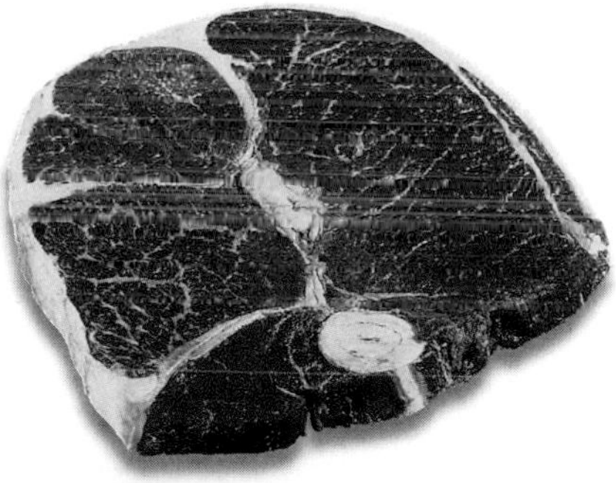

Beef round steak

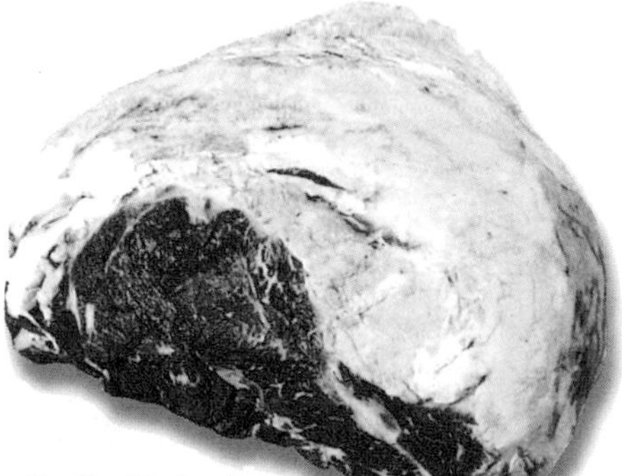

Beef inside (top) round

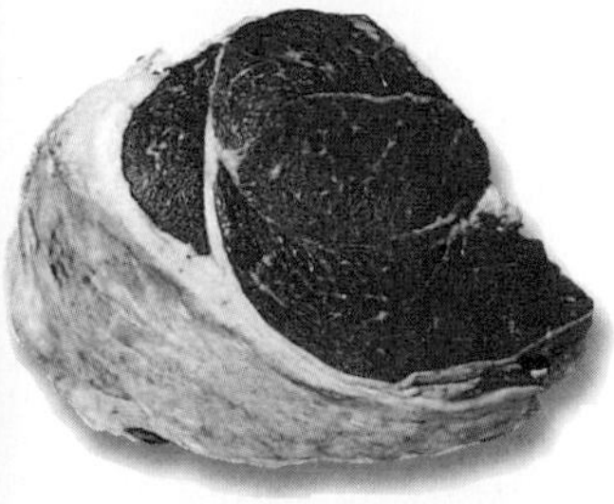

Beef knuckle, untrimmed

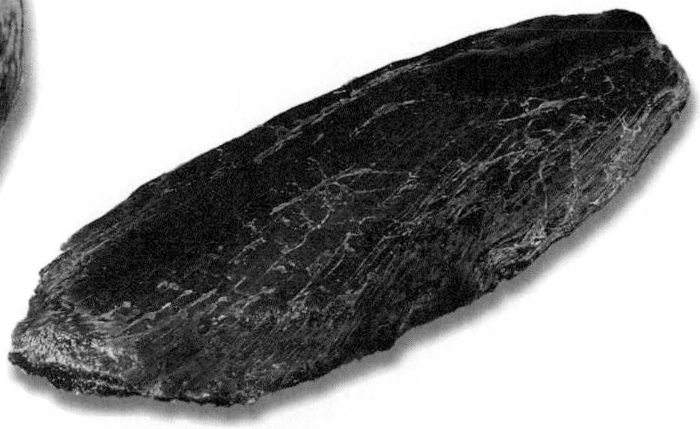

Beef flank steak

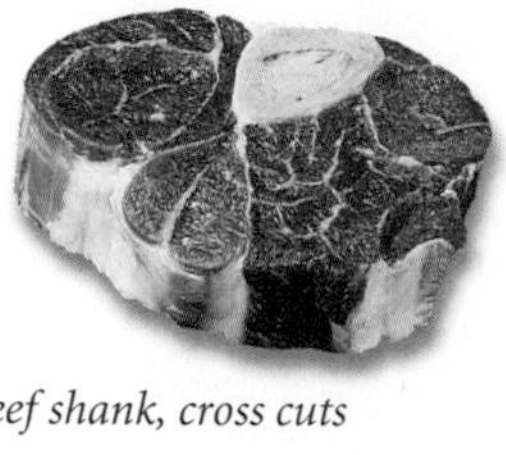

Beef shank, cross cuts

Figure 10.4 Veal.

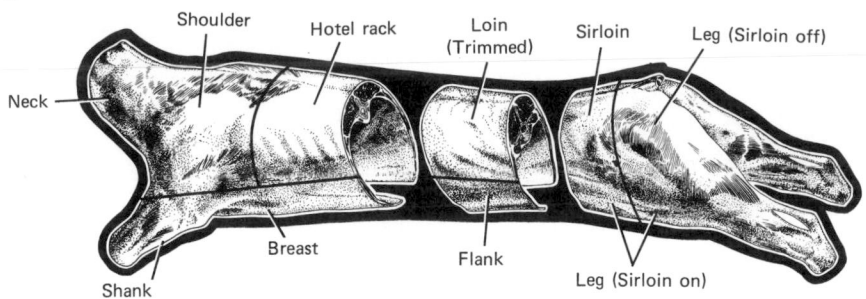

Figure 10.4a Primal (wholesale) veal meat cuts.
(Courtesy National Live Stock and Meat Board.)

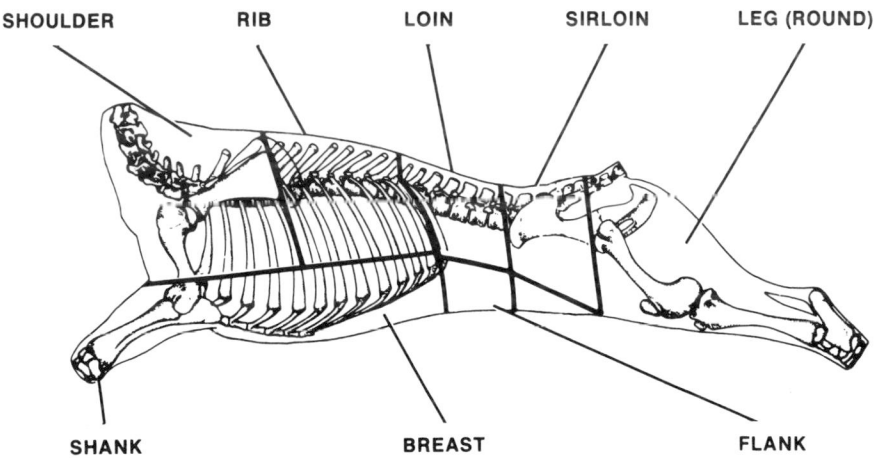

Figure 10.4b Primal (wholesale) veal cuts and their bone structure.
(Courtesy National Live Stock and Meat Board.)

Veal rib roast

Veal breast

Figure 10.5 Lamb.

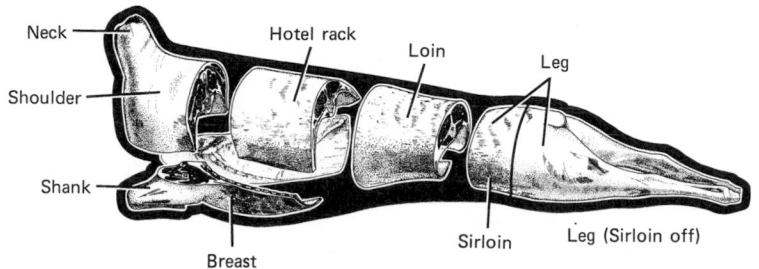

Figure 10.5a Primal (wholesale) lamb meat cuts.
(Courtesy National Live Stock and Meat Board.)

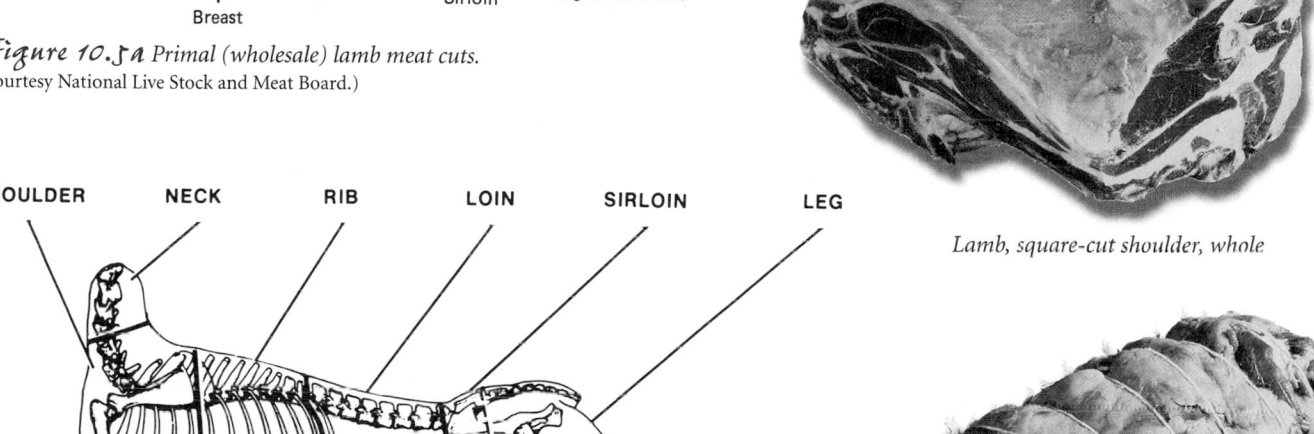

Figure 10.5b Primal (wholesale) lamb cuts and their bone structure.
(Courtesy National Live Stock and Meat Board.)

Lamb, square-cut shoulder, whole

Lamb, boneless shoulder, rolled and tied

Lamb arm chop

Lamb blade chop

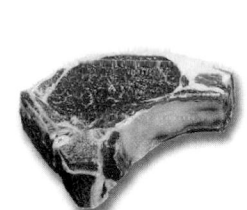

Lamb rib chop

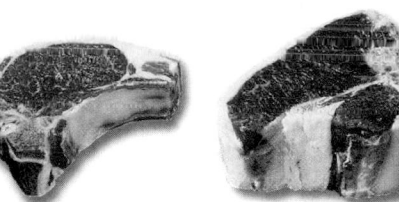

Lamb loin chop

Lamb loin roast

Lamb, whole leg

Lamb foreshank

Figure 10.6 Pork.

Boston butt
Fat back
Loin
Jowl
Ham
Foot
Foot
Hock
Shoulder
(Picnic)
Bacon side
(Belly)
Spareribs

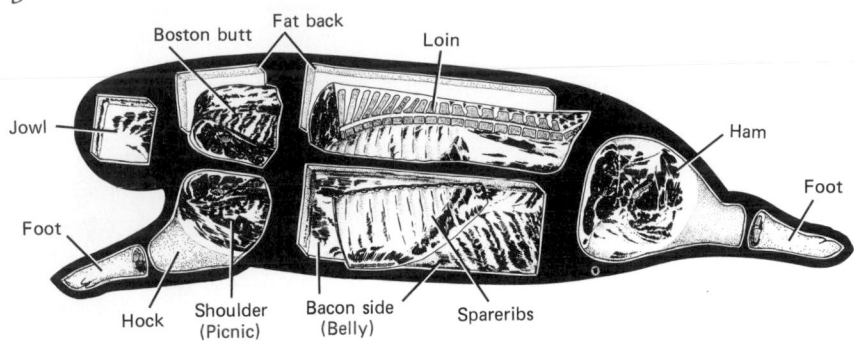

Figure 10.6a Primal (wholesale) pork meat cuts.
(Courtesy National Live Stock and Meat Board.)

BLADE BOSTON
SHOULDER
CLEAR PLATE
FAT BACK
LOIN
LEG (FRESH OR SMOKED HAM)
JOWL
PICNIC SHOULDER
SPARERIBS
BACON (SIDE PORK)

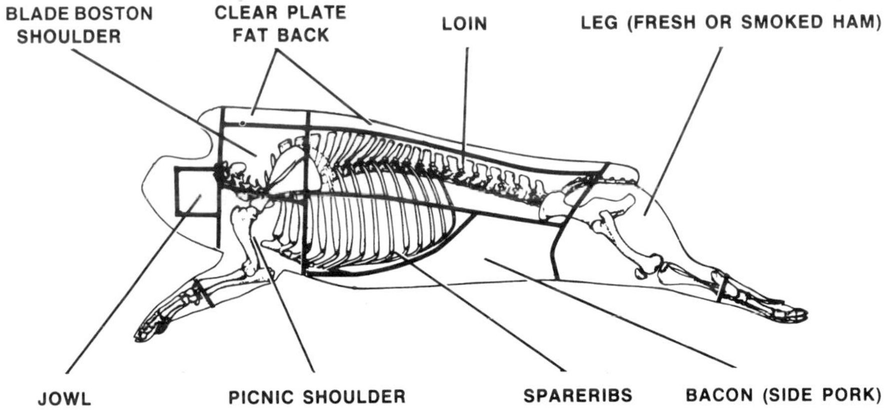

Figure 10.6b Primal (wholesale) pork cuts and their bone structure.
(Courtesy National Live Stock and Meat Board.)

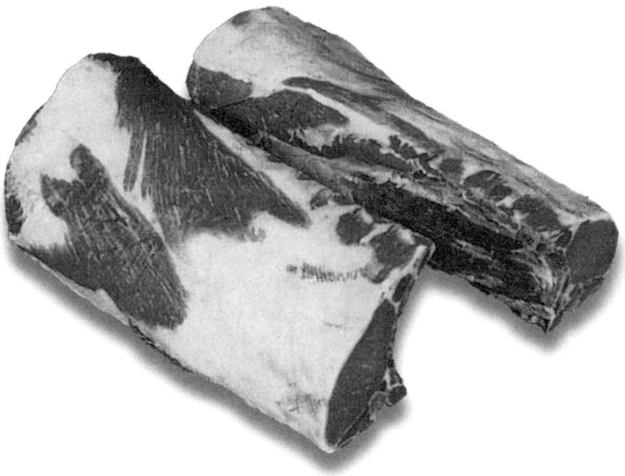

Pork rib half and loin half roasts

Pork butt

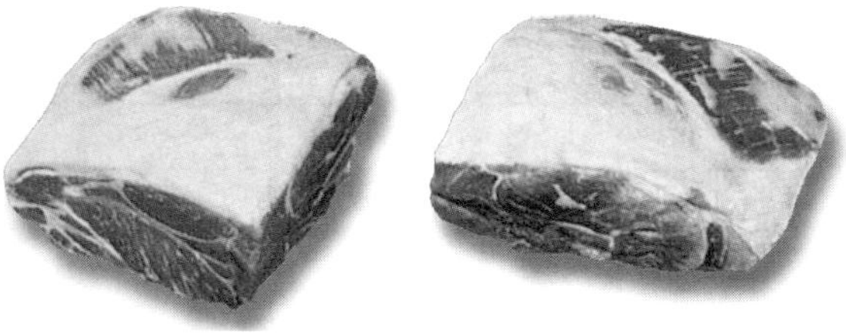

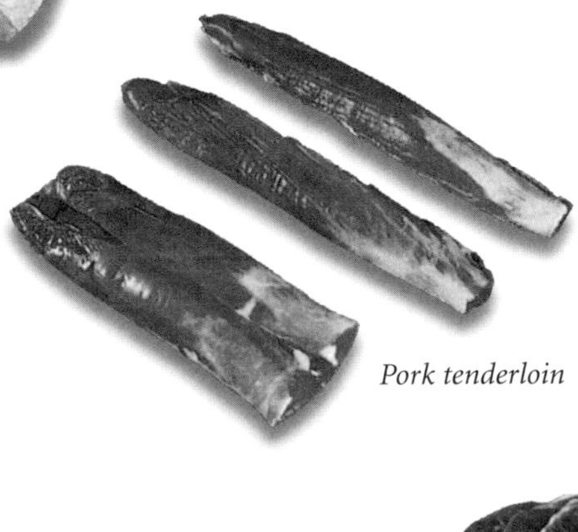

Pork tenderloin

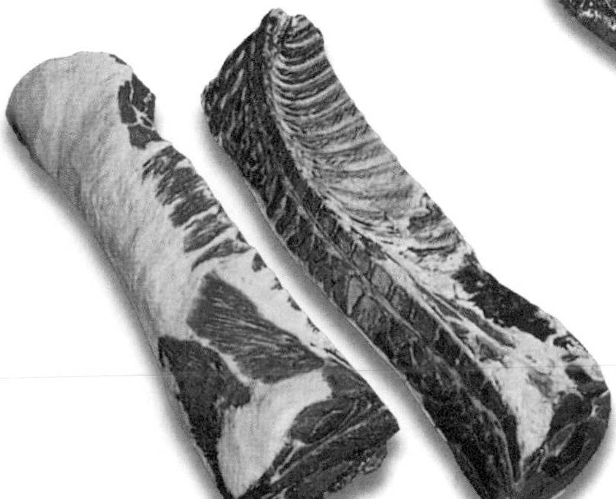

Full pork loin (includes ribs)

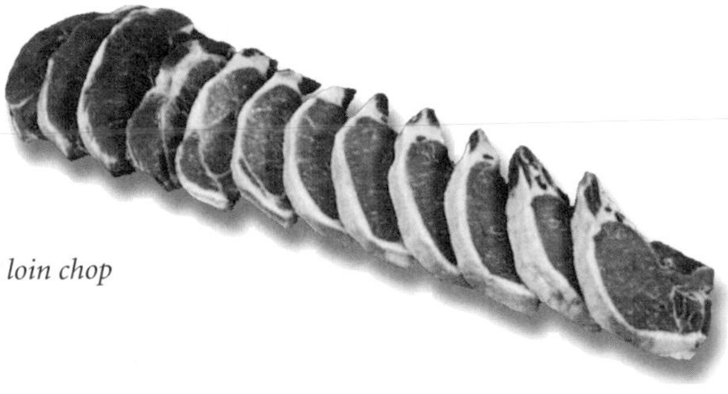

Pork loin chop

Figure 10.7 Beef bone structure.
(Courtesy National Live Stock and Meat Board.)

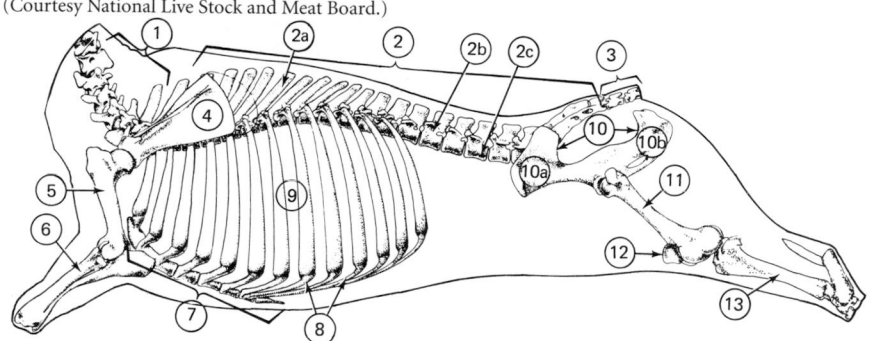

1. Neck bone
2. Backbone
   2a. Feather bone
   2b. Finger bone
   2c. Chine bone
3. Tailbone
4. Blade bone
5. Arm bone
6. Foreshank bone
7. Breastbone
8. Rib cartilage
9. Ribs
10. Pelvis
    10a. Hip bone
    10b. Rump or aitch bone
11. Leg or round bone
12. Knee cap
13. Hindshank bone

Beef, Lamb, Veal, and Pork Cuts

Beef Primal Cuts and Fabricated Cuts

Primal	Major Bones	Common Fabricated Cuts	Primary Cooking Methods
Forequarter			
Chuck (square cut)	Ribs 1–5 Blade bone Backbone (including chine and feather bones) Neck bones Arm bone	Shoulder clod Triangle Boneless inside chuck Chuck tender Chuck short ribs Cubed steaks Stew meat Ground chuck	Moist heat
Brisket	Rib bones Rib cartilage Breast bone	Boneless brisket and corned beef brisket Ground beef	Moist heat
Shank	Shank bone	Stew meat Ground beef	Moist heat

Note: Square-cut chuck, brisket, and shank, in one piece, are called *cross-cut chuck.*

Rib	Ribs 6–12 Backbone (chine and feather bones)	Rib roasts (prime rib) Rib steaks Short ribs	Dry heat Moist heat
Short plate	Rib bones Tip of breastbone Rib cartilage	Short ribs Stew meat Ground beef	Moist heat
Hindquarter (Full loin)		Full tenderloin (to have tenderloin in one piece, it must be stripped out of loin before loin is split into short loin and sirloin)	Dry heat
Short loin	Rib 13 Backbone [chine, feather bones, finger bones (see note 1)]	Club steaks T-bone steaks Porterhouse steaks Strip loin Strip loin steaks Short tenderloin	Dry heat
Sirloin	Backbone Hip bone (part of pelvis)	Top sirloin butt Bottom sirloin butt Butt tenderloin	Dry heat
Flank	Tip of rib 13	Flank steak Ground beef	Moist heat (exception: flank steak cooked as London broil)
Round	Round (leg) bone Aitch bone (part of pelvis) Shank bone Tailbone	Knuckle (sirloin tip) Inside (top) round Outside (bottom) round Eye of round (part of outside round) Rump Hind shank	Moist heat and dry heat

Note 1: Finger bones are the short horizontal bones attached to those chine bones that have no ribs attached. They are stems of the Ts in T-bones.

Lamb Primal Cuts and Fabricated Cuts

Primal	Major Bones	Common Fabricated Cuts	Primary Cooking Methods
Foresaddle			
Shoulder	Ribs 1–4 or 1–5 (see note 2) Arm Blade Backbone (chine and feather bones) Neck bones	Shoulder roasts Shoulder chops Stew meat Ground lamb	Moist heat and dry heat
Breast and shank	Rib bones Breastbone Shank bone	Riblets Breast Stew meat Ground lamb	Moist heat
Hotel rack	Ribs 5–12 or 6–13 (see note 2) Backbone	Rib roast (rack) Crown roast Rib chops	Dry heat
Hindsaddle			
Loin (with or without flank)	Rib 13 (optional; see note 2) Backbone (chine, feather bones, finger bones)	Loin roast Loin chops	Dry heat
Leg	Backbone Tailbone Pelvis (hip bone, aitch bone) Round bone Hind shank	Leg roast Leg chops Sirloin chops Shank	Dry heat Moist heat

Note: Hotel rack and loin attached are called lamb back; used mostly for chops.

Note 2: Lamb foresaddles are divided between ribs 4 and 5, unlike beef and veal, which are divided between ribs 5 and 6. Thus, the rack or rib section of lamb has 8 ribs; beef and veal, 7 ribs. In the new, optional style of cutting, the carcass is divided into foresaddle and hindsaddle after the 13th rib, and the foresaddle is divided between ribs 5 and 6. The rack thus contains ribs 6–13

Veal Primal Cuts and Fabricated Cuts

Primal	Major Bones	Common Fabricated Cuts	Primary Cooking Methods
Foresaddle			
Shoulder (square cut)	Ribs 1–5 Blade bone Backbone (chine and feather bones) Neck bones Arm bone	Shoulder roasts Shoulder chops Shoulder clod steaks Cubed steaks Stew meat Ground veal	Moist heat and dry heat
Breast	Rib bones Rib cartilage Breastbone	Boneless breast Cubed steaks Ground veal	Moist heat
Shank	Shank bone	Shank cross-cuts (osso buco)	Moist heat
Hotel rack	Ribs 6–12 Backbone (chine and feather bones)	Rib roast (rack) Rib chops	Dry heat and moist heat

Note: Hotel rack plus connecting portions of breast is called a *bracelet.*

Primal	Major Bones	Common Fabricated Cuts	Primary Cooking Methods
Hindsaddle			
Loin (with or without flank)	Rib 13 Backbone (chine, feather bones, finger bones)	Saddle (loin roast) Loin chops	Dry heat and moist heat
Leg	Backbone Tailbone Pelvis (hip bone, aitch bone) Round bone Hind shank	Leg roasts Scaloppine or cutlets Shank cross-cut (osso buco)	Dry heat Moist heat

Note: Hotel rack and loin attached are called veal back; used mostly for chops.

Pork Primal Cuts and Fabricated Cuts

Primal	Major Bones	Common Fabricated Cuts	Primary Cooking Methods
Shoulder picnic	Shoulder (arm) bone Shank bone	Fresh and smoked picnic Hocks Ground pork Sausage meat	Moist heat
Boston butt	Blade bone (rib bones, back, and neck bones are removed)	Butt steaks Shoulder roasts Daisy (smoked) Ground pork Sausage meat	Dry heat and moist heat
Loin	Rib bones (see note 3) Backbone (chine, feather bones, finger bones) Hip bone	Loin roast Loin and rib chops Boneless loin Country-style ribs Canadian-style bacon (smoked)	Dry heat and moist heat
Ham	Aitch bone Leg bone Hind shank bone	Fresh ham Smoked ham Ham steaks	Dry heat and moist heat
Belly	None	Bacon	Dry heat and moist heat
Spareribs	Rib bones Breast bone	Spareribs	Moist heat
Fatback and clear plate	None	Fresh and salt fatback Salt pork Lard	(Used as cooking fats)
Jowl	None	Jowl bacon	Moist and dry heat
Feet	Foot bones		Moist heat

Note 3: Pork has more than 13 ribs (unlike beef, lamb, and veal) due to special breeding to develop long loins.

Selecting Meats for Your Operation

DECIDING WHICH FORMS TO PURCHASE

Whether you buy whole carcasses, fabricated cuts, or anything in between, depends on four factors:

1. How much meat-cutting skill you or your staff has
2. How much work and storage space you have
3. Whether or not you can use all cuts and lean trim on your menu
4. Which form gives you the best *cost per portion* after figuring in labor costs

Meat purveyors can usually cut meat more economically than food service operators because they deal in large volume. Carcasses or primal cuts cost less per pound than fabricated cuts, but they have more waste (fat and bone) and require more labor (which costs money). However, some operators still do some of their own cutting, depending on how they can answer the four questions above. They feel that cutting their own meat gives them greater control over quality.

Some compromises are available. If you want the quality of freshly cut steaks, for example, you might buy boneless strip loins and cut your own steaks to order. You need not buy primal loins.

SPECIFICATIONS

When buying meat, you will need to indicate the following specifications:

1. **Item name.**
   Include IMPS/NAMPS number, if applicable.
   Example: 173 Beef Short Loin, Regular
2. **Grade.**
   Example: U.S. Choice
   (You may also want to specify division of grade, such as the upper half or lower half of U.S. Choice.)

3. **Weight range for roasts and large cuts.**
   Portion weight or *thickness* (not both) for steaks and chops.

4. **State of refrigeration: chilled or frozen.**

5. **Fat limitations, or average thickness of surface fat.**
   Example: ¾ inch average, 1 inch maximum.
   (Does not apply to veal.)

Cooking and Handling Meats

Tenderness and Appropriate Cooking Methods

The heat of cooking affects tenderness in two ways:

1. It tenderizes connective tissue if moisture is present and cooking is slow.

2. It toughens protein. Even meats low in connective tissue can be tough and dry if cooked at excessively high heats for too long.

THE PRINCIPLE OF LOW-HEAT COOKING

1. High heat toughens and shrinks protein and results in excessive moisture loss. Therefore, low-heat cooking should be the general practice for most meat cooking methods.

2. Broiling seems to be a contradiction to this rule. The reason that carefully broiled meat stays tender is that it is done quickly. It takes time for the heat to be conducted to the interior of the meat, so the inside never gets very hot. Meat broiled well done, however, is likely to be dry.

3. Roasts cooked at low temperatures have better yields than those roasted at high heat. That is, they shrink less and lose less moisture.

4. Because both liquid and steam are better conductors of heat than air, moist heat penetrates meat quickly. Therefore, to avoid overcooking, meat should be simmered, never boiled.

BREAKING DOWN CONNECTIVE TISSUE

Remember that connective tissue is highest in muscles that are more frequently exercised and in more mature animals.

Look again at the principal cooking methods (column 4) in the table of meat cuts (p. 221). You should detect a pattern of tender cuts, cooked primarily by dry heat; slightly less tender cuts, cooked sometimes by dry and sometimes by moist heat; and least tender cuts, cooked almost always by moist heat.

1. **Rib and loin cuts.**
   Always the most tender cuts, used mostly for roasts, steaks, and chops.

   Beef and lamb. Because these meats are often eaten rare or medium done, the rib and loin are used almost exclusively for roasting, broiling, and grilling.

   Veal and pork. Pork is generally eaten well done, and veal is most often eaten well done, although many people prefer it slightly pink in the center. Therefore, these meats are occasionally braised, not to develop tenderness but to help preserve juices. Veal chops, which are very low in fat, may be broiled if great care is taken not to overcook them and dry them out. A safer approach is to use a method with fat, such as sautéing or pan-frying, or to use moist heat.

2. **Leg or round.**

   Beef. The cuts of the round are less tender and are used mostly for braising.

   Top grades, such as U.S. Prime, U.S. Choice, Canada Prime, and Canada AAA, can also be roasted. The roasts are so large that, roasted at low temperatures for a long time, the beef's own moisture helps dissolve collagen. Inside round (top round) is favored for roasts because of its size and relative tenderness.

   Beef round is very lean. It is best roasted rare. Lack of fat makes well-done round taste dry.

   Veal, lamb, and pork. These meats are from young animals and therefore are tender enough to roast.

   Legs make excellent roasts because large muscles with few seams and uniform grain allow easy slicing and attractive portions.

   Figure 10.8 shows the muscle structure of the round in cross section. A center-cut steak from a whole round of beef, lamb, veal, or pork has this same basic structure.

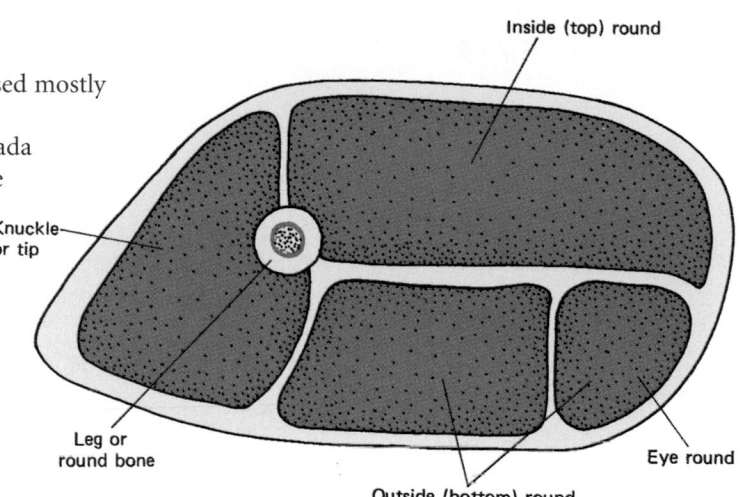

Figure 10.8 Location of the muscles in a whole center-cut round steak of beef, veal, lamb, or pork.

3. **Chuck or shoulder.**

   Beef. Beef chuck is a tougher cut that is usually braised.

   Veal, lamb, and pork. These are most often braised but are young enough to be roasted or cut into chops for broiling. Shoulder roasts are not the most desirable because they consist of many small muscles running in several directions. Therefore, they do not produce attractive, solid slices.

4. **Shanks, breast, brisket, and flank.**

   These are the least tender cuts, even on young animals, and are almost always cooked by moist heat.

   Shanks are desirable for braising and simmering because their high collagen content is converted into much gelatin that gives body to braising liquids and good eating quality to the meat.

   Beef flank steaks can be broiled (as London broil) if they are cooked rare and cut across the grain into thin slices. This cuts the connective tissue into chewable pieces (see mechanical tenderization, p. 211).

5. **Ground meat, cubed steaks, and stew meat.**

   These can come from any primal cut. They are usually made from trimmings, although whole chucks are sometimes ground into chopped meat. Ground meat and cubed steaks can be cooked by dry or moist heat because they have been mechanically tenderized. Stew meat is, of course, cooked by moist heat.

OTHER FACTORS INFLUENCING CHOICE OF COOKING METHODS

1. **Fat content.**

   Meats high in fat, such as Prime beef or lamb, are generally cooked without added fat, such as by roasting or broiling.

   Meats low in fat, such as veal, are often cooked with added fat to prevent dryness. Sautéing, pan-frying, or braising is generally preferable to broiling for veal chops that are cooked well done.

   Fat can be added to lean meats in two ways:

   - *Barding.* Tying slices of fat, such as pork fatback, over meats with no natural fat cover to protect them while roasting.
   - *Larding.* Inserting strips of fat with a larding needle into meats low in marbling.

   These two techniques were developed in Europe when meats were much leaner and not as tender. They are not often used with today's tender, grain-fed meats. These techniques are useful, however, when cooking lean game such as venison.

2. **Developing tenderness is not the only goal of cooking.**
   Other goals are

   • Developing flavor.
   • Preventing excessive shrinkage and nutrient loss.
   • Developing appearance.

   You will often have to compromise to get a balanced result. For example, preliminary browning of a roast at high heat increases shrinkage but may be desirable for some roasts to develop flavor and appearance.

SEARING AND "SEALING"

Searing

The purpose of searing meats at high heat is to create desirable flavor and color by browning the meats' surfaces. It was long believed that searing the surface of meat "seals the pores," keeping in juices.

This does not actually happen. Meat does not have pores but rather an open network of fibers. Think of the surface of a steak as resembling the cut end of a thick rope. There are no pores to seal. It is true that heavy browning creates a kind of crust on the surface of the meat, but this crust is no more waterproof than an unbrowned surface.

You can easily demonstrate that this is true. Place a steak or chop on a hot griddle or grill and sear it well. Turn it over and continue cooking. As it cooks, you will see meat juices driven up through the seared top surface. Everyone who has cooked a steak has seen this demonstration that searing doesn't seal.

Roasts cooked from the start at a low temperature retain more juices than roasts that are seared at high heat first.

Steaks, chops, and cutlets cooked very quickly at high heat retain more moisture at first because the intense heat instantly evaporates the juices from the surface of the meat and forces internal juices further into the meat. This permits browning, because moisture would create steam and inhibit browning. However, overcooked steaks are dry whether or not they were seared.

Blanching and "Sealing"

Dropping meat into boiling water doesn't seal the pores either. What actually happens is this: Many proteins dissolve in cold water. When heated, these proteins coagulate and become froth or scum on the surface of the water. When meat is placed into boiling water, some of the protein coagulates inside that meat and not as much is carried out of the meat with the lost moisture. Prolonged cooking shrinks meat as much if started in boiling water as if started in cold water.

COOKING FROZEN MEATS

Some sources recommend cooking some meats from the frozen state, without thawing, in order to eliminate drip loss that occurs during defrosting. However, it is usually better to thaw before cooking because of the following reasons:

1. Frozen meats lose no moisture from defrosting but lose more during cooking. The total loss is about the same as for thawed meats. Besides, the perception of juiciness depends as much or more on fat content than on moisture content.

2. Cooking frozen meats complicates the cooking process and requires adjustments in procedure. It is possible for roasts to be cooked on the outside but still be frozen in the center. Frozen steaks, too, are more difficult to cook evenly than thawed steaks. Thawed meats, on the other hand, are handled like fresh meats.

3. Cooking frozen meats requires extra energy, and energy is expensive. A hard-frozen roast may take 3 times as long to cook as a thawed roast.

DEFINITIONS

The meaning of the term *doneness* depends on whether the cooking method uses dry heat or moist heat.

1. **Dry heat.**
   Meat is "done" when the proteins have reached the desired degree of coagulation (see p. 52), as indicated by internal temperature.

2. **Moist heat.**
   Meat is "done" when connective tissues have broken down enough for the meat to be palatable. With a few exceptions, meat cooked by moist heat is always well done.

DRY-HEAT COOKING

The object of dry-heat cooking is to achieve the desired degree of doneness (protein coagulation) while preserving natural tenderness and juiciness.

Degree of Doneness

As meat cooks, its pigments change color. These color changes indicate degrees of doneness.

Red meat (beef and lamb) changes from red to pink to gray or gray-brown.

* Rare: browned surface; thin layer of cooked (gray) meat; red interior
* Medium: thicker layer of gray; pink interior
* Well done: gray throughout

(Of course, there are stages in between.)

White meat (veal and pork) changes from pink or gray-pink to white or off-white. It is generally cooked well done, although many cuts of veal may be considered done when still slightly pink in the center.

As explained on page 18, trichinosis is a disease caused by a parasite that lives in the muscle tissue of hogs as well as of some wild animals. In countries in which this disease is a problem, pork must be cooked long enough to eliminate this danger. This parasite is killed at 137°F (58°C) but, to be safe, pork should be cooked to at least 150° to 155°F (66° to 68°C). At this stage, pork is only medium to medium-well done. Most people prefer pork to be cooked slightly more than this. On the other hand, it is not necessary to cook pork to 185°F (85°C), as older guidelines said. At this temperature, pork is overcooked and dry. Perhaps the best doneness range is 160° to 170°F (71° to 77°C).

Testing Doneness

Determining doneness is one of the most difficult and critical aspects of meat cooking. Anyone can put a steak on the grill or a roast in the oven. But it takes experience and skill to take it off the fire at the right time.

Color change cannot be used by the cook to test doneness because it would be necessary to cut the meat. Piercing the meat and examining the color of the juices is not a reliable method.

Internal Temperature

Testing the interior of meat with a meat thermometer is the most accurate method of testing doneness. Thermometers are of two types: *standard*, which are inserted before roasting and left in the roast; and *instant-read*, which are inserted at any time, read as soon as the needle stops moving, and pulled out. Whatever thermometer you use, make sure it is *clean* and *sanitary* before inserting it in the meat.

The tip of the thermometer should be inserted into the center of the thickest part of the flesh, not touching fat or bone. Table 10.2 gives internal temperatures of meats at various degrees of doneness.

In general, regional traditions of eating well-done or overcooked meats are decreasing, and more people are eating meat cooked rare. For decades, meats cooked to an internal temperature

TABLE 10.2

Interior Temperatures of Cooked Meats

Meat	Rare	Medium	Well Done
Beef	130°F (54°C)	140°–145°F (60°–63°C)	160°F (71°C)
Lamb	130°F (54°C)	145°F (63°C)	160°F (71°C)
Veal	—	145°–150°F (63°–66°C)	160°F (71°C)
Pork	—	—	165°–170°F (74°–77°C)

of 140°F (60°C) were called rare, but by today's standards, this is more like medium. Current preferences are reflected in the temperatures given in Table 10.2.

It should be stated that the U.S. Department of Agriculture and other agencies caution that meats may contain harmful bacteria and parasites. Although studies are still being done, these agencies suggest that meats should be cooked to at least 140°F (60°C) in order to be completely safe. The USDA requires that beef precooked for food service sale (such as precooked roast beef for sandwiches) be heated to an internal temperature of at least 145°F (63°C) when it is processed.

Whether or not 140°F (60°C) is the lowest safe temperature for cooking meats, it is not really accurate to call it rare. In any case, tastes vary from region to region. You should be guided by the preferences of your customers.

Carry-over Cooking

Internal temperature continues to rise even after the meat is removed from the oven. This is because the outside of roasting meat is hotter than the inside. This heat continues to be conducted into the meat until the heat is equalized throughout the roast.

Carry-over cooking can raise internal temperatures from 5°F (3°C) for small cuts to as much as 25°F (14°C) for very large roasts, such as a steamship round. The usual range is 10°F to 15°F (6°C to 8°C) for average roasts. Exact temperature change depends on the size of the cut and on the oven temperature.

Remove roasts from the oven when internal temperature is 10° to 15°F (6° to 8°C) below desired reading. Let the roast stand 15 to 30 minutes before slicing. For example, a beef rib roast cooked rare should be removed from the oven when the thermometer reads about 115° to 120°F (46° to 49°C). Carry-over cooking will bring the temperature to 130°F (54°C) after the roast has stood for 30 minutes.

Touch

The small size of steaks and chops makes using a thermometer impractical. The cook must depend on his or her sense of touch.

Meat gets firmer as it cooks. Pressing it lightly with the finger indicates its doneness. Press the center of the lean part, not the fat.

Rare. Feels soft, gives to pressure, though not as soft and jellylike as raw meat.
Medium. Feels moderately firm and resilient, springs back readily when pressed.
Well done. Feels firm, does not give to pressure.

Time-Weight Ratio

Many charts give roasting times per pound of meat. However, these can be approximate only and should be used in estimating and planning cooking times, not in determining doneness.

Many factors other than weight and oven temperature determine cooking time:

1. Temperature of meat before roasting.
2. Amount of fat cover (fat acts as an insulator).
3. Bones (bones conduct heat faster than flesh, so boneless roasts cook more slowly than bone-in roasts of the same weight).
4. Size, type, and contents of oven.
5. Number of times oven door is opened.
6. Shape of the cut (a flat or a long, thin cut cooks more quickly per pound than a round, compact cut).

You can see why roasting requires experience and judgment. To be really accurate and useful, a complete roasting chart that took all variables into consideration, including all meat cuts, sizes, oven temperatures, and so on, would be the size of a small book.

Point 6 above is a key point. It is the *thickness* of a cut, *not its weight*, that determines cooking time—the time needed for the heat to penetrate to the center. Half a pork loin roasts in about the same time as a whole pork loin, even though it weighs half as much. The thickness is the same.

Perhaps the most useful roasting time charts are those you make yourself. When you regularly roast the same cuts in the same way with the same equipment and find that they always take the same time, then you may use those times as indicators of doneness. Many food service operators have developed charts based on their own practices, and the correct times are indicated on their individual recipe cards.

MOIST-HEAT COOKING

Meat cooked by moist heat is cooked well done, and actually beyond well done. Doneness is indicated by tenderness, not by temperature.

Piercing with a meat fork is the usual test for doneness. When the prongs of the fork go in and slide out easily, the meat is done.

Low temperatures—no higher than simmering—are essential to avoid toughening protein in moist-cooked meats. Oven temperatures of 250° to 300°F (120° to 150°C) are usually sufficient to maintain a simmer.

JUICINESS

Three main factors determine the juiciness—or, more accurately, the *perception* of juiciness—in cooked meat. Despite the myths about basting with stock and about searing meat to "seal in the juices," the following are the only factors that have any significant effect on juiciness.

1. Internal fat.

   Fat makes meat taste juicy. This is why well-marbled meats taste juicier than lean meats. We understand the health effects of too much fat in the diet, but there is no getting around the fact that high fat content makes meat taste juicier. When lean meats are cooked, other measures (such as using sauces and, especially, avoiding overcooking) are used to increase palatability.

2. Gelatin.

   This factor is most important in braised meats. Gelatin, converted from connective tissue, helps to bind water molecules and hold them in the meat. Also, the texture of the gelatin improves the texture of the meat in the mouth. This is why braised beef shank tastes so much juicier than braised bottom round.

3. Protein coagulation.

   As you know, as protein coagulates or is cooked, it breaks down and begins to lose water. The more it is cooked, the more it contracts and forces out moisture. No matter how much you try to "sear to seal in the juices," this moisture will be lost. The only way to minimize this loss is to avoid overcooking.

Cooking Variety Meats

Variety meats, also known as *offal*, include various organs, glands, and other meats that don't form a part of the dressed carcass of the animal.

For cooking purposes, we can divide the most popular variety meats into two groups:

Glandular meats	*Muscle meats*
Liver	Heart
Kidneys	Tongue
Sweetbreads	Tripe
Brains	Oxtails

Glandular meats do not consist of muscle tissue like regular meats but instead are internal organs or glands. This fact is important for two reasons.

First, because they do not consist of bundles of muscle fibers, the texture of glandular meats is unlike that of regular meats. Because they are not muscle tissue, they are naturally tender and do not need long, slow cooking like muscular variety meats do. If organ meats are dry and tough, it is usually because they have been overcooked.

Second, glandular meats are much more perishable than muscle meats. While some muscle meats, especially beef, benefit from aging, organ meats must be very fresh to be of the best quality. Liver, sweetbreads, and brains must be used within a day or two after purchase. If brains or sweetbreads must be kept longer, they should be blanched as described below so that they will keep another day or two.

Heart, tongue, oxtails, and tripe are made of muscle tissue, just like other meats from the carcass. They are all tough, however, and must be cooked for a long time by simmering or braising in order to be made tender.

LIVER

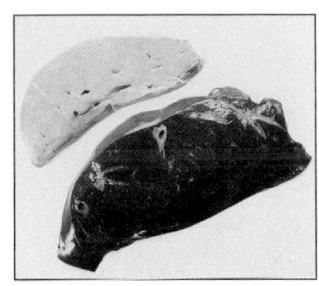

Top: calf's liver slice. Bottom: beef liver slice.

Calf's liver is the most prized because it is tender and delicate in flavor. It is easily recognized by its pale, pinkish color. Most calf's liver is served pan-fried, sautéed, or broiled.

Beef liver is darker in color (see accompanying photo), stronger in flavor, and tougher than calf's liver. It is also pan-fried or broiled, and it is frequently braised.

Pork liver is also available, but it is used mostly in pâtés and sausages.

Preparation

- Remove outer skin.
- Slice on the bias about ¼ inch (½ cm) thick. Slicing is easier if liver is partially frozen.
- Remove tough membranes.

Cooking

- Cook to order. Do not cook ahead.
- To broil: Brush with (or dip in) oil or melted butter. Broil according to basic procedure for meats.
- To pan-fry, griddle, or sauté: Dredge in seasoned flour. Cook in desired fat over moderately high heat.
- *Do not overcook*, unless customer requests well done. To be moist, liver must be slightly pink inside. Liver cooked well done is very dry.
- Serve with bacon, French-fried or smothered onions, or seasoned butter.

KIDNEYS

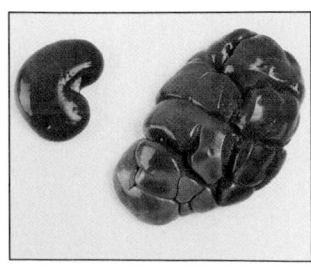

Left: lamb kidney. Right: veal kidney.

Veal and lamb kidneys are the most popular, especially in the more upscale restaurants. They are usually prepared by sautéing and broiling. Beef kidneys are tougher and more strongly flavored. They are often cooked by braising and served in specialty items like steak and kidney pie. Pork kidneys are not often used.

Veal kidneys weigh about 8 to 12 oz (225 to 350 g) each. Lamb kidneys are very small, about 1½ to 3 oz (40 to 85 g) each. If you purchase whole lamb or veal carcasses, you will find a pair of kidneys inside the cavity, attached to the small of the back in the region of the tenderloin and surrounded by a heavy layer of fat or suet.

Preparation

If the kidney is encased in fat, pull the fat away with your hands and use a knife to cut it away from the core area where the ducts emerge from inside the kidney.

Lamb kidneys are usually broiled and served two or three per portion, or as part of a mixed grill. Butterfly them by splitting them almost in half, starting at the curved or convex side. Spread them open and skewer them to hold them open during cooking.

Veal kidneys can be broiled like lamb kidneys, but they are most often cut up, sautéed, and served in a sauce. To prepare them for sautéing, first split them in half. Remove the white ducts from the center. Then cut into large dice or thick slices.

Cooking

There are two main pitfalls to cooking kidneys. First, they become tough and rubbery if over-cooked. Properly cooked, they are pink in the middle and still tender and juicy. Cooking time is very short.

Second, they have a high moisture content, which can interfere with proper sautéing. Make sure the pan is very hot before adding the kidneys, and do not overcrowd the pan. Failure to do this results in kidneys that are boiled in their juices rather than sautéed.

To avoid overcooking when sautéing over high heat, do not try to brown the kidneys too heavily. Brown them only lightly and remove them from the pan when they are still somewhat rare. Set them aside while you deglaze the pan and prepare the sauce. During this time, some juices will be released from the kidneys. Drain this juice and add it to the sauce if desired, or discard it if you feel that the flavor is too strong. Finally, add the kidneys to the sauce and warm them gently. Do not let them simmer long. Serve at once.

SWEETBREADS

Sweetbreads are the thymus glands of calves and young beef animals. (The gland gradually disappears as the animal matures.) They are considered a delicacy and are often expensive. Sweetbreads are mild in flavor and delicate in texture. They are usually braised or breaded and sautéed in butter.

Before cooking, sweetbreads should be prepared according to the following procedure (see Figure 10.9):

1. Soak in several changes of cold water for several hours or overnight. This removes blood, which would darken the meat when cooked.

2. Blanch in simmering salted water for 10 minutes. Some chefs like to add a little lemon juice or vinegar to the water to preserve whiteness and make the meat firmer.

3. Refresh under cold water and peel off membranes and connective tissue.

4. Press between two trays, with a light weight on top, and refrigerate for several hours.

Figure 10.9 Preparing sweetbreads.

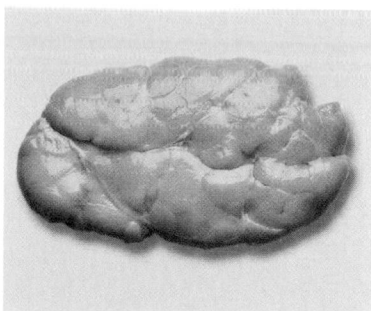

(a) Raw sweetbreads.

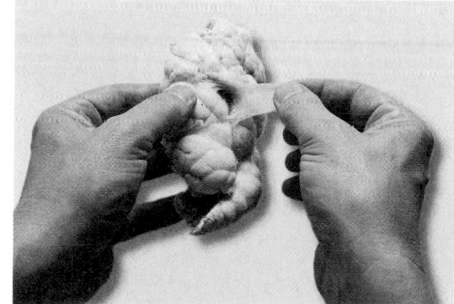

(b) After the sweetbread has been blanched, peel off the membrane.

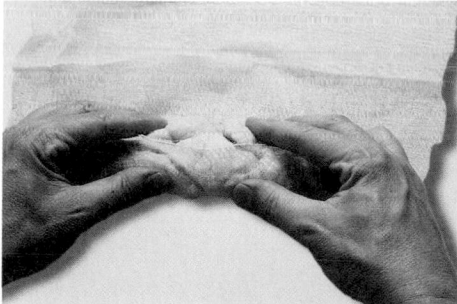

(c) Wrap the sweetbreads in clean cheesecloth.

(d) Tie the ends securely.

(e) Place in a hotel pan or other flat pan and top with another pan.

(f) Place weights in the top pan and refrigerate for several hours.

5. Prepare for cooking:
   - For braising, leave whole or cut into large dice.
   - For breading and sautéing, split in half horizontally. Pass through Standard Breading Procedure (p. 121) or dredge in flour.

BRAINS

Brains are not a popular item, but they are delicate in both flavor and texture. Calf's brains are the most frequently used.

Brains are very perishable and should be cooked as soon as possible. They are also fragile and must be handled carefully.

Brains must be pre-prepared according to the following procedure. They may then be served hot with Black Butter (p. 152) or cooled, then dipped in batter, deep-fried, and served with tomato sauce.

1. Soak in fresh water, as for sweetbreads.
2. Peel off outer membrane (this may be done before or after poaching).
3. Poach 20 minutes in court bouillon made of 1 oz (25 mL) lemon juice or vinegar per pint (500 mL) salted water, plus a bouquet garni.
4. Drain and serve immediately, or cool in fresh, cold water.

HEART

Heart, usually from veal or beef, is very tough and lean. It can be braised or simmered, or it may be ground and added to chopped meat for casserole dishes and meatloaf.

Before cooking, trim coarse fibers and veins inside and at top.

TONGUE

Cooked beef *tongue* is popular as a cold, sliced meat for sandwiches. It may be fresh, cured, or smoked. Veal and lamb tongues are also available.

After simmering, remove the skin and trim the gristle at the base of the tongue before slicing.

OXTAILS

Oxtails contain flavorful meat and a rich gelatin content, making them highly desirable for soups and stews.

To disjoint oxtails, cut into sections at the joints with a French knife or butcher knife. Do not use a cleaver, or you may splinter the bones.

TRIPE

Tripe is the muscular stomach lining of meat animals. Although lamb and pork tripe are sometimes available, beef tripe is by far the most widely used. Because cattle have four stomachs, there are four kinds of beef tripe. Honeycomb tripe, from the second stomach, is the kind most widely available. Other kinds, however, can be substituted in recipes that call for honeycomb tripe. In France, another type of beef tripe, known as *gras-double*, is popular; it is smooth rather than honeycombed.

Most tripe that comes from the market has been partially cooked, but it still requires several hours of simmering to be made tender. Undercooked tripe is chewy and somewhat rubbery, but tripe that has simmered long enough is tender, with a pleasant gelatinous texture.

To prepare, first remove any lumps of fat by pulling or cutting them off. Next, blanch the tripe, if desired. Although it is already partially cooked when purchased, blanching freshens it. Place it in a pot with cold, salted water. Bring to a boil, simmer 5 to 10 minutes, drain, and rinse under cold water.

OTHER VARIETY MEATS

Intestines

The most common use for intestines is to make sausage casings. These are discussed in Chapter 22.

Chitterlings are pork intestines that are treated like tripe. They are blanched or simmered, then braised or fried. Chitterlings are generally available in 10-pound pails. Because they shrink a great deal when simmered, this quantity yields only 3 pounds or less of finished product.

Caul

Pig's *caul* is a fatty membrane covering the animal's stomach. It looks somewhat like a delicate piece of lace. Its main uses are to line terrines and to wrap forcemeats and other foods so that they hold their shape during cooking and do not dry out. Sausage patties wrapped in caul are called *crepinettes* (see p. 656). The advantage of using caul instead of fatback to line terrines is that the caul is so thin that it melts almost completely away during cooking.

Feet

Feet are exceptionally rich in gelatin. For this reason, they are added to soups, stews, and stocks to add richness and body. Indeed, some stews made with feet, such as Tripes à la Môde de Caen, may be so rich in gelatin that not only do they solidify when cold but they can even be unmolded and sliced like cold cuts.

Pig's feet are readily available in most markets. Calf's feet and ox feet are also available, but often only on the wholesale market. The feet from older animals have less gelatin. If a recipe calls for a calf's foot but none is available, in most cases, you can substitute two pig's feet.

Game and Specialty Meats

The term *game* is used to refer to poultry and meat animals normally found in the wild. However, much of the "wild" game that has become so popular on restaurant menus is actually from farm-raised animals. Venison farms, in particular, have become numerous and productive, supplying a growing demand.

Farm-raised game birds are discussed along with other poultry in Chapter 12. This section is concerned with furred game.

Although a great variety of game, large and small, can be found on hunters' tables, the supply of game for the restaurant and retail markets is more limited. Venison is the most popular game item and is the main subject of this section. Other products, such as boar and hare, are occasionally available as well. In addition, domestic rabbit is considered here, although its meat has little in common with true game.

The French terms for various game meats are often used on menus and in various cooking manuals and references. To clarify these terms, a list of those most commonly used follows:

Chevreuil: often translated as "venison," but refers specifically to the roe deer, the most prized European variety
Cerf: red deer; often farm raised
Daim: fallow deer; often farm raised
Marcassin: young boar, especially boar under six months of age
Sanglier: boar

Lapin: rabbit
Lapereau: young rabbit
Lièvre: hare
Levraut: young hare
Venaison: usually translated as "venison," the term in fact refers to the meat of any game animal

VENISON

Several varieties of deer are raised on farms for use as meat, including the red deer and the smaller fallow deer. An important advantage of farm-raised venison, besides its year-round availability, is that the cook can be assured that it is from young, tender animals. In the wild, young animals less than two years old are likely to have tender meat, but the meat rapidly becomes tough as the animal matures and ages. The tradition of marinating game for several days in strong wine marinades originates, in large part, from efforts to tenderize hunted game enough to make it palatable.

Marination, Flavor, and Tenderness

The first thing to be said about farm-raised venison is that it is milder in flavor than venison hunted in the wild. It has little, if any, of the strong, gamy flavor usually associated with wild game. In fact, a farm-raised venison steak tastes rather like an especially flavorful, lean cut of beef. Those who enjoy strong, gamy flavors may even find farmed venison a little bland.

Although it does have some tenderizing effect, marination is not necessary to tenderize commercially raised venison because the meat is already tender. Nevertheless, marinating is widely used as a flavoring technique. Much of the flavor traditionally associated with venison, in fact, is due less to its gaminess than to the red wine marinades that were invariably used.

To retain more of the natural flavor of the meat, cook without marination, or let it marinate for only a short period (30 minutes to 3 or 4 hours) with the desired seasonings and flavoring ingredients. Modern quick marinades are often simple and may contain a few ingredients only.

Fat Content

Venison, like other game, is very low in fat. This makes it especially popular with health-conscious diners. It also makes the meat likely to become dry unless the cook takes great care.

The loin and leg, being tender, are best cooked by dry-heat methods and served rare or medium done. If cooked longer, they will dry out. Roast these cuts whole, either bone-in or boned out, or cut them into steaks, cutlets, and medallions, and sauté, pan-fry, or broil them, taking care not to overcook.

Whole leg of venison, completely boned, seamed, and vacuum packed, is available. Weights range from 5 to 10 pounds (2 to 4.5 kg). Whole bone-in saddle weighs from 5 to 20 pounds (2.3 to 9 kg), while the loin muscle weighs about half that after boning and trimming.

Tougher cuts, chiefly the shoulder, neck, and breast, are braised, stewed, or made into ground meat or sausage. These cuts are also lean, but because they are higher in connective tissue and gelatin, they take more readily to stewing and braising.

To generalize, farm-raised venison can be treated like very lean beef. Take care not to cook it to the point of dryness.

BOAR

Boar is a type of wild pig. Its meat is somewhat similar to pork, except that it is leaner and its flavor is fuller and richer. Boar is now raised commercially on a few farms and is available in limited quantities.

Boar is somewhat more difficult to cook than venison and other game because, like pork, it must be cooked until well done. At the same time, it is leaner and less tender than domestic pork, so that it often tends to be somewhat dry and chewy. Special care must be taken to cook it adequately with overcooking. Because boar is usually tougher than farm-raised venison, its legs or hams are better suited for braising or slow roasting, while the loins can be used for roasts or cut into medallions and sautéed.

Traditionally, boar is handled much like venison, and typical recipes call for red wine marinades. Although marinating a white meat in red wine may seem strange at first, this treatment actually works very well with boar. The red wine accentuates the more pronounced flavor of boar (as compared with pork) and makes it taste more like game.

OTHER LARGE GAME

Various other meats are sometimes found in food-service kitchens. *Elk, caribou, moose,* and *antelope* are all similar to venison and are handled in much the same way. The first three of these, especially moose, are larger than deer, so it may be necessary to allow for longer cooking times when using venison recipes for them.

Buffalo, or *American bison,* is raised on ranches in the western United States and Canada and is handled like beef. Flavor and cooking characteristics are similar to those of beef, but the meat is somewhat richer in flavor and has less fat and cholesterol than beef.

RABBIT

Domestic rabbit is a versatile meat that can be cooked in most of the same ways as chicken. In fact, in some countries it is classified as poultry. Some typical recipes for rabbit are included in Chapter 11, but nearly any chicken recipe can be used for domestic rabbit as well. In addition, many recipes for veal or pork are adaptable to rabbit.

Rabbit's light, delicate meat is often compared to chicken, but there are some differences. It is somewhat more flavorful than chicken, with a mild but distinctive taste that is not exactly like that of other poultry or meat. Also, it is very lean (more like chicken or turkey breast than legs) and can become dry if overcooked.

Figure 10.10 Cutting rabbit for stews and sautés.

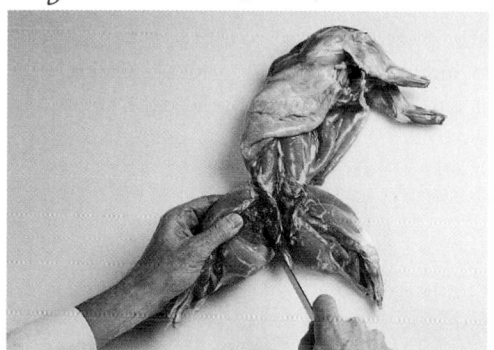

(a) Cut off the hind legs, separating them at the hip joint.

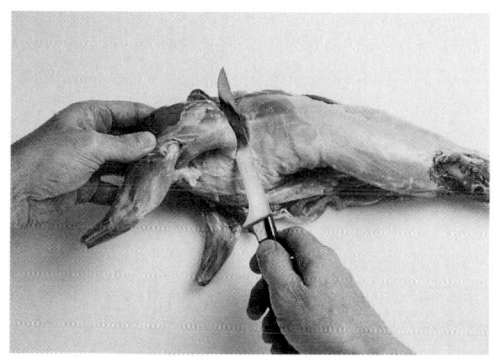

(b) Cut off the forelegs by cutting under the shoulder blade.

(c) Cut off the hip bone.

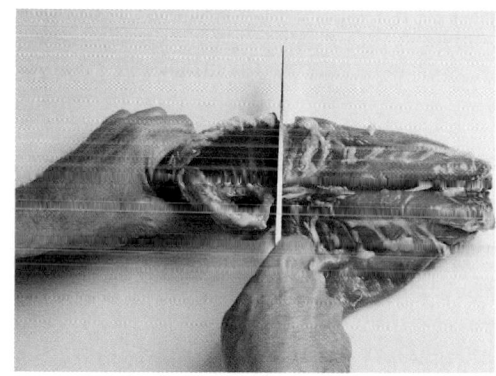

(d) Cut through the backbone to separate the bony rib section from the meaty loin or saddle.

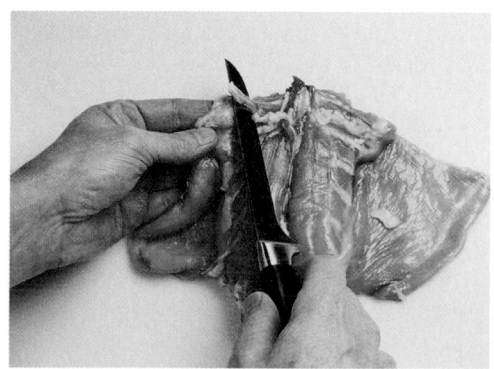

(e) Carefully separate the remaining rib bones from the loin and remove them. The saddle can then be cut crosswise through the backbone into pieces if desired.

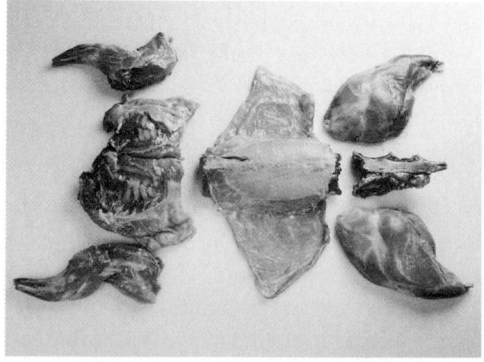

(f) This is the cut up rabbit, with the forelegs and rib section on the left, the saddle in the center, and the hind legs and hip bone on the right.

Rabbit takes well to marination and, of course, it can also be cooked without prior marination. Either way, it can be cooked by long, slow simmering, braising, or stewing, or it can be quickly cooked by sautéing, grilling, or roasting.

The structure of rabbit, of course, is like that of other land mammals rather than like that of poultry. Cutting methods divide the meaty hind legs, the bonier forelegs, and the choice saddle or back section (*râble* in French). The whole carcass, cut up, is used for stews and sautés, while the saddle alone is often roasted. It may be boned or bone-in. (See Figure 10.10.)

Small rabbits, 3 pounds (1.5 kg), or less, are the best for cooking. Mature rabbits, weighing about 4 to 5 pounds (about 2 kg), tend to be tougher and drier.

HARE

Hare is a wild cousin of the rabbit. (Please note that rabbits and hares are different animals; the American jackrabbit, for example, is actually a hare, not a rabbit.) Unlike domestic rabbit, with its light-colored, delicate meat, hare has flesh that is dark reddish-brown and gamy.

Hares seven to eight months old and weighing about 6 pounds (2.7 kg) make the best eating. Larger ones, more than 8 pounds (3.6 kg), are likely to be tough and stringy.

Because its structure is the same, hare is cut the same way as rabbit.

Roast Saddle of Hare

Like other game, hare is very lean and therefore becomes dry if overcooked. If roasted, it should be removed from the oven while rare or at least still pink. Rare roast hare has an attractive, deep red color. A typical classic preparation of saddle of hare is as follows. Note that this is also the classic treatment for roast venison.

1. Marinate the saddle of hare in a red wine marinade (such as the venison marinade on p. 255).

2. Brown it on top of the stove and roast it rare or medium done, about 15 minutes at 425°F (220°C).

3. Remove the loin muscles from the bone and cut lengthwise into thin slices. Remove the tenderloins from the underside of the saddle and leave whole or slice as desired.

4. Serve it with a poivrade sauce (p. 149).

Storage of Meats

The quality of the finished product depends not only on proper selection and cooking of meats but also on proper storage as well. Fresh meat is highly perishable. The high cost of meat makes it essential to avoid spoilage.

FRESH MEATS

1. Check purchases on arrival to ensure that purchased meat is of good quality.

2. Do not wrap tightly. Bacteria and mold thrive in moist, stagnant places. Air circulation inhibits their growth. Store loosely to allow air circulation between pieces, but cover cut surfaces to prevent excessive drying.

3. Do not open vacuum-packed meats until ready to use.

4. Store at 32° to 36°F (0° to 2°C). Meat does not freeze until about 28°F (–2°C).

5. Keep meats separated in cooler (and on worktable) to avoid cross-contamination.

6. Use as soon as possible. Fresh meats keep well for only two to four days. Ground meats keep even less well because so much surface area is exposed to bacteria. Cured and smoked products may keep up to one week.
    Frequent deliveries are better than long storage.

7. Do not try to rescue meats that are going bad by freezing them. Freezing will not improve the quality of spoiling meat.

8. Keep coolers clean.

FROZEN MEATS

1. Wrap frozen meats well to prevent freezer burn.

2. Store at 0°F (−18°C) or colder.

3. Rotate stock—first in, first out. Frozen meats do not keep indefinitely. Recommended shelf life at 0°F (−18°C) for beef, veal, and lamb: 6 months; for pork: 4 months (pork fat turns rancid easily in the freezer).

4. Defrost carefully. Tempering in the refrigerator is best. Defrosting at room temperature encourages bacterial growth.

5. Do not refreeze thawed meats. Refreezing increases loss of quality.

6. Keep freezers clean.

Terms for Review

coagulation	yield grade	fabricated cuts	sweetbreads
marbling	green meat	portion-controlled cuts	tripe
connective tissue	aging	barding	gras-double
collagen	Cryovac	larding	caul
elastin	Institution Meat Purchase	doneness	venison
inspection	Specifications	carry-over cooking	boar
grading	primal cuts	variety meats	hare

Questions for Discussion

1. Many people assume that the leaner a meat is, the better it is. Do you agree? Explain.

2. What is connective tissue? Why is it important for the cook to understand connective tissue?

3. Flank steak (beef) is high in connective tissue, yet it is often broiled and served in thin slices as London broil. How is this possible?

4. You are in charge of a large hospital food service. Why might you choose USDA Select grade beef for making pot roast and stew?

5. Why are portion-controlled meats so widely used in food service, even though their per-pound cost is higher?

6. Can you explain why veal loin, a tender cut, is sometimes braised, while veal shoulder, a less tender cut, is sometimes roasted?

7. Which of the following cuts are you more likely to braise? Which might you roast? Beef chuck, lamb shanks, veal rib, beef rib, pork shoulder, corned beef brisket, ground pork, beef strip loin, lamb leg.

8. Table 10.2 indicates the internal temperature of rare roast beef as 130°F (54°C). Why, then, would you remove a roast rib from the oven when the temperature on the meat thermometer reads 115°F (46°C)?

9. Why are weight-time roasting charts inadequate for determining the doneness of roast meats?

10. Describe the fat content of game meats such as venison, boar, and elk. Explain how the fat content affects how game meats are handled and cooked.

11. How does farm-raised venison differ from wild venison?

chapter 11

Cooking Meats and Game

This chapter presents basic cooking methods as they apply to beef, lamb, veal, pork, and game such as venison. It is important that you have read and understood the basic material in Chapter 10, especially the sections on matching particular cuts to appropriate cooking methods and on testing for doneness. If necessary, please review those sections as well as the discussion of basic cooking methods in Chapter 4.

The procedures given here are general. Be aware that they may be modified slightly in specific recipes. Nevertheless, the basic principles still hold. In addition, your instructors may wish to show you variations or methods that differ from those presented here.

The recipes that follow each of the procedures for roasting, sautéing, braising, and so on are intended to illustrate the basic techniques. Each time you prepare one of these recipes, you should be thinking not just about that one product but about the techniques you are using and how they can be applied to other products. It is helpful to compare the recipes in each section, to see how they are alike and how they are different. This way you will be learning to cook, not just to follow recipes.

After reading this chapter,
you should be able to

1. Cook meats by roasting
   and baking.

2. Cook meats by broiling,
   grilling, and pan-broiling.

3. Cook meats by
   sautéing, pan-frying,
   and griddling.

4. Cook meats by
   simmering.

5. Cook meats by braising.

6. Cook variety meats.

Roasting and Baking

Remember the definitions of *roast* and *bake* (Chapter 4): to cook foods by surrounding them with hot, dry air, usually in an oven. Roasting is a dry-heat method. No water is used, and the meat is not covered so that steam can escape.

In principle, roasting meats is a simple procedure. The prepared cut of meat is placed in an oven at a selected temperature, and it is removed when done. What could be easier?

However, there are many variables, and chefs often disagree about proper roasting procedures, especially when it comes to the fine points. In this section, you will learn a roasting procedure that you can apply to most meats. But first we discuss in more detail several of the points of disagreement and some of the possible variations.

SEASONING

Salt added to the surface of meat just before roasting will penetrate the meat only a fraction of an inch during cooking. The same is true of the flavors of herbs and spices. In the case of a beef rib roast, where most of the surface is either fat or bone, there will be no penetration at all. You will have salty fat, salty bones, and salty pan drippings, but the meat will be unseasoned. Also, salt added just before roasting retards browning because the salt draws moisture to the surface.

There are several alternatives to seasoning just before cooking:

1. Season several hours or a day in advance to give the seasonings time to penetrate.
2. Season the roast after cooking.
3. Don't season at all, but carefully season the gravy or juices (jus) that are served with the meat.

With smaller cuts of meat, such as beef tenderloin and rack of lamb, the chef may season just before roasting because the meat is not as thick and each customer receives a larger share of seasoned, browned surface.

TEMPERATURE

Low-Temperature Roasting

As we discussed on page 226, it was once thought that starting the roast at a high temperature "seals the pores" by searing the surface, thus keeping in more juices.

We now know that this is not the case. Repeated tests have shown that *continuous roasting at a low temperature* gives a superior product with

1. Less shrinkage.
2. More flavor, juiciness, and tenderness.
3. More even doneness from outside to inside.
4. Greater ease in carving.

   Low roasting temperatures generally range from 250° to 325°F (120° to 160°C), depending on

1. The size of the cut. The larger the cut, the lower the temperature. This ensures that the outer portion is not overcooked before the inside is done.
2. The operation's production schedule. Lower temperatures require longer roasting times, which may or may not be convenient for a particular operation.

Searing

If a well-browned, crusted surface is desired for appearance, such as when the roast is to be carved in the dining room, a roast may be started at high temperature (400° to 450°F/200° to 230°C) until it is browned. The temperature should then be lowered to the desired roasting temperature and the meat roasted until done, as for low-temperature roasting.

High-Temperature Roasting

Very small pieces of meat that are to be roasted rare may be cooked at a high temperature, from 375° to 450°F (190° to 230°C). The effect is similar to broiling: a well-browned, crusted exterior and a rare interior. The meat is in the oven for so short a time that there is little shrinkage.

Examples of cuts that may be roasted at a high temperature are rack of lamb and beef tenderloin.

Convection Ovens

If a convection oven is used for roasting, the temperature should be reduced about 50°F (25°C). Many chefs prefer not to use convection ovens for large roasts because the drying effect of the forced air seems to cause greater shrinkage. On the other hand, convection ovens are effective in browning and are good for high-temperature roasting.

FAT SIDE UP OR FAT SIDE DOWN

Roasting meats fat side up provides continuous basting as the fat melts and runs down the sides. This method is preferred by perhaps the majority of chefs, although there is not complete agreement.

In this book, we use the fat side up method. In the classroom, you should be guided by the advice of your instructor.

BASTING

Basting is unnecessary if the meat has a natural fat covering and is roasted fat side up. For lean meats, *barding* has the same effect. Barding is covering the surface of the meat with a thin layer of fat, such as sliced pork fatback or bacon.

If a roast is basted by spooning pan drippings over it, use only the fat. Fat protects the roast from drying, while moisture washes away protective fat and allows drying. Juices used in basting will not soak into the meat.

Basting with drippings or juices may be used to increase the appetite appeal of the roast because it enhances browning. Gelatin and other solids dissolved in the juices are deposited on the surface of the meat, helping to form a flavorful brown crust. This does not increase juiciness, however. Some cookbooks claim that basting forms a waterproof coating that seals in juices, but this is not the case.

Basting sometimes produces more tender roasts for an unexpected reason: Frequent basting interrupts and slows down the cooking. Every time the oven door is opened, the temperature in the oven drops considerably, so the roasting time is longer and more connective tissue breaks down. Thus, it is not the basting but the lower temperature that increases tenderness.

USE OF MIREPOIX

Mirepoix is often added during the last part of the roasting time to flavor the roast and to add extra flavor to the pan juices.

Many chefs feel, however, that the mirepoix adds little flavor, if any, to the roast and that it is actually harmful because the moisture of the vegetables creates steam around the roast. Mirepoix can be more easily added when the gravy is being made. If no gravy or juice is to be served, there may be no need for mirepoix at all.

The use of mirepoix is more important for white meats—veal and pork—which, because they are usually cooked well done, lose more juices and need a good gravy or jus to give them moistness and flavor.

GRAVY AND JUS

The general procedures for making pan gravy are given in Chapter 8 (p. 157). Read or review this section if necessary. The procedure for making jus, given here in the recipe for roast prime ribs of beef au jus, is the same except that no roux or other thickening agents are used. In other words, use the methods for making pan gravy (p. 158) but eliminate steps 5 and 6 from Method 1 and step 3 from Method 2.

Basic Procedure for Roasting Meats

1. Collect all equipment and food supplies.
    Select roasting pans that have low sides (so moisture vapor does not collect around the roast) and that are just large enough to hold the roast. If pans are too large, drippings will spread out too thin and burn.

2. Prepare or trim meat for roasting. Heavy fat coverings should be trimmed to about ½ inch (1 cm) thick.

3. If desired, season meat several hours ahead or the day before.

4. Place meat fat side up on a rack in the roasting pan. The rack holds the roast out of the drippings. Bones may be used if no rack is available. Bone-in rib roasts need no rack because the bones act as a natural rack.

5. Insert a meat thermometer (clean and sanitary) so that the bulb is in the center of the meat, not touching bone or fat. (Omit this step if you are using an instant-read thermometer.)

6. Do not cover or add water to the pan. Roasting is a dry-heat cooking method.

7. Place meat in oven, which has been preheated to desired temperature.

8. If desired, add mirepoix to the pan during the last half of the cooking period.

9. Roast to desired doneness, allowing for carry-over cooking.

10. Remove roast from oven and let stand in a warm place 15 to 30 minutes. This allows the juices to be reabsorbed through the meat so that less juice is lost when the meat is sliced. Also, resting the meat makes slicing easier.

11. If the meat must be held, place it in an oven or warmer set no higher than the desired internal temperature of the roast.

12. While the roast is resting, prepare jus or pan gravy from the drippings. Mirepoix may be added to the drippings now if it was not added in step 8.

13. Slice the roast as close as possible to serving time. In almost all cases, slice the meat against the grain for tenderness.

Roast Rib of Beef au Jus

Yield: 10 lb (4.5 kg) boneless, trimmed meat Portions: 25 Portion size: 6½ oz (175 g)
    20   8 oz (225 g)
        1½ (50 mL) jus

U.S.	Metric	Ingredients	PROCEDURE
20 lb	9 kg	Beef rib, roast ready, bone in (one average-size rib roast)	1. Place the meat fat side up in a roasting pan.
2. Insert a meat thermometer so that the bulb is in the center of the meat, not touching bone or fat.
3. Place in a preheated 300°F (150°C) oven. Roast until rare or medium done, as desired, *allowing for carryover cooking.*
Thermometer readings:
Rare: 120°F (49°C)
Medium: 130°F (54°C)
(Outer slices will be more done than center.)
Roasting time will be at least 3–4 hours.
4. Remove the meat from the pan and let stand in a warm place 30 minutes before carving.
		Mirepoix:	5. Drain off all but about 3–4 oz (100 g) of the fat from the roasting pan. Be careful to retain any juices in the pan. Add the mirepoix to the pan (see Figure 11.1).
8 oz	250 g	Onions	
4 oz	125 g	Carrots	6. Set the pan over high heat and cook until mirepoix is brown and moisture has evaporated, leaving only fat, mirepoix, and browned drippings.
4 oz	125 g	Celery	7. Pour off any excess fat.
2 qt	2 L	Brown stock	8. Pour about 1 pint (500 mL) of stock into the roasting pan to deglaze it. Stir over heat until brown drippings are dissolved.
to taste	to taste	Salt	9. Pour the deglazing liquid and mirepoix into a saucepot with the remaining stock. Simmer until mirepoix is soft and liquid is reduced by about one-third.
to taste	to taste	Pepper	10. Strain through a china cap lined with cheesecloth into a bain-marie. Skim fat carefully. Season to taste with salt and pepper.
11. For service, stand the roast on its widest end. Cut down beside the bones to free the meat, and slice the meat across the grain.
12. Serve each portion with 1½ oz (50 mL) jus.

Per 6½ ounces:
Calories, 810; Protein, 52 g; Fat, 65 g (74% cal.); Cholesterol, 180 mg; Carbohydrates, 0 g; Fiber, 0 g; Sodium, 150 mg.

VARIATIONS

Roast rib-eye roll, top round, sirloin, or strip loin
These cuts may be roasted by the same procedure; roast them on a rack.

Roast Beef with Gravy
Roast desired cut of beef according to the basic recipe. Prepare gravy according to the following recipe.

Roast Beef Gravy

Yield: approx. 1½ qt (1.5 L)   **Portions:** 25   **Portion size:** 2 oz (60 mL)

U.S.	Metric	Ingredients	PROCEDURE
as needed	as needed	Pan drippings from roast beef (previous recipe)	1. After removing the roast, add the mirepoix to the drippings in the roasting pan.
		Mirepoix:	2. Set the pan over high heat and cook until mirepoix is brown and moisture has evaporated, leaving only fat, mirepoix, and browned drippings (see Figure 11.1).
8 oz	250 g	Onions	
4 oz	125 g	Carrots	
4 oz	125 g	Celery	3. Pour off and save the fat.
2 qt	2 L	Brown stock	4. Deglaze the pan with some of the stock. Pour the deglazing liquid and mirepoix into a saucepot with the remaining stock. Add the tomato purée. Bring to a boil and reduce heat to a simmer.
4 oz	125 g	Tomato purée	
4 oz	125 g	Flour	5. Make a brown roux with the flour and 4 oz (125 g) of the reserved fat. Cool the roux slightly and beat it into the simmering stock to thicken it.
to taste	to taste	Salt	
to taste	to taste	Pepper	6. Simmer 15–20 minutes, until all raw flour taste is cooked out and liquid is reduced slightly.
to taste	to taste	Worcestershire sauce	
			7. Strain through a china cap into a bain-marie.
			8. Season to taste with salt, pepper, and Worcestershire sauce.

Per serving:
Calories, 35; Protein, 1 g; Fat, 1.5 g (40% cal.); Cholesterol, 5 mg;
Carbohydrates, 4 g; Fiber, 0 g; Sodium, 10 mg.

VARIATION

Jus Lié
Omit tomato paste and roux. Thicken liquid with 1½ oz (50 g) cornstarch or arrowroot blended with ½ cup (100 mL) cold water or stock.

Figure 11.1 Preparing pan jus.
(a) After removing the cooked meat from the roasting pan, degrease the pan. Add mirepoix to the pan and brown on the stovetop or in the oven.

(b) Deglaze with brown stock.

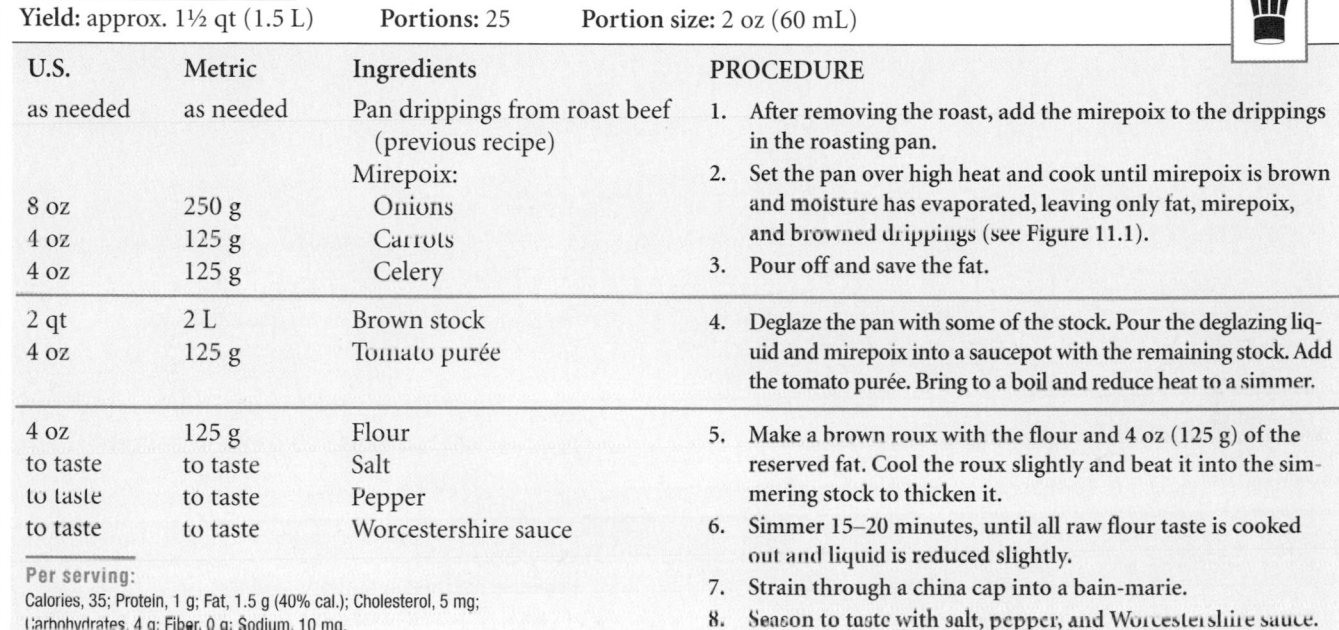

(a)

(b)

(c) Pour the mirepoix and deglazing liquid into a saucepan. Simmer for the desired time.

(d) Strain through a fine chinois or through a china cap lined with cheesecloth.

(c)

(d)

Roast Stuffed Shoulder of Lamb

Portions: 10   Portion size: 5 oz (150 g) meat and stuffing
                                 2 oz (60 mL) gravy

U.S.	Metric	Ingredients	PROCEDURE
		Stuffing:	1. Sauté the onion and garlic in oil until soft. Remove from heat and cool.
4 oz	125 g	Onion, fine dice	
1 tsp	5 mL	Garlic, chopped fine	2. Combine onion and garlic with the remaining stuffing ingredients and mix lightly.
2 oz	60 g	Olive oil, vegetable oil, *or* butter	
3 oz (about 2 cups)	100 g	Soft, fresh bread crumbs	
⅓ cup	80 mL	Chopped parsley	
½ tsp	2 mL	Rosemary	
¼ tsp	1 mL	Black pepper	
½ tsp	2 mL	Salt	
1	1	Egg, beaten	
1	1	Boneless lamb shoulder, about 4 lb (1.8 kg)	3. Lay the lamb shoulder out flat, fat side down.
as needed	as needed	Oil	4. Spread the lamb with the stuffing and roll it up. Tie the roll tightly.
as needed	as needed	Salt	5. Rub the meat with oil, salt, pepper, and rosemary.
as needed	as needed	Pepper	6. Place the meat on a rack in a roasting pan. Insert a meat thermometer into the thickest part of the meat (not into the stuffing).
as needed	as needed	Rosemary	
			7. Place in a 325°F (165°C) oven. Roast the meat about 1½ hours.
		Mirepoix:	8. Place the mirepoix in the bottom of the roasting pan. Baste the meat with fat and continue to roast until the thermometer reads 160°F (71°C). Total cooking time is about 2½ hours.
4 oz	125 g	Onions, chopped	
2 oz	60 g	Carrots, chopped	
2 oz	60 g	Celery, chopped	9. Remove the roast from the pan and let stand in a warm place.
2 oz	60 g	Flour	10. Set the roasting pan over high heat to clarify the fat and finish browning the mirepoix. Drain off about three-fourths of the fat.
1 qt	1 L	Brown beef stock or lamb stock	
4 oz	125 g	Tomatoes, canned	11. Add the flour to the pan to make a roux, cooking it until it is brown.
to taste	to taste	Salt	12. Stir in the stock and tomatoes and bring to a boil. Simmer, while stirring, until the gravy is thickened and reduced to about 1½ pints (750 mL).
to taste	to taste	Pepper	
			13. Strain and skim excess fat.
			14. Season to taste with salt and pepper.
			15. Slice the roast crosswise, so that each slice contains stuffing in the center. When slicing, be careful to keep the slices from falling apart. Serve each portion with 2 oz (60 mL) gravy.

Per serving:
Calories, 390; Protein, 31 g; Fat, 25 g (57% cal.); Cholesterol, 120 mg;
Carbohydrates, 11 g; Fiber, 1 g; Sodium, 275 mg.

VARIATIONS

Roast Boneless Shoulder of Lamb

Roast tied, boneless lamb shoulder as in basic recipe, without stuffing.

Roast Leg of Lamb

Prepare leg of lamb for roasting as shown in Figure 11.2. Rub with oil, salt, pepper, rosemary, and garlic. Roast as in basic recipe (without stuffing) to rare, medium, or well-done stage. Leg of lamb may be served with natural juices (au jus) instead of thickened gravy, if desired. Approximate yield: 8 lb (3.6 kg) AP leg of lamb yields about 3½ lb (1.6 kg) cooked meat. Yield is less if cooked well done. See Figure 11.3 for carving technique.

Roast Leg of Lamb Boulangère

1½ hours before lamb is done, transfer the meat to a rack over a pan of Boulangère Potatoes (p. 496) and finish cooking.

Figure 11.2 *Preparing a leg of lamb for roasting. Fresh hams may be prepared using the same basic technique.*

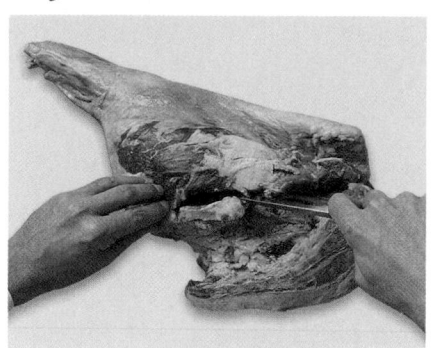

(a) Begin by removing the hip and tail bones.

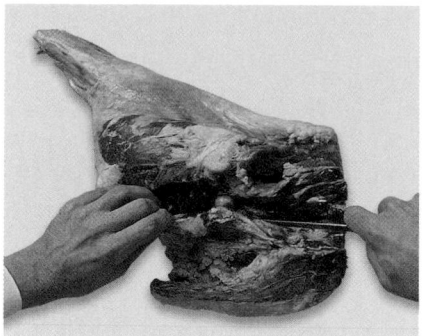

(b) With a sharp-pointed boning knife, cut along the hip bone to separate bone from meat. Always cut against the bone.

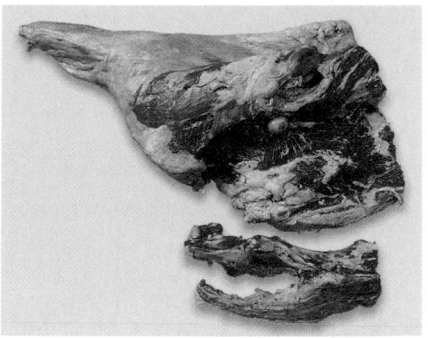

(c) Continue until the hip bone and tailbone are completely removed. Note the round ball joint at the end of the leg bone in the center of the meat.

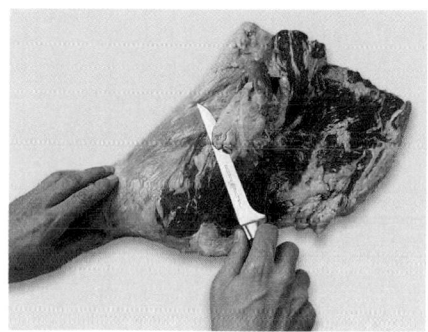

(d) Trim off excess external fat, leaving a thin covering.

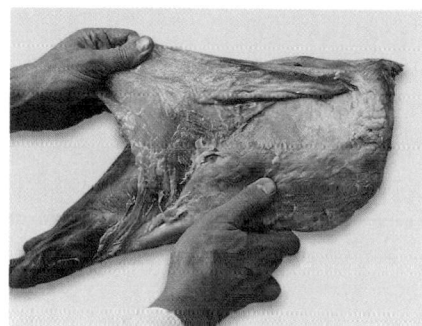

(e) Pull off the skin or fell on the outside of the leg.

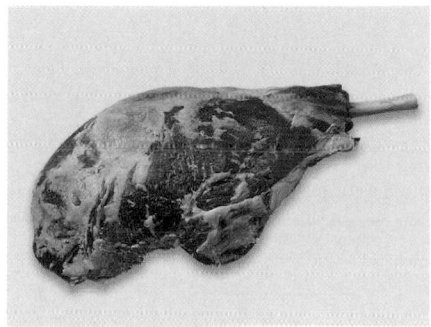

(f) Full leg of lamb, ready for roasting. The end of the shank bone and part of the shank meat have been removed.

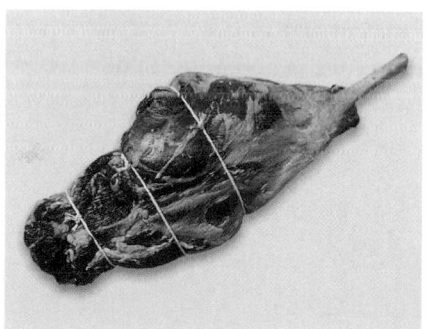

(g) The leg may be tied into a more compact shape.

(h) The sirloin portion may be cut off and used for another purpose, such as shish kebabs.

Figure 11.3 Carving a leg of lamb. Hams and other leg roasts may be carved using the same basic technique shown here.

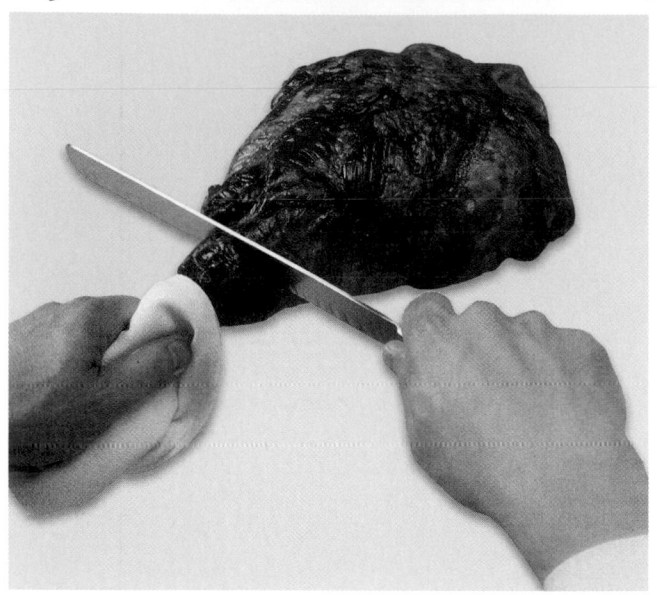

(a) Place the roast on a clean, sanitary cutting board. Begin by making a vertical cut through to the bone about 1 inch (2.5 cm) from the end of the shank meat. The small collar of shank meat forms a guard to protect the hand in case the knife slips.

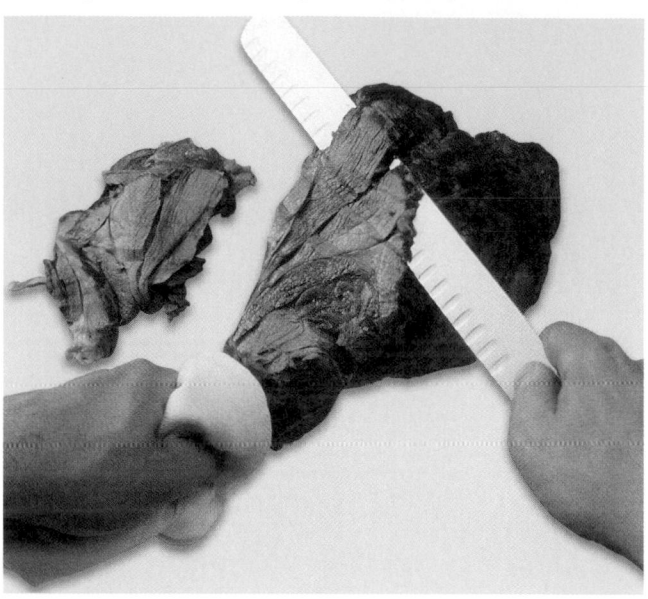

(b) Using long, smooth strokes, cut thin slices on a slight bias as shown.

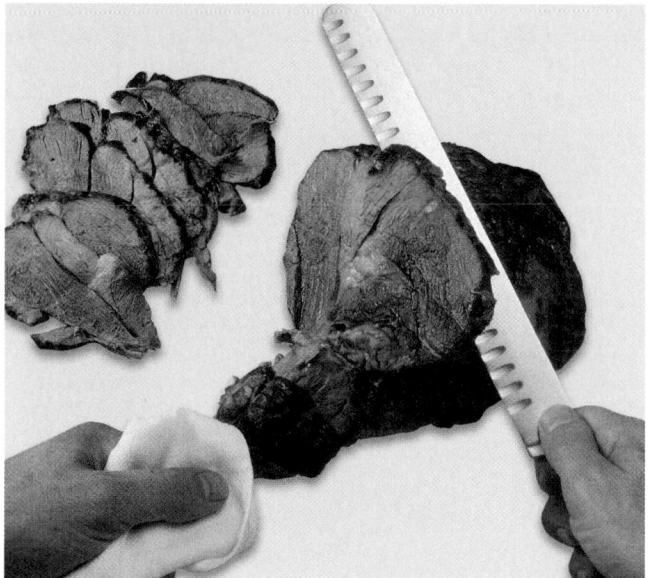

(c) When slices become too large, angle the knife.

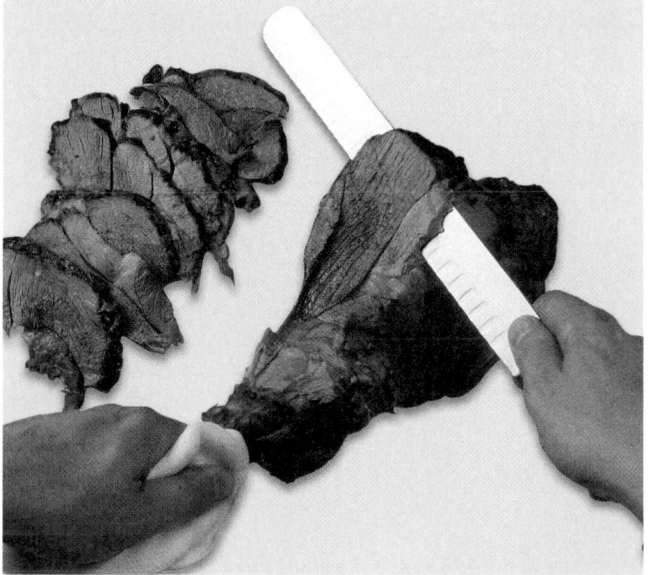

(d) Then take alternating slices from different sides of the roast as shown. When the top of the roast has been completely sliced, turn over and repeat the procedure on the bottom of the roast.

Roast Rack of Lamb

Portions: 8	Portion size: 2 chops 1 oz (30 mL) jus		

U.S.	Metric	Ingredients	PROCEDURE
2	2	Racks of lamb, 8 ribs each	1. Prepare lamb for roasting as shown in Figure 11.4.
to taste	to taste	Salt	2. Place any trimmed-off bones in the bottom of a roasting pan. Place the meat fat side up on top of the bones. Season with salt, pepper, and thyme.
to taste	to taste	Pepper	
to taste	to taste	Thyme	
			3. Place in hot oven (450°F/230°C) and roast to desired doneness. Rack of lamb is usually roasted rare or medium. Test doneness with a meat thermometer or by the touch method, as for steaks. Total time will be about 30 minutes.
			4. Remove the lamb from the roasting pan and hold in a warm place. Leave bones in pan.
			5. Set the roasting pan over moderate heat to caramelize the juices and clarify the fat. Pour off the fat.
2 cloves	2 cloves	Garlic, chopped	6. Add the garlic to the pan and cook 1 minute.
1 pt	500 mL	White or brown veal stock	7. Deglaze the pan with the stock and reduce by half. Strain, degrease, and season to taste.
			8. Cut the meat between the ribs into chops. Serve 2 chops per portion with 1 oz (30 mL) jus.

Per serving:
Calories, 280; Protein, 19 g; Fat, 22 g (72% cal.); Cholesterol, 75 mg; Carbohydrates, 0 g; Fiber, 0 g; Sodium, 70 mg.

VARIATIONS

Rack of Lamb aux Primeurs (with Spring Vegetables)

Place the racks on one or two heated serving platters. Garnish the platters with an assortment of spring vegetables, cooked separately: tournéed carrots, tournéed turnips, buttered peas, green beans, rissolé potatoes. Pour the jus into a warm gooseneck or sauceboat. Carve and serve the meat, vegetables, and jus in the dining room.

Rack of Lamb Persillé

Prepare as in basic recipe. Combine the ingredients for Persillade (pear-see-yahd), listed below. Before carving and serving, spread the top (fat side) of each rack with 1 tbsp (15 g) soft butter. Pack the persillade onto the top of the racks and brown under the salamander.

Persillade

4 cloves garlic, minced
2 oz (60 g) fresh bread crumbs (about 1 cup)
⅓ cup (80 mL) chopped parsley

Roast Rack of Lamb; White Beans Bretonne and Steamed Brussels Sprout Leaves

Figure 11.4 Preparing a rack of lamb for roasting.

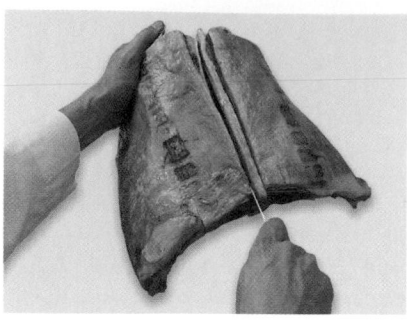

(a) Begin by cutting down on both sides of the feather bones all the way to the chine bone.

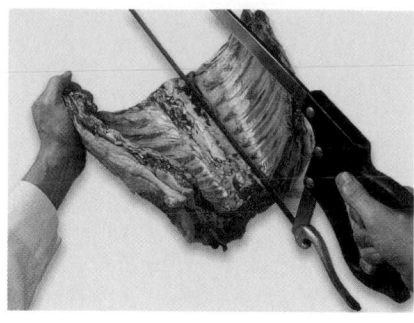

(b) If a meat saw is available, turn the rack over and cut through the rib bones at the points where they attach to the chine bone.

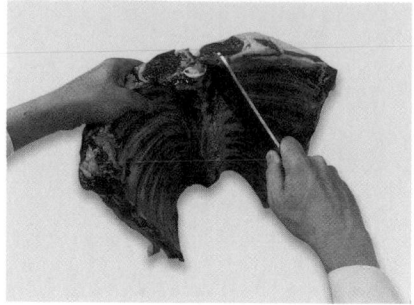

(c) If a meat saw is not available, use a cleaver. Stand the roast up on end and cut through the rib bones at the point where they join the chine bone. This will separate one rack.

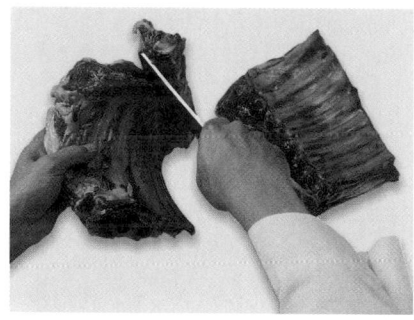

(d) Repeat the procedure on the other side of the chine.

(e) The two halves are separated from the chine.

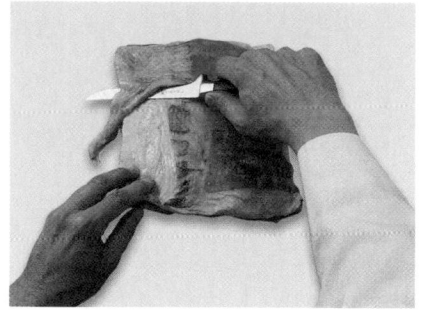

(f) Trim excess fat from the top of the meat, leaving a thin protective covering. During this step, you should also remove the shoulder blade cartilage, which is embedded in the layers of fat.

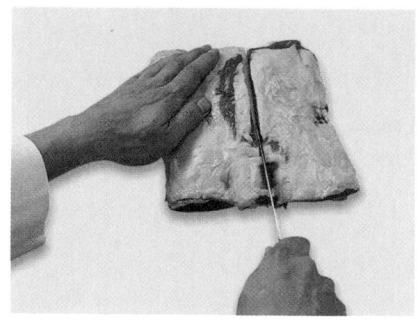

(g) To trim the fat and meat from the ends of the bones (called frenching the bones), first cut through the fat in a straight line down to the bone, keeping the cut about 1 inch (2.5 cm) from the tip of the eye muscle.

(h) Score the membrane covering the rib bones. Pull and cut the layer of fat from the bones.

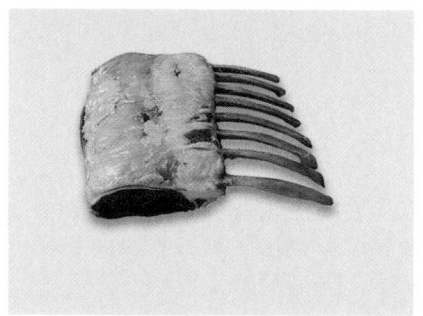

(i) The roast is trimmed and ready to cook.

Roast Loin of Pork with Sage and Apples

Portions: 25   Portion size: 1 chop, about 6 oz (175 g) with bone
                              2 oz (60 mL) gravy

U.S.	Metric	Ingredients	PROCEDURE
14½ lb	6.6 kg	Pork loins, center cut, bone in	1. With a meat saw, cut off the chine bones so that the loins can be carved into chops after roasting.
1 tsp	5 mL	Salt	2. Rub the pork with salt, pepper, and sage.
½ tsp	2 mL	Pepper	3. Place the chine bones in a roasting pan. Place the pork loins fat side up on top of the bones. Insert a meat thermometer into the thickest part of the muscle.
1 tbsp	15 mL	Sage	
		Mirepoix:	
8 oz	250 g	Onion	4. Place in oven at 325°F (165°C) and roast for 1 hour.
4 oz	125 g	Carrot	5. Place the mirepoix and the apples in the bottom of the pan and continue to roast until the thermometer reads 160°F (71°C). Total cooking time is about 2 to 2½ hours.
4 oz	125 g	Celery	
8 oz	250 g	Apples, peeled, cored, and diced	6. Remove the roast from the pan and hold in a warm place.
2½ qt	2.5 L	Chicken stock, veal stock, or pork stock	7. Set the roasting pan over moderate heat and cook until moisture has evaporated and mirepoix is well browned. Drain off and reserve fat.
5 oz	150 g	Flour	8. Deglaze the pan with the stock and pour the contents into a saucepot. Skim well.
to taste	to taste	Salt	9. Make a browned roux with the flour and 5 oz (150 g) of the pork fat. Thicken the gravy with the roux and simmer 15 minutes, until thickened and slightly reduced.
to taste	to taste	Pepper	
8	8	Tart apples	10. While the gravy is simmering, core the apples. They may be peeled or not, as desired. Cut the apples crosswise into slices about 3/8 inch (1 cm) thick. Sauté the slices in a little butter over moderately high heat. Sprinkle them with sugar as they cook. Continue to sauté on both sides until browned and caramelized.
2 oz	60 g	Butter	
1 tbsp	15 mL	Sugar	
			11. Strain the gravy and adjust the seasonings.
			12. Cut the roast into chops between the rib bones. Serve each portion with 2 oz (60 mL) gravy. Garnish with caramelized apple slices.

Per serving:
Calories, 420; Protein, 40 g; Fat, 22 g (48% cal.); Cholesterol, 105 mg;
Carbohydrates, 13 g; Fiber, 2 g; Sodium, 210 mg.

VARIATIONS

Other pork cuts may be roasted as in basic recipe: full loin, loin ends, boneless loin, fresh ham, shoulder.

Roast Loin or Rack of Veal with Sage and Apples

Substitute loin or rack of veal for pork in the basic recipe. Use brown stock instead of white stock.

Barbecued Spareribs

Portions: 24   Portion size: 10 oz (300 g)

U.S.	Metric	Ingredients	PROCEDURE
18 lb	8.5 kg	Fresh pork spareribs	1. Weigh the spareribs and cut them into 12-oz (350-g) portions.
2½ qt	2.5 L	Barbecue Sauce (p. 163) or Chile Barbecue Sauce (p. 164)	2. Place the ribs in roasting pans with the inside of the ribs down.
			3. Place the ribs in a slow oven (300°F/150°C). Bake for 1 hour (see note).
			4. Drain the fat from the pans. Spoon about 1 cup (250 mL) sauce over the ribs to coat them with a thin layer. Turn them over and coat with more sauce.
			5. Bake 45 minutes. Turn and coat the ribs with the remaining sauce. Bake until tender, about 30–60 minutes more.
			6. Serve the portions whole or cut into 1- or 2-rib pieces for easier eating.

Per serving:
Calories, 515; Protein, 47 g; Fat, 35 g (63% cal.); Cholesterol, 140 mg;
Carbohydrates, 0 g; Fiber, 0 g; Sodium, 150 mg.

Note: Spareribs are often covered with boiling water and simmered for 30 minutes before baking. This is not necessary to cook the ribs and may result in the loss of some flavor and nutrients, but it does speed the cooking time. If ribs are simmered, omit the preliminary baking (step 3). Ribs may also be finished on a grill or under a broiler.

Roast Pork Tenderloin with Leeks and Whole Grain Mustard Sauce

Portions: 12   Portion size: about 8 oz (250 mL) meat
                      2 oz (60 mL) sauce

U.S.	Metric	Ingredients	PROCEDURE
4 lb	1.8 kg	Leek, white part only, cut julienne	1. Sweat the julienned leek in the butter. Season to taste. Cover and keep warm.
3½ oz	100 g	Butter	2. Trim the pork fillets and season with salt and pepper.
to taste	to taste	Salt	3. Brown in a little oil. Transfer to an oven preheated to 475°F (250°C) for 10 minutes. Remove the pork fillets, cover with aluminum foil, and set aside to rest. Remove most of the fat from the pan.
to taste	to taste	Pepper	
5 lb	2.4 kg	Pork tenderloins	
as needed	as needed	Oil	
3½ oz	100 g	Shallots, chopped	4. Add the shallots to the pan. Sweat the shallots, then deglaze with the dry vermouth. Reduce by two-thirds.
5 oz	150 mL	Dry vermouth	
1 pt 4 oz	600 mL	Crème fraîche	5. Add the cream. Bring to a boil, then strain through a fine sieve. Season to taste, then add the mustard. Once the mustard has been added, do not allow the mixture to boil.
2½ oz	75 g	Whole grain mustard	
		Chervil sprigs for garnish	6. Slice the pork. Spoon the leeks onto the center of the dinner plates, then arrange the sliced pork around the leeks. Pour 2 oz (60 mL) sauce around the meat. Garnish with sprigs of chervil.

Per serving:
Calories, 640; Protein, 46 g; Fat, 37 g (53% cal.); Cholesterol, 160 mg;
Carbohydrates, 26 g; Fiber, 4 g; Sodium, 300 mg.

Roasted Loin of Pork with Ginger

Portions: 12   Portion size: 1 chop, about 6½ oz (190 g) with bone
                      2 oz (60 mL) sauce

U.S.	Metric	Ingredients	PROCEDURE
8 lb	3.6 kg	Pork loin, center cut, bone in	1. Trim the pork racks of excess fat and sinews. With a meat saw, cut off the chine bones so that the loin can be cut into chops after cooking. French the bones if desired (see Figure 11.4). The trimmed loin should weigh about 6-6½ lb (2.8 kg). Reserve the trimmings (except for the fat).
3½ oz	100 mL	Oil	
3½ oz	100 mL	Soy sauce	
2½ oz	75 g	Ginger root, fine dice	
to taste	to taste	Salt	2. Mix together the oil, soy sauce, ginger, and seasonings. Marinate the pork with its trimmings for at least 1 hour.
to taste	to taste	Pepper	
12 oz	350 g	Onion, diced	3. Remove the pork rack from the marinade, leaving any pieces of ginger adhering to the meat. Place in an oiled roasting pan and place in an oven preheated to 350°F (175°C).
3½ oz	100 g	Carrot, diced	
12 cloves	12 cloves	Garlic, peeled, left whole	
			4. After 10 minutes of roasting, add the bones and trimmings, the onion, carrot, and garlic cloves, and continue roasting until the pork is done, about 1 hour 20 minutes to 1 hour 50 minutes in all.
			5. Remove the roast from the pan and hold in a warm place.
1 tbsp	25 g	Tomato paste	6. Place the roasting pan on the stovetop. Add the tomato paste and cook for a few minutes, then add the chicken stock. Cook for 15 minutes, then strain. Reserve the garlic cloves. Skim off any fat.
1 qt	1 L	Chicken stock	
3½ fl. oz	100 mL	Honey (preferably acacia honey)	
7 oz	200 mL	Cider vinegar	7. Combine the honey with the vinegar in a saucepan and cook until lightly caramelized.
to taste	to taste	Salt	8. Add the strained cooking liquid and cook for a few minutes, then add the garlic cloves. Reduce until the sauce is thickened enough to lightly coat the back of a spoon. Strain, pressing the garlic cloves well. Season to taste.
to taste	to taste	Pepper	

Per serving:
Calories, 410; Protein, 45 g; Fat, 18 g (40% cal.); Cholesterol, 100 mg;
Carbohydrates, 16 g; Fiber, 1 g; Sodium, 170 mg.

9. Serve the pork sliced with the sauce around.

Note: A mixture of caramelized sugar and vinegar is called a *gastrique*. It is used as the base of many sweet and savory sauces, such as orange sauce for roast duck and other sauces with fruit, because it gives a good balance of sweetness and acidity.

Baked Pork Chops with Prune Stuffing

Portions: 25   Portion size: 1 chop
                2 oz (60 mL) gravy

U.S.	Metric	Ingredients	PROCEDURE
25	25	Prunes, pitted	1. Soak the prunes in hot water 15 minutes. Drain and cool.
1½ lb	750 g	Basic Bread Stuffing (p. 357)	2. Prepare the stuffing and add the prunes. Keep refrigerated until ready to use.
25	25	Pork chops, cut thick (at least ¾ inch/2 cm)	3. Cut a pocket in the pork chops as shown in Figure 11.5.
as needed	as needed	Oil	4. Stuff the pockets with the prune stuffing, using 1 prune per chop. Fasten the openings with picks or skewers.
to taste	to taste	Salt	5. Oil a baking pan and place the chops in it. Brush them with oil and season with salt and pepper.
to taste	to taste	Pepper	6. Place the chops under the broiler just until lightly browned.
			7. Transfer the pan to an oven at 350°F (175°C) and bake for about ½ hour, until chops are cooked through.
			8. Remove the chops from the pan and place in a hotel pan for holding. *Remove picks.*
8 oz	250 mL	Water or white wine	9. Deglaze the baking pan with the water or wine, degrease, and strain the liquid into the hot brown sauce.
3½ pt	1.75 L	Brown sauce or demiglaze	10. Bring to a boil and reduce the sauce slightly to bring to the proper consistency.
2 oz	60 mL	Sherry (optional)	11. Add the sherry (if using) and adjust seasoning.
			12. Serve 1 chop per portion with 2 oz (60 mL) gravy.

Per serving:
Calories, 500; Protein, 49 g; Fat, 26 g (47% cal.); Cholesterol, 125 mg;
Carbohydrates, 16 g; Fiber, 1 g; Sodium, 290 mg.

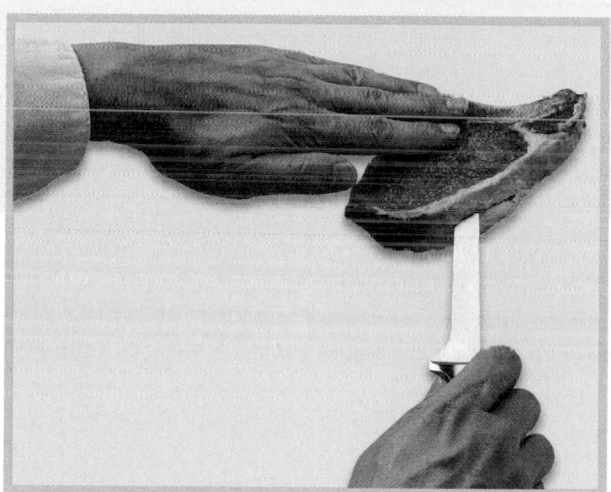

Figure 11.5 *For stuffed pork chops, cut a pocket in the chops as shown.*

Glazed Ham with Cider Sauce

Portions: 25   Portion size: 5 oz (150 g) ham
                                    2 oz (60 mL) sauce

U.S.	Metric	Ingredients	PROCEDURE
15 lb	7 kg	Smoked ham	1. Place the ham(s) in a stockpot with enough water to cover. Bring to a boil and reduce heat to a simmer. Simmer for 1 hour. Drain.
			2. Cut off skin and excess fat. Leave fat covering about ½ inch (1 cm) thick. Score the fat with a knife.
3–4 tbsp	45–60 mL	Prepared mustard	3. Place the ham fat side up in a roasting or baking pan. Spread with a thin layer of prepared mustard. Mix the sugar and cloves and sprinkle over the ham.
6 oz	175 g	Brown sugar	
¼ tsp	1 mL	Ground cloves	4. Bake at 350°F (175°C) about 1 hour. (*Caution:* Sugar burns easily, so check ham after 30–45 minutes.)
1½ qt	1.5 L	Apple cider	5. Place cider, raisins, sugar, nutmeg, and lemon rind in a saucepan and simmer 5 minutes.
8 oz	250 g	Raisins, seedless (optional)	
3 oz	100 g	Brown sugar	6. Mix cornstarch with a little cold water or cold cider and stir into the sauce. Simmer until thickened.
½ tsp	2 mL	Nutmeg	
1 tsp	5 mL	Grated lemon rind	7. Add salt to taste.
6 tbsp	50 g	Cornstarch	8. Slice ham (as for leg of lamb, Figure 11.3). Serve 5-oz (150-g) portion with 2 oz (60 mL) sauce on the side.
to taste	to taste	Salt	

Per serving:
Calories, 300; Protein, 32 g; Fat, 7 g (21% cal.); Cholesterol, 70 mg;
Carbohydrates, 26 g; Fiber, 1 g; Sodium, 1680 mg.

Note: The amount of cooking required depends on type of ham. *Aged country hams* must be soaked 24 hours in cold water, scrubbed, and simmered about 20 minutes per pound (500 g). Hams labeled "tenderized" or "ready to cook" may be baked without simmering (starting with step 2) or may be just blanched before baking (place in cold water, bring to a boil, and drain).

VARIATIONS

Ham with Brown Cider Sauce
When ham is baked, drain fat from pan and deglaze with 1½ pt (750 mL) cider. Add 1½ qt (1.5 L) demiglaze or espagnole and simmer until reduced and thickened. Flavor to taste with mustard and a little sugar.

Fruit-Glazed Ham
Omit mustard-sugar glaze. During last half of baking, spoon fruit preserves (apricot, pineapple, or peach) over ham to glaze.

Lamb Fillet Cooked in a Salt Crust

Portions: 8   **Portion size:** one-half lamb loin plus vegetable garnish and 1½–2 oz (45–60 mL) jus

U.S.	Metric	Ingredients	PROCEDURE
2	2	Small lamb saddles or double loins (see note)	1. Bone out the lamb loins, removing each loin eye and each tenderloin in a single piece. Trim well of fat, tendons, and silverskin, saving the trimmings. Chop up the bones.
as needed	as needed	Oil	
		Mirepoix:	2. Brown the bones and trimmings in a little oil, along with the carrot, onion, celery, crushed garlic, bouquet garni, and the stems from the fresh herbs used in step 3. Add just enough water to cover—about 1 qt (1 L)—and allow to simmer, skimming occasionally. Do not allow to reduce by more than half.
7 oz	200 g	Carrots, coarsely chopped	
8 oz	250 g	Onions, coarsely chopped	
4 oz	125 g	Celery, coarsely chopped	
3 cloves	3 cloves	Garlic, crushed	
1	1	Bouquet garni	
1 lb 6 oz	660 g	Sea salt or kosher salt	3. Combine the salt, water, flour, egg, egg yolks, and herbs. Mix to form a dough. Wrap and set aside. (Note that this is a coarse, rather crumbly dough and a little difficult to handle. If you find it too difficult to roll thin enough (step 6), you may need to make extra dough.)
8 oz	240 mL	Water	
1 lb 8 oz	720 g	Flour	
3	3	Whole eggs	
3	3	Egg yolks	
4 tsp	10 g	Fresh rosemary, chopped	
2 tsp	5 g	Fresh thyme	
2 tsp	5 g	Fresh basil, chopped	
2 tsp	5 g	Parsley, chopped	
10 oz	300 g	Fresh bread crumbs	4. Combine the bread crumbs, herbs and seasonings, and soft butter. Set aside.
2 tsp	5 g	Fresh thyme	
2 tsp	5 g	Fresh basil, chopped	
2 tsp	5 g	Parsley, chopped	
to taste	to taste	Salt	
to taste	to taste	White pepper	
8 oz	240 g	Soft butter	
to taste	to taste	Salt	5. Lightly season the boneless lamb and brown quickly in butter in a sauté pan without letting the interior of the meat cook. Set aside to rest.
to taste	to taste	White pepper	
as needed	as needed	Butter	6. Divide the salt dough into 4 pieces. For each 2 portions, roll out a piece of dough into a rectangle a little longer than the lamb loin and about 3 times as wide. It should be about ¼ inch thick (6 mm)
as needed	as needed	Beaten egg for glazing	
			7. Place the lamb loin on top of the tenderloin so that the meat is of fairly uniform thickness. Position in the middle of the rolled-out dough. Top with some of the herbed bread crumb mixture. Wrap in the rectangle of dough by folding the sides over the top of the meat, trimming off excess dough, and sealing the seams. If desired, decorate the top with cutouts from the leftover scraps of dough. Brush the top with beaten egg to glaze.
			8. Bake in an oven preheated to 500°F (250°C) for 8–10 minutes, depending on the size of the lamb fillets. Set aside in a warm place until ready to serve.
8 portions	8 portions	Vegetable Tagliatelle (p. 460)	9. Strain the jus (from step 2) and season to taste.
8 oz	250 g	Fresh Tomato Coulis with Garlic (p. 151)	10. Serve with vegetable tagliatelle and about 1 oz (30 g) tomato coulis for garnish, and the jus on the side. For plating and presentation, see the following note.

Per serving:
Calories, 500; Protein, 11 g; Fat, 36 g (63% cal.); Cholesterol, 90 mg; Carbohydrates, 36 g; Fiber, 6 g; Sodium, 560 mg.

Note: Try to use loins from small lambs for this preparation so that the portion size will not be too large and there will be enough dough to cover them.

There are two ways to serve this dish. Although the salt crust is not edible, the meat is served with the crust in order to preserve the presentation.

The first approach is to cut each fillet in half crosswise, then cut each half into 3 thick slices. Then reconstruct the slices on the plate. The client can use his or her knife and fork to separate the slices and spear the meat out of the crust.

The other approach is to cut the fillet in half, then cut around the side in order to remove the top of the crust in a single piece. Carefully remove and slice the fillet (carefully, because the filling is very delicate), then place the sliced fillet back in the bottom half of the crust. Place the top slightly off center in order to show the sliced meat.

Home-Style Meatloaf

Portions: 25   Portion size: 4 oz (125 g)

U.S.	Metric	Ingredients	PROCEDURE
1 lb	500 g	Onions, fine dice	1. Sauté the onions and celery in oil until tender. Remove from pan and cool thoroughly.
8 oz	250 g	Celery, fine dice	
2 oz	60 mL	Oil	2. In a large bowl, soak the bread crumbs in the liquid.
12 oz	375 g	Soft bread crumbs	3. Add the sautéed vegetables, the meat, eggs, salt, and pepper. Mix *gently* until evenly combined. Do not overmix.
12 oz	375 mL	Tomato juice, stock, or milk	
2½ lb	1.25 kg	Ground beef	4. Form the mixture into 2 or 3 loaves in a baking pan, or fill loaf pans with the mixture.
2½ lb	1.25 kg	Ground pork	
2½ lb	1.25 kg	Ground veal	5. Bake at 350°F (175°C) about 1–1½ hours, until done. Test with a meat thermometer for internal temperature of 165°F (74°C).
5	5	Eggs, beaten slightly	
1 tbsp	15 mL	Salt	
½ tsp	2 mL	Black pepper	
3 pt	1.5 L	Tomato sauce, Spanish sauce, Creole sauce, or sour cream sauce	6. For service, cut the loaves into 4-oz (125-g) slices. Serve with 2 oz (60 mL) sauce per portion.

Per serving:
Calories, 360; Protein, 27 g; Fat, 21 g (53% cal.); Cholesterol, 135 mg;
Carbohydrates, 15 g; Fiber, 2 g; Sodium, 680 mg.

VARIATIONS

Home-Style All-Beef Meatloaf

In place of the mixture of beef, pork, and veal, use 7½ lb (3.75 kg) ground beef.

Italian-Style Meatloaf

Add the following ingredients to the basic mix:

4 tsp (20 mL) chopped garlic, sautéed with the onion
1 oz (30 g) parmesan cheese
⅔ cup (150 mL) chopped parsley
1½ tsp (7 mL) basil
1 tsp (5 mL) oregano

Salisbury Steak

Divide meat mixture for all-beef meatloaf into 6-oz (175-g) portions. Form into thick, oval patties and place on sheet pan. Bake at 350°F (175°C) for about 30 minutes.

Baked Meatballs

Divide basic meat mixture or Italian-Style Meatloaf mixture into 2½-oz (75-g) portions using a No. 16 scoop. Form into balls and place on sheet pans. Bake at 350°F (175°C). May be served with tomato sauce over pasta.

Loin or Rack of Venison Grand Veneur

Portions: 8   Portion size: ¼ loin or rack (2 chops)

U.S.	Metric	Ingredients	PROCEDURE
2	2	Loins or racks of venison (2½–3 lb/1.1–1.4 kg each)	1. Trim the venison, removing all silverskin. Because venison is very lean, there will be very little fat to remove.
2 qt	2 L	Red Wine Marinade for Game (below)	2. Marinate the venison for 2 days, using enough marinade to cover the meat completely. (The quantity indicated is approximate.)
12 oz	350 g	Pork fatback for barding (quantity approximate)	3. Cut the fatback into thin sheets on a slicing machine. Bard the venison by covering the meat with the sheets of fat and tying them in place.
			4. Roast the meat at 450°F (230°C) until rare, about 30–45 minutes.
1 pt	500 mL	Poîvrade Sauce (p. 149)	5. When the meat is done, set it aside in a warm place for 15 minutes. Degrease the roasting pan and deglaze it with a little of the marinade. Reduce slightly and strain it into the poîvrade sauce.
1 oz	30 g	Red currant jelly	
3 oz	90 mL	Heavy cream	6. Heat the sauce with the jelly until the jelly is melted and dissolved.
1 lb	480 g	Chestnut purée (fresh or canned), thinned to a soft texture with a little demiglaze and cream	7. Temper the cream with a little of the sauce, then add to the rest of the sauce.
			8. Cut the meat into chops, or else cut the meat from the bones in one piece and slice into medallions.

Per serving:
Calories, 990; Protein, 67 g; Fat, 65 g (60% cal.); Cholesterol, 345 mg; Carbohydrates, 8 g; Fiber, 1 g; Sodium, 200 mg.

9. Serve each portion with 2 oz (60 mL) sauce and garnish with 2 oz (60 g) chestnut purée.

VARIATION

Leg of Venison Grand Veneur

Leg of venison can be prepared and served in the same way. A whole leg of venison weighing 4–5 lb (about 2 kg) yields 8–10 portions. This larger cut should be marinated slightly longer, 2–3 days.

Red Wine Marinade for Game

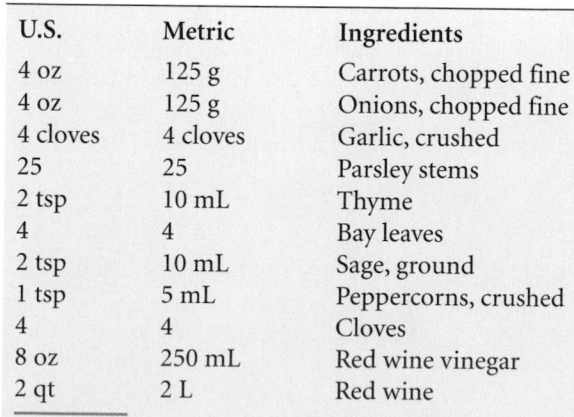

Yield: 2 qt (2 L)

U.S.	Metric	Ingredients	PROCEDURE
4 oz	125 g	Carrots, chopped fine	1. Combine all ingredients in a nonreactive container (e.g. stainless steel, glass, plastic; do not use aluminum).
4 oz	125 g	Onions, chopped fine	
4 cloves	4 cloves	Garlic, crushed	2. Marinate meat as desired or as indicated in recipe. Marinating times may vary from a few hours to several days. After marinating, use the liquid as a cooking medium and as the base for a sauce.
25	25	Parsley stems	
2 tsp	10 mL	Thyme	
4	4	Bay leaves	
2 tsp	10 mL	Sage, ground	
1 tsp	5 mL	Peppercorns, crushed	
4	4	Cloves	
8 oz	250 mL	Red wine vinegar	
2 qt	2 L	Red wine	

Per 1 ounce:
Calories, 25; Protein, 0 g; Fat, 0 g (0% cal.); Cholesterol, 0 mg; Carbohydrates, 23 g; Fiber, 5 g; Sodium, 200 mg.

Roast Loin of Rabbit with Risotto

Portions: 8   Portion size: 5–6 oz (140–160 g) rabbit, 4 oz (125 g) risotto, plus sauce and garnish

U.S.	Metric	Ingredients	PROCEDURE
2½–3 lb	1.1–1.3 kg	Boneless saddles of rabbit	1. Trim the meat as necessary, leaving the meat in whole pieces.
as needed	as needed	Oil	2. Heat the oil in a sauté pan. Add the rabbit meat and brown on all sides.
			3. Transfer to an oven heated to 450°F (230°C) and roast for 5–10 minutes, until medium done (slightly pink in center). Remove the meat from the pan and keep warm.
2 oz	60 g	Shallots, chopped fine	4. Add the shallots, carrots, mushrooms, and garlic. Brown lightly.
2 oz	60 g	Carrots, chopped fine	5. Add the vermouth or wine and reduce by half.
4 oz	125 g	Mushrooms, chopped fine	6. Add the stock and reduce by half.
1 clove	1 clove	Garlic, chopped fine	7. Strain. Season to taste with salt.
4 oz	125 g	Dry white vermouth or white wine	
1 pt	500 mL	Rabbit stock or chicken stock, rich and concentrated	
to taste	to taste	Salt	
2 lb	1 kg	Risotto alla Parmigiana (p. 511)	8. Place a mound of risotto in the center of each plate.
as desired	as desired	Steamed, buttered spinach	9. Cut the rabbit meat into thick slices and arrange around the risotto.
as desired	as desired	Carrots, small dice, cooked, hot	10. Arrange small mounds of spinach between the slices of meat.
as desired	as desired	Zucchini, small dice, cooked, hot	11. Place a few pieces of diced carrot and zucchini on the plate.
			12. Spoon the sauce onto the plate around the meat.

Per serving:
Calories, 510; Protein, 38 g; Fat, 24 g (42% cal.); Cholesterol: 105 mg;
Carbohydrates, 33 g; Fiber, 5 g; Sodium, 280 mg.

Broiling, Grilling, and Pan-broiling

Broiling and grilling are dry-heat cooking methods, which use very high heat to cook meat quickly. Properly broiled meats have a well-browned, flavorful crust on the outside, and the inside is cooked to the desired doneness and still juicy.

It may be helpful to think of broiling and grilling as browning techniques rather than cooking techniques. This is because the best, juiciest broiled meats are those cooked to the rare or medium-done stage. Because of the intense heat, it is difficult to broil meats to the well-done stage and still keep them juicy. Pork and veal, which are usually eaten well done, are generally better griddled, sautéed, or braised than broiled or grilled. (Veal can be broiled successfully if the customer prefers it still a little pink inside.)

For best results, only high-quality, tender cuts with a good fat content should be broiled.

TEMPERATURE CONTROL

The object of broiling is not just to cook the meat to the desired doneness but also to form a brown, flavorful, crusty surface.

The goal of the broiler cook is to create the right amount of browning—not too much or too little—by the time the inside is cooked to the desired doneness. To do this, he or she must broil the item at the right temperature.

In general, *the shorter the cooking time, the higher the temperature,* or else the meat won't have time to brown. The longer the cooking time, the lower the temperature, or the meat will brown too much before the inside is done.

Cooking time depends on two factors:

1. The desired doneness.
2. The thickness of the cut.

In other words, a well-done steak should be cooked at a lower heat than a rare one. A thin steak cooked rare must be broiled at a higher temperature than a thick one cooked rare.

To control the cooking temperature of a broiler, raise or lower the rack. On a grill, set different areas for different temperatures and grill meats in the appropriate area.

SEASONING

As for roasting, chefs disagree on when to season. Some feel that meats should not be seasoned before broiling. This is because salt draws moisture to the surface and retards browning. Others feel that seasoning before broiling improves the taste of the meat because the seasonings become part of the brown crust rather than something sprinkled on afterward.

Generally, if you have a professional broiler that has been properly preheated, it is not difficult to brown meat that has been salted. Low-powered broilers such as those found in home kitchens, on the other hand, do not get as hot. In such cases, it is better to salt after broiling, not before.

One way around this problem is to serve the meat with a *seasoned butter* (p. 153). Another option is to marinate the meat in seasoned oil 30 minutes before broiling.

Procedure for Broiling or Grilling Meats

In a broiler, the heat source is above the food. In a grill, the heat is below the food. Except for this difference, the basic procedure is the same for both.

Make sure you understand how to test broiled meats for doneness (p. 228) before starting.

1. Collect and prepare all equipment and food supplies. If necessary, score the fatty edges of meats to prevent curling.

2. Preheat the broiler or grill.

3. Brush the meat with oil, or dip it in oil and let the excess drip off. Place the item on the broiler or grill. The oil helps prevent sticking and keeps the product moist. It may be unnecessary for meats high in fat. Using too much oil can cause grease fires.

4. When one side is brown and the meat is cooked halfway, turn it over with a fork (piercing only the fat, *never the meat*, or juices will be lost) or with tongs. Figure 11.6 illustrates the technique for grill-marking steaks and other meats.

5. Cook the second side until the meat is cooked to the desired doneness.
   If the meat is to be brushed with a glaze or sauce, such as a barbecue sauce, it is usually best to wait until the product is partially cooked on each side before applying the first coat. Many glazes or sauces burn if cooked too long. After the item has cooked on both sides and is one-half to three-fourths done, brush the top with a light coat of the sauce. Turn over and repeat as necessary.

6. Remove from broiler or grill and serve immediately.

Figure 11.6 Grill-marking steaks.

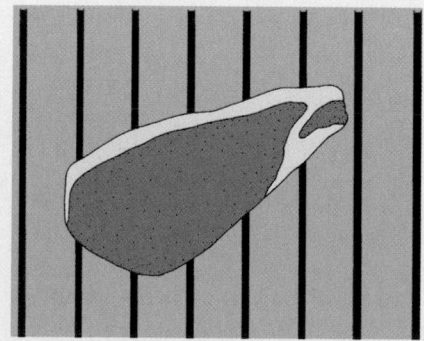

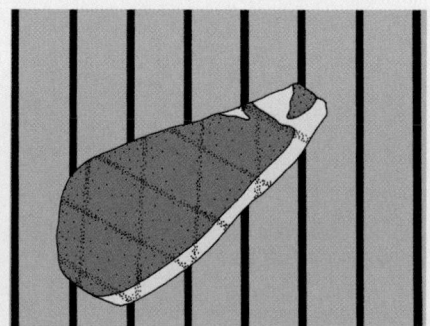

(a) Place the meat on a preheated grill at an angle as shown.

(b) When the meat is about one-fourth done, turn the meat about 60 to 90 degrees, as shown. Do not turn it over.

(c) When the steak is about half done, turn it over. The grill marks will appear as shown.

SAUCES AND ACCOMPANIMENTS FOR GRILLED AND BROILED MEATS

Many kinds of sauces and accompaniments are appropriate for grilled meats, including compound butters, butter sauces such as béarnaise; brown sauce variations such as Bercy, mushroom, and bordelaise; tomato sauce variations; and salsas and relishes. For other examples, see the recipes in this section. Note that, unlike pan sauces made by deglazing sauté pans (see p. 264), all these sauces are prepared in advance because broiling or grilling does not give you the opportunity to deglaze a pan.

Part of the appeal of broiled and grilled meats is their brown, crisp surface. For this reason, it is best not to cover the item with the sauce. Also, less sauce is usually served with grilled items than with sautéed items. Serve the sauce on the side or around the meat or, at most, in a thin ribbon across only part of the meat.

Similarly, vegetables and accompaniments for broiled and grilled meats should, in most cases, not be heavily sauced. Grilled vegetables are often good choices as accompaniments.

PAN-BROILING

Broiling very thin steaks (minute steaks) to the rare stage is difficult because the heat is not high enough to form a good brown crust without overcooking the inside.

Pan-broiling in a heavy iron skillet is an answer to this problem.

Procedure for Pan-Broiling Meats

1. Preheat an iron skillet over a high flame until it is very hot. Do not add fat. (The pan should, of course, be well seasoned.)

2. Proceed as for grilling. Pour off any fat that accumulates during cooking if necessary.

Broiled Strip Loin Steak Maître d'Hôtel

Yield: 10 portions

U.S.	Metric	Ingredients	PROCEDURE
10	10	Strip loin steaks, boneless, 10–12 oz (300–350 g) each	1. Trim steaks as necessary, leaving a thin layer of fat on the edge.
to taste	to taste	Salt	2. Season the steaks to taste with salt and pepper. Brush lightly with oil.
to taste	to taste	Black pepper	3. Place the steaks on a preheated grill or broiler.
as needed	as needed	Vegetable oil	4. When the steak is about one-fourth done, turn it about 60–90 degrees to grill-mark it (see Figure 11.6).
			5. When the steak is half-done, turn it over and complete the cooking to the desired doneness. If turning with a fork, pierce the fat, not the meat, or juices will be lost.
5 oz	150 g	Maître d'Hôtel Butter (p. 154)	6. Remove the steaks from the broiler and immediately place on a hot plate. Top each steak with a ½-oz (15-g) slice of seasoned butter.

Per 8 ounces:
Calories, 550; Protein, 60 g; Fat, 33 g (55% cal.); Cholesterol, 185 mg; Carbohydrates, 0 g; Fiber, 0 g; Sodium, 250 mg.

VARIATIONS

Other steaks may be cooked by the same method, including *rib steak, rib eye steak, tenderloin, club steak, porterhouse, T-bone, and sirloin. Chopped beef patties* may also be prepared using this recipe.

Other seasoned butters and sauces make good accompaniments to broiled steaks, including:

Garlic butter	Chasseur sauce	Mushroom sauce (brown)	Béarnaise sauce
Anchovy butter	Madeira sauce	Bercy sauce (brown)	Foyot sauce
Bordelaise sauce	Perigueux sauce	Lyonnaise sauce	Choron sauce
Marchand de vin sauce			

Broiled Lamb Chops
Prepare as for broiled steaks, using rib, loin, or shoulder chops.

Charbroiled Minute Steak with Blue Cheese Butter

Portions: 12   Portion size: 1 steak, 6 oz (175 g)

U.S.	Metric	Ingredients	PROCEDURE
7 oz	200 g	Unsalted butter, softened	1. Prepare the compound butter (see p. 153): Thoroughly combine the butter and cheese in a bowl, then roll in greaseproof paper or foil into cylinders, 1½ inches (4 cm) in diameter. Chill until firm. Cut into slices ½ inch (.75 cm) thick.
2½ oz	75 g	Blue cheese	
12	12	Sirloin steaks, 6–7 oz (180–200 g) each	2. Remove all fat and sinew from the steaks and flatten between oiled sheets of greaseproof paper or plastic film to a thickness of ½ inch (¾ cm). Season the steaks with salt and pepper.
to taste	to taste	Salt	
to taste	to taste	Pepper	3. Lightly oil the steaks and cook rapidly on a hot charbroiler, allowing approximately 30 seconds on each side. Garnish with watercress and serve immediately, topped with 2–3 slices of butter per portion.
4 oz	125 mL	Oil	
as needed	as needed	Watercress sprigs for garnish	

Per serving:
Calories, 470; Protein, 40 g; Fat, 34 g (66% cal.); Cholesterol, 155 mg;
Carbohydrates, 0 g; Fiber, 0 g; Sodium, 170 mg.

London Broil

Portions: 24   Portion size: 5 oz (150 g)

U.S.	Metric	Ingredients	PROCEDURE
10 lb	4.75 kg	Flank steak (5 steaks)	1. Trim all fat and connective tissue from beef.
		Marinade:	2. Combine the marinade ingredients in a hotel pan. Place the steaks in the pan and turn them so they are coated with oil. Cover and refrigerate at least 2 hours.
1 pt	500 mL	Vegetable oil	
2 oz	60 mL	Lemon juice	3. Remove the meat from the marinade and place in a preheated broiler or grill. Broil at high heat about 3–5 minutes on each side, until well browned outside but rare inside (see note).
2 tsp	10 mL	Salt	
2 tsp	10 mL	Black pepper	4. Remove from broiler and let rest 2 minutes before slicing.
1 tsp	5 mL	Thyme	5. Slice the meat very thin on a sharp angle across the grain (see Figure 11.7).
1½ qt	1.5 L	Mushroom Sauce (brown) (p. 149)	6. Weigh 5-oz (150-g) portions. Serve each portion with 2 oz (60 mL) sauce.

Per serving:
Calories, 520; Protein, 41 g; Fat, 37 g (65% cal.); Cholesterol, 110 mg;
Carbohydrates, 3 g; Fiber, 0 g; Sodium, 370 mg.

Note: Flank steak should be broiled rare. If cooked well done, it will be tough and dry.

VARIATIONS

Thick-cut steaks from the round or chuck are sometimes used for London broil.

Teriyaki-Style London Broil

Marinate the steaks in a mixture of the following ingredients: 2½ cups (600 mL) Japanese soy sauce, 6 oz (200 mL) vegetable oil, 4 oz (125 mL) sherry, 6 oz (175 g) chopped onion, 2 tbsp (30 g) sugar, 2 tsp (10 mL) ginger, 1 crushed clove garlic. Marinate at least 4 hours or, preferably, overnight. Broil as in basic recipe.

Figure 11.7 Slicing London broil flank steak.

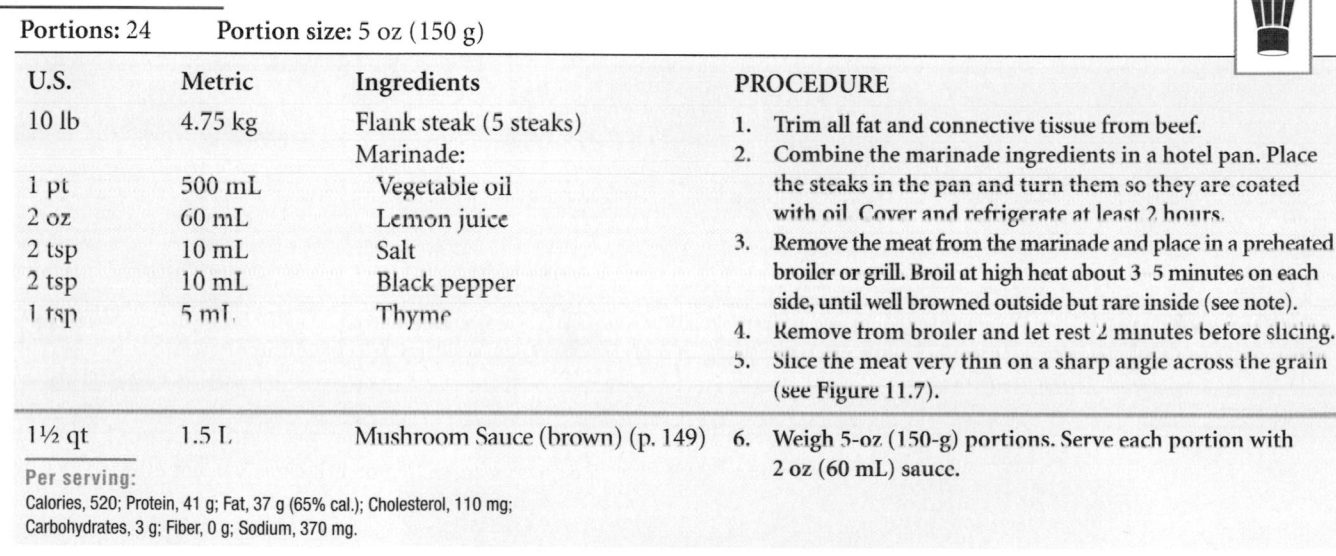

(a) Holding the knife at a sharp angle, slice the meat in very thin slices across the grain. Use a table fork or kitchen fork to hold the meat steady. Some chefs slice the meat toward the fork.

(b) Others prefer to slice away from the fork. The result is the same.

Broiled Smoked Pork Chop with Flageolet Beans and Wilted Arugula

Portions: 15   Portion size: 1 pork chop, 8 oz (250 g)
                 about 5 oz (150 g) vegetable

U.S.	Metric	Ingredients	PROCEDURE
15	15	Smoked pork loin chops, bone-in, about 8 oz each	1. Brush the chops very lightly with oil. Place on a preheated grill or broiler until grill-marked on both sides and heated through. Smoked pork chops are fully cooked, so it is necessary only to heat them through.
as needed	as needed	Vegetable oil	2. Serve each chop with 5 oz (150 g) of the beans with arugula.
4 lb 12 oz	2.2 kg	Flageolet Beans with Wilted Arugula (see note)	

Per serving:
Calories, 620; Protein, 67 g; Fat, 26 g (39% cal.); Cholesterol, 110 mg;
Carbohydrates, 26 g; Fiber, 9 g; Sodium, 3110 mg.

Note: The quantity of beans and arugula required for this recipe is equal to the yield of the recipe on p. 463.

Broiled Smoked Pork Chop with Flageolet Beans and Wilted Arugula

Grilled Chopped Lamb "Steaks" with Rosemary and Pine Nuts

Portions: 25   Portion size: 5 oz (150 g)

U.S.	Metric	Ingredients	PROCEDURE
6 oz	175 g	Onions, chopped fine	1. Sauté the onion in oil until tender. Do not brown. Cool thoroughly.
2 oz	60 g	Salad oil	
6½ lb	3.25 kg	Ground lamb	2. Combine all ingredients except bacon in a bowl. Mix gently until evenly combined. Do not overmix.
8 oz	250 g	Soft, fresh bread crumbs	
8 oz	250 g	Toasted pine nuts	3. Scale the meat into 5-oz (150-g) portions. Form the portions into thick patties, about ¾ inch (2 cm) thick.
10 oz	300 mL	Milk	
½ cup	30 g	Chopped parsley	4. Wrap a strip of bacon around each patty and fasten with picks.
2 tsp	10 mL	Rosemary	
2½ tsp	12 mL	Salt	5. Grill or broil the patties under moderate heat until done, turning once (see note).
1 tsp	5 mL	White pepper	
25 strips	25 strips	Bacon	6. Remove picks before serving.

Per serving:
Calories, 460; Protein, 25 g; Fat, 37 g (72% cal.); Cholesterol, 95 mg;
Carbohydrates, 7 g; Fiber, 1 g; Sodium, 520 mg.

Note: Patties may be browned under the broiler, arranged on a sheet pan, and finished in the oven at 375°F (190°C).

VARIATIONS

Ground beef or veal may be used instead of lamb.

Grilled Chopped Beef "Steaks" with Marjoram

Substitute ground beef for ground lamb. Substitute marjoram for the rosemary. Omit the pine nuts.

Grilled Marinated Pork Tenderloin with Sweet Potato Purée and Warm Chipotle Salsa

Portions: 10   **Portion size:** 5 oz (150 g) meat

U.S.	Metric	Ingredients	PROCEDURE
4 lb	2 kg	Pork tenderloin	1. Trim fat and membranes from the tenderloins (see Figure 11.8).
2 oz	60 g	Onion, chopped fine	2. Mix together the onion, garlic, powdered chile, salt, oregano, cumin, cinnamon, lime juice, and oil.
1 clove	1 clove	Garlic, chopped fine	3. Coat the meat with this mixture. Wrap and refrigerate several hours or overnight.
2 tbsp	30 mL	Powdered red New Mexico chile (see note)	
1 tsp	5 mL	Salt	
½ tsp	2 mL	Oregano	
¼ tsp	1 mL	Ground cumin	
⅛ tsp	0.5 mL	Cinnamon	
2 oz	60 mL	Lime juice	
1 oz	30 mL	Olive oil	
1 clove	1 clove	Garlic, unpeeled	4. Roast the garlic and tomatoes in an oven preheated to 450°F (230°C) for 10 minutes.
1 lb	500 g	Plum tomatoes or other small tomatoes	5. Remove the skins from the tomatoes and garlic. Place them in a blender.
2	2	Whole chipotle chiles in adobo (canned)	6. Carefully cut open the chiles. Scrape out and discard the seeds. Chop the chiles.
½ tsp	2 mL	Salt	7. Add the chiles, salt, and the sauce from the chiles to the blender. Blend to make a coarse purée. Add more salt if needed.
2–3 tsp	10–15 mL	Sauce from the canned chiles	
3 lb	1.5 kg	Sweet potatoes	8. Bake the sweet potatoes at 400°F (200°C) until soft. Cut in half and scoop out the flesh. Pass through a food mill to purée. Season lightly.
to taste	to taste	Salt	9. Scrape the onions and garlic off the meat (they will burn if left on).

Per serving:
Calories, 410; Protein, 41 g; Fat, 10 g (22% cal.); Cholesterol, 110 mg;
Carbohydrates, 38 g; Fiber, 5 g; Sodium, 630 mg.

10. Grill the meat until just well done. Be careful not to overcook, or the meat will be dry.

11. To serve, place 3 oz (90 g) sweet potato purée on the plate. Slice the meat across the grain into medallions. Arrange 5 oz (150 g) meat on top of the sweet potato. Drizzle with 1½ oz (45 mL) tomato chipotle salsa.

Note: For a slightly different flavor, or if powdered New Mexico chile is not available, use a regular chile powder blend.

Grilled Marinated Pork Tenderloin with Warm Chipotle Salsa

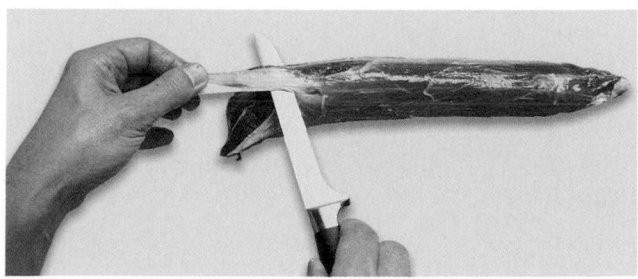

Figure 11.8 Trimming a pork tenderloin.

Shish Kebab

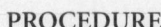

Portions: 25   Portion size: 6 oz (175 g)

U.S.	Metric	Ingredients	PROCEDURE
10 lb	4.5 kg	Lamb leg, boneless, trimmed	1. A day before cooking, trim any remaining fat and connective tissue from the lamb. Cut into 1-inch (2½-cm) cubes. Keep all the cubes the same size for even cooking.
		Marinade:	
1 qt	1 L	Olive oil, or part olive and part vegetable oil	2. Combine the marinade ingredients and pour over the lamb in a hotel pan. Mix well. Refrigerate overnight.
½ cup	125 mL	Lemon juice	3. Drain the meat and weigh out 6-oz (175-g) portions. Thread each portion onto a skewer.
5 cloves	5 cloves	Garlic, crushed	
4 tsp	20 mL	Salt	4. Place skewers on a grill or broiler rack and broil at moderate heat until medium done, turning over once when they are half cooked.
1½ tsp	7 mL	Pepper	5. To serve, place each portion on a bed of Rice Pilaf (p. 509). The skewers should be removed by the waiter in the dining room or by the cook in the kitchen.
1 tsp	5 mL	Oregano	

Per serving:
Calories, 280; Protein, 37 g; Fat, 14 g (46% cal.); Cholesterol, 115 mg; Carbohydrates, 0 g; Fiber, 0 g; Sodium, 125 mg.

Note: Shish kebabs are sometimes made with vegetables (onions, green peppers, cherry tomatoes, mushrooms) on the same skewer with the meat. However, it is easier to control cooking times if vegetables are broiled on separate skewers. Also, the meat is less likely to steam in the moisture from the vegetables.

Broiled Lamb Kidneys with Bacon

Portions: 10   Portion size: 2 kidneys
                                   2 strips bacon

U.S.	Metric	Ingredients	PROCEDURE
20	20	Bacon strips	1. Cook the bacon on a griddle or in the oven on a sheet pan until crisp. Drain fat and keep bacon warm.
20	20	Lamb kidneys	2. Split the kidneys in half lengthwise and cut out the white fat and gristle in center.
as needed	as needed	Melted butter or oil	3. Arrange the kidneys on skewers, 4 half kidneys per skewer.
to taste	to taste	Salt	4. Brush the kidneys well with melted butter or oil and season with salt and pepper.
to taste	to taste	Pepper	5. Broil the kidneys under high heat, turning once, until browned on the outside but still slightly rare. (Test by pressing with finger, as for testing steaks.)
			6. Serve immediately with 2 slices of bacon per portion. Mustard is often served with kidneys.

Per serving:
Calories, 410; Protein, 26 g; Fat, 33 g (73% cal.); Cholesterol, 515 mg; Carbohydrates, 1 g; Fiber, 0 g; Sodium, 580 mg.

Grilled Venison with Lime Butter

Portions: 8   Portion size: 3–4 oz (90–125 g)

U.S.	Metric	Ingredients	PROCEDURE
2 lb	1 kg	Boneless, trimmed venison (see step 1)	1. Select a piece or pieces of venison suitable for broiling and slicing in the manner of London broil. Make sure the venison is well trimmed of all silverskin.
1 tsp	5 mL	Sichuan peppercorns, toasted	2. Rub the meat with Sichuan peppercorns. Sprinkle with lime juice and salt. Let marinate for 30 minutes.
1 oz	30 mL	Lime juice	
to taste	to taste	Salt	
2 oz	60 g	Butter	3. Soften the butter and mix in the crushed peppercorns, lime zest, lime juice, and salt. Refrigerate until needed.
½ tsp	2 mL	Sichuan peppercorns, toasted and crushed	4. Grill or broil the venison until rare or medium rare. Remove from the heat and let rest for a few minutes.
2 tsp	10 mL	Grated lime zest	5. Cut on the bias, across the grain, into thin slices, like London broil.
½ tsp	2 mL	Lime juice	6. Arrange the slices on plates. Top each portion with a small slice of lime butter, about 1½ tsp (8 g).
to taste	to taste	Salt	

Per serving:
Calories, 190; Protein, 26 g; Fat, 9 g (43% cal.); Cholesterol, 110 mg; Carbohydrates, 1 g; Fiber, 0 g; Sodium, 115 mg.

Grilled Veal Chop with Roasted Onions

Portions: 12		Portion size: 1 chop plus garnish	

U.S.	Metric	Ingredients	PROCEDURE
12	12	Veal rib chops, 10–12 oz (300–350 g) each	1. Trim the chops of excess fat.
6 oz	175 mL	Olive oil	2. Combine the oil, sage, rosemary, thyme, garlic, and salt to make a marinade.
1 tsp	5 mL	Sage, dried	3. Coat the chops with the marinade and refrigerate for 4–6 hours.
1 tsp	5 mL	Rosemary, dried	
½ tsp	2 mL	Thyme, dried	
1½ tsp	7 mL	Garlic, chopped fine	
1½ tsp	7 mL	Salt	
2 lb	1 kg	Roasted Onions (p. 473)	4. Prepare the onions and keep warm.
1 lb	500 g	Sweet potatoes	5. Peel the sweet potatoes. Cut into very thin, uniform slices on a mandoline or electric slicer, as for making potato chips. Deep-fry the slices at 350°F (175°C) until lightly colored and crisp. Do not allow to become too brown.
			6. Remove the veal chops from the marinade. Grill or broil to desired doneness.
			7. For each portion, place 2½ oz (75 g) onions on a plate. Place a chop on the onions. Garnish the plate with a few sweet potato chips.

Per serving:
Calories, 690; Protein, 70 g; Fat, 31 g (42% cal.); Cholesterol, 225 mg; Carbohydrates, 27 g; Fiber, 1 g; Sodium, 640 mg.

Sautéing, Pan-frying, and Griddling

If you review the general definitions of sautéing, pan-frying, and griddling in Chapter 4, you will see that the differences among these methods are largely a matter of degree. Sautéing uses high heat and a small amount of fat and is usually used for small pieces of food. Pan-frying uses moderate heat, a moderate amount of fat, and is usually employed with larger items, such as chops. But at what point does moderate heat become high heat and a small amount of fat become a moderate amount of fat? It is impossible to draw an exact dividing line between sautéing and pan-frying.

Each time you cook a piece of meat, you must judge how much heat and how much fat to use to do the job best. This depends on the kind of food and the size of the pieces. Following are guidelines to help you make the right judgments.

Guidelines for Sautéing, Pan-frying, and Griddling

1. Use only tender cuts for sautéing.
2. Smaller or thinner pieces of meat require higher heat. The object is to brown or sear the meat in the time it takes to cook it to the desired doneness. Very small or thin pieces cook in just a few moments.
3. If large or thick items are browned over high heat, it may be necessary to finish them at lower heat to avoid burning them.
4. The amount of fat needed is the amount required to conduct the heat to all surfaces so that the item cooks evenly. Flat items need much less fat than irregularly shaped items like chicken pieces.
   Sautéing small pieces of meat requires little fat because the items are tossed or flipped so that all sides come in contact with the hot pan.
5. When sautéing small pieces of food, do not overload the pan, and do not flip or toss the food more than necessary. This will cause the temperature to drop too much and the meat will simmer in its own juices instead of sauté.
6. Use clarified butter or oil or a mixture for sautéing. Whole butter burns easily.
7. Dredging meats in flour promotes even browning and helps prevent sticking. Flour meats immediately before cooking, not in advance, or the flour will get pasty. Also, shake off excess flour before adding meat to the pan.
8. Meats to be pan-fried are often breaded. Review page 121 for Standard Breading Procedure.
9. When pan-frying several batches, strain or skim the fat between batches. Otherwise, burned food particles from previous batches may mar the appearance of the meat.
10. Griddling and pan-frying are preferable to broiling and grilling for cooking pork and veal chops because the lower temperatures keep these meats moister when cooked well done. Hamburgers cooked well done are also moister if cooked on a griddle.

DEGLAZING THE PAN

A sauce made by *deglazing* the pan often accompanies sautéed meats. To *deglaze* means to swirl a liquid in a sauté or other pan to dissolve cooked particles of food remaining on the bottom. (Review discussions of deglazing in Chapter 4, p. 59, and in Chapter 8, p. 131 and p. 140). The deglazing liquid can be used to flavor a sauce in one of two ways:

1. Add the reduced deglazing liquid to a prepared sauce. The deglazing liquid adds flavor and color to the sauce.

2. Use the deglazing liquid to make a freshly prepared sauce. Add stock or other liquids and other flavoring and thickening ingredients and finish the sauce as indicated in the recipe.

General Procedures for Sautéing and Pan-frying Meats

The following procedures are presented side by side so that you can compare them. Keep in mind that these are the two extremes and that many recipes require a procedure that falls somewhere between the two.

The procedure for pan-frying applies to *griddling* as well, although only a small amount of fat can be used on a griddle.

Sautéing

1. Collect all equipment and food supplies.

2. Prepare meats as required. This may include dredging with flour.

3. Heat a small amount of fat in a sauté pan until very hot.

4. Add the meat to the pan. Do not overcrowd the pan.

5. Brown the meat on all sides, flipping or tossing it in the pan as necessary so that it cooks evenly.

6. Remove meat from pan. Drain excess fat, if any.

7. Add any sauce ingredients to be sautéed, such as shallots or mushrooms, as indicated in the recipe. Sauté them as necessary.

8. Add liquid for deglazing, such as wine or stock. Simmer while swirling and scraping the pan to release food particles on the bottom so that they can dissolve in the liquid. Reduce the liquid.

9. Add a prepared sauce or other sauce ingredients and finish the sauce as indicated in the recipe.

10. Serve the meat with the sauce, or return the meat to the sauce to reheat *briefly* and coat it with the sauce. Do not let the meat cook in the sauce. Serve.

Pan-frying

1. Collect all equipment and food supplies.

2. Prepare meats as required. This may include breading or dredging with flour.

3. Heat a moderate amount of fat in a sauté pan or skillet until hot.

4. Add the meat to the pan.

5. Brown the meat on one side. Turn it with a spatula and brown the other side. Larger pieces may need to be finished at reduced heat after browning. Or, if required, they may finish cooking, uncovered, in the oven.

6. Serve immediately.

Breaded Veal Cutlets

Portions: 24   **Portion size:** 4 oz (125 g)

U.S.	Metric	Ingredients	PROCEDURE
6 lb	3 kg	Veal cutlets (scaloppine): 24 pieces, 4 oz (125 g) each. (See Figure 11.9 for preparation of veal.)	1. Lightly flatten each piece of veal with a meat mallet. Do not pound too hard, or you may tear the meat.
to taste	to taste	Salt	2. Season the meat with salt and pepper and pass through Standard Breading Procedure (see p. 121).
to taste	to taste	Pepper	
		Standard Breading Procedure (see note):	3. Heat about ¼ inch (½ cm) oil or butter in a large sauté pan. Place the cutlets in the pan and pan-fry until golden brown. Turn and brown the other side. Remove from the pan and place on hot plates.
4 oz	125 g	Flour	
4	4	Eggs	
1 cup	250 mL	Milk	
1½ lb	750 g	Bread crumbs, dry or fresh	
8 oz	250 mL	Oil or clarified butter, or a mixture of oil and butter	
12 oz	375 g	Butter	4. Heat the butter in a small saucepan or sauté pan until lightly browned. Pour ½ oz (15 g) brown butter over each portion.

Per serving:
Calories, 550; Protein, 31 g; Fat, 38 g (63% cal.); Cholesterol, 165 mg; Carbohydrates, 19 g; Fiber, 1 g; Sodium, 380 mg.

Note: Quantities given for breading materials are only guidelines. You may need more or less, depending on the shapes of the meat pieces, the care used in breading, and other factors. In any case, you will need enough so that even the last piece to be breaded can be coated easily and completely.

VARIATIONS

Veal Cutlet Sauté Gruyère
Top each cooked cutlet with 1 or 2 thin slices of tomato and a slice of Gruyère cheese. Pass under a broiler to melt cheese. Serve with tomato sauce placed under the cutlet or in a ribbon (cordon) around the cutlet.

Schnitzel à la Holstein
Top each portion with a fried egg and 4 anchovy fillets placed around the edge of the egg.

Veal Cutlet Viennese Style (Wiener Schnitzel)
Top each cutlet with 1 peeled lemon slice and 1 anchovy fillet rolled around a caper. Garnish the plate with chopped hard-cooked egg white, sieved egg yolk, and chopped parsley.

Veal Parmigiana
Top each cutlet with 2 oz (60 mL) tomato sauce, a slice of mozzarella cheese, and 2 tbsp (30 mL) parmesan cheese. Pass under a broiler to melt cheese.

Veal Cordon Bleu
Use 2 thin 2-oz (60-g) cutlets per portion. Sandwich 1 thin slice ham and 1 thin slice Swiss cheese between 2 cutlets. Pound edges lightly to seal. Bread and fry as in basic recipe.

Breaded Pork Cutlets
Cutlets from pork leg or loin may be breaded and pan-fried like veal. They must be cooked well done.

Veal Cutlet Viennese Style

Veal Scaloppine alla Marsala

Portions: 10   Portion size: 4 oz (125 g)

U.S.	Metric	Ingredients	PROCEDURE
2½ lb	1.25 kg	Small veal scaloppine: 20 pieces, 2 oz (60 g) each. (See Figure 11.9 for preparation of veal.)	1. Lightly flatten each piece of veal with a meat mallet. Do not pound hard, or you may tear the meat.
to taste	to taste	Salt	2. Dry the meat, season it with salt and pepper, and dredge in flour. Shake off excess. (Do not do this step until immediately before cooking.)
to taste	to taste	White pepper	3. Heat the oil in a large sauté pan until very hot. Add the veal and sauté over high heat just until lightly browned on both sides. (If necessary, sauté the meat in several batches.)
for dredging	for dredging	Flour	
2 oz	60 mL	Oil	4. Remove the meat from the pan and drain the excess oil.
4 oz	125 mL	Marsala wine	5. Add the Marsala to the pan and deglaze.
8 oz	250 mL	Strong white stock, veal or chicken (see note)	6. Add the stock and reduce over high heat by about half.
2 oz	60 g	Butter, cut in pieces	7. Add the pieces of butter and swirl the pan until they are melted and blended with the sauce.
2 tbsp	30 mL	Chopped parsley	8. Add the veal to the pan and bring just to the simmer. Turn the meat to coat it with the sauce.
			9. Serve immediately, 2 pieces per portion, sprinkled with chopped parsley.

Per serving:
Calories, 360; Protein, 27 g; Fat, 26 g (65% cal.); Cholesterol, 115 mg; Carbohydrates, 2 g; Fiber, 0 g; Sodium, 120 mg.

Note: Brown sauce may be used instead of white stock. However, the stock makes a more delicate product without masking the flavor of the veal.

VARIATIONS

Veal Scaloppine with Sherry

Substitute sherry for the Marsala.

Veal Scaloppine with Lemon

Substitute 3 oz (90 mL) lemon juice for the 4 oz (125 mL) wine. After plating, top each piece of veal with 1 lemon slice and sprinkle with chopped parsley.

Veal Scaloppine à la Crème

Prepare as in basic recipe but omit the wine. Deglaze the pan with the stock. Add 1 cup (250 mL) heavy cream and reduce until thickened. Omit the butter. Season the sauce with a few drops of lemon juice. Taste carefully for salt.

Veal Scaloppine with Mushrooms and Cream

Prepare as for Veal Scaloppine à la Crème, but sauté ½ lb (250 g) sliced mushrooms in butter in the sauté pan before deglazing.

Figure 11.9 Trimming and cutting veal for scaloppine.

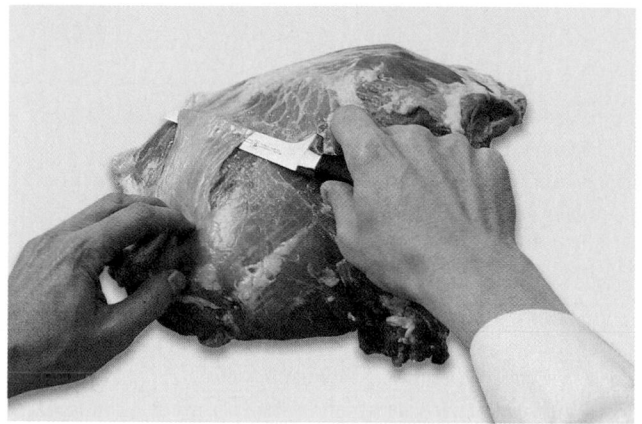

(a) *Remove all tendons and connective tissue (silverskin) from the veal. Slip the point of a thin boning knife under the skin. Angle the edge of the blade upward against the skin and cut it away carefully without cutting through the meat.*

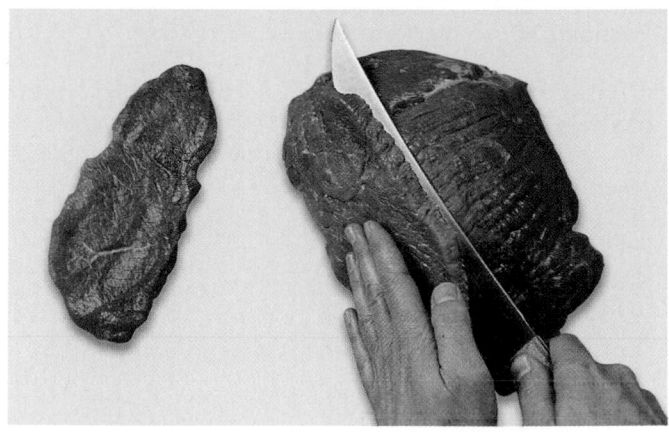

(b) *Holding the blade of the knife at an angle if necessary to get a broader slice, cut* across the grain *of the meat as shown to make thin slices.*

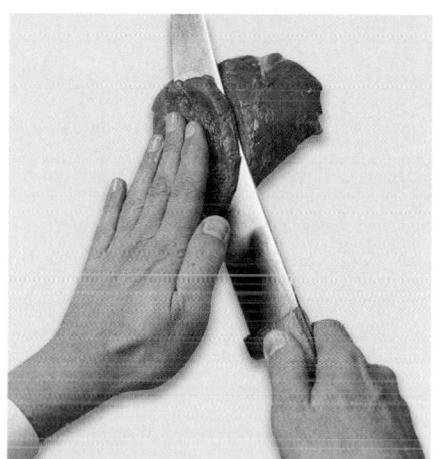

(c) *Broader slices can be cut from narrower pieces of meat by butterflying. Cut the slice almost through the meat but...*

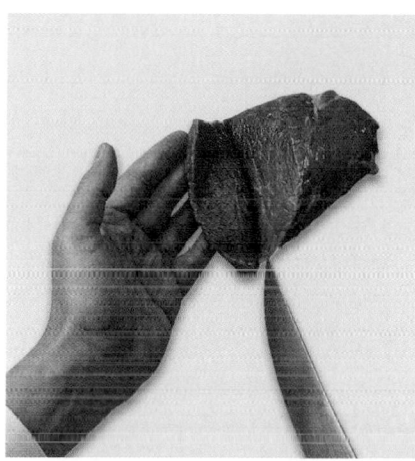

(d) *...leave it attached*

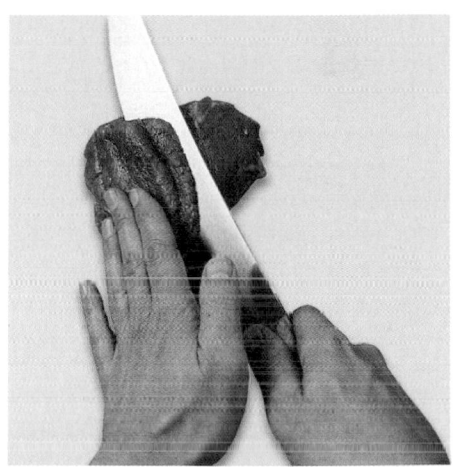

(e) *Then cut a second slice the same way, but cut all the way through.*

(f) *A butterflied scaloppine is twice as large as a single slice. Unfortunately, it has a seam in the center that often detracts from the appearance of the finished dish, unless the veal is breaded or covered with a topping.*

(g) *If desired, pound the cutlet to an even thickness with a cutlet mallet. This helps to disguise the seam in a butterflied cutlet.*

Pork Chops Charcutière

Portions: 24   Portion size: 6 oz (175 g) chop
                                2 oz (60 mL) sauce

U.S.	Metric	Ingredients	PROCEDURE
24	24	Pork chops, 6 oz (175 g) each	1. Trim excess fat from chops if necessary.
as needed	as needed	Oil	2. Add enough oil to a skillet or sauté pan or to a griddle to make a thin film. Heat over moderate heat.
			3. Place the chops in the hot pan or on griddle and cook until browned and about half done. Turn over and cook until well done and browned on the second side.
1½ q	1.5 L	Charcutière Sauce (p. 149)	4. Place the chops on hot dinner plates for service (or place them in a hotel pan if they must be held).
			5. Spoon a ribbon of sauce (2 oz/60 mL) around each plated chop.

Per serving:
Calories, 260; Protein, 28 g; Fat, 13 g (46% cal.); Cholesterol, 90 mg;
Carbohydrates, 4 g; Fiber, 0 g; Sodium, 180 mg.

VARIATIONS

Pork Chops Robert
Use Robert sauce instead of charcutière sauce.

Pork Chops Piquante
Use piquante sauce.

Veal Chops
These may be cooked by the same basic procedure and served with an appropriate sauce, such as a well-seasoned demiglaze or a mixture of demiglaze and cream. Other suggestions: ivory sauce, Hungarian sauce, mushroom sauce (white), aurora sauce

Sautéed Veal Chop; Zucchini with Tomatoes

Entrecôte Sauté Bordelaise (Sirloin Steak with Red Wine and Shallot Sauce)

Portions: 12   Portion size: 1 steak, 6 oz (175 g)
                                3 oz (95 mL) sauce

U.S.	Metric	Ingredients	PROCEDURE
12	12	Strip loin steaks, 6–7 oz (180–200 g) each	1. Season the steaks and sear in a hot sauté pan with the oil. Cook until rare and rest the steaks in a warm place. Degrease the pan.
5 oz	150 mL	Oil	
3 oz	90 g	Butter	2. For the sauce, add the first quantity of butter to the pan and gently sauté the shallots until lightly golden. Add the wine and reduce by 90 percent. Add the stock and continue to reduce by another 50 percent.
1 lb 4 oz	600 g	Shallots, chopped fine	
1 pt 4 oz	600 mL	Red wine	
2½ pt	1.2 L	Brown stock	
1½ oz	50 g	Butter (optional)	3. Season the sauce to taste with salt and pepper and, if desired, finish with the second amount of butter to add a gloss to the sauce.
5 oz	150 g	Bone marrow, poached and diced (optional)	
1 oz	30 g	Chopped parsley	4. Rewarm the steaks and place on hot plates with the sauce around. Place the warm diced bone marrow on top of the steaks and garnish with chopped parsley.

Per serving:
Calories, 400; Protein, 29 g; Fat, 27 g (61% cal.); Cholesterol, 90 mg;
Carbohydrates, 9 g; Fiber, 0 g; Sodium, 135 mg.

Tournedos Vert-Pré

Portions: 1   Portion size: 5–6 oz (150–175 g)

U.S.	Metric	Ingredients	PROCEDURE
1 oz	30 g	Clarified butter	1. Heat the butter in a small sauté pan over moderately high heat.
2	2	Tournedos (see note), 2½–3 oz (75–90 g) each	2. Place the tournedos in the pan and cook until well browned on the bottom and about half cooked.
2 slices	2 slices	Maître d'Hôtel Butter (p. 154)	3. Turn the meat over and continue to cook until rare or medium done, according to customer's request.
as needed	as needed	Watercress	
as needed	as needed	Allumette Potatoes (p. 501)	4. Place the tournedos on a hot dinner plate and top each with a slice of maître d'hôtel butter. Garnish the plate with a portion of allumette potatoes and a generous bunch of watercress. Serve immediately, while the butter is still melting.

Per serving:
Calories, 640; Protein, 27 g; Fat, 59 g (83% cal.); Cholesterol, 185 mg; Carbohydrates, 0 g; Fiber, 0 g; Sodium, 410 mg.

Note: Tournedos (TOOR-nuh-doe; singular form: one tournedos) are small tenderloin steaks cut about 1½ inches (4 cm) thick. The same recipe may be used for fillet steaks, which are larger but thinner cuts from the tenderloin. See Figure 11.10 for cutting tenderloin.

VARIATIONS

Tournedos Béarnaise
Pan-fry tournedos as in basic recipe and serve with béarnaise sauce.

Tournedos Bordelaise
Pan-fry as in basic recipe. Top each steak with 1 slice poached beef marrow and coat lightly with bordelaise sauce.

Tournedos Chasseur
Pan-fry as in basic recipe. Plate the steaks and deglaze the sauté pan (drained of cooking fat) with ½ oz (15 mL) white wine. Add 2 oz (60 mL) chasseur sauce, bring to a simmer, and pour around the tournedos.

Tournedos Rossini
Pan-fry as in basic recipe. Set the tournedos on croutons (rounds of bread cut the same size as the steaks and fried in butter until golden). Top each steak with 1 slice pâté de foie gras (goose liver pâté) and 1 slice truffle (if available). Coat lightly with Madeira sauce.

Tournedos Rossini; Berny Potatoes and Braised Lettuce

Figure 11.10 Preparing beef tenderloin.

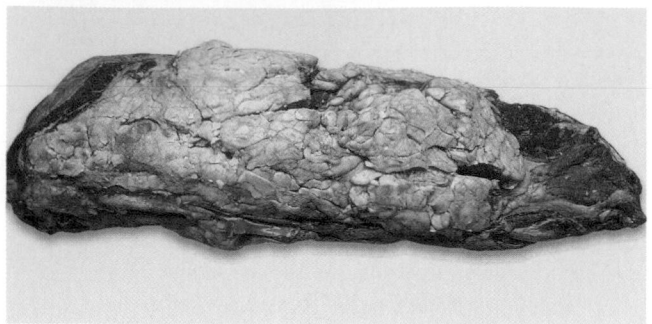

(a) A whole, untrimmed beef tenderloin.

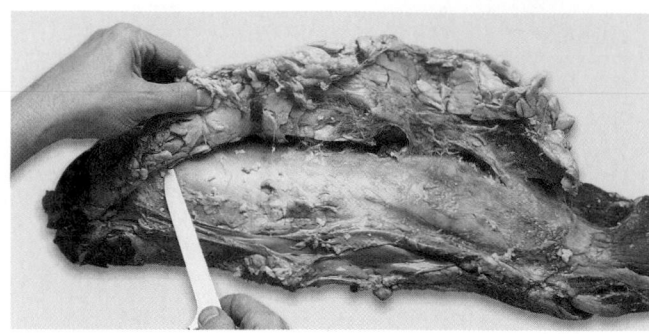

(b) Pull off the heavy fat from the outside of the tenderloin, freeing it with a knife as necessary.

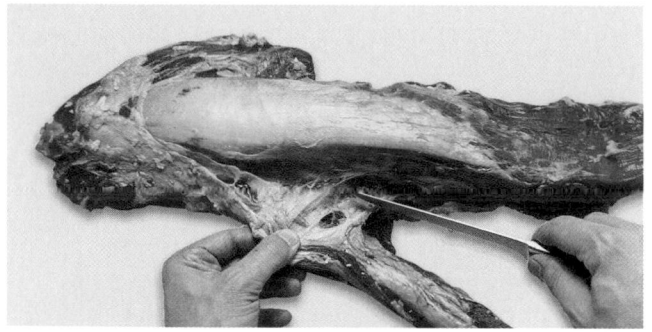

(c) Separate the strip of gristly meat, or chain, from the side of the tenderloin. Use this piece for ground meat.

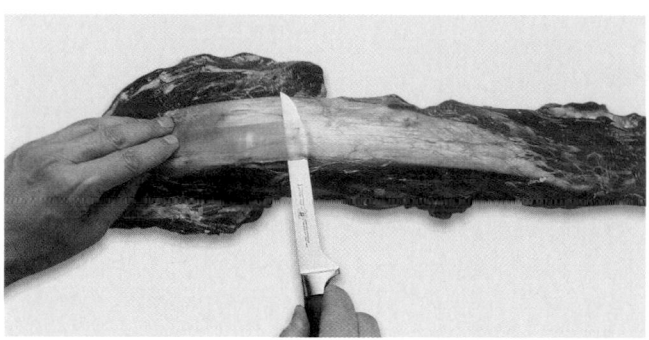

(d) Carefully remove the silverskin.

(e) The fully trimmed tenderloin before cutting.

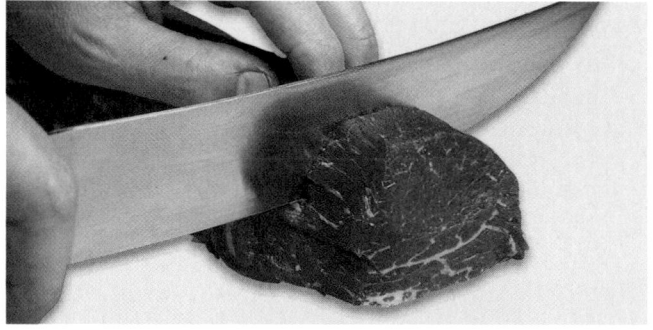

(f) Cut into steaks of the desired size.

(g) This tenderloin has been cut into a variety of steaks as a demonstration. From left to right: four fillet steaks, two large pieces for chateaubriand, two tournedos, four filets mignons. In front: trimmings from both ends.

Medallions of Beef with Two Peppers

Portions: 12   Portion size: 1 steak, about 6½ oz (185 g) each
                  2½ oz (70 mL) sauce

U.S.	Metric	Ingredients	PROCEDURE
12	12	Beef tenderloin steaks, about 6½–7 oz (180–200 g) each	1. Sauté the steak in the oil or butter. Remove from the pan and keep warm.
5 oz	150 mL	Oil or clarified butter	2. Drain off the excess fat from the pan and add the shallots. Sauté the shallots with the black peppercorns, then deglaze the pan with the cognac or brandy.
3½ oz	100 g	Shallots, chopped fine	
1 oz	30 g	Black peppercorns, crushed	
5 oz	150 mL	Cognac or brandy	3. Stir in the stock and bring to the boil. Cook until the liquid is reduced by half. Add the cream, then season to taste with salt.
1½ qt	1.5 L	Brown veal stock	
10 oz	300 mL	Heavy cream	
to taste	to taste	Salt	4. Drain the green peppercorns of brine. Add them to the sauce.
1½ oz	45 g	Green peppercorns packed in brine	
36	36	Potato Croquettes with Peppers (p. 502)	5. Place the steaks on hot plates, spoon the sauce around, and garnish with 3 potato croquettes per person.

Per serving:
Calories, 860; Protein, 40 g; Fat, 65 g (68% cal.); Cholesterol, 195 mg;
Carbohydrates, 21 g; Fiber, 3 g; Sodium, 300 mg.

Côte de Veau Grandmère (Veal Chops with Bacon, Mushrooms, and Onions)

Portions: 12   Portion size: 1 chop
                  Plus 5 oz (150 g) vegetable garnish

U.S.	Metric	Ingredients	PROCEDURE
1 lb 5 oz	650 g	Pearl onions	1. Peel the pearl onions and place in a pan large enough to cook in a single layer.
1 oz	30 g	Butter	
1 tbsp	15 g	Sugar	2. Add the butter and sugar and add enough water to cover. Cover with a round of parchment paper and cook until all the water has evaporated and the onions are coated with a fine glaze. Continue cooking, constantly moving the onions, until they are evenly colored.
1 lb 2 oz	550 g	Slab bacon	3. Cut the bacon into small cubes. Blanch in water and drain.
1 oz	30 g	Butter	4. Brown in melted butter.
1 oz	30 g	Butter	5. Heat the butter and cook the mushrooms until the liquid has evaporated. Strain and set aside.
1 lb 5 oz	650 g	Button mushrooms	
4 lb	1.8 kg	Potatoes	6. Tourné the potatoes into small olive shapes. Rinse and pat dry. Cook in very hot oil, moving often. After about 5 minutes, add the butter to finish cooking. (Adding the butter too early will soften the potatoes and make them stick to the pan, causing them to break up.) Strain off excess oil and season with salt.
8 oz	250 mL	Oil	
1½ oz	45 g	Butter	
to taste	to taste	Salt	7. Toss the onions, bacon, mushrooms, and potatoes together.
12	12	Veal rib chops, about 7–8 oz (200–250 g) each	8. Pan-fry the veal chops in a little oil and butter.
as needed	as needed	Oil	9. Remove from the pan and keep warm.
as needed	as needed	Butter	10. Degrease the pan and deglaze with the stock. Reduce until thick enough to coat the back of a spoon. Season with salt, pepper, and a few drops of lemon juice.
1 qt	900 mL	Brown stock	
to taste	to taste	Salt	
to taste	to taste	Pepper	11. Serve the chop on the center of the plate and spoon the mixed vegetables and bacon around. Coat the chop with the sauce and sprinkle with chopped parsley.
to taste	to taste	Lemon juice	
3 tbsp	20 g	Chopped parsley	

Per serving:
Calories, 740; Protein, 29 g; Fat, 52 g (64% cal.); Cholesterol, 150 mg;
Carbohydrates, 37 g; Fiber, 4 g; Sodium, 510 mg.

Sautéed Tenderloin Tips with Mushrooms in Red Wine Sauce

Portions: 10   Portion size: 7 oz (200 g)

U.S.	Metric	Ingredients	PROCEDURE
2½ lb	1.2 kg	Beef tenderloin tips, trimmed of all fat	1. Cut the beef into thin slices, cutting across the grain on the bias.
2 oz	60 mL	Oil	2. Heat the oil in a sauté pan over high heat until almost to the smoke point. Sauté the beef quickly, until well browned but not overcooked. It should be still pink inside. If necessary, sauté in several batches or in more than one pan to avoid overcrowding the pan.
			3. Remove the meat from the pan and discard excess fat.
2 oz	60 g	Clarified butter	4. Heat the clarified butter in the sauté pan and sauté the mushrooms until lightly browned. Remove from pan.
1 lb	500 g	Mushrooms, sliced thick	
4 oz	125 mL	Red wine, dry	5. Deglaze the pan with the red wine and reduce by about half.
1½ pt	750 mL	Demiglaze or brown sauce, hot	6. Add the demiglaze or brown sauce. Also, add any juices that have collected under the meat and the mushrooms.
to taste	to taste	Salt	
to taste	to taste	Pepper	7. Bring the sauce to a boil and cook briefly until reduced to desired consistency. Season.
			8. Add the beef and mushrooms to the sauce and bring just to a simmer. Remove from heat and serve immediately in casserole dishes. Garnish with toast points (p. 707).

Per serving:
Calories, 340; Protein, 27 g; Fat, 23 g (60% cal.); Cholesterol, 100 mg;
Carbohydrates, 6 g; Fiber, 1 g; Sodium, 180 mg.

Note: Less tender cuts of beef may be used if the meat is simmered in the sauce until tender. The item will then be braised rather than sautéed.

VARIATIONS

À la Carte Service: Preprep: Sauté mushrooms and add to demiglaze. Deglaze mushroom pan with wine and add to sauce. For each order: Sauté 4 oz (125 g) beef and combine with 3 oz (100 mL) sauce.

Beef Tenderloin Tips Chasseur

Prepare as in basic recipe, except omit mushrooms; use white wine instead of red; and use chasseur sauce instead of demiglaze.

Beef Sauté à la Deutsch

Prepare as in basic recipe, except, during preprep, sauté the following in butter and add to the demiglaze: 12 oz (375 g) onions, cut julienne; 6 oz (175 g) green peppers, cut julienne; and ½ tsp (2 mL) chopped garlic. (For à la carte service, the mushrooms may also be added at this point, although they will be a little fresher if cooked at the last minute.)

Beef Stroganoff

Use 8 oz (250 g) mushrooms instead of 1 lb (500 g). Sauté 4 oz (125 g) onions, cut brunoise, with the mushrooms. Substitute white wine for the red wine. Add 1 oz (30 g) tomato paste and 2 tsp (10 mL) prepared mustard to the mushroom mixture before adding the demiglaze. Finish the sauce by stirring in 1¼ cups (300 mL) sour cream. Serve with noodles or spaetzle.

Lamb Medallions with Thyme and Garlic Cream

Portions: 8   Portion size: ½ lamb rack

U.S.	Metric	Ingredients	PROCEDURE
40 cloves	40 cloves	Garlic, peeled	1. Simmer the peeled garlic cloves in the milk for 3–4 minutes.
10 oz	300 mL	Milk	
10 oz	300 g	Crème fraîche	2. Add the crème fraîche and finish cooking at a simmer until soft (the cloves should give easily when pressed with the back of a spoon).
to taste	to taste	Salt	
to taste	to taste	White pepper	3. Purée in a blender until smooth. Season to taste.
4 racks	4 racks	Lamb (2 hotel racks)	4. Bone the lamb racks. Trim the meat of excess fat and connective tissue. Rub the meat with a little olive oil and coat lightly with fresh thyme. Allow to marinate for several hours or overnight.
as needed	as needed	Olive oil	
2 tbsp	30 mL	Fresh thyme leaves	
		Optional ingredients (see step 5):	5. If you have a good-quality brown lamb stock on hand, simmer 1 qt (1 L) of it until reduced to a rich syrup and reserve. If you do not have lamb stock on hand, use the bones from the racks to make the jus, following steps 6–9.
as needed	as needed	Oil	
5 oz	150 g	Carrots, chopped	
5 oz	150 g	Onions, chopped	6. Chop the bones. Heat some oil in a deep pan. Add the bones and trimmings and brown.
2 stems	2 stems	Celery, chopped	
2 cloves	2 cloves	Garlic, chopped	7. Add the vegetables and bouquet garni. Stir, coating well with the oil. Cook for a few minutes.
1 lb	500 g	Tomatoes, chopped	
1	1	Bouquet garni	8. Deglaze with the white wine or water and stir to dissolve the caramelized cooking juices. Cook until almost completely reduced.
3½ oz	100 mL	White wine (optional)	
		Water	9. Reduce to a simmer and cook for 30 minutes, skimming regularly. If the jus reduces too quickly, add more water. Strain and degrease further if necessary and continue to reduce until syrupy.
to taste	to taste	Salt	10. Season the lamb with salt and pepper. Brown in the oil and butter in a sauté pan. Finish cooking at reduced heat on top of the stove or, for more even cooking, in the oven at 400°F (200°C) for about 6 minutes, until rare or medium rare. Allow to rest 10 minutes. Slice each piece into 6 medallions.
to taste	to taste	Pepper	
3 oz	90 mL	Oil	
2 oz	60 mL	Butter	
8 portions	8 portions	Zucchini and Tomato Tian (p. 477; optional)	
			11. To serve, pour a little garlic cream sauce on the plate and arrange the medallions on top. Drizzle with a little of the reduced lamb jus. Serve each portion with a vegetable tian on a side dish.

Per serving:
Calories, 470; Protein, 20 g; Fat, 40 g (76% cal.); Cholesterol, 105 mg;
Carbohydrates, 8 g; Fiber, 0 g; Sodium, 150 mg.

Fillet of Lamb with Mint and Cilantro Jus

Portions: 12   Portion size: 6½ oz (185 g) meat
                                 2½ oz (70 mL) sauce

U.S.	Metric	Ingredients	PROCEDURE
9 lb	4.5 kg	Spinach	1. Carefully pick and wash the spinach. Drain well. Set aside.
1 lb	500 g	Large tomatoes	2. Peel, seed, and chop the tomatoes. Set aside.
4	4	Hotel racks of lamb (or 8 single racks)	3. Remove the eye meat from the racks of lamb. Trim well. Reserve the bones for making stock if desired.
as needed	as needed	Oil	4. Gently sauté the eye meat (fillets) to the point of still just pink, taking care to brown them on all sides. Remove from the pan and hold in a warm place.
6 large	6 large	Shallots, chopped	
1½ qt	1.5 L	Brown veal stock	5. Degrease the pan. Add the shallots and lightly sauté before adding the stock. Reduce to about 14 oz (850 mL) and season to taste. Finish with the chopped cilantro and mint.
to taste	to taste	Salt	
1 oz	30 g	Fresh cilantro, chopped	
1 oz	30 g	Fresh mint, chopped	
3½ oz	100 mL	Hazelnut oil	6. Heat a clean sauté pan. Add the hazelnut oil and quickly cook the spinach until just wilted. Drain and season.
10 oz	300 g	Pine nuts, toasted	7. For each portion, place a ring mold, about 2½–3 inches (6–8 cm) in diameter, on the center of a plate. Pack the spinach into the mold and remove the ring.

Per serving:
Calories, 390; Protein, 27 g; Fat, 26 g (57% cal.); Cholesterol, 40 mg;
Carbohydrates, 17 g; Fiber, 9 g; Sodium, 240 mg.

8. Slice the rested lamb fillet and arrange neatly on the bed of spinach. Surround with the herb jus and sprinkle with the chopped tomatoes and pine nuts.

*Fillet of Lamb
with Mint and
Cilantro Jus*

Calf's Liver Lyonnaise

Portions: 10   Portion size: 1 slice liver
                                 1½ oz (50 g) onion garnish

U.S.	Metric	Ingredients	PROCEDURE
2 lb	1 kg	Onions	1. Peel and slice the onions.
3 oz	90 g	Butter	2. Heat the butter in a sauté pan and add the onions. Sauté them over medium heat until tender and golden brown.
1 cup	250 mL	Demiglaze or strong brown stock	3. Add the demiglaze or stock and cook a few minutes, until the onions are nicely glazed. Season to taste.
to taste	to taste	Salt	
to taste	to taste	Pepper	4. Place in a bain-marie and keep warm for service.
10 slices	10 slices	Calf's liver, ¼ inch (6 mm) thick, about 4 oz (125 g) each	5. Season the liver and dredge in flour. Shake off excess flour.
as needed	as needed	Salt	6. Pan-fry the liver in butter or oil over moderate heat until browned on both sides and slightly firm to the touch. Do not overcook or use high heat.
as needed	as needed	Pepper	
as needed	as needed	Flour	7. Serve each portion with 1½ oz (50 g) onion mixture.
as needed	as needed	Clarified butter or oil	

Per serving:
Calories, 310; Protein, 24 g; Fat, 19 g (54% cal.); Cholesterol, 445 mg;
Carbohydrates, 13 g; Fiber, 1 g; Sodium, 250 mg.

Medallions of Venison Poîvrade with Cassis

Portions: 8   Portion size: 2 medallions, 2–3 oz (60–90 g) each

U.S.	Metric	Ingredients	PROCEDURE
16	16	Medallions of venison, cut from the loin, ¾ inch (2 cm) thick, about 2–3 oz (60–90 g) each	1. Season the meat with salt and pepper. Sauté in butter or oil, keeping the meat rare.
to taste	to taste	Salt	2. Remove the meat from the sauté pan and set it aside in a warm place.
to taste	to taste	Pepper	
as needed	as needed	Butter or oil	
4 oz	125 mL	Chicken stock	3. Degrease the sauté pan. Deglaze it with the chicken stock and reduce the stock by half.
12 oz	375 mL	Poîvrade Sauce (p. 149)	
1 oz	30 mL	Crème de cassis (black currant liqueur)	4. Add the sauce and the cassis to the pan and bring to a simmer. Strain the sauce.
			5. Serve 2 medallions per portion. Spoon the sauce around the meat, using about 1½ oz (45 mL) per portion. Garnish the plate with appropriate seasonal vegetables.

Per serving:
Calories, 260; Protein, 28 g; Fat, 11 g (39% cal.); Cholesterol, 120 mg;
Carbohydrates, 4 g; Fiber, 2 g; Sodium, 150 mg.

VARIATION

Medallions of Boar Poîvrade with Cassis

Prepare as in the basic recipe, substituting loin of boar for the venison. Cook the meat until it is almost well done but still a little pink inside. Do not overcook, or the meat will be dry.

Sautéed Veal Sweetbreads with Shiitake Mushrooms and Port Wine Sauce

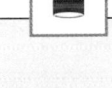

Portions: 10   Portion size: 4 oz sweetbreads, plus sauce and garnish

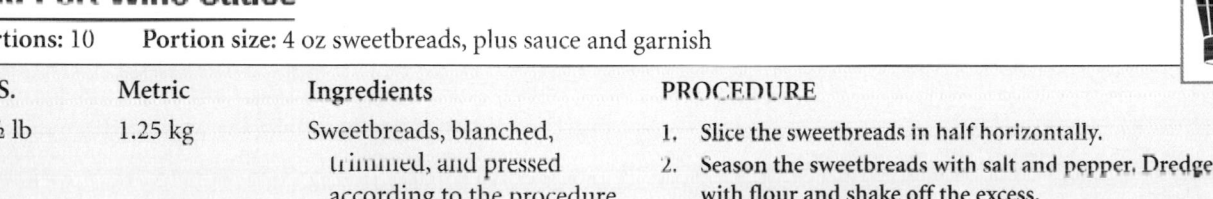

U.S.	Metric	Ingredients	PROCEDURE
2½ lb	1.25 kg	Sweetbreads, blanched, trimmed, and pressed according to the procedure on page 231	1. Slice the sweetbreads in half horizontally.
to taste	to taste	Salt	2. Season the sweetbreads with salt and pepper. Dredge them with flour and shake off the excess.
to taste	to taste	Pepper	3. Heat the butter in a sauté pan over moderately high heat. Sauté the sweetbreads until golden brown on both sides. Place on hot dinner plates.
as needed	as needed	Flour	
as needed	as needed	Clarified butter	
as needed	as needed	Clarified butter	4. Heat additional butter in the sauté pan and quickly sauté the mushrooms over high heat just until tender, about 1 minute. Add salt and pepper to taste.
1¼ lb	625 g	Shiitake mushrooms, caps only, cut into strips	
to taste	to taste	Salt	5. Spoon the sauce around (not over) the sweetbreads. Distribute the mushrooms around the sweetbreads.
to taste	to taste	Pepper	
1 pt	500 mL	Port Wine Sauce (p. 149)	6. Serving suggestion: A green vegetable, such as small green beans, makes a good additional complement to the plate.

Per serving:
Calories, 330; Protein, 23 g; Fat, 16 g (43% cal.); Cholesterol, 340 mg;
Carbohydrates, 17 g; Fiber, 1 g; Sodium, 270 mg.

VARIATION

Instead of dredging the sweetbreads in flour, bread them using the Standard Breading Procedure (p. 121). Omit the port wine sauce and top each portion with a little beurre noisette.

Veal Sweetbread and Morel Mushroom Fritters

Portions: 12   Portion size: 4 oz (125 g) plus 2½ oz (75 g) vegetable garnish

U.S.	Metric	Ingredients	PROCEDURE
		Aromatic oil:	1. To prepare the aromatic oil, combine all ingredients and let infuse 3–4 days. Strain before use.
8 oz	200 mL	Peanut oil	
2 oz	50 mL	Oriental sesame oil	
2 oz	50 mL	Olive oil	
2 oz	50 mL	Hazelnut oil	
2 oz	50 mL	Walnut oil	
1 tbsp	5 g	Pink peppercorns	
3	3	Bay leaves	
2	2	Thyme sprigs	
2	2	Rosemary sprigs	
1 tsp	5 g	Rock salt	
2 tsp	5 g	Black peppercorns, crushed	
1	1	Orange, zest only	
3 lb	1.5 kg	Veal sweetbreads	2. Soak the sweetbreads in cold water overnight (see p. 231 for preparation of sweetbreads).
1 lb 4 oz	600 g	Mirepoix	3. Prepare the vegetable stock by simmering the mirepoix and bouquet garni in 1½ qt (1.5 L) water for 30 minutes.
3	3	Bouquet garni	4. Simmer the sweetbreads in the stock for 20 minutes or until a thermometer pierced to the center of them reads about 160°–165°F (70°–75°C).
			5. Drain the sweetbreads, cool, and clean off the heavy membrane. Slice into medallions, ¼-inch (½ cm) thick.
3 oz	90 g	Fresh morel mushrooms (see note)	6. Quarter, rinse, and sweat the morels in the butter with the shallots, add the cream, and reduce until thick. Season and allow to cool.
1 oz	30 g	Butter	7. Sandwich together 2 veal sweetbread slices with the morel mixture, continuing until all the sweetbread slices are used. Some stuffing will be left over; reserve this for the sauce.
2½ oz	75 g	Shallots	
12 oz	350 mL	Heavy cream	8. Bread the sweetbread sandwiches by passing them through flour, egg, and bread crumbs (see p. 121). Either deep-fry or shallow-fry until golden brown. (Deep-frying gives an overall better finish.)
12 oz	350 mL	Heavy cream	9. Reheat the leftover mushroom mixture. Thin it with the remaining cream.
		Vegetable garnish:	
5 oz	150 g	Snow peas	10. Blanch the snow peas, cabbage, green beans, and fava beans, refresh under cold water, and drain. Reheat by gently sautéing in some of the aromatic oil.
5 oz	150 g	Cabbage, cut chiffonade	
5 oz	150 g	Green beans	
5 oz	150 g	Fava beans, shucked, blanched, and peeled (see note)	11. Plate the sweetbreads, distribute the vegetables around them, and drizzle the sauce around the sweetbreads. Garnish with 1 tablespoon (15 mL) tomato concassé and the chervil.
7 oz	200 g	Tomato concassé	
as needed	as needed	Tiny chervil sprigs	

Per serving:
Calories, 570; Protein, 28 g; Fat, 39 g (61% cal.); Cholesterol, 425 mg;
Carbohydrates, 28 g; Fiber, 1 g; Sodium, 410 mg.

Note: Dried morels can be substituted for fresh. Use one-fourth the quantity indicated in the recipe, or ¾ ounce (22 g). Soak in hot water until soft, then remove from the water and proceed with step 6. Decant the soaking liquid to leave behind any sediment, then reduce until nearly dry and add this reduction to the sauce in step 9.

See page 439 for preparation of fava beans. If not available, omit or substitute tender lima beans.

Simmering

Simmering is not a frequently used cooking method for meats. Part of the reason that simmered meats are not as popular may be that they lack the kind of flavor produced by browning with dry heat.

However, simmering is used effectively for certain less tender cuts for which browning is not desired or not appropriate. Popular examples of simmered meats are cured products such as ham and corned beef, fresh or cured tongue, fresh beef brisket, and white stews such as veal blanquette.

The term *stewing* means cooking small pieces of meat by simmering or braising (a composite method that includes both browning and simmering). Stews cooked by braising are covered in the next section.

One difference between stews and many other simmered meats is that stews are served in a sauce or gravy made of the cooking liquid.

LIQUIDS AND FLAVORING INGREDIENTS FOR SIMMERED MEATS

The kind of meat to be cooked determines the kind and amount of cooking liquid to use as well as the kinds of flavorings and seasonings to use.

- For fresh meats, use enough liquid to cover the meat completely, but don't use too much, as flavors will be diluted. Water is the main cooking liquid, but other liquids, such as wine, can be added to flavor the meat. Use herbs, spices, and a generous amount of mirepoix to give a good flavor to the meat.

- For cured meats, especially meats that are heavily salted or smoked, use a generous amount of water to help draw excess salt or smoky flavor from the meat. In some cases, such as country hams, the water may even have to be changed during cooking to remove salt from the meat. Heavily seasoned cured meats, such as corned beef, are often simmered in pure, unseasoned water, but milder cured meats may be simmered with mirepoix and herbs. Do not add salt, however, because cured meats already contain a great deal of salt.

Basic Procedure for Simmering Meats

1. Collect all equipment and food supplies.

2. Prepare meat for cooking. This may include cutting, trimming, or tying.

3. Prepare the cooking liquid:
    - For fresh meats, start with boiling liquid, usually seasoned.
    - For cured and smoked meats, start with cold, unsalted liquid to help draw out some of the salt from the meats.
    - For both kinds of meats, use enough liquid to cover the meat completely.
    - Add mirepoix and seasonings as desired. (See the discussion of seasonings and flavorings above.)

4. Place the meat in the cooking liquid and return (or bring) to a boil.

5. Reduce heat to a simmer and skim the surface. Meat must never boil for any length of time. Simmering results in a more tender, juicier product.

6. Simmer until the meat is tender, skimming as necessary. To test for doneness, insert a kitchen fork into the meat. The meat is tender if the fork slides out easily. This is called *fork tender*.

7. If the meat is to be served cold, cool it in its cooking liquid to retain moistness. Cool rapidly in a cold-water bath, as for stocks.

Simmered Fresh Beef Brisket ("Boiled Beef")

Portions: 25   Portion size: 4 oz (125 g)

U.S.	Metric	Ingredients
10 lb	5 kg	Fresh beef brisket, well trimmed
		Mirepoix:
8 oz	250 g	Onion, coarsely chopped
4 oz	125 g	Carrot, coarsely chopped
4 oz	125 g	Celery, coarsely chopped
2 cloves	2 cloves	Garlic
1	1	Bay leaf
½ tsp	2 mL	Peppercorns
2	2	Whole cloves
6	6	Parsley stems
to taste	to taste	Salt

Per serving:
Calories, 280; Protein, 35 g; Fat, 15 g (49% cal.); Cholesterol, 110 mg; Carbohydrates, 0 g; Fiber, 0 g; Sodium, 90 mg.

PROCEDURE

1. Place beef in a stockpot with enough boiling water to cover. Return the water to a boil, reduce heat to a simmer, and skim the scum carefully.
2. Add the mirepoix and seasonings.
3. Simmer until the meat is tender when tested with a fork.
4. Transfer the meat to a steam table pan and add enough of the broth to barely cover (to keep the meat moist), or cool the meat with some of the broth in a cold-water bath and refrigerate.
5. To serve, cut the meat into thin slices across the grain. Slice at an angle to make the slices broader. Serve each portion with Horseradish Sauce (p. 147), prepared horseradish, or mustard and with boiled vegetables, such as carrots, potatoes, or turnips.
6. Strain the broth and save for soups or sauces. If desired, use some of the broth to make horseradish sauce to accompany the meat.

VARIATIONS

Beef tongue (fresh, cured, or smoked), beef shank, various cuts of beef chuck, beef short ribs, fresh or smoked ham, pork shoulder, and lamb shoulder or leg may be cooked using the same method.

Simmered Pork Shoulder with Cabbage

Cook fresh or smoked pork shoulder or pork butt as in basic recipe. Cut 5 lb (2.3 kg) cabbage (for 25 portions) into wedges and simmer in some of the pork broth. Serve each portion of meat with a cabbage wedge. For 25 portions, 4 oz (125 g) each, use about 15 lb (7.5 kg) bone-in, skin-on shoulder.

Simmered Pork Shoulder; Braised Red Cabbage, Kasha Pilaf with Parsley, Roasted Onions

New England Boiled Dinner

Portions: 16   Portion size: 3 oz (90 g) meat, plus assorted vegetables

U.S.	Metric	Ingredients
5½ lb	2.75 kg	Corned beef brisket
2 heads	2 heads	Green cabbage
2 lb	1 kg	Turnips
2 lb	1 kg	Carrots
30	30	Pearl onions
30	30	Baby beets
30	30	Small red-skinned potatoes
as needed	as needed	Horseradish Sauce (p. 147) or prepared horseradish

PROCEDURE

1. Trim excess fat from corned beef if necessary.
2. Place the beef in a stockpot or steam kettle. Cover with cold water.
3. Bring to a boil and reduce heat to a simmer. Simmer until the meat feels tender when pierced with a fork. Cooking time will be about 2–3 hours.
4. To hold and serve hot, place the cooked meat in a steam table pan and add some of the cooking liquid to keep it moist.
5. Prepare the vegetables: Cut each cabbage into 8 wedges; pare the turnips and carrots and cut them into serving-size pieces; peel the onions; scrub the beets and potatoes.
6. Cook the cabbage, carrots, onions, and potatoes separately in a little of the beef cooking liquid.
7. Steam the beets, then peel them.
8. To serve, cut the meat across the grain into slices, holding the knife at an angle to get broader slices. Serve with horseradish sauce or prepared horseradish.

Per serving:
Calories, 560; Protein, 31 g; Fat, 24 g (38% cal.); Cholesterol, 85 mg; Carbohydrates, 57 g; Fiber, 12 g; Sodium, 400 mg.

VARIATION

To serve the corned beef cold, cool the beef, with some of its cooking liquid to keep it moist, in a cold-water bath. When cool, remove from the liquid and refrigerate, covered. Cold corned beef may be reheated in its cooking liquid.

Blanquette of Veal

Portions: 25   Portion size: 5 oz (150 g)

U.S.	Metric	Ingredients	PROCEDURE
10 lb	5 kg	Boneless, trimmed veal breast, shoulder, or shank	1. Cut the veal into 1-inch (2½-cm) dice. 2. Blanch the meat: Place in a saucepot and cover with cold water. Bring to a boil, drain, and rinse the meat under cold water (see note).
1	1	Medium onion stuck with 2 cloves	3. Return the meat to the pot and add the onion stuck with cloves, bouquet garni, and salt.
1	1	Bouquet garni	4. Add enough stock to just cover the meat.
4 tsp	20 mL	Salt	5. Bring to a boil, skim, cover, and lower heat to a slow simmer.
2½ qt (approximately)	2.5 L (approximately)	White veal stock	6. Simmer until meat is tender, about 1½ hours. Skim when necessary. 7. Strain the stock into another pan. Reserve the meat and discard the onion and bouquet garni
		Roux:	8. Reduce the stock to about 2½ pt (1.25 L).
4 oz	125 g	Butter, clarified	9. Meanwhile, prepare a white roux with the butter and flour. Beat into the stock to make a velouté sauce and simmer until thickened and no raw flour taste remains.
4 oz	125 g	Flour	
		Liaison:	
5	5	Egg yolks	10. Remove the sauce from the heat. Beat the egg yolks and cream together, temper with a little of the hot sauce, and stir into the sauce.
1 pt	500 mL	Heavy cream	
to taste	to taste	Lemon juice	11. Combine the sauce and meat. Heat gently but do not boil.
pinch	pinch	Nutmeg	12. Season to taste with a few drops of lemon juice, a pinch of nutmeg and white pepper, and more salt if needed.
pinch	pinch	White pepper	

Per serving:
Calories, 350; Protein, 35 g; Fat, 21 g (55% cal.); Cholesterol, 230 mg;
Carbohydrates, 4 g; Fiber, 0 g; Sodium, 550 mg.

Note: Blanching eliminates impurities that discolor the sauce. This step can be omitted, but the product will have a less attractive appearance.

VARIATIONS

Blanquette of Lamb
Prepare as in basic recipe, using lamb shoulder or shank.

Blanquette of Pork
Prepare as in basic recipe, using pork shoulder or butt.

Irish Lamb Stew

Portions: 16   Portion size: 8 oz (250 g) meat, vegetables, and broth

U.S.	Metric	Ingredients	PROCEDURE
3½ lb	1.75 kg	Lean, boneless lamb shoulder or shanks	1. Cut meat into 1-inch (2½-cm) cubes.
3 pt (approximately)	1.5 L (approximately)	Water or white lamb stock	2. Bring the water to a boil in a large, heavy saucepot. Add the lamb. There should be just enough liquid to cover the meat; add more liquid if necessary.
1	1	Small onion stuck with 2 cloves	3. Return to a boil, reduce heat to a simmer, and skim the scum carefully.
		Sachet:	4. Add the onion stuck with cloves, the sachet ingredients tied in a piece of cheesecloth, and salt to taste. Simmer 1 hour.
1	1	Bay leaf	
1 clove	1 clove	Garlic	
4	4	Whole peppercorns	
6	6	Parsley stems	
¼ tsp	1 mL	Thyme	
to taste	to taste	Salt	
1 lb	500 g	Onions, sliced thin	5. Add the onion, leek, and potatoes. Continue to simmer until the meat is tender and the vegetables are cooked. The potatoes should break down somewhat and thicken the stew.
8 oz	250 g	Leeks (white part), sliced	
2 lb	1 kg	Potatoes, peeled and sliced thin	6. Remove and discard the sachet and the onion stuck with cloves. Correct the seasoning.
		Chopped parsley	7. Garnish each portion with chopped parsley.

Per serving:
Calories, 200; Protein, 18 g; Fat, 7 g (33% cal.); Cholesterol, 60 mg;
Carbohydrates, 14 g; Fiber, 2 g; Sodium, 55 mg.

VARIATION

Carrots and white turnips may be cooked with the stew or cooked separately and added as a garnish.

Tripes à la Mode de Caen

Yield: approx. 5 lb (2.4 kg)   Portions: 8   Portion size: 10 oz (300 g)

U.S.	Metric	Ingredients	PROCEDURE
4 lb 8 oz	2.2 kg	Beef tripe	1. Trim all fat from the tripe. Put the tripe in a pot of cold water and bring it to a boil. Simmer 5 minutes. Drain and rinse in cold water. Cut the tripe into 1½-inch (4-cm) squares.
2	2	Calf's feet (see note)	
8 oz	250 g	Onion, medium dice	2. Cut the feet into pieces with a meat saw as necessary so that they fit into the braising pan.
6 oz	185 g	Carrots, sliced	
6 oz	185 g	Leek, sliced	3. Combine all the ingredients, except the Calvados, in a braising pan or other heavy pot. Salt lightly. Bring to a boil, cover tightly, and put in an oven at 325°F (160°C). Cook 5 hours or longer, until the tripe is very tender.
		Sachet:	
12	12	Peppercorns, lightly crushed	
2	2	Bay leaf	4. Remove the feet and bone them out. Dice the skin and meat and return it to the pot. Discard the bone, fat, and connective tissue.
12	12	Parsley stems	
½ tsp	2 mL	Thyme	
4	4	Whole cloves	5. Stir in the Calvados. Adjust the seasoning. Simmer a few minutes to blend in the flavor of the Calvados.
2 pt	1 L	Dry white wine	
1 pt	500 mL	White stock	6. Serve with boiled potatoes.
to taste	to taste	Salt	
3 oz	90 mL	Calvados (apple brandy)	

Per serving:
Calories, 640; Protein, 159 g; Fat, 28 g (40% cal.); Cholesterol, 345 mg;
Carbohydrates, 8 g; Fiber, 1 g; Sodium, 200 mg.

Note: If calf's feet are not available, substitute twice the number of pig's feet. Do not omit, or the tripe stew will not have enough gelatin to give it the proper texture.

This dish is from the Normandy region of France, famed for, among other things, its apples. The traditional recipe calls for hard cider, but white wine is an acceptable substitute.

Braising

Braising is a combination of dry-heat and moist-heat cooking methods. Meats are first browned or seared in fat or in a hot oven, then simmered in a flavorful liquid until tender.

The popularity of properly braised items is due to the flavor imparted by the browning and by the sauce made from the braising liquid. Clearly, the quality of a braised meat depends greatly on the quality of the stock the meat is cooked in. Other liquids used in braising include wine, marinades, tomato products, and, occasionally, water.

POPULAR TYPES OF BRAISED MEAT DISHES

1. **Large cuts.**
   Large cuts of meat braised whole, sliced, and served with a sauce or gravy are sometimes called *pot roasts*.

2. **Individual portion cuts.**
   Meats may be cut into portion sizes before braising instead of afterward. When portion cuts of beef round are braised in a brown sauce, the process is sometimes called *swissing*, and the product is called Swiss steak.

   Other braised portion cut meats include short ribs, lamb shanks, and pork chops.

3. **Stews.**
   Stews are made of meats cut into small pieces or cubes. Most stews are made by braising, but some are cooked by simmering only, without first browning or searing the meat.

Stews are usually made with enough liquid or gravy to cover the meat completely while cooking. However, so-called dry stews are braised in their own juices or in a very little added liquid.

Brown stews are made by browning the meat thoroughly before simmering. *Fricassées* are white stews made by cooking white meat in fat over low heat without letting it brown, then adding liquid. Compare this to a *blanquette*, which is a white stew made by simmering the meat in stock without first cooking it in fat. The cooking method for blanquettes, therefore, is simmering rather than braising.

Note: This use of the term *fricassée* is its traditional or classical usage. Today the word is often used for many kinds of stews.

Many other dishes can be classified as braised stews, even if we don't normally think of them that way. Chili, for example, is a braised dish made of finely cut or ground beef or pork. Even meat sauce for spaghetti (p. 516) is actually a braised meat or a stew.

Many chefs prefer to use the term *braising* only for large cuts of meat. However, the basic cooking method—using first dry heat, then moist heat—is the same for small cuts as well.

Guidelines for Braising Meats

The basic principle of braising is a combination of searing or browning and then simmering. This process accomplishes two things: *it cooks the meat*, and *it produces a sauce.* (You will use some of your sauce-making techniques when you braise meats.)

Before giving basic procedures that apply to most popular braised meats, we discuss factors that affect the quality of the finished product.

1. Seasoning.

The meat may be seasoned before browning, or it may receive its seasonings from the cooking liquid while braising. But remember that salt on the surface of meat retards browning. Also, herbs may burn in the high heat necessary for browning.

Marinating the meat for several hours or even several days before browning is an effective way to season because the seasonings have time to penetrate. The marinade is often included as part of the braising liquid.

2. Browning.

Dry the meat thoroughly before browning. Small pieces for stew may be dredged in flour for better browning. In general, red meats are well browned; white meats are browned less heavily, usually until they are golden.

3. Amount of braising liquid.

The amount of liquid to be added depends on the type of preparation and on the amount of sauce required for serving. Do not use more liquid than necessary, or the flavors will be less rich and less concentrated.

Pot roasts usually require about 2 oz (60 mL) sauce per portion, and this determines the amount of liquid needed. The size of the braising pot used should allow the liquid to cover the meat by one-third to two-thirds.

Stews usually require enough liquid to cover the meat.

Some items are braised with no added liquid. They are browned, then covered, and the item cooks in its own moisture, which is trapped in by the pan lid. Pork chops are frequently cooked in this way. If roasted, sautéed, or pan-fried items are covered during cooking, they become, in effect, braised items.

4. Vegetable garnish.

Vegetables to be served with the meat may be cooked along with the meat or cooked separately and added before service.

If the first method is used, the vegetables should be added just long enough before the end of cooking for them to be cooked through but not overcooked.

5. Adjusting the sauce.

Braising liquids may be thickened by a roux either before cooking (Method 2) or after cooking (Method 1). In some preparations, the liquid is left unthickened or is naturally thick, such as tomato sauce.

In any case, the sauce may require further adjustment of its consistency by

* Reducing.
* Thickening with roux or beurre manié or other thickening agent.
* The addition of a prepared sauce, such as demiglace or velouté.

Basic Procedures for Braising Meats

Method 1: Braising in Unthickened Liquid

1. Collect all equipment and food supplies.

2. Cut or trim meat as required. Dry it thoroughly. For stews, the meat may be dredged with flour.

3. Brown the meat thoroughly on all sides in a heavy pan with a small amount of fat, or in an oven.

4. Remove the meat from the pan and brown mirepoix in the fat left in the pan.

5. Return the meat to the pan and add the required amount of liquid.

6. Add a sachet or other seasonings and flavorings.

7. Bring liquid to a simmer, cover the pot tightly, and simmer in the oven or on top of the range until the meat is tender.
   Oven braising provides more uniform heat. Temperatures of 250° to 300°F (120° to 150°C) are sufficient to maintain a simmer. Do not let boil.

8. Remove meat from the pan and keep it warm.

9. Prepare a sauce or gravy from the braising liquid. This usually includes the following:
   - Skim fat.
   - Prepare a brown roux with this fat or with another fat if desired.
   - Thicken the braising liquid with the roux. Simmer until the roux is cooked thoroughly.
   - Strain and adjust seasonings.

10. Combine the meat (sliced or whole) with the sauce.

Method 2: Braising in Thickened Liquid

1. Collect all equipment and food supplies.

2. Prepare meat for cooking, as required.

3. Brown meat thoroughly in a heavy pan with fat or in a hot oven.

4. Remove meat from pan (if required) and brown mirepoix in remaining fat.

5. Add flour to make a roux. Brown the roux.

6. Add stock to make a thickened sauce. Add seasonings and flavorings.

7. Return meat to pan. Cover and simmer in oven or on range until meat is tender.

8. Adjust sauce as necessary (strain, season, reduce, dilute, etc.).

Method 3: Classic Fricassées

1. Follow Method 2, *except:*
   - Do not brown the meat. Cook it gently in the fat without browning.
   - Add flour to the meat in the pan and make a blond roux.

2. Finish the sauce with a liaison of egg yolks and cream.

Beef Pot Roast

Portions: 25   **Portion size:** 4 oz (125 g) meat
2 oz (60 mL) sauce

U.S.	Metric	Ingredients	PROCEDURE
10 lb	5 kg	Beef bottom round, well trimmed (see note)	1. Dry the meat so that it will brown more easily. Heat the oil in a brazier over high heat and brown the meat well on all sides. Remove from pan. (Alternative method: Brown meat in a very hot oven.)
4 oz	125 mL	Oil	
		Mirepoix:	2. Add the mirepoix to the brazier and brown it.
8 oz	250 g	Onions, medium dice	3. Add the tomato product, the stock, and the sachet ingredients tied in cheesecloth. Bring to a boil, cover, and place in a preheated oven set at 300°F (150°C), or just hot enough to maintain a simmer.
4 oz	125 g	Celery, medium dice	
4 oz	125 g	Carrots, medium dice	
6 oz	175 g	Tomato purée	4. Braise the meat until tender, about 2–3 hours.
		or	5. Remove meat from pan and keep warm for service in a covered pan. Discard sachet. (See alternate method of service given below.)
12 oz	375 g	Tomatoes, canned	
2½ qt	2.5 L	Brown stock	
		Sachet:	
1	1	Bay leaf	
pinch	pinch	Thyme	
6	6	Peppercorns	
1 clove	1 clove	Garlic	
4 oz	125 g	Bread flour	6. Skim the fat from the braising liquid and reserve 4 oz (125 g) of it.
			7. Make a brown roux with the flour and the reserved fat. Cool the roux slightly.
			8. Bring the braising liquid to a simmer and beat in the roux. Simmer the sauce at least 15–20 minutes, until thickened and reduced slightly.
			9. Strain the sauce and adjust the seasonings.
			10. Slice the meat across the grain. The slices should not be too thick. Serve each 4-oz (125-g) portion with 2 oz (60 mL) sauce.

Per serving:
Calories, 320; Protein, 38 g; Fat, 15 g (45% cal); Cholesterol, 90 mg; Carbohydrates, 4 g; Fiber, 0 g; Sodium, 70 mg.

Note: Other cuts of beef from the round, or from the chuck or brisket, may be used instead of bottom round. Braised round makes the best slices, but it tends to be dry. Chuck and brisket are moister when braised because they have a higher fat content.
    For quicker, more uniform cooking and easier handling, cut meats for braising into 5–7 lb (2–3 kg) pieces.

VARIATIONS

Alternative Method of Service: Cool beef as soon as cooked. For service, slice cold meat on electric slicer and arrange in hotel pans. Add sauce, cover pans, and reheat in oven or steamer. Individual portions may also be reheated to order in the sauce.

Braised Beef Jardinière
Garnish the finished product with 1 lb (500 g) each carrots, celery, and turnips, all cut batonnet and boiled separately, and 1 lb (500 g) pearl onions, boiled and sautéed until brown.

Braised Lamb Shoulder
Prepare boned, rolled shoulder of lamb according to the basic recipe. Use either regular brown stock or brown lamb stock.

Swiss Steak

Portions: 25   Portion size: 5 oz (150 g) meat
2 oz (60 mL) sauce

U.S.	Metric	Ingredients	PROCEDURE
25	25	Beef round steaks, 5 oz (150 g) each	1. Dry the meat so it will brown more easily.
8 oz	250 mL	Oil	2. Heat the oil in a heavy skillet until very hot. Brown the steaks well on both sides. Transfer the browned steaks to a braising pan or baking pan.
10 oz	300 g	Onion, cut brunoise	3. Add the onion to the fat in the skillet and sauté until lightly browned.
5 oz	150 g	Bread flour	4. Stir in the bread flour to make a roux. Cook until the roux is browned.
2½ qt	2.5 L	Brown stock	
5 oz	150 mL	Tomato purée	5. Stir in the stock and tomato purée and simmer until the sauce thickens. Add the bay leaves and season to taste with salt and pepper.
2	2	Bay leaves	
to taste	to taste	Salt	6. Pour the sauce over the steaks. Cover and braise in the oven at 300°F (150°C) until tender, about 2 hours.
to taste	to taste	Pepper	7. Transfer the steaks to a hotel pan for service.

Per serving:
Calories, 299; Protein, 29 g; Fat, 17 g (52% cal.); Cholesterol, 55 mg;
Carbohydrates, 6 g; Fiber, 0 g; Sodium, 70 mg.

8. Strain the sauce (optional). Degrease. Adjust the seasoning and consistency and pour over the steaks.

VARIATIONS

Steaks and other variations may be braised in a prepared brown sauce or espagnole instead of a specially made sauce. Omit steps 3, 4, and 5.

Swiss Steaks in Tomato Sauce

Reduce flour to 2½ oz (75 g). For braising liquid, use 2½ pt (1.25 L) brown stock, 2½ lb (1.25 kg) chopped canned tomatoes with their juice, and 1¼ lb (625 g) tomato purée. Season with bay leaf, oregano, and basil. After removing cooked steaks, reduce sauce to desired consistency. Do not strain. Garnish each portion with chopped parsley.

Swiss Steaks with Sour Cream

Prepare as in basic recipe. When steaks are cooked, finish the sauce with 1 pt (500 mL) sour cream, 2½ oz (75 mL) Worcestershire sauce, and 2 tbsp (30 g) prepared mustard.

Swiss Steaks in Red Wine Sauce

Prepare as in basic recipe, but add 1 pt (500 mL) dry red wine to the braising liquid.

Braised Short Ribs

Allow 1 piece weighing 10 oz (300 g) per portion. Tie (see Figure 11.11). Braise as in basic recipe, but add 5 oz (150 g) each celery and carrot to the onion to make 1¼ lb (600 g) mirepoix. If desired, replace the tomato purée with 1 lb (500 g) chopped canned tomatoes.

Braised Oxtails

Allow 1 lb (500 g) oxtails per portion. Cut into sections at joints. Prepare like Braised Short Ribs.

Braised Lamb Shanks

Allow 1 lamb shank per portion. Prepare like Braised Short Ribs. Add chopped garlic to mirepoix if desired.

Figure 11.11 Tie short ribs as shown so that the meat will stay on the bone during cooking.

Beef Stew

Portions: 25　　　**Portion size:** 8 oz (250 g)

U.S.	Metric	Ingredients	PROCEDURE
6 lb	3 kg	Beef chuck, boneless and well trimmed of fat	1. Cut the meat into 1-inch (2½-cm) cubes.
4 oz	125 mL	Oil	2. Heat the oil in a brazier until very hot. Add the meat and brown well, stirring occasionally to brown all sides. If necessary, brown the meat in several small batches to avoid overcrowding the pan.
1 lb	500 g	Onion, fine dice	
2 tsp	10 mL	Garlic, chopped	3. Add the onion and garlic to the pan and continue to cook until onion is lightly browned.
4 oz	125 g	Flour	4. Add the flour to the meat and stir to make a roux. Continue to cook over high heat until the roux is slightly browned.
8 oz	250 g	Tomato purée	
2 qt	2 L	Brown stock	5. Stir in the tomato purée and stock and bring to a boil. Stir with a kitchen spoon as the sauce thickens.
		Sachet:	
1	1	Bay leaf	6. Add the sachet. Cover the pot and place in an oven at 325°F (165°C). Braise until the meat is tender, about 1½–2 hours.
pinch	pinch	Thyme	
small sprig	small sprig	Celery leaves	
1 lb	500 g	Celery, EP	7. Cut the celery and carrots into large dice.
1½ lb	750 g	Carrots, EP	8. Cook the celery, carrots, and onions separately in boiling salted water until just tender.
1 lb	500 g	Small pearl onions, EP	
8 oz	250 g	Tomatoes, canned, drained, and coarsely chopped	9. When meat is tender, remove the sachet and adjust seasoning. Degrease the sauce.
8 oz	250 g	Peas, frozen, thawed	10. Add celery, carrots, onions, and tomatoes to the stew.
to taste	to taste	Salt	11. Immediately before service, add the peas. Alternatively, garnish the top of each portion with peas.
to taste	to taste	Pepper	

Per serving:
Calories, 240; Protein, 27 g; Fat, 9 g (34% cal.); Cholesterol, 60 mg;
Carbohydrates, 13 g, Fiber, 2 g, Sodium, 150 mg.

Note: For more elegant service, remove the cooked meat from sauce before adding the vegetables. Strain the sauce and pour it back over the meat.

VARIATIONS

Vegetables for garniture may be varied, as desired.

Beef Stew with Red Wine

Prepare as in basic recipe, but use 2½ pt (1.25 L) dry red wine and 1½ pt (750 mL) brown stock instead of 2 qt (2 L) brown stock.

Boeuf Bourguignon

Prepare Beef Stew with Red Wine, using rendered salt pork or bacon fat instead of oil. (Cut the pork into batonnet shapes, sauté until crisp, and save the cooked pork for garnish.) Increase garlic to 2 tbsp (30 mL). Omit vegetable garnish (celery, carrots, pearl onions, tomatoes, and peas) indicated in basic recipe, and substitute lardons (cooked salt pork or bacon pieces), small mushroom caps browned in butter, and boiled pearl onions browned in butter. Serve with egg noodles.

Navarin of Lamb (Brown Lamb Stew)

Prepare as in basic recipe, using lamb shoulder instead of beef chuck. Increase garlic to 2 tbsp (30 mL).

Brown Veal Stew

Prepare as in basic recipe, using veal shoulder or shank.

Brown Veal with White Wine

Prepare Brown Veal Stew, replacing 1 pt (500 mL) stock with white wine.

Beef Pot Pie

Fill individual casserole dishes with stew and vegetable garnish. Top with pie pastry (p. 755). Bake in a hot oven (400°–450°F/200°–225°C) until crust is brown.

Boeuf à la Mode

Portions: 15 **Portion size:** 5½ (175 g) meat
2 oz (60 mL) sauce

U.S.	Metric	Ingredients	PROCEDURE
1 lb 4 oz	600 g	Fatback	1. Cut the fatback into long, thin strips to fit a larding needle (Figure 11.12). Marinate in the cognac and season with salt and pepper.
1½ oz	50 mL	Cognac or brandy	
to taste	to taste	Salt	2. Trim the rump roast well, removing as much fat and sinew as possible. Reserve the trimmings.
to taste	to taste	Pepper	
8 lb	4 kg	Beef rump roast (in one or more pieces)	3. Lard the roast, piercing lengthwise in 3 rows. The strips of fat should be about 1–1½ inches (3–4 cm) apart. Stagger the rows so that the fat is evenly distributed.
as needed	as needed	Oil	4. Heat some oil in a braising pan and brown the rump roast along with the trimmings.
1 lb 10 oz	800 g	Carrot, diced	5. Once evenly browned, remove the roast and add the carrot, celery, and garlic. Sweat for a few minutes.
7 oz	200 g	Celery, diced	
2 oz	70 g	Garlic, diced	6. Add the tomatoes and the tomato paste. Cook for a few minutes.
1 lb	500 g	Tomatoes, cut into quarters	
1 tbsp	15 mL	Tomato paste	7. Deglaze with the cognac and white wine. Reduce by half. Add the veal stock and water.
1 oz	30 mL	Cognac or brandy	
10 oz	300 mL	White wine	8. Return the meat to the pot and add the bouquet garni and blanched calf's foot. Bring to a boil, then cover and place in a 350°F (175°C) oven. Cook for about 3 hours. (If the liquid evaporates too quickly, add more water.)
1 qt	1 L	Brown veal stock	
1 qt	1 L	Water	
1	1	Bouquet garni	
1	1	Calf's foot, blanched (see note)	
to taste	to taste	Salt	9. Once cooked, remove the meat and set aside. Remove the calf's foot, debone, and cut the meat and skin into small dice.
to taste	to taste	Pepper	
3 tbsp	20 g	Chopped parsley	10. Strain the braising liquid and discard the solids. Reduce the liquid until it is thick enough to lightly coat the back of a spoon. Season to taste, then add the diced calf's foot.
			11. Serve sliced, coated with the sauce, sprinkled with some chopped parsley.

Per serving:
Calories, 740; Protein, 56 g; Fat, 51 g (63% cal.); Cholesterol, 190 mg;
Carbohydrates, 8 g; Fiber, 2 g; Sodium, 150 mg.

Note: The purpose of the calf's foot is to provide gelatin to add body and texture to the sauce. If a calf's foot is not available, use 2 pig's feet.

VARIATION

Beef Stew with Carrots

Omit the fatback and both quantities of cognac. Use beef chuck, cut for stew, instead of the beef rump. Add 2½ lb (1.2 kg) chopped onion with the celery and carrot and reduce the garlic to ½ oz (15 g). Use half the quantity of stock and omit the water. Braise as in the basic recipe. Serve with Glazed Carrots (p. 465), cut tourné rather than sliced.

Figure 11.12 Larding meat using a large needle.

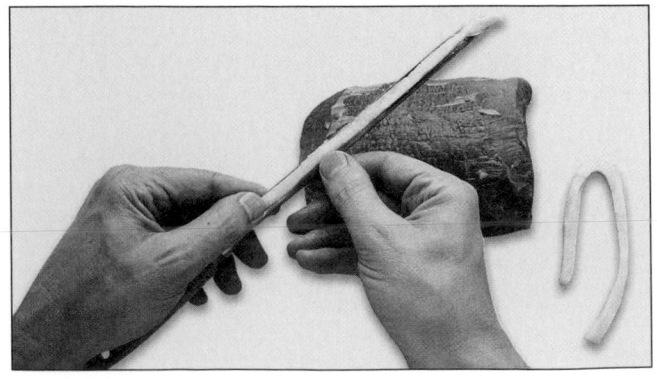

(a) Cut a strip of fatback to fit inside the needle.

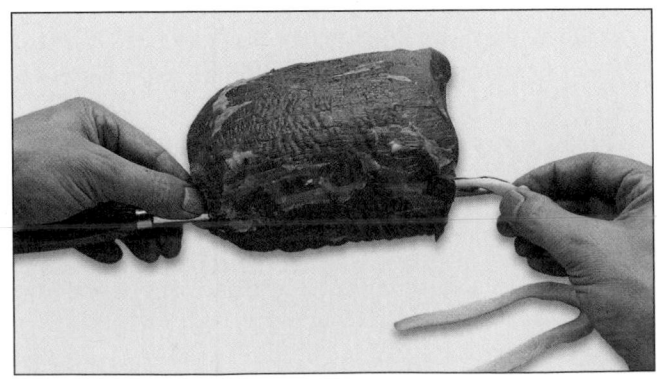

(b) Insert the needle through the meat. Pull out the needle, holding the strip of fat so that it stays inside the meat.

Chile con Carne

Portions: 24   Portion size: 8 oz (250 g)

U.S.	Metric	Ingredients	PROCEDURE
2½ lb	1.25 kg	Onion, small dice	1. Sauté the onion, pepper, and garlic in oil in a heavy sauce-pot until tender but not browned. Remove from the pot.
1¼ lb	625 g	Green pepper, small dice	
1 oz	30 g	Garlic, chopped	2. Add the meat to the pot and brown over high heat, breaking up the meat with a spoon as it browns. Drain off the fat.
4 oz	125 g	Oil	
5 lb	2.5 kg	Ground beef	3. Return the vegetables to the pot and add the remaining ingredients.
1 No. 10 can	1 No. 10 can	Tomatoes	
10 oz	300 g	Tomato paste	4. Simmer uncovered until the chili has reduced to desired thickness, about 45-60 minutes. Stir occasionally during the cooking period.
2½ pt	1.25 L	Brown stock	
3 oz	90 g	Chili powder	
to taste	to taste	Salt	
to taste	to taste	Pepper	

Per serving:
Calories, 310; Protein, 20 g; Fat, 19 g (54% cal.); Cholesterol, 55 mg; Carbohydrates, 16 g; Fiber, 4 g; Sodium, 380 mg.

VARIATION

Chile with Beans

Add 4 lb (2 kg) (drained weight) cooked or canned and drained kidney beans or pinto beans about 15 minutes before end of cooking.

Braised Pork Loin with Olives

Portions: 12   Portion size: 1 chop, about 6½ oz (190 g) with bone
                              2 oz (60 mL) sauce

U.S.	Metric	Ingredients	PROCEDURE
8 lb	3.6 kg	Pork loin, center cut, bone in	1. Trim the pork racks of excess fat and sinews. With a meat saw, cut off the chine bones so that the loin can be cut into chops after cooking. French the bones if desired (see Figure 11.4). The trimmed loin should weigh about 6–6½ lb (2.8 kg). Reserve the trimmings.
as needed	as needed	Oil	
to taste	to taste	Salt	
to taste	to taste	Pepper	2. Heat a little oil in a braising pan. Season the racks and brown along with the trimmings. Remove the racks and trimmings and set aside.
5 oz	150 g	Carrot, chopped	
5 oz	150 g	Onion, chopped	3. Add the carrots and onion and sweat. Add the tomatoes and the sliced olives.
1 lb	450 g	Tomatoes, chopped	
2 oz	60 g	Pitted black olives, sliced	4. Mix in the flour and cook for a few minutes. Deglaze with the white wine and reduce until almost dry.
2 oz	60 g	Pitted green olives, sliced	
2½ tbsp	20 g	Flour	5. Add the veal stock, the pork racks, trimmings, and the bouquet garni. Bring to a boil, then cover and place in a 350°F (175°C) oven to cook for around 1½–2 hours, until tender.
15 oz	450 mL	White wine	
1½ qt	1.5 L	Brown veal stock	
1	1	Bouquet garni	
to taste	to taste	Salt	6. Remove the racks and set aside. Strain the braising liquid and discard the solids.
to taste	to taste	Pepper	
2 oz	60 g	Pitted black olives, sliced into rings and blanched	7. Reduce the liquid until it coats the back of a spoon, then season to taste.
2 oz	60 g	Pitted green olives, sliced into rings and blanched	8. Add the sliced blanched olives. 9. Cut the rack into chops. Serve coated with the sauce and sprinkled with chopped parsley.
2 tbsp	15 g	Chopped parsley	

Per serving:
Calories, 510; Protein, 51 g; Fat, 30 g (54% cal.); Cholesterol, 150 mg; Carbohydrates, 6 g; Fiber, 1 g; Sodium, 415 mg.

Daube d'Agneau Provençale (Braised Lamb Provençale)

Portions: 12   Portion size: 4 oz (125 g)
2 oz (60 mL) sauce

U.S.	Metric	Ingredients	PROCEDURE
8 lb	3.8 kg	Lamb shoulder (see note)	1. Trim the lamb shoulder of excess fat and sinews.
to taste	to taste	Salt	2. Season the lamb with salt and pepper. Brown in hot oil in a braising pan.
to taste	to taste	Pepper	
as needed	as needed	Oil	3. Add the carrot, onion, shallot, and garlic. Sweat the vegetables.
4 oz	125 g	Carrot, large dice	
3 oz	90 g	Onion, large dice	4. Add the herbs. Deglaze the pan with the red wine, cover, and place in the oven to cook at 350°F (175°C) for 2½–3 hours.
1½ oz	45 g	Shallot, large dice	
1 oz	30 g	Garlic cloves, halved	
2 tsp	5 g	Marjoram	5. Remove from the pan and strain the cooking liquid.
4 tsp	10 g	Basil	
4 tsp	10 g	Rosemary	
1½ qt (2 bottles)	1.5 L (2 bottles)	Heavy red wine	
10 oz	300 g	Onion, chopped fine	6. Sweat the onion and garlic in olive oil. Add the diced tomato and the tomato paste. Stir well and cook for a few minutes. Add the chopped olives, season, and cook until thick.
1 oz	30 g	Garlic, chopped fine	
1½ oz	50 mL	Olive oil	
1 lb 10 oz	800 g	Tomatoes, peeled, seeded, and diced	7. Degrease the lamb cooking liquid. Mix in the tomato mixture. Cook for a few minutes to allow the flavors to blend.
1 tsp	5 g	Tomato paste	
4 oz	125 g	Finely chopped black olives	8. Adjust the seasoning.
to taste	to taste	Salt	9. Serve the lamb sliced, with the sauce on top.
to taste	to taste	Pepper	

Per serving:
Calories, 370; Protein, 34 g; Fat, 17 g (41% cal.); Cholesterol, 80 mg;
Carbohydrates, 11 g; Fiber, 2 g; Sodium, 190 mg.

Note: This recipe specifies bone-in lamb shoulder. The lamb is sliced from the bone after cooking. If desired, substitute 4½ lb (2 kg) trimmed, boneless lamb shoulder for ease in handling. The result will be somewhat less flavorful, however, because the bones contribute to flavor and to the texture of the sauce.

Veal Fricassée
Pork Fricassée

See Chicken Fricassée variations, page 344.

Veal Shank with Orange

Portions: 12   **Portion size:** 8 oz (250 g) cooked weight
2½ oz (70 mL) sauce

U.S.	Metric	Ingredients
3½ oz	100 mL	Oil
1 oz	30 g	Butter
12 pieces	12 pieces	Veal shank, cut crosswise into thick slices, about 11 oz (320–350 g) each
12 oz	350 g	Carrot, chopped
12 oz	350 g	Onion, chopped
3 oz	90 g	Garlic, chopped
8 oz	250 g	Tomatoes, cut into quarters
2½ tbsp	20 g	Flour
10 oz	300 mL	White wine
1 pt 4 oz	600 mL	Fond Lié (p. 148) or espagnole
1	1	Bouquet garni
4 tbsp	50 g	Sugar
2 oz	60 mL	Wine vinegar
¾ oz	20 g	Orange zest, cut brunoise and blanched
¾ oz	20 g	Lemon zest, cut brunoise and blanched
1 oz	30 g	Carrot, cut brunoise
1 oz	30 g	Onion, cut brunoise
1 tbsp	15 mL	Chopped parsley

Per serving:
Calories, 470; Protein, 62 g; Fat, 15 g (29% cal.); Cholesterol, 170 mg;
Carbohydrates, 17 g; Fiber, 2 g; Sodium, 310 mg.

PROCEDURE

1. Heat the oil and butter. Season the veal and brown. Remove and set aside.
2. Add the carrot, onion, garlic, and tomato. Sweat briefly.
3. Add the flour and cook for a few minutes. Deglaze with the white wine. Reduce until almost dry.
4. Add the stock and bouquet garni. Return the veal to the pan. Cover and cook in a 350°F (175°C) oven for 1¼–1¾ hours, until the veal is tender.
5. Remove the veal. Strain the braising liquid and skim off the fat.
6. Combine the sugar and vinegar in a stainless-steel pan. Cook until lightly caramelized (see note). Once colored, stop the cooking by adding the strained cooking liquid. Reduce until it coats the back of a spoon.
7. Strain and add the blanched orange and lemon zest, the carrot, and the onion. Simmer for a few minutes. Season to taste and mix in the chopped parsley before serving.

Note: A mixture of caramelized sugar and vinegar is called a *gastrique.* It is used as the base of many sweet and savory sauces, such as orange sauce for roast duck and other sauces with fruit, because it gives a good balance of sweetness and acidity.

Veal Shank with Orange

Cotelettes d'Agneau Champvallon
(Braised Lamb Cutlets with Potatoes and Onions)

Portions: 12   Portion size: 1 8-oz (250-g) cutlet
3½ oz (100 g) potatoes

U.S.	Metric	Ingredients	PROCEDURE
12	12	Lamb shoulder cutlets or chops, 8 oz (250 g) each	1. Season the meat and place in a hot pan containing the oil. Sear until lightly golden brown. Remove from the pan and reserve in a warm place. Degrease the pan.
to taste	to taste	Salt	
to taste	to taste	Pepper	2. Sweat the onion and garlic in the butter in the same pan until soft. Remove from the heat and cool.
5 oz	150 mL	Oil	
1½ lb	675 g	Onion, sliced thin	
2 cloves	2 cloves	Garlic, chopped	
6 oz	175 g	Butter	
3 lb	1.5 kg	Potatoes, starchy or all-purpose	3. Reserve 6–8 potatoes of similar shape and size. Slice the remainder thinly and evenly and mix gently with the onion. Season well with salt and pepper.
2	2	Bouquets garni	4. Place half of this mixture in a casserole dish, lay in the lamb pieces, and cover with the remaining potato mixture. Bury the bouquet garni in the center of the dish. Add enough stock to cover by about three-fourths.
1½ qt (approximately)	1.5 L (approximately)	White lamb stock or chicken stock	
as needed	as needed	Melted butter	5. Slice the reserved potatoes to an even thickness, as before, and arrange neatly on top of the lamb, overlapping the slices by 50 percent. Place in a moderate oven, 325°F (160°–170°C) for 1–1½ hours, until the lamb is very tender and the potatoes on top are golden and crisp. Finish with a glaze of melted butter and the parsley.
3 tbsp	20 g	Chopped parsley	

Per serving:
Calories, 670; Protein, 30 g; Fat, 50 g (67% cal.); Cholesterol, 150 mg; Carbohydrates, 25 g; Fiber, 3 g; Sodium, 230 mg.

Hungarian Goulash (Veal, Beef, or Pork)

Portions: 25   Portion size: 8 oz (250 g)

U.S.	Metric	Ingredients	PROCEDURE
7½ lb	3.75 kg	Boneless, lean meat: Veal (shoulder, shank, or breast), or beef (chuck), or pork (shoulder or butt)	1. Cut the meat into 1-inch (2½-cm) cubes.
			2. Heat the fat in a brazier and sauté the meat until lightly seared on all sides.
5 oz	150 mL	Oil, lard, or rendered beef suet	3. Add the onions and cook over moderate heat to sweat the onions. Continue to cook until most of the liquid that forms is reduced.
2½ lb	1.25 kg	Onions, fine dice	
5 tbsp	75 mL	Hungarian paprika	
2 tsp	10 mL	Garlic, crushed	4. Add the paprika, garlic, and caraway seeds and stir.
½ tsp	2 mL	Caraway seeds	
10 oz	300 g	Chopped, drained canned tomato or tomato purée	5. Add the tomato and stock, cover, and simmer until the meat is almost tender, about 1 hour in the oven (325°F/165°C) or on the range.
2½ qt	2.5 L	White stock	
2½ lb	1.25 kg	Potatoes, medium dice	6. Add the potatoes and continue to cook until the meat and potatoes are tender.
to taste	to taste	Salt	

Per serving:
Calories, 250; Protein, 27 g; Fat, 10 g (35% cal.); Cholesterol, 85 mg; Carbohydrates, 14 g; Fiber, 2 g; Sodium, 120 mg.

7. The potatoes will thicken the sauce slightly but, if necessary, reduce the sauce slightly. Degrease and season to taste.

8. Serve with spaetzle or noodles.

Fricassée of Veal with Peppers

Portions: 12   Portion size: about 10 oz (300 g)

U.S.	Metric	Ingredients	PROCEDURE
14 oz	400 g	Red peppers	1. Trim and cut the peppers into batonnets. Cook gently in olive oil, covered with a round of parchment paper.
14 oz	400 g	Green peppers	
14 oz	400 g	Yellow peppers	
3½ oz	100 mL	Olive oil	
6 lb 8 oz	3 kg	Veal shoulder	2. Trim the meat and cut into small cubes weighing around 1 oz (50 g) each.
3½ oz	100 mL	Peanut oil	3. Brown the meat lightly in hot oil and butter. Remove the meat and set aside.
2 oz	50 g	Butter	
4 tsp	20 g	Garlic, chopped	4. Add the garlic and onion. Sweat. Add the tomatoes, then season with salt and pepper. Add the bouquet garni, cayenne, quatre épices, and basil.
10 oz	300 g	Onions, chopped	
1 lb	500 g	Tomatoes, peeled, seeded, and chopped	5. Return the veal and sprinkle with the flour. Stir. Cook for a few minutes. Deglaze the pan with the rosé wine and reduce by one-third.
to taste	to taste	Salt	
to taste	to taste	Pepper	
1	1	Bouquet garni	
1 pinch	1 pinch	Cayenne	
2 pinches	2 pinches	Quatre épices (see p. 657)	
1½ tbsp	10 g	Fresh basil leaves, chopped	
8 tsp	20 g	Flour	
1 bottle	1 bottle (750 mL)	Dry rosé wine	
1 pt 4 oz	600 mL	Veal stock	6. Add the veal stock and the bouquet garni, and cook over low heat for about 1 hour. Mix in the cooked peppers. Simmer for around 10 minutes.
1	1	Bouquet garni	7. Serve garnished with basil leaves
as needed	as needed	Fresh basil leaves for garnish	

Per serving:
Calories, 470; Protein, 33 g; Fat, 29 g (55% cal.); Cholesterol, 150 mg; Carbohydrates, 13 g; Fiber, 2 g; Sodium, 170 mg.

Rabbit with Mustard

Portions: 8   Portion size: approximately 8 oz (250 g), including sauce

U.S.	Metric	Ingredients	PROCEDURE
4–5 lb	2 kg	Rabbit	1. Clean and cut up the rabbit for stewing.
as needed	as needed	Oil	2. Brown the rabbit in oil in a heavy pan.
			3. Remove the rabbit pieces from the pan and keep them warm. Degrease the pan.
½ oz	15 g	Butter	4. Add the butter to the pan. Sweat the shallots in the butter, but do not brown.
1 oz	30 g	Shallots, chopped	
2 oz	60 g	Prepared mustard, Dijon-style or grainy	5. Add the mustard, salt, pepper, thyme, wine, and stock to the pan and return the browned rabbit to the pan. Cover and braise slowly over low heat or in a low oven until the meat is cooked.
to taste	to taste	Salt	
to taste	to taste	Pepper	6. Remove the rabbit from the liquid and set aside.
¼ tsp	1 mL	Thyme	
8 oz	250 mL	White wine	
8 oz	250 mL	Chicken stock	
8 oz	250 mL	Heavy cream	7. Reduce the cooking liquid by about one-third. Skim any excess fat from the top.
			8. Temper the heavy cream and add it to the reduced liquid. Simmer and reduce until the sauce is lightly thickened. Adjust the seasonings. Return the rabbit pieces to the sauce.

Per serving:
Calories, 450; Protein, 39 g; Fat, 28 g (58% cal.); Cholesterol, 150 mg; Carbohydrates, 2 g; Fiber, 0 g; Sodium, 260 mg.

Sauerbraten

Portions: 25   Portion size: 4 oz (125 g)
                              2 oz (60 mL) sauce

U.S.	Metric	Ingredients	PROCEDURE
10 lb	5 kg	Beef bottom round, trimmed (see note)	1. Place the trimmed beef in a nonmetallic crock or barrel.
		Marinade:	2. Add all the marinade ingredients to the crock. If the meat is not completely covered by the liquid, add equal parts vinegar and water until it is. Cover.
1 qt	1 L	Red wine vinegar	
1 qt	1 L	Water	3. Refrigerate for 3–4 days. Turn the meat in the marinade every day.
1 lb	500 g	Onion, sliced	
8 oz	250 g	Carrots, sliced	
2 cloves	2 cloves	Garlic, chopped	
2 oz	60 g	Brown sugar	
2	2	Bay leaves	
3	3	Whole cloves	
1 tsp	5 mL	Peppercorns, crushed	
2 tsp	10 mL	Salt	
as needed	as needed	Vegetable oil, if needed for browning meat	4. Remove the meat from the marinade. Dry the meat thoroughly with towels.
			5. Brown the meat on all sides. This may be done on the range in an iron skillet, on a very hot griddle, under the broiler, or in a brazier in a hot oven.
			6. Place the meat in a braising pan. Strain the marinade. Add the vegetables to the meat and enough of the liquid to cover the meat by half. Cover and braise in a 300°F (150°C) oven until the meat is tender, about 2–3 hours.
			7. Remove the meat from the braising liquid and transfer to a hotel pan. Set aside.
8 oz	250 mL	Red wine	8. Strain 2 qt (2 L) of the braising liquid into a saucepan and skim off fat. Bring to a boil. Reduce to about 1½ qt (1.5 L).
4 oz	125 g	Gingersnap crumbs	9. Add wine and boil another 2–3 minutes.
			10. Reduce heat to a simmer and stir in the gingersnap crumbs. Simmer another 3–4 minutes. Remove from heat and let stand 5 minutes to allow the crumbs to be completely absorbed.
			11. Slice the meat across the grain. Serve 4 oz (125 g) meat per portion, overlapping the slices on the plate. Ladle 2 oz (60 mL) sauce over the meat.

Per serving:
Calories, 260; Protein, 37 g; Fat, 9 g (32% cal.); Cholesterol, 80 mg; Carbohydrates, 4 g; Fiber, 0 g; Sodium, 110 mg.

Note: If you are preparing this item in large quantities and are using whole bottom round (called gooseneck), separate the eye of round from the bottom round, and cut the bottom round in half lengthwise, so that two pieces are about the size of the eye of round.

Brisket or chuck may also be used for sauerbraten. They will not make attractive slices, but the eating quality will be very good.

VARIATION

Sauerbraten with Sour Cream Gravy

Marinate and braise meat as in basic recipe. Prepare gravy through step 8. Thicken the sauce with a roux made of 4 oz (125 g) butter or beef fat, 4 oz (125 g) flour, and 2 oz (60 g) sugar. Cook the roux until well browned and thicken the sauce. Omit wine and add 8 oz (250 mL) sour cream.

Braised Sweetbreads

Portions: 10   Portion size: 3½ oz (100 g) sweetbreads (cooked weight)
                    2 oz (60 mL) sauce

U.S.	Metric	Ingredients	PROCEDURE
3 lb	1.5 kg	Sweetbreads	1. Prepare (blanch and trim) sweetbreads according to the procedure on page 231. Leave them whole or cut into uniform serving pieces.
2 oz	60 g	Butter	
		Mirepoix:	
6 oz	175 g	Onion, medium dice	2. Heat the butter in a large sauté pan (straight-sided). Add the mirepoix and cook over medium heat until lightly browned.
3 oz	90 g	Carrot, medium dice	
3 oz	90 g	Celery, medium dice	
3½ pt	750 mL	Demiglaze, hot	3. Place the sweetbreads on top of the mirepoix and pour in the demiglaze.
			4. Cover tightly and place in oven at 325°F (165°C), until the sweetbreads are very tender and well flavored with the sauce, about 45–60 minutes.
			5. Remove the sweetbreads from the sauce and place in a hotel pan.
			6. Bring the sauce to a rapid boil and reduce slightly. Strain and adjust seasoning. Pour over sweetbreads.

Per serving:
Calories, 500; Protein, 21 g; Fat, 42 g (75% cal.); Cholesterol, 350 mg;
Carbohydrates, 10 g; Fiber, 1 g; Sodium, 340 mg.

Swedish Meatballs

Portions: 25   Portion size: 3 meatballs, 5 oz (150 g) cooked weight
                    2 oz sauce (60 mL)

U.S.	Metric	Ingredients	PROCEDURE
10 oz	300 g	Onion, chopped fine	1. Sauté the onions in oil until tender but not brown. Cool thoroughly.
2 oz	60 mL	Oil	
10 oz	300 g	Dry bread crumbs	2. Combine the bread crumbs with the milk and egg and let soak for 15 minutes.
2½ cups	625 mL	Milk	
10	10	Eggs, beaten	
5 lb	2.5 kg	Ground beef	3. Add the cooked onion and the crumb mixture to the meat in a mixing bowl. Add the spices and salt and mix gently until well combined.
1¼ lb	625 g	Ground pork	
2½ tsp	12 mL	Dill weed	
½ tsp	2 mL	Nutmeg	4. Portion the meat with a No. 20 scoop into 2-oz (60-g) portions. Roll into balls and place on a sheet pan.
½ tsp	2 mL	Allspice	
2 tbsp	30 g	Salt	5. Brown in a 400°F (200°C) oven.
2 qt	2 L	Brown sauce, hot	6. Remove meatballs from sheet pan and place in baking pans in a single layer.
2½ cups	625 mL	Light cream, hot	7. Add the hot cream and dill to the hot brown sauce and pour over the meatballs.
1 tsp	5 mL	Dill weed	8. Cover the pans and bake at 325°F (165°C) for 30 minutes, until the meatballs are cooked.
			9. Skim fat from sauce.
			10. Serve 3 meatballs and 2 oz (60 mL) sauce per portion.

Per serving:
Calories, 440; Protein, 27 g; Fat, 29 g (61% cal.); Cholesterol, 180 mg;
Carbohydrates, 15 g; Fiber, 1 g; Sodium, 810 mg.

Veal Curry with Mangoes and Cashews

Portions: 25   Portion size: 8 oz (250 g)

U.S.	Metric	Ingredients	PROCEDURE
9 lb	4.5 kg	Boneless, lean veal (shoulder, shank, or breast)	1. Cut the veal into 1-inch (2½-cm) cubes.
8 oz	250 mL	Oil	2. Heat the oil in a brazier over medium heat and add the meat. Cook the meat in the fat, stirring occasionally, until seared on all sides but only lightly browned.
2½ lb	1.25 kg	Onions, medium dice	3. Add the onions and garlic to the pan. Sauté until softened, but do not brown.
2 tbsp	30 mL	Garlic, chopped	
5 tbsp	75 mL	Curry powder (see note)	4. Add the spices and salt and stir. Cook 1 minute.
1 tbsp	15 mL	Coriander, ground	
2½ tsp	12 mL	Paprika	
1 tsp	5 mL	Ground cumin	
1 tsp	5 mL	Pepper	
½ tsp	2 mL	Cinnamon	
2	2	Bay leaves	
2 tsp	10 mL	Salt	
4 oz	125 g	Flour	5. Stir in the flour to make a roux and cook another 2 minutes.
2 qt	2 L	White stock	6. Add the stock and tomatoes. Bring to a boil while stirring.
10 oz	300 g	Tomato concassé	7. Cover and simmer slowly in the oven (300°F/150°C) or on top of the range until the meat is tender, 1–1½ hours.
8 oz	250 mL	Heavy cream, hot	8. Degrease, discard the bay leaf, and add the cream. Adjust the seasonings.
4–5	4–5	Mangoes	9. Peel the mangoes with a paring knife or vegetable peeler. Cut the mango flesh from the stone in thick slices. Cut into medium dice.
as needed	as needed	Boiled or steamed rice	
8 oz	250 g	Cashews, coarsely chopped	10. To serve, place a bed of rice on a plate. Spoon the curry onto the center of the rice. Top with diced mango. Sprinkle with chopped cashews and chopped parsley.
½ cup	125 mL	Chopped parsley	

Per serving:
Calories, 430; Protein, 31 g; Fat, 26 g (54% cal.); Cholesterol, 95 mg;
Carbohydrates, 18 g; Fiber, 2 g; Sodium, 330 mg.

Note: If desired, increase curry powder to taste and omit other spices (except bay leaf).

VARIATIONS

In place of the mango and cashews, serve meat curries with an assortment of other condiments, such as raisins, chutney, peanuts, chopped scallions or onions, diced pineapple, diced banana, diced apple, shredded coconut, and poppadums.

Lamb Curry

Substitute lean boneless lamb shoulder, breast, or leg for the veal.

Terms for Review

persillade	stroganoff	pot roast	navarin
London broil	stew	Swiss steak	sauerbraten
shish kebab	New England boiled	fricassée	goulash
tournedos	dinner	blanquette	

Questions for Discussion

1. List four advantages of roasting at a low temperature.
2. When might you use high temperatures for roasting?
3. What is the purpose of basting?
4. In the recipe for Home-Style Meatloaf (p. 254), why are the sautéed vegetables cooled after cooking in step 1?
5. Which steaks require the highest broiler heat, thick ones or thin ones? Steaks to be cooked rare or steaks to be cooked well done?
6. Why is it important not to overload the pan when sautéing meats?
7. Why is the menu term "boiled beef" inaccurate?

chapter 12

Understanding Poultry and Game Birds

The versatility, the popularity, and the relatively low cost of poultry items make them ideal for all kinds of food service operations, from elegant restaurants to cafeterias and fast-food restaurants. Also, chicken and turkey are popular among diet-conscious people because they are lower in fat and cholesterol than other meats.

Game birds, such as pheasant, are also increasing in popularity and availability because they are now raised domestically by many producers. Farm-raised game birds are similar, in many ways, to chicken, so learning techniques for cooking and handling chicken teaches you a great deal about handling these other birds as well.

Learning about poultry is, in some ways, easier than learning about meats like beef and lamb. Because chickens, turkeys, and other poultry are much smaller, they are not cut up in such detail.

However, poultry has its own cooking problems, so it is important that the student observe both the similarities and the differences between meat and poultry.

Composition and Structure

The flesh of poultry is muscle tissue, as is the flesh of beef, lamb, veal, and pork. Its composition and structure are essentially the same as those of meat.

Review the section on meat composition and structure (Chapter 10, pp. 210-211). Remember that muscle tissue is composed of

Water (about 75 percent)
Protein (about 20 percent)
Fat (up to 5 percent)
Other elements, including carbohydrate, in small quantities

Remember that muscles consist of *muscle fibers* held together in bundles by *connective tissue*.

After reading this chapter, you should be able to

1. Explain the differences between light meat and dark meat, and describe how these differences affect cooking.

2. Describe four techniques that help keep chicken or turkey breast moist while roasting.

3. Define the following terms used to classify poultry: *kind, class,* and *style*.

4. Identify popular types of farm-raised game birds and the cooking methods appropriate to their preparation.

5. Store poultry items.

6. Determine doneness in cooked poultry, both large roasted birds and smaller birds.

7. Truss poultry for cooking.

8. Cut chicken into parts.

MATURITY AND TENDERNESS

We learned in Chapter 10 that the tenderness of a piece of meat—or poultry—is related to *connective tissue* and that connective tissue increases with

- Use or exercise of the muscle.
- Maturity or age of the animal or bird.

1. Use or exercise is of less concern in poultry. Most poultry is so young that it is relatively tender throughout. However, there are some differences, discussed in the next section, between "light meat" and "dark meat."

2. *Maturity* is a major consideration when selecting poultry. Young, tender birds are cooked by dry-heat methods, such as broiling, frying, and roasting, as well as by moist-heat methods. Older, tougher birds need slow, moist heat to be made palatable.

Maturity is the major factor in categorizing each kind of poultry (see p. 301).

Skin color is determined by diet and is not related to the flavor or tenderness of the poultry.

FREE-RANGE CHICKENS

Most chickens on the market are produced by large operations that house their poultry indoors in carefully controlled environments and feed them scientifically monitored diets. This process enables the industry to raise healthy chickens quickly and in large numbers to meet the great demand. Many people feel that these chickens lack flavor because they are not allowed to move around outdoors. Some farmers, in response, offer *free-range chickens*, which are allowed to move around freely and eat outdoors in a more natural environment.

It is important to note that there is no legal definition of "free-range," and that free-range chickens are considerably more expensive than ordinary chickens. Many people, however, feel that free-range chickens are more flavorful and are worth the extra cost. Because quality varies from producer to producer, it is necessary to do careful taste-testing to determine whether you want to purchase free-range poultry for your operation.

A term related to free-range is *organic*, which also has no legal definition. In general, a poultry item with this designation has been raised without various chemical growth enhancers or without certain antibiotics. The label "organic" guarantees none of this, however.

"LIGHT MEAT" AND "DARK MEAT"

Poultry is not divided into many small cuts as are meats. Chicken and turkey, however, are usually thought of as consisting of two kinds of parts, depending on the color of the meat. These color differences reflect other differences:

"Light meat"—breast and wings
   Less fat
   Less connective tissue
   Cooks faster

"Dark meat"—legs (drumsticks and thighs)
   More fat
   More connective tissue
   Takes longer to cook

Duck, goose, and squab have all dark meat, but the same differences in connective tissue hold true.

The cook must observe these differences when preparing poultry.

1. **Cooking whole birds.**

   Everyone has tasted chicken or turkey breast so dry it was difficult to swallow. In fact, light meat is overcooked more often than not because it cooks faster than the legs and is done first. In addition, the breast has less fat than the legs, so it tastes much drier when cooked (or overcooked).

   A major problem in roasting poultry is cooking the legs to doneness without overcooking the breast. Chefs have devised many techniques to help solve this problem. Here are some of them.

   - Roasting breast down for part of the roasting period. Gravity draws moisture and fat to the breast rather than away from it.
   - Basting with fat only, not with water or stock. Fat protects from drying, but moisture washes away protective fat.
   - Barding, or covering the breast with a thin layer of pork fat. This is usually done with lean game birds.
   - Separating breast from leg sections and roasting each for a different length of time. This is often done with large turkeys.

2. **Cooking poultry parts.**

   Many recipes have been devised especially for certain poultry parts, such as wings, drumsticks, and boneless chicken breasts. These recipes take into account the different cooking characteristics of each part. For example, flattened boneless chicken breasts can be quickly sautéed and remain juicy and tender. Turkey wings, when braised, release enough gelatin to help make a rich sauce.

   Many of these items have especially high customer appeal, especially boneless chicken breast, and are served in the most elegant restaurants.

   Several of the chicken and turkey recipes in Chapter 13 are for specific parts. Those that use cut-up whole chickens can easily be adapted for specific parts. For example, you may want to buy whole chickens, braise the leg sections, and reserve the breasts for other preparations.

Inspection and Grading

Like meat, poultry is subject to federal inspection and grading. (*Note:* Unlike for meats, poultry inspection and grading stamps are not stamped on the birds but are printed on tags and packing cases.)

INSPECTION

1. A guarantee of wholesomeness (fit for human consumption).
2. Indicated by a round stamp (Figure 12.1).
3. Required by U.S. law.

GRADING

1. Based on quality.
2. Indicated by a shield stamp and letter grade (Figure 12.2).
3. Not required by U.S. law.

   U.S. grades are A, B, and C (A being the best). They are based on

   Shape of carcass (lack of defects)
   Amount of flesh
   Amount of fat
   Pinfeathers (present or absent)
   Skin tears, cuts, broken bones
   Blemishes and bruises

   Most poultry used in food service is Grade A. Lower grades are used by canners and processors.

Figure 12.1 USDA inspection stamp for poultry.

Figure 12.2 USDA grade stamp for poultry.

Classification and Market Forms

The following terms are used to classify poultry:

Kind—the species, such as chicken, turkey, or duck.
Class—the subdivision of kind, depending on age and sex.
Style—the amount of cleaning and processing.
    Live: almost never purchased in food service.
    Dressed: killed, bled, and plucked. Also rarely seen in food service.
    Ready to cook: dressed and eviscerated, with head and feet removed.

- Whole.
- Cut up, or parts.

State of refrigeration—chilled or frozen.

Table 12.1 describes the kinds and classes of domestic poultry. *Chicken* is the most common kind of poultry in the kitchen. As indicated in the table, age or maturity determines the differences among the various classes of chicken. *Rock Cornish game hens* (usually called Cornish hens), *broilers*, and *fryers* are young, tender chickens suitable for sautéing, broiling, or frying, while *roasters* and *capons* are larger chickens that are usually roasted. Older *hens* and (rarely marketed) *roosters* must be simmered or braised to make them tender.

In addition to the common classes of chicken listed in the table, you may also find *poussin* (poo-san) on the market in certain localities. Similar to Rock Cornish game hen but often smaller, a poussin is a young chicken weighing a pound (450 g) or less. It commands a fairly high price because of the special techniques required for raising it.

Turkeys are larger birds that are usually roasted, although the cooking of turkey parts is increasingly common. For example, legs may be stewed or braised for special dishes (see, for example, Mole Poblano, p. 736), while breasts are cut into cutlets or scaloppine and sautéed like veal cutlets.

Ducks and **geese** also are usually roasted, although duck parts are sometimes cooked separately. Boneless breast of duck is sautéed or broiled and served rare, sliced into small medallions, and the legs may be braised. Ducks and geese have a thick layer of fat under the skin. Compared with chicken and turkey, they have a low yield. For example, a 4-pound duck yields about 1 pound raw lean meat, and a 4-pound chicken yields about 2 pounds raw lean meat.

Most ducks marketed in North America are a breed called *White Pekin*; this includes the well-known Long Island duck. A specialty item available in some markets is *magret* (mah-gray). This is the boneless breast of a breed of duck called *moulard*. It is thicker and meatier than the breast of a regular Pekin.

Guineas are a domestically raised descendent of the pheasant. They taste like a flavorful chicken and are usually cooked and handled like young chickens.

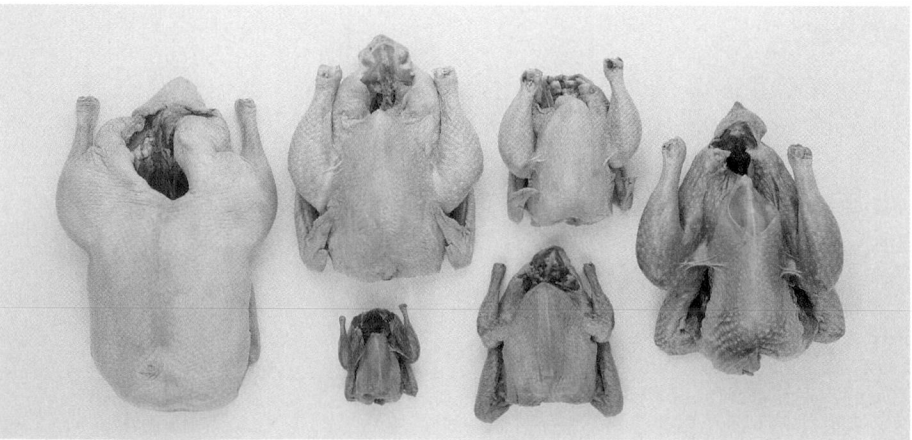

Clockwise from left: duckling, free-range chicken, poussin, guinea fowl, squab, quail.

TABLE 12.1

Domestic Poultry Classes and Characteristics

Kind/Class	Description	Age	Weight Range
Chicken			
Rock Cornish game hen	Special breed of young chicken, very tender and delicate.	5–6 weeks	¾–2 lb (0.34–0.9 kg)
Broiler or fryer	Young chicken of either sex. Tender flesh and flexible cartilage. Smooth skin.	9–12 weeks	Broiler: 1½–2½ lb (0.7–1.1 kg) Fryer: 2½–3½ lb (1.1–1.6 kg)
Roaster	Young chicken of either sex. Tender flesh and smooth skin, but less flexible cartilage.	3–5 months	3½–5 lb (1.6–2.3 kg)
Capon	Castrated male chicken. Flesh very tender and well flavored. Large breast. Expensive.	Under 8 months	5–8 lb (2.3–3.6 kg)
Hen or fowl	Mature female. Tough flesh and coarse skin. Hardened breastbone cartilage.	Over 10 months	3½–6 lb (1.6–2.7 kg)
Cock or rooster	Mature male. Coarse skin. Tough, dark meat.	Over 10 months	4–6 lb (1.8–2.7 kg)
Turkey			
Fryer-roaster	Young bird of either sex. Tender flesh, smooth skin, and flexible cartilage.	Under 16 weeks	4–9 lb (1.8–4 kg)
Young turkey (hen or tom)	Young turkeys with tender flesh but firmer cartilage.	5–7 months	8–22 lb (3.6–10 kg)
Yearling turkey	Fully matured turkey that is still reasonably tender.	Under 15 months	10–30 lb (4.5–14 kg)
Mature turkey or old turkey (hen or tom)	Old turkey with tough flesh and coarse skin.	Over 15 months	10–30 lb (4.5–14 kg)
Duck			
Broiler or fryer duckling	Young tender duck with soft bill and windpipe.	Under 8 weeks	2–4 lb (0.9–1.8 kg)
Roaster duckling	Young tender duck with bill and windpipe that are just starting to harden.	Under 16 weeks	4–6 lb (1.8–2.7 kg)
Mature duck	Old duck with tough flesh and hard bill and windpipe.	Over 6 months	4–10 lb (1.8–4.5 kg)
Goose			
Young goose	Young bird with tender flesh.	Under 6 months	6–10 lb (2.7–4.5 kg)
Mature goose	Tough old bird.	Over 6 months	10–16 lb (4.5–7.3 kg)
Guinea			
Young guinea	Domestic relatives of the pheasant. Young birds are tender, old ones are tough.	About 6 months	¾–1½ lb (0.34–0.7 kg)
Mature guinea		Up to 12 months	1–2 lb (0.45–0.9 kg)
Pigeon			
Squab	Very young pigeons with light, tender meat.	3–4 weeks	Under 1 lb (0.45 kg)
Pigeon	Older pigeons with tough, dark meat.	Over 4 weeks	1–2 lb (0.45–0.9 kg)

Squabs are young, domestically raised pigeons, usually weighing less than a pound (450 g). Their rich, dark meat, which is usually cooked slightly rare to avoid dryness, has a slightly gamy flavor that combines well with flavorful brown sauces.

GAME BIRDS AND SPECIALTY PRODUCTS

In recent years, the availability of such birds as quail and squab has increased dramatically, and they are seen regularly on restaurant menus. While the poultry items discussed in this section are classified as game birds, they are all, in fact, raised domestically. While farm-raised pheasants and partridge lack the full gamy flavor of their wild cousins, they do have a richer, somewhat gamelike taste when compared to chicken. With bland, factory-raised chickens dominating the market, cooks and eaters are turning more and more to exotic poultry and are willing to pay the higher price.

Traditionally, true wild game is hung and allowed to age, usually before plucking and dressing. The purpose is essentially the same as for aging beef, namely to allow the natural enzymes in the meat to tenderize it and to develop flavor. Often, game is hung until it becomes "high," to the point where spoiled meat is mistaken for aged meat. With today's farm-raised game birds, this procedure is not appropriate. Anyway, most customers prefer a fresh taste to a strong, gamy one.

Quails are small, weighing about 4 to 5 ounces (110 to 140 g) each. A normal portion is two birds. They have meaty breasts for their size, but not much meat on the legs. Quails are richly flavored without being gamy. The French name is *caille.*

Partridges are about the size of Rock Cornish game hens, weighing about 1 pound (450 g) each. It is important to look for young, tender birds because mature partridge is likely to be tough. They have excellent flavor, but not as delicate as squab or pheasant. The French names are *perdreau* (young partridge) and *perdrix* (mature partridge).

Pheasant is a popular game bird, and farm-raised pheasant is widely available. Most pheasant sold weighs from 2 to 2½ pounds (900 to 1200 g), but young pheasant weighing 1 pound (450 g) or less is also available. This bird has delicate, light-colored meat with subtle flavor similar to that of chicken. Most recipes for chicken are also suitable for pheasant, but the simplest preparations are usually the best, because the flavor stands well on its own and is easily covered by too many spices. Pheasant can be very dry if overcooked. The French name is *faisan.*

Many varieties of **wild duck** are eaten, but mallard is the most common. Farm-raised mallards weigh from 1½ to 3 pounds (700 to 1400 g). Unlike domestic duck, wild duck is very lean. It has dark, flavorful flesh.

Handling game birds is easy if you remember that their structure is basically the same as the structure of chickens. All the cutting and trussing techniques that you learn for chicken can be applied to these other birds.

Because farm-raised game birds are usually young and tender, they can be roasted, sautéed, grilled, and barbecued. The most important thing to remember about them is that they are usually very lean. Therefore, they are best served slightly rare. If cooked to well done, they become dry. This is especially true of wild duck, which is almost inedible if overcooked. Wild duck is usually left rarer than the other birds discussed here. Its meat is then red and juicy.

Pheasant is also very dry if well done. Its light-colored meat is best if still slightly pink at the bone. Quail doesn't become as dry, but it too has the best flavor if still slightly pink at the bone.

Another category of farm-raised birds increasing in popularity is the category technically known as *ratites.* **Ostrich** and **emu** are the most familiar members of this category. Meat from both birds is widely available. It is lean and red and resembles venison or very lean beef in appearance, although it is slightly lighter in color than venison.

Because ostrich and emu are so lean, they are best cooked to the medium rare or, at most, medium stage to avoid dryness. Maximum recommended internal temperature is 150° to 160°F (65° to 71°C). Grilling, sautéing, and pan-frying are the best cooking methods for small, tender cuts, while larger tender cuts can be roasted. Moist-heat methods, especially braising, are sometimes recommended for less tender cuts, but this often results in excessively dry meat because it is so lean. Take care to avoid overcooking if you braise ostrich or emu. Another option is to grind the less tender cuts. Mixed with seasonings and added moisture, ground emu and ostrich can make excellent burgers, meatballs, and meatloaf.

Ostrich and emu are best cooked like other lean red meats and game. Recipes for venison, in particular, are often excellent when applied to these meats, as are recipes for grilled or sautéed beef. Ostrich producers often recommend cooking their product like veal. This may be slightly misleading because veal is often cooked medium well or well done. Nevertheless, grilled, sautéed, and roast veal recipes can often be used for ostrich and emu as well, as long as the meat is not overcooked. See page 327 for a sample of a recipe developed specifically for ostrich and emu. For other cooking ideas, look for appropriate recipes in Chapter 11 based on the guidelines just described.

Handling and Storage

FRESH POULTRY

1. Fresh poultry is extremely perishable. It should arrive packed in ice and be kept in ice until used.

2. Ideally, use poultry within 24 hours of receiving. Never hold it for more than 4 days.

3. Poultry often carries salmonella bacteria. Wash all equipment and cutting surfaces after handling poultry to avoid contamination of other foods.

FROZEN POULTRY

1. Store frozen poultry at 0°F (−18°C) or lower until ready to thaw.

2. Thaw in original wrapper in refrigerator, allowing 1 to 2 days for chickens, 2 to 4 days for larger birds. If pressed for time, thaw in cold, running water in original wrapper.

3. Do not refreeze thawed poultry.

Doneness

Domestic poultry is almost always cooked well done (except squab and sautéed or grilled duck breast). Many cooks, however, cannot tell the difference between well done and overcooked. Chicken and turkey are low in fat, so they quickly become dry and unpalatable when overcooked. Even duck and goose, which are very fatty, taste dry and stringy if cooked too long.

Skilled chefs with years of experience can often tell the doneness of a roast chicken or turkey just by looking at it. Until you have gained that much experience, you should rely on other methods.

FOR LARGE ROASTED BIRDS

An *internal temperature* of 180°F (82°C), tested with a thermometer, is the most accurate guide. The thermometer should be inserted into the thickest muscle of the inner part of the thigh, away from the bone.

The thigh is tested rather than the breast because the thigh is the last part of the bird to become fully cooked.

FOR SMALLER BIRDS, COOKED BY ANY METHOD

Doneness of smaller birds is determined in the following ways.

1. Looseness of joints. The leg moves freely in its socket.

2. Clear juices. Juices inside the cavity of a roasted bird are clear yellow rather than cloudy and red or pink.

3. Flesh separating from bone. Muscles begin to pull away from bones, especially breastbone and leg bones. Excessively shrunken flesh means it's overcooked and dry.

4. Firmness to touch. Test with finger pressure as you would a steak (see p. 228). This method is especially useful for sautéed boneless chicken breasts.

Not recommended: Do not test by piercing deeply with a fork and twisting the flesh. Too many valuable juices will be lost.

Trussing Methods

Trussing means tying the legs and wings against the body to make a compact, solid unit. It has two main purposes:

1. Even cooking. Extended legs and wings cook too quickly.
2. More attractive appearance, especially when presented or served whole or carved in the dining room.

One of many trussing methods is illustrated in Figure 12.3. Your instructor may wish to show you other methods.

Figure 12.3 Trussing chicken.

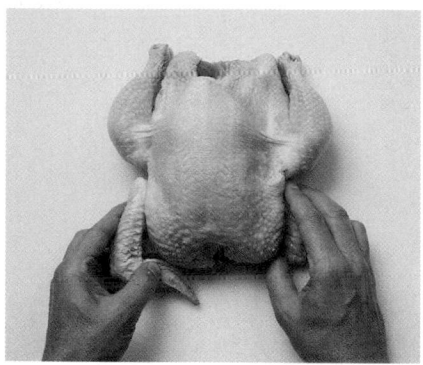

(a) Place the chicken breast up with the neck end toward you. Tuck the first joint of the wings behind the back.

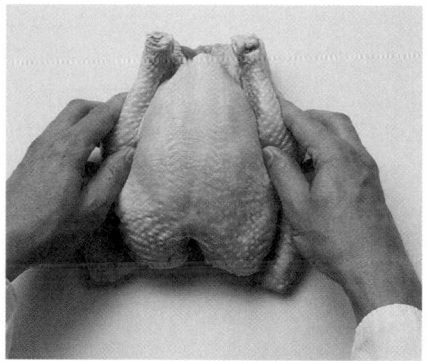

(b) Press the legs forward and down against the body.

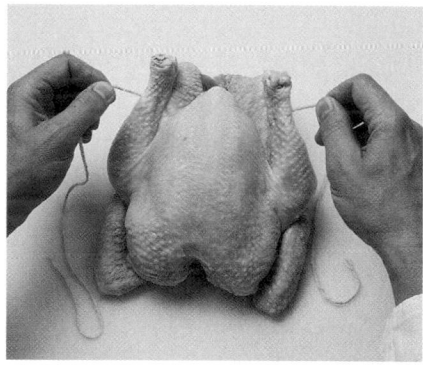

(c) Pass the center of a length of twine under the hip bone just ahead of the tail.

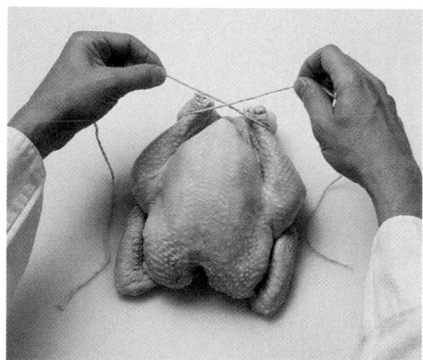

(d) Bring the twine up and across the ends of the legs.

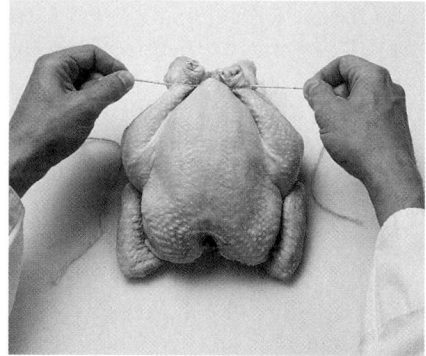

(e) Pass the twine under the ends of the legs as shown and pull tight.

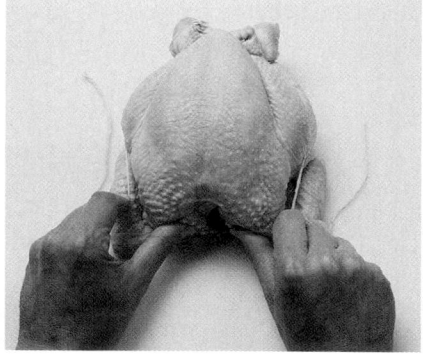

(f) Bring the ends of the twine toward the neck end of the bird. Pull firmly on the twine while pressing on the breast portion with the thumbs as shown.

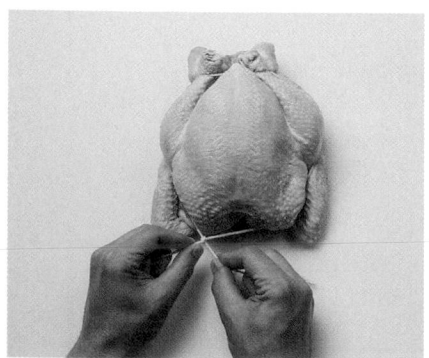

(g) Tie the twine tightly.

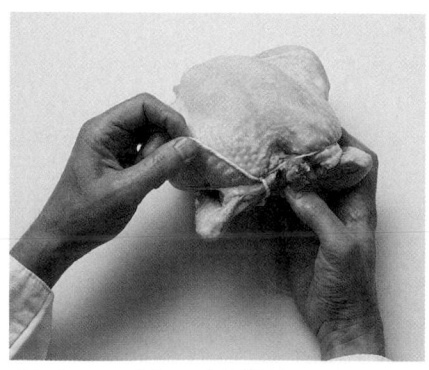

(h) The stub of the neck holds the twine in place, preventing it from slipping behind the back.

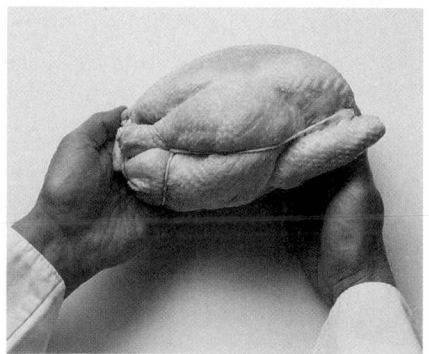

(i) The trussed chicken.

Cutting Up Chicken

There are many ways to cut up chickens. Every chef has his or her own preferred methods. Some of these methods are illustrated, step by step, in Figures 12.4, 12.5, and 12.6. They show how to split a chicken for broiling and how to cut whole chickens into quarters and eighths, for both bone-in parts and semiboneless pieces.

As for meats, it is important to know the bone structure of chicken in order to cut it up. The best way to learn this is to practice cutting chickens.

Figure 12.4 Splitting chicken for broiling.

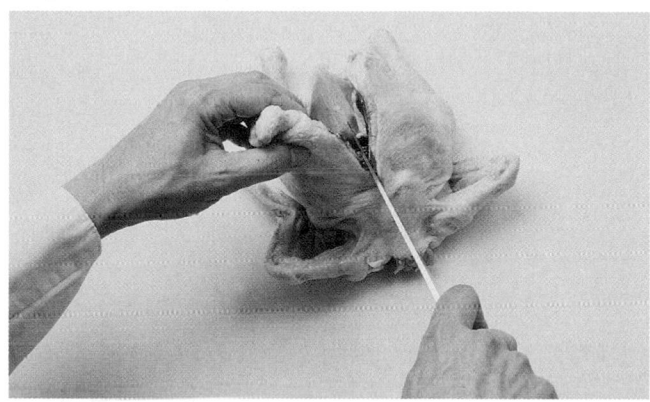

(a) Hold the chicken up by the tail. Cut through the bones to one side of the backbone, all the way to the neck.

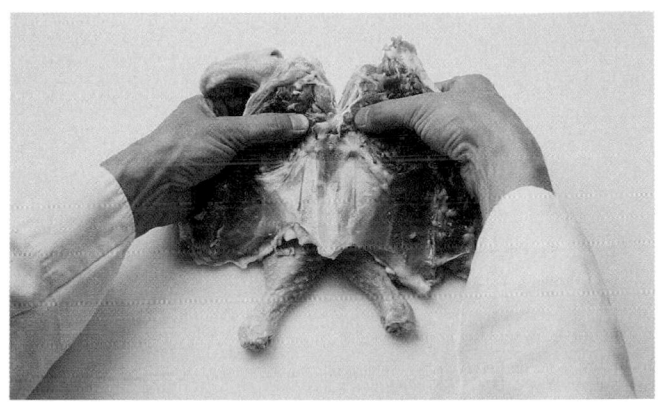

(b) Split the chicken open.

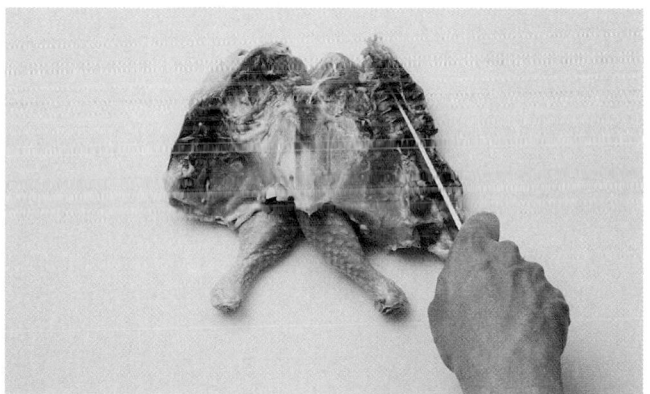

(c) Cut off the backbone as shown.

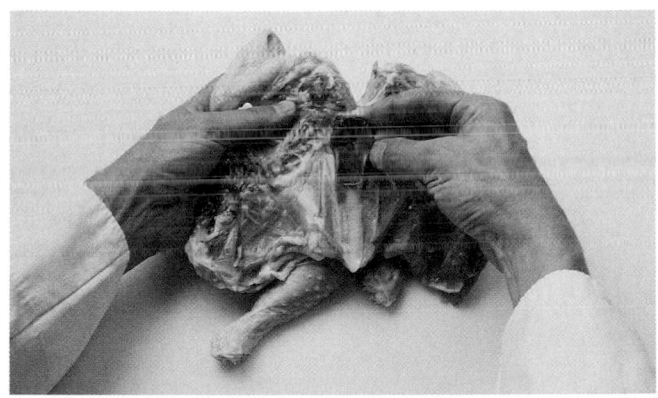

(d) Pull out the breastbone or keel bone. This helps the chicken lie flat and cook evenly.

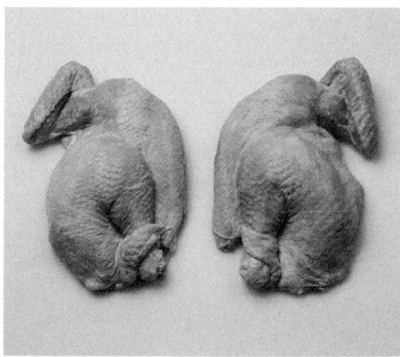

(e) For a portion size of one-half chicken, cut the chicken in half down the center of the breast. Make a split in the skin below the leg and slip the end of the leg through it as shown to hold the chicken in shape.

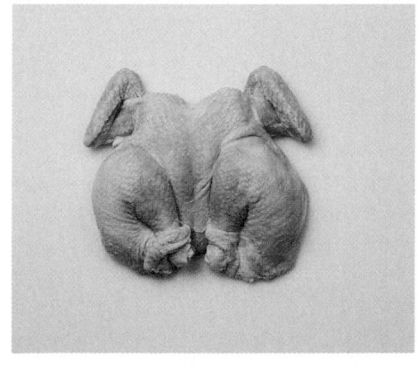

(f) Portion-size Cornish game hens are left whole.

Figure 12.5 Cutting chicken into quarters and eighths, bone in.

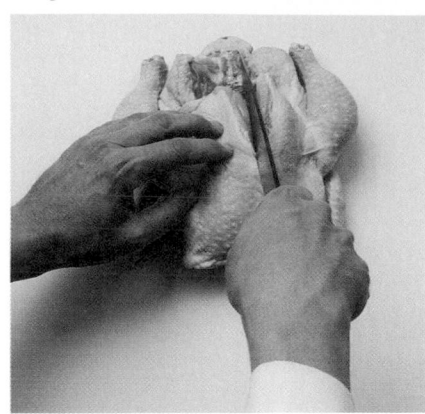

(a) Place the chicken on the cutting board breast up. Split the chicken down the center of the breast with a heavy knife as shown.

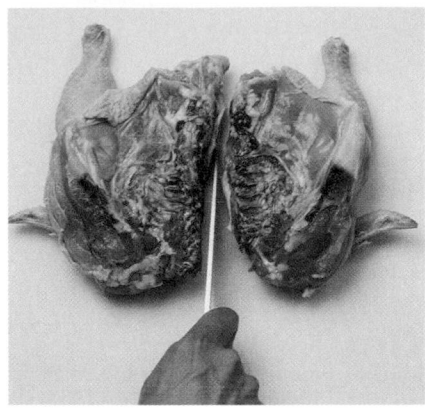

(b) Spread the chicken open and cut through the bones on one side of the backbone.

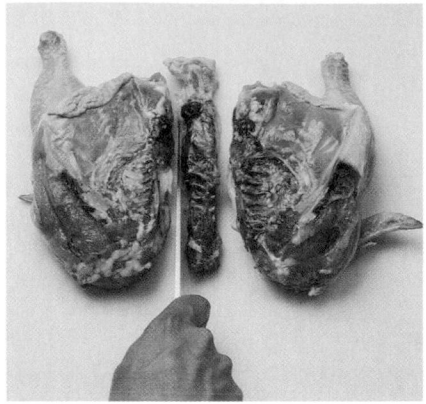

(c) Cut off the backbone completely. Save for stocks.

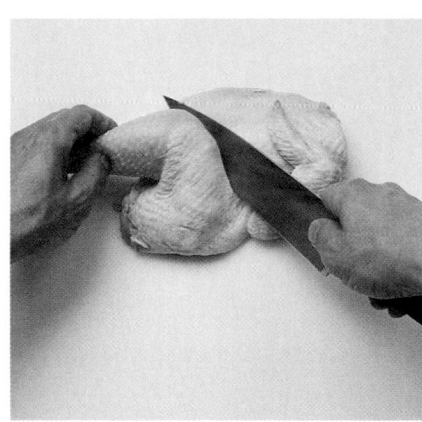

(d) Cut through the skin between the leg and the breast.

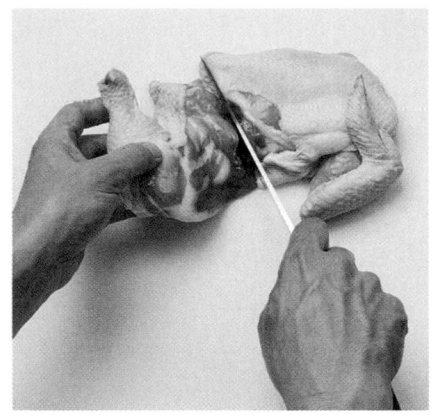

(e) Pull the leg back and cut off the entire leg section. Repeat with the other half. The chicken is now in quarters.

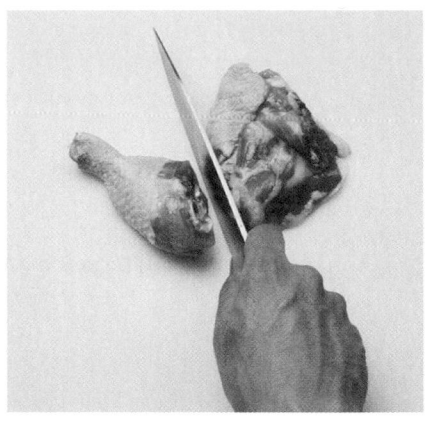

(f) To cut into eighths, cut the drumstick and thigh apart at the joint.

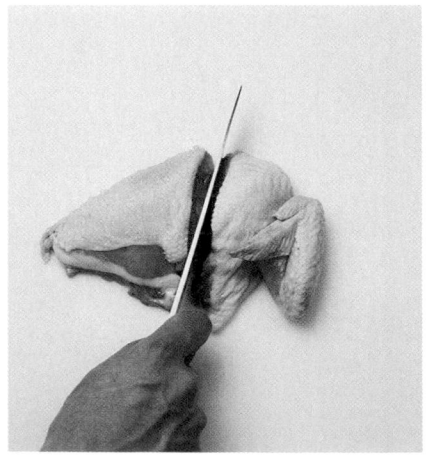

(g) Cut the breast and wing quarter into two equal pieces. (Another method is simply to cut off the wing.)

(h) The chicken cut into eighths. Note that the first joint of each wing has been cut off.

Figure 12.6 *Cutting up chickens, semiboneless.*

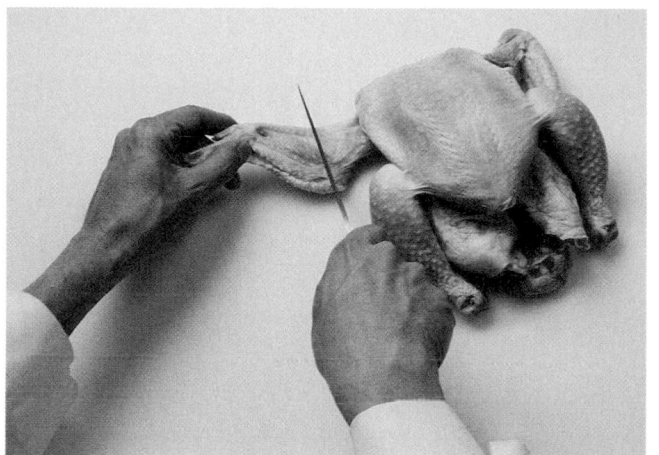

(a) Cut off the wings at the second joint. Save for stocks.

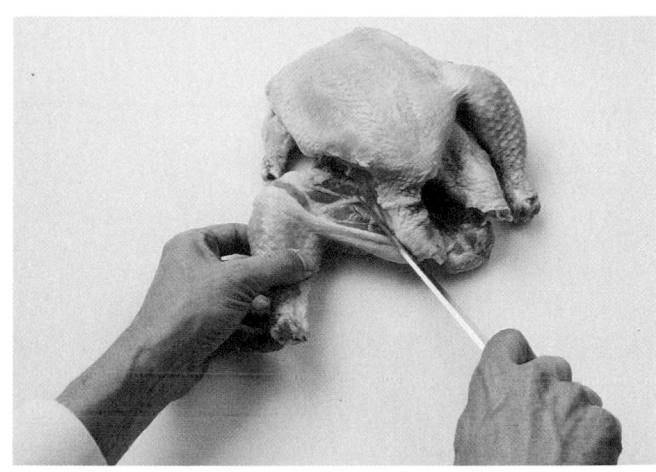

(b) Cut through skin between the leg and body.

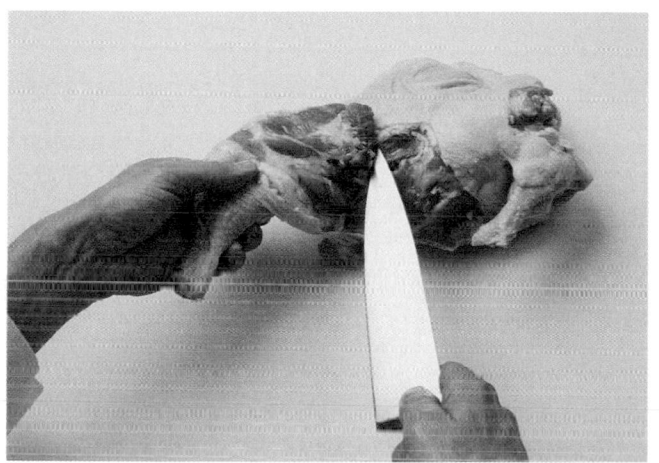

(c) Turn the chicken on its side and pull the leg back. Carefully start to cut the flesh from the bone, being sure to get the "oyster," the little nugget of tender meat in the hollow of the hip bone. Cut through the ligaments at the hip joint.

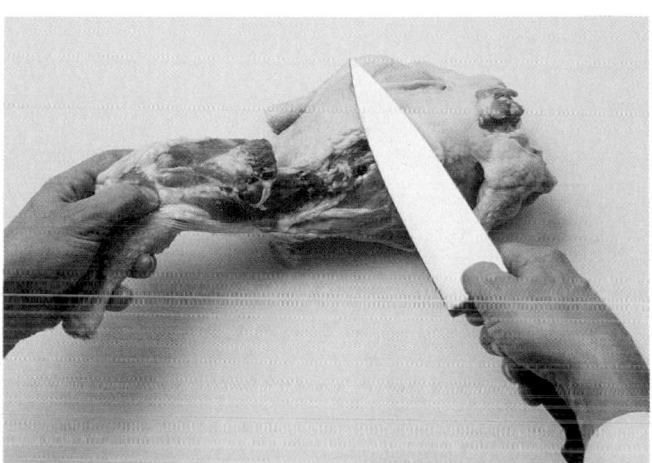

(d) Holding the chicken steady with the knife, pull off the leg. Repeat with the other leg.

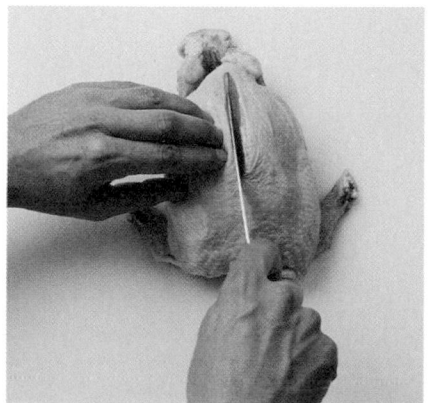

(e) Turn the breast portion upright. Cut down along one side of the ridge of the breastbone to separate the breast meat from the bone.

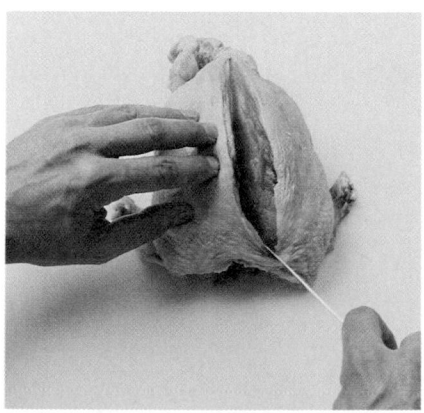

(f) Continue the cut along the wishbone to the wing joint.

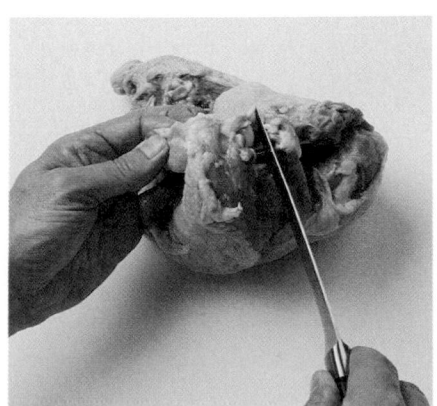

(g) Holding the chicken by the wing, cut through the wing joint.

(Continued)

Figure 12.6 (Continued)

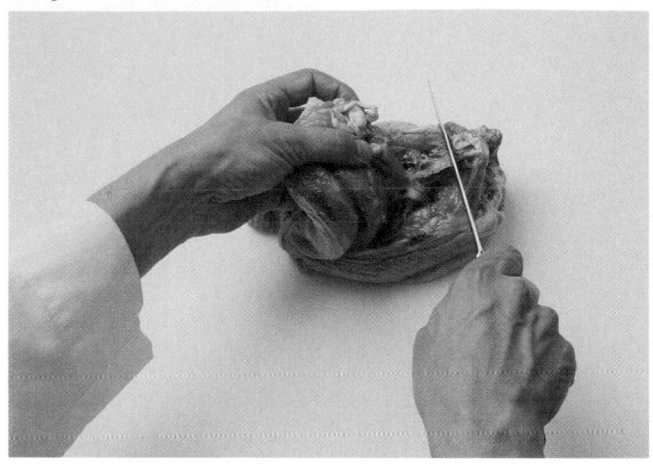

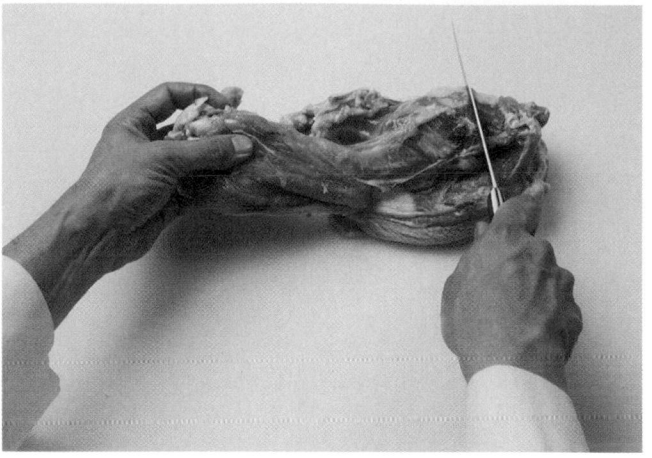

(h) Holding the carcass steady with the knife, pull back on the wing and breast meat.

(i) Pull the breast meat completely off the bone. Be sure to hold on to the small "tenderloin" muscle inside the breast so that it doesn't separate from the rest of the meat. Repeat with the other side.

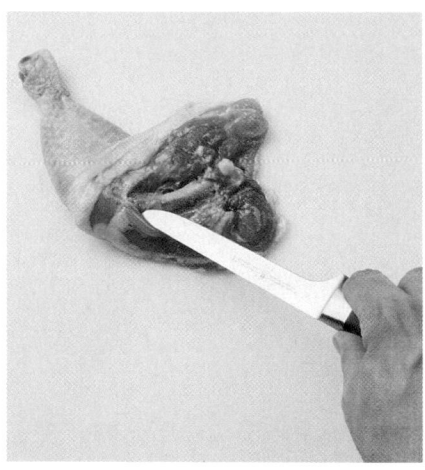

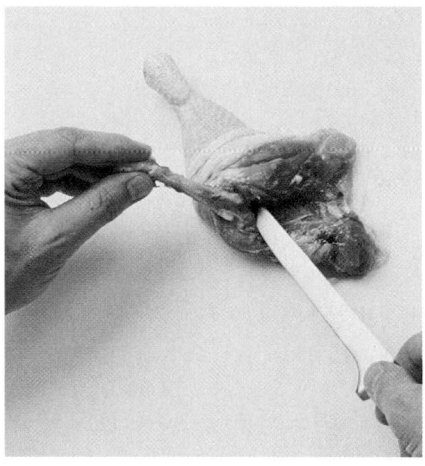

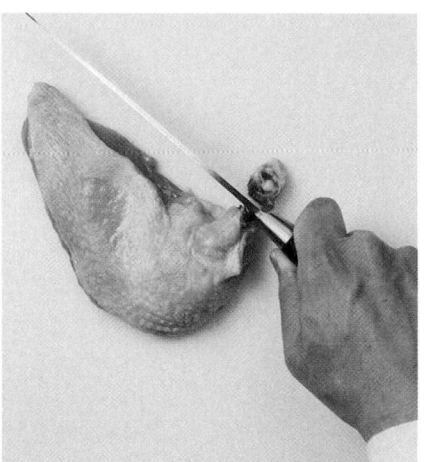

(j) If desired, remove the thigh bone. Cut down along both sides of the bone to separate it from the meat.

(k) Lift out the bone and cut it off at the joint.

(l) For a neater appearance, chop off the end of the wing bone with the heel of the knife.

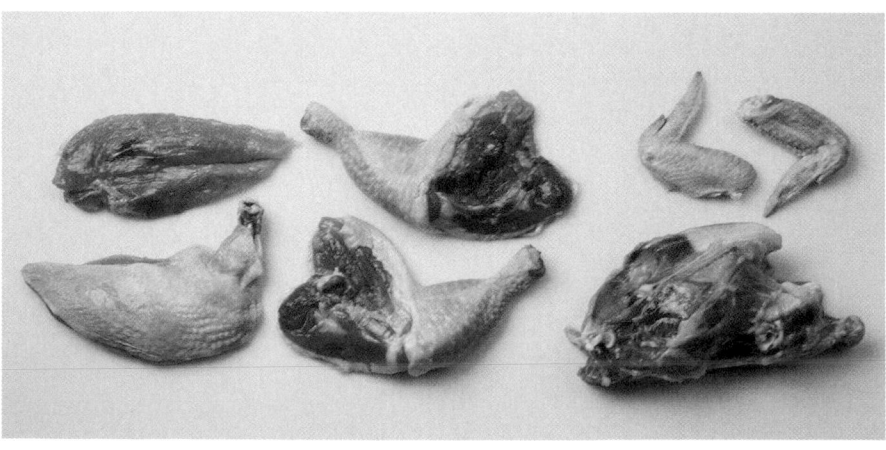

(m) The cut-up chicken. From left: breast portions without and with wing bone; leg portions without and with thigh bone; wing sections and carcass for stockpot. The drumstick and thigh (bone-in) may be cut apart at the joint, as in Figure 12.5.

Terms for Review

maturity	class	fowl	quail
light and dark meat	style	White Pekin	trussing
free-range	broiler/fryer	magret	partridge
organic	roaster	moulard	pheasant
inspection	capon	guinea	ostrich
grading	hen	squab	emu
kind			

Questions for Discussion

1. Why are hens or fowl not roasted in commercial kitchens?

2. Why is the breast section so often dry when whole chickens and turkeys are roasted? Can you suggest ways to remedy this problem?

3. Give a brief description of each of the following classes of poultry. Be sure to mention relative tenderness and approximate size.

Capon	Young tom turkey
Roaster duckling	Rock Cornish hen
Broiler/fryer	Yearling turkey
Roaster	Hen or fowl

4. How should fresh and frozen poultry be stored?

5. Describe five methods for determining doneness in poultry items.

6. What is the purpose of trussing poultry?

7. Why are most game birds better if not cooked until well done?

Cooking Poultry and Game Birds

The muscle tissue of domestic poultry and game birds, as we have said, has basically the same structure as the muscle tissue of meat animals. In particular, the breast meat of chicken and turkey is so similar to veal that they are interchangeable in many recipes.

Imaginative cooks realize that even when two meats are quite different—chicken and beef, for example—interesting new dishes can be made by making substitutions that might seem unusual. For example, it is possible to make a delicious chili from chicken or turkey meat, a preparation that has the added advantage of having a lower food cost than beef chili.

Because the basic cooking methods for poultry are the same as for meat, they are not repeated here. But you may want to review them before proceeding with any of the recipes in this chapter. Also, please review the discussion of light and dark meat (pp. 298–299) in the previous chapter, as well as the methods for testing doneness (p. 303).

Roasting and Baking

The general procedures for roasting and baking meats also apply to poultry, as illustrated by the following recipes. However, there are some differences in the ways poultry items are handled. The guidelines below should be observed.

Remember that poultry items are almost always cooked well done (except for squab and game birds).

After reading this chapter, you should be able to

1. Cook poultry by roasting and baking.

2. Cook poultry by broiling and grilling.

3. Cook poultry by sautéing, pan-frying, and deep-frying.

4. Cook poultry by simmering and poaching.

5. Cook poultry by braising.

6. Identify the safety, quality, and practicality concerns associated with preparing dressings and stuffings.

7. List basic ingredients for dressings and stuffings.

8. Prepare dressings and stuffings.

SEASONING AND BASTING

1. Seasonings and, if desired, a little mirepoix or a bouquet garni should be placed inside the cavity. You need to season the skin only if it is to be served and eaten, as the seasonings will not penetrate the skin.

2. Oil the skin before roasting to help in browning and to protect against drying. The skin may be basted with *fat only* during roasting, but this is unnecessary if the bird is roasted breast down (and turned breast up just to brown at the end of the roasting period).

   Basting is beneficial for large turkeys, which must be subjected to dry heat for several hours. If you baste large poultry during roasting, do it every 20 to 30 minutes. More frequent basting results in the loss of a great deal of heat from the oven because the door is opened so frequently.

3. Basting is unnecessary for duck and goose, which have a great deal of fat under the skin. These birds are usually roasted breast up for that reason.

TEMPERATURE

Selection of roasting temperature depends on the product being roasted.

1. *Low-temperature roasting* is best for large items such as turkeys and capons. It results in a tender juicy product. Review pages 224 and 240 for a discussion of low-temperature roasting.

   Large turkeys may be roasted at 250° to 325°F (120° to 165°C). For most operations, however, cooking times at the lower end of this range will be too long. In addition, if a turkey is stuffed (see pp. 356–357), it is not advisable to roast it at a very low temperature because the interior temperature will take too long to rise, providing a good breeding ground for bacteria.

   Some recipes call for starting large turkeys at a high temperature for 15 to 30 minutes in order to brown them. This is usually not necessary because they will likely brown anyway during the long cooking times.

   Smaller items such as roasting chickens are usually roasted at 325° to 375°F (165° to 190°C). Small items roasted at low temperatures may not brown well by the time they are done. In such cases, the heat can be turned up for a few minutes when they are almost done in order to brown them.

2. The *searing* method may be used for chickens under 4 to 5 pounds (2 kg) and for baked chicken parts. That is, start at 450°F (230°C) for 15 minutes, then reduce to 250° to 325°F (120° to 160°C). These small items cook so quickly that continuous roasting at a low temperature would produce very little browning.

   Ducks and geese also may be started at a high temperature in order to melt off some of the heavy fat layer under the skin and to make the skin brown and crisp.

3. *High-temperature roasting* is used for small items such as squab and game birds, which are often served rare. Cornish hens and other small poultry under 3 pounds (1.35 kg) may also be flash-roasted. Great care is necessary when roasting at high temperatures, however, because the poultry will quickly become overcooked if left in the oven only a few minutes too long. For example, a 2½-lb (1.2-kg) chicken or guinea hen roasted at 450°F (230°C)

may be perfectly cooked and nicely browned after 45 minutes but overcooked and dry if left another 10 minutes.

Ducks may also be roasted at a continuously high temperature (400° to 425°F/200° to 220°C) because their fat content protects them from drying. Great care should be used to prevent overcooking, however, because this can happen very quickly at these temperatures.

BAKED POULTRY

Roasting and baking are the same process. Cutting up the chicken doesn't change the cooking method. Baked chicken or turkey parts are treated like roasted poultry.

Chicken parts are sometimes coated with seasoned crumbs or flour and rolled in fat before baking. Such products are sometimes misleadingly called "oven-fried," because of their resemblance to breaded fried chicken.

Baked Chicken

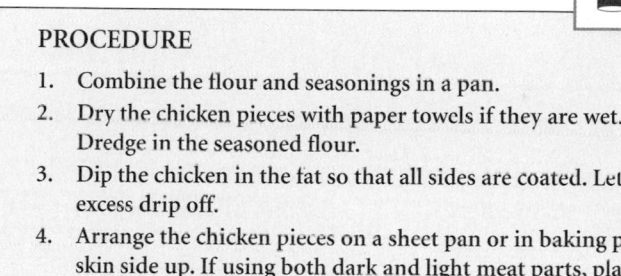

Portions: 24   **Portion size:** ¼ chicken

U.S.	Metric	Ingredients	PROCEDURE
8 oz	250 g	Flour	1. Combine the flour and seasonings in a pan.
5 tsp	25 mL	Salt	2. Dry the chicken pieces with paper towels if they are wet. Dredge in the seasoned flour.
½ tsp	2 mL	White pepper	
2 tsp	10 mL	Paprika	3. Dip the chicken in the fat so that all sides are coated. Let excess drip off.
½ tsp	2 mL	Thyme	
15 lb	7 kg	Fryer chicken parts or quarters (see note)	4. Arrange the chicken pieces on a sheet pan or in baking pans, skin side up. If using both dark and light meat parts, place them on separate pans.
1 lb	500 g	Melted butter, oil, or a mixture of butter and oil	5. Bake the chicken at 350°F (175°C) until done, about 1 hour.

Per serving:
Calories, 450; Protein, 38 g; Fat, 30 g (61% cal.); Cholesterol, 150 mg;
Carbohydrates, 6 g; Fiber, 0 g; Sodium, 590 mg.

Note: If you are starting with whole chickens, cut them into quarters or eighths, as shown in Figure 12.5. Any chicken parts may be used for this recipe. For example, you might bake just the legs and use the breasts and wings for other preparations.

VARIATIONS

Baked Herbed Chicken

Add 1 tbsp (15 mL) tarragon, 1 tsp (5 mL) marjoram, 2 tbsp (30 mL) chives, and 2 tbsp (30 mL) dry parsley to the flour mixture. Omit paprika.

Baked Rosemary Chicken

Prepare as in basic recipe. After placing chicken parts in baking pans, sprinkle with rosemary, about 4 tsp (20 mL) for 24 portions. Fifteen minutes before chicken is done, sprinkle with 3–4 oz (90–125 mL) lemon juice.

Baked Chicken Parmesan

Instead of flour for dredging, use 1 cup (100 g) parmesan cheese mixed with 1½ cups (150 g) fine dry bread crumbs. Season as in basic recipe.

Roast Chicken with Natural Gravy

Portions: 24   Portion size: ¼ chicken
                              2 oz (60 mL) jus

U.S.	Metric	Ingredients	PROCEDURE
6	6	Chickens, 3–3½ lb (1.4–1.6 kg) each	1. Remove giblets from chickens. Check inside cavities to make sure they have been well cleaned. Reserve giblets for other use.
to taste	to taste	Salt	2. Season the insides of the chickens with salt and pepper.
to taste	to taste	Pepper	3. Truss the chickens (see Figure 12.3).
as needed	as needed	Oil or butter	4. Rub the outside of the chickens with oil or butter (butter promotes faster browning). Season the skin with salt and pepper, as it will be served with the meat.
		Mirepoix:	5. Place the mirepoix in a roasting pan. Place a rack over the mirepoix, and place the chickens breast down on the rack.
6 oz	175 g	Onion, medium dice	6. Place the chickens in an oven preheated to 450°F (230°C). After 15 minutes (not longer), turn the heat down to 325°F (165°C).
3 oz	90 g	Carrots, medium dice	
3 oz	90 g	Celery, medium dice	7. When the chickens have been in the oven for 45–60 minutes, turn them breast side up. Baste with the fat in the roasting pan and finish roasting. Total cooking time is about 1½ hours.
			8. Remove the chickens from the roasting pan and hold them in a warm place for service.
3 qt	3 L	Strong chicken stock	9. Set the roasting pan on the range over high heat and brown the mirepoix well, but do not let it burn. Pour off the fat.
2 oz	60 g	Cornstarch or arrowroot	10. Add the stock to deglaze the pan. Boil until the gravy is reduced by about one-third. Degrease carefully. See Figure 13.1.
2 oz	60 mL	Cold water or stock	
to taste	to taste	Salt	11. Stir the starch with the cold water or stock. Stir it into the gravy. Bring to a boil and simmer until thickened.
to taste	to taste	Pepper	12. Strain into a bain-marie, using a china cap lined with cheesecloth. Season carefully with salt and pepper.
			13. Quarter the chickens, or carve them as shown in Figure 13.2. Serve a quarter chicken with 2 oz (60 mL) gravy.

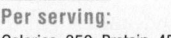

Per serving:
Calories, 350; Protein, 45 g; Fat, 17 g (45% cal.); Cholesterol, 105 mg; Carbohydrates, 2 g; Fiber, 0 g; Sodium, 140 mg.

Roast Chicken with Natural Gravy; Whipped Potatoes, Glazed Root Vegetables, Roasted Garlic, Peas

VARIATIONS

Roast Herbed Chicken

Place 3–4 parsley stems and a pinch each of tarragon and marjoram in the cavity of each bird. After turning the chicken breast up in the roasting pan, rub the skin with chopped parsley, tarragon, and marjoram.

Roast Chicken with Gravy

Save 4 oz (125 g) of the fat skimmed from the juices and make a blond roux with the fat and 4 oz (125 g) bread flour. Beat the roux into the juices and simmer until thickened.

Roast Chicken with Cream Gravy

Prepare as in basic recipe, but use only 1½ qt (1.5 L) chicken stock. Boil until reduced to 1 qt (1 L) and strain (step 9). Add 1 qt (1 L) hot milk and thicken with 8 oz (250 g) blond roux. Finish with 4 oz (125 mL) heavy cream.

Figure 13.1 Preparing pan gravy.

(a) Remove the rack of cooked poultry from the roasting pan.

(b) If the mirepoix is not already browned, set it over a burner to brown it. Degrease the pan.

(c) Deglaze the pan with stock.

(d) Bring to a simmer and cook until reduced by about one-third. Stir in a starch slurry or a roux to thicken. Simmer until the desired texture is reached.

(e) Strain the gravy.

Figure 13.2 Carving roast chicken.

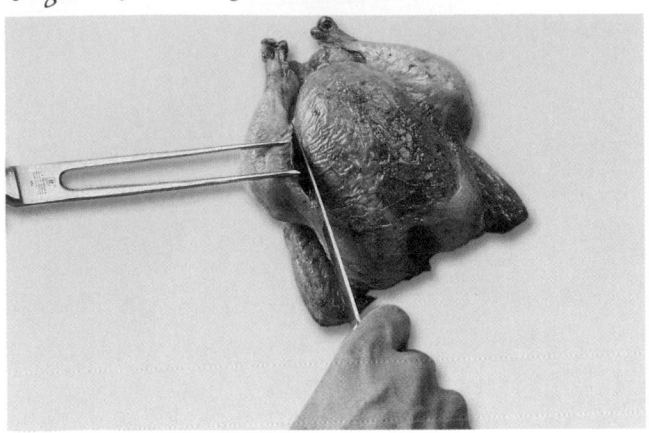

(a) Place the chicken on a clean, sanitary cutting board. Cut through the skin between the leg and the breast sections.

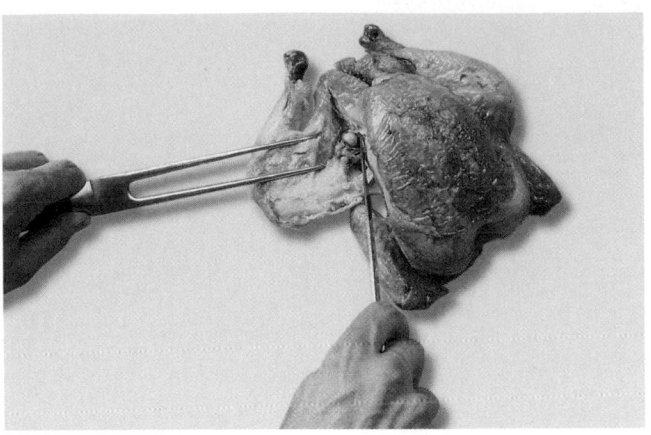

(b) Pull the leg away from the body of the chicken with the fork. Using the knife, cut between the thigh bone and the hip to separate the leg completely.

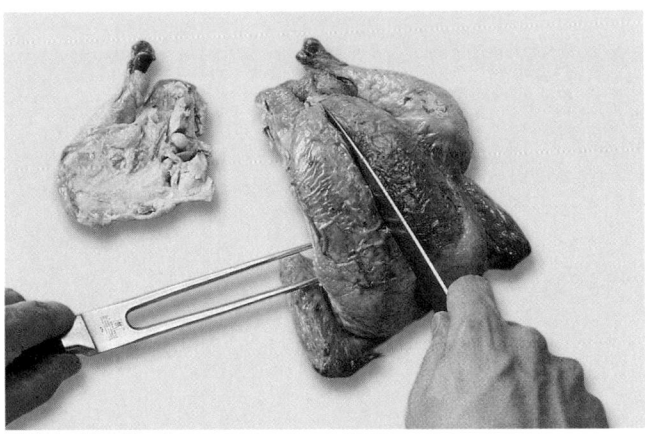

(c) Hold the chicken steady by bracing the backbone with the fork. Cut through the breast between the two halves, just to one side of the keel bone.

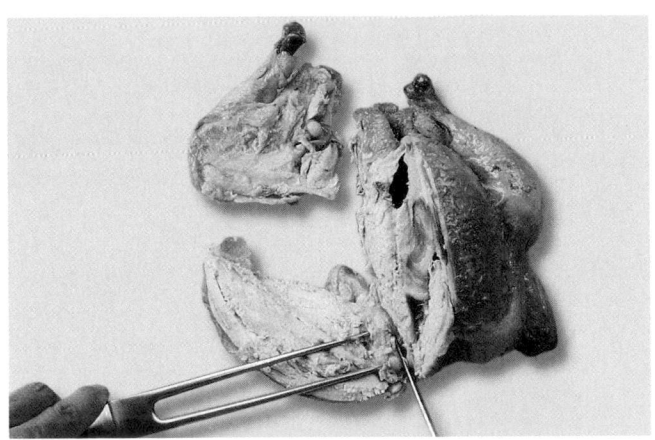

(d) Pull the breast section away from the bone. With the knife, cut through the joint where the wing bone is attached to the body. Separate the breast and wing section completely from the carcass. Repeat steps (a) through (d) on the other side of the chicken.

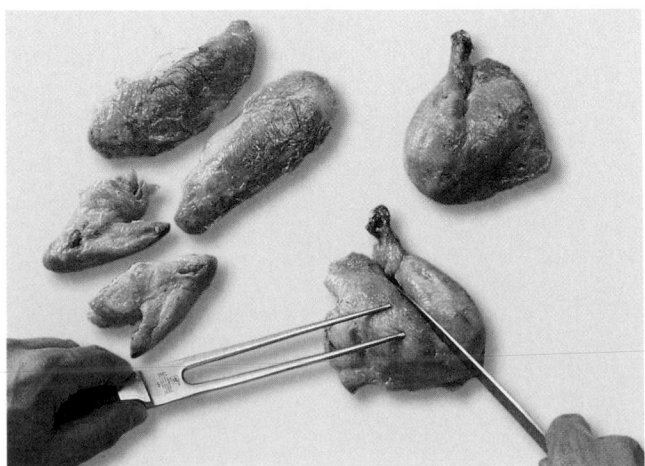

(e) Cut the wings from the breast portions and cut the drumsticks apart from the thighs.

Roast Turkey with Giblet Gravy

Yield: about 7 lb (3.5 kg) sliceable meat

	Portions:	Portion size:
	22	5 oz (150 g)
	28	4 oz (125 g)
	36	3 oz (100 g)

U.S.	Metric	Ingredients	PROCEDURE
1	1	Turkey, dressed, 20 lb (10 kg)	1. Remove the giblets from the cavity of the turkey. Check inside the turkey to make sure it has been well cleaned. Lock the wings in place by twisting the wing tips behind the back of the turkey.
to taste	to taste	Salt	2. Season the inside of the turkey with salt and pepper. Rub the skin thoroughly with oil.
to taste	to taste	Pepper	3. Place the turkey on one side in a roasting pan, on a rack if possible (see note).
as needed	as needed	Oil	4. Place in an oven preheated to 325°F (165°C). (Lower temperatures are preferable if production schedule permits. See p. 312 for explanation.)
			5. Roast for 1½ hours. Turn the turkey on the other side. Roast another 1½ hours. Baste turkey with drippings (fat only) every 30 minutes.
			6. While turkey is roasting, place turkey heart, gizzard, and neck in a saucepan. (Reserve the liver for another use, or add it to bread dressing.) Cover the giblets with water and simmer until very tender, about 2–3 hours. Reserve the broth and the giblets for gravy.
		Mirepoix:	7. Turn the turkey breast up. Place the mirepoix in the pan.
8 oz	250 g	Onions, chopped medium	8. Return the turkey to the oven and continue to roast. Baste occasionally by spooning the fat in the pan over the turkey.
4 oz	125 g	Carrots, chopped medium	9. The turkey is done when a thermometer inserted into the thickest part of the inside of the thigh reads 180°F (82°C). Total roasting time is about 5 hours. (See Chapter 12 for a discussion of how to determine doneness.)
4 oz	125 g	Celery, chopped medium	10. Remove the turkey from the roasting pan and let stand in a warm place at least 15 minutes before carving.
3 qt	3 L	Chicken stock, hot	11. Drain off and save the fat from the roasting pan.
6 oz	175 g	Bread flour	12. Set the roasting pan with the mirepoix and drippings on the range to reduce the moisture and brown the mirepoix. Brown lightly if a light gravy is desired. Brown heavily if a dark gravy is desired.
to taste	to taste	Salt	13. Deglaze the pan with about 1 quart (1 L) of the chicken stock. Pour into a saucepan with the rest of the stock and the giblet broth (from step 6). Bring to a simmer. Degrease well.
to taste	to taste	Pepper	14. Make a blond roux with the flour and 6 oz (175 g) of the fat from the roasting pan. Beat the roux into the gravy to thicken it.
			15. Simmer at least 15 minutes, until the gravy is smooth and no raw flour taste remains. Strain and season.
			16. Chop or dice the giblets very fine and add to the gravy.
			17. Slice the turkey and serve desired portion with 2 oz (60 mL) gravy. See Figure 13.3 for slicing techniques. For quantity service, see procedures demonstrated in Figure 13.4.

Per 5 ounces:
Calories, 460; Protein, 68 g; Fat, 16 g (33% cal.); Cholesterol, 135 mg;
Carbohydrates, 6 g; Fiber, 0 g; Sodium, 170 mg.

Note: Because of the difficulty of handling large turkeys, many chefs do not use a rack. Also, large turkeys are easier to turn if they are placed first on one side, then on the other, rather than breast down.

For more even cooking, separate leg and thigh sections from breast section. Roast dark and light meat on separate pans, if many turkeys are being prepared. Remove each part from oven when done.

VARIATIONS

Roast Capons and Large Chickens
Prepare like roast turkey. Reduce roasting time, depending on size of bird. A 6-lb (2.7-kg) bird requires about 3 hours at 325°F (165°C).

Roast Turkey, Chicken, or Capon with Cream Gravy
Prepare as in basic recipe, but use half stock and half milk for the gravy instead of all stock. When gravy is finished, add 8 oz (250 mL) heavy cream.

Figure 13.3 Carving roast turkey.

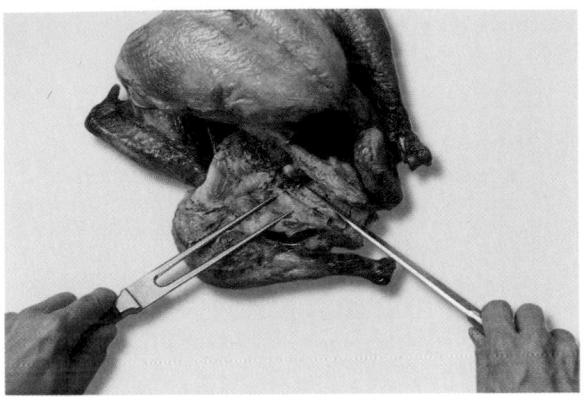

(a) Place the turkey on a clean, sanitary cutting board. Cut through the skin between the leg and the body. Pull the leg outward with a fork. The leg should pull off easily, but use the knife as necessary to separate the thigh from the hip.

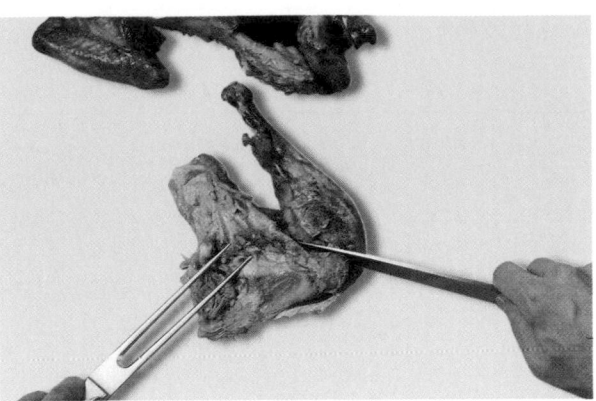

(b) Cut the drumstick and thigh apart at the joint. Repeat with the other leg.

(c) Cut the meat from the drumstick and thigh in thin slices.

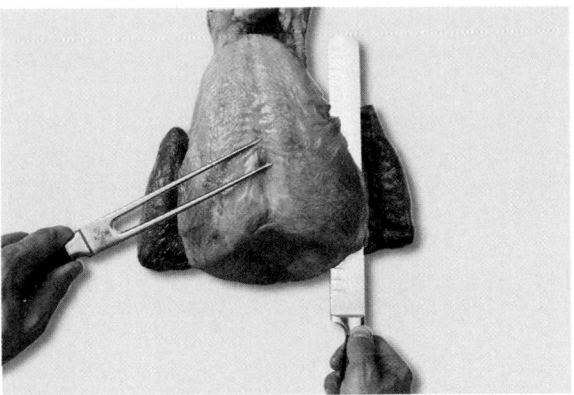

(d) Make a horizontal cut just above the wing, cutting all the way through to the bones of the body cavity. This cut helps the breast slices separate evenly.

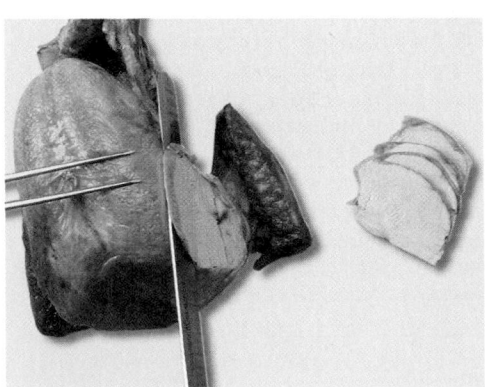

(e) With long, smooth strokes, cut the breast into thin slices.

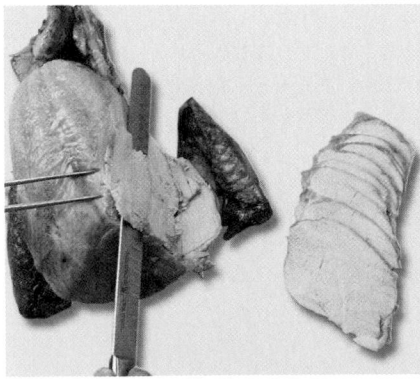

(f) When the slices become too large, change the angle of the knife slightly as shown. Continue until both sides of the breast are completely sliced.

(g) An alternative method is to cut off an entire half breast in one piece. This piece can then be sliced as shown. Cut across the grain, holding the knife at an angle to get broader slices.

Figure 13.4 Quantity service of roast turkey and dressing.

(a) Using a scoop, place measured portions of baked dressing in hotel pans as shown or on sheet pans.

(b) Place measured portions of dark meat slices on top of the mounds of dressing.

(c) Place light meat slices on last, using the best-looking slices for the tops. Cover the pans. Refrigerate if they are to be held for later service. To serve, ladle a small amount of stock over the portions to keep them moist, and reheat, covered, in a moderate oven. Ladle 2 oz (60 mL) gravy over the portions when served.

Roast Duckling with Caramelized Apples

Portions: 12   **Portion size:** ¼ duckling
                            2 oz (60 mL) sauce

U.S.	Metric	Ingredients	PROCEDURE
3	3	Ducklings, about 4½ lb (2 kg) each	1. Clean the ducklings well. Season them inside and out with salt and pepper. Place the orange zest inside the cavities. Truss the ducks.
to taste	to taste	Salt	
to taste	to taste	Pepper	2. Heat some oil in a roasting pan. Brown the ducks well. Place in an oven preheated to 425°F (220°C). Roast for 45 minutes or until done.
1 oz	30 g	Orange zest	
as needed	as needed	Oil	
2½ oz	75 g	Sugar	3. Place the sugar and vinegar in a casserole and bring to a boil. Cook until light caramel in color. Deglaze with the orange and lemon juices. Reduce until syrupy. Add two-thirds of the brown stock. Reduce by one-third.
5 oz	150 mL	Red wine vinegar	
9 oz	275 mL	Orange juice	
2½ oz	75 mL	Lemon juice	4. Once the ducks are cooked, remove and discard the excess fat in the pan. Place on the stovetop and deglaze the pan using the remaining brown stock. Add the deglazing liquid to the other sauce.
1 qt	1 L	Brown stock	
4 tsp	10 g	Potato starch	
1 oz	30 mL	Orange liqueur (optional)	
1½ oz	45 g	Orange zest, cut julienne, blanched	5. Dilute the potato starch with a little water and, if desired, the orange liqueur. Bring the sauce to a boil and add a little to the diluted potato starch before mixing into the sauce. Season and strain. Add the julienned zest.
¾ oz	25 g	Lemon zest, cut julienne, blanched	
2½ lb	1.2 kg	Apples	6. Peel, core, and slice the apples into thin wedges.
3 oz	90 g	Clarified butter	7. Heat the clarified butter in a sauté pan. Add the apples and toss until well coated. Sprinkle with the sugar and cook until lightly caramelized.
2 oz	60 g	Sugar	

Per serving:
Calories, 740; Protein, 40 g; Fat, 52 g (63% cal.); Cholesterol, 145 mg;
Carbohydrates, 28 g; Fiber, 2 g; Sodium, 200 mg

8. Remove the string from the duck and carve. Serve the sliced duck with the apples neatly arranged on the plate. Spoon the sauce around.

Duckling in Paprika

Portions: 12   Portion size: ¼ duck
                  2 oz (60 mL) sauce

U.S.	Metric	Ingredients	PROCEDURE
3	3	Ducklings, about 4½ lb (2 kg) each	1. Clean the ducklings well. Rub them with the paprika and season them inside and out with salt and pepper. Reserve any trimmings, including neck, heart, and gizzard.
4 tsp	10 g	Paprika	
to taste	to taste	Salt	2. Heat the oil in a roasting pan. Brown the ducks well. Place in an oven preheated to 425°F (220°C). Roast for 45 minutes or until done, basting often.
to taste	to taste	Pepper	
3 oz	90 mL	Oil	
4 oz	125 g	Onions, diced	3. Remove the ducks from the pan and set aside. Drain off most of the fat.
4 oz	125 g	Carrots, diced	
2½ oz	75 g	Celery, diced	4. Place the roasting pan on the stovetop and add the onions, carrots, celery, and duck trimmings. Brown the vegetables, then drain off the excess fat thoroughly.
1 tsp	3 g	Paprika	
10 oz	300 mL	White wine (see note)	5. Add the paprika. Mix well and cook for a few minutes. Deglaze with the white wine and reduce a few minutes before adding the brown stock. Reduce until thick enough to coat the back of a spoon. Skim off any fat from the surface. Strain and season.
2½ pt	1.2 L	Brown stock	
to taste	to taste	Salt	
to taste	to taste	Pepper	6. Carve the duckling and serve the sauce around.

Per serving:
Calories, 630; Protein, 40 g; Fat, 49 g (71% cal.); Cholesterol, 130 mg;
Carbohydrates, 1 g; Fiber, 0 g; Sodium, 135 mg.

Note: If you do not wish to use wine in this recipe, substitute water or stock for deglazing. Adjust the flavor balance of the finished sauce with a little fresh lemon juice.

Herb-Roasted Squab

Portions: 8   Portion size: 1 squab
                 1 oz (30 mL) jus

U.S.	Metric	Ingredients	PROCEDURE
2 tbsp	15 g	Chopped parsley	1. Mix the chopped herbs into the soft butter and season with salt and pepper.
2 tbsp	15 g	Chopped tarragon	
2 tbsp	15 g	Chopped chervil	2. Trim the squab by removing the wing tips and setting aside. Loosen the skin of the squab, being careful not to break it. Using a piping bag, pipe a small amount of the herb butter underneath the skin. Using your fingertips, spread the butter evenly under the skin. Truss for roasting.
4 oz	125 g	Soft butter	
to taste	to taste	Salt	
to taste	to taste	Pepper	
8	8	Squab	
2 oz	60 mL	Oil	3. Heat the oil in a braising pan or roasting pan. Brown the squab and finish cooking in the oven at 425°F (220°C). Start on the side and roast for about 5 minutes, then turn over onto the other leg and roast another 5 minutes. Finally, turn the *squab* on their backs and finish cooking for 10 to 20 minutes. Total cooking time for squab is about 20–30 minutes, depending on size. The breast should still be pink inside, or it will be dry.
2½ oz	75 g	Carrots, chopped	4. Remove the *squab* and set aside in a warm place. Degrease the pan and add the trimmings, carrot, onion, celery, and garlic. Cook until lightly browned. Deglaze with white wine, then add the water and bouquet garni. Reduce by two-thirds. Strain and skim. Season to taste.
2½ oz	75 g	Onions, chopped	
2 oz	60 g	Celery, chopped	
2–3 cloves	2–3 cloves	Garlic, chopped	
4 oz	125 mL	White wine	5. The squab may be served halved or whole but, in any case, remove the backbone first, using a pair of shears.
1½ pt	750 mL	Water	
1	1	Bouquet garni	
to taste	to taste	Salt	
to taste	to taste	Pepper	

Per serving:
Calories, 1120; Protein, 64 g; Fat, 94 g (76% cal.); Cholesterol, 335 mg;
Carbohydrates, 1 g; Fiber, 0 g; Sodium, 310 mg.

Breast of Guinea Fowl en Croûte with Madeira Sauce

Portions: 12   **Portion size:** ½ breast
2 oz (60 mL) sauce

U.S.	Metric	Ingredients	PROCEDURE
6	6	Guinea fowl, about 2¼ lb (1 kg) each	1. Remove and reserve the skinless, boneless breasts from the guinea fowl (see Figure 12.6). Chop the carcasses. Reserve the legs for another use.
2 oz	60 mL	Oil	
2 oz	60 mL	Butter	2. Heat the oil in a wide pan and sear the breasts for 1 minute on each side. Cool and refrigerate.
4½ oz	140 g	Shallots, chopped fine	
3 cloves	3 cloves	Garlic, crushed	3. Pour off any excess oil from the pan and heat the butter in the same pan. Sweat the shallots and garlic gently until soft. Add the chopped mushrooms. Cook until dry. Season and cool.
1 lb 8 oz	750 g	Mushrooms, chopped fine	
to taste	to taste	Salt	
to taste	to taste	Pepper	
		Sauce (see note):	4. To make the sauce, heat the remaining oil in a pan and sauté the chopped guinea-fowl bones and onions until golden brown. Pour off any excess fat and deglaze the pan with the Madeira, reducing this to a syrup. Add the stock to the pan and reduce again by 50 percent, skimming often. Strain and season.
2 oz	60 mL	Oil	
8 oz	250 g	Onions, chopped	
2½ pt	1.2 L	Madeira	
3 pt	1.5 L	Brown stock	
to taste	to taste	Salt	
to taste	to taste	Pepper	
as needed	as needed	Flour for dusting	5. Lightly dust a work surface and roll out the puff pastry about ⅛ inch (2–3 mm) thick. Cut out 12 rectangles about ½ inch (1 cm) longer than a guinea fowl breast and about 3 times the width.
2 lb 10 oz	1.2 kg	Puff Pastry (p. 855)	
2	2	Eggs	
			6. Lightly press some of the mushroom mixture on top of each breast. Wrap the breast in a rectangle of pastry, sealing the edges well. Chill for 20 minutes, then brush with beaten egg to glaze.
			7. Place the breasts on a sheet pan and bake at 400°F (200°C) for 25 minutes, checking that the bottoms are browned.
as needed	as needed	Chervil sprigs	8. Strain the sauce into a clean pan and reheat. Serve each breast with 2 oz (60 mL) sauce and garnish with sprigs of chervil.

Per serving:
Calories, 1570; Protein, 130 g; Fat, 94 g (49% cal.); Cholesterol, 420 mg;
Carbohydrates, 52 g; Fiber, 3 g; Sodium, 660 mg.

Note: As an alternative, prepare a Madeira sauce as on page 149.

VARIATION

Breast of Chicken en Croûte
Substitute chicken breast for the guinea fowl.

Smoke-Roasted Spiced Chicken Breasts with Fruit Salsa

Portions: 12   Portion size: 1 chicken breast
                                       3 oz (90 g) vegetable garnish
                                       2 oz (60 g) salsa

U.S.	Metric	Ingredients	PROCEDURE
2 tbsp	30 mL	Paprika	1. Combine the paprika, cumin, thyme, coriander, salt, and pepper.
1½ tsp	7 mL	Ground cumin	
¾ tsp	4 mL	Thyme, dried	2. Coat the chicken breasts with the spice mixture.
1½ tsp	7 mL	Ground coriander	3. Brush lightly with oil. Allow to marinate, refrigerated, for 3 to 4 hours.
1½ tsp	7 mL	Salt	
¾ tsp	4 mL	Pepper	4. Set up a smoke-roasting system as shown in Figure 4.1. Heat the pan of wood chips or sawdust on top of the stove until smoke starts to appear. Lay the chicken breasts on the rack, cover, and turn the heat to medium-low. Smoke-roast for 10 minutes.
12	12	Chicken breasts, boneless and skinless, about 5 oz (150 g) each	
as needed	as needed	Vegetable oil	5. Transfer the pan to an oven preheated to 400°F (200°C) and continue roasting for another 10 minutes.
2 lb 4 oz	1.1 kg	Wheat Berries with Pecans and Poblanos (p. 512)	6. For each portion, place a 3-oz (90-g) portion of wheat berries on the center of a plate. Slice a chicken breast on the diagonal and arrange the slices, overlapping, on top of the wheat berries. Spoon 2 oz (60 g) salsa around the chicken and wheat berries.
24 oz	725 g	Fruit Salsa (p. 164)	
as needed	as needed	Cilantro sprigs for garnish	

Per serving:
Calories, 200; Protein, 29 g; Fat, 6 g (27% cal.); Cholesterol, 80 mg;
Carbohydrates, 7 g; Fiber, 1 g; Sodium, 360 mg.

Quail Baked with Prosciutto and Herbs

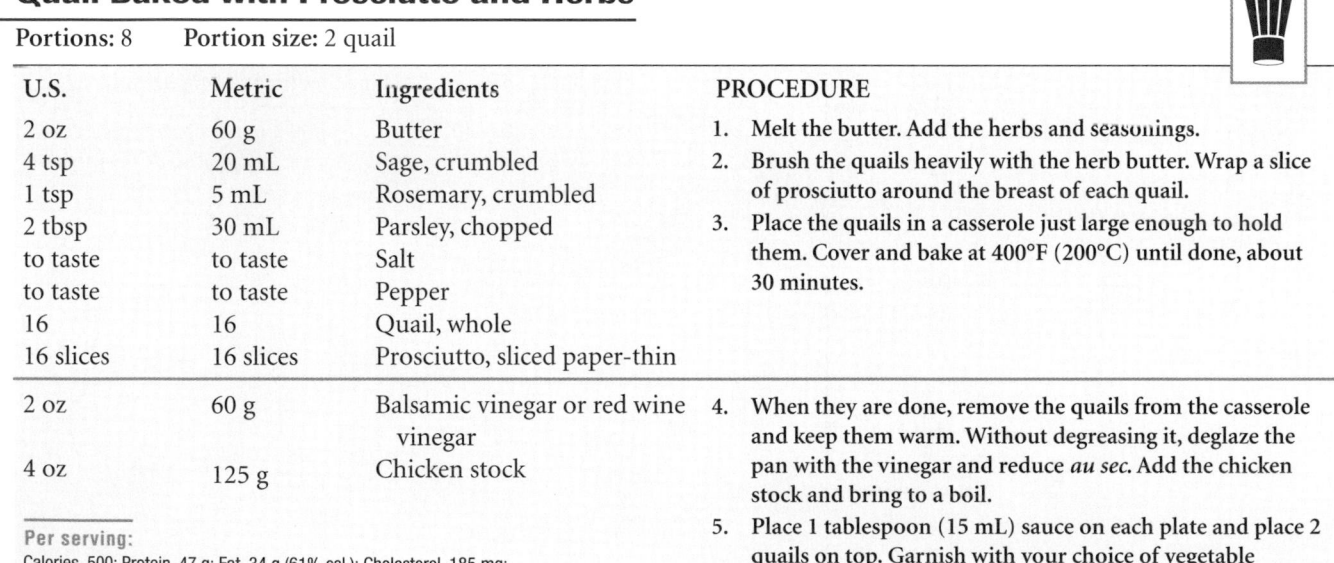

Portions: 8   Portion size: 2 quail

U.S.	Metric	Ingredients	PROCEDURE
2 oz	60 g	Butter	1. Melt the butter. Add the herbs and seasonings.
4 tsp	20 mL	Sage, crumbled	2. Brush the quails heavily with the herb butter. Wrap a slice of prosciutto around the breast of each quail.
1 tsp	5 mL	Rosemary, crumbled	
2 tbsp	30 mL	Parsley, chopped	3. Place the quails in a casserole just large enough to hold them. Cover and bake at 400°F (200°C) until done, about 30 minutes.
to taste	to taste	Salt	
to taste	to taste	Pepper	
16	16	Quail, whole	
16 slices	16 slices	Prosciutto, sliced paper-thin	
2 oz	60 g	Balsamic vinegar or red wine vinegar	4. When they are done, remove the quails from the casserole and keep them warm. Without degreasing it, deglaze the pan with the vinegar and reduce *au sec*. Add the chicken stock and bring to a boil.
4 oz	125 g	Chicken stock	
			5. Place 1 tablespoon (15 mL) sauce on each plate and place 2 quails on top. Garnish with your choice of vegetable accompaniment.

Per serving:
Calories, 500; Protein, 47 g; Fat, 34 g (61% cal.); Cholesterol, 185 mg;
Carbohydrates, 1 g; Fiber, 0 g; Sodium, 900 mg.

VARIATIONS

Chicken, squab, and guinea hens can be cooked using this recipe. Cut them into pieces, brush each piece with the herb butter, and wrap with a slice of prosciutto. If desired, the skin can be removed before the pieces are brushed with the herb butter.

Broiling and Grilling

Tender, young poultry items may be cooked on the grill or broiler using the same procedure as for steaks and chops.

Use lower temperatures than for meats. The outside can be burned easily before the inside is cooked through. Poultry skin, in particular, browns and then burns very easily. For quantity production, broiled chicken is sometimes finished in the oven on sheet pans, preferably on racks.

Start poultry pieces skin side down. This helps to keep flavorful juices from dripping out. Brush generously with melted butter or other fat before and during broiling.

Because the skin of broiled chicken is often eaten, it may be seasoned before cooking.

Large or thick poultry items are not well suited to broiling and grilling because it would take so long for the heat to penetrate to the center and cook them through. For example, turkey thighs could be broiled if you kept the heat low enough, but, in practice, this is rarely done. On the other hand, if you boned them out and flattened them lightly with a cutlet mallet, you would make them more suitable for broiling and grilling.

Grilled meat and poultry items are fairly simple, straightforward dishes, without the variety of ingredients and components that you find in, for example, stews. However, there are several ways you can give variety to grilled poultry:

1. **Marinate the poultry or rub it with seasonings before cooking.**
   Keep in mind that marinade ingredients such as sugar and tomato burn easily, so use these with care. Also, herbs on the surface of the poultry burn easily. Charred rosemary can give a pleasant aroma to the food, but herbs such as parsley, if used in large quantity and allowed to burn, may end up tasting like burned leaves.

2. **Baste with seasoned butter, marinade, or other flavorings during broiling.**
   Again, be careful with ingredients that burn easily. Use them only toward the end of cooking.

3. **Serve with an appropriate sauce or seasoned butter.**
   Flavored butters can be placed on top of the grilled poultry, but sauces should be underneath or on the side so that they don't detract from the crisp, browned skin.

4. **Select vegetable garnishes for variety and interest.**
   Well-chosen and carefully plated garnishes should be thought of as part of the whole presentation, not just as something served on the side.

Broiled Chicken

Portions: 10   Portion size: ½ chicken

U.S.	Metric	Ingredients	PROCEDURE
5	5	Broiler chickens, about 2 lb (900 g) each	1. Split the chickens in half and prepare for broiling, as shown in Figure 12.4.
4 oz	125 mL	Melted butter (or oil)	2. Brush the chickens on both sides with melted butter. Season with salt and pepper.
to taste	to taste	Salt	3. Place the chickens skin side down on broiler rack (or on grill). Broil at moderately low heat until the chicken is half cooked and well browned on one side.
to taste	to taste	Pepper	4. Turn the chickens over. (Use tongs or fork, but do not pierce the flesh with the fork.) Continue to broil until the chicken is done (no pink near thigh bone) and well browned on second side. (See first variation below for oven method.)
			5. Remove from broiler. To serve, place half a chicken on dinner plate, skin side up.

Per serving:
Calories, 600; Protein, 59 g; Fat, 39 g (60% cal.); Cholesterol, 215 mg;
Carbohydrates, 0 g; Fiber, 0 g; Sodium, 270 mg.

VARIATIONS

Broiled Chicken, Quantity Method

For large quantities, or for bigger chickens (quartered instead of halved), use slightly higher heat (set the broiler rack higher), and broil until browned on both sides, as in basic recipe. Remove from broiler and place in baking pans or on sheet pans. Finish cooking in the oven at 325°–350°F (165°–175°C).

Broiled Rock Cornish Game Hen

Remove backbones from hens and prepare for broiling (see Figure 12.4f). Broil as in the basic recipe for any of the variations. Serve 1 hen per portion.

Broiled Tarragon Chicken

Before brushing with melted butter, rub each chicken half with ¼ tsp (1 mL) tarragon and 1–2 tsp (5–10 mL) chopped fresh parsley. Broil as in basic recipe.

Chicken Paillard with Grilled Vegetables

Portions: 12   Portion size: 1 chicken breast, about 6 oz (175 g)

U.S.	Metric	Ingredients	PROCEDURE
12	12	Boneless, skinless chicken breasts, about 6 oz (175 g) each	1. Place each chicken breast between sheets of plastic film. With a meat mallet, carefully pound to a uniform thickness of about ¼ inch (6 mm).
3 cloves	3 cloves	Garlic, chopped	2. Combine the garlic, rosemary, salt, and pepper. Lightly rub the flattened chicken breasts on both sides with the mixture. Sprinkle both sides with the lemon juice, then with the olive oil. Let marinate for 2–4 hours in the refrigerator.
1 tbsp	15 mL	Fresh rosemary, chopped	
1½ tsp	7 mL	Salt	
½ tsp	2 mL	Pepper	
3 oz	90 mL	Lemon juice	3. Preheat a grill or broiler to very hot. Place the chicken breasts on the grill, skin side (that is, the side that had the skin on) down, and grill until about one-fourth done. Rotate on the grill, as in Figure 11.6, to mark. Continue to cook until about half done. Turn over and continue to grill until just cooked through.
3 oz	90 mL	Olive oil	
as desired	as desired	Grilled Vegetable Medley (p. 479)	
12	12	Fresh rosemary sprigs	4. Plate and serve at once with an assortment of grilled vegetables. Garnish each portion with a sprig of rosemary.

Per serving:
Calories, 250; Protein, 34 g; Fat, 11 g (41% cal.); Cholesterol, 95 mg;
Carbohydrates, 1 g; Fiber, 0 g; Sodium, 370 mg.

Broiled Poussin or Cornish Hens with Mustard Crust

Portions: 10   Portion size: 1 hen
                               1½ oz (40 mL) sauce

U.S.	Metric	Ingredients	PROCEDURE
10	10	Poussins or Cornish hens, about 1 lb (450 g) each	1. Lift the neck skin of each chicken and remove the wishbone by scraping the meat from the bone with a small sharp knife. Remove the backbone and split open, as shown in Figure 12.4f. Tuck each wing tip behind the breast as shown. Push a skewer through a middle wing joint, through the breast, and through the second middle wing joint. Push another skewer through from one thigh to the other. Place skin side up on an oiled tray.
8 oz	250 g	Melted butter	
to taste	to taste	Salt	
to taste	to taste	Pepper	
7 oz	225 g	Dijon mustard	2. Brush with butter (reserve remaining butter for step 3) and season with salt and pepper. Broil at a low heat to lightly color the skin. Transfer to the oven set at 375°F (180°C) and cook for 30 minutes.
4 oz	125 g	Fresh white bread crumbs	
10	10	Broiled tomato halves	3. When the Cornish hens have been in the oven for 30 minutes, spread the mustard evenly over the skin. Sprinkle with the bread crumbs and drizzle with the remaining butter. Broil (grill) at high heat to golden brown and crisp.
10 oz	300 g	Broiled mushrooms	4. Remove the chicken from the broiler, remove the skewers, and place a whole chicken on a dinner plate, skin side up. Garnish with 1 broiled tomato half and 1 oz (30 g) broiled mushrooms.

Per serving:
Calories, 920; Protein, 81 g; Fat, 60 g (59% cal.); Cholesterol, 300 mg;
Carbohydrates, 12 g; Fiber, 2 g; Sodium, 1630 mg.

Grilled Spiced Squab with Couscous and Fig Compote

Portions: 12   Portion size: 1 squab, plus garnish

U.S.	Metric	Ingredients	PROCEDURE
12	12	Whole squab	1. Split the squab for broiling, as shown in Figure 12.4f, leaving the birds in one piece.
1 tbsp	15 mL	Salt	
1 tbsp	15 mL	Quatre épices (p. 657)	2. Combine the salt, spices, and thyme. Rub the squab with the spice mixture. Refrigerate for several hours.
¾ tsp	3 mL	Thyme, dried	
¾ tsp	3 mL	Black pepper	3. Brush the squab lightly with olive oil. Place on the grill or broiler, starting skin side down. Grill or broil, turning as necessary, until the breast portion is medium rare.
as needed	as needed	Olive oil	
3 pt	750 mL	Water	4. Combine the water and salt in a saucepan and bring to a boil. Stir in the couscous. Cover and let stand for 5 minutes. Remove the cover and fluff with a kitchen fork.
1½ tsp	7 mL	Salt	
12 oz	375 g	Instant couscous (uncooked)	
1 lb	500 g	Tender, young salad greens, such as mesclun	5. Wash and drain the salad greens. Toss with the vinaigrette. Place a small mound of the greens at the top of each dinner plate. Top with the halved cherry tomatoes.
6 oz	175 mL	Basic vinaigrette (p. 572) made with red wine vinegar and olive oil	6. At the bottom center of each plate, place a small mound of couscous. In the center of the plate, above the couscous, place 1 oz (30 g) fig compote.
36	36	Cherry tomatoes, cut in half	7. Split the squabs in half. Place 1 half squab on each side of the couscous.
12 oz	360 g	Fig Compote (p. 167)	

Per serving:
Calories, 1300; Protein, 69 g; Fat, 94 g (66% cal.); Cholesterol, 325 mg;
Carbohydrates, 42 g; Fiber, 5 g; Sodium, 1180 mg.

VARIATION

Grilled Spiced Cornish Hen
Prepare and grill Cornish hens using the same procedure as in the basic recipe, except make sure that the chicken is more thoroughly cooked.

Grilled Chicken with Garlic and Ginger

Portions: 8   Portion size: approximately 12 oz (375 g), bone in

U.S.	Metric	Ingredients	PROCEDURE
6–8 lb	2.8–3.6 kg	Chicken parts or halves, or whole Cornish hens	1. Cut the chickens into parts or halves for broiling. If using Cornish hens, split down the back and flatten, or cut into halves.
6 oz	180 mL	Lemon or lime juice	2. Combine the lemon or lime juice, oil, ginger, garlic, salt, and pepper to make a marinade.
2 oz	60 mL	Vegetable oil	
1 oz	30 g	Fresh ginger, grated	3. Marinate the chicken for 3-4 hours.
2 tsp	10 mL	Garlic, chopped fine	
to taste	to taste	Salt	
to taste	to taste	Pepper	
as needed	as needed	Melted butter	4. Remove the chicken from the marinade. Broil or grill the chicken until done. Baste with the marinade several times during cooking.
to taste	to taste	Ginger oil (p. 160), optional	5. Shortly before the chicken is done, brush the pieces once or twice with melted butter.
			6. If desired, drizzle a few drops of ginger oil around the chicken after plating.

Per serving:
Calories, 430; Protein, 42 g; Fat, 27 g (59% cal.); Cholesterol, 140 mg;
Carbohydrates, 1 g; Fiber, 0 g; Sodium, 150 mg.

VARIATIONS

Substitute any of the following for the chicken parts in the above recipe or in any of the following variations:

Chicken or turkey brochettes (cubes of boneless meat on skewers)
Boneless chicken breast
Turkey cutlets (thick slices of turkey breast)
Turkey paillards (broad slices of turkey breast pounded thin)
Chicken or turkey thighs, boned out and lightly pounded

Southwestern Grilled Chicken

Substitute the following ingredients for the marinade in the basic recipe:

4 oz	120 g	Tomato, puréed
4 tsp	20 mL	Jalapeño, chopped very fine
4 tbsp	60 mL	Cilantro, chopped
3 oz	90 mL	Red wine vinegar

Spicy Barbecue Style Grilled Chicken

Substitute the following ingredients for the marinade in the basic recipe. Toss the chicken pieces by hand so that they are well coated.

2 oz	60 mL	Worcestershire sauce
1 oz	30 mL	Red wine vinegar
4 tsp	20 mL	Paprika
2 tsp	10 mL	Chili powder
1 tsp	5 mL	Dry mustard
1 tsp	5 mL	Garlic, crushed
½ tsp	2 mL	Black pepper
1 tsp	5 mL	Salt

Grilled Chicken Oriental Style

Substitute the following ingredients for the marinade in the basic recipe. Brush the chicken with the marinade frequently during grilling.

8 oz	250 mL	Soy sauce
2 oz	60 mL	Rice wine or sherry
2 oz	60 mL	Chicken stock or water
1 oz	30 mL	Lemon juice
2 tsp	10 mL	Sugar
4 tsp	20 mL	Ginger root, grated

Grilled Chicken Marinated in Yogurt and Spices

Substitute the following ingredients for the marinade in the basic recipe. Marinate the chicken overnight.

8 oz	250 g	Unflavored yogurt
2 oz	60 g	Onion, grated
½ tsp	2 mL	Garlic, crushed
½ tsp	2 mL	Ginger root, grated
1 tsp	5 mL	Ground cumin
½ tsp	2 mL	Ground cardamom
pinch	pinch	Mace
½ tsp	2 mL	Cayenne
½ tsp	2 mL	Black pepper
1 tsp	5 mL	Salt

Grilled Quail Marinated in Soy Barbecue Sauce

Portions: 12   **Portion size:** 2 quails

U.S.	Metric	Ingredients	PROCEDURE
24	24	Quails	1. Remove the backbones and split open the quails, as shown in Figure 12.4. Keep each quail in one piece.
1 qt	1 L	Soy Barbecue Sauce (p. 164)	2. Marinate the quails in the barbecue sauce for 2 hours. Drain.
			3. Place the quails on a preheated broiler or grill. Cook, turning as necessary, until they are browned and the breast meat is medium done. Do not overcook, or the breast meat will be dry.

Per serving:
Calories, 790; Protein, 58 g; Fat, 53 g (61% cal.); Cholesterol, 215 mg; Carbohydrates, 14 g; Fiber, 0 g; Sodium, 1780 mg.

Grilled Ostrich or Emu with Adobo Spices

Portions: 8   **Portion size:** 4 oz (125 g)

U.S.	Metric	Ingredients	PROCEDURE
		Spice rub:	1. Combine the ingredients for the spice rub. (*Note:* The quantities given are enough to mildly spice the meat. For a spicier product, double the quantities.)
1 tbsp	15 mL	Powdered ancho or pasilla chiles	
½ tsp	2 mL	Salt	2. Rub the spices over both sides of the steaks to lightly but evenly coat them.
¼ tsp	1 mL	Oregano	3. Refrigerate for 1 hour or longer.
¼ tsp	1 mL	Ground cumin	4. Grill or broil until medium rare or medium done, no longer.
¼ tsp	1 mL	Black pepper	5. Cut into thin slices across the grain.
8	8	Ostrich or emu steaks or fillets, 4 oz (125 g) each	

Per serving:
Calories, 130; Protein, 25 g; Fat, 3 g (21% cal.); Cholesterol, 85 mg; Carbohydrates, 0 g; Fiber, 0 g; Sodium, 230 mg.

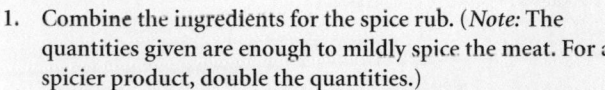

Sautéing, Pan-frying, and Deep-frying

Because chicken and turkey are lean, tender meats, cooking in fat is an appropriate and a popular way to prepare them. The procedures for sautéing and pan-frying meats apply to chicken as well. Also, please note the following guidelines that apply particularly to poultry items.

SAUTÉING

1. Boneless chicken breasts, thin slices of turkey breast, and other quick-cooking items are ideal for sautéing.

2. Larger items, such as bone-in chicken cut into eighths, are harder to cook to doneness by sautéing because they need longer cooking times. Such items are often browned by sautéing, then finished by another method, such as baking or braising.

3. In classical cuisine, there are preparations for chicken called sautés, many of which are actually made by braising. The basic procedure for sautéing meats is used, except that the chicken is only partially cooked by sautéing. It is then finished by simmering briefly in the sauce made by deglazing the pan. Recipes for this kind of preparation are included under "Braising."

PAN-FRYING

1. Pan-fried chicken is usually breaded or floured before cooking for even browning and crispness.

2. About ¼ inch (½ cm) or more of fat in the pan is needed to pan-fry chicken.

3. The side that is to be face up on the plate should be browned first for best appearance. This is called the *presentation side*. For chicken pieces, this is usually the skin side.

4. After browning on all sides over moderately high heat, lower the heat so that the chicken will cook to doneness without overbrowning. Pan-fried chicken takes about 30 to 45 minutes to cook.

DEEP-FRYING

1. The procedure for deep-frying is like that for pan-frying, except that the item doesn't have to be turned because it is submerged in the hot fat. Review page 60 for deep-frying instructions.

2. Pieces from small chickens (under 2½ lb/1 kg) are best for deep-frying. Larger pieces require such a long cooking time that the surface may brown too much.
   If necessary, fried items may be finished in the oven.

3. Fry chicken at 325° to 350°F (160° to 175°C) for even cooking.

Pan-Fried Chicken

Portions: 24   Portion size: ½ chicken
            48   ¼ chicken

U.S.	Metric	Ingredients	PROCEDURE
12	12	Chickens, 2½ lb (1.1 kg) each	1. Cut chickens into 8 pieces, as shown in Figure 12.5.
1 lb	450 g	Flour	2. Place the flour in a small hotel pan and season with salt and pepper.
5 tsp	25 mL	Salt	3. Pour about ¼ inch (½ cm) oil into enough heavy iron skillets to hold all the chicken pieces in a single layer. Heat over moderately high heat.
1 tsp	5 mL	White pepper	4. Dredge the chicken pieces in the seasoned flour and shake off excess.
			5. Place the pieces skin side down in the hot oil. Let the pieces fall away from you to avoid splashing hot oil on yourself.
			6. Fry the chicken until golden brown on the bottom. Turn the pieces with tongs and brown the other side.
			7. Lower the heat slightly to avoid overbrowning. Continue to cook the chickens, turning once or twice more, until cooked through. Breast meat cooks faster than leg meat—remove it when it is done. Total cooking time will be 20–40 minutes, depending on the size of the chickens and the temperature of the fat.
			8. Remove the chicken from the pan and drain well. Place on hot dinner plates or hold for service in counter pans. Do not cover pans or hold too long, or chicken will lose its crispness.

Per ½ chicken:
Calories, 820; Protein, 75 g; Fat, 51 g (57% cal.); Cholesterol, 235 mg;
Carbohydrates, 11 g; Fiber, 0 g; Sodium, 580 mg.

VARIATIONS

For slightly crustier, browner chicken, dip in milk before dredging in flour.

Alternative Method, Quantity Service: Brown chickens in hot oil as in basic recipe. Place on sheet pans or in baking pans skin side up, and finish cooking in a 350°F (175°C) oven.

Country-Style Fried Chicken

Fry chickens as in basic recipe. For 24 portions: Pour all but 4 oz (125 g) fat from the pans. Add 4 oz (125 g) flour and make a blond roux. Stir in 2½ qt (2.5 L) milk and bring to a boil. Stir constantly as the gravy thickens. Simmer a few minutes to eliminate all raw starch taste, and season with salt and white pepper. Adjust the consistency with stock, water, or additional milk, if necessary. Strain. Serve the chicken with gravy and mashed potatoes.

Sautéed Boneless Breast of Chicken with Mushroom Sauce

Portions: 10   Portion size: 1 chicken breast, about 4 oz (125 g)
                   2 oz (60 mL) sauce

U.S.	Metric	Ingredients	PROCEDURE
2 oz	60 g	Clarified butter	1. Add enough clarified butter to a sauté pan to just cover the bottom with a thin film. Place on the range over moderate heat.
10	10	Boneless, skinless chicken breasts from 5 chickens, 3½ lb (1.6 kg) each	2. While the pan is heating, season the chicken breasts and dredge in flour. Shake off excess flour.
to taste	to taste	Salt	3. Place the breasts in the hot pan, presentation side (that is, the side that had the skin) down.
to taste	to taste	White pepper	4. Sauté over moderate heat until lightly browned and about half cooked. The heat must be regulated so that the chicken doesn't brown too fast.
2 oz	60 g	Flour for dredging	5. Turn the chicken over and complete the cooking.
			6. Remove the chicken from the pan and place on hot dinner plates for service. Keep warm.
10 oz	300 g	Mushrooms (white), sliced	7. Add the mushrooms to the pan and sauté briefly. After a few seconds, before the mushrooms start to darken, add the lemon juice. Toss the mushrooms in the pan as they sauté.
1 oz	30 mL	Lemon juice	8. Add the suprême sauce to the pan and simmer for a few minutes, until reduced to the proper consistency. (The juices from the mushrooms will dilute the sauce.)
2½ cups	600 mL	Suprême sauce, hot	9. Ladle 2 oz (60 mL) sauce over each portion and serve immediately.

Per serving:
Calories, 360; Protein, 36 g; Fat, 20 g (51% cal.); Cholesterol, 145 mg; Carbohydrates, 8 g; Fiber, 1 g; Sodium, 200 mg.

VARIATIONS

Alternative (Quick) Method: Sauté the chicken as in basic recipe. Plate and ladle 2 oz (60 mL) prepared Mushroom Sauce (p. 147, made with suprême sauce as a base) over each portion.

Other sauces based on chicken stock may be used in place of mushroom sauce to serve with sautéed chicken breasts, including suprême, aurora, Hungarian, and ivory.

Sautéed Chicken Breast with Ivory Sauce; Broccoli, Parisienne Potatoes

Deep-Fried Chicken

Portions: 24   Portion size: ½ chicken

U.S.	Metric	Ingredients	PROCEDURE
12	12	Chickens, about 2 lb (900 g) each	1. Cut chickens into 8 pieces, as shown in Figure 12.5.
		Standard Breading Procedure (see note):	2. Set up breading station: seasoned flour, egg wash, and crumbs (see p. 121).
8 oz	250 g	Flour	3. Pass the chicken through the Standard Breading Procedure.
2 tsp	10 mL	Salt	
1 tsp	5 mL	White pepper	4. Heat the fat in a deep fryer to 325°–350°F (165°–175°C).
2	2	Eggs	5. Fry the chicken until golden brown and cooked through. Fry light meat and dark meat pieces in separate baskets, as the light meat cooks faster.
2½ cups	600 mL	Milk	
1½ lb	750 g	Dry bread crumbs	6. Remove from the fat, drain well, and serve immediately.

Per serving:
Calories, 880; Protein, 63 g; Fat, 58 g (61% cal.); Cholesterol, 205 mg;
Carbohydrates, 22 g; Fiber, 1 g; Sodium, 520 mg.

Note: Quantities given for breading materials are only guidelines. You may need more or less, depending on the shapes of the chicken pieces, the care used in breading, and other factors. In any case, you will need enough so that even the last piece to be breaded can be coated easily and completely.

VARIATION

Alternative Method: For larger chickens or for quantity service, brown the chicken in the deep fryer. Drain, place on sheet pans, and finish in the oven at 350°F (175°C).

Fried Chicken Maryland

Fry the chicken as in basic recipe. Serve each portion with the following sauce and garnish:

2 oz (60 mL) cream sauce, suprême sauce, or horseradish sauce made with béchamel, placed on the plate under the chicken

2 strips crisp bacon (p. 627), placed in a cross on top of the chicken

2 corn fritters (p. 482)

2 banana quarters, breaded and fried

Turkey Scaloppine with Shiitake Mushrooms and Roasted Shallots

Portions: 10   **Portion size:** 4 oz (125 g) plus garnish

U.S.	Metric	Ingredients
2½ lb	1.25 kg	Boneless, skinless turkey breast
15 oz	450 g	Shiitake mushrooms, caps only
to taste	to taste	Salt
to taste	to taste	White pepper
for dredging	for dredging	Flour
2 oz	60 mL	Oil
½ oz	15 g	Butter
30	30	Roasted shallots (prepared using the recipe for Roasted Winter Vegetables, p. 473)

PROCEDURE

1. Cut the turkey breast across the grain into 20 scaloppine, about 2 oz (60 g) each, using the procedure for cutting veal (Figure 11.9).
2. Lightly flatten each piece of turkey with a meat mallet.
3. Refrigerate until ready to cook.
4. Slice the mushroom caps into strips about ¼ inch (5 mm) wide.
5. Dry the meat, season it with salt and pepper, and dredge in flour. Shake off excess. (Do not do this step until immediately before cooking.)
6. Heat the oil in a large sauté pan until very hot. Add the turkey in a single layer and sauté over high heat just until lightly browned on both sides. (If necessary, sauté the meat in several batches.)
7. Remove the meat from the pan and keep warm. Drain any excess oil from the pan.
8. Add the butter to the pan. When it is hot, add the mushrooms and sauté for about 1 minute, just until the mushrooms are cooked. Adjust the seasoning.
9. Place the meat on hot dinner plates and top with the mushrooms. Arrange 3 roasted shallots on each plate.

Per serving:
Calories, 280; Protein, 31 g; Fat, 11 g (36% cal.); Cholesterol, 85 mg; Carbohydrates, 13 g; Fiber, 1 g; Sodium, 140 mg.

Turkey Scaloppine with Shiitake Mushrooms and Roasted Shallots

Quail with Balsamic Glaze

Portions: 12 (see note)   **Portion size:** 1 quail plus garnish

U.S.	Metric	Ingredients	PROCEDURE
1 pt	500 mL	Balsamic vinegar	1. Combine the balsamic vinegar and rosemary in a stainless-steel pan. Reduce to about 2 oz (60 mL), until syrupy. Strain.
½ tsp	2 mL	Rosemary, dried	
1 lb	500 g	Dried black-eyed peas	2. Soak and simmer the black-eyed peas until cooked. See page 450 for information on cooking dried beans. The black-eyed peas may be cooked ahead of time and cooled.
3 oz	90 mL	Olive oil	
1½ oz	45 mL	Lemon juice	3. Heat the olive oil in a saucepan. Add the peas and cook until heated through. Add the lemon juice. Season to taste with salt and pepper.
to taste	to taste	Salt	
to taste	to taste	Pepper	
1 oz	30 mL	Olive oil	4. In another saucepan or sauté pan, heat the olive oil and add the garlic. Cook briefly.
4 cloves	4 cloves	Garlic, chopped	
1½ lb	750 g	Swiss chard, greens only (reserve the thick stalks for another use)	5. Add the chard leaves. Stir while cooking over high heat to wilt the greens and evaporate excessive moisture. Cook just until tender.
to taste	to taste	Cayenne	6. Season to taste with cayenne, salt, and pepper.
to taste	to taste	Salt	
to taste	to taste	Pepper	
12	12	Quails	7. Cut each quail into four semiboneless parts, as shown in Figure 12.6. Leave the third wing joint in the breast sections. Season lightly with salt and pepper.
to taste	to taste	Salt	
to taste	to taste	Pepper	8. Heat the oil in a sauté pan or pans. Add the legs and pan-fry until well browned and slightly crisp on the outside.
3 oz	90 mL	Oil	
4 oz	125 mL	Balsamic vinegar	9. When the legs are almost cooked, add the breast sections, skin side down, and pan-fry until medium rare, turning as necessary to brown both sides.
12 oz	375 mL	Red Bell Pepper Coulis (p. 161)	
			10. Remove the quail from the pan and degrease. Return to the pan and add the balsamic vinegar (not the reduced vinegar from step 1). Cook over moderate heat, turning the pieces until they are lightly glazed.
			11. For each portion, make a bed of Swiss chard on the center of the plate. Top with black-eyed peas. Arrange 2 leg portions and 2 breast portions on top of the peas.
			12. Drizzle 1 oz (30 mL) coulis around the arrangement. Then drizzle 1 tsp (5 mL) reduced balsamic glaze around the arrangement.

Per serving:
Calories, 600; Protein, 37 g; Fat, 36 g (54% cal.); Cholesterol, 110 mg; Carbohydrates, 33 g; Fiber, 5 g; Sodium, 200 mg.

Note: One quail per portion is suitable for a first-course portion. For main courses, use 2 quails per portion.

Chicken Sauté with Tomatoes and Mushrooms

Portions: 12   Portion size: ½ chicken

U.S.	Metric	Ingredients	PROCEDURE
3	3	Chickens, about 2¾ lb (1.3 kg) each	1. Cut each chicken into 8 pieces, reserving and chopping the backbone and wingtips.
2½ qt	2.4 L	Brown stock	2. Roast the reserved bones in a moderately hot oven until golden brown. Degrease the pan and deglaze with a little of the stock. Place the bones and the deglazing liquid with the bouquet garni in a deep pan with the remaining stock and cook for approximately 1 hour.
1	1	Bouquet garni	
3 oz	90 g	Beurre manié	
			3. Remove and discard the bones from the pan and lightly thicken the liquid with the beurre manié. Cook for a further 10 minutes before straining.
6 oz	175 g	Shallots, chopped fine	4. In another pan, sweat the shallots, garlic, and mushrooms in the butter until soft. Deglaze the pan with cognac and wine, then reduce by half. Add the tomato paste and mix. Pour in the strained, thickened stock and simmer 10 minutes. Season to taste.
3 cloves	3 cloves	Garlic, chopped	
1½ lb	750 g	Button mushrooms, sliced thin	
2 oz	60 g	Butter	
3⅓ oz	100 mL	Cognac or brandy	
10 oz	300 mL	White wine	
3 oz	90 g	Tomato paste	
to taste	to taste	Salt	5. Season and sauté the chicken pieces slowly in a little oil in a shallow pan until golden on all sides, particularly the skin side, in order to melt the fat and crisp the skin. This must be done slowly so that the chicken can be cooked completely without scorching.
to taste	to taste	Pepper	
as needed	as needed	Oil	
6 slices	6 slices	Firm white bread	
as needed	as needed	Clarified butter	
as needed	as needed	Water or stock	6. To prepare the garnish, cut the slices of bread into heart shapes with a cutter (or see Figure 24.7) and fry until golden.
1½ lb	750 g	Tomato concassé	
2 oz	60 g	Fines herbes: chopped parsley, tarragon, and chervil	7. When the chicken pieces are cooked, remove and drain. Degrease the pan and deglaze with a little water or stock and strain into the sauce. Finish the sauce with the tomato concassé and fines herbes. Serve 2 chicken pieces on each plate with the sauce around, garnishing with the potatoes and croutons.
48 pieces	48 pieces	Cocotte Potatoes (p. 499)	

Per serving:
Calories, 810; Protein, 50 g; Fat, 36 g (40% cal.); Cholesterol, 160 mg; Carbohydrates, 66 g; Fiber, 7 g; Sodium, 480 mg.

Chicken Pojarski Princesse

Portions: 12   Portion size: 2 pieces, 2 oz (55 g) each

U.S.	Metric	Ingredients	PROCEDURE
2 lb 4 oz	1 kg	Chicken breast, boneless and skinless	1. Ensure the chicken is thoroughly trimmed of all tendons. Chop finely, either by hand or in a grinder fitted with a large plate. Do not use a food processor, as it will not create the proper texture.
15 oz	450 mL	Heavy cream	2. Mix the cream into the chicken, adding a little at a time, only as fast as it is absorbed. Season well with salt and pepper. The mixture will be very soft. Keep it as cold as possible. (Test the seasoning by pan-frying a small bit and tasting.)
to taste	to taste	Salt	
to taste	to taste	Pepper	
7 oz	200 g	Fresh white bread crumbs	3. Divide the mixture into 24 equal amounts and drop each into the bread crumbs, rolling to cover completely. Mold, while still in the bread crumbs, into cutlet shapes.
as needed	as needed	Oil or clarified butter	
12 oz	350 g	Asparagus tips, cooked	4. Fry the cutlets gently in the clarified butter or oil until golden brown. Allow 2 pieces per person and serve garnished with the asparagus tips.

Per serving:
Calories, 190; Protein, 4 g; Fat, 16 g (75% cal.); Cholesterol, 50 mg; Carbohydrates, 8 g; Fiber, 1 g; Sodium, 80 mg.

Sautéed Chicken Breasts with Lemongrass and Three Peppers

Portions: 12   Portion size: 1 chicken breast
4 oz (125 g) vegetable garnish
2½ oz (75 mL) sauce

U.S.	Metric	Ingredients	PROCEDURE
2 stalks	2 stalks	Lemongrass	1. Cut the bulbous bases (the bottom 2½–3 inches/5–7 cm) from the lemongrass; discard the tops. Crush the lemongrass bases and chop fine. Tie in a square of cheesecloth (see note).
2 oz	50 mL	Olive oil	
12 oz	350 g	Yellow pepper, cut brunoise	
12 oz	350 g	Green pepper, cut brunoise	2. Heat the olive oil in a saucepan over moderate heat. Add the brunoise of peppers. Sauté briefly.
12 oz	350 g	Red pepper, cut brunoise	
1 oz	30 g	Garlic, chopped fine	3. Add the garlic, onion, ginger, cilantro, and the sachet of lemongrass. Sauté briefly.
7 oz	200 g	Onion, chopped fine	
1½ oz	40 g	Fresh ginger, chopped fine	4. Mix in the dry mustard and add the chicken stock. Simmer for 20 minutes.
2 oz	50 g	Cilantro, chopped fine	
4 tsp	10 g	Dry mustard	5. Strain the vegetables, reserving both the vegetables and the cooking liquid. Discard the lemongrass.
1 pt 4 oz	600 mL	Chicken stock	
12	12	Boneless chicken breasts, about 7 oz (200 g) each	6. Season the chicken breasts with salt and pepper.
			7. Over moderate heat, pan-fry the chicken breasts in clarified butter until well browned and cooked through. (Alternatively, brown them on top of the stove, then finish cooking them in a hot oven.)
to taste	to taste	Salt	
to taste	to taste	Pepper	
3 oz	90 g	Clarified butter	
5 oz	150 g	Peanut butter	8. Place the reserved cooking liquid from step 5 in a blender. Add the peanut butter and blend to mix well.
5 oz	150 mL	Peanut oil or sesame oil	
to taste	to taste	Salt	9. Add the oil and blend until emulsified. Add salt and pepper to taste.
to taste	to taste	Pepper	
			10. To serve, make 3 quenelles, about 1 oz (40 g) each, of the vegetable garnish (see Figure 24.8) and place at the top of a dinner plate. Slice the chicken breast and fan out with a little sauce just below.

Per serving:
Calories, 610; Protein, 48 g; Fat, 41 g (61% cal.); Cholesterol, 140 mg;
Carbohydrates, 12 g; Fiber, 2 g; Sodium, 230 mg.

Note: Most lemongrass is too fibrous to be eaten, so it must be removed after it has been used as seasoning. If you have access to tender, edible lemongrass, simply chop it fine and add it with the other chopped herbs.

Sautéed Chicken Breast with Lemongrass and Three Peppers

Goujons of Chicken in Salad with Sesame Seeds

Portions: 12   **Portion size:** 4 oz (125 g) meat
2½–3 oz (80 g) salad/garnish

U.S.	Metric	Ingredients	PROCEDURE
3½ lb	1.6 kg	Chicken breast, skinless and boneless	1. Prepare the chicken by cutting into strips (*goujons*).
9 oz	275 mL	Sesame oil	2. Mix the sesame oil, vinegar, soy sauce, ginger root, and garlic together in a bowl. Add the strips of chicken and stir well to coat. Cover and marinate while preparing the remaining ingredients
1½ oz	40 mL	Cider vinegar	
4 tsp	20 mL	Soy sauce	
3½ oz	100 g	Ginger root, peeled, chopped fine	
12 cloves	12 cloves	Garlic, crushed	
		Sauce:	3. Process all the sauce ingredients in a blender or food processor until smooth.
3 cloves	3 cloves	Garlic	
2 oz	60 g	Ginger root, peeled, chopped fine	
10 oz	300 mL	Light soy sauce	
6 oz	175 mL	Sesame oil	
pinch	pinch	Sugar	
1 lb	500 g	Carrots, cut batonnet	4. For the garnish, put the carrots into a pan and just cover with water. Add the honey and simmer until the water has evaporated and the carrots are tender and lightly caramelized. Allow to cool.
2 oz	20 mL	Honey	
10 oz	300 g	Flour, seasoned with salt and pepper	5. Remove the strips of chicken from the marinade and dry on paper towels. Toss in seasoned flour, beaten eggs, and then the sesame seeds. Deep-fry in hot oil.
3	3	Eggs, beaten	6. Separate the lettuce leaves and wash. Dress the lettuce with a little sauce and place in the center of individual plates. Top with the remaining sauce and the cooked goujons and carrots. Garnish with cilantro leaves.
10 oz	300 g	Sesame seeds	
2 heads	2 heads	Boston lettuce	
as needed	as needed	Cilantro for garnish	

Per serving:
Calories, 600; Protein, 33 g; Fat, 41 g (61% cal.);
Cholesterol, 80 mg; Carbohydrates, 27 g; Fiber, 4 g;
Sodium, 1280 mg.

Goujons of Chicken in Salad with
Sesame Seeds

Chicken Stir-Fry with Walnuts

Portions: 12   Portion size: 6 oz (175 g)

U.S.	Metric	Ingredients	PROCEDURE
2½ lb	1.2 kg	Boneless, skinless chicken meat	1. Remove all fat from the chicken. Cut into ½-inch (1-cm) dice.
1 lb	450 g	Green or red peppers	2. Cut the peppers in half and remove the core and seeds. Cut into strips ¼ inch (½ cm) wide.
1 lb	450 g	Scallions	3. Cut off the roots and withered parts of the green tops of the scallions. Split the scallions in half lengthwise and cut into 1-inch (2½-cm) pieces. Combine with the green peppers.
3 tbsp	45 mL	Cornstarch	
4 oz	125 mL	Soy sauce	4. Stir the cornstarch with the soy sauce until smooth.
4 oz	125 g	Walnut pieces (or unsalted peanuts)	5. Have the remaining ingredients ready in separate containers. Everything must be ready before starting to cook because cooking takes only a few minutes.
¼ tsp	1 mL	Ground ginger	
⅛ tsp	0.5 mL	Cayenne	
1½ cups	350 mL	Chicken broth or water	
2 oz	60 mL	Oil	6. Heat half the oil in a large sauté pan or skillet until very hot, almost smoking.
			7. Add the peppers and scallions and sauté rapidly for about 2 minutes, until the vegetables are only slightly cooked. Remove from the pan.
			8. Add the remaining oil to the pan and again get it very hot.
			9. Add the chicken and sauté rapidly until no longer pink. If the chicken sticks to the pan, use a spatula to stir.
			10. Add the nuts, ginger, and cayenne and sauté another minute.
			11. Quickly stir the cornstarch mixture (the starch settles out) and add it and the stock or water to the pan. Stir to deglaze the pan and bring to a simmer.
			12. Add the sautéed vegetables and simmer just until heated through. Correct the seasonings.
			13. Serve immediately with boiled or steamed rice.

Per serving:
Calories, 270; Protein, 22 g; Fat, 16 g (53% cal.); Cholesterol, 60 mg;
Carbohydrates, 10 g; Fiber, 2 g; Sodium, 610 mg.

Chicken Breasts Parmesan

Portions: 10   Portion size: 1 chicken breast, about 4 oz (125 g)

U.S.	Metric	Ingredients	PROCEDURE
3 oz	90 g	Flour	1. Place the flour in a small counter pan and season with salt and white pepper.
1 tsp	5 mL	Salt	
½ tsp	2 mL	White pepper	2. Beat the eggs in a bowl and mix in the parmesan cheese and milk. Place the bowl next to the seasoned flour when ready for service.
4	4	Eggs	
3 oz	90 g	Parmesan cheese	
1 oz	30 mL	Milk	
10	10	Boneless, skinless chicken breasts from 5 chickens, 3½ lb (1.6 kg) each	3. Flatten the chicken breasts lightly with a meat mallet.
			4. If cooking to order, select a sauté pan just large enough to hold in a single layer the number of portions being cooked. If cooking all the chicken breasts at once, use a very large skillet or enough sauté pans to hold all the breasts in a single layer.
4 oz	125 mL	Clarified butter	5. Place the pan (or pans) over moderate heat and add enough clarified butter to just cover the bottom.
			6. Dip the chicken breasts in the flour and shake off excess. Dip in the cheese batter, turning the pieces to coat both sides.
			7. Cook over moderate heat until the bottom is golden. Turn the pieces over. Reduce the heat to low and continue to cook until the chicken is cooked through. It should feel somewhat firm when done.
20	20	Lemon slices	8. Place each portion on a hot plate and top with 2 lemon slices. Serve immediately.

Per serving:
Calories, 350; Protein, 40 g; Fat, 18 g (47% cal.); Cholesterol, 190 mg;
Carbohydrates, 5 g; Fiber, 0 g; Sodium, 510 mg.

VARIATION

Alternative Method: As soon as the first side is browned, turn the pieces over, cover the pans, and place in an oven at 350°F (175°C) for 8–10 minutes. This procedure requires less attention from the cook, an advantage in a busy kitchen.

Simmering and Poaching

Simmering and poaching are both methods of cooking in a liquid. The major difference is the temperature. In simmering, the liquid is a little below the boiling point and bubbling very gently. In poaching, the temperature is even lower, and the liquid is not really bubbling. Also, less liquid is usually used for poaching.

SIMMERING

1. The simmering method is used to cook fowl and other tough items, which require long cooking in moist heat to be made tender. Cooking time is about 2½ hours.
2. The cooking liquid is usually water, seasoned with salt and, most often, with mirepoix and herbs.
3. Simmered fowl yields a rich, flavorful broth. The meat can be used for soups, creamed dishes, casseroles, salads, and similar preparations.
4. Start the fowl in *cold water* if a flavorful soup is your main objective. Start with *hot water* to retain more flavor in the meat.

POACHING

1. The poaching method is used to gently cook tender poultry in order to retain moisture and to develop a light, subtle flavor. Cooking time is usually short because the product is naturally tender.
2. The cooking liquid is usually stock, sometimes with the addition of wine and other flavorings and seasonings. Cold liquid is added to the poultry product in the pan to cover partway, and the pan must be covered to retain steam. Covering also helps to prevent drying and discoloration.
3. After cooking, the liquid may be used to make a sauce, such as suprême sauce, to serve with the cooked product.
4. It is important to drain the poultry well after cooking, or any remaining liquid may spoil the appearance of the sauce on the plate.
5. Poaching may be done on the rangetop or in the oven. Oven poaching provides more even heat.

"Boiled" Fowl

This preparation and the variation that follows are usually not served as is. Instead, they are the basis for several of the other recipes in this section that call for simmered or cooked chicken or turkey and for chicken or turkey stock or velouté. The cooked meat can also be used for chicken or turkey salads.

Yield: about 4½–5 lb (2–2.3 kg) cooked meat

U.S.	Metric	Ingredients	PROCEDURE
3	3	Fowls, about 5 lb (2.3 kg) each	1. Truss the fowls. This step is optional but recommended because it keeps the chicken from falling apart, especially if you are cooking more than one in the pot.
		Mirepoix:	
8 oz	250 g	Onion, coarsely chopped	2. Place the fowls in a stockpot.
4 oz	125 g	Celery, coarsely chopped	3. Add boiling water to cover and return to a boil. Skim the scum carefully.
4 oz	125 g	Carrots, coarsely chopped	
		Sachet:	4. Add the mirepoix and sachet.
1	1	Bay leaf	5. Simmer until the fowls feel tender when pressed on the thigh, about 2½ hours.
6	6	Parsley stems	
¼ tsp	1 mL	Peppercorns	6. If the meat and broth are to be used immediately for another preparation, remove the fowl from the liquid. Place in another pan and keep covered until needed. Strain the broth.
2	2	Whole cloves	
1 tsp	5 mL	Salt	7. If the meat and broth are not needed right away, leave the fowls in the broth and cool quickly in a cold-water bath, as for cooling stocks (pp. 129–130). When completely cool, remove the fowls and refrigerate, covered. Strain the broth and refrigerate.

Per 1 ounce:
Calories, 70; Protein, 10 g; Fat, 2.5 g (36% cal.); Cholesterol, 30 mg;
Carbohydrates, 0 g; Fiber, 0 g; Sodium, 65 mg.

8. To use, disjoint the fowls, remove all bones and skin, and dice or cut as required.

VARIATION

Simmered Chicken or Turkey

Simmer young chickens or turkey as in basic recipe. They may be whole or disjointed. A 3-lb (1.4-kg) chicken will take about 45–60 minutes. Turkey will take about 1½–3 hours, depending on size. Do not overcook young poultry, and do not let the liquid boil.

Chicken or Turkey Pot Pie

Portions: 25   **Portion size:** 3 oz (90 g) meat
2 oz (60 g) vegetables
4 oz (125 mL) sauce

U.S.	Metric	Ingredients	PROCEDURE
5 lb	2.3 kg	Cooked chicken or turkey meat (light and dark meat)	1. Cut the chicken or turkey into ¾-inch (1-cm) dice.
12 oz	350 g	Potatoes, medium dice	2. Cook the vegetables separately in boiling salted water. Drain and cool.
12 oz	350 g	Carrots, medium dice	3. Season the velouté to taste with salt and pepper. Add the tarragon.
12 oz	350 g	Tiny white onions, peeled	
12 oz	350 g	Peas	4. Prepare the pastry and cut out circles to cover the tops of casserole serving dishes. You will need about 2 oz (60 g) pastry per portion.
3 qt	3 L	Chicken velouté	
to taste	to taste	Salt	5. Divide the light and dark meat evenly among individual serving casseroles (3 oz/90 g per portion).
to taste	to taste	Pepper	
2 tsp	10 mL	Tarragon, dried	6. Divide the vegetables evenly among the casseroles (about ½ oz/15 g per portion of each vegetable).
25	25	Flaky pie pastry covers (p. 844)	
			7. Ladle about 4 oz (125 mL) velouté into each casserole.
			8. Top the dishes with the pastry. Cut holes in the centers to allow steam to escape.
			9. Place the dishes on a sheet pan. Bake at 400°F (200°C) until the crust is well browned.

Per serving:
Calories, 520; Protein, 25 g; Fat, 32 g (55% cal.); Cholesterol, 80 mg;
Carbohydrates, 34 g; Fiber, 5 g; Sodium, 430 mg.

VARIATIONS

Vegetable ingredients may be varied as desired. Other vegetables that may be used include celery, mushroom caps, and lima beans.

Chicken or Turkey Stew

Prepare the meat, vegetables, and velouté as in basic recipe. Omit pastry. Combine the ingredients in a saucepot and bring to a simmer. Hold for service.

Poached Chicken Breast Princesse

Portions: 24   Portion size: ½ chicken breast
2 oz (60 mL) sauce, plus garnish

U.S.	Metric	Ingredients	PROCEDURE
24	24	Boneless, skinless half chicken breasts from 12 chickens, 3 lb (1.2 kg) each	1. Select a baking pan just large enough to hold the chicken breasts in a single layer. Butter the inside of the pan.
as needed	as needed	Butter	2. Season the chicken breasts with salt and pepper. Place them in the pan, presentation side (that is, the side that had the skin on) up.
as needed	as needed	Salt	
as needed	as needed	White pepper	3. Sprinkle with the lemon juice and add enough chicken stock to barely cover the chicken.
¼ cup	60 mL	Lemon juice	4. Cover the chicken with a buttered piece of parchment or waxed paper.
1½ qt (approximately)	1.5 L (approximately)	Chicken stock, cold	5. Bring to a simmer on top of the stove. Finish poaching in a 325°F (165°C) oven or over low heat on the stove. Cooking time will be 5–10 minutes.
			6. Remove the chicken breasts from the liquid. Place them in a hotel pan, cover, and keep them warm.
		Beurre manié:	7. Reduce the poaching liquid over high heat to about 2½ pt (1.1 L).
3 oz	90 g	Butter, softened	8. Knead the butter and flour together to make a beurre manié (p. 138).
3 oz	90 g	Flour	
2½ cups	600 mL	Heavy cream, hot	9. With a wire whip, beat the beurre manié into the simmering stock to thicken it. Simmer a minute to cook out any starchy taste.
to taste	to taste	Salt	10. Add the hot cream to the sauce. Season to taste.
72	72	Asparagus tips, cooked, hot	11. Place each chicken breast, well drained, on a plate and coat with 2 oz (60 mL) sauce. Garnish with 3 asparagus tips. Serve immediately.

Per serving:
Calories, 330; Protein, 37 g; Fat, 17 g (47% cal.); Cholesterol, 140 mg; Carbohydrates, 6 g; Fiber, 1 g; Sodium, 140 mg.

VARIATIONS

Alternative Method: Poach the chicken as in basic recipe. Plate immediately and coat with prepared suprême sauce. Save poaching liquid for next day's sauce.

Other sauces may be used to coat poached chicken breasts, including:

Allemande
Aurora
Hungarian
Ivory
Mushroom

Poached Chicken Breast Florentine

Poach the chicken as in basic recipe. Place each portion on a bed of buttered spinach (well drained). Coat with Mornay sauce. *Optional:* Sprinkle with parmesan cheese and brown under the broiler.

Chicken Blanquette I

Portions: 25   **Portion size:** 5 oz (150 g)

U.S.	Metric	Ingredients	PROCEDURE
5 lb	2.5 kg	Cooked chicken meat, 1-inch (2½-cm) dice	1. Combine the chicken with the sauce and bring to a simmer.
2½ pt	1.1 L	Chicken velouté	2. Remove from the heat. Beat the egg yolks and cream together. Temper with a little of the hot sauce, and stir into the sauce.
		Liaison:	
5	5	Egg yolks	3. Return the pot to the heat and bring to just below the simmer. Do not boil.
1 pt	500 mL	Heavy cream	
to taste	to taste	Lemon juice	4. Season to taste with a few drops of lemon juice and a pinch each of nutmeg, white pepper, and salt.
pinch	pinch	Nutmeg	
pinch	pinch	White pepper	
pinch	pinch	Salt	

Per serving:
Calories, 240; Protein, 21 g; Fat, 16 g (60% cal.); Cholesterol, 135 mg;
Carbohydrates, 3 g; Fiber, 0 g; Sodium, 160 mg.

VARIATIONS

Chicken Blanquette II

Follow the recipe for Veal Blanquette, page 279. Use 12 lb (6 kg) disjointed chicken (raw) in place of the 10 lb veal. Use chicken stock instead of veal stock.

Chicken Blanquette à l'Ancienne (Ancient Style)

Garnish each portion with 2 cooked pearl onions and 1 cooked mushroom cap, fluted if possible (see p. 705).

Chicken Blanquette Brunoise

Add to the sauce: 4 oz (125 g) each of carrot, celery, and leeks or onions, all cut brunoise and sautéed lightly in butter.

Chicken Blanquette Argenteuil

Garnish each portion with 3 cooked asparagus tips.

Stuffed Chicken Breasts Doria

Portions: 12   Portion size: 1 stuffed chicken breast
1½–2 oz (50 mL) sauce

U.S.	Metric	Ingredients	PROCEDURE
3½ oz	100 g	Shallots, chopped fine	1. To make the stuffing, sweat the shallots in the butter until soft. Allow to cool. Process the chicken leg meat in a food processor for a few seconds. Add the cooled shallots, egg whites, crème fraîche, herbs, and bread crumbs. Process briefly to combine. Season and chill.
2 oz	60 g	Butter	
1 lb	500 g	Chicken leg meat	
2	2	Egg whites	
7 oz	200 mL	Crème fraîche	
3 tbsp	25 g	Mixed fresh herbs, chopped fine	2. Flatten the chicken breasts and the smaller fillets that come with them. Cut a pocket in each breast and stuff with the filling. This can be done easily by piping the stuffing in with a pastry bag. Place the smaller fillet over the top and wrap each breast in foil or nonstick paper, securing the ends with string. Cover with the stock and poach gently for 20–25 minutes. Leave in the hot stock.
1 oz	50 g	Fresh white bread crumbs	
12	12	Chicken breasts, boneless, about 6 oz (175 g) each	
2	2	Cucumbers	3. Cut the cucumbers into 1½-inch (4-cm) lengths and into quarters, removing the seeds. Turn (tourné) into barrel shapes (see Figure 18.1). Blanch in boiling water for 1–2 minutes, then drain and refresh under cold water. Drain and set aside.
1 tbsp	15 g	Butter	4. Sauté the cucumber in the remaining butter until tender, but do not let it brown. Unwrap the chicken and cut into slices. Arrange on plates and spoon the sauce around the chicken. Garnish with the cucumber and chives.
1–1½ pt	600 mL	Yogurt Sour Cream Sauce (p. 162)	
as needed	as needed	Chives, chopped, for garnish	

Per serving:
Calories, 410; Protein, 45 g; Fat, 21 g (47% cal.); Cholesterol, 165 mg;
Carbohydrates, 7 g; Fiber, 1 g; Sodium, 220 mg.

Stuffed Chicken Breasts Doria

Chicken Stew with Sorrel

Portions: 12 Portion size: ¼ chicken
2½ oz (75 mL) sauce
vegetable garnish

U.S.	Metric	Ingredients	PROCEDURE
36	36	Baby carrots	1. Trim and peel the baby vegetables. Poach in chicken stock. Cool. Reserve the vegetables and the stock.
36	36	Baby turnips	2. Peel the cherry tomatoes (optional).
36	36	Baby leeks	3. Shred the sorrel. Cook in butter until wilted.
36	36	Pearl onions	
36	36	Snow pea pods	
as needed	as needed	Chicken stock	
36	36	Cherry tomatoes	
7 oz	200 g	Sorrel	
1 oz	30 g	Butter	
3	3	Chickens, about 3¼ lb (1.5 kg) each	4. Cut the chickens into 8 pieces each (see Figure 12.6).
2 qt	2 L	Chicken stock	5. Simmer in the chicken stock until cooked.
5 oz	150 mL	Heavy cream, hot	6. Remove the chicken from the stock and keep warm.
		Liaison:	7. Strain the stock and measure out 1½ pt (750 mL), reserving the remainder for another purpose.
5 oz	150 mL	Heavy cream	8. Add the hot cream to the hot stock and bring to a simmer.
5	5	Egg yolks	9. Mix the egg yolks and the cream to make a liaison. Temper with a little of the hot stock, then add the mixture back to the stock. Also add the sorrel. Cook over low heat until lightly thickened, but do not allow to boil. Season to taste.
to taste	to taste	Salt	10. Reheat the tomatoes and the baby vegetables in their stock, then drain.
to taste	to taste	Pepper	11. Plate the chicken and coat lightly with the sauce. Arrange the vegetables around the chicken.

Per serving:
Calories, 620; Protein, 50 g; Fat, 37 g (53% cal.); Cholesterol, 270 mg; Carbohydrates, 24 g; Fiber, 5 g; Sodium, 320 mg.

Braising

A moist-heat cooking method, braising may be used to tenderize tough poultry products. Also, as for veal and pork, it can be used to provide moistness and flavor to tender poultry items. Coq au vin, the well-known braised chicken in red wine, was originally made with tough old rooster (*coq*), but today the same recipe is applied to tender young chicken.

Poultry products are braised using the same procedures as for meats, except that mirepoix is frequently omitted. Other flavoring ingredients may be used instead, depending on the recipe. Methods 1 and 2 (p. 282) are used when the chicken is to be browned. Method 3 is used for fricassées, white stews in which the chicken is sautéed without browning.

BRAISED "SAUTÉS"

If you review the procedure for sautéing meats (p. 264), you will see that if the product is not completely cooked when browned in step 5, then finished cooking by simmering it in the sauce in step 10, the result is a braised item. This procedure may be used for classical "sautés," which are often braised items. (An alternative method is to finish cooking the chicken or meat in a covered pan in the oven while you are making the sauce. This is also braising because the cover holds in moisture.)

Chicken Fricassée

Portions: 24   Portion size: ¼ chicken
                              3 oz (90 mL) sauce

U.S.	Metric	Ingredients	PROCEDURE
6	6	Chickens, 2½–3 lb (1.1–1.4 kg) each	1. Cut the chicken into 8 pieces each. Season with salt and white pepper.
to taste	to taste	Salt	2. Melt the butter in a brazier over moderate heat.
to taste	to taste	White pepper	3. Add chicken and onion. Sauté very lightly so that the chicken is seared on all sides, but *do not brown*.
6 oz	175 g	Butter	
12 oz	350 g	Onion, cut brunoise	
6 oz	175 g	Flour	4. Add the flour and stir so that it combines with the fat to make a roux. Cook another 2 minutes, without browning.
3 qt (approximately)	3 L (approximately)	Chicken stock	5. Gradually stir in enough stock to cover the chicken. Bring to a simmer, stirring, until the sauce thickens.
		Sachet:	
1	1	Bay leaf	6. Add the herbs, tied in cheesecloth (sachet).
1	1	Small piece of celery	7. Cover and place in a slow oven (300°F/150°C) or over very low heat on the range. Cook until tender, about 30–45 minutes.
4	4	Parsley stems	
¼ tsp	1 mL	Thyme	
		Liaison:	8. Remove the chicken from the sauce and keep it warm in a covered pan.
5	5	Egg yolks, beaten	9. Degrease the sauce. Reduce it over high heat to proper thickness. You should have about 2 qt (2 L) sauce. Strain through cheesecloth.
1 pt	500 mL	Heavy cream	
2 tbsp	30 mL	Lemon juice	10. Combine the egg yolks and cream. Temper with a little hot sauce, and add the liaison to the sauce. Bring to just below the simmer. Do not boil.
to taste	to taste	Salt	
to taste	to taste	White pepper	11. Season to taste with lemon juice, salt, white pepper, and nutmeg. Pour the sauce over the chicken.
to taste	to taste	Nutmeg	

Per serving:
Calories, 440; Protein, 39 g; Fat, 27 g (56% cal.); Cholesterol, 175 mg;
Carbohydrates, 8 g; Fiber, 0 g; Sodium, 180 mg.

VARIATIONS

Chicken Fricassée with Tarragon
Add 1 tbsp (15 mL) tarragon to the sachet.

Chicken Fricassée à l'Indienne
Add 4 tbsp (60 mL) curry powder when making the roux.

Fricassée of Turkey Wings
Prepare as in basic recipe, using 1 or 2 turkey wings per portion, depending on size. Cut large turkey wings into 2 pieces.

Veal Fricassée
Prepare as in basic recipe, using 10 lb (4.5 kg) boneless veal shoulder, cut into large dice. Use white veal stock.

Pork Fricassée
Use 10 lb (4.5 kg) boneless, diced pork and pork, veal, or chicken stock.

Fricassée à l'Ancienne

Fricassée Brunoise   } Use same garnishes as Chicken Blanquette variations (p. 341).

Fricassée Argenteuil

Chicken Chasseur

Portions: 10   Portion size: ½ chicken
                    3 oz (90 mL) sauce

U.S.	Metric	Ingredients	PROCEDURE
5	5	Chickens, 2–2¼ lb (0.9–1 kg) each (see note)	1. Cut the chickens into 8 pieces. Season the chicken with salt and pepper.
to taste	to taste	Salt	2. Heat the oil in a brazier or large sauté pan. Brown the chicken well on all sides.
to taste	to taste	Pepper	3. Remove the chickens from the pan. Cover and keep them hot.
2 oz	60 mL	Oil	
2 oz	60 g	Shallots or onions, cut brunoise	4. Add the shallots and mushrooms to the pan and sauté lightly without browning.
8 oz	250 g	Mushrooms, sliced	5. Add the white wine and reduce by three-fourths over high heat.
8 oz	250 mL	White wine	
1½ pt	750 mL	Demiglaze	6. Add the demiglaze and tomatoes and bring to a boil. Reduce slightly. Season with salt and pepper.
8 oz	250 g	Tomato concassée, fresh *or*	7. Place the chickens in the sauce. Cover and simmer slowly on the stove or in the oven at 325°F (165°C), about 20–30 minutes, until done.
4 oz	125 g	Drained, chopped canned tomatoes	8. When the chicken is done, remove it from the pan and reduce the sauce slightly over high heat. Add the chopped parsley and check the seasonings.
to taste	to taste	Salt	
to taste	to taste	Pepper	9. Serve ½ chicken (2 pieces dark meat and 2 pieces light meat) per portion. Cover with 3 oz (90 mL) sauce.
2 tbsp	30 mL	Chopped parsley	

Per serving:
Calories, 780; Protein, 76 g; Fat, 47 g (55% cal.); Cholesterol, 250 mg;
Carbohydrates, 7 g; Fiber, 1 g, Sodium, 290 mg.

Note: Large chickens may be used, if desired. For 3½-lb (1.6-kg) chickens, use ¼ chicken per portion (1 piece dark meat and 1 piece light meat).

VARIATIONS

Alternative Method: Brown chickens as in basic recipe. Drain excess fat. Add 1 qt (1 L) prepared chasseur sauce and finish cooking the chickens as in basic method.

Chicken Bercy

Method 1: Prepare as in basic recipe, but omit the mushrooms and tomato.
Method 2: Brown chickens as in basic recipe. Add 1 qt (1 L) prepared Bercy sauce and simmer the chickens until done.

Chicken Portugaise

Method 1: Prepare as in basic recipe, but omit the mushrooms and wine. Use 4 oz (125 g) onions, cut brunoise, and add 1 tsp (5 mL) chopped garlic. Substitute tomato sauce for the demiglaze.
Method 2: Brown chicken as in basic recipe. Add 1 qt (1 L) portugaise sauce and simmer the chicken until done.

Chicken Hongroise

Prepare as in basic recipe, but sauté chicken only lightly. Do not brown. Omit mushrooms and wine. Use Hungarian (hongroise) sauce instead of demiglaze. When the chicken is cooked, add 4–6 oz (125–175 mL) heavy cream (tempered or heated) to the sauce. Omit parsley garnish. Serve with rice pilaf.

Braised Duckling with Sauerkraut

Portions: 12   Portion size: ¼ duckling
                4 oz (125 g) kraut

U.S.	Metric	Ingredients	PROCEDURE
3	3	Ducklings, 5 lb (2.2 kg) each	1. Cut the ducklings into 8 pieces, the same way you would disjoint a chicken. (See Figure 12.5.) Trim off all excess fat.
2 oz	60 mL	Oil	2. Heat the oil in a sauté pan or brazier. Place the duck pieces in the pan skin side down, and cook over moderately high heat until the skin is well browned. A great deal of fat will render out.
			3. Turn the pieces over and continue to brown on all sides.
			4. Drain off all the fat from the pan. Turn the duck pieces skin side up.
		Sachet:	5. Tie the herbs in a cheesecloth bag and place in the pan with the duck.
1	1	Bay leaf	6. Cover the pan and place in a 325°F (165°C) oven for about 30 minutes. Do not add any liquid. The duck will cook in its own juices.
½ tsp	2 mL	Thyme	
6–8	6–8	Parsley stems	
½ recipe (about 3 lb)	½ recipe (about 1.5 kg)	Braised Sauerkraut (p. 470)	7. While the duck is cooking, prepare the sauerkraut, but cook it only 30 minutes.
			8. Remove the duck from its pan and bury it in the partially cooked sauerkraut. Carefully degrease the duck pan without losing any of the juices. Pour the juices over the duck and sauerkraut.
			9. Cover and continue braising the duck and sauerkraut for another hour.
			10. When done, remove the duck and place in a hotel pan or on a serving platter. Remove the sauerkraut with a slotted spoon and place in another hotel pan, or around the duck on the platter.
			11. Degrease the juices. Pour some of the juices over the duck and some over the sauerkraut.

Per serving:
Calories, 680; Protein, 45 g; Fat, 53 g (71% cal.); Cholesterol, 145 mg;
Carbohydrates, 4 g; Fiber, 2 g; Sodium, 600 mg.

VARIATION

Braised Duckling with Cabbage

Prepare as in basic recipe, but substitute ½ recipe Braised Green or White Cabbage (p. 469) for the ½ recipe Sauerkraut.

Paprika Chicken

Portions: 24 Portion size: ¼ chicken
3 oz (90 mL) sauce

U.S.	Metric	Ingredients	PROCEDURE
4 oz	125 mL	Oil	1. Heat the oil in a skillet and brown the chicken lightly on all sides.
6	6	Chickens, disjointed, 3–3½ lb (1.4–1.6 kg) each	2. Remove the chicken from the pan and place in a brazier.
1½ lb	700 g	Onions, chopped fine	3. Add the onion and green pepper to the fat in the pan. Sauté until soft but not browned.
1 lb	450 g	Green pepper, small dice	
2 oz	60 g	Flour	4. Add the flour and stir to make a roux. Cook the flour slowly for a few minutes.
6 tbsp	90 mL	Hungarian paprika	5. Add the paprika and stir to blend in.
1 pt	500 mL	Chicken stock	6. Stir in the chicken stock, tomatoes, and salt. Bring to a boil. The sauce will be very thick at this point.
1 lb	450 g	Canned tomatoes, crushed	
2 tsp	10 mL	Salt	7. Pour the sauce over the chicken. Cover and simmer over very low heat or in a 325°F (165°C) oven until the chicken is tender, about 30–40 minutes.
1 pt	500 mL	Sour cream	8. When the chicken is tender, remove it from the sauce and place in a hotel pan.
			9. Degrease the sauce. Stir in the sour cream. Simmer a minute, but do not boil. Adjust the seasonings.
			10. Pour the sauce over the chicken in the hotel pan.
			11. Serve with egg noodles, spaetzle (p. 529), or rice.

Per serving:
Calories, 440; Protein, 46 g; Fat, 24 g (50% cal.); Cholesterol, 120 mg;
Carbohydrates, 8 g; Fiber, 1 g; Sodium, 370 mg.

Poulet Sauté Basquaise (Basque-Style Chicken)

Portions: 12 Portion size: ¼ chicken or 2 pieces (about 8 oz or 250 g)

U.S.	Metric	Ingredients	PROCEDURE
3	3	Chickens, about 2¾–3 lb (1.3 kg) each	1. Cut each chicken into 8 pieces (see Figure 12.5) and season with salt and pepper. Heat the oil in a large pan and sauté, skin side down first, in batches until lightly browned.
to taste	to taste	Salt	
to taste	to taste	Pepper	
as needed	as needed	Oil	2. Remove the chicken from the pan and drain on kitchen paper. Discard the excess fat in the pan.
5 oz or as needed	150 mL or as needed	Olive oil	3. Place the pan back over a low heat and gently sauté the onion, peppers, garlic, and tomatoes. Cook for 10 minutes, uncovered. Add the wine and cook for a further 30 minutes.
1 lb 4 oz	600 g	Onion	
1 lb 12 oz	800 g	Green peppers	
1 lb 12 oz	800 g	Red peppers	
9 cloves	9 cloves	Garlic, chopped	4. Return the browned chicken pieces to the pan and simmer until done. Check that the juices on the chicken are running clear. Check the seasoning.
1½ lb	750 g	Tomatoes, peeled, seeded, and quartered	
10 oz	300 mL	White wine	5. Pan-fry the prosciutto lightly in butter.
8 oz	250 g	Prosciutto, cut batonnet	6. Serve the chicken coated with the sauce and topped with the ham and the buttery juices in the pan.
as needed	as needed	Butter	

Per serving:
Calories, 570; Protein, 48 g; Fat, 33 g (52% cal.); Cholesterol, 125 mg;
Carbohydrates, 16 g; Fiber, 3 g; Sodium, 610 mg.

Poulet Sauté au Vinaigre
(Lyonnaise-Style Chicken with Tomatoes and Vinegar)

Portions: 12   Portion size: ¼ chicken

U.S.	Metric	Ingredients	PROCEDURE
3	3	Chickens, about 2½ lb (1.2 kg) each	1. Cut each chicken into 8 pieces. Season with salt and pepper.
to taste	to taste	Salt	2. Heat the oil in a large pan and sauté the chicken pieces until golden brown, skin side first. You may have to do this in batches. Remove excess oil from the pan.
to taste	to taste	Pepper	
3½ oz	100 mL	Oil	
1 pt 4 oz	600 mL	Tarragon vinegar	3. Add *half* the vinegar to the pan with the chicken and simmer, covered, for 10 minutes. Turn the pieces over and cook for a further 10 minutes. Check that the chicken is cooked by ensuring the juices run clear when pricked with a fork.
3 oz	90 g	Beurre manié	
3 lb 12 oz	1.7 kg	Tomatoes, peeled, seeded, and chopped	4. While the chicken is cooking, heat the rest of the vinegar in a second pan and boil for 4 minutes. Whisk the beurre manié into the reduced vinegar. Add this to the pan containing the chicken pieces, together with the tomatoes. Simmer for 10 minutes. Check the seasoning.
as needed	as needed	Tarragon sprigs for garnish	5. Serve the chicken on hot plates and pour the sauce over the meat. Garnish with the tarragon. This dish should be served with rice.

Per serving:
Calories, 450; Protein, 38 g; Fat, 28 g (56% cal.); Cholesterol, 125 mg;
Carbohydrates, 12 g; Fiber, 2 g; Sodium, 150 mg.

Pheasant en Cocotte

Portions: 4   Portion size: ½ pheasant (see note)

U.S.	Metric	Ingredients	PROCEDURE
4 oz	110 g	Tiny white onions	1. Peel the onions and potatoes.
8 oz	220 g	Small new potatoes	2. Brown the onions and potatoes in the butter, then cover them and let them steam over low heat until they are about half cooked. They will finish cooking with the pheasant.
½ oz	15 g	Butter	
2	2	Pheasants, 2 lb (900 g) each (see note)	3. Season the pheasants with salt and pepper. Truss them.
to taste	to taste	Salt	4. In a casserole just large enough to hold the birds, brown the pheasants well in butter over moderate heat, making sure that all sides are well browned.
to taste	to taste	Pepper	
1 oz	25 g	Butter	5. If the butter has burned during the browning, wipe out the casserole or transfer the birds to a clean casserole and add a little fresh butter.
1 oz	25 g	Brandy (optional)	6. Add brandy, if it is being used. Also add the onions and potatoes. Cover tightly and place in a 375°F (190°C) oven. Cook until done, about 30–45 minutes, or 15–30 minutes if you have substituted baby pheasants. Halfway through the cooking time, remove the cover and baste with butter. Replace the cover.
4 oz	110 g	Brown stock or demiglaze	7. When the pheasant is done, remove it from the casserole and keep it warm. Deglaze the casserole with the stock and reduce lightly.
			8. The pheasant, with its vegetable garnish and sauce, may be sent to the dining room in its own casserole, to be carved and plated by the dining room staff. Alternatively, it can be carved like chicken (see p. 316) and plated in the kitchen. Plate the pheasant with the vegetable garnish and moisten with a spoonful of the sauce.

Per serving:
Calories, 850; Protein, 92 g; Fat, 46 g (49% cal.); Cholesterol, 305 mg;
Carbohydrates, 14 g; Fiber, 1 g; Sodium, 250 mg.

Note: Very small pheasants of 1 lb (each) may be substituted, using 1 pheasant per portion.

VARIATIONS

Other birds, such as partridges, guinea fowl, small chickens, and Cornish hens, may be prepared using this recipe.

Other garnishes may be used in place of the onions and potatoes, such as:

Mushrooms
Cabbage, blanched and sautéed with a little pork fat
Whole chestnuts, cooked separately
Peas
Sliced artichoke bottoms

Fricassee de Volaille Vallée d'Auge
(Fricassée of Chicken with Apples and Cider)

Portions: 12   **Portion size:** ¼ chicken
4 oz (125 g) sauce and mushrooms

U.S.	Metric	Ingredients	PROCEDURE
3	3	Chickens, about 2¾ lb (1.3 kg) each	1. Cut each chicken into 8 pieces and season with salt and pepper.
to taste	to taste	Salt	2. Heat the oil in a large pan, add the butter, and sauté the
to taste	to taste	Pepper	chicken skin side down in batches until lightly browned.
2½ oz	75 mL	Oil	Discard the excess fat.
2½ oz	75 g	Butter	3. Add the Calvados to the chicken in the pan and ignite to
7 oz	200 mL	Calvados	burn off the alcohol.
5 oz	150 g	Shallots	4. Add the shallots and cook gently until they have softened,
1½ qt	1.5 L	Fermented cider (see note)	then pour in the cider. Cover and barely simmer for 20–25 minutes. Turn the chicken pieces after 15 minutes.
1 lb	500 g	Mushrooms	5. Sauté the mushrooms in the butter in another pan, covered, for 5 minutes. Five minutes before the end of the
1½ oz	50 g	Butter	cooking time for the chicken, add the mushrooms and
1½ pt	750 mL	Heavy cream	their juices to the chicken. Also add the cream.
			6. When cooked, remove the chicken from the pan and keep warm. Reduce the sauce until it coats the back of a spoon. Adjust the seasoning, then return the chicken pieces to the pan and simmer until they are thoroughly heated through.
1 lb 4 oz	600 g	Apples, Golden Delicious	7. To prepare the apples, core but do not peel. Cut across into
5 oz	150 g	Clarified butter	slices about ¼ inch (¼–½ cm) thick and fry in the clarified
1½ oz	40 g	Chopped parsley	butter until golden on both sides. Serve with the chicken and garnish with parsley.

Per serving:
Calories, 890; Protein, 43 g; Fat, 63 g (63% cal.); Cholesterol, 260 mg; Carbohydrates, 22 g; Fiber, 2 g; Sodium, 330 mg.

Note: If fermented cider is not available, substitute 1 qt (1 L) apple juice (unsweetened) plus 1 pt (500 mL) dry white wine.

Turkey and Cilantro Roulade with Turmeric and Almonds

Portions: 12   Portion size: 4 oz (125 g) meat
                              2 oz (60 mL) sauce

U.S.	Metric	Ingredients
10 oz	300 g	Whole blanched almonds
1½ qt	1.5 L	Strong chicken stock
3 lb	1.5 kg	Turkey breast
7 oz	200 g	Cilantro leaves
to taste	to taste	Salt
to taste	to taste	Pepper
1 oz	50 mL	Vegetable oil
1 oz	30 g	Turmeric

PROCEDURE

1. Place the almonds in a deep pan and add the stock. Simmer for 45–60 minutes to soften.
2. Slice the turkey into 12 large, thin slices and flatten between sheets of plastic film. Lay the cilantro leaves over the turkey, reserving some of the best leaves for garnish. Season with salt and pepper and roll up into roulades, securing with string.
3. Sear the roulades briefly in the hot oil. Drain and roll in the turmeric.
4. Add the roulades to the pan with the almonds and stock, cover, and cook in an oven at 350°F (180°C).
5. Remove the roulades from the liquid. Cover to prevent from drying out and rest in a warm place.
6. Place the almonds in a blender with a little of the stock. Purée until smooth. Add more stock until the mixture has the consistency of a light sauce. Check seasoning and adjust if necessary.
7. Slice the roulades and arrange on hot plates with the sauce around the slices. Garnish with the reserved cilantro leaves.

Per serving:
Calories, 310; Protein, 35 g; Fat, 16 g (46% cal.); Cholesterol, 85 mg; Carbohydrates, 7 g; Fiber, 3 g; Sodium, 65 mg.

Turkey and Cilantro Roulade with Turmeric and Almonds

Chicken en Cocotte with Côte du Rhône

Portions: 12   **Portion size:** ¼ chicken
2½ oz (75 mL) sauce

U.S.	Metric	Ingredients	PROCEDURE
3	3	Chickens, about 4½ lb (2 kg) each	1. Cut each chicken into 8 pieces. Season the chicken with salt and pepper.
to taste	to taste	Salt	2. Brown the chicken in the clarified butter. Remove the chicken from the pan.
to taste	to taste	Pepper	
1½ oz	50 g	Clarified butter	3. Add the shallots to the pan. Sweat, then sprinkle with the flour and mix well to make a roux. Cook for a few minutes.
2½ oz	75 g	Shallots	
⅔ oz	20 g	Flour	
1 pt 5 oz	650 mL	Red wine, preferably Côte du Rhône	4. Deglaze with the red wine. Reduce by two-thirds, then add the chicken stock.
1 qt	1 L	Chicken stock	5. Return the chicken pieces to the pan, cover, and cook in the oven at 400°F (200°C) until the chicken is cooked.
4 oz	125 mL	Cream, hot	6. Remove the chicken from the cooking liquid and strain. Skim off any fat from the surface, then reduce until it coats the back of a spoon.
3 tbsp	50 g	Black olive purée	
2 tbsp	6 g	Chopped basil	7. Add the cream and reduce again.
3 tbsp	50 g	Butter	8. Mix in the olive purée and half of the chopped basil.
to taste	to taste	Salt	9. Swirl in the butter (monter au beurre) and check the seasoning.
to taste	to taste	Pepper	
as needed	as needed	Basil leaves for garnish	10. Just before serving, mix in the remaining chopped basil.
			11. Decorate with a few leaves of basil.

Per serving:
Calories, 630; Protein, 67 g; Fat, 33 g (48% cal.); Cholesterol, 190 mg;
Carbohydrates, 4 g; Fiber, 0 g; Sodium, 290 mg.

Ballotine de Poulet Grandmère
(Stuffed Boneless Chicken Legs with Mushrooms, Onion, and Bacon)

Portions: 12 **Portion size:** 1 chicken leg
6–7 oz (195 g) sauce and vegetables

U.S.	Metric	Ingredients	PROCEDURE
12	12	Chicken legs, about 10 oz (300 g) each, skin on	1. Carefully remove the bones from both thigh and drumstick of the chicken legs, following the procedure shown in Figure 13.5. Be sure to remove all cartilage. Chop and reserve the bones.
3 oz	90 g	Shallot, chopped fine	
1½ oz	45 g	Carrot, cut brunoise	2. Sweat the shallot, carrot, and celery in butter until soft. Cool. Bind with bread crumbs and just enough egg to make a soft but not too wet consistency. Season.
1½ oz	45 g	Celery, cut brunoise	
2 oz	60 g	Butter	
6 oz	175 g	Fresh white bread crumbs	
3 (approximately)	3 (approximately)	Eggs, beaten	3. Fill the bone cavity of the chicken legs with this stuffing, then roll up the legs to enclose the filling. If caul is available, roll neatly in pork caul and tie to secure. Alternatively, simply tie the rolls securely without the caul.
to taste	to taste	Salt	
to taste	to taste	Pepper	
12 pieces	12 pieces	Pork caul, approximately 13 oz (375 g) total (see note)	
2 oz	60 mL	Oil	4. Heat the oil in large, shallow pan and brown the legs. Remove from the pan.
12 oz	350 g	Mirepoix, small dice	5. Add the chopped chicken bones and the mirepoix to the pan. Cook until golden. Deglaze with the wine and reduce by 90 percent. Stir in the tomato paste and the stock. Bring to the boil and thicken lightly with beurre manié.
5 oz	150 mL	White wine (see note)	
1½ oz	45 g	Tomato paste	
1½ qt	1.5 L	Brown stock	
5 oz	150 g	Beurre manié	
to taste	to taste	Salt	6. Place the chicken legs in the pan, ensuring that the liquid comes only halfway up them. Bring to the boil, then continue cooking, uncovered, in the oven at 350°F (180°C) for about 30 minutes. During this time, baste with the braising liquid to give the legs a glaze.
to taste	to taste	Pepper	
			7. Remove the chicken legs from the liquid and keep warm. Strain the liquid into a clean pan, degrease, and season with salt and pepper, adjusting consistency if necessary.
12 oz	350 g	Slab bacon	8. Prepare the garnish. Cut the bacon into lardons (batonnet). Blanch the lardons by placing them in cold water and bringing to the boil, cooking for 5 minutes in total, then frying them in a sauté pan until golden brown. Sauté the mushrooms and onions in the bacon fat until glazed and golden. Combine all three.
10 oz	300 g	Pearl onions	
1 lb	500 g	Button mushrooms	
		Parsley sprigs for garnish	
			9. Remove the strings from the chicken legs, slice neatly, and serve on hot plates with the sauce around. Sprinkle the mixed garnish over the chicken and finish with parsley sprigs.

Per serving:
Calories, 680; Protein, 46 g; Fat, 46 g (61% cal.); Cholesterol, 205 mg;
Carbohydrates, 19 g; Fiber, 2 g; Sodium, 610 mg.

Note: Caul is a thin, lacy membrane of fat surrounding the abdominal cavity of pigs and other animals. Wrapping in caul helps maintain the shape of the roll and prevent the stuffing from escaping, and it melts away almost entirely during cooking. If it is not available, simply omit.

If you do not wish to use wine in this recipe, substitute water or stock for deglazing. Adjust the flavor balance of the finished sauce with a little fresh lemon juice.

Ballotine de Poulet Grandmère

Figure 13.5 Boning and stuffing a chicken leg.

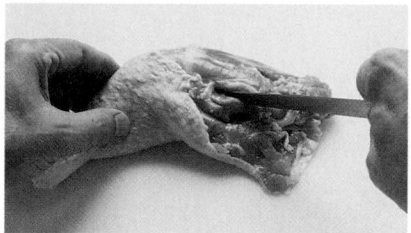

(a) Make a shallow cut along the thigh bone.

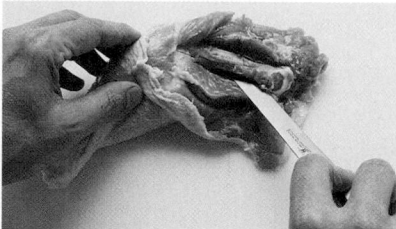

(b) Continue to cut along the bone to free it from the meat.

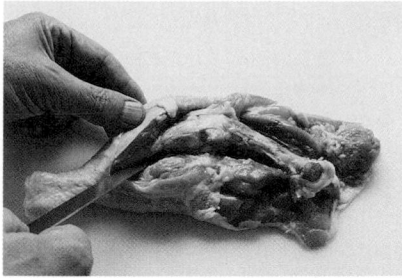

(c) Continue the cut along the entire length of the leg bone to expose all the bone.

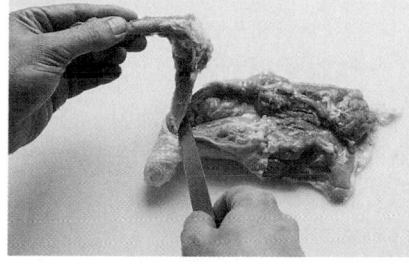

(d) Remove the bone completely from the meat.

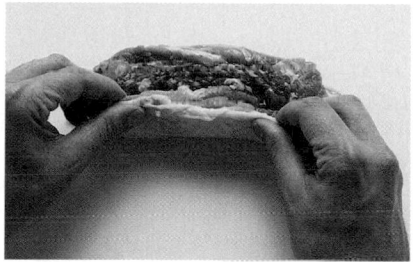

(e) Place a portion of the stuffing along the length of the meat and roll the leg into a cylinder to enclose the stuffing.

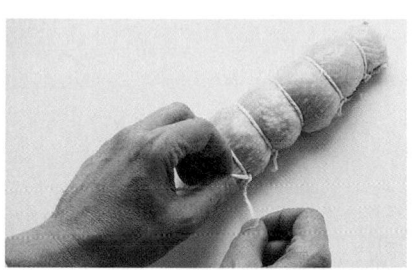

(f) Tie securely.

Salmis of Partridge

Portions: 4   Portion size: 1 partridge

U.S.	Metric	Ingredients	PROCEDURE
4	4	Partridges, about 1 lb (450 g) each (see variations)	1. Season the birds with salt and pepper and brush them with melted butter. 2. Roast them in a hot oven (475°F/250°C), keeping them rare.
as needed	as needed	Salt	3. Cut off the legs. Put them under the broiler for a few minutes with the insides toward the heat and broil until well done.
as needed	as needed	Pepper	4. Carefully cut each side of the breast from the carcass in one piece. Set aside and keep warm.
as needed	as needed	Butter, melted	5. Chop the carcasses.
1 oz	30 g	Shallots	6. Sauté the chopped carcasses and the shallots in butter for a few minutes.
½ oz	15 g	Butter	
3–4	3–4	Peppercorns, crushed	7. Add the peppercorns and red wine. Reduce by two-thirds.
10 oz	300 mL	Red wine	8. Add the demiglaze and bring to a boil. Strain through a fine sieve, pressing down on the solids to squeeze out as much liquid as possible.
6 oz	180 mL	Demiglaze	
to taste	to taste	Salt	9. Combine the breasts and the sauce in a saucepan and heat gently until the meat is hot and cooked to the desired degree. It should remain pink on the inside.
2 oz	60 g	Butter	10. Strain the sauce again. Season with salt. Finish the sauce by setting over low heat and swirling in the butter.
			11. Serve the breasts with the sauce, and garnish with the broiled legs.

Per serving:
Calories, 920; Protein, 118 g; Fat, 21 g (26% cal.); Cholesterol, 435 mg; Carbohydrates, 5 g; Fiber, 0 g; Sodium, 390 mg.

Note: A *salmis* (sahl mee) is a dish, usually of game or poultry, prepared by roasting the item partway and finishing it in a sauce. The sauce is usually made with red or white wine and flavored by adding the juices from the carcass or by simmering the carcass in the sauce. The meat may then be simply reheated with the sauce or simmered in it for a longer time.

VARIATIONS

This recipe can be prepared with any of the following in place of the partridge. The number of birds to use will depend on their size.

Pheasant   Squab   Wild duck   Guinea hen

Coq au Vin

Portions: 12   **Portion size:** ¼ chicken
2½ oz (75 mL) sauce

U.S.	Metric	Ingredients	PROCEDURE
12 oz	350 g	Salt pork or slab bacon	1. Cut the salt pork or bacon into batonnet shapes, 1 × ¼ × ¼ inch (2 × ½ × ½ cm).
1 oz	30 mL	Oil	2. Place the bacon pieces in a saucepan. Cover with cold water. Bring to a boil and drain.
			3. Add the oil to a large sauté pan and place over moderate heat. When hot, add the blanched bacon. Sauté until lightly browned. Remove with a slotted spoon and set aside.
3	3	Chickens, 3½ lb (1.6 kg) each, cut into 8 pieces	4. Increase the heat to high. Add the chickens to the fat remaining in the pan and brown well on all sides. Remove the chicken from the pan.
24	24	Tiny white onions, peeled and parboiled	5. Add the onions and mushrooms to the pan and sauté until browned. Remove with a slotted spoon and set aside with the bacon pieces. Pour off the fat from the pan.
1½ lb	700 g	Small mushroom caps	
1 qt	1 L	Red wine (dry)	6. Add the wine and stock to the pan and bring to a boil.
1 pt	500 mL	Chicken stock	7. Add the thyme, bay leaf, and garlic, tied in a piece of cheesecloth.
		Sachet:	8. Return the chicken to the pan. Bring the liquid back to a boil. Cover and cook in a 300°F (150°C) oven or over very low heat on top of the stove until chicken is done, about 30–40 minutes.
½ tsp	2 mL	Thyme	
1	1	Bay leaf	
4	4	Large garlic cloves, crushed	
		Beurre manié:	9. Remove the chicken from the cooking liquid and place in a heated pan or on a serving platter. Garnish with the mushrooms, onions, and bacon pieces.
2 oz	60 g	Butter, softened	10. Degrease the cooking liquid carefully.
2 oz	60 g	Flour	11. Place over high heat and boil until the liquid is reduced to about 1 qt (1 L).
as needed	as needed	Chopped parsley	12. Mix the butter and flour to make beurre manié. Beat in the beurre manié a little at a time, just enough to thicken the sauce lightly. Strain the sauce over the chicken and garnish.
			13. At service time, sprinkle each portion with a little chopped parsley.

Per serving:
Calories, 690; Protein, 56 g; Fat, 41 g (54% cal.); Cholesterol, 165 mg;
Carbohydrates, 10 g; Fiber, 2 g; Sodium, 480 mg.

Arroz con Pollo (Spanish Rice with Chicken)

Portions: 24   Portion size: ¼ chicken
                5 oz (150 g) rice

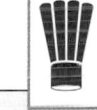

U.S.	Metric	Ingredients	PROCEDURE
6	6	Chickens, 3 lb (1.4 kg) each	1. Cut the chickens into 8 pieces each.
3 oz	90 mL	Olive oil	2. Heat the olive oil in a large sauté pan. Brown the chickens on all sides. Transfer the pieces to a brazier as they are browned. Drain off and discard about one-third of the fat in the pan.
1 lb	500 g	Onion, small dice	3. Place the onion, green pepper, and garlic in the sauté pan in which the chicken was browned. Sauté over medium heat until the vegetables are almost tender.
1 lb	500 g	Green peppers, medium dice	
4 tsp	20 mL	Garlic, chopped fine	
2 tsp	10 mL	Paprika	4. Add the paprika and rice and stir until the grains are coated with fat.
1 qt	1 L	Long-grain rice, raw	
3 pt	1.5 L	Chicken stock	5. Add the stock and tomatoes. Bring to a boil. Season the liquid to taste with salt and pepper.
2 lb	900 g	Fresh tomatoes, 1-inch (2½-cm) dice	6. Pour the contents of the pan over the chicken in the brazier. Cover and place in a 325°F (165°C) oven until the rice and chicken are cooked, about 20–30 minutes.
		or	
1½ lb	700 g	Canned tomatoes, diced	
to taste	to taste	Salt	
to taste	to taste	Pepper	
1¼ lb	600 g	Frozen peas, thawed	7. At service time, stir in the peas and garnish the top with pimiento strips.
4 oz	125 g	Pimientos, cut into thin strips	

Per serving:
Calories, 580; Protein, 49 g; Fat, 26 g (41% cal.); Cholesterol, 145 mg;
Carbohydrates, 35 g; Fiber, 3 g; Sodium, 180 mg.

Duck Confit

Portions: 8 (see note)

U.S.	Metric	Ingredients	PROCEDURE
8 lb	3.6 kg	Duck parts, preferably legs	1. Trim off excess fat from the duck and reserve.
			2. If you are using duck legs (the ideal part for this preparation), leave the thigh attached to the drumstick.
1 oz	30 g	Salt	
1 tsp	5 mL	White pepper	3. Rub the duck pieces with the salt and spices. Refrigerate overnight.
½ tsp	2 mL	Nutmeg	
½ tsp	2 mL	Powdered bay leaf	4. Render the trimmed fat plus as much extra fat as needed. You will need enough rendered fat to completely cover the duck pieces.
pinch	pinch	Ground cloves	
as needed	as needed	Extra duck fat	5. Put the duck and the rendered fat in a brazier, large saucepan, or casserole. Simmer gently in the fat over low heat or in a 300°F (150°C) oven until very tender, about 1½–2 hours.
			6. Remove the cooked duck from the fat and pack into a clean crock or other container. Pour the melted fat over the meat so that it is completely covered, but be careful not to pour in any of the juices. (The degreased juices may be used for another purpose, such as cooking beans.)
			7. Remove pieces and use as needed. For best storage, remaining pieces must be kept covered by the fat. For serving, the confit is usually browned in a little of the fat until it is heated through and the skin is crisp. Serve with such accompaniments as braised cabbage, cooked white beans, or sautéed potatoes with garlic, or on a bed of salad greens.

Per serving:
Calories, 620; Protein, 35 g; Fat, 52 g (77% cal.); Cholesterol, 155 mg;
Carbohydrates, 0 g; Fiber, 0 g; Sodium, 1480 mg.

Note: The exact weight of the finished confit can vary considerably.

Dressings and Stuffings

Stuffing chickens and turkeys is usually not practical in production kitchens. Baking the "stuffing" separately gives better results, for these reasons:

1. **Safety.**
   Stuffing inside a bird is an ideal breeding ground for bacteria that cause food poisoning.

2. **Quality.**
   Additional roasting time is needed to heat the stuffing through. The result is often overcooked poultry.

3. **Practicality.**
   Filling poultry with stuffing and removing it after roasting is impractical, time-consuming, and messy.

Stuffing that is baked separately is usually called *dressing*.

Is poultry ever stuffed? Yes. Small birds served whole as one or two portions can be stuffed and often are. Stuffed Cornish hens or small game birds such as quails are popular items.

BASIC INGREDIENTS OF DRESSINGS

1. Starch base, such as bread or rice.

2. Aromatic vegetables, generally onions and celery.

3. Fat, such as butter or chicken fat, for sautéing the vegetables and for providing richness.
   Dressings for chicken and turkey, which are lean, may require more fat than dressings for duck and goose, which are fatty.

4. Liquid, usually stock, to provide moisture.

5. Seasonings, herbs, and spices.

6. Eggs, sometimes added as a binder, but not always necessary.

7. Other ingredients for flavor, character, and bulk, such as:

Sausage	Chestnuts
Oysters	Fruits
Giblets	Nuts

Guidelines for Making Dressings

1. All ingredients that require cooking must be completely cooked before combining with other dressing ingredients. They will cook very little more during baking or roasting.

2. Cool all ingredients before combining to avoid growth of dangerous bacteria.

3. Never let baked or unbaked dressing stay in the Food Danger Zone (40° to 140°F/4° to 60°C) longer than 1 hour.
   - Refrigerate unbaked dressing if not to be baked immediately.
   - Hold baked dressing above 140°F (60°C) for service or chill as rapidly as possible.
   - Reheat baked dressing rapidly in oven or steamer to an internal temperature of 180°F (82°C).

4. Bake dressing in shallow pans (2 inches/5 cm deep) for rapid cooking, to get it above the Danger Zone quickly.

5. Do not overmix bread dressings, or they will become pasty. Toss ingredients together lightly.

6. For light texture, do not pack dressings into baking pans; instead, spoon loosely.

7. If you stuff poultry instead of baking the dressing separately, fill the birds loosely. Do not pack. Stuffings expand during cooking.

Basic Bread Dressing

Yield: about 4 lb (2 kg)

U.S.	Metric	Ingredients	PROCEDURE
1 lb	500 g	Onion, small dice	1. Sauté the onion and celery lightly in the fat until tender but not browned. Cool thoroughly.
½ lb	250 g	Celery, small dice	
½ lb	250 g	Fat such as butter, chicken fat, or bacon fat	2. Cut the bread into small cubes. If desired, crusts may be trimmed first.
2 lb	1 kg	White bread, 2 days old	3. Combine the bread and cooked vegetables in a large stainless-steel bowl. Add the herbs and seasonings and toss gently until all ingredients are well mixed.
1 oz	30 g	Chopped parsley	
1 tsp	5 mL	Sage	
½ tsp	2 mL	Thyme	4. Add the stock a little at a time, and mix the dressing lightly after each addition. Add just enough to make the dressing slightly moist, neither dry nor soggy. Adjust the seasonings.
½ tsp	2 mL	Marjoram	
½ tsp	2 mL	White pepper	
2 tsp	10 mL	Salt	5. Place in a greased baking pan and bake at 375°F (190°C) until hot at the center, about 1 hour.
1–2 pt	0.5–1 L	Chicken stock, cold	

Per 1 ounce:
Calories, 70; Protein, 1 g; Fat, 3.5 g (47% cal.); Cholesterol, 10 mg;
Carbohydrates, 8 g; Fiber, 0 g; Sodium, 175 mg.

VARIATIONS

Sausage Dressing

Cook 1 lb (500 g) crumbled pork sausage meat, drain, and cool. Use some of the drained fat to cook the vegetables for the dressing. Add the cooked sausage to the dressing before adding the stock.

Chestnut Dressing

Reduce the bread to 1½ lb (750 g). Add 1 lb (500 g) cooked, coarsely chopped chestnuts to the dressing before adding the stock.

Mushroom Dressing

Cook 2 lb (1 kg) sliced mushrooms with the onion and celery. Proceed as in basic recipe.

Giblet Dressing

Add ½ lb (250 g) cooked, chopped chicken or turkey gizzards and hearts to the dressing before adding the stock

Cornbread Dressing

Substitute cornbread for all or part of the white bread in Basic Bread Dressing or Sausage Dressing.

Questions for Discussion

1. Describe the three roasting methods discussed in this chapter: low-temperature roasting, searing, and high-temperature roasting. When are they used?

2. True or false: Chicken should be broiled at a lower temperature than steaks. Explain your answer.

3. What is meant by the term "presentation side"?

4. Why is it difficult to cook large chicken pieces by deep-frying? How can this problem be solved?

5. What are the differences between simmering and poaching as applied to poultry?

6. Give three reasons for baking dressing in a separate pan rather than stuffing it into roast poultry.

Understanding Fish and Shellfish

At one time, fresh fish was enjoyed only in limited areas—along the seacoast and, to a lesser extent, around lakes and rivers. Today, thanks to modern refrigeration and freezing technology, fish products are enjoyed much more widely.

For the cook, the difficulties of understanding fish and shellfish are, in some ways, the reverse of those for meat. With meat, we are presented with only a few animals, but a bewildering array of cuts from each. With fish, there are only a few cuts but hundreds of species, each with its own characteristics and cooking requirements.

For this reason, it is especially important that students learn the basic principles of structure, handling, and cooking so that they can utilize the many varieties of seafood in a systematic way.

Fish products are divided into two categories: fin fish, or fish with fins and internal skeletons, and shellfish, or fish with external shells but no internal bone structure. Because they have many differences, it is helpful to look at them separately, as we do in this chapter.

After reading this chapter, you should be able to:

1. Explain how the cooking qualities of fish are affected by the lack of connective tissue.

2. Determine doneness in cooked fish.

3. Demonstrate the appropriate cooking methods for fat and lean fish.

4. List seven basic market forms of fish.

5. Dress and fillet round fish and flatfish.

6. List and describe common varieties of salt-water and freshwater fin fish used in North American food service.

7. Identify the characteristics of fresh fish, and contrast them with characteristics of not-so-fresh fish.

8. Store fish and fish products.

9. Identify the popular varieties of shellfish and discuss their characteristics.

10. Outline the special safe handling and cooking procedures for shellfish.

11. Open clams and oysters, split lobster, and peel and devein shrimp.

Fin Fish

Composition and Structure

The edible flesh of fish, like that of meat and poultry, consists of water, proteins, fats, and small amounts of minerals, vitamins, and other substances. The differences, however, are perhaps more important than the similarities.

Fish has very little connective tissue. This is one of the most important differences between fish and meat. It means that

1. *Fish cooks very quickly*, even at low heat (just enough heat to coagulate the proteins).
2. *Fish is naturally tender.* Toughness is the result not of connective tissue but of the toughening of the protein by high heat.
3. *Moist-heat cooking methods* are used not to create tenderness but to preserve moistness and provide variety.
4. *Cooked fish must be handled very carefully* or it will fall apart.

Special Problems in Cooking Fish

DONENESS AND FLAKING

When fish is cooked, the flesh breaks apart into its natural separations. This is called "flaking." Most books, somewhat misleadingly, say that fish is done when it flakes *easily*. Unfortunately, some cooks interpret this as meaning "nearly falling apart." Because fish continues to cook in its retained heat even when removed from the fire, it is often dreadfully overcooked by the time it reaches the customer. *Fish is very delicate and is easily overcooked.*

Observe these tests for doneness:

1. The *fish just separates* into flakes; that is, it is beginning to flake but does not yet fall apart easily.
2. If bone is present, the flesh separates from the bone, and the bone is no longer pink.
3. The flesh has turned from translucent to opaque (usually white, depending on the kind of fish).

Remember, the major flaw in fish preparation is *overcooking*.

COOKING FAT FISH AND LEAN FISH

The fat content of fish ranges from 0.5 percent to 20 percent.

Lean fish are those that are low in fat. Examples: Flounder, sole, cod, red snapper, bass, perch, halibut, pike.

Fat fish are those that are high in fat. Examples: Salmon, tuna, trout, butterfish, mackerel.

Cooking Lean Fish

Because lean fish has almost no fat, it can easily become dry, especially if overcooked. It is often served with sauces to enhance moistness and give richness.

Moist-heat methods. Lean fish is especially well suited to poaching. This method preserves moistness.

Dry-heat methods. Lean fish, if it is broiled or baked, should be basted with butter or oil. Take special care not to overcook, or the fish will be dry.

Dry-heat methods with fat. Lean fish may be fried or sautéed. The fish gains palatability from the added fat.

Cooking Fat Fish

The fat in these fish enables them to tolerate more heat without becoming dry.

Moist-heat methods. Fat fish, like lean fish, can be cooked by moist heat. Poached salmon and trout are very popular.

Dry-heat methods. Fat fish are well suited to broiling and baking. The dry heat helps eliminate some excessive oiliness.

Dry-heat methods with fat. Large fat fish, like salmon, and stronger-flavored fish, like bluefish and mackerel, may be cooked in fat, but care should be taken to avoid excessive greasiness. Smaller ones, like trout, are often pan-fried. Drain the fish well before serving.

Cutting Fish

MARKET FORMS

Fish are available in several forms, as illustrated in Figure 14.1. Or they may be cut by the cook into these forms, depending on how they are to be cooked.

BUYING PROCESSED FISH VERSUS CUTTING THEM YOURSELF

Most food service establishments purchase fish in the forms in which they intend to cook them. They find it less expensive to pay the purveyor to do the cutting than to hire and train the personnel and to allocate the storage and work space to do it in-house.

Some restaurants still buy whole fish. Here are a few reasons why they do:

1. Their clientele demands it. Some high-priced luxury restaurants stake their reputations on using only the freshest, most unprocessed ingredients. They are able to charge enough to cover their high labor costs.

2. They are in the heart of a fresh fish market, where fresh whole fish, delivered daily, are economical. They can best take advantage of seasonal bargains.

3. They are high-volume specialty restaurants and find it more economical to clean the fish themselves and watch the market for the best prices every day.

4. They make fish stocks and use the bones.

5. They serve the whole fish. Examples: sautéed or poached trout presented whole; whole cold poached fish as a buffet display.

Your purchasing decisions will depend on what you plan to do with the fish and what forms are most economical for those purposes.

Figure 14.1 Market forms of fish.

(a) Whole or round: completely intact, as caught.

(b) Drawn: viscera removed.

(c) Dressed: viscera, scales, head, tail, and fins removed.

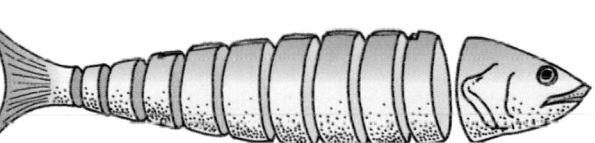

(d) Steaks: cross-section slices, each containing a section of backbone.

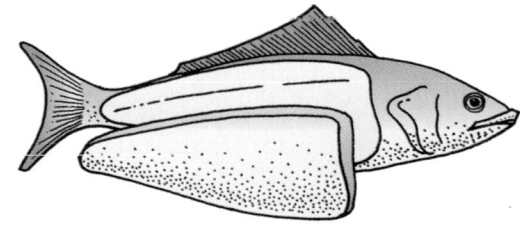

(e) Fillets: boneless sides of fish, with skin on or off.

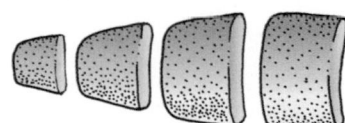

(f) Sticks: cross-section slices of fillets.

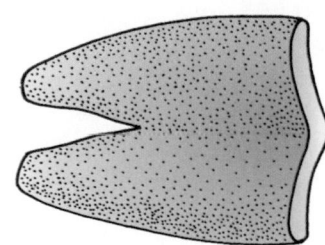

(g) Butterflied fillets: both sides of a fish still joined, but with bones removed.

Figure 14.2 Dressing a fish.

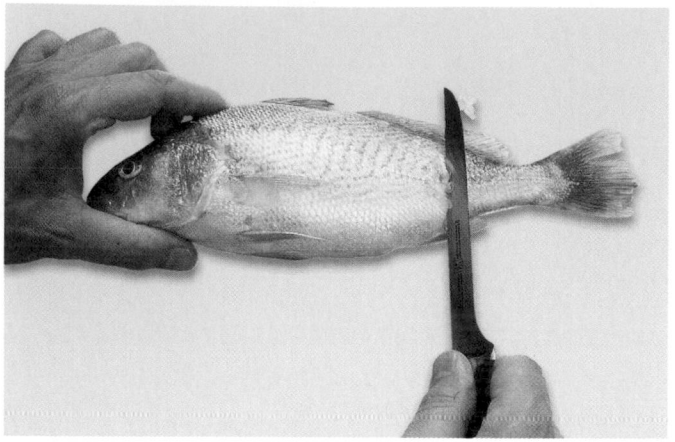

(a) Scale the fish. Lay the fish flat on work surface. Rub a scaling tool or the back of a knife against the scales from tail to head. Repeat until all scales are removed. Rinse. (Exceptions: Trout, with very tiny scales, and scaleless fish, like catfish, are not scaled.)

DRESSING AND FILLETING

Although most of you will work with ready-to-cook fish products, you should know how to clean and fillet whole fish.

1. **Dressing.**
    Figure 14.2 illustrates how to dress a whole fish.

2. **Filleting.**
    There are two basic shapes of fish: flatfish (like flounder and sole) and round fish (like cod and trout). They are filleted differently. Flatfish have four fillets; round fish have two. Figures 14.3 and 14.4 show the two methods for filleting these fish.

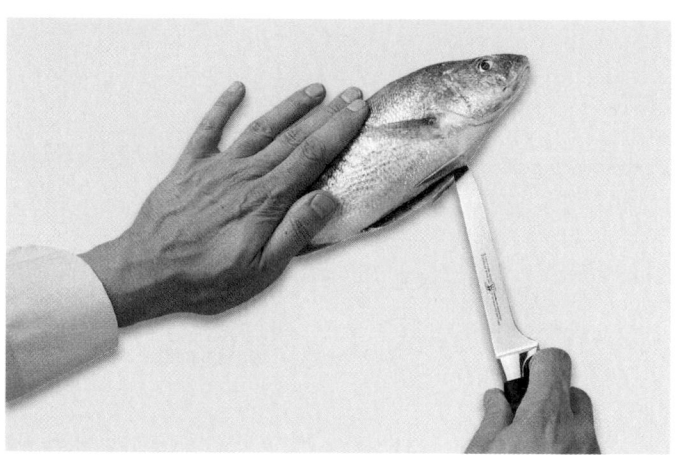

(b) Eviscerate. Slit the belly and pull out viscera. Rinse cavity.

(c) Cut off tail and fins. Scissors are easiest to use.

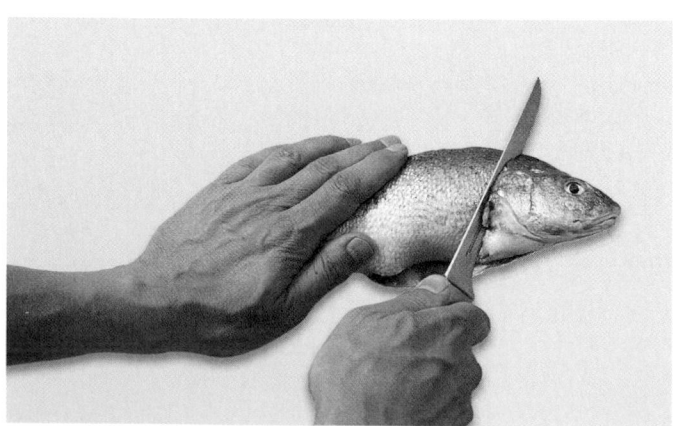

(d) Remove head. Cut through flesh just behind gills. Cut or break backbone at the cut and pull off head.

(e) The fish is dressed.

Figure 14.3 Filleting flatfish.

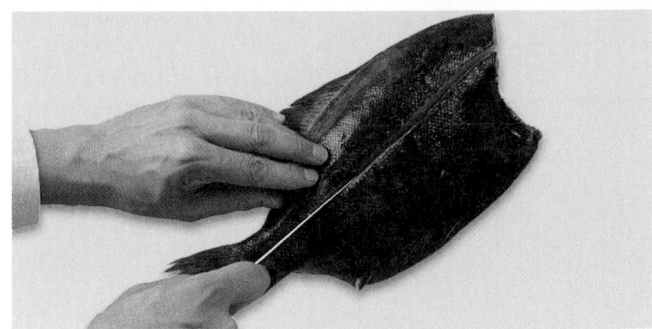

(a) Use a thin-bladed, flexible knife. Cut off the head, just behind the gills. (This step is optional.)

(b) Make a cut from head to tail just to one side of the center line, down to the backbone.

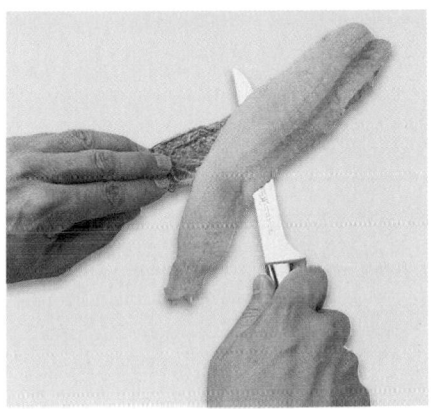

(c) Turn the knife so that it is almost parallel to the table. Making long, smooth cuts, cut horizontally against the backbone toward the outer edge of the fish. Gently separate the fillet from the bone.

(d) Remove the fillet completely. Repeat to remove the three remaining fillets.

(e) To skin, place the fillet skin side down on the work surface with the tail pointing toward you. Holding the skin at the tail end, slide the knife between the skin and flesh, scraping against the skin to avoid cutting into the fillet. Note: Dover or English sole is skinned before filleting. Cut through the skin at the tail. Holding the tail with one hand, peel off the skin toward the head. Caution: Do not do this with flounder. You will tear the flesh.

Figure 14.4 Filleting round fish.

(a) Cut into the top of the fish along one side of the backbone from head to tail. Cut against the bone with smooth strokes of the knife to separate the flesh from the bone.

(b) Cut under the flesh toward the tail; detach it.

(c) Cut along the curved rib bones and finish detaching the fillet at the head end. Turn the fish over and repeat to remove the second fillet. Lightly run your finger along the flesh side of the fillets to see if any bones remain in them. Pull out any you find. Skin the fillets as for flatfish.

Varieties and Characteristics

Hundreds of varieties of fish are eaten around the world. However, relatively few species account for the majority of the fish used in food service in the U.S. and Canada. Following are some of the most common varieties that are used fresh. Some of these are illustrated in the following photographs.

SALTWATER FISH—FLATFISH

These are all popular in commercial kitchens. Flatfish have lean, white flesh and a mild, delicate flavor. They are all very flat, oval in shape, with both eyes on one side of the head.

Flounder

Flounder
Type: Lean.
Varieties: Winter flounder, lemon sole, gray sole, sand dab.
Characteristics: White flesh; fine flakes; mild, sweet flavor.
Weight: ½ to 5 lb (0.2 to 2.3 kg).

Sole (Dover sole or English sole)
Type: Lean.
Characteristics: Narrower, more elongated than flounder. Flesh similar to flounder, but firmer in texture. One of the most prized of all fish. Expensive.
Weight: 1 to 2 lb (0.5 to 1 kg).

Dover sole

Halibut
Type: Lean.
Characteristics: Looks like a giant flounder, with thicker flesh, delicate flavor. Cut into steaks and fillets.
Weight: 4 to 100 lb and up (2 to 45 kg).

Turbot
Type: Lean.
Characteristics: Large, broad flatfish. White, firm, delicate flesh.
Weight: 1 to 25 lb (0.5 to 11 kg).

SALTWATER FISH—ROUND FISH

Black Sea Bass
Type: Lean.
Characteristics: Small, black-skinned fish with firm, delicate, sweet white flesh.
Weight: Up to 3 lb (1.5 kg).

Black sea bass

Bluefish
Type: Fat.
Characteristics: Flavorful, oily flesh that is bluish when raw, grayish when cooked. Abundant and inexpensive.
Weight: 1 to 10 lb (0.5 to 4.5 kg).

Bluefish

Cod

Type: Lean.

Varieties: Small, young cod is called *scrod*.

Characteristics: Lean, white, delicately flavored flesh with large flakes. Most important food fish in North America. Most fish sticks and similar items are made from cod.

Weights: Scrod: 1 to 2½ lb (0.5 to 1 kg).
Cod: 2½ to 25 lb and up (1 to 11 kg).

Cod

Grouper

Type: Lean.

Characteristics: Many varieties with varying shape and skin color. Firm white fish, similar in texture and flavor to red snapper. Tough skin.

Weight: Up to 700 lb (300 kg), but most groupers on the market weigh 5 to 15 lb (2.3 to 7 kg).

Grouper

Haddock

Type: Lean.

Varieties: Finnan haddie is smoked haddock, not a separate kind of fish.

Characteristics: Similar to cod, but generally smaller.

Weight: 1 to 5 lb (0.5 to 2.3 kg).

Jack

Type: Fat.

Varieties: Members of the jack family include kingfish, blue runner, yellowtail, amberjack, and golden thread. The best-known jack is the pompano, listed separately.

Characteristics: Smooth, shiny skin; firm, oily flesh; strong flavor. Some varieties are much stronger than others.

Weight: Varies greatly depending on variety.

Blue runner, a type of Jack

Jack

John Dory

Also known as St. Peter's fish, St. Pierre.

Type: Lean.

Characteristics: Identified by the characteristic black spot ("St. Peter's thumbprint") on each side of the body behind the head. Firm, sweet, white flesh with fine flakes; broad, thin fillets.

Weight: About 2 lb (900 g) average.

Mackerel

Type: Fat.

Varieties: Spanish and Boston mackerel are the most common small varieties. King mackerel is larger, usually cut into steaks.

Characteristics: Fat, firm flesh with rich flavor and slightly dark color.

Weight: ½ to 5 lb (0.2 to 2.3 kg).

Boston mackerel

Spanish mackerel

Mahi-mahi

Also known as dorado, dolphinfish (not related to the mammal called dolphin).

Type: Lean.

Characteristics: Firm, fine-textured pinkish flesh with rich, sweet taste. Becomes very dry when overcooked, so best cooked with moist heat or with fat or served with a sauce.

Weight: 5 to 40 lb (2.3 to 18 kg).

Mahi-mahi

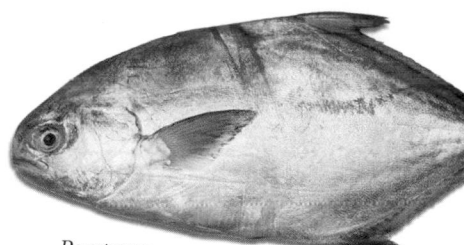

Monkfish

Also known as lotte, anglerfish, bellyfish.

Type: Lean.

Characteristics: Large, ugly fish, but only tail is used. White, very firm flesh with fine texture, somewhat like lobster. Rich flavor. Holds up well in soups and stews, but dries out easily if cooked dry without fat.

Weight: 5 to 50 lb (2.3 to 23 kg).

Ocean Perch

Type: Lean.

Varieties: Many. Red-skinned varieties (redfish) are especially popular and more expensive.

Characteristics: Mild, somewhat bony.

Weight: Depends on variety, but typically about 1 lb (0.5 kg).

Monkfish

Orange Roughy

Type: Lean.

Characteristics: A South Pacific fish available in some markets. Texture and flavor similar to red snapper.

Weight: ¾ to 2 lb (0.3 to 1 kg).

Pompano

Type: Fat.

Characteristics: Small fish with rich, sweet-flavored flesh. Expensive.

Weight: ¾ to 2 lb (0.3 to 1 kg).

Pompano

Porgy

Type: Lean.

Characteristics: Small, oval fish. Sweet and mild, but quite bony.

Weight: Up to 2 lb (1 kg).

Porgy

Red Mullet

Also known as rouget barbet (roo-zhay bar-bay), rouget.

Type: Lean.

Varieties: A member of the goatfish family. In addition to the Mediterranean variety discussed here, similar varieties are found in North American waters.

Characteristics: Mediterranean fish resembling a small red snapper. Rich flavor with a slight taste of shrimp or lobster. Always cooked with skin on, because much of the desired flavor comes from the skin.

Weight: Usually 12 oz or less (350 g or less).

Two red mullets

Red Snapper

Type: Lean.

Characteristics: Firm, delicate, sweet white flesh with large flakes. Large, coarse bones. Skin is red. Highly prized, and popular in restaurants.

Weight: 1 to 15 lb (0.5 to 7 kg).

Red snapper

Salmon

Type: Fat.

Varieties: Atlantic, chinook, sockeye, coho, chum, humpback.

Characteristics: Rich, pink-to-red flesh with somewhat meaty texture and flavor. One of the most prized of all fish. Much is canned or smoked.

Weight: 4 to 25 lb (2 to 11 kg).

Note: Salmon may also be classed as a freshwater fish because it swims upriver to spawn.

Salmon

Shad

Type: Fat.

Characteristics: Oily, rich flavor and very many bones in several rows in each fillet. Its roe (egg sacs) are especially prized. Fresh shad is highly seasonal (February to June).

Weight: 1½ to 5 lb (0.7 to 2.3 kg).

Shark

Type: Fat.

Varieties: Mako shark is the variety usually used.

Characteristics: Firm texture, similar to swordfish, but softer and a little moister and with finer grain; less expensive. Has cartilage skeleton, no bones. Usually cut into steaks.

Weight: 25 to 40 lb (11 to 18 kg).

Skate

Also known as ray.

Type: Lean.

Characteristics: May be sold whole, but often, only the triangular wings are marketed. Skeleton is cartilage, not bone; tough skin, gray on top, white on bottom. Flesh consists of sweet, white, gelatinous strips of meat extending the width of the wings; two fillets per wing, one above and one below the cartilage.

Weight: Some varieties weigh up to a ton, but most sold for food weigh 1 to 4 lb (0.5 to 2 kg) per wing.

Skate wings, top view (left) and bottom view (right)

Striped Bass

Type: Lean.

Characteristics: Firm, white, delicately flavored fish with large flakes.

Weight: 1 to 10 lb (0.5 to 4.5 kg).

Striped bass

Swordfish

Type: Fat.

Characteristics: Very large, fat fish with dense meaty, not flaky, texture. High yield. Sold mostly as steaks. Expensive.

Weight: Up to 1000 lb (450 kg).

Tilefish

Type: Lean.

Characteristics: Firm, sweet, mild white flesh, pinkish when raw. Used mostly for steaks, but smaller ones can be filleted or poached whole.

Weight: 4 to 8 lb (1.8 to 3.6 kg).

Tilefish

Triggerfish

Type: Lean.

Characteristics: Tough-skinned fish with firm, meaty, white to gray-white flesh. Low yield Low yield because of large head.

Weight: about 2 lb (900 g) average.

Triggerfish

Tuna

Type: Fat.

Varieties: Yellowfin and bluefin have red flesh, gray when cooked. Albacore has pink flesh, off-white when cooked. Some other varieties are also available.

Characteristics: Meaty texture and appearance. Belly cuts much fattier than back ("loin"). Red-fleshed varieties often served raw as sashimi or sushi. When cooked, usually cut into steaks and grilled. Should not be cooked well done, or will be very dry.

Weight: Depends on variety. May be several hundred pounds (100 kg and up).

Weakfish

Also called sea trout.

Type: Lean.

Characteristics: Mild, light-gray flesh with soft texture.

Weight: Up to 10 lb (4.5 kg).

Weakfish

Whiting

Type: Lean.

Characteristics: Fragile, white flesh with mild flavor. Fillets must be handled carefully or they will break up.

Weight: ¼ to 3 lb (0.1 to 1.4 kg).

Whiting

FRESHWATER FISH

Catfish

Type: Lean to fat.

Varieties: Bullhead is similar but is not the same species.

Characteristics: Firm flesh with abundant flavor. Layer of fat directly under skin. Catfish has no scales and is usually skinned before frying or pan-frying. Farmed catfish is milder and usually leaner than wild catfish.

Weight: 1 to 8 lb (0.5 to 3.6 kg).

Catfish

Perch

Type: Lean.

Varieties: Yellow perch is the most common. Walleyed pike is actually a perch, not a pike.

Characteristics: Mild-flavored, flaky, white flesh with firm texture and fine grain.

Weight: ½ to 5 lb (0.2 to 2.3 kg).

Pike

Type: Lean.

Varieties: Northern pike is most common in North America. Walleyed pike or walleye is not a pike but a perch.

Characteristics: Firm white flesh similar to perch but not as thick, and with many small bones.

Weight: 2 to 12 lb (1 to 5.4 kg).

Tilapia

Type: Lean.

Characteristics: Nearly always from aquafarms because wild tilapia often taste muddy. Firm, mild white flesh.

Weight: up to 3 lb (1.4 kg), usually about 1½ lb (700 g).

Tilapia

Trout

Type: Fat.

Varieties: Lake trout, river trout, brook trout, rainbow trout, many local varieties.

Characteristics: Soft, fine-textured flesh with rich, delicate flavor. Color of flesh may be white, pink, or reddish.

Weight: Lake trout: 4 to 10 lb (2 to 4.5 kg). Others: ½ to 3 lb (0.2 to 1.4 kg).

Whitefish

Type: Fat.

Characteristics: Flaky, white flesh with somewhat sweet flavor.

Weight: 1½ to 6 lb (0.7 to 2.7 kg).

Trout

Whitefish

Handling and Storage

Fish and shellfish are some of the most perishable foods you will handle. It is especially important to store them carefully and use them quickly. The fishy taste that turns many people away from fish is actually a sign of decomposition. Fresh fish should taste and smell sweet and fresh.

Guidelines for checking fish quality are summarized in Table 14.1.

STORING FRESH FISH

Objectives

1. To maintain temperature of 30° to 34°F (−1° to +1°C).
2. To keep the fish moist.
3. To prevent fish odors and flavors from being transferred to other foods.
4. To protect the delicate flesh from being bruised or crushed.

TABLE 14.1

Checklist for Fish Freshness

Characteristics	Fresh Fish	Not-so-fresh Fish
Odor	Fresh and mild, no off odors	Strong fishy odor
Eyes	Clear, shiny, bulging	Cloudy, sunken
Gills	Red or pink	Gray or brown
Texture of flesh	Firm, elastic	Soft, dents easily
Scales	Shiny, tight on skin	Loose, not shiny

Note: Because most fish is not purchased whole or dressed but as fillets, steaks, or other portions, odor must be your primary check for freshness.

Methods

1. On crushed ice—the preferred method. Use drip pans to allow for drainage of melted ice. Change ice daily. Cover container or store in separate box away from other foods.

   Whole fish should be drawn as soon as possible because the entrails deteriorate quickly. Whole or drawn fish are not wrapped. Cut fish (fillets, steaks, portions) should be wrapped or left in original moistureproof wrap.

2. In refrigerated box at 30° to 34°F (–1° to +1°C)—if crushed ice storage is not available or practical. Wrap all fish or leave in original moistureproof wrap.

Storage Time

Fresh fish may be stored for 1 or 2 days. If it must be kept longer, you may (1) wrap and freeze it immediately or (2) cook and then refrigerate it for later use in recipes calling for cooked fish.

Check stored fish for freshness just before you use it. Even if it was fresh when received, it may not be fresh after a few days in storage.

FROZEN, CANNED, AND OTHER PROCESSED FISH

Figure 14.5 Seafood PUFI seal (U.S.).

Federal Inspection

In the United States, the National Oceanic and Atmospheric Administration (NOAA) and the Department of Commerce conduct voluntary seafood inspection programs to promote the safety of processed fish and shellfish. Processors who wish to take part in the programs must pay for the service, but they may then use official seals or marks on their product packaging and in advertising, including the PUFI seal (Processed Under Federal Inspection) (Figure 14.5) and the U.S. Grade A shield (Figure 14.6). The PUFI seal indicates that the product is packed under federal inspection and is safe and wholesome, of good quality, and properly labeled. In addition, companies that operate with a written HACCP quality management program (see p. 24) may take advantage of the Department of Commerce's HACCP-based inspection program.

Frozen Fish

Frozen seafood products account for more of the fish served today than does fresh. If it were not for the wide availability of these frozen seafood products, commercial kitchens would serve much less fish than they do.

Figure 14.6 Seafood grade shield (U.S.).

Checking Quality

1. Frozen products should be frozen when received, not thawed.

2. Look for fresh, sweet odor or none at all. Strong, fishy odor means poor handling.

3. Items should be well wrapped, with no freezer burn.

4. Some frozen fish is *glazed* with a thin layer of ice to prevent drying. Check for shiny surface to make sure glaze has not melted off or evaporated.

Storage

1. Store at 0°F (–18°C) or colder.

2. Keep well wrapped to prevent freezer burn.

3. Maximum storage time:
   Fat fish: 2 months.
   Lean fish: 6 months.

4. Rotate stock—first in, first out.

Thawing and Handling

1. *Frozen raw fish.*

   • Thaw in refrigerator, never at room temperature. Allow 18 to 36 hours, depending on size. Alternative method, if pressed for time: Keep in original moistureproof wrapper and thaw under cold running water.

- Small pieces (fillets, steaks, portions) up to 8 oz (250 g) can be cooked from frozen state to make handling easier and to prevent excessive drip loss. Large fish should be thawed for more even cooking from surface to interior.
- Fillets or other portions that are to be breaded or prepared in some other way before cooking may be partially thawed (for example, for a few seconds in a microwave), then prepped and cooked. They will be easier to handle than if fully thawed.
- Handle thawed fish as you would fresh fish.
- Do not refreeze.

2. *Breaded and battered fish, fully prepared entrées, and other frozen, prepared fish items.*
   - Read and follow package directions.
   - Most of these items are cooked from the frozen state, usually in the deep-fryer, oven, microwave, or steamer.

Canned Fish

1. Check cans for signs of damage. Discard swollen cans (or return to the supplier).
2. Store, like other canned goods, in a cool, dry place.
3. Opened canned fish should be placed in covered containers, labeled with the contents and date, and refrigerated. It will keep for 2 or 3 days.

Shellfish

Shellfish are distinguished from fin fish by their hard outer shells and their lack of backbones or internal skeletons.

There are two classifications of shellfish:

1. *Mollusks* are soft sea animals that fall into three main categories:
   - *Bivalves*, which have a pair of hinged shells (such as clams and oysters)
   - *Univalves*, which have a single shell (such as abalone and conch)
   - *Cephalopods* (such as octopus, squid, and cuttlefish).

   (From the scientist's point of view, there are other mollusks as well, but they do not concern us here.)
2. *Crustaceans* are animals with segmented shells and jointed legs.

Mollusks

The most important mollusks in commercial kitchens are oysters, clams, mussels, scallops, squid, and octopus.

OYSTERS

Characteristics

1. Oysters have rough, irregular shells. The bottom shell is slightly bowl shaped. The top shell is flat.
2. The flesh of the oyster is extremely soft and delicate and contains a high percentage of water.
3. Oysters are available all year, even in months without an *R* in their names, but they are at their best in the fall, winter, and spring.
4. There are four main varieties in the United States and Canada, depending on their origin. Note in particular that the dozens of varieties of Eastern oysters are all the same species; they all have different flavors, however, depending on the environment in which they grew.

   Eastern: Known by many local names, depending on their place of origin.
   Olympia: Very small, from the Pacific coast.
   Belon: European oyster now grown in North America. Shells are flatter than those of Eastern oysters.
   Japanese or Pacific: Large oysters from the Pacific coast.

Market Forms

1. Live, in the shell.

2. Shucked—fresh or frozen. Shucked oysters are graded by size as follows.

Grade	Number per Gallon (3.8 liters)
Extra Large or Counts	160 or fewer
Large or Extra Selects	161 to 210
Medium or Selects	211 to 300
Small or Standards	301 to 500
Very Small	Over 500

3. Canned—rarely used in food service.

Checking Freshness

1. Oysters in the shell must be alive to be good to eat. Tightly closed shells, or shells that close when jostled, indicate live oysters. Discard dead ones.

2. Live oysters and shucked oysters should have a very mild, sweet smell. Strong odors indicate spoilage.

Opening Oysters

1. Scrub shells thoroughly before opening.

2. Oysters to be served raw must be opened in a way that leaves the bottom shell intact and the tender oyster undamaged. The technique illustrated in Figure 14.7 is one common way of opening oysters. Your instructor may wish to show you another method.

3. Oysters to be cooked may be opened by spreading them on a sheet pan and placing them in a hot oven just until the shells open. Remove from shells and cook immediately. Discard any that do not open.

Figure 14.7 Opening oysters.

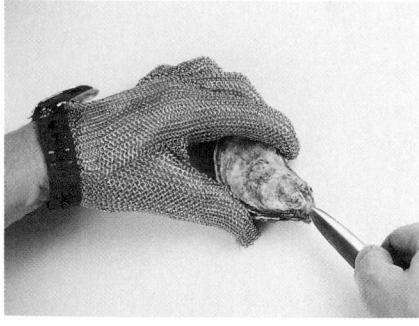

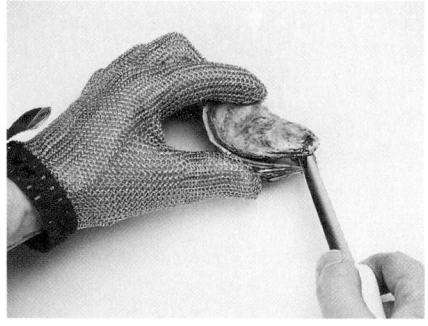

(a) Examine the shell to see that it is tightly closed, indicating a live oyster. Rinse the shell under cold, running water. Hold oyster in left hand, as shown. (Left-handers will hold oyster in right hand.) Hold the oyster knife near the tip as shown. Insert the knife between the shells near the hinge.

(b) Twist the knife to break the hinge.

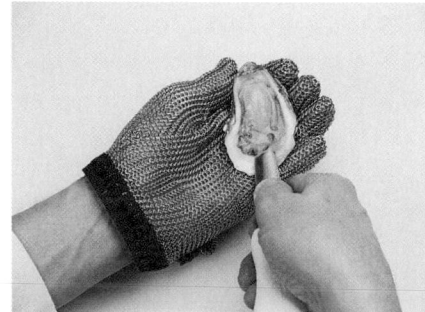

(c) Slide the knife under the top shell and cut through the adductor *muscle (which closes the shells) near the top shell. Try not to cut the flesh of the oyster, or it will lose plumpness. Remove the top shell.*

(d) Carefully cut the lower end of the muscle from the bottom shell to loosen oyster. Remove any particles of shell from the oyster before serving.

Storage

1. Keep live oysters in a cold, wet place in the cartons or sacks in which they arrived. They should keep at least 1 week.

2. Store fresh shucked oysters in the original container in refrigerator at 30° to 34°F (−1° to 1°C). They will keep up to 1 week.

3. Keep frozen oysters in freezer, at 0°F (−18°C) or colder, until ready for use. Thaw in refrigerator for 24 hours or more, depending on size of container.

Cooking Oysters

1. Cook just enough to heat through to keep oysters juicy and plump. Overcooking makes them shrunken and dry.

2. Cooking methods: Poaching, deep-frying, baking on the half shell with toppings, in soups and stews.

CLAMS

Characteristics

There are two major kinds of clams from the east coast of North America: *hard shell* and *soft shell.* The West Coast also has some local varieties.

1. Hard-shell clams or quahogs. These go by different names, depending on size.

   Littlenecks are the smallest. They are the most tender for eating raw or for steaming.

   Cherrystones are medium-sized, and perhaps the most common. They can be eaten raw and are good for steaming, though tougher than littlenecks.

   Chowders, the largest, are also called *quahogs* in the Northeast. Rather tough, they are chopped for cooking in chowders or cut into strips for frying.

2. Soft-shell clams. These are sometimes called *longnecks* because of the long tube that protrudes from between the shells. They have very thin shells that do not close completely.

   They are also called *steamers* because the usual way to serve them is to steam them and serve them with their own broth and with melted butter for dipping.

Clams, clockwise from top left: steamers, littlenecks, cherrystones, chowder clams.

Market Forms (Hard–Shell Clams)

1. Live, in the shell.
2. Shucked, fresh or frozen.
3. Canned, whole or chopped.

Checking Freshness

Same as for oysters. Clams in the shell must be alive. Live and shucked clams should smell fresh.

Opening Clams

1. Scrub shells thoroughly before opening.

2. Hard-shell clams are sometimes sandy inside, and soft-shell clams nearly always are. They can be flushed as follows:
   - Make a salt brine, using ⅓ cup salt per gallon of water (20 mL salt per liter).
   - Soak the clams in the brine for 20 minutes.
   - Drain and repeat until the clams are sand free.
   - Some chefs put cornmeal in the water and refrigerate the clams in it for a day. The clams eat the cornmeal and expel the sand.
   - Rinse in fresh water before using.

Figure 14.8 Opening clams.

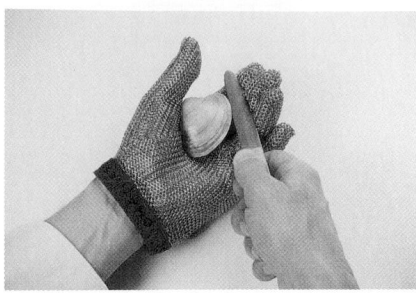

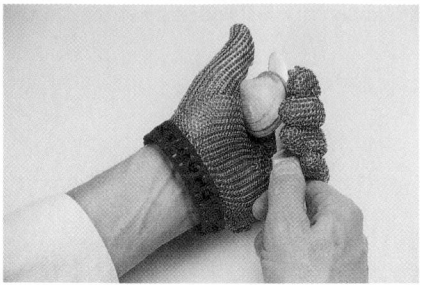

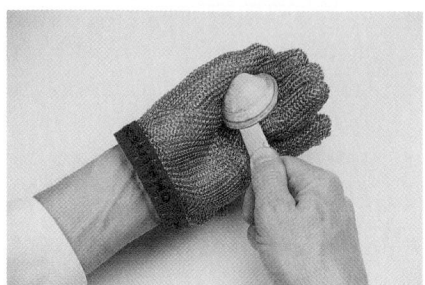

(a) Examine the shell to see that it is tightly closed, indicating a live clam. Rinse the shell under cold, running water. Avoid jostling the clam too much, or it will "clam up" tighter. Hold clam in left hand as shown (or in right hand if you are left handed). Place the sharp edge of the clam knife against the crack between the shells.

(b) Squeeze with the fingers of the left hand, forcing the knife between the shells.

(c) Change the angle of the blade as shown in the illustration and slide the knife against the top shell to cut the adductor muscles (clams have two; oysters have only one). Be careful not to cut or pierce the soft clam.

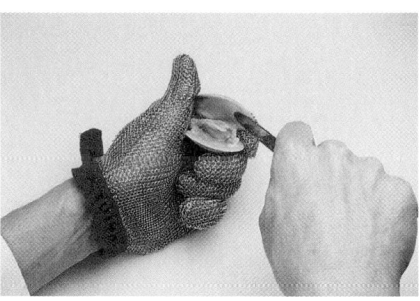

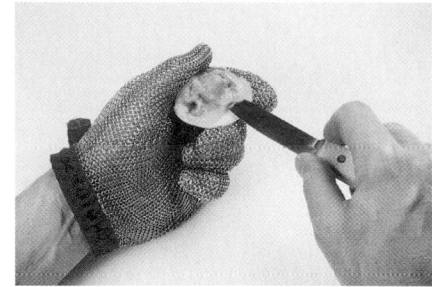

(d) Open the clam and finish detaching the meat from the upper shell.

(e) Cut the muscles against the lower shell to loosen the clam completely. Discard the top shell. Remove any particles of shell from the clam before serving.

3. Opening hard-shell clams is different from opening oysters. This technique is illustrated in Figure 14.8.
4. Like oysters, clams to be cooked may be opened by spreading on sheet pans and placing in a hot oven just until the shells open. Discard any that do not open.

Storage
Same as for oysters.

Cooking Clams
1. Clams become very tough and rubbery if overcooked. Cook just enough to heat through.
2. When steaming clams in the shell, steam just until shells open.
3. Cooking methods: Steaming, poaching, deep-frying, baking on the half shell with toppings, simmering in soups and chowders.

MUSSELS

Characteristics
The most common mussels resemble small black or dark-blue clams. Their shells are not as heavy as clamshells. Their flesh is yellow to orange in color and firm but tender when cooked. Mussels are harvested worldwide and are also extensively farmed.

Mussels, left to right: green, blue (wild), blue (farm-raised)

Green mussels, from New Zealand and Southeast Asia, are larger and have a lighter colored gray or tan shell with a green edge. Green mussels often command premium prices.

Market Forms
Most mussels are sold live, in the shell. Many are also sold shucked and packed in brine.

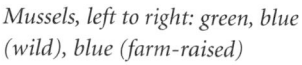

Checking Freshness

1. Like oysters and clams, mussels must be alive to be good to eat. Check for tightly closed shells or shells that just close when jostled.

2. Discard any mussels that are very light in weight or seem to be hollow. Also, discard any that are much too heavy—they are probably full of sand.

Cleaning

1. Clean shells thoroughly:
   - Scrub well under cold running water.
   - Scrape off barnacles, if any, with a clam knife.
   - Remove the beard, a fibrous appendage protruding from between the shells (see Figure 14.9).

2. Mussels may be sandy inside if not commercially grown. They may be soaked in brine and flour or cornmeal like clams (see previous section) to rid them of sand.

Figure 14.9 When cleaning mussels, pull off the fibrous beard that extends from between the shells.

Storage

Keep refrigerated (32° to 35°F/0° to 2°C) and protect from light. Store in original sack and keep sack damp.

Cooking

Unlike oysters and clams, mussels are almost never served raw. They are usually steamed and served in their cooking broth, in soups, or chilled and served with mayonnaise-type sauces. Cook only until shells open and mussels are heated through. Do not overcook. Discard any that are not open after cooking.

SCALLOPS

Characteristics

1. Scallops are almost always sold shucked. The only part we usually eat is the adductor muscle, which closes the shell. If live scallops in the shell are available, leave the orange, crescent-shaped coral attached to the adductor muscle when shucking.

2. There are two main kinds of scallops:

    Bay scallops: small, with delicate flavor and texture; expensive; 32 to 40 per pound (70 to 88 per kilogram) on average.

    Sea scallops: larger, not as delicate as bay scallops, but still tender unless overcooked; 10 to 15 per pound (22 to 33 per kilogram) on average.

3. Scallops are creamy white in color and have a sweet flavor.

4. They are available all year.

Market Forms

1. Fresh, shucked. Sold by volume or weight.
2. Frozen.
   - IQF (individually quick frozen).
   - In 5-lb (2.3-kg) blocks.

Scallops with roe or coral

Checking Freshness

A sweet, clean smell is a sign of freshness. Strong fishy odor or a brownish color is a sign of age or spoilage.

Handling

1. Shucked scallops can be cooked without any further preparation. They are improved, however, if you pull off the small, tough tendon or sinew on the side of each scallop.

2. Large sea scallops are sometimes cut into smaller pieces before cooking.

Storage

Keep scallops covered and refrigerated (30° to 34°F/−1° to 1°C). Do not let them rest directly on ice, or they will lose flavor and become watery.

Cooking Scallops

Scallops are cooked in almost every way that fish are cooked. The most popular methods are sautéing, deep-frying, broiling, and poaching.

Cephalopods

The term *cephalopod* means "head-foot," referring to the fact that these animals have tentacles or "legs" attached to the head, surrounding the mouth. The most important cephalopods in the North American kitchen are squid and octopus. A third type, cuttlefish, is similar to squid but is usually seen only in limited markets.

SQUID

Squid, usually referred to on menus by their Italian name, *calamari*, are classified as mollusks, even though they have no external shell. They are soft-bodied animals somewhat resembling octopus, but they have 10 tentacles, 2 of them longer than the others.

Squid must be skinned and eviscerated. The head, beak, and the internal plasticlike quill are discarded. The hollow body and tentacles are eaten. Figure 14.10 illustrates how to clean squid.

Somewhat chewy, squid are cut up and either fried quickly or simmered for about 45 minutes in a seasoned liquid or sauce.

Note: The similar *cuttlefish* has a shorter, thicker body than does squid. Instead of a thin, transparent interior quill, it has a hard, chalky cuttlebone.

OCTOPUS

Octopus (the name means "eight feet") range in size from less than an ounce to many pounds. All sizes are firm-textured, even chewy, but the larger sizes are usually considered too tough to eat. Because of its texture, octopus requires either mechanical tenderization (such as pounding with a mallet) or long, slow cooking in a court bouillon.

Like squid, octopus is cleaned by cutting off the tentacles, discarding the head and beak, and eviscerating the body cavity. Pull the skin off the body pouch and tentacles; it may be necessary to parboil the octopus for a few minutes to loosen the skin. The skin is reddish gray, turning purple-red when cooked.

Figure 14.10 Cleaning squid.

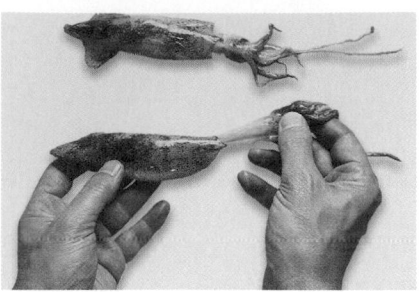

(a) Pull off the head. The interior organs will come out with it.

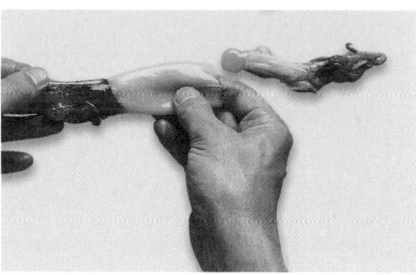

(b) Pull off the skin.

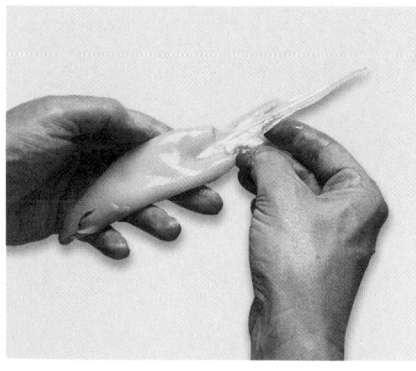

(c) Pull out the plasticlike quill from the body sac. Rinse out the sac to clean it well.

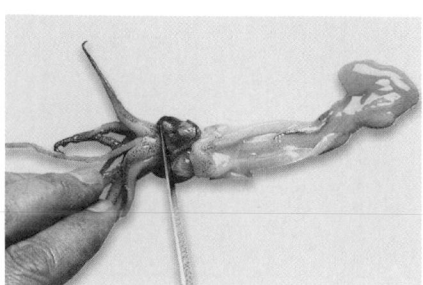

(d) Cut off the tentacles just above the eyes. Discard the head and organs.

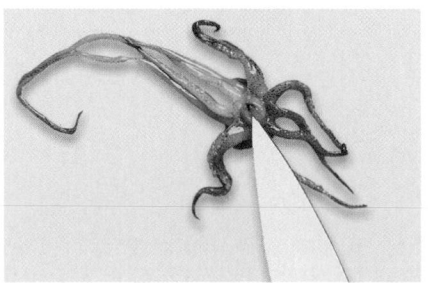

(e) Be sure to remove the hard beak, which is found at the center of the tentacle cluster, as shown by the tip of the knife in this picture.

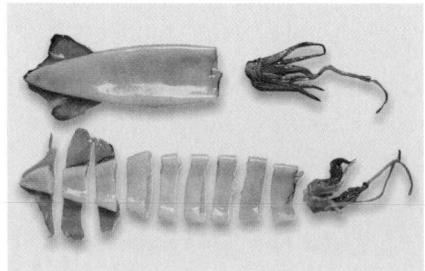

(f) The body sac may be left whole for stuffing or cut into rings for frying, sautéing, or stewing.

Crustaceans

The most important crustaceans in commercial kitchens are lobsters, rock lobsters or langoustes, shrimp, and crabs.

LOBSTERS

Characteristics

1. The northern lobster is perhaps the most prized of all shellfish. It has a large, flexible tail, four pairs of legs, and two large claws. Its shell is dark green or bluish green but turns red when cooked.

2. Meat from the tail, claws, and legs is eaten. It is white and sweet, with a distinctive taste. Claw meat is considered especially good. The *coral* (roe or eggs), which is dark green when raw and red when cooked, and the green *tomalley* (liver) in the thorax or body portion are also eaten.

3. Lobsters are classified by weight.

Chicken	1 lb (450 g)
Quarters	1¼ lb (575 g)
Selects	1½ to 2¼ lb (675 to 1025 g)
Jumbos	over 2½ lb (1130 g)

4. Lobsters weighing over 20 lb (9 kg) have been caught, but they are rare.

5. Yield: A 1-lb lobster yields about ¼ lb of cooked meat, or a 500-g lobster yields about 125 g of cooked meat.

6. Sometimes customers request female lobsters in order to get the coral, so you should be able to tell females from males. Look at the pairs of tiny legs (called *swimmerets*) under the tail. If the pair closest to the front is soft and flexible, the lobster is female. If it is hard, the lobster is male.

Market Forms

1. Live.

2. Cooked meat, fresh or frozen.

Checking Freshness

1. Live lobster must be alive when cooked. This is indicated by movement of the legs and claws and by a tightly curled tail.

2. If the lobster is dead when cooked, the meat will fall apart. If alive, the meat will be firm and the tail will spring back when straightened.

3. "Sleepers" (dying lobsters) should be cooked immediately so that the meat will still be usable.

4. Cooked lobster meat (fresh or thawed) should smell fresh and sweet.

Handling

1. Live lobsters are either cooked live or cut up before cooking (as for broiling or sautéing). Live lobsters are plunged head first into boiling water to kill them instantly. They are then simmered for 5 to 6 minutes per pound (500 g). If served hot, they are drained well and split in half, and the claws are cracked.

2. Splitting and cutting up live lobsters is necessary for certain preparations. Figure 14.11 shows splitting a lobster for broiling. Figure 14.12 shows cutting up a lobster for sautés and stews. Note that the methods are somewhat different.

3. The thorax section contains three parts you should recognize. Figure 14.13 shows their location.
   - The stomach or sac, located just behind the eyes, is often sandy and should be discarded.
   - The tomalley, or liver, is pale green. It is eaten plain or removed, mashed, and added to sauces that accompany the lobster.
   - The coral or roe is red when cooked and dark green when raw. It is present only in females. Like the tomalley, it is considered a delicacy.

(Text continues on p. 381)

Figure 14.11 Splitting a lobster for broiling.

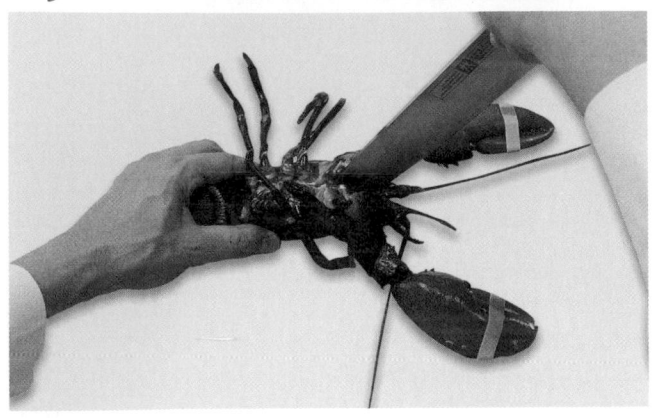

(a) Place the lobster on its back on a cutting board. With a firm thrust of a French knife, pierce the head.

(b) Bring the knife down firmly through the center of the lobster to split it in half.

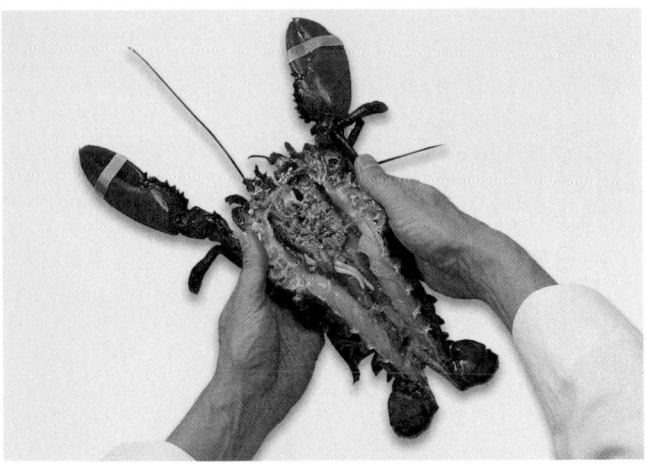

(c) With the hands, crack the back of the shell by spreading the lobster open.

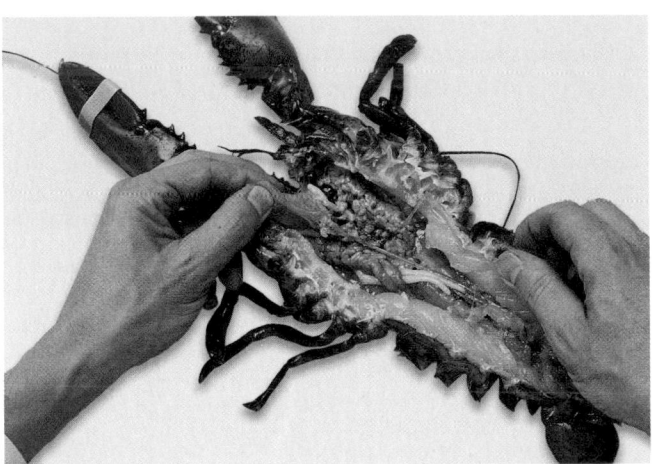

(d) Pull out and discard stomach, a sac just behind the eyes.

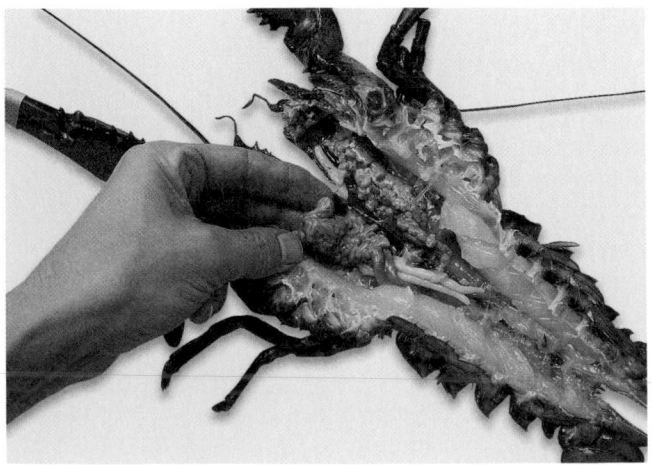

(e) If desired, remove the tomalley for use in the crumb stuffing.

(f) With a sharp blow of the back of the knife, crack the claws.

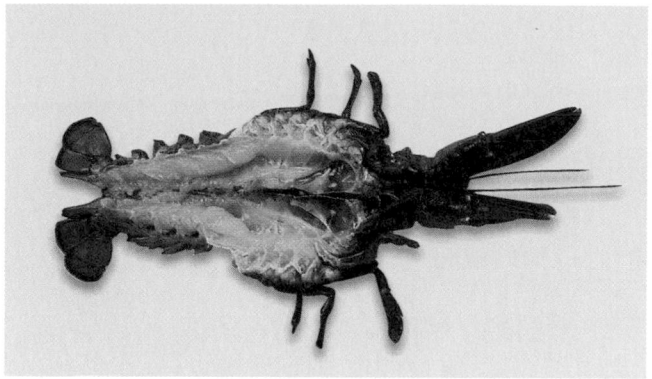

(g) The lobster is ready for broiling. If it is broiled as shown, the end of the tail should be weighted down to keep it from curling.

(h) You may also split the tail all the way through and curl up the two sides as shown. In this position, weighting the tail is not necessary. Note that the claws have been broken off and placed beside the lobster.

Figure 14.12 Cutting a lobster for sautés and stews.

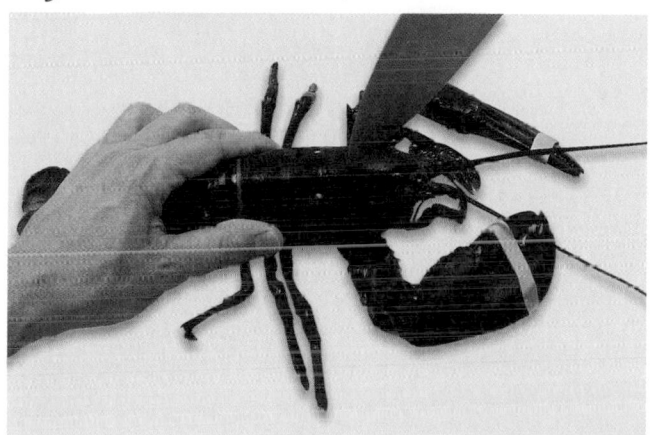
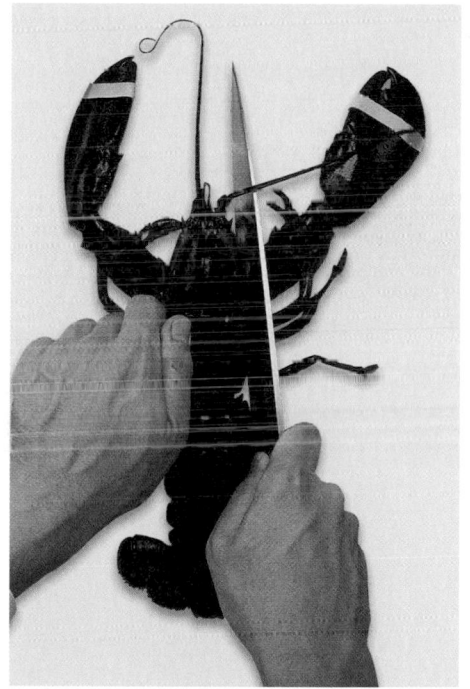

(a) Place the lobster on the cutting board. Pierce the head with a firm thrust of the knife point to kill the lobster quickly.

(b) Cut off the legs and claws.

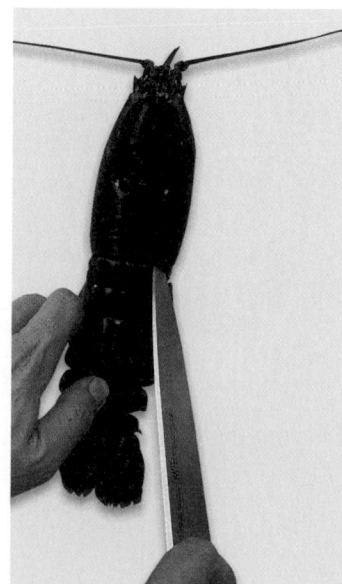

(c) Remove the tail section from the thorax, either by breaking it off or by inserting the knife behind the thorax as shown and cutting through the flesh.

Figure 14.12 (Continued)

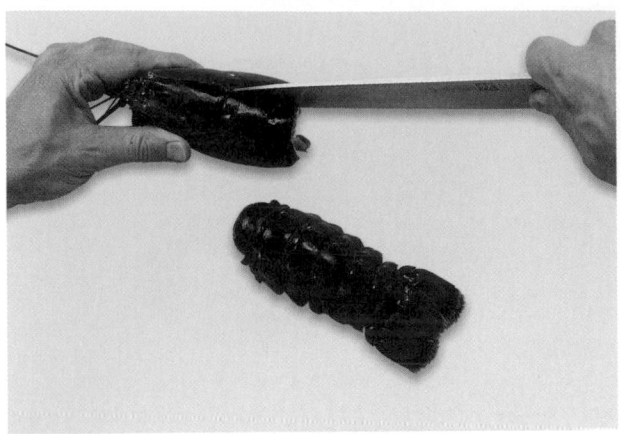

(d) Cut the thorax in half lengthwise.

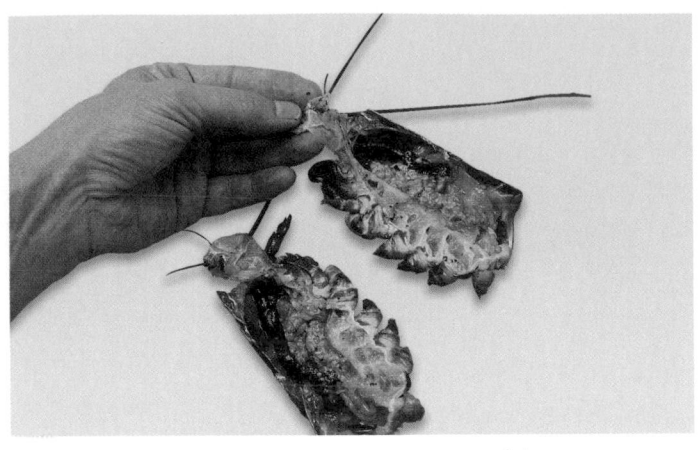

(e) Remove and discard the stomach, a sac just behind the eyes.

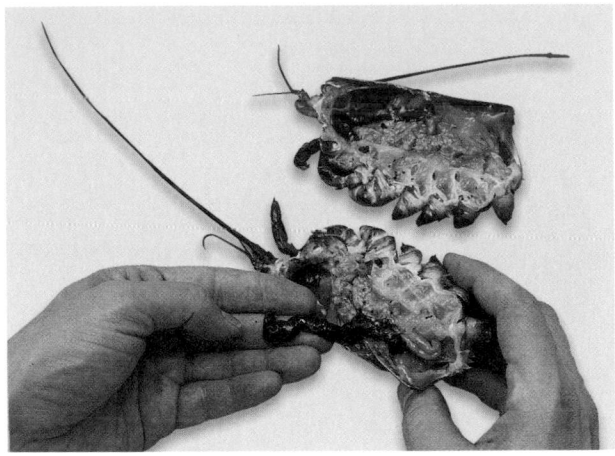

(f) Remove the tomalley and coral for use in the sauce to accompany the lobster.

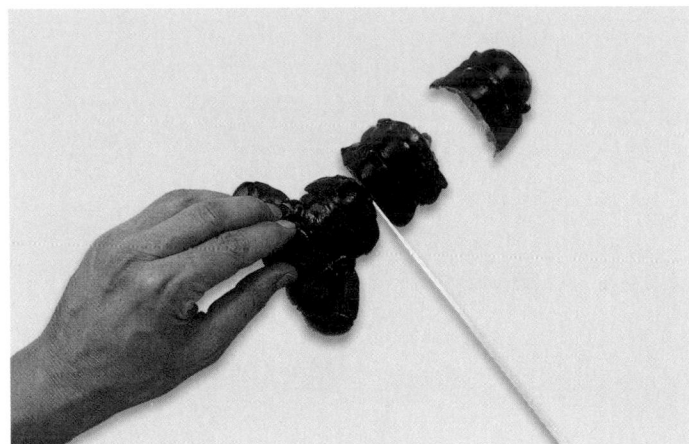

(g) Cut the tail into pieces where the segments join. This is a small lobster. Large tails should be cut into more pieces (at least four or five) so that each piece is not too large.

(h) The cut-up lobster, ready to cook.

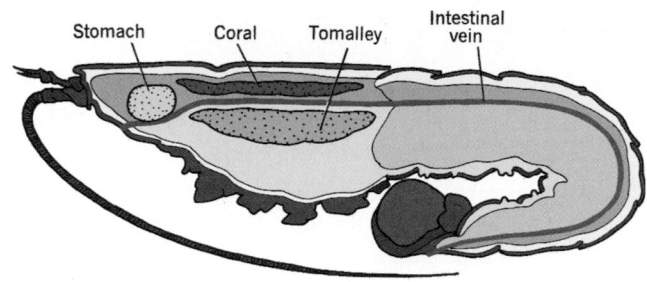

Figure 14.13 Cross section of a female lobster showing the location of the stomach, tomalley, coral, and vein.

Storage

1. Live lobsters can be kept in two ways:
   - Packed in moist seaweed or in moist, heavy paper, kept in a cool place.
   - In saltwater. Special lobster tanks are used in restaurants for display and for allowing customers to select their own lobster. Air must be bubbled through the water to keep the lobsters alive.

2. Cooked lobster meat must be covered and refrigerated at 30° to 34°F (−1° to 1°C). It is very perishable and should be used in 1 or 2 days.

Cooking Lobsters

1. Lobster meat becomes tough if cooked at too high a temperature or for too long. Boiling too long will also make the meat dry. Whole lobster is usually cooked by dropping into boiling water and then simmering for 5 to 6 minutes per pound (500 g). For jumbo lobsters, reduce the cooking time slightly.

2. Whole or cut-up lobster can be cooked by simmering in water or court bouillon, simmering in sauce or soup, sautéing, baking, or broiling.

ROCK LOBSTERS

Characteristics

1. Rock lobsters are also known as *spiny lobsters* or *langoustes*. They are warm-water relatives of northern lobsters but have no claws. Only the tails are marketed, sold as *lobster tails*.

2. The flesh of the rock lobster tail is similar to that of the northern or Maine lobster, but it is drier and coarser, with less flavor.

3. Rock lobster tails weigh from 2 to 12 oz (60 to 340 g).

4. *Langoustines* or *langostinos* are smaller relatives of the rock lobster. These small shellfish are often marketed as *rock shrimp*. When out of the shell, they look like shrimp, but their flavor is milder and sweeter than that of shrimp. The term *scampi* (plural form of *scampo*) refers not to shrimp but to a variety of langoustine from Italian waters. The name *scampi* is often used, incorrectly, for large shrimp broiled with butter and garlic.

Market Forms

Nearly all rock lobster tails are sold IQF (individually quick frozen).

Handling and Cooking

1. Rock lobsters are handled and cooked much like northern lobsters. Most common cooking methods are steaming, simmering, and broiling.

2. Tails to be broiled will be moister if poached for 5 minutes before splitting and broiling.

3. Tails steamed or simmered whole should have the shells split before serving as a convenience to the customer.

SHRIMP

Characteristics

1. Shrimp are small crustaceans that look somewhat like tiny, clawless lobsters. Only the tail is marketed and eaten, as a rule.

2. Shrimp come in many varieties, depending on where they are caught, but the particular variety is usually of little importance to the cook.

3. Shrimp are classified by count per pound—the higher the count, the smaller the shrimp. (For example, 16/20 means 16 to 20 per pound.) Classification systems differ by market. That is, in different markets a given size shrimp may have different names.

4. Large shrimp are more expensive per pound, but they require less work to peel and devein.

5. Yield: 1 lb raw shrimp (tails) in the shell yield about ½ lb peeled, cooked shrimp.

6. The term *prawn* is sometimes used for large shrimp, sometimes for langoustines (see p. 381). Use of the term varies from region to region.

Market Forms

1. *Green shrimp* are raw shrimp in the shell.

    Fresh: Not widely available, except near source of supply.
    Frozen: In 5-lb (2.3-kg) blocks.

2. P/D (peeled, deveined): Usually IQF (individually quick frozen).

3. PDC (peeled, deveined, and cooked): Usually IQF.

Note: IQF shrimp are usually glazed (see p. 370).

Checking Freshness

1. Frozen shrimp should be solidly frozen when received.

2. Glazed shrimp should be shiny, with no freezer burn.

3. All shrimp should smell fresh and sweet. A strong fishy or iodine smell indicates age or spoilage.

Storing

1. Like other frozen fish, shrimp should be kept frozen at 0°F (–18°C) or lower until ready for use.

2. Thaw in refrigerator, allowing sufficient slack time.

3. Fresh or thawed shrimp in the shell are stored on crushed ice, like whole fish.

4. Peeled shrimp lose soluble nutrients and flavor when stored unwrapped on ice. They should be wrapped before placing on ice or covered and simply refrigerated.

Handling

1. Shrimp served hot must normally be peeled and deveined before cooking. Figure 14.14 shows how.

2. Shrimp to be served cold may be peeled after cooking to preserve flavor.

3. Large shrimp are sometimes butterflied, as shown in Figure 14.14f. This is done for appearance (makes shrimp seem larger, with more surface area for breading) and to speed cooking by reducing thickness.

Cooking Shrimp

Like most shellfish, shrimp become tough and rubbery when cooked at too high a heat. Shrimp can be cooked by simmering, deep-frying, sautéing, broiling, and baking.

Figure 14.14 Peeling and deveining shrimp.

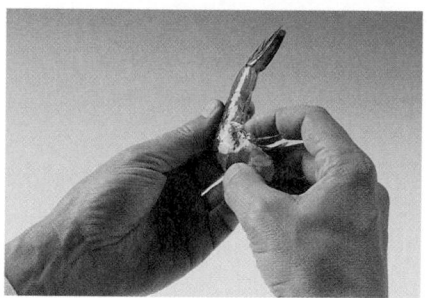

(a) Pull off the legs with your forefinger.

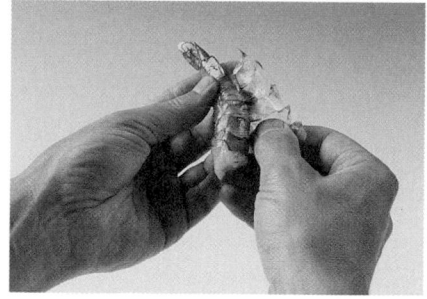

(b) Peel back the shell as shown and remove.

(c) For deep-fried and broiled shrimp, leave on the tail section of the shell for appearance. This also gives you something to hold when dipping the shrimp in batter.

CRABS

Six kinds of crabs are important in commercial kitchens.

1. **Alaskan king crab.**
    Largest of the crabs, weighing from 6 to 20 lb (2.7 to 9 kg). The meat can be removed in large chunks, making it especially attractive to serve in restaurants. It is expensive.

2. **Alaskan snow crab.**
    Smaller than the king crab. Often used as a less expensive substitute.

3. **Dungeness crab.**
    Another West Coast crab, weighing 1½ to 4 lb (0.7 to 1.8 kg). The meat is very sweet.

4. **Blue crab.**
    Small crab from the East coast, weighing about 5 oz (140 g). Most frozen crab-meat is from blue crabs.

5. **Soft-shell crab.**
    Actually a molting blue crab, harvested before the new shell has hardened. It is sautéed or fried and eaten shell and all; only the gills and head are removed.
    Soft-shell crabs must be cleaned before being cooked. The procedure is shown in Figure 14.15.

6. **Stone crab.**
    Popular in the Southeast. Only the claws are eaten.

Market Forms

1. Live. Crabs taste best when fresh, but very few (except soft-shell crabs) are purchased live because of the labor required to pick the meat. An average blue crab yields less than an ounce (30 g) of meat.

2. Cooked, frozen, in the shell.
    King crab legs, whole and split.
    Snow and stone crab claws.
    Soft-shell crabs, whole.

3. Cooked, frozen meat. All varieties.

Freshness and Storage

1. Live crabs should be kept alive until cooked. They are packed in damp seaweed and kept cool.

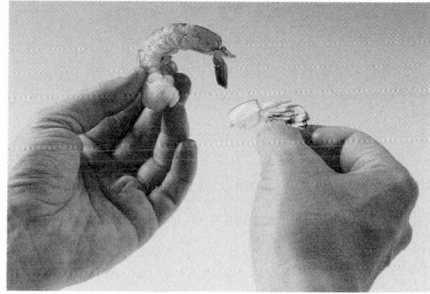

(d) For most other preparations, remove the tail section of the shell.

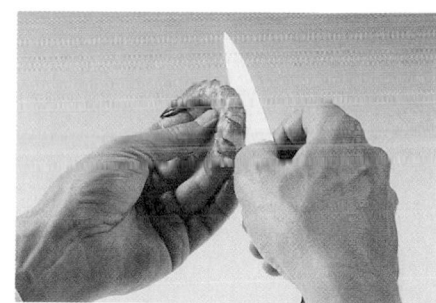

(e) With a paring knife, make a shallow cut down the back of the shrimp and pull out the intestinal vein, which is just below the surface.

(f) To butterfly shrimp, make the cut in step (e) deeper so that the shrimp can be spread open as shown.

Figure 14.15 *Cleaning soft-shell crabs.*

(a) Soft-shell crabs, seen from the bottom and top.

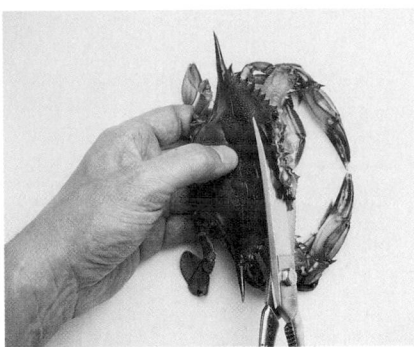

(b) Cut off the head just behind the eyes.

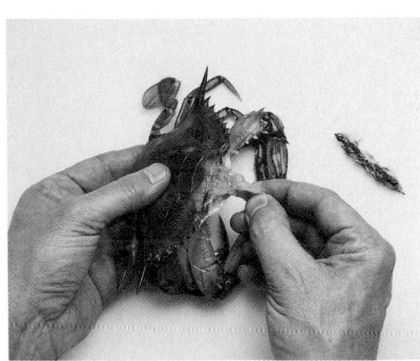

(c) Pull out the stomach sac.

2. Frozen crabmeat should be treated like any other frozen fish. It is very perishable when thawed.

Handling and Cooking

1. Hard-shell crabs are picked of their meat after cooking.
   - Simmer 10 to 15 minutes in salted water (½ cup salt per gallon or 30 mL per liter). Cool rapidly in ice water.
   - Break off the pointed shell on the underside (called the *apron*) and remove the top shell.
   - Remove and discard the spongy gills and the stomach, which is just behind the eyes.
   - Pick out the body meat.
   - Crack the legs and claws with a mallet or the back of a heavy knife and pick out the meat.

2. Soft-shell crabs.
   - With a knife or shears, cut off the head section, just behind the eyes.
   - Lift the pointed, outside corners of the top shell and pull out the spongy gills.
   - Cut off the apron, the small flap on the underside.
   - Dredge the crab in flour for sautéing, or bread or batter it for deep-frying.

3. Frozen crabmeat.
   - Crabmeat is usually watery. You may need to squeeze out excess moisture before cooking. Whenever possible, save the liquid for use in sauces and soups.
   - Frozen crabmeat is already cooked. It needs only to be heated through to be prepared for serving.

CRAYFISH

Crayfish or *crawfish* (the preferred term in the southern United States) are freshwater relatives of the lobster. Not long ago, they were used almost exclusively in Southern regional cuisine and in French restaurants. With the spreading popularity of Southern cuisines, including Creole and Cajun, they have become more widely available.

Crayfish are marketed live and frozen (peeled tail meat or whole).

(d) Pull back one side of the soft top shell to reveal the feathery gills.

(e) Pull off the gills. Repeat on the other side.

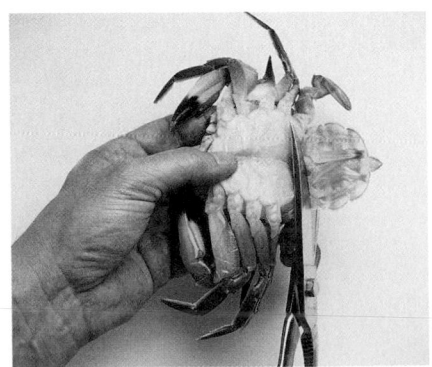

(f) Cut off the apron on the underside. The wide apron indicates that this is a female crab. Males have a much narrower apron.

Miscellaneous Seafood

Several other seafood items play a role in food service kitchens. They are classified with fish, even though some of them spend part or all of their lives on land, like frogs and snails.

Snails or *escargots* are popular hors d'oeuvres when baked in their shells with a highly seasoned butter. Fresh snails require long, slow cooking before being baked with escargot butter, but canned snails are fully cooked and ready to prepare. Canned snails can be improved, however, by first simmering them in white wine and seasonings.

Frogs' legs are often compared to chicken in taste and texture (but then, so are a lot of things). Only the hind legs are used, and they are sold in pairs. They may be sautéed, deep-fried, or poached and served with a sauce.

Surimi is a processed seafood product made by grinding lean, inexpensive, white fish, combining it with flavorings, and forming it into various shapes. The most popular shapes are shredded crab and crab leg segments, but other items, such as lobster claws, are also available. Coloring is added for a realistic appearance. Originally from Japan, surimi has found growing acceptance in North America because of the reasonably good quality of the product and the high cost of crab and lobster.

Terms for Review

fin fish	flatfish and round fish	calamari	scampi
shellfish	mollusks	cuttlefish	prawn
flaking	crustaceans	adductor muscle	soft-shell crab
lean and fat fish	bivalve	coral	crayfish
drawn	univalve	tomalley	surimi
dressed	cephalopod	langoustine	
fillet	squid	rock shrimp	

Questions for Discussion

1. Fish has very little connective tissue. How does this affect the ways in which you handle it and cook it?

2. Based on what you learned about fat and lean fish and about individual species of fish, can you suggest at least one cooking method for each of the following?

Mackerel	Salmon
Cod	Perch
Flounder	Swordfish
Trout	Whitefish
Red snapper	Halibut

3. List and describe the major market forms of fresh fish.

4. What are the differences between filleting flatfish and round fish? Describe or demonstrate.

5. You have just received delivery of fresh whole red snapper and fresh cod fillets. What should you check before accepting the shipment? After accepting them, what do you do with them?

6. You are making a casserole of shrimp with a prepared Newburg sauce and frozen, glazed cooked shrimp. When you add the frozen shrimp to the sauce, it thins out so much it is no longer usable. Why did this happen, and how could you have prevented it?

7. What is the most important indication of freshness in fresh oysters, clams, lobsters, and crabs? Describe how you would preserve this freshness.

8. How does opening oysters differ from opening clams, and how is it similar?

9. What happens to most kinds of shellfish when they are overcooked?

chapter 15

Cooking Fish and Shellfish

Because most fish and shellfish have very little connective tissue, the procedures for cooking them are somewhat different from those for cooking meats and poultry. When we cook meats, we are often concerned with tenderizing the product. Fish is naturally tender, however, and cooking—especially overcooking—is more likely to toughen the product and dry it out.

In this chapter, we apply basic cooking principles to the preparation of fish dishes. Our goals are to cook the product just to doneness, to preserve moisture and texture, and to preserve and enhance natural flavors.

Of course, your study of these procedures depends on your understanding of the basic information on fish in the previous chapter. In particular, you may want to review the sections on testing for doneness and on fat and lean fish and their appropriate cooking methods.

After reading this chapter, you should be able to

1. Cook fish and shellfish by baking.

2. Cook fish and shellfish by broiling.

3. Cook fish and shellfish by sautéing and pan-frying.

4. Cook fish and shellfish by deep-frying.

5. Cook fish and shellfish by poaching in court bouillon.

6. Cook fish and shellfish by poaching in fumet and wine.

7. Cook fish and shellfish by mixed cooking techniques.

8. Prepare dishes made of raw seafood.

Baking

Whole fish and fish portions may be cooked by baking in an oven. Although large whole fish may be baked, this is usually not practical in volume food service. The method is more often used with steaks and fillets and with small fish. It is also a popular method for preparing shellfish such as stuffed clams or oysters.

Baking is often combined with other cooking methods. For example, partially broiled fish can be finished by baking. Baked fish casseroles are usually made with cooked fish.

Whole fish or portions of fish baked in the oven may also be referred to as "roasted," as is currently the fashion. The term "roasting" may be applied both to basic baking and to moist baking, discussed below.

Guidelines for Baking Fish

1. Fat fish are best for baking because they are less likely to dry out.

2. Lean fish may be baked successfully if great care is taken not to overcook them. Basting with butter or oil helps prevent drying.

3. In most cases, baking temperatures are from 350° to 400°F (175° to 200°C). Large fish are best baked at the lower end of this range so that they will bake more evenly.

   It is also possible to bake thin fillets or slices of fillets (cut like scaloppine) at very high temperatures. Great care must be used in this case because the fish may cook in a minute or less, and a few seconds too long might ruin the fish. The effect of the high heat is almost like broiling, and the normal guidelines for broiling thin fish fillets should be followed, as explained in the next section.

4. It is not possible to give specific baking times because fish vary so much in shape and composition. Different ingredients and types of baking pans also affect the baking time. The following guideline is helpful, however: Measure the thickness of the fish at the thickest point. At 400°F (200°C), baking time will be about 10 minutes per inch (2.5 cm) of thickness.

5. Serving baked fish with a sauce or seasoned butter enhances its moistness and improves palatability. Serving with lemon also enhances the fish.

6. If fish is baked with a moist topping or sauce, strictly speaking, it is no longer being cooked by a dry-heat method. However, because the basic procedure is the same, the fish is treated as if it were.

Procedure for Baking Fish

1. Collect all equipment and food supplies.

2. Prepare and season fish (whole, steaks, fillets) as directed in the recipe.

3. Place the fish on oiled or buttered baking sheets. Brush tops with oil or butter.
   Alternative method: Dip fish in oil or melted butter to coat both sides. Place on baking sheets.

4. Apply toppings, if desired. Examples: seasoned bread crumbs, lemon slices, mushrooms or other vegetable garnish, and sauces.

5. Bake at 350° to 400°F (175° to 200°C) until done. If the fish is lean and doesn't have a moist topping, baste with oil or butter during baking.

MOIST BAKING OR BRAISING

As we noted above, if fish is baked with moist ingredients or with liquids, strictly speaking, the method is no longer a dry-heat method, although such preparations are included in this section. In French cooking, baking fish—usually whole fish or large pieces—with vegetables and liquid is called *braising*. To avoid confusion with the braising method as applied to meats, however, we avoid that term and refer to such dishes as *baked*.

This procedure is the same as the basic procedure for baking fish as described above, with the following special features:

1. The baking pan should be just large enough to hold the fish so that you will not need too much liquid.

2. The bottom of the pan is buttered or oiled, then covered with a layer of sliced or chopped vegetables, such as carrots, onions, shallots, and mushrooms. The vegetables may be raw or first sautéed gently in butter or oil. The fish is then placed on top of the vegetables.

3. A small amount of liquid is frequently added, such as equal parts wine and fish stock. Just enough liquid is used to cover the fish about halfway or less. During baking, the fish is basted with this liquid.

4. The fish may be baked uncovered or covered only lightly. It should not be covered tightly, however, because the liquid must be able to reduce somewhat so that it will become more concentrated and more flavorful. Remember also that more liquid will be released from the fish, diluting the cooking liquid.

5. For service, the fish is removed from the dish. The liquid is strained, degreased, reduced, and finished in various ways, such as by adding butter, cream, or velouté sauce.

You can see that this is a sort of combination technique. Because it often uses wine and other liquids, the method is, in some ways, similar to poaching in wine, as explained on page 412.

Baked Cod Fillets Portugaise

Portions: 24 **Portion size:** 5 oz (150 g) fish
2 oz (60 mL) sauce

U.S.	Metric	Ingredients	PROCEDURE
24	24	Cod fillets, 5-oz (150-g) portions	1. Place cod fillets on a well-oiled baking sheet or baking pan, flesh side up (that is, skin side down).
⅓ cup	75 mL	Lemon juice	2. Brush the fish lightly with lemon juice. Then brush generously with the butter or oil and season lightly with salt and pepper.
8 oz	250 mL	Melted butter or oil	3. Place the pan in a preheated 350°F (175°C) oven until done, about 10–15 minutes.
to taste	to taste	Salt	
to taste	to taste	White pepper	4. Halfway through the cooking time, check the fish and, if the tops appear to be drying out, brush with more butter or oil.
1½ qt	1.5 L	Portuguese Sauce (p. 151)	5. Serve each portion with 2 oz (60 mL) sauce. Nap the sauce across the center of the portion. Do not cover the entire fillet.

Per serving:
Calories, 170; Protein, 16 g; Fat, 10 g (53% cal.); Cholesterol, 60 mg; Carbohydrates, 4 g; Fiber, 1 g; Sodium, 250 mg.

VARIATIONS

Many other fish may be baked according to the basic recipe, such as

Haddock (fillets or steaks)	Pike (fillets)	Halibut (steaks or fillets)	Salmon (fillets or steaks)
Snapper (fillets)	Perch (fillets)	Bluefish (fillets)	Swordfish (steaks)
Bass (fillets)	Flounder (fillets)	Mackerel (fillets)	Whitefish (fillets)

Other appropriate sauces may be used, such as

Melted butter
Beurre noisette
Maître d'hôtel butter

Tomato and tomato-based sauces such as Creole (not for salmon or for very delicate fish like flounder)
Mustard (for strong-flavored fish only, such as mackerel or bluefish)
Curry (not for salmon or other fat fish)

Baked Fish with Tomatoes and Mushrooms

Portions: 10   Portion size: 1 fish

U.S.	Metric	Ingredients	PROCEDURE
10	10	Small whole fish, about 12 oz (375 g) each (see note)	1. Scale and clean the fish but leave the heads on. Season the fish inside and out with salt and pepper, and put a small pinch of thyme and a sprig of parsley in the cavity of each.
to taste	to taste	Salt	
to taste	to taste	Pepper	
pinch	pinch	Thyme	
10	10	Parsley sprigs	
as needed	as needed	Olive oil	2. Select as many baking pans as necessary to just hold the fish in a single layer. Oil the pans with a little olive oil.
8 oz	250 g	Onion, small dice	
1 oz	30 g	Shallots, minced	3. Sauté the onions and shallots in a little olive oil for about 1 minute. Add the mushrooms and sauté lightly.
8 oz	250 g	Mushrooms, chopped	
1 lb	500 g	Tomato concassé	4. Put the sautéed vegetables and the tomatoes in the bottoms of the baking pans.
8 oz	250 mL	Dry white wine	5. Put the fish in the pans. Oil the tops lightly. Pour in the wine.
			6. Bake at 400°F (200°C) until the fish is done. The time will vary but will average 15–20 minutes. Baste often with the liquid in the pan.
			7. Remove the fish and keep them warm until they are to be plated.
			8. Remove the vegetables from the pans with a slotted spoon and check for seasonings. Serve a spoonful of the vegetables with the fish, placing it under or alongside each fish.
			9. Strain, degrease, and reduce the cooking liquid slightly. Just before serving, moisten each portion with 1–2 tablespoons (15–30 mL) of the liquid.

Per serving:
Calories, 350; Protein, 55 g; Fat, 9 g (24% cal.); Cholesterol, 120 mg;
Carbohydrates, 6 g; Fiber, 1 g; Sodium, 210 mg.

Note: Many types of fish can be used, including sea bass, red snapper, porgy, perch, and trout. As an alternative, use thick steaks or thick pieces of fillet from larger fish such as cod or tilefish.

VARIATION

Baked Fish à la Menagère

Use butter instead of olive oil. Substitute sliced leeks for part or all of the onion. Omit the tomatoes. Add 4 oz (125 g) sliced carrot and cook it with the leek. Slice the mushrooms instead of chopping them, and add them to the pan raw. Add 1 cup (250 mL) fish stock along with the wine. After straining and reducing the cooking liquid in step 9, thicken it very lightly with a little beurre manié. Enrich the sauce with a little raw butter or cream.

Baked Stuffed Mackerel

Portions: 10   Portion size: 1 fish, with stuffing

U.S.	Metric	Ingredients	PROCEDURE
10	10	Mackerel, about 8–12 oz (250–375 g) each, or other small fish	1. Fillet the fish (see p. 363, Figure 14.4), but leave the skin on.
8 oz	250 g	Bread crumbs, fresh	2. Combine the crumbs, butter, and herbs in a bowl. Toss lightly until mixed.
3 oz	90 mL	Melted butter	
1 tbsp	15 mL	Chopped parsley	3. Mix the beaten egg, lemon zest, and lemon juice. Add to the crumbs and mix gently. Season to taste.
½ tsp	2 mL	Thyme	
1	1	Egg, beaten	
¼ tsp	1 mL	Grated lemon zest	
2 oz	60 mL	Lemon juice	
to taste	to taste	Salt	
as needed	as needed	Oil or melted butter	4. Place 10 fillets (that is, half of each fish) on a well-oiled baking sheet, skin side down.
			5. Top each fillet with 1½ oz (50 g) stuffing. (Portion with a No. 24 scoop.) Shape the stuffing to fit the length of the fish.
			6. Place the second fillet on top and press down lightly.
			7. Brush fish with oil or melted butter.
			8. Bake at 350°F (175°C) until done, about 15–20 minutes.

Per serving:
Calories, 600; Protein, 43 g; Fat, 41 g (63% cal.); Cholesterol, 165 mg; Carbohydrates, 12 g; Fiber, 1 g; Sodium, 330 mg.

Baked Clams Oreganata

Portions: 10   Portion size: 3 clams (appetizer portion)

U.S.	Metric	Ingredients	PROCEDURE
30	30	Cherrystone clams	1. Open the clams (see Figure 14.8 for technique). Catch the juice in a bowl.
			2. Remove the clams from the shell. Place them in a strainer over the bowl of juice. Let them drain 15 minutes in the refrigerator. Save the 30 best half-shells.
			3. Chop the clams into small pieces.
2 oz	60 mL	Olive oil	4. Heat the oil in a sauté pan. Add the onion and garlic. Sauté about 1 minute but do not brown.
1 oz	30 g	Onions, shallots, or scallions, chopped fine	5. Add *half* the clam juice and reduce by three-fourths over high heat.
1 tsp	5 mL	Garlic, chopped fine	
1 oz	30 mL	Lemon juice	6. Remove from the heat and add the lemon juice, crumbs, parsley, oregano, and white pepper. Mix gently to avoid making the crumbs pasty.
10 oz	300 g	Bread crumbs, fresh	
1 tbsp	15 mL	Chopped parsley	7. Taste and adjust seasonings if necessary. (Clams are usually very salty.)
¾ tsp	3 mL	Oregano	
⅛ tsp	0.5 mL	White pepper	8. Cool the mixture. Mix in the chopped clams.
⅓ cup	25 g	Parmesan cheese	9. Fill the 30 clam shells with the mixture. Sprinkle with parmesan cheese and (very lightly!) with paprika.
as needed	as needed	Paprika	
			10. Place on a sheet pan and refrigerate until needed.
10	10	Lemon wedges	11. For each order, bake 3 clams in a hot oven (450°F/230°C) until they are hot and the top is brown.
			12. Garnish with lemon wedge.

Per serving:
Calories, 180; Protein, 10 g; Fat, 8 g (41% cal.); Cholesterol, 20 mg; Carbohydrates, 16 g; Fiber, 1 g; Sodium, 230 mg.

Note: Clams and oysters are often baked on a bed of rock salt to hold them steady. The rock salt also holds heat well.

Smoke-Roasted Salmon Fillet with Pepper Salad

Portions: 12   Portion size: 4 oz (125 g) fish
                           4 oz (125 g) garnish

U.S.	Metric	Ingredients	PROCEDURE
3 lb	1.5 kg	Salmon fillets	1. Cut the salmon fillets into 4-oz (125-g) portions.
1 oz	30 mL	Vegetable oil	2. Brush the salmon lightly with oil.
¾ tsp	3 mL	Ground coriander	3. Combine the spices and salt. Sprinkle over the fish to coat them in a light, even layer.
¾ tsp	3 mL	Ground cumin	
¼ tsp	1 mL	Ground cloves	4. Set up a smoke-roasting system as shown in Figure 4.1. Heat the pan of wood chips or sawdust on top of the stove until smoke starts to appear. Lay the salmon fillets on the rack, cover, and turn the heat to medium-low. Smoke-roast for 2 minutes.
½ tsp	2 mL	Ground fennel	
½ tsp	2 mL	Black pepper	
1 tsp	5 mL	Salt	
			5. Transfer the pan to an oven preheated to 400°F (200°C) and continue roasting for another 8–10 minutes, until the fish is just cooked through.
3 lb	1.5 kg	Basque-Style Pepper Salad (p. 548)	6. Arrange the salmon fillets and the pepper salad on plates. Serve immediately.

Per serving:
Calories, 370; Protein, 22 g;
Fat, 29 g (70% cal.); Cholesterol, 70 mg;
Carbohydrates, 6 g; Fiber, 2 g;
Sodium, 250 mg.

Smoke-Roasted Salmon Fillet with Pepper Salad

Roasted Monkfish Wrapped in Prosciutto

Portions: 12   Portion size: 6 oz (175 g) fish
2⅓ oz (70 g) relish

U.S.	Metric	Ingredients	PROCEDURE
6 oz	175 g	Sugar	1. To prepare a syrup, dissolve the sugar in the water over low heat, bring to the boil, then remove from the heat. Add the lemon zest and rosemary sprigs and let stand to cool.
10 oz	300 mL	Water	
1½	1½	Lemons, zest only	
3	3	Rosemary sprigs	2. Brush the monkfish with the syrup and lay on the prosciutto ham. Roll the ham around the fish and tie securely with string.
4 lb 8 oz	2.2 kg	Monkfish fillets	
1 lb	500 g	Prosciutto, sliced	
as needed	as needed	Olive oil	3. Brush with olive oil and sear under a broiler or salamander. Finish cooking in a moderately hot oven (375°F/190°C). Remove from the oven and allow to rest a few minutes.
5 oz	150 g	Black olives, pitted, coarsely chopped	4. Prepare a relish by mixing together the olives, tomato, capers, chives, and olive oil.
12 oz	375 g	Tomatoes, peeled, seeded, and chopped	5. Slice the rested monkfish into thick slices resembling tournedos, allowing 3 per person. Arrange on plates. Spoon the relish around the fish. Garnish with whole chives laid across the plate.
4 oz	125 g	Capers	
½ oz	15 g	Chives, chopped	
7 oz	200 mL	Olive oil	
as needed	as needed	Whole chives for garnish	

Per serving:
Calories, 460; Protein, 36 g; Fat, 29 g (55% cal.); Cholesterol, 70 mg;
Carbohydrates, 17 g; Fiber, 1 g; Sodium, 1260 mg.

Roasted Monkfish Wrapped in Prosciutto

Baked Oysters with Balsamic Vinegar, Arugula, and Pine Nuts

Portions: 12   Portion size: 3 oysters (appetizer portion)

U.S.	Metric	Ingredients	PROCEDURE
36	36	Oysters	1. Open the oysters as shown in Figure 14.7. Arrange the oysters on a sheet pan.
½ oz	15 mL	Balsamic vinegar	
1 oz	30 g	Pine nuts, toasted	2. Top each oyster with a few drops of balsamic vinegar, then with a little chopped arugula, a few pine nuts, and, finally, about ¼ tsp (1.2 mL) olive oil. If the oysters are not salty, you may wish to add a little salt.
1 oz	30 g	Arugula, chopped	
1½ oz	45 mL	Olive oil	
			3. Bake at 450°F (230°C) for a few minutes, just until the oysters are hot. Serve immediately.

Per serving:
Calories, 70; Protein, 3 g; Fat, 6 g (77% cal.); Cholesterol, 15 mg;
Carbohydrates, 2 g; Fiber, 0 g; Sodium, 75 mg.

Broiling

Broiled and grilled seafood items, like grilled meats, are increasingly popular. Customers perceive them as simpler and more healthful and, because they are prepared quickly, as fitting the faster pace of modern life.

Grilled dishes are, in their purest form, simple and straightforward, but they lend themselves to many variations in presentation. By varying the sauces, vegetable accompaniments, and garnishes, you can offer a great assortment of grilled fish on the menu. And, because the sauces and accompaniments are generally prepared ahead of time, these dishes are still quick to prepare, even if the presentation is elaborate.

A slightly crisped, browned, or grill-marked surface is important to the appeal of grilled or broiled fish. Do not cover the item with sauce, and do not serve too much sauce. A small piece of seasoned butter or a drizzle of a flavorful condiment or sauce can be used to decorate the top of the item. In most other cases, it is better to place sauces on the side. Healthful sauces that are appropriate include vegetable coulis and salsas. For richer dishes, beurre blanc is a good accompaniment, especially for lean fish like halibut.

Another popular approach is to serve the fish without a sauce, except perhaps for a small dab of a condiment such as a relish or chutney, and to complement the fish with an attractive variety of vegetables.

Guidelines for Broiling Fish

1. Because of the intense heat of the broiler, great care is needed to avoid overcooking the fish.

2. Use small slices or fillets for broiling.

3. Fat fish is best for broiling because it doesn't get as dry as lean fish. However, all fish (fat or lean) should be coated with a fat before broiling to reduce drying.

4. Lean fish may be dredged in flour before dipping in oil or melted butter. The flour helps form a flavorful browned crust.

5. Instead of being dredged with flour, fish may be coated with fat and then with bread crumbs or cornmeal. Use caution, however, as bread crumbs burn very easily. Use this technique only with items that cook quickly.

6. If the fish has an attractive skin (such as red snapper and black sea bass), the skin may be left on and used as the presentation side. This enhances appearance and also helps hold the delicate flesh together. Make sure the fish is thoroughly scaled. To prevent splitting during cooking, score the skin with a sharp knife, making a series of parallel cuts across the fish or cutting in a diamond pattern for larger fish. For small fillets, scoring may not be necessary.

7. Broil fish to order and serve immediately.

8. Broiled fish may be garnished *lightly* with paprika if more color is desired. But don't overdo it. One of the most common faults in broiling or baking fish is coating them with a heavy layer of paprika, which ruins the delicate flavor of the fish.

9. Thick cuts should be turned once during broiling in order to cook evenly. Thin pieces may be arranged on an oiled pan and broiled on one side only. Lobster is also broiled without turning.

Procedure for Broiling Fish

1. Collect all equipment and food supplies.
2. Prepare the fish as required: season and coat with oil or butter, with flour and then fat, or with fat and then bread crumbs.
3. Preheat broiler.
4. Broil thick cuts on both sides, turning once. Broil thin pieces on one side only.
5. Serve immediately, with appropriate sauce and garnish.

Broiled Fish Steaks Maître d'Hôtel

Portions: as needed   **Portion size:** 5–6 oz (150–175 g)

U.S.	Metric	Ingredients	PROCEDURE
as needed	as needed	Fish steaks, 5–6 oz (150–175 g) each (see note)	1. Season the steaks with salt and pepper. 2. Place the oil or melted butter in a small pan. Dip both sides of the steaks in it to coat completely.
to taste	to taste	Salt	3. Place on the rack of a preheated broiler. Broil under medium heat until half cooked. Turn over with a spatula. At this point, it may be necessary to brush the tops of the steaks with more oil or butter if they are becoming dry.
to taste	to taste	White pepper	
as needed	as needed	Oil or melted butter	4. Complete the cooking on the second side.
as needed	as needed	Maître d'hôtel butter	5. Plate the fish. Place a slice of seasoned butter on top of each steak. Garnish the plate with a lemon wedge. Serve immediately.
as needed	as needed	Lemon wedges	

Per serving:
Calories, 320; Protein, 27 g; Fat, 22 g (63% cal.); Cholesterol, 105 mg; Carbohydrates, 2 g; Fiber, 1 g; Sodium, 2460 mg.

Note: Salmon, tuna, and swordfish steaks are ideal for broiling, but they are also expensive. Other fish steaks that may be broiled include cod, haddock, halibut, king mackerel, and large bluefish.

Fillets may also be broiled using this recipe if they are thick or firm enough to avoid breaking up on the grill.

VARIATIONS

For lean white fish (halibut, cod, etc.), dredge in flour and shake off excess before dipping in the melted butter or oil. Broil as in basic recipe.

Other compound butters may be used in place of maître d'hôtel butter.

For fat fish, omit the butter and serve the fish with a small quantity of flavorful vinaigrette.

Grilled Tuna with Sauce Vierge and Spinach

Portions: 12   Portion size: 5 oz (150 g) tuna
4 oz (125 g) spinach
1⅓ oz (40 mL) sauce

U.S.	Metric	Ingredients	PROCEDURE
7 oz	200 mL	Olive oil	1. Combine the olive oil, garlic, basil, chile, salt, and pepper to make a marinade.
⅔ oz	20 g	Garlic, chopped	
1½ tsp	10 g	Basil, chopped	2. Marinate the tuna for 1 hour.
1	1	Small chile, such as cayenne	
to taste	to taste	Salt	
to taste	to taste	Pepper	
12	12	Tuna steaks, 5 oz (150 g) each	
3 lb	1.5 kg	Cooked spinach, buttered	3. Grill the tuna steaks, keeping them medium rare.
1 pt	500 mL	Sauce Vierge (p. 162)	4. For each portion, place 4 oz (125 g) hot spinach on a plate. Place the tuna steak on top. Drizzle the sauce around.

Per serving:
Calories, 500; Protein, 35 g; Fat, 39 g (68% cal.); Cholesterol, 75 mg; Carbohydrates, 6 g, Fiber, 3 g; Sodium, 210 mg.

Grilled Tuna with Sauce Vierge and Spinach

Broiled Mako Shark Steaks with Browned Garlic Vinaigrette

Portions: 10   Portion size: 6 oz (175 g)

U.S.	Metric	Ingredients	PROCEDURE
15–20 cloves	15–20 cloves	Garlic	1. Cut the garlic cloves crosswise into thick slices.
8 oz	250 mL	Olive oil	2. Heat the oil in a small sauté pan over moderate heat. Add the garlic and sauté gently until light golden brown. Do not allow the garlic to become too dark or it will be bitter.
			3. Remove the browned garlic with a slotted spoon. Reserve the garlic and the oil separately.
10	10	Mako shark steaks, about 6 oz (175 g) each	4. Brush the shark steaks with about half the garlic-flavored oil from step 3. Season to taste with salt and pepper.
to taste	to taste	Salt	5. Place the steaks on a heated broiler or grill and broil until just done. Do not overcook or the steaks will be dry.
to taste	to taste	Pepper	
4 oz	125 mL	Olive oil	6. Beat the remaining oil from step 3 with the additional oil and the vinegar to make a basic vinaigrette. Season to taste with salt and pepper.
2 oz	60 mL	Red wine vinegar	
to taste	to taste	Salt	
to taste	to taste	Pepper	7. Plate the shark steaks and top with the browned garlic from step 3. Drizzle about 1 oz (30 mL) vinaigrette around the fish. Sprinkle with chopped parsley.
2 tbsp	30 mL	Chopped parsley	

Per serving:
Calories, 530; Protein, 36 g; Fat, 42 g (71% cal.); Cholesterol, 85 mg; Carbohydrates, 2 g; Fiber, 0 g; Sodium, 135 mg.

VARIATIONS

Substitute other firm fish steaks, such as swordfish or tuna, for the shark.

Broiled Lobster

Portions: 1   Portion size: 1 lobster

U.S.	Metric	Ingredients	PROCEDURE
1	1	Live lobster, 1–1½ lb (450–700 g)	1. Split the lobster as shown in Figure 14.11. Remove and discard the stomach (just behind the eyes) and the vein that runs through the tail. The liver and coral may be left in or removed and added to the stuffing (step 3), as desired.
1 tsp	5 mL	Shallot, chopped fine	2. Sauté the onion in the butter just until it starts to become tender.
1 tbsp	15 g	Butter	3. Optional step: Chop the lobster coral and liver (tomalley) and add to the pan. Sauté just until firm, about 10–20 seconds.
1 oz	30 g	Bread crumbs, dry	4. Add the bread crumbs and brown them lightly in the butter. Remove from the heat.
3 tbsp	45 mL	Chopped parsley	5. Add the parsley. Season the crumbs with salt and pepper.
to taste	to taste	Salt	
to taste	to taste	Pepper	
as needed	as needed	Melted butter	6. Place the lobster shell side down on a small sheet pan or in a shallow baking pan. Fill the body cavity with the crumb mixture. Do not put the crumbs over the tail meat.
			7. Brush the tail well with melted butter.
			8. Place a few of the legs on top of the stuffing. If the lobster was split by the first method, shown in Figure 14.11g, weight the end of the tail down to keep it from curling.
			9. Place the lobster under the broiler at least 6 inches (15 cm) from the heat. Broil until the crumbs are well browned.
			10. At this point, the lobster will probably not be completely cooked, unless it is very small and the broiler heat very low. Place the pan with the lobster in a hot oven to finish cooking.
2 oz	60 mL	Melted butter	11. Remove the lobster from the heat and serve immediately with a small cup of melted butter and with lemon garnish.
as needed	as needed	Lemon wedges	

Per serving:
Calories, 760; Protein, 12 g; Fat, 71 g (82% cal.); Cholesterol, 210 mg;
Carbohydrates, 22 g; Fiber, 1 g; Sodium, 1090 mg.

VARIATION

Broiled Rock Lobster Tail

Rock lobster is usually dry if broiled like lobster. A better method is to poach it in salted water (see pp. 411–412) until just cooked. Then split the tails, brush with butter, and run under the broiler for 1–2 minutes.

Broiled Shrimp, Scampi Style

Portions: 10   Portion size: 4½ oz (125 g)

U.S.	Metric	Ingredients	PROCEDURE
50	50	Shrimp, size 16/20	1. Peel, devein, and butterfly the shrimp, as shown in Figure 14.14. Leave tails on. 2. Place shrimp in individual service casserole dishes or in a shallow baking pan, tails up and cut side down. (Shrimp will curl more when cooked, so tails will stand up as shrimp are broiled.) 3. Keep refrigerated until needed.
6 oz	175 g	Butter	4. Heat butter and oil in a saucepan until the butter is melted.
½ cup	125 mL	Oil, preferably olive oil (see note)	5. Add the garlic, lemon juice, parsley, salt, and pepper. 6. Pour the butter sauce over the shrimp.
1 tbsp	15 mL	Garlic, chopped very fine	7. Place under the broiler at medium heat. Broil until the tops are lightly browned. (Don't worry if the tips of the tails burn a little; this is normal.)
1 oz	30 mL	Lemon juice	
2 tbsp	30 mL	Chopped parsley	8. Transfer the shrimp to the oven above the broiler for a few minutes to finish cooking.
to taste	to taste	Salt	
to taste	to taste	Pepper	

Per serving:
Calories, 250; Protein, 7 g; Fat, 25 g (88% cal.); Cholesterol, 95 mg;
Carbohydrates, 1 g; Fiber, 0 g; Sodium, 210 mg.

Note: All butter may be used, instead of a mixture of butter and oil. Or, if you are using a good-quality olive oil, use more oil and less butter or all olive oil.

Serve this dish with rice or with plenty of bread to soak up the flavorful butter.

VARIATIONS

The shrimp can be marinated for 1–2 hours in the oil, chopped garlic, lemon juice, and seasonings. Add the butter at cooking time. Or omit the butter when cooking, and serve small cups of garlic butter on the side.

Shrimp Brochettes

Marinate the shrimp as indicated above. Put the shrimp on skewers and broil, basting several times with the marinade and melted butter.

Broiled Scallops

Place the scallops in individual service casseroles (5–6 oz/150–175 g per portion). Top each portion with 1 tbsp (15 mL) dry bread crumbs. Pour the butter sauce over the scallops and broil as in basic recipe.

Broiled Fish Fillets or Steaks with Garlic Butter

Use fillets or steaks of any lean, white fish. Place fish on sheet pans and prepare according to procedure for Broiled Scallops, using the bread crumbs.

Marinated Fillets of Red Snapper with Crispy Potato Scales and Tapenade

Portions: 12   Portion size: 3–4 oz (100 g)

U.S.	Metric	Ingredients	PROCEDURE
12	12	Small red snapper fillets, scaled but with skin on, about 3–4 oz (100 g) each (see note)	1. Rinse and dry the fillets. Place on a baking sheet and season. Combine the olive oil and orange zest and brush over the fillets. Chill, preferably overnight.
10 oz	300 mL	Olive oil	2. Cut the potatoes into ½-inch (1-cm) cylinders and cut into very thin slices. Sauté just to soften in the clarified butter (note that after slicing, the potato should not be placed in water). Arrange the potato "scales" neatly over the skin side of the fish.
3	3	Oranges, zest only	
1 lb	450 g	Potatoes, peeled	
as needed	as needed	Clarified butter	
		Tapenade:	3. Combine all the ingredients for the tapenade in a food processor until finely chopped.
6 oz	150 g	Pitted black olives (see note)	4. Broil the fillets of fish until the potato scales are golden and the fish just cooked through (see note). Adjust the height of the broiler rack as necessary so that the potatoes are not too heavily browned before the fish is cooked.
1 oz	25 g	Capers	
1 oz	25 g	Anchovy fillets	
1 clove	1 clove	Garlic	5. Serve with quenelles of tapenade, made by shaping the olive paste into oval shapes with two spoons (see Figure 24.8).
2 oz	50 mL	Olive oil	

Per serving:
Calories, 450; Protein, 24 g; Fat, 36 g (72% cal.); Cholesterol, 55 mg; Carbohydrates, 8 g; Fiber, 1 g; Sodium, 360 mg.

Note: This recipe is originally for rouget or red mullet, which is not widely available in North America. These fish are usually very small, with fillets weighing about 2 oz (60 g) or less; 2 or 3 fillets are often served per portion. For this recipe, small, thin fillets are important so that they cook properly. If small snapper fillets are not available, substitute another small, firm fish with thin fillets, such as sea bream or pompano.

As an alternative, slightly thicker fillets can be cooked by starting the fish on top of the stove to cook the bottoms, then transferring to a salamander to complete the cooking and brown the potatoes.

It is essential to use Mediterranean-style cured black olives, such as kalamata, for this recipe. Canned California black olives do not have sufficient flavor.

Oysters Casino

Portions: 12   **Portion size:** 3 oysters (appetizer portion)

U.S.	Metric	Ingredients	PROCEDURE
36	36	Oysters	1. Open oysters as shown in Figure 14.7. Discard top shell.
			2. Place oysters on a sheet pan or in a shallow baking pan (see note).
½ lb	225 g	Butter	3. Place the butter in the bowl of a mixer and beat with the paddle attachment until soft and smooth.
2 oz	60 g	Green pepper, chopped fine	
1 oz	30 g	Pimiento, chopped fine	4. Add the green pepper, pimiento, shallots, parsley, and lemon juice. Mix until evenly combined. Season to taste with salt and pepper. (Casino butter can be rolled in parchment, refrigerated or frozen, and sliced to order.)
1 oz	30 g	Shallots, chopped fine	
¼ cup	60 mL	Chopped parsley	
1 oz	30 mL	Lemon juice	
to taste	to taste	Salt	
to taste	to taste	White pepper	
9 strips	9 strips	Bacon	5. Cook the bacon in the oven or on the griddle until about half cooked. Drain.
			6. Cut each strip into 4 pieces.
			7. Place about 2 tsp (10 mL) butter mixture on top of each oyster.
			8. Top each oyster with a piece of bacon.
			9. Run the oysters under the broiler until the bacon is brown and the oysters are hot. Do not overcook.

Per serving:
Calories, 610; Protein, 26 g; Fat, 51 g (75% cal.); Cholesterol, 230 mg;
Carbohydrates, 12 g; Fiber, 0 g; Sodium, 860 mg.

Note: Broiled or baked oysters and clams are often placed on beds of rock salt to hold them steady.

VARIATION

Clams Casino

Prepare as in basic recipe, using cherrystone or littleneck clams.

Sautéing and Pan-frying

As in meat cookery, the exact distinction between sautéing and pan-frying fish is impossible to draw. For many purposes, the two terms are used interchangeably.

A classic method for sautéing fish is called *à la meunière* (mun yair). In this preparation, the product is dredged in flour and sautéed in clarified butter or oil. It is then plated and sprinkled with lemon juice and chopped parsley, and freshly prepared, hot brown butter (beurre noisette) is poured over it. When the hot butter hits the lemon juice, it creates a froth. The fish should then be served at once.

Other sautéed fish preparations call for Standard Breading Procedure or for dredging the fish with a product other than flour, such as cornmeal. Also, a variety of garnishes may be used.

The procedures and variations just described apply to most popular sautéed and pan-fried fish recipes. In general, because most types of fin fish are so delicate, especially if filleted, they do not lend themselves to a great many sautéing variations. On the other hand, firm shellfish, like shrimp and scallops, are easy to sauté, and there is a greater variety of recipes for them.

Guidelines for Sautéing and Pan-frying Fish and Shellfish

1. Lean fish are especially well suited to sautéing because the cooking method supplies fat that the fish lack.

   Fat fish may also be sautéed, as long as you take care not to get the fish too greasy.

2. Sautéed fish is usually given a coating of flour, breading, or other starchy product before sautéing. This forms a crust that browns attractively, enhances the flavor, and helps hold the fish together and prevent sticking.

3. Fish may be soaked in milk briefly before dredging in flour. This helps the flour form a better crust.

4. Clarified butter and oil are the preferred fats for sautéing and pan-frying. Whole butter is likely to burn, unless the fish items are very small.

5. Use a minimum of fat. About ⅛ inch (3 mm), or enough to cover the bottom of the pan, is enough.

6. Small items, such as shrimp and scallops, are sautéed over high heat. Larger items, such as whole fish, require lower heat to cook evenly.

7. Very large fish may be browned in fat, then finished in the oven, uncovered.

8. Brown the most attractive side—the presentation side—first. For fillets, this is usually the flesh side or the side against the bone, not the skin side.

9. Handle fish carefully during and after cooking to avoid breaking the fish or the crisp crust.

10. Sauté or fry to order and serve immediately.

Procedure for Cooking Fish à la Meunière

1. Collect all equipment and food supplies.

2. Heat a small amount of clarified butter in a sauté pan.

3. Season the fish and dredge in flour. Shake off excess.

4. Place the fish in the pan, presentation side down.

5. Sauté the fish, turning once with a spatula, until both sides are brown and the fish is just cooked through.

6. Remove the fish from the pan with a spatula and place on serving plate, presentation side up.

7. Sprinkle fish with lemon juice and chopped parsley.

8. Heat some raw butter in the sauté pan until it turns light brown. Pour it over the fish immediately.

9. Serve at once.

Fillets of Sole Meunière

Portions: 10   Portion size: 4 oz (125 g)

U.S.	Metric	Ingredients	PROCEDURE
20	20	Sole fillets, 2 oz (60 g) each	1. Have all ingredients ready, but do not season and flour the fish until immediately before cooking.
to taste	to taste	Salt	
to taste	to taste	White pepper	2. Unless you are cooking to order, use as many sauté pans as necessary to hold all the fillets, or cook them in several batches. Place the sauté pans over medium heat so that they will be ready as soon as the fish is floured.
3 oz	90 g	Flour	
6 oz	175 g	Clarified butter or oil, or a mixture of butter and oil	3. Season the fillets with salt and pepper. Place the clarified butter in the hot pans to heat. Dredge the fish in flour and shake off excess. Place the fish in the pans flesh side (presentation side) down.
			4. Sauté until lightly browned. Turn over with a spatula and brown the other side. Be careful not to break the fillets when turning.
			5. Remove the fillets from the pan with a spatula, being careful not to break them. Plate the fish on hot dinner plates.
1 oz	30 mL	Lemon juice	6. Sprinkle the fish with lemon juice and chopped parsley.
¼ cup	60 mL	Chopped parsley	7. Heat the butter in a small saucepan or sauté pan until it turns light brown (beurre noisette).
5 oz	150 g	Butter	
20	20	Slices of peeled lemon	8. Pour the hot butter over the fish.
			9. Quickly place a lemon slice on top of each fillet and serve immediately.

Per serving:
Calories, 370; Protein, 20 g; Fat, 29 g (71% cal.); Cholesterol, 130 mg; Carbohydrates, 7 g; Fiber, 0 g; Sodium, 370 mg.

VARIATIONS

Other white fish fillets, as well as shellfish such as scallops and shrimp, may be cooked by the same procedure.

Placing fish in milk before dredging in flour helps form an attractive, well-browned crust. However, the fish must be drained well before flouring, or the flour coating may be heavy and pasty.

Fillets of Fish Doré

Sauté the fish as in the basic recipe, but serve without the lemon juice, chopped parsley, and beurre noisette. Garnish the plate with lemon and parsley sprig. (*Doré* means "golden.")

Trout Meunière

Prepare whole, drawn trout as in basic recipe. Dip fish in milk before dredging in flour to form a better crust.

Fish Sauté Amandine

Prepare as in basic recipe. Brown sliced almonds in the butter used for garnishing. Omit garnish of lemon slices, and garnish plate with lemon wedges.

Fish Sauté Grenobloise

Prepare as in basic recipe. Garnish the fish with capers and diced, peeled lemon sections in addition to the chopped parsley before pouring on the brown butter.

Sautéed Soft-Shell Crabs

Prepare as in basic recipe. Serve 2 per portion. Chopped parsley and lemon slices may be omitted.

Scallops Meunière

Sautéed Scallops with Tomato, Garlic, and Parsley

Portions: 10   Portion size: 4 oz (125 g)

U.S.	Metric	Ingredients	PROCEDURE
2½ lb	1.25 kg	Bay or sea scallops	1. If you are using sea scallops and they are very large, cut them in halves or quarters. Dry the scallops with paper towels.
2 oz	60 mL	Olive oil	
2 oz	60 mL	Clarified butter	
2 tsp	10 mL	Garlic, chopped fine	2. Heat the oil and butter in a large sauté pan until it is very hot.
4 oz	125 g	Drained, chopped canned or fresh tomato	3. Place the scallops in the sauté pan and sauté quickly. Shake the pan often to keep the scallops from sticking.
¼ cup	60 mL	Chopped parsley	4. When the scallops are about half cooked, add the garlic. Continue to sauté until the scallops are lightly browned.
to taste	to taste	Salt	5. Add the tomato and parsley and sauté a few seconds, just enough to heat the tomato.
			6. Add salt to taste and serve immediately.

Per serving:
Calories, 160; Protein, 9 g; Fat, 13 g (73% cal.); Cholesterol, 35 mg;
Carbohydrates, 2 g; Fiber, 0 g; Sodium, 310 mg.

VARIATIONS

Omitting the tomato makes a slightly different but equally good dish.

Sautéed Shrimp

Use peeled, deveined shrimp. Sauté as in basic recipe.

Escalope of Salmon with Sorrel

Portions: 12   Portion size: 3½–4 oz (115–120 g) salmon
                                        2 oz (60 mL) sauce

U.S.	Metric	Ingredients	PROCEDURE
2 lb	1 kg	Sorrel	1. Wash and stem the sorrel. Cut into chiffonade.
½ oz	15 g	Butter	2. Over low heat, cook the sorrel with the butter until very soft, about 2–5 minutes.
1 pt	500 mL	Heavy cream	
1 pt	500 mL	Fish stock	3. Add the cream and simmer for 1 minute. Set aside.
to taste	to taste	Salt	4. Reduce the fish stock by four-fifths. Add the sorrel and cream mixture.
to taste	to taste	Pepper	5. Place in a blender and blend until smooth. Strain into a saucepan and reheat. Season to taste and keep warm.
3 lb	1.5 kg	Salmon fillets, boneless and skinless	6. Slice the salmon fillets into thin escalopes weighing 4 oz (125 g) each (see Figure 15.1).
as needed	as needed	Oil	7. Heat a little oil over high heat in a sauté pan. Sauté the salmon slices about 1–2 minutes on each side. Remove and drain briefly on paper towels to absorb excess oil.
			8. To serve, cover the bottom of a warm plate with sauce and place a salmon escalope on top.

Per serving:
Calories, 380; Protein, 23 g; Fat, 28 g (66% cal.); Cholesterol, 130 mg;
Carbohydrates, 10 g; Fiber, 1 g; Sodium, 95 mg.

Figure 15.1 Cutting escalopes of salmon.

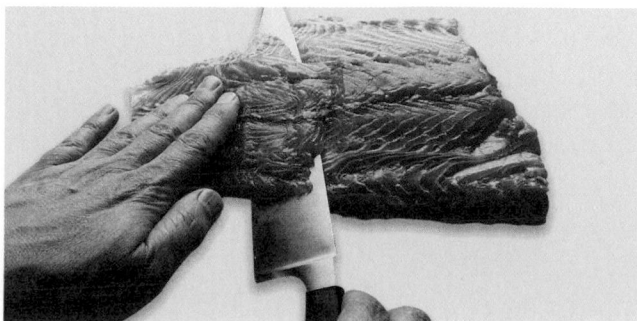

(a) Holding the knife at a sharp angle, cut a thin slice of the fillet, slicing toward the tail or thin end.

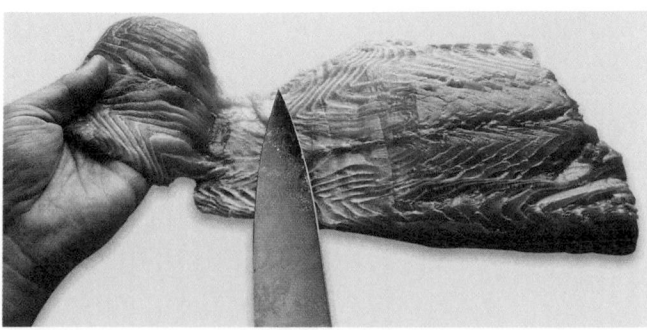

(b) The cut slice. Weigh the slice to check for accuracy of cutting, then continue making slices.

Crispy Sea Bass with Spices and Coriander Jus

Portions: 12   Portion size: 4 oz (125 g) fish
4 oz (125 g) vegetable
1½ oz (40 mL) sauce

U.S.	Metric	Ingredients	PROCEDURE
3 lb	1.5 kg	Sea bass fillets (see step 1 for size)	1. Cut the sea bass fillets into 4-oz (125-g) pieces and score the skin. Keep chilled until ready to use.
3½ lb	1.8 kg	Green or savoy cabbage, with outer leaves removed	2. Shred the cabbage and blanch well in boiling salted water. Drain.
5 oz	150 g	Butter	3. In a sauté pan over medium heat, toss the cabbage in the butter with the thyme until hot. Season to taste with salt and pepper.
2 tsp	5 g	Thyme, fresh	
to taste	to taste	Salt	
to taste	to taste	Pepper	
2 oz	60 g	Shallots, chopped	4. Sweat the shallot in the first quantity of butter, then deglaze with white wine. Reduce until almost dry, then add the stocks. Reduce by about one-fourth. Then add about three-fourths of the shredded cilantro.
4 tsp	20 g	Butter	
10 oz	300 mL	White wine	
10 oz	300 mL	Chicken stock	
10 oz	300 mL	Brown veal stock	5. Remove from the heat, leave to infuse a few minutes, then strain. Swirl in the second quantity of butter (monter au beurre), then stir in the remaining cilantro.
1 oz	25 g	Cilantro, shredded	
1½ oz	40 g	Butter	
2 tbsp	18 g	Ground mace	6. Mix together the mace, ginger, coriander, cinnamon, quatre épices, and salt, and sprinkle onto the fish. Sprinkle with just enough spices to lightly color the flesh of the fish. (You will probably not need all the spice mixture; reserve leftover for later use.)
2 tbsp	18 g	Ground ginger	
2 tbsp	18 g	Ground coriander	
1 tbsp	9 g	Cinnamon	
1 tbsp	9 g	Quatre épices (p. 657)	
2½ oz	70 g	Salt	7. Pan-fry the fish in olive oil over medium high heat, starting with the flesh side down. After a few minutes, turn over and finish cooking until the skin is crisp and the fish is just cooked.
3½ oz	100 mL	Olive oil	
as needed	as needed	Cilantro sprigs for garnish	8. For each serving, place an oval or round ring mold, about 3 inches (8 cm) in diameter, on the center of the plate. Mold the cabbage into this mold, then lift off the ring. Top with a piece of fish. Drizzle the sauce around and decorate with sprigs of cilantro.

Per serving:
Calories, 350; Protein, 20 g; Fat, 25 g (64% cal.); Cholesterol, 80 mg;
Carbohydrates, 8 g; Fiber, 3 g; Sodium, 1370 mg.

Salmon with an Almond Crust

Portions: 12   Portion size: 5½ oz (165 g)

U.S.	Metric	Ingredients	PROCEDURE
3½ oz	100 g	Ground almonds	1. Mix together the almonds, bread crumbs, and chopped parsley. Add the egg and mix gently.
3½ oz	100 g	Bread crumbs	
1 oz	30 g	Chopped parsley	2. Add the soft butter and mix until incorporated.
2	2	Eggs, beaten	3. Season to taste with salt and white pepper.
4 oz	125 g	Softened butter	
to taste	to taste	Salt	
to taste	to taste	White pepper	
4 lb	1.8 kg	Salmon fillets	4. Cut the salmon fillets into 5-oz (150-g) portions.
3 oz	90 g	Clarified butter	5. Pan-fry the salmon in butter, starting with the flesh side down. Brown lightly. Turn over and continue cooking skin side down. Do not cook the fish completely, as it will continue cooking with the almond crust. It should still be somewhat rare inside.
1 pt 4 oz	600 mL	Red Wine Butter Sauce for Fish (p. 155)	
			6. Spread a layer of the almond crust mixture over the salmon.
			7. Place under a salamander or broiler to brown the crust and finish cooking the salmon. Adjust the height of the broiler rack so that the crust is not too browned before the salmon is cooked.
			8. Plate the salmon. Ladle the sauce around it, not over it.

Per serving:
Calories, 770; Protein, 33 g; Fat, 62 g (72% cal.); Cholesterol, 250 mg; Carbohydrates, 9 g; Fiber, 1 g; Sodium, 590 mg.

VARIATIONS

This recipe works well with other firm-fleshed fish.

Crab Cakes with Roasted Pepper Rémoulade

Portions: 16   Portion size: 4 oz (125 g)

U.S.	Metric	Ingredients	PROCEDURE
3 lb	1.4 kg	Crabmeat	1. Pick over the crabmeat to remove any bits of shell.
4 oz	125 g	Fresh bread crumbs	2. Mix together the bread crumbs, mayonnaise, eggs, mustard, Worcestershire sauce, salt, pepper, parsley, and scallions. Fold in the crabmeat.
6 oz	175 g	Mayonnaise	
4	4	Eggs, beaten	
2 tsp	10 mL	Prepared mustard	3. Form by hand into round cakes. For each portion, allow 1 large cake, about 4 oz (125 g), or 2 small cakes, about 2 oz (60 g) each (see note).
2 tsp	10 mL	Worcestershire sauce	
2 tsp	10 mL	Salt	
½ tsp	2 mL	White pepper	4. Pan-fry the cakes in butter until browned on both sides and cooked through.
3 tbsp	45 mL	Chopped parsley	
8	8	Scallions, chopped fine	5. Cut the roasted peppers into brunoise. Mix into the rémoulade.
as needed	as needed	Clarified butter, for cooking	
3 oz	90 g	Roasted red peppers, peeled, cored, and seeded (see Figure 16.12)	6. Serve each crab cake with 1 oz (30 mL) sauce and 1 lemon wedge.
1 pt	500 mL	Rémoulade Sauce (p. 165)	
16	16	Lemon wedges	

Per serving:
Calories, 440; Protein, 21 g; Fat, 36 g (72% cal.); Cholesterol, 145 mg; Carbohydrates, 7 g; Fiber, 0 g; Sodium, 1070 mg.

Note: This mixture has very little bread filler, so it may be somewhat difficult to handle. If desired, add more bread crumbs to make a firmer mixture that will pack more easily into cakes. The texture of the crabmeat may also affect the texture of the cakes and the quantity of bread crumbs needed.

Cornmeal-Crusted Soft-Shell Crabs with Cornmeal Pancakes and Roasted Tomatoes

Portions: 10   Portion size: 1 crab
1 pancake
2 tomato halves

U.S.	Metric	Ingredients	PROCEDURE
10	10	Plum tomatoes	1. Cut the tomatoes in half lengthwise. Carefully squeeze the tomatoes to remove most of the seeds. Place the tomatoes cut side down on an oiled sheet pan. Bake at 250°F (120°C) for 1½ hours or until they are soft and shriveled but not browned.
10	10	Pancakes (p. 625), made without sugar and with half white flour and half cornmeal	2. Prepare the pancakes. Keep both the pancakes and the tomatoes warm.
10	10	Soft-shell crabs	3. Clean the crabs, as shown in Figure 14.15.
8 oz	250 mL	Milk	4. Dip the crabs in milk. Drain, then dredge in cornmeal. Discard leftover milk.
5 oz	150 g	Cornmeal	
4 oz	125 mL	Oil	5. Heat the oil and butter in enough sauté pans to hold the crabs in a single layer (or pan-fry in separate batches). Place the crabs in the pan upside down and cook over moderate heat until lightly browned. Salt lightly to taste while the crabs are cooking. Turn over and brown the other side. Remove from the pan and drain for a few seconds on paper towels to remove excess fat.
6 oz	175 g	Butter	
to taste	to taste	Salt	
5 oz	150 mL	Rémoulade Sauce (p. 165)	6. For each portion, place 1 pancake in the center of a plate. Top with 2 tomato halves, cut side up. Top with a crab. Place a tablespoon (15 mL) of rémoulade sauce on the plate beside the crab.

Per serving:
Calories, 420; Protein, 16 g; Fat, 27 g (57% cal.); Cholesterol, 120 mg;
Carbohydrates, 30 g; Fiber, 2 g; Sodium, 580 mg.

Peppered Haddock with Garlic Whipped Potatoes and Parsley Sauce

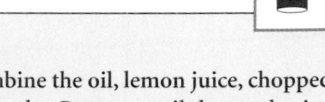

Portions: 12   Portion size: 5 oz (150 g) plus garnish

U.S.	Metric	Ingredients	PROCEDURE
10 oz	300 mL	Olive oil	1. Prepare the sauce: Combine the oil, lemon juice, chopped parsley, and salt in a blender. Process until the parsley is puréed.
1 oz	30 mL	Lemon juice	
½ cup	125 mL	Chopped parsley	
½ tsp	2 mL	Salt	
3 lb 12 oz	1.8 kg	Haddock fillets, cut into 5-oz (150-g) portions	2. Coat the fish fillets evenly with a light sprinkling of crushed peppercorns. Season with salt.
2 tbsp	30 mL	Crushed black peppercorns	3. Heat the olive oil in as many sauté pans as necessary to hold the fish in a single layer.
1 tsp	5 mL	Salt	4. Place the fish in the pans, presentation side down, and sauté over moderate heat until lightly browned and about half cooked. Turn over and finish the cooking.
2 oz	60 mL	Olive oil	
2 lb 4 oz	1.1 kg	Garlic Whipped Potatoes (p. 491)	5. Place a 3-oz (90-g) portion of potatoes in the center of each plate. Top with the fish fillet. Drizzle about 1 ounce (30 mL) sauce in a circle around the fish.

Per serving:
Calories, 480; Protein, 28 g; Fat, 33 g (62% cal.); Cholesterol, 95 mg; Carbohydrates, 17 g; Fiber, 2 g; Sodium, 420 mg.

VARIATIONS

Other firm-fleshed white fish, such as cod, sea bass, striped bass, red snapper, or grouper, may be substituted.

Peppered Haddock with Purée of Flageolet Beans

Substitute Purée of Flageolet Beans with Garlic (p. 463) for the potatoes.

Peppered Haddock with Purée of Flageolet Beans and Fried Parsley

Spicy Shrimp or Scallop Sauté

Portions: 10   Portion size: 4 oz (125 g)

U.S.	Metric	Ingredients
1 tsp	5 mL	Paprika
¼ tsp	1 mL	Cayenne
¼ tsp	1 mL	Black pepper
½ tsp	2 mL	White pepper
¼ tsp	1 mL	Thyme
¼ tsp	1 mL	Basil
¼ tsp	1 mL	Oregano
½ tsp	2 mL	Salt
2½ lb	1.25 kg	Peeled, deveined shrimp, or scallops
6 oz	175 g	Onion, sliced
1 clove	1 clove	Garlic, chopped
as needed	as needed	Clarified butter

PROCEDURE

1. Mix together the spices, herbs, and salt.
2. If the shrimp or scallops are wet, dry them with paper towels. If you are using sea scallops and they are large, cut them into halves or quarters.
3. Toss the shrimp or scallops with the dry seasonings.
4. Sauté the onion and garlic in a little clarified butter until they are tender and only lightly browned. Remove them from the pan and set them aside.
5. Add a little more butter to the pan and sauté the seafood just until it is cooked.
6. Return the onion and garlic to the pan and toss to combine. Serve immediately, accompanied by white rice.

Per serving:
Calories, 160; Protein, 18 g; Fat, 9 g (50% cal.); Cholesterol, 185 mg;
Carbohydrates, 2 g; Fiber, 0 g; Sodium, 390 mg.

VARIATION

For spicy fish fillets, season them well with the dry seasoning mix in the basic recipe. Then dredge them in flour and sauté as for meunière.

Spicy Shrimp Sauté; Steamed Rice; Sautéed Grated Zucchini

Deep-frying

Deep-frying is perhaps the most popular method of preparing fish in North America. While fried fish may not be the most subtle or refined preparation, it can be of very high quality if the fish is fresh and not overcooked, the frying fat is of good quality, and the item is served without delay after cooking.

Lean fish—either small whole fish or small portions such as fillets or sticks—and shellfish such as shrimp, clams, oysters, and scallops are best for deep-frying.

Fish to be fried is breaded or battered to protect the fish from the frying fat and to protect the frying fat from the fish. Also, the breading or batter provides a crisp, flavorful, and attractive coating.

Frozen breaded fish portions are widely used. They should be fried without thawing.

Fried fish is usually served with lemon and/or a cold sauce such as tartar, rémoulade, or cocktail sauce on the side.

Frying and breading procedures were discussed in detail in Chapter 7. There is no need to repeat them here, but you should review those sections if necessary. Also, the batter recipes on page 481 are suitable for fish as well as for vegetables.

Fried Breaded Fish Fillets

Portions: 25   Portion size: 4 oz (125 g)

U.S.	Metric	Ingredients	PROCEDURE
		Standard Breading Procedure (see note):	1. Set up a breading station (see p. 121): Place the flour in one pan, the eggs beaten with milk in a shallow bowl, and the bread crumbs in another pan.
4 oz	125 g	Flour	
4	4	Whole eggs, beaten	
1 cup	250 mL	Milk	
1¼ lb	625 g	Bread crumbs, dry	
25	25	4-oz (125-g) fillets of lean, white fish, such as	2. Season the fish lightly with salt and white pepper.
		Haddock	3. Bread the fish fillets by passing them through the flour, egg wash, and crumbs. Press the crumbs on firmly. (See p. 121 for detailed breading instructions.)
		Perch	
		Pike	4. Fry the fillets in deep fat heated to 350°F (175°C) until golden brown.
		Bass	
		Sole	
		Flounder	
to taste	to taste	Salt	
to taste	to taste	White pepper	
25	25	Parsley sprigs	5. Drain and serve immediately. Garnish each portion with a parsley sprig and a lemon wedge. Serve with 1 oz (25 mL) tartar sauce.
25	25	Lemon wedges	
25 oz	750 mL	Tartar sauce	

Per serving:
Calories, 490; Protein, 25 g; Fat, 36 g (66% cal.); Cholesterol, 115 mg; Carbohydrates, 16 g; Fiber, 1 g; Sodium, 430 mg.

Note: Quantities given for breading materials are only guidelines. You may need more or less, depending on the shapes of the fish pieces, the care used in breading, and other factors. In any case, you will need enough so that even the last piece to be breaded can be coated easily and completely.

VARIATIONS

Breaded fish fillets may also be pan-fried in butter or oil (see previous section).

Fried Breaded Scallops

Prepare as in basic recipe. Use wire baskets in the breading station to simplify the procedure, as explained on page 121.

Fried Breaded Shrimp

Peel, devein, and butterfly shrimp, as shown in Figure 14.14. Leave tails on. Bread and fry as in basic recipe.

Fried Oysters or Clams

Prepare like scallops.

Cod Cakes

Portions: 25   Portion size: 2 cakes, 2½ oz (75 g) each

U.S.	Metric	Ingredients	PROCEDURE
4 lb	1.8 kg	Cooked cod	1. Flake the fish until it is well shredded.
4 lb	1.8 kg	Potato purée (p. 490)	2. Combine with the potato, egg, and egg yolk. Mix well.
3	3	Whole eggs	3. Season to taste with salt, pepper, and a little ground ginger.
2	2	Egg yolks	4. Scale the mixture into 2½-oz (75-g) portions. Shape into round, slightly flattened cakes.
to taste	to taste	Salt	5. Pass the cakes through Standard Breading Procedure.
to taste	to taste	White pepper	6. Deep-fry at 350°F (175°C) until golden brown.
pinch	pinch	Ginger	
		Standard Breading Procedure:	
as needed	as needed	Flour	
as needed	as needed	Egg wash	
as needed	as needed	Bread crumbs	
as desired	as desired	Tomato sauce *or* tartar sauce	7. Serve 2 cakes per portion. Accompany with tomato sauce or tartar sauce.

Per serving:
Calories, 280; Protein, 23 g; Fat, 6 g (19% cal.); Cholesterol, 110 mg;
Carbohydrates, 33 g; Fiber, 2 g; Sodium, 360 mg.

VARIATION

Salmon or Tuna Cakes

Prepare as in basic recipe, using well-drained canned salmon or tuna.

If you have duchesse potato mixture on hand, simply combine equal parts fish and duchesse mixture. No additional eggs are needed, as the potatoes already contain eggs.

Deep-Fried Calamari with Spicy Tomato Sauce and Aioli

Portions: 12   Portion size: 6 oz (175 g) squid
                             2 oz (60 mL) each sauce

U.S.	Metric	Ingredients	PROCEDURE
4½ lb	2.25 kg	Small cleaned squid (see Figure 14.10)	1. Slice the body sacs of the squid crosswise into rings. Leave the tentacle sections whole, or cut them in half if they are large.
4 oz	125 mL	Lemon juice	2. Combine the squid with the lemon juice and marinate, refrigerated, for 2–3 hours.
1 lb	500 g	Flour	3. Mix the flour and salt.
3 tbsp	45 mL	Salt	4. Drain the squid and dry on clean towels. Immediately before cooking, toss the squid with the flour, then shake in a large strainer to remove excess flour.
			5. Deep-fry at 350°F (175°C) just until lightly golden. Remove from the fryer and drain.
1½ pt	750 mL	Tomato Sauce for Pasta (p. 516)	6. Heat the tomato sauce and season to taste with the hot pepper sauce.
to taste	to taste	Hot red pepper sauce	7. Heap the fried squid in the center of the serving plates, accompanied by 2 oz (60 mL) of each of the sauces in small cups.
1½ pt	750 mL	Aioli I (p. 165) or Aioli II (p. 576)	

Per serving:
Calories, 700; Protein, 30 g; Fat, 50 g (64% cal.); Cholesterol, 395 mg;
Carbohydrates, 33 g; Fiber, 2 g; Sodium, 1710 mg.

VARIATIONS

For other versions of deep-fried calamari, bread the squid (see Standard Breading Procedure) or dip in batter, using one of the batter recipes for Onion Rings (p. 481); the recipe for Beer Batter is recommended. Follow steps 6–8 in the Onion Ring recipe for battering and frying.

Poaching and Simmering

Poaching is cooking in a liquid at very low heat. Fillets and other small portions are sometimes cooked in a small amount of fish fumet and/or wine and served with a sauce made of the poaching liquid. Whole fish and thick steaks may be cooked in a seasoned liquid called a court bouillon. The liquid is not used to make a sauce, and the fish may be served hot or cold. Because these are two distinct procedures, we discuss them separately.

These two methods are illustrated in their most basic form in the recipes on pages 414 and 416. In addition, this section contains recipes using a variety of techniques for preparing fish dishes by cooking in flavorful liquids.

POACHING AND SIMMERING IN COURT BOUILLON

Court bouillon may be defined as water containing seasonings, herbs, and usually an acid, used for cooking fish. The name means "short broth" in French, so called because it is made quickly, unlike stocks.

In quantity food service, this method is perhaps used most often for cooking large whole fish that are to be decorated and served cold on a buffet. Slightly higher simmering temperatures are used for cooking crustaceans, such as lobster, crab, and shrimp.

The famous preparation called *truit au bleu* (blue trout) is made by poaching trout that are alive until cooking time. The fish must be alive and must not be washed in order for the fish to turn blue. Live fish have a protective slippery coating on the skin, and the blue color results from the vinegar in the court bouillon reacting with this coating.

Guidelines for Poaching Fish in Court Bouillon

1. Both fat and lean fish may be cooked by this method.
2. Seasoned liquid for cooking fish may be as simple as salted water. More often, however, it contains flavoring ingredients such as spices, herbs, and mirepoix, and acid ingredients such as lemon juice, vinegar, and white wine.
3. Cook flavoring ingredients in court bouillon to extract the flavors before cooking the fish.
4. Cooking temperature is 160° to 180°F (70° to 80°C), well below boiling. A temperature of 160°F is sufficient to cook fish, and it reduces the likelihood of overcooking. Higher temperatures are harmful to the delicate texture and flavor of fish.
   Lobsters, crabs, and shrimp may be cooked at a *simmer* because their textures are less fragile. The terms "boiled lobster" and "boiled fish" are often used but inaccurate. Lobster and fish should never be boiled.
5. Start shellfish, small fish, and portion cuts in hot liquid to preserve flavors. Start large fish in cold liquid to cook more evenly and to avoid sudden contractions that would split the skin and spoil the appearance.
6. Special fish poachers with racks are best for poaching. They allow the fish to be removed from the liquid without damage. If these utensils are not available, wrap fish in cheesecloth so it can be lifted out easily, or tie the fish loosely to a board.
7. Serve poached fish with an appropriate sauce, such as hollandaise for hot fish and a mayonnaise-based sauce for cold fish. Mild vinaigrettes go well with both hot and cold poached fish.

Procedure for Poaching Fish in Court Bouillon

1. Collect all equipment and food supplies.
2. Prepare court bouillon.
3. Place the fish in a suitable pan with liquid to cover.
   Start small fish and portions in simmering liquid.
   Start shellfish in boiling liquid.
   Start large fish in cold liquid.
4. Cook fish at below the simmer, 160° to 180°F (70° to 80°C). Lobsters, crabs, and shrimp may be cooked at a gentle simmer.
5. If fish is to be served hot, remove from liquid and serve immediately.
6. If fish is to be served cold, stop the cooking by adding ice to the liquid, and cool the fish in the court bouillon to retain moisture.

POACHING IN FUMET AND WINE

Fish poached in white wine is rightly considered one of the stars of classical cuisine. If well prepared, it can be one of the most exquisite dishes on the menu.

This method of preparation is best for lean, delicate white fish, such as sole, halibut, turbot, haddock, cod, pike, and perch. It is also used for salmon and trout. The fish is always served with a sauce made from the poaching liquid.

The procedure and recipe given here are for fillets of sole au vin blanc (in white wine). This is the basic preparation, and most other classical poached fish recipes are variations on it. Many of the variations involve only different garnishes.

Because of the delicacy of flavors, this preparation requires good-quality fish and well-made stock, and the wine should have a good flavor. A cheap, bad tasting wine will spoil the dish.

Procedure for Poaching Fish in Fumet and Wine

1. Collect all equipment and food supplies. Select a pan just large enough to hold the fish portions in a single layer. This will enable you to use a minimum amount of poaching liquid. Also, use a pan with low, sloping sides. This makes it easier to remove the fragile cooked fish from the pan.

2. Butter the bottom of the pan and sprinkle with chopped shallots.

3. Arrange the fish portions in the pan in a single layer. Season them lightly.

4. Add enough fish fumet and white wine to almost cover the fish. Use no more liquid than necessary so the flavor will be more concentrated and less reduction will be required later.

5. Cover the fish with a piece of buttered parchment or other paper and cover the pan with a lid. The paper holds in the steam to cook the top of the fish. It is sometimes omitted if the pan has a tight lid, but it does help to cook more evenly.

6. Bring the liquid just to a simmer and finish poaching in the oven at moderate heat. Thin fillets will cook in just a few minutes. Fish may be poached on top of the range, but the oven provides more even, gentle heat from both top and bottom.

7. Drain the liquid into a wide pan and keep the fish warm. After a few minutes of standing, more liquid will drain from the fish. Add this to the rest.

8. Reduce the poaching liquid over high heat to about one-fourth its volume.

9. Add fish velouté and heavy cream and bring to a boil. Adjust seasoning with salt, white pepper, and lemon juice.

10. Strain the sauce.

11. Arrange the fish on plates for service, coat with the sauce, and serve immediately.

Variations in Sauce Production

Using a prepared velouté, as in the standard method just given, makes the sauce production very quick, and the procedure can easily be used for cooking to order.

An alternative method may be used if no velouté is available or if a large quantity of fish is being poached for banquet service:

1. Use a larger quantity of fumet and wine for cooking the fish and reduce it only by about half, depending on the amount of sauce needed.

2. Thicken the liquid with roux or beurre manié and simmer until no raw starch taste remains.

3. Finish the preparation as in the basic method.

Another method, which has recently become popular, uses no starch thickener. Instead, the reduced poaching liquid is lightly bound with heavy cream or raw butter:

- To bind the sauce with cream, add about 2 oz (60 mL) or more heavy cream per portion to the reduced cooking liquid and continue to reduce until the sauce is lightly thickened.

- To bind with butter, whip raw butter into the reduced cooking liquid as for *monter au beurre* (p. 141). Use about ½ oz (15 g) butter or more per portion.

A further variation is known as *à la nage*, which means "swimming." To serve poached seafood à la nage, reduce the cooking liquid only slightly; season, and strain it carefully. If desired, enrich the liquid with a very small quantity of butter, or leave it unenriched. Serve the seafood with the liquid in a soup plate or other plate deep enough to hold the juices.

Finally, in one recipe in this section, the fish is steamed above the wine rather than poached in it. But the dish is finished by making a sauce from the wine and fumet in a fairly traditional manner (even though the wine is red rather than white!).

GLAZING

Poached fish is sometimes glazed before serving. This is done as follows:

1. According to the particular recipe, combine the finished sauce with egg yolk, hollandaise sauce, and/or lightly whipped cream. Alternatively, combine the reduction of the cooking liquid with Mornay sauce instead of fish velouté.

2. Coat the fish with the sauce and run the plate or platter under the salamander or broiler for a few seconds, until golden brown.

   Note: It's a good idea to test a little of the sauce under the salamander before coating the fish to make sure it will brown.

Court Bouillon for Fish

Yield: 1 gal (4 L)

U.S.	Metric	Ingredients	PROCEDURE
1 gal	4 L	Water	1. Combine all ingredients in a stockpot or saucepot and bring to a boil.
8 oz	250 mL	White vinegar, wine vinegar, *or* lemon juice	2. Reduce heat and simmer 30 minutes.
8 oz	250 g	Onions, sliced	3. Strain and cool.
4 oz	125 g	Celery, sliced	
4 oz	125 g	Carrots, sliced	
2 oz	60 g	Salt	
½ tsp	2 mL	Peppercorns, crushed	
1	1	Bay leaf	
¼ tsp	1 mL	Thyme	
10–12	10–12	Parsley stems	

Per 1 ounce:
Calories, 0; Protein, 0 g; Fat, 0 g (0% cal.); Cholesterol, 0 mg;
Carbohydrates, 0 g; Fiber, 0 g; Sodium, 170 mg.

Sole Vin Blanc (Poached Fillets of Sole in White Wine Sauce)

Portions: 25 Portion size: 4 oz (125 g) fish
2 oz (60 mL) sauce

U.S.	Metric	Ingredients	PROCEDURE
6¼ lb	3 kg	Sole fillets: 50 fillets, 2 oz (60 g) each	1. Fold the fillets in half or roll them up, starting with the large end (see Figure 15.2). Be sure that the skin side of the fillet is on the inside of the fold or the roll (called *paupiette*).
3 oz	90 g	Butter	2. Butter the inside of shallow hotel pans or baking pans. Sprinkle with the shallots. Lay the fillets on top of the shallots in a single layer.
3 oz	90 g	Shallots, fine dice	3. Pour the wine into the pan and add enough stock to almost cover the fish.
10 oz	300 mL	White wine	4. Butter a piece of parchment or waxed paper cut the same size as the pan. Cover the fish closely with it, buttered side down. Cover the pan.
2½ cups or as needed	600 mL or as needed	Fish stock	5. Set the pan on the range and bring just barely to a simmer. DO NOT BOIL.
			6. Place the pan in a hot oven (400°F/200°C) and cook the fish until it is just barely done, about 5 minutes.
			7. Drain the poaching liquid into a broad sauté pan. Keep the fish covered in a warm, not hot, place. If more liquid collects under the fish as it stands, add this to the rest.
3½ pt	1.75 L	Fish velouté	8. Reduce the poaching liquid over high heat to about one-fourth its volume.
3	3	Egg yolks	9. Add the velouté and bring to a simmer. Reduce to about 1 qt (1 L).
8 oz	250 mL	Heavy cream	10. Beat the egg yolks, then mix in the cream to make a liaison.
2 oz	60 g	Butter	11. Whip in a little of the hot velouté to temper the liaison. Stir the tempered liaison into the sauce.
as needed	as needed	Lemon juice	12. Swirl in the raw butter (monter au beurre). Season to taste with salt, pepper, and a few drops of lemon juice if necessary. Strain.
to taste	to taste	Salt	13. To serve, place 2 fillets on a dinner plate and coat with 2 oz (60 mL) sauce.
to taste	to taste	White pepper	

Per serving:
Calories, 260; Protein, 25 g; Fat, 14 g (51% cal.); Cholesterol, 125 mg; Carbohydrates, 4 g; Fiber, 0 g; Sodium, 190 mg.

VARIATIONS

Any lean white fish may be poached using this recipe or any of the variations below, including:

Halibut	Cod	Perch
Turbot	Pike	Scallops
Haddock		

For a sauce that is lower in fat, omit the liaison and the final monter au beurre. Finish the sauce with the desired amount of heavy cream, 6–12 oz (175–350 mL).

À la Carte Service, Fast Method: Poach fish as in basic recipe. Plate the fish as soon as it is cooked. Coat it with a *preprepared white wine sauce*. The poaching liquid may be reused throughout the service period, then used to make velouté for the next day's sauce. Other sauces based on fish velouté or béchamel may be used instead of white wine sauce:

Bercy	Normandy	Nantua
Herb	Mushroom	Mornay

Glazed Poached Fish

Prepare as in basic recipe. Immediately before serving, fold 1 pt (500 mL) hollandaise and 8 oz (250 mL) heavy cream, whipped, into the sauce. Coat the fish and brown it quickly under the salamander.

Sole Vin Blanc (Poached Fillets of Sole in White Wine Sauce) *(Continued)*

Paupiettes of Sole Dugléré; Buttered Spinach, Steamed Potatoes

Poached Fish Bonne Femme

Add 1½ lb (700 g) sliced mushrooms to the shallots in the poaching pan. Poach as in basic recipe. Omit egg yolks. Do not strain the sauce.

Poached Fish Duglére

Add 1½ lb (700 g) tomato concassée (p. 445) and 4 tbsp (60 mL) chopped parsley to the pan when poaching the fish. Poach as in basic recipe. Omit liaison, but stir 5 oz (150 g) raw butter into the sauce before serving. Do not strain.

Poached Fish Mornay

Strain the reduced poaching liquid (after step 8) and add a little of it to a thick Mornay Sauce for Glazing (p. 145), just enough to thin it to the desired consistency. Coat the fish with the sauce and brown under the salamander or broiler.

Note: Scallops are often prepared à la Mornay and served in scallop shells with a duchesse potato border. The dish is called *Coquille St. Jacques Mornay.* (*St. Jacques* is the French term for scallop, and *coquille* means "shell.")

Poached Fish Florentine

Prepare like Poached Fish Mornay, but place the cooked fish on beds of cooked, buttered spinach before coating with sauce.

Seafood à la Nage

Double the quantity of fish stock. Omit the velouté, liaison, and final butter. After poaching, reduce the cooking liquid only slightly. Season carefully and strain. Serve the seafood with the broth.

Figure 15.2 Rolling and folding sole fillets.

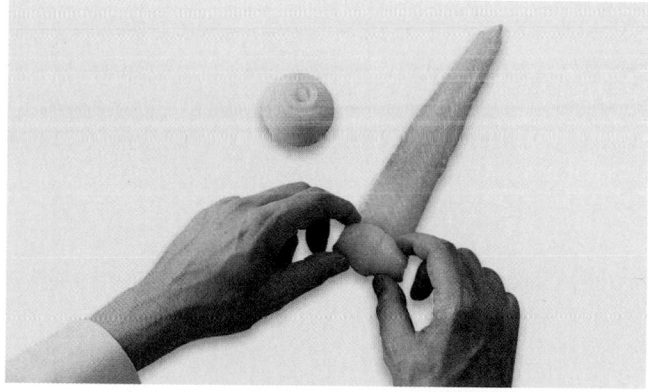

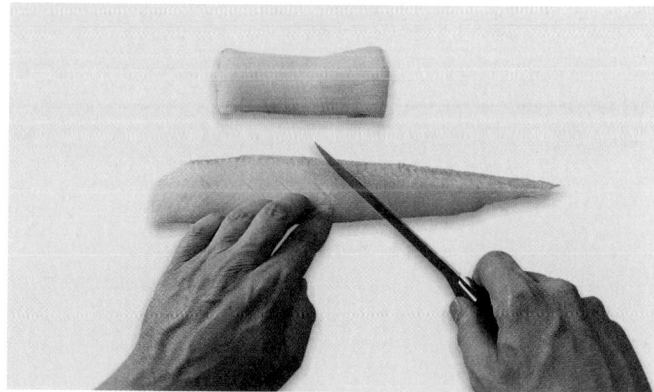

(a) To make paupiettes, or rolled fillets of sole, lay the fillets on the work surface, skin side up. Starting at the large end, roll tightly. As the fish cooks, the connective tissues on the skin side shrink and keep the roll tight. If you roll the fillet skin side out, it unrolls as it cooks.

(b) If the fillets are to be poached flat or folded, first make a series of very shallow cuts in the skin side as shown. This helps keep the tissues from shrinking and deforming the fillet. Fold so that flesh side is out (skin side on the inside).

Poached Whole Fish

Portions: 10   Portion size: 4 oz (125 g)

U.S.	Metric	Ingredients	PROCEDURE
5 lb 4 lb 3 qt or as needed	2.5 kg 2 kg 3 L or as needed	Drawn fish or Dressed fish (1 large or 2 or more smaller fish; see note) Court bouillon, cold	1. Place the clean dressed or drawn fish on the lightly oiled rack of a fish poacher. If a rack is unavailable, wrap the fish in cheesecloth or tie it loosely on a board so that it can be lifted out when cooked. 2. Place the fish in the poaching pan and pour in enough cold court bouillon to cover the fish completely. 3. Set the pan over moderately low heat and slowly bring barely to a simmer. 4. Reduce heat to very low and cook the fish at below the simmering point until done. The fish will feel firm, not mushy, at its thickest part, and the backbone, as seen inside the cavity, will no longer be pink. Total cooking time will vary from 5 to 20 minutes, depending on the size of the fish and exact cooking temperature. In general, plan on about 8–10 minutes for every inch of thickness at the thickest point.
		Suggested sauces: Hollandaise Mousseline Beurre noisette Herb vinaigrette	5. For serving hot: Remove fish from liquid, drain well, and serve immediately with choice of sauce. For serving cold: Add ice to the court bouillon to stop the cooking. Cool the fish rapidly in the liquid and refrigerate. Drain when chilled.

Per serving:
Calories, 220; Protein, 47 g; Fat, 2 g (9% cal.); Cholesterol, 140 mg;
Carbohydrates, 0 g; Fiber, 0 g; Sodium, 320 mg.

Note: For attractive presentations, such as for buffet work, fish is often poached with the head on. Suggested fish for poaching whole:

Haddock	Red snapper	Striped bass
Cod	Salmon	Trout

VARIATIONS

Poached Fish Steaks

Prepare as in basic recipe, except start with boiling court bouillon. Drain the cooked fish, remove skin and center bone, and serve immediately with selected sauce. Suggested fish steaks: cod, haddock, halibut, turbot, salmon.

"Boiled" Shellfish (Lobster, Crab, Shrimp)

Prepare as for fish steaks using *salted water, court bouillon,* or *acidulated water* (4 oz lemon juice and ½ oz salt per quart of water/125 mL lemon juice and 15 g salt per liter). Water may simmer when cooking shellfish.

Poached Fingers of Salmon and Turbot with Saffron and Julienne of Vegetables

Portions: 10   Portion size: 5 oz (150 g) fish
2 oz (60 mL) broth

U.S.	Metric	Ingredients	PROCEDURE
8 oz	250 g	Leeks	1. Cut the leeks, carrots, and celery or celery root into julienne and keep the trimmings.
8 oz	250 g	Carrots	
8 oz	250 g	Celery or celery root	2. Place the trimmings into a deep pan with the onion and cover with the water. Bring slowly to the boil and skim to remove any impurities.
8 oz	250 g	Onion, sliced thin	
2½ qt	2.5 L	Cold water	3. Simmer for 30 minutes, then strain into a shallow poaching pan and keep barely simmering to reduce to 1½ qt (1.5 L). Season.
to taste	to taste	Salt	
to taste	to taste	Pepper	
2 lb 4 oz	1 kg	Turbot fillets	4. Skin the fillets. Cut the fish into pieces, 1 × 4 inches (2 × 6 cm), and add to the cooking liquid with the vegetable strips and saffron.
2 lb 4 oz	1 kg	Salmon fillets	
large pinch	large pinch	Saffron threads	5. Simmer for 5 minutes. Check the seasoning. Serve in broad soup plates with the cooking liquid. Sprinkle with chopped chives.
to taste	to taste	Salt	
to taste	to taste	Pepper	
1 oz	30 g	Chopped chives	

Per serving:
Calories, 280; Protein, 36 g; Fat, 11 g (37% cal.); Cholesterol, 110 mg;
Carbohydrates, 7 g; Fiber, 2 g; Sodium, 240 mg.

Poached Fingers of Salmon and Turbot with Saffron and Julienne of Vegetables

Poached Salmon with Lentils in Cream

Portions: 12   Portion size: 4 oz (125 g) salmon
5 oz (150 g) lentils
2 oz (60 mL) sauce

U.S.	Metric	Ingredients	PROCEDURE
3 lb	1.5 kg	Salmon fillets	1. Cut the salmon fillets into 4-oz (125-g) portions.
as needed	as needed	Court bouillon	2. Poach in the court bouillon until just cooked, about 10 minutes.
3 lb 12 oz	1.8 kg	Lentils in Cream (p. 462)	3. For each portion, cover the center of a plate with 5 oz (150 g) lentils. Place the salmon on top.
1½ pt	750 mL	White Wine Cream Sauce for Fish (p. 161)	4. Dot with the sauce and serve.

Per serving:
Calories, 640; Protein, 31 g; Fat, 46 g (64% cal.); Cholesterol, 175 mg;
Carbohydrates, 20 g; Fiber, 8 g; Sodium, 420 mg.

Sole Fillets Steamed in Beaujolais

Portions: 12 Portion size: 4 oz (125 g) fish
1½–2 oz (50 mL) sauce

U.S.	Metric	Ingredients	PROCEDURE
3 lb	1.5 kg	Sole fillets: 24 fillets, 2 oz (60 g) each	1. Fold the fillets in half. Be sure that the skin side of the fillet is on the inside of the fold.
1½ pt	750 mL	Beaujolais wine	2. Place the wine on to boil in a wide pan. Place a round rack above the wine. Arrange the fish on the rack in a single layer, cover, and cook in the steam of the boiling wine (the side of the fish exposed to the steam will take on a light color).
1½ pt	750 mL	Fish stock	
10 oz	300 g	Butter	
to taste	to taste	Salt	3. Set the fish aside and keep warm. Reduce the wine to a glaze.
to taste	to taste	Pepper	4. Add the fish stock. Reduce until the sauce is thick enough to lightly coat the back of a spoon. Swirl in the butter (monter au beurre). Strain. Season to taste.
as needed	as needed	Chervil sprigs for garnish	
			5. To serve, ladle some sauce onto the plate and arrange the sole in the center. Garnish with a sprig of chervil.

Per serving:
Calories, 300; Protein, 24 g; Fat, 21 g (64% cal.); Cholesterol, 110 mg;
Carbohydrates, 0 g; Fiber, 0 g; Sodium, 290 mg.

Bourride of Monkfish

Portions: 12 Portion size: about 5 oz (150 g) fish
2 oz (60 g) vegetables
2½ oz (70 mL) sauce

U.S.	Metric	Ingredients	PROCEDURE
2 large	2 large	Baking potatoes	1. Bake the potatoes. While they are still hot, peel them and pass through a food mill to purée.
5 cloves	5 cloves	Garlic	
to taste	to taste	Salt	2. Peel and chop the garlic. Crush to a fine paste with a little salt and pepper.
to taste	to taste	Pepper	
7 oz	200 mL	Olive oil	3. Mix the garlic into the potato purée.
7 oz	200 mL	Peanut oil	4. A little at a time, whip the olive oil and peanut oil into the potato as though making mayonnaise. It is important to add just a few drops at a time at first to get a smooth mixture.
4 oz	125 g	Onion, cut julienne	5. Sweat the onion, carrot, and leek in the olive oil over low heat, covered, until tender. Set aside.
8 oz	250 g	Carrot, cut julienne	
4 oz	125 g	Leek, cut julienne	6. Cook the peas in boiling salted water until tender. Drain, cool under cold water, drain again, and set aside.
1 oz	30 mL	Olive oil	
12 oz	375 g	Peas	
1½ pt	750 mL	White wine	7. Reduce the white wine by half, then add the fish stock. Simmer for 5 minutes.
1 pt 6 oz	700 mL	Fish stock	
5 lb	2.5 kg	Monkfish fillets, boneless and skinless	8. Cut the monkfish fillets into 48 equal pieces.
			9. Butter the inside of a braising pan large enough to hold the monkfish in a single layer. Season the monkfish and place in the braising pan.
as needed	as needed	Butter	
to taste	to taste	Salt	10. Pour the hot fish stock over the fish and simmer for 5–8 minutes or until done.
to taste	to taste	Pepper	
			11. Remove the fish. Add it to the julienned vegetables and set aside.
			12. Bring the cooking liquid to a boil and reduce by half (about 20 oz/600 mL), skimming regularly.
			13. If the fish has cooled, reheat it and the vegetables briefly in the reduced cooking liquid. Strain again.
			14. Whip the cooking liquid into the potato garlic mixture from step 4. Adjust the seasoning as necessary. Strain through a fine sieve.
			15. Arrange the fish, julienned vegetables, and peas on plates (allowing 4 pieces of fish per portion) or on a serving platter. Pour the strained sauce over the fish.

Per serving:
Calories, 750; Protein, 31 g; Fat, 64 g (77% cal.); Cholesterol, 135 mg;
Carbohydrates, 10 g; Fiber, 2 g; Sodium, 110 mg.

Mixed Cooking Techniques

The recipes in this section are included here because they are difficult to classify as one of the basic cooking methods, although they are all based on moist-heat methods. Most of the recipes have two characteristics in common:

1. The item cooks in its own juices and, usually, a small amount of added liquid.

2. The item is served with its flavorful cooking liquid.

In some cases, enough liquid is added to barely cover, and the item simmers. In other cases, little liquid is added and the item cooks in the steam trapped by the pot lid.

The French term *étuver* (ay too vay) is used for this kind of procedure. The word is usually translated as "stew," but this may be misleading. More precisely, it means "to cook or steam in its own juices" or "to sweat."

In addition, this section includes two traditional recipes for dishes made with cooked seafood.

Variations

Note the following three variations represented by the recipes in this section.

1. The product is cooked for a few minutes in fat over low heat, along with mirepoix or onion, to begin extracting juices. A little liquid is then added, the pot is covered, and the item is cooked. Example: Fisherman's Stew.

2. The product is sautéed over high heat. Then other ingredients and liquids are added and the item is cooked, covered, over low heat. Examples: Lobster à l'Americaine and Fricassée of Lobster.

3. The product is simply placed in a pot with liquids and flavoring ingredients. The pot is covered, and the item is steamed or simmered. Example: Moules Marinière.

COOKING EN PAPILLOTE

An unusual version of variation 3 just cited is called *cooking en papillote* (on poppy-yote), or in paper. The fish item, plus flavoring ingredients and sauce, is tightly enclosed in a piece of parchment so that steam cannot escape. When it is heated, the item steams in its own moisture. All the juices, flavors, and aromas are held inside the paper, which is not opened until it is placed before the customer.

Sometimes a starch-thickened sauce is used in cooking fish en papillote. In this case, the fish is usually precooked (poached) so that it will not exude juices that would dilute and spoil the sauce. The problem with this method is that the fish is often overcooked by the time it reaches the customer.

COMPARTMENT STEAMING

Several precautions should be observed if you cook fish and shellfish in a compartment steamer.

1. Watch the cooking time carefully. Fish cooks quickly, especially in the high heat of a steamer, and is easily overcooked.

2. Avoid pressure-steaming of fish and shellfish, if possible. The high temperatures toughen fish protein very quickly. Such items as lobster tails can become rubbery.

3. Use solid pans to retain juices, and use the juices for sauces and soups.

Lobster à l'Americaine

Portions: 2   Portion size: ½ lobster

U.S.	Metric	Ingredients	PROCEDURE
1	1	Live lobster, about 1½ lb (700 g)	1. Cut up the lobster, as shown in Figure 14.12.
1 oz	30 g	Butter, softened	2. Remove the tomalley (liver) and coral (if any). Mash them in a small bowl with the soft butter.
2 oz	60 mL	Oil	3. Heat the oil in a sauté pan and add the lobster pieces. Sauté over high heat until the shells turn red.
1 tbsp	15 mL	Shallot, chopped fine	
½ tsp	2 mL	Garlic, chopped fine	4. Drain off the oil by tilting the pan and holding the lobster in with the pan lid.
2 oz	60 mL	Brandy	5. Add the shallot and garlic to the pan. Sauté for a few seconds.
6 oz	200 mL	White wine	
4 oz	125 mL	Fish stock	6. Remove from the heat (to avoid burning yourself if the brandy flares up) and add the brandy. Return to the heat and add the wine, fish stock, tomato, chopped parsley, tarragon, and cayenne.
4 oz	125 g	Tomato concassé	
		or	
2 oz	60 g	Tomato purée	7. Cover the pan and simmer until the lobster is cooked, about 10–15 minutes.
1 tbsp	15 mL	Chopped parsley	8. Remove the lobster from the cooking liquid and place it on a serving platter or in broad soup plates for service. The meat may be left in the shell or removed from the shell, as desired.
¼ tsp	1 mL	Tarragon	
pinch	pinch	Cayenne	
			9. Reduce the cooking liquid over high heat to about 6 oz (175 mL).
			10. Remove from the heat and stir in the mixture of butter, tomalley, and coral from step 2. Heat the sauce gently for a minute, but do not boil or it will curdle. Adjust the seasoning.
			11. Strain the sauce and pour it over the lobster. Serve immediately.

Per serving:
Calories, 340; Protein, 7 g; Fat, 26 g (67% cal.); Cholesterol, 50 mg; Carbohydrates, 5 g; Fiber, 1 g; Sodium, 230 mg.

VARIATIONS

Lobster Newburg

(*Note:* See p. 424 for Seafood Newburg using cooked shellfish.) Prepare through step 4. Omit remaining ingredients. Instead, add 1 tbsp (15 mL) brandy, 3 tbsp (45 mL) sherry or Marsala or Madeira wine, and 3 oz (100 mL) fish stock. Cover and simmer as in basic recipe. Remove lobster meat from shells and discard shells. Reduce cooking liquid by half and add 1 cup (250 mL) heavy cream *or* light cream sauce. Reduce the sauce slightly and finish by adding the mixture of butter, tomalley, and coral (step 10 of basic recipe). If desired, flavor with more sherry. Pour sauce over the lobster meat.

Shrimp à l'Americaine or Shrimp Newburg

Shrimp may be cooked using the main recipe or the variation. They should be shelled before combining with the finished sauce.

Moules Marinière (Steamed Mussels)

Portions: 10

U.S.	Metric	Ingredients	PROCEDURE
7 lb	3.2 kg	Mussels, in shells	1. Scrub the mussels well with a stiff brush and remove the beards. Clean them well by soaking them according to the procedure given in Chapter 14.
3 oz	90 g	Shallots or onions, chopped fine	
6	6	Parsley stems	2. Place the mussels in a stockpot or large saucepot. Add the onions or shallots, parsley stems, pepper, and wine.
¼ tsp	1 mL	Pepper	
1 cup	250 mL	White wine	3. Cover the pot and set it over moderately high heat. Cook until the mussels open, about 5 minutes.
¼ cup	60 mL	Chopped parsley	4. Drain the mussels and strain the liquid through cheesecloth into a broad saucepan. Bring to a boil.
3 oz	90 g	Butter	
to taste	to taste	Salt	5. Add the parsley and butter. Swirl the liquid in the pan until the butter is melted. Season to taste with salt and a few drops of lemon juice.
to taste	to taste	Lemon juice	
			6. For service, remove the top shells of the mussels (or leave them on, if desired). Place the mussels in broad soup plates and pour the sauce over them.

Per serving:
Calories, 220; Protein, 20 g; Fat, 11 g (44% cal.); Cholesterol, 65 mg; Carbohydrates, 8 g; Fiber, 0 g; Sodium, 540 mg.

VARIATIONS

Steamed Mussels (without wine)

Substitute water for the wine and add 2 oz (60 mL) lemon juice. Increase the onion or shallot to 6 oz (175 g) and add 3 oz (90 g) sliced celery.

Mussels in Cream

Prepare the basic recipe. Reduce the cooking liquid by half and add 1 cup (250 mL) heavy cream or a liaison of 2 egg yolks and 1 cup (250 mL) heavy cream.

Moules Marinière

Fricassée of Lobster with Cardamom and Cilantro

Portions: 12   Portion size: 2½ oz (65 g) lobster meat
2½ oz (65 mL) sauce

U.S.	Metric	Ingredients	PROCEDURE
6	6	Lobsters, 1–1¼ lb (about 500 g) each	
5 oz	150 mL	Corn oil	
to taste	to taste	Salt	
to taste	to taste	Pepper	
3 tbsp	10 g	Cardamom pods, crushed	
3 oz	90 g	Butter	
1½ oz	40 g	Carrot, chopped fine	
1½ oz	40 g	Celery root, chopped fine	
1½ oz	40 g	Leek, sliced thin	
2 tbsp	20 g	Garlic, chopped fine	
1½ oz	40 g	Ginger root, chopped fine	
1½ oz	40 g	Cilantro stems	
10 oz	300 g	Tomatoes, chopped	
8 oz	250 mL	Shellfish stock (from step 2)	
8 oz	250 mL	Heavy cream	
		Garnish:	
1 lb 4 oz	600 g	Fine noodles (such as vermicelli), cooked	
10 oz	300 g	Green beans, cooked	

PROCEDURE

1. Cut up the lobster (catching all the juices); follow the procedure in Figure 14.12, but leave the tail in one piece and the head halved, cleaned, and chopped.

2. Reserve the tail and claws and use the remaining shells and legs to make a shellfish stock, following the procedure for Fish Fumet (p. 132), using the shells in place of the fish bones.

3. Heat the oil in a large pan until smoking and add the lobster tails and claws. Cover and fry until well seared. Drain off excess oil. Season the lobster with salt and pepper. Add the cardamom pods.

4. Add the butter to the pan, melt, and add the carrot, celery root, leek, garlic, ginger, and cilantro stems. Lower the heat, replace the lid, and soften the vegetables without allowing them to color.

5. Move the pan to one side of the stove and add the tomatoes, leaving them for a few minutes to infuse. Return to the stove and add the shellfish stock. Simmer gently.

6. When the lobster is cooked, take the pieces out of the pan and gently remove the meat from the shells, carefully keeping the pieces as whole as possible. Cut the tails in half lengthwise.

7. Add the cream to the pan and heat gently. Check the seasoning and strain the sauce through a chinois. Serve the sauce around the lobster, and garnish the plate with the cooked noodles and beans.

Per serving:
Calories, 260; Protein, 5 g; Fat, 25 g (84% cal.); Cholesterol, 55 mg; Carbohydrates, 6 g; Fiber, 1 g; Sodium, 140 mg.

Figure 15.3 *Preparing foods en papillote.*

(a) Cut out a heart-shaped piece of parchment by folding a parchment sheet in half and cutting half a heart from the folded side. Oil or butter the parchment and place on the work surface, oiled side down.

(b) Place the fish fillet or other item plus any sauce, topping, or seasoning, on one side of the heart.

Mackerel en Papillote

Portions: 1   Portion size: 4 oz (125 g)

U.S.	Metric	Ingredients	PROCEDURE
1	1	Mackerel fillet, 4 oz (125 g) (see note)	1. Cut out a piece of parchment in a heart shape, as shown in Figure 15.3. (Foil may be used instead of parchment.) The piece must be big enough to hold the fish and still have room for crimping the edges. Oil the parchment and place on the work bench oiled side down. (If using foil, place it oiled side up.)
2 tsp	10 mL	Melted butter	
to taste	to taste	Salt	
to taste	to taste	White pepper	
2 tsp	10 mL	Chopped parsley	2. Place the fillet on one side of the heart. Brush with melted butter and sprinkle with salt, pepper, parsley, marjoram, and chopped shallot. Lay the lemon slices on top.
pinch	pinch	Marjoram	
1 tsp	5 mL	Shallots, chopped very fine	
2	2	Thin lemon slices	3. Fold and crimp the parchment, as shown in the illustration, to enclose the fish tightly.

4. Place the folded package in a sauté pan or, if several orders are being done at once, on a sheet pan. Set on the range to start the cooking.

5. As soon as the paper begins to puff, place the pan in a hot oven (450°F/230°C). Bake until the parchment is puffed and browned, about 5–8 minutes. (If the paper doesn't brown, you may run it under the broiler for a second.)

6. Serve immediately. The parchment should be cut open in front of the customer.

Per serving:
Calories, 290; Protein, 20 g; Fat, 23 g (71% cal.); Cholesterol, 85 mg;
Carbohydrates, 1 g; Fiber, 0 g; Sodium, 150 mg.

Note: Pompano or bluefish may be used.

VARIATION

Instead of the parsley, shallots, and lemon slices, top fillets with a thin layer of Duxelles (p. 468).

(c) Fold over the other half of the heart. Starting at the top of the fold, make a small crimp in the edges as shown.

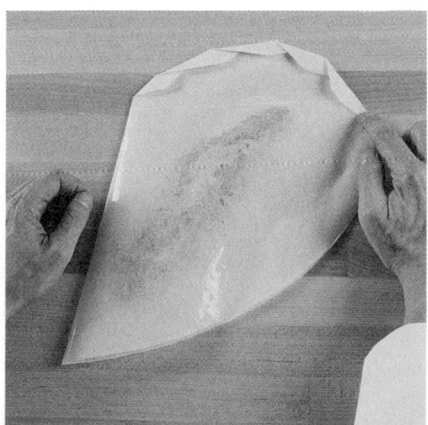

(d) Continue crimping around the edge. Each crimp holds the previous one in place.

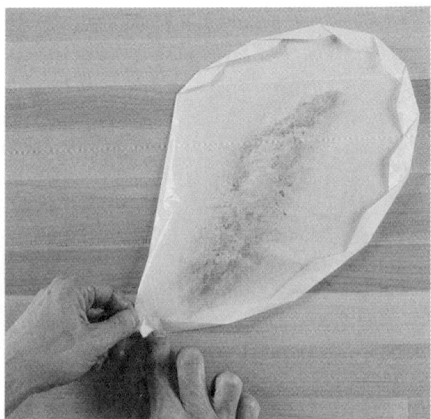

(e) When you reach the bottom of the heart, fold the point under to hold it in place. The papillote is now ready for cooking.

Seafood Newburg

Portions: 25   **Portion size:** 7 oz (200 g)

U.S.	Metric	Ingredients	PROCEDURE
2½ lb	1.2 kg	Cooked sea scallops	1. If the sea scallops are large, cut them in halves or quarters.
2½ lb	1.2 kg	Cooked crabmeat	2. Pick over the crabmeat to make sure there are no pieces of shell. If there are large pieces of meat, cut them into ½-inch (1-cm) dice.
1¼ lb	600 g	Cooked, peeled shrimp	
4 oz	125 g	Butter	3. Cut the shrimp in half lengthwise.
2½ tsp	12 mL	Paprika	4. Heat the butter in a large saucepan or sauté pan. Add the paprika and the seafood. Sauté over moderate heat until heated through and coated lightly with butter.
8 oz	250 mL	Sherry	
2½ qt	2.5 L	Cream sauce, hot	5. Add sherry and simmer for a minute.
to taste	to taste	Salt	6. Add the cream sauce and bring to a simmer. Season to taste with salt and white pepper.
to taste	to taste	White pepper	7. Serve with rice or in patty shells.

Per serving:
Calories, 330; Protein, 26 g; Fat, 19 g (53% cal.); Cholesterol, 145 mg;
Carbohydrates, 11 g; Fiber, 0 g; Sodium, 550 mg.

VARIATIONS

Different proportions of seafood may be used. Lobster meat may also be included.

Seafood Curry

Omit paprika and sherry. Substitute curry sauce (made with fish velouté) for the cream sauce. Garnish with toasted, sliced almonds, if desired.

Fisherman's Stew

Portions: 10   **Portion size:** (see step 9)

U.S.	Metric	Ingredients	PROCEDURE
2 lb	900 g	Fish steaks or fillets (see note for suggested fish)	1. Cut the fish into 3-oz (90-g) serving pieces.
			2. Scrub the clams and mussels well.
10	10	Clams, in shell	3. Cut the lobster tails in half lengthwise with a heavy chef's knife. Remove the intestinal vein.
20	20	Mussels, in shell (or 10 more clams)	
5	5	Lobster tails, small (or use 10 large shrimp)	
4 oz	125 mL	Olive oil	4. Heat the oil in a heavy saucepot or large straight-sided sauté pan.
8 oz	250 g	Onions, sliced	
8 oz	250 g	Leeks, cut julienne	5. Add the onions, leeks, garlic, and fennel. Sweat them in the oil for a few minutes.
2 tsp	10 mL	Garlic, chopped	
¼ tsp	1 mL	Fennel seed	6. Add the pieces of fish and the lobster tails (or shrimp). Cover and cook over low heat for a few minutes to begin extracting juices from the fish.
12 oz	350 g	Tomato concassé or drained, chopped canned tomato	
2 qt	2 L	Fish stock	7. Remove the cover and add the clams and mussels.
4 oz	100 mL	White wine (optional but recommended)	8. Add the tomato, fish stock, wine, bay leaves, parsley, thyme, salt, and pepper. Cover and bring to a boil. Reduce heat and simmer about 15 minutes, until the clams and mussels are open.
2	2	Bay leaves	
2 tbsp	30 mL	Chopped parsley	
¼ tsp	1 mL	Thyme	
2 tsp	10 mL	Salt	
¼ tsp	1 mL	Pepper	
20–30	20–30	French bread slices, dry or toasted	9. To serve, place 2 or 3 thin slices of French bread in the bottoms of soup plates. For each portion, place 1 piece of fish, 1 clam, 2 mussels, and half of 1 lobster tail in each plate. Ladle 8 oz (250 mL) broth over the fish.

Per serving:
Calories, 470; Protein, 32 g; Fat, 26 g (51% cal.); Cholesterol, 90 mg;
Carbohydrates, 25 g; Fiber, 2 g; Sodium, 910 mg.

Note: Any firm fish may be used, such as halibut, cod, haddock, sea bass or striped bass, red snapper, or mackerel. Avoid delicate fish like flounder or sole, which break up easily during cooking.

If desired, reduce or eliminate shellfish from the recipe and increase the quantity of fish.

Seafood Casserole au Gratin

Portions: 25   Portion size: 6 oz (175 g)

U.S.	Metric	Ingredients	PROCEDURE
3¾ lb	1.7 kg	Cooked, flaked cod or other firm, white fish	1. Pick over the fish and shellfish to make sure it contains no bones or pieces of shell.
2½ lb	1.1 kg	Cooked crabmeat, shrimp, scallops, or lobster meat, or a mixture of any of these	2. Heat the butter in a wide saucepan or straight-sided sauté pan. Add the fish and shellfish. Sauté lightly over moderate heat until the fish is heated through and coated with butter.
4 oz	125 g	Butter	3. Add the mornay sauce and bring just to a simmer. Taste and adjust seasonings.
2 qt	2 L	Mornay sauce, hot	4. Ladle 6-oz (175-g) portions into individual service casseroles. Sprinkle with parmesan cheese.
4 oz	125 g	Parmesan cheese	5. Heat under the broiler at low heat until the tops are lightly browned.

Per serving:
Calories, 330; Protein, 33 g; Fat, 18 g (51% cal.); Cholesterol, 120 mg; Carbohydrates, 6 g; Fiber, 0 g; Sodium, 520 mg.

VARIATIONS

Other combinations of seafood may be used. If desired, use all fish or all shellfish.

Other sauces may be used instead of mornay, including

> Cream sauce
> Cheddar cheese sauce
> Nantua sauce
> White wine sauce
> Mushroom sauce (made from fish velouté)

Salmon or Tuna Casserole

Use drained, canned salmon or tuna, and use cream sauce, cheddar cheese sauce, or mushroom sauce (made with fish velouté) instead of Mornay sauce. Combine the parmesan cheese with an equal quantity of buttered bread crumbs before topping. If desired, prepare in a baking pan instead of individual casseroles.

Seafood Served Raw

Raw oysters and clams have long been enjoyed in North American restaurants as well as in homes. Smoked salmon, too, has always been a popular raw seafood item, although many people don't think of it as raw fish because it has been processed.

More recently, with the popularity of Japanese sushi and sashimi, many more people enjoy eating items made with raw fish, and chefs are experimenting with new ways to serve raw seafood items. Because of the danger of contamination from polluted fishing waters, however, many health officials advise against serving raw seafood. Nevertheless, these items remain popular. If you choose to serve raw seafood, observe the following guidelines:

1. Use only the freshest possible fish.
2. Buy the fish from a reliable purveyor.
3. Use only saltwater seafood from clean waters. Do not use freshwater fish, which may contain parasites.
4. Observe the strictest sanitation procedures.
5. Keep the fish cold and handle it as little as possible.

Two kinds of raw fish recipes are included in this chapter. *Fish tartar* is a mixture of chopped raw fish mixed with various condiments and seasonings. *Fish carpaccio* is a dish consisting of very thin slices of firm, meaty fish such as tuna, served with various garnishes and usually with a piquant sauce such as a vinaigrette. *Carpaccio* (karpachio) is the Italian word for a dish of thin slices of raw beef, served the same way.

Chapter 25 includes procedures for making sushi, which is seasoned rice that is usually, but not always, garnished with raw fish.

Tartar of Sea Bass and Salmon

Yield: 3 lb (1.5 kg)   Portions: 12   Portion size: 4 oz (125 g)

U.S.	Metric	Ingredients	PROCEDURE
1 lb 4 oz	600 g	Salmon fillet, skinless and boneless	1. Chop the fish with a knife. Refrigerate until ready to mix and serve.
12 oz	375 g	Sea bass fillet, skinless and boneless	2. Whip together the lemon juice, mustard, and shallots. Gradually whip in the oil until well emulsified. Season to taste, then mix in the chopped herbs.
3 oz	90 mL	Lemon juice	3. Mix into the chopped fish.
2½ oz	75 g	Dijon mustard	4. Cut a small brunoise of tomato.
3½ oz	100 g	Shallots, chopped	5. The tartar can be presented either in quenelles (see Figure 24.8) or molded in a ring mold (see Figure 24.9). Sprinkle the plate with the tomato and decorate with sprigs of chervil.
6 oz	175 mL	Olive oil	
to taste	to taste	Salt	
to taste	to taste	Pepper	
7 tbsp	40 g	Chopped parsley	
4 tbsp	25 g	Chopped chervil	
3 tbsp	17 g	Chopped chives	
12 oz	375 g	Tomato, peeled and seeded	
as needed	as needed	Chervil sprigs	

Per serving:
Calories, 250; Protein, 16 g; Fat, 19 g (68% cal.); Cholesterol, 40 mg;
Carbohydrates, 4 g; Fiber, 1 g; Sodium, 190 mg.

Tartar of Sea Bass and Salmon

Tuna Carpaccio with Sheep's Milk Cheese

Portions: 12   Portion size: 5 oz (150 g) tuna
2½ oz (70 g) garnish
1½ oz (45 mL) sauce

U.S.	Metric	Ingredients	PROCEDURE
7 oz	200 mL	Lime juice	1. Combine the lime juice, shallots, and olive oil to make a marinade, seasoning it with salt and pepper.
3 oz	80 g	Shallots, chopped	
12 oz	375 mL	Olive oil	2. Slice the tuna into paper-thin slices, using a slicing machine. Marinate, refrigerated, for 2 hours.
to taste	to taste	Salt	
to taste	to taste	Pepper	
4½ lb	2 kg	Fresh tuna	
1 lb	500 g	Sheep's milk cheese (see note)	3. Cut the cheese into very thin slices.
3½ oz	100 g	Red pepper	4. Cut the peppers into a small brunoise. Blanch and refresh. Drain well on paper towel.
3½ oz	100 g	Green pepper	5. Thinly slice the scallions.
7 oz	200 g	Scallions	6. Chop the basil.
⅔ oz (3 tbsp)	20 g	Basil	7. Drain the tuna, reserving the marinade. Cut out rounds using a round cutter. Do the same with the cheese. Arrange in a single layer on a plate, alternating cheese and tuna, with the rounds slightly overlapping.
			8. Sprinkle with the chopped scallions, peppers, and chopped basil.
			9. Whisk the marinade until emulsified and drizzle over. Decorate with whole basil leaves.

Per serving:
Calories, 620; Protein, 50 g; Fat, 44 g (64% cal.); Cholesterol, 120 mg;
Carbohydrates, 6 g; Fiber, 1 g; Sodium, 200 mg.

Note: The cheese used for this recipe is a hard cheese, with a smooth texture, golden color, and nutty flavor. It is similar in flavor to Edam. Substitute a similar cheese as necessary.

Terms for Review

meunière	au bleu	étuver	fish tartar
court bouillon	à la nage	en papillote	fish carpaccio

Questions for Discussion

1. What major precaution must be taken when baking or broiling lean fish?
2. Describe the procedure for cooking fish à la meunière.
3. Which side of a fish fillet is the presentation side?
4. What techniques can you use for lifting whole poached fish out of court bouillon without breaking it or damaging its appearance?
5. What temperatures are best for poaching fish?
6. What is one advantage of using the oven to poach fish fillets?
7. Describe two methods for making a finished sauce out of the cooking liquid (fumet and wine) used for poaching fish fillets.
8. Discuss the precautions a cook should take to ensure that raw fish is safe to eat.

chapter 16

Understanding Vegetables

Vegetables were, at one time, abused and neglected, relegated to the minor role of unimportant side dishes, to be taken or left, or not even noticed on the table.

Today, however, lowly vegetables are much more appreciated, not only for their nutritional importance but for the variety, flavor, eye appeal, and even elegance and sophistication that they bring to the menu. Modern cooks owe it to themselves and their customers to treat vegetables with understanding, respect, and imagination.

Because they are so perishable, vegetables require extra care from receiving to service. *Freshness* is their most appealing and attractive quality, and one must be especially careful to preserve it. The goals of proper vegetable cookery are to preserve and enhance fresh flavor, texture, and color, to prepare and serve vegetables that are not just accepted but sought after.

Controlling Quality Changes During Cooking

As a cook, you have a choice of many kinds of vegetables and many cooking methods. Not surprisingly, then, you are also faced with the necessity of learning many rules for cooking vegetables.

Many guides to vegetable cookery simply present a long list of rules to memorize. You should be able to understand the principles more easily, however, if you first learn how vegetables change as they are cooked and how to control those changes. In other words, we suggest that you not just memorize what to do but understand why you do it.

Cooking affects vegetables in four ways. It changes the following:

1. Texture.   3. Color.
2. Flavor.   4. Nutrients.

How much these four characteristics change determines whether your final product is attractive and delicious to the customer or whether it ends up in the garbage. You can control these changes if you understand how they happen.

Unfortunately, there is still legitimate controversy among chefs about proper vegetable cooking techniques. Modern technology has not yet solved all the problems that experienced chefs tackle successfully every day in the kitchen.

Controlling Texture Changes

Changing the texture is one of the main purposes of cooking vegetables.

FIBER

The fiber structures of vegetables (including cellulose and pectins) give them shape and firmness. Cooking softens some of these components.

The *amount of fiber* varies

1. In different vegetables. Spinach and tomatoes have less than carrots and turnips, for example.
2. In different examples of the same vegetables. Old, tough carrots have more fiber than young, fresh carrots.
3. In the same vegetable. The tender tips of asparagus and broccoli have less fiber than their tougher stalks.

Fiber is made *firmer* by

1. **Acids.**
   Lemon juice, vinegar, and tomato products, when added to cooking vegetables, extend the cooking time.

2. **Sugars.**
   Sugar strengthens cell structure. You will use this principle primarily in fruit cookery. For firm poached apples or pears, for example, cook in a heavy syrup. For applesauce, cook apples until soft before sweetening.

Fiber is *softened* by

1. **Heat.**
   In general, longer cooking means softer vegetables.

2. **Alkalis.**
   Do not add baking soda to green vegetables. Not only does it destroy vitamins but it also makes the vegetables unpleasantly mushy.

After reading this chapter, you should be able to:

1. Describe the factors that influence texture, flavor, color, and nutritional changes when cooking vegetables.

2. Cook vegetables to their proper doneness.

3. Judge quality in cooked vegetables based on color, appearance, texture, flavor, seasonings, and appropriateness of combination with sauces or other vegetables.

4. Perform the pre-preparation tasks for fresh vegetables.

5. Calculate yields based on trimming losses.

6. Determine the quality of frozen, canned, and dried vegetables.

7. Prepare vegetables using the batch cooking method and the blanch-and-chill method.

8. Store both fresh and processed vegetables.

STARCH

Starch is another vegetable component that affects texture.

1. *Dry starchy foods* like dried legumes (beans, peas, lentils), rice, and macaroni products must be cooked in sufficient water so that the starch granules can absorb moisture and soften. Dried beans are usually soaked before cooking to replace lost moisture.

2. *Moist starchy vegetables* like potatoes and sweet potatoes have enough moisture of their own, but they must still be cooked until the starch granules soften.

DONENESS

A vegetable is said to be done when it has reached the desired degree of tenderness. This stage varies from vegetable to vegetable. Some, such as winter squash, eggplant, and braised celery, are considered properly cooked when they are quite soft. Most vegetables, however, are best cooked very briefly, until they are crisp-tender or *al dente* (firm to the bite). At this stage of tenderness, they not only have the most pleasing texture but also retain maximum flavor, color, and nutrients.

Guidelines for Achieving Proper Doneness in Vegetables

1. Don't overcook.

2. Cook as close to service as possible. Holding vegetables in a steam table continues to cook them.

3. If vegetables must be cooked in advance, slightly undercook them, cool rapidly in cold water, drain, and refrigerate, then reheat to order.

4. For uniform doneness, cut vegetables into pieces of uniform size before cooking.

5. Vegetables with both tough and tender parts need special treatment so that the tender parts are not overcooked by the time the tougher parts are done.

   For example,

   Peel the woody stalks of asparagus.

   Peel or split broccoli stalks.

   Pierce the base of brussels sprouts with a sharp knife.

   Remove the heavy center stalks of lettuce leaves before braising.

6. Don't mix batches of cooked vegetables. They are likely to be cooked to slightly different levels of doneness.

Controlling Flavor Changes

COOKING PRODUCES FLAVOR LOSS

Many flavors are lost during cooking, by dissolving into the cooking liquid and by evaporation. The longer a vegetable is cooked, the more flavor it loses.

Flavor loss can be controlled in several ways:

1. Cook for as short a time as possible.

2. Use boiling salted water. Starting vegetables in boiling water shortens cooking time. The addition of salt helps reduce flavor loss.

3. Use just enough water to cover to minimize leaching. Note that this rule contradicts rule 1 in that adding vegetables to a small quantity of water lowers the temperature more, so cooking time is extended. Save your questions on this until you have finished reading the sections on color and nutritional changes.

4. Steam vegetables whenever appropriate. Steam cooking reduces leaching out of flavor and shortens cooking time.

Strong-flavored Vegetables

With certain strong-flavored vegetables, it is desirable to lose some of the flavor to make them more appealing to the taste. These include the onion family (onions, garlic, leeks, shallots), the cabbage family (cabbage, brussels sprouts, cauliflower, broccoli), and some root vegetables (turnips, rutabagas).

When cooking strong-flavored vegetables, leave uncovered to allow these flavors to escape, and use larger amounts of water.

COOKING PRODUCES FLAVOR CHANGES

Cooked vegetables do not taste like raw vegetables because cooking produces certain chemical changes. As long as the vegetables are not overcooked, this change is desirable. It produces the flavors one looks for in vegetable dishes.

Overcooking produces undesirable changes in members of the cabbage family. They develop a strong, unpleasant flavor. Cabbage and its relatives should be cooked quickly, uncovered.

COOKING AND SWEETNESS

Young, freshly harvested vegetables have a relatively high sugar content that makes them taste sweet. As they mature, or as they sit in storage, the sugar gradually changes to starch. This is especially noticeable in corn, peas, carrots, turnips, and beets.

To serve sweet-tasting vegetables:

1. Try to serve young, fresh vegetables that have been stored for as short a time as possible.

2. For older vegetables, especially those just listed, add a small amount of sugar to the cooking water to replace lost sweetness.

Controlling Color Changes

It is important to preserve as much natural color as possible when cooking vegetables. Because customers may reject or accept a vegetable on the basis of its appearance, it can be said that its visual quality is as important as its flavor or nutritional value.

Pigments are compounds that give vegetables their color. Different pigments react in different ways to heat and to acids and other elements that may be present during cooking, so it is necessary to discuss them one at a time. Table 16.1 summarizes this information.

WHITE VEGETABLES

White pigments, called *flavones*, are the primary coloring compounds in potatoes, onions, cauliflower, and white cabbage and in the white parts of such vegetables as celery, cucumbers, and zucchini.

TABLE 16.1

Vegetable Color Changes During Cooking

Color	Examples of Vegetables	Cooked with Acid	Cooked with Alkali	Overcooked
White	Potatoes, turnips, cauliflower, onions, white cabbage	White	Yellow	Yellowish, gray
Red	Beets, red cabbage (not tomatoes, whose pigment is like that in yellow vegetables)	Red	Blue or blue-green	Greenish blue, faded
Green	Asparagus, green beans, lima beans, broccoli, brussels sprouts, peas, spinach, green peppers, artichokes, okra	Olive green	Bright green	Olive green
Yellow (and orange)	Carrots, tomatoes, rutabagas, sweet potatoes, squash, corn	Little change	Little change	Slightly faded

White pigments stay white in acid and turn yellow in alkaline water. To keep vegetables such as cauliflower white, add a little lemon juice or cream of tartar to the cooking water. (Don't add too much, though, as this may toughen the vegetable.) Covering the pot also helps keep acids in.

Cooking for a short time, especially in a steamer, helps maintain color (and flavor and nutrients as well). Overcooking or holding too long in a steam table turns white vegetables dull yellow or gray.

RED VEGETABLES

Red pigments, called *anthocyanins*, are found in only a few vegetables, mainly red cabbage and beets. Blueberries also are colored by these red pigments. (The red color of tomatoes and red peppers is due to the same pigments that color carrots yellow or orange.)

Red pigments react very strongly to acids and alkalis.

Acids turn them a brighter red.
Alkalis turn them blue or blue-green (not a very appetizing color for red cabbage).

Red beets and red cabbage, therefore, have their best color when cooked with a small amount of acid. Red cabbage is often cooked with tart apples for this reason.

When a strongly acidic vegetable is desired, such as Harvard beets or braised red cabbage, add just a small amount of acid at first. Acids toughen vegetables and prolong cooking time. Add the rest when the vegetables are tender.

Red pigments dissolve easily in water. This means

1. Use a short cooking time. Overcooked red vegetables lose a lot of color.
2. Use only as much water as is necessary.
3. Cook beets whole and unpeeled, with root and an inch of stem attached, to protect color. Skins easily slip off cooked beets.
4. When steaming, use solid pans instead of perforated pans to retain the red juices.
5. Whenever possible, serve the cooking liquid as a sauce with the vegetable.

GREEN VEGETABLES

Green coloring, or *chlorophyll,* is present in all green plants. Green vegetables are common in the kitchen, so it is important to understand the special handling required by this pigment.

Acids are enemies of green vegetables. Both *acid* and *long cooking* turn green vegetables to a drab olive green.

Protect the color of green vegetables by

1. Cooking uncovered to allow plant acids to escape.
2. Cooking for the shortest possible time. Properly cooked green vegetables are tender-crisp, not mushy.
3. Cooking in small batches rather than holding for long periods in a steam table.

Steaming is rapidly becoming the preferred method for cooking green vegetables. Steam cooks food rapidly, lessens the dissolving out of nutrients and flavor, and does not break up delicate vegetables. Overcooking, however, can occur rapidly in steamers.

Do not use baking soda to maintain green color. Soda destroys vitamins and makes texture unpleasantly mushy and slippery.

How much water should be used when boiling? A large quantity of water helps dissolve plant acids, helps preserve colors, and speeds cooking. But some cooks feel that an excessive amount of nutrients are lost. See the next section for further discussion.

YELLOW AND ORANGE VEGETABLES

Yellow and *orange* pigments, called *carotenoids,* are found in carrots, corn, winter squash, rutabaga, sweet potatoes, tomatoes, and red peppers. These pigments are very stable. They are little affected by acids or alkalis. Long cooking can dull the color, however. Short cooking not only prevents dulling of the color but also preserves vitamins and flavors.

Controlling Nutrient Losses

Vegetables are an important part of our diets because they supply a wide variety of essential nutrients. They are our major sources of vitamins A and C and are rich in many other vitamins and minerals. Unfortunately, many of these nutrients are easily lost.

Six factors are responsible for most nutrient loss:

1. High temperature.
2. Long cooking.
3. Leaching (dissolving out).
4. Alkalis (baking soda, hard water).
5. Plant enzymes (which are active at warm temperatures but are destroyed by high heat).
6. Oxygen.

Some nutrient loss is inevitable because it is rarely possible to avoid all of these conditions at the same time. For example,

- Pressure steaming shortens cooking time, but the high temperature destroys some vitamins.
- Braising uses low heat, but the cooking time is longer.
- Baking eliminates the leaching out of vitamins and minerals, but the long cooking and high temperature cause nutrient loss.
- Boiling is faster than simmering, but the higher temperature can be harmful and the rapid activity can break up delicate vegetables and increase loss through leaching.
- Cutting vegetables into small pieces decreases cooking time, but it increases leaching by creating more exposed surfaces.
- Even steaming allows some leaching out of nutrients into the moisture that condenses onto the vegetables and then drips off.

COOKING IN A LITTLE LIQUID VERSUS A LOT OF LIQUID

This is an area of controversy with good arguments on both sides.

1. Using a lot of liquid increases vitamin loss by leaching. Use just enough liquid to cover. Save the cooking liquid for reheating the vegetables or for stocks or soups.
2. Using a little liquid increases cooking time. When the vegetables are combined with the small quantity of boiling water, the temperature is lowered greatly and the vegetables must sit in warm water while it again heats up. Also, plant enzymes may destroy some vitamins before the water again becomes hot enough to destroy them.

Tests have shown that, for these reasons, no more nutrients are lost when vegetables are cooked in a lot of water than when vegetables are cooked in just enough water to cover.

When cooking green vegetables, there is an added advantage to using a lot of water. Plant acids are more quickly diluted and driven off, better preserving the color.

The best cooking methods, nutritionally, are usually those that produce the most attractive, flavorful products.

- They are more likely to be eaten. Discarded vegetables benefit no one, no matter how nutritious they are.
- Factors that destroy nutrients are often those that also destroy color, flavor, and texture.

General Rules of Vegetable Cookery

Now that you understand *how* vegetables change as they cook, let's summarize that information in some general rules. You should now be able to explain the reasons for each of these rules.

- Don't overcook.
- Cook as close to service time as possible and in small quantities. Avoid holding for long periods on a steam table.
- If the vegetable must be cooked ahead, undercook slightly and chill rapidly. Reheat at service time.

- Never use baking soda with green vegetables.
- Cut vegetables uniformly for even cooking.
- Start with boiling, salted water when boiling vegetables.
- Cook green vegetables and strong-flavored vegetables uncovered.
- To preserve color, cook red and white vegetables in a slightly acidic (not strongly acidic) liquid. Cook green vegetables in a neutral liquid.
- Do not mix batches of cooked vegetables.

Standards of Quality in Cooked Vegetables

1. **Color.**
    Bright, natural colors.
    Green vegetables, in particular, should be a fresh, bright green, not olive green.

2. **Appearance on plate.**
    Cut neatly and uniformly. Not broken up.
    Attractively arranged or mounded on plate or dish.
    Not swimming in cooking water.
    Imaginative and appropriate combinations and garnishes are always well received.

3. **Texture.**
    Cooked to the right degree of doneness.
    Most vegetables should be crisp-tender, not overcooked and mushy, but not tough or woody either.
    Vegetables intended to be soft (potatoes, squash, sweet potatoes, tomatoes, vegetable purées) should be cooked through, with a pleasant, smooth texture.

4. **Flavor.**
    Full, natural flavor and sweetness, sometimes called "garden-fresh" flavor. Strong flavored vegetables should be pleasantly mild, with no off flavors or bitterness.

5. **Seasonings.**
    Lightly and appropriately seasoned. Seasonings should not be too strong and not mask the natural "garden" flavors.

6. **Sauces.**
    Butter and seasoned butters should be fresh and not used heavily; vegetables should not be greasy.
    Cream sauces and other sauces should not be too thick or too heavily seasoned. As with seasonings, sauces should enhance, not cover up.

7. **Vegetable combinations.**
    Interesting combinations attract customers.
    Flavors, colors, and shapes should be pleasing in combination.
    Vegetables should be cooked separately and then combined to allow for different cooking times.
    Acid vegetables (like tomatoes) added to green vegetables will discolor them. Combine just before service.

Handling Vegetables

Fresh Vegetables

WASHING

1. Wash all vegetables thoroughly.
2. Root vegetables that are not peeled, such as potatoes for baking, should be scrubbed very well with a stiff vegetable brush.

3. Wash green, leafy vegetables in several changes of cold water. Lift the greens from the water so that the sand can sink to the bottom. Pouring off into a colander dumps the sand back onto the leaves.
4. After washing, drain well and refrigerate lightly covered. The purpose of covering is to prevent drying, but covering too tightly cuts off air circulation. This can be a problem if the product is stored more than a day because mold is more likely to grow in a damp, closed space. Use a drain insert in the storage container to allow drainage.

SOAKING

1. With a few exceptions, do not soak vegetables for long periods. Flavor and nutrients leach out.
2. Cabbage, broccoli, brussels sprouts, and cauliflower may be soaked for 30 minutes in cold salted water to eliminate insects, if necessary.
3. Limp vegetables can be soaked briefly in cold water to restore crispness.
4. Dried legumes are soaked for several hours before cooking to replace moisture lost in drying. Dried beans absorb their weight in water.

PEELING AND CUTTING

1. Peel most vegetables as thinly as possible. Many nutrients lie just under the skin.
2. Cut vegetables into uniform pieces for even cooking.
3. Peel and cut vegetables as close to cooking time as possible to prevent drying and loss of vitamins through oxidation.
4. For machine paring, sort vegetables for evenness of size to minimize waste.
5. Treat vegetables that brown easily (potatoes, eggplant, artichokes, sweet potatoes) with an acid, such as lemon juice, or an antioxidant solution, or hold under water until ready to use (some vitamins and minerals will be lost).
6. Save edible trim for soups, stocks, and vegetable purées.

TRIMMING LOSS: CALCULATING YIELDS AND AMOUNTS NEEDED

Table 16.2 lists, in the last column, the percentage yield for each vegetable. This figure indicates, on the average, how much of the AP (as purchased) weight is left after pre-prep to produce the ready-to-cook item, or EP (edible portion) weight. You can use this figure to do two basic calculations.

1. Calculating yield.
   Example. You have 10 lb AP brussels sprouts. Percentage yield after trimming is 80%. What will your EP weight be?

   First, change the percentage to a decimal number by moving the decimal point two places to the left.
   $$80\% = 0.80$$

   Multiply the decimal by your AP weight to get EP yield.
   $$10 \text{ lb} \times 0.80 = 8 \text{ lb}$$

2. Calculating amount needed.
   Example. You need 10 lb EP brussels sprouts. How much untrimmed vegetables do you need?

   Change the percentage to a decimal number.
   $$80\% = 0.80$$

   Divide the EP weight needed by this number to get the AP weight.
   $$\frac{10 \text{ lb}}{0.80} = 12.5 \text{ lb}$$

TABLE 16.2

Fresh Vegetable Pre-preparation

Note: Because fruits are handled in the pantry more than in the vegetable kitchen, the table of fruit pre-preparation is included in Chapter 19.

Product	Quality Indicators (Q.I.) and Pre-preparation (Prep.)	Percentage Yield
Artichokes, globe	**Q.I.:** Compact, tight leaves; heavy for size; few or no brown blemishes. **Prep.:** Wash. Cut 1 inch (2–3 cm) off tops. Cut off stem and lower leaves. Scrape out choke (fuzzy center) with melon ball cutter. (Remove choke before or after cooking.) Dip in lemon juice immediately. To prepare bottoms, see Figures 16.1 and 16.2.	80% (whole, trimmed) 30% (bottoms only)

(Continued)

Figure 16.1 Trimming artichoke bottoms.

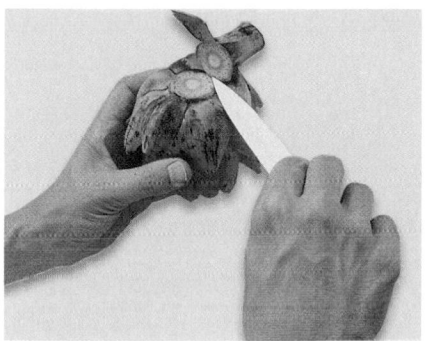

(a) Cut or break off the stem flush with the bottom of the artichoke, as shown.

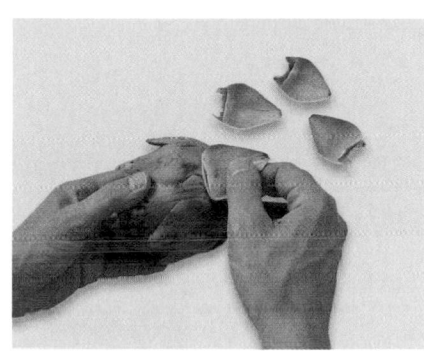

(b) Break off the outer leaves.

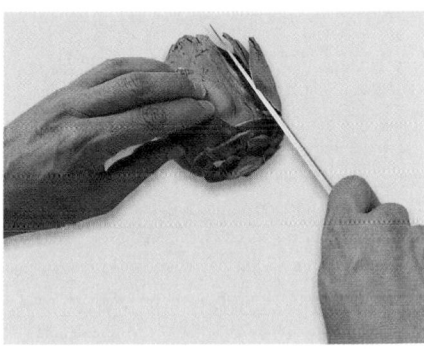

(c) Alternatively, trim the outer leaves with a knife as shown, being careful not to cut into the base of the artichoke.

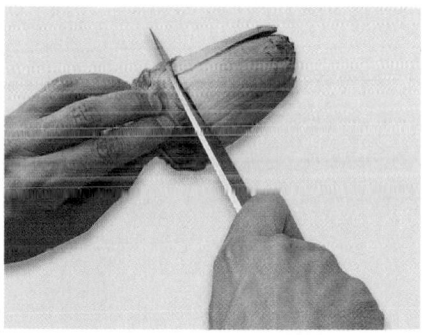

(d) Cut off the remaining leaves above the base.

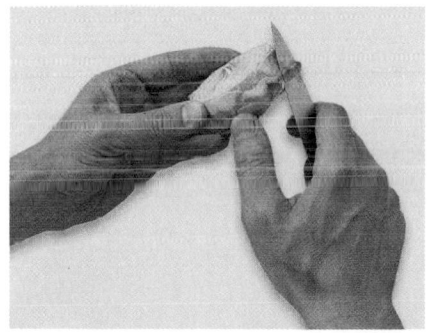

(e) With a paring knife, trim off the green outer peel to give the base a smooth, neat appearance.

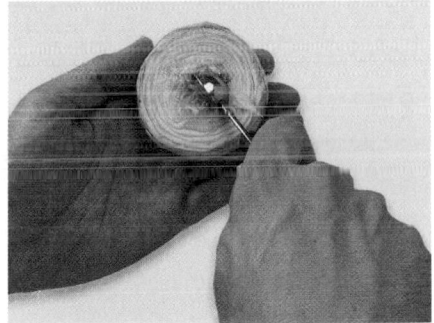

(f) With a ball cutter or tablespoon, scrape out the fuzzy choke.

(g) A trimmed artichoke bottom on the left; a trimmed whole artichoke on the right. Note that the points of the leaves have been cut off and the center choke removed.

Figure 16.2 To keep the cut stem end of an artichoke from darkening during steaming or boiling, tie a slice of lemon over the cut surface.

TABLE 16.2

Fresh Vegetable Pre-preparation *(Continued)*

Product	Quality Indicators (Q.I.) and Pre-preparation (Prep.)	Percentage Yield
Artichokes, Jerusalem	Wash and peel off brown skin.	80%
Asparagus	**Q.I.:** Tightly closed tips; firm, not withered, stalks. **Prep.:** Break off woody lower ends. Remove lower scales, which may harbor sand, or peel lower part of stalk. Figure 16.3 shows an alternative method. Cut tips to uniform lengths and/or tie them in bundles for cooking.	55%
Avocado	**Q.I.:** Two main types: with rough green skin that turns black when ripe; with smoother skin that stays green. Fresh appearance, heavy for size, turning soft when ripe. Avoid soft spots and bruises. **Prep.:** Ripen at room temperature, 2–5 days. Cut in half lengthwise and remove pit (see Figure 16.4). Peel (skin pulls away easily from ripe fruit). Dip or rub with lemon juice immediately to prevent browning.	75%

(Continued)

Figure 16.3 Trimming asparagus.

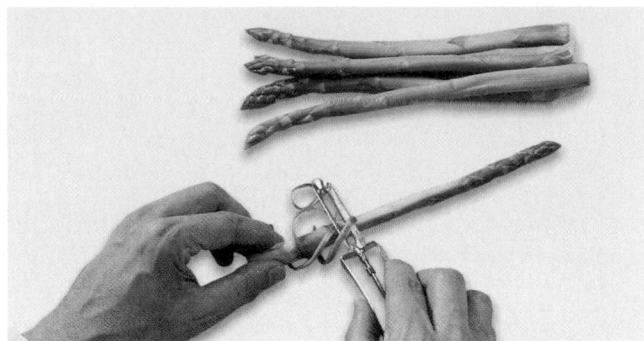

(a) With a vegetable peeler, pare the stalk from about 2 inches (5 cm) below the tip down to the base.

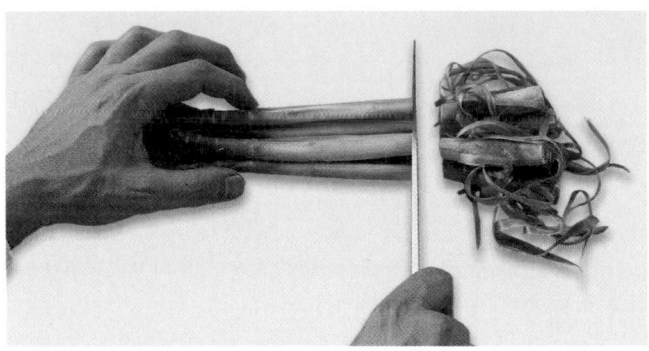

(b) Cut or break off the hard, woody bottoms of the stems.

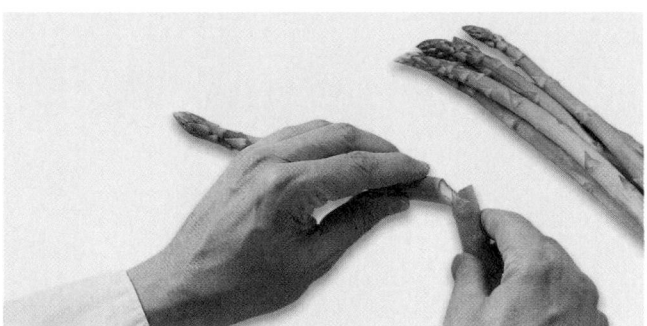

(c) Another method used by many chefs is to break off the stems first…

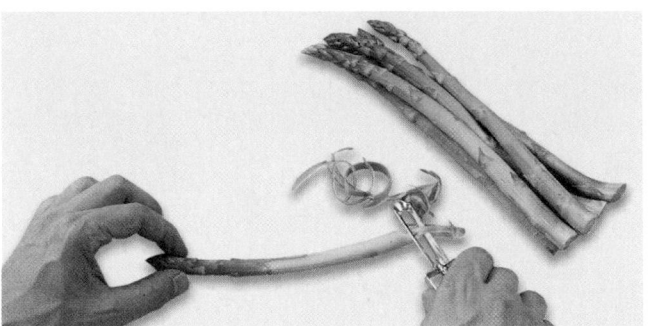

(d) …and then peel the stem.

Figure 16.4 Preparing avocados.

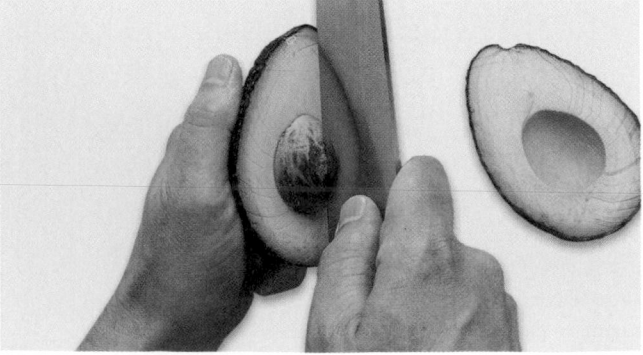

(a) To remove the pit or seed from the cut avocado, strike it sharply (but carefully) with the heel of a chef's knife.

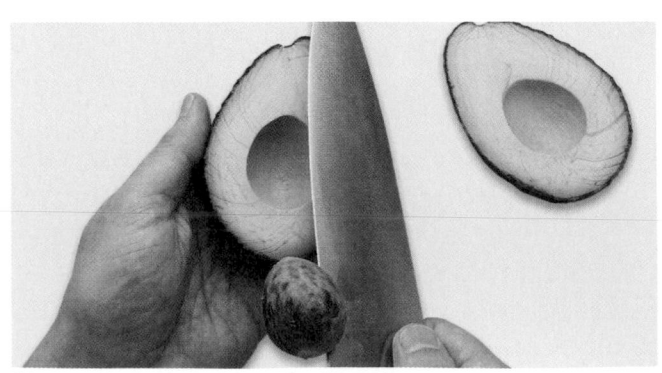

(b) Twist the knife slightly and pull out the pit.

T A B L E   16.2

Fresh Vegetable Pre-preparation *(Continued)*

Product	Quality Indicators (Q.I.) and Pre-preparation (Prep.)	Percentage Yield
Beans, dried	**Prep.:** Pick over to remove bad beans and foreign particles. Soak overnight in 3 times their volume of cold water.	
Beans, fava	**Q.I.:** Select small to medium pods that are fresh green in color, not overly large. Yellowing pods may be too mature. Some spots on pods are normal. **Prep.:** Shell the beans, parboil, then peel off skins or husks (Figure 16.5).	15–20%
Beans, green or wax	**Q.I.:** Firm and straight, with few shriveled ends; even color, without blemishes. Should be tender and crisp enough to break when bent to a 45-degree angle. Enclosed seeds should be small, not large and bulging. **Prep.:** Wash. Cut or snap off ends. Remove any spots. Leave whole or cut into desired lengths.	88%
Beans, lima	**Q.I.:** Shelled beans should be plump, with tender skins. **Prep.:** Shell, wash, and drain.	40%
Beets	**Q.I.:** Firm, round, uniform size; smooth skin. Tops, if any, should be fresh or just wilted, but not yellow or deteriorated. Large, rough beets are often woody. **Prep.:** Cut off tops, leaving 1 inch (2–3 cm) of stem attached to beets. Leave roots on. Scrub well. Steam or boil before peeling.	40–45% (75% if purchased without tops)
Broccoli	**Q.I.:** Dark-green, tightly closed buds. **Prep.:** Wash well. Soak in salted water 30 minutes if necessary to remove insects. Split large stalks into smaller sizes for portioning. Split thick stalks partway for faster cooking, or cut tops from stalks. Tougher stalks may be peeled (Figure 16.6).	65–75%

(Continued)

Figure 16.5 Preparing fava beans.

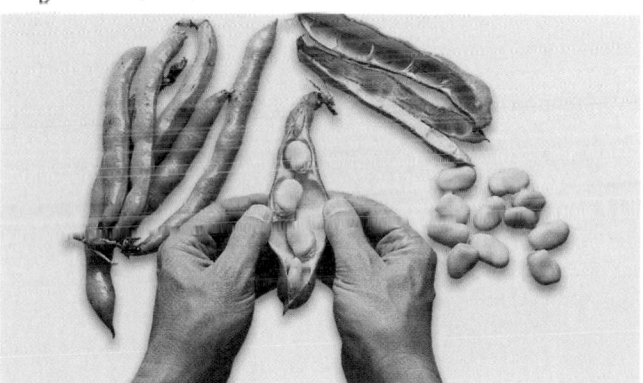

(a) Split open the pods and remove the beans.

(b) Blanch the beans for a few minutes. This cooks the beans and loosens the skins. Peel off the outer skins. Unpeeled beans are on the left, peeled beans on the right.

Figure 16.6 Prepare tough bottoms of broccoli stalks by pulling off the fibrous peel, as shown.

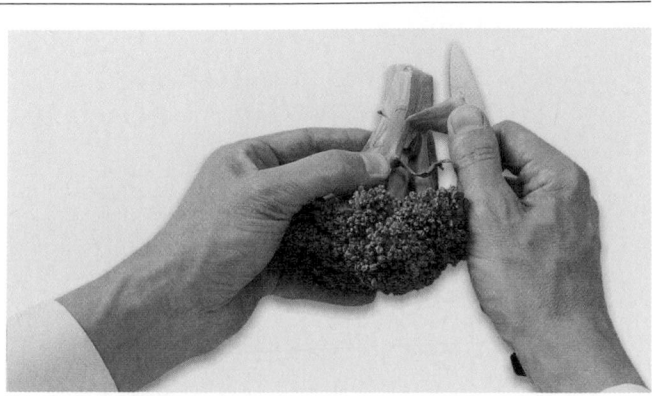

TABLE 16.2

Fresh Vegetable Pre-preparation *(Continued)*

Product	Quality Indicators (Q.I.) and Pre-preparation (Prep.)	Percentage Yield
Brussels sprouts	Q.I.: Bright-green; tight heads; uniform size. Prep.: Trim bottom ends and remove yellowed outer leaves (but don't cut off too much of the bottom or you will lose too many leaves). For more even cooking, pierce base with sharp knife point. Rinse well. Rinse in cold salted water 30 minutes if necessary to remove insects.	80%
Cabbage, white, green, or red	Q.I.: Firm head, heavy for size. Good color. Crisp leaves, finely ribbed. Prep.: Remove coarse or discolored outer leaves. Remove core and rinse whole, or cut into quarters and then remove core. For wedges, core is left in, but with bottom trimmed, to hold sections together. (See Figure 16.7)	80%
Carrots	Q.I.: Bright orange color; crisp, straight, and well shaped; smooth surface. Large carrots are sometimes woody. Prep.: Trim top and bottom ends. Pare with hand peeler or in machine.	75–80%
Cauliflower	Q.I.: White color, not yellow or brownish; fine-grained, tightly closed buds; fresh green, well-trimmed leaves. Prep.: Remove leaves and trim tough part of stalk. Cut away discolored parts. Wash. Soak in salted water 30 minutes if necessary to remove insects. Separate into florets, leaving portion of center stalk attached to each one to minimize trim loss. If cooking whole, cut out center of stalk for more even cooking.	55%
Celery	Q.I.: Straight, compact, well trimmed; fresh green color. Prep.: Cut off root end. Separate stems and scrub well. Reserve leaves and tough outer stems for stocks, soups, mirepoix. Ribbed outer side of stems may be peeled to remove strings.	75%
Celery root (knob celery or celeriac)	Q.I.: Firm and heavy. Large ones are often soft and spongy in the center. Prep.: Wash well, peel, and cut as desired.	75%
Corn (on cob)	Q.I.: Fresh, moist husks, not dry; no worm damage; kernels well filled, tender, and milky when punctured. Prep.: Strip off husks, remove silk, and cut off bottom stump. Cut into 2 or 3 sections as desired. Keep refrigerated and use as soon as possible.	28% (after husking and cutting from cob)
Cucumbers (slicing type)	Q.I.: Firm, crisp, dark green, well shaped. Yellow color means overmature. Prep.: Wash. Trim ends. Peel if skin is tough or has been waxed.	75–95% depending on peeling
Eggplant	Q.I.: Shiny, dark purple color; heavy and plump; without blemishes or soft spots. Prep.: Wash. Trim off stem end. Peel if skin is tough. Cut just before use. Dip in lemon juice (or antioxidant solution) to prevent discoloration.	90% (75% if peeled)

(Continued)

Figure 16.7 Cutting and shredding cabbage.

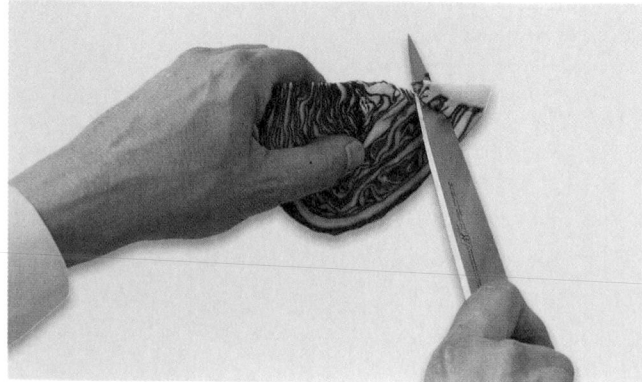

(a) Cut the cabbage head into quarters. Then cut out the core as shown.

(b) With a French knife, cut into thin shreds.

TABLE 16.2

Fresh Vegetable Pre-preparation (*Continued*)

Product	Quality Indicators (Q.I.) and Pre-preparation (Prep.)	Percentage Yield
Fennel	**Q.I.:** Bright, pale-green color with few or no brown spots. Fresh green tops, not wilted or spoiled. Compact, heavy for size. **Prep.:** Trim stems and feathery leaves. Split through the base and cut out core, as for cabbage.	80%
Garlic	**Q.I.:** Skin may be white or pink. No brown spots, soft spots, or spoilage; dry skin; no green shoots. **Prep.:** Separate cloves as needed, or strike whole bulb with heel of hand to separate. To peel cloves, crush slightly with side of heavy knife. Peel and trim root end. (See Figure 16.8)	88%
Kohlrabi	**Q.I.:** Uniform light-green color; 2–3 inches (5–8 cm) in diameter. Crisp and firm. No woodiness. **Prep.:** Peel like turnips, being sure to remove full thickness of skin.	55%
Leeks	**Q.I.:** Fresh green leaves; 2–3 inches (5–8 cm) of white. White part should be crisp and tender, not fibrous. **Prep.:** Cut off roots and green tops. Cut deeply through white part, separate the layers slightly, and wash carefully to remove all embedded soil. (See Figure 16.9)	50%
Lettuce	See Chapter 19 for full descriptions of salad greens.	75%

(*Continued*)

Figure 16.8 Peeling and crushing garlic.

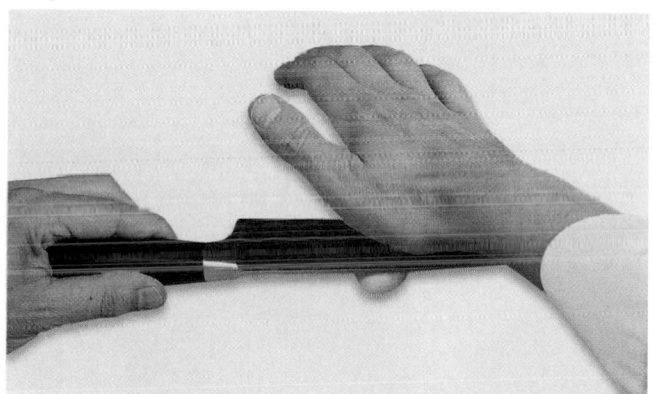

(a) Place the garlic on the worktable. Hold a broad knife blade over it as shown and strike it firmly with the palm of the hand.

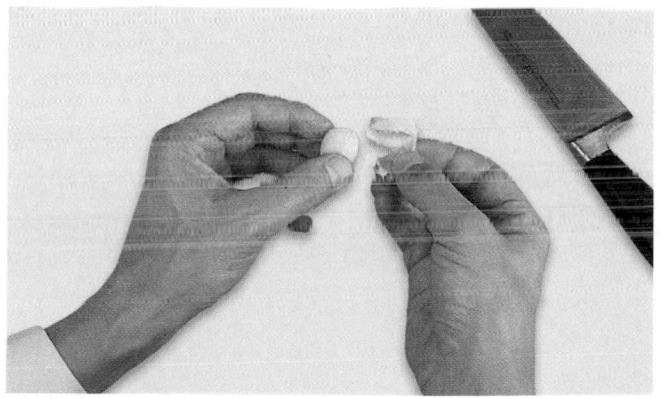

(b) You can now peel the garlic easily.

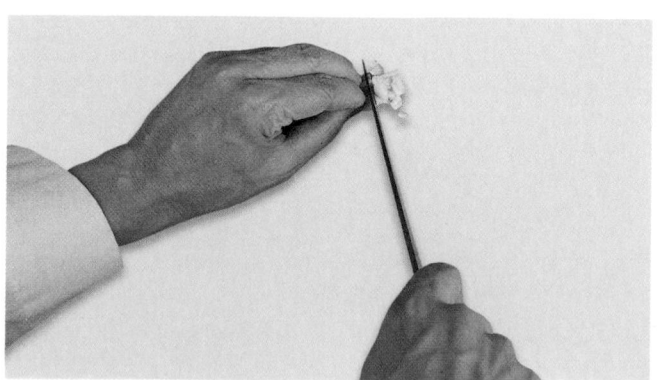

(c) Chop or mince the garlic.

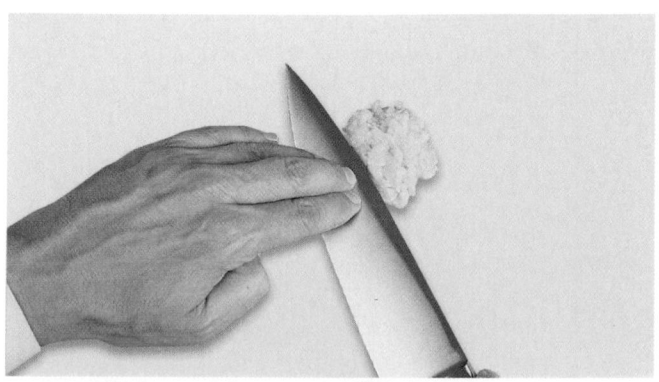

(d) To make a paste of the garlic, sprinkle it with salt and mash it firmly with the back of the knife blade.

TABLE 16.2

Fresh Vegetable Pre-preparation *(Continued)*

Product	Quality Indicators (Q.I.) and Pre-preparation (Prep.)	Percentage Yield
Mushrooms, white	**Q.I.:** Firm, white caps, closed at the stem. Stems should be relatively short. No dark spots, bruises, or mold. **Prep.:** Trim bottoms of stems. Just before cooking, wash quickly in cold water; drain well. If you desire to keep the mushrooms white, add a small amount of acid (lemon juice, vinegar, ascorbic acid) to the rinse water.	90%
Okra	**Q.I.:** Tender, full pods, not dry or shriveled. Ridges should be soft. Seeds should be soft and white. Uniform green color. **Prep.:** Wash. Trim ends (see Figure 16.10). Slice or leave whole.	82%
Onions, dry	**Q.I.:** Clean, hard, well shaped; no mold or black fungus; no green shoots. Skins should be very dry. **Prep.:** Cut off root and stem ends. Peel. Wash. Cut or slice as needed. (See Figure 7.11.)	90%
Onions, green (scallions)	**Q.I.:** Fresh, crisp green tops; little or no bulb formation at white part. **Prep.:** Cut off roots and wilted ends of green tops. Amount of green left on varies with recipe or use.	60–70%
Parsley	**Q.I.:** Bright green, unwilted leaves with no rot. **Prep.:** Wash well and drain. Remove yellow leaves and large stems (save stems for stocks). Separate into sprigs for garnish, or chop leaves.	85%
Parsnips	**Q.I.:** Firm, smooth, well shaped, with light, uniform color. Large ones are often woody. **Prep.:** Refrigerating for 2 weeks develops sweetness. Trim ends and peel. Rinse.	70–75%
Pea shoots or pea greens	**Q.I.:** These are the tender tips, with leaves, of pea vines (see Figure 16.11), usually snow peas. Fresh, medium-green leaves and tender, not woody, stems. **Prep.:** Wash well, trim ends of stems, especially if they are tough. Cook like spinach.	90–95%

(Continued)

Figure 16.9 Cleaning leeks.

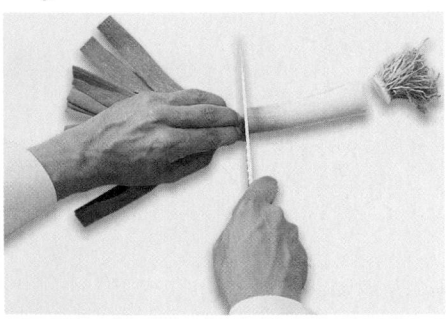 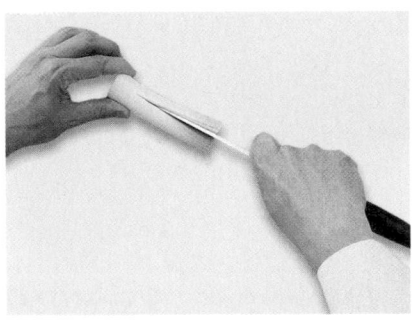 

(a) Trim off the root end and as much of the green as desired.

(b) Make one or two deep cuts to within 1 inch (2.5 cm) of the root end.

(c) Spread apart the layers, as shown. Carefully wash out all embedded dirt under running water.

Figure 16.10 To prepare okra, cut off the stem ends.

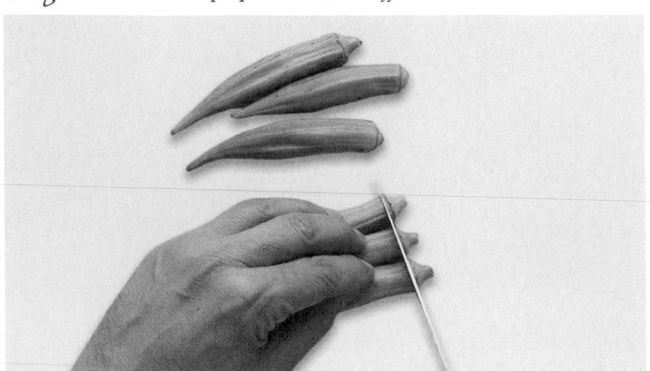

Figure 16.11 Pea shoots are the tender tips of pea vines, usually snow peas.

TABLE 16.2

Fresh Vegetable Pre-preparation *(Continued)*

Product	Quality Indicators (Q.I.) and Pre-preparation (Prep.)	Percentage Yield
Peas (green and black-eyed)	**Q.I.:** Firm, fresh, moderately filled-out pods. **Prep.:** Shell and rinse. (Peas are not often purchased in the pod by food service operations because of the labor required for shelling.)	40%
Peas, edible pod	**Q.I.:** Fresh green color, crisp pods, no blemishes. **Prep.:** Remove stem end. Pull off strings at side veins. (Both the flat, Chinese snow peas and the full-pod variety called sugar snap peas are available. Expensive.)	90%
Peppers, sweet (green, red, yellow, orange, purple)	**Q.I.:** Shiny color; well shaped; no soft spots or shriveling. **Prep.:** Wash. Cut in half lengthwise and remove core, seeds, and white membranes. Or leave whole (as for stuffed peppers) and cut out core from the end. Peppers are often roasted and peeled as preparation for use in various recipes; see Figure 16.12.	82%
Peppers, hot (chile peppers or chiles)	**Q.I.:** See sweet peppers above. **Prep.:** Larger fresh chile peppers, such as ancho, mulato, New Mexico, and Anaheim, are usually roasted and prepared like sweet peppers (see above). Small peppers, such as cayenne, jalapeño, and serrano, are usually chopped or sliced and used as seasoning. Remove core, veins, and seeds carefully; wear rubber gloves if you are sensitive to the hot oils.	80–90%
Potatoes, white	See Chapter 18.	80%

(Continued)

Figure 16.12 Roasting peppers.

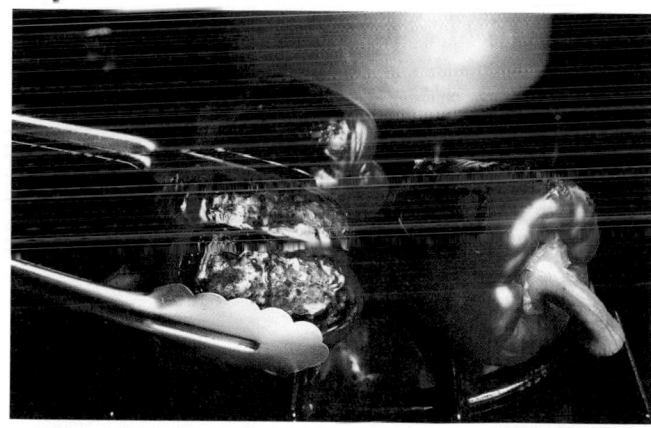

(b) Wrap the peppers in plastic film while they are still hot. This helps loosen the skins.

(a) Roast the peppers over an open flame until the skins blacken. For large quantities, you may do this under a broiler or in a hot oven. In this case, the skins will not darken as much but can still be peeled off.

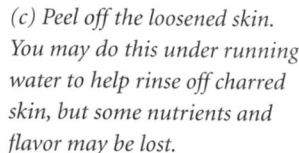

(c) Peel off the loosened skin. You may do this under running water to help rinse off charred skin, but some nutrients and flavor may be lost.

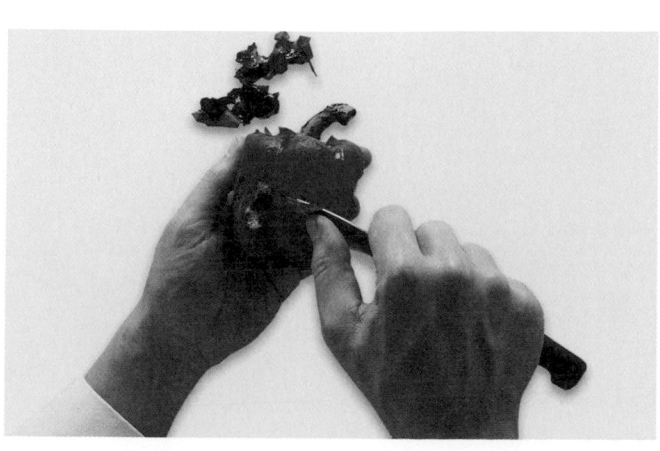

TABLE 16.2

Fresh Vegetable Pre-preparation *(Continued)*

Product	Quality Indicators (Q.I.) and Pre-preparation (Prep)	Percentage Yield
Potatoes, sweet (including "yams")	**Q.I.:** Clean, dry surface. Firm, not shriveled or blemished. Fat, regular shapes are preferable because of less waste in trimming and portioning. **Prep.:** Scrub, boil or steam, then peel. May be peeled before cooking but must be dipped in antioxidant to prevent discoloring. Machine paring is wasteful with irregular shapes. *Note:* There are two basic varieties of sweet potatoes. The variety that has a moister, deeper orange flesh is sometimes referred to, inaccurately, as the yam. The two varieties are interchangeable for most purposes. True yams are an entirely different vegetable, with starchy white flesh. They are not often seen in North America, except in Hispanic and some other specialty markets.	80%
Radishes	**Q.I.:** Firm, tender, and crisp, with good shape and color. **Prep.:** Cut off root and stem ends. Wash.	90%
Rutabagas	See turnips.	
Spinach and other greens	**Q.I.:** Fresh, crisp, dark-green leaves. No rot or slime or badly bruised leaves. Short stems. **Prep.:** Remove stems and damaged leaves (Figure 16.13). Wash in several changes of water. Use large quantity of water and lift spinach up and down to float off sand and dirt. Lift from water and drain well.	50–70%
Squash, summer (including zucchini)	**Q.I.:** Firm, heavy, and crisp; tender skins, no blemishes. **Prep.:** Wash or scrub well. Trim ends.	90%
Squash, winter	**Q.I.:** Heavy and firm. Hard rind. No blemishes. **Prep.:** Wash. Cut in half. Scrape out seeds and fibers. Cut into portion sizes. For puréed or mashed squash, either steam or bake, then remove peel; or peel, dice, then steam.	65–85%
Swiss chard	**Q.I.:** Fresh, dark-green color, not wilted. Crisp, not wilted or rubbery stalks. Two varieties: with white stalks and ribs, and with red stalks and ribs (like large beet greens). **Prep.:** Wash thoroughly. Trim ends of stalks. Remove leafy greens from stalks by cutting along the margins of the stalk down the center of the leaf. Stalks may be cooked separately like asparagus.	85%
Tomatoes	**Q.I.:** Firm but not hard, with little or no green core. Smooth, without bruises, blemishes, cracks, or discoloration. If underripe, let stand 2–3 days at room temperature. **Prep.:** For use with skin on: wash, remove core. To peel: plunge into boiling water for 10–20 seconds (riper tomatoes take less time). Cool immediately in ice water. Slip skins off and remove core. See Figure 16.14 for further techniques	90% (peeled)

(Continued)

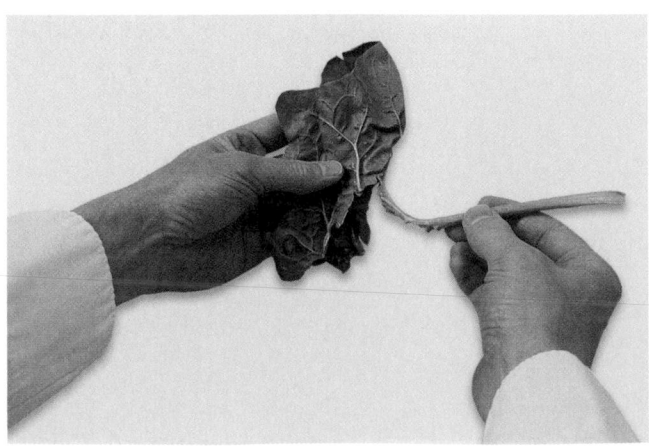

Figure 16.13 When trimming spinach leaves, remove the heavy center rib along with the stem.

TABLE 16.2

Fresh Vegetable Pre-preparation (*Continued*)

Product	Quality Indicators (Q.I.) and Pre-preparation (Prep.)	Percentage Yield
Turnips and rutabagas	**Q.I.:** Firm and heavy, with good color and no blemishes. White turnips over 2½ inches (6–7 cm) in diameter may be woody or spongy. **Prep.:** Peel heavily by hand or in machine to remove thick skin (see Figure 16.15). Rinse.	75–80%
Watercress	**Q.I.:** Bright green, crisp, unbruised leaves. **Prep.:** Wash well. Remove heavy stems and discolored leaves.	90%

Figure 16.14 Preparing tomato concassé.

(*a*) Blanch and peel the tomato and cut it in half crosswise. Gently squeeze out the seeds, as shown.

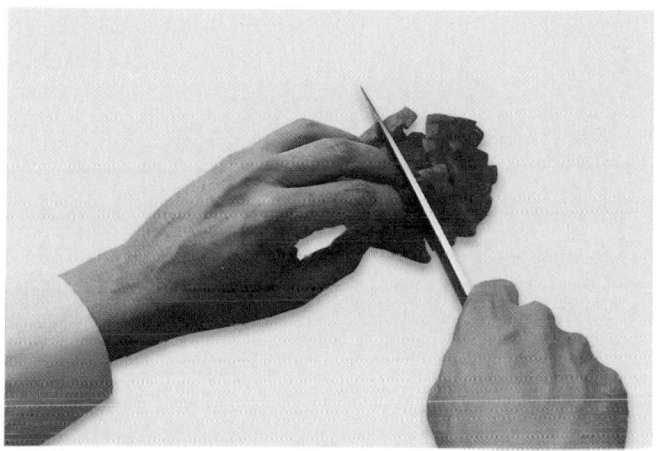

(*b*) Dice the seeded tomato or chop it coarsely.

Figure 16.15 Peel rutabagas and turnips deeply enough to remove the full thickness of skin, as pointed out in this photograph.

CLASSIFYING VEGETABLES

Many people are bothered by the fact that tomatoes are referred to as vegetables when they are, in fact, fruits. Yes, tomatoes are fruits, and carrots are roots, and spinach is a leaf, and they are all vegetables.

To a botanist, the term *fruit* refers to a specific part of a plant. A fruit is defined as the ripened ovary or ovaries of a seed-bearing plant, and it contains the seeds. In other words, if it has seeds, it's a fruit. We shouldn't be misled by the fact that a few fruits are sweet. Many, if not most, fruits in nature are not sweet at all. Some examples of fruits used in the vegetable kitchen are tomatoes, eggplant, peppers, green beans, okra, cucumbers, squash, pea pods, walnuts, and avocados.

There are many ways of classifying vegetables. Some are more helpful to the cook than others. Putting vegetables into groups based on their botanical origin is not always helpful. For example, okra and eggplant are both fruits, but they are handled and cooked so differently that this information doesn't really help us.

The following vegetable categories are based, in part, on how the vegetables are used in the kitchen. For example, the vegetables listed under roots and tubers come from several unrelated families, but they all have fairly solid, uniform textures and are handled in similar ways. This is not a scientific classification, and it is not the only way to group vegetables.

Note that the first three categories are all fruits.

- **The gourd family:** cucumber, winter and summer squashes
- **Seeds and pods:** beans, peas, corn, okra
- **Other tender-fruited vegetables:** avocado, eggplant, sweet and hot peppers, tomato
- **Roots and tubers:** beet, carrot, celery root, parsnip, radish, turnip, rutabaga, Jerusalem artichoke, potato, sweet potato
- **The cabbage family:** cabbage, broccoli, cauliflower, brussels sprouts, kohlrabi
- **The onion family:** onion, scallion, leek, garlic, shallot
- **Leafy greens:** spinach, beet greens, lettuces, endive and chicory, Swiss chard, watercress
- **Stalks, stems, and shoots:** globe artichoke, asparagus, celery, fennel
- **Mushrooms**

MUSHROOMS, A SPECIAL TOPIC

Because of the great interest today in exotic mushrooms, and because eating some poisonous species of wild mushrooms can be fatal, it is important for the cook to be familiar with at least the most popular varieties of exotic mushrooms, both cultivated and wild.

Although hundreds of mushroom varieties are edible, until recently, only the common cultivated button mushroom was used with any frequency in most commercial kitchens. Now, however, many varieties are available. Some of these mushrooms, especially the wild ones, are expensive, but the demand always seems to exceed the supply.

Strictly speaking, the term *wild* should be used only for those mushrooms that are not cultivated but that are hunted and gathered in the wild. In the kitchen and on menus, however, exotic cultivated varieties, such as shiitakes, are often referred to as *wild mushrooms* because they are seen as rare and unusual, like true wild mushrooms, and they are generally more flavorful than the button mushroom.

One important advantage of cultivated exotic mushrooms is that they are available all year, while certain wild mushrooms may be in season for only a few weeks annually.

Cultivated Exotic Mushrooms

1. **Shiitake.**
   Sometimes known as *Black Forest mushroom* or *golden oak mushroom*, the shiitake is also available in dried form as *Chinese black mushroom.* The fresh mushroom is golden brown to dark brown. It has a firm, fleshy texture and a broad, dome-shaped cap with creamy white gills. The stem is rather tough, so it is trimmed off and chopped fine or used in stocks.

2. **Oyster mushroom.**
Also called *pleurotte*, it is a light tan or cream-colored, fan-shaped mushroom with a short stem at the side. Tender, with delicate flavor, it is best prepared simply so that its mild flavor is not overwhelmed by stronger-tasting ingredients. (*Note:* The name *oyster* refers to the shape of the mushroom, not its taste.)

3. **Enoki mushroom.**
Also called *enokitake* or *enokidake*, this mushroom has a tiny white cap on a long, slender stem, and grows in clusters or bunches that are attached at the base. The base is trimmed off before use. The enoki mushroom has a crisp texture and a fruity, slightly acidic but sweet flavor. It is often used raw (for example, in salads or as garnish) or in clear soups. When used in cooked dishes, it should be added in the last few minutes so as not to be overcooked.

4. **Cremini mushroom.**
The cremini is a variety of the common cultivated button mushroom, but it has a brown or tan skin. It may have a slightly more robust flavor than white cultivated mushrooms.

5. **Portobello mushroom.**
This is a mature cremini in which the cap has opened and spread into a broad, flat disk. It may be 6 inches (15 cm) or more across. Portobello (note the correct spelling) are often grilled, brushed with olive oil, and served plain as a first course.

Wild Mushrooms

Of the many varieties of edible wild mushrooms, those described here are among the most prized as well as the most likely to be found on menus. As a rule, they are expensive and of limited availability.

Wild mushrooms should be carefully examined for spoilage or insect infestation. Cut away any damaged parts.

The four varieties described here are also available dried (see p. 451). Dried mushrooms have a high price per pound but are more economical to use than fresh wild mushrooms because they are equivalent to about 7 or 8 times their weight of fresh mushrooms. In addition, they have a more intense, concentrated flavor, so a little goes a long way.

Caution: Never eat any wild mushroom that has not been identified by an expert. Many mushrooms are poisonous and some are deadly. Many species are difficult to identify, and some poisonous varieties resemble edible ones.

1. **Morel.**
Several varieties exist, including black, golden, and nearly white. The morel is shaped somewhat like a conical sponge, with a pitted surface, on a smooth stem. It is completely hollow. The most prized of spring mushrooms, it is usually sautéed in butter or cooked in a sauce and is especially good with cream.

2. **Bolete.**
Other names for this mushroom include *cep, cèpe* (sepp; the French term), *porcino* (por chee no; the Italian term; the plural is *porcini* [por chee nee]), and *steinpilz* (shtine pilts; the German term). It is a brown-capped mushroom with a light-colored, bulbous stem. The interior flesh is creamy white. The underside of the cap has no gills but many tiny pores. With a meaty but smooth texture and rich, earthy flavor, it is often sautéed or braised with garlic and olive oil or butter. It is available late summer to fall.

3. **Chanterelle.**
Also called *girolle*, the chanterelle is yellow to orange in color and shaped like an umbrella that has turned inside out. The underside of the cone-shaped cap has ridges instead of gills. It has a rich, woodsy aroma and flavor and is best cooked simply, such a sautéed in butter, perhaps with garlic. It is available summer and fall.

4. **Black trumpet.**
This mushroom is closely related to the chanterelle but is black in color and has much thinner flesh. It is also called *black chanterelle, horn of plenty,* and *trompette de la mort* (French name, meaning "trumpet of death," so called because of its black color). In spite of this French name, it is edible and delicious.

Processed Vegetables

It is generally agreed that the quality of frozen or canned vegetables can never equal that of the best-quality fresh product at its peak of maturity, prepared properly, and cooked while still fresh. However, because of the high perishability of fresh produce, seasonal variations in availability and price, and the amount of labor required to handle fresh produce in commercial kitchens, food service relies, to a great extent, on processed vegetables. Therefore, it is important to know how to handle processed foods properly. Your goal should be to make them as close as possible in quality to the best fresh produce.

The quality of processed vegetables varies greatly. For example, frozen cauliflower always lacks the slightly crunchy texture of properly cooked fresh cauliflower. In fact, most frozen vegetables are a bit mushier than fresh because cell walls rupture during freezing. On the other hand, frozen peas are almost universally accepted, not just for their convenience but for their dependably high quality in comparison with the highly perishable fresh product.

In the section of Chapter 7 called "Handling Convenience Foods," we learned that convenience foods are products that have been partially or completely prepared or processed by the manufacturer. This means that you should treat frozen and canned vegetables as though they are partially or fully cooked fresh vegetables, which deserve the same care in handling, heating, seasoning, and presentation.

HANDLING FROZEN VEGETABLES

Checking Quality

Examine all frozen products when received to make sure there has been no loss of quality. Check in particular for the following:

1. **Temperature.**
   Check the temperature inside the case with a thermometer. Is it still 0°F (−18°C) or below, or have the vegetables begun to thaw during shipment?

2. **Large ice crystals.**
   A little frost is normal, but lots of ice means poor handling.

3. **Signs of leaking on the carton.**
   This is another obvious sign of thawing.

4. **Freezer burn.**
   Open a package and check the vegetables themselves. Is the color bright and natural, or is there any yellowing or drying on the surface?

Cooking

Frozen vegetables have been partially cooked, so final cooking time is shorter than for fresh products.

Cook from the frozen state. Most vegetables need no thawing. They can go directly into steamer pans or boiling salted water.

Exceptions: Corn on the cob and vegetables that freeze into a solid block, such as spinach and squash, should be thawed in the cooler first for more even cooking.

Seasoning: Most frozen vegetables are slightly salted during processing, so add less salt than you would to fresh products.

HANDLING CANNED VEGETABLES

Checking Quality

1. **Reject damaged cans on receipt.**
   Puffed or swollen cans indicate spoilage. Small dents may be harmless, but large dents may mean that the can's protective lining has been damaged. Avoid rusted or leaking cans.

2. **Know the drained weight.**

   This varies with different grades of different vegetables and should be specified when ordering. Typical drained weights are 60 to 65 percent of total contents. You must know this drained weight in order to calculate the number of servings the can contains.

   Some canned products, such as tomato sauce and cream-style corn, have no drained weight because the entire contents are served.

3. **Check the grade.**

   Grades are determined by the packers or by federal inspectors. They are based on factors like color, absence of defects, and sieve size (size of individual pieces). Check to make sure you receive the grade you ordered (and paid for).

   In the United States, the federal grades are

   U.S. Grade A or Fancy.
   U.S. Grade B or Extra Standard (for vegetables) or Choice (for fruits).
   U.S. Grade C or Standard.

   In Canada, the grades are

   Canada Fancy.
   Canada Choice.
   Canada Standard.

Cooking

1. Wipe the top of the can clean before opening. Use a clean can opener.

2. Drain the vegetable and place half the liquid in cooking pot. Bring it to a boil. This shortens the heating time of the vegetable.

3. Add the vegetable and heat to serving temperature. *Do not boil for a long time.* Canned vegetables are fully cooked—in fact, usually overcooked. They need only to be reheated.

   (*Note:* Health officials recommend holding vegetables at 190°F/88°C for 10 minutes or more—20 to 30 minutes for nonacid vegetables like beets, green beans, or spinach—to eliminate the danger of botulism. See Chapter 2.)

4. Heat as close to serving time as possible. Do not hold in steam table for long periods.

5. Season and flavor with imagination. Canned vegetables require more creativity in preparation than fresh because they can be pretty dreary when just served plain.

6. Season the liquid while it is coming to a boil, before you add the vegetable. This will give the flavors of the herbs and spices time to blend.

7. Butter enhances the flavor of most vegetables and it carries the flavors of other seasonings that you choose to add.

8. Dress up the vegetables with added flavors and garnishes, such as beets or sauerkraut with caraway, limas or green beans with crisp crumbled bacon, corn with sautéed minced onion and green or red pepper, carrots with butter and tarragon, or with orange juice and brown sugar.

   The combinations suggested in the table in Chapter 17 apply to canned vegetables as well as to fresh and frozen.

HANDLING DRIED VEGETABLES

There are two basic kinds of dried vegetables.

Dried Legumes

Dried beans and peas have been used as food for thousands of years, and they continue to be important foods even today. In fact, with today's increased interest in healthful eating and in vegetables of all sorts, many more interesting varieties of beans are widely available now than only a few years ago. Some of these varieties are shown in the illustrations.

The three most important types of dried legumes are kidney beans, peas, and lentils. Most of the many-colored beans in the illustrations are types of kidney beans. Their flavors vary slightly, but their cooking and handling characteristics are similar, although some may require longer cooking times than others. Dried peas are usually husked and split to speed cooking time. Lentils are small, lens-shaped legumes that have shorter cooking times than kidney beans. Other types of dried beans include chickpeas or garbanzos, fava beans, and lima beans.

Top row: navy beans, garbanzo beans or chickpeas, Great Northern beans. Bottom row: baby lima beans, cannelini beans or white kidney beans, rice beans.

Top row: black turtle beans, dried fava beans. Bottom row: Swedish brown beans, calypso beans, flageolet beans.

Top row: red kidney beans, pink beans, appaloosa beans. Bottom row: cranberry beans or borlotti, Christmas lima beans, pinto beans.

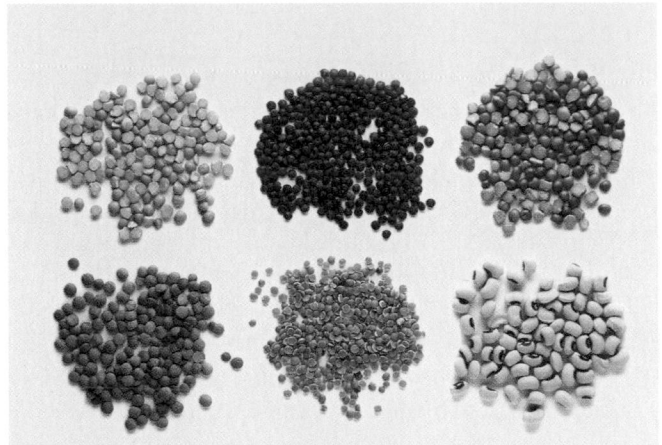

Top row: yellow split peas, green lentils, green split peas. Bottom row: brown lentils, red lentils, black-eyed peas.

Procedure for Preparing Dried Legumes

1. Pick over to remove any foreign particles and rinse well.

2. Soak overnight in 3 times their volume of water. (Split peas and some lentils do not require soaking. Check package directions.)

3. Simmer, covered, until tender. Do not boil, or the vegetables may toughen. Some beans require up to 3 hours of simmering.

4. If you forget to soak beans overnight, an alternative method can be used. Put the beans in a cooking pot with 3 times their volume of cold water. Bring to a boil. When water boils, cover tightly and remove from the heat. Let stand 1 hour. Then proceed with step 3 above.

Freeze-dried and Other Dehydrated Vegetables

Drying has always been an important method for preserving vegetables, especially before modern canning and freezing techniques were developed. Modern technology has developed additional methods for drying foods, so a great variety of dried products is on the market, including dried potatoes, onions, carrots, celery, beans, peppers, tomatoes, and mushrooms.

Follow manufacturers' directions for reconstituting these products. Many need to be soaked in cold or warm water for specific lengths of time. They continue to absorb water as they are simmered.

Dried mushrooms, clockwise from top left: morels, porcini, shiitake, chanterelles.

Instant dried products, especially potatoes, require only the addition of a boiling liquid and seasonings to be ready to serve. Again, manufacturers' directions vary with their brands.

An important category of dried vegetables is dried mushrooms. Many flavorful wild mushrooms are in season for only a short time and are in limited supply at high prices. They are available year round in dried form, however. The most popular types—morels, chanterelles, and porcini—are illustrated, along with dried shiitake, a cultivated mushroom that originated in Japan and China.

Dried mushrooms should be soaked in hot water until soft, then drained and lightly squeezed before being cooked. The flavorful soaking liquid is strained and used as a flavoring for cooking liquids and sauces.

Production and Holding Problems in Quantity Cooking

We have emphasized throughout this chapter that vegetables should be cooked as close as possible to serving time. They lose quality rapidly when held in a steam table.

In quantity cooking, however, it is rarely possible to cook individual vegetable portions to order. After 20 to 30 minutes at steam table temperatures, even carefully prepared vegetables are usually overcooked.

Two systems have been devised to help solve this problem. *Batch cooking* is especially well suited to set meal service, and the *blanch-and-chill* method is most helpful in extended meal service. Needs vary from institution to institution, and you will probably find both techniques useful in one kitchen.

BATCH COOKING

Rather than cooking all your vegetables in one batch large enough for the entire meal service, this method (described in Chapter 7, p. 111) involves dividing the food into smaller batches and cooking them one at a time, as needed.

Procedure for Batch Cooking

1. Steamers and small tilting trunnion kettles behind the service line are the most useful kinds of equipment for vegetable batch cooking.

2. Divide each vegetable into batches small enough to be served within 20 to 30 minutes. Arrange in steamer pans ready to be placed in steamers or in containers ready for pouring into the kettles.

3. Keep the prepped vegetables in the cooler until needed.

4. Cook batches as needed. In planning, allow time for loading and unloading the equipment, for cooking, for finishing the product with desired seasoning, sauce, or garnish, and for carrying to the serving line.

5. Undercook slightly if the vegetable must be held before serving.

6. Have all your seasonings, sauces, and garnishes ready for finishing the dish.

7. Do not mix batches. They will be cooked to different degrees, and colors and textures usually will not match.

BLANCH-AND-CHILL METHOD

It is usually impractical to cook vegetables completely to order. Too much time is required. But if the vegetables have been partially cooked, the time needed to finish them to order is short.

Partially cooking, chilling, and finish-cooking is not as good, nutritionally, as cooking completely to order, but it is almost as good. It's certainly better than holding vegetables for hours at serving temperature, and it gives the cook complete control over the degree of doneness when served.

Procedure for Blanching and Chilling

1. Steam or simmer the vegetable until partially cooked to desired degree. (In the case of French fries, blanch by deep frying.)

The amount of cooking required depends on the vegetable and on the method by which it will be reheated or finished. Frozen vegetables need less cooking than fresh. Often, they need only be thawed.

2. Chill immediately in ice water. (Needless to say, French fries are an exception.)

3. Drain and keep chilled until needed.

4. Finish to order by desired cooking method.

For example, one or more portions can be placed in a strainer and lowered briefly into a ready pot of boiling water. Sautéing in butter is a popular method for finishing such items as peas, green beans, and carrots.

Potato croquettes are an example of a more complicated application of this same method. The potatoes are boiled or steamed, puréed, seasoned, formed, and breaded in advance. They are then deep-fried to order.

Storage

FRESH VEGETABLES

1. Potatoes, onions, and winter squash are stored at cool temperatures (50°–65°F/10°–18°C) in a dry, dark place.

2. Other vegetables must be refrigerated. To prevent drying, they should be kept covered or wrapped, or the humidity in the cooler must be high. Allow for some air circulation to help prevent mold.

3. Peeled and cut vegetables need extra protection from drying and oxidation. Cover or wrap, and use quickly to prevent spoilage. Potatoes, eggplant, and other vegetables that brown when cut should be treated with an acid or antioxidant. As an alternative, they can be blanched to destroy the enzymes that cause browning. Raw, cut potatoes are sometimes held in cold water for a short time.

4. Store all fresh vegetables for as short a time as possible. They lose quality rapidly. Peas and corn lose sweetness even after a few hours in storage.

5. Keep refrigerators and storage areas clean.

FROZEN VEGETABLES

1. Store at 0°F (−18°C) or colder, in original containers, until ready for use.
2. Do not refreeze thawed vegetables. Quality will be greatly reduced.

DRIED VEGETABLES

1. Store in a cool (less than 75°F/24°C), dry, well-ventilated place.
2. Keep well sealed and off the floor.

CANNED VEGETABLES

1. Keep in a cool, dry place, away from sunlight and off the floor.
2. Discard cans that show signs of damage or spoilage (swollen, badly dented, or rusted cans). "When in doubt, throw it out."

LEFTOVERS

1. The best way to store leftovers is not to create them in the first place. Careful planning and small batch cooking reduce leftovers.
2. Don't mix batches.
3. Store leftover creamed vegetables for 1 day only. Then either use or discard. Before storing, cool rapidly by placing the container on ice.

Terms for Review

al dente	anthocyanins	trimming loss	sieve size
pigment	carotenoids	AP weight	batch cooking
plant acids	chlorophyll	EP weight	blanch and chill
flavones			

Questions for Discussion

1. Give two reasons for not adding baking soda to the cooking water for green vegetables.
2. Besides appearance, why is proper, uniform cutting of vegetables important?
3. What are some advantages of steam cooking vegetables over boiling or simmering?
4. You are trying a recipe for blueberry muffins. When you break open a finished muffin, you see that the baked dough around each berry is green. What caused this? How can you correct it? (Hint: The batter is made with buttermilk and leavened with baking soda.)
5. Discuss the reasons for cooking green vegetables in a large quantity of water and in just enough water to cover.
6. You are to prepare buttered, steamed asparagus and must produce 50 portions of 3 ounces each (or 90-gram portions if you use metric measures). How much untrimmed fresh asparagus will you need?

chapter 17

Cooking Vegetables

Now that you have studied the whys and wherefores of vegetable cooking, you should be able to proceed to actual preparation with a clear understanding of what you are doing.

This chapter outlines briefly the basic methods of vegetable preparation. Successful performance of these methods relies on your knowledge of the principles we have discussed.

The recipes given here reinforce your understanding through actual practice. The emphasis is on the method rather than on the particular vegetable used because each method applies to many vegetables. For this reason, variations are listed after basic recipes rather than presented as separate complete recipes. As in other chapters, recipes for sauces that appear in Chapter 8 and are used in these vegetable preparations are not repeated here.

Most of the recipes are applicable to fresh, frozen, or canned vegetables, even though variations are not listed for each. You have learned how to handle these products in order to make proper substitutions. Review pages 448 to 4451 if necessary.

Potatoes and other starchy foods, such as rice and pasta, are covered in the next chapter. However, the basic cooking methods here apply to potatoes as well as to other vegetables.

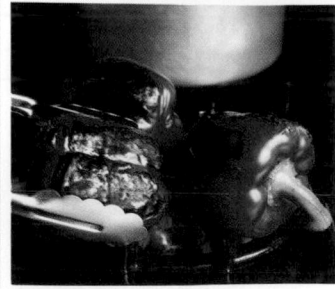

Boiling and Steaming

Nearly all vegetables may be cooked by boiling or by steaming, and these are the two most frequently used methods because they are easy, economical, and can be adapted to a great variety of preparations.

Boiling and steaming are basic cooking methods. In most cases, additional steps are required after the basic cooking is completed in order to make the product ready for serving. These steps include adding butter, seasonings, flavorings, and sauces.

Unless they are to be served immediately, boiled or simmered vegetables are drained as soon as they are cooked and then cooled quickly under cold water. This is called *shocking* or *refreshing*. This prevents the vegetables from being overcooked in their retained heat. Normally, they are then reheated quickly by sautéing in butter or other fat. Seasonings and sauces can be added at this stage. We classify this cooking method as boiling even though the vegetables are finished by sautéing to reheat them. This section includes recipes for boiled vegetables finished with a variety of sauces, flavorings, and seasonings.

In other cases, the product is only partially cooked by boiling or steaming and is finished by another cooking method, such as sautéing or baking. Recipes of this sort are usually included under the *final* cooking method.

We speak of the cooking method as boiling even though, in many cases, simmering is a more appropriate term. Green vegetables are generally boiled so that they cook quickly, preserving color and nutrients. In many cases, however, the agitation and high temperature of boiling break up delicate vegetables, and simmering is more appropriate.

Steaming as a method for cooking vegetables is becoming more and more widely used, especially as more varieties of advanced equipment become available. It may be the ideal method for cooking certain vegetables, such as broccoli, that easily break or turn watery or mushy when simmered.

Procedure for Boiling Vegetables

1. Collect all equipment and food products.

2. Trim, peel, and cut vegetables as required. See Table 16.2 for pre-prep requirements.

3. Add the required amount of water to the pot (saucepot, steam-jacketed kettle, tilting skillet, or whatever equipment you are using).

    Most vegetables are cooked in just enough water to cover, but many green vegetables and strong-flavored vegetables may be cooked in a large quantity of water (2 or 3 times their volume). See pages 433–434 for discussion.

4. Add salt (approximately 1½ to 2 tablespoons per gallon of water/6 to 8 grams per liter) and bring to a boil.

5. Place the vegetables in the pot and return the water to a boil.

6. Reduce heat to a simmer and cook the vegetables, covered or uncovered, as indicated, to required doneness.
    * Green vegetables and strong-flavored vegetables are cooked uncovered.
    * Other vegetables are cooked covered.

7. Drain the vegetable quickly to avoid overcooking.

8. If the vegetable is to be served at once, complete the recipe and serve.

9. If the vegetable is not to be served at once, cool the vegetable (except potatoes) in cold water, drain, and refrigerate until needed.

Variation

In some instances, the vegetable may be placed in a cooking utensil and boiling salted water added to it, as when broccoli is cooked in steam table pans (see recipe, p. 459). The advantage of this procedure is that you don't have to estimate how much water is needed to cover the vegetable, as in step 3. The disadvantages are that two pots are required instead of one, and that boiling water is dangerous to pour.

After reading this chapter, you should be able to

1. Identify vegetables that are well suited to the different vegetable cooking methods.

2. Cook vegetables by boiling and steaming.

3. Cook vegetables by sautéing and pan-frying.

4. Cook vegetables by braising.

5. Cook vegetables by baking.

6. Cook vegetables by broiling and grilling.

7. Cook vegetables by deep-frying.

Procedure for Steaming Vegetables

This method is used both for pressurized and nonpressurized compartment steam cookers and for simple rangetop steamers that consist of a perforated basket over a pot of boiling water.

1. Know your equipment. Read all operating instructions supplied with your equipment. Every model is a little different.
2. Collect all equipment and food products.
3. Trim and cut vegetables as required.
4. Preheat the steamer.
5. Arrange vegetables in pans or baskets for cooking. Make shallow, even layers for uniform cooking.
   - Use perforated pans for best steam circulation.
   - Use solid pans if cooking liquid must be retained.
6. Insert pans or baskets in steamer and close door or lid.
7. Steam for required time. Consult timing charts supplied with your model of steamer.
8. Remove vegetable from steamer. If it is a pressure steamer, *pressure must return to zero before door is opened.*
9. Finish vegetable according to recipe and serve at once, or cool quickly for later use.

   Vegetables that form compact layers do not steam well. They do not allow the steam to circulate, so they cook unevenly. Examples: spinach and other greens, peas, whole kernel corn, frozen puréed squash.

Peas, Carrots, and Pearl Onions with Tarragon Butter

Portions: 15   Portion size: 3 oz (100 g)

U.S.	Metric	Ingredients	PROCEDURE
12 oz	375 g	Pearl onions	1. Blanch the onions for 20 seconds in boiling water. (Blanching makes them easier to peel.) Drain, refresh under cold water, and drain again. Peel the onions.
1 lb	500 g	Carrots	2. Bring salted water to a boil in a saucepan. Add the onions, return to a boil, reduce heat to a simmer, and simmer until tender. Drain, refresh under cold water, and drain again.
1 lb 8 oz	750 g	Peas, frozen	3. Peel the carrots and cut into batonnet.
2 oz	60 g	Butter	4. Bring salted water to a boil in a saucepan. Add the carrots, return to a boil, reduce heat to a simmer, and simmer until tender. Drain, refresh briefly, and drain again.
1½ tsp	7 mL	Tarragon, dried	5. Bring a third pan of salted water to a boil. Add the frozen peas. Return to a boil, reduce heat, and simmer until tender. Frozen peas have already been blanched and need very little cooking. Drain, refresh, and drain again.
1 tbsp	15 mL	Chopped parsley	6. Mix together the three vegetables.
to taste	to taste	Salt	7. Heat the butter in as many sauté pans as necessary to hold the vegetables without overcrowding.
to taste	to taste	White pepper	8. Add the vegetables and the tarragon. Toss over heat until the vegetables are hot and coated with the butter. Add the parsley and toss to mix.
			9. Season to taste with salt and white pepper.

Per serving:
Calories, 90; Protein, 3 g; Fat, 3.5 g (34% cal.); Cholesterol, 10 mg; Carbohydrates, 12 g; Fiber, 3 g; Sodium, 90 mg.

Quantity preparation: Cook and drain the vegetables and combine in a steam table pan. Heat the butter with the herbs and ladle over the vegetables. Season and serve.

(Continued)

Peas, Carrots, and Pearl Onions with Tarragon Butter *(Continued)*

VARIATIONS

Herbs may be omitted for a simpler preparation, if desired.

Buttered Vegetables

The following vegetables may be cooked by simply boiling or steaming method and dressed with butter for service, as in basic recipe:

Asparagus	Cabbage	Parsnips
Beans, green or yellow	Carrots	Peas
Beans, lima	Cauliflower *(see note)*	Rutabagas
Beets	Celery	Spinach
Broccoli (see note)	Corn (on cob or whole kernel)	Turnips
Brussels sprouts	Kohlrabi	

Note: Dress each portion of broccoli spears with butter just when served. Butter runs off broccoli quickly. Do not sauté for à la carte service. Reheat in boiling water, then add butter. Other large vegetables, such as cauliflower, may also be prepared like broccoli.

Herbed Vegetables

Season buttered vegetables with fresh chopped parsley or other appropriate fresh or dried herbs (see table on p. 483). Dried herbs should be heated a few minutes with the vegetable to release flavor.

Amandine

Especially for green beans, broccoli, celery, cauliflower. For each 2 lb (900 g) EP of vegetable, sauté 2 oz (60 g) slivered or sliced almonds in 2–3 oz (60–90 g) butter until lightly browned. (Caution: Almonds darken quickly.) Combine with cooked vegetable.

Hollandaise

Especially for broccoli, asparagus, cauliflower, brussels sprouts, leeks, and artichoke hearts or bottoms. At service time, nap each portion of vegetable with 2 oz (60 mL) hollandaise sauce.

Polonaise

Especially for cauliflower, broccoli, brussels sprouts, and, sometimes, asparagus and green beans. For each 5 lb (2.3 kg) EP of vegetable, sauté 1½ pt (750 mL) fresh bread crumbs in about 6 oz (175 g) butter until golden. Chop the whites and yolks of 2–4 hard-cooked eggs separately. Combine the crumbs, chopped egg, and 4 tbsp (60 mL) chopped parsley. Sprinkle this mixture over the cooked vegetable immediately before serving.

Puréed Butternut Squash

Portions: 25   **Portion size:** 3 oz (90g)

U.S.	Metric	Ingredients	PROCEDURE
7½ lb	3.5 kg	Butternut squash	1. Peel the squash, cut in half, and scrape out seeds. Cut into large dice.
6 oz	175 g	Butter	
3 oz	90 g	Brown sugar	2. Place in perforated steamer pan. Steam until tender. (Alternative method: Place in heavy pot. Add 1 inch (3 cm) water, cover, and cook slowly until tender. Drain well.)
2 tsp	10 mL	Salt	
to taste	to taste	White pepper	
to taste	to taste	Nutmeg or ginger	3. Purée the squash with a food mill. Add the butter, sugar, and seasonings. Whip until light, but do not overwhip or squash will become watery.

Per serving:
Calories, 90; Protein, 1 g; Fat, 6 g (51% cal.); Cholesterol, 15 mg;
Carbohydrates, 12 g; Fiber, 2 g; Sodium, 250 mg.

Note: If squash is too wet, cook out some of the moisture in a shallow pan over medium heat.

VARIATIONS

Add 3–4 oz (90–125 mL) heavy cream, heated. Sugar may be reduced or omitted if the squash has a good flavor.

Mashed Rutabagas or Yellow Turnips

Prepare as in basic recipe. If desired, add a small amount of whipped potato.

Creamed Spinach

Portions: 25   Portion size: 3½ oz (100 g)

U.S.	Metric	Ingredients	PROCEDURE
10 lb AP	4.5 kg AP	Spinach, fresh	1. Trim spinach and wash carefully in several changes of water. Drain.
2½ pt	1.2 L	Cream sauce, hot	
to taste	to taste	Nutmeg	2. Place 2 inches (5 cm) water in a heavy pot, cover, and bring to a boil. Add the spinach. Stir several times so that it cooks evenly.
to taste	to taste	Salt	
to taste	to taste	White pepper	3. As soon as the spinach is thoroughly wilted, drain in a colander, pressing with the back of a kitchen spoon to squeeze out excess liquid.
			4. Chop the spinach coarsely.
			5. Combine with the cream sauce in a hotel pan. Season to taste with nutmeg, salt, and pepper. (The spinach must not taste strongly of nutmeg.)

Per serving:
Calories, 120; Protein, 6 g; Fat, 7 g (50% cal.); Cholesterol, 20 mg; Carbohydrates, 10 g; Fiber, 3 g; Sodium, 150 mg.

Note: For frozen chopped spinach, partially thaw 2½ packages (2½ lb/1.1 kg each). Cover with boiling salted water and break spinach apart. Cook only until hot and drain. Squeeze out excess liquid and combine with cream sauce.

VARIATION

Creamed Vegetables

The following vegetables, cut into small pieces if necessary, may be cooked by boiling or steaming and combined with cream sauce, as in basic recipe. For 25 portions, use 5–6 lb (about 2½ kg) EP vegetables and 2½–3½ pt (1.2–1.7 L) cream sauce.

Asparagus	Broccoli	Carrots	Kohlrabi
Beans, green or yellow	Brussels sprouts	Cauliflower	Okra
Beans, lima	Cabbage	Celery	Onions, small white
			Peas

Broccoli Mornay

Portions: 24   Portion size: 3½ oz (100 g) broccoli
2 oz (60 mL) sauce

U.S.	Metric	Ingredients	PROCEDURE
7½ lb	3.4 kg	Broccoli	1. Trim and wash broccoli. Separate large pieces into smaller serving pieces. Split or peel stems for even cooking.
1½ qt	1.5 L	Mornay sauce, hot	2. Arrange broccoli in hotel pan with flowers to the outside, stems in center.
			3. Pour in boiling salted water to partially cover. Cover with clean, wet towels and set on rangetop.
			4. Simmer until blossom parts are nearly tender. Fold back towels from edges to uncover blossoms. This releases steam and helps avoid overcooking. Leave stems covered and continue to simmer until stems feel tender but *al dente* when pierced with a knife. Drain well.
			5. Nap each portion with 2 oz (60 mL) Mornay sauce at service time. Ladle the sauce across the stems without covering the blossoms.

Per serving:
Calories, 160; Protein, 9 g; Fat, 10 g (53% cal.); Cholesterol, 30 mg; Carbohydrates, 11 g; Fiber, 4 g; Sodium, 180 mg.

Note: This method of cooking in a shallow pan is used to prevent damaging the blossom ends, which are easily broken. Other delicate vegetables, such as asparagus, are also sometimes cooked in shallow water in hotel pans or sauté pans.

Broccoli may be cooked in a steamer, following basic steaming method.

VARIATIONS

Other vegetables may be served with cheese sauce, such as cauliflower and brussels sprouts.

Broccoli with Cheddar Cheese Sauce

Prepare as in basic recipe, but substitute cheddar cheese sauce for the Mornay sauce.

Vegetable Tagliatelle

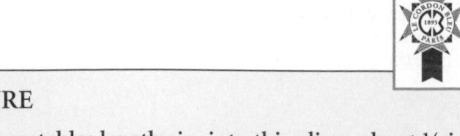

Portions: 16   Portion size: about 4 oz (125 g)

U.S.	Metric	Ingredients	PROCEDURE
1 lb 8 oz	800 g	Zucchini, trimmed	1. Cut the vegetables lengthwise into thin slices, about ⅛ inch (3 mm) thick, then cut into long, thin strips so that the vegetables resemble flat noodles (tagliatelle).
1 lb 8 oz	800 g	Carrots, peeled and trimmed	
1 lb 8 oz	800 g	Celery root, peeled	
2 oz	60 g	Butter	2. Blanch each vegetable separately in boiling salted water. Vegetables should be tender but still firm. Refresh under cold water and drain.
			3. Just before serving, heat the butter in a saucepan over moderate heat. Add the vegetables and toss in the butter until hot.

Per serving:
Calories, 70; Protein, 1 g; Fat, 3 g (40% cal.); Cholesterol, 10 mg;
Carbohydrates, 9 g; Fiber, 3 g; Sodium, 100 mg.

Cauliflower au Gratin

Portions: 25   Portion size: 3 oz (90 g) cauliflower
1½ oz (45 g) sauce and topping

U.S.	Metric	Ingredients	PROCEDURE
5 lb EP	2.3 kg EP	Cauliflower	1. Separate the cauliflower into florets.
1 tbsp	15 mL	Lemon juice (see note)	2. Place the cauliflower and lemon juice into boiling, salted water. Return to boil, lower heat, and cover. Simmer until just tender. Do not overcook, as it will cook further in the sauce. Drain.
1 qt 6 oz	1.2 L	Béchamel or Mornay sauce, hot	
1½ oz	45 g	Dry bread crumbs	3. Butter the bottom of a baking pan or hotel pan and place the cauliflower in it about 2 inches (5 cm) deep. (Individual ovenproof serving dishes may be used instead.)
1½ oz	45 g	Parmesan cheese, grated	
2½ oz	75 g	Butter, melted	4. Cover with the hot sauce.
			5. Mix together the bread crumbs and cheese and sprinkle evenly over the top. Drizzle melted butter over the top.
			6. Bake at 350°F (175°C) for about 20 minutes to heat through. Brown the top under the broiler or salamander.

Per serving:
Calories, 60; Protein, 3 g; Fat, 3.5 g (50% cal.); Cholesterol, 10 mg;
Carbohydrates, 5 g; Fiber, 2 g; Sodium, 80 mg.

Note: Adding lemon juice to cooking water helps to keep white vegetables white. It may be omitted if desired.

VARIATIONS

Substitute cheddar cheese sauce for the béchamel or Mornay, and use grated cheddar cheese instead of parmesan for topping.

Other vegetables may be prepared au gratin, such as asparagus, Belgian endive, broccoli, brussels sprouts, celery, celery root, leeks, and turnips.

Green Beans Basquaise

Portions: 12   Portion size: 4 oz (110 g)

U.S.	Metric	Ingredients	PROCEDURE
1 lb 12 oz	800 g	Green beans, trimmed	1. Boil the green beans in salted water until tender but firm. Drain and cool under cold water. Drain.
4 oz	125 mL	Olive oil	
6 oz	175 g	Green pepper, cut brunoise	2. Heat the olive oil over medium heat. Add the peppers and sweat.
6 oz	175 g	Red pepper, cut brunoise	
6 oz	175 g	Yellow pepper, cut brunoise	3. Add the green beans and toss in the hot oil until the beans are hot.
to taste	to taste	Salt	
to taste	to taste	Pepper	4. Season to taste.

Per serving:
Calories, 120; Protein, 2 g; Fat, 10 g (69% cal.); Cholesterol, 0 mg;
Carbohydrates, 8 g; Fiber, 2 g; Sodium, 0 mg.

Mixed Vegetables with Herbs

Portions: 16   Portion size: 4 oz (125 g)

U.S.	Metric	Ingredients	PROCEDURE
2 lb	1 kg	Asparagus	1. Trim and peel the asparagus (see Figure 16.3). Cook in boiling salted water until tender but firm. Refresh under cold water and set aside.
1 lb 6 oz	600 g	Zucchini	
14 oz	400 g	Celery root	
14 oz	400 g	Turnips	2. Trim the zucchini, celery root, and turnips as necessary. Cut into batonnet. Cook each vegetable separately in boiling salted water. Refresh under cold water and drain.
4 oz	125 g	Butter	3. Melt the butter in a large sauté pan and sweat the shallots with some salt, lemon juice, and 2 tablespoons (30 mL) water.
6	6	Shallots, chopped	
1½ oz	45 mL	Lemon juice	
1 oz	30 mL	Water	4. Add the vegetables. When hot, mix in the herbs.
to taste	to taste	Salt	
2 tbsp	30 mL	Chopped parsley	
2 tbsp	30 mL	Chopped chives	

Per serving:
Calories, 80; Protein, 2 g; Fat, 6 g (67% cal.); Cholesterol, 15 mg; Carbohydrates, 7 g; Fiber, 3 g; Sodium, 105 mg.

Compote of Carrots and Onions

Portions: 12   Portion size: 3½–4 oz (110–120 g)

U.S.	Metric	Ingredients	PROCEDURE
3 lb 8 oz	1.6 kg	Carrots	1. Trim and peel the carrots. Cut them in half lengthwise, then cut them into slices. In a large pan, cook the onions over low heat in the olive oil for about 5 minutes.
14 oz	400 g	Onions, chopped	
1 tbsp	15 mL	Olive oil	
12 oz	350 mL	Water	2. Add the carrots and water. Season to taste with salt, pepper, and ground ginger. Cover and cook over medium heat for about 20 minutes. Check from time to time to make sure that the liquid hasn't evaporated and that the vegetables aren't scorching. This could happen if the cover is loose or if the heat is too high.
to taste	to taste	Salt and pepper	
to taste	to taste	Ground ginger	
			3. Remove the cover and cook another 5–10 minutes to allow the moisture to evaporate, stirring occasionally, until the desired consistency is reached. Adjust the seasoning if necessary and serve.

Per serving:
Calories, 80; Protein, 2 g; Fat, 1.5 g (16% cal.); Cholesterol, 0 mg; Carbohydrates, 16 g; Fiber, 4 g; Sodium, 80 mg.

Lentils in Cream

Yield: 3 lb 12 oz (1.8 kg)   **Portions:** 12   **Portion size:** 5 oz (150 g)

U.S.	Metric	Ingredients	PROCEDURE
1 lb 4 oz	600 g	Small green lentils	1. Blanch the lentils and drain.
7 oz	200 g	Carrots, cut in large chunks	2. Return to the pan and cover with enough cold water to cover by at least 2 inches (5 cm).
7 oz	200 g	Onion, cut in large chunks	
7 oz	200 g	Celery, cut in large chunks	3. Add the carrot, onion, celery, bacon, garlic, and bouquet garni.
7 oz	200 g	Bacon	
6 cloves	6 cloves	Garlic	4. Simmer until tender but still firm. Drain, reserving the liquid. Discard the vegetables, bacon, and bouquet garni.
1	1	Bouquet garni	
2 oz	60 g	Onion, cut brunoise	5. Sweat the onion, carrot, and celery in the clarified butter.
2 oz	60 g	Carrot, cut brunoise	
1 oz	30 g	Celery, cut brunoise	6. Add the lentils along with 10 oz (300 mL) of the cooking liquid. Bring to a boil and cook for a few minutes.
1 oz	30 g	Clarified butter	
4 oz	125 mL	Heavy cream, hot	7. Add the cream, return to a simmer, and stir in the butter, then the mustard and chopped parsley. Season to taste.
2 oz	60 g	Butter	
2 tbsp	30 mL	Dijon mustard	
1 oz	30 g	Chopped parsley	
to taste	to taste	Salt	
to taste	to taste	Pepper	

Per serving:
Calories, 320; Protein, 12 g; Fat, 20 g (54% cal.); Cholesterol, 40 mg;
Carbohydrates, 26 g; Fiber, 12 g; Sodium, 200 mg.

Brussels Sprouts Paysanne

Portions: 24   **Portion size:** 6 oz (175 g)

U.S.	Metric	Ingredients	PROCEDURE
4 lb 8 oz	2 kg	Brussels sprouts	1. Clean the brussels sprouts and cook in boiling salted water until tender.
1 lb 4 oz	600 g	Carrot	
1 lb 4 oz	600 g	Celery	2. Cut the vegetables into paysanne as follows: Cut the carrot and celery into 1/16-inch (2-mm) slices. Cut each slice into strips, 1/4 inch (6 mm) wide. Cut the strips into triangles. Cut the leek and onion into triangles approximately the same size.
1 lb 4 oz	600 g	Leek	
1 lb 4 oz	600 g	Onion	
7 oz	200 g	Prosciutto	
			3. Cut the prosciutto into julienne.
5 oz	150 g	Butter	4. Sweat the paysanne vegetables in the butter. Once cooked, add the ham and the brussels sprouts. Cook for around 10 minutes, then mix in the chopped parsley. Adjust the seasoning if necessary.
to taste	to taste	Salt	
3 tbsp	20 g	Chopped parsley	

Per serving:
Calories, 130; Protein, 6 g; Fat, 7 g (41% cal.); Cholesterol, 20 mg;
Carbohydrates, 17 g; Fiber, 5 g; Sodium, 310 mg.

VARIATION

Substitute bacon for the prosciutto. Render the bacon, then use the bacon fat instead of the butter for sweating the vegetables.

Artichokes Gribiche

Portions: 10   Portion size: 1 artichoke
                             2½ oz (80 mL) sauce

U.S.	Metric	Ingredients	PROCEDURE
10	10	Artichokes	1. Trim the artichokes for cooking whole, as shown in Figure 16.1.
3	3	Lemons	2. Cut the lemons into ¼-inch (5-mm) slices. Tie a slice of lemon to the base of each artichoke to prevent discoloration (see Figure 16.2).
			3. Cook in gently simmering water until tender, about 30–40 minutes.
1½ pt	800 mL	Sauce Gribiche (p. 573)	4. Serve warm or cooled, with the sauce on the side, for dipping.

Per serving:
Calories, 480; Protein, 6 g; Fat, 45 g (82% cal.); Cholesterol, 65 mg;
Carbohydrates, 16 g; Fiber, 7 g; Sodium, 310 mg.

Purée of Flageolet Beans with Garlic

Yield: 4 lb (2 kg)   Portions: 16   Portion size: 4 oz (125 g)

U.S.	Metric	Ingredients	PROCEDURE
1½ lb	750 g	Dried flageolet beans	1. Rinse and drain the beans. Soak overnight in enough cold water to cover by several inches (5 cm or more).
1	1	Sachet (p. 127)	
3 pt	1.5 L	Water or light vegetable stock	2. Drain. Add the sachet and the water or stock. Simmer until the beans are tender, about 45 minutes. Discard the sachet.
6–8 cloves	6–8 cloves	Garlic, peeled and chopped	3. Mash the chopped garlic with the salt.
2 tsp	10 mL	Salt	4. Drain the beans. Place the beans in a food processor with the garlic and olive oil. Blend to a purée.
12 oz	375 mL	Olive oil	
3 oz	90 mL	Lemon juice	5. With the motor running, pour in the lemon juice. The purée should have the consistency of soft mashed potatoes.
to taste	to taste	Additional salt	6. Adjust seasoning to taste with salt and pepper if necessary.
to taste	to taste	Pepper	7. Serve warm as a vegetable accompaniment (reheat as necessary) or cold as a dip.

Per serving:
Calories, 320; Protein, 9 g; Fat, 22 g (60% cal.); Cholesterol, 0 mg;
Carbohydrates, 24 g; Fiber, 8 g; Sodium, 290 mg.

VARIATIONS

Other beans, such as white kidney beans and pinto beans, may be substituted.

Flageolet Beans with Wilted Arugula

Cook the beans as in the basic recipe but do not purée. Use 3 cloves garlic and 4 oz (125 mL) olive oil. Chop the garlic and sauté in the olive oil. Add 1 lb (500 g) coarsely chopped arugula and sauté just until wilted. Add this mixture to the drained, hot beans. Season to taste.

Artichokes Clamart

Portions: 10   **Portion size:** 1 artichoke heart
                              1 oz (30 g) peas

U.S.	Metric	Ingredients	PROCEDURE
10	10	Artichokes, large	1. Prepare artichoke bottoms by trimming, as shown in Figure 16.1. Rub the cut surfaces with the lemon as you work to keep them from darkening.
1	1	Lemon, cut in half	
1 oz	30 g	Flour	2. Mix the flour with a little water, then add it to the remaining water in a saucepan. Add the lemon juice and salt. Bring to a boil. This mixture is called a *blanc*. It helps keep the artichokes white as they cook.
3 pt	1.5 L	Cold water	
1½ oz	50 mL	Lemon juice	
1 tbsp	15 mL	Salt	3. Add the artichokes to the *blanc* and simmer until just tender, about 30 minutes. Drain.
10 oz	300 g	Peas, frozen	4. Place the peas in a saucepan with boiling salted water and simmer until just heated through. Drain.
3 oz	90 g	Butter	
to taste	to taste	Salt	5. Heat 1 oz (30 g) of the butter in a sauté pan and sauté the peas briefly. Season with salt, pepper, and basil, tossing over heat briefly so that the basil can release its flavor.
to taste	to taste	White pepper	
pinch	pinch	Basil	
			6. At the same time, heat the remaining 2 oz (60 g) butter in another sauté pan. Place the cooked artichoke bottoms in the pan and sauté over medium heat until the artichokes are well coated with butter and are hot. Season with salt and pepper.
			7. Arrange artichokes in a hotel pan and fill with the peas. (Do not do this in advance because the lemon juice in the artichokes will discolor the peas.)

Per serving:
Calories, 150; Protein, 6 g; Fat, 7 g (38% cal.); Cholesterol, 20 mg;
Carbohydrates, 20 g; Fiber, 9 g; Sodium, 560 mg.

VARIATIONS

Artichoke bottoms can be filled with other vegetables, such as asparagus tips, tiny tournéed carrots, tournéed turnips, or mushrooms. They may also be used as containers for a sauce served with grilled meat items. Either way, they are used mostly as garnish for meats.

White Beans, Bretonne Style

Yield: about 6 lb (3 kg)   **Portions:** 20   **Portion size:** 5 oz (150 g)

U.S.	Metric	Ingredients	PROCEDURE
2 lb	1 kg	Dried white beans	1. Soak the beans overnight in cold water.
1	1	Carrot, small	2. Drain the beans and place in a pot with enough water to cover by 1 inch (2.5 cm). Add the carrot, celery, onion, and sachet. Simmer until the beans are tender but not soft or broken (1–3 hours, depending on the beans). Drain but save the liquid. Discard the vegetables and sachet.
1 stem	1 stem	Celery	
1	1	Onion, small, peeled	
		Sachet (tied in cheesecloth):	
1	1	Bay leaf	
6–8	6–8	Parsley stems	
3–4	3–4	Peppercorns	
1	1	Clove	
pinch	pinch	Thyme	
4 oz	125 g	Butter	3. Heat the butter in a large saucepot or brazier. Sauté the onion and garlic until soft. Add the tomatoes and cook a few minutes to reduce liquid.
8 oz	250 g	Onion, diced	
2 cloves	2 cloves	Garlic, chopped	
1 lb	500 g	Canned tomatoes, with juice, coarsely chopped	4. Add the beans to this mixture and stir carefully. Simmer until heated through and flavors are blended. If too dry, add some of the bean cooking liquid. Add pan drippings, if you are using them. Season to taste.
as needed	as needed	Pan juices from roast lamb (optional; see note)	
to taste	to taste	Salt	**Per serving:**
to taste	to taste	Pepper	Calories, 200; Protein, 11 g; Fat, 5 g (22% cal.); Cholesterol, 10 mg; Carbohydrates, 29 g; Fiber, 7 g; Sodium, 90 mg.

Note: This preparation is often served with roast leg of lamb or other lamb roast. If so, the pan drippings may be used to flavor the beans.

Glazed Root Vegetables

Portions: 25   Portion size: 3 oz (90 g)

U.S.	Metric	Ingredients	PROCEDURE
3 lb	1.4 kg	Carrots	1. Trim and peel the carrots, parsnips, and turnips. Tournéed root vegetables (see Figure 18.1) are often prepared by this method.
1½ lb	600 g	Parsnips	
2½ lb	1 kg	Turnips	
3 oz	90 g	Butter	2. Place the vegetables in a saucepan with boiling salted water to cover. Simmer until tender. Drain.
2 oz	60 g	Sugar	
to taste	to taste	Salt	3. Heat the butter in a sauté pan. Add the vegetables and sprinkle with the sugar. Season to taste with salt. Sauté until the vegetables are well glazed.

Per serving:
Calories, 90; Protein, 1 g; Fat, 3 g (30% cal.); Cholesterol, 5 mg;
Carbohydrates, 15 g; Fiber, 4 g; Sodium, 85 mg.

VARIATIONS

Single vegetables as well as other combinations of vegetables may be glazed by this method, including celery root, pearl onions, rutabagas, and chestnuts, in addition to carrots, parsnips, and turnips.

Glazed Carrots (Carrots Vichy)

Portions: 25   Portion size: 3 oz (90 g)

U.S.	Metric	Ingredients	PROCEDURE
6½ lb	3 kg	Carrots	1. Trim, peel, and slice the carrots.
as needed	as needed	Water (see note)	2. Place them in a saucepan or straight-sided sauté pan. Add water to barely cover the carrots. Add the butter, sugar, and salt.
5 oz	150 g	Butter	
2 tbsp	30 g	Sugar	
2 tsp	10 mL	Salt	3. Bring to a boil. Lower heat and simmer until the carrots are tender and the water is nearly evaporated. If done properly, these should happen at the same time. Toss the carrots so that they are well coated with the glaze that is left in the pan.
to taste	to taste	White pepper	
as needed	as needed	Chopped parsley	

Per serving:
Calories, 100; Protein, 2 g; Fat, 5 g (43% cal.); Cholesterol, 10 mg;
Carbohydrates, 13 g; Fiber, 2 g; Sodium, 240 mg.

4. Garnish with chopped parsley.

Note: Sometimes Vichy water or other bottled mineral water is used, but it is not necessary.

Sautéing and Pan-frying

Remember that the main differences between sautéing and pan-frying are in the amount of fat used and in the cooking time. Sautéing means cooking quickly in a small amount of fat. The product is often tossed or flipped in the pan over high heat. Pan-frying means cooking in a larger amount of fat, usually for a longer time at lower heat, and the product is not tossed or flipped. In practice, the two methods are often similar, and the distinction between them is hard to draw.

Both methods may be used for finish-cooking precooked or blanched vegetables as well as for completely cooking vegetables from the raw state. Sautéing in butter is especially popular for finishing precooked and chilled vegetables for service.

Stir-frying is a quick-cooking technique used in Asian cookery. In effect, it is similar to sautéing, except that the pan is left stationary and the items being cooked are stirred and flipped in hot fat with spatulas or other tools.

Procedure for Sautéing Vegetables

This method is used for precooked or blanched vegetables and for tender, small-cut vegetables that cook quickly.

1. Collect all equipment and food products.
2. Prepare vegetables as required.
3. Place sauté pan on high heat.
4. When the pan is hot, add a small amount of clarified butter, oil, or other fat, enough to coat the bottom of the pan. (Clarified butter is used because the milk solids in whole butter burn quickly at the high heat necessary for sautéing.)
5. As soon as the fat is hot, add the vegetable. DO NOT overload the pan, or the temperature will be lowered too much and the vegetables will simmer instead of sauté.
6. After the heat has had time to recover, flip the pan a few times to turn and toss the vegetables (see Figure 17.1). Let the pan set again over the heat.

Flipping action of wrist

Figure 17.1 To flip foods in a sauté pan, give the handle a sharp twist upward with the wrist. Be sure to move the pan back far enough to catch the foods as they come down.

7. Continue to flip the vegetables as often as necessary for them to cook or heat evenly and become coated with the cooking fat. (Don't flip more than necessary, however. It may be fun and a good way to show off, but it's a waste of time and accomplishes nothing except breaking fragile vegetables. Also, the heat must have time to recover between flips.)
8. As soon as the vegetables are cooked, or heated through if precooked, remove from the pan and serve. Browning may or may not be desirable, depending on the vegetable and the particular preparation.

Procedure for Pan-frying Vegetables

Note: A griddle is often used for this procedure if only a small amount of fat is required.

1. Collect all equipment and food products.
2. Prepare vegetables as required.
3. Place a sauté pan or cast-iron skillet on moderately high heat. Add required amount of fat to the pan and let it heat.
4. Place prepared vegetables in the pan. Adjust the heat so that the product cooks through with the desired amount of browning, but without burning the outside.
5. Turn vegetables with a spatula and continue to cook until done.
6. Remove from pan. If necessary, drain on absorbent paper to eliminate excess fat.

Pan-fried Eggplant with Tomato Sauce

Portions: 24	Portion size: 3½ oz (100 g) eggplant 2 oz (60 mL) sauce			
U.S.	Metric	Ingredients		PROCEDURE
6½ lb	3 kg	Eggplant Breading:		1. Wash and trim eggplants. Pare if skins are tough. Cut crosswise into ¼-inch (½-cm) slices.
6 oz	175 g	Flour		2. Hold in strongly salted cold water up to 30 minutes. (This step may be omitted, but it helps prevent darkening and eliminates some bitter flavors.)
1½ tsp	7 mL	Salt		
½ tsp	2 mL	White pepper		3. Set up breading station, seasoning the flour with the salt and pepper.
1 pt	500 mL	Egg wash		4. Drain the eggplants and dry them well. Pass through Standard Breading Procedure (see p. 121).
1¼ lb	600 g	Bread crumbs		
as needed	as needed	Oil for frying		5. Heat ¼ inch (½ cm) oil in a heavy iron skillet or sauté pan. Pan-fry the breaded eggplant on both sides until browned. Remove from pan with slotted spatula and drain on absorbent paper.
1½ qt	1.5 L	Tomato sauce		6. Serve 2–3 slices per portion, depending on size. Nap each portion with 2 oz (60 mL) tomato sauce. Ladle the sauce in a band across the eggplant; do not cover completely.

Per serving:
Calories, 260; Protein, 7 g; Fat, 13 g (44% cal.); Cholesterol, 70 mg; Carbohydrates, 30 g; Fiber, 4 g; Sodium, 490 mg.

VARIATIONS

Instead of Standard Breading Procedure, simply dredge slices in seasoned flour and pan-fry.

Pan-fried Eggplant Creole

Use Creole sauce instead of tomato sauce.

Eggplant Parmigiana

Pan-fry as in basic recipe. Top each fried slice with a thin slice of mozzarella cheese. Arrange in layers in a baking pan, covering each layer with tomato sauce and sprinkling with parmesan cheese. Bake 30 minutes at 350°F (175°C).

Zucchini Sauté Provençale

Portions: 25   Portion size: 3½ oz (100 g)

U.S.	Metric	Ingredients	PROCEDURE
6 lb	2.7 kg	Zucchini	1. Wash and trim the zucchini. Cut crosswise into thin slices.
6 oz	175 mL	Olive oil	2. Heat the oil in two or three sauté pans (or sauté in several batches—do not overload the pans). Add the shallot or onion and the garlic. Sauté until soft but not browned.
6 oz	175 g	Shallots or onions, minced	
4–6 cloves	4–6 cloves	Garlic, chopped	3. Add the zucchini and sauté until slightly browned but still somewhat crisp.
to taste	to taste	Parsley, chopped	4. Add the parsley and toss to mix. Season to taste.
to taste	to taste	Salt	
to taste	to taste	White pepper	

Per serving:
Calories, 80; Protein, 1 g; Fat, 7 g (72% cal.); Cholesterol, 0 mg;
Carbohydrates, 5 g; Fiber, 1 g; Sodium, 5 mg.

VARIATIONS

Cut the zucchini into other shapes, but keep them small enough to cook quickly. Examples: batonnet, julienne, dice, and shredded on a coarse grater.

Shredded Zucchini with Shallots

Shred the zucchini on a coarse grater. Sauté with shallots as in basic recipe, but without browning. Omit the garlic and parsley.

Zucchini with Tomatoes

Sauté as in basic recipe. When half cooked, add 2½ pt (1.2 L) drained, chopped, canned tomatoes or fresh tomatoes concassé (p. 455). Finish cooking. Season with oregano and basil.

Zucchini with Cream

Shred zucchini on grater. Salt lightly and let stand in a colander for 30 minutes. Press out excess liquid. Sauté as in basic recipe, but without browning. Add 2½ cups (600 mL) heavy cream and simmer 2 minutes.

Black Bean Cakes with Salsa

Yield: 20 cakes, 2 oz (60 g) each   Portions: 10   Portion size: 2 cakes
1½ oz (45 mL) salsa

U.S.	Metric	Ingredients	PROCEDURE
1 oz	30 mL	Olive oil	1. Heat the olive oil in a sauté pan over moderately low heat.
1 lb	500 g	Onion, cut brunoise	2. Add the onions and garlic and sweat until very soft. Do not brown.
2–4 cloves	2–4 cloves	Garlic, chopped	
1–2	1–2	Jalapeño peppers, seeded and cut brunoise	3. Add the jalapeño and ground cumin. Cook slowly another few minutes.
2 tsp	10 mL	Ground cumin	4. Add the beans and oregano. Cook until heated through.
2 lb	1 kg	Cooked black beans (see note)	
1 tsp	5 mL	Oregano	
to taste	to taste	Salt	5. Transfer the mixture to a food processor and process to form a coarse purée. The mixture should be thick enough to hold its shape but not too dry. If necessary, moisten with a little water.
to taste	to taste	Pepper	
3 oz	100 mL	Olive oil	6. Taste and adjust the seasoning with salt and pepper.
1 pt	450 mL	Salsa Cruda (p. 733)	7. Divide the mixture into 2-oz (60-g) portions. Form into small, flat cakes.
			8. Brown the cakes lightly on both sides in hot olive oil in a sauté pan. They will be very soft; handle carefully.
			9. Serve 2 cakes per portion with 1½ oz (45 mL) salsa.

Per serving:
Calories, 260; Protein, 9 g; Fat, 12 g (41% cal.); Cholesterol, 0 mg;
Carbohydrates, 30 g; Fiber, 9 g; Sodium, 180 mg.

Note: Canned black beans may be used, but they should be drained and rinsed.

Corn Sauté Mexicaine

Portions: 25   Portion size: 3 oz (90 g)

U.S.	Metric	Ingredients	PROCEDURE
5 lb	2.2 kg	Corn, frozen whole kernel	1. Place the corn in a saucepot with boiling salted water. Simmer until heated through. Drain well. Cool if the corn is to be held for later service.
4 oz	100 g	Butter	
8 oz	200 g	Green pepper, chopped fine	
4 oz	100 g	Pimiento (canned), chopped fine	2. Heat the butter in a sauté pan and sauté the green pepper about 1 minute.
to taste	to taste	Salt	3. Add the corn and pimiento. Sauté until hot and well blended. Season to taste.
to taste	to taste	White pepper	

Per serving:
Calories, 110; Protein, 3 g; Fat, 4 g (30% cal.); Cholesterol, 10 mg;
Carbohydrates, 18 g; Fiber, 3 g; Sodium, 45 mg.

Note: Canned corn may be used, but it does not need to be simmered first. Just drain well and add to sauté pan.

VARIATIONS

Corn O'Brien

Prepare as in basic recipe, but sauté 6 oz (175 g) chopped onion with the green pepper. Cook 8 oz (250 g) diced bacon until crisp and add at service time. Bacon fat may be used instead of butter for sautéing if desired.

Corn and Zucchini Sauté

Prepare as in basic recipe, but replace green pepper with 2½ lb (1.1 kg) zucchini, cut in ¼-inch (½-cm) dice. Omit pimiento.

Sautéed Mushrooms

Portions: 25   Portion size: 3½ oz (100 g)

U.S.	Metric	Ingredients	PROCEDURE
6½ lb	3 kg	Mushrooms, fresh	1. Rinse the mushrooms quickly and dry them with towels. Trim off the bottoms of the stems and slice the mushrooms.
10 oz	300 g	Clarified butter, or half oil, half butter	
to taste	to taste	Salt	2. Heat two or three sauté pans over high heat (or sauté in several batches—do not overload pans). Add the fat to the pans. Place the mushrooms in the pan and sauté over high heat until browned. Do not overcook, or the mushrooms will shrivel and lose a great deal of moisture.
to taste	to taste	Pepper	
			3. Season with salt and pepper.

Per serving:
Calories, 120; Protein, 2 g; Fat, 11 g (80% cal.); Cholesterol, 30 mg;
Carbohydrates, 4 g; Fiber, 2 g; Sodium, 115 mg.

Note: If mushrooms must be kept light in color, add lemon juice to the pan when the mushrooms are added. Use about 1 oz (30 mL) lemon juice per pound (500 g) of mushrooms.

VARIATIONS

Garnish with chopped parsley.

Instead of slicing, leave small mushroom caps whole, or cut in halves or quarters.

Creamed Mushrooms

Prepare as in basic recipe, using lemon juice to keep light color. Combine with 2½ pt (1.2 L) hot cream sauce. Season with a little nutmeg.

Duxelles

Chop mushrooms very fine. Squeeze out moisture in a towel. Sauté in butter with 3 oz (90 g) minced shallot or onion until dry. Season with salt, pepper, nutmeg. Used in vegetable and meat stuffings. May be moistened with heavy cream or stretched with bread crumbs.

Braising

Braising, as you know, is a slow, moist-heat cooking method using a small amount of liquid. When meats are braised, they are seared or browned in fat before any liquid is added. Braised vegetables are not always cooked in fat before liquid is added, although some kind of fat is used in the preparation.

Braised vegetable preparations tend to be more complex than boiled or steamed vegetables, and the cooking times are longer. Unfortunately, there are so many variations of braised vegetables that it is not possible to prescribe a single basic procedure. Instead, we discuss the procedures in general terms and use the recipes to illustrate them.

Characteristics of Vegetable Braising Procedure

1. Fat is added to a braising or baking pan or a saucepan and heated. Finely diced mirepoix or other flavoring ingredients may be cooked briefly in the fat. The fat contributes to flavor and eating quality.

2. The vegetable (blanched or raw) is placed in the pan. It may or may not be cooked in the fat before the liquid is added, depending on the recipe.

3. Liquid is added—stock, water, wine, or a combination of liquids. The liquid generally covers the vegetable only partway.

4. The pot or saucepan is covered and the vegetable is cooked slowly in the oven or on the rangetop.

5. The flavorful cooking liquid is served with the vegetable. It is sometimes drained off and reduced over high heat before serving in order to concentrate flavor.

Braised Red Cabbage

Portions: 25   Portion size: 5 oz (150 g)

U.S.	Metric	Ingredients	PROCEDURE
6 lb	3 kg	Red cabbage	1. Remove the outer leaves of the cabbage and cut it into quarters. Remove the core and shred the cabbage with a knife (Figure 16.7) or a power shredder attachment. Do not chop; cabbage should be in long, fine shreds.
12 oz	375 g	Bacon, diced	
1 lb	500 g	Onions, sliced	
1 oz	30 g	Sugar	
1½ pt	750 mL	White stock (chicken, pork, veal) or water	2. Render the bacon in a large, heavy pot. Add the onions and sugar and cook until the onion is soft.
1 lb	500 g	Apples (unpeeled), cored and diced	3. Add the cabbage and stir over heat until it is coated with fat.
4	4	Cloves	4. Add the stock, apples, and the spices, tied in a cheesecloth bag. Cover and simmer until cabbage is nearly tender, about 30 minutes.
6	6	Whole allspice	
1	1	Cinnamon stick	
4 oz or more	125 mL	Cider vinegar or red wine vinegar	5. Add the vinegar and red wine and simmer another 10 minutes. Remove spice bag.
1 cup	250 mL	Red wine (or more vinegar)	6. Taste and correct seasoning. If not tart enough or color is not red enough, add more vinegar.
to taste	to taste	Salt	
to taste	to taste	Pepper	

Per serving:
Calories, 130; Protein, 3 g; Fat, 8 g (54% cal.); Cholesterol, 10 mg;
Carbohydrates, 11 g; Fiber, 3 g; Sodium, 110 mg.

VARIATIONS

Substitute lard, salt pork, or chicken fat for the bacon. Vegetable oil may be used, but it does not contribute to flavor.

Eliminate cinnamon, cloves, and allspice. Add 1 tablespoon (15 mL) caraway seeds to onions when sautéing them.

Braised Green or White Cabbage

Prepare as in the basic recipe, but season with 1 bay leaf, 6–8 parsley stems, 6 peppercorns, and a pinch of thyme instead of the cinnamon, cloves, and allspice. Omit sugar, apples, wine, and vinegar. Butter may be used as cooking fat if desired.

Sauerkraut

Portions: 25   Portion size: 4½ oz (125 g)

U.S.	Metric	Ingredients	PROCEDURE
1 No. 10 can	1 No. 10 can	Sauerkraut	1. Rinse the sauerkraut in cold water. Drain and press out water. Taste and rinse again if still too briny. (See Appendix 2, p. 892, for can sizes and substitutions.)
2 oz	60 g	Lard or bacon fat	
1 lb	500 g	Onions, sliced	
1 pt	500 mL	Dry white wine (optional)	
1½ qt	1.5 L	Chicken stock	2. Heat the lard in a heavy pot and sauté the onions until soft. Add the sauerkraut, wine (if used), and enough stock so that the sauerkraut is covered by about three-fourths. Tie the spices and garlic in cheesecloth and add to the pot.
(approximately)	(approximately)		
5	5	Juniper berries	
2	2	Bay leaves	
2	2	Whole cloves	3. Cover and simmer for 1½ hours on the rangetop or in a slow oven (300°F/150°C).
1 tsp	5 mL	Caraway or cumin seed	
2	2	Garlic cloves	4. Remove the spice bag. Taste the sauerkraut and adjust seasoning.
to taste	to taste	Salt	

Per serving:
Calories, 50; Protein, 2 g; Fat, 2.5 g (38% cal.); Cholesterol, 5 mg;
Carbohydrates, 7 g; Fiber, 3 g; Sodium, 790 mg.

VARIATION

Choucroute Garni

Double quantities per portion. Cook a variety of fresh and smoked pork products and sausages in the sauerkraut. Add each item at the proper time so that it is in the sauerkraut for its correct cooking time. Suggestions: fresh or smoked pork chops, slab bacon, bratwurst, frankfurters, smoked pork shoulder. Serve as a main course. Accompany with boiled potatoes.

Peas à la Française

Portions: 16   Portion size: 3 oz (90 g)

U.S.	Metric	Ingredients	PROCEDURE
3 oz	90 g	Butter	1. Heat the butter in a saucepan. Add the onions and sauté lightly.
2 oz	60 g	Onion, chopped, or whole tiny pearl onions, peeled	
2½ lb	1.1 kg	Peas, frozen	2. Add the peas, lettuce, parsley, salt, and sugar. Cook over moderate heat, stirring a few times, until the vegetables begin to steam.
8 oz	225 g	Lettuce, shredded	
2 tbsp	30 mL	Chopped parsley	
1 tsp	5 mL	Salt	3. Add the stock or water. Bring to a boil, cover, and simmer over low heat or in oven until peas are tender.
2 tsp	10 mL	Sugar	
4 oz	125 mL	Chicken stock or water, hot	
1 tbsp	15 mL	Beurre manié	4. Stir in a little beurre manié to thicken the cooking liquid and simmer another 2–3 minutes. Adjust seasoning. (For larger quantities, drain off liquid and thicken separately.)

Per serving:
Calories, 100; Protein, 4 g; Fat, 5 g (43% cal.); Cholesterol, 15 mg;
Carbohydrates, 11 g; Fiber, 4 g; Sodium, 250 mg.

Braised Celery

Portions: 25   Portion size: 3 oz (90 g)

U.S.	Metric	Ingredients	PROCEDURE
6 lb	3 kg	Celery	1. Trim and wash the celery. If it is very stringy, peel the outside of the ribs, or use the tender inner stems and save the outside ones for the mirepoix. Cut into 1½-inch (4-cm) lengths. Split broad pieces lengthwise so all pieces are about the same size.
4 oz	125 g	Butter	
3 pt (approximately)	1.5 L (approximately)	Brown stock or chicken stock	2. Heat the butter in a braising pot and add the celery. Cook over moderate heat until the celery is just beginning to soften.
to taste	to taste	Salt	
to taste	to taste	Pepper	3. Add enough stock to cover the celery by about two-thirds. Cover and cook slowly in the oven or on the rangetop until tender, about 20–30 minutes.
as needed	as needed	Optional: beurre manié	4. Drain the celery and keep it warm in a steam table pan. Reduce the stock over high heat to about 2½ pt (1.25 L). If desired, thicken slightly with beurre manié. Adjust the seasonings and pour the sauce over the celery.

Per serving:
Calories, 50; Protein, 1 g; Fat, 4 g (64% cal.); Cholesterol, 10 mg; Carbohydrates, 4 g; Fiber, 2 g; Sodium, 130 mg.

VARIATIONS

Bacon fat may be used instead of butter. For extra flavor, add finely diced mirepoix to the fat in the pan before adding celery.

Braised Celery Hearts

Prepare as in basic recipe, but use celery hearts (the tender inner stalks, connected at the root), cut into wedges.

Braised Celery with Brown Sauce

Add 2½ pt (1.25 L) brown sauce or demiglaze to the reduced cooking liquid and reduce again to reach desired consistency. Add to celery.

Braised Celery Root

Prepare as in basic recipe, using sliced, blanched knob celery (celeriac).

Braised Lettuce

Blanch romaine lettuce to wilt leaves. Fold leaves into neat, portion-size bundles. Arrange on finely cut sautéed mirepoix and braise as in basic recipe, without sautéing the lettuce.

Carrots with Orange and Cumin

Portions: 12   Portion size: 3½ oz (100 g)

U.S.	Metric	Ingredients	PROCEDURE
3 lb 4 oz	1.5 kg	Carrots	1. Trim and peel the carrots. Cut into thin slices.
3½ oz	100 g	Butter	2. Sweat the carrots in the butter for a few minutes, then add the cumin and salt and pepper to taste.
⅛ tsp	1 g	Cumin seed	
¼ tsp	2 g	Ground cumin	3. Add the orange juice. Cook, loosely covered, over low heat until tender. Remove the cover and continue to cook until most of the liquid has evaporated.
to taste	to taste	Salt	
to taste	to taste	White pepper	
10 oz	300 mL	Orange juice	

Per serving:
Calories, 120; Protein, 2 g; Fat, 7 g (51% cal.); Cholesterol, 20 mg; Carbohydrates, 13 g; Fiber, 2 g; Sodium, 70 mg.

VARIATION

Carrot Purée with Orange and Cumin

Transfer the cooked carrots to the bowl of a food processor or a food mill. Purée until smooth. Place back on the heat to remove any excess moisture. Mix in 3–4 oz (100 g) butter (monter au beurre). Adjust the seasoning.

Ratatouille

The method for this preparation is unlike that for the other braised vegetables in this section because no liquid is added. It is classified as a braised item because the vegetables are first sautéed in fat, then simmered in their own juices.

Portions: 20   **Portion size: 4 oz (125 g)**

U.S.	Metric	Ingredients	PROCEDURE
1 lb	500 g	Zucchini	1. **Prepare the vegetables:** Cut the zucchini into ½-inch (1-cm) slices. Peel the eggplant and cut into large dice. Slice the onions. Remove the cores and seeds of the peppers and cut into 1-inch (2½-cm) dice. Chop the garlic. Peel and seed the tomatoes and cut into large dice (leave canned tomatoes whole; they will break up during cooking).
1 lb	500 g	Eggplant	
1 lb	500 g	Onions	
4	4	Green peppers	
4 cloves	4 cloves	Garlic	
2 lb	1 kg	Tomatoes (canned may be used if necessary)	
6 oz or more as needed	200 mL or more as needed	Olive oil	2. Sauté the zucchini in a little of the olive oil until it is about half cooked. Remove from pan.
½ cup	125 mL	Chopped parsley	3. Sauté the eggplant in olive oil until half cooked. Remove from pan.
1	1	Bay leaf	4. Sauté the onions and peppers until half cooked. Add the garlic and sauté another minute.
¼ tsp	1 mL	Thyme	5. Combine all vegetables and seasonings in a brazier or heavy saucepan. Cover and cook in a slow oven (325°F/160°C) for about 30 minutes, until vegetables are tender and flavors are well blended. If the vegetables are too juicy, cook uncovered on a rangetop for a few minutes to reduce. Be careful not to scorch the vegetables on the bottom.
to taste	to taste	Salt	
to taste	to taste	Pepper	6. **Adjust seasonings.** Serve hot or cold.

Per serving:
Calories, 110; Protein, 1 g; Fat, 9 g (67% cal.); Cholesterol, 0 mg;
Carbohydrates, 9 g; Fiber, 2 g; Sodium, 5 mg.

Baking

You could, if you wished, cook carrots by placing them in a pot of boiling water, placing the pot in a hot oven, and cooking until tender. This is not a different cooking technique, however. It's plain old simmering. You'd just be using the heat of the oven rather than the rangetop to simmer the water.

When we talk about baking vegetables, we usually mean one of two things:

1. Cooking starchy vegetables, such as potatoes, winter squash, and sweet potatoes, and other moist, dense-textured vegetables such as tomatoes, beets, eggplant, onions, and turnips, from the raw to the finished state. Starch vegetables are baked because the dry heat produces a desirable texture. Baked potatoes, for example, do not have the same texture as boiled or steamed potatoes.

   In some areas, it is fashionable to refer to such baked vegetables as "roasted."

   In theory, any vegetable with enough moisture could be baked like potatoes, but the drying effects of the oven and the long cooking time make it undesirable for most small vegetables, such as peas and green beans.

2. Finishing certain vegetable combinations, sometimes known as casseroles. The vegetables in these items are usually parcooked by simmering or steaming before they are baked.

   Vegetable casseroles are baked for either of two reasons:

   - The slow, all-around heat allows the product to cook undisturbed. The agitation and stirring of rangetop cooking is not always desirable. Baked beans could be finished on top of the range, but they would be mushier and more broken. Custard-based timbales would be pourable, not firmly set.

   - The dry heat produces desirable effects, such as browning and caramelizing of sugars. For example, you could put a pan of candied sweet potatoes in a steamer, but the moist heat would not allow a glaze to form.

Procedure for Baking Vegetables

1. Collect all equipment and food products.

2. Prepare vegetables as required.

3. Place in appropriate pan and set in preheated oven.

4. Bake to desired doneness.

Baked Acorn Squash

Portions: 24   Portion size: ½ squash

U.S.	Metric	Ingredients
12	12	Acorn squash, small
as needed	as needed	Butter, melted
5 oz	150 g	Brown sugar
2½ tsp	12 mL	Salt
2 oz	60 mL	Sherry (optional)

PROCEDURE

1. Wash and cut squash in half lengthwise. Scrape out seeds. (If using large squash, cut into portion sizes.)
2. Brush cut surfaces and cavity with melted butter. Place close together cut side down on baking sheet. (This helps squash cook faster without drying by retaining steam.)
3. Bake at 350°F (175°C) until almost tender, about 30–40 minutes.
4. Turn the squash cut side up and brush again with butter. Sprinkle the cavities with sugar and salt. Add a few drops of sherry to each if desired.
5. Bake 10–15 minutes more, until surface is glazed.

Per serving:
Calories, 130; Protein, 2 g; Fat, 2 g (13% cal.); Cholesterol, 5 mg;
Carbohydrates, 28 g; Fiber, 3 g; Sodium, 270 mg.

VARIATIONS

Hubbard, buttercup, and other winter squash varieties may be cut into portion sizes and baked as in basic recipe.

Gingered Squash

Mix 1½ tsp (7 mL) powdered ginger with the sugar in basic recipe.

Puréed Squash

Bake cut Hubbard squash until tender. Remove from shell and purée in food mill. Add butter, salt, and pepper to taste.

Roasted Winter Vegetables

Portions: 16   Portion size: 4 oz (125 g)

U.S.	Metric	Ingredients
12 oz	375 g	Carrots, peeled
12 oz	375 g	Celery root, peeled
8 oz	250 g	Turnips, peeled
8 oz	250 g	Parsnips, peeled
12 oz	375 g	Waxy potatoes, peeled
8 oz	250 g	Butternut squash, peeled and seeded
12	12	Shallots, peeled
12 whole cloves	12 whole cloves	Garlic, peeled
4 oz	125 mL	Olive oil
1½ tsp	7 mL	Thyme, dried
1½ tsp	7 mL	Coarse salt
1 tsp	5 mL	Coarsely ground black pepper

PROCEDURE

1. Cut the carrots, celery root, turnips, parsnips, potatoes, and squash into 1-inch (2.5-cm) dice.
2. Place these cut vegetables, plus the shallots and garlic cloves, in a baking pan.
3. Pour the olive oil over the vegetables and sprinkle with the thyme, salt, and pepper. Toss or mix until the vegetables are well coated with oil. Add more oil if necessary.
4. Bake at 375°F (190°C) for about 45 minutes, until the vegetables are tender and lightly browned. Turn or stir the vegetables several times during baking so that they cook evenly. Do not allow them to become too browned, or they may be bitter.

Per serving:
Calories, 120; Protein, 1 g; Fat, 7 g (51% cal.); Cholesterol, 0 mg;
Carbohydrates, 14 g; Fiber, 3 g; Sodium, 230 mg.

VARIATIONS

Vegetable proportions may be varied as desired. Other vegetables, such as sweet potatoes, stalk celery, onions, and rutabagas, may be added.

Roasted Onions

Substitute 4 lb (2 kg) onions, sliced ¼ inch (5 mm) thick, for all the vegetables in the basic recipe. Bake as in the basic recipe, cooking until the onions are browned and caramelized. Onions lose a lot of moisture during baking, so total yield is only about 2¼ lb (1.1 kg).

Roasted Summer Vegetables

Omit the parsnips, turnips, celeriac, and butternut squash. Substitute an assortment of summer vegetables in desired proportions, such as eggplant, summer squash, fennel, bell peppers, cherry tomatoes, and baby turnips. Season with fresh chopped basil and parsley. For another version of Roasted Summer Vegetables, see Provençale Vegetables Confit, p. 475.

Roasted Garlic

Yield: approximately 6 oz (175 g) garlic pulp

U.S.	Metric	Ingredients	PROCEDURE
6 heads	6 heads	Garlic, whole	1. Preheat an oven to 400°F (200°C).
1 oz	30 mL	Olive oil	2. Rub the heads of garlic with olive oil.
			3. Place on a sheet pan in the oven. Roast for about 30 minutes, until soft.
			4. Remove from the oven and cool slightly.
			5. For roasted garlic pulp, cut the heads in half crosswise and squeeze out the pulp.
			6. For roasted garlic cloves to use as garnish, separate the cloves. Serve peeled or unpeeled.

Per 1 ounce:
Calories, 90; Protein, 2 g; Fat, 5 g (48% cal.); Cholesterol, 0 mg;
Carbohydrates, 10 g; Fiber, 1 g; Sodium, 5 mg.

VARIATION

For whole roasted heads of garlic to use as garnish, cut off the tops (the pointed end) of the heads before rubbing with oil.

Glazed Sweet Potatoes

Portions: 25   Portion size: 5 oz (150 g)

U.S.	Metric	Ingredients	PROCEDURE
8 lb	3.6 kg	Sweet potatoes	1. Scrub the sweet potatoes and boil or steam until nearly tender. Do not overcook.
			2. Spread the potatoes on a sheet pan to cool.
			3. Peel the potatoes when they are cool enough to handle. Remove dark spots. Cut into neat, uniform pieces for easy portioning. Arrange in a buttered baking pan.
6 oz	175 mL	Water	4. Place the water, syrup, and sugar in a saucepan. Stir over heat until sugar is dissolved. Add the remaining ingredients and boil until the mixture is reduced to about 1½ pt (700–800 mL) and forms a heavy syrup.
1½ cups	350 mL	Light corn syrup or maple syrup	
6 oz	175 g	Brown sugar	
8 oz	250 mL	Orange juice	5. Pour the syrup over the potatoes.
2 oz	60 mL	Lemon juice	6. Bake at 350°F (175°C) until potatoes are thoroughly cooked and glazed, about 45–60 minutes. Baste with the syrup several times during baking.
2 oz	60 g	Butter	
1 tsp	5 mL	Cinnamon	
¼ tsp	1 mL	Ground cloves	
½ tsp	2 mL	Salt	

Per serving:
Calories, 190; Protein, 2 g; Fat, 2 g (9% cal.); Cholesterol, 5 mg;
Carbohydrates, 44 g; Fiber, 2 g; Sodium, 100 mg.

Spinach Timbales

Portions: 15   Portion size: 3 oz (90 g)

U.S.	Metric	Ingredients	PROCEDURE
2 lb	1 kg	Cooked spinach	1. Purée the spinach in a food processor. Season to taste with salt, white pepper, and nutmeg.
to taste	to taste	Salt	
to taste	to taste	White pepper	2. Add the eggs and process another few seconds to mix well.
to taste	to taste	Nutmeg	3. Add the cream and mix in.
6	6	Eggs	4. Pass the mixture through the fine disk of a food mill.
4 oz	125 mL	Heavy cream	5. Butter the insides of 4-oz (125-mL) timbale molds. Place 3 oz (90 g) spinach mixture in each mold. Rap each one sharply on the worktable to remove air bubbles.
as needed	as needed	Butter	
			6. Set the molds in a hot-water bath and bake at 375°F (190°C) until set, about 25–40 minutes.
			7. When set, remove them from the oven. Let stand 10 minutes to allow them to settle.
			8. The timbales can be kept warm for a short time in the water bath. At service time, unmold and serve at once.

Per serving:
Calories, 80; Protein, 4 g; Fat, 6 g (66% cal.); Cholesterol, 100 mg;
Carbohydrates, 3 g; Fiber, 1 g; Sodium, 85 mg.

Southwestern Corn and Pinto Bean Gratin

Portions: 10   Portion size: 4 oz (125 g)

U.S.	Metric	Ingredients	PROCEDURE
4 oz	125 g	Onion, small dice	1. Over low heat, sweat the onion in the oil until soft but not browned.
2 oz	60 mL	Oil	
1–2 tbsp	15–30 mL	Chili powder	2. Stir in the chili powder and cook another minute.
4 oz	125 g	Red bell peppers, small dice	3. Add the red and green peppers and continue to sweat just until they begin to soften.
4 oz	125 g	Green bell peppers, small dice	
1 lb	500 g	Whole kernel corn (see note)	4. Add the corn and beans and mix. Adjust the seasoning with salt and pepper. If the mixture seems dry (the beans may absorb a lot of moisture), moisten with a little water or stock.
1 lb	500 g	Cooked pinto beans (see note)	
to taste	to taste	Salt	5. Transfer the vegetables to a shallow baking pan or gratin dish. Top with a thin layer of bread crumbs.
to taste	to taste	Pepper	
as needed	as needed	Water or chicken stock	6. Bake at 375°F (190°C) until the mixture is very hot and the top is lightly browned. If necessary, brown the top lightly under a salamander or broiler.
4 oz	125 g	Fresh white bread crumbs	

Per serving:
Calories, 190; Protein, 6 g; Fat, 7 g (0% cal.); Cholesterol, 0 mg;
Carbohydrates, 29 g; Fiber, 6 g; Sodium, 70 mg.

Note: Use either frozen corn (thawed) or fresh corn cut from the cob. If you use canned beans, first rinse them under cold water and drain well.

VARIATION

Substitute roasted fresh chiles, such as poblanos or New Mexico peppers, for all or part of the bell peppers.

Provençale Vegetables Confit

Portions: 24   Portion size: about 4 oz (125 g)

U.S.	Metric	Ingredients	PROCEDURE
1 lb	450 g	Eggplant	1. Cut the eggplant, zucchini, peppers, and fennel into batonnet. (Peel the eggplant if desired.)
1 lb 6 oz	625 g	Zucchini	
1 lb	450 g	Red bell peppers, seeded	2. Halve the cherry tomatoes and set them aside.
7 oz	200 g	Green bell peppers, seeded	3. Mix the vegetables, except the tomatoes, together with the onions, garlic, shallots, chopped basil, and thyme. Spread out on the bottom of a roasting pan and drizzle with the olive oil. Mix well until the vegetables are well coated.
1 lb 2 oz	525 g	Fennel bulb	
1 lb	450 g	Cherry tomatoes	
1 lb 8 oz	725 g	Pearl onions, peeled	
3 oz	90 g	Garlic, finely chopped	4. Cook gently at 300°F (150°C) for 1 hour.
3½ oz	100 g	Shallots, chopped	5. Add the tomatoes, then cook another 10 minutes.
1½ oz	45 g	Basil, finely chopped	6. Season to taste and serve.
2 tbsp	30 mL	Fresh thyme, finely chopped	
10 oz	300 mL	Olive oil	

Per serving:
Calories, 160; Protein, 2 g; Fat, 12 g (66% cal.); Cholesterol, 0 mg;
Carbohydrates, 12 g; Fiber, 3 g; Sodium, 80 mg.

Vegetable Strudels

Portions: 12   Portion size: 5 oz (150 g)

U.S.	Metric	Ingredients	PROCEDURE
2 oz	60 mL	Vegetable oil	1. Heat the oil in a large pan and sauté the onion until soft. Sprinkle the curry powder over the onion and mix in thoroughly.
8 oz	250 g	Onion, chopped fine	
2 tsp	5 g	Mild curry powder	
3½ oz	100 g	Carrot, chopped fine	2. Add the carrot, parsnip, turnip, and celery root to the onion in the pan and toss over high heat for 2 minutes.
7 oz	200 g	Parsnip, chopped fine	
7 oz	200 g	Turnip, chopped fine	3. Add the remaining vegetables and continue to cook for another 2 minutes. Remove from the heat, season well, and stir in the bread crumbs. Set aside.
12 oz	350 g	Celery root, chopped fine	
4 oz	125 g	Green beans, cut into ½-inch (1-cm) lengths	
8 oz	250 g	Cauliflower, cut in tiny florets	
3½ oz	100 g	Leek, white part only, finely sliced	
5 oz	150 g	Broccoli, in tiny florets	
to taste	to taste	Salt	
to taste	to taste	Pepper	
¾ oz	20 g	White bread crumbs, fresh	
12 sheets	12 sheets	Phyllo pastry	4. Cut a sheet of phyllo pastry in half crosswise and brush with melted butter. Lay one piece on top of the other; cut in half again. Repeat the buttering and layering to make a four-layered rectangle of the same proportions as the original sheet but one-fourth the size.
5 oz	150 g	Melted butter	
			5. Scatter evenly with some of the vegetable filling and roll up, tucking in the ends as you go.
			6. Repeat to use all the phyllo pastry and filling, making 12 rolls in all.
			7. Brush the strudels with melted butter and bake in a preheated oven at 375°F (190°C) for 15–20 minutes or until golden and crisp on the bases.

Per serving:
Calories, 240; Protein, 4 g; Fat, 16 g (56% cal.); Cholesterol, 26 mg; Carbohydrates, 24 g; Fiber, 4 g; Sodium, 250 mg.

Note: The variety of vegetables used can be seasonally adjusted. Sauté the vegetables in the appropriate order, according to cooking times. One large strudel can be made instead of individual ones, if desired.

Eggplants Bayaldi

Portions: 24 as a first course
12 as vegetarian main course

Portion size: ½ eggplant, about 8 oz (250 g)
Portion size: 1 eggplant

U.S.	Metric	Ingredients	PROCEDURE
12	12	Small eggplants, about 8 oz (250 g) each	1. Cut the eggplants in half lengthwise. Using a knife, carefully dig out the flesh without puncturing the skin. Set aside the flesh until you have around 2½ lb (1.2 kg).
to taste	to taste	Salt	
to taste	to taste	Cayenne	2. Place the eggplant skins on a baking sheet. Season and lightly drizzle with oil. Cook for about 5–10 minutes in the oven at 400°F (200°C). They should hold their shape but be somewhat tender.
to taste	to taste	Olive oil	
3½ oz	100 g	Garlic, chopped	3. Sweat the garlic in the olive oil. Add the eggplant flesh and cook until soft. Add 3 tbsp (20 g) chopped basil. Season to taste.
1½ oz	50 mL	Olive oil	
1½–2 oz	50 g	Basil, chopped	
to taste	to taste	Salt	
to taste	to taste	Pepper	
4 oz	125 g	Shallots	4. Sweat the shallots in the olive oil and add the tomato. Cook until thick, then mix in the remaining basil (from step 3). Season to taste with salt and cayenne.
1½ oz	50 mL	Olive oil	
4 lb 6 oz	2 kg	Tomatoes, peeled, seeded, and chopped	
to taste	to taste	Salt	
to taste	to taste	Cayenne	
12	12	Small tomatoes about 1 oz (30 g) each	5. Thinly slice the tomatoes.
14 oz	400 g	Grated Swiss cheese	6. Spread some of the tomato sauce in the bottom of the cooked eggplant skins. Top with the cooked eggplant flesh. Top with overlapping slices of tomato and sprinkle with the grated cheese. Place in a hot oven until the cheese is melted and golden brown.

Per serving:
Calories, 200; Protein, 7 g; Fat, 14 g (60% cal.); Cholesterol, 15 mg; Carbohydrates, 14 g; Fiber, 4 g; Sodium, 55 mg.

Tomato and Zucchini Tian

Portions: 12   **Portion size:** 3½ oz (100 g)

U.S.	Metric	Ingredients	PROCEDURE
1 lb 4 oz	600 g	Zucchini, large	1. Trim the ends off the zucchini and cut into very thin rounds. Quickly blanch in boiling salted water.
1 lb 8 oz	700 g	Small tomatoes (about the same diameter as the zucchini)	2. Core the tomatoes but do not peel. Cut the tomatoes in rounds the same thickness as the zucchini.
to taste	to taste	Salt	3. Place 12 ring molds, 4 inches (10 cm) in diameter, on an oiled baking sheet (see note). Inside the ring molds, alternately place the zucchini and tomato in overlapping circles. Season and drizzle with olive oil. Sprinkle with the bread crumbs. Lift off the rings and bake the vegetables in the oven for 10 minutes at 350°F (180°C).
to taste	to taste	White pepper	
2–3 oz	60–90 mL	Olive oil	
1½ oz	40 g	Fresh bread crumbs	

Per serving:
Calories, 70; Protein, 1 g; Fat, 5 g (62% cal.); Cholesterol, 0 mg; Carbohydrates, 6 g; Fiber, 1 g; Sodium, 25 mg.

Note: If you have only one ring mold, simply fill it as directed, lift off, and repeat for the remaining tians.

Baked Beans, New England Style

Portions: 20   Portion size: 4½ oz (125 g)

U.S.	Metric	Ingredients	PROCEDURE
2 lb	900 g	Dried beans, navy or Great Northern	1. Soak the beans overnight in enough water to cover by 2 inches (5 cm).
		Bouquet garni:	2. Place the beans and liquid in a pot and add the bouquet garni. Bring to a boil and skim foam. Reduce heat to a simmer. Cover
1	1	Bay leaf	and simmer 45 minutes–1 hour or until beans are just tender
6–8	6–8	Parsley stems	but not soft. Add more water if necessary during cooking.
¼ tsp	1 mL	Thyme	3. Drain the beans, reserving the cooking liquid. Discard the
		A few celery tops	bouquet garni.
1 cup	250 mL	Molasses	4. Mix together the molasses, brown sugar, dry mustard, salt, and 1 qt (1 L) of the bean cooking liquid. If there is not
2 oz	60 g	Brown sugar	enough bean liquid, add water to make up the difference.
1 tbsp	15 mL	Dry mustard	5. Mix the beans, molasses mixture, and salt pork in a 4-qt
1 tbsp	15 mL	Salt	(4-L) pot or deep baking pan.
8 oz	225 g	Salt pork, medium dice	6. Bake, covered, at 300°F (150°C) for 2–2½ hours. Add more liquid if necessary during baking.

Per serving:
Calories, 290; Protein, 10 g; Fat, 10 g (31% cal.); Cholesterol, 10 mg; Carbohydrates, 41 g; Fiber, 7 g; Sodium, 520 mg.

VARIATION

Michigan Baked Beans

Reduce molasses to ¼ cup (60 mL) and add 2 cups (500 mL) tomato sauce or tomato purée.

Broiling and Grilling

Grilled quick-cooking vegetables such as peppers, zucchini, large mushroom caps, and eggplant are pleasant accompaniments to grilled and roasted meats and poultry. Cut the vegetables into broad slices, brush with oil, and grill until lightly cooked and lightly browned. Heavy browning may produce an unpleasant burned taste. Grilled vegetables are often dressed with vinaigrette.

Broiling is also used to finish cooked or partially cooked vegetables by browning or glazing them on top. Bread crumbs are sometimes used to give a pleasing brown color and to prevent drying. Casseroles or gratin dishes that do not brown sufficiently in the oven may be browned for a few seconds under the broiler or salamander.

Broiled Tomato Slices

Portions: 10   Portion size: about 2 slices
                                    3–4 oz (100 g)

U.S.	Metric	Ingredients	PROCEDURE
2½ lb	1.1 kg	Tomatoes	1. Wash the tomatoes, cut out the core ends, and slice cross-
2 oz	60 g	Butter, melted (or olive oil)	wise into ½-inch (1-cm) slices.
to taste	to taste	Salt	2. Place the slices in a single layer on an oiled baking sheet.
to taste	to taste	White pepper	3. Drizzle melted butter or oil over the tomatoes and sprinkle
			with salt and pepper.
			4. Place in a broiler, 4 inches (10 cm) from the heat, and broil
			just until bubbling and hot but still firm enough to hold
			shape.
			5. Serve 2 slices per portion, depending on size.
		Optional topping:	To use optional ingredients, cook tomatoes halfway.
1 cup	100 g	Dry bread crumbs	Combine topping ingredients and sprinkle over tomatoes.
4 oz	100 g	Melted butter or olive oil	Brown under broiler.
1 oz	30 g	Onion, minced very fine	

Per serving:
Calories, 60; Protein, 1 g; Fat, 5 g (65% cal.); Cholesterol, 10 mg;
Carbohydrates, 5 g; Fiber, 1 g; Sodium, 55 mg.

VARIATIONS

Herbed Broiled Tomatoes

Top tomatoes with ¼ cup (60 mL) chopped parsley and ½ tsp (2 mL) basil or oregano before broiling, or mix herbs with crumb topping.

Parmesan Broiled Tomatoes

Add ½ cup (125 mL) grated parmesan cheese to crumb topping.

Grilled Vegetable Medley

Yield: about 3 lb (1.5 kg)   Portions: 9   Portion size: 5 oz (150 g)

U.S.	Metric	Ingredients	PROCEDURE
3 3½ lb	1.5–1.75 kg	Assorted vegetables:	1. Prepare the vegetables: Trim off the stem ends of the eggplants
		Small eggplants	and cut them lengthwise into thick slices. If they are very
		Zucchini	small, just cut them in half lengthwise. Trim the stem ends of
		Yellow summer squash	the zucchini and yellow squash. Cut lengthwise into thick
		Bell peppers	slices. Core and seed the peppers and cut into quarters length-
		Radicchio	wise. Remove any bruised outer leaves of the radicchio and cut
		Large onions	in halves or quarters through the base, leaving the core in to
			hold the leaves together. Cut the onion into thick slices, hold-
as needed	as needed	Olive oil	ing the rings of each slice together with a bamboo skewer.
to taste	to taste	Salt	2. Brush the vegetables with olive oil and sprinkle them with
as needed	as needed	Balsamic vinegar	salt.
			3. Grill the vegetables over medium heat, turning as necessary,
			until they are tender and lightly grill-marked. Cooking time
			will vary for different vegetables. Regulate the heat or distance
			from the flame so that the vegetables cook without browning
			too much.
			4. Remove from the grill and brush with a little balsamic vinegar,
			and, if desired, a little more olive oil. Serve warm.

Per serving:
Calories, 180; Protein, 1 g; Fat, 16 g (78% cal.); Cholesterol, 0 mg;
Carbohydrates, 9 g; Fiber, 2 g; Sodium, 10 mg.

VARIATIONS

Other vegetables and vegetable assortments may be grilled in the same manner. Suggestions include large mushroom caps, Belgian endive, blanched potatoes, fennel, asparagus, leeks, and scallions.

Grilled vegetables may be served with various sauces, such as aioli, sauce Vierge, salsa cruda, and vinaigrette variations.

Deep-frying

The principles of deep-frying that you have already learned are applied to vegetables as well as to other foods.

- Review "Deep-frying," Chapter 4, page 60.
- Review "Breadings" and "Batters," Chapter 7, pages 120–122.

Potatoes (covered in the next chapter) and onion rings are the most popular fried vegetables, but many others may be fried, too.

Deep-fried vegetables may be divided into five categories:

1. Vegetables dipped in batter and fried.

2. Vegetables breaded and fried.

3. Vegetables fried without a coating.

   Potatoes are the obvious example. Other starchy vegetables, such as sweet potatoes, may be fried without breading or batter if they are cut thin to reduce cooking time. The sugar in them burns easily if they are cooked too long.

   Thin slices and shavings of vegetables, deep-fried until light and crisp, make attractive and interesting garnish for many dishes. Root vegetables, such as beets, celery root, and parsnips, can be sliced thin and fried like potato chips (slice long roots like parsnips lengthwise). Other vegetables, such as leeks and celery, can be cut into thin shreds or julienne and fried. These may be dusted in flour before frying.

4. Small vegetables or cuts mixed with a batter and dropped with a scoop into hot fat. The term *fritter* is used for this preparation, as well as for that in category 1.

5. *Croquettes:* thick vegetable purées or mixtures of small pieces of vegetable and a heavy béchamel or other binder, formed into shapes, breaded, and fried.

Procedure for Deep-Frying Vegetables

1. Collect all equipment and food products.

2. Preheat fryer to proper temperature.
   Most vegetables are fried at 325° to 350°F (160° to 175°C).

3. Prepare food items as required. Apply breading or batter if necessary.

4. Place proper amount of food in fryer—do not overload.

5. Fry to desired doneness.

6. Remove food from fryer and let fat drain from it.

7. Serve at once, or, if necessary, hold uncovered in a warm place for the shortest possible time.

VEGETABLES FOR DEEP-FRYING

Most vegetables large enough to coat with breading or batter may be fried. Tender, quick-cooking vegetables can be fried raw. Others may be precooked by simmering or steaming briefly to reduce the cooking time they need in the frying fat.

Raw vegetables for frying in breading or batter:

Eggplant	Peppers
Mushrooms	Tomatoes
Onion rings	Zucchini

Blanched or precooked vegetables for frying in breading or batter:

Artichoke hearts	Celery
Asparagus	Celery root
Beans, green and yellow	Cucumbers
Broccoli	Fennel
Brussels sprouts	Okra
Carrots	Parsnips
Cauliflower	Turnips

Onion Rings

Portions: 20   Portion size: 3 oz (90 g), 8–10 pieces

U.S.	Metric	Ingredients	PROCEDURE
2	2	Eggs, beaten	1. Combine the eggs and milk in a bowl.
1 pt	500 mL	Milk	2. Mix the flour, baking powder, salt, and paprika together and add to the milk. Mix well. The batter should have the consistency of a thin pancake batter.
10 oz	300 g	Cake flour	
2 tsp	10 mL	Baking powder	
½ tsp	2 mL	Salt	
½ tsp	2 mL	Paprika (optional: for color)	
3 lb	1.4 kg	Large onions	3. Peel the onions and cut crosswise into ¼-inch (½-cm) slices. Separate into rings (save unusable pieces for another purpose).
as needed	as needed	Flour	4. Place the onions in cold water if they are not used immediately to maintain crispness.
			5. Drain and dry the onions thoroughly.
			6. Dredge with flour and shake off excess. (This step isn't always necessary, but it helps the batter adhere.)
			7. Dip a few pieces at a time in the batter and fry in deep fat (350°F/175°C) until golden brown.
			8. Drain and serve immediately.

Per serving:
Calories, 130; Protein, 3 g; Fat, 6 g (40% cal.); Cholesterol, 20 mg; Carbohydrates, 17 g; Fiber, 1 g, Sodium, 95 mg.

VARIATIONS

Beer Batter

Substitute light beer for the milk. Omit baking powder because the carbonation of the beer acts as a leavener.

Buttermilk Batter

Substitute buttermilk for the milk and use 1 tsp (5 mL) baking soda instead of the 2 tsp (10 mL) baking powder.

Other Fried Vegetables

Any of the vegetables on the list at the beginning of this section may be fried in these batters.

Pea Fritters with Sesame

Yield: about 2 lb (1 kg)   Portions: 10   Portion size: 4 fritters, about ¾ oz (25 g) each

U.S.	Metric	Ingredients	PROCEDURE
3 lb	1.5 kg	Peas, fresh or frozen	1. Bring a large pan of water to a boil and simmer the peas for 8 minutes or until tender. Drain thoroughly and process in a food processor or blender to a very thick paste. Push through a fine sieve to remove the skins.
4 tsp	20 g	Butter, softened	
3	3	Egg yolks	
3 tbsp	20 g	Fresh mint leaves, chopped fine	
to taste	to taste	Salt	2. Beat the softened butter and egg yolks into the pea mixture and add the chopped mint. Season well to taste and chill until firm.
to taste	to taste	Pepper	
6 oz	175 g	Flour	3. Shape the pea mixture into slightly flattened patties, approximately 2 inches (5 cm) in diameter.
to taste	to taste	Salt	
to taste	to taste	White pepper	4. Prepare a Standard Breading Procedure, seasoning the flour with salt and white pepper and mixing the sesame seeds with the bread crumbs.
3	3	Whole eggs, beaten	
4 oz	125 g	Sesame seeds	
4 oz	125 g	Dry bread crumbs	5. Pass the pea patties through the breading procedure. Chill for 30 minutes.
as needed	as needed	Mint leaves for garnish	6. Deep-fry the fritters in batches at 350°F (180°C) until golden. Drain and serve warm, garnished with mint leaves.

Per serving:
Calories, 360; Protein, 13 g; Fat, 18 g (45% cal.); Cholesterol, 115 mg; Carbohydrates, 37 g; Fiber, 9 g; Sodium, 110 mg.

Celery Leaf Fritters

Portions: 12   Portion size: about 4 oz (125 g)

U.S.	Metric	Ingredients	PROCEDURE
8 oz	250 g	Flour	1. Mix together the flour, salt, and melted butter.
1 tsp	5 g	Salt	2. Gradually mix in the cold water until a thin batter forms. It should be about the consistency of a crêpe batter.
2¾ oz	80 mL	Butter, melted	
12–13 oz	400 mL	Cold water	3. Fold in the beaten egg whites.
4	4	Egg whites, beaten to stiff peaks	
96 pieces (8 per portion)	96 pieces (8 per portion)	Leafy celery tops	4. Dip the celery leaves into the batter, then drop into a deep fryer heated to 350°F (180°C).
			5. Serve immediately.

Per serving:
Calories, 130; Protein, 3 g; Fat, 8 g (55% cal.); Cholesterol, 10 mg; Carbohydrates, 12 g; Fiber, 1 g; Sodium, 220 mg.

Vegetable Fritters

Portions: 20   Portion size: 3 oz (90 g)
2 pieces

U.S.	Metric	Ingredients	PROCEDURE
		Batter:	1. Combine the eggs and milk.
6	6	Eggs, beaten	2. Mix together the flour, baking powder, salt, and sugar. Add to the milk and eggs and mix until smooth.
1 pt	500 mL	Milk	
1 lb	500 g	Flour	3. Let the batter stand for several hours in a refrigerator.
2 tbsp	30 mL	Baking powder	
1 tsp	5 mL	Salt	
1 oz	30 g	Sugar	
1½ lb EP	700 g EP	Vegetables: Choice of corn, cooked diced carrots, baby lima beans, diced asparagus, diced celery or celery root, turnip, eggplant, cauliflower, zucchini, parsnips	4. Stir the cold, cooked vegetables into the batter.
			5. Drop with a No. 24 scoop into deep fat at 350°F (175°C). Hold the scoop just above the hot fat when dropping. Fry until golden brown.
			6. Drain well and serve.

Per serving:
Calories, 140; Protein, 4 g; Fat, 6 g (37% cal.); Cholesterol, 45 mg; Carbohydrates, 19 g; Fiber, 1 g; Sodium, 230 mg.

VARIATIONS

For lighter fritters, beat egg whites separately and fold into batter.

Fruit Fritters

Increase sugar to 2 oz (60 g). Use fresh, frozen, or canned fruits such as blueberries, diced pineapple, or apple. Fruit must be well drained. Dust each portion with powdered sugar at service time. (Batter may be seasoned with cinnamon, vanilla, brandy, or other appropriate flavoring.)

Some Suggested Vegetable Seasonings, Flavorings, and Combinations

Asparagus	Lemon juice, brown butter, mustard sauce, parmesan cheese; hard-cooked egg, peas, artichokes, mushrooms
Beans, green	Dill, basil, tarragon, oregano, garlic, brown butter, soy sauce; almonds, sesame seed, onion, tomato, celery, mushrooms, bacon
Beans, lima	Oregano, sage, thyme, sour cream, cheddar cheese; corn, peas, onions, mushrooms, pimiento, bacon
Beets	Lemon, allspice, caraway, cloves, dill, ginger, horseradish, bay leaf, orange, sour cream, onion
Broccoli	Lemon, mustard sauce, almonds, buttered toasted bread crumbs, hard-cooked egg
Brussels sprouts	Caraway, dill, parmesan cheese, cheddar cheese, chestnuts
Cabbage	Caraway, celery seed, dill, mustard, nutmeg, garlic; bacon, ham, carrots, onion
Carrots	Parsley, dill, fennel, tarragon, ginger, nutmeg, bay leaves, caraway, mint, orange; celery, peas, zucchini
Cauliflower	Dill, nutmeg, mustard, curry, cheese, tomato sauce; hard-cooked egg, peas, almonds
Celery	Parsley, tarragon, onion, green or red pepper, potatoes
Corn	Chili powder, mild cheddar or jack cheese, tomato, bacon, lima beans
Cucumber	Dill, garlic, mint, tarragon; peas
Eggplant	Garlic, marjoram, oregano, parsley, parmesan cheese; tomato, chopped walnuts
Mushrooms	Nutmeg, parsley, lemon, paprika, dill, sherry, parmesan cheese, cayenne, heavy cream; peas, spinach, artichokes, green beans
Okra	Garlic, coriander, sage; tomatoes, corn
Onions	Nutmeg, sage, thyme, cheese sauce, sour cream; peas
Peas	Mint, basil, dill, sage; mushrooms, pearl onions, turnips, potatoes, carrots, water chestnuts, Jerusalem artichokes
Spinach	Nutmeg, garlic, heavy cream; mushrooms, hard-cooked egg, cheese
Squash, summer (including zucchini)	Cumin, basil, oregano, mustard seed, rosemary, garlic, parmesan cheese, parsley; tomato, carrots (with zucchini), onion, almonds, walnuts
Squash, winter	Cinnamon, nutmeg, allspice, cloves, ginger; apples, bacon, pecans
Sweet potatoes	Allspice, cinnamon, cloves, nutmeg, ginger, brandy, orange; almonds, apples, bananas
Tomatoes	Basil, bay leaf, garlic, celery seed, oregano, thyme, rosemary, chili powder; peppers, black olives
Turnips	Parsley, chives, nutmeg; mushrooms, potatoes, peas

Questions for Discussion

1. Which of the following vegetables would you simmer uncovered?

Asparagus	Cauliflower
Green beans	Peas
Beets	Sweet potatoes
Brussels sprouts	Rutabagas
Carrots	Turnips

2. Why are greens such as spinach not well suited to cooking in a compartment steamer?

3. In the recipe for Peas, Carrots, and Pearl Onions (p. 457), why could you not save a step and cook the three vegetables together in one pot?

4. Why is it important to drain vegetables well before combining with a cream sauce?

5. Which of the two methods for making glazed root vegetables (see Glazed Root Vegetables, p. 465, and Glazed Carrots, p. 465) might be more appropriate for à la carte service, or cooking to order? Why?

6. We have learned that green vegetables are supposed to be cooked in a neutral liquid because acids destroy green pigments. But the recipe for artichokes says to cook them with lemon juice. What's going on here?

7. Describe briefly how you would make breaded, fried onion rings rather than onion rings with batter.

chapter 18

Potatoes and Other Starches

The eating habits of most nations place a great deal of importance on a category of foods we call starches. In North America and Europe, the most important of these foods are potatoes, rice, pasta, and bread. It is true that we do not depend on these high-carbohydrate foods as much as many of the world's people do who eat far less meat than we do. Nevertheless, starches appear at nearly all our meals.

Because we eat them often and have devised a great many ways of preparing them, starchy foods require extra study beyond that which we have given to other vegetables. In this chapter, we turn our attention primarily to the preparation of potatoes, rice, and pasta, and we also take a short detour to look at other grains as well as a group of products called dumplings.

Potatoes

The potato is in the strange position of being one of the most popular foods and, at the same time, one of the most neglected. The potato is among the most important staple foods in our kitchens. And because it functions both as a vegetable and as a starch, it appears in all three meals more often than any other food.

Sadly, however, the potato is so often taken for granted that it is nothing more than the second half of the phrase "meat and potatoes," something everyone wants plenty of but no one pays much attention to. So instead of steaming, snowy-white baked potatoes and crispy, golden, flavorful hashed browns, we are often served heavy, soggy, gray baked potatoes and burned, greasy, tasteless hashed browns.

Because potatoes are so popular, the experienced cook knows how to gain the enthusiasm of customers with well-prepared potato items. Because they can be prepared in so many ways, they add variety to the menu. Offer your customers something in addition to the same old "baked, French fries, and mashed."

Understanding Potatoes

TYPES

Potatoes are classified according to their starch content. The amount of starch determines the use for which they are most suitable.

1. **Waxy or new potatoes.**
   High moisture content, high sugar content, low starch content.

   Usually small and round in shape, but some varieties can be large, and some may be elongated in shape. Flesh is white, yellow, or even blue or purple. Skin is white, red, yellow, or blue.

   Hold shape well when cooked. Firm, moist texture.

   Use for boiling whole, for salads, soups, hashed browns, and any preparation where the potato must hold its shape.

   Do not use for deep-frying. High sugar content will cause dark streaks and poor texture.

2. **Mature or starchy potatoes.**
   High starch content, low moisture and sugar. Light, dry, and mealy when cooked.

   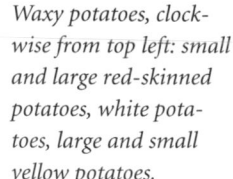

   - **Russets or Idahos.**
     Long, regularly shaped potatoes with slightly rough skin.

     Ideal for baking. Best potato for French fries because the high starch content produces an even, golden color and good texture. Also, the regular shape means little trimming loss.

Waxy potatoes, clockwise from top left: small and large red-skinned potatoes, white potatoes, large and small yellow potatoes.

After reading this chapter, you should be able to

1. Classify potatoes into two types, describe the general properties of each type, and identify the most suitable cooking method for each type.

2. Identify characteristics of high-quality potatoes and describe how to store them.

3. Cook potatoes by boiling and steaming.

4. Prepare potato purée.

5. Cook potatoes by baking, sautéing, pan-frying, and deep-frying.

6. Distinguish five major types of rice.

7. Prepare rice by boiling and steaming and by the pilaf and risotto methods.

8. Distinguish the major kinds and shapes of commercial pasta and determine their quality.

9. Identify the ingredients in the best commercial pastas and identify the common characteristics of these pastas.

10. Prepare fresh and commercial pasta, and list the steps involved in the alternate steamtable method of its preparation.

May be used for mashing, but is generally too expensive.

Sizes are indicated by count per 50-pound carton. For example, 100s average 8 oz each.

- **All-purpose** (sometimes called *chef potatoes*).

  Not always as dry and starchy as russets.

  Irregularly shaped, less expensive than russets.

  Suitable for most purposes except baking (due to shape). Especially useful for puréeing or mashing, or any preparation in which the shape of the whole potato is not important.

  Note: Very knobby potatoes are wasteful when pared in a mechanical peeler.

CHECKING FOR QUALITY

Look for these signs of high-quality potatoes:

1. Firm and smooth, not soft or shriveled.
2. Dry skins.
3. Shallow eyes.
4. No sprouts. Sprouting potatoes are high in sugar.
5. No green color. Green areas develop on potatoes stored in light. These areas contain a substance called *solanine*, which has a bitter taste and is poisonous in large quantities. All green parts should be cut off before cooking.
6. Absence of cracks, blemishes, and rotten spots.

Starchy potatoes, left to right: russet potatoes, all-purpose or chef potatoes.

STORING

Keep in a cool, dry, dark place, ideally at 55° to 60°F (13° to 16°C). If they will be used quickly, you may keep them at room temperature.

Do not refrigerate. Temperatures below 45°F (7°C) convert potato starch to sugar. Refrigerated potatoes must be stored at 50°F (10°C) for two weeks to change the sugar back to starch.

New potatoes do not keep well. Purchase only one week's supply at a time.

MARKET FORMS

The demands of time and labor have made processed potato products widely used, and many forms are available. Many of these products are very good, and there is no doubt that they save time. However, for best quality, there is no substitute for fresh potatoes, *if they are well prepared.*

1. **Fresh, unprocessed.**
2. **Peeled. Treated to prevent browning.**
   Keep refrigerated (below 40°F/4°C) for five to seven days.
3. **Canned whole, cooked.**
4. **French fries. Blanched in deep fat and frozen.**
   Available in wide variety of sizes and cuts. Cook from the frozen state.
   Refrigerated French fries are also available.
5. **Other frozen, prepared products.**
   Available as hashed browns, puffs, stuffed baked, and croquettes; in casseroles with a variety of sauces.
6. **Dehydrated.**
   Granules or flakes for mashed potatoes to be reconstituted with hot water or milk and butter or other desired flavorings.
   Other products: many varieties and preparations. May need soaking in water before cooking.

Cooking Potatoes

Some potato recipes are simple, but many are complex and use a combination of cooking methods. For example, to make potato croquettes, you must first boil or steam the potatoes, purée them and combine the purée with other ingredients, shape them, bread them, and, finally, deep-fry them.

Cooking methods are essentially the same as the methods for vegetables in the previous chapter. If necessary, review these methods before proceeding with the following recipes.

BOILING AND STEAMING POTATOES

These methods for cooking potatoes are given in the first recipe in this section. Boiled or steamed potatoes are served as is and are also the basis for many other preparations.

Two points should be noted:

1. Boiled potatoes are generally started in cold water rather than hot. This allows for more even cooking and heat penetration from outside to inside during the relatively long cooking time required.

2. Potatoes are never cooled in cold water, unlike most vegetables. This would make them soggy.

Figure 18.1 Tournéing potatoes and other root vegetables.

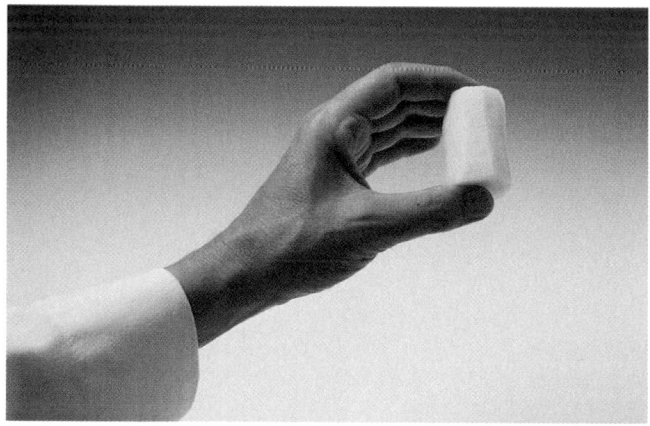

(a) Cut the potatoes roughly into pieces slightly larger than the final size desired. Cut off the top and bottom of each piece so that they are flat and parallel.

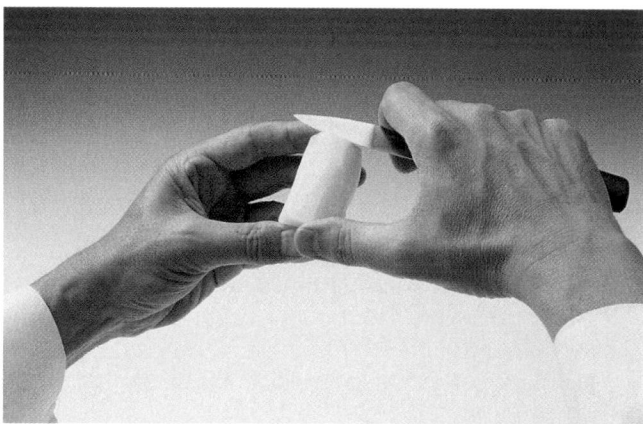

(b) Hold the potato between the thumb and forefinger and place the paring knife against the top edge as shown and the thumb of the cutting hand firmly against the potato. Your hand should be far enough up on the blade to maintain steady control.

(c) Cut downward toward your thumb with a curving movement of the blade.

(d) Turn the potato slightly (one-seventh of a full turn, to be exact) and repeat the motion.

(e) The finished product. If perfectly done, the potato has seven sides (but customers rarely count them).

Figure 18.2 Cutting parisienne potatoes.

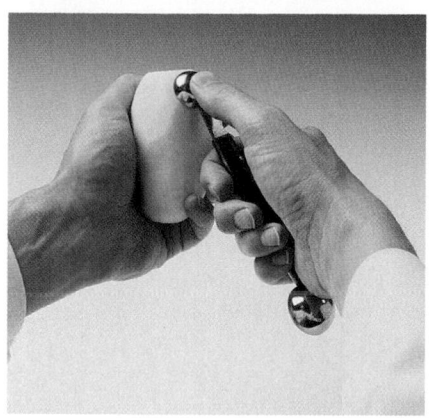

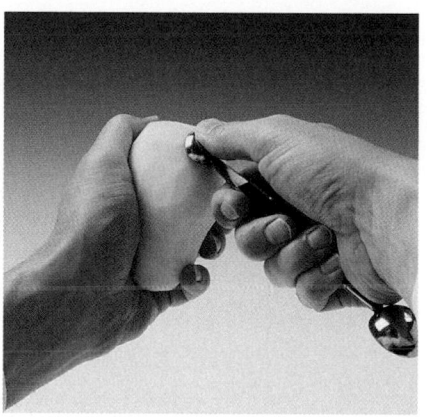

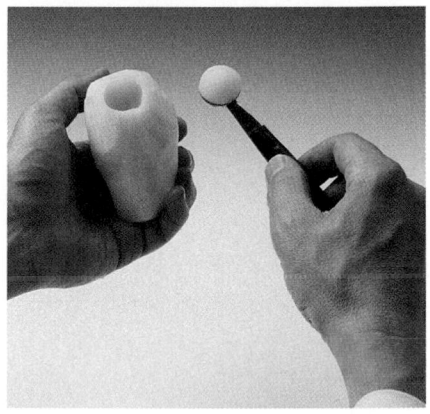

(a) Place the ball cutter against the potato as shown.

(b) With the thumb, press the cutter firmly into the potato as far as it will go.

(c) Lift the handle of the cutter outward, twist the cutter around, and remove the ball.

 ## Boiled Potatoes (Pommes Natures)

Portions: 25   **Portion size:** 5 oz (150 g)

U.S.	Metric	Ingredients
10 lb	4.5 kg	Potatoes

PROCEDURE

1. Peel and eye potatoes. Be sure that all traces of dark peel are removed.
2. Cut potatoes into 25 uniform portions, 1 or 2 pieces per portion. Trim pieces to shape (see note). Save the trimmings for other use.
3. Place in a pot and cover with salted water. Bring to boil, lower heat, and simmer until tender.
4. Drain and let the potatoes steam dry in the colander for 1 minute.
5. Serve immediately or place in a hotel pan, cover with a clean, damp towel, and hold for service.

Per serving:
Calories, 140; Protein, 3 g; Fat, 0 g (0% cal.); Cholesterol, 0 mg; Carbohydrates, 32 g; Fiber, 3 g; Sodium, 10 mg.

Note: Potatoes may be cut, shaped, or trimmed as desired. They may be left in neat but irregular shapes, trimmed or tournéed into large, medium, or small sizes (see Figure 18.1), or cut with a ball scoop (see Figure 18.2) for parisienne boiled potatoes. Allow for greater trimming loss if preparing tournéed or parisienne potatoes.

VARIATIONS

Steamed Potatoes (Pommes Vapeurs)

Prepare as in basic recipe, but steam in perforated pan instead of boiling.

Parsley Potatoes

Prepare as in basic recipe. Brush or pour 4 oz (125 mL) melted butter onto the potatoes and sprinkle with chopped parsley.

New Potatoes

Prepare as in basic recipe, using small new potatoes. Scrub well but do not peel. Serve 1–3 per portion, depending on size. Optional: Peel a narrow band around potato before cooking to prevent skin from splitting.

Creamed Potatoes

Prepare new potatoes or all-purpose potatoes as in basic recipe. Cut or slice to desired size, or leave small new potatoes whole. Combine with 2 qt (2 L) hot cream sauce. Heat over low heat, but do not boil, and hold for service.

Hungarian Potatoes

Portions: 25   Portion size: 4 oz (125 g)

U.S.	Metric	Ingredients	PROCEDURE
4 oz	125 g	Butter	1. Heat the butter in a large saucepan and add the onion and paprika. Cook until onion is soft.
8 oz	250 g	Onion, chopped	
2 tsp	10 mL	Paprika	2. Add the tomatoes and potatoes. Pour in enough stock just to cover the potatoes. Add a small amount of salt (about 2 tsp/10 mL), but undersalt because liquid will reduce.
1 lb	500 g	Tomatoes, peeled, seeded, diced	
5 lb	2.5 kg	Potatoes, peeled and cut into thick slices	3. Simmer until potatoes are cooked and liquid is mostly evaporated or absorbed. Stir gently from time to time.
1 qt (approximately)	1 L (approximately)	Chicken or beef stock, hot	4. Season to taste.
to taste	to taste	Salt	5. Garnish with chopped parsley at service time.
to taste	to taste	Pepper	
½ cup	125 mL	Chopped parsley	

Per serving:
Calories, 110; Protein, 2 g; Fat, 4 g (31% cal.); Cholesterol, 10 mg;
Carbohydrates, 18 g; Fiber, 2 g; Sodium, 45 mg.

VARIATION

Bouillon Potatoes

Prepare as in basic recipe but omit paprika and tomatoes. Slice onion instead of chopping it, and sauté 6 oz (175 g) carrot, cut julienne, with the onion. Trim the potatoes into portion-size pieces instead of slicing them.

POTATO PURÉE

Potato purée is an important product in most kitchens, even though it is not served as is. It is the basis of many popular preparations, including mashed or whipped potatoes, duchesse potatoes, and potato croquettes. (Please note that this usage of the term is different from classic European usage, where *purée de pommes de terre* means mashed or whipped potatoes.)

In order to prepare these products successfully, you must first understand the method for making a basic purée.

Procedure for Making Potato Purée

1. Select starchy potatoes rather than new or waxy potatoes.

2. Wash, peel, and eye carefully.

3. Cut into uniform sizes for even cooking.

4. Simmer or steam until tender. Potatoes for purée must be thoroughly cooked or the purée will be grainy. But they must not be overcooked, or they will be watery.

5. Drain in a colander (if simmered). Set the colander on a sheet pan and place in an oven for several minutes to dry out the potatoes. If potatoes are too moist, they will be too loose or slack when additional liquid is added later.

6. Pass the potatoes through a food mill or ricer to purée. A mixer with the paddle attachment may be used to break up the potatoes for whipped potatoes, but there is no guarantee that it will remove all lumps.

   Equipment used for puréeing should not be cold, or it will cool the potatoes too much. Heat equipment under hot water before use.

Duchesse Potatoes

Portions: 25   Portion size: 4 oz (100 g)

U.S.	Metric	Ingredients	PROCEDURE
7 lb	3 kg	Potatoes, peeled and quartered	1. Steam the potatoes or simmer them in salted water until tender. Drain in a colander and let dry in an oven for several minutes.
4 oz	100 g	Butter, melted	2. Pass the potatoes through a food mill or ricer.
to taste	to taste	Salt	3. Add butter and mix to a smooth paste. Season to taste with salt, pepper, and just a little nutmeg (the potatoes should not taste strongly of nutmeg).
to taste	to taste	White pepper	
to taste	to taste	Nutmeg	4. If the potatoes are very moist, stir over a low flame to stiffen. *They must be much stiffer than mashed potatoes.*
10	10	Egg yolks	5. Add the egg yolks (off the fire) and beat until smooth.
			6. Put the mixture in a pastry bag with a star tube and bag out into desired shapes on sheet pans or as platter borders (see Figure 18.3). Cone-shaped spiral mounds are most popular for individual portion service.
as needed	as needed	Egg wash (optional)	7. If desired, brush lightly with egg wash for greater browning.
			8. At service time, place potatoes in hot oven (400°–425°F/200°–230°C) until lightly browned. Platter borders may be browned under the salamander.

Per serving:
Calories, 150; Protein, 3 g; Fat, 6 g (34% cal.); Cholesterol, 95 mg;
Carbohydrates, 23 g; Fiber, 2 g; Sodium, 45 mg.

VARIATION

Duchesse potato mixture is also used as the base for Potato Croquettes (p. 502) and is considered one of the basic hot kitchen preparations.

Whipped or Mashed Potatoes

Portions: 25   Portion size: 5 oz (150 g)

U.S.	Metric	Ingredients	PROCEDURE
9 lb	4 kg	Potatoes	1. Peel and eye the potatoes and cut them into uniform sizes. Simmer in salted water to cover until tender.
6 oz	175 g	Butter	2. Drain well and let the potatoes steam dry for a few minutes.
1 cup	250 mL	Light cream, hot	3. Pass the potatoes through a food mill or ricer into the bowl of a mixer. Alternative method: Place potatoes in mixer with paddle attachment. Mix until well broken up. Replace paddle with whip and beat until well puréed. Do not over-whip, or potatoes will become pasty.
as needed	as needed	Milk, hot	
to taste	to taste	Salt	4. Beat in butter, then cream.
to taste	to taste	White pepper	5. Add enough hot milk to bring potatoes to proper consistency. They should be soft and moist, but firm enough to hold their shape, not runny.
			6. Add salt and white pepper to taste.
			7. Whip *briefly* at high speed until potatoes are light and fluffy. Do not overwhip.

Per serving:
Calories, 190; Protein, 3 g; Fat, 8 g (36% cal.); Cholesterol, 20 mg;
Carbohydrates, 29 g; Fiber, 3 g; Sodium, 65 mg.

VARIATIONS

Garlic Whipped Potatoes

Method 1: Simmer 6–8 whole, peeled cloves of garlic with the potatoes. Purée the garlic and the potatoes together.
Method 2: Purée 1 or 2 heads roasted garlic (p. 474) and mix into the potatoes before adding cream.

Ancho Whipped Potatoes

Add Ancho Sauce (p. 734) to taste to whipped potatoes before adding milk. Reduce the quantity of milk as necessary to achieve the proper consistency.

Figure 18.3 Using the pastry bag: duchesse potatoes.

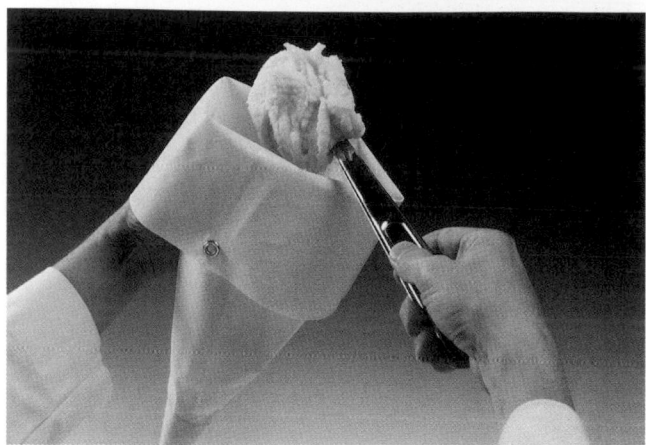

(a) *Turn down the top of the pastry bag as shown. Slip your hand under this collar and hold the top open with your thumb and forefinger while you fill it with duchesse potato mixture.*

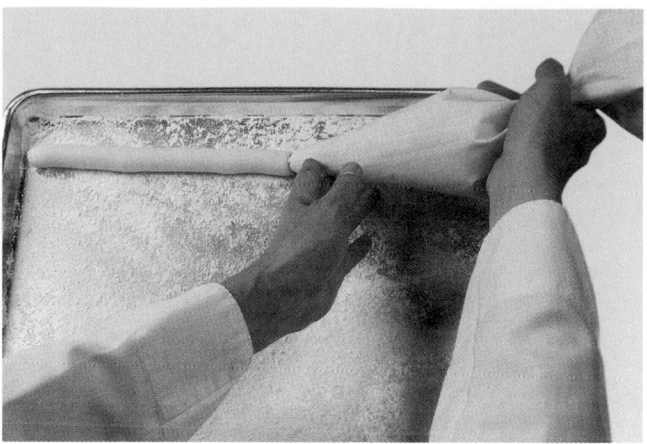

(b) *Turn the top of the bag up again and gather the loose top together again as shown. Hold the bag shut with your thumb and forefinger. To force out the potatoes, squeeze the top of the bag in the palm of your hand. Use your free hand to guide the tip or hold the item being filled or decorated. You can make potato croquettes quickly by forcing out the potato mixture in long strips, using a large plain tube. Cut the strips into 2-inch (5-cm) lengths with a knife.*

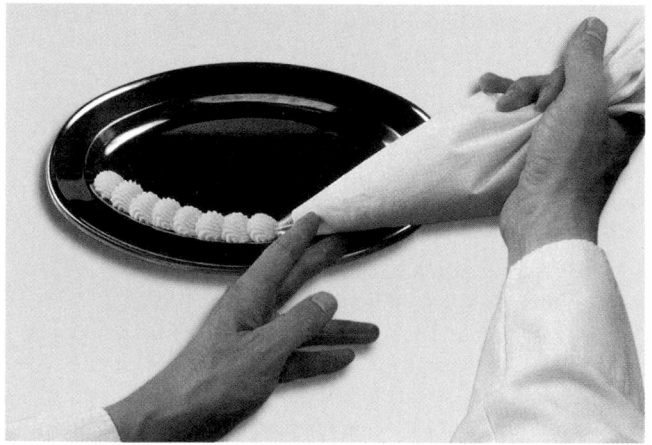

(c) *Duchesse potatoes are often used to decorate platters, as in this illustration. This technique is also used in decorating cakes and desserts with icing, whipped cream, or meringue.*

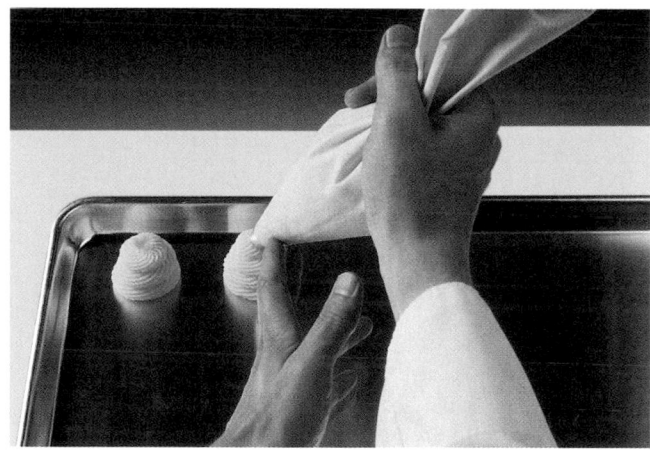

(d) *Single portions of duchesse potatoes are usually piped out into a tall spiral shape. They are then browned in the oven.*

(e) *Dauphine and Lorette Potatoes (see recipes, p. 502) may be bagged out into many shapes, such as these small stars. Some cookies are also shaped this way.*

BAKING

Preparing baked potatoes is a simple procedure, which, for some reason, is widely misunderstood and needlessly complicated. Properly baked potatoes are white, fluffy, mealy, and steamy. Poorly baked potatoes, unfortunately common, are gray and soggy.

Procedure for Baking Potatoes

1. Select russet potatoes or other regularly shaped starchy potatoes.
2. Scrub well and pierce the ends with a fork or skewer so steam can escape.
3. For crisp skins, rub lightly with oil. For more tender skins, leave dry.
4. Place on sheet pans or on sheet pan racks in a preheated 400°F (200°C) oven and bake until done, about 1 hour. To test doneness, squeeze gently. Done potatoes yield to gentle pressure.
    Note: Using sheet pan racks eliminates the hard spot that forms where the potato is in contact with the sheet pan.
5. Remove from oven.
6. To hold for service, keep warm and uncovered so the potatoes will not be made soggy by trapped steam. Hold no more than 1 hour, if possible, though they will keep longer with some loss of quality.
    Note that nothing was said about wrapping potatoes in foil. Foil-wrapped potatoes do not bake but rather steam in their own moisture. The texture of a steamed potato is entirely different from that of a baked potato. Save yourself the trouble and expense of wrapping in foil and serve a better product.

Baked Potatoes

Portion size: 1 potato

U.S.	Metric	Ingredients	PROCEDURE
as needed	as needed	Idaho or baking potatoes	1. Scrub the potatoes well and pierce the ends with a skewer or fork to allow steam to escape.
as needed	as needed	Vegetable oil (optional)	2. Leave potatoes dry or oil them lightly if a crisp skin is desired.
			3. Place on sheet pan in 400°F (200°C) oven. Bake until done, about 1 hour. Test for doneness by squeezing a potato gently.

Per serving:
Calories, 130; Protein, 3 g; Fat, 0 g (0% cal.); Cholesterol, 0 mg; Carbohydrates, 31 g; Fiber, 3 g; Sodium, 10 mg.

Stuffed Baked Potatoes

Portions: 10   Portion size: 1 potato

U.S.	Metric	Ingredients	PROCEDURE
10	10	Baking potatoes, about 7–8 oz (200–225 g) each	1. Bake the potatoes according to the basic method.
2 oz	60 g	Butter, melted	2. Remove from the oven. Cut a slice off the top of each potato and scoop out the pulp, leaving a shell about ¼ inch (½ cm) thick.
4 oz	100 mL	Light cream or milk, hot	3. Pass the pulp through a food mill or ricer. Beat in the butter and enough cream or milk to make a smooth purée. Season to taste. (Note that this preparation is basically the same as whipped potatoes.)
to taste	to taste	Salt	
to taste	to taste	White pepper	4. Fill the potato shells with the purée, using a pastry bag or kitchen spoon. (A pastry bag is faster and neater.) Place them on a baking sheet.
3 tbsp	45 mL	Dry bread crumbs	5. Mix the bread crumbs and parmesan cheese and top the potatoes with this mixture. Sprinkle with melted butter.
3 tbsp	45 mL	Parmesan cheese, grated	
1 oz	30 g	Butter, melted	6. Place in hot oven (400°F/200°C) until potatoes are heated through and tops are browned, about 15 minutes.

Per serving:
Calories, 270; Protein, 5 g; Fat, 10 g (32% cal.); Cholesterol, 30 mg; Carbohydrates, 42 g; Fiber, 4 g; Sodium, 140 mg.

(Continued)

Stuffed Baked Potatoes *(Continued)*

VARIATIONS

For each variation listed, add the indicated ingredients to the potato purée mixture. Proportions are for about 2½–3 lb (1.1–1.4 kg) purée.

1. 2 oz (60 g) grated parmesan cheese
2. 8 oz (225 g) minced onion, sautéed in butter
3. 4 oz (100 g) cooked ham, small dice
   4 oz (100 g) mushrooms, chopped and sautéed in butter
4. 8 oz (225 g) bacon, diced and cooked crisp
   1 green pepper, chopped and sautéed in butter or bacon fat

Macaire Potatoes

Scoop out the pulp completely and discard the skins. Mash the pulp with a kitchen fork or break it up with the paddle of a mixer. Omit the melted butter and cream or milk. Instead, mix in 7 oz (200 g) soft butter. Season. Form into small cakes and pan-fry in clarified butter until golden brown on both sides.

Oven Roast Potatoes

Portions: 25   Portion size: 4 oz (125 g)

U.S.	Metric	Ingredients	PROCEDURE
10 lb AP	4.5 kg	Potatoes	1. Peel and eye potatoes. Cut into 25 uniform portions and trim pieces to shape. Save the trimmings for other use.
as needed	as needed	Vegetable oil or olive oil	2. Dry the potatoes well and rub with oil. Place in oiled baking pan and season with salt and pepper.
to taste	to taste	Salt	3. Place in 400°F (200°C) oven and bake until browned and cooked through, about 1 hour. Halfway through baking time, turn potatoes and brush with additional oil.
to taste	to taste	White pepper	

Per serving:
Calories, 160; Protein, 3 g; Fat, 2.5 g (14% cal.); Cholesterol, 0 mg; Carbohydrates, 32 g; Fiber, 3 g; Sodium, 10 mg.

BAKED "EN CASSEROLE"

A number of preparations call for potatoes baked in a baking pan or casserole, with or without liquid added. The best-known is scalloped potatoes. A characteristic of most of these preparations is that they are baked uncovered at least part of the time so that a brown crust forms on top. (Note that two versions of Gratin Dauphinois are included here. The first is a modern version, while the second is a more traditional version.)

Gratin Dauphinois I

Portions: 24   Portion size: 4½–5 oz (130–150 g)

U.S.	Metric	Ingredients	PROCEDURE
5 lb	2.5 kg	Firm-fleshed potatoes	1. Peel the potatoes and cut into thin slices (as for potato chips). Do not place the sliced potatoes in water.
1 oz	30 g	Salt	2. Toss the potatoes in the salt and chopped garlic and arrange in an even layer in a buttered roasting pan. Marinate for 15 minutes.
2 oz	60 g	Garlic, chopped	
1½ qt	1.5 L	Cream	3. Mix together the cream and milk and lightly season with pepper. Pour over the potatoes. Bring the liquid to a boil, then place the pan in the oven at 400°F (200°C) for about 30 minutes or until the potatoes are tender and the sauce is thick.
1 pt	500 mL	Milk	
to taste	to taste	White pepper	

Per serving:
Calories, 300; Protein, 4 g; Fat, 23 g (67% cal.); Cholesterol, 85 mg; Carbohydrates, 21 g; Fiber, 2 g; Sodium, 490 mg.

Gratin Dauphinois II

Portions: 15   Portion size: 5 oz (150 g)

U.S.	Metric	Ingredients	PROCEDURE
3 lb	1.4 kg	Potatoes	1. Peel and eye the potatoes. Cut into very thin slices.
to taste	to taste	Salt	2. Place some of the potatoes in a layer in a buttered baking pan. Season with salt, pepper, and a very small amount of nutmeg. Sprinkle with a little of the cheese. Repeat until all the potatoes and about three-fourths of the cheese are used up.
to taste	to taste	White pepper	
to taste	to taste	Nutmeg	
½ lb	225 g	Gruyère cheese, grated	
1 pt	500 mL	Milk	3. Combine the milk and half the cream and heat to a simmer. Beat the egg yolks with the remaining cream. Slowly stir in the hot milk mixture.
1 cup	250 mL	Heavy cream	4. Pour the milk mixture over the potatoes. Top with remaining cheese.
3	3	Egg yolks	5. Bake uncovered at 350°F (175°C) until done, about 45–60 minutes.

Per serving:
Calories, 220; Protein, 8 g; Fat, 13 g (53% cal.); Cholesterol, 85 mg;
Carbohydrates, 18 g; Fiber, 1 g; Sodium, 80 mg.

VARIATION

Savoyarde Potatoes

Prepare as above, but use chicken stock instead of milk.

Scalloped Potatoes

Portions: 25   Portion size: 5 oz (150 g)

U.S.	Metric	Ingredients	PROCEDURE
2½ qt	2.5 L	Milk	1. Make a thin white sauce (béchamel) using the ingredients listed (see p. 145). Keep hot while preparing the potatoes.
3 oz	90 g	Butter	
3 oz	90 g	Flour	
2 tsp	10 mL	Salt	
to taste	to taste	White pepper	
7½ lb	3.5 kg	Potatoes	2. Peel and eye the potatoes. Cut into slices ⅛ inch thick (3 mm).
			3. Place the potatoes in a buttered baking pan, making several layers.
			4. Pour in the white sauce. Lift the potatoes slightly so that the sauce can run between the layers.
			5. Cover with foil or greased paper and place in oven at 350°F (175°C) for 30 minutes.
			6. Uncover and continue to bake until top is lightly browned and potatoes are tender.

Per serving:
Calories, 200; Protein, 6 g; Fat, 6 g (27% cal.); Cholesterol, 20 mg;
Carbohydrates, 31 g; Fiber, 2 g; Sodium, 270 mg.

Note: Unthickened milk may be used instead of a thin white sauce, but the milk is more likely to curdle. The roux helps prevent curdling.

VARIATIONS

Scalloped Potatoes with Onions

Add 1¼ lb (600 g) sliced onions to baking pan with the potatoes.

Scalloped Potatoes with Cheese

Add 1 lb (500 g) shredded cheddar cheese to baking pan with potatoes. Top with additional cheese before browning.

Scalloped Potatoes with Ham

Add 2½ lb (1.4 kg) diced ham.

Boulangère Potatoes

Portions: 25   Portion size: 5 oz (150 g)

U.S.	Metric	Ingredients	PROCEDURE
2½ lb	1.1 kg	Onions, sliced	1. Sauté the onions in butter or fat until they are translucent and just beginning to brown.
5 oz	150 g	Butter or fat drippings from roast (see note)	2. Add the potatoes and toss until coated with fat.
7½ lb	3.5 kg	Potatoes, peeled and cut into thick slices	3. Place in a baking pan or in a roasting pan under a partially cooked roast. Pour in the hot stock. Season.
1 qt	1 L	Stock, chicken or lamb (if available), hot	4. Bake 1–1½ hours at 350°F (175°C) or at the roasting temperature of lamb, until potatoes are done. Add additional stock during cooking if necessary to keep potatoes from drying out.
to taste	to taste	Salt	
to taste	to taste	Pepper	

Per serving:
Calories, 160; Protein, 3 g; Fat, 5 g (27% cal.); Cholesterol, 15 mg;
Carbohydrates, 28 g; Fiber, 3 g; Sodium, 55 mg.

Note: Boulangère potatoes may be cooked separately, but they are usually cooked with a roast, especially leg of lamb (see p. 244). If the potatoes are cooked with a roast, they must be added to the pan at the right time so that they will be done at the same time as the meat.

Potatoes au Gratin

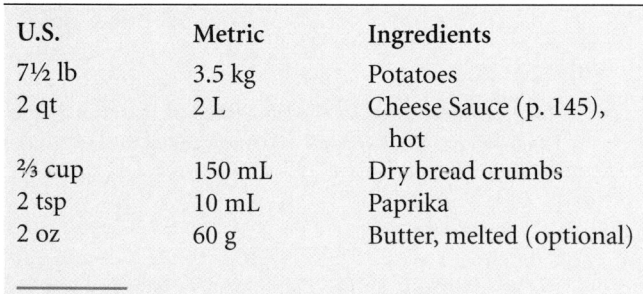

Portions: 25   Portion size: 6 oz (175 g)

U.S.	Metric	Ingredients	PROCEDURE
7½ lb	3.5 kg	Potatoes	1. Scrub the potatoes and simmer or steam them until tender but still firm.
2 qt	2 L	Cheese Sauce (p. 145), hot	2. Drain and spread on sheet pan to cool.
⅔ cup	150 mL	Dry bread crumbs	3. When the potatoes are cool enough to handle, peel and cut them into uniform ⅜-inch (1-cm) dice.
2 tsp	10 mL	Paprika	4. Combine with the hot cheese sauce in a baking pan.
2 oz	60 g	Butter, melted (optional)	5. Mix the bread crumbs and paprika and sprinkle over the potatoes. Drizzle the butter evenly over the top.
			6. Bake at 350°F (175°C) about 30 minutes, until hot and browned.

Per serving:
Calories, 190; Protein, 7 g; Fat, 6 g (29% cal.); Cholesterol, 20 mg;
Carbohydrates, 26 g; Fiber, 2 g; Sodium, 150 mg.

Note: Cream sauce may be used instead of cheese sauce. Grated cheese (cheddar or parmesan) may be sprinkled over the potatoes before topping them with bread crumbs.

Anna Potatoes

Portions: 10   Portion size: 5 oz (150 g)

U.S.	Metric	Ingredients
4 lb AP	1.8 kg	Boiling potatoes
12 oz	350 g	Butter
to taste	to taste	Salt
to taste	to taste	White pepper

PROCEDURE

1. Select round, uniformly sized potatoes. The appearance of this dish is important, so the slices should be neat and even.
2. Peel and eye the potatoes and cut into thin slices. Hold in cold water until ready to use.
3. Clarify the butter (see p. 152).
4. Heat about ¼ inch (½ cm) butter in a heavy 9-inch (23-cm) cast iron skillet. The skillet must be well seasoned so that the potatoes will not stick. Remove from heat.
5. Drain the potatoes and dry them well. Select the most uniform slices for the bottom layer. Arrange the slices in circles in the bottom of the pan. Shingle the slices and reverse the direction of each circle. See Figure 18.4 for illustration of this technique. Season this layer with salt and pepper and ladle some clarified butter over it.
6. Continue making layers, seasoning and buttering each layer, until the ingredients are used up. The potatoes will be mounded over the top of the pan, but they will compress as they cook. There will be a great deal of butter in the pan, but it will be drained after cooking and can be reused.
7. Place the pan over a moderate fire and heat until the pan is sizzling. Shake the pan lightly to make sure the potatoes are not sticking.
8. Cover with foil and bake in a hot oven (450°F/230°C) for about 40 minutes, until potatoes are tender. Test for doneness by piercing center with paring knife. Remove the foil and bake 10 minutes more.
9. Drain off excess butter (remember that it's hot!) and carefully invert the potato cake onto a baking sheet. The potatoes should have stayed intact in a round cake, but if any slices fall off, put them back in place. Set the potatoes back in the oven if necessary for even browning.
10. Cut into wedges for service.

Per serving:
Calories, 200; Protein, 3 g; Fat, 14 g (47% cal.); Cholesterol, 35 mg;
Carbohydrates, 32 g; Fiber, 3 g; Sodium, 150 mg

Note: Small molds may be used instead of the large pan for individual service.

VARIATION

Voisin Potatoes

Prepare as in basic recipe, but sprinkle each layer of potatoes with grated Swiss cheese.

Figure 18.4
Anna Potatoes.

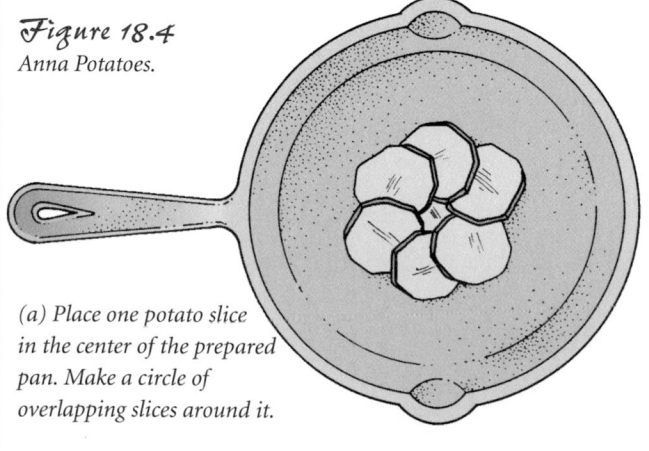

(a) Place one potato slice in the center of the prepared pan. Make a circle of overlapping slices around it.

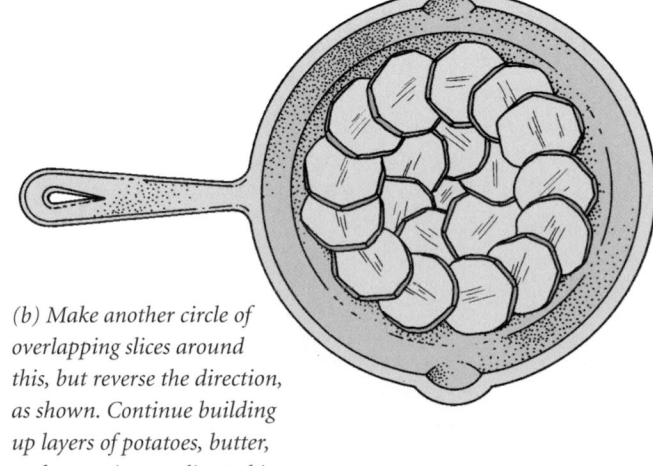

(b) Make another circle of overlapping slices around this, but reverse the direction, as shown. Continue building up layers of potatoes, butter, and seasonings as directed in the recipe.

SAUTÉING AND PAN-FRYING

The procedures for sautéing and pan-frying potatoes are basically the same as for other vegetables (p. 466).

There are many varieties of sautéed and pan-fried potato preparations. Some are made with raw potatoes, others with precooked or blanched potatoes. Many of these recipes are especially useful because they are excellent ways to utilize leftover boiled potatoes.

This group of recipes may be divided into two categories based on production technique.

1. **Potatoes mixed or tossed while cooking.**
   The procedure for sautéing vegetables, page 466, is used for these preparations. The potatoes are cut into pieces or into small shapes and cooked in a small amount of fat. They are turned or tossed in the pan so that they brown on all sides. This category includes rissolé, parisienne, noisette, château, and American fried or home-fried potatoes.

2. **Potatoes cooked and served in compact cakes.**
   The procedure for pan-frying vegetables, page 466, is the basic method used for these preparations. The potatoes are not mixed while cooking but are made into cakes, which are browned on both sides. This category includes hashed browns and variations, as well as potato pancakes and macaire potatoes (see p. 494).

Hashed Brown Potatoes

Portions: 25		Portion size: 4½ oz (125 g)	

U.S.	Metric	Ingredients	
7½ lb	3.4 kg	Boiled potatoes, cooled and peeled	
10 oz	275 g	Oil, clarified butter, or a mixture of oil and clarified butter	
to taste	to taste	Salt	
to taste	to taste	Pepper	

PROCEDURE

1. Chop the potatoes into small pieces.
2. Ladle a thin layer of oil or butter into a well-seasoned 6-inch (15-cm) sauté pan and set it over high heat. A griddle may also be used for this preparation.
3. When the fat is hot, add 1 portion of potatoes and flatten them into a round cake. Shake the pan back and forth to keep the potatoes from sticking.
4. When the potatoes are well browned on the bottom, flip them over or turn them with an offset spatula. Try to keep the potato cake unbroken. Season with salt and pepper.
5. When the second side is done, tilt the pan to drain off any excess fat for reuse, holding the potatoes in the pan with the spatula. Slide the potatoes out of the sauté pan onto a plate.
6. Repeat with remaining portions.

Per serving:
Calories, 180; Protein, 2 g; Fat, 7 g (35% cal.); Cholesterol, 0 mg; Carbohydrates, 27 g; Fiber, 2 g; Sodium, 5 mg.

VARIATIONS

Any of the following can be added to the potatoes to vary the flavor: chopped parsley, chives, bacon, hard-cooked egg, grated cheese, and garlic.

Roesti Potatoes

Shred boiled potatoes on the large holes of a hand grater, or use a machine. Prepare as in basic recipe. Potatoes should be very crisp. (These are sometimes called "hashed brown potatoes" but, strictly speaking, hashed browns are made with chopped potatoes, as *hash* means "to chop.")

Lyonnaise Hashed Browns

Combine 1¼ lb (600 g) onion, chopped and sautéed in butter, with the chopped or shredded potatoes before pan-frying.

Rissolé or Cocotte Potatoes

Portions: 25   Portion size: 4 oz (125 g)

U.S.	Metric	Ingredients
14 lb	7 kg	Potatoes (see note)
10 oz	300 g	Clarified butter
to taste	to taste	Salt
to taste	to taste	White pepper

PROCEDURE

1. Peel and eye the potatoes and trim or tourné them into small oval shapes about 1½ inches (4 cm) long. (See Figure 18.1 for technique.)
2. Place the potatoes in a saucepan, cover with salted water, and bring to a boil. Reduce heat and simmer 7–8 minutes or until about three-fourths cooked.
3. Drain and turn out onto a sheet pan to steam dry.
4. Heat the clarified butter in a large sauté pan. Add the potatoes and sauté over moderate heat until golden brown and fully cooked. (Potatoes may also be browned in deep fat if speed of service is critical.)
5. Season with salt and pepper.

Per serving:
Calories, 290; Protein, 4 g; Fat, 11 g (34% cal.); Cholesterol, 30 mg; Carbohydrates, 45 g; Fiber, 4 g; Sodium, 125 mg.

Note: The quantity of potatoes needed varies, depending on how heavily they are trimmed. Save trimmings for purées or other uses.

VARIATIONS

Alternative Method: Potatoes may be sautéed without prior blanching. Sauté over low heat and keep covered during the first half or three-fourths of the cooking period so that the potatoes will cook fully without becoming overbrowned. Potatoes cooked this way absorb more butter than those that are blanched first. Thus they are tastier, but they also are higher in calories.

Parisienne and Noisette Potatoes

Prepare as in basic recipe, but cut potatoes with melon ball cutter. Parisienne potatoes are cut with a scoop slightly larger than 1 inch (about 3 cm). Noisette potatoes are smaller than 1 inch (about 2½ cm). Blanch for 3–5 minutes or cook from raw state.

Château Potatoes

Prepare as in basic recipe, but tourné the potatoes into larger ovals, about 2 inches (5 cm) long.

Lyonnaise Potatoes

Portions: 25   Portion size: 4½ oz (125 g)

U.S.	Metric	Ingredients
6½ lb	3 kg	Boiled potatoes, cooled and peeled
1½ lb	700 g	Onions
8 oz	225 g	Clarified butter, vegetable oil, or mixture of oil and butter
to taste	to taste	Salt
to taste	to taste	White pepper

PROCEDURE

1. Cut the potatoes into slices about ¼ inch (½ cm) thick.
2. Peel the onions, cut in half lengthwise, and slice into julienne.
3. Heat half the fat in a sauté pan and sauté the onions until they are golden. Remove from the pan with a slotted spoon and set aside.
4. Put the rest of the fat into the pan. Set the pan on high heat and add the potatoes.
5. Sauté the potatoes, tossing them in the pan until well browned on all sides.
6. Add the onions and continue to sauté for another minute, until onions and potatoes are well mixed and the flavors are blended.
7. Season to taste.

Per serving:
Calories, 190; Protein, 2 g; Fat, 9 g (42% cal.); Cholesterol, 25 mg; Carbohydrates, 26 g; Fiber, 2 g; Sodium, 95 mg.

Note: This preparation may be made on a griddle instead of in a sauté pan.

VARIATIONS

Home Fries or American Fries
Prepare as in basic recipe, but omit onions.

Potatoes O'Brien
Cook 10 oz (300 g) diced bacon until crisp. Remove bacon from pan. Sauté 10 oz onion (300 g), cut in fine dice, and 10 oz (300 g) green pepper, cut in fine dice, in bacon fat. Sauté 6½ lb (3 kg) diced potatoes as in basic recipe and add vegetables. Add the crisp bacon and 4 oz (125 g) diced pimiento to finish, and season to taste.

Potato Pancakes

Portions: 20   Portion size: 2 pancakes, about 2 oz (60 g) each

U.S.	Metric	Ingredients	PROCEDURE
6 lb	2.7 kg	Potatoes	1. Peel the potatoes and onions. Grate them together into a stainless-steel bowl. Juice the lemons, add the juice to the potatoes to prevent discoloration, and toss to mix.
1 lb	450 g	Onions	
2	2	Lemons	
6	6	Eggs	2. Place the potatoes in a china cap and squeeze out the excess liquid. Hold the liquid and let the starch settle out. Drain off the liquid from the starch.
¼ cup	60 mL	Chopped parsley (optional)	
2 tsp	10 mL	Salt	3. Return the potatoes to a stainless-steel bowl and add the potato starch.
½ tsp	2 mL	White pepper	4. Beat in the eggs, parsley, salt, and pepper.
2 oz or more	60 g or more	Flour (see note)	5. Stir in enough flour to bind the potato mixture. (If the batter is too thin, the pancakes will fall apart in the pan. Test-fry a little first, and add more flour if necessary.)
as needed	as needed	Oil for pan-frying	6. Pour about ¼ inch (½ cm) oil into a heavy iron skillet. Heat the oil over moderately high heat. The oil should reach about 325°F/160°C.
			7. Measuring with a solid kitchen spoon, place portions of the batter in the pan to make individual pancakes.
			8. Pan-fry, turning once, until golden brown on both sides.
			9. Remove from the pan with a slotted spoon or spatula and drain briefly on absorbent paper.
			10. Alternative method: Lightly brown in oil and place in one layer on a sheet pan. Finish in the oven (375°F/190°C) until brown and crisp.

Per serving:
Calories, 220; Protein, 5 g; Fat, 10 g (40% cal.); Cholesterol, 65 mg; Carbohydrates, 29 g; Fiber, 3 g; Sodium, 260 mg.

Note: Matzoh meal or dried potato starch may be used instead of flour for binding the batter.

DEEP-FRYING

All the rules of deep-frying that you learned in Chapter 4 apply to potatoes. Review page 60 if you need to refresh your memory.

There are two kinds of deep-fried potato preparations:

1. **Potatoes fried raw.**
   These are potatoes that are simply cut into various shapes and deep-fried until golden and crisp. They include all the varieties of French fries as well as potato chips.
   Russet or Idaho potatoes are most suitable for frying because of their high starch content and their regular shape, which permits less trimming loss.

2. **Preparations made from cooked, puréed potatoes.**
   Most of these products are made from duchesse potato mixture. They include potato croquette variations, Dauphine potatoes, and Lorette potatoes.
   Starchy potatoes are used for these recipes, as they are for duchesse potatoes, because they make a good dry, mealy purée.

FRENCH FRIES

Because French fries, or deep-fried potatoes, are one of the most popular items in American food service, you must know how to prepare them well. Most French fries served are made from blanched, frozen products, but it is also important to know how to make them from fresh potatoes.

The recipe on page 501 gives the complete procedure for preparing French fries. Note that they are fried in two stages. It is possible to cook them in one step, but this is impractical in a volume operation because of the long cooking time. The more common practice is to blanch them in frying fat. This is done at a lower temperature so that they will cook through without becoming brown. They are then drained and refrigerated until service time. Portions can then be finished to order in a few minutes.

Frozen products have been prepared through step 5 in the recipe and then frozen. To use them, it is only necessary to begin with step 6.

French Fries

Portions: as needed (2¼ lb AP/1 kg AP potatoes will yield about 1 lb/450 g cooked potatoes)

U.S.	Metric	Ingredients	PROCEDURE
as needed	as needed	Idaho potatoes	1. Peel and eye the potatoes. 2. Cut the potatoes into strips ⅜ inch (1 cm) square and about 3 inches (7½ cm) long. (See Figure 7.10 for cutting procedure.) Hold the cut potatoes in cold water until needed, to prevent discoloration. 3. Line sheet pans with several layers of brown paper and have them ready by the deep fryer. 4. Drain and dry the potatoes well. Deep-fry in fat heated to 325°F (160°C) until they are just beginning to turn a pale golden color. At this point, they should be cooked through and soft. 5. Remove the potatoes from the fryer and turn them out onto the sheet pans in a single layer to drain. Refrigerate. 6. At service time, fry the potatoes in small quantities in fat heated to 350°–375°F (175°–190°C) until brown and crisp. 7. Drain well. Salt them lightly *away from the fryer* or let customers salt their own. Serve immediately.

Per 3.2 ounces:
Calories, 290; Protein, 4 g; Fat, 15 g (46% cal.); Cholesterol, 0 mg; Carbohydrates, 36 g; Fiber, 3 g; Sodium, 200 mg.

VARIATIONS

Pont-Neuf Potatoes

Prepare as in basic recipe, but cut the potatoes in thicker strips, about ½ inch (1¼ cm) square or slightly larger. Blanching time will be slightly longer.

Allumette Potatoes (Shoestring or Matchstick Potatoes)

Cut the potatoes into thin strips, slightly less than ¼ inch thick (about ½ cm). Because they are so thin, they are usually fried in one step (without blanching) until very crisp.

Straw Potatoes

Cut into very thin strips, about ⅛ inch (3 mm) thick. Fry in one step in hot fat (375°F/190°C).

Steakhouse Fries

Scrub but do not peel potatoes. Cut in half lengthwise, then cut each half lengthwise into 4–6 wedges, depending on size. Prepare as in basic recipe.

Potato Chips

Cut potatoes into very thin slices, less than ⅛ inch (3 mm) thick. Fry in one step in hot fat (375°F/190°C).

Waffle or Gaufrette Potatoes

Set the fluted blade of a mandoline (a special slicer) so that it cuts very thin slices. Cut potatoes into round slices, turning the potato about 90 degrees between slices so that you cut waffle shapes (see Figure 18.5). Fry like potato chips.

Figure 18.5 Gaufrette Potatoes.

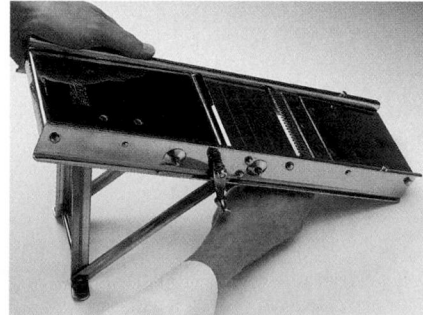

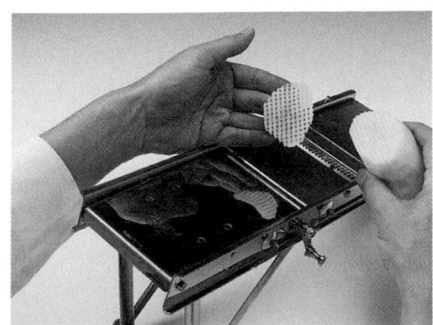

(a) Set the fluted blade of the mandoline so that it cuts very thin slices.

(b) Slice the potatoes, turning the potato about 90 degrees between slices so that the ridges on the two sides of each slice cross each other.

(c) You may need to adjust the thickness of the cut after the first slice or two. The slices should be thin enough to have holes.

Potato Croquettes

Note: These are made from duchesse potato mixture. The procedure for duchesse potatoes is repeated here for the sake of convenience.

Portions: 20   **Portion size:** 3 pieces, 1½ oz (40 g) each

U.S.	Metric	Ingredients	PROCEDURE
7 lb	3 kg	Potatoes, peeled and quartered	1. Steam the potatoes or simmer in salted water until tender. (Steaming is preferable because it results in a drier product.) Drain in a colander (if simmered) and let dry in an oven for a few minutes.
4 oz	100 g	Butter	2. Pass the potatoes through a food mill or ricer.
to taste	to taste	Salt	3. Add the butter and mix to a smooth paste. Season to taste with salt, pepper, and nutmeg.
to taste	to taste	White pepper	
to taste	to taste	Nutmeg	4. Set over moderate fire and stir the mixture to dry it out well. If it is not dry enough, the croquettes will not hold their shape. Alternative method: Add enough cornstarch or dry potato starch to absorb excess moisture and stiffen the mixture.
10	10	Egg yolks	
			5. Remove from the fire, add the egg yolks, and beat in thoroughly.
			6. To shape croquettes, two methods are available: (a) Spread the mixture out to cool in a pan, cover with plastic or buttered paper to keep a crust from forming, and refrigerate. Dust hands with flour and shape potatoes by hand into cylinders the shape of corks, about 2 inches (5 cm) long. They should be about 1½ oz (40 g) each. (b) Dust sheet pans with flour. Place the warm potato mixture in a pastry bag fitted with a large, plain tip. Bag out the potatoes into long strips on the pans (see Figure 18.3). With a knife, cut the strips into 2-inch (5-cm) lengths.
		Standard Breading Procedure:	7. Set up the breading station and pass the potatoes through Standard Breading Procedure (p. 121).
as needed	as needed	Flour	8. At service time, fry croquettes in deep fat at 350°F (175°C) until golden brown. Drain well.
as needed	as needed	Egg wash	
as needed	as needed	Bread crumbs	9. Serve immediately, 3 pieces per portion.

Per serving:
Calories, 430; Protein, 9 g; Fat, 20 g (42% cal.); Cholesterol, 155 mg;
Carbohydrates, 54 g; Fiber, 3 g; Sodium, 315 mg.

VARIATIONS

Other shapes may be used as desired.

Add 8 oz (225 g) of any one of the following to the potato mixture:

Grated cheese   Minced, sautéed onion   Chopped, sautéed mushrooms
Chopped ham   Finely chopped nuts

Berny Potatoes

Shape into small balls. Bread with finely slivered almonds instead of bread crumbs. (In classical cuisine, minced truffles are added to the potato mixture.)

Dauphine Potatoes

Method 1: For each pound of duchesse or croquette potato mixture, add ⅓ lb Pâte à Choux or cream puff paste (p. 860), made without sugar and with half the amount of butter. To fry, bag out into desired shapes on greased brown paper. Slide into hot fat. Remove paper when potatoes float loose. **Method 2:** Hold pastry bag over deep fryer. Force out potato mixture and cut off short lengths with the back of a knife, letting them drop into the hot fat.

Lorette Potatoes

Prepare like Dauphine Potatoes and add 1 oz grated parmesan cheese per pound of mixture (60 g per kg). Shape as desired (the classic shape is a small crescent) and fry without breading.

Potato Croquettes with Peppers

Yield: 36 pieces

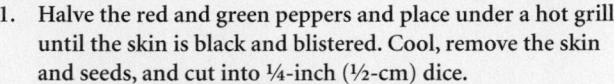

U.S.	Metric	Ingredients	PROCEDURE
3	3	Small red bell peppers	1. Halve the red and green peppers and place under a hot grill until the skin is black and blistered. Cool, remove the skin and seeds, and cut into ¼-inch (½-cm) dice.
3	3	Small green bell peppers	
1 lb 7 oz	700 g	Potatoes, peeled	2. Boil the potatoes and prepare a basic potato purée as explained on page 490.
1 oz	25 g	Butter, softened	3. Mix the peppers gently with the mashed potato, butter, and egg yolk. Season well.
1	1	Egg yolk	
		Standard Breading Procedure	4. With flour-dusted hands, shape the potato mixture into 36 balls. Set up Standard Breading Procedure (p. 121) and bread the croquettes.

Per piece:
Calories, 270; Protein, 6 g; Fat, 12 g (40% cal.); Cholesterol, 55 mg;
Carbohydrates, 34 g; Fiber, 2 g; Sodium, 240 mg.

5. Just before service, deep-fry the croquettes at 350°F (175°C). Drain well.

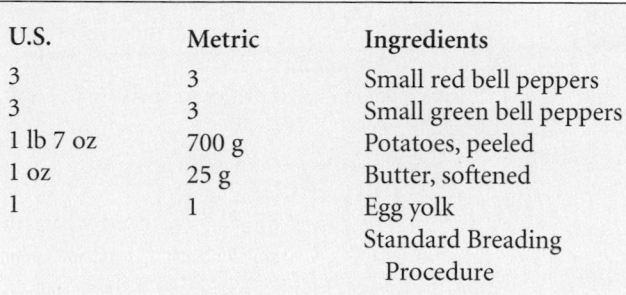

Rice and Other Grains

Understanding Rice

TYPES AND CHARACTERISTICS

Regular Milled White Rice

This rice has been milled to remove the outer bran coating. This process removes some vitamins and minerals, but it produces a white, lighter-textured product that most people prefer.

Enriched rice has received a coating of vitamins to compensate for some of the nutrients lost in milling.

Short-grain and medium-grain rice have small, round kernels that become sticky when cooked. They are used for such preparations as rice pudding and rice molds. In addition, the regular boiled rice used in Japanese cuisine for everyday eating and for making sushi is short-grain rice.

Long-grain rice has long, slender grains that stay separate and fluffy when properly cooked. It is used for side dishes, entrées, casseroles, and so on.

Parboiled or Converted Rice

This is a specially processed long-grain rice. It has been partially cooked under steam pressure, redried, then milled or polished. This process results in a higher vitamin and mineral content.

Parboiled rice is the most widely used in food service. The grains stay firm, separate, and light, and the product holds well in the steam table without becoming mushy or sticky. However, the flavor and texture are not like those of regular long-grain rice, so it is not always preferred by all customers.

Converted rice takes slightly more liquid and time to cook.

Instant Rice

This product has been precooked and dried so that it can be prepared quickly. It does not hold well after cooking and the grains quickly lose their shape and become mushy.

Top row: basmati rice, glutinous rice, plain long-grain rice. Bottom row: Japanese short-grain rice, jasmine rice, arborio rice.

Top row: true wild rice, wehani rice, cultivated wild rice. Bottom row: parboiled or converted rice, brown long-grain rice.

Brown Rice

This rice has had the bran layer left on, giving it a light brown color, slightly coarse, crunchy texture, and nutty flavor. Brown rice is available as short, medium, or long grain.

Brown rice takes about twice as long to cook as white rice.

Specialty Rices

A number of types of rice are used in various international cuisines. Perhaps the most important to us are the following five types.

Arborio rice is one of several Italian varieties of a type of short-grain rice that is essential for making the highest-quality risotto (see p. 510). It is the variety most often found here and the one specified in recipes.

Basmati rice is an extra-long-grain rice widely used in India and surrounding countries. It has a unique nutty flavor.

Jasmine rice is a long-grain white rice from Thailand and other parts of Southeast Asia. It is very fragrant, a little like basmati rice but more delicate or floral.

Wehani rice is another aromatic rice, red in color, with a rich, earthy flavor.

Glutinous rice is a sweet-tasting short-grain rice that becomes quite sticky and chewy when cooked. It is used for a number of special dishes, including desserts, in Chinese and Japanese cuisines. Contrary to what you may read elsewhere, however, it is not the rice used for sushi, which is made with regular Japanese short-grain rice.

HANDLING AND STORAGE

Washing

Regular milled rice should be rinsed in cold water before boiling or steaming. This removes the excess starch that makes rice sticky.

The American rice industry recommends *not* washing rice because it washes off some of the vitamin coating of enriched rice. But that's probably a small price to pay for a more attractive product. This is a decision you will have to make in your own operation.

Do not buy low-grade rice, which tends to be dirty, or rice that has been coated with talc.

Rice cooked by the pilaf method (p. 508) does not need to be washed (unless it is dirty) because the fat coating each kernel helps keep the grains separate and reduces stickiness.

Converted rice and instant rice do not need to be washed.

Storing

Keep raw rice at room temperature in a dry place and in a tightly sealed container to keep out moisture and insects. White rice will keep for many months. Brown rice is somewhat more perishable.

Other Grains and Grain Products

Several other cereal products can be served as side dishes to add variety to your menu. Many of these can be prepared using the basic cooking methods for rice, although cooking times and amount of liquid needed vary. These grain products, as well as a few other related items, are briefly summarized.

WILD RICE

Wild rice is not actually rice but is harvested from a kind of grass native to the northern United States and Canada. The grains are long, slender, hard, and dark brown or nearly black in color. Because of its unique nutty flavor, its scarcity, and its high price, wild rice is considered a luxury food.

Wild rice is now widely cultivated, but the cultivated type is slightly different from that which is harvested in the wild. Grains of cultivated wild rice are generally larger and firmer, but the texture of the cooked rice is coarser and the flavor less complex. Cultivation has helped reduce the price of wild rice, however.

Wild rice should always be washed before cooking. It is simmered in three times its volume of water, for example, 3 pints water per pint of grain for 45 minutes. The grains burst open when cooked.

Wild rice may be mixed with long-grain white rice, cooked *separately*, to decrease the cost per serving.

BARLEY

Pearl barley has been milled to remove the outer bran layers. It is commonly used in soups, but it can also be cooked by the pilaf method and served like rice, although it has a longer cooking time.

WHEAT PRODUCTS

Whole wheat grains that have been cut into smaller pieces are called *cracked wheat*. This product also can be cooked like pilaf. *Whole wheat berries* are the whole grain minus the hulls. They are generally cooked by boiling or simmering, but cooking time can be several hours. Soaking overnight reduces the cooking time to about 1 hour.

Bulgur is a type of cracked wheat that has been partially cooked or parched. It is usually available in coarse, medium, and fine granulations. Its cooking time is shorter than regular cracked wheat and, in fact, the fine granulations can be prepared simply by pouring boiling water over them and letting them stand for a half hour. This type of bulgur is often served cold, mixed with lemon juice, olive oil, chopped scallions, and fresh herbs.

Other wheat or wheat-type products include *farro*, which is actually an ancestor of modern wheat, available in whole-grain form; *spelt*, which is similar to, if not the same as, farro (authorities disagree); and *green wheat*, which can be cooked like cracked wheat. *Couscous* (koose koose) is not actually a grain, although it resembles one. It is made from wheat and is sort of a granular pasta. It is cooked by soaking and then steaming, using a fairly time-consuming process. *Instant couscous* is prepared simply by adding the dry product to hot or boiling water and letting it stand 5 minutes.

Top row: Egyptian green wheat, hulled whole wheat berries.
Bottom row: couscous, kasha, farro.

Top row: quinoa, triticale, pearl barley. Bottom row: blue corn-meal, pozole, bulgur wheat.

CORN PRODUCTS

Polenta is Italian-style cornmeal. Polenta has become popular in North America in recent years. Its preparation and uses are explained and illustrated in Chapter 25 (see p. 740). *Hominy* is corn that has been treated with lye. When it is cracked into a coarse meal, it becomes *grits,* popular in the southern United States and wherever the foods of the South are appreciated. Hominy in whole-grain form is known in Mexican cuisine as *pozole* (poh soh leh). It requires several hours of simmering. *Blue corn,* usually available as blue cornmeal, is derived from early varieties of corn grown by Native Americans.

KASHA AND SPECIALTY GRAINS

Kasha refers to whole buckwheat groats, which are especially popular in Eastern European and Jewish cooking. Kasha is also cooked like pilaf, requiring 2 pints liquid per pint of grain and 15 minutes cooking time. Sometimes eggs are added (2 eggs per pint [500 mL] of grain) while the kasha is being sautéed in the fat.

Chefs continue to experiment with a variety of other unusual grains, such as amaranth, quinoa, and triticale, but these products are still of minor importance, and most people are unfamiliar with them.

Cooking Rice

There seems to be very little agreement among chefs regarding the best ways to cook rice. The methods outlined here have been shown to produce good results. Your instructor may have developed other methods or variations. In any case, consult your instructor if you have questions.

BOILING AND STEAMING RICE

Below are basic procedures for preparing plain boiled or steamed rice on top of the range, in the oven, or in a steamer.

Everyone agrees that the key to properly cooked rice is correct proportions of rice to water and correct cooking times. Unfortunately, no one agrees on what those proportions and times should be.

The proportions given here indicate slightly less liquid than has been used in the past. Even so, they produce a very moist product. Apparently American-grown rice is less dry than it used to be. *You may wish to reduce the quantity of liquid as much as 25 percent.*

The proportion of liquid needed depends on

1. Tightness or looseness of the cover (degree of moisture loss during cooking).
2. Desired moistness of the finished product.
3. Variety, age, and moisture content of the rice used.

Boiled and Steamed Rice

Yield: about 3 lb (1.4 kg)	Portions: 10	Portion size: 4½–5 oz (140 g)
	12	4 oz (115 g)
	16	3 oz (90 g)

PROPORTIONS	U.S.	Metric
Regular long-grain white rice		
Rice	1 lb	475 g
Water	1 qt	1 L
Salt	1 tsp	5 mL
Butter	1 oz	30 g
Parboiled long-grain rice		
Rice	1 lb	475 g
Water	4½ cups	1.1 L
Salt	1 tsp	5 mL
Butter	1 oz	30 g
Medium-grain white rice		
Rice	18 oz	525 g
Water	1 qt	1 L
Salt	1 tsp	5 mL
Butter	1 oz	30 g
Brown rice		
Rice	12 oz	350 g
Water	1 qt	1 L
Salt	1 tsp	5 mL
Butter	1 oz	30 g

PROCEDURES

Rangetop

1. Wash rice in cold water until water is clear (optional step; see p. 504 for note on washing rice).
2. Combine all ingredients in a heavy pot. Bring to boil. Stir. Cover and cook over very low heat.

   Cooking times:
   Long- and medium-grain: 15–20 minutes
   Parboiled: 20–25 minutes
   Brown: 40–45 minutes

3. Test rice for doneness. Cook 2–4 minutes more if necessary.
4. Turn rice out into a hotel pan. Fluff with fork or slotted spoon to let steam escape.

Oven

1. Wash rice in cold water until water is clear (optional step; see p. 504 for note on washing rice).
2. Bring salted water to boil. Combine all ingredients in a shallow steamer pan. Cover with foil or tight lid. Place in 375°F (175°C) oven.

   Cooking times:
   Long- and medium-grain: 25 minutes
   Parboiled: 30–40 minutes
   Brown: 1 hour

3. Test rice for doneness. Bake 2–4 minutes more if necessary.
4. Fluff rice with fork or slotted spoon to let steam escape.

Steamer

1. Wash rice in cold water until water is clear (optional step; see p. 504 for note on washing rice).
2. Bring salted water to boil. Combine all ingredients in a shallow steamer pan. Place uncovered pan in steamer for cooking time recommended by equipment manufacturer.

   Cooking times:
   Depend on type of steamer.

3. Test rice for doneness. Steam 2–4 minutes more if necessary.
4. Fluff rice with fork or slotted spoon to let steam escape.

Per 4½–5 oz (140g) serving:
Calories, 200; Protein, 4 g; Fat, 2.5 g (12% cal.); Cholesterol, 5 mg; Carbohydrates, 39 g; Fiber, 1 g; Sodium, 260 mg.

Figure 18.6 Making rice pilaf.

(a) Sweat the onion or shallot.

(b) Add the rice and sauté briefly.

THE PASTA METHOD

Rice may be cooked in a large quantity of boiling water like pasta (see p. 515). This method is good for producing separate, unsticky grains. However, some nutrients are lost in the cooking water, so chefs disagree about the value of this method.

1. Drop rice into a large pot of boiling, salted water, 4 quarts per pound of rice (4 liters per 500 grams).
2. When just tender, pour rice into a strainer and drain well.
3. Place in a hotel pan. Cover and steam dry in oven for 5 to 10 minutes, or leave uncovered and place in a steamer to steam dry.

THE PILAF METHOD

This is equivalent to braising. The rice is first sautéed in fat, then cooked in liquid—preferably in the oven for uniform heating—until the liquid is absorbed (see Figure 18.6). The fat helps keep the grains separate and adds flavor.

It is normal to measure the rice by volume when making pilaf, as the proportions are based on volume measure. One pint of raw rice weighs about 14 ounces, or 1 pound measures about 2¼ cups (1 liter weighs about 875 grams, or 1 kilogram measures 1.15 liters). Regarding exact measurements, see the note following the pilaf recipe.

REHEATING AND STORING COOKED RICE

To Reheat Cooked Rice

Add 4 ounces water per quart of cooked rice (125 mL per liter). Cover and heat slowly in oven or on range. Or reheat in a steamer, uncovered, without additional water.

To Store Cooked Rice

Cover tightly and refrigerate.

(c) Pour in the hot stock or other liquid.

(d) Bring to a boil and cover. Cook at low heat on top of the stove or in the oven for the required time.

(e) The finished pilaf.

Rice Pilaf

Yield: about 3 lb (1.4 kg)	Portions: 10	Portion size: 5 oz (150 g)
	12	4 oz (125 g)
	16	3 oz (90 g)

U.S.	Metric	Ingredients	PROCEDURE
2 oz	60 g	Butter	1. Heat the butter in a heavy saucepan. Add the onion and sauté until it begins to soften. Do not brown.
3 oz	90 g	Onions, fine dice	
1 pt (see note)	500 mL (see note)	Long-grain rice	2. Add the rice, without washing. Stir over heat until the rice is completely coated with butter.
1½–2 pt (see note)	750 mL–1 L (see note)	Chicken stock or water, boiling	3. Pour in the boiling liquid. Return the liquid to a boil with the rice. Taste and adjust seasonings; cover tightly.
to taste	to taste	Salt	4. Place in a 350°F (175°C) oven and bake for 18–20 minutes, until liquid is absorbed and rice is dry and fluffy. Taste the rice and, if it is not done, replace in oven 3–5 minutes.
			5. Turn out into a hotel pan and fluff the rice with a fork. This releases steam and prevents further cooking. Keep hot for service.
			6. If desired, additional raw butter may be stirred into finished rice.

Per 5 oz (150 g) serving:
Calories, 190; Protein, 4 g; Fat, 5 g (23% cal.); Cholesterol, 15 mg;
Carbohydrates, 33 g; Fiber, 1 g; Sodium, 50 mg.

Note: Rice for pilaf is measured by volume rather than by weight. Use 1½–2 times its volume in stock or water (1¾ times is the normal proportion for long-grain rice). For example, use 2 pints liquid per pint of rice if you desire a moister product or if you are using parboiled rice. Use 1½ pints liquid if you desire a drier product and if your cover is tight enough to retain most of the steam.

VARIATIONS

Tomato Pilaf

Prepare as in basic recipe, using 12–16 oz (375–500 mL) chicken stock and 1½ lb (700 g) chopped canned tomatoes with juice.

Spanish Rice

Prepare like Tomato Pilaf, but use bacon fat and sauté 6 oz (175 g) diced green pepper, 1 crushed clove garlic, and 1 tbsp (15 mL) paprika with the onion.

Turkish Pilaf

Sauté ¼ tsp (1 mL) turmeric with the rice. To finished rice, add 4 oz (125 g) tomato concassé or drained, chopped canned tomatoes, 4 oz (125 g) cooked peas, and 4 oz (125 g) raisins (soaked and drained). Let stand 10–15 minutes before serving.

Cracked Wheat Pilaf

Prepare as in basic recipe, using cracked wheat instead of rice.

Orzo Pilaf

Prepare as in basic recipe, using orzo (rice-shaped pasta) instead of rice.

Barley Pilaf

Prepare as in basic recipe, using pearled barley instead of rice. Use 2½ pints (1.25 L) stock and bake 45 minutes. Mushrooms are often added to barley pilaf.

Additions to rice pilaf

Pimiento	Peas	Ham, diced or cut julienne
Chopped nuts	Green pepper, diced	Raisins or currants
Celery, diced	Spinach, chopped	Water chestnuts
Carrot, diced or grated	Mushrooms	Bacon
Scallions	Olives, chopped or sliced	

RISOTTO

Risotto is a classic Italian preparation made by a special procedure that is like neither the boiling method nor the pilaf method. After sautéing the rice, add a small amount of stock and stir until the liquid is absorbed. Repeat this procedure until the rice is cooked but still firm. Risotto should be served quickly and does not hold well. The finished product has a creamy consistency due to the starch that is cooked out of the rice. The grains are not fluffy and separate.

Because of the labor required, the risotto served in restaurants is not always cooked by the true risotto method. Instead, chefs often prepare a basic pilaf with the special Italian arborio rice and finish it with extra stock, butter, and cheese.

The restaurant method appears after the basic recipe below. The true risotto method (Figure 18.7) is given here because, if you are going to make an imitation risotto, you first have to know what you are imitating. Otherwise, you won't know how good your imitation is. Anyway, risotto is a preparation you should be familiar with as a professional cook.

Figure 18.7 Making risotto.

(a) Sauté the onion or shallot until soft.

(b) Add the rice. Sauté until coated with the fat.

(c) Add a ladleful of stock to the rice. Stir until it is absorbed.

(d) Continue adding stock and stirring until the rice is cooked.

(e) For Risotto Milanese, add saffron steeped in hot stock near the end of the cooking period.

(f) Finish by stirring in parmesan cheese and butter.

Risotto alla Parmigiana

Portions: 10 Portion size: 5 oz (150 g)

U.S.	Metric	Ingredients	PROCEDURE
1 oz	30 g	Butter	1. Heat the butter and oil in a large, straight-sided sauté pan. Add the onion and sauté until soft. Do not brown.
1 oz	30 mL	Vegetable oil	
1 oz	30 g	Onion, chopped fine	2. Add the rice and sauté until well coated with the fat.
1 lb	450 g	Italian Arborio rice	3. Using a 6-oz (150-mL) ladle, add one ladle of stock to the rice. Stir the rice over medium heat until the stock is absorbed and the rice is almost dry.
1½ qt (approximately)	1.4 L (approximately)	Chicken stock, hot	4. Add another ladle of stock and repeat procedure. Do not add more than one ladleful of stock at a time.
			5. Stop adding stock when the rice is tender but still firm. It should be very moist and creamy, but not runny. The cooking should take about 30 minutes.
1 oz	30 g	Butter	6. Remove from the heat and stir in the raw butter and parmesan cheese. Salt to taste.
3 oz	90 g	Parmesan cheese, grated	
to taste	to taste	Salt	

Per serving:
Calories, 260; Protein, 7 g; Fat, 11 g (38% cal.); Cholesterol, 25 mg;
Carbohydrates, 34 g; Fiber, 3 g; Sodium, 210 mg.

VARIATIONS

Restaurant Method: Prepare basic pilaf (p. 509) using 1 lb Italian Arborio rice to 1 qt chicken stock (500 g rice to 1 L stock). To finish for service, place desired number of portions in a sauté pan and moisten with additional stock. Simmer until slightly moist and creamy, as in basic recipe. Finish with raw butter and parmesan cheese.

Risotto Milanese
Prepare as in basic recipe, but add ¼–½ tsp (1–2 mL) saffron soaked in 1 cup (200 mL) stock near the end of cooking.

Risotto with Mushrooms
Add 4–8 oz (100–200 g) mushrooms, chopped and sautéed in butter, near the end of cooking time.

Risi Bisi
Add 1 lb (450 g) cooked peas and ¼ cup (60 mL) chopped parsley to basic risotto. (This is not authentic Risi Bisi, which is considered a thick soup in Italy. However, it is similar.)

Risotto Milanese

Bulgur Pilaf with Lemon

Portions: 12 Portion size: 2½ oz (75 g)

U.S.	Metric	Ingredients	PROCEDURE
1 oz	30 g	Butter	1. Heat the butter in a saucepan. Add the chopped onion and sauté gently without browning until the onion is soft.
4 oz	125 g	Onion, chopped fine	
8 oz	250 g	Bulgur, coarse	2. Add the bulgur. Stir to coat with butter. Stir over heat for 1 minute to lightly toast the grain.
4 tsp	20 mL	Grated lemon zest	3. Add the grated lemon zest and stir to mix.
1½ pt	750 mL	Chicken stock, hot	4. Stir in the hot chicken stock. Add salt and pepper to taste. Bring to a simmer.
to taste	to taste	Salt	
to taste	to taste	Pepper	5. Cover the pot and cook over low heat or in an oven heated to 350°F (175°C) until the bulgur is tender, about 20 minutes.
4 tbsp	60 mL	Chives, chopped	6. Uncover and fluff the grain with a kitchen fork. Add the chives and toss to mix in.

Per serving:
Calories, 90; Protein, 3 g; Fat, 2 g (20% cal.); Cholesterol, 5 mg;
Carbohydrates, 15 g; Fiber, 4 g; Sodium, 25 g.

Wheat Berries with Pecans and Poblanos

Portions: 12   Portion size: 4 oz (125 g)

U.S.	Metric	Ingredients	PROCEDURE
1 lb 8 oz	750 g	Whole wheat berries, rinsed and soaked overnight in cold water (see note)	1. Drain the soaking water from the wheat berries. Add the wheat berries to the cold water in a pot. Bring to a boil. Reduce heat to a simmer, cover, and simmer until the wheat berries are tender but still slightly crunchy. This will take about 1 hour. Remove from heat and allow to stand, covered, for 10 minutes. Drain.
2 qt	2 L	Cold water	
2 oz	60 mL	Olive oil	2. Heat the olive oil in a sauté pan. Add the pecans and diced poblano peppers. Sauté about 1 minute.
3 oz	90 g	Chopped pecans	3. Add the cooked wheat berries. Toss over heat until the mixture is hot. Season to taste.
3 oz	90 g	Roasted poblano pepper, diced	
to taste	to taste	Salt	

Per serving:
Calories, 280; Protein, 8 g; Fat, 10 g (31% cal.); Cholesterol, 0 mg;
Carbohydrates, 42 g; Fiber, 7 g; Sodium, 0 mg.

Note: This recipe was developed using soft wheat berries with the bran left on. Other types of wheat berries may be used, but the yields and cooking times will vary. For example, the white wheat berries shown in the illustration on page 505 cook in less than 30 minutes and yield 3 times their dry weight (about 4½ lb/2.25 kg for this recipe). When using a new type of product, test cooking time and yield with a small quantity before adapting it to production.

VARIATIONS

Substitute any green chile or any sweet bell pepper for the poblanos.

Brown Rice, Barley, Farro, or Cracked Wheat with Pecans and Poblanos
Substitute cooked brown rice, cooked barley, cooked farro, or cracked wheat pilaf for the cooked wheat berries.

Barley with Wild Mushrooms and Ham

Portions: 10   Portion size: 3½ oz (110 g)

U.S.	Metric	Ingredients	PROCEDURE
1 oz	30 g	Dried porcini mushrooms	1. Soak the dried porcini in hot water until they are soft. Drain the mushrooms and squeeze them out, reserving all the soaking liquid. Strain or decant the liquid to remove any sand or grit. Chop the mushrooms.
4 oz	125 mL	Hot water	
1 oz	30 mL	Oil	2. Heat the oil in a heavy pot. Add the onion and celery. Sauté briefly.
4 oz	125 g	Onions, small dice	3. Add the barley and sauté briefly, as for making rice pilaf.
4 oz	125 g	Celery, small dice	4. Add the stock and the mushroom liquid. Bring to a boil. Stir in the chopped mushrooms and the ham. Add salt to taste.
10 oz	300 g	Barley	
1 pt 4 oz	600 mL	Brown stock, chicken stock, or vegetable broth	5. Cover tightly. Cook on top of the stove over low heat or in the oven at 325°F (160°C) until the barley is tender and the liquid is absorbed, about 30–45 minutes.
4 oz	125 g	Cooked ham, small dice	
to taste	to taste	Salt	

Per serving:
Calories, 170; Protein, 7 g; Fat, 6 g (30% cal.); Cholesterol, 10 mg;
Carbohydrates, 24 g; Fiber, 6 g; Sodium, 125 mg.

VARIATIONS

Add other vegetables to the barley, such as diced carrots, turnips, fennel, or parsnips. Add them at the same time as the onion and celery, or cook them separately and add them at the end of cooking.

Pasta and Dumplings

Understanding Pasta

Macaroni products, or pastas, are popular alternatives to other starch foods. The word *pasta* is Italian for "paste," so called because pasta is made from a mixture of wheat flour and water and, sometimes, eggs.

Not so many years ago, many of us knew only spaghetti with tomato sauce and elbow macaroni with cheese, among all pasta products. Today, thanks to the influence of Italian cooks, we have a choice of a great variety of pasta dishes.

KINDS, CHARACTERISTICS, AND QUALITY FACTORS

1. Commercial pasta is made from dough that has been shaped and dried.

    Macaroni refers to pastas made from flour and water. These include spaghetti, lasagne, elbow macaroni, and many other shapes.

    Egg pastas contain at least 5½ percent egg solids in addition to the flour and water. They are usually sold as flat noodles of various widths.

    Checking quality. The best dried macaroni pastas are made from *semolina*, a high-protein flour from the inner part of durum wheat kernels. Lower-quality products are made from farina, a softer flour.

    Look for a good yellow color, not gray-white. The product should be very hard, brittle, and springy, and it should snap with a clean, sharp-edged break. When cooked, it should be firm and hold its shape well. Poor-quality pastas are soft and pasty when cooked.

2. Fresh egg pasta is made from flour and eggs and, sometimes, a small quantity of water and/or oil. Use a regular all-purpose or bread flour. Hard semolina flour, used for factory-made spaghetti and macaroni, is not appropriate for fresh egg pasta. Softer flour makes a more tender pasta. Soft egg noodle products are also available fresh and frozen from manufacturers. They take less time to cook than dried macaroni products.

SHAPES AND THEIR USES

Pasta is made in hundreds of shapes and sizes. Each shape is appropriate for different kinds of preparations because of the way different kinds of sauce cling to them or the way their textures complement the texture of the topping. The illustrations show some of the most popular kinds. Table 18.1 describes the most common shapes and gives suggestions for use.

Top row: elbow macaroni, pepe bucato, radiatore, ziti, conchiglie.
Middle row: fettuccine; spaghettini; fusilli; (three small piles, from top to bottom) orzo, stelline, and ditalini; lasagne; spaghetti; (two small piles, from top to bottom) gemelli and rigatoni.
Bottom row: bow ties (farfalle), penne, manicotti.

TABLE 18.1

Commercial Pasta Shapes and Uses

Name	Description	Suggested Uses
Spaghetti	Long, round	With great variety of sauces, especially tomato sauces
Spaghettini	Thin, long, round	Like spaghetti, especially with olive oil and seafood sauces
Vermicelli	Very thin	With light, delicate sauces and, broken, in soups
Linguine	Looks like slightly flattened spaghetti	Like spaghetti; popular with clam sauces
Fusilli	Long, shaped like a corkscrew	Thick, creamy sauces
Macaroni	Long, hollow, round tubes	Especially good with hearty meat sauces
Elbow macaroni	Short, bent macaroni	Cold, in salads; baked, in casseroles
Penne or mostaccioli	Hollow tubes, cut diagonally; may be smooth or ridged	Baked, with meat sauce or with tomato sauce and cheese; or freshly cooked, with tomato sauce
Ziti	Short, hollow tubes, cut straight	
Rigatoni	Larger tubes, with ridges	
Manicotti	Large hollow tubes, sometimes with ridges (sometimes called cannelloni, which are actually rolled from fresh egg noodle dough)	Stuff with cheese or meat filling
Fettuccine	Flat egg noodles	Rich cream sauces or meat sauces
Lasagne	Broad, flat noodles, often with rippled edges	Bake with meat, cheese, or vegetable fillings
Conchiglie	Shell shaped	With seafood or meat sauces; small sizes can be used in salads
Bow ties or farfalle		With sauces containing chunks of meat, sausage, or vegetables
Pastina (little pasta)		In soups; cold, in salads; buttered, as a side dish
Ditalini	Very short, hollow tubes	
Orzo	Rice shaped	
Stelline	Tiny stars	
Acini di pepe	"Peppercorns"	
Pepe bucato	"Peppercorns" with holes	

Remember that fresh egg pasta and factory-made spaghetti and macaroni are different products. It makes no sense to say that one type is better than the other. Italian cooks use fresh and dried pasta in different ways, with different recipes for each type.

Cooking Pasta

DONENESS

Pasta should be cooked *al dente*, or "to the tooth." This means that cooking should be stopped when the pasta still feels firm to the bite, not soft and mushy. Much of the pleasure of eating pasta is its texture (that's why there are so many shapes), and this is lost if it is overcooked.

Testing Doneness

Many suggestions have been made for testing doneness, but none is more reliable than breaking off a very small piece and tasting it. As soon as the pasta is *al dente*, the cooking must be stopped at once. Half a minute extra is enough to overcook it.

Cooking times differ for every shape and size of pasta. Timing also depends on the kind of flour used and the moisture content. Times indicated on the package are often too long.

Fresh egg pasta, if it has not been allowed to dry, takes only 1 to 1½ minutes to cook after the water has returned to a boil.

Pasta is best if cooked and served immediately. Whenever possible, you should try to cook pasta to order. Fresh pasta, in particular, cooks so quickly that there is little reason to cook it in advance. In volume operations, however, commercial pasta may have to be cooked ahead of time. The following procedures are used for quantity cookery.

Procedure for Cooking Pasta

1. Use at least 4 quarts boiling, salted water per pound of pasta (4 L per 500 g). Use about 1½ tablespoons (25 g) salt per 4 quarts (4 L) water.

2. Have the water boiling rapidly and drop in the pasta. As it softens, stir gently to keep it from sticking together and to the bottom.

3. Continue to boil, stirring a few times.

4. As soon as it is *al dente*, drain immediately in a colander and rinse with cold running water until the pasta is completely cooled. Otherwise, it would continue to cook and become too soft. (If you are cooking just a few portions to serve immediately, just drain well and do not cool. Sauce and serve without a moment's delay.)

   If the pasta is to be used cold in a salad, it is ready to be incorporated into the recipe as soon as it has cooled.

5. If the pasta is to be held, toss gently with a small amount of oil to keep it from sticking.

6. Measure portions into mounds on trays. Cover with plastic film and refrigerate until service time. (Do not store pasta in cold water. The pasta will absorb water and become soft, as though it had been overcooked.)

7. To serve, place the desired number of portions in a china cap and immerse in simmering water to reheat. Drain, plate, and add sauce.

Alternative Method: Steam Table Service

Pasta gradually becomes soft and mushy when kept hot for service, but it will hold reasonably well for 30 minutes. It will not be as good as if freshly cooked, however.

1. Follow steps 1 to 3 above.

2. Drain the pasta while still slightly undercooked. Rinse briefly in cool water, enough to stop the cooking and rinse off starch but not enough to cool the pasta. Pasta should still be quite warm.

3. Transfer to steam table pan and toss with oil to prevent sticking.

4. Hold for up to 30 minutes.

Yields

One pound (450 g) uncooked dried pasta yields about 3 pounds (1.4 kg) cooked pasta. This is enough for four to six main-course portions or eight to ten side-dish or first-course portions.

One pound (450 g) uncooked fresh pasta yields about 2 to 2½ pounds (900 to 1100 g) cooked pasta.

Tomato Sauce for Pasta

Yield: 3 qt (3 L)   Portions: 24   Portion size: 4 oz (125 g)

U.S.	Metric	Ingredients	PROCEDURE
1 pt	500 mL	Olive oil	1. Heat the olive oil in a large saucepot. Add the onions, carrots, and celery and sauté lightly for a few minutes. Do not let them brown.
½ lb	225 g	Onion, chopped fine	
½ lb	225 g	Carrot, chopped fine	
½ lb	225 g	Celery, chopped fine	2. Add remaining ingredients. (See Appendix 2 for can sizes and substitutions.) Simmer, uncovered, about 45 minutes, until reduced and thickened.
1 No. 10 can	1 No. 10 can	Whole tomatoes	
2	2	Garlic cloves, minced	3. Pass through a food mill. Taste and adjust seasonings.
1 oz	30 g	Salt	
1 tbsp	15 mL	Sugar	

Per serving:
Calories, 190; Protein, 1 g; Fat, 18 g (82% cal.); Cholesterol, 0 mg;
Carbohydrates, 8 g; Fiber, 2 g; Sodium, 660 mg.

Note: Except for meat sauce, most Italian sauces are cooked less than American-style tomato sauce and have fewer ingredients. As a result, they have a more pronounced fresh tomato taste.

VARIATIONS

Meat Sauce

Brown 2 lb (1 kg) ground beef, ground pork, or a mixture of beef and pork, in oil or rendered pork fat. Add 8 oz (250 mL) red wine, 2 qt (2 L) tomato sauce, 1 qt (1 L) beef or pork stock, and parsley, basil, and oregano to taste. Simmer 1 hour, uncovered.

Tomato Cream Sauce

Use butter instead of olive oil in basic recipe. At service time, add 1 cup heavy cream per quart of tomato sauce (250 mL per liter). Bring to simmer and serve.

Tomato Sauce with Sausage

Slice 3 lb (1.4 kg) fresh Italian sausage and brown in oil. Drain and add to basic tomato sauce. Simmer 20 minutes.

Tomato Sauce with Sausage and Eggplant

Prepare like Tomato Sauce with Sausage, but use 1½ lb (700 g) each sausage and peeled, diced eggplant.

Tomato Sauce with Ham and Rosemary

Cook 1 lb (450 g) ham, cut into fine dice, and 2 tbsp (30 mL) dried rosemary leaves in a little olive oil for a few minutes. Add to basic tomato sauce (after it has been passed through the food mill) and simmer 5 minutes.

Fresh Egg Pasta

Yield: 1½ lb (700 g)

U.S.	Metric	Ingredients	PROCEDURE
1 lb	450 g	Bread flour	1. Put the flour in a mound on a work surface. Make a well in the center and add the eggs, oil, and salt.
5	5	Eggs	2. Working from the center outward, gradually mix the flour into the eggs to make a dough.
½ oz	15 mL	Olive oil	3. When it is firm enough to knead, begin kneading the dough, incorporating more flour. If the dough is still sticky when all the flour has been incorporated, add more flour, a little at a time. Knead well for at least 15 minutes.
pinch	pinch	Salt	4. Cover the dough and let it rest for at least 30 minutes.

5. Cut the dough into 3–5 pieces. Set the rollers of a pasta machine at the widest opening. Pass the pieces of dough through the machine, folding them in thirds after each pass and dusting them lightly with flour to keep them from getting sticky. Continue passing each piece through the machine until it is smooth. See Figure 18.8.

6. Working with one piece of dough at a time, decrease the width between the rollers one notch and pass the dough through them again. After each pass, turn the rollers one notch narrower, dust the dough with flour, and pass it through again. Continue until the dough is as thin as desired. The pasta is now ready to cut into desired shapes and to cook. See below for cutting instructions.

Per 1 ounce:
Calories, 90; Protein, 4 g; Fat, 2 g (20% cal.); Cholesterol, 45 mg; Carbohydrates, 14 g; Fiber, 0 g; Sodium, 20 mg.

VARIATIONS

Cutting Instructions

Fettuccine or Taghatelle: Roll dough thin and cut with wide cutting rollers.

Taglierini: Roll dough thin and cut with narrow cutting rollers.

Papardelle: Cut by hand, using a fluted cutting wheel, into long noodles about ¾ inch (18 mm) wide.

Tonnarelli: Roll dough to the same thickness as the width of the narrow cutting roller. Cut with the narrow cutting rollers. The result is like square spaghetti.

Bow ties: Cut into rectangles about 1½ × 3 inches (4 × 8 cm). Pinch in the middle to make a bow.

Lasagne: Cut by hand into broad strips about 8–12 inches (20–30 cm) long.

Spinach Pasta

Clean 1 lb (450 g) AP spinach, discarding stems. Simmer 5 minutes in salted water. Drain, rinse in cold water, and squeeze dry. Chop as fine as possible. Incorporate in basic pasta recipe, adding it to the flour at the same time as the eggs. Reduce the quantity of eggs to 4.

Other Colored Pastas

Other colored vegetables, in small quantities, cooked until tender and puréed or chopped fine, can be substituted for spinach to color pasta. For example, try experimenting with beets, red bell peppers, and carrots.

Figure 18.8 Working with fresh egg pasta.

(a) Set the rollers of the machine at their widest setting. Pass the piece of dough through the rollers, fold in thirds, and repeat until the dough is smooth.

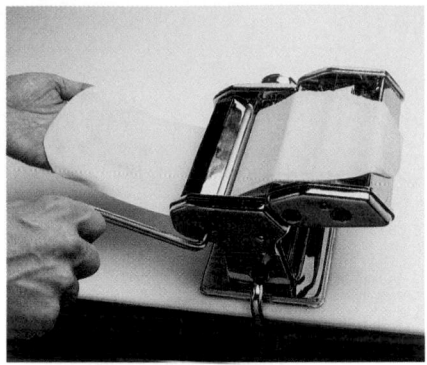

(b) Decrease the opening between the rollers one notch at a time and pass the dough through them to roll to desired thickness.

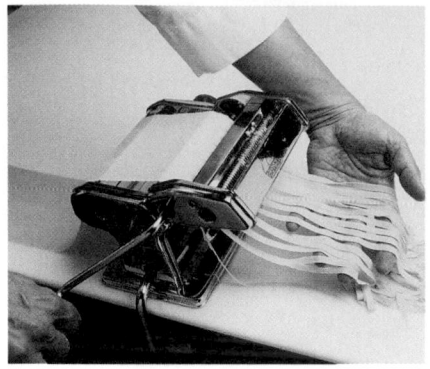

(c) Pass the rolled-out dough through the appropriate cutters to make pasta of desired size and shape.

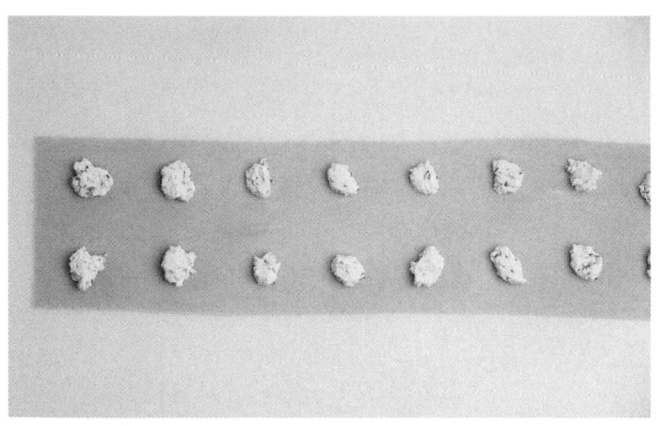

(d) To make ravioli, lay a thin sheet of pasta on the workbench. Deposit portions of filling on the dough using a spoon, small scoop, or pastry bag.

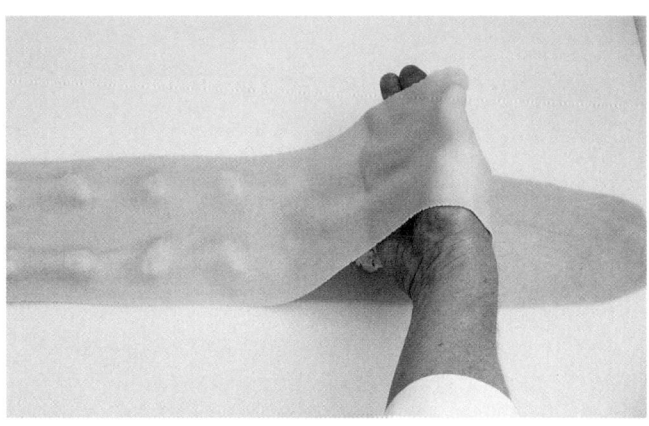

(e) Cover with another sheet of pasta.

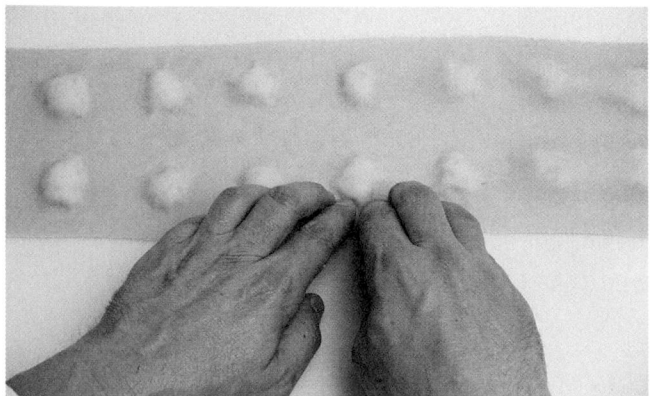

(f) Press down between the mounds of filling to seal the layers of pasta together. Try to remove air bubbles from between the layers.

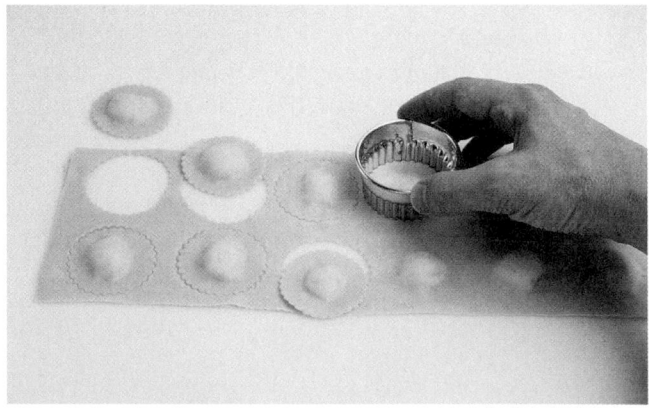

(g) Cut out the ravioli with cutters, or cut them apart with a pastry wheel.

Fettuccine Alfredo

Portions: 10   **Portion size:** 6–7 oz (175–200 g)

U.S.	Metric	Ingredients	PROCEDURE
1 cup	250 mL	Heavy cream	1. Combine the cream and butter in a sauté pan. Bring to a simmer, reduce by one-fourth, and remove from heat.
2 oz	60 g	Butter	
1½ lb	700 g	Fresh fettuccine	2. Drop the noodles into boiling salted water, return to a full boil, and drain. The noodles must be slightly undercooked because they will cook further in the cream.
1 cup	250 mL	Heavy cream	3. Put the drained noodles in the pan with the hot cream and butter. Over low heat, toss the noodles with two forks until they are well coated with the cream.
6 oz	175 g	Freshly grated parmesan cheese	4. Add the remainder of the cream and the cheese and toss to mix well. (If the noodles seem dry at this point, add a little more cream.)
to taste	to taste	Salt	5. Add salt and pepper to taste.
to taste	to taste	Pepper	6. Plate and serve immediately. Offer additional grated cheese at the table.

Per serving:
Calories, 500; Protein, 17 g; Fat, 32 g (58% cal.); Cholesterol, 195 mg; Carbohydrates, 35 g; Fiber, 1 g; Sodium, 430 mg.

VARIATIONS

Fettuccine with Vegetables I (Fettuccine Primavera)

Fresh, lightly cooked vegetables can be added to fettuccine to make a great variety of dishes. In the basic recipe, use about half the quantity of cream and one-third to one-half the quantity of cheese. Select 4–6 fresh vegetables, cook them al dente, cut into appropriately small sizes and shapes, and add them to the pasta when it is being tossed in the cream. The following are examples of appropriate vegetables:

Fettuccine with Vegetables II

Mushrooms	Tiny green beans
Peas	Asparagus
Broccoli	Artichoke hearts
Red or green bell pepper	Zucchini

Small quantities of finely diced ham, prosciutto, or bacon can also be added as a flavor accent.

Fettuccine with Vegetables II

Prepare like Fettuccine with Vegetables I, but omit all butter and cream. Instead, toss the freshly cooked fettuccine and cooked vegetables with olive oil. Add parmesan cheese as desired.

Fettuccine with Seafood

Use half the quantity of cream and cheese in the basic recipe. Prepare like Fettuccine with Vegetables I, adding only 1–3 types of vegetables. At the same time, add desired quantity of cooked seafood, such as shrimp, scallops, crab, or lobster. For a fuller flavor, reduce a small amount of fish stock and white wine with the cream in the first step.

Fettuccine with Gorgonzola

Prepare as in basic recipe, except use light cream instead of heavy cream in the first step. Omit the second quantity of heavy cream, and instead add 6 oz (175 g) gorgonzola cheese (Italian blue cheese). Reduce the quantity of parmesan cheese to 2 oz (60 g).

Pesto (Fresh Basil Sauce)

Yield: about 3 cups (750 mL)   **Portions:** 12   **Portion size:** 2 oz (60 mL)

U.S.	Metric	Ingredients	PROCEDURE
2 qt	2 L	Fresh basil leaves	1. Wash the basil leaves and drain well.
1½ cups	375 mL	Olive oil	2. Put the basil, oil, nuts, garlic, and salt in a blender or food processor. Blend to a paste, but not so long that it is smooth. It should have a slightly coarse texture.
2 oz	60 g	Walnuts or pine nuts (pignoli)	
6 cloves	6 cloves	Garlic	3. Transfer the mixture to a bowl and stir in the cheese.
1½ tsp	7 mL	Salt	
5 oz	150 g	Freshly grated parmesan cheese	4. To serve, cook pasta to order according to the basic procedure. Just before the pasta is done, stir a little of the hot cooking water into the pesto to thin it, if desired. Toss the drained pasta with the pesto and serve immediately. Pass additional grated cheese.
1½ oz	50 g	Freshly grated romano cheese	

Per 1 ounce:
Calories, 350; Protein, 8 g; Fat, 35 g (88% cal.); Cholesterol, 15 mg;
Carbohydrates, 3 g; Fiber, 1 g; Sodium, 550 mg.

Spaghettini Puttanesca

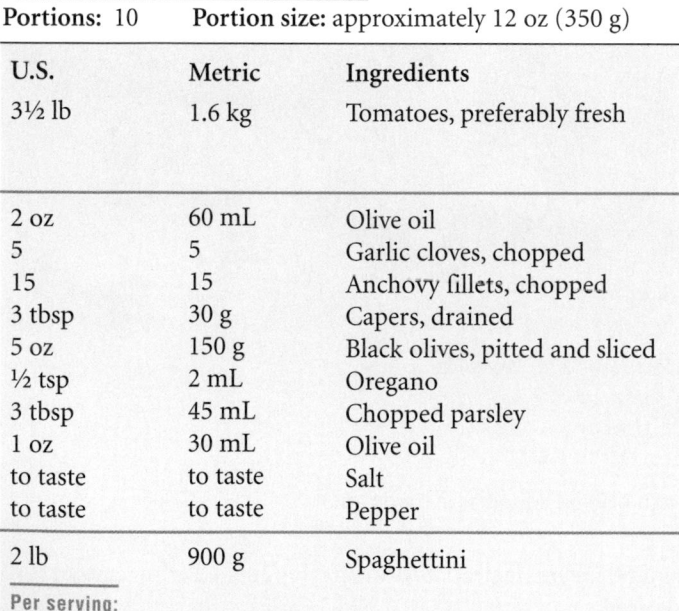

Portions: 10   **Portion size:** approximately 12 oz (350 g)

U.S.	Metric	Ingredients	PROCEDURE
3½ lb	1.6 kg	Tomatoes, preferably fresh	1. Peel, seed, and dice the tomatoes, and let them stand in a colander. If using canned tomatoes, drain them and chop them coarsely.
2 oz	60 mL	Olive oil	2. Heat the olive oil in a sauté pan over moderate heat. Add the garlic and sauté for a minute.
5	5	Garlic cloves, chopped	
15	15	Anchovy fillets, chopped	3. Add the anchovy fillets and sauté for a few seconds.
3 tbsp	30 g	Capers, drained	4. Add the tomatoes, capers, and olives. Bring to a boil. Cook 2–3 minutes.
5 oz	150 g	Black olives, pitted and sliced	
½ tsp	2 mL	Oregano	5. Remove from heat. Add the oregano, the parsley, and the second quantity of olive oil. Season to taste with salt and pepper.
3 tbsp	45 mL	Chopped parsley	
1 oz	30 mL	Olive oil	
to taste	to taste	Salt	
to taste	to taste	Pepper	
2 lb	900 g	Spaghettini	6. Boil the spaghettini, drain, toss with the sauce, and serve immediately. Grated cheese is usually not served with this dish.

Per serving:
Calories, 500; Protein, 16 g; Fat, 13 g (23% cal.); Cholesterol, 5 mg;
Carbohydrates, 80 g; Fiber, 9 g; Sodium, 460 mg.

Linguine with White Clam Sauce

Portions: 10   **Portion size:** approximately 12 oz (350 g)

U.S.	Metric	Ingredients	PROCEDURE
4 dozen	4 dozen	Cherrystone clams	1. Open the clams. Strain and reserve 1 pt (500 mL) of their juice. Chop the clams coarsely.
1 cup	250 mL	Olive oil	2. Heat the olive oil in a large sauté pan. Add the garlic and brown it very lightly. Do not let it get too brown, or it will be bitter.
4–6 cloves	4–6 cloves	Garlic, sliced thin	
½ tsp	2 mL	Red pepper flakes	3. Add the red pepper and then, very carefully, add the wine. (If the pan is very hot, you may want to cool it a little first to prevent dangerous spattering when the liquid is added.) Reduce the wine by half.
½ cup	125 mL	Dry white wine (optional)	
2 tsp	10 mL	Oregano	4. Add the reserved clam juice and reduce by half.
			5. Add the oregano.
2 lb	900 g	Linguine	6. Drop the linguine into boiling, salted water and boil al dente. Drain and plate.
4 tbsp	60 mL	Chopped parsley	7. While the linguine is boiling, add the chopped clams and the parsley to the olive oil mixture. Heat gently, just until the clams are hot. Do not overcook them, or they will be tough.
to taste	to taste	Black pepper	
			8. Add pepper to taste. (Because clams are salty, the sauce will probably not need any salt, but taste to make sure.)
			9. Spoon the sauce over the hot linguine and serve at once.
			10. Many people prefer this dish without parmesan cheese, but provide it on the side to those who want it.

Per serving:
Calories, 600; Protein, 21 g; Fat, 24 g (36% cal.); Cholesterol, 25 mg;
Carbohydrates, 74 g; Fiber, 7 g; Sodium, 40 mg.

Baked Lasagne

Portions: 24   Portion size: 8 oz (225 g)

U.S.	Metric	Ingredients	PROCEDURE
1½ lb	700 g	Ricotta cheese	1. Mix together the ricotta, parmesan, and eggs. Season to taste with salt and pepper.
2 oz	60 g	Parmesan cheese	
2	2	Eggs	
to taste	to taste	Salt	
to taste	to taste	Pepper	
2 lb	900 g	Fresh pasta or spinach pasta	2. Cut the fresh pasta into lasagne noodles. Cook them in boiling salted water, drain, and rinse in cold water. Lay them out in a single layer on oiled sheet pans.
3 qt	3 L	Meat sauce (p. 516)	3. Ladle a little meat sauce into a standard hotel pan, 12 × 20 inches (20 × 50 cm). Spread it across the bottom.
1½ lb	700 g	Mozzarella cheese, shredded	4. Arrange a layer of noodles in the pan. Then add a layer of the ricotta mixture, a layer of noodles, a layer of sauce, and a layer of mozzarella.
4 oz	125 g	Parmesan cheese	5. Continue making layers of noodles, ricotta, sauce, and mozzarella until all ingredients are used. Top with parmesan cheese.
			6. Bake at 375°F (190°C) for about 45 minutes. Cover lightly with foil at first to keep it from drying out, but remove the foil for the last 15 minutes of baking time.

Per serving:
Calories, 450; Protein, 26 g; Fat, 25 g (50% cal.); Cholesterol, 150 mg;
Carbohydrates, 29 g; Fiber, 2 g; Sodium, 590 mg.

VARIATIONS

Other ingredients can be added to lasagne, such as sliced, cooked meatballs, sausages, zucchini, eggplant, and so forth. It is best to add only one or two ingredients so that the lasagne doesn't seem like a catchall for leftovers.

If meat items are added to the lasagne, you may use plain tomato sauce instead of meat sauce. The ricotta mixture may also be omitted, especially if other protein items are added or if the quantity of mozzarella is increased.

Vegetable Ravioli in Lemongrass Broth

Portions: 12   **Portion size:** 4 oz (125 g) (uncooked weight)
plus 2 oz (60 mL) broth

U.S.	Metric	Ingredients	PROCEDURE
1 lb	500 g	Chinese cabbage	1. Cut the Chinese cabbage into fine shreds.
6	6	Scallions	2. Trim and slice the scallions.
6 oz	175 g	Snow peas	3. Trim the snow peas and cut diagonally into thin julienne.
4 oz	125 g	Carrots	4. Trim, peel, and grate the carrot.
4 oz	125 g	Mushrooms, trimmed	5. Chop the mushrooms coarsely.
2 oz	60 mL	Vegetable oil	6. Heat the oil in a large sauté pan. Add the vegetables and sauté until wilted.
1 oz	30 mL	Soy sauce	7. Add the soy sauce. Lower the heat to moderate and continue to cook until the vegetables are tender and there is no liquid in the pan.
1 tsp	5 mL	Sesame oil	8. Remove from the heat and cool. Add the sesame oil and the cilantro. Adjust the seasoning with salt.
2 tbsp	30 mL	Chopped cilantro	
to taste	to taste	Salt	
1 lb 8 oz	750 g	Fresh pasta dough	9. Roll the pasta dough into thin sheets. Lay half the sheets on the worktable.
as needed	as needed	Water or egg wash	10. Place mounds of the vegetable mixture about 3–4 inches (8–10 cm) apart on the pasta, using about ½ oz (15 g) for each mound. This quantity makes about 60 ravioli, or 5 per portion.
			11. Brush the exposed pasta with water or egg wash. Top with the remaining sheets of pasta. Press the layers of pasta together to seal them, at the same time pressing around the vegetable mounds to eliminate air bubbles. Cut into round or square ravioli.
4 stalks	4 stalks	Lemongrass	12. Trim off and discard the tops of the lemongrass stalks. Crush the bases, then chop coarsely.
1 oz	30 g	Ginger root, sliced	13. Combine the lemongrass, ginger, scallions, and water in a saucepan. Simmer 10–15 minutes, until the water is lightly flavored. Strain and season to taste with salt.
4	4	Scallions, sliced	
1 qt	1 L	Water	14. Drop the ravioli into boiling salted water. Reduce the heat and simmer about 3 minutes, until the pasta is cooked.
to taste	to taste	Salt	15. Remove the ravioli with a skimmer and drain well.
as needed	as needed	Cilantro leaves for garnish	16. Arrange the ravioli in broad soup plates and pour the lemongrass broth over them. Garnish with a few leaves of cilantro.

Per serving:
Calories, 250; Protein, 9 g; Fat, 9 g (33% cal.); Cholesterol, 90 mg; Carbohydrates, 32 g; Fiber, 3 g; Sodium, 190 mg.

Ravioli with Cheese Filling

Portions: 25   Portion size: 5 oz (150 g) uncooked
or approx.
7 oz (200 g) cooked

U.S.	Metric	Ingredients	PROCEDURE
3 lb	1.4 kg	Ricotta cheese	1. Mix together the ricotta, parmesan, egg yolks, parsley, and seasonings.
8 oz	250 g	Parmesan cheese	
5	5	Egg yolks	
¾ cup	50 g	Chopped parsley	
½ tsp	2 mL	Nutmeg	
to taste	to taste	Salt	
to taste	to taste	White pepper	
4½ lb	2 kg	Fresh pasta	2. Roll the pasta into thin sheets.

3. Over half the pasta, make small mounds of the cheese filling about 1 tsp (5 mL) each, arranging them in a checkerboard pattern about 1½–2 inches (4–5 cm) apart.

4. Lay the remaining pasta over the top and press down between the mounds of cheese to seal well (see Figure 18.8). While doing this, try to avoid sealing large air bubbles inside the ravioli. Note: If the pasta is fresh and moist, the layers will seal together if pressed firmly. If it is dry, moisten the bottom layer lightly between the mounds of cheese, using a brush dipped in water. Do not get the pasta too wet.

5. Cut the ravioli apart with a pastry wheel. Check each piece to be sure it is completely sealed.

6. The cheese filling does not keep well, so the ravioli should be cooked the same day they are made. They can be held briefly on sheet pans covered with dry, clean towels; turn them over from time to time so that they do not stick. Alternatively, cook them immediately in boiling salted water, keeping them slightly underdone. Drain and rinse under cold water, drain, and toss with oil or melted butter. Spread in a single layer on a sheet pan and refrigerate. They can then be reheated to order by sautéing them briefly in butter or oil or by dipping them in boiling water.

7. Serve with your choice of sauce, such as tomato sauce, meat sauce, tomato cream sauce, or just melted butter and parmesan cheese.

Per serving:
Calories, 410; Protein, 21 g; Fat, 17 g (38% cal.); Cholesterol, 205 mg; Carbohydrates, 42 g; Fiber, 1 g; Sodium, 270 mg.

Rigatoni or Penne with Sausage and Clams

Portions: 8   **Portion size:** approximately 10 oz (300 g) pasta and sauce, plus 3 clams

U.S.	Metric	Ingredients
1 oz	30 mL	Olive oil
8 oz	250 g	Italian sausage, cut into ½-inch (1-cm) slices
4 oz	125 g	Onion, chopped
4 oz	125 g	Green bell pepper, diced
4 oz	125 g	Red bell pepper, diced
6 oz	180 g	Tomatoes, peeled, seeded, chopped
pinch	pinch	Saffron
to taste	to taste	Hot red pepper flakes
24	24	Littleneck clams, well scrubbed
to taste	to taste	Salt
to taste	to taste	Pepper
1 lb	500 g	Rigatoni or penne
8 tsp	40 mL	Chopped parsley

PROCEDURE

1. Heat the oil in a sauté pan. Add the sausage and sauté until just cooked. Remove with a slotted spoon.
2. Add the onion and diced peppers to the fat in the pan. Sauté briefly until just starting to get tender.
3. Add the tomatoes, saffron, and hot pepper. Simmer about 5 minutes.
4. Meanwhile, add the penne or rigatoni to boiling salted water and boil al dente.
5. Shortly before the pasta is cooked, return the sausage to the pan with the vegetable mixture. Set over moderately high heat. Add the clams and cover. Cook just until the clams open. Do not overcook, or they will be tough. Season with salt and pepper.
6. Drain the pasta and immediately transfer to pasta bowls for serving.
7. Top with the contents of the pan, dividing the clams, sausage, and vegetables evenly among the servings.
8. Sprinkle with chopped parsley. Serve immediately.

Per serving:
Calories, 340; Protein, 18 g; Fat, 9 g (24% cal.); Cholesterol, 30 mg; Carbohydrates, 47 g; Fiber, 6 g; Sodium, 170 mg.

VARIATIONS

Mussels may be substituted for clams. Adjust the quantity as desired. If neither clams nor mussels are available, the dish can be made with shrimp, although its flavor and character will be quite different.

Rigatoni or Penne with Sausage, Peppers, and Tomatoes

Omit the seafood from the recipe and double the quantity of sausage.

Fettuccine with Chiles and Grilled Chicken

Portions: 8   Portion size: approximately 12 oz (360 g)

U.S.	Metric	Ingredients	PROCEDURE
1 lb	450 g	Chicken breasts, boneless and skinless	1. Season the chicken breasts lightly with chili powder and salt. Coat with oil. Marinate in the refrigerator until ready to cook.
to taste	to taste	Chili powder	
to taste	to taste	Salt	
as needed	as needed	Olive oil or corn oil	
4 oz	120 mL	Sour cream	2. Mix together the sour cream and lime juice. Refrigerate until needed.
1 oz	30 mL	Lime juice	
12 oz	360 g	Tomatoes, peeled, seeded, and chopped	3. Warm the tomatoes and garlic gently in the oil. Add the pepper strips. Season to taste with salt.
1 tsp	5 mL	Garlic, minced	4. Grill the chicken.
2 oz	60 mL	Olive oil or corn oil	
4 oz	120 mL	Mild green chiles (see note), roasted, peeled (p. 443), and cut into small strips	
to taste	to taste	Salt	
10–12 oz	300-360 g	Fresh fettuccine (see note)	5. Cook the pasta in boiling water. Drain and immediately toss together with the tomato mixture.
8 oz	240 g	Monterey jack cheese, grated	
6 oz	180 g	Avocado, sliced	6. Add the cheese and toss lightly. Check for seasonings and add more salt if necessary. Put into pasta bowls or serving plates.
			7. Slice the grilled chicken. Arrange the sliced chicken and sliced avocado on top of the paste.
			8. Drizzle with the sour cream mixture. Serve at once.

Per serving:
Calories, 440; Protein, 24 g; Fat, 27 g (55% cal.); Cholesterol, 65 mg; Carbohydrates, 25 g; Fiber, 3 g; Sodium, 260 mg.

Note: Green bell peppers may be substituted for the chiles if desired.

To add to the character of the dish, prepare fresh egg pasta according to the recipe on page 517, adding 5 tbsp (75 mL) chili powder for each pound (450 g) of flour.

VARIATION

To serve as a main course, increase the quantity of chicken as desired.

Macaroni and Cheese

Portions: 15	Portion size: 6 oz (175 g)		

U.S.	Metric	Ingredients	PROCEDURE
1 lb	450 g	Elbow macaroni	1. Cook macaroni according to basic method for boiling pasta. Drain and rinse in cold water.
1 qt	1 L	Medium Béchamel, hot (p. 145)	2. Flavor the white sauce with the dry mustard and Tabasco.
1 tsp	5 mL	Dry mustard	3. Mix the macaroni with the cheese. Combine with the béchamel.
dash	dash	Tabasco	4. Pour into a buttered half-size hotel pan. Sprinkle with bread crumbs and paprika.
1 lb	450 g	Cheddar cheese, grated	5. Bake at 350°F (175°C) until hot and bubbling, about 30 minutes.
		Garnish:	
as needed	as needed	Bread crumbs	
as needed	as needed	Paprika	

Per serving:
Calories, 330; Protein, 14 g; Fat, 17 g (46% cal.); Cholesterol, 50 mg; Carbohydrates, 31 g; Fiber, 1 g; Sodium, 290 mg.

Note: Cheese sauce may be used instead of béchamel. If you do so, reduce grated cheese to 4 oz (100 g) or omit.

Dumplings

Dumplings are starch products made from soft doughs or batters and cooked by simmering or steaming. They are served as side dishes and in soups and stews. Many national cuisines have their own kinds of dumplings. (For Chinese filled dumplings or wontons, see p. 731.)

Potato Dumplings

Portions: 10	Portion size: 5 oz (150 g)		

U.S.	Metric	Ingredients	PROCEDURE
2½ lb	1.1 kg	Boiled potatoes, peeled, cold	1. Grate the potatoes into a mixing bowl.
12 oz	350 g	Flour	2. Add the flour and salt and mix lightly until just combined.
2 tsp	10 mL	Salt	3. Add the eggs and mix well to form a stiff dough. Work in more flour if necessary.
2	2	Eggs	4. Divide the dough into 20 equal portions. Roll each piece into a ball. Refrigerate 1 hour. Dumplings may be made ahead up to this point.
4 oz	125 g	Butter	5. Heat the butter in a sauté pan and add the bread crumbs. Sauté for a few minutes, until the crumbs are toasted and brown. Set aside.
4 oz	125 g	Dry bread crumbs	6. Place the dumplings into a pot of boiling salted water. Stir so that they rise to the top and don't stick to the bottom of the pan. Simmer 10 minutes.
			7. Remove with a slotted spoon and place in a single layer in a hotel pan (or onto serving plates).
			8. Top with the toasted buttered bread crumbs. Serve 2 pieces per order. (Dumplings may also be served with melted butter or with pan gravy.)

Per serving:
Calories, 360; Protein, 8 g; Fat, 11 g (28% cal.); Cholesterol, 65 mg; Carbohydrates, 57 g; Fiber, 3 g; Sodium, 680 mg.

VARIATIONS

One or more of the following may be added to the dough: ¼ cup (60 mL) chopped parsley; 4 oz (125 g) diced bacon, cooked crisp; 2 oz (60 g) onion, chopped fine and sautéed in butter or bacon fat.

Potato Gnocchi with Tomato Sauce

Portions: 16   Portion size: 4½ oz (140 g)

U.S.	Metric	Ingredients	PROCEDURE
4 lb	2 kg	All-purpose potatoes	1. Wash the potatoes but do not peel. Boil until tender.
1 lb	500 g	Flour	2. Peel the potatoes while they are still hot, and force them through a food mill.
			3. Add about three-fourths of the flour to the potatoes and knead to make a soft, sticky mixture. Continue to work in more flour to form a soft, smooth dough. It should still be somewhat sticky. You may not need all the flour.
			4. Divide the dough into smaller pieces. Roll each piece into a sausage shape about ½ inch (1.5 cm) thick. Cut into pieces about ¾ inch (2 cm) long.
			5. To shape the gnocchi, pick up one piece of the dough and press it with the fingertip against the tines of a fork. Then flip the piece with the finger and allow it to drop on the worktable. This will give the piece grooves on one side and an indentation on the other side.
3 pt	1.5 L	Tomato Sauce for Pasta (p. 516)	6. Drop the gnocchi into a large quantity of boiling salted water. When they float to the surface, let them boil 10–15 seconds, then remove with a skimmer or slotted spoon.
1½ cup	350 mL	Grated parmesan cheese	7. Plate the gnocchi. Top each portion with 2 oz (60 mL) tomato sauce and 1 tbsp (15 mL) grated parmesan cheese.

Per serving:
Calories, 380; Protein, 10 g; Fat, 17 g (40% cal.); Cholesterol, 5 mg; Carbohydrates, 47 g; Fiber, 4 g; Sodium, 680 mg.

VARIATIONS

Gnocchi may be served with other pasta sauces, such as pesto, or simply with melted butter and grated cheese.

Spaetzle

Portions: 15   Portion size: 4 oz (125 g)

U.S.	Metric	Ingredients	PROCEDURE
6	6	Eggs	1. Beat the eggs in a bowl and add the milk or water, salt, nutmeg, and pepper.
1½ cups	375 mL	Milk or water	2. Add the flour and beat until smooth. You should have a thick batter. If it is too thin, beat in a little more flour.
1 tsp	5 mL	Salt	
⅛ tsp	0.5 mL	Nutmeg	3. Let the batter stand 1 hour before cooking to relax the gluten.
⅛ tsp	0.5 mL	White pepper	
1 lb or more	450 g or more	Flour	4. Set a colander (or a spaetzle machine, if available) over a large pot of boiling salted water. The colander should be high enough so that the steam doesn't cook the batter in the colander.
as needed	as needed	Butter, for service	5. Place the batter in the colander and force it through the holes with a spoon.
			6. After the spaetzle float to the top of the water, let them simmer 1–2 minutes, then remove them with a skimmer. Cool quickly in cold water and drain well.
			7. Cover and refrigerate until service.
			8. Sauté portions to order in butter until hot. Serve immediately.

Per serving:
Calories, 260; Protein, 7 g; Fat, 15 g (52% cal.); Cholesterol, 120 mg; Carbohydrates, 24 g; Fiber, 1 g; Sodium, 310 mg.

Terms for Review

waxy potato	long-grain rice	couscous	pasta
russet	parboiled rice	farro	macaroni
solanine	instant rice	spelt	egg noodle
duchesse potatoes	wild rice	polenta	semolina
hashed	basmati rice	hominy	al dente
enriched rice	jasmine rice	kasha	dumpling

Questions for Discussion

1. True or false: French fries made from fresh potatoes are always better than French fries made from frozen, blanched potato strips. Explain.

2. If mature, starchy potatoes are best for puréeing (mashed, duchesse, etc.), then why doesn't everyone use russets or Idahos, which are the starchiest?

3. Why is it not a good idea to put parisienne potatoes on your menu unless you are also serving a puréed potato product?

4. Many of the potato recipes in this chapter do not indicate what type of potato to use. For each of those recipes, indicate whether you would select all-purpose, russet, or waxy potatoes.

5. Should rice be washed before cooking? Always, sometimes, or never? Discuss.

6. Can wild rice and long-grain rice be cooked together to decrease the portion cost of wild rice? Explain.

7. What are the factors that determine how much water is needed to cook rice?

8. Describe the procedure for making cheese ravioli, starting with a freshly made piece of pasta dough.

chapter 19

Salads and Salad Dressings

In the days before modern refrigeration, the pantry was the storeroom where food products were kept before being brought into the kitchen. Because this room was cooler than the kitchen, it was especially suited as a work area for the production of cold food, especially aspics, chaud-froids, and other elaborate buffet preparations. In kitchens around the world, this department is often referred to by its French name, *garde manger* (gard mawn zhay).

Today, the pantry is the department responsible for cold foods and related items. This does not mean that no cooking is done in the pantry. On the contrary, garde manger chefs must be masters of a wide range of cooking techniques. In addition, they should have artistic judgment as well as the patience and dexterity to perform a great many hand operations quickly and efficiently.

This chapter deals with two groups of items prepared in the pantry: salads and salad dressings.

Salads

Because the number and variety of salad combinations is nearly endless, it is helpful to divide salads into categories in order to understand how they are produced. For the pantry chef, the most useful way to classify salads is by ingredients: green salads, vegetable salads, fruit salads, and so on. This is because production techniques are slightly different for each kind. We use this kind of classification when we discuss specific recipes later in this chapter.

Before the pantry chef can produce the salads, first he or she has to decide exactly what salads should be made. Therefore, you should know what kinds of salads are best for which purposes. For this reason, salads are also classified according to their function in the meal. Keep in mind that there are no exact dividing lines between the types of salads discussed below. For example, a salad that is suitable as the first course of a dinner may also be an excellent main course on a luncheon menu.

Types of Salads

APPETIZER SALADS

Many establishments serve salads as a first course, often as a substitute for a more elaborate first course. Not only does this ease the pressure on the kitchen during service but it also gives the customers a satisfying food to eat while their dinners are being prepared.

In addition, more elaborate composed salads are popular as appetizers (and also as main courses at lunch) in many elegant restaurants. These often consist of a poultry, meat, or fish item, plus a variety of vegetables and garnishes, attractively arranged on a bed of greens.

Appetizer salads should stimulate the appetite. This means they must have fresh, crisp ingredients; a tangy, flavorful dressing; and an attractive, appetizing appearance.

Preportioned salads should not be so large as to be filling, but they should be substantial enough to serve as a complete course in themselves. (Self-service salad bars, of course, avoid this problem.) Tossed green salads are especially popular for this reason, as they are bulky without being filling.

The combination of ingredients should be interesting, not dull or trite. Flavorful foods like cheese, ham, salami, shrimp, and crab meat, even in small quantities, add appeal. So do crisp raw or lightly cooked vegetables. A bowl of poorly drained iceberg lettuce with a bland dressing is hardly the most exciting way to start a meal.

Attractive arrangement and garnish are important because visual appeal stimulates appetites. A satisfying, interesting starter puts the customer in a good frame of mind for the rest of the meal.

ACCOMPANIMENT SALADS

Salads can also be served with the main course. They serve the same function as other side dishes (vegetables and starches).

Accompaniment salads must balance and harmonize with the rest of the meal, like any other side dish. For example, don't serve potato salad at the same meal at which you are serving French fries or another starch. Sweet fruit salads are rarely appropriate as accompaniments, except with such items as ham or pork.

Side-dish salads should be light and flavorful, not too rich. Vegetable salads are often good choices. Heavier salads, such as macaroni or high-protein (meat, seafood, cheese, etc.) salads are less appropriate, unless the main course is light. Combination salads with a variety of elements are appropriate accompaniments to sandwiches.

MAIN-COURSE SALADS

Cold salad plates have become popular on luncheon menus, especially among nutrition- and diet-conscious diners. The appeal of these salads is in variety and freshness of ingredients.

After reading this chapter, you should be able to:

1. Identify and describe five different salad types, and select appropriate recipes for use as an appetizer, accompaniment, main course, separate course, or dessert salad.

2. Identify a dozen popular salad greens; list six categories of other salad ingredients, and recognize several examples from each category.

3. Judge the quality of fruit and complete the pre-preparation procedures for fruit.

4. Identify the four basic parts of a salad.

5. Prepare and arrange salads that achieve maximum eye appeal.

6. Set up an efficient system for producing salads in quantity.

7. Prepare the following types of salads: green, vegetable, cooked, fruit, combination, and gelatin.

8. Set up a successful salad bar and buffet service.

9. Identify the major salad dressing ingredients.

10. Prepare the following: oil and vinegar dressings, mayonnaise and mayonnaise-based dressings, cooked dressings, and specialty dressings.

Main-course salads should be large enough to serve as a full meal and should contain a substantial portion of protein. Meat, poultry, and seafood salads, as well as egg salad and cheese, are popular choices.

Main-course salads should offer enough variety on the plate to be a balanced meal, both nutritionally and in flavors and textures. In addition to the protein, a salad platter should offer a variety of vegetables, greens, and/or fruits. Examples are chef's salad (mixed greens, raw vegetables, and strips of meat and cheese), shrimp or crab meat salad with tomato wedges and slices of avocado on a bed of greens, and cottage cheese with an assortment of fresh fruits.

The portion size and variety of ingredients give the chef an excellent opportunity to use imagination and creativity to produce attractive, appetizing salad plates. Attractive arrangements and good color balance are important.

SEPARATE-COURSE SALADS

Many finer restaurants serve a refreshing, light salad after the main course. The purpose is to cleanse the palate after a rich dinner and to refresh the appetite and provide a pleasant break before dessert.

Salads served after the main course were the rule rather than the exception many years ago, and the practice deserves to be more widespread. A diner who may be satiated after a heavy meal is often refreshed and ready for dessert after a light, piquant salad.

Separate-course salads must be very light and in no way filling. Rich, heavy dressings, such as those made with sour cream and mayonnaise, should be avoided. Perhaps the ideal choice is a few delicate greens, such as Bibb lettuce or Belgian endive, lightly dressed with vinaigrette. Fruit salads are also popular choices.

DESSERT SALADS

Dessert salads are usually sweet and may contain items such as fruits, sweetened gelatin, nuts, and cream. They are often too sweet to be served as appetizers or accompaniments and are best served as dessert or as part of a buffet or party menu.

Ingredients

Freshness and variety of ingredients are essential for quality salads. Lettuce, of course, is the first choice for most people, but many other foods can make up a salad.

The following tables list, by category, most of the ingredients used in popular salads. You will be able to think of others. Add them to the lists as they occur to you or as they are suggested by your instructors. The lists will be useful to you when you are creating your own salad ideas.

Following these lists are detailed descriptions of two groups of foods that have not been covered in previous chapters and belong especially in the pantry: salad greens and fresh fruits (Table 19.1).

SALAD GREENS

Iceberg lettuce	Escarole	Spinach
Romaine lettuce	Chicory or curly endive	Dandelion greens
Boston lettuce	Belgian endive	Watercress
Bibb or limestone lettuce	Chinese cabbage or celery	Arugula
Loose-leaf lettuce	cabbage	Radicchio

VEGETABLES, RAW

Avocado	Celery	Onions and scallions
Bean sprouts	Celeriac (celery root)	Peppers, red, green, and
Broccoli	Cucumbers	yellow
Cabbage, white, green, and red	Jerusalem artichokes	Radishes
Carrots	Kohlrabi	Tomatoes
Cauliflower	Mushrooms	

VEGETABLES, COOKED, PICKLED, AND CANNED

Artichoke hearts
Asparagus
Beans (all kinds)
Beets
Carrots
Cauliflower

Corn
Cucumber pickles (dill, sweet, etc.)
Hearts of palm
Leeks
Olives

Peas
Peppers, roasted and pickled
Pimientos
Potatoes
Water chestnuts

STARCHES

Dried beans (cooked or canned)

Potatoes
Macaroni products

Rice
Bread (croutons)

FRUITS, FRESH, COOKED, CANNED, OR FROZEN

Apples
Apricots
Bananas
Berries
Cherries
Coconut
Dates
Figs
Grapefruit

Grapes
Kiwi fruit
Mandarin oranges and tangerines
Mangoes
Melons
Oranges
Papayas
Peaches and nectarines

Pears
Persimmons
Pineapple
Plums
Prunes
Pomegranates
Raisins

PROTEIN FOODS

Meats (beef, ham)
Poultry (chicken, turkey)

Fish and shellfish (tuna, crab, shrimp, lobster, salmon, sardines, anchovies, herring, any fresh cooked fish)

Salami, luncheon meats, etc.
Bacon
Eggs, hard-cooked
Cheese, cottage
Cheese, aged or cured types

MISCELLANEOUS

Gelatin (plain or flavored)   Nuts

LETTUCE AND OTHER SALAD GREENS

Iceberg Lettuce

The most popular salad ingredient. Firm, compact head with crisp, mild-tasting, pale-green leaves. Valuable for its texture because it stays crisp longer than other lettuces. Can be used alone but is best mixed with more flavorful greens such as romaine because it lacks flavor itself. Keeps well.

Iceberg lettuce

Romaine or Cos Lettuce

Elongated, loosely packed head with dark-green, coarse leaves. Crisp texture, with full, sweet flavor. Keeps well and is easy to handle. Essential for Caesar salad. For elegant service, the center rib is often removed.

Romaine or cos lettuce

Boston Lettuce

Small, round heads with soft, fragile leaves. Deep green outside shading to nearly white inside. The leaves have a rich, mild flavor and delicate, buttery texture. Bruises easily and does not keep well. Cup-shaped leaves excellent for salad bases.

Boston lettuce

Bibb or Limestone Lettuce

Similar to Boston lettuce, but smaller and more delicate. A whole head may be only a few inches (less than 10 cm) across. Color ranges from dark green outside to creamy yellow at the core. Its tenderness, delicate flavor, and high price make it a luxury in some markets. The small, whole leaves are often served by themselves, with a light vinaigrette dressing, as an after-dinner salad.

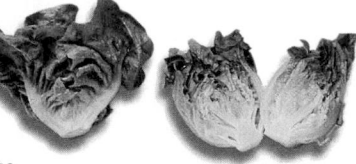

Bibb or limestone lettuce

Loose-leaf Lettuce

Forms bunches rather than heads. Soft, fragile leaves with curly edges. May be all green or with shades of red. Wilts easily and does not keep well, but is inexpensive and gives flavor, variety, and interest to mixed green salads.

Loose-leaf lettuce

Escarole or Broad-leaf Endive

Broad, thick leaves in bunches rather than heads. Texture is coarse and slightly tough, and flavor is somewhat bitter. Mix with sweeter greens to vary flavor and texture, but do not use alone because of the bitterness. Escarole is frequently braised with olive oil and garlic and served as a vegetable in Italian cuisine.

Escarole or broad-leaf endive

Chicory or Curly Endive

Narrow, curly, twisted leaves with firm texture and bitter flavor. Outside leaves are dark green; core is yellow or white. Attractive when mixed with other greens or used as a base or garnish, but may be too bitter to be used alone.

Chicory or curly endive

Frisée

Frisée

Frisée is the same plant as curly endive or chicory, except that it is grown in a way that makes it more tender and less bitter. Except for the outer layer, the leaves are pale yellow, slender, and feathery, with a distinct but mild taste.

Belgian Endive or Witloof Chicory

Narrow, lightly packed, pointed heads resembling spearheads, 4 to 6 inches (10 to 15 cm) long. Pale yellow-green to white in color. Leaves are crisp, with a waxy texture and pleasantly bitter flavor. Usually expensive. Often served alone, split in half or into wedges, or separated into leaves, accompanied by a mustard vinaigrette dressing.

Belgian endive or witloof chicory

Chinese Cabbage

Elongated, light-green heads with broad, white center ribs. Available in two forms: narrow, elongated head, often called *celery cabbage*, and thicker, blunt head, called *napa cabbage*. Tender but crisp, with a mild cabbage flavor. Adds excellent flavor to mixed green salads. Also used extensively in Chinese cooking.

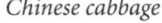

Chinese cabbage

Spinach

Spinach

Small, tender spinach leaves are excellent salad greens, either alone or mixed with other greens. A popular salad is spinach leaves garnished with sliced, raw mushrooms and crisp, crumbled bacon. Spinach must be washed thoroughly and the coarse stems must be removed.

Watercress

Most commonly used as a garnish, watercress is also excellent in salads. Small, dark-green, oval leaves with a pungent, peppery flavor. Remove thick stems before adding to salads.

Watercress

Arugula or rocket

Arugula

Also known as *rugula* or *rocket*, these pungent, distinctively flavored greens are related to mustard and watercress. They are tender and perishable, and they often are sandy, so they must be washed carefully. Arugula was once found almost exclusively in Italian restaurants, but it has since become more widely available and is increasingly popular.

Mesclun

Mesclun is a mixture of tender, baby lettuces. It is available as a mixture, but some chefs prefer to buy individual baby lettuces and make their own mixture.

Tatsoi

Tatsoi is a small, dark-green, round leaf. Its flavor has a pleasant bite similar to that of arugula and watercress and other members of the mustard family. It is sometimes included in mesclun mixtures, although it is not actually a lettuce.

Tatsoi

Mesclun

Mâche

Also called corn salad, lamb's lettuce, lamb's tongue, and field salad, mâche is a small, very tender green with spoon-shaped leaves. It has a delicate, nutty flavor.

Radicchio

Radicchio (ra dik ee oh), a red-leafed Italian variety of chicory, has creamy white ribs or veins and generally comes in small, round heads. It has a crunchy texture and a slightly bitter flavor. Radicchio is expensive, but only a leaf or two are needed to add color and flavor to a salad.

Mâche

Radicchio

Treviso

Treviso is a red-leafed plant like radicchio, but with elongated leaves somewhat like Belgian endive. Like radicchio and endive, it belongs to the chicory family and has a slightly bitter flavor.

Dandelion Greens

The familiar lawn ornament is also cultivated for use in the kitchen. Only young, tender leaves may be used. Older leaves are coarse and bitter, though cultivated varieties are milder than wild dandelion. Best in spring.

Treviso

Precleaned, Precut Salad Greens

Precut greens are sold in large, sealed plastic bags. They save labor costs in large operations but are more perishable than unprocessed greens. Keep refrigerated, and do not open until ready to use. Unopened bags will keep for two or three days. Taste before serving to make sure the greens do not have too much antioxidant on them, making them bitter.

TABLE 19.1

Fresh Fruit Pre-preparation

Note: This chart is a continuation of Table 16.2: Fresh Vegetable Pre-preparation

Product	Quality Indicators (Q.I.) and Pre-preparation (Prep.)	Percentage Yield
Apples	**Q.I.:** Mature apples have fruity aroma, brown seeds, and slightly softer texture than unripe fruit. Overripe or old apples are soft and sometimes shriveled. Avoid apples with bruises, blemishes, decay, or mealy texture. Summer varieties (sold until fall) do not keep well. Fall and winter varieties keep well and are available until summer. **Prep.:** Wash. Pare (if desired), quarter and remove core, or leave whole and core with special coring tool. Use stainless-steel knife for cutting. After paring, dip in solution of lemon juice (or other tart fruit juice) or ascorbic acid to prevent browning.	75%
Apricots	**Q.I.:** Accept only tree-ripened fruits, golden yellow, firm, and plump. Avoid fruit that is too soft or with blemishes, cracks, or decay. **Prep.:** Wash, split in half, and remove pit. Do not need to be peeled.	94%
Bananas	**Q.I.:** Plump and smooth, without bruises or spoilage. Avoid overripe fruit. **Prep.:** Ripen at room temperature for 3–5 days (full ripe fruit is all yellow with small brown flecks and no green). Do not refrigerate, or fruit will discolor. Peel and dip in fruit juice to prevent browning.	70%
Berries (blackberries, blueberries, cranberries, currants, raspberries, strawberries)	**Q.I.:** Full, plump and clean, with bright, fully ripe color. Watch for mold or spoiled fruits. Wet spots on carton indicate damaged fruit. **Prep.:** Refrigerate in original container until ready to use. Except for cranberries, berries do not keep well. Sort out spoiled berries and foreign materials. Wash with gentle spray and drain well. Remove stems from strawberries. Handle carefully to avoid bruising.	92–95%
Cherries	**Q.I.:** Plump, firm, sweet, and juicy, with uniform dark red to almost black color (except Royal Anne variety, which is creamy white with red blush). No blemishes or bruises. **Prep.:** Refrigerate in original container until ready to use. Remove stems and damaged fruit. Rinse and drain well. Remove pits with special cherry-pitting tool	82% (pitted)
Coconuts	**Q.I.:** Shake to hear liquid inside. Avoid cracked fruits and fruits with wet eyes. **Prep.:** Pierce eyes with ice pick or nail and drain liquid (which may be used in curries and similar dishes). Crack with a hammer and remove meat from shell (easier if placed in 350°F (175°C) oven for 10 to 15 minutes). Peel off brown skin with paring knife or vegetable peeler.	50%
Figs	**Q.I.:** Plump, soft fruits without spoilage or sour odor. Calimyrna figs are light green when ripe; Missions are nearly black. **Prep.:** Rinse and drain (handle carefully). Remove stem ends. Very perishable. Store as short a time as possible.	95% (80–85% if peeled)
Grapefruit	**Q.I.:** Firm, smooth skins, heavy for size. Avoid puffy, soft fruits and those with pointed ends. Cut and taste for sweetness. **Prep.:** For grapefruit halves, cut in half crosswise and free flesh from membranes with grapefruit knife. For sections and slices, peel and section or slice as illustrated in Figure 7.12.	45–50% (flesh without membrane); 40–45% (juiced)
Grapes	**Q.I.:** Firm, ripe, well-colored fruits in full bunches that are firmly attached to stems and do not fall off when shaken. Watch for shriveling or rotting at stem ends. **Prep.:** Refrigerate in original container. Wash and drain. Leave on bunches if desired for dining room presentation, or pull from stems. Cut in half and remove seeds (except for seedless variety).	90%
Kiwi fruit	**Q.I.:** Firm but slightly soft to touch when ripe. No bruises or excessively soft spots. **Prep.:** Pare thin outer skin with paring knife. Cut crosswise into slices.	80%
Kumquats	**Q.I.:** These look like tiny, elongated oranges about the size of an olive. Avoid shriveled or soft fruit. **Prep.:** Wash, drain well, and cut as desired. Skins and even seeds can be eaten. Skin is sweet, while pulp and juice are tart.	95–100%

(Continued)

Fresh Fruit Pre-preparation (*Continued*)

Product	Quality Indicators (Q.I.) and Pre-preparation (Prep.)	Percentage Yield
Lemons and limes	**Q.I.:** Firm, smooth skins. Color may vary: limes may be yellow, and lemons may have some green on skin. **Prep.:** Cut in wedges, slices, or other shapes for garnish, or cut in half crosswise for juicing.	40–45% (juiced)
Mangoes	**Q.I.:** Plump and firm, with clear color and no blemishes. Avoid rock-hard fruits, which may not ripen properly. **Prep.:** Let ripen at room temperature until slightly soft. Peel and cut flesh away from center stone, or cut in half before peeling, working a thin-bladed knife around both sides of the flat stone.	75%
Melons	**Q.I.:** Cantaloupes: Smooth scar on stem end, with no trace of stem (called *full slip*, meaning melon was picked ripe). Yellow rind, with little or no green. Heavy, with good aroma. Honeydew: Good aroma, slightly soft, heavy, creamy white to yellowish rind, not green. Large sizes have best quality. Crenshaws, casabas, Persians: Heavy, with rich aroma and slightly soft blossom end. Watermelon: Yellow underside, not white. Firm and symmetrical. Large sizes have best yield. Velvety surface, not too shiny. When cut, look for hard, dark-brown seeds and no white heart (hard white streak running through center). **Prep.:** Hollow types: Wash, cut in half, and remove seeds and fibers. Cut into portion-size wedges or cut balls with ball cutter. Watermelon: Wash. Cut into desired portions, or cut in half and cut balls with ball cutter.	Watermelons: 45%; other: 50–55%
Nectarines	Same as for peaches, except do not need to be peeled.	86%
Oranges and mandarins (including tangerines)	**Q.I.:** Oranges: Same as for grapefruit. Mandarins: May feel puffy, but should be heavy for size. **Prep.:** Peel by hand and separate sections. Discard fibers between sections.	60–65% (sections with no membranes); 50% (juiced)
Papayas	**Q.I.:** Firm and symmetrical, without bruises or rotten spots. Avoid dark-green papayas, which may not ripen properly. **Prep.:** Let ripen at room temperature, until slightly soft and nearly all yellow, with only a little green. Wash. Cut in half lengthwise and scrape out seeds. Peel, if desired, or serve like cantaloupe.	65%
Passion fruit	**Q.I.:** Select large fruit (size of large eggs or larger) that is heavy for size. Heavily wrinkled skin indicates ripeness. If skin is smooth, let ripen at room temperature. **Prep.:** Cut in half, taking care not to lose any juice. Scrape out seeds, juice, and pulp. Seeds can be eaten, so do not discard.	40–45%
Peaches	**Q.I.:** Plump and firm, without bruises or blemishes. Avoid green fruits, which are immature and will not ripen well. Select freestone varieties; clingstone varieties require too much labor.	75%

(*Continued*)

Arrangement and Presentation

THE STRUCTURE OF A SALAD

The four basic parts of a salad are base, body, garnish, and dressing. Salads may or may not have all four parts.

Base or Underliner

Leafy greens usually form the base of a salad. They add greatly to the appearance of some kinds of salads, which would look naked on a bare plate. Bound salads and many vegetable and fruit salads are usually more appealing when made with a base or under liner. Tossed green salads, salads served in a bowl rather than on a plate, and many kinds of combination salads and main-course salads are usually made without a base.

T A B L E   19.1

Fresh Fruit Pre-preparation *(Continued)*

Product	Quality Indicators (Q.I.) and Pre-preparation (Prep.)	Percentage Yield
Peaches *(Continued)*	**Prep.:** Let ripen at room temperature, then refrigerate in original container. Blanch in boiling water about 10–20 seconds, until skins slip off easily, and cool in ice water. Peel, cut in half, remove pits, and drop into fruit juice, sugar syrup, or ascorbic acid solution to prevent darkening.	
Pears	**Q.I.:** Clean, firm, and bright; no blemishes or bruises. **Prep.:** Wash. Peel, if desired, cut in half or quarters, and remove core.	75% (peeled and cored)
Persimmons	**Q.I.:** Firm, plump, and smooth, with good red color and stem cap attached. **Prep.:** Ripen at room temperature until very soft, then refrigerate (unripe fruits make your mouth feel as though hair is growing in it). Remove stem cap, cut as desired, and remove seeds, if any.	80%
Pineapples	**Q.I.:** Plump and fresh looking, orange-yellow color, abundant fragrance. Avoid soft spots, bruises, and dark, watery spots. Large sizes have best yield. **Prep.:** Store at room temperature for a day or two to allow some tartness to disappear, then refrigerate. May be cut in many ways. For slices, chunks, and dice, cut off top and bottom and pare like a grapefruit (see Figure 7.12), using stainless-steel knife. Remove all eyes. Cut into quarters lengthwise and cut out hard center core. Slice or cut as desired.	50%
Plums	**Q.I.:** Plump and firm but not hard, with good color and no bruises or blemishes. **Prep.:** Wash, cut in half and remove pits, or serve whole.	95% (pitted only)
Pomegranates	**Q.I.:** Good red color, firm but not hard, with no bruises **Prep.:** Lightly score the skin without cutting into the seeds. Carefully break into sections and separate the seeds from the membranes.	55%
Prickly pear or cactus pear	**Q.I.:** Good skin color, ranging from magenta to greenish red. Tender but not mushy, with no rotten spots. **Prep.:** If the fruit is hard, ripen at room temperature. Pare off ends and sides as for grapefruit, but holding the fruit with a fork, not with the hands, to avoid getting stung with any tiny thorns that may remain on the skin. Cut the red pulp as desired, or force it through a sieve to purée it and remove the seeds.	70%
Quince	**Q.I.:** Pear-shaped fruits are normally lumpy but should have firm or hard flesh and yellow skin with, at most, only a few small blemishes. **Prep.:** Pare, quarter, and remove core and seeds. Fruit is always cooked, usually in a sugar syrup, as raw fruit is hard, dry, and astringent. Fruit will turn slightly pink when cooked with sugar.	75%
Rhubarb	**Q.I.:** Firm, crisp, tender, with thick stalks, not thin and shriveled. Rhubarb is not actually a fruit but a stem. **Prep.:** Cut off all traces of leaf (which is poisonous). Trim root end if necessary. Cut into desired lengths.	85–90% (no leaves)

Cup-shaped leaves of iceberg or Boston lettuce make attractive bases. They give height to salads and help to confine loose pieces of food.

A layer of loose, flat leaves (such as romaine, loose-leaf, or chicory) or of shredded lettuce may be used as a base. This kind of base involves less labor and food cost, as it is not necessary to separate whole cup-shaped leaves from a head.

Body

This is the main part of the salad and, as such, receives most of our attention in this chapter.

Garnish

A garnish is an edible decorative item that is added to a salad to give eye appeal, though it often adds to the flavor as well. It should not be elaborate or dominate the salad. Remember this basic rule of garnishing: Keep it simple.

Garnish should harmonize with the rest of the salad ingredients and, of course, be edible. It may be mixed with the other salad ingredients (for example, shreds of red cabbage mixed into a tossed green salad), or it may be added at the end.

Often, the main ingredients of a salad form an attractive pattern in themselves, and no garnish is necessary. In the case of certain combination salads and other salads with many ingredients or components, there may be no clear distinction between a garnish and an attractive ingredient that is part of the body.

Nearly any of the vegetables, fruits, and protein foods listed on pages 533–534, cut into simple, appropriate shapes, may be used as garnish.

Dressing

Dressing is a seasoned liquid or semiliquid that is added to the body of the salad to give it added flavor, tartness, spiciness, and moistness.

The dressing should harmonize with the salad ingredients. In general, use tart dressings for green salads and vegetable salads and use slightly sweetened dressings for fruit salads. Soft, delicate greens like Boston or Bibb lettuce require a light dressing. A thick, heavy dressing will turn them to mush.

Dressings may be added at service time (as for green salads), served separately for the customer to add, or mixed with the ingredients ahead of time (as in potato salad, tuna salad, egg salad, and so on). A salad mixed with a heavy dressing, like mayonnaise, to hold it together is called a *bound salad.*

Remember: Dressing is a *seasoning* for the main ingredients. It should accent their flavor, not overpower or drown them. Review the rules of seasoning in Chapter 4.

ARRANGING THE SALAD

Perhaps even more than with most other foods, the appearance and arrangement of a salad is essential to its quality. The colorful variety of salad ingredients gives the chef an opportunity to create miniature works of art on the salad plate.

Unfortunately, it is nearly as difficult to give rules for arranging salads as it is for painting pictures because the principles of composition, balance, and symmetry are the same for both arts. It is something you have to develop an eye for, by experience and by studying good examples.

Guidelines for Arranging Salads

1. **Keep the salad off the rim of the plate.**
Think of the rim as a picture frame and arrange the salad within this frame. Select the right plate for the portion size, not too large or too small.

2. **Strive for a good balance of colors.**
Plain iceberg lettuce looks pale and sickly all by itself, but it can be livened up by mixing in some darker greens and perhaps a few shreds of carrot, red cabbage, or other colored vegetable. On the other hand, don't go overboard. Three colors are usually enough, and sometimes just a few shades of green will create a beautiful effect. Too many colors may look messy.

3. **Height helps make a salad attractive.**
Ingredients mounded on the plate are more interesting than if they are spread flat. Lettuce cups as bases add height. Often just a little height is enough. Arrange ingredients like fruit wedges or tomato slices so that they overlap or lean against each other rather than lay them flat on the plate.

4. **Cut ingredients neatly.**
Ragged or sloppy cutting makes the whole salad look sloppy and haphazard.

5. **Make every ingredient identifiable.**
Cut every ingredient into large enough pieces so that the customer can recognize each immediately. Don't pulverize everything in the buffalo chopper or VCM. Bite-size pieces are the general rule, unless the ingredient can be cut easily with a fork, such as tomato slices. Seasoning ingredients, like onion, may be chopped fine.

6. **Keep it simple.**
A simple, natural arrangement is pleasing. An elaborate design, a gimmicky or contrived arrangement, or a cluttered plate is not pleasing. Besides, elaborate designs take too long to make.

Recipes and Techniques

Thorough mise en place is extremely important in salad making. Little cooking is involved, but a great deal of time-consuming handwork is. Salads can be made quickly and efficiently only if the station is set up properly.

Procedure for Quantity Salad Production

(a) Prepare all ingredients ahead. Arrange cold salad plates on trays for easy refrigeration.

(b) Place lettuce bases on all plates.

When salads are made in quantity, an assembly-line production system is most efficient. Figure 19.1 illustrates this technique.

1. Prepare all ingredients. Wash and cut greens. Prepare cooked vegetables. Cut all fruits, vegetables, and garnish. Mix bound and marinated salads (egg salad, potato salad, three-bean salad, etc.). Have all ingredients chilled.

2. Arrange salad plates on worktables. Line them up on trays for easy transfer to refrigerator.

3. Place bases or underliners on all plates.

4. Arrange body of salad on all plates.

5. Garnish all salads.

6. Refrigerate until service. Do not hold more than a few hours or salads will wilt. Holding boxes should have high humidity.

7. Do not add dressing to green salads until service or they will wilt.

(c) Place body of salad (in this case, potato salad) on all plates.

(d) Garnish all salads. Refrigerate until service.

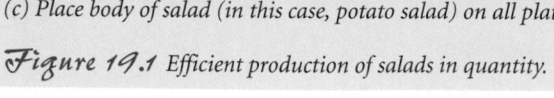

Figure 19.1 *Efficient production of salads in quantity.*

GREEN SALADS

Principles

Salad greens must be fresh, clean, crisp, cold, and well drained, or the salad will be of poor quality. Good greens depend on proper preparation.

Moisture and air are necessary to keep greens crisp.

1. Leaves wilt because they lose moisture. Crispness can be restored by washing and refrigeration. The moisture that clings to the leaves after thorough draining is usually enough. Too much water drowns them and dissolves out flavor and nutrients.

2. Air circulation is essential for the greens to breathe. Do not seal washed greens too tightly or pack too firmly. Refrigerate in colanders covered with clean, damp towels, or in specially designed perforated plastic bins. These protect from drying while still allowing air circulation.

Browning or rusting occurs when cut greens are held too long. This can be partially avoided by rinsing them in a mild antioxidant and by using stainless-steel knives. Better yet, plan purchasing and production so that you don't need to hold them too long.

Basic Procedure for Green Salads

1. **Wash greens thoroughly.**

Remove core from head lettuce by striking the core gently against the side of the sink and twisting it out. Do not smash it or you'll bruise the entire head. Cut through the core of other greens or separate the leaves so that all traces of grit can be removed. Wash in several changes of cold water, until completely clean. For iceberg lettuce, run cold water into the core end (after removing core), then turn over to drain.

2. **Drain greens well.**

Lift greens from the water and drain in a colander. Tools and machines are available that quickly spin-dry greens. Poor draining results in a watered-down dressing and a soupy, soggy salad.

3. **Crisp the greens.**

Refrigerate greens in a colander covered with damp towels or in a perforated storage bin to allow air circulation and complete drainage.

4. **Cut or tear into bite-size pieces.**

Many people insist on tearing leaves instead of cutting, but this is a slow method if you have a large quantity to do. Also, you are more likely to crush or bruise the leaves.

Use sharp stainless-steel knives for cutting. Bite-size pieces are important as a convenience to the customer. It is difficult to eat or cut large leaves with a salad fork.

5. **Mix the greens.**

Toss *gently* until uniformly mixed. Nonjuicy raw vegetable garnish such as green pepper strips or carrot shreds may be mixed in at this time. Just make sure the vegetables are not cut into compact little chunks that will settle to the bottom of the bowl. Broad, thin slices or shreds stay better mixed.

For tossed salads to be served immediately, add the dressing to the greens in the bowl. Toss to coat the greens with the dressing. Plate (step 6) and serve immediately. For preplated salads, proceed with steps 6 through 9.

6. **Plate the salads (including underliners, if used).**

Cold plates, please. Don't use plates right out of the dishwasher.

Avoid plating salads more than an hour or two before service, or they are likely to wilt or dry.

7. **Garnish.**

Exceptions: (a) Garnish that is tossed with the greens in step 5. (b) Garnish that will not hold well (croutons will get soggy, avocado will discolor, etc.). Add these at service time.

8. **Refrigerate.**

9. **Add dressing immediately before service, or serve it on the side.**

Dressed greens wilt rapidly.

Mixed Green Salad

Portions: 25   Portion size: 2½–3 oz (70–90 g)

U.S.	Metric	Ingredients	PROCEDURE
2 heads	2 heads	Iceberg lettuce	1. Review guidelines and method for preparing green salads (p. 542).
2 heads	2 heads	Romaine	2. Wash and drain the greens thoroughly. Chill in refrigerator.
½ head	½ head	Curly endive (chicory)	3. Cut or tear the greens into bite-size pieces.
1 bunch	1 bunch	Watercress	4. Place the greens in a large mixing bowl and toss gently until uniformly mixed.
			5. Plate the salads on cold salad plates or in bowls.
			6. Refrigerate until service.
			7. Serve with any appropriate dressing. Serve the dressing in a separate container or add it just before service.

Per serving:
Calories, 15; Protein, 1 g; Fat, 0 g (0% cal.); Cholesterol, 0 mg; Carbohydrates, 2 g; Fiber, 2 g; Sodium, 10 mg.

VARIATIONS

Any combination of salad greens may be used. The number of heads needed will vary because the size of the heads is not always the same. Plan on 2½–3 oz (70–90 g) EP per serving. For 25 portions, you will need about 4½ lb (2 kg) trimmed greens.

Vegetable ingredients, if they are not juicy, may be tossed with the greens. See pages 533–534 for a listing. Shredded carrot and red cabbage are useful because a small amount gives an attractive color accent.

Garnishes may be added after the salads are plated, such as

Tomato wedges   Cherry tomatoes   Cucumber slices   Radishes
Pepper rings   Croutons   Hard-cooked egg wedges or slices

Service Variation

Instead of plating and holding the salads, toss the greens with dressing immediately before service. For 25 portions, use about 1½ pt (700 mL) dressing. Use a vinaigrette variation or emulsified French. Mayonnaise dressings are too thick for tossing. Plate and serve immediately.

Spinach Salad

Portions: 25   Portion size: 3 oz (90 g)

U.S.	Metric	Ingredients	PROCEDURE
3 lb	1.4 kg	Spinach leaves, trimmed (no stems)	1. Wash the spinach in several changes of cold water until there is no trace of sand on them. Drain well. Chill in the refrigerator.
12 oz	350 g	Bacon	2. Cook the bacon on a griddle or in the oven on a sheet pan until crisp. Drain and let cool.
			3. Crumble the bacon.
1 lb	450 g	Fresh white mushrooms	4. Wash the mushrooms and dry them well. Trim the bottoms of the stems. Cut the mushrooms into thin slices.
6	6	Hard-cooked eggs	5. Chop the eggs coarsely.
			6. Place the spinach in a large bowl. Tear large leaves into smaller pieces. Smaller leaves may be left whole.
			7. Add the mushrooms. Toss to mix thoroughly.
			8. Portion the salad onto cold salad plates.
			9. Sprinkle the salads with the chopped eggs.
			10. Hold for service in refrigerator.
			11. At serving time, sprinkle with the crumbled bacon.
			12. Serve with a vinaigrette variation or with emulsified French dressing.

Per serving:
Calories, 60; Protein, 5 g; Fat, 3.5 g (50% cal.); Cholesterol, 55 mg; Carbohydrates, 3 g; Fiber, 2 g; Sodium, 130 mg.

Note: Bacon may be added to salads when they are assembled (step 9). However, it will be less appetizing because the fat congeals in the refrigerator. For best quality, cook the bacon as close to serving time as possible.

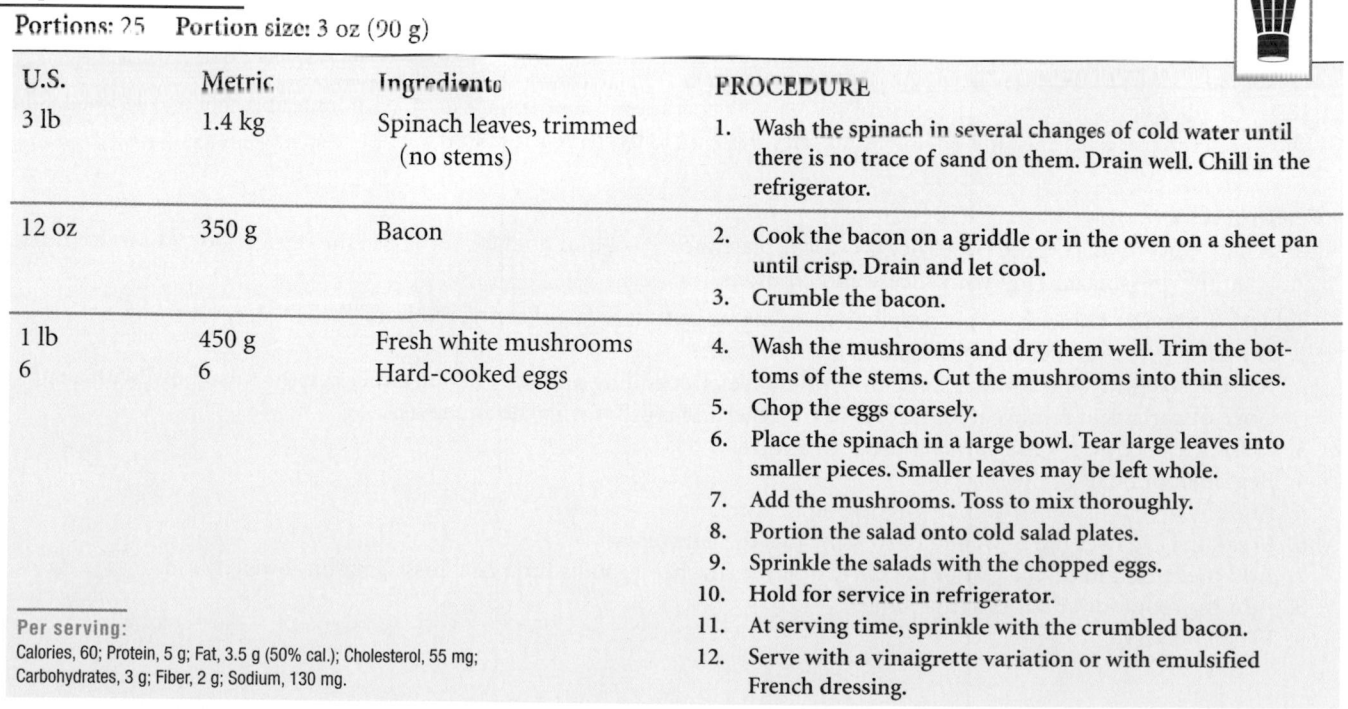

Caesar Salad

This famous salad is frequently prepared at the customer's table by the waiter, and most recipes are written for à la carte service. The recipe included here is adapted for kitchen preparation so that larger quantities can be prepared if desired. The ingredients are traditional, even if the method is not.

Portions: 25   **Portion size: 3 oz (90 g) lettuce, plus dressing**

U.S.	Metric	Ingredients	PROCEDURE
5 lb	2.3 kg	Romaine leaves	1. Wash and drain the greens thoroughly. Chill in the refrigerator.
12 oz	350 g	White bread	2. Trim the crusts from the bread. Cut the bread into small cubes measuring about ⅜ inch (1 cm).
2–4 oz	60–125 mL	Olive oil	3. Heat a thin layer of olive oil in a sauté pan over moderately high heat. Add the bread cubes and sauté in the oil until golden and crisp. Add more oil as needed.
			4. Remove the croutons from the pan and hold for service. Do not refrigerate.
		Dressing:	5. Mash the anchovies and garlic together to make a paste.
25	25	Anchovy fillets (optional)	6. Beat in the eggs and lemon juice until smooth.
2 tsp	10 mL	Garlic, crushed	7. Beating constantly with a wire whip, slowly add the olive oil.
4	4	Eggs, beaten (see note)	
6 oz	175 mL	Lemon juice	
2½ cups	600 mL	Olive oil	
to taste	to taste	Salt	
2 oz	60 g	Parmesan cheese, grated	8. Season the dressing to taste.
			9. Cut or tear the romaine into bite-size pieces. Place in a large bowl.
			10. Immediately before service, pour the dressing over the greens and sprinkle with the parmesan cheese. Toss until all the leaves are coated with the dressing.
			11. Add the croutons and toss again.
			12. Plate and serve immediately.

Per serving:
Calories, 290; Protein, 5 g; Fat, 26 g (80% cal.); Cholesterol, 35 mg; Carbohydrates, 10 g; Fiber, 2 g; Sodium, 125 mg.

Note: Coddled eggs are often used instead of raw eggs. To coddle eggs, simmer in water for 1 minute and cool in cold water. Some chefs prefer to use yolks only. It is advisable, for safety reasons, to use pasteurized eggs.

VARIATION

Alternative Method: If speed of service is critical, plate the lettuce and hold for service in the refrigerator. At service time, ladle on the dressing and top with cheese and croutons.

Tableside Service: Using the same proportions of ingredients, use the following method:
1. Have the lettuce and croutons prepared ahead of time.
2. Ask the customers how much garlic they would like. Depending on their answer, either rub the salad bowl with a cut clove of garlic and remove it, or leave it in the bowl and crush it with the anchovies.
3. Mash the anchovies (and garlic, if used) to a paste.
4. Beat in about half of the olive oil.
5. Add the greens and toss to coat with the oil mixture.
6. Break the egg over the bowl and drop it in. Toss the lettuce well.
7. Add the lemon juice, the rest of the oil, the parmesan cheese, and a little salt. Toss again until well mixed.
8. Add the croutons and toss a final time.
9. Plate and serve.

Garden Salad

Portions: 25   **Portion size:** 3 oz (90 g) plus garnish

U.S.	Metric	Ingredients	PROCEDURE
3½ lb	1.6 kg	Mixed salad greens	1. Include some firm-textured, crisp lettuce in the mixed greens, such as romaine or iceberg.
8 oz	250 g	Cucumbers	2. Wash and drain the greens thoroughly. Chill in the refrigerator.
4 oz	125 g	Celery	3. Score the cucumbers lengthwise with a fork (see p. 704). Peel them if they have been waxed. Cut into thin slices.
4 oz	125 g	Radishes	4. Cut the celery into thin slices on the bias.
4 oz	125 g	Scallions	5. Trim the radishes and cut into thin slices.
4 oz	125 g	Carrots	6. Trim the roots and wilted tops of the scallions. Cut in half crosswise. Then slice lengthwise into thin shreds.
1½ lb	700 g	Tomatoes	7. Trim and peel the carrots. Shred on a medium grater.
			8. Remove the core end of the tomatoes. Cut into wedges, 8–10 per tomato, depending on size.
			9. Cut or tear the lettuce and other greens into bite-size pieces.
			10. Place all ingredients except tomatoes in a large mixing bowl. Toss until evenly mixed.
			11. Plate the salads on cold plates or bowls.
			12. Garnish with tomato wedges.
			13. Hold for service in refrigerator.
			14. Serve with an appropriate dressing.

Per serving:
Calories, 25; Protein, 2 g; Fat, .5 g (14% cal.); Cholesterol, 0 mg;
Carbohydrates, 5 g; Fiber, 2 g; Sodium, 25 mg.

VEGETABLE SALADS

Principles

Vegetable salads are salads whose main ingredients are vegetables other than lettuce or other leafy greens. Some vegetables are used raw, such as celery, cucumbers, radishes, tomatoes, and green peppers. Some are cooked and chilled before including in the salad, such as artichokes, green beans, beets, and asparagus. See pages 533–534 for lists of vegetables that can be used.

Sometimes cooked pasta or a protein item such as meat, poultry, fish, or cheese is added to a vegetable salad. If the proportion of these ingredients is high, the salad may be more like the cooked salads discussed in the next section. There is no exact dividing line between these types of salads. It helps to keep the guidelines for both types of salads in mind when you are preparing these recipes.

Guidelines for Making Vegetable Salads

1. Neat, accurate cutting of ingredients is important because the shapes of the vegetables add to eye appeal. The design or arrangement of a vegetable salad is often based on different shapes, such as long, slender asparagus and green beans, wedges of tomato, slices of cucumber, strips or rings of green pepper, and radish flowers.

2. Cut vegetables as close as possible to serving time, or they may dry or shrivel at the edges.

3. Cooked vegetables should have a firm, crisp texture and good color. Mushy, overcooked vegetables are unattractive in a salad. See Chapter 16 for vegetable cooking principles.

4. After cooking, vegetables must be thoroughly drained and chilled before being included in the salad.

5. Vegetables are sometimes *marinated*, or soaked in a seasoned liquid, before being made into salads, as for Three-Bean Salad and Mushrooms à la Grecque. The marinade is usually some form of oil and vinegar dressing that also serves as the dressing for the salad. Do not plate marinated salads too far ahead of time, or the lettuce base will wilt. Use crisp, sturdy greens (such as iceberg, romaine, or chicory) as bases, as they do not wilt as quickly.

Cucumber and Tomato Salad

Portions: 25   Portion size: about 3 oz (90 g)

U.S.	Metric	Ingredients	PROCEDURE
10	10	Tomatoes, medium size	1. Wash the tomatoes and cut out the core at the stem end. Cut each tomato into 5 slices of uniform thickness.
3	3	Cucumbers	2. Wash the cucumbers. Score them lengthwise with a fork or flute them with a channel knife (see Figure 22.1). If the cucumbers have been waxed, peel them.
25	25	Lettuce leaves for underliners	3. Cut the cucumbers on the bias into slices ⅛ inch (3 mm) thick.
½ cup	125 mL	Chopped parsley	4. Arrange the washed, crisped lettuce leaves on cold salad plates.
			5. On the lettuce, overlap 2 slices of tomato alternating with 2 slices of cucumber. Make sure the most attractive side of each slice is facing up.
			6. Sprinkle the salads with chopped parsley.
			7. Hold for service in refrigerator.
1⅔ cups	400 mL	Vinaigrette	8. At service time, dress each salad with 1 tbsp (15 mL) dressing.

Per serving:
Calories, 110; Protein, 1 g; Fat, 11 g (83% cal.); Cholesterol, 0 mg; Carbohydrates, 4 g; Fiber, 1 g; Sodium, 125 mg.

VARIATIONS

Tomato and Cucumber Salad with Capers
Omit chopped parsley and sprinkle the salads with capers.

Tomato Salad
Omit cucumbers. Use 15 tomatoes and serve 3 slices per portion, overlapping on the plate.

Tomato and Spinach Salad
Prepare like Tomato Salad, but use spinach leaves instead of lettuce as the salad base.

Tomato and Watercress Salad
Prepare like Tomato Salad, but use watercress instead of lettuce as the salad base.

Tomato and Onion Salad
Substitute sweet Bermuda onion for the cucumber in the basic recipe. Alternate slices of tomato and onion on the plate.

Tomato and Green Pepper Salad
Substitute green peppers for the cucumber in the basic recipe. Alternate slices of tomato and pepper (rings) on the plate.

Tomato and Avocado Salad
Substitute avocado for the cucumber. Dip avocado slices in vinaigrette or lemon juice to keep them from darkening. Alternate slices of tomato and avocado on the plate.

Coleslaw

Portions: 25   **Portion size:** 3 oz (100 g)

U.S.	Metric	Ingredients	PROCEDURE
1½ pt	750 mL	Mayonnaise	1. Combine the mayonnaise, vinegar, sugar, salt, and pepper in a stainless-steel bowl. Mix until smooth.
2 oz	60 mL	Vinegar	
1 oz	30 g	Sugar (optional)	2. Add the cabbage and mix well.
2 tsp	10 mL	Salt	3. Taste and, if necessary, add more salt and/or vinegar.
½ tsp	2 mL	White pepper	
4 lb EP	2 kg EP	Cabbage, shredded	
25	25	Lettuce cups for under-liners	4. Arrange the lettuce leaves on cold salad plates.
			5. Using a No. 12 scoop, place a mound of coleslaw in the center of each plate.
			6. Hold for service in refrigerator.

Per serving:
Calories, 230; Protein, 2 g; Fat, 24 g (89% cal.); Cholesterol, 25 mg; Carbohydrates, 5 g; Fiber, 2 g; Sodium, 270 mg

VARIATIONS

1. Use Cooked Salad Dressing (p. 578) instead of mayonnaise. Reduce or omit vinegar.
2. Substitute sour cream for *half* of the mayonnaise.
3. Substitute heavy cream for 1 cup (250 mL) mayonnaise.
4. Substitute lemon juice for the vinegar.
5. Use 1 pt (500 mL) basic vinaigrette and omit mayonnaise and vinegar. Flavor with 2 tsp (10 mL) celery seed and 1 tsp (5 mL) dry mustard.
6. Add 2 tsp (10 mL) celery seed to the basic mayonnaise dressing.

Mixed Cabbage Slaw

Use half red cabbage and half green cabbage.

Carrot Coleslaw

Add 1 lb (500 g) shredded carrots to the basic recipe. Reduce cabbage to 3½ lb (1.7 kg).

Garden Slaw

Add the following ingredients to the basic recipe: 8 oz (250 g) carrots, shredded; 4 oz (125 g) celery, chopped or cut julienne; 4 oz (125 g) green pepper, chopped or cut julienne; 2 oz (60 g) scallions, chopped. Reduce cabbage to 3½ lb (1.7 kg).

Coleslaw with Fruit

Add the following ingredients to the basic recipe: 4 oz (125 g) raisins, soaked in hot water and drained; 8 oz (250 g) unpeeled apple, cut in small dice; 8 oz (250 g) pineapple, cut in small dice. Use sour cream dressing (dressing variation 2 above) and use lemon juice instead of vinegar.

Salad of Mixed Cabbage and Apples

Yield: 7½ lb (3.5 kg)   Portions: 24   Portion size: 5 oz (150 g)

U.S.	Metric	Ingredients	PROCEDURE
2 lb	900 g	Red cabbage	1. Finely shred the two cabbages, using a mandoline, a slicing machine, or the shredding blade of a food processor.
2 lb	900 g	Green cabbage	
1 lb 12 oz	800 g	Granny Smith apples	2. Peel and core the apples, then cut them into a fine julienne. Toss in the lemon juice.
1½ oz	45 mL	Lemon juice	
1 pt 4 oz	600 mL	Cider vinegar	3. To make the vinaigrette, whisk together the vinegar and cream, then whisk in the oil. Season to taste.
4 oz	125 mL	Cream	
8 oz	250 mL	Salad oil	
to taste	to taste	Salt	
to taste	to taste	White pepper	
1½–2 oz	50 g	Chives, chopped	4. Toss the cabbage and apples together and season with the vinaigrette. Leave to marinate 2–3 hours before serving.
			5. Just before serving, mix in the chopped chives.

Per serving:
Calories, 140; Protein, 1 g; Fat, 12 g (69% cal.); Cholesterol, 5 mg; Carbohydrates, 11 g; Fiber, 3 g; Sodium, 15 mg.

Basque-Style Pepper Salad

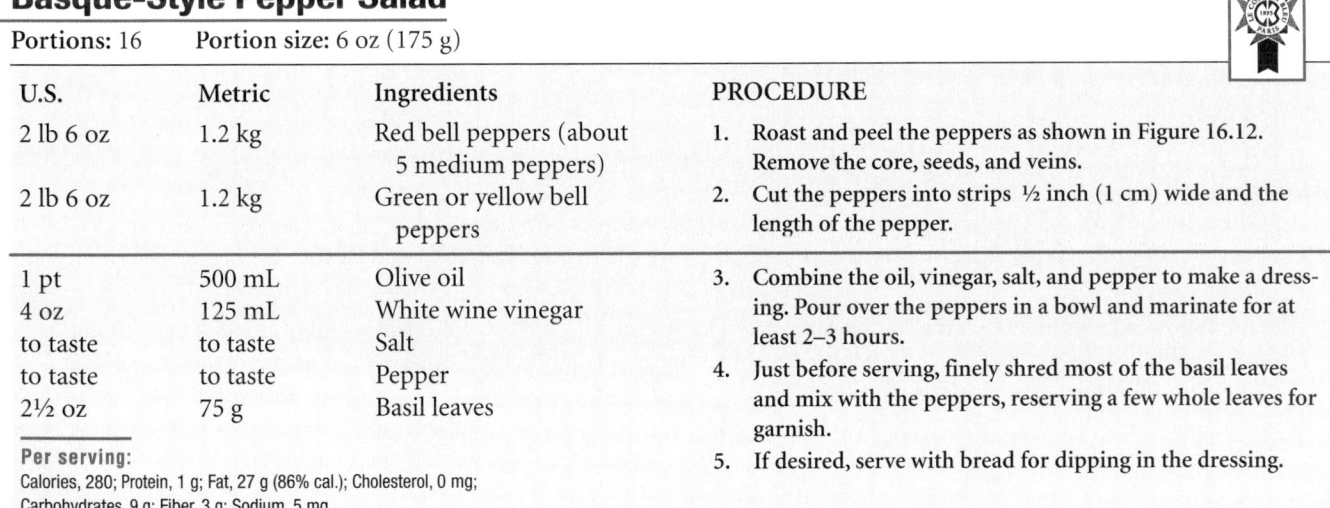

Portions: 16   Portion size: 6 oz (175 g)

U.S.	Metric	Ingredients	PROCEDURE
2 lb 6 oz	1.2 kg	Red bell peppers (about 5 medium peppers)	1. Roast and peel the peppers as shown in Figure 16.12. Remove the core, seeds, and veins.
2 lb 6 oz	1.2 kg	Green or yellow bell peppers	2. Cut the peppers into strips ½ inch (1 cm) wide and the length of the pepper.
1 pt	500 mL	Olive oil	3. Combine the oil, vinegar, salt, and pepper to make a dressing. Pour over the peppers in a bowl and marinate for at least 2–3 hours.
4 oz	125 mL	White wine vinegar	
to taste	to taste	Salt	
to taste	to taste	Pepper	4. Just before serving, finely shred most of the basil leaves and mix with the peppers, reserving a few whole leaves for garnish.
2½ oz	75 g	Basil leaves	
			5. If desired, serve with bread for dipping in the dressing.

Per serving:
Calories, 280; Protein, 1 g; Fat, 27 g (86% cal.); Cholesterol, 0 mg; Carbohydrates, 9 g; Fiber, 3 g; Sodium, 5 mg.

Cucumber Salad with Dill and Yogurt

Portions: 10   Portion size: 3½ oz (100 g)

U.S.	Metric	Ingredients	PROCEDURE
1½ lb	750 g	Cucumbers	1. Cut the cucumbers in half lengthwise. Scoop out the seeds and discard. Slice across into half-moon shapes, ¼ inch (½ cm) thick.
½ oz	15 g	Salt	
1 lb	500 g	Plain yogurt	2. Place the cucumber slices in a colander, sprinkle with the salt, and set aside for 30 minutes.
1½–2 oz	50 g	Fresh dill, chopped	
to taste	to taste	Freshly ground pepper	3. Rinse off the salt under cool running water, drain, and pat dry.
			4. Mix with the yogurt and dill, then season to taste with pepper.

Per serving:
Calories, 40; Protein, 2 g; Fat, 1.5 g (36% cal.); Cholesterol, 5 mg;
Carbohydrates, 4 g; Fiber, 1 g; Sodium, 570 mg.

White Bean Salad

Portions: 12   Portion size: about 6 oz (175 g)

U.S.	Metric	Ingredients	PROCEDURE
1 lb	500 g	White beans	1. Soak the beans overnight in cold water.
1	1	Carrot	2. Rinse the beans and place in a large pot with 6 qt (6 L) fresh water. Add the carrot, the onion stuck with the whole cloves, and the bouquet garni. Bring to a boil and simmer 1–2 hours or until tender. After cooking for 45 minutes, add some salt. Strain and allow to cool for 10 minutes. Discard the carrot, onion with cloves, and bouquet garni.
1	1	Onion	
2	2	Whole cloves	
1	1	Bouquet garni	
to taste	to taste	Salt	
5 tbsp plus 1 tsp	80 mL	Vinegar	3. Whisk together the vinegar, salt and pepper to taste, shallots, and chopped herbs.
to taste	to taste	Salt	4. Gradually whisk in the oil.
to taste	to taste	Pepper	5. Peel, seed, and dice the tomatoes. Mix into the vinaigrette.
6	6	Shallots, finely chopped	6. Once the beans have cooled to lukewarm, mix in the vinaigrette and place in the refrigerator to cool completely.
2 oz	60 g	Chopped mixed herbs (chives, parsley, chervil)	7. Grate the carrots and squeeze out the juices. Discard the juice or save for another use. Mix the carrots into the beans.
11 oz	325 mL	Oil	
24 oz	750 g	Tomatoes	8. Shred the radicchio. Line plates with the shredded radicchio. Portion the bean salad onto the plates.
4 oz	125 g	Carrots	
2 heads	2 heads	Radicchio	

Per serving:
Calories, 380; Protein, 10 g; Fat, 27 g (62% cal.); Cholesterol, 0 mg;
Carbohydrates, 28 g; Fiber, 7 g; Sodium, 20 mg.

Green Bean Salad

Portions: 25   Portion size: 3 oz (90 g)

U.S.	Metric	Ingredients	PROCEDURE
5 lb	2.3 kg	Green beans (see note)	1. Trim the ends of the green beans. Cut the beans into 2-inch (5-cm) lengths. 2. Cook the beans, uncovered, in boiling salted water until just tender. 3. Cool the beans thoroughly under cold running water or in ice water. Drain well.
1½ pt	700 mL	Mustard Vinaigrette (p. 572) or Italian dressing	4. Combine the beans, dressing, chives, and garlic. Mix well. 5. Refrigerate for 2–4 hours (see note).
4 tbsp	60 mL	Chives	
½ tsp	2 mL	Garlic, chopped fine	
6 oz	175 g	Red onions	6. Peel the onions and cut into very thin slices. Separate into rings.
25	25	Lettuce leaves for underliners	7. Line salad plates with lettuce leaves. 8. Just before service, place a 3-oz (90-g) portion of marinated green beans on each lettuce underliner, using a solid spoon. 9. Garnish the tops of the salads with a few onion rings. 10. Keep chilled, but serve as soon as possible so that the lettuce doesn't wilt.

Per serving:
Calories, 210; Protein, 2 g; Fat, 20 g (83% cal.); Cholesterol, 0 mg;
Carbohydrates, 7 g; Fiber, 3 g; Sodium, 220 mg.

Note: Frozen or canned green beans may be used. Canned green beans need no further cooking. Just drain and mix with the dressing.

Green vegetables should be served the same day they are placed in the marinade. If held too long, they begin to turn brown.

VARIATIONS

Portion the beans with a slotted spoon. Place a tablespoon of mayonnaise on each salad.

Other *cooked vegetables* may be marinated in vinaigrette and served using the same procedure:
  Artichoke hearts
  Asparagus
  Beets
  Carrots
  Cauliflower
  Leeks
  Dried beans: white beans, chickpeas, etc., alone or in combination (see next variation).

Three Bean Salad

Use only 1½ lb (700 kg) green beans. After beans are cooked, add 1½ lb (700 g) drained, canned kidney beans; 1½ lb (700 g) drained, canned chickpeas; 4 oz (125 g) onion, cut in small dice; 2 oz (60 g) green pepper, cut in small dice; and 2 oz (60 g) drained chopped pimiento. Proceed to step 4 as in basic recipe.

Mushrooms à la Grecque

Portions: 25   Portion size: 2½ oz (75 g)

U.S.	Metric	Ingredients	PROCEDURE
4½ lb	2 kg	Small whole mushrooms	1. Wash and dry the mushrooms. Trim the bottoms of the stems. Leave the mushrooms whole. (If only large ones are available, cut them into quarters.)
1 qt	1 L	Water	2. Place the water, olive oil, lemon juice, celery, and salt in a stainless-steel saucepan. Tie the sachet ingredients in cheesecloth and add to the pan.
1 pt	500 mL	Olive oil	
6 oz	175 mL	Lemon juice	
1 rib	1 rib	Celery	3. Bring to a boil. Simmer 15 minutes to extract flavors from the spices.
2 tsp	10 mL	Salt	
		Sachet:	4. Add the mushrooms. Simmer 5 minutes.
2	2	Garlic cloves, crushed	5. Remove from heat. Cool the mushrooms in the liquid.
1½ tsp	7 mL	Peppercorns, lightly crushed	6. Remove the celery and the sachet. Marinate the mushrooms overnight in the refrigerator. (The mushrooms will keep several days in the marinade.)
2 tsp	10 mL	Coriander seeds	
1	1	Bay leaf	
1 tsp	5 mL	Thyme, dried	
25	25	Lettuce cups for underliners	7. Arrange the lettuce leaves on cold salad plates.
¼ cup	60 mL	Chopped parsley	8. Just before service, place a 2½-oz (75-g) portion of mushrooms in each lettuce cup, using a slotted spoon.
			9. Sprinkle with chopped parsley.

Per serving:
Calories, 180; Protein, 3 g; Fat, 19 g (88% cal.); Cholesterol, 0 mg;
Carbohydrates, 3 g; Fiber, 1 g; Sodium, 190 mg.

VARIATIONS
Other vegetables may be prepared à la Grecque, using this recipe. Increase cooking time as necessary, but keep the vegetables crisp.

Artichoke hearts   Leeks
Carrots, sliced or diced Pearl onions
Cauliflower, florets

Carrot Salad

Portions: 25   Portion size: 3 oz (100 g)

U.S.	Metric	Ingredients	PROCEDURE
5 lb	2.5 kg	Carrots	1. Peel the carrots. Shred them on a coarse grater.
1½ cups	375 mL	Mayonnaise	2. Combine the mayonnaise and vinaigrette. Mix until smooth.
1 cup	250 mL	Vinaigrette	3. Add the carrots and mix. Season to taste with salt.
to taste	to taste	Salt	
25	25	Lettuce cups	4. Arrange the lettuce cups on cold salad plates.
13	13	Pitted black olives	5. Using a No. 12 scoop, place a mound of carrot salad in each lettuce cup.
			6. Cut the olives in half lengthwise. Garnish the top of each salad with an olive half.

Per serving:
Calories, 200; Protein, 1 g; Fat, 18 g (79% cal.); Cholesterol, 10 mg;
Carbohydrates, 10 g; Fiber, 3 g; Sodium, 200 mg.

VARIATIONS
Carrot Raisin Salad
Simmer 8 oz (250 g) raisins in water for 2 minutes. Cool, then drain. Mix raisins with the carrots.
Carrot Pineapple Salad
Mix 12 oz (375 g) drained pineapple tidbits with the carrots.
Carrot Celery Salad
Reduce the carrots to 3½ lb (1.7 kg). Mix 1½ lb (750 g) celery (cut julienne) or celery root (shredded) with the carrots.
Celery Salad
Use celery or celery root instead of carrots in basic recipe. Cut stalk celery into thin slices instead of shredding it.
Add 2 tbsp (30 mL) French or Dijon-type mustard to the dressing.

Pacific-Rim Salad with Beef

Portions: 25   Portion size: 5 oz (150 g)

U.S.	Metric	Ingredients	PROCEDURE
2 lb	900 g	Bean sprouts	1. Mix together the bean sprouts, snow peas, carrots, water chestnuts, scallions, and almonds. Hold in the refrigerator.
1 lb	450 g	Snow peas, trimmed and blanched	
8 oz	225 g	Carrots, cut julienne	
12 oz	350 g	Water chestnuts, sliced	
4 oz	125 g	Scallions, chopped	
4 oz	125 g	Slivered almonds, toasted	
1½ lb	700 g	Cold roast beef	2. Slice the beef about ¼ inch (6 mm) thick, then cut into thin strips.
1¾ pt	800 mL	Oriental Vinaigrette (p. 574)	3. About 2 hours before serving, marinate the beef in the vinaigrette for 30–60 minutes.
			4. Add the mixed vegetables to the beef and vinaigrette mixture. Toss to mix well.
1½ lb	700 g	Chinese cabbage, shredded	5. Place a bed of shredded Chinese cabbage on salad plates.
50	50	Orange wedges	6. Portion the salad mixture onto the plates.
			7. Garnish each salad with 2 orange wedges.

Per serving:
Calories, 330; Protein, 11 g; Fat, 27 g (72% cal.); Cholesterol, 25 mg;
Carbohydrates, 13 g; Fiber, 4 g; Sodium, 200 mg.

VARIATIONS

Substitute chicken, turkey, ham, or duck meat for the beef.

Mixed Vegetable Salad with Pasta

Portions: 25   Portion size: 4 oz (125 g)

U.S.	Metric	Ingredients	PROCEDURE
1½ lb	700 g	Cooked ditalini pasta, cold	1. Combine the pasta, beans, vegetables, and cheese in a large bowl. Toss to mix.
1 lb	450 g	Cooked chickpeas or other dried beans, cold	2. No more than 1–2 hours before service, add the dressing and toss.
12 oz	350 g	Zucchini, medium dice, raw or blanched	
12 oz	350 g	Green beans, cooked, cut into ½-inch (1-cm) lengths	
8 oz	250 g	Red onions, diced	
6 oz	175 g	Small pitted black olives	
6 oz	175 g	Celery, diced	
4 oz	125 g	Green pepper, diced	
4 oz	125 g	Red pepper, diced	
¼ cup	60 mL	Capers, drained	
4 oz	125 g	Parmesan cheese	
1½ pt	700 mL	Italian dressing	
25	25	Lettuce leaves for underliners	3. Arrange the lettuce leaves on cold salad plates.
25	25	Tomato wedges or cherry tomatoes	4. Just before service, place a 4-oz (125-g) portion of the salad on each lettuce leaf.
			5. Garnish each salad with a tomato wedge.

Per serving:
Calories, 290; Protein, 6 g; Fat, 22 g (67% cal.); Cholesterol, 5 mg;
Carbohydrates, 18 g; Fiber, 4 g; Sodium, 420 mg.

VARIATIONS

Add 1 lb (450 g) diced or sliced salami, pepperoni, or mozzarella cheese to the salad mixture.

COOKED SALADS

Principles

Cooked salads are those whose main ingredients are cooked foods, usually meat, poultry, fish, eggs, or starch products, and, occasionally, vegetables. They are different from combination salads and from vegetable salads using cooked vegetables in that the cooked product is usually mixed with a thick dressing, generally mayonnaise, during preparation.

A salad that is mixed with a thick dressing to bind it together is called a *bound salad*. Some bound salads, such as tuna, egg, or chicken salad, can also be used as sandwich fillings.

Popular choices for cooked salads are the following:

Chicken	Lobster
Turkey	Eggs
Ham	Potatoes
Tuna	Pastas
Salmon	Rice
Crab	Mixed vegetables
Shrimp	

Guidelines for Making Cooked Salads

1. Cooked ingredients must be thoroughly cooled before being mixed with mayonnaise, and the completed salad mixture must be kept chilled at all times. Mayonnaise-type salads are ideal breeding grounds for bacteria that cause food poisoning.

2. Cooked salads are good ways to use leftovers such as chicken, meat, or fish, but the ingredient must have been handled according to the rules of good sanitation and food handling. The product will not be cooked again to destroy any bacteria that might grow in the salad and cause illness.

3. Potatoes for salads should be cooked whole, then peeled and cut, in order to preserve nutrients.

4. Don't cut ingredients too small, or the final product will be like mush or paste, with no textural interest.

5. Crisp vegetables are usually added for texture. Celery is the most popular, but other choices are green peppers, carrots, chopped pickles, onions, water chestnuts, and apples. Be sure that the flavors go together, however.

6. Bland main ingredients, such as potatoes and some seafoods, may be marinated in a seasoned liquid such as vinaigrette before being mixed with the mayonnaise and other ingredients. Any marinade not absorbed should be drained first to avoid thinning the mayonnaise.

7. Fold in thick dressings gently to avoid crushing or breaking the main ingredients.

8. Bound salads are usually portioned with a scoop. This has two advantages: (a) It provides portion control. (b) It gives height and shape to the salad.

9. Choose attractive, colorful garnishes. A scoop of potato or chicken salad looks pale and uninteresting without a garnish.

Macedoine of Vegetables Mayonnaise

Portions: 25   Portion size: 4 oz (125 g)

U.S.	Metric	Ingredients	PROCEDURE
2 lb	1 kg	Cooked carrots, ¼-inch (½-cm) dice	1. Chill all ingredients before combining.
2 lb	1 kg	Cooked white turnips, ¼-inch (½-cm) dice	2. Place all ingredients in a bowl and mix until evenly combined. Use just enough mayonnaise to bind. Season to taste with salt and white pepper.
1 lb	500 g	Cooked green beans, sliced in ¼-inch (½-cm) pieces	
1 lb	500 g	Cooked green peas	
1 pt or as needed	500 mL or as needed	Mayonnaise	
to taste	to taste	Salt	
to taste	to taste	White pepper	
25	25	Lettuce cups for underliners	3. Place lettuce bases on cold salad plates.
25	25	Tomato wedges	4. Using a No. 10 scoop, place a mound of salad on each plate. Garnish with 1 tomato wedge.

Per serving:
Calories, 180; Protein, 3 g; Fat, 14 g (68% cal.); Cholesterol, 10 mg;
Carbohydrates, 12 g; Fiber, 4 g; Sodium, 150 mg.

Chicken or Turkey Salad

Portions: 25   Portion size: 3½ oz (100 g)

U.S.	Metric	Ingredients	PROCEDURE
3 lb	1.4 kg	Cooked chicken or turkey, ½-inch (1-cm) dice	1. Combine all ingredients in a mixing bowl. Toss gently until thoroughly mixed.
1½ lb	700 g	Celery, ¼-inch (½-cm) dice	
1 pt	500 mL	Mayonnaise	
2 oz	60 mL	Lemon juice	
to taste	to taste	Salt	
to taste	to taste	White pepper	
25	25	Lettuce cups for underliners	2. Arrange lettuce on cold salad plates.
as needed	as needed	Parsley or watercress sprigs	3. Using a No. 10 scoop, place a mound of chicken salad on each plate. Garnish with parsley or watercress.
			4. Hold for service in refrigerator.

Per serving:
Calories, 260; Protein, 15 g; Fat, 22 g (74% cal.); Cholesterol, 60 mg;
Carbohydrates, 2 g; Fiber, 1 g; Sodium, 170 mg.

VARIATIONS

Additions to Chicken Salad: Add any of the following ingredients to the basic recipe:
1. 6 oz (175 g) broken walnuts or pecans
2. 6 hard-cooked eggs, chopped
3. 8 oz (225 g) seedless grapes, cut in half, and 3 oz (90 g) chopped or sliced almonds
4. 8 oz (225 g) drained, diced pineapple
5. 8 oz (225 g) diced avocado
6. 1 lb (450 g) peeled, seeded, diced cucumber, *substituted for* 1 lb of the celery
7. 8 oz (225 g) sliced water chestnuts

Egg Salad

Substitute 28 diced hard-cooked eggs for the chicken in the basic recipe.

Tuna or Salmon Salad

Substitute 3 lb (1.4 kg) drained, flaked canned tuna or salmon for the chicken in the basic recipe. Add 2 oz (60 g) chopped onion. Optional ingredient: 4 oz (100 g) chopped pickles or drained capers.

Potato Salad

Portions: 25   Portion size: 4 oz (125 g)

U.S.	Metric	Ingredients	PROCEDURE
5 lb AP	2.5 kg AP	Waxy potatoes (see note)	1. Scrub the potatoes. Steam or boil until tender, but do not overcook. 2. Drain the potatoes. Leave in the colander or spread out on a sheet pan until cool enough to handle.
1½ cups 1½ tsp ¼ tsp	375 mL 7 mL 1 mL	Basic Vinaigrette (p. 572) Salt White pepper	3. Peel the warm potatoes. Cut into ½-inch (1-cm) dice. 4. Combine the dressing, salt, and pepper. Add the potatoes and mix carefully to avoid breaking or crushing them. 5. Marinate until cold. For the purpose of food safety, chill the potatoes in the refrigerator before proceeding with the next step.
12 oz 4 oz	375 g 125 g	Celery, small dice Onion, chopped fine (Optional ingredients—see variations below)	6. If any vinaigrette has not been absorbed by the potatoes, drain it off. 7. Add the celery, onion, and, if desired, any of the optional ingredients listed below. Mix gently.
1 pt	500 mL	Mayonnaise	8. Add the mayonnaise. Mix carefully until evenly blended. 9. Keep refrigerated until ready to use.
25 50	25 50	Lettuce cups for underliners Pimiento strips	10. Arrange the lettuce on cold salad plates. 11. Using a No. 11 scoop, place a 4-oz (125-g) mound of potato salad on each plate. 12. Garnish each salad with 2 strips pimiento placed crosswise on top. 13. Hold for service in refrigerator.

Per serving:
Calories, 290; Protein, 2 g; Fat, 24 g (74% cal.); Cholesterol, 10 mg;
Carbohydrates, 17 g; Fiber, 2 g; Sodium, 360 mg.

Note: See pages 487–488 for explanation of potato types. Do not use starchy, mealy potatoes for salad because they will not hold their shape.

VARIATIONS

Optional ingredients, to be added in step 7:

4–6 hard-cooked eggs, diced
2 oz (60 g) green peppers, small dice
2 oz (60 g) pimientos, small dice
4 oz (125 g) chopped pickles or capers or sliced olives
¼ cup (60 mL) chopped parsley

Vinaigrette marination (steps 4–5) may be omitted if necessary. In this case, chill the potatoes before mixing with the dressing. Add 2 oz (60 mL) vinegar to the mayonnaise and check carefully for seasonings. Refrigerate for 2 hours or more before serving.

French Potato Salad

Portions: 25 **Portion size: 4 oz (125 g)**

U.S.	Metric	Ingredients	PROCEDURE
7 lb	3.5 kg	Waxy potatoes	1. Scrub the potatoes. Steam or boil until tender, but do not overcook. 2. Drain the potatoes. Leave in the colander or spread out on a sheet pan until cool enough to handle.
8 oz	250 mL	Salad oil	3. Peel the potatoes while still hot. Cut into slices ¼-inch (½-cm) thick or into ½-inch (1-cm) dice.
6 oz	200 mL	Wine vinegar (white or red)	4. Mix the potatoes with the remaining ingredients. Allow to stand at least 15 minutes while the potatoes absorb the dressing.
4 oz	125 g	Onions or shallots, chopped fine	
¼ tsp	1 mL	Garlic, chopped fine	
¼ cup	60 mL	Chopped parsley	5. Serve warm or cold. This salad is a popular accompaniment to hot cooked sausages.
1 tbsp	15 mL	Tarragon	
to taste	to taste	Salt	
to taste	to taste	Pepper	

Per serving:
Calories, 180; Protein, 2 g; Fat, 9 g (46% cal.); Cholesterol, 0 mg;
Carbohydrates, 22 g; Fiber, 2 g; Sodium, 5 mg.

VARIATION

Hot German Potato Salad

Omit oil and tarragon from basic recipe. Cook 8 oz (250 g) diced bacon until crisp. Add the bacon, the bacon fat, and 1 cup (250 mL) hot chicken stock to the dressing ingredients. (More stock may be needed if the potatoes absorb a great deal.) Place the mixed salad in a hotel pan, cover, and heat in a 300°F (150°C) oven for about 30 minutes. Serve hot.

Dilled Shrimp Salad

Portions: 25 **Portion size: 3½ oz (100 g)**

U.S.	Metric	Ingredients	PROCEDURE
3 lb	1.4 kg	Cooked, peeled, deveined shrimp	1. Cut the shrimp into ¼-inch (1-cm) pieces. (If the shrimp are very small, leave them whole.)
1½ lb	700 g	Celery, small dice	2. Combine the celery and shrimp in a bowl.
1 pt	500 mL	Mayonnaise	3. Mix together the mayonnaise, lemon juice, dill, and salt.
2 tbsp	30 mL	Lemon juice	
2 tsp	10 mL	Dried dill weed (or 2 tbsp/30 mL chopped fresh dill)	4. Add the dressing to the shrimp mixture. Mix in thoroughly.
½ tsp	2 mL	Salt	
25	25	Lettuce cups for underliners	5. Arrange the lettuce leaves on cold salad plates.
50	50	Tomato wedges	6. Using a No. 10 scoop, place a mound of shrimp salad on each plate. 7. Garnish with tomato wedges, using 2 per salad.

Per serving:
Calories, 200; Protein, 12 g; Fat, 15 g (67% cal.); Cholesterol, 115 mg;
Carbohydrates, 5 g; Fiber, 1 g; Sodium, 300 mg.

VARIATIONS

Crab or Lobster Salad

Prepare as in basic recipe, using crab or lobster meat instead of shrimp.

Crab, Shrimp, or Lobster Louis

Use Louis Dressing (p. 576) instead of the mixture of mayonnaise, lemon juice, and dill. Serve on shredded lettuce. If food cost permits, omit celery and increase shellfish to 4½ lb/2 kg.

Rice and Shrimp Salad

Reduce shrimp in basic recipe to 1 lb (450 g) and add 2 lb (900 g) cooked rice.

Curried Rice Salad with Shrimp

Prepare Rice and Shrimp Salad but omit the dill. Instead, flavor the dressing with 1 tsp (5 mL) curry powder heated lightly in a teaspoon (5 mL) of oil and cooled. Optional: Substitute diced green pepper for half the celery.

FRUIT SALADS

Principles

As their name indicates, fruit salads have fruits as their main ingredients. They are popular as appetizer salads, as dessert salads, and as part of combination luncheon plates, often with a scoop of cottage cheese or other mild-tasting protein food.

Guidelines for Making Fruit Salads

1. Fruit salads are often arranged rather than mixed or tossed because most fruits are delicate and easily broken. An exception is the Waldorf salad, made of firm apples mixed with nuts, celery, and a mayonnaise-based dressing.

2. Broken or less attractive pieces of fruit should be placed on the bottom of the salad, with the more attractive pieces arranged on top.

3. Some fruits discolor when cut and should be dipped into an acid such as tart fruit juice. See pages 537–539 for pre-preparation guidelines for individual fruits.

4. Fruits do not hold as well as vegetables after being cut. If both vegetable and fruit salads are being prepared for a particular meal service, the vegetable salads should usually be prepared first.

5. Drain canned fruits well before including them in the salad, or the salad will be watery and sloppy. The liquid from the canned fruit may be reserved for using in fruit salad dressing or other preparations.

6. Dressings for fruit salads are usually slightly sweet, but a little tartness is usually desirable as well. Fruit juices are often used in dressings for fruit salad.

Waldorf Salad

Portions: 25   Portion size: 3 oz (90 g)

U.S.	Metric	Ingredients	PROCEDURE
1½ cups	350 mL	Chantilly Dressing (p. 576)	1. Prepare the dressing. Place it in a large stainless-steel bowl and have it ready in the refrigerator.
4 lb AP	1.8 kg AP	Crisp, red eating apples	2. Core the apples and dice them to ½ inch (1 cm) without peeling them.
1 lb	450 g	Celery, small dice	3. As soon as the apples are cut, add them to the dressing and mix in to prevent darkening.
4 oz	100 g	Walnuts, coarsely chopped	4. Add the celery and walnuts. Fold in until evenly mixed.
25	25	Lettuce cups for underliners	5. Arrange the lettuce bases on cold salad plates.
		Optional garnish:	6. Using a No. 12 scoop, place a mound of salad on each plate.
2 oz	60 g	Chopped walnuts	7. If garnish is desired, sprinkle each salad with about 1 tsp (5 mL) chopped nuts.
			8. Hold for service in refrigerator.

Per serving:
Calories, 150; Protein, 1 g; Fat, 12 g (69% cal.); Cholesterol, 10 mg; Carbohydrates, 11 g; Fiber, 2 g; Sodium, 40 mg.

Note: Plain mayonnaise may be used instead of Chantilly dressing.

VARIATIONS

Any of the following ingredients may be added to the basic Waldorf mixture. If any of these changes is made, the item should no longer be called simply Waldorf Salad. Change the menu name to indicate that the product contains other ingredients. For example: Pineapple Waldorf Salad or Apple Date Salad.

1. 8 oz (225 g) diced pineapple
2. 4 oz (100 g) chopped dates, *substituted* for the walnuts
3. 4 oz (100 g) raisins, plumped in hot water and drained
4. 1 lb (450 g) shredded cabbage or Chinese cabbage, *substituted* for the celery

Fresh Fruit Chantilly

Portions: 25   Portion size: 4 oz (125 g)

U.S.	Metric	Ingredients	PROCEDURE
1½ lb	750 g	Orange sections	1. Prepare orange and grapefruit sections as shown in Figure 7.12. Be sure to save the juice. Cut the grapefruit sections in half.
1¼ lb	625 g	Grapefruit sections	
1 lb	500 g	Diced apples	2. Drain the orange and grapefruit in a china cap or strainer and collect the juice in a stainless-steel bowl.
1 lb	500 g	Sliced bananas	
12 oz	375 g	Grapes	3. Place the apples and bananas in the citrus juice as soon as they are cut to prevent darkening.
			4. Cut the grapes in half lengthwise. If they are not seedless, remove the seeds.
1 cup	250 mL	Heavy cream	5. Just before service, whip the cream until it forms soft peaks.
1 cup	250 mL	Mayonnaise	6. Stir about one-fourth of the cream into the mayonnaise to lighten it. Then fold in the rest of the cream.
			7. Drain the fruits well and fold into the dressing.
25	25	Lettuce leaves for underliners	8. Arrange the lettuce leaves on cold salad plates.
as needed	as needed	Suggested garnish (one only):	9. Place a 4-oz (125-g) portion of fruit salad on each plate. Garnish as desired.
		Mint sprigs	10. Serve immediately, or hold in refrigerator up to 30 minutes.
		Strawberries	
		Red or black grapes	
		Fresh cherries	

Per serving:
Calories, 160; Protein, 1 g; Fat, 11 g (61% cal.); Cholesterol, 20 mg;
Carbohydrates, 15 g; Fiber, 2 g; Sodium, 55 mg.

Note: Other fresh fruits in season may be used. The fruits here were chosen because they are available all year. Canned or frozen fruits may be used, but the word "fresh" must then be removed from the menu title.

COMBINATION SALADS

Principles

Combination salads get their name because they are combinations of kinds of ingredients. They may even consist of two or more salads in an attractive arrangement—for example, chicken salad and sliced cucumber and tomato salad arranged on a bed of greens. Probably the most popular combination salad is the chef's salad, mixed greens with strips of turkey, ham, and cheese, and usually several raw vegetables such as tomato and green pepper.

Because they are more elaborate and can usually be quite substantial in size, combination salads are often served as main courses. Because combination salads are often made up of other kinds of salads, there are really only two guidelines for their production:

1. Observe the guidelines for preparing the salad's components, such as greens, vegetables, cooked salads, and fruit salads.

2. Observe the guidelines for attractive salad arrangement.

Chef's Salad

Portions: 25

U.S.	Metric	Ingredients	PROCEDURE
6 lb	3 kg	Mixed salad greens, washed, trimmed, and crisped	1. Place the greens in cold salad bowls, approximately 4 oz (125 g) per portion.
1½ lb	700 g	Turkey breast, cut into thin strips	2. Arrange the turkey, ham, and cheese strips neatly on top of the greens. Keep the items separate—do not mix them all together.
1½ lb	700 g	Pullman ham, cut into thin strips	3. Arrange the remaining items attractively on the salad.
1½ lb	700 g	Swiss cheese, cut into thin strips	4. Hold for service. If salads must be held for over 1 hour, they should be covered so that the meats and cheese don't dry out.
50	50	Tomato wedges or cherry tomatoes	5. Serve with any appropriate salad dressing, served on the side in a separate container.
50	50	Hard-cooked egg quarters	
25	25	Radishes	
8 oz	225 g	Carrots, cut batonnet	
25	25	Green pepper rings	

Per serving:
Calories, 400; Protein, 37 g; Fat, 25 g (54% cal.); Cholesterol, 485 mg;
Carbohydrates, 10 g; Fiber, 3 g; Sodium, 570 mg.

VARIATIONS

Other vegetable garnish may be used in addition to or in place of the items in the basic recipe. See lists on pages 533–534.

Shrimp in Avocado

Portions: 24   Portion size: ½ avocado

U.S.	Metric	Ingredients	PROCEDURE
3 lb	1.4 kg	Cooked, peeled, deveined shrimp	1. Cut the shrimp into ½-inch (1-cm) pieces or, if they are very small, leave them whole.
12 oz	350 g	Mayonnaise	2. Combine the shrimp, mayonnaise, and lemon juice in a bowl. Mix until evenly combined. Add salt to taste.
2 oz	60 mL	Lemon juice	3. Keep refrigerated until needed.
to taste	to taste	Salt	
12	12	Avocados, ripe	4. Wash the avocados. As close as possible to serving time, cut them in half lengthwise. Remove the pits. (Do not peel.)
4 oz (or as needed)	125 mL (or as needed)	Lemon juice	5. Dip the cut sides of the avocados in lemon juice to prevent darkening.
2 heads	2 heads	Leaf lettuce, washed, trimmed, and crisped	6. Line cold salad plates with lettuce leaves.
6	6	Tomatoes	7. Place an avocado half on each plate. Top with a 2½-oz (75-g) portion of the shrimp mixture.
			8. Cut each tomato into 8 wedges. Place 2 wedges on each plate. Serve.

Per serving:
Calories, 330; Protein, 15 g; Fat, 27 g (70% cal.); Cholesterol, 120 mg;
Carbohydrates, 11 g; Fiber, 6 g; Sodium, 220 mg.

VARIATIONS

Crab meat may be used instead of shrimp for avocado filling. Alternatively, use Dilled Shrimp Salad (p. 556) or any of its variations.

Vinaigrette may be used instead of mayonnaise.

Salade Niçoise

Portions: 25

U.S.	Metric	Ingredients	PROCEDURE
3 lb	1.4 kg	Waxy potatoes, scrubbed	1. Cook the potatoes in boiling salted water until just tender. Drain and let cool. Peel. Cut into thin slices. Hold in refrigerator, covered.
3 lb	1.4 kg	Green beans, washed and trimmed	2. Cook the beans in boiling salted water. Drain and cool under cold running water. Cut into 2-inch (5-cm) pieces. Hold in refrigerator.
3 heads	3 heads	Leaf lettuce or Boston lettuce, washed, trimmed, and crisped	3. Line the bottoms of cold salad bowls with the lettuce leaves (see note).
1 60-oz can	1 1700-g can	Tuna, solid pack or chunk	4. Combine the potatoes and green beans. Divide the mixture among the salad bowls, about 3 oz (90 g) per portion.
25	25	Anchovy fillets	5. Drain the tuna and break it into chunks. Place a 1½-oz (50-g) portion in the center of each salad.
50	50	Olives, black or green	6. Arrange the anchovy fillets, olives, egg quarters, and tomato wedges attractively on the salads.
50	50	Hard-cooked egg quarters	7. Sprinkle the salads with chopped parsley.
100	100	Tomato wedges	8. Hold for service in refrigerator.
½ cup	60 mL	Chopped parsley	
		Vinaigrette:	9. Combine the dressing ingredients and mix well. Just before service, mix again and dress each salad with 1½ oz (50 mL) dressing.
1 qt	1 L	Olive oil	
1 cup	250 mL	Wine vinegar	
1 tsp	5 mL	Garlic, chopped fine	
1 tbsp	15 mL	Salt	
½ tsp	2 mL	Pepper	

Per serving:
Calories, 710; Protein, 37 g; Fat, 53 g (67% cal.); Cholesterol, 440 mg;
Carbohydrates, 22 g; Fiber, 5 g; Sodium, 890 mg.

Note: Salade Niçoise (nee-swahz) may be plated on large platters or in bowls to serve 2–6 portions each.

Chicken Breast Salad with Walnuts and Blue Cheese

Portions: 10

U.S.	Metric	Ingredients	PROCEDURE
10	10	Boneless, skinless chicken breasts, about 4 oz (125 g) each	1. Poach the chicken breasts in a flavorful, seasoned chicken stock, using just enough to cover them. (See Chapter 13 for information on poaching chicken.) When they are just done but still juicy, remove from the heat and cool in the poaching liquid.
as needed	as needed	Chicken stock	
1 lb	450 g	Fresh white mushrooms	2. Shortly before serving, slice the mushrooms. Toss them with about 4 oz (125 mL) vinaigrette and with the parsley so that they are lightly coated with the dressing.
1 pt	500 mL	Mustard vinaigrette, made with olive oil	
2 tbsp	30 mL	Chopped parsley	
1 lb 4 oz	575 g	Mixed salad greens (see note)	3. Arrange the greens on large salad plates or dinner plates.
2–3 heads	2–3 heads	Belgian endive	4. Cutting across the grain, slice each chicken breast on the slant into slices about ¼ inch (6 mm) thick. On one side of each salad plate, arrange a sliced breast single-fashion, fanning out the slices.
3 oz	90 g	Walnuts, coarsely chopped	
3 oz	90 g	Blue cheese, crumbled	

Per serving:
Calories, 530; Protein, 31 g; Fat, 43 g (72% cal.); Cholesterol, 75 mg; Carbohydrates, 7 g; Fiber, 3 g; Sodium, 570 mg.

5. Separate the endive into leaves. Arrange some of the leaves on the other half of each plate.

6. Place a small mound of the mushroom slices on the endive.

7. Sprinkle the salads with the nuts and the blue cheese.

8. Just before serving, spoon about 1 oz (30 mL) dressing over each salad.

Chicken Breast Salad with Walnuts and Blue Cheese

VARIATION

When plating the salads to order, toss the mixed salad greens with some of the salad dressing before plating.

Salad of Seared Sea Scallops with Oriental Vinaigrette

Portions: 10   Portion size: 3 oz (90 g) scallops
1½ oz (45 g) greens
1½ oz (45 mL) vinaigrette

U.S.	Metric	Ingredients	PROCEDURE
1 lb	500 g	Mesclun or other delicate mixed greens	1. Wash and drain the salad greens.
1 pt	500 mL	Oriental Vinaigrette (p. 574)	2. Prepare the vinaigrette.
2 lb	1 kg	Sea scallops	3. Trim the scallops by removing the small, tough side muscle. If any scallops are very large, cut them in half crosswise. Dry them well.
as needed	as needed	Butter	4. Heat a little butter in a nonstick sauté pan. Sear a few scallops at a time until they are browned on top and bottom.
30	30	Orange segments (free of membranes)	5. Toss the mesclun with half the vinaigrette.
			6. Mound the mesclun in the center of the plates.
			7. Arrange the orange segments so that they are leaning against the mound of salad greens. Use 3 per portion.
			8. Arrange the scallops around the salads.
			9. Drizzle the remaining vinaigrette around the scallops.

Per serving:
Calories, 360; Protein, 9 g; Fat, 33 g (80% cal.); Cholesterol, 20 mg; Carbohydrates, 9 g; Fiber, 2 g; Sodium, 460 mg.

Salad of Seared Sea Scallops with Oriental Vinaigrette

Salad of Belgian Endive, Scallops, and Walnuts

Portions: 8   Portion size: 3–4 scallops (3 oz/90 g)
                           plus 5 oz (150 g) salad

U.S.	Metric	Ingredients	PROCEDURE
14 oz	400 g	Belgian endive	1. Remove any damaged outer leaves of the Belgian endive. Then remove some undamaged leaves and set aside for the presentation (step 8).
10 oz	300 g	Radicchio	
7 oz	200 g	Carrot	2. Thinly slice the remaining endive. Thinly slice the radicchio. Peel and trim the carrots and cut into a fine julienne.
1 oz	30 g	Chives	
3½ oz	100 g	Walnuts	3. Set aside some of the whole chives, then mince the remaining chives.
			4. Chop the walnuts.
3½ oz	100 mL	Balsamic vinegar	5. Make the vinaigrette. Whisk the vinegar with salt and white pepper to taste. Whisk in the two oils until the sauce is thick and well emulsified.
to taste	to taste	Salt	
to taste	to taste	White pepper	
5 oz	150 mL	Peanut oil	6. Toss the endive, radicchio, carrot, chives, and walnuts together with a little of the vinaigrette.
5 oz	150 mL	Walnut oil	
1 lb 10 oz	725 g	Sea scallops	7. Season the scallops and sear them in hot olive oil.
to taste	to taste	Salt	8. Make a dome of salad in the center of a plate. Arrange 3–4 scallops around the salad. Between the scallops, place a leaf of endive, cut in half lengthwise, and place a length of chive on top. Top each scallop with a little vinaigrette and serve.
to taste	to taste	White pepper	
3½ oz	100 mL	Olive oil	

Per serving:
Calories, 590; Protein, 11 g; Fat, 57 g (85% cal.); Cholesterol, 15 mg;
Carbohydrates, 11 g; Fiber, 4 g; Sodium, 220 mg.

Chicory and Smoked Chicken Salad with Mustard Vinaigrette

Portions: 10   Portion size: 8 oz (250 g)

U.S.	Metric	Ingredients	PROCEDURE
10 heads	10 heads	Belgian endive	1. Remove the outer leaves from the Belgian endive. For plated service, cut the base of each leaf to a point so that they fit together neatly and arrange radially on plates. For buffet presentation, omit cuts in stem and use leaves to line a bowl. Cut the remainder of the Belgian endive into julienne.
2 small heads	2 small heads	Frisée or curly endive, washed	
2 oz	60 mL	White wine vinegar	
10 oz	300 mL	Salad oil	
2 oz	60 mL	Whole grain mustard	2. Break the curly endive into bite-size pieces and mix gently with the julienne of Belgian endive.
to taste	to taste	Salt	
to taste	to taste	Pepper	3. Briskly combine the white wine vinegar, salad oil, and whole grain mustard with salt and pepper to taste.
2 lb	1 kg	Smoked chicken, boneless, with or without skin as desired	4. Toss the mixed curly endive and Belgian endive julienne with the vinaigrette and pile onto the arranged plates.
			5. Dice the smoked chicken and sprinkle over the endives.

Per serving:
Calories, 410; Protein, 15 g; Fat, 34 g (75% cal.); Cholesterol, 40 mg;
Carbohydrates, 10 g; Fiber, 9 g; Sodium, 180 mg.

Crab and Asparagus Charlotte with Orange and Tomato Vinaigrette

Portions: 12   Portion size: 5 oz (140 g)
                                    2½ oz (70 mL) vinaigrette

U.S.	Metric	Ingredients	PROCEDURE
5 lb	2.5 kg	Asparagus	1. Peel and cook the asparagus. Drain and cool under cold water. Drain well.
as needed	as needed	Oil	
1 pt	500 mL	Mayonnaise (see note)	2. Lightly oil 12 timbale molds, 5 oz (140 mL) in capacity. Cut the asparagus tips the same length as the height of the molds. Line the molds with the asparagus tips, placing the points of the asparagus at the bottom.
3 tbsp	45 mL	Ketchup	
2 lb 4 oz	1 kg	Crab meat (see note)	
			3. Neatly dice the remaining asparagus stalks and reserve for garnish.
			4. Color the mayonnaise with the ketchup. Fold in the crab meat.
			5. Pack the crab mixture into the molds and chill thoroughly.
1 pt 14 oz	850 mL	Orange and Tomato Vinaigrette (p. 573)	6. Turn out the molds onto the center of plates. Spoon the vinaigrette around the charlottes. Scatter the asparagus dice around. Garnish additionally with the salmon roe and tiny sprigs of dill.
1 oz	30 g	Salmon roe	
2 oz	50 g	Dill sprigs	

Per serving:
Calories, 810; Protein, 25 g; Fat, 76 g (82% cal.); Cholesterol, 110 mg;
Carbohydrates, 13 g; Fiber, 3 g; Sodium, 490 mg.

Note: For best results, use freshly made mayonnaise (see p. 576). Use good-quality claw crab meat rather than the brownish body meat.

Warm Goat Cheese Salad

Portions: 12

U.S.	Metric	Ingredients	PROCEDURE
12 slices	12 slices	Sandwich bread	1. Cut the sandwich bread into ¼-inch (½-cm) slices. Toast, then cut each slice into 4 triangles.
12	12	Small goat cheeses, about 2½ oz (75 g) each (see note)	2. Cut the goat cheese in half horizontally. Place under a broiler or salamander until just beginning to melt and lightly colored.
8 oz	250 g	Frisée	3. Wash and drain the frisée, radicchio, and mâche. Tear the frisée and mâche into bite-size pieces.
8 oz	250 g	Radicchio	
4 oz	125 g	Mâche	
14 oz	400 mL	Walnut Herb Vinaigrette (p. 573)	4. Toss the salad greens with the vinaigrette and the chopped walnuts.
1½ oz	45 g	Chopped walnuts	5. Place a small mound of the salad greens in the center of the plate and arrange 4 pieces of toast on top, close together. Place 2 pieces of the toasted cheese on top of the toast. Decorate with whole walnut halves and sprigs of chervil.
as desired	as desired	Walnut halves	
as desired	as desired	Chervil sprigs	

Per serving:
Calories, 600; Protein, 20 g; Fat, 50 g (73% cal.); Cholesterol, 55 mg;
Carbohydrates, 22 g; Fiber, 2 g; Sodium, 540 mg.

Note: The cheese used in testing this recipe is Crottin de Chavignol, a small, slightly aged goat cheese. If this or a similar small goat cheese is not available, substitute a log-shaped goat cheese cut into portion sizes.

Stuffed Tomatoes Chinoise

Portions: 12   **Portion size:** 1 tomato with about 3½ oz (100 g) filling

U.S.	Metric	Ingredients	PROCEDURE
12	12	Tomatoes, about 7–8 oz (200–250 g) each	1. Remove the stems from the tomatoes. Slice the top third of the tomatoes, keeping the tops. Remove the seeds and ribs of the tomatoes. Season the interior with salt and overturn on paper towels. Set aside in the refrigerator for at least 30 minutes.
to taste	to taste	Salt	
1⅓ oz	40 g	Ginger root, grated	2. Place the grated ginger, rice vinegar, sesame oil, soy oil, soy sauce, and sugar to taste in a blender. Blend until well mixed.
2 oz	60 mL	Rice vinegar	
2 oz	60 mL	Sesame oil	3. Strain the vinaigrette into a small bowl. Set aside.
1 oz	30 mL	Soybean oil or vegetable oil	
1 oz	30 mL	Soy sauce	
to taste	to taste	Sugar	
7 oz	200 g	Carrot	4. Cut the carrot, celery, and onion into a fine julienne.
3½ oz	100 g	Celery	5. Blanch the vegetables in boiling salted water for 30 seconds, then refresh in ice water. Strain and squeeze out any excess water. Spread on paper towels and keep chilled until ready to use.
3½ oz	100 g	Onion	
1 lb	500 g	Bean sprouts	
1 lb	500 g	Shelled, cooked small shrimp	6. Repeat the procedure for the bean sprouts.
3 tbsp	45 mL	Chopped cilantro	7. Combine the vegetables, shrimp, and chopped cilantro in a bowl. Add the vinaigrette and toss to mix.
2	2	Cucumbers	8. Channel the cucumbers (see Figure 24.1), then cut into thin slices.
			9. Arrange the cucumber slices into circles on plates.
			10. Fill the tomatoes with the vegetable and shrimp mixture. Place in the center of the cucumber circles and place the tops on the tomatoes.

Per serving:
Calories, 170; Protein, 12 g; Fat, 8 g (39% cal.); Cholesterol, 75 mg, Carbohydrates, 16 g; Fiber, 4 g; Sodium, 250 mg.

Stuffed Tomato Chinoise

GELATIN SALADS

Principles

Gelatin salads have a distinguished history. Their ancestors are aspics, the highly ornamented appetizers and elaborate buffet pieces made with meat and fish stocks rich in natural gelatin extracted from bones and connective tissue. Aspics are part of the glory of classical cuisine and still an important part of modern buffet work. (See Chapter 23.)

It's no longer necessary to extract gelatin from bones in your kitchen. Purified, granular gelatin and gelatin sheets have long been available for use in the pantry. Many excellent gelatin-based salads can be made with little labor using these products. However, most gelatin products today are made with sweetened prepared mixes whose high sugar content and heavy reliance on artificial color and flavor make their appropriateness as salads somewhat questionable. (Often, in a cafeteria line, you will see in the salad section little squares of gelatin with a lettuce leaf underneath and a dab of mayonnaise on top, and in the dessert section the identical product, without the lettuce leaf and with a dab of whipped cream in place of the mayo.)

Nevertheless, as a professional cook, you need to know how to prepare these products because your customers will expect them. You should also know how to prepare salads using unflavored gelatin, relying on fruit juices and other ingredients for flavor. Unflavored gelatin is especially valuable for preparing molded vegetable salads because shredded cabbage and other vegetables make a poor combination with a highly sweetened dessert gelatin.

Guidelines for Making Gelatin Salads

1. It is important to use the right amount of gelatin for the volume of liquid in the recipe. Too much gelatin makes a stiff, rubbery product. Too little makes a soft product that will not hold its shape.

Basic proportions for unflavored gelatin are 2½ ounces dry gelatin per gallon of liquid (19 g per liter) BUT you will almost always need more than this because of acids and other ingredients in the recipe. Basic proportions for sweetened, flavored gelatin are 24 ounces per gallon of liquid (180 g per liter).

Acids, such as fruit juices and vinegar, weaken the gelatin set, so a higher proportion of gelatin to liquid is needed, sometimes as much as 4 ounces or more per gallon (30 g per liter). The setting power is also weakened by whipping the product into a foam and by adding a large quantity of chopped foods. It is impossible to give a formula for how much gelatin to use, as it varies with each recipe. Test each recipe before using it.

2. Gelatin dissolves at about 100°F (38°C), but higher temperatures will dissolve it faster.

To dissolve unflavored gelatin, stir it into cold liquid to avoid lumping and let it stand for 5 minutes to absorb water. Then heat it until dissolved, or add hot liquid and stir until dissolved.

To dissolve sweetened, flavored gelatin, stir it into boiling water. It will not lump because the gelatin granules are held apart by sugar granules, much the way starch granules in flour are held separate by the fat in a roux.

3. To speed setting, dissolve the gelatin in up to half of the liquid and add the remainder cold to lower the temperature. For even faster setting, add crushed ice in place of an equal weight of cold water. Stir until the ice is melted.

4. Do not add raw pineapple or papaya to gelatin salads. They contain enzymes that dissolve the gelatin. If cooked or canned, however, these fruits may be included.

5. Add solid ingredients when the gelatin is partially set—very thick and syrupy. This will help keep them evenly mixed rather than floating or settling.

6. Canned fruits and other juicy items must be well drained before being added or they will dilute the gelatin and weaken it.

7. For service, pour into pans and cut into equal portions when set, or pour into individual molds.

8. To unmold gelatin:

- Run a thin knife blade around the top edges of the mold to loosen.
- Dip the mold into hot water for 1 or 2 seconds.
- Quickly wipe the bottom of the mold and turn it over onto the salad plate (or invert the salad plate over the mold and flip the plate and mold over together). Do not hold in the hot water for more than a few seconds or the gelatin will begin to melt.
- If it doesn't unmold after a gentle shake, repeat the procedure. You may also wrap a hot towel (dipped in hot water and wrung out) around the mold until it releases, but this is more time-consuming.

9. Refrigerate gelatin salads until service to keep them firm.

Jellied Coleslaw

Portions: 25   Portion size: 4 oz (125 g)

U.S.	Metric	Ingredients	PROCEDURE
2 oz	60 g	Unflavored gelatin	1. Stir the gelatin into the cold water. Let stand for 5 minutes.
1 cup	250 mL	Water, cold	2. Add the boiling water, sugar, and salt. Stir until the gelatin and sugar are dissolved.
1 pt	500 mL	Water, boiling	3. Cool until syrupy but not set.
2 oz	60 g	Sugar	
1 tbsp	15 mL	Salt	
4 oz	125 mL	Vinegar	4. Add the vinegar, mayonnaise, and white pepper to the gelatin. Beat with a wire whip or in a mixing machine until thoroughly mixed.
1 pt	500 mL	Mayonnaise	5. Fold in the cabbage and scallions.
½ tsp	2 mL	White pepper	6. Pour the mixture into individual half-cup (125-mL) molds. Chill until set.
3½ lb	1.6 kg	Shredded cabbage	
2 oz	60 g	Chopped scallions	
as needed	as needed	Lettuce for lining plates	7. When firm, unmold and place on salad plates lined with lettuce. Garnish the tops with pimiento strips or small parsley sprigs.
as needed	as needed	Pimiento strips or parsley for garnish	

Per serving:
Calories, 160; Protein, 3 g; Fat, 14 g (76% cal.); Cholesterol, 10 mg; Carbohydrates, 7 g; Fiber, 2 g; Sodium, 400 mg.

Jellied Fruit Salad

Portions: 25   Portion size: 4 oz (125 g)

U.S.	Metric	Ingredients	PROCEDURE
1 No. 2 can	1 No. 2 can	Pineapple cubes	1. Drain the pineapple and reserve the juice. You should have about 12 oz (350 g) drained fruit.
8 oz	250 g	Grapefruit sections	2. Cut the grapefruit and orange sections into ½-inch (1-cm) dice. (See p. 117 for cutting citrus sections.)
12 oz	375 g	Orange sections	3. Cut the grapes in half. Remove seeds, if any.
8 oz	250 g	Grapes	4. Place the fruit in a colander or strainer over a bowl and hold in the refrigerator.
2 oz	60 g	Unflavored gelatin	5. Stir the gelatin into the cold water and let stand at least 5 minutes.
1 cup	250 mL	Water, cold	6. Add enough fruit juice (or part juice and part water) to the liquid from the pineapple to measure 3½ pt (1.75 L).
as needed	as needed	Fruit juice: grapefruit, orange, or pineapple	7. Bring the fruit juice to a boil in a stainless-steel pan. Remove from heat.
6 oz	175 g	Sugar	8. Add the sugar, salt, and softened gelatin. Stir until gelatin and sugar are dissolved.
¼ tsp	1 g	Salt	9. Cool the mixture. Add the lemon juice.
3 oz	90 mL	Lemon juice	10. Chill until thick and syrupy but not set.
			11. Fold the drained fruits into the gelatin mixture.
			12. Pour into individual molds or into a half-size hotel pan. Chill until firm.
25	25	Lettuce leaves for underliners	13. Line cold salad plates with lettuce leaves.
1⅔ cups	400 mL	Chantilly Dressing (p. 576)	14. Unmold the salads or, if a hotel pan was used, cut 5 × 5 into rectangles.
			15. Place a gelatin salad on each plate. Hold for service in the refrigerator.
			16. At service time, top each salad with 1 tablespoon (15 mL) dressing.

Per serving:
Calories, 170; Protein, 3 g; Fat, 10 g (49% cal.); Cholesterol, 15 mg; Carbohydrates, 20 g; Fiber, 1 g; Sodium, 55 mg.

Basic Flavored Gelatin with Fruit

Portions: 25		Portion size: 4 oz (125 g)	

U.S.	Metric	Ingredients	PROCEDURE
12 oz	375 g	Flavored gelatin mix	1. Place the gelatin in a bowl.
1 qt	1 L	Water, boiling	2. Pour in the boiling water. Stir until dissolved.
1 qt	1 L	Water or fruit juice, cold	3. Stir in the cold water or juice.
			4. Chill until thick and syrupy but not set.
2 lb	1 kg	Fruit, well drained	5. Fold the fruit into the gelatin mixture.
			6. Pour into molds or into a half-size hotel pan.
			7. Chill until firm.
			8. Unmold. If using a hotel pan, cut 5 × 5 into portions.

Per serving:
Calories, 70; Protein, 1 g; Fat, 0 g (0% cal.); Cholesterol, 0 mg;
Carbohydrates, 18 g; Fiber, 0 g; Sodium, 40 mg.

VARIATIONS

The number of combinations of fruits and flavored gelatin is nearly limitless. The following suggestions are only a few possibilities. *Note:* When using canned fruits, use the syrup from the fruits as part of the liquid in step 3.

1. Lime-flavored gelatin; pear halves or slices.
2. Black cherry-flavored gelatin; Bing cherries.
3. Raspberry-flavored gelatin; peach slices or halves.
4. Strawberry, raspberry, or cherry-flavored gelatin; canned fruit cocktail.
5. Orange-flavored gelatin; equal parts sliced peaches and pears.
6. Cherry-flavored gelatin; equal parts crushed pineapple and Bing cherries.
7. Lime-flavored gelatin; grapefruit sections.

SALAD BARS AND BUFFET SERVICE

Salad bars have become regular fixtures in restaurants and are popular with both customer and restaurateur. The customer enjoys being able to custom make a salad with selections from a large bowl of greens, smaller containers of assorted condiments, and a variety of dressings. The restaurateur likes them because they take some of the pressure off the dining room staff during service. Many restaurants have designed unique salad bars that have become almost a trademark.

For successful salad bar service, it is important to keep several points in mind:

1. Keep the salad bar attractive and well stocked from the beginning until the end of service. Refill containers before they begin to look depleted, wipe the edges of dressing containers, and clean up debris that has been scattered by customers.

2. Keep the components simple but attractive. Elaborately arranged salad bowls lose their effect as soon as two or three customers have dug into them.

3. Select a variety of condiments to appeal to a variety of tastes. Try both familiar and unusual items to make your salad bar something different. There is no reason to restrict yourself to the same old stuff everyone else is serving.

There are two basic kinds of salad bar condiments:

- **Simple ingredients.** Nearly any item in the salad ingredient list on pages 533–534 might be selected. Your choice will depend on balance of flavors and colors, customer preference, and cost.

- **Prepared salads.** Marinated vegetable salads, such as three-bean salad, and cooked salads, like macaroni salad, are especially suitable. The choice is large.

4. Arrange the salad bar in the following order (see Figure 19.2):

   - Plates.
   - Mixed greens.
   - Condiments (put the expensive ones at the end).
   - Dressings.
   - Crackers, breads, etc., if desired.

5. Make sure your setup conforms to your state health department regulations.

6. Some portion control can be achieved by selecting the right size plates, condiment servers, and dressing ladles.

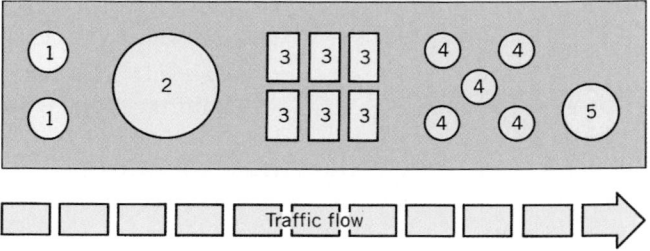

Figure 19.2 Suggested arrangement of a salad bar. Key: (1) plates; (2) large bowl of salad greens; (3) condiments; (4) dressings; (5) crackers, breads, etc.

Salad Dressings

Salad dressings are liquids or semiliquids used to flavor salads. They are sometimes considered cold sauces and they serve the same functions as sauces—that is, they flavor, moisten, and enrich.

Most of the basic salad dressings used today can be divided into three categories:

1. Oil and vinegar dressings (most unthickened dressings).

2. Mayonnaise-based dressings (most thickened dressings).

3. Cooked dressings (similar in appearance to mayonnaise dressings, but more tart, and with little or no oil content).

A number of dressings have as their main ingredient such products as sour cream, yogurt, and fruit juices. Many of these are designed specifically for fruit salads or for low-calorie diets.

Ingredients

Because the flavors of most salad dressings are not modified by cooking, their quality depends directly on the quality of the ingredients.

Most salad dressings are made primarily of an oil and an acid, with other ingredients added to modify the flavor or texture.

OILS

Kinds

Corn oil is widely used in dressings. It has a light golden color and is nearly tasteless, except for a very mild cornmeal-type flavor.

Cottonseed oil, soybean oil, canola oil, and *safflower oil* are bland, nearly tasteless oils. *Vegetable oil* or *salad oil* is a blend of oils and is popular because of its neutral flavor and relatively low cost.

Peanut oil has a mild but distinctive flavor and may be used in appropriate dressings. It is somewhat more expensive.

Olive oil has a distinctive, fruity flavor and aroma and a greenish color. The best olive oils are called *virgin* or *extra-virgin*, which means they are made from the first pressing of the olives. Because of its flavor, olive oil is not an all-purpose oil but may be used in specialty salads such as Caesar salad.

Walnut oil has a distinctive flavor and a high price. It is occasionally used in fine restaurants featuring specialty salads. Other nut oils, such as *hazelnut oil*, are sometimes used.

Quality Factors

All-purpose oils for dressings should have a mild, sweet flavor. Strongly flavored oils can make excellent salad dressings but are not appropriate with every food.

Winterized oil should be used with dressings that are to be refrigerated. These oils have been treated so they remain a clear liquid when chilled.

Rancidity is a serious problem with oils because even a hint of a rancid flavor can ruin an entire batch of dressing. A thin film of oil, such as might be left on containers through careless washing, becomes rancid very quickly. Clean all dressing containers thoroughly, and never pour a fresh batch into a jar containing older dressing.

VINEGAR

Kinds

Cider vinegar is made from apples. It is brown in color and has a slightly sweet apple taste.
White or *distilled vinegar* is distilled and purified so that it has a neutral flavor.
Wine vinegar may be white or red, and it has, naturally, a winey flavor.
Flavored vinegars have had another product added to them, such as tarragon, garlic, or raspberries.
Sherry vinegar is made from sherry wine and, consequently, has the distinctive flavor of that wine.
Balsamic vinegar is a special wine vinegar that has been aged in wooden barrels. It is dark brown in color and has a noticeably sweet taste.
Other specialty vinegars include *malt vinegar*, *rice vinegar*, and vinegars flavored with fruits, such as raspberry.

Quality Factors

Vinegars should have a good, clean, sharp flavor for their type.

Strength of acidity determines the tartness of the vinegar—and of the dressing made from it. Most salad vinegars are about 5 percent acidity, but some range as high as 7 or 8 percent. Read the label for this information. Vinegar that is too strong should be diluted with a little water before it is measured for a recipe.

White vinegar is used when a completely neutral flavor is desired for a dressing. Other vinegars are used for their characteristic flavors. Wine vinegars are usually preferred for the best-quality oil-and-vinegar dressings.

LEMON JUICE

Fresh lemon juice may be used in place of or in addition to vinegar in some preparations, when its flavor is desired.

EGG YOLK

Egg yolk is an essential ingredient in mayonnaise and other emulsified dressings. For safety, pasteurized eggs should be used (see pp. 614 and 897), and the finished product should be refrigerated to guard against spoilage.

SEASONINGS AND FLAVORINGS

Nearly any herb or spice can be used in salad dressings. Remember that dried herbs and spices need extra time to release their flavors if they are not heated in the product. This is why most dressings are best made at least 2 or 3 hours before serving. Review Chapter 4 to refresh your memory on the use of herbs and spices.

Other ingredients added for flavoring include mustard, catsup, Worcestershire sauce, and various kinds of cheeses.

A note on blue cheese and Roquefort cheese: Many restaurants sell what they call Roquefort dressing when it is actually blue cheese dressing. Roquefort is a brand name for a special kind of blue cheese made in Roquefort, France. It is made of sheep's milk, has a distinctive taste, and is expensive. Never use the term *Roquefort* for blue cheese dressings unless you are actually using this brand of cheese.

Emulsions in Salad Dressings

As you know, oil and water do not normally stay mixed but separate into layers. Salad dressings, however, must be evenly mixed for proper service, even though they are made primarily of oil and vinegar. A uniform mixture of two unmixable liquids is called an *emulsion*. One liquid is said to be in *suspension* in the other.

TEMPORARY EMULSIONS

A simple oil and vinegar dressing is called a temporary emulsion because the two liquids always separate after being shaken.

The harder the mixture is beaten or shaken, the longer it takes for it to separate. This is because the oil and water are broken into smaller droplets, so the droplets take longer to recombine with each other so that the oil and water can separate. (When milk is homogenized, the milk fat or cream is broken into such tiny droplets that they stay in suspension.)

The disadvantage of oil and vinegar dressings is that they must be shaken or stirred before each use.

PERMANENT EMULSIONS

Mayonnaise is also a mixture of oil and vinegar, but the two liquids do not separate. This is because the formula also contains egg yolk, which acts as an emulsifier. This means that the egg yolk forms a layer around each of the tiny droplets and holds them in suspension.

The harder the mayonnaise is beaten to break up the droplets, the more stable the emulsion becomes. Also, all emulsions, whether permanent or temporary, form more easily at room temperature, because a chilled oil is harder to break up into small droplets.

Other stabilizers are used in some preparations. Cooked dressing uses starch in addition to eggs. Commercially made dressings may use such emulsifiers as gums, starches, and gelatin.

Oil and Vinegar Dressings

Basic French Dressing, the first recipe in this section, is a simple mixture of oil, vinegar, and seasonings. It can be used as is, but it is usually the base for other dressings, such as the variations that follow.

Incidentally, the thickened, sweet tomato-based dressing often served as "French Dressing" is unknown in France. This is not to say that the product cannot be a good one. But to avoid confusion and to help standardize food service terminology, it would be helpful if it were called by another name, such as "Tomato French" or "American French."

The ratio of oil to vinegar in Basic French Dressing is 3 parts oil to 1 part vinegar. This is not a divine law, however, and the proportions may be changed to taste. Some chefs prefer a 2:1 ratio, while others prefer a 4:1 or even 5:1 ratio. Less oil makes the dressing more tart, while more oil makes it taste milder and oilier.

A very strong vinegar, more than 5 percent acid, may have to be diluted with water before being measured and added to the recipe.

Vinaigrette or Basic French Dressing

Yield: 2 qt (2 L)

U.S.	Metric	Ingredients	PROCEDURE
1 pt	500 mL	Wine vinegar	1. Combine all ingredients in a bowl and mix well.
2 tbsp	30 mL	Salt	2. Mix or stir again before using.
2 tsp	10 mL	White pepper	
3 pt	1.5 L	Salad oil	

Per 1 ounce:
Calories, 180; Protein, 0 g; Fat, 20 g (100% cal.); Cholesterol, 0 mg;
Carbohydrates, 0 g; Fiber, 0 g; Sodium, 220 mg.

VARIATIONS

Substitute olive oil for all or part of the salad oil.

Mustard Vinaigrette

Add 2–4 oz (60–125 g) prepared mustard (French or Dijon type) to the basic recipe. Mix with vinegar before adding oil.

Herbed Vinaigrette

Add to the basic recipe or to the Mustard Vinaigrette variation 1 cup (60 g) chopped parsley and 4 tsp (20 mL) of one of the following dried herbs: basil, thyme, marjoram, tarragon, chives.

Italian Dressing

Use all or part olive oil. Add to the basic recipe 1 tbsp (15 mL) minced garlic, 2 tbsp (30 mL) oregano, ½ cup (125 mL) chopped parsley.

Piquante Dressing

Add to the basic recipe 4 tsp (20 mL) dry mustard, ¼ cup (60 mL) finely chopped onion, 4 tsp (20 mL) paprika.

Chiffonade Dressing

Add to the basic recipe the following ingredients, all chopped fine: 4 hard-cooked eggs, 8 oz (250 g) cooked or canned beets (drained), 4 tbsp (60 mL) parsley, 2 oz (60 g) onion or scallion.

Avocado Dressing

Add 2 pt (1 kg) puréed avocado to basic recipe or to Herbed Vinaigrette. Beat until smooth. Increase salt to taste.

Blue Cheese or Roquefort Dressing

Mix 8 oz (250 g) crumbled blue or Roquefort cheese and 8 oz (250 mL) heavy cream in a mixer with paddle attachment. Gradually beat in 3 pt (1.5 L) basic vinaigrette.

Low-Fat Vinaigrette

Prepare basic vinaigrette or any of the variations, substituting a *jus lié* (see p. 148) made with a white stock, vegetable stock, or vegetable juice for *two-thirds* of the oil.

Walnut Herb Vinaigrette

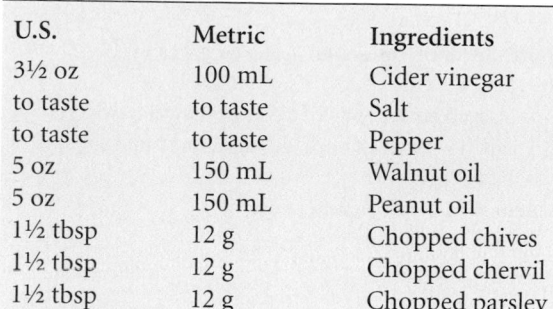

Yield: 14 oz (400 mL)

U.S.	Metric	Ingredients	PROCEDURE
3½ oz	100 mL	Cider vinegar	1. Season the vinegar with salt and pepper.
to taste	to taste	Salt	2. Whip in the oils, a little at a time.
to taste	to taste	Pepper	3. Mix in the herbs. Check the seasoning and adjust as
5 oz	150 mL	Walnut oil	necessary.
5 oz	150 mL	Peanut oil	
1½ tbsp	12 g	Chopped chives	
1½ tbsp	12 g	Chopped chervil	
1½ tbsp	12 g	Chopped parsley	

Per 1 ounce:
Calories, 180; Protein, 0 g; Fat, 20 g (98% cal.); Cholesterol, 0 mg;
Carbohydrates, 1 g; Fiber, 0 g; Sodium, 0 mg.

Orange and Tomato Vinaigrette

Yield: 2 pt 10 oz (1.3 L)

U.S.	Metric	Ingredients	PROCEDURE
3	3	Oranges	1. Zest the oranges (see p. 119), then juice them.
1 pt 8 oz	750 mL	Olive oil	2. Combine the zest, juice, and olive oil. Season to taste.
to taste	to taste	Salt	3. Add the shallots and tomato.
to taste	to taste	Pepper	
3	3	Shallots, chopped	
10 oz	300 g	Tomato concassé	

Per 1 ounce:
Calories, 230; Protein, 0 g; Fat, 25 g (97% cal.); Cholesterol, 0 mg;
Carbohydrates, 2 g; Fiber, 0 g; Sodium, 0 mg.

Sauce Gribiche

Yield: 1½ pt (800 mL)

U.S.	Metric	Ingredients	PROCEDURE
3½ oz	100 mL	White wine vinegar	1. Prepare a basic vinaigrette with the vinegar and oil.
1 pt	500 mL	Salad oil	Season with salt and pepper.
to taste	to taste	Salt	2. Add the gherkins, capers, onion, and sieved cooked eggs.
to taste	to taste	Pepper	Stir gently to combine.
2 oz	65 g	Gherkins or cornichons, chopped	
2 oz	65 g	Capers, chopped	
2 oz	65 g	Onion, chopped	
3	3	Hard-cooked eggs, forced through a sieve	

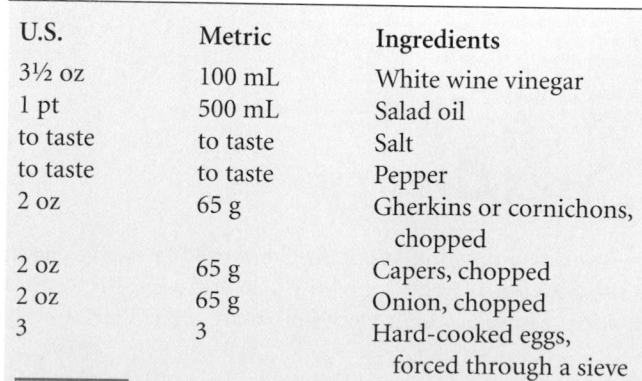

Per 1 ounce:
Calories, 170; Protein, 1 g; Fat, 19 g (96% cal.); Cholesterol, 25 mg;
Carbohydrates, 1 g; Fiber, 0 g; Sodium, 80 mg.

American French or Tomato French Dressing

Yield: 2 qt (2 L)

U.S.	Metric	Ingredients	PROCEDURE
4 oz	125 g	Onion	1. Grate the onion on a hand grater or grind in a food chopper.
1 qt	1 L	Salad oil	2. Combine all ingredients in a stainless-steel bowl.
12 oz	375 mL	Cider vinegar	3. Mix with a wire whip until well combined and sugar is dissolved. Chill.
2½ cups	625 mL	Catsup	4. Beat or stir again before serving.
4 oz	125 g	Sugar	
1 tsp	5 mL	Garlic, mashed	
1 tbsp	15 mL	Worcestershire sauce	
1 tsp	5 mL	Paprika	
¼ tsp	1 mL	Hot pepper sauce (such as Tabasco)	
½ tsp	2 mL	White pepper	

Per 1 ounce:
Calories, 140; Protein, 0 g; Fat, 14 g (86% cal.); Cholesterol, 0 mg;
Carbohydrates, 5 g; Fiber, 0 g; Sodium, 115 mg.

Oriental Vinaigrette

Yield: 1½ pt (750 mL)

U.S.	Metric	Ingredients	PROCEDURE
¾ cup	200 mL	Rice vinegar or white vinegar	1. Combine all ingredients except salt in a bowl and mix well.
¼ cup	60 mL	Soy sauce	2. Taste the dressing and add salt if necessary (the soy sauce may contain enough salt).
1¾ cups	425 mL	Salad oil	3. Mix or stir again before using.
¼ cup	60 mL	Sesame oil	
1 tbsp	15 mL	Grated fresh ginger root	
2 tsp	10 mL	Pepper	
¼ tsp	1 mL	Garlic, crushed	
½ tsp	2 mL	Hot pepper sauce	
as needed	as needed	Salt	

Per 1 ounce:
Calories, 160; Protein, 0 g; Fat, 18 g (100% cal.); Cholesterol, 0 mg;
Carbohydrates, 0 g; Fiber, 0 g; Sodium, 150 mg.

Emulsified Dressings

Mayonnaise is the most important emulsified dressing. It is sometimes used by itself as a salad dressing but more often serves as the base for a wide variety of other dressings. Mayonnaise-based dressings are generally thick and creamy. In fact, many of them are made with the addition of sour cream.

Emulsified French Dressing is similar to Basic French Dressing, except that egg yolk has been added to keep the oil and vinegar from separating. Its preparation is similar to that of mayonnaise. Emulsified French Dressing is given a red-orange color and a subtle flavoring through the addition of Spanish paprika.

PREPARATION OF MAYONNAISE

Good-quality prepared mayonnaise is readily available on the market, and few establishments make their own. But it is such a basic preparation and, like the mother sauces you studied in Chapter 8, the foundation of many others. Therefore, it is important to know how to make it.

Homemade mayonnaise is not as stable as the commercial product, which is prepared with special equipment that creates a finer emulsion and which may have added stabilizers to increase its shelf life. Also, the commercial product is usually less expensive. Nevertheless, making mayonnaise in your operation takes only minutes with a power mixer and, by carefully selecting your ingredients, you can make a superior-tasting product.

To make mayonnaise, you must observe several conditions in order to get an emulsion. Study these guidelines before proceeding with the recipe.

Guidelines for Making Mayonnaise

1. **Use fairly bland ingredients if the mayonnaise is to be used as a base for other dressings.**
   The mayonnaise will be more versatile as a base if it has no strong flavors. Olive oil and other ingredients with distinctive flavors may be used for special preparations.

2. **Use the freshest eggs possible for the best emulsification. For safety, use pasteurized eggs.**

3. **Have all ingredients at room temperature.**
   Cold oil is not easily broken into small droplets, so it is harder to make an emulsion.

4. **Beat the egg yolks well in a bowl.**
   Thorough beating of the yolks is important for a good emulsion.

5. **Beat in the seasonings.**
   It is helpful to add a little of the vinegar at this time as well. The emulsion will be easier to form because the acidity of the vinegar helps to prevent the curdling of the egg yolk proteins. Also, the vinegar helps to disperse the spices and dissolve the salt.

6. **Begin to add the oil very slowly, beating constantly.**
   It is critical to add the oil slowly at first, or the emulsion will break. When the emulsion has begun to form, the oil may be added more quickly. But never add more oil at once than the amount of mayonnaise that has already formed in the bowl, or the emulsion may break.

7. **Gradually beat in the remaining oil alternately with the vinegar.**
   The more oil you add, the thicker the mayonnaise gets. Vinegar thins it. Add a little vinegar whenever the mayonnaise gets too thick to beat.
   Beating with a power mixer using the wire whip attachment makes a more stable emulsion than beating by hand.

8. **Add no more than 8 ounces (240 mL) oil per large egg yolk, or no more than 1 quart (950 mL) per 4 yolks.**
   The emulsion may break if more oil is added than the egg yolks can handle.

9. **Taste and correct the seasonings.**
   Finished mayonnaise should have a smooth, rich, but neutral flavor, with a pleasant tartness. Its texture should be smooth and glossy, and it should be thick enough to hold its shape.

10. **If the mayonnaise breaks, it can be rescued.**
    Beat an egg yolk or two or some good prepared mayonnaise in a bowl, and very slowly begin to beat in the broken mayonnaise, as in step 6. Continue until all the mayonnaise has been added and re-formed.

Mayonnaise

Yield: 2 qt (2 L)

U.S.	Metric	Ingredients	PROCEDURE
8	8	Egg yolks, preferably pasteurized	1. Review guidelines for making mayonnaise on page 575.
2 tbsp	30 mL	Vinegar	2. Place the egg yolks in the bowl of a mixer and beat with the whip attachment until well beaten.
2 tsp	10 mL	Salt	3. Add 2 tbsp (30 mL) vinegar and beat well.
2 tsp	10 mL	Dry mustard	4. Mix together the dry ingredients and add to the bowl. Beat
pinch	pinch	Cayenne	until well mixed.
3¼ pt	1.7 L	Salad oil	5. Turn the mixer to high speed. Very slowly, almost drop by drop, begin adding the oil. When the emulsion forms, you
4 tbsp	60 mL	Vinegar	can add the oil slightly faster.
3–4 tbsp	50–60 mL	Lemon juice	6. When the mayonnaise becomes thick, thin with a little of the vinegar.
			7. Gradually beat in the remaining oil alternately with the vinegar.
			8. Adjust the tartness and the consistency by beating in a little lemon juice.

Per 1 ounce:
Calories, 220; Protein, 0 g; Fat, 25 g (100% cal.); Cholesterol, 25 mg;
Carbohydrates, 0 g; Fiber, 0 g; Sodium, 75 mg.

Mayonnaise-based Dressings

For each of the following dressings, add the listed ingredients to *2 qt (2 L) mayonnaise* as indicated.

Thousand Island Dressing

1 pt (500 mL) chili sauce, 2 oz (60 g) minced onion, 4 oz (125 g) finely chopped green pepper, 4 oz (125 g) chopped drained pimiento, and (optional ingredient) 3 chopped hard-cooked eggs.

Louis Dressing

Prepare Thousand Island Dressing without the chopped eggs. Add 1 pt (500 mL) heavy cream.

Russian Dressing

1 pt (500 mL) chili sauce or catsup, ½ cup (125 mL) drained horseradish, 2 oz (60 g) minced onion, and (optional ingredient) 1 cup (500 mL) lumpfish or whitefish caviar.

Chantilly Dressing

1 pt (500 mL) heavy cream, whipped. Fold the whipped cream into the mayonnaise carefully to retain volume. Do this as close as possible to service time.

Blue Cheese Dressing

½ cup (125 mL) white vinegar, 2 tsp (10 mL) Worcestershire sauce, a few drops of hot red pepper sauce, and 1 lb (500 g) crumbled blue cheese. Thin to desired consistency with 1–2 cups (250–500 mL) heavy cream or half-and-half.
Variation: Substitute sour cream for up to half of the mayonnaise.

Ranch Dressing

1½ qt (1.5 L) sour cream, 2½ pt (1.25 L) buttermilk, 8 oz (250 mL) wine vinegar, 6 oz (175 mL) lemon juice, 6 oz (175 mL) Worcestershire sauce, 6 tbsp (90 mL) chopped parsley, 4 tbsp (60 mL) chopped chives, 6 crushed garlic cloves, 4 chopped scallions, 2 oz (60 mL) prepared mustard, 1 tbsp (15 mL) celery seed.

Aioli II

Mash 2–4 oz (60–125 g) garlic with the salt in the basic recipe. Add this to the egg yolks. Use olive oil or one-half olive oil and one-half salad oil. For another version of Aioli, see page 165.

Emulsified French Dressing

Yield: 2 qt (2 L)

U.S.	Metric	Ingredients	PROCEDURE
2	2	Eggs, preferably pasteurized	1. Place the eggs in the bowl of a mixer and beat with the whip attachment until well beaten.
1 tbsp	15 mL	Salt	2. Mix together the dry ingredients and add to the bowl. Beat until well mixed.
1 tbsp	15 mL	Paprika	
1 tbsp	15 mL	Dry mustard	3. Turn the mixer to high speed. *Very slowly* begin adding the oil, as when making mayonnaise.
½ tsp	2 mL	White pepper	4. When the dressing becomes thick, thin with a little of the vinegar.
3 pt	1.4 L	Salad oil	
8 oz	250 mL	Cider vinegar	5. Gradually beat in the remaining oil alternatively with the vinegar.
4 oz	125 mL	Lemon juice	6. Beat in the lemon juice.
as needed	as needed	Vinegar, lemon juice, or water	7. The dressing should be pourable, not thick like mayonnaise. If it is too thick, *taste for seasonings first*. If the dressing is not tart enough, thin with a little vinegar or lemon juice. If it is tart enough, thin with water.

Per 1 ounce:
Calories, 190; Protein, 0 g; Fat, 21 g (100% cal.); Cholesterol, 5 mg;
Carbohydrates, 0 g; Fiber, 0 g; Sodium, 110 mg.

Other Dressings

Cooked salad dressing is similar in appearance to mayonnaise, but it has a more tart flavor, while mayonnaise is richer and milder. Cooked dressing is made with little or no oil and with a starch thickener. It may be made in the kitchen or purchased ready prepared. Formerly, it was little used in commercial kitchens because of its strong flavor and tartness, but now it is preferred to mayonnaise in some regions.

You will find in many cookbooks a great variety of other dressings based on neither mayonnaise nor oil and vinegar. They include dressings based on sour cream, on fruit juice and yogurt (for fruit salads), and low-calorie dressings that appeal to the dieter. The important thing to remember is that these dressings should have well balanced flavors with a pleasant tartness, and that they should harmonize with and complement the salad with which they are served.

Sour Cream Fruit Salad Dressing

Yield: About 2½ pt (1.25 L)

U.S.	Metric	Ingredients	PROCEDURE
4 oz	125 g	Currant jelly	1. Place the jelly and lemon juice in a stainless-steel bowl. Set over hot water or low heat and stir until melted.
4 oz	125 mL	Lemon juice	
2 pt	1 L	Sour cream	2. Remove from heat and beat in the sour cream a little at a time. Chill the dressing.

Per 1 ounce:
Calories, 60; Protein, 1 g; Fat, 5 g (74% cal.); Cholesterol, 10 mg;
Carbohydrates, 3 g; Fiber, 0 g; Sodium, 15 mg.

VARIATION

Yogurt Fruit Salad Dressing
Prepare as in basic recipe, using 1 cup (250 mL) sour cream and 3 cups (750 mL) plain yogurt.

Cooked Salad Dressing

Yield: 2 qt (2 L)

U.S.	Metric	Ingredients	PROCEDURE
4 oz	125 g	Sugar	1. Mix the sugar, flour, salt, mustard, and cayenne in a stainless-steel bowl.
4 oz	125 g	Flour	
2 tbsp	30 mL	Salt	2. Add the eggs and yolks and beat until smooth.
2 tbsp	30 mL	Dry mustard	3. Place the milk in a saucepan and bring to a simmer. Be careful not to scorch it.
¼ tsp	1 mL	Cayenne	
4	4	Eggs	4. Gradually beat about half the milk into the egg mixture. Then return the mixture to the saucepan.
4	4	Egg yolks	5. Cook over low heat, stirring constantly, until very thick and no raw flour taste remains.
3 pt	1.5 L	Milk	
4 oz	125 g	Butter	6. Remove from heat and stir in the butter.
12 oz	375 mL	Cider vinegar	7. When the butter is melted and mixed in, stir in the vinegar.
			8. Immediately transfer the dressing to a stainless-steel container. Cover and cool.

Per 1 ounce:
Calories, 50; Protein, 2 g; Fat, 3 g (49% cal.); Cholesterol, 35 mg;
Carbohydrates, 5 g; Fiber, 0 g; Sodium, 250 mg.

Honey Lemon Dressing

Yield: 1 pt (500 mL)

U.S.	Metric	Ingredients	PROCEDURE
1 cup	250 mL	Honey	1. Mix honey and lemon juice together until thoroughly mixed.
1 cup	250 mL	Lemon juice	2. Serve with fruit salads.

Per 1 ounce:
Calories, 70; Protein, 0 g; Fat, 0 g (0% cal.); Cholesterol, 0 mg;
Carbohydrates, 19 g; Fiber, 0 g; Sodium, 0 mg.

VARIATIONS

Honey Cream Dressing
Mix 1 cup (250 mL) heavy cream with the honey before adding the lemon juice.

Honey Lime Dressing
Use lime juice instead of lemon juice.

Fruit Salad Dressing

Yield: 1 qt (1 L)

U.S.	Metric	Ingredients	PROCEDURE
6 oz	175 g	Sugar	1. Mix the sugar and cornstarch in a stainless-steel bowl.
1 oz	30 g	Cornstarch	2. Add the eggs and beat until the mixture is smooth.
4	4	Eggs	
1 cup	250 mL	Pineapple juice	3. Heat the fruit juices in a saucepan and bring to a boil.
1 cup	250 mL	Orange juice	4. Gradually beat the hot juices into the egg mixture.
½ cup	125 mL	Lemon juice	5. Return the mixture to the saucepan and bring to a boil, stirring constantly.
			6. When the mixture has thickened, immediately pour it out into a stainless-steel bowl or bain-marie and chill.
1 cup	250 mL	Sour cream	7. Beat the sour cream into the chilled fruit mixture.

Per 1 ounce:
Calories, 60; Protein, 1 g; Fat, 2 g (31% cal.); Cholesterol, 30 mg;
Carbohydrates, 9 g; Fiber, 0 g; Sodium, 10 mg.

Terms for Review

appetizer salad	full slip	cooked salad	winterized oil
accompaniment salad	four parts of a salad	fruit salad	vinegar strength
main-course salad	bound salad	combination salad	Roquefort
separate-course salad	green salad	gelatin salad	emulsion
dessert salad	vegetable salad	marinated	French dressing

Questions for Discussion

1. List three or four salads that may be served as appetizers, as accompaniments, as main dishes, as separate-course salads, and as desserts. Give reasons for your choices.

2. What is the effect of salad dressings on the crispness of salad greens, and what are some ways to solve this problem?

3. You are asked to prepare 250 Waldorf salads for a banquet. Explain the procedure you will use for the preparation. List each step, from raw ingredients to plated salads. (You may refer to the recipe on p. 557.)

4. How can you ensure that salad greens will be crisp?

5. You are making mixed green salads and have the following ingredients to choose from. Which would you toss together and which would you add after plating or at service time? Why?

Iceberg lettuce	Chicory
Shredded red cabbage	Avocado slices
Carrot strips or shreds	Tomato wedges
Watercress	Romaine lettuce
Sliced celery	

6. You are preparing tossed green salads, potato salads, and avocado and grapefruit salads for luncheon service. How will you plan your preparation (what will you do first, second, and so on)?

7. You are trying a new recipe for a molded vegetable salad using unflavored gelatin. After evaluating the flavor, you decide it isn't tart enough and more vinegar should be added. Should you make any other adjustments?

8. When you are making mayonnaise, you should take are a number of precautions to make sure a good emulsion is formed. Name as many as you can. If you forget one of these and your mayonnaise breaks, what can you do?

Sandwiches and Hors d'Oeuvres

The sandwich is a favorite and convenient lunchtime food. It is quickly made and served and adaptable to so many variations that it satisfies nearly every taste and nutrition requirement.

Sandwiches have long been the domain of the pantry department, along with salads and other cold preparations. However, when you consider that the most popular sandwich today is the hamburger, you realize that sandwich preparation is as much the responsibility of the short-order cook as it is of the pantry cook.

Preparing hot and cold sandwiches to order is one of the fundamental skills required in modern food service. In this chapter, we start by looking at the fundamentals of sandwich making, the basic ingredients and basic sandwich types. We then look at the setup of the sandwich station and methods for efficient production.

The subject of sandwiches leads us to the study of another category of foods that are handled by the pantry department: hors d'oeuvres. One of the most important types of hors d'oeuvre is the canapé, which is actually a tiny, open-faced sandwich. In the last part of this chapter, we discuss not only canapés but also other basic kinds of hors d'oeuvres.

Sandwiches

Breads

One of the functions of the bread in a sandwich is to provide an edible casing for the food inside. Ideally, though, the bread should do more than this. Good-quality breads provide variety, texture, flavor, and eye appeal to sandwiches, as well as providing bulk and nutrients.

TYPES

Pullman or sandwich loaves of white bread are most frequently used. These are long, rectangular loaves that provide square slices of specified thickness, from ⅜ inch to ⅝ inch (10 mm to 16 mm) thick.

Commercial sandwich bread should be of fine rather than coarse texture and firm enough to spread well. Supermarket white bread is unsuitable because it is too soft for spreading and for holding most fillings, and it becomes pasty in the mouth.

Because of its neutral flavor, white bread is suitable for the largest variety of fillings.

Other kinds of breads add variety and interest, provided that they harmonize with the filling. The following are some possibilities:

Rolls, including hard and soft rolls, hamburger and hot dog rolls, long rolls for submarine sandwiches
French or Italian bread, split horizontally
Whole wheat
Cracked wheat
Rye and pumpernickel
Pita bread
Raisin bread
Cinnamon bread
Fruit and nut breads
Focaccia

STORAGE

Fresh bread is essential for top-quality sandwiches. Stale or dry bread is undesirable. The following measures can be taken to ensure freshness.

1. Daily delivery, or as frequent as possible, depending on your location. Bread stales rapidly, and day-old bread has lost much of its freshness.

2. Keep bread tightly wrapped in moistureproof wrapping until it is used. This prevents drying and guards against absorption of odors.

3. French bread and other hard-crusted breads should not be wrapped, or the crusts will soften. These breads stale rapidly and should be used the day they are baked.

4. Store at room temperature, away from ovens or hot equipment. Do not refrigerate, because refrigerated bread becomes stale faster.

5. If bread must be kept more than 1 day, it may be frozen. Thaw frozen bread without unwrapping.

6. Day-old bread may be used for toasting without loss of quality.

After reading this chapter, you should be able to

1. Select, store, and serve fresh, good-quality breads for sandwiches.

2. Use sandwich spreads correctly.

3. Identify the most popular types of sandwich fillings.

4. Set up an efficient sandwich station.

5. Prepare the major types of sandwiches to order.

6. Prepare simple, cold sandwiches in quantity.

7. Prepare canapés and other popular categories of hors d'oeuvres.

Spreads

PURPOSES OF SPREADS

1. To protect the bread from soaking up moisture from the filling.
2. To add flavor.
3. To add moisture or mouthfeel.

BUTTER

Butter should be soft enough to spread easily without tearing the bread. It may be softened by whipping in a mixer or by simply letting it stand at room temperature for half an hour.

Whipping gives the butter greater volume, and this cuts food cost. However, whipped butter does not keep as well because the incorporated air speeds the development of rancidity.

Some operators whip a small amount of water or milk into the butter. This not only increases spreadability but also increases volume. However, it adds nothing to the quality of the sandwich and increases the likelihood of soaking the bread.

Margarine is sometimes used instead of butter, if food costs require it or if customers request it.

Flavored butters, such as those listed on page 594, may be used with appropriate fillings.

MAYONNAISE

Mayonnaise is often preferred to butter as a spread because it contributes more flavor. However, it does not protect the bread from moisture as well as butter does.

Because of the danger of food-borne disease, sandwiches made with mayonnaise should be served immediately or refrigerated at once and kept refrigerated until served.

Fillings

The filling is the heart of the sandwich. As we have already said, nearly any kind of food may be served between two slices of bread. The following are some possible fillings, which may be used separately or in combination.

MEATS AND POULTRY

Most meats for sandwiches are precooked, though some are cooked to order. Sliced meats dry out and lose flavor, so avoid slicing farther ahead than necessary and keep sliced meats covered or wrapped.

Leftovers may be used, but only if they are of good quality and have been properly handled and stored to avoid contamination.

Thin slices are more tender, and sandwiches made with them are easier to eat. Also, many thin slices make a thicker sandwich than one or two thick slices of the same total weight.

1. Beef

Sliced roast beef, hot or cold	Corned beef
Hamburger patties	Pastrami
Small steaks	Tongue, fresh or smoked

2. Pork products

Roast pork	Bacon
Ham, all kinds	Canadian bacon

3. **Poultry**
    Turkey breast   Chicken breast

4. **Sausage products**
    Salami   Liverwurst
    Frankfurters   Luncheon meats
    Bologna

CHEESE

Like meats, cheese dries out rapidly when unwrapped and sliced. When slicing is done ahead, the slices should remain covered until service time. See Chapter 21 for a summary of cheese varieties.

The most popular sandwich cheeses are

Cheddar types   Cream cheese
Swiss types   Process cheese
Provolone   Cheese spreads

FISH AND SHELLFISH

Most seafood fillings for sandwiches are highly perishable and should be kept well chilled at all times.
Some popular seafood fillings are

Tuna   Shrimp
Sardines   Anchovies
Smoked salmon   Fried fish portions
  and lox

MAYONNAISE-BASED SALADS

Refer to page 553 for preparation of cooked salads. The most popular salads for sandwich fillings are tuna salad, egg salad, chicken or turkey salad, and ham salad.

VEGETABLE ITEMS

Lettuce, tomato, and onion are indispensable in sandwich production. In addition, nearly any vegetables used in salads may also be included in sandwiches. See pages 533–534 for a listing.

MISCELLANEOUS

Peanut butter   Fruits, fresh or dried
Jelly   Nuts (such as sliced almonds)
Hard-cooked egg

Types of Sandwiches

HOT SANDWICHES

1. *Simple hot sandwiches* consist of hot fillings, usually meats, between two slices of bread or two halves of a roll. They may also contain items that are not hot, such as a slice of tomato or raw onion on a hamburger.
    Hamburgers and hot dogs and all their variations are the most popular hot sandwiches.

2. *Open-faced hot sandwiches* are made by placing buttered or unbuttered bread on a serving plate, covering it with hot meat or other filling, and topping with a sauce, gravy, cheese, or

Figure 20.1 Cutting a club or multidecker sandwich.

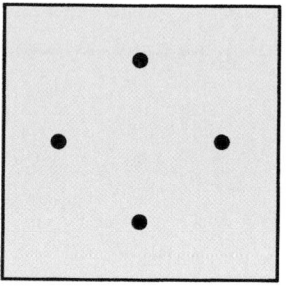

(a) Place four picks in the
sandwich in the location
shown by the dots in the
illustration.

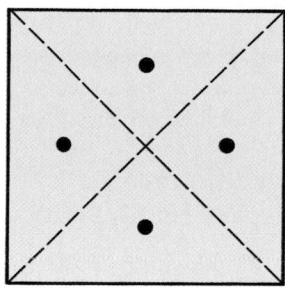

(b) Cut the sandwiches into quarters from corner to corner. Plate the
sandwich with the points up.

other topping. Some versions are browned under the broiler before serving. This type of
sandwich is eaten with a knife and fork.

3. *Grilled sandwiches*, also called *toasted sandwiches*, are simple sandwiches that are buttered
   on the outside and browned on the griddle or in a hot oven. Sandwiches containing cheese
   are popular for grilling.

4. *Deep-fried sandwiches* are made by dipping sandwiches in beaten egg and, sometimes, in
   bread crumbs and then deep-frying. This type of sandwich is often cooked on a griddle or
   in a hot oven instead, as deep-frying makes it greasy.

COLD SANDWICHES

1. *Simple cold sandwiches* are those made with two slices of bread or two halves of a roll, a
   spread, and a filling. They are called simple because they are made with just two slices of
   bread, not because they are necessarily simple in construction. Simple cold sandwiches
   range from a single slice of cheese or meat between two slices of buttered bread to complex
   constructions like the submarine sandwich (also called a hero sandwich or grinder), a long
   Italian roll filled with salami, ham, capocollo, mortadella or bologna, provolone cheese,
   peppers, onions, olives, tomatoes, and more.

   Most popular sandwiches fall into this category.

2. *Multidecker sandwiches* are made with more than two slices of bread (or rolls split into
   more than two pieces) and with several ingredients in the filling.

   The *club sandwich* is a popular multidecker sandwich, made of three slices of toast and
   filled with sliced chicken or turkey breast, mayonnaise, lettuce, tomato, and bacon. It is cut
   into four triangles, as shown in Figure 20.1.

3. *Open-faced sandwiches* are made with a single slice of bread, like large canapés, which is
   what they are. Like canapés, the filling or topping should be attractively arranged and garnished. Canapé ingredients and method are discussed later in this chapter.

4. *Tea sandwiches* are small, fancy sandwiches generally made from light, delicate ingredients
   and bread that has been trimmed of crusts. They are often cut into fancy shapes. Fillings
   and spreads can be the same as those for canapés.

5. *Wraps* are sandwiches in which the fillings are wrapped, like a Mexican burrito, in a large
   flour tortilla or similar flatbread. They may be served whole or cut in half if large.

Making Sandwiches

The preparation of sandwiches requires a great deal of handwork. Many individual motions
may be required, especially if the sandwiches are multideckers or have several ingredients.
Whether you are making sandwiches in quantity or to order, your goal must be to reduce your
motions to make the production as efficient and quick as possible.

SETTING UP THE STATION FOR PREPARED-TO-ORDER SANDWICHES

A station setup depends on the menu and on the available equipment and space, so there is no single correct way to set up.

Any setup involves two elements: ingredients and equipment.

Ingredients

This phase of the setup has two parts:

1. **Prepare ingredients.**
    Mix fillings, prepare spreads, slice sandwich meats and cheeses, separate lettuce leaves, slice tomatoes, prepare garnishes, and so on. In other words, have everything ready ahead of time, so nothing is left to do but put the ingredients together.

2. **Arrange or store ingredients for maximum efficiency.**
    To reduce your movements to a minimum, the ideal setup has everything you need within easy reach of both hands. Depending on the kitchen layout, this may not be possible, especially if the sandwich menu is very large. But try to get as close to it as possible.

    Arrange ingredients so you can use both hands. For example, while the left hand reaches for the bread, the right hand reaches for the butter spreader. Then, while the right hand puts the spreader back, the left reaches for the sliced ham. The right hand, on its way back from the butter, picks up a slice of cheese and so on. On a busy sandwich station, every second counts.

Two other considerations are important while we're talking about ingredients:

1. **Sanitation.**
    Because cold sandwiches are subjected to a lot of handling and are not cooked, it is especially important that ingredients be properly refrigerated and protected at all times. A refrigerated table—sort of a cold version of a steam table—is usually used. Refrigerated drawers or under-the-counter reach-ins are used for less frequently needed items.

2. **Portion control.**
    Sliced items are portioned by the count and by weight. If portioning is by the count, you must take care, during pre-prep, to slice to the proper thickness. If done by weight, each portion can be placed on squares of waxed paper and stacked in a container.

Equipment

The equipment needed for a sandwich station depends, of course, on the menu and the size of the operation.

1. *Storage equipment* for ingredients includes refrigeration equipment for cold ingredients and a steam table for hot ingredients, such as roasted meats.
2. *Hand tools* are basic requirements for sandwich making and are often the only tools necessary. These include spreaders, spatulas, and knives, including a serrated knife and a sharp chef's knife for cutting the finished sandwich. A cutting board, of course, is also required. A power slicer may be necessary for any slicing not done ahead.
3. *Portion control equipment* includes scoops for fillings and a portion scale for other ingredients.
4. *Cooking equipment* is necessary for most hot sandwiches. Griddles, grills, broilers, and deep fryers are all used for cooking sandwich ingredients to order. Microwave ovens are sometimes used to heat ingredients or finished sandwiches.

SETTING UP AND PREPARING SANDWICHES IN QUANTITY

Once the ingredients are prepared and the hand tools assembled, all that's needed for a complete sandwich station is a large table.

Assembly line production is the most efficient method because it simplifies movements. This is the same method applied to producing salads in quantity in Chapter 19.

Procedure for Making Simple Cold Sandwiches in Quantity

1. Prepare and assemble all ingredients.

2. Assemble necessary equipment, including wrapping materials.

3. Arrange bread slices in rows on the tabletop.

4. Spread each slice with butter or whatever spread is required.

5. Place fillings evenly and neatly on alternate slices, leaving the other slices plain. Fillings should not hang over the edges of the bread. If the filling is spreadable, spread it evenly to the edges. See Figure 20.2 for spreading technique.

6. Top the filled slices with the plain buttered slices.

7. Stack two or three sandwiches and cut with a *sharp* knife.

8. To hold, do one of the following:
   - Wrap separately in plastic, waxed paper, or sandwich bags.
   - Place in storage pans, cover tightly with plastic wrap, and cover with clean, damp towels. The towels must not touch the sandwiches; their purpose is to provide a moisture barrier to help prevent drying.

9. Refrigerate immediately and hold until served.

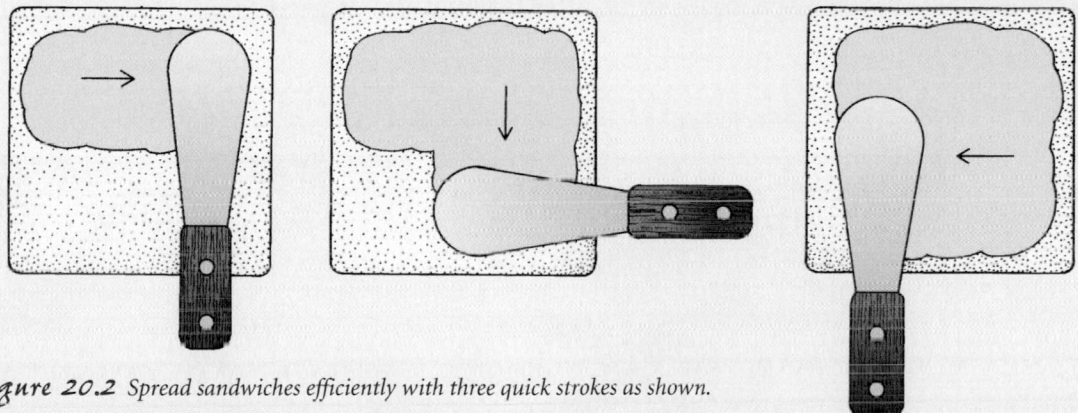

Figure 20.2 Spread sandwiches efficiently with three quick strokes as shown.

SERVICE

With a few exceptions, such as hamburgers and hot dogs, sandwiches are cut before serving. Cutting serves two purposes: It makes the sandwich easier to handle and eat, and it makes possible a more attractive presentation.

The first purpose is usually accomplished by simply cutting the sandwich in half or, if it is very large or thick, into thirds or quarters.

The second purpose can be served by displaying the cut edges rather than the crust edges to the outside. If the sandwich was neatly made, of good ingredients, and tastefully garnished (see Chapter 24), it will be appetizing and attractive. Little purpose is served by cutting and arranging the sandwich in complicated ways. That sort of presentation is seen more often in textbooks than in busy kitchens.

Hamburgers and other uncut sandwiches may be presented open faced to display the attractive ingredients. For example, a hamburger version often called a California Burger is presented with the meat on the bottom half of the bun and, alongside, a lettuce leaf and a slice of tomato on the top half of the bun.

Figure 20.3 shows examples of sandwich presentation.

COLD SANDWICH COMBINATIONS

The following suggestions are only a few of the many sandwiches that can be made from the ingredients listed in the first part of this chapter.

1. Roast beef on rye bread spread with a mixture of softened cream cheese and horseradish.
2. Beef tongue, lettuce, and tomato on onion roll; mayonnaise.
3. Bologna, provolone cheese, tomatoes, and chopped pimiento on hard roll; mayonnaise.
4. Liverwurst, onion slices, and sour pickles on pumpernickel; mayonnaise or butter.
5. Corned beef or ham, Swiss cheese, mustard, and dill pickle slices on rye; mayonnaise or butter.
6. Corned beef, coleslaw (well drained), and Swiss cheese on rye; mayonnaise or butter.
7. Ham, salami, tomato slice, Russian dressing, and lettuce on rye toast.
8. Chicken or turkey, ham, Swiss cheese, and lettuce on white or whole wheat toast; mayonnaise.
9. Chicken and cucumber slices on whole wheat; mayonnaise.
10. Turkey, bacon, Swiss cheese, and lettuce on white or whole wheat toast; mayonnaise.
11. Deviled ham, pineapple slice, and lettuce on white toast.
12. Tuna salad, lettuce, tomato, and shredded cheddar cheese on white toast.
13. Sardines and onion slices on dark rye spread with cream cheese; served open faced.

Figure 20.3 Sandwich presentation need not be elaborate to be attractive.

(a) California Burger.

(b) Tuna Salad Sandwich with an assortment of fruits.

(c) Club Sandwich.

(d) Monte Cristo Sandwich with Tomato and Cucumber Salad.

California Burger

Yield: 1 sandwich

U.S.	Metric	Ingredients	PROCEDURE
1	1	Hamburger patty, 4 oz (125 g)	1. Cook the hamburger patty on a griddle or grill to desired doneness.
1	1	Hamburger roll	2. While the meat is cooking, prepare the roll. Butter the bottom half very lightly. Spread the top half with mayonnaise.
as needed	as needed	Butter	
2 tsp	10 mL	Mayonnaise	3. Place the halves of the roll side by side on a serving plate.
1	1	Lettuce leaf	4. On the top half, place the lettuce leaf, the onion slice (if used), and the tomato slice.
1	1	Thin slice of onion (optional)	
1	1	Tomato slice	5. When the hamburger patty is cooked, place it on the bottom half of the roll. Serve immediately, open faced.

Per serving:
Calories, 480; Protein, 24 g; Fat, 32 g (61% cal.); Cholesterol, 85 mg;
Carbohydrates, 23 g; Fiber, 2 g; Sodium, 370 mg.

VARIATIONS

California Cheeseburger
Prepare as in basic recipe, except place a slice of cheddar or American cheese on the hamburger patty 1 minute before it is done. Cook until the cheese melts.

Cheeseburger (plain)
Omit mayonnaise, lettuce, onion, and tomato, but add the slice of cheese as in California Cheeseburger.

Cheeseburger with Bacon
Prepare like a Cheeseburger, but place 2 half-strips of bacon on the cheese.

California Cheeseburger Deluxe
Prepare like a California Cheeseburger, but place 2 half-strips of bacon on the cheese.

Submarine Sandwich

Yield: 1 sandwich

U.S.	Metric	Ingredients	PROCEDURE
1	1	Submarine roll	1. Split the roll horizontally, but leave it hinged on one side.
2 tbsp	30 mL	Mayonnaise	2. Spread the roll with mayonnaise.
1 oz	30 g	Salami, cut in thin slices	3. Arrange the meats and cheese in the sandwich in layers. If the slices of meat are too wide to fit, fold them in half.
1 oz	30 g	Ham, cut in thin slices	
1 oz	30 g	Bologna, cut in thin slices	4. Arrange the tomato, onion, and pepper slices on top of the meats and cheese.
1 oz	30 g	Provolone cheese, cut in thin slices	
2	2	Tomato slices	5. Close the sandwich. Leave it whole or cut it in half for service.
2	2	Onion slices, very thin	
3	3	Green pepper rings	6. Serve the sandwich with mustard and olives or pickles on the side.

Per serving:
Calories, 770; Protein, 28 g; Fat, 51 g (60% cal.); Cholesterol, 85 mg;
Carbohydrates, 50 g; Fiber, 5 g; Sodium, 1650 mg.

Club Sandwich

Yield: 1 sandwich

U.S.	Metric	Ingredients
3 slices	3 slices	White bread, toasted
as needed	as needed	Mayonnaise
2 leaves	2 leaves	Lettuce
2 slices	2 slices	Tomato, about ¼ inch (½ cm) thick
3 strips	3 strips	Bacon, cooked crisp
2 oz	60 g	Sliced turkey or chicken breast

PROCEDURE

1. Place the 3 slices of toast on a clean work surface. Spread the tops with mayonnaise.
2. On the first slice, place 1 lettuce leaf, then 2 slices of tomato, then 3 strips of bacon.
3. Place the second slice of toast on top, spread side down.
4. Spread the top with mayonnaise.
5. On top of this, place the turkey or chicken, then the other lettuce leaf.
6. Top with the third slice of toast, spread side down.
7. Place frilled picks on all 4 sides of the sandwich, as shown in Figure 20.1.
8. Cut the sandwich from corner to corner into 4 triangles. Each triangle will have a pick through the center to hold it together.
9. Place on a plate with the points up. The center of the plate may be filled with potato chips, French fries, or other garnish or accompaniment.

Per serving:
Calories, 580; Protein, 32 g; Fat, 25 g (40% cal.); Cholesterol, 75 mg;
Carbohydrates, 53 g; Fiber, 3 g; Sodium, 910 mg.

VARIATION

Bacon, Lettuce, and Tomato Sandwich (BLT)

Using only 2 slices of toast, prepare basic recipe through step 3. Omit remaining ingredients. Cut sandwich in half diagonally for service.

Grilled Cheese Sandwich

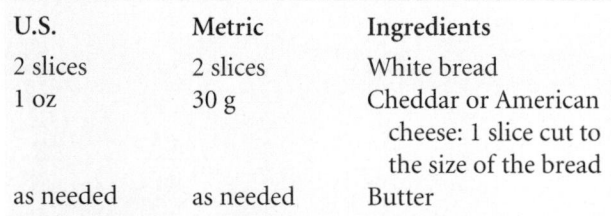

Yield: 1 sandwich

U.S.	Metric	Ingredients
2 slices	2 slices	White bread
1 oz	30 g	Cheddar or American cheese: 1 slice cut to the size of the bread
as needed	as needed	Butter

PROCEDURE

1. Place the slice of cheese between the slices of bread.
2. Butter the outsides of the sandwich and place on a griddle preheated to 350°–375°F (175°–190°C).
3. Cook until golden brown on one side. Turn over and cook until the second side is golden brown and the cheese starts to melt.
4. Remove the sandwich from the griddle. Cut in half diagonally and serve immediately.

Per serving:
Calories, 360; Protein, 13 g; Fat, 20 g (49% cal.); Cholesterol, 55 mg;
Carbohydrates, 34 g; Fiber, 1 g; Sodium, 580 mg.

VARIATIONS

Grilled Ham and Swiss Sandwich

Make the sandwich with a ½-oz (15-g) slice of Swiss cheese and a 1-oz (30-g) slice of ham. Griddle as in basic recipe.

Grilled Cheese and Bacon Sandwich

Make the sandwich with 1 oz (30 g) cheddar or American cheese and 2 strips of crisp cooked bacon. Griddle as in basic recipe.

Reuben Sandwich

Yield: 1 sandwich

U.S.	Metric	Ingredients	PROCEDURE
2 slices	2 slices	Dark rye bread	
4 tsp	20 mL	Russian or Thousand Island dressing	
2 oz	60 g	Corned beef, sliced very thin	
1 oz	30 g	Sauerkraut, well drained	
1 oz	30 g	Swiss cheese (1 or 2 slices)	
as needed	as needed	Butter	

1. Place the slices of bread on a clean work surface.
2. Spread each slice with about 2 tsp (10 mL) dressing.
3. On one of the slices, place the corned beef, then the sauerkraut, then the cheese.
4. Place the second slice of bread on top, spread side down.
5. Butter the top of the sandwich and place buttered side down on a preheated griddle. Immediately butter the other side of the sandwich, which is now on top. (This method is less messy than buttering both sides before placing it on the griddle.)
6. Griddle the sandwich, turning once, until browned on both sides and hot through.
7. Cut the sandwich into halves and serve immediately.

Per serving:
Calories, 590; Protein, 25 g; Fat, 39 g (59% cal.); Cholesterol, 105 mg;
Carbohydrates, 35 g; Fiber, 4 g; Sodium, 1580 mg.

Monte Cristo Sandwich

Yield: 1 sandwich

U.S.	Metric	Ingredients	PROCEDURE
2 slices	2 slices	White bread	
as needed	as needed	Butter	
1 oz	30 g	Sliced turkey or chicken breast	
1 oz	30 g	Sliced ham	
1 oz	30 g	Sliced Swiss cheese	
1	1	Egg, beaten	
2 tbsp	30 mL	Milk	

1. Place the bread on a clean work surface. Spread the tops with butter.
2. Place the turkey, ham, and cheese slices on one of the pieces of bread. Top with the remaining slice of bread, buttered side down.
3. Secure the sandwich with 2 picks placed in opposite corners.
4. Beat the egg and milk together.
5. Dip the sandwich in the batter until it is completely coated and the liquid has partially soaked into the bread.
6. Fry the sandwich in deep fat at 375°F (190°C) until golden brown.
7. Cut in half and serve immediately.

Per serving:
Calories, 570; Protein, 35 g; Fat, 30 g (48% cal.); Cholesterol, 285 mg;
Carbohydrates, 37 g; Fiber, 1 g; Sodium, 850 mg.

Alternative Method: Omit the picks and cook on a griddle until browned on both sides.

Barbecued Pork or Beef Sandwich

Portions: 20   **Portion size:** 1 sandwich with 4 oz (115 g) filling

U.S.	Metric	Ingredients	PROCEDURE
3 lb	1.3 kg	Cooked pork or beef	
2¼ pt	1 L	Barbecue Sauce (p. 163)	
20	20	Hamburger rolls	
as needed	as needed	Butter	

1. Using a slicing machine or chef's knife, cut the meat into very thin slices.
2. Combine the meat and sauce in a saucepan. Simmer uncovered over low heat for 10–15 minutes, until the meat has absorbed some of the flavor of the sauce and the liquid has reduced and thickened slightly.
3. Keep the meat hot for service.
4. For each order, butter a hamburger roll. Place a 4-oz (115-g) portion of the meat mixture on the bottom half of the roll. Close the sandwich and serve immediately.

Per serving:
Calories, 400; Protein, 20 g; Fat, 24 g (54% cal.); Cholesterol, 65 mg;
Carbohydrates, 26 g; Fiber, 2 g; Sodium, 300 mg.

Turkey BLT Wrap

Yield: 1 sandwich

U.S.	Metric	Ingredients	PROCEDURE
1	1	Flour tortilla, 10 inches (25 cm) in diameter	1. Spread the tortilla with the mayonnaise, leaving a ½-inch (15-mm) border around the outside unspread. (For a richer, moister sandwich, double the quantity of mayonnaise.)
½ oz	15 g	Mayonnaise	
½–1 oz	15–30 g	Lettuce leaves	2. Arrange the lettuce leaves in the center of the tortilla, leaving a border of about 2 inches (5 cm) uncovered.
3	3	Tomato slices, thin	3. Arrange the tomato, bacon, and turkey on top of the lettuce.
1 oz	30 g	Cooked bacon, crumbled	
2 oz	60 g	Turkey breast, in thin slices	4. To roll the wrap, first fold the uncovered rim of the tortilla on opposite edges of the circle toward the center. This closes the ends of the roll to hold in the filling. Then roll the tortilla tightly. The mayonnaise on the edge of the tortilla helps seal it closed.

Per serving:
Calories, 610; Protein, 32 g; Fat, 35 g (52% cal.); Cholesterol, 75 mg; Carbohydrates, 42 g; Fiber, 3 g; Sodium, 920 g.

5. Serve whole or cut in half on the diagonal.

Vegetarian Wrap with White Beans

Yield: 1 sandwich

U.S.	Metric	Ingredients	PROCEDURE
1	1	Flour tortilla, 10 inches (25 cm) in diameter	1. Lay the tortilla flat on the workbench. Brush it very lightly with olive oil.
as needed	as needed	Olive oil	2. Arrange the lettuce leaves in the center of the tortilla, leaving a border of about 2 inches (5 cm) uncovered.
½–1 oz	15–30 g	Lettuce leaves	
3 oz	90 g	White Bean Salad (p. 549)	3. Place the bean salad in a sieve to drain excess vinaigrette, reserving the vinaigrette. Mix together the bean salad and the rice. If the mixture is dry, add enough of the dressing back to the mixture so that it is just sufficiently moistened.
1½ oz	45 g	Cooked rice, white or brown, cold	
½ oz	15 g	Green pepper, diced	4. Mix in the diced pepper.

Per serving:
Calories, 510; Protein, 13 g; Fat, 21 g (38% cal.); Cholesterol, 0 mg; Carbohydrates, 65 g; Fiber, 6 g; Sodium, 360 mg.

5. Place the bean mixture on the tortilla in an oblong mound. Roll and wrap the tortilla tightly around the filling as in the recipe for Turkey BLT Wrap above.

Hors d'Oeuvres

In addition to salads and salad dressings, the pantry or *garde manger* department is generally responsible for the small food items known as *appetizers* or *hors d'oeuvres*. The function of these foods is to enliven the appetite before dinner, often to the accompaniment of drinks, so they are generally small in size and spicy or piquant in flavor.

There is some confusion as to the distinction, if any, between the terms *appetizer* and *hors d'oeuvre*. Most books prescribe definitions of these words. The trouble is, everyone has different definitions for them, and they rarely correspond to the general way most people use the terms.

In general, the first course of a multicourse meal is called an *appetizer*, and the finger foods served at receptions and with cocktails are called *hors d'oeuvres*. In some regions, however, the terms are used interchangeably.

This section deals not with first courses but with special kinds of foods that are usually encountered away from the dinner table—foods that are the special domain of the pantry chef. They include finger foods such as canapés and relishes, indispensable accompaniments to receptions and parties.

The French expression *hors d'oeuvre* literally translates as "outside the work," meaning "apart from the main meal or main part of the meal." Incidentally, in French, the term is not spelled or pronounced with an *s* at the end to make it plural, so you will often see the plural form spelled the same as the singular. In English-language dictionaries, the plural is spelled and pronounced with a final *s*.

Canapés

Canapés may be defined as bite-size open-faced sandwiches. The variety of possible combinations is nearly unlimited. Most canapés consist of three parts: base, spread, and garnish.

BASE

Canapé bases may be made from several items:

Bread cutouts	Melba toasts
Toast cutouts	Tiny unsweetened pastry shells
Crackers	Profiteroles (miniature unsweetened cream puff shells, pp. 860–861)

Many of these items, such as crackers and melba toasts, can be purchased ready made, but bread and toast cutouts are the most widely used and offer the lowest food cost, though they require more labor.

Untoasted bread for canapés should be firm enough to allow the finished product to be handled easily. It may be cut thick and flattened slightly with a rolling pin to make it firmer. Toast is, of course, firmer, and it gives a pleasing texture and crispness to the canapés.

Procedures for Preparing Canapés From Toast

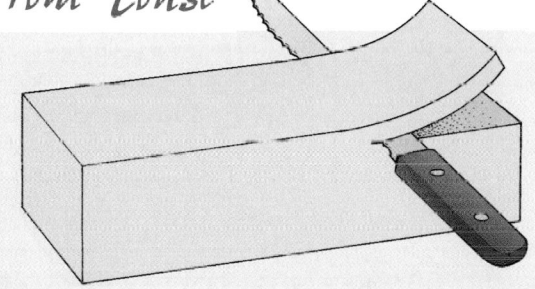

Method 1

1. You may use ready-sliced bread (after trimming the crusts), but it is usually most efficient to use long, unsliced pullman loaves. Cut the crusts from all sides (save for bread crumbs). Cut the bread horizontally into slices ¼ inch (6 mm) thick, as shown in Figure 20.4.

2. Toast the slices in the oven or in a large toaster.

3. Let the toasts cool.

4. Cover with a thin, even layer of the chosen spread and cut into desired shapes with a knife (see Figure 20.5). Make the cuts neat and uniform.

   Alternatively, cut the toasts into desired shapes with small cutters and reserve the trim for bread crumbs. Spread each cutout with desired topping. (This method is more time-consuming, but it may be used with round or odd-shaped cutters if you desire to save food cost by not losing spread on unused trimmings.)

5. Garnish the cutouts as desired.

Figure 20.4 For canapés, trim the crusts from a pullman loaf. With a serrated knife, cut horizontally into thin slices.

Method 2

1. Cut bread slices as in step 1 above.

2. Cut into desired shapes. Brush both sides of each cutout with melted butter and arrange on sheet pans. Place in a hot oven (450°F/230°C) until golden brown and very crisp, about 6 to 8 minutes.

3. Let the bases cool.

4. Assemble the canapés.

This method is more costly but gives a crisper base that holds up better with a moist spread.

Figure 20.5 Bread slices for canapés can be cut into several basic shapes with no waste.

SPREAD

Canapé spreads may be as simple as butter or softened cream cheese, but it is better to use a more highly flavored spread because sharp or spicy flavors are better for stimulating the appetite.

The spread should be thick enough so that it clings well to the base and so that the garnish sticks to it without falling off.

Spreads may be divided into three basic categories, as follows.

Flavored Butters

Basic procedures for making flavored or compound butters are explained in Chapter 8 (see recipes on pp. 153–154). Most flavored butters are made simply by blending the flavoring ingredients with the softened butter until completely mixed. Solid ingredients should be puréed or chopped very fine so that the butter can be spread smoothly.

Proportions of flavoring ingredients to butter can be varied widely, according to taste. For example, to make anchovy butter, you could double the quantity of anchovies indicated in the recipe on page 154 to get a stronger flavor, or you could decrease it to get a milder flavor. Because of this variability, and because the basic procedure is so simple, you should be able to make many kinds of flavored butters without individual recipes. Use the recipes in Chapter 8 and the following list as guides. Popular and versatile flavors for butter spreads include

Lemon	Caviar	Shrimp
Parsley	Mustard	Olive
Tarragon	Horseradish	Shallot or scallion
Chive	Pimiento	Curry
Anchovy	Blue cheese	Caper

Flavored Cream Cheese

Flavored cream cheese spreads are made like flavored butters, except that you substitute cream cheese for the butter. You can also use a mixture of cream cheese and butter, blended together well. Flavor variations are the same as those listed above for butter.

In addition, cream cheese is often blended with sharper, more flavorful cheeses that have been mashed or grated. Adding cream cheese to firmer cheese helps make the latter more spreadable. A liquid such as milk, cream, or port wine may be added to make the mixture softer. Such cheese spreads are often flavored with spices and herbs such as paprika, caraway seeds, dry mustard, parsley, or tarragon.

Meat or Fish Salad Spreads

You can use many cold meat or fish mixtures, such as cooked salads, to make canapé spreads. Popular examples include tuna salad, salmon salad, shrimp salad, chicken salad, deviled ham, and liver pâté.

To convert a salad recipe (see pp. 553–555) to a spread recipe, you may need to make one or more of the following modifications:

1. Chop the solid ingredients until very fine, or grind or purée them, so that the mixture is spreadable and not chunky.

2. Do not add the liquid ingredients and mayonnaise all at once. Add them a little at a time, just until the mixture reaches a thick, spreadable consistency.

3. Check the seasonings carefully. You may want to increase the seasonings to make the spread more stimulating to the appetite.

GARNISH

The garnish of a canapé is any food item or combination of items placed on top of the spread. It may be a major part of the canapé, such as a slice of ham or cheese, or it may be a small tidbit that is selected for color, design, texture, or flavor accent, such as a pimiento cutout, a slice of radish, a caper, or a dab of caviar. Even the spread can be used as a garnish. For example, you may make a canapé with a mustard butter spread and a slice of ham, then decorate the ham with a border or design of mustard butter piped on with a paper cone.

Here are some of the many food items that may be used alone or in combination to decorate canapés:

Vegetables, Pickles, and Relishes

Radish slices
Olives
Pickles
Capers
Pimiento

Pickled onions
Chutney
Asparagus tips
Cucumber slices

Cherry tomato slices or halves
Watercress leaves
Marinated mushrooms
Parsley

Fish

Smoked oysters
 and clams
Smoked salmon
Smoked trout
Herring

Shrimp
Rolled anchovy
 fillets
Caviar

Salmon or tuna flakes
Crab meat
Lobster chunks or slices
Sardines

Meats

Ham
Salami

Chicken or turkey
 breast

Smoked tongue
Roast beef

Other

Cheese

Hard-cooked egg slices

Guidelines for Assembling Canapés

1. **Good mise en place is essential.**
Preparing thousands of canapés for large functions can be tedious work, so it is essential that all bases, spreads, and garnishes be prepared ahead of time in order that final assembly may go quickly and smoothly.

2. **Assemble as close as possible to serving time.**
Bases quickly become soggy and spreads and garnish dry out easily. As trays are completed, they may be covered lightly with plastic and held for a short time under refrigeration. Be sure to observe all rules for safe food handling and storage, as you learned in Chapter 2.

3. **Select harmonious flavor combinations in spreads and garnish.**
For example, caviar and chutney or anchovy and ham are not appealing combinations, but these combinations are:

Mustard butter and ham
Lemon butter and caviar
Pimiento cream cheese and sardine
Horseradish butter and smoked salmon or
 smoked tongue
Tuna salad and capers
Anchovy butter, hard-cooked egg slice, and olive

4. **Be sure that at least one of the ingredients is spicy or pronounced in flavor.**
A bland canapé has little value as an appetizer.

5. **Use quality ingredients.**
Canapés can be a good way to utilize leftovers, but only if the leftovers have been carefully handled and stored to retain freshness.

6. **Keep it simple.**
Simple, neat arrangements are more attractive than elaborate, overworked designs. Besides, you don't have time to get too fancy. Also, be sure that the canapés hold together and do not fall apart in the customers' hands.

7. **Arrange the canapés carefully and attractively on trays.**
Much of the attraction of canapés is eye appeal, and the customer never sees just one at a time, but a whole trayful. Each tray should carry an assortment of various flavors and textures, so there is something for every taste.
Figure 20.6 shows a tray of simple, attractive canapés.

Figure 20.6 Assorted canapés, from left: Row 1: mustard butter, ham, sour pickle. Row 2: lemon butter, salmon caviar. Row 3: chive butter, liver pâté, black olive. Row 4: lemon butter, shrimp, fresh dill. Row 5: curry butter, cucumber, pimiento. Row 6: shallot butter, hard-cooked egg slice, caviar. Row 7: chive cream cheese, smoked salmon, stuffed olive slice.

Cocktails

The term *cocktail* is used not only for alcoholic beverages and vegetable and fruit juices but also for a group of appetizers made of seafood or fruit, usually with a tart or tangy sauce. Such cocktails are always served well chilled, often on a bed of crushed ice.

Oysters and clams on the half-shell are popular seafood cocktails, as are shrimp, crab meat, lobster, and firm, flaked white fish with an appropriate sauce. Recipes for a standard tomato-based cocktail sauce and for a lighter sauce called Mignonette are included in Chapter 8.

Fresh oysters and clams on the half-shell should be opened just before they are served (see pp. 372–374) and arranged on flat plates, preferably on a bed of ice. Provide cocktail sauce in a small cup in the center or at the side of the plate. Lemon wedges should also be provided.

Cocktails of shrimp and other cooked seafood are generally served in a stemmed glass or in a small, cup-shaped bowl, which may be nestled in a bed of ice. The cocktail sauce may be put in the glass first and the seafood then arranged on top, partially immersed. Or the cocktail sauce may be added to the seafood as a topping. A third alternative is to serve the sauce separately in a small cup, as for raw oysters. Garnish the dish attractively with lettuce or other salad greens and with lemon wedges.

Fruit cups served as cocktails should be pleasantly tart and not too sweet. Many fruit salads (see Chapter 19) may be served as cocktails. Adding fresh lemon or lime juice to fruit mixtures or serving with a garnish of lemon or lime wedges provides the necessary tartness. A simple wedge of melon with lime is a refreshing cocktail.

A few drops of a flavored liqueur can also be used to perk up the flavor of a fruit cocktail.

Relishes

The term *relish* covers two categories of foods: raw vegetables, and pickled items.

RAW VEGETABLES

These are also known as *crudités* (croo dee tays; *cru* in French means "raw").

Any vegetable that can be eaten raw may be cut into sticks or other attractive, bite-size shapes and served as relishes. Most popular are celery, carrots, and radishes. Other good choices are green and red peppers, zucchini, cucumber, scallions, cauliflower and broccoli florets, peeled broccoli stems, peeled kohlrabi, cherry tomatoes, and Belgian endive leaves. Crudités are often served with an appropriate dip (see the next section).

Raw vegetables must be served crisp and well chilled, just as in salads. Use the freshest, most attractive vegetables possible. If they are a little wilted, they can be recrisped by holding them for a short time in ice water. Serving vegetables embedded in crushed ice will maintain their crispness.

An imaginative pantry chef can make an attractive, colorful bouquet of raw vegetables.

PICKLED ITEMS

A wide variety of items such as dilled cucumber pickles, gherkins, olives, watermelon pickles, pickled peppers, spiced beets, and other preserved vegetables and fruits are served as relishes. These items are rarely made in-house but are purchased already prepared. Like raw vegetables, they should be served chilled.

Dips

Savory dips are popular accompaniments to potato chips, crackers, and raw vegetables.

Proper consistency is important for any dip you prepare. It must not be so thick that it cannot be scooped up without breaking the chip or cracker, but it must be thick enough to stick to the items used as dippers. Proper consistency means thickness at *serving temperature*. Most dips become thicker when held in the refrigerator.

Many mixtures used as spreads (see "Canapés") can also be used as dips. Thin or soften them by adding a little mayonnaise, cream, or other appropriate liquid.

The recipes here are examples of typical dips. Many other sauces and salad dressings can be used as dips. Salsas (pp. 164 and 733) and aioli (pp. 165 and 576) are two popular examples.

Blue Cheese Dip

Yield: 1 qt (1 L)

U.S.	Metric	Ingredients	PROCEDURE
12 oz	375 g	Cream cheese	1. In a mixer with the paddle attachment, beat the cream cheese at low speed until soft and smooth.
5 oz	150 mL	Milk	2. With the machine running, slowly beat in the milk.
6 oz	175 g	Mayonnaise	3. Add the rest of the ingredients and blend in well.
1 oz	30 mL	Lemon juice	4. Taste and adjust seasonings. Chill.
1 oz	30 g	Onion, minced	
½ tsp	2 mL	Hot red pepper sauce	
½ tsp	2 mL	Worcestershire sauce	
10 oz	300 g	Blue cheese, crumbled	

Per 1 ounce:
Calories, 110; Protein, 3 g; Fat, 11 g (86% cal.); Cholesterol, 20 mg;
Carbohydrates, 1 g; Fiber, 0 g; Sodium, 190 mg.

VARIATIONS

Cheddar Cheese Dip

Substitute grated sharp cheddar cheese for the blue cheese. If desired, add chopped chives.

Garlic Cheese Dip

Add mashed garlic to taste to Cheddar Cheese Dip.

Bacon Cheese Dip

Add crumbled crisp bacon to Cheddar Cheese Dip.

Cheese and Chile Dip

Flavor Cheddar Cheese Dip with canned green chiles, chopped.

Romesco

Yield: 1 pt (500 mL)

U.S.	Metric	Ingredients	PROCEDURE
1 oz	30 g	White bread	1. Sauté the bread in olive oil until golden.
½ oz	15 mL	Olive oil	2. Toast the almonds in an oven at 350°F (175°C) for about 15 minutes or in a skillet over moderately low heat until light golden, not dark brown. Remove from the pan as soon as they are golden so they do not brown further.
3 oz	90 g	Blanched almonds	
2 tsp	10 mL	Garlic, chopped	3. Combine the bread, almonds, and garlic in a food processor. Grind until fine.
10 oz	300 g	Tomatoes, peeled	4. Add the tomatoes, paprika, and cayenne. Process to a paste.
2 tsp	10 mL	Spanish paprika	5. With the machine running, gradually add the vinegar and then the oil in a slow stream.
⅛ tsp	0.5 mL	Cayenne	6. Adjust the seasonings with salt and pepper. Add more vinegar if required. The sauce should not be too acidic but should have a definite sharpness.
1½ oz	45 mL	Red wine vinegar	
3–4 oz	90–120 mL	Olive oil	
to taste	to taste	Salt	
to taste	to taste	Pepper	

Per 1 ounce:
Calories, 100; Protein, 2 g; Fat, 9 g (80% cal.); Cholesterol, 0 mg;
Carbohydrates, 3 g; Fiber, 1 g; Sodium, 15 mg.

Hummus (Chickpea Dip)

Yield: 1 qt (1 L)

U.S.	Metric	Ingredients	PROCEDURE
1 lb	500 g	Cooked or canned chickpeas, drained	1. Purée the chickpeas with the tahini, garlic, lemon juice, and olive oil.
8 oz	250 g	Tahini (sesame paste)	2. If necessary, thin the purée with a little water or additional lemon juice, depending on the taste.
¼ oz	8 g	Garlic, crushed	
4 oz	125 mL	Lemon juice	3. Season with salt to taste and with cayenne.
1 oz	30 mL	Olive oil	4. Chill for at least 1 hour to allow the flavors time to blend.
to taste	to taste	Salt	
pinch	pinch	Cayenne	
1–2 oz	30–50 mL	Olive oil	5. Spoon the hummus into serving bowls. Drizzle additional olive oil over each bowl before serving.

Per 1 ounce:
Calories, 80; Protein, 3 g; Fat, 6 g (63% cal.); Cholesterol, 0 mg;
Carbohydrates, 5 g; Fiber, 2 g; Sodium, 0 mg.

VARIATION

Babaganouj

Substitute eggplant purée for the chickpeas. Make the eggplant purée as follows. Toast whole eggplants under a broiler, over a gas burner, or directly on a flattop range until the skin is charred and the eggplant is soft. Peel off the charred skin under running water and cut off the tops. Remove large clumps of seeds if desired. Let stand in a china cap or sieve to let excess moisture drain, then purée the pulp. Reduce the lemon juice to 2–3 oz (60–90 mL) and the tahini to 4 oz (125 g). Double the olive oil.

Guacamole

Yield: approximately 1 qt (1 L)

U.S.	Metric	Ingredients	PROCEDURE
4	4	Ripe avocados, medium size	1. Pit and peel the avocados. Mash the pulp coarsely. The purée should be slightly lumpy rather than smooth.
2 oz	60 g	Onion, grated	
1	1	Small, hot green chile such as jalapeño, minced	2. Mix in the onion, minced chile, lime or lemon juice, olive oil, and salt to taste.
1 oz	30 mL	Lime or lemon juice	3. If desired, peel, seed, and dice the tomato and mix it into the avocado.
1 oz	30 mL	Olive oil	
to taste	to taste	Salt	4. Cover tightly with plastic wrap placed on the surface of the guacamole. This is to protect it from air, which will darken it. For the same reason, guacamole should not be made too long before serving time. Chill the guacamole until ready to serve.
12 oz	375 g	Fresh tomato (optional)	

Per 1 ounce:
Calories, 45; Protein, 1 g; Fat, 4 g (75% cal.); Cholesterol, 0 mg;
Carbohydrates, 2 g; Fiber, 2 g; Sodium, 0 mg.

Note: If fresh chiles are not available, used canned chiles or a few dashes of hot red pepper sauce.

VARIATION

Sour Cream Avocado Dip

Use 1 oz (30 g) onion. Omit the olive oil and tomato. Mash the avocado to a smooth purée. Add ½–¾ pt (250–375 mL) sour cream.

Miscellaneous Hors d'Oeuvres

A great variety of other foods, both hot and cold, can be served as hors d'oeuvres. If they are to be served away from the dinner table, it is best if they can be eaten with the fingers or speared with a pick. At a cocktail reception at which many hors d'oeuvres are served, it is all right if a few of them must be eaten with forks from small plates, but finger food is much easier for the guests, who are likely to be standing and holding a wineglass or cocktail glass while eating.

Of course, there are many thousands of hors d'oeuvre recipes, including many that have been adapted from the cuisines of other lands. Those included here are a sampling of some popular types.

Many of the recipes given elsewhere in this book can be adapted as hors d'oeuvre recipes. In most cases, unit size or portion size should be decreased. For example, meatballs should be made small enough to be eaten in one or two bites. Among the items most readily adapted are the following (check the Index or Recipe Table of Contents for page numbers):

Barbecued Spareribs
Shish Kebab
Deep-fried Chicken (using wing sections)
Baked Clams Oreganata
Broiled Shrimp, Scampi Style
Broiled Scallops
Fried Breaded Scallops, Shrimp, Oysters, or Clams
Steamed Mussels (served on the half-shell, with a sauce)
Cod Cakes or other fish cakes
Vegetable Fritters
Many salads
Quiche
Cheese Wafers and Straws
Sushi

Italian cuisine is particularly rich in hors d'oeuvres, or *antipasti*, as they are called (singular form: *antipasto*). Many books give a recipe for a mixed salad called antipasto. This is misleading, however, because the Italian term does not refer to a specific recipe but to any typically Italian hors d'oeuvre, hot or cold.

Many menus of Italian-style restaurants offer a cold antipasto plate or platter comprising an assortment of flavorful tidbits. Typical components include the following:

Cured meats, such as salami, prosciutto, bologna, and boiled ham.
Seafood items, especially canned or preserved items such as sardines, anchovies, and tuna.
Cheese, such as provolone and mozzarella.
Hard-cooked eggs and stuffed eggs.
Relishes, such as raw carrots, celery, fennel, radishes, cauliflower, and tomatoes, and cooked or pickled items, such as olives, artichoke hearts, small hot peppers, and onions.
Mushrooms and other vegetables prepared à la grecque (p. 551).
Cooked dried beans and other firm vegetables in a piquant vinaigrette.

Spinach Boreks

Yield: 50 pieces

U.S.	Metric	Ingredients	PROCEDURE
2 lb	900 g	Spinach	1. Trim, wash, and steam or boil the spinach just until it is thoroughly wilted. 2. Drain, cool under cold running water, and squeeze dry. Chop fine.
4 oz	100 g	Butter	3. Heat the butter in a sauté pan. Sauté the onions and scallions over low heat until soft.
4 oz	100 g	Onion, chopped fine	
1 oz	30 g	Scallions, chopped fine	4. Remove from the heat and add the spinach and dill. Mix to coat the spinach lightly with butter.
1 oz	30 g	Fresh dill weed, chopped	
1 lb	450 g	Feta cheese, crumbled	5. Mix in the cheese.
to taste	to taste	Salt	6. Season to taste with salt and pepper.
to taste	to taste	Pepper	
25 sheets	25 sheets	Phyllo dough (about 1 lb/450 g)	7. Thaw the phyllo if it is frozen. Unwrap and unfold the stack of sheets and cut them in half lengthwise. Keep them covered to prevent drying.
8 oz approximately	225 g approximately	Melted butter	8. Taking one sheet at a time, brush each lightly with melted butter. Fold the sheet in half lengthwise and butter it again. 9. Put a small mound (about ½–⅔ oz/15–20 g) of the spinach mixture toward the bottom of the strip and a little to one side, as shown in Figure 20.7. 10. Fold into triangular packets as indicated in the illustration. 11. Arrange the triangles on baking sheets with the loose ends of the phyllo on the bottom. Brush the tops with melted butter. 12. Bake at 375°F (190°C) until golden brown and crisp, about 20–25 minutes. 13. Serve warm.

Per 1 piece:
Calories, 110; Protein, 2 g; Fat, 8 g (69% cal.); Cholesterol, 25 mg;
Carbohydrates, 6 g; Fiber, 1 g; Sodium, 210 mg.

VARIATIONS

Many other fillings can be baked wrapped in phyllo, as long as they are not too juicy. The following are some suggestions:

Diced ham, cheddar cheese, and prepared mustard

Gruyère cheese, blue cheese, walnuts

Feta and cream cheese (2 parts feta to 1 part cream cheese) mixed together, plus 1 egg yolk per 12 oz (350 g) cheese

Sautéed mushrooms and onions, crumbled bacon, parsley, parmesan cheese

Diced cooked chicken, mozzarella cheese, sun-dried tomatoes, basil

Crab meat, sautéed shellfish, cream cheese, hot pepper sauce

Ratatouille (p. 472)

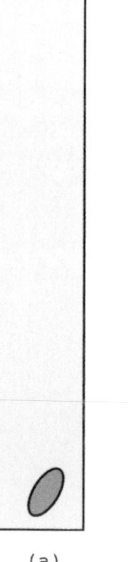
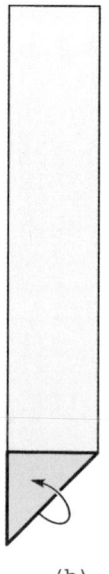
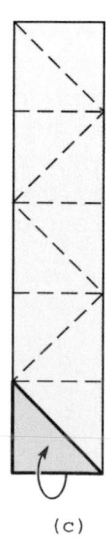
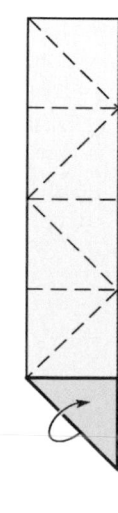

Figure 20.7 Folding phyllo dough triangles.
(a) Place the filling at the bottom of the strip of buttered phyllo dough and a little to one side.
(b) Fold the bottom corner over at a 45-degree angle to form a tri-angle.
(c, d) Continue folding the triangle as shown in the diagram.

(a)   (b)   (c)   (d)

Stuffed Mushrooms with Cheese

Yield: 36 pieces

U.S.	Metric	Ingredients	PROCEDURE
15 oz	425 g	Onion	1. Finely chop the onion, shallot, garlic, parsley, and chives.
2 oz	60 g	Shallot	2. Sweat the onion, shallot, and garlic in the olive oil. Once cooked, add the herbs and bread crumbs. Season to taste.
⅔ oz	20 g	Garlic	
⅓ oz	10 g	Italian parsley (flat-leaf)	
1½ oz	45 g	Chives	
5 oz	150 mL	Olive oil	
3 oz	90 g	Fresh bread crumbs	
36	36	Large mushrooms	3. Remove the stems from the mushrooms and reserve for another use, such as stock or duxelles (alternatively, chop and sauté them with the ingredients in step 2). Place the mushrooms in a pot of water and add the lemon juice, butter, and salt. Bring to a boil and allow to boil for a few minutes. Remove the pan from the heat and leave the mushroom caps in the hot liquid to finish cooking.
3 oz	90 mL	Lemon juice	
1 oz	30 mL	Butter	
as needed	as needed	Kosher or sea salt	
5 oz	150 g	Swiss cheese, grated	4. Once cool enough to handle, remove the mushroom caps and drain. Arrange hollow side up on a sheet pan. Fill with the onion mixture, then sprinkle with the grated cheese. Brown under a salamander or broiler until hot and the cheese has melted.

Per 1 piece:
Calories, 70; Protein, 2 g; Fat, 6 g (69% cal.); Cholesterol, 5 mg; Carbohydrates, 4 g; Fiber, 1 g; Sodium, 25 mg.

Smoked Salmon Rolls

Yield: about 4 lb (2 kg)

U.S.	Metric	Ingredients	PROCEDURE
4 oz	125 g	Carrot, cut brunoise	1. Quickly blanch the carrot and celery in boiling salted water.
8 oz	250 g	Celery, cut brunoise	
5 oz	150 g	Cooked shrimp	2. Finely chop the cooked shrimp and crab.
3 oz	90 g	Crab meat	3. Blanch the bean sprouts.
1 lb 6 oz	700 g	Bean sprouts	4. Spread the blanched vegetables on paper towels to remove as much excess moisture as possible.
½ oz	15 g	Chives	
2 tsp	10 mL	Lemon zest	5. Mix together the vegetables, the crab, shrimp, chives, lemon zest, and mayonnaise. Mix in the Worcestershire sauce. Season to taste.
6 oz	175 g	Mayonnaise	
2½ tsp	12 mL	Worcestershire sauce	
to taste	to taste	Salt	
to taste	to taste	Pepper	
1 lb 4 oz	600 g	Smoked salmon (about 14 slices, 1½ oz or 40–50 g each)	6. Place 2 slices of smoked salmon slightly overlapping each other on plastic film. Place some of the filling on top, roll, and twist the ends tightly so that the filling holds. When ready to serve, cut to desired length and remove the plastic.
as needed	as needed	Oriental Vinaigrette (p. 574)	7. To serve as hors d'oeuvre, pass with picks and with Oriental Vinaigrette as dipping sauce.

Per 1 ounce:
Calories, 120; Protein, 3 g; Fat, 12 g (87% cal.); Cholesterol, 10 mg; Carbohydrates, 11 g; Fiber, 0 g; Sodium, 290 mg.

Fried Chicken Wings

Yield: 72 pieces

U.S.	Metric	Ingredients	PROCEDURE
36	36	Chicken wings	1. Prepare the chicken wings. Cut off the wing tip and discard or save for stock. Cut at the joint. Loosen the skin at the narrow end of the wing drumstick (the thicker piece) and scrape and pull the skin and flesh toward the opposite joint. The result should look like half of a barbell. Cut the other half of the wing at one end, cutting off the joint. Scrape and pull the skin and flesh as for the drumstick. Disengage the smaller of the two bones and discard or save for stock.
2 oz	60 mL	Oil	
3 oz	90 mL	Soy sauce	
1 oz	30 g	Ginger root, grated	
½ oz	15 g	Garlic, chopped	
			2. Whisk together the oil, soy sauce, ginger, and chopped garlic.
			3. Toss the wings in the marinade and allow to marinate overnight, stirring occasionally.
		Standard Breading Procedure	4. Bread the chicken wings. Deep-fry at 325°F (160°C).
		Tomato Sauce (p. 150)	5. Serve with Tomato Sauce for dipping.

Per 1 piece:
Calories, 90; Protein, 5 g; Fat, 6 g (63% cal.); Cholesterol, 20 mg;
Carbohydrates, 3 g; Fiber, 0 g; Sodium, 40 mg.

Eggplant Caviar

Yield: about 2½ lb (1.2 kg)

U.S.	Metric	Ingredients	PROCEDURE
3 lb 12 oz	1.7 kg	Eggplants	1. Cut the eggplants in half lengthwise and season. Brush with oil (reserving the remaining oil for step 4) and bake for 25 minutes at 400°F (200°C) or until soft.
to taste	to taste	Salt	
10 oz	300 mL	Olive oil	
3½ oz	100 g	Pitted black olives, chopped	2. Drain the eggplants briefly to get rid of excess liquid and scrape out the flesh. Mash with a fork.
2 cloves	2 cloves	Garlic, crushed	
1 oz	30 g	Chives, chopped fine	3. Add the olives, garlic, and chives.
2 tsp	5 g	Paprika	4. Mix in the olive oil slowly, along with the paprika. Season to taste. Refrigerate for 1 hour before serving.
as needed	as needed	Additional chopped olives and chives for garnish	5. To serve, place the caviar into a chilled bowl. Decorate with additional olives and chives. Serve with melba toasts for dipping.

Per 1 ounce:
Calories, 80; Protein, 0 g; Fat, 7 g (84% cal.); Cholesterol, 0 mg;
Carbohydrates, 3 g; Fiber, 1 g; Sodium, 25 mg.

Prosciutto and Melon Balls

Yield: as desired

U.S.	Metric	Ingredients	PROCEDURE
as needed	as needed	Melon (cantaloupe, honeydew, crenshaw, etc.)	1. Using a ball cutter, cut the melon into small balls.
to taste	to taste	Lime juice	2. Sprinkle the melon balls with lime juice and let stand 10 minutes.
as needed	as needed	Prosciutto ham	3. Using a slicing machine, cut the ham into paper-thin slices. Cut large slices in half crosswise.
			4. Shortly before serving, wrap each melon ball in a slice of ham and fasten with a pick.

Per serving:
Calories, 20; Protein, 2 g; Fat, 1 g (43% cal.); Cholesterol, 5 mg;
Carbohydrates, 1 g; Fiber, 0 g; Sodium, 175 mg.
One serving equals 0.5 ounce of melon with 0.25 ounce of prosciutto.

VARIATIONS

Other fruits may be substituted for the melon, such as pineapple sticks or chunks, fresh figs (whole, halved, or quartered), fresh pear or peach slices. Pears and peaches must be coated with lime or lemon juice to prevent darkening.

Apple Slices with Curried Chicken and Mango

Yield: 36–40 pieces, about 1½–2 oz (50–60 g) each

U.S.	Metric	Ingredients	PROCEDURE
1 lb	500 g	Apples	1. Peel and core the apples. Cut into brunoise. Toss with the lemon juice.
1½ oz	45 mL	Lemon juice	
8 oz	250 g	Mango, flesh only	2. Cut the mango into brunoise. Mix with the apples.
1 lb 8 oz	750 g	Cooked chicken breast meat, cooled	3. Cut the chicken breast into fine dice. Mix with the mango and apples. Mix in the chopped cilantro.
2 tbsp	15 g	Chopped cilantro	4. Season the mayonnaise with curry powder.
1 pt	500 mL	Mayonnaise	5. Mix enough mayonnaise into the chicken mixture so that it holds together well. (You may have some mayonnaise left over.) Keep refrigerated until ready to use.
2 tsp	10 mL	Curry powder	
3–4	3–4	Apples	6. Wash the apples and core them. Channel the apples (see Figure 24.1) from top to bottom at ½-inch (1-cm) intervals. Cut the apples in half vertically, then cut crosswise into slices about ¼ inch (½ cm) thick. Rub with lemon juice.
as needed	as needed	Lemon juice	
as needed	as needed	Paprika	
as needed	as needed	Cilantro leaves	7. Form quenelles (see Figure 24.8) of the chicken mixture and place on top of each slice of apple. Decorate with paprika and cilantro.

Per 1 piece:
Calories, 60; Protein, 6 g; Fat, 2 g (29% cal.); Cholesterol, 15 mg;
Carbohydrates, 5 g; Fiber, 1 g; Sodium, 15 mg.

VARIATIONS

The chicken mixture can also be used to fill savory tart shells and vegetables such as leaves of Belgian endive and cucumber shells.

Smoked Chicken Purses with Sun-dried Tomatoes

Yield: 36 pieces, about ¾ oz (22 g) each

U.S.	Metric	Ingredients	PROCEDURE
3½ oz	100 mL	Olive oil or oil from sun-dried tomatoes	1. Place the oil and sun-dried tomatoes in a blender. Blend until smooth. Strain through a fine strainer.
1 oz	25 g	Sun-dried tomatoes packed in oil, drained	2. In a stainless-steel bowl, whip together the egg yolk, salt, pepper, and mustard. Gradually add the flavored oil in a steady stream, whipping constantly to make a stiff mayonnaise.
1	1	Egg yolk	
pinch	pinch	Salt	
pinch	pinch	Pepper	
1 tbsp	15 mL	Dijon mustard	
7 oz	200 g	Smoked chicken breast	3. Coarsely chop the smoked chicken. Coarsely chop the sun-dried tomatoes.
2 oz	60 g	Sun-dried tomatoes packed in oil, drained	
1 oz	30 g	Chopped basil	4. Mix together the chicken, tomatoes, chopped basil, and the mayonnaise from step 2. Taste and adjust seasoning if necessary.
36	36	Crêpes (recipe follows)	5. Using a 4-inch (10-cm) round cutter, cut out a circle from the center of each crêpe.
1–2 bunches	1–2 bunches	Chives	6. Place about 2 tsp (10–12 g) chicken mixture in the center of each circle. Gather the edges to form small purses and tie with a length of chive.

Per 1 piece:
Calories, 110; Protein, 5 g; Fat, 7 g (57% cal.); Cholesterol, 50 mg;
Carbohydrates, 7 g; Fiber, 0 g; Sodium, 125 mg.
Analysis is based on smoked turkey as nutrient information for smoked chicken was unavailable.

Crêpes

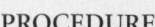

Yield: about 36 crêpes

U.S.	Metric	Ingredients	PROCEDURE
8 oz	250 g	Flour	1. Whisk together the flour, salt, and eggs. Gradually mix in the milk to make a smooth batter, about the consistency of heavy cream.
1 tsp	5 g	Salt	
6	6	Eggs	2. Strain the batter through a fine sieve and whisk in the browned butter.
1 pt	500 mL	Milk	
1½ oz	50 g	Browned butter	3. Cover with plastic wrap and set aside to rest at least 30 minutes at room temperature.
as needed	as needed	Oil	4. Heat a 5½-inch (14-cm) crêpe pan over moderate heat. Lightly oil the pan. Add about 2–3 tbsp (30–45 mL) batter and swirl to coat the bottom of the pan with a thin layer; pour any excess batter back into the bowl. Cook until the edges are brown and the bottom is golden. Flip over and cook another minute.
			5. Place the crêpe on a wire rack to cool. Repeat the procedure to make additional crêpes, overlapping but not stacking them on the rack.

Per 1 crêpe:
Calories, 70; Protein, 2 g; Fat, 4 g (53% cal.); Cholesterol, 40 mg; Carbohydrates, 6 g; Fiber, 0 g; Sodium, 90 mg.

Chicken Satay

Yield: 36 pieces, about ¾–1 oz (25 g) each

U.S.	Metric	Ingredients	PROCEDURE
2 cloves	2 cloves	Garlic, crushed	1. Soak 36 bamboo skewers, 6 inches (15 cm) long, in cold water overnight (to prevent burning when grilling).
2 oz	60 g	Ginger root, grated	
2 oz	60 g	Brown sugar	2. Place the garlic, ginger, brown sugar, sesame oil, and soy sauce in a blender and blend until smooth.
3 oz	90 mL	Sesame oil	
1 oz	30 mL	Soy sauce	3. Cut the chicken into thin strips lengthwise. Place them in a bowl. Pour the marinade mixture (from step 1) over the chicken and stir to coat well. Cover and refrigerate for 2 hours or more.
1 lb	900 g	Boneless, skinless chicken breasts	
4 oz	125 mL	Water	4. Prepare a dipping sauce: Bring the water to a boil and add the chopped garlic. Simmer for 1 minute.
3 cloves	3 cloves	Garlic, finely chopped	
8 oz	250 g	Peanut butter	5. Add the peanut butter and coconut milk. Cook over medium heat for 2–3 minutes until smooth and thick.
4 oz	125 mL	Coconut milk	
2 tbsp plus 2 tsp	40 mL	Honey	6. Stir in the honey, lemon juice, soy sauce, and hot pepper sauce. Remove from the heat. Cool.
2 tbsp plus 2 tsp	40 mL	Lemon juice	
2 tbsp plus 2 tsp	40 mL	Soy sauce	
to taste	to taste	Hot pepper sauce	
			7. Thread the marinated chicken onto the soaked skewers.
			8. Grill under a salamander or over a charbroiler for approximately 2 minutes on each side, brushing with the leftover marinade.
			9. Serve with the dipping sauce.

Per 1 piece:
Calories, 80; Protein, 4 g; Fat, 5 g (58% cal.); Cholesterol, 5 mg; Carbohydrates, 4 g; Fiber, 0 g; Sodium, 125 mg.

Beef Teriyaki Skewers

Yield: 36 pieces, ⅓–½ oz (12–13 g) each

U.S.	Metric	Ingredients	PROCEDURE
1½ oz	45 mL	Vegetable oil	1. Mix together the oil, soy sauce, ginger, and garlic.
1½ oz	45 mL	Soy sauce	2. Cut the beef into small cubes, about ¾ inch (2 cm) on a side. Marinate in the soy sauce mixture 2–3 hours, refrigerated.
1 oz	30 g	Ginger root, grated	
2 cloves	2 cloves	Garlic, chopped	3. Thread each meat cube on a wooden cocktail skewer. Cook quickly under a salamander or broiler. Serve hot.
1 lb	500 g	Beef tenderloin	

Per 1 piece:
Calories, 30; Protein, 3 g; Fat, 2 g (60% cal.); Cholesterol, 10 mg;
Carbohydrates, 0 g; Fiber, 0 g; Sodium, 75 mg.

Smoked Salmon and Trout Logs on Pumpernickel

Yield: 36 pieces, about ⅓ oz (8–10 g) each

U.S.	Metric	Ingredients	PROCEDURE
3 oz	90 g	Smoked trout	1. Remove the skin and any bones from the smoked trout.
3 oz	90 g	Cream cheese	2. Place the trout and the cream cheese in the bowl of a food processor. Process until smooth. Season with salt and pepper if necessary. Mix in the chives.
to taste	to taste	Salt	
to taste	to taste	Pepper	
⅔ oz	20 g	Chives, chopped	3. Transfer to a bowl and refrigerate until needed.
9 slices	9 slices	Pumpernickel bread	4. Beat the trout mixture to soften. Spread the bread with a thin layer of the trout mixture.
8 oz	200–250 g	Smoked salmon, sliced	5. On a sheet of plastic wrap, arrange the smoked salmon slices in a row, overlapping them slightly.
as needed	as needed	Chervil or parsley for garnish	6. Beat the trout mixture and spread onto the smoked salmon. Roll to form a log, twist the ends of the plastic wrap, and knot or secure with kitchen string. Place in the freezer for 10–15 minutes or until firm. Cut into slices ½ inch (1 cm) thick.
			7. Trim the crusts off the bread and cut each slice into 4 triangles.
			8. Place 1 slice of the trout log cut side up on each triangle. Garnish each piece with a tiny sprig of chervil or a parsley leaf.

Per 1 piece:
Calories, 35; Protein, 2 g; Fat, 1.5 g (40% cal.); Cholesterol, 5 mg;
Carbohydrates, 3 g; Fiber, 0 g; Sodium, 100 mg.

Prosciutto, Blue Cheese, and Walnut Parcels

Yield: 36 pieces, about ⅓ oz (18–20 g) each

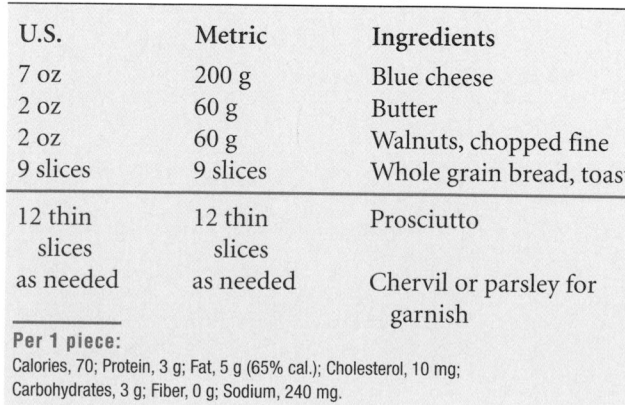

U.S.	Metric	Ingredients	PROCEDURE
7 oz	200 g	Blue cheese	1. Mix the blue cheese and butter in a food processor until smooth. Transfer to a bowl and mix in the walnuts.
2 oz	60 g	Butter	
2 oz	60 g	Walnuts, chopped fine	2. Remove the crust from the bread and spread a little of the cheese mixture on each slice. Cut each slice into 4 squares.
9 slices	9 slices	Whole grain bread, toasted	
12 thin slices	12 thin slices	Prosciutto	3. Cut each slice of the prosciutto into 3 squares, 3 inches (7–8 cm) per side.
as needed	as needed	Chervil or parsley for garnish	4. Using a piping bag, pipe about ½ tbsp (8 g) filling in the center of each square. Fold the edges over the center to make a square parcel.
			5. Place on the prepared squares of bread and decorate each with a tiny sprig of chervil or a parsley leaf.

Per 1 piece:
Calories, 70; Protein, 3 g; Fat, 5 g (65% cal.); Cholesterol, 10 mg;
Carbohydrates, 3 g; Fiber, 0 g; Sodium, 240 mg.

Cucumber Roundels with Smoked Trout Pâté

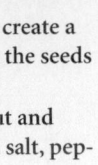

Yield: 36 pieces, about 1 oz (30 g) each

U.S.	Metric	Ingredients	PROCEDURE
2 (approximately)	2 (approximately)	Cucumbers	1. Channel the cucumbers (see Figure 24.1). Trim the ends and cut into slices ½ inch (1 cm) thick. You will need enough cucumbers to make 36 slices.
6 oz	175 g	Smoked trout fillet	
6 oz	175 g	Cream cheese	2. Using a melon baller, scoop out the seed area to create a shallow depression, being careful not to remove the seeds completely.
to taste	to taste	Salt	
to taste	to taste	Pepper	
to taste	to taste	Lemon juice	3. In the bowl of a food processor, process the trout and cream cheese until smooth. Season to taste with salt, pepper, and lemon juice.
12–15	12–15	Pitted black olives, sliced into rings	
as needed	as needed	Chervil or parsley for garnish	4. Transfer to a piping bag fitted with a medium star tip. Lightly salt the cucumber and fill the cavity of the cucumber slices with the trout pâté (about 2 tsp/10 mL per piece).
			5. Garnish each with an olive slice and a tiny sprig of chervil or a parsley leaf.

Per 1 piece:
Calories, 30; Protein, 1 g; Fat, 2 g (69% cal.); Cholesterol, 10 mg; Carbohydrates, 1 g; Fiber, 0 g; Sodium, 50 mg.

Feuilleté Chorizo

Yield: 72 pieces, about ⅓ oz (9–10 g) each

U.S.	Metric	Ingredients	PROCEDURE
1 lb 4 oz	600 g	Puff pastry	1. Roll out the puff pastry to about 1/12 inch (2 mm) thick. Cut into 72 squares, 2 inches (5 cm) per side. Refrigerate.
8 oz	250 g	Chorizo (or other spicy sausage)	2. Remove the skin from the chorizo. Grind the chorizo in a meat grinder fitted with a medium blade.
1	1	Egg	3. Beat the egg with a pinch of salt.
pinch	pinch	Salt	4. Brush each square with the egg wash and place a small mound (about ½ tsp/3 g) of the ground chorizo in the center. Fold over to form a triangle. Press the edges to seal.
			5. Place on a baking sheet and brush with the egg wash. Set aside for 15 minutes, then brush with a second coating of egg wash.
			6. Bake at 350°F (180°C) or until lightly browned, about 8–10 minutes.

Per 1 piece:
Calories, 60; Protein, 1 g; Fat, 4.5 g (67% cal.); Cholesterol, 5 mg; Carbohydrates, 4 g; Fiber, 0 g; Sodium, 60 mg.

Crab Beignets with Lime and Ginger Chutney

Yield: 36 pieces, about ¾ oz (20–22 g) each

U.S.	Metric	Ingredients	PROCEDURE
3 oz	90 g	Flour	1. Sift the flour, potato starch, baking powder, and salt into a bowl. Whisk in the oil and then the water.
2½ oz	70 g	Potato starch	
1 tsp	6 g	Baking powder	2. Strain through a sieve. Set aside to rest for at least 30 minutes.
pinch	pinch	Salt	
2 tsp	10 mL	Oil	
5 oz	150 mL	Water	
1¾ oz	50 g	Onion, chopped fine	3. Sweat the onion in the olive oil.
1 tbsp	15 mL	Olive oil	4. Add the brunoise of red pepper and sweat with the onion until soft.
1¾ oz	50 g	Red pepper, cut brunoise	
1	1	Egg	5. Set aside in a large bowl to cool.
3 tbsp plus 1 tsp	50 mL	Heavy cream	6. Beat the egg with the cream and add to the cooled onion and pepper mixture. Add the chives and mix well.
½ oz	15 g	Chives, chopped fine	7. Stir in the crab, then add the fresh bread crumbs. Mix well and season to taste.
6 oz	175 g	Crab meat	
6 oz	175 g	Fresh bread crumbs	8. Make the mixture into tightly packed balls of about ½ oz (18 g) each.
8 oz	250 g	Lime and Ginger Chutney (p. 166)	9. Dip in the batter and deep-fry at 400°F (200°C) until golden brown, about 2–3 minutes. Remove and place on paper towels to drain.
			10. Serve with the Lime and Ginger Chutney on the side.

Per 1 piece:
Calories, 60; Protein, 2 g; Fat, 2 g (33% cal.); Cholesterol, 10 mg;
Carbohydrates, 7 g; Fiber, 0 g; Sodium, 65 mg.

Mushrooms Stuffed with Tapenade

Yield: 50 pieces

U.S.	Metric	Ingredients	PROCEDURE
8 oz	250 g	Pitted Mediterranean or Greek black olives	1. In a blender or food processor, purée the olives, capers, anchovies, tuna, mustard, oil, lemon juice, and herbs.
1 oz	30 g	Capers, drained	2. Chill the mixture several hours to let the flavors blend.
1 oz	30 g	Anchovies, drained	
1 oz	30 g	Tuna, drained	
1 tsp	5 mL	Dijon-style mustard	
2½ oz	75 mL	Olive oil	
1 tsp	5 mL	Lemon juice	
2 tbsp	30 mL	Chopped parsley	
pinch	pinch	Thyme	
to taste	to taste	Salt	
to taste	to taste	Pepper	
50	50	Small to medium fresh white mushrooms	3. Remove the stems from the mushrooms and clean the caps.
as needed	as needed	Pimiento	4. Fill each cap with a small spoonful of the tapenade.
			5. Garnish the top of each with a dot of pimiento.

Per 1 piece:
Calories, 30; Protein, 1 g; Fat, 2.5 g (74% cal.); Cholesterol, 0 mg;
Carbohydrates, 1 g; Fiber, 0 g; Sodium, 110 mg.

Deviled Eggs

Yield: 50 pieces

U.S.	Metric	Ingredients	PROCEDURE
25	25	Hard-cooked eggs	1. Halve the eggs lengthwise and remove the yolks.
½ pt	250 mL	Mayonnaise	2. Mash the yolks or force them through a sieve.
1 oz	30 mL	Lemon juice or vinegar	3. Add the remaining ingredients (except the garnish) and mix to a smooth paste.
1 tsp	5 mL	Dry mustard	
1 tsp	5 mL	Worcestershire sauce	4. Using a pastry bag with a star tip, fill the egg white halves.
to taste	to taste	Salt	5. Using a variety of garnishes, decorate the top of each egg.
to taste	to taste	White pepper	
to taste	to taste	Cayenne	
as needed	as needed	Assorted garnish, such as:	
		Chopped parsley	
		Tiny dill sprigs	
		Capers	
		Diced pimiento	
		Sliced stuffed olives	
		Paprika	
		Red or black caviar	

Per 1 piece:
Calories, 70; Protein, 3 g; Fat, 7 g (84% cal.); Cholesterol, 110 mg;
Carbohydrates, 0 g; Fiber, 0 g; Sodium, 45 mg.

VARIATIONS

Vary the flavor of stuffed eggs by adding any of the following ingredients to the egg yolk mixture in the basic recipe.

Anchovy: 2–3 oz (60–90 g) anchovy paste.

Curry: 2 tbsp (30 mL) curry powder, heated very gently with a little oil and cooled.

Blue cheese: 6 oz (175 g) mashed blue cheese.

Parmesan: 3 oz (90 g) grated parmesan cheese.

Tarragon: Use tarragon vinegar in the filling and add 2 tsp (10 mL) tarragon.

Tuna: 6 oz (175 g) well-mashed, drained tuna.

Miniature Gougère Puffs

Yield: about 160 pieces

U.S.	Metric	Ingredients	PROCEDURE
2½ lb	1.1 kg	Éclair paste (p. 860)	1. Mix together the éclair paste and the cheese.
8 oz	225 g	Gruyère cheese, grated	2. Using a pastry bag with a small, plain tip, pipe small mounds of about 1 tablespoon (15 mL) each onto sheet pans lined with parchment. See page 861 for guidelines on making tiny cream puff shells or profiteroles, which is essentially what these are.
as needed	as needed	Egg wash	
			3. Bake at 400°F (200°C) until puffed and brown, about 20–30 minutes.
			4. Make a little slit in the side of each to allow steam to escape. Put the puffs in a warm oven until they are dry.
			5. Serve warm or at room temperature.

Per 1 piece:
Calories, 25; Protein, 1 g; Fat, 1.5 g (63% cal.); Cholesterol, 15 mg;
Carbohydrates, 1 g; Fiber, 0 g; Sodium, 25 mg.

Chicken Liver Pâté

Yield: 2½ lb (1.2 kg)

U.S.	Metric	Ingredients	PROCEDURE
2 lb	1 kg	Chicken livers	1. Trim fat and sinews from the livers.
to taste	to taste	Salt	2. Sprinkle the livers lightly with salt. Add milk to cover and let stand overnight, refrigerated. This step is optional, but it results in a slightly milder flavor and lighter color.
as needed	as needed	Milk	
4 oz	125 g	Onion, chopped	3. Sauté the onion lightly in the butter until tender but not brown.
3 oz	90 g	Butter	
½ tsp	2 mL	Oregano	4. Add the livers (drained and rinsed), herbs, and spices. Brown the livers lightly and cook them until they are still slightly pink in the center. Remove from the heat and cool.
¼ tsp	1 mL	White pepper	
pinch	pinch	Nutmeg	
pinch	pinch	Ground ginger	
pinch	pinch	Ground cloves	
1 tsp	5 mL	Salt	
12 oz	375 g	Cream cheese	5. Grind the livers and onions in a grinder or buffalo chopper.
1–2 oz	30–60 mL	Brandy, Madeira, or port (optional)	6. Add cream cheese and continue to process to obtain a uniformly mixed paste.
to taste	to taste	Salt	7. Add brandy or wine to taste. Add additional salt if necessary.
			8. Pack the mixture into containers and chill overnight.

Per 1 ounce:
Calories, 60; Protein, 3 g; Fat, 5 g (74% cal.); Cholesterol, 75 mg;
Carbohydrates, 1 g; Fiber, 0 g; Sodium, 105 mg.

Terms for Review

pullman loaf	wrap	cocktail
simple sandwich (hot or cold)	tea sandwich	crudité
open-faced sandwich (hot or cold)	hors d'oeuvre	dip
club sandwich	canapé	antipasto

Questions for Discussion

1. If you cannot get daily bread delivery, what are some measures you can take to ensure that the bread in the sandwiches you serve is always fresh?

2. What precautions must you take when using mayonnaise as a sandwich spread?

3. Briefly describe the setup of a short-order sandwich station.

4. How does a setup for preparing sandwiches in quantity differ from a short-order sandwich setup?

5. Why are most sandwiches cut before serving?

6. How can you avoid soggy canapé bases?

7. In order to use a ham salad recipe to make a ham spread, you may need to change the recipe slightly. What are three modifications that you may need to make?

8. What is the difference between a fruit salad and a fruit cocktail?

9. What is the proper consistency or thickness for a dip?

Breakfast Preparation, Dairy Products, and Coffee and Tea

When we speak of breakfast cookery, we are not just talking about a particular meal. We are referring to a particular small group of foods that appears on perhaps every breakfast menu. These items not only appear on breakfast menus but also are popular for brunches, snacks, and late suppers. Many establishments offer a breakfast menu all day long.

Eggs, of course, are the most popular breakfast food and are the primary subject of this chapter. In addition, this chapter examines the preparation of other breakfast staples: pancakes, waffles, French toast, and breakfast meats. We then turn our attention to dairy products, specifically milk, cream, butter, and cheese. Finally, we study the preparation of two items essential not only at breakfast but at every meal: coffee and tea.

Eggs

Contrary to popular opinion, there is no law that says one must have eggs or cereal or pancakes or pastries for breakfast and must not have shrimp curry or chili or spaghetti and meatballs. Although most of us would think these last suggestions rather strange for the morning meal, there is probably no food that someone, somewhere, does not enjoy for breakfast. No doubt many Japanese, who have soybean soup, sour pickles, and rice for their first meal of the day, think Western breakfast habits are strange.

However, the egg remains a favorite breakfast food, even as we become more adventurous and explore ethnic cuisines. For such apparently simple items, eggs are used in many ways in the kitchen and require special study. We examine not only the usual breakfast preparation but other egg dishes as well, such as soufflés and custards.

Understanding Eggs

COMPOSITION

A whole egg consists primarily of a yolk, a white, and a shell. In addition, it contains a membrane that lines the shell and forms an air cell at the large end, and two white strands called *chalazae* that hold the yolk centered. Figure 21.1 is a cross-sectional diagram that shows the location of these features.

1. The *yolk* is high in both fat and protein, and it contains iron and several vitamins. Its color ranges from light to dark yellow, depending on the diet of the chicken.

2. The *white* is primarily albumin protein, which is clear and soluble when raw but white and firm when coagulated. The white also contains sulfur.

   The white has two parts: a thick portion that surrounds the yolk, and a thinner, more liquid portion outside of this.

3. The *shell* is not the perfect package, in spite of what you may have heard. Not only is it fragile but it is also porous, allowing odors and flavors to be absorbed by the egg and allowing the egg to lose moisture even if unbroken.

GRADES AND QUALITY

Grades

In the United States, eggs are graded for quality by the U.S. Department of Agriculture. The three grades are AA, A, and B.

The best grade (AA) has a firm yolk and white that stand up high when broken onto a flat surface and do not spread over a large area. In the shell, the yolk is well centered, and the air sac is small.

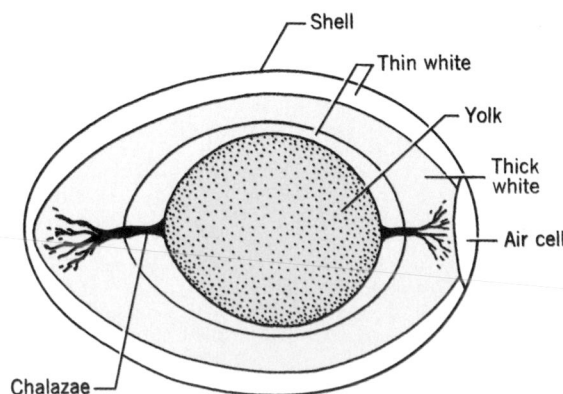

Figure 21.1 The parts of an egg. The diagram shows, in simplified form, the location of the parts of an unbroken egg, as described in the text.

Figure 21.2 Egg grades.

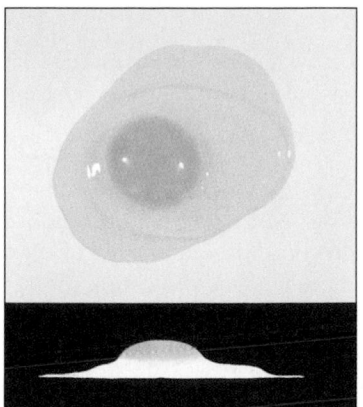
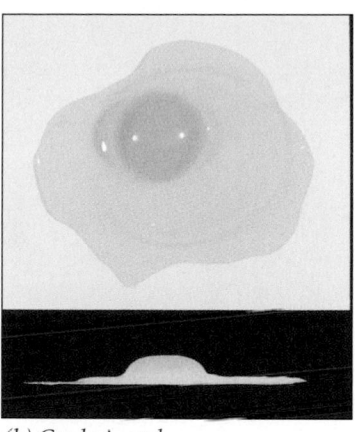
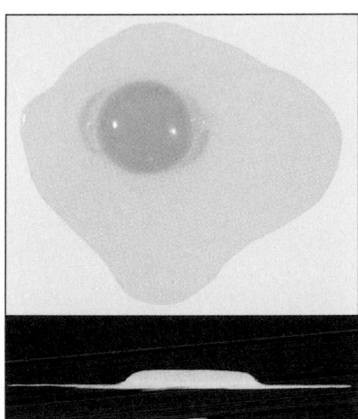

(a) Grade AA,

(b) Grade A, and

(c) Grade B eggs, as seen from the top and side. Note how the white and yolk lose thickness and spread more in the lower grades.

As eggs age, they lose density. The thin part of the white becomes larger, and the egg spreads over a larger area when broken. Also, the air sac becomes larger as the egg loses moisture through the shell. Figure 21.2 shows the differences among grades AA, A, and B.

Maintaining Quality

Proper storage is essential for maintaining quality. Eggs keep for weeks if held at 36°F (2°C) but lose quality quickly if held at room temperature. In fact, they can lose a full grade in one day at warm kitchen temperatures. There's no point in paying for Grade AA eggs if they are Grade B by the time you use them.

Store eggs away from other foods that might pass on undesirable flavors or odors.

Grades and Use

One glance at Figure 21.2 will show you why Grade AA is the best to use for fried or poached eggs. Lower grades spread out too much to produce a high-quality product.

For hard-cooked eggs, use either Grade A eggs or Grade AA that have been held a few days in the refrigerator. Very fresh eggs are difficult to peel when cooked in the shell.

Grade B eggs are suitable for use in baking. If you are certain they have developed no strong flavors, they may be used for scrambled eggs, where the firmness of the whole egg is less important.

SIZE

Eggs are also graded by size. Table 21.1 gives the minimum weight per dozen (including shell) according to size category. Note that each size differs from the next by 3 ounces or 85 grams.

Most food service operations use large eggs, and recipes are based on this size.

MARKET FORMS

1. **Fresh eggs or shell eggs.**
   These are most often used for breakfast cookery and are the main subject of this section.

2. **Frozen eggs.**
   - Whole eggs
   - Whites
   - Yolks
   - Whole eggs with extra yolks

   Frozen eggs are usually made from high-quality fresh eggs and are excellent for use in scrambled eggs, omelets, French toast, and in baking. They are pasteurized and are usually purchased in 30-pound (13.6-kg) cans. These take at least two days to thaw at refrigerator temperatures.

TABLE 21.1

Egg Size Classifications

Size	Minimum Weight per Dozen	
	U.S.	Metric
Jumbo	30 oz	850 g
Extra large	27 oz	765 g
Large	24 oz	680 g
Medium	21 oz	595 g
Small	18 oz	510 g
Peewee	15 oz	425 g

3. **Dried eggs.**
   - Whole eggs
   - Yolks
   - Whites

Dried eggs are used primarily for baking. They are not suggested for use in breakfast cookery. Unlike most dehydrated products, dried eggs are not shelf stable and must be kept refrigerated or frozen, tightly sealed.

Sanitation

In recent years, cases of *salmonella* food poisoning have been caused by raw or undercooked eggs. As a result, cooks have been made more aware of sanitation concerns with the use of eggs. Pasteurized egg products are used in more operations. For a more detailed discussion of eggs and food safety, see Appendix 5, page 897.

Figure 21.3 Whipping egg whites.

(a) The whites are just beginning to whip into a foam.

(b) The whites have reached the soft-peak stage.

(c) The whites have reached the firm-peak stage. Note the smooth texture. Whipping beyond this stage will cause the foam to break.

GENERAL COOKING PRINCIPLES

The most important rule of egg cookery is simple: *Avoid high temperatures and long cooking times.* In other words, do not overcook. This should be a familiar rule by now.
Overcooking produces tough eggs, causes discoloration, and affects flavor.

Coagulation

Eggs are largely protein, so the principle of coagulation (p. 52) is important to consider.
Eggs coagulate at the following temperatures:

Whole eggs, beaten	about 156°F (69°C)
Whites	140° to 149°F (60° to 65°C)
Yolks	144° to 158°F (62° to 70°C)
Custard (whole eggs plus liquid)	175° to 185°F (79° to 85°C)

Note that whites coagulate or cook before yolks do. This is why it is possible to cook eggs with firm whites but soft yolks.
Note also that when eggs are mixed with a liquid, they become firm at a higher temperature. However, 185°F (85°C) is still much lower than the temperature of a sauté pan or skillet over high heat. As the temperature of coagulation is reached, the eggs change from semiliquid to solid, and they become opaque. If their temperature continues to rise, they become even firmer. *An overcooked egg is tough and rubbery.* Low temperatures produce the best-cooked eggs.
If egg-liquid mixtures such as custards and scrambled eggs are overcooked, the egg solids separate from the liquids, or *curdle.* This is often seen in tough, watery scrambled eggs.

Sulfur

The familiar green ring that you often see in hard-cooked eggs is caused by cooking at high temperatures or cooking too long. The same green color appears in scrambled eggs that are overcooked or held too long in the steam table.
This ring results when the sulfur in the egg whites reacts with the iron in the yolk to form iron sulfide, a compound that has a green color and a strong odor and flavor. The best way to avoid green eggs is to use *low temperatures and short cooking and holding times.*

Foams

Beaten egg whites are used to give lightness and rising power to soufflés, puffy omelets, cakes, some pancakes and waffles, and other products. The following guidelines will help you handle beaten egg whites properly (see Figure 21.3).

1. **Fat inhibits foaming.**
   When separating eggs, be careful not to get any yolk in the whites. Yolks contain fats. Use very clean equipment when beating whites.

2. **Mild acids help foaming.**
   A small amount of lemon juice or cream of tartar gives more volume and stability to beaten egg whites. Use about 2 teaspoons cream of tartar per pound of egg whites (20 mL per kg).

3. **Egg whites foam better at room temperature.**
   Remove them from the cooler 1 hour before beating.

4. **Do not overbeat.**
   Beaten egg whites should look moist and shiny. Overbeaten eggs look dry and curdled and have lost much of their ability to raise soufflés and cakes.

5. **Sugar makes foams more stable.**
   When making sweet puffed omelets and dessert soufflés, add some of the sugar to the partially beaten whites and continue to beat to proper stiffness. (This will take longer than when no sugar is added.) The soufflé will be more stable before and after baking.

Cooking Eggs

SIMMERING IN THE SHELL

The term "hard-boiled egg" is not a good one to use because eggs should be simmered instead of boiled.

Eggs may be simmered in water to the soft-, medium-, or hard-cooked stage according to the following methods.

Procedures for Simmering Eggs in the Shell

Method 1

1. Collect equipment and food items.

2. Bring eggs to room temperature by (a) removing them from cooler 1 hour before cooking, or (b) placing them in warm water for 5 minutes and draining. Cold eggs are more likely to crack when placed in boiling water.

3. Place eggs in boiling water and return the water to a simmer.

4. Simmer, do not boil, for the required time:

Soft cooked	3 to 4 minutes
Medium cooked	5 to 7 minutes
Hard cooked	12 to 15 minutes

   Exact cooking time depends on temperature of eggs, size of eggs, and amount of water used.

5. Drain immediately and cool under cold running water to stop the cooking. Cool just a few seconds if eggs are to be served hot. Cool further if they are to be held for later use.

6. To peel, crack the shell and pull it away, starting at large end (where the air sac is located). For easier peeling, peel while still warm, and hold under running water to help loosen shell. Very fresh eggs are hard to peel. Eggs for cooking in the shell should be several days old.

Method 2

1. Collect equipment and food items.

2. Place eggs in saucepan and cover with cold water.

3. Bring water to a boil.

4. Reduce heat and simmer for the required time:

Soft cooked	1 minute
Medium cooked	3 to 5 minutes
Hard cooked	10 minutes

Method 3, for Hard-Cooked Eggs Only

Proceed as in Method 2, but remove pan from heat and cover as soon as it comes to a boil. Let stand off heat for 20 minutes.

Standards of Quality for Hard-Cooked Eggs

1. Evenly coagulated whites and yolks.
2. Whites glossy and firm but tender, not tough or rubbery.
3. No dark color on outside of yolk.
4. Pleasing flavor.

POACHING

The principles of cooking eggs in the shell are applicable to poached eggs. The only difference between the two items is the shell.

This difference, of course, complicates the cooking process, as emphasized in the following procedure. The object is to keep the eggs egg-shaped—that is, in a round, compact mass rather than spread all over the pan.

Procedure for Poaching Eggs

1. Collect equipment and food items.

2. Use the freshest Grade AA eggs whenever possible for best results. These maintain their shape best because the yolks and whites are firm.

3. If eggs are not very fresh, add 1 teaspoon salt and 2 teaspoons distilled vinegar per quart of water (5 mL salt and 10 mL vinegar per liter). The vinegar helps coagulate the egg white faster so that it keeps a better shape.

   Vinegar is not necessary if very fresh eggs are used. Omit in this case because whites will be tougher and not as shiny if cooked with vinegar.

4. Bring water to a simmer.

   If water is boiling, eggs will toughen and may be broken up by the agitation.

   If water is not hot enough, eggs will not cook quickly enough and will spread.

5. Break eggs, one at a time, into a dish or a small plate and slide into the simmering water. Eggs will hold their shape better if they slide in against the edge of the pan.

6. Simmer 3 to 5 minutes, until whites are coagulated and yolks are still soft.

7. Remove eggs from pan with slotted spoon or skimmer.

8. To serve immediately, drain very well. For better appearance, trim off ragged edges.

9. To hold for later service, plunge immediately into cold water to stop the cooking. At service time, reheat briefly in hot water.

Standards of Quality for Poached Eggs

1. Bright, shiny appearance.
2. Compact, round shape, not spread or flattened.
3. Firm but tender whites; warm, liquid yolks.

Eggs Benedict

Yield: 1 portion (see note)

U.S.	Metric	Ingredients	PROCEDURE
½	½	English muffin	1. Toast the muffin half. Spread it with butter and place on a serving plate.
as needed	as needed	Butter	
1	1	Egg, fresh Grade AA	2. Poach the egg according to the basic procedure given in this section.
1 slice	1 slice	Canadian bacon or ham, cooked (about 2 oz/60 g)	3. While the egg is poaching, heat the Canadian bacon or ham for 1 minute on a hot griddle or in a sauté pan. Place the meat on the toasted muffin.
1½ oz	50 mL	Hollandaise Sauce (p. 159)	
			4. Drain the poached egg well and place it on the Canadian bacon.
			5. Ladle Hollandaise Sauce over the top. Serve immediately.

Per serving:
Calories, 660; Protein, 19 g; Fat, 58 g (79% cal.); Cholesterol, 480 mg; Carbohydrates, 15 g; Fiber, 1 g; Sodium, 1260 mg.

Note: To prepare Eggs Benedict in quantity, the eggs may be poached ahead of time, cooled in cold water, and refrigerated. At service time, reheat the eggs in simmering water for 30–60 seconds. Drain, plate, and serve.

VARIATIONS

Eggs Florentine

Instead of the muffin and bacon, place the egg on a bed of hot, buttered cooked spinach (about 2 oz/60 g). Cover with Mornay sauce instead of hollandaise. Optional: Sprinkle with parmesan cheese and brown under the salamander or broiler.

Eggs Bombay

Instead of the muffin and bacon, place the egg on a bed of hot rice pilaf (about 2 oz/60 g). Cover with curry sauce instead of hollandaise.

FRYING

Fried eggs are an especially popular breakfast preparation. They should always be cooked to order and served immediately. For best quality, observe each step in the following procedure.

Choice of cooking fat is a matter of taste and budget. Butter has the best flavor, but margarine or oil may be used. Use bacon fat only if that flavor is desired by customer.

Procedure for Frying Eggs to Order

1. Collect all equipment and food items.

Eggs may be fried in small, individual sauté pans (omelet pans) or on the griddle. Griddled eggs are not as attractive because they tend to spread more. See page 619 for the procedure for conditioning sauté pans to avoid sticking.

2. Select very fresh Grade AA eggs for best results.

3. Add about ⅛ inch (2 mm) of fat to the sauté pan and set it over moderate heat, or preheat the griddle to 325°F (165°C) and ladle on a small quantity of fat. Too much fat will make the eggs greasy. Not enough will cause them to stick, unless a pan with a nonstick coating is used.

4. Break the eggs into a dish. This lessens the chance of breaking the yolks.

5. When the fat is hot enough so that a drop of water sizzles when dropped into it, slide the eggs into the pan (or onto the griddle).

If the fat is not hot enough, the eggs will spread too much and may stick. If it is too hot, the eggs will become tough or even crisp.

6. Reduce heat to low (if using sauté pan) and cook the eggs to order as indicated below. See Figures 21.4 and 21.5 for flipping and turning techniques.

- **Sunny side up.** Cook slowly without flipping until white is completely set and yolk is still soft and yellow. Heat must be low or bottom will toughen or burn before top is completely set.
- **Basted.** Do not flip. Add a few drops of water to pan and cover so steam cooks the top. A thin film of coagulated white will cover the yolk, which should remain liquid. *Note:* This preparation is sometimes called *country style*. The term "basted" is used because the same effect may be achieved by spooning hot fat over the egg as it fries. This method may make the eggs excessively greasy, however.
- **Over easy.** Fry and flip over. Cook just until the white is just set and the yolk is still liquid.
- **Over medium.** Fry and flip over. Cook until the yolk is partially set.
- **Over hard.** Fry and flip over. Cook until the yolk is completely set.

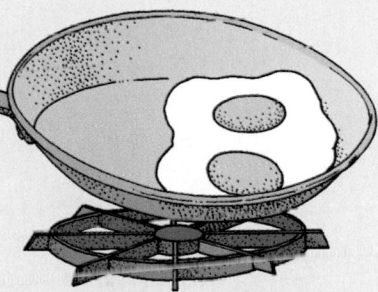

Figure 21.4 *Flipping eggs in a pan.*

(a) Lift the handle of the pan and slide the eggs to the far edge with a quick jerk.

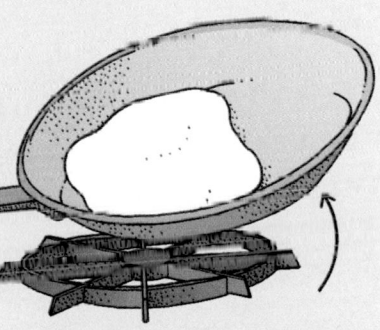

(b) With a quick flip of the wrist, as shown by the arrow, turn the eggs over. Do not flip the eggs too hard, or the yolks may break when they land.

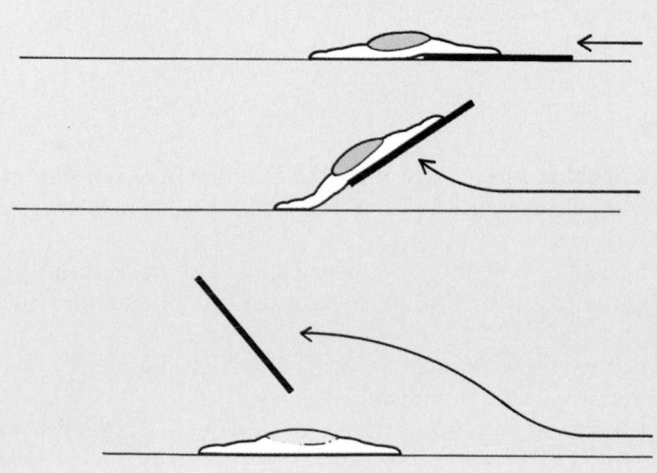

Figure 21.5
When frying eggs on a griddle, turn them with one smooth motion of the spatula, as shown. The left corner of the egg never actually leaves the surface of the griddle.

Standards of Quality for Fried Eggs

1. White should be shiny, uniformly set, and tender, not browned, blistered, or crisp at edges.
2. Yolk should be set properly according to desired doneness. Sunny-side-up yolks should be yellow and well rounded. In other styles, the yolk is covered with a thin layer of coagulated white.
3. Relatively compact, standing high. Not spread out and thin.

SHIRRED EGGS

Shirred eggs resemble fried eggs, except that they are baked in individual serving dishes rather than fried.

They may also be baked with or garnished with a variety of meats and sauces, as indicated in the variations that follow.

Procedure for Making Shirred Eggs

1. Collect equipment and food items.
2. Butter individual portion casseroles or baking dishes.
3. Break eggs into dish.
4. Set over moderate heat until the eggs begin to coagulate on the bottom.
5. Place in oven at 350°F (175°C) and cook to desired doneness.
6. Serve in the same dish or casserole.

SHIRRED EGG VARIATIONS

Any of the following may be placed in the buttered shirred egg dish *before* adding the egg:

Ham or Canadian bacon, thin slice, lightly browned on griddle or in sauté pan
Bacon, cooked crisp, 3 or 4 half-strips
Corned beef hash, beef hash, or ham hash
Cheese, such as cheddar, Swiss, or Gruyère, grated
Diced chicken in cream sauce
Tomato concassé, sautéed in butter

Any of the following may be added to shirred eggs *after baking*. Place solid garnish to one side. Spoon sauces around the outside. Do not cover the yolk.

Heavy cream, hot
Brown sauces such as bordelaise, Madeira, or demiglaze
Tomato sauce
Soubise sauce
Sautéed chicken livers and brown sauce
Small grilled sausages
Mushrooms sautéed in butter or cream sauce
Asparagus tips

SCRAMBLED EGGS

Like other egg preparations, scrambled eggs are best if cooked to order. However, they may be made in larger quantities. They should be undercooked if they are to be held for volume service, as they will cook more in the steam table.

If scrambled eggs must be held over 30 minutes, they will be more stable if the eggs are mixed with a medium white sauce (béchamel) before cooking. Use about 8 ounces sauce per quart of eggs (250 mL per liter).

Do not overcook scrambled eggs or hold them too long. Overcooked eggs are tough and watery, and they eventually turn green in the steam table.

Scrambled eggs should be soft and moist, unless the customer requests "scrambled hard."

Procedure for Scrambling Eggs

1. Collect equipment and food items.

2. Break eggs into a stainless-steel bowl and beat until well blended. Season with salt and white pepper.
   Do not use aluminum, which may discolor the eggs.

3. If desired, add a small amount of milk or cream, about 1 to 1½ tablespoons (15 to 20 mL) for 2 eggs, or 8 to 12 ounces per quart of eggs (250 to 375 mL per liter).
   Too much liquid may make cooked eggs watery and dilutes the flavor. Heavy cream adds richness but also adds cost.

4. Heat butter in a small sauté pan (for cooking to order) or in a large skillet, as for fried eggs.
   Note: Steam kettles or tilting skillets may be used for scrambling large quantities of eggs.

5. When fat is just hot enough to make a drop of water sizzle, pour in eggs.

6. Cook over low heat, stirring gently from time to time as the eggs coagulate. Lift portions of coagulated egg so that uncooked egg can run underneath.
   Too much stirring breaks up eggs into very small particles.
   Do not let the eggs brown. Keep heat low.

7. When eggs are set but still soft and moist, remove from heat. Turn out onto plate or into steam table pan.

Additions to Scrambled Eggs

Flavor variations may be created by adding any of the following ingredients to scrambled eggs before serving:

Chopped parsley and/or other herbs	Sautéed diced onion and green pepper
Grated cheese (cheddar, Swiss, parmesan)	Diced smoked salmon
Diced ham	Sliced cooked breakfast sausage
Crumbled bacon	

OMELETS

Making omelets is like riding a bicycle. When you are learning, it seems difficult, and you can't imagine how anyone can do it. But once you have mastered the technique, it seems easy, and you don't understand how anyone could have trouble doing it.

We are talking about the plain or French omelet. There are several kinds, as described below, but the French omelet remains the most popular. Making it is a technique worth mastering.

French Omelet

Omelets may be described as sophisticated scrambled eggs. The first part of the technique is similar to that for making scrambled eggs. But the similarities end there, and the omelet emerges from the pan not as a shapeless pile of curds but an attractive oval with a light, delicate texture.

Two elements are necessary for making omelets:

1. High heat. This seems like a contradiction to our basic principle of low temperature egg cookery. But the omelet cooks so fast that its internal temperature never has time to get too high.

2. A conditioned omelet pan. First, the pan must have sloping sides and be the right size so that the omelet can be shaped properly. Second, it must be well seasoned or conditioned to avoid sticking.

Procedure for Conditioning an Omelet Pan

The following method is only one of many. Your instructor may show you another. The object is to seal the surface of the metal with a layer of baked-on oil.

1. Rub the clean pan with a thin film of vegetable oil.

2. Set the pan over moderately high heat until it is very hot.

3. Remove from heat and let cool.

4. Do not scour the pan or wash with a detergent after use. Rub with salt, which will scour the pan without harming the primed surface. Rinse only after pan has cooled, or wipe with a clean towel.

5. Reseason as often as necessary, or after each day's use.

Procedure for Making a French Omelet

Figure 21.6 *Making a French omelet. Read the accompanying text for a full description of the steps shown here.*

(a) As soon as the eggs are added to the hot pan, shake the pan back and forth with one hand and stir the eggs in a circular motion with a fork.

(b) When the eggs are almost set, tilt the pan and shake the eggs down to the opposite side of the pan. Rapping the handle sharply helps move the eggs.

(c) Spoon the filling, if used, across the center.

See Figure 21.6 for illustration of technique.

1. Collect all equipment and ingredients.
2. Beat 2 or 3 eggs in a small bowl just until well mixed. Do not whip until frothy. Season with salt and pepper.

    If desired, 1 tablespoon (15 mL) of water may be added to make the omelet lighter.

    For extended service, beat a large quantity of eggs. Measure each portion with a ladle.
3. Place an omelet pan over high heat.
4. When the pan is hot, add about 1 tablespoon (15 mL) clarified butter and swirl it around to coat the inside of the pan. Give it a second to get hot.

    Raw butter may be used, but great care is necessary to keep it from burning.
5. Add the eggs to the pan. They should begin to coagulate around the edges and on the bottom in a few seconds.
6. With one hand (the left, if you are right handed), vigorously shake the pan back and forth. At the same time, stir the eggs with a circular motion with the bottom side of a fork, but do not let the fork scrape the pan.

    This is the difficult part. The most common errors are not shaking and stirring vigorously enough and using heat that is too low. The purpose of this action is to keep the eggs in motion so that they coagulate uniformly.
7. Stop shaking and stirring when the eggs are almost set but still very moist. If you continue stirring, you will have scrambled eggs instead of an omelet.
8. Tilt the handle up and shake the pan so that the omelet slides to the opposite side of the pan and begins to climb up the opposite slope.
9. For a filled omelet, spoon the filling across the center of the egg, perpendicular to the handle.
10. With the fork, fold the sides of the omelet over the center. The omelet should now be resting in the corner of the pan and have an approximately oval shape.
11. Grasp the handle of the pan with your palm underneath and tilt the omelet out onto a plate so that it inverts and keeps an oval shape.

    The whole procedure should take less than 1 minute.

    The finished omelet should be moist on the inside, tender on the outside, and yellow or only slightly browned.

(d) Fold over the side of the omelet to make an oval shape.

(e) Grasp the handle of the pan with your palm underneath and tilt the omelet onto a plate.

(f) The finished omelet should have a neat, oval shape. Some chefs prefer omelets that are lightly browned. Others feel that they should not be browned at all.

Suggested Omelet Fillings

Cheese	Sautéed onions and diced potatoes
Sautéed or creamed mushrooms	Seafood Newburg or in a cream sauce
Creamed or curried chicken	Red caviar
Creamed or buttered spinach	Thick Spanish Sauce (p. 151)
Sautéed onions, with or without bacon	Ratatouille (p. 472)

American-Style or Folded Omelet

This style of omelet is often called a French omelet, but it is not a French omelet. It was probably devised by cooks who hesitated to tackle the French method.

It is made somewhat like a French omelet, except that low heat is used and the eggs are not stirred or agitated. Instead, the edges of the cooked portion are lifted with a fork or spatula, allowing the uncooked portion to flow underneath. The finished omelet may be folded in half or like a French omelet.

The advantage of this method is that it is easier to learn.

The disadvantages are that the omelet is not as light or delicate in texture, and that the method is much slower—a serious disadvantage in a busy kitchen.

Fluffy Omelet or Soufflé Omelet

These omelets are made by beating the egg whites separately and folding them into the beaten yolks, which may have some milk added. The mixture is poured into a hot, buttered omelet pan and the omelet is finished in the oven. It is folded in half for service.

Fluffy omelets are not often made in food service because of the time they take to make.

Frittatas and Other Flat Omelets

A frittata is a flat omelet that originated in Italy. The same basic techniques are used for many popular American preparations. Flat omelets are made by mixing beaten eggs with a variety of ingredients, such as vegetables, meats, or cheese, and cooking the mixture over low heat without stirring. To finish, it is either flipped over or run under the broiler or into the oven until the top is set.

A popular American frittata (actually derived from the Chinese egg foo yung) is the Western omelet, containing diced sautéed onion, green pepper, and ham.

SOUFFLÉS

Soufflés are not normally featured on breakfast menus. However, they are important basic egg preparations with which you should be familiar.

Soufflés are often considered by amateur cooks to be difficult to make. Actually, they are relatively easy preparations. Many restaurants have no difficulty turning out large numbers of soufflés to order. The only hard part is making sure the waiter picks up the order when it is ready.

A standard entrée soufflé consists of three elements:

1. Base—usually a heavy béchamel sauce.
2. Flavor ingredient—cheese, vegetables, seafood, etc.
3. Egg whites, beaten.

General Procedure for Preparing Entrée Soufflés

1. Prepare a heavy béchamel sauce.
2. Combine the sauce with egg yolks.
3. Prepare the flavor ingredient—grate cheese, cook and chop vegetables, and so on.
4. Combine the base and the flavor ingredient.
5. Beat egg whites and fold in.
6. Bake in a soufflé dish that has been buttered and dusted with parmesan cheese.
7. Serve immediately.

À la Carte Service

Prepare through step 4 and hold in refrigerator.

If several flavors are offered, prepare a single large batch of base and keep the flavor ingredients separate.

For each order, beat egg whites and combine with measured amount of base.

Cheese Soufflé

Portions: 12   Portion size: 4 oz (125 g)

U.S.	Metric	Ingredients	PROCEDURE
as needed	as needed	Butter	1. Select three 1½-qt (1½-L) soufflé dishes (4 portions each) or two 2-qt (2-L) dishes (6 portions each). Butter the insides of the dishes well. Sprinkle with cheese or crumbs so that the bottom and sides are completely coated.
as needed	as needed	Parmesan cheese or dry bread crumbs	
		Roux:	2. Make a white roux with the butter and flour. Cook the roux a few minutes.
2½ oz	75 g	Butter	
2½ oz	75 g	Flour	3. Beat in the hot milk. Bring to a boil, while stirring. Cool and stir until very thick and smooth.
1½ pt	750 mL	Milk, hot	
1½ tsp	7 mL	Salt	4. Remove from the heat. Stir in the salt, pepper, cayenne, and nutmeg.
1 tsp	5 mL	White pepper	
pinch	pinch	Cayenne	
pinch	pinch	Nutmeg	
12	12	Egg yolks	5. Add the egg yolks to the hot sauce and quickly mix in with a wire whip.
10 oz	300 g	Gruyère cheese, coarsely grated (see note)	6. Stir in the cheese.
12–15	12–15	Egg whites	7. Beat the egg whites with the salt until they form stiff peaks. (The larger number of egg whites will make a lighter soufflé.)
¼ tsp	1 mL	Salt	
			8. Fold the egg whites into the cheese mixture.
			9. Pour the mixture into the prepared soufflé dishes.
			10. Place the dishes in a preheated 375°F (190°C) oven. Bake for 40 minutes without opening the oven door. After this time, check for doneness by *very gently* shaking the dishes. If the centers are firm and do not jiggle, the soufflés are done. If necessary, bake another 5–10 minutes.
			11. Remove from oven and serve *immediately*.

Per serving:
Calories, 290; Protein, 17 g; Fat, 21 g (65% cal.); Cholesterol, 265 mg;
Carbohydrates, 8 g; Fiber, 0 g; Sodium, 600 mg.

Note: Other cheeses may be used: sharp cheddar, Swiss, a mixture of Swiss and Gruyère, or a mixture of Swiss or Gruyère and parmesan.

VARIATIONS

À la Carte Service: Prepare basic recipe through step 6. Chill mixture quickly and hold in refrigerator. For each order, scale off 3½ oz (100 g) of the mixture. Beat 1 egg white and fold in. Bake in an individual soufflé dish about 20–30 minutes.

Spinach Soufflé
Reduce cheese to 5 oz (150 g). Add 5 oz (150 g) well-drained, chopped cooked spinach.

Spinach and Ham Soufflé
Add 2 oz (60 g) ground or finely chopped ham to Spinach Soufflé.

Mushroom Soufflé
Reduce cheese to 5 oz (150 g). Add 4 oz (125 g) cooked chopped mushrooms.

Other Vegetable Soufflés
Follow the procedure for Spinach Soufflé, using chopped cooked vegetables such as broccoli, asparagus, or carrots.

Salmon Soufflé
Make the sauce base with milk plus liquid from canned salmon. Add 1½ oz (45 g) tomato paste to the base. Reduce cheese to 4 oz (125 g) and add 8 oz (250 g) flaked canned salmon.

CUSTARDS

A *custard* is a liquid that is thickened or set by the coagulation of egg protein.

There are two basic kinds of custards:

1. *Stirred custard*, which is stirred as it cooks and remains pourable when cooked.

2. *Baked custard*, which is not stirred and which sets firm.

One basic rule governs the preparation of both custards: *Do not heat custards higher than an internal temperature of 185°F (85°C).*

This temperature, as you know, is the point at which egg-liquid mixtures coagulate. If they are heated more than this, they tend to curdle. An overbaked custard becomes watery because the moisture separates from the toughened protein.

Most custards are sweet. These preparations are covered in the baking and dessert section of this book. You may have already encountered a savory custard in the recipe for Spinach Timbales (p. 474).

The *quiche* (keesh), which is a custard baked in a pastry shell, is probably the most popular form of savory custard. The following recipe illustrates the technique for preparing savory custards.

Quiche au Fromage (Cheese Tart)

Yield: four 8-inch (20 cm) tarts   **Portion:** 24   **Portion size:** ⅙ of tart
                                                  16   ¼ of tart

U.S.	Metric	Ingredients	PROCEDURE
2 lb	900 g	Mealy Pie Dough (p. 844)	1. Scale the dough into 4 pieces, 8 oz (225 g) each.
			2. Roll the dough into 4 circles, ⅛ inch (3 mm) thick.
			3. Fit the dough into four 8-inch (20-cm) pie pans or tart pans.
			4. Hold the pie shells in the refrigerator until needed (see note).
1 lb	450 g	Swiss or Gruyère cheese, grated	5. Sprinkle 4 oz (110 g) cheese into the bottom of each tart shell.
12	12	Eggs, beaten	
1 pt	500 mL	Heavy cream	6. Beat together the eggs, cream, milk, and seasonings. Pour into the tart shells.
2 pt	950 mL	Milk	
2 tsp	10 mL	Salt	7. Place the tarts in a 375°F (190°C) oven on the bottom shelf or, if using a deck oven, directly on the deck.
¼ tsp	1 mL	White pepper	
⅛ tsp	0.5 mL	Nutmeg	8. Bake until the filling is set, about 20–30 minutes.
			9. Serve hot or cold. Cut into wedges of desired size.

Per serving.
Calories, 370; Protein, 12 g; Fat, 30 g (69% cal.); Cholesterol, 155 mg;
Carbohydrates, 18 g; Fiber, 3 g; Sodium, 450 mg.

Note: Pastry shells may be partially baked before filling if uncooked bottoms tend to be a problem. This is sometimes the case if you are using shiny aluminum pie pans or if the bottom heat of the oven isn't strong enough. See page 847 for procedure.

VARIATIONS

Quiche Lorraine
Dice 1 lb (450 g) bacon strips and cook until crisp. Drain and add to pie shell in step 5. Omit cheese or leave it in, as desired. (Quiche Lorraine was originally made without cheese.)

Onion Quiche
Sauté 2 lb (900 g) sliced onions very slowly in 2 oz (60 g) butter until golden and tender. Cool and add to empty pie shells. Reduce cheese to 8 oz (225 g).

Spinach Quiche
Sauté 3 oz (90 g) chopped onion in 3 oz (90 g) butter until soft. Add 1½ lb (700 g) cooked, drained chopped spinach. Sauté until most of the liquid has evaporated. Cool and add to empty pie shell. Omit cheese.

Mushroom Quiche
Sauté 2 lb (900 g) sliced mushrooms and 3 oz (90 g) chopped onion in 3 oz (90 g) butter. Add 1 tbsp (15 mL) lemon juice to keep the mushrooms white. Cook until juices have evaporated. Cool and add to the empty pie shell. Omit cheese.

Seafood Quiche
Substitute 8 oz (225 g) cooked diced shrimp and 8 oz (225 g) cooked diced crabmeat for the cheese. Add 3 oz (90 mL) sherry and 2 oz (60 g) tomato paste to the egg mixture.

Breakfast Breads, Cereals, and Meats

Bread items probably play a more important role at breakfast than even eggs. Hardly an order of eggs is sold without an order of toast on the side. And for the diner who prefers a continental breakfast, coffee and a bread item such as a roll or pastry constitute the entire breakfast.

Except for toast, few breakfast breads are prepared to order. Most operations purchase such items ready made. These products include muffins, doughnuts, Danish pastries, sweet rolls, and regional favorites such as bagels and corn bread.

In this section, we consider three items that are made to order: pancakes, waffles, and French toast. You may not think of pancakes and waffles as breads, but they are actually a form of quick bread, a category of foods that we consider in more detail in the baking section of this book.

Pancakes and Waffles

Waffles and pancakes, also called griddle cakes and hot cakes, are made from pourable batters. Pancakes are made on a griddle, while waffles are made on a special tool called a waffle iron.

Both items should be cooked to order and served hot. Waffles lose their crispness very quickly, and pancakes toughen as they are held. However, batters may be prepared ahead and are often mixed the night before.

Serve with butter and with maple syrup or syrup blends (pure maple syrup is expensive). Other condiments that may accompany these items are fruit syrups, jams and preserves, applesauce, and fruits such as strawberries or blueberries.

INGREDIENTS AND PROCEDURES

Instead of presenting these items in the usual recipe format, we list the ingredients and methods in parallel columns so you can see the similarities and differences at a glance.

Note how much alike the batters are, with some important exceptions:

1. Waffle batter contains more fat.
2. Waffle batter contains less liquid, so it is slightly thicker.
3. Waffles are given extra lightness by beating the egg whites separately and folding into the batter. (Some recipes omit this step.)

A standard-size pancake requires ¼ cup (60 mL) batter. The amount of batter needed for waffles depends on the size of the waffle iron.

PRE-PREPARATION FOR VOLUME SERVICE

Pancake and waffle batters leavened by *baking powder only* may be mixed the night before and stored in the cooler. Some rising power may be lost, so baking powder may have to be increased.

Batters leavened by baking soda should not be made too far ahead because the soda will lose its power. Mix dry ingredients and liquid ingredients ahead and combine just before service.

Batters using beaten egg whites and baking powder may be partially made ahead, but *incorporate the egg whites just before service.*

Pancakes and Waffles

Ingredients for 3½ pt (1.75 L) batter

	Pancakes		Waffles	
	U.S.	Metric	U.S.	Metric
Dry ingredients:				
Flour	1 lb 4 oz	625 g	1 lb 4 oz	625 g
Sugar	2 oz	60 g	—	—
Salt	1 tsp	5 mL	1 tsp	5 mL
Baking powder	2 tbsp	30 mL	2 tbsp	30 mL
Liquid ingredients:				
Eggs, beaten	4	4	—	—
Egg yolks, beaten	—	—	6	6
Milk	1 qt	1 L	1½ pt	750 mL
Melted butter or oil	4 oz	125 g	8 oz	250 g
Egg whites	—	—	6	6
Sugar	—	—	2 oz	60 g

Buttermilk pancakes and waffles: Use buttermilk instead of milk. Reduce baking powder to 1 tbsp (15 mL) and add 2 tsp (10 mL) baking soda. Buttermilk makes a thick batter. You may need to thin the batter with a little plain milk.

PROCEDURES

Pancakes

1. Sift together dry ingredients.
2. Combine liquid ingredients.
3. Add liquid ingredients to dry ingredients. Mix just until dry ingredients are thoroughly moistened. Do not overmix. Overmixing causes toughness by developing the gluten in the flour (see p. 761).
4. Using a 2-oz ladle or No. 16 scoop, measure ¼ cup (60 mL) portions onto a greased, preheated griddle (375°F/190°C), allowing space for spreading.
5. Griddle the pancakes until the tops are full of bubbles and begin to look dry and the bottoms are golden brown. Turn and brown other side.
6. Remove from griddle and serve.

Per 1 2-ounce pancake:
Calories, 140; Protein, 4 g; Fat, 5 g (33% cal.); Cholesterol, 45 mg; Carbohydrates, 19 g; Fiber, 1 g; Sodium, 250 mg.

Waffles

1. Sift together dry ingredients.
2. Combine liquid ingredients.
3. Add liquid ingredients to dry ingredients. Mix just until dry ingredients are thoroughly moistened. Do not overmix. Overmixing causes toughness by developing the gluten in the flour (see p. 761).
4. Beat the egg whites until they form soft peaks. Add sugar and beat until stiff peaks form. Fold the egg white foam into the batter.
5. Pour enough batter onto a lightly greased, preheated waffle iron to almost cover the surface with a thin layer. Close the iron.
6. Cook waffles until signal light indicates they are done or until steam is no longer emitted.
7. Remove from iron and serve.

Per 1 2-ounce waffle:
Calories, 170; Protein, 4 g; Fat, 9 g (47% cal.); Cholesterol, 65 mg; Carbohydrates, 19 g; Fiber, 1 g; Sodium, 280 mg.

French Toast

Different versions of French toast are popular in many regions, and they have the added advantage of being an excellent way to utilize day-old bread.

Basic French toast consists of slices of bread dipped in a batter of eggs, milk, a little sugar, and flavorings. French toast is cooked on a griddle like pancakes.

Variations may be created by changing the basic ingredients:

Bread. White pullman bread is standard. Specialty versions can be made with French bread, rich egg bread, or whole grain breads.

Batter. Milk is the usual liquid, mixed with egg in various proportions. Deluxe versions may include cream or sour cream.

Flavorings. Vanilla, cinnamon, and nutmeg are popular choices. Other possibilities are grated lemon and orange rind, ground anise, rum, and brandy.

The most common fault in making French toast is not soaking the bread long enough to allow the batter to penetrate. If the bread is just dipped in the batter, the final product is just dry bread with a little egg on the outside.

French toast is dusted with powdered sugar and served, like pancakes, with accompanying butter, syrups, preserves, or fruits.

Cereals

HOT, COOKED CEREALS

Cooked cereals are of two types:

1. Whole, cracked, or flaked cereals, such as oatmeal (rolled oats), Scotch oatmeal (cracked oats), and cracked wheat. The particles are large and can be added to boiling water without lumping.

2. Granular cereals, such as farina and cornmeal. The particles are small and tend to lump when added to boiling water.

Procedure for Cooking Whole, Cracked, or Flaked Cereals

1. Collect equipment and ingredients.

2. Measure the correct amount of water and salt into a pot and bring to a boil. Read package directions for quantities.
   Using milk or part milk makes a richer cereal, but a more expensive one. Be careful not to scorch the milk if you use it.

3. Measure the correct amount of cereal.

4. Add the cereal slowly, stirring constantly.

5. Stir until some thickening takes place, then stop stirring. Too much stirring makes cereal gummy.

6. Reduce heat to a slow simmer, cover, and cook until desired doneness and consistency are reached. Cooking times vary greatly.

7. Keep covered until served to prevent drying.

Procedure for Cooking Granular Cereal

The procedure is the same as above, except that the cereal is mixed with a little cold water before being added to boiling water. This separates the grains and prevents lumping. The cold water must be calculated as part of the total amount of liquid.

COLD CEREALS

Cold, dry cereals are purchased ready prepared and need no preparation by the kitchen. Like hot cereals, they are served with accompanying milk or cream, sugar, and, sometimes, fruit such as berries or sliced bananas.

Breakfast Meats

Meats and meat cooking methods are covered in previous chapters, but we mention them again because three meats in particular—bacon, sausage, and ham—appear on most breakfast menus.

BACON

Bacon is a cured, smoked pork product. It is available in whole slabs but is almost always purchased sliced. Thickness of slices is specified by number of slices per pound, usually 18 to 22 (40 to 48 per kilogram).

Low-temperature cooking applies to bacon as well as to other meats. Bacon is about 70 percent fat and shrinks a great deal. However, cooking at low temperatures minimizes shrinkage. The oven is most often used for cooking bacon in quantity, though a griddle or sauté pan may also be used.

To cook in the oven, lay out the bacon strips on sheet pans in a single layer, or, even better, on racks over sheet pans. (Bacon may be purchased already laid out on parchment.) Bake at 300° to 350°F (150° to 175°C) until about three-fourths done. Remove from the oven, being careful not to spill the hot fat. Finish individual portions to order on the griddle or in the oven, cooking them until crisp.

HAM

Ham for breakfast service is almost always precooked. Slices in 3- to 4-ounce (90- to 115-g) portions need only be heated and browned slightly on a griddle or under the broiler.

Canadian bacon is boneless pork loin that is cured and smoked like ham. It is handled like ham in the kitchen.

SAUSAGE

Breakfast sausage is simply fresh pork that has been ground and seasoned. It is available in three forms: patties, links, and bulk.

Because it is fresh pork, sausage must be cooked well done. This does not mean, however, that it should be cooked until it is just hard, dry, shrunken little nuggets, as it often is.

Most kitchens cook sausages by the same methods as bacon. For volume service, it is partially cooked in the oven and then finished to order. Link sausages hold better than patties because the links are protected from drying by their casings.

Dairy Products

Milk and Cream

CATEGORIES AND DEFINITIONS

1. **Fresh milk.**

    Whole milk is fresh milk as it comes from the cow, with nothing removed and nothing (except vitamin D) added. It contains 3½ percent fat (known as *milk fat* or *butterfat*), 8½ percent nonfat milk solids, and 88 percent water.

    Fresh milk is available in several forms:

    Pasteurized milk has been heated to kill disease-producing bacteria, then cooled. Most milk and cream products on the market have been pasteurized.

    Raw milk is milk that has not been pasteurized. It is not often used and, in fact, is generally not legal.

    Certified milk is produced by disease-free herds under very strict sanitary conditions. It may be raw or pasteurized.

    Homogenized milk has been processed so that the cream doesn't separate out. This is done by forcing the milk through very tiny holes, which breaks the fat into particles so small they stay distributed in the milk.

The above terms apply not just to whole milk but to most of the following forms:

Skim or *nonfat milk* has had most or all of the fat removed. Its fat content is 0.5 percent or less.

Low-fat milk has a fat content of 0.5 to 3 percent. Its fat content is usually indicated.

Fortified nonfat or *low-fat milk* has had substances added to increase its nutritional value, usually vitamins A and D and extra nonfat milk solids.

Flavored milks, such as *chocolate milk*, have had flavoring ingredients added. A label such as *chocolate milk drink* or *chocolate-flavored drink* indicates that the product does not meet the standards for regular milk. Read ingredient labels.

2. **Cream.**

Whipping cream has a fat content of 30 to 40 percent. Within this category, you may find *light whipping cream* (30 to 35 percent) and *heavy whipping cream* (36 to 40 percent). Whipping cream labeled *ultrapasteurized* keeps longer than regular pasteurized cream. Pure ultrapasteurized cream does not whip as well as regular pasteurized cream, so it may contain additives such as vegetable gums to make it more whippable.

Light cream, also called *table cream* or *coffee cream*, contains 16 to 22 percent fat, usually about 18 percent.

Half-and-half has a fat content of 10 to 12 percent, too low for it to be called cream.

Crème fraîche is a slightly aged, cultured heavy cream. It is widely used for sauce making in Europe because of its pleasant, slightly tangy flavor and its ability to blend easily into sauces. Unlike regular heavy cream, it usually doesn't require tempering and can be added directly to hot sauces. It is available commercially but is expensive. A close approximation can be made by warming 1 quart (1 L) heavy cream to about 100°F (38°C), adding 1½ ounces (50 mL) buttermilk, and letting the mixture stand in a warm place until slightly thickened, about 6 to 24 hours.

3. **Fermented milk products.**

Sour cream has been cultured or fermented by added lactic acid bacteria, which makes it thick and slightly tangy in flavor. It has about 18 percent fat.

Buttermilk is fresh, liquid milk, usually skim milk, which has been cultured or soured by bacteria. It is usually called *cultured buttermilk* to distinguish it from the original buttermilk, which was the liquid left after butter making. Buttermilk is used in recipes calling for *sour milk*.

Yogurt is milk (whole or low-fat) cultured by special bacteria. It has a custardlike consistency. Most yogurt has additional milk solids added, and some of it is flavored and sweetened.

4. **Milk products with water removed.**

Evaporated milk is milk, either whole or skim, with about 60 percent of the water removed. It is then sterilized and canned. Evaporated milk has a somewhat cooked flavor.

Condensed milk is whole milk that has had about 60 percent of the water removed and is heavily sweetened with sugar. It is available canned and in bulk.

Dried whole milk is whole milk that has been dried to a powder. *Nonfat dry milk* is skim milk that has been dried in the same way. Both are available in regular form and in instant form, which dissolves in water more easily.

ARTIFICIAL DAIRY PRODUCTS

A wide variety of imitation cream and dessert topping products are made from various fats and chemicals, which are listed on the label. They are used in some institutions because they keep longer and are generally less expensive than dairy products. Some people feel they are acceptable, but many find their flavors objectionable.

PROBLEMS IN COOKING MILK AND CREAM PRODUCTS

Curdling

Curdling is a process by which milk proteins solidify and separate from the whey. Curdling is usually caused by acids, tannins, salt, and heat. The mild acids in many vegetables and the tannins in potatoes are often enough to curdle milk.

Starches partially stabilize milk and cream. This is why it is possible to make soups and sauces with both milk or cream and acid ingredients. Avoid combining milk or cream with strong acids unless a starch is present.

Reducing temperatures and cooking times also helps. Curdling is more likely at high heat or with prolonged cooking.

Salt lightly, unless the milk has been stabilized by starch.

When adding milk or cream to a hot liquid, heat it first in a separate pot, or temper it by stirring a little of the hot liquid into it first.

Reconstituted dry milk is more likely to curdle than fresh milk.

Scorching

Scorching occurs when milk that is being heated coagulates on the bottom of the pan due to high heat. This deposit is likely to burn if cooking continues.

To avoid scorching, heat milk in a double boiler, steamer, or steam-jacketed kettle rather than over direct heat.

Skin Formation

Formation of scum or skin on top of heated milk or milk sauces is caused by coagulation of proteins in contact with air. Prevent by covering the utensil or by coating the surface with a layer of melted fat.

WHIPPING CREAM

Cream with a fat content of 30 percent or more can be whipped into a foam (see Figure 21.7). One quart or liter of cream produces up to 2 quarts or liters of whipped cream.

For the best results, observe the following guidelines:

1. Have cream and all equipment well chilled.

2. Do not sweeten until the cream is whipped. Sugar decreases stability and makes the cream harder to whip. Use powdered sugar instead of granulated sugar for best stability.

3. Do not overwhip. Stop beating when the cream forms stiff peaks. If it is whipped longer, it first becomes granular and then turns into butter and whey.

4. Cream to be folded into other ingredients should be underbeaten because the action of folding it in whips it more and may overwhip it.

Figure 21.7 Whipping cream.

(a) The cream has begun to thicken.

(b) The cream has reached the soft-peak stage. Stop at this stage if the cream is to be folded into a batter or other mixture.

(c) The cream has reached the firm-peak stage. Whipping beyond this stage causes the cream to break or separate.

BUTTER CHARACTERISTICS AND GRADES

Fresh butter consists of about 80 percent milk fat. The remainder is milk solids and water.

In the United States, butter is graded according to USDA standards for flavor, body, color, and salt content, although grading is not mandatory. Grades are AA, A, B, and C. Most operations use grades AA and A because the lower grades may have off flavors.

Most butter on the market is lightly *salted*. *Sweet*, or *unsalted*, butter is more perishable but has a fresher, sweeter taste.

Because of its flavor, butter is the preferred cooking fat for most purposes. It has no equal in sauce making and is used as a sauce itself, as is discussed in Chapter 8.

Clarified butter (see p. 152 for production procedure) is used as a cooking fat more often than whole butter because the milk solids in whole butter burn easily.

The smoke point of butterfat is only 260° to 265°F (127° to 130°C), so another product, such as vegetable oil, should be used when high cooking temperatures are required.

STORING

Have you ever been served butter that tasted like onions? Butter absorbs odors and flavors easily, so it should be kept well wrapped and away from other foods that might transfer odors to it in the refrigerator.

Best storage temperature is 35°F (2°C).

MARGARINE

Margarine is a manufactured product that is intended to resemble butter in taste, texture, and appearance. It is made from various vegetable and animal fats, plus flavoring ingredients, emulsifiers, coloring agents, preservatives, and added vitamins. Like butter, it is about 80 percent fat.

Flavors of different brands should be evaluated carefully because they vary considerably. Margarine should have a reasonably clean, fresh flavor, although you should not expect even the best to taste like high-grade butter.

Margarines that include an emulsifier called lecithin foam and brown like butter when heated. Those without lecithin do not. In all other respects, margarine is handled and stored like butter.

COMPOSITION

Cheese is a food produced by separating milk solids from whey by curdling or coagulation. This curdling is brought about by introducing selected bacteria or an enzyme called *rennet* into the milk. The resulting curds are drained, processed, and cured or aged in a variety of ways.

Processing techniques are so numerous that from a single basic ingredient (milk from cows, sheep, or goats) it is possible to produce hundreds of kinds of cheese, from cottage cheese to parmesan, from cheddar to Swiss, from blue to Limburger. Variables that produce these differences include the type of milk used, the method of curdling and the temperatures during curdling, the method of cutting and draining the curd, the way the curds are heated, pressed, or handled, and all the conditions of ripening or curing.

Ripening is the process that converts freshly made curds into distinctive, flavorful cheeses. This ripening is brought about by certain bacteria or molds that are introduced during manufacture. Much of a cheese's final character is determined by the kind of ripening agent and the way it acts on the cheese.

Cheeses can be classified by the kind of ripening agent and by whether the cheese ripens from the inside or the outside.

Bacteria ripened, from inside: Cheddar, Swiss, Gouda, parmesan.
Bacteria ripened, from outside: Limburger, Liederkranz.
Mold ripened, from inside: Blue cheeses, including Roquefort and Stilton.
Mold ripened, from outside: Brie, Camembert, St. André.
Unripened: Cottage, cream, baker's cheese.

The three major components of cheese are water, fat, and protein. The water content of cheese ranges from about 80 percent for a fresh, soft cheese like cottage cheese to about 30 percent for a very hard, aged cheese like parmesan.

The fat content of cheese, when it is listed on a label, generally refers to the percentage of solids. In other words, if a cheddar cheese has a 50 percent fat content, this means that the cheese would be 50 percent fat if all the moisture were removed. In fact, the cheese may have a moisture content of about 40 percent, and its actual fat content may be about 30 percent of the total.

Double-crème (at least 60 percent fat) and triple-crème (at least 75 percent fat, dry weight) are very rich cheeses. Most of these styles of cheese originated in France, but they have become very popular and are now made in many countries. Most of them fall into the unripened, soft-ripened, or blue-veined categories, discussed below.

VARIETIES

Only a few of the many hundreds of the world's cheeses find their way into commercial kitchens. The following are the most frequently used. See also the accompanying photographs.

Unripened Cheeses
These are soft, white, freshly made cheeses.

Cottage cheese is a moist, loose-curd cheese that may or may not have cream added. *Baker's cheese* or *pot cheese* is similar but drier. Baker's cheese is used in cheesecakes and pastry.

Ricotta cheese is sometimes called *Italian cottage cheese,* but it is smoother, moister, and sweeter.

Cream cheese is a smooth, mild cheese with a high fat content. It is extensively used in making sandwiches, canapés, and hors d'oeuvres and in baking.

Neufchâtel is similar to cream cheese but has less fat. An Italian cream cheese called *mascarpone* is very soft and rich, and it looks almost like whipped cream. It has a slightly tangy taste that goes well with fruits as a dessert.

Mozzarella is a soft, mild cheese made from whole milk or part skim milk. It has a stringy texture that comes from being pulled and stretched during production. It is widely used in pizzas and Italian-style dishes. The freshly made mozzarella one finds in Italian neighborhoods is moister and more tender than the packaged varieties.

Mozzarella di bufala, made from the milk of water buffaloes, is imported from Italy and is available in some areas at a somewhat high price. It is much softer and more delicate in texture than regular mozzarella, and it has a slightly acidic flavor that is refreshing.

Feta is a crumbly, curdy cheese from Greece and other Balkan countries. Instead of being aged or cured, it is pickled in brine. This, plus the fact that it is generally made from goat's or sheep's milk, gives it a distinctive salty flavor.

Semisoft Cheeses
Bel Paese and *fontina* from Italy, *Port Salut* from France, and American *munster* and *brick* cheeses are the best known of a larger group of cheeses that range from bland and buttery when young to more earthy and full flavored when older. They are often used as dessert cheeses and as hors d'oeuvres.

France produces many soft cheeses, often with orange rinds and with flavors that range from mild to pungent. Among the better-known ones are *Pont l'Evêque* and *Livarot* from Normandy and *Muenster* from Alsace. (These cheeses might also be categorized as soft ripened cheeses, below.)

Soft Ripened Cheeses

These cheeses ripen from the outside toward the center. When very young, they are firm and cakey and have little flavor. As they mature, they gradually become softer and, when fully ripe, may be actually runny.

Brie and *Camembert* from France are ripened by mold. They are made in flat, round shapes and are covered with a crust that varies in color from white to straw. When ripe, these cheeses are creamy and flavorful, but they develop a sharp odor of ammonia when overripe.

Liederkranz, made in the United States, and its Belgian cousin, *Limburger*, are ripened by bacteria rather than mold, but they also become softer as they age. They are widely misunderstood because of their aroma. Actually, when not overripe, these cheeses are not nearly as strong as most people expect, and they have a pleasant, smooth texture. Liederkranz and Limburger are served as dessert cheeses, like *Brie* and *Camembert.*

Many rich double- and triple-crème cheeses fall in this category, including *Explorateur, Brillat-Savarin, St. André, Boursault,* and *Boursin* (which may be flavored with pepper or with garlic and herbs). *Chaource* is similar in texture and appearance to a double-crème cheese but is actually closer in composition to Brie, having a fat content of 45 to 50 percent.

Hard Ripened Cheeses

These are cured cheeses with a firm texture and varying degrees of mildness or sharpness, depending on their age.

Cheddar is an English invention, but American versions of it are so popular in the United States that it is often thought of as a distinctly American cheese. It ranges in flavor from mild to sharp and in color from light yellow to orange. Cheddar is eaten as is and is also widely used in cooking. *Colby* and *Monterey jack* are similar to very mild cheddars. Monterey jack is usually sold when quite young. In this case, it is more like American munster and belongs in the semi-soft category.

Swiss-type cheeses are also popular. Swiss-type cheeses are produced in many countries, but the original Swiss cheese from Switzerland, *Emmenthaler,* is perhaps the most flavorful. These are very firm, slightly rubbery cheeses with a nutty taste. Their large holes are caused by gases formed during ripening. *Gruyère* is another Swiss-type cheese from either Switzerland or France. It has smaller holes and a sharper, earthier flavor. Gruyère is important in cooking and it, plus Emmenthaler, are widely used for sauces, soufflés, fondue, and gratinéed items. Other cheeses related to Swiss are *Comté* from France, *Appenzeller* and *Raclette* from Switzerland, and *Jarlsberg* from Norway.

Edam and *Gouda* are the familiar round Dutch cheeses with the yellow and red wax rinds. Hard in texture, with a mellow, nutlike flavor, they are often seen on buffet platters and among dessert cheeses.

Provolone is an Italian cheese that resembles mozzarella when very young, but it becomes sharper as it ages. It is also available smoked.

Blue-Veined Cheeses

These cheeses owe their flavor and appearance to the blue or green mold that mottles their interiors. The most famous of the blue cheeses is *Roquefort,* made in France from sheep's milk and cured in limestone caves near the town of Roquefort. *Stilton,* from England, is a mellower, firmer blue cheese that the English call "Roquefort with a college education." Italy's *gorgonzola* is a soft, creamy cheese with an unmistakable pungency. Less expensive than these three, and thus more widely used, are a number of blue cheeses made in the United States and in Denmark.

Less widely known but worth seeking out are a number of special blues, including *Bleu de Bresse, Fourme d'Ambert,* and *Pipo Crem'* from France, *Saga* from Denmark, and *Bavarian Blue* and *Blue Castello* from Germany. The last four of these are double- or triple-crèmes.

Goat Cheeses

Cheeses made from goat's milk are produced in dozens of varieties in France, where this type of cheese, called *chèvre,* is very popular. It has also become well known in the United States, which now has several producers. With a few exceptions, most goat cheeses are small, ranging in size from tiny buttons to logs, cakes, cones, and pyramids weighing up to 5 or 6 ounces (140 to 170 g).

An assortment of cheeses. Back row, left to right: Port Salut, Danish Blue, Jarlsberg, New York cheddar, Edam. Center: large Brie. Front, left to right: Limburger, slightly aged domestic chèvre, fresh chèvre coated with dill, Crottin de Chavignol, Camembert, Explorateur, Chaource, Saga.

Clockwise from top: Emmenthaler, Gorgonzola, Provolone, Gruyère, Gouda, Locatelli Romano, Pont l'Evêque, Baby Gouda. Lower center: Livarot.

Fresh, unaged chèvres are the most popular and the mildest in flavor. Their paste is very white, with a soft but interestingly dry texture. They have a distinctive peppery, slightly acidic taste. The most widely available fresh French chèvre is probably the cylindrical *Montrachet*, either plain or with a coating of ash. Other fresh goat cheeses, both domestic and imported, may be available in different localities, and many may have no name other than *chèvre*.

As goat cheese ages, it becomes firmer, and the peppery, acidic flavor becomes stronger. Cheeses two or three months old can be quite powerful, while the youngest might taste almost like the unaged ones. Some names of chèvres are *Boucheron*, *Banon* (wrapped in chestnut leaves), *Pyramide*, *Crottin de Chavignol*, *Chabis*, *Rocamadour*, and *Saint-Marcellin* (part cow's milk).

Hard Grating Cheeses

The hard grating cheeses, typified by Italian *parmesan*, are called *grana* cheeses, referring to their grainy textures. The best of all granas is called *Parmigiano Reggiano*. It is the true parmesan, aged at least two years, and is very expensive. It is imitated widely around the world, and the imitations vary from bad to very good. Another Italian grana is *Romano*. Italian romanos are made with sheep's milk, but American versions are usually made with cow's milk. Romano is stronger and saltier than parmesan.

These cheeses are often sold already grated. This is a convenience for commercial kitchens, of course, but, unfortunately, pregrated cheese has much less flavor than freshly grated cheese. A merchant was once arrested for selling what he claimed was grated parmesan cheese but was actually grated umbrella handles. A large share of pregrated cheese sold today resembles grated umbrella handles in flavor.

Process Cheeses

Up to now, we have been talking about so-called natural cheeses, made by curdling milk and ripening the curds. Process cheese, by contrast, is manufactured by grinding one or more natural cheeses, heating and blending them with emulsifiers and other ingredients, and pouring the mixture into molds to solidify. Process cheese is a uniform product that does not age or ripen like natural cheese. Thus, it keeps very well. It is usually mild in flavor and gummy in texture.

Because of its melting quality and low price, it is often used in cooking. However, it is not as good a value as its price implies. Because it is relatively flavorless, you have to use much more of it to get the same flavor as from a smaller quantity of sharp cheddar.

In addition to its price and keeping qualities, its chief advantages are that it melts easily and its blandness appeals to many people who don't like a more flavorful cheese.

The term *American cheese* usually refers to process cheese, although some people use this name for cheddar. In the United States, most process cheeses are made from cheddar, while European process cheeses more often contain Swiss-type cheeses. Among them is a process cheese called *Gruyère*, which bears little resemblance to true *Gruyère*.

Process cheese food and *process cheese spread* contain a lower percentage of cheese and more moisture than a product labeled simply *process cheese*. *Cold pack* or *club cheese*, on the other hand, is not heated and pasteurized like process cheese but is simply ground and mixed with flavorings and seasonings to a spreadable consistency. Some brands are fairly flavorful.

STORAGE AND SERVICE

Storing

Keeping qualities of cheese vary considerably. In general, *the firmer and more aged the cheese, the longer it will keep.* Cottage cheese must be used within a week, while a whole, uncut parmesan may keep a year or more.

Soft ripened cheeses like Brie, Camembert, and Liederkranz deteriorate rapidly once they reach maturity. They are difficult cheeses to purchase because in their whole lifespan there may be only one week when they are neither underripe nor overripe.

Other ripened cheeses are not as fussy, as long as you store them under refrigeration and well wrapped to prevent drying. Cut cheeses dry especially quickly, so they must be wrapped in plastic at all times.

Serving

Serve cheese at room temperature. This is the single most important rule of cheese service. Only at room temperature will the full flavors develop. (This does not apply to unripened cheese like cottage cheese.)

Cut cheese just before service to prevent drying. Better yet, set out whole cheeses and large pieces when possible so that portions can be cut to order by the customer or the service personnel.

COOKING WITH CHEESE

Three varieties of cheese account for the majority of cheese used in cooking. *Cheddar* is the most frequently used in American dishes, especially in sauces, as casserole ingredients, and as a melted or gratinéed topping. *Swiss-type* cheeses are used more often in European-style dishes. Emmenthaler and Gruyère are essential ingredients for fondue, Mornay sauce, gratinéed dishes, soufflés, and quiches. *Parmesan-type* cheeses are used in grated form for toppings and for seasoning and flavoring purposes.

Many other varieties are called for in specialized recipes, such as mozzarella and ricotta in Italian-style dishes.

Guidelines for Cooking With Cheese

1. Use low temperatures. Cheese contains a high proportion of protein, which toughens and becomes stringy when heated too much. Sauces containing cheese should not be boiled.

2. Use short cooking times, for the same reasons. Cheese should be added to a sauce at the end of cooking. Stirring it into the hot sauce *off the heat* is usually enough to melt it.

3. Grate cheese for faster and more uniform melting.

4. Aged cheeses melt and blend into foods more easily than young cheeses.

5. Aged cheese adds more flavor to foods than young, mild cheeses, so you need less of it.

Welsh Rabbit

Portions: 25   Portion size: 4 oz (125 g)

U.S.	Metric	Ingredients	PROCEDURE
3 tbsp	45 mL	Worcestershire sauce	1. Mix the Worcestershire sauce and spices in a heavy saucepan.
2 tsp	10 mL	Dry mustard	2. Add the beer or ale. Heat almost to a simmer.
pinch	pinch	Cayenne	3. Set the pan over very low heat. Add the grated cheese, a little at
2½ cups	625 mL	Beer or ale	a time. Stir constantly. Continue to stir over low heat until the
5 lb	2.5 kg	Sharp cheddar cheese, grated	mixture is smooth and thick.
			4. Remove from heat. The mixture may be kept warm in a steam table or bain-marie, but it is better if served immediately.
25 slices	25 slices	White bread	5. Toast the bread.
			6. For each portion, place a slice of hot toast on a plate. Ladle 4 oz (125 mL) cheese mixture over the toast. Serve.

Per serving:
Calories, 470; Protein, 26 g; Fat, 31 g (60% cal.); Cholesterol, 85 mg; Carbohydrates, 19 g; Fiber, 1 g; Sodium, 750 mg.

Note: This dish is sometimes called Welsh Rarebit, although Rabbit is the original name.

Swiss Fondue

Portions: 4   Portion size: 8 oz (250 g)

U.S.	Metric	Ingredients	PROCEDURE
1 clove	1 clove	Garlic	1. Cut the garlic clove in half. Rub the inside of a 1½-qt (1½-L) fondue pot or casserole with the garlic.
1 pt	500 mL	Dry white wine	
1 lb	500 g	Swiss Emmenthaler cheese, or half Emmenthaler and half Gruyère, grated	2. Add the wine to the pot and set over moderate heat. Heat the wine until it is hot but not simmering. Do not boil.
			3. Add the cheese to the wine, about one-fourth at a time. Stir well between each addition.
1 tsp	5 mL	Cornstarch	4. Dissolve the cornstarch in the kirsch. Stir into the cheese mixture. Stir over very low heat until smooth and slightly thickened.
3 tbsp	45 mL	Kirsch (see note)	
to taste	to taste	Salt	
to taste	to taste	White pepper	5. Season to taste with salt, white pepper, and just a trace of nutmeg.
to taste	to taste	Nutmeg	
2	2	Small loaves French bread, cut into bite-size pieces	6. Set the casserole over a chafing dish heating element for service. Serve the bread cubes in baskets. To eat fondue, the diner spears a cube of bread on a special fondue fork and swirls it in the cheese mixture, which is kept hot over the heating element.

Per serving:
Calories, 870; Protein, 43 g; Fat, 35 g (36% cal.); Cholesterol, 105 mg; Carbohydrates, 70 g; Fiber, 3 g; Sodium, 1000 mg.

Note: Kirsch is a white (that is, clear) alcoholic beverage distilled from cherries. While it is traditional in Swiss fondue, it may be omitted if unavailable. In this case, dissolve the cornstarch in cold water or mix it with the grated cheese.

Sirniki (Russian Fried Cheese Cakes)

Portions: 25   Portion size: 3½ oz (100 g)

U.S.	Metric	Ingredients	PROCEDURE
5 lb	2.3 kg	Pot cheese	1. Place the pot cheese in a strainer lined with cheesecloth. Fold the overhanging cloth over the top of the cheese so that it is covered. Set the strainer over a bowl and refrigerate for 24 hours to drain the cheese.
6 oz	175 g	Bread flour	2. Force the cheese through a sieve or food mill into the bowl of a mixer.
8	8	Egg yolks	3. Add the flour, egg yolks, salt, and sugar.
½ tsp	2 mL	Salt	4. With the paddle attachment, mix until smooth.
2 oz	60 g	Sugar	5. Divide the dough into 3 parts. Roll each part into a cylinder about 3 inches (7½ cm) thick. Wrap in plastic film. Refrigerate 2 hours or more.
as needed	as needed	Butter for frying	6. At service time, cut the cheese rolls into cakes about ¾ inch (2 cm) thick.
			7. Heat about ⅛ inch (3 mm) butter in a heavy sauté pan. Pan-fry the cakes over low heat until golden brown on both sides. Turn very carefully with a spatula.
as needed	as needed	Confectioners' sugar	8. Plate the cakes and sprinkle lightly with confectioners' sugar. Place about 1½ tbsp (20 mL) sour cream on the plate next to the cake. Serve immediately.
2½ pt	1.2 L	Sour cream	

Per serving:
Calories, 350; Protein, 18 g; Fat, 23 g (63% cal.); Cholesterol, 130 mg;
Carbohydrates, 12 g; Fiber, 0 g; Sodium, 480 mg.

Note: This dish is often served as the main course for brunch or lunch. In this case, portion sizes may be increased. Sirniki may also be served with strawberry or other preserves.

Cheese Wafers

Yield: about 150 wafers

U.S.	Metric	Ingredients	PROCEDURE
1 lb	500 g	Sharp cheddar cheese, grated	1. Combine all ingredients in the bowl of a mixer. Mix at low speed with the paddle attachment until the mixture forms a dough.
8 oz	250 g	Butter, softened	2. Remove from the mixer and knead lightly on a floured board until the dough holds together well.
12 oz	375 g	Bread flour	3. Divide the dough into 4 or 5 pieces. Roll each piece into a cylinder 1 inch (2½ cm) in diameter. Wrap in waxed paper or plastic film and chill.
½ tsp	2 mL	Salt	4. Slice the dough into thin rounds a little less than ¼ inch (½ cm) thick. Place on greased baking sheets.
¼ tsp	1 mL	White pepper	5. Bake at 450°F (230°C) about 10 minutes, until crisp and lightly browned.
			6. Serve hot or cold as an hors d'oeuvre or as a soup accompaniment.

Per 1 wafer:
Calories, 30; Protein, 1 g; Fat, 2.5 g (65% cal.); Cholesterol, 5 mg;
Carbohydrates, 2 g; Fiber, 0 g; Sodium, 40 mg.

VARIATION

Cheese Straws

Roll out the dough like pie dough, slightly less than ¼ inch (½ cm) thick. Cut into strips, ¼ × 3 inches (½ × 7½ cm). Bake as in basic recipe.

Coffee and Tea

Coffee

Many people judge a restaurant by its coffee. Regardless of the quality of the food, one of the things they are most likely to remember about an establishment is whether the coffee is good or bad.

Whether or not that seems fair to you, it is at least a clear signal that you ought to learn to make coffee properly. Coffee making is basically a simple procedure. All you do is pass hot water through ground coffee. The care with which you perform this operation, with attention to all the details, makes the difference between a rich, aromatic, satisfying beverage and a bitter, unpleasant liquid.

VARIETIES, ROASTS, AND BLENDS

Coffee beans are the berries of a tropical shrub. Coffee is grown in many tropical countries, and each producing area is known for certain quality and flavor characteristics. Many connoisseurs feel that the finest coffee comes from Colombia. Excellent coffees are grown in Brazil, Venezuela, Mexico, and nations in Africa, the Middle East, and Indonesia.

Most ground coffees are blends of several varieties. Blending enables the processor to combine desirable quantities from a number of beans to produce a well-balanced beverage.

Coffee beans are roasted to develop their flavor. The degree of roasting—light, medium, dark—affects the flavor. Americans generally prefer medium roast, while dark roast coffees are popular in Europe and are often served as after-dinner beverages in French and Italian restaurants.

The most important fact about coffee varieties for you to know as a professional cook is that many blends at different prices and quality levels are available. You do have a choice—all coffee is not alike. Your selection will be based on your own taste evaluation, the needs of your establishment, the preferences of your customers, and your cost constraints.

In addition to the standard American blends, the following coffee varieties are sometimes served.

1. **Instant coffee** is a powdered, soluble extract from coffee beans. To simplify somewhat, instant coffee is made by brewing regular coffee and drying it. In the process, the coffee loses a portion of its flavor and aroma. Most coffee lovers agree that it does not taste as good as freshly brewed coffee. Instant coffee is rarely used in food service, with the major exception of decaffeinated coffee.

2. **Decaffeinated coffee.** Caffeine is a chemical stimulant that occurs naturally in coffee, tea, and chocolate. Decaffeinated coffee is coffee from which the caffeine has been removed by solvents. It is often specially requested by some customers. In the past, most restaurants offered decaffeinated coffee only in the instant form. Recently, however, due to increased demand, more and more restaurants are serving freshly brewed decaffeinated coffee.

3. **Espresso or expresso** is a strong, dark coffee made from beans roasted until they are almost black and ground to a powder. It is brewed in special machines (like the one shown in the photograph) that force water through the ground coffee under steam pressure. Espresso is served in small cups as an after-dinner beverage.

4. **Demitasse** means "half cup." It refers to strong, black coffee served in small cups after dinner.

5. **Cappuccino** is a combination of equal parts espresso and frothy, steamed milk. It is served in tall cups, often topped with whipped cream and cinnamon.

6. **Iced coffee** is made double strength to compensate for dilution by melting ice.

An espresso maker.
(Courtesy of Cecilware)

Basic Principles of Coffeemaking

Coffee is made by extracting flavors from ground coffee by dissolving them in hot water. The essence of making good coffee is to extract enough of these solids to make a flavorful beverage, but not to brew so long as to extract those solids that make the coffee bitter.

With this principle in mind, study the following guidelines for making good coffee. The list is long, and every item is important.

1. Use fresh coffee.

Once it is ground, coffee loses flavor and aroma rapidly. To maintain freshness, store coffee, tightly sealed, in a cool, dry place. Even with the best storage, however, you should not use coffee more than a week old. Vacuum-packed coffee keeps longer, but it too deteriorates as soon as it is opened. If you can't grind your own coffee daily (some restaurants do), at least you can arrange for frequent delivery.

2. Use the right grind and the right brewing time.

A coarse grind requires more time for extraction than a fine grind. You must use the grind that is suited to your equipment.

Grind	Extraction Time
Fine or vacuum	2 to 4 minutes
Drip or urn	4 to 6 minutes
Regular (percolator)	6 to 8 minutes

3. Use the right proportions.

Always measure. Recommended proportions are 1 pound of coffee and 1¾ to 2½ gallons of water, or 500 grams of coffee and 7.5 to 10.5 liters of water, depending on the strength desired.

To make weaker coffee, add more hot water after removing the used grounds. Using more water while actually making the coffee extends the brewing time, resulting in overextraction and bitterness. In fact, many experts feel that passing no more than 2 gallons of water through 1 pound of ground coffee (8 liters to 500 grams) and then diluting to taste is the surest way to avoid bitterness.

Coffee strength is a matter of customer preference and varies from region to region. For example, people in New York generally prefer stronger coffee than people in Chicago. In some areas, the preferred ratio is 1 pound (500 g) coffee to 3 gallons (12 liters) water.

4. Use fresh water.

Fresh, cold water brought to a boil contains dissolved air. Water that has been kept hot for a long time does not, so it tastes flat, and it makes flat-tasting coffee.

Tap water is usually best to use. Special filtration systems are available for tap water that has off flavors or is heavily chlorinated. Do not use chemically softened water.

5. Use water at the right brewing temperature: 195° to 200°F (90° to 93°C).

Water that is too hot extracts bitter solids. Water that is too cold does not extract enough flavor and yields coffee that is too cool for serving.

6. Use a good brewing procedure.

Most operations use either urns, for large volume, or automatic drip makers, which make one pot at a time, as shown in the photograph. These machines can make excellent coffee because water passes through the grounds only once.

Percolator-type coffee makers should not be used. They boil the coffee as it is being brewed and pass it through the grounds repeatedly.

7. Use clean equipment.

Urns and coffee makers must be cleaned every day. Coffee leaves oily deposits that quickly turn rancid or bitter and that can ruin the next batch of coffee.

8. Use good filters.

Good filters are the only way to ensure sparkling, clear coffee. Most operations use paper filters, which are discarded after use. If cloth filters are used, they must be perfectly clean and free from odors.

9. Use proper holding procedures.

Proper holding temperature is 185° to 190°F (85° to 88°C). Higher temperatures decompose the coffee quickly. Lower temperatures mean that the customer gets cold coffee.

Do not hold coffee more than 1 hour. After an hour, loss of flavor is considerable. Loss of customers might also be considerable. Plan production so that coffee is always fresh. Discard old coffee.

Twin urn.

(Courtesy of Cecilware)

Procedure for Making Coffee in an Urn

1. Be familiar with your equipment. Models differ in details.

2. Check to make sure the urn holds sufficient fresh water at the proper temperatures for brewing.

3. Fit the filter securely in place.

4. Spread a measured amount of coffee evenly in the filter. An even bed is necessary for uniform extraction.

5. Pass the correct amount of water through the ground coffee. If the urn is manual, pour the water slowly in a circular motion. If it is automatic, all you need to do is make sure the nozzle is in place.

6. Keep the top covered during brewing to retain heat.

7. Remove the filter with the used grounds as soon as brewing has been completed. Leaving the grounds in the urn results in overextraction and bitterness.

8. Mix the coffee. Because the coffee at the bottom is stronger, you must draw out some of it—about 1 gallon (4 liters) per pound (500 grams) of coffee—and pour it back into the top of the urn.

9. Hold at 185° to 190°F (85° to 88°C) for up to 1 hour.

10. Clean the urn thoroughly after use.

    Using special urn brushes, clean the inside of the urn as well as inside spigots and glass gauges. Rinse and fill with several gallons of fresh water if the urn is to stand for a time. Empty and rinse with hot water before next use.

    Twice a week, clean thoroughly with urn cleaning compound, following manufacturer's instructions.

Decanter-type automatic drip coffee maker.
(Courtesy of Cecilware)

Tea

Tea is one of the world's most popular beverages and is widely drunk even in coffee-drinking countries. In many regions, tea is a much more popular beverage in the home than in the restaurant. Part of the difference may be due to mishandling in the restaurant and indifference on the part of restaurateurs.

    Food service professionals would do well to pay more attention to tea. First of all, it is much less expensive to serve. One pound (500 grams) of tea yields 200 servings, as compared with 40 from 1 pound (500 grams) of coffee. Moreover, tea is one of the simplest of beverages to serve and does not require the equipment or the labor of coffee service.

VARIETIES

All the world's varieties of tea are produced from one species of evergreen shrub. Most of the differences among varieties are the results of growing conditions and modifications in processing techniques.

    As in the case of coffee, different regions produce teas of different quality and flavor characteristics. Most of the tea consumed in the United States is imported from India and Sri Lanka (Ceylon).

    Variations in processing produce three categories of tea. *Black tea* is fermented by allowing the freshly harvested leaves to oxidize in a damp place. *Green tea* is dried without fermenting. *Oolong tea* is partially fermented to a greenish-brown color. Specialty teas and flavored teas are also available.

    Black teas are graded by leaf size according to a rather complicated system. This is important to remember because most people think of orange pekoe as a variety of tea, whereas it is actually a specific leaf size of any black variety.

After grading, teas are blended to ensure consistency and uniformity. A blend may contain as many as 30 individual teas.

Many excellent blends are available from many purveyors. A smart food service operator would do well to shop around rather than serve the same mediocre blend that the competition serves.

PACKAGING AND MARKET FORMS

Tea is packaged in bulk as loose tea and in tea bags of various sizes. Standard cup-size bags are packaged 200 to the pound (500 grams), while the pot-sized bag (that is, individual service pot) is packaged at 150 to 175 per pound (500 grams). This is important for you to know if you are purchasing tea because the larger bags would not be as economical if the service in your establishment is by the cup.

Larger tea bags that contain 1 or 2 oz (30 to 60 g) of tea are available for brewing larger quantities, especially for iced tea.

Instant tea is a soluble extraction made by brewing a very strong tea, using lesser grades, and drying the liquid to obtain a powder. This product is used primarily for iced tea because the processing results in the loss of much of the flavor and aroma essential to a good hot tea.

PREPARING TEA

In most restaurants, it seems, when one orders tea, one receives a cold cup, a tea bag in a little package, and a pot of warm water that has been standing in an urn for hours. This is absolutely the worst possible way to serve tea, with the possible exception of brewing a large quantity and keeping it warm all day. No wonder most people don't order tea.

Here is the right way:

Procedure for Making Hot Tea

1. Use proper proportions of tea and water. One teaspoon (5 mL) of loose tea or one single-service tea bag makes a 6-oz (175-mL) cup.

2. Rinse the teapot with hot water to warm it. Use china, glass, or stainless steel. Other metals may give an off flavor.

3. Bring fresh, cold water to a boil. Water that has been kept warm for a time makes flat-tasting tea.

4. Place the loose tea or tea bag in the pot and pour the water directly over it.

5. Let the tea steep 3 to 5 minutes. Then remove the tea bag or strain off the tea from the loose leaves.
   Establishments specializing in tea service present the customer with the pot of tea and a pot of hot water so that they can dilute the tea to taste.

6. Serve immediately. Tea does not hold well.

Procedure for Making Iced Tea

The following method makes 1 gallon (4 L). The tea is brewed stronger to allow for melting ice.

1. Place 2 ounces (60 g) of tea in a pot.

2. Bring 1 quart (1 L) of water to a boil and pour over the tea.

3. Steep 5 minutes. Remove tea bags, or strain out loose leaves.

4. Add 3 quarts (3 L) cold tap water.

5. Hold at room temperature up to 4 hours. Refrigeration may make the tea cloudy.

6. Serve over ice.

Terms for Review

sunny side up	breakfast sausage	sour cream	triple-crème cheese
over easy	pasteurized	buttermilk	chèvre
shirred egg	homogenized	yogurt	process cheese
conditioned pan	skim milk	evaporated milk	instant coffee
frittata	whipping cream	condensed milk	espresso
soufflé	light cream	nonfat dry milk	demitasse
custard	half-and-half	ripened cheese	
quiche	crème fraiche	double-crème cheese	

Questions for Discussion

1. Which grade of eggs would you choose to prepare poached eggs? hard-cooked eggs? fried eggs? scrambled eggs? Why?

2. Is it possible to prepare hard-cooked eggs in a pressure steamer? Give reasons for your answer.

3. When separating eggs, many chefs advise breaking them one by one over a small bowl, then transferring each white to the larger bowl as it is separated. Can you give a reason for this advice?

4. Give two reasons for being careful not to add too much vinegar to egg poaching water.

5. In the recipe for waffles, what is the purpose of beating the sugar into the egg whites rather than combining it with the other dry ingredients?

6. What special precautions might you take if you were making French toast from thick slices of French bread?

7. What is curdling, and how can you prevent it when cooking with milk?

8. Why does cheese combine more smoothly with a sauce at low heat than at high heat?

9. Why is using the proper grind important in making coffee?

10. Describe the proper method for making tea.

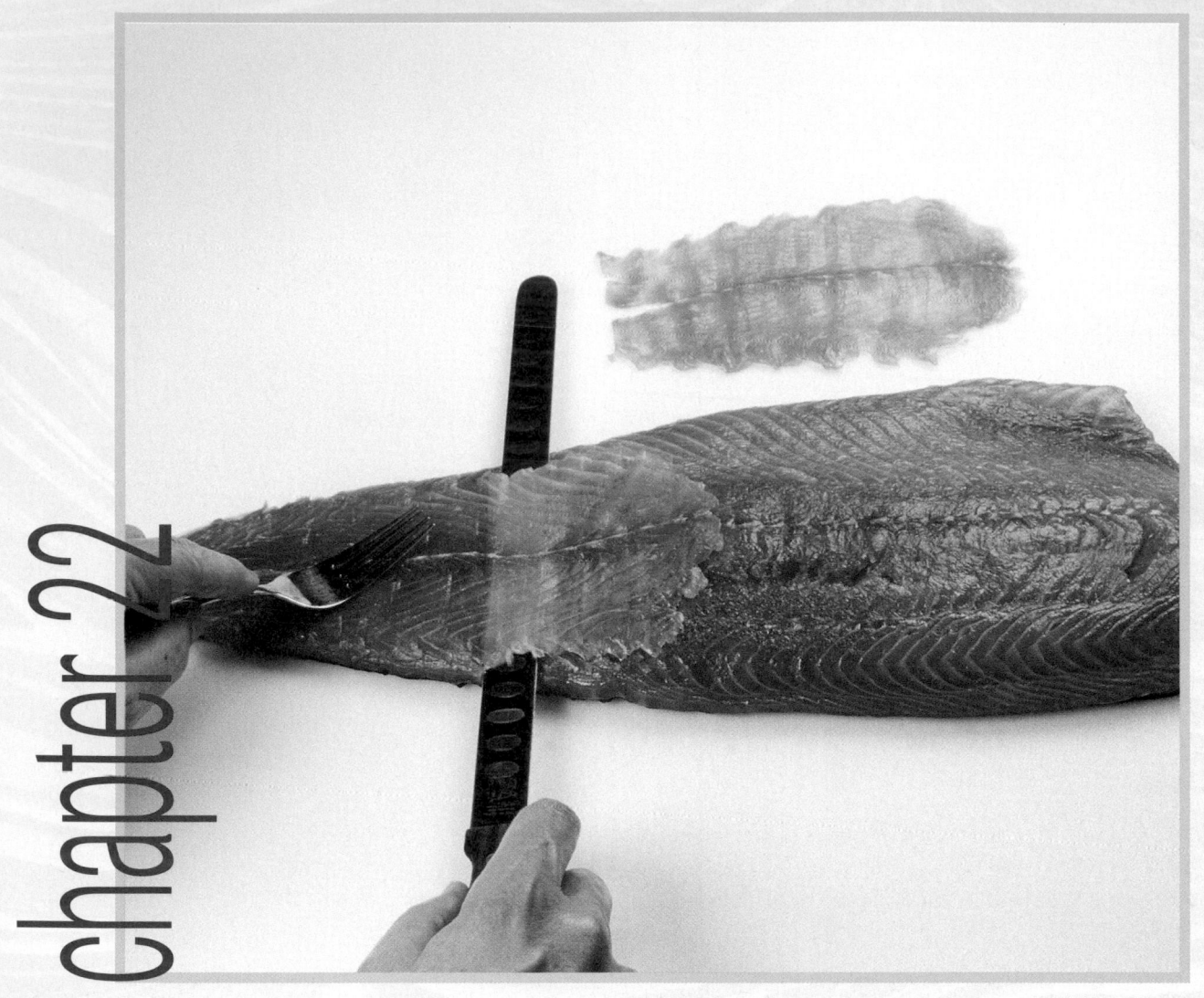

chapter 22

Sausages and Cured Foods

Sausages have been popular since ancient times. They were first made to utilize and preserve trimmings and less desirable cuts from a meat carcass. Most people have heard the expression about using "every part of the hog except the squeal." The preparation of sausages is an important part of this process.

The French term *charcutier* (shar koo tyay; the feminine form is *charcutière* [shar koo tyair]) means one who prepares cooked meat products, usually pork. The art of the charcutier is called *charcuterie* (shar koo tree). We use this term more generally to refer to the production of sausages, pâtés, and smoked ham and other cured and smoked products.

The main part of this chapter is devoted to the production of fresh sausages, which are easily prepared in any kitchen with relatively simple equipment. We also introduce the subject of cured and smoked sausages with an overview of curing and smoking. Preparing smoked hams and cured, air-dried meat products is an advanced subject that is beyond the scope of this book. However, reading the first section of this chapter will enable you to understand how these items are produced. A small sampling of recipes gives you some experience with curing and smoking before you proceed to the main section on sausages.

Curing and Smoking

Curing and smoking have been important methods for preserving foods, especially protein foods, since prehistoric times. Before the days of modern preservation techniques such as canning, freezing, and refrigeration, curing and smoking, as well as drying, have enabled people to store food in times of abundance for use in times of scarcity. Today we use these techniques for their contribution to flavor perhaps even more than their preservative qualities. We smoke foods because we like the taste, not because we must in order to preserve them.

Nevertheless, it is important to understand how curing works to preserve foods so that we can avoid spoilage and food-borne disease that can result from improper curing or improper handling of cured foods.

INGREDIENTS FOR CURING FOODS

Ingredients used in cures fill two main functions: preserving the food, and changing its flavor and texture. The following discussion of cure ingredients and processes is somewhat simplified, but it introduces the most important principles.

Salt

Salt has been one of the most important food preservatives throughout most of human history. When a food comes in direct contact with salt, a two-way process takes place in an effort to make the salt concentrations inside and outside the food more nearly equal. Moisture from inside the cell walls of the food is drawn out and dilutes the salt used for the cure. At the same time, dissolved salt is absorbed into the cells to increase the salt concentration there. The result is foods that have less moisture and are saltier. Both the moisture reduction and the increased salt content make the food less hospitable to bacteria that cause spoilage and disease.

Of course, the reduced moisture and the increased salt content also change the flavor and texture of the food.

Clockwise from top: table salt, curing salt, kosher salt.

Nitrites and Nitrates

Some foods, especially meats, are susceptible to contamination by the bacteria that cause botulism (see p. 17). Nitrites and nitrates are added to the cures for these foods to make them safe from botulism infection. Sodium nitrite ($NaNO_2$) is the most important of these chemicals. Even in the very small quantities in which it is used, sodium nitrite has strong preservative powers. In addition, it keeps meats red or pink, which is why products like cured ham, corned beef, and certain sausages have their characteristic color.

Nitrites gradually break down inside the cured foods, but by the time they lose their effectiveness, the curing and, in some cases, smoking procedures are finished, the food is cooked or refrigerated, and the food remains safe. On the other hand, when the food is raw and air-dried, as in the case of prosciutto and various salamis, a stronger chemical, sodium nitrate ($NaNO_3$) is used. Nitrates break down more slowly than nitrites and therefore are effective for a longer time. (Potassium nitrate, or saltpeter, is sometimes used in cures, but it is not as safe and is strongly regulated. It should be avoided.)

Nitrates and nitrites are the subject of controversy regarding their safety. Substances called *nitrosamines* form when foods containing nitrates or nitrites are subjected to very high heat, such as when bacon is fried. Nitrosamines are known to cause cancer. Using only nitrites to cure foods usually avoids this problem because the nitrites break down quickly and are not usually a factor when the food is cooked. Nitrates, on the other hand, because they remain in meats longer, should not be used for curing bacon for this reason.

Some people feel that all use of nitrites and nitrates should be avoided because of the nitrosamine factor. However, if only nitrites and not nitrates are used in foods that will be exposed to extreme heat, the risk is low—much lower than the risk of botulism. So far, we know of no adequate substitute for these chemicals in curing pork and other meats.

Two special mixtures are employed that make it easy to add nitrites and nitrates in very low but sufficient concentration:

1. **Prague Powder #1**, or *curing salt*, is a blend of 6 percent sodium nitrite and 94 percent sodium chloride, or regular table salt. It is colored pink so that it will not be confused with regular salt, and thus it is often called *tinted curing mix* (TCM). It is also sold under various trade names, such as InstaCure I.

2. **Prague Powder #2** is similar to Prague Powder #1 except that it contains nitrates in addition to nitrites. It is used in curing products that have a long curing and drying period, as explained above. Prague Powder #2 is not used in any of the recipes in this chapter. Air-dried cured meats require advanced procedures that are beyond the scope of this book.

Fish and seafood are usually cured without the use of nitrites. Fish is almost always cured under refrigeration and the salt cure is sufficient to protect it, even when it is cold smoked (p. 646).

The quantity of nitrite to be added to meats depends on several factors, including the type of meat, the type of cure, and the length of curing time. For cooked sausage, the U.S. Department of Agriculture recommends 156 parts nitrite per million parts meat. This is equivalent to 1 ounce (30 g) nitrite per 400 pounds (192 kg) meat. To translate this to quantities similar to those used in this chapter, 10 pounds (4.5 kg) cooked sausage requires about 0.025 ounces (0.7 g) nitrite. This is the amount of nitrite contained in 0.4 ounces or 2 teaspoons (11 g or 10 mL) Prague Powder #1.

Keep in mind, however, that not all the nitrite specified in a recipe may be absorbed into the meat. In the case of the basic dry cures and brine cures (described below), part of the curing medium is discarded after the cure is complete. Therefore, enough nitrite must be used so that the portion that is absorbed is adequate for the cure. The only exception is the case of sausages, in which all of the curing medium is mixed directly with the meat. The recipes in this book contain appropriate quantities of nitrite to cure the product.

Sugars

Ordinary white sugar (sucrose) and other forms of sugar, including corn syrup, honey, and maple syrup, are used in some cures. Sugars modify the flavor of the food and counteract some of the harsh flavor of the highly concentrated salt in the cure. Also, because salt extracts so much moisture, sugar adds to the perception of moistness in the cured product. Using less sweet forms of sugar, such as corn syrup and dextrose, provides the advantages of sugar without adding too much sweetness.

Herbs, Spices, and Other Flavorings

Nearly any spice or flavoring that can be used in cooking can be used in curing. Traditional recipes, of course, use traditional seasonings. Most of our most familiar cured sausages, for example, are of European origin and use such seasonings as garlic, pepper, coriander, caraway, nutmeg, and dry mustard. In addition, many chefs today are experimenting with unusual ingredients to give a modern accent to cured meats, poultry, fish, and sausages.

CURING METHODS

The two basic types of cures are *dry cures* and *brines*. With both of these methods, the food item remains in contact with the curing mixture, which contains salt plus any of the other ingredients discussed above, until the curing medium has penetrated the food uniformly. The difference between the methods is that in brines, the salt is dissolved in water, whereas in dry cures, it is not.

Dry Cures

In a dry cure, the cure ingredients (salt, plus seasonings and, in many cases, sugar and Prague Powder) are mixed together and packed or rubbed over the food product to coat it completely.

The length of time required to dry-cure meats depends on their thickness. Lean meat 1 inch (2.5 cm) thick requires 3 to 8 hours, while a whole ham needs about 45 days. During a long cure, the food is repeatedly turned and rubbed with the cure mixture in order to maintain uniform contact. It is important that the entire surface area be coated.

The curing procedure for sausages could be considered a dry cure. However, in this case, the cure is mixed directly with the meat. Because no time is required for the cure to penetrate to the center of the meat, the curing process takes place very quickly, although the products may be air-dried or smoked for a longer period before being consumed.

Brine Cures

A brine is a solution of salt and other curing ingredients in water. The simplest way to use a brine is to immerse the meat in the brine and let it soak until the cure is complete. Compared with dry cures, brines are especially useful for poultry items, which are difficult to coat evenly with a dry cure because of their shape. Items that float, such as poultry, must be held down with a weight so that they are completely submerged in the brine.

Simple brine soaking is used for small meat items, but because the brine takes time to penetrate to the center of large items such as hams, another method is used to speed the process. Brine is pumped or injected into the meat to make sure that it penetrates evenly. After injection, the meat may then be soaked in brine as well. Commercial operations use a variety of high-speed equipment for injecting brine. In addition, small pumps are available for brining by hand.

The length of time required for brining depends on the size and thickness of the item. Of course, meats that have been injected with brine need less time in the brine soak.

Fresh brine should be made for each batch of cured meats. Do not reuse brines because they are diluted and contaminated with juices from the first batch of meats.

SMOKING

Smoking has been used as a way of drying and preserving foods since prehistoric times. Smoking does have some preservative effects but, for modern cooking, it is more important for the flavors that it gives to meats, poultry, and seafood. Even smoked cheeses and vegetables are enjoyed for their special flavors.

The first rule of smoking foods is *do not smoke meats, poultry, and fish that have not been cured.* The reason for this rule is a matter of food safety. During smoking, foods spend a period of time in the Food Danger Zone (p. 15), that is, at a temperature that is favorable for the growth of bacteria. Without the preservative effects of curing, smoking could be unsafe. (This rule does not apply to *smoke roasting* and *barbecuing* (pp. 57–58), which are more properly considered cooking methods rather than smoking methods because they take place at higher temperatures.)

After meats, poultry, and fish are cured, they should be allowed to dry slightly before being smoked. So that air can circulate all around the foods, place them on racks or hang them from hooks under refrigeration until the surface is dry to the touch. This preliminary drying allows the smoke to penetrate the foods more effectively.

The two basic types of smoking are *cold smoking* and *hot smoking*. In cold smoking, the temperature inside the smokehouse is kept at or below 85°F (30°C). At these temperatures, the foods take on the flavor of the smoke but are not cooked.

In hot smoking, the temperature inside the smokehouse may be as high as 165°F (74°C) for sausage and meats, or as high as 200°F (93°F) for fish and poultry. These temperatures are high enough to cook the foods being smoked. Higher temperatures are usually avoided because they result in excessive shrinkage. Foods may be hot smoked until they reach an internal temperature of 150° to 165°F (65° to 74°C) to ensure that they are fully cooked. Alternatively, they may be hot smoked for a shorter period and then poached until they reach this internal temperature. This second method is used when a less intense smoke flavor is desired. No matter which method is used, hot-smoked foods are always sold fully cooked.

A typical smoker consists of the following elements:

- An enclosed chamber for holding the foods to be smoked
- A source of smoke

- A means to circulate the smoke around the food and then to exhaust it
- A way of controlling the temperature inside the chamber

The smoke source consists of a receptacle for wood chips or sawdust plus a heating element, usually electric. If the smoker is to be used for cold smoking, the smoke generator should be outside the main chamber that holds the food. If the smoke generator is inside the food chamber, as in some less expensive smokers, the temperature will rise too high for cold smoking. This type of smoker is used only for hot smoking. Foods to be smoked are arranged on racks or hung from hangers with enough space between them so that the smoke circulates freely around all surfaces. Commercially made smokers are safest to use, as improperly built smokers may present a fire hazard. In addition, if a smoker is used indoors, it is essential to provide for ventilation of the exhausted smoke to the outdoors.

Hickory is perhaps the most popular wood for smoking, but other hardwoods that may be used include oak, mesquite, and fruitwoods such as apple and cherry. Soft woods, like pine, are not used because they release bitter, tarry components when burned. It is important to use woods from a reliable source. Pressure-treated woods should never be used, as they contain toxic chemicals such as arsenic.

To summarize, the smoking process consists of the following steps:

1. Curing (dry cure or brine cure)
2. Air-drying
3. Smoking (hot smoking or cold smoking)

Gravlax

Yield: 1 lb 14 oz (850 g) without skin

U.S.	Metric	Ingredients
2½ lb	1.2 kg	Salmon fillet, skin on
4 oz	125 g	Coarse salt
4 oz	125 g	Sugar
¼ tsp	1 mL	White pepper
2 oz	60 g	Fresh dill sprigs

Per 1 ounce:
Calories, 70; Protein, 8 g; Fat, 4 g (50% cal.); Cholesterol, 20 mg; Carbohydrates, 1 g; Fiber, 0 g; Sodium, 240 mg.

PROCEDURE

1. Pass the fingertips over the surface of the salmon fillet to locate any bones. Pull them out with needlenose pliers.
2. Mix together the salt, sugar, and pepper.
3. Select a stainless-steel, glass, ceramic, or other nonreactive pan to hold the salmon for curing. Sprinkle a little of the salt mixture on the bottom of the pan and lay the salmon on it skin side down. Cover the flesh side of the fillet completely with a layer of the salt mixture. Then top with the dill, again covering the fillet completely.
4. If you are doubling this recipe and curing 2 fillets, salt the second fillet in the same manner and invert it on top of the first so that the dill is sandwiched between the fillets and the skin side of each fillet is toward the outside.
5. Cover the pan well and refrigerate for 1 day. Turn the fillet or fillets over and refrigerate for another day (for a total of 2 days). Note: Some instructions say to place a weight on the fish during the cure. This is optional. Weighting the fish produces a slightly drier, firmer finished product.
6. After 2 days, drain off any liquid that has accumulated in the pan. Carefully scrape all the dill and curing mixture from the fish.
7. To serve, cut on a sharp diagonal—that is, with the knife almost parallel to the table—into broad, paper-thin slices (Figure 22.1).

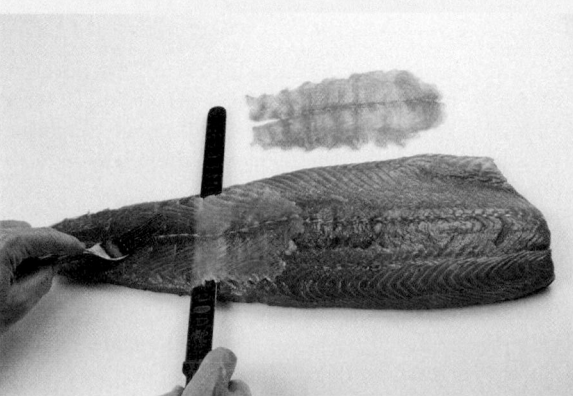

Figure 22.1 Slice gravlax and smoked salmon on the diagonal into paper-thin slices. Cut toward the tail end.

Smoked Salmon

Yield: 1 lb 14 oz (850 g) without skin

U.S.	Metric	Ingredients	PROCEDURE
2½ lb	1.2 kg	Salmon fillet, skin on	
6 oz	180 g	Coarse salt	
3 oz	90 g	Sugar	
2 tsp	10 mL	Coarse black pepper	
1 tsp	5 mL	Dry mustard	
½ tsp	2 mL	Allspice, ground	
¼ tsp	1 mL	Cayenne	
2 oz	60 g	Onion, chopped fine	

1. Pass the fingertips over the surface of the salmon fillet to locate any bones. Pull them out with needlenose pliers.
2. Mix together the salt, sugar, pepper, dry mustard, allspice, and cayenne.
3. Select a stainless-steel, glass, ceramic, or other nonreactive pan to hold the salmon for curing. Sprinkle a little of the salt mixture on the bottom of the pan and lay the salmon on it skin side down. Cover the flesh side of the fillet completely with a layer of the salt mixture. Then top with the chopped onion, distributing it evenly over the fillet.
4. If you are doubling this recipe and curing 2 fillets, salt the second fillet in the same manner and invert it on top of the first so that the onion is sandwiched between the fillets and the skin side of each fillet is toward the outside.
5. Cover the pan well and refrigerate for 12–24 hours.
6. Remove the fillet from the pan and rinse off all the salt mixture and onion. Place on a rack set on a sheet pan, skin side down, and allow to dry, uncovered, in the refrigerator until a thin, dry skin has formed on the surface of the flesh.
7. Cold smoke at 86°F (30°C).
8. To serve, cut on a sharp diagonal—that is, with the knife almost parallel to the table—into broad, paper-thin slices.

Per 1 ounce:
Calories, 70; Protein, 8 g; Fat, 4 g (53% cal.); Cholesterol, 25 mg;
Carbohydrates, 0 g; Fiber, 0 g; Sodium, 240 mg.

Smoked Trout

Yield: 10 fillets, 6–7 oz (180–200 g) each

U.S.	Metric	Ingredients	PROCEDURE
2 qt	2 L	Water	
8 oz	250 g	Salt	
2 oz	60 g	Light brown sugar	
4	4	Bay leaves	
2 tsp	10 mL	Black peppercorns	
1 tsp	5 mL	Whole coriander seed	
½ tsp	2 mL	Whole allspice	
½ tsp	2 mL	Dry mustard	

1. Prepare the brine: Combine the water, salt, sugar, bay leaves, peppercorns, coriander, allspice, and mustard in a pot. Bring to a simmer, stirring until the salt and sugar are dissolved.
2. Cool, then chill the brine.

U.S.	Metric	Ingredients	PROCEDURE
10	10	Trout fillets, about 8 oz (250 g) each	

3. Place the trout fillets in a stainless-steel, plastic, or other nonreactive pan in a single layer. Add enough cold brine to completely cover the fillets. Place a light weight on top of the fish to keep them submerged.
4. Refrigerate for 6–8 hours.
5. Remove from the brine and rinse in cold water. Blot dry.
6. Arrange on racks and allow to dry for several hours in the refrigerator.
7. Hot smoke at 185°F (85°C) until the internal temperature of the fish reaches 145°F (63°C), about 1–1½ hours. Cool, then refrigerate.

Per serving:
Calories, 320; Protein, 47 g; Fat, 12 g (36% cal.); Cholesterol, 135 mg;
Carbohydrates, 2 g; Fiber, 0 g; Sodium, 3420 mg.

Smoked Duck

Yield: 2 smoked ducks

U.S.	Metric	Ingredients	PROCEDURE
1½ gal	6 L	Water	1. Prepare the brine. Heat the water in a pot until it is warm. Add the salt, sugar, and Prague Powder and stir until they are dissolved. Add the bay leaves and onion powder.
12 oz	360 g	Salt	
6 oz	180 g	Sugar	
3 oz	90 g	Prague Powder #1	2. Cool, then chill the brine.
3	3	Bay leaves	
2 tsp	10 mL	Onion powder	
2	2	Small ducks, about 4 lb (1.8 kg) each	3. Place the ducks in a stainless-steel, plastic, or other nonreactive container. Pour enough brine over them to cover them completely. Weight them to keep them submerged.
			4. Allow to cure in the refrigerator for 2 days. (Note: Large ducks take 3–4 days to cure.)
			5. Remove the ducks from the brine and rinse well.
			6. Place on a rack and let dry in the refrigerator for at least 8 hours.
			7. Hot smoke at 185°F (85°C) until the internal temperature of the duck reaches 165°F (74°C).

Per serving:
Calories, 510; Protein, 79 g; Fat, 17 g (32% cal.); Cholesterol, 305 mg; Carbohydrates, 4 g; Fiber, 0 g; Sodium, 4330 mg.

VARIATIONS

Smoked Turkey or Chicken

Brine the turkey or chicken as in the basic recipe. Turkey requires 4–6 days to cure in the brine, depending on the size. Chickens require 2–4 days, depending on their size.

Sausages

A sausage is a mixture of ground meat, usually pork, and seasonings stuffed into a casing. The term *sausage* may also be used for the meat mixture itself, without the casing. Reduced to its simplest form, sausage meat may be nothing more than ground pork seasoned with salt.

Although there are hundreds or even thousands of kinds of sausages, the majority are based on the same few basic principles. These principles are simple enough that we can make a wide variety of sausages in the kitchen and not have to rely entirely on commercially made ones. Furthermore, it is not necessary to restrict ourselves to traditional sausage recipes. Many chefs are experimenting with ingredients and seasonings to add variety to the menu.

CATEGORIES OF SAUSAGES

Sausages can be classified into three basic groups:

Fresh sausages
Cured sausages
Smoked sausages

A *fresh sausage*, by USDA definition, is one that contains no nitrates or nitrites. It is basically a mixture of ground meat, seasonings, and flavorings. Although they are often raw, fresh sausages may contain cooked ingredients, or they may even be fully cooked before being sold. Any fresh raw sausage containing pork, of course, must be fully cooked before being served and eaten.

A *cured sausage* is one that contains nitrites or nitrates of sodium. These chemicals help prevent spoilage and food-borne disease, as explained in the first part of this chapter, and, incidentally, they also keep the meat red or pink, even when cooked. Cured sausages may be sold raw or cooked, soft and moist like fresh sausages, semidried and firm, or dried and hard like salami.

Pork salamis, which are Italian in origin, and similar cured, dried sausages are raw, but the curing, aging, and drying process renders them safe to eat. As explained on page 644, air-dried sausages that are intended to be eaten raw are made with nitrates in addition to nitrites for a longer lasting cure.

Smoked sausages may be hot smoked and, therefore, cooked, or cold smoked. Smoking may be light or heavy, depending on the sausage. Sausages, like other smoked meats, are cured before being smoked. The cure mixture is mixed directly with the sausage meat.

BASIC SAUSAGE INGREDIENTS

The basic ingredients of sausage meat are the following:

Lean pork
Pork fat, preferably hard fatback, ground with the meat
Salt
Spices, herbs, and other seasonings and flavorings

In the case of cured sausage, curing mixes containing nitrites or nitrates are added to the above list.

The Meat

Pork is the most commonly used meat in sausage making, but other meats or mixtures of meat may be used. Beef, veal, lamb, chicken, turkey, duck, liver, rabbit, and venison all find their way into sausages. Mixtures of pork plus one or more of these meats are often used. More exotic sausages may include such ingredients as sweetbreads and brains.

Certified pork, that is, pork that is certified to be free of trichinosis, is used for sausages that are to be air-dried and eaten uncooked.

The Fat

Pork fat or other fat, such as the beef fat used in all-beef sausages, is an important ingredient. Because our impression of juiciness in any cooked meat is largely due to the meat's fat content, some fat is included in sausage mixtures. Without it, the texture of the cooked sausage would be very dry.

In most traditional sausages, fat makes up 25 to 50 percent of the total weight, with 33 percent fat being the norm. In other words, proportions of fat to lean range from 3 parts lean plus 1 part fat (the leanest sausages) to 1 part lean plus 1 part fat (rich, fatty sausages). Varying the proportions changes the character of the sausage.

Hard fatback is preferred over other fats for pork sausage. Softer fats are more likely to melt out of the sausage during cooking. A quick and easy way to make pork sausages without worrying about the ratio of fat to lean is to use whole pork butt. The ratio of fat to lean in this cut is very good for sausages.

In today's diet-conscious atmosphere, it may make sense to try to create low-fat sausages. But be advised that extra care is required when making sausages with less than 25 percent fat. Lean sausages should never be overcooked, as overcooking makes them dry. Keep the meat mixture cold to avoid damage to the texture of the meat and fat. With care, it is possible to make tasty sausages with a fat content as low as 10 or 15 percent. One should not expect, however, that the eating qualities of lean sausages be the same as those of fattier sausages.

Cereal ingredients and fillers (rice, barley, bread crumbs, and so on) can be used to help reduce fat content. Because these starches absorb and retain moisture, they enhance the total moisture content of low-fat sausages.

Seasonings

Herbs, spices, and other flavorings account for the primary differences among sausages. Many, if not most, of the world's fresh sausages are made of nothing more than ground pork and seasonings. It is the seasonings that give them their characteristic flavor. A glance at the recipes in this section will confirm this.

Some of the major spices and herbs used in sausage making are

Allspice	Cumin	Paprika
Caraway seeds	Fennel seed	Parsley
Cayenne or	Ginger	Pepper, black and white
hot red pepper	Mace	Sage
Cinnamon	Marjoram	Tarragon
Cloves	Mustard	Thyme
Coriander	Nutmeg	

Other important ingredients include

Garlic	Chives	Vinegar
Onion	Wine, white	Eggs
Shallots	and red	

Standardized spice mixtures are often used to season sausages, pâtés, and similar items. One of the most common is *quatre épices* (French for "four spices"), a mixture that exists in many versions. It can usually be obtained commercially, or it can be homemade, using recipes such as those on page 657.

Cure Mixes

Sausages that are to be air-dried are cured with both nitrate and nitrite, as explained on page 644. For other cured sausages, only nitrite, usually in the form of Prague Powder #1, is used. Other ingredients, such as dextrose and additional salt, may be combined with the Prague Powder to make the cure mix. The cure mix may be incorporated into the sausage in one of two ways:

1. It may be mixed with the meat after it is diced. The diced meat is then chilled thoroughly before being ground.

2. It may be combined with the remaining spices and seasonings and mixed into the ground meat.

Refer to individual recipes for more detailed instructions on making and incorporating cure mixes.

Other Ingredients

A number of sausages are characterized by unusual or exotic ingredients. Some of these are traditional and time-honored, such as the black truffles included in some regional French sausages and the chestnuts or raisins in other specialty sausages.

Other unusual sausages are modern innovations by creative chefs. It is no longer uncommon, when reading today's restaurant menus, to come across sausages with such ingredients as sun-dried tomatoes or fresh vegetables like sweet bell peppers and spinach. In theory, there is no limit to what can be stuffed into sausage casings. The main requirement is that the ingredients complement or enhance one another, just as the meat, seasonings, and vegetable garnish on a dinner plate should complement one another.

CASINGS

Natural casings are made from the intestines of meat animals. *Sheep casings* are the smallest, ranging from ¾ inch (18 mm) to more than 1 inch (25 mm) in diameter. They are used for breakfast links, frankfurters, and similar sausages. *Hog casings* are medium-sized, about 1 to 1½ inches (3 to 4 cm) in diameter, depending on what part of the intestines they are taken from. They are used for many popular fresh sausages, such as Italian sausages and fresh bratwurst. *Beef casings* range in size from the so-called *beef round*, about 1¾ inches (45 mm) in diameter, through *beef middles*, 2½ inches (63 mm), to the large *beef bung*, more than 4 inches (100 mm) in diameter.

Natural casings are often sold packed in salt. Because of the preservative effect of the salt, the casings keep indefinitely as long as they are refrigerated. Natural casings are easy to use if they are handled correctly. Before being stuffed, they must be untangled, rinsed, and flushed, and examined for holes according to the following procedure.

Procedure for Preparing Natural Casings

1. Carefully remove the casings, one at a time, from the salt pack and unravel them. Because a single casing may be 12 feet (4 meters) long, it is easiest to do this on a large workbench. Separate the individual lengths and keep them separate in their own little stacks on the bench. When unraveling them, do not pull hard, because this may cause knotting.

   Unravel slightly more casing than you think you will need. It is easier to return unused casings to the salt pack than it is to separate and flush additional casings when you run out before you have stuffed your whole batch of meat.

2. Partially fill a large bowl with clean water and set it in a sink under the faucet. Take hold of the end of one casing and drop the rest of it into the bowl of water. Open the end of the casing and run cold water into it, enough to fill about 12 inches (30 cm) of it. Holding the casing at both ends of this "water sausage," allow the water to flush through the casing from one end to the other.

   This accomplishes two purposes. It rinses out the inside of the casing, and it identifies any holes that might be present. Pinpoint-size holes are no problem, but if a large hole is found, simply cut the casing in two at that point. Short pieces may be discarded for the sake of efficiency. Refer to Figure 22.2, page 654.

3. If you are making a small quantity of sausages and stuffing them immediately, each casing can be put on the stuffing horn as it is rinsed. If this is not the case, they must be stored for later use. Select a container with a cover and fill it about three-fourths full of cold water. Drop in the casing and let one end hang over the edge.

   Repeat with remaining casings. Fill the container to the top with cold water, cover, and refrigerate until needed. By letting the ends of the casings hang over the edge, you can remove one at a time from the container without tangling them. If the end of the casing dries out, simply cut it off.

Because the supply of natural casings is not nearly large enough to accommodate all the sausages produced, other types of casings have come into wide use. *Collagen casings* are molded from animal materials and are completely edible, like natural casings. Unlike natural casings, they are uniform in size, making portion control easier. Various types are manufactured for different uses. Some are used only for fresh sausages, as they are not strong enough to hold the weight of the sausages if they are hung for smoking. Other types are stronger and intended to be used for smoked sausages. Most collagen casings must be refrigerated to keep them from becoming dry and brittle. To use, dip them in water for a few seconds to soften them if they are dry, then put them on the sausage stuffing nozzle.

Synthetic fibrous casings are made from a plastic material and are not edible. They are widely used for salamis and luncheon meats, and the casing is peeled off before or after slicing. These casings are nonperishable and need no refrigeration. They must be soaked in water before using to make them flexible. Soaking time varies, and the manufacturer should specify the recommended time.

EQUIPMENT

Most fresh sausages can be made with no special equipment other than a meat grinder and a device for getting the meat into the casings.

The working parts of a meat grinder are a rotating blade and a selection of dies in various sizes. The size of the die determines the fineness of the grind. A screw forces the meat from the feed tube to the blade, and the blade chops the meat as it is forced through the holes of the die.

Before grinding meat, it is important to be sure of the following two points:

1. The equipment must be clean and sanitary. Make sure that there is no trace of food from previous jobs hiding in the many nooks and crannies of the grinder, blades, and dies.

2. The equipment must be cold in order to avoid warming the meat. Refrigerate the grinder parts or set them in ice water before use.

The sausage stuffer is the second piece of equipment necessary for making sausages. The simplest stuffer resembles a funnel. The casings are pushed over the narrow end and the meat is pushed through the wide end by hand or with a wooden plunger. These are adequate for making a few pounds of sausage but are not suitable for larger batches.

Larger stuffers have detachable nozzles or horns of various sizes for different sizes of casings. The nozzle is attached to a cylindrical reservoir that holds the meat, which is pushed through by a piston. On smaller machines, the piston is simply pushed through by hand. These machines are suitable for small-scale production such as might be done in a small to medium-size restaurant. For large-scale commercial production, larger machines are used. The piston in a large machine is operated by means of a crank and a sequence of gears.

THE GRIND

The grind of the meat determines the texture of the sausage. We can divide sausage meat into two categories based on grind. Most common sausages are made simply of meat and fat ground to varying degrees of fineness or coarseness, mixed with seasonings, and stuffed into casings. We refer to these as *basic grind* sausages. Some sausages, on the other hand, including familiar ones like frankfurters, mortadella, and bologna, are made with meat and fat ground to a smooth purée and blended with a little liquid, such as water or milk. We refer to these as *emulsified* or *emulsion grind* sausages because of the added liquid content and the emulsion of the fat with the meat and liquid.

Basic Grind

The fineness or coarseness of the grind is an important characteristic of any sausage. For example, one identifying feature of Toulouse Sausages (p. 658) is their coarse texture. The meat is chopped by hand rather than ground. On the other hand, typical breakfast sausages have a fairly fine grind.

To grind meat, cut it into pieces small enough to fit easily into the feed tube of the grinder, then chill it well. Control the coarseness of the grind by selecting the proper die, as indicated in the recipe. In some cases, fine grinds are made by grinding the meat once through the large die and a second time through the fine die. As indicated in the procedure below, the meat, fat, and seasonings are mixed until uniformly blended after the meat is ground.

The meat mixture must be kept cold during grinding. When the mixture gets too warm, the fat becomes soft and begins to lose its structure. As a result, it may melt out too readily when the sausage is cooked, resulting in excessive shrinkage, poor texture, and dryness. If the kitchen is warm, return the meat to the refrigerator to chill it thoroughly after cutting it up and before grinding it. If it must be ground more than once, return it to the refrigerator between grindings.

Additional textural variation in basic grind sausages can be created by mixing chunks or dice of meat or other ingredients into a more finely ground forcemeat, as is often done in pâtés.

When following any recipe, adhere closely to the grinding and processing directions in order to achieve the proper texture and character of the sausage.

Procedure for Making Fresh and Cured Basic Grind Sausages

Figure 22.2 Stuffing sausages.

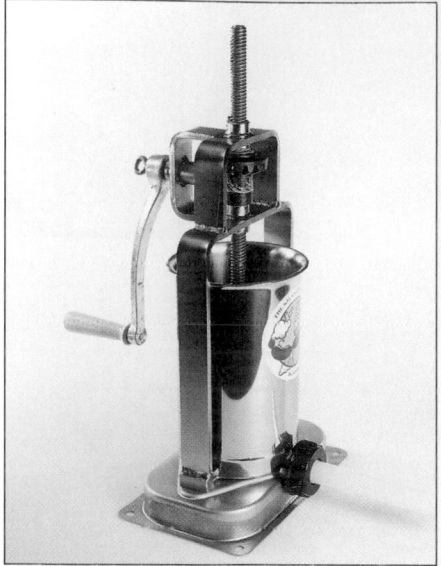

(a) A small sausage stuffer fitted with a medium nozzle. This stuffer holds 5 pounds (2.3 kg) meat at a time.

(b) Flush out the casings with fresh, cold water, while looking for holes.

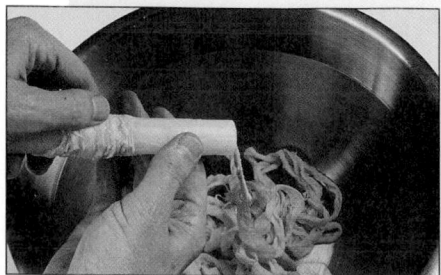

(c) Slide the casings onto the proper size nozzle.

1. Weigh the meats and fat. Cut them into chunks small enough to fit into the grinder.

2. If the sausages are to be cured, toss the cure mix with the diced meat at this point. Alternatively, combine the cure mix with the salt and spices in step 4.

3. Chill the meat well before proceeding.

4. Measure the salt and spices.

5. Grind the meat and fat, following the directions in the recipe to achieve the proper fineness or coarseness of grind.

6. Chill the meat well. Ideally, the meat should be chilled to 32° to 35°F (0° to 2°C) before mixing and stuffing.

7. Combine the meat, salt, and spices and mix thoroughly. This is best done by hand in a large tub or other container. It can also be done with a mixing machine using the paddle attachment.

    If the recipe calls for cold water or other liquid, mix the salt and spices with the water first, then mix this combination with the meat. This facilitates a better distribution of the spices than mixing them dry with the meat.

    Many recipes say to refrigerate the meat overnight after it is mixed to allow the meat to absorb the seasonings and the flavors to blend. However, it is easier to stuff the sausages immediately after mixing. If the salted meat mixture is allowed to stand, it becomes firmer and thus harder to force through the stuffer. Stuffing immediately allows the casings to be filled more uniformly and with fewer air bubbles. Besides, the meat can absorb the seasonings just as well in the casings as in the meat tub.

8. Test for seasonings. Do not taste the raw meat. Rather, make a small ball or patty and cook it in a small sauté pan or poach it in water. Then cool the meat slightly and taste. If more salt or other seasoning is needed, add it to the sausage mixture.

9. Place the meat in the stuffer, one handful at a time. Pack each handful firmly into the stuffer to eliminate air bubbles.

10. Slide the casings onto the nozzle. To help the casings slide on easily, moisten both them and the stuffer nozzle with water.

11. Stuff the sausages, following the directions for your particular equipment (see Figure 22.2). The sausages will pull the casings off the nozzle as the meat flows through it, but it is best to hold your hand at the end of the nozzle to help control the rate at which the casing is pulled from the nozzle. From time to time, as the casing is filled, it is necessary to push the bunched-up, unfilled casing toward the end of the nozzle so that it will slide off more easily. Do not stuff the casings too tightly. If the meat is packed too tightly, it will be difficult to twist the sausage into links.

12. After all the meat is stuffed into casings, remove any air bubbles by pricking the casing and pressing the surface to expel the air.

13. Twist the sausage into links of uniform size.

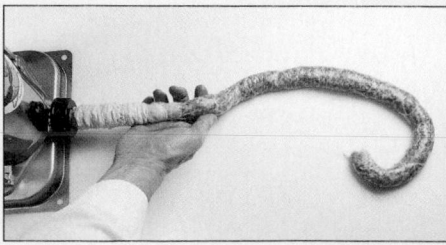

(d) When stuffing the casings, use the hand to guide the casing as it slides off the nozzle.

(e) Pinch and twist the sausage into links of the desired size.

Emulsified Grind

In the finest-textured sausages, the meat is actually puréed to a smooth paste. Puréed raw meat is capable of absorbing a good deal of moisture, and water or milk is usually added to improve the texture. For sausages that include milk, a recipe may indicate either liquid milk or water plus dried milk solids. The dried milk is added at the same time as the spice mixture.

Because grinding meat to a smooth paste generates heat, water is added in the form of ice to keep the temperature low. If liquid milk is called for, freeze the milk into chunks.

Because a meat grinder is not capable of grinding sausage to this texture, the grinding procedure is done in two stages. First, grind the meat and fat separately using the fine die on the meat grinder. Keep the two separate and chill them after this grinding. Second, grind the meat to a smooth paste with a food chopper (buffalo chopper) or food processor. Place the lean meat in the bowl of the chopper and run it a few seconds. Then add the ice and continue to grind until smooth. Monitor the temperature carefully and do not allow it to rise above 50°F (10°C). Add the fat and continue to grind to blend it in. Continue to monitor the temperature. Do not allow it to rise above 58°F (14°C).

Emulsified sausages are usually cooked in water, then chilled in cold water after stuffing. If they are to be smoked, they are smoked first and then cooked.

Procedure for Making Fresh and Cured Emulsified Sausages

1. Keeping the meat and fat separate, grind them with the fine die of a meat grinder, following steps 1 through 6 of the basic sausage-making procedure above. Chill well.

2. If indicated in the recipe, mix the seasonings with the lean meat. (Alternatively, add the seasonings at the same time as the ice in step 3.)

3. Place the lean meat in the bowl of a food chopper or food processor. Run the chopper a few turns, then add the ice. Continue to chop to a fine paste. Do not allow the temperature to rise above 50°F (10°C).

4. Add the fat and continue to grind to blend it in. Continue to monitor the temperature and do not allow it to rise above 58°F (14°C).

5. Follow steps 8 through 12 in the procedure above to test the seasonings and stuff the casings.

SMOKING SAUSAGES

The procedure for smoking sausages is the same as for smoking other meats (see Figure 22.3). Refer to page 646 for basic information on smoking and follow the instructions in individual recipes. Note in particular the following points:

1. Only cured sausages should be smoked.

2. The sausages should be dried briefly before being smoked, like other smoked foods (see p. 646). Hang them so that air can circulate around them and allow to dry for about 1½ hours or as indicated in the recipe.

3. Hot smoke or cold smoke as indicated in the recipe. Air-dried sausages to be eaten raw are cold smoked. Sausages that are sold cooked are generally hot smoked. After smoking, they are usually poached to an internal temperature of 160° to 165°F (71° to 74°F), then cooled quickly in ice water and blotted dry.

COOKING SAUSAGES

Although sausages are sometimes ingredients or components of more elaborate dishes, they are also popular as stand-alone menu items like other meats. Preparation of sausages before

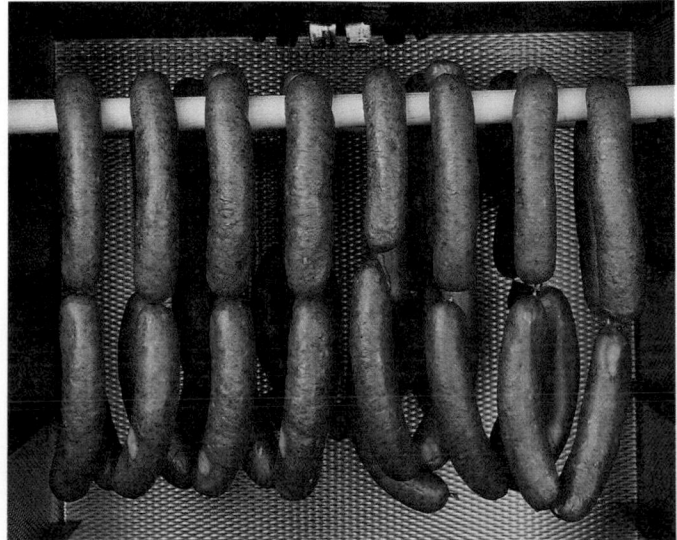

Figure 22.3 Finished sausages before removing from the smoker.

cooking is minimal. In most cases, sausages may be considered ready to cook—or, in the case of fully cooked sausages, ready to heat. Fresh raw sausages containing pork must be fully cooked before serving, like other fresh pork products. If a fresh sausage contains no pork, such as the lamb sausage on page 660, it may be served somewhat less done. Removing it from the heat when still pink inside helps to retain juices.

Fully cooked sausages need only be heated through before serving. Cooking times, however, are nearly the same as for raw sausages. In other words, the time it takes for the heat to penetrate to the center is about the same.

The following cooking methods are most often used for sausages.

Simmering

Place sausages in a pan with enough salted water to cover. Bring to a simmer and simmer until completely cooked. Do not let the water boil. This is likely to make the sausages burst or shrink excessively.

Time depends on the thickness of the sausage. Sausages in hog casings take about 20 minutes to cook; smaller ones may take as little as 10 minutes, larger ones 30 minutes or more.

Raw sausages may be simmered until cooked through, then finished by one of the following methods.

Sautéing and Pan-frying

Sausages are sautéed or pan fried using the same techniques as for other meats. For many kinds of sausages, the browning that results makes them more appetizing than simmered ones.

If the sausages are not raw, it is necessary only to cook them until they are lightly browned and heated through. If they are raw, lower heat is necessary so that they have time to become completely cooked by the time they are browned.

Sautéing and pan-frying are used not only for sausages in casings but also for patties and *crépinettes*, which are sausage patties wrapped in caul fat (see p. 658). Do not press on the patties with the spatula while cooking. This forces out juices and makes them dry.

Braising

Because fresh raw sausages may require long cooking times, braising is often the preferred cooking method. The sausages are browned by sautéing them over moderate heat for up to 5 minutes, then finished using a moist-heat cooking method. Cooking with moisture may take any of several forms, including the four methods listed below. These methods are suitable not only for fresh sausages but also for fully cooked and smoked sausages that are served hot.

- Covering the pan to hold in steam.
- Adding a small amount of liquid (water, stock, wine, and so on), covering the pan, and cooking until done.
- Glazing—that is, adding a small amount of stock and continuing to cook. The pan may be covered or left uncovered at the beginning, but the last part of cooking takes place with the cover off. The sausages are basted with the stock as it reduces, giving them a glaze. Any stock remaining in the pan after the sausages are cooked will be reduced and thickened, and it may be served with the sausages as a sauce. This cooking method is especially suitable for patties and crépinettes.
- Cooking the sausages in a casserole or stew after they are browned. Sauerkraut, bean dishes, and gumbos are examples.

Broiling and Grilling

Brush the sausages with oil to prevent sticking, and broil or grill as for other meats. Moderate heat is usually best. High heat may brown the sausages too much before they are fully cooked and is more likely to cause splitting.

ABOUT THE SAUSAGE RECIPES

Before proceeding to the sausage recipes that follow, please take note of the following points.

1. Refer to the general procedures for making sausages on pages 654–655. Some of these points are not repeated in each recipe.

2. Ratios of fat to lean are not specified in most of the recipes. Refer to the explanation of fat-lean ratios on page 650 and adjust the amount of fat in the recipes as desired.

Quatre Épices I

Yield: 1¼ oz (37 g)

U.S.	Metric	Ingredients
4 tbsp	25 g	Ground white or black pepper
2 tsp	4 g (10 mL)	Nutmeg
2 tsp	4 g (10 mL)	Ground cloves
2 tsp	4 g (10 mL)	Cinnamon

PROCEDURE

1. Combine ingredients and mix well.
2. Store in a tightly sealed container.

Per 1 ounce:
Calories, 90; Protein, 3 g; Fat, 2 g (13% cal.); Cholesterol, 0 mg;
Carbohydrates, 19 g; Fiber, 8 g; Sodium, 10 mg.

Quatre Épices II

Yield: 1¼ oz (34 g)

U.S.	Metric	Ingredients
10 tsp	20 g	Ground white pepper
3 tsp	6 g (15 mL)	Nutmeg
3 tsp	6 g (15 mL)	Powdered ginger
1 tsp	2 g (5 mL)	Ground cloves

PROCEDURE

1. Combine ingredients and mix well.
2. Store in a tightly sealed container.

Per 1 ounce:
Calories, 100; Protein, 3 g; Fat, 3 g (21% cal.); Cholesterol, 0 mg;
Carbohydrates, 18 g; Fiber, 7 g; Sodium, 5 mg.

Pork Sausage

Yield: 6 lb (3 kg)

U.S.	Metric	Ingredients	PROCEDURE
6 lb	3 kg	Pork and pork fat	1. Cut the meat and fat into cubes small enough to fit into the grinder. Chill thoroughly.
2 tbsp	30 g	Salt	
2 tsp	4 g (10 mL)	Quatre épices	2. Grind the meat once with the large die and again with the small die. If necessary, chill the meat between grindings.
6 oz	200 mL	Cold water	3. Mix the salt and spices with the water. Add to the ground meat and mix thoroughly by hand.
			4. Stuff into hog casings or sheep casings.

Per 1 ounce:
Calories, 70; Protein, 5 g; Fat, 5 g (69% cal.); Cholesterol, 20 mg;
Carbohydrates, 0 g; Fiber, 0 g; Sodium, 160 mg.

VARIATIONS

Toulouse Sausage

Use the ingredients specified in the recipe, but grind the meat coarsely. This can be done in three ways, with slightly different results for each method:

1. Chop the meat coarsely with a knife.
2. Grind only once using the large die of the grinder.
3. Grind very briefly in a food processor, just until achieving a coarse texture.

Stuff into hog casings.

Toulouse sausages should have a fat content of at least 33 percent—that is, 1 part fat to 2 parts lean.

Crépinettes

Weigh out 3½-oz (100-g) portions of sausage meat. Shape it into oval patties. Cut squares of caul fat (p. 233) and wrap the sausage portions in the squares. Cook by pan-frying, glazing (see p. 656), or grilling.

Other ingredients are often mixed with the sausage meat. Classic additions include blanched, peeled pistachios (2–3 oz per lb of sausage meat/125–175 g per kg); chopped, cooked chestnuts (4 oz per lb/250 g per kg); or fresh, diced truffle (whatever quantity the budget allows).

Other sausage mixtures, such as those in the other recipes in this section, may be used to make crépinettes.

French Garlic Sausage

Yield: 7 lb (3.5 kg)

U.S.	Metric	Ingredients	PROCEDURE
6 lb	3 kg	Pork and pork fat	1. Cut the meat and fat into cubes small enough to fit into the grinder. Chill thoroughly.
1 lb	500 g	Pork rind	
2 tbsp	30 g	Salt	2. Simmer the pork rind in salted water at least 2 hours, until very tender. Chill thoroughly.
1½ tsp	3 g (7 mL)	Black pepper	
2 tsp	8 g	Garlic, crushed	3. Grind the meat once with the large die and again with the medium die. If necessary, chill the meat between grindings.
½ tsp	2 mL	Ground sage	
½ tsp	2 mL	Marjoram	4. Repeat this grinding procedure with the pork rind. Mix the ground pork rind with the ground meat.
½ tsp	2 mL	Thyme	
4 oz	125 mL	Dry white wine	5. Mix the salt and spices with the wine. Add to the ground meat and mix thoroughly by hand.
			6. Stuff into hog casings.

Per 1 ounce:
Calories, 70; Protein, 5 g; Fat, 5 g (69% cal.); Cholesterol, 20 mg;
Carbohydrates, 0 g; Fiber, 0 g; Sodium, 150 mg.

Veal or Beef Sausage

Yield: 6 lb (3 kg)

U.S.	Metric	Ingredients	PROCEDURE
4 lb	2 kg	Pork and pork fat	1. Cut the meat into cubes small enough to fit into the grinder. Chill the meat thoroughly.
2 lb	1 kg	Veal or beef, lean	
2 tbsp	30 g	Salt	2. Grind the meat once with the large or medium die for coarse sausage. For a finer texture, grind once more with the small die. If necessary, chill the meat between grindings.
2 tsp	4 g (10 mL)	Quatre épices	
6 oz	200 mL	Cold water	3. Mix the salt and spices with the water. Add to the ground meat and mix thoroughly by hand.
			4. Stuff into hog casings.

Per 1 ounce:
Calories, 60; Protein, 5 g; Fat, 4 g (64% cal.); Cholesterol, 20 mg;
Carbohydrates, 0 g; Fiber, 0 g; Sodium, 170 mg.

VARIATIONS

Instead of the meat ratios given in the main recipe, use 3 lb (1.5 kg) pork and pork fat and 3 lb (1.5 kg) veal or beef. These proportions make a somewhat leaner sausage with more of the flavor of the veal or beef.

Venison Sausage
Prepare as in the basic recipe or the first variation above, substituting venison for the veal or beef. Add 4 juniper berries, crushed to a powder, to the spice mixture. Substitute chilled red wine for the cold water.

Hot Italian Sausage

Yield: 6 lb (3 kg)

U.S.	Metric	Ingredients	PROCEDURE
6 lb	3 kg	Pork and pork fat	1. Cut the meat into cubes small enough to fit into the grinder. Chill the meat thoroughly.
2 tbsp	30 g	Salt	
2 tsp	10 mL	Black pepper	2. Grind once with the medium die.
2 tsp	10 mL	Fennel seeds	3. Mix the salt and spices with the cold water. Add to the ground meat and mix thoroughly by hand.
4 tsp	20 mL	Paprika	
2 tsp	10 mL	Crushed red pepper	4. Stuff into hog casings.
1 tsp	5 mL	Ground coriander	
2 tsp	10 mL	Sugar	
6 oz	200 mL	Cold water	

Per 1 ounce:
Calories, 70; Protein, 5 g; Fat, 5 g (69% cal.); Cholesterol, 20 mg;
Carbohydrates, 0 g; Fiber, 0 g; Sodium, 160 mg.

VARIATIONS

Mild Italian Sausage
Omit the paprika, crushed red pepper, and coriander.

Spicy Garlic Sausage
Omit the fennel and coriander. Add 2 tsp (10 mL) oregano and 1–2 tsp (5–10 mL) chopped garlic.

Fresh Bratwurst

Yield: 6 lb (3 kg)

U.S.	Metric	Ingredients	PROCEDURE
6 lb	3 kg	Pork and pork fat	1. Cut the meat and fat into cubes small enough to fit into the grinder. Chill thoroughly.
2 tbsp	30 g	Salt	
3 tsp	15 mL	White pepper	2. Grind the meat once with the large die and again with the small die. If necessary, chill the meat between grindings.
¼ tsp	1 mL	Mace	
1 tsp	5 mL	Ground coriander	3. Mix the salt and spices with the water. Add to the ground meat and mix thoroughly by hand.
½ tsp	2 mL	Ginger	
6 oz	200 mL	Cold water	4. Stuff into hog casings.

Per 1 ounce:
Calories, 70; Protein, 5 g; Fat, 5 g (69% cal.); Cholesterol, 20 mg;
Carbohydrates, 0 g; Fiber, 0 g; Sodium, 160 mg.

VARIATION

Following the procedure on page 655, make an emulsified grind instead of a basic grind. Omit the water indicated in the recipe and add 12 oz (400 g) ice as indicated in the procedure.

Lamb Sausages

Yield: 6 lb (3 kg)

U.S.	Metric	Ingredients	PROCEDURE
6 lb	3 kg	Lamb shoulder (see note)	1. Cut the meat and fat into cubes small enough to fit into the grinder. Chill thoroughly.
2 tbsp	30 g	Salt	2. Grind the meat once with the medium die.
4 tsp	20 mL	Garlic, chopped	3. Mix the salt and spices with the water. Add to the ground meat and mix thoroughly by hand.
2 tbsp	30 mL	Paprika	4. Stuff into hog casings.
1 tsp	5 mL	Cayenne	
1 tsp	5 mL	Black pepper	
2 tbsp	30 mL	Ground cumin	
2 tsp	10 mL	Oregano	
1 tsp	5 mL	Cinnamon	
4 tbsp	60 mL	Cilantro, chopped	
6 oz	200 mL	Cold water	

Per 1 ounce:
Calories, 80; Protein, 5 g; Fat, 6 g (73% cal.); Cholesterol, 20 mg;
Carbohydrates, 0 g; Fiber, 0 g; Sodium, 160 mg.

Note: Include some fat with the lean or, if desired, include some pork fat. If pork fat is used, the finished sausage must be cooked to the well-done stage. If all lamb is used, the sausage may be served slightly rare.

VARIATIONS

For a simpler, more straightforward flavor, omit the oregano, cinnamon, and cilantro.

Herbed Lamb Sausage

The flavor of the sausages made by the main recipe is characteristic of the Middle East and parts of North Africa. For a lamb sausage of a more European or North American character, omit the paprika, cumin, oregano, cinnamon, and cilantro. Add 2 tsp (10 mL) thyme, 2 tsp (10 mL) rosemary, and 1 oz (30 g) chopped shallot.

Duck Sausages

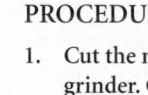

Yield: 6 lb (3 kg)

U.S.	Metric	Ingredients	PROCEDURE
6 lb	3 kg	Boneless duck meat and fat	1. Cut the meat and fat into cubes small enough to fit into the grinder. Chill thoroughly.
2 tbsp	30 g	Salt	2. Grind the meat once with medium die.
2 tsp	10 mL	Quatre épices	3. Mix the salt, spices, nuts, and sun-dried tomatoes. Add to the ground meat and mix thoroughly by hand.
6 oz	185 g	Pine nuts, toasted, or pistachios, blanched and peeled	4. Stuff into small hog casings.
6 oz	185 g	Marinated sun-dried tomatoes, drained and chopped	
½ tsp	2 mL	Thyme	

Per 1 ounce:
Calories, 160; Protein, 3 g; Fat, 17 g (91% cal.); Cholesterol, 25 mg;
Carbohydrates, 1 g; Fiber, 0 g; Sodium, 160 mg.

Mortadella

Yield: 5 lb (2.4 kg)

U.S.	Metric	Ingredients	PROCEDURE
2 lb 8 oz	1.2 kg	Pork, lean	1. Cut the pork into cubes small enough to fit into the grinder.
1 tsp	5 mL	Prague Powder #1	2. Toss the meat with the Prague Powder, salt, and wine and refrigerate for several hours or overnight.
5 tsp	25 mL	Salt	
1½ oz	45 mL	Dry white wine	3. Cut the pork fat into cubes. Refrigerate several hours or overnight.
1 lb 6 oz	660 g	Firm pork fat, such as fatback	
		Garnish:	4. Prepare the garnish. Cut the fatback into small dice. Blanch in boiling water for 2 minutes. Drain. Refrigerate.
6 oz	180 g	Pork fatback	
2 oz	60 g	Pistachios, peeled	5. Pick over the pistachios to be sure they are all peeled and in good condition.
14 oz	400 g	Ice	6. Grind the lean pork using the small die of the grinder. Place it in a food chopper.
1½ tsp	7 mL	White pepper	
1½ tsp	7 mL	Paprika	7. Grind the fat from step 3 (not the fat for the garnish) through the small die and set it aside. Refrigerate it if the kitchen is warm, even though you will be using it in a few minutes.
1 tsp	5 mL	Mace	
1 tsp	5 mL	Quatre épices	
1 tsp	5 mL	Ground coriander	8. Start the food chopper and run a few seconds. Add the ice, the spices, and the milk powder and continue to chop the meat to a fine paste. Check the temperature of the meat. Do not let it rise above 50°F (10°C).
¼ tsp	1 mL	Ground cloves	
2 oz	60 g	Nonfat dry milk powder	
			9. Add the ground fat and continue to run the chopper. Stop the machine from time to time and stir briefly by hand if necessary for even mixing. Process to a fine, uniform paste. Do not let the temperature rise above 58°F (14°C).
			10. Remove the meat mixture from the chopper and place in a stainless-steel bowl set over ice. Add the garnish (diced pork and pistachios) and mix them into the meat purée.
			11. Stuff into large beef casings or artificial casings.
			12. Allow to dry for several hours in the refrigerator. This step is not essential, but it gives the sausage time to take on the desired pink color.
			13. Poach the sausage in water over very low heat, using a thermometer to ensure that the temperature of the water stays at 165°F (74°C). Cook until the internal temperature of the sausage reaches 152°F (67°C).
			14. Remove the sausage from the cooking water and cool it in 2 steps. First, place it in room-temperature water for 5–10 minutes. Next, place it a tub of cold running water until completely cooled.
			15. Refrigerate.

Per 1 ounce:
Calories, 110; Protein, 4 g; Fat, 10 g (82% cal.); Cholesterol, 15 mg; Carbohydrates, 1 g; Fiber, 0 g; Sodium, 190 mg.

VARIATION

Bologna

Omit the garnish of diced fat and pistachios. Omit the wine. After stuffing the casings and drying the sausage, hot smoke at 165°F (74°C) for 1 hour. Remove from the smoker and immediately poach as in the basic recipe.

Boudin Blanc (White Sausage)

Yield: 7 lb (3.6 kg)

U.S.	Metric	Ingredients	PROCEDURE
1 lb 8 oz	750 g	Chicken breast, boneless and skinless	1. Cut the chicken, pork, and fat into cubes small enough to fit into the grinder. Combine the chicken with the lean pork, but keep the pork fat separate.
2 lb	1 kg	Lean, white pork	2. Grind the meat once with the large die, then once with the small die. Chill.
1 lb 8 oz	750 g	Pork fat	3. Grind the fat once with the large die, then once with the small die. Chill.
12 oz	375 g	Onion, chopped	4. Simmer the onions in the milk until they are tender. Pour this mixture over the bread crumbs in a bowl. Cool, then set in the freezer until partly frozen.
1 pt	500 mL	Milk	
8 oz	250 g	Fresh bread crumbs	5. Place the ground meat in the bowl of a food chopper or food processor. Chop a few seconds, then add the partially frozen milk mixture. Grind until the mixture is uniformly blended.
4	4	Eggs	6. Beat together the eggs, salt, pepper, mace, and parsley (if used). Add to the meat in the grinder and continue to grind to a smooth paste. Check the temperature to make sure it does not rise above 50°F (10°C). If necessary, chill before continuing.
3 tbsp	45 mL	Salt	
2 tsp	10 mL	White pepper	
½ tsp	2 mL	Mace	7. Add the fat to the grinder and continue to grind until the mixture is smooth and uniform. Do not let the temperature rise above 58°F (14°C).
1 oz	30 g	Chopped parsley (optional)	8. Stuff into hog casings.
			9. Poach the sausages by simmering them slowly in water until cooked through, about 20 minutes. Drain and plunge into ice water to cool. Drain again and refrigerate.

Per 1 ounce:
Calories, 90; Protein, 4 g; Fat, 7 g (72% cal.); Cholesterol, 25 mg;
Carbohydrates, 2 g; Fiber, 0 g; Sodium, 210 mg.

VARIATIONS

Other white meats, such as veal or rabbit, can be used instead of chicken.

Smoked Garlic Sausage

Yield: 5 lb 12 oz (2750 g)

U.S.	Metric	Ingredients	PROCEDURE
6 lb	3 kg	Pork and pork fat	1. Cut the pork and fat into cubes.
1¼ tsp	6 mL	Prague Powder #1	2. Mix together the Prague Powder, salt, and sugar.
5 tsp	25 mL	Salt	3. Add this mixture to the diced meat and fat and mix well. Refrigerate for several hours.
1 tsp	5 mL	Sugar	
1 tsp	5 mL	White pepper	4. Grind the meat mixture using the medium die of the grinder.
1 tsp	5 mL	Quatre épices	5. Add the remaining ingredients to the meat and mix thoroughly.
2 tsp	10 mL	Garlic, crushed	
6 oz	180 mL	Dry white wine or water	6. Stuff into large hog casings.
			7. Hang the sausages in the refrigerator, if possible, or arrange on towel-covered sheet pans so that they are not touching each other. Refrigerate for 24 hours to dry the sausages before smoking.
			8. Hot smoke at 160°F (71°C) for 1½ hours, then poach in water at 165°F (74°C) until the internal temperature is 152°F (67°C).
			9. Cool the sausages in cold water, then drain, dry, and refrigerate.

Per 1 ounce:
Calories, 70; Protein, 5 g; Fat, 5 g (68% cal.); Cholesterol, 20 mg;
Carbohydrates, 0 g; Fiber, 0 g; Sodium, 170 mg.

VARIATIONS

For a darker color and heavier smoke flavor, leave the sausages in the hot smoke until their internal temperature is 152°F (67°C), and do not poach them. Spray them with cold water after removing them from the smoker to keep them from shriveling.

Cured Garlic Sausage

Dry the sausages for 24–48 hours (step 7). Omit the hot smoking and simply poach, cool, and refrigerate them as described in steps 8 and 9.

Cajun-Style Sausage

Yield: 6 lb (3 kg)

U.S.	Metric	Ingredients	PROCEDURE
6 lb	3 kg	Pork and pork fat	1. Cut the pork and fat into cubes.
1¼ tsp	6 mL	Prague Powder #1	2. Mix together the Prague Powder, salt, and sugar.
2 tsp	10 mL	Salt	3. Add this mixture and the water to the diced meat and fat and mix well. Refrigerate for several hours.
1 tsp	5 mL	Sugar	
4 oz	125 mL	Cold water	
4 tsp	20 mL	Salt	4. Grind the meat mixture using the large die of the grinder.
4 tsp	20 mL	Garlic, crushed	5. Add the remaining ingredients to the meat and mix thoroughly.
1 tbsp	15 mL	Black pepper	6. Stuff into large hog casings
1 tsp	5 mL	Cayenne	7. Hang the sausages in the refrigerator, if possible, or arrange on towel-covered sheet pans so that they are not touching each other. Refrigerate for 24 hours to dry the sausages before smoking.
1 tsp	5 mL	Ground bay leaf	
½ tsp	2 mL	Ground cumin	
1 tsp	5 mL	Chili powder	8. Cold smoke at 80°F (27°C) for 4 hours.
1 tbsp	15 mL	Paprika	9. At this point, the sausages are still raw and should be treated the same way as fresh sausages. They may be sold this way but must be cooked (by poaching, sautéing, grilling, etc.) before being eaten. Alternatively, they may be poached to an internal temperature of 152°F (67°C) immediately after smoking.

Per 1 ounce:
Calories, 70; Protein, 5 g; Fat, 5 g (69% cal.); Cholesterol, 20 mg; Carbohydrates, 0 g; Fiber, 0 g; Sodium, 190 mg.

VARIATION

Andouille

Prepare the sausage meat as in the basic recipe, but omit the seasonings added in step 5, substituting the seasonings and quantities listed to the right. Cold smoke for 12 hours. After smoking, again hang the sausages in the refrigerator, if possible, or arrange on towel-covered sheet pans so that they are not touching each other. Allow to cure another 24 hours in the refrigerator.

4 tsp	20 mL	Salt
3 tbsp	50 mL	Garlic, crushed
1 tsp	5 mL	Black pepper
1 tbsp	15 mL	Cayenne
¼ tsp	1 mL	Ground bay leaf
1 tsp	5 mL	Paprika
½ tsp	2 mL	Thyme
½ tsp	2 mL	Sage
½ tsp	2 mL	Mace
½ tsp	2 mL	Ground allspice

Terms for Review

charcutier	curing salt	hot smoking	quatre épices
charcuterie	tinted curing mix	sausage	natural casing
sodium nitrite	nitrosamine	fresh sausage	collagen casing
sodium nitrate	dry cure	cured sausage	basic grind
Prague Powder #1	brine cure	smoked sausage	emulsified grind
Prague Powder #2	cold smoking	certified pork	

Questions for Discussion

1. Explain how salt helps to preserve meats.
2. Nitrites and nitrates are both used to cure meats. Explain how their use differs. Against which food-borne disease are they important in protecting cured foods?
3. Explain why smoked meats are first cured.
4. Describe the basic differences between fresh, cured, and smoked sausages.
5. What are the four basic kinds of ingredients in sausage meat? List ways that this basic formula can be changed to create different types of sausages.
6. Why should sausage meat be kept cold when it is being ground and processed?
7. Describe the procedure for preparing natural sausage casings for stuffing.

chapter 23

Pãtés, Terrines, and Other Cold Foods

The techniques and procedures presented in this chapter belong to the culinary department known as *garde manger* (gard mawn zhay), a term whose basic meaning is "larder" or "food storage place." As explained in Chapter 19 (p. 531), this area, because of its cooler temperature, was traditionally used for the preparation of cold foods. Thus, the work carried out in the storage area, or garde manger, became known by the same name.

The art of garde manger includes the techniques of cold food decoration, cold platter design and presentation, and the design and planning of whole buffets. Garde manger is an intricate and complex discipline that is the subject of whole books and of extended courses of study.

This book is primarily concerned with à la carte cooking. Buffet service is beyond its scope. Nevertheless, à la carte restaurants have inherited from classical garde manger a number of special food preparations that can be served in single portions as well as on butter platters. Pâtés, terrines, galantines, and mousses are not only ideal for buffets, they are also popular in many restaurants. This chapter serves as an introduction to these preparations.

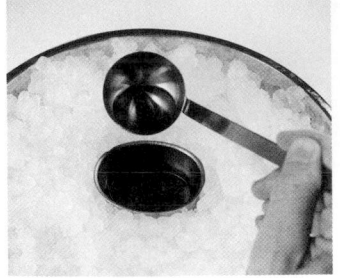

The Handling and Service of Cold Dishes

Because the dishes featured in this chapter are served cold, various factors relating to their handling and service require special consideration. These have to do with sanitation and presentation.

After reading this chapter, you should be able to:

1. Prepare and use aspic jellies.

2. Prepare and use classic chaud-froid and mayonnaise chaud-froid.

3. Prepare livers for use in forcemeats.

4. Prepare basic meat and poultry forcemeats.

5. Prepare pâtés and terrines using basic forcemeats.

6. Prepare galantines.

7. Prepare mousseline forcemeats and make terrines based on them.

8. Prepare specialty terrines and other molded dishes based on aspics and mousses.

9. Handle raw foie gras and prepare foie gras terrines.

10. Prepare baked liver terrines.

11. Prepare rillettes.

SANITATION AND STORAGE

Hot foods that have been handled in a sanitary manner and that are served at or above a temperature that kills microorganisms can usually be considered safe and sanitary to eat. Cold foods, on the other hand, present special problems because they have been stored and handled after cooking. During this time, they may be exposed to disease-causing organisms. Because these foods are not subjected to further cooking, the organisms will not be destroyed.

For this reason, it is particularly important to follow all the rules of safe food handling. Make sure tools, containers, and work surfaces are clean and sanitary. Keep ingredients refrigerated when they are not being worked on, and keep the finished product refrigerated until service time.

The length of time terrines and other cold foods can be stored in the refrigerator depends on the ingredients, the type of item, and the method of preparation. Uncut meat terrines sealed with a layer of fat (see p. 679) may keep as long as several weeks (although the quality may start to decline after a week or so), while seafood and vegetable terrines may keep no more than two or three days, or even less. Pâtés en croûte (see p. 676) do not keep as well as terrines because the pastry loses its freshness. Aspics should be kept covered or wrapped to prevent them from drying out.

PRESENTATION

Attractive plating or presentation of foods is, of course, always important, but it could be argued that it is even more important for cold foods than for hot foods. Foods presented hot and steaming, directly from the sauté pan or carving board, have an immediate appeal to the nose as well as the eye, but cold foods must rely more completely on visual impact to make their first impression.

Furthermore, because the urgency in getting the plate from the kitchen to the dining room before the food cools down is absent, the cook has more time to arrange cold foods on the plate. This does not mean, however, that the most elaborate or intricate presentation is the best. "Keep it simple" is a good rule of thumb. Food is not made more appetizing by excessive handling.

Arrangements should be kept neat, but this does not mean that they must always be symmetrical or regular. As in the case of salads, a deliberate casualness in the arrangement can be appetizing when it suggests that the dish has been freshly assembled with minimum handling and rushed to the table.

In the case of pâtés and terrines, careful handling is essential to the presentation. Slice these items carefully and plate each slice with the best side up. To make neat slices, use a sharp, thin-bladed slicing knife. Before each slice, wipe off any residue from the previous slice and dip the blade in hot water. Slice the pâté with a gentle sawing motion, using the full length of the blade. Don't force the knife straight down or make little jagged cuts; this will make the cut surface uneven rather than smooth.

If the cut end of the pâté has discolored somewhat from exposure to air, plate the first slice with this side down. In contrast to pâtés for buffet presentation, slices of pâté for à la carte service are often garnished with greens or other colorful items, which enliven the sometimes drab appearance of a plain meat pâté. In addition, greens and other vegetable garnish provide a pleasant flavor contrast to the somewhat rich, processed flavor of the pâté or terrine.

Tart or piquant garnishes and accompaniments, as well as tart sauces such as vinaigrette and mayonnaise variations, help to counter the richness of pâtés, which are often rather fatty. This is why sour pickles and mustard are classic accompaniments for these foods.

Consideration must be given to the serving temperature of cold foods such as aspics, pâtés, and terrines. A common error is to serve these items too cold. At refrigerator temperature, their flavors are masked. Furthermore, their textures are too firm; the fat in pâtés and the gelatin in aspics are firmly congealed. A little warmer temperature is necessary to enable them to melt pleasantly in the mouth.

To bring them to suitable serving temperature, remove individual portions from refrigeration and let stand at room temperature for about 5 or 10 minutes, but no longer. Remember the sanitation guidelines discussed earlier. This period is long enough to let them warm slightly but not long enough to give microorganisms time to start multiplying. Keep in mind, too, that this short period of tempering applies only to those portions to be served right away. Whole pâtés from which portions were cut, for example, should be returned immediately to refrigeration.

Aspic and Chaud-Froid

Aspic jelly or *gelée* (zhuh lay) is clarified stock that contains enough gelatin that it solidifies when cold. The gelatin may be naturally extracted from bones or added from a package. Good stock naturally contains a certain amount of gelatin but, in most cases, it must be supplemented with additional unflavored, packaged gelatin.

Aspic jelly may be nearly colorless ("white" aspic) or various shades of amber. Most often, however, it must be crystal clear. This is achieved by clarifying it like a consommé. White or light-colored aspic is used when the natural colors of the foods and decorations must show through. Amber or golden aspic enhances the brown color of foods such as roasted meats and poultry

Aspic is used as a coating for foods and as a binding ingredient. When it is used as a coating, it has three main purposes:

1. To protect foods from the air, which would dry them out and discolor them.
2. To improve appearance and give shine.
3. To add flavor. This last purpose is, of course, best accomplished if the stock is of high quality

As a binding ingredient, aspic is used in mousses, terrines, and aspic molds, as discussed later in this chapter. It is also the binding agent in chaud-froid sauce (see p. 668). *Note:* When aspic is used as a binding agent, it need not be perfectly clarified.

In addition, when congealed and chopped or cut into various shapes, aspic jelly is used as a garnish for platters or servings of pâtés, terrines, and other cold items.

PREPARING ASPIC JELLY

The best aspic is a well-made, naturally gelatinous stock. It has a superior texture and flavor, but it is time-consuming to make because a separate batch of stock must be made in addition to the normal stock production. Consequently, most aspics are made by reinforcing regular stock with gelatin. Aspic powders and mixes are available, but the flavor of aspic made from them does not compare with that made from stock. They can be useful in an emergency, however, or for pieces used purely for display or decoration.

Classic Aspic Jelly
Prepare classic aspic jelly as you would white or brown veal stock, but with the addition of products that release a good deal of gelatin, such as split calves' feet or pigs' feet, pork skin, and veal knuckle bones. If enough of these items are used, the stock will contain enough natural gelatin to be used as an aspic jelly.

Follow basic stock-making procedures, except do not brown the added feet and pork skin when making brown stock. When the stock is made, use the following procedure to convert it to aspic jelly.

Procedure for Preparing Classic Aspic Jelly

1. Test the stock for gelatin content. Ladle a small amount of cooled stock onto a small plate or saucer and refrigerate.

- If the stock becomes firm, no additional gelatin is needed.
- If it sets but is not firm enough, add about ½ oz or 2 tbsp (15 g) powdered gelatin per quart (liter) of stock, or 2 oz (60 g) per gallon (4 liters).
- If it does not set at all (which is unlikely if the stock is properly made) but merely becomes thicker, add about 1 oz or 4 tbsp (30 g) powdered gelatin per quart (liter), or 4 oz (125 g) per gallon (4 liters). In this case, you will actually be making *regular aspic jelly* (see next section) rather than classic aspic jelly.

  Add the gelatin by first stirring it gradually into a little cold water, avoiding making lumps, and letting it soften. Then add the softened gelatin to the stock.

2. Clarify the stock as for consommé. For white aspic (made with white stock), omit the carrots in the mirepoix.

3. After the stock is clarified, remove all traces of fat. The aspic jelly is now ready to use.

Regular Aspic Jelly

This is normal meat, poultry, or fish stock reinforced with gelatin and clarified. Regular stock rarely has enough natural gelatin to enable it to be used as a jelly, so extra gelatin must be added. To test the stock for gelatin content and to convert it to aspic jelly, follow the same procedure as for classic aspic jelly, described earlier. However, note that if the stock contains very little gelatin and stays watery when chilled, more than 4 oz (125 g) gelatin may be needed per gallon (4 liters).

Aspic Powder

Aspic powder is unflavored gelatin mixed with a powdered stock base. To prepare it, follow the instructions on the container. Additional unflavored gelatin may be needed for some purposes.

Procedures for using aspic jelly are discussed following a brief consideration of a related topic, chaud-froid sauce.

CHAUD-FROID

Described in simplest terms, *chaud-froid* sauce is a white sauce containing enough gelatin that it sets like an aspic. The name *chaud-froid* is French for "hot-cold." The sauce is so called because the classic version is made hot but eaten cold.

Today, chaud-froid sauce is rarely used except for display pieces on buffets. Its main purpose there is to provide a smooth, uniformly white background for colored decorations. Because it is not eaten in these cases, it does not have to have a good flavor, and it may be made out of a simple béchamel sauce thickened with a roux made with white shortening.

Nevertheless, chaud-froid sauce finds occasional use in cold dishes—for example, as a component of some aspic molds and terrines. A brief discussion is warranted without going into the kind of detail found in books on garde manger.

Many kinds of white sauces may be used as a base for chaud-froid, including cream sauces, white stocks enriched with cream or cream and egg yolks, veloutés, and mayonnaise. There are also colored chaud-froid sauces, but they are not often used. Red sauce can be made with the addition of tomato paste and, sometimes, paprika. Green sauce is colored with spinach and watercress, puréed with some of the hot sauce, and strained. Brown chaud-froid can be made by combining glace de viande, tomato sauce, and aspic jelly in equal proportions.

Preparing Chaud-Froid Sauce

Two basic types of chaud-froid sauce are considered here, one based on white stock and cream, the other on mayonnaise. Both of these are of good eating quality and can be used for first-class cold foods. Heavier types based on roux-thickened sauces may be economical to make but are more appropriate for inedible display pieces.

Two recipes for chaud-froid are given here. Classical chaud-froid is essentially an aspic jelly with the addition of cream or a cream and egg yolk liaison. In fact, it can be made by combining aspic jelly and cream, but this mixture would have to be reinforced with extra gelatin because of the quantity of cream.

Mayonnaise chaud-froid, also called *mayonnaise collée*, which means something like "glued mayonnaise," is simply a mixture of aspic jelly and mayonnaise. It is easy to make and, if the two ingredients are of good quality, is a tasty and useful chaud-froid.

The basic proportion is equal parts aspic jelly and mayonnaise. The proportion can be varied to taste, however, from one-third aspic and two-thirds mayonnaise to one-third mayonnaise and two-thirds aspic jelly.

Using a commercially-made mayonnaise is recommended. If you are using a homemade mayonnaise, it is best to prepare the chaud-froid at the last minute and use it at once. Reheating it to melt it could cause the mayonnaise to break. Commercial mayonnaise, on the other hand, can generally be melted without damage, but it is still best to use the sauce as soon it is made.

Classical Chaud-Froid

Yield: 2 qt (2 L)

U.S.	Metric	Ingredients	PROCEDURE
½ –1 oz	15–30 g	Gelatin powder, unflavored (see note)	1. Soften the gelatin in the heavy cream.
8 oz	250 mL	Heavy cream	
1 qt	1 L	White stock (veal, chicken, or fish)	2. Bring the stock to a simmer. 3. Add the gelatin mixture to the stock and heat until the gelatin is dissolved. Do not boil.
2–4	2–4	Egg yolks (optional)	4. If the egg yolks are used, beat them with the remaining cream to make a liaison. Stir a little of the stock mixture into the liaison to temper it, then add it back to the hot stock. Heat the mixture carefully to cook the egg yolks, but do not let it simmer, or the yolks will curdle.
1 pt 8 oz	750 mL	Heavy cream	5. If the yolks are not used, simply temper the remaining cream with a little of the hot stock, then add it to the rest of the stock.
			6. Strain through a cheesecloth.

Per 1 ounce:
Calories, 50; Protein, 1 g; Fat, 5 g (69% cal.); Cholesterol, 20 mg;
Carbohydrates, 0 g; Fiber, 0 g; Sodium, 5 mg.

Note: If the stock is firmly set when cold, use the smaller quantity of gelatin. If the stock sets but is not firm when cool, use the larger quantity.

Mayonnaise Chaud-Froid

Yield: 1 qt (1 L)

U.S.	Metric	Ingredients	PROCEDURE
1 pt	500 mL	Mayonnaise	1. Stir the mayonnaise, if necessary, so that it is smooth. If it has just been removed from the refrigerator, let it warm to cool room temperature. If it is too cold, the first drops of aspic may congeal as soon as they hit it, causing lumps.
1 pt	500 mL	Aspic jelly	2. Melt the aspic over a hot water bath. Cool it to thicken slightly (see below for cooling aspic). It should be at about the same temperature as the mayonnaise or just slightly warmer.
			3. Using a stirring whip (not a balloon whip, used for whipping in air), stir the aspic into the mayonnaise. Stir carefully to avoid making bubbles. If the gelatin begins to set before the mixing is complete, carefully remelt over the hot water bath.
			4. Set the chaud-froid over ice to thicken (see below). When ready to use, it should be about the consistency of heavy cream. Use at once.

Per 1 ounce:
Calories, 100; Protein, 0 g; Fat, 11g (100% cal.); Cholesterol, 10 mg; Carbohydrates, 0 g; Fiber, 0 g; Sodium, 80 mg.

USING ASPIC JELLY AND CHAUD-FROID SAUCE

As discussed earlier, aspic and chaud-froid are used to enhance both the appearance and the flavor of cold foods. For best results, the aspic and chaud-froid, as well as the foods to be coated, should be prepared and handled in specific ways. The following sections offer general procedures for handling these products. Specific applications, such as recipes for aspic-based terrine molds, are included later in the chapter.

Aspic jelly must be cooled to just above congealing temperature before it is used to coat foods. If it is too warm, it will not have enough body to coat and will just run off.

Procedure for Cooling Aspic Jelly

The following procedure is used for chaud-froid as well as aspic jelly.

1. If the jelly is congealed, it must first be melted. Set the pan or container of jelly in a hot water bath. Stir it gently from time to time until it is completely melted.

2. Place the warm aspic jelly in a stainless-steel bowl.

3. At all times, be careful not to make any bubbles. Bubbles in the jelly may get transferred to the surface of your food item and mar its appearance.

4. Select a ladle that fits the curve of the bowl. Set the bowl in crushed ice, pushing it in so that it sits in a well of ice. With the edge of the ladle against the inside of the bowl, rotate the bowl so that the ladle continually scrapes the inside of the bowl. This method prevents the formation of lumps that occur when jelly touching the cold bowl solidifies too quickly.

5. Continue to rotate the bowl until the jelly is thick and syrupy but not yet set. The jelly is now ready for use. Remove from the ice bath and work quickly, because it will set very fast.

6. Remelt and recool the jelly as necessary.

Procedure for Coating Foods with Aspic Jelly

1. Chill the food to be coated. For best results, the surface of the item should be as smooth and as free of fat as possible.

2. Place the item on a wire rack over a tray or sheet pan. Excess aspic that falls onto the tray can be remelted and reused.

3. Cool the aspic jelly according to the procedure on page 670.

4. Use the aspic as soon as it is ready. Various methods can be used to coat foods with aspic, depending on the size and shape of the item.

- For smooth, regularly shaped items, use a large ladle and nap them with a single smooth stroke, as illustrated in Figure 23.1. Working too slowly may produce an uneven, bumpy coat.

- Large items and items with steep sides or irregular shapes are harder to coat. Using a ladle, coat the sides first and then the top for best results.

- For small items, it may be more convenient to use a kitchen spoon than a ladle.

- A pastry brush can be used to coat small items. A brush is often used for small portions, such as canapés, that need only a light glaze rather than a perfectly smooth coating of aspic.

5. Chill the items until the jelly is thoroughly set.

6. Repeat with additional coats, if necessary, until the aspic is of the desired thickness.

7. To decorate, dip pieces of decoration in liquid aspic and place on the product in the desired pattern. Some items appropriate to use for decorating aspic are

Leek leaves
Fresh herbs, especially flat-leaf parsley and tarragon
Black olives
Truffles, real or artificial
Tomato peels
Carrots

As appropriate, cut the items for decoration into very thin slices and then into desired shapes. For most vegetable decorations, such as carrots and leek leaves, blanch to make them more limber and to intensify the color.

8. If decorations have been used, cover the decorated item with a final layer of aspic jelly to protect the design.

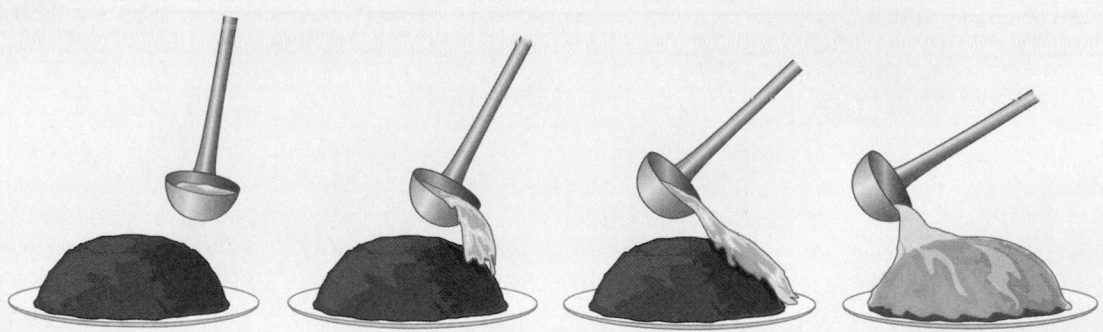

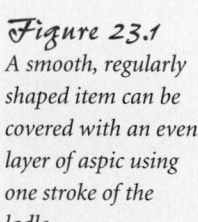

Figure 23.1
A smooth, regularly shaped item can be covered with an even layer of aspic using one stroke of the ladle.

Coating with Chaud-Froid

Apply chaud-froid sauce according to the same procedure as for aspic. Because most chaud-froid is thicker than aspic, it is usually kept a little warmer when poured.

If the first layer of chaud-froid is too transparent or not thick enough, apply one or two additional layers.

After the chaud-froid has chilled and set, apply decorations if desired. Finish with a layer of aspic for best appearance.

Procedure for Lining a Mold with Aspic Jelly

Figure 23.2 Lining a mold with aspic jelly.

(a) *Bury the mold up to the rim in crushed ice.*

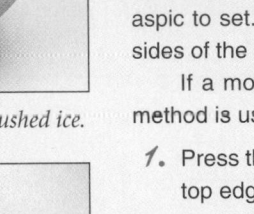

(b) *Fill the mold with liquid aspic.*

Many instructions for lining molds say to chill the mold, then pour in a little liquid aspic jelly and turn and tilt the mold until the bottom and sides are coated. This method works and is suitable for some purposes, but it does not produce a smooth, even layer of aspic.

It is not always necessary to line a mold with aspic. Many aspic molds are made by first pouring a thin layer of aspic into the bottom of the mold, chilling it, then adding layers of ingredients (vegetables, meats, mousses, and so on) and covering each layer with a little aspic. The mold is chilled after each layer is added to allow the aspic to set. As long as the layers of solid ingredients are not allowed to touch the sides of the mold, the liquid aspic will fill in these spaces and, in effect, line the mold.

If a mold must be lined with a perfectly even thickness of jelly, the following method is used (see Figure 23.2):

1. Press the mold into a bed of crushed ice so that the ice comes all the way to the top edge.

2. Fill the mold with cooled liquid aspic jelly. Leave the mold in place for 10 seconds. Immediately remove the mold from the ice and quickly dump out the jelly that is still liquid. If the layer of jelly remaining inside the mold is too thin, repeat. If it is too thick, remove it, clean the mold, and repeat the procedure, leaving the mold on ice for less time.

3. Decorate the inside of the mold as desired by dipping decorations in liquid aspic and arranging them in place. Chill. Then fill the mold with the selected food product.

(c) *After 10 seconds, quickly but smoothly pour out the aspic that is still liquid.*

(d) *An even layer of aspic jelly lines the mold, as can be seen by comparing it with an empty mold.*

(e) *At this point, you can decorate the mold by dipping vegetable cutouts in liquid aspic and carefully setting them in place in the mold.*

Special Forcemeat Dishes

This section is concerned with classic meat and poultry dishes called *pâtés, terrines,* and *galantines.* Some terrines are based on vegetables and other items rather than meats, but these are the subject of a later section. The main ingredients of the items discussed here are a *forcemeat* and, usually but not always, a *garnish.*

A forcemeat may be defined as a mixture of seasoned, ground meats used as a stuffing or filling. The name comes from the French word *farce,* which means stuffing.

The garnish in a pâté or terrine is not just a decoration but a major ingredient that adds body, flavor, and nutritional value as well as appearance. Garnish usually consists of meats or other foods cut in dice, strips, or other shapes, or left whole if they are small. Classic pâté garnishes include:

Ham	Foie gras	Pistachios
Veal	Game	Truffles
Chicken, duck, or turkey breast	Fresh pork fatback	
Chicken, duck, or goose livers	Tongue	

TYPES OF FORCEMEATS

The following are the three basic types of forcemeats:

1. Straight forcemeat (including country-style forcemeats).
   This is a mixture of seasoned ground meats. As such, it is basically a form of sausage meat, except that the grind is generally, but not always, finer. Consequently, many of the guidelines for making and handling sausage meat, discussed in Chapter 22, apply here as well. It may be helpful to read or to review pages 650–655 in conjunction with this discussion. Straight forcemeats are the basis of most traditional pâtés and terrines and are the major focus of this chapter.

   A *country-style forcemeat* is made the same way except that the grind is coarser. Most country-style forcemeats are made from pork and pork fat and contain some liver.

2. Gratin forcemeat.
   This type of forcemeat differs from a straight forcemeat in that a portion of the meat is seared, and thus partially cooked, and cooled before it is ground. Because the partial cooking eliminates some of the binding power of the meat protein, gratin forcemeats usually contain a starch binder called a *panada* (also called *panade*). This type of forcemeat is not used as often as straight or mousseline forcemeats and is not covered in this book.

3. Mousseline forcemeat.
   This type of forcemeat consists of white meat (usually poultry or veal) or seafood processed to a purée and combined with heavy cream and egg. See page 682 for a discussion.

STRAIGHT FORCEMEATS

A basic straight forcemeat consists of the following:

50 to 65 percent lean meat
35 to 50 percent fat
Seasonings

The many variations on this basic formula depend on the ingredients used and how they are combined.

Meat

Pork is the basic ingredient, but many other meats can be included in addition to or instead of pork, including veal, chicken, turkey, ham, duck, rabbit, and game of all kinds.

Liver

Chicken, goose, duck, or pork liver is often included in forcemeats. Liver gives flavor and also acts as a binder.

Fat

The classic proportion in forcemeats is equal parts fat and meat. Many forcemeats, however, contain less than 50 percent fat, especially in recent years, as people have become more attentive to nutrition and dietary considerations (see the discussion of the fat content of sausages on page 650). Nevertheless, a certain amount of fat is necessary for both moisture and flavor. A pâté with too little fat tastes dry. Hard fat, such as pork fatback, gives best results. Heavy cream is sometimes used to add fat as well as liquid to a forcemeat.

Note that this discussion of fat content refers only to the solid fat specifically added as a measured ingredient. There is, of course, some fat in the lean meat as well.

Other Ingredients

Eggs or egg whites may be added as a binder. Flour or other starches may be added for the same purpose. Extra binders are not absolutely necessary in a forcemeat made purely of meat and fat because the meat proteins are sufficient to bind the product when cooked. On the other hand, when brandy, cream, and other liquids are added to the forcemeat, extra binders may be needed or at least may be beneficial.

The Grind

Forcemeat may be ground coarse, medium, or fine. Country-style pâté, or *pâté de campagne* (cawm pah nyuh), is characterized by a coarse texture. Galantines, on the other hand, are usually made from finely ground forcemeats.

Preparing Straight Forcemeats

Many, if not most, pâté and terrine forcemeats contain some liver. Chicken livers or other poultry livers, both economical and widely available, are the most often used. For the best results, livers should be soaked in milk and then cleaned according to the following procedures. Pork liver and other larger livers can be cut into pieces and prepared in the same way.

Procedure for Preparing Poultry Livers for Forcemeats

1. Rinse the livers in cold water, drain, then soak for 24 hours in enough milk to cover.

2. Drain and rinse thoroughly in cold water. Drain again.

3. Remove all fat and connective tissue. At this point, the livers are ready to be used whole as garnish for pâtés and terrines. If they are to be added to forcemeats, continue with steps 4 and 5.

4. Blend in a blender until liquid.

5. Strain through a fine china cap or strainer to remove all traces of connective tissue.

The following recipe can be used with many garnishes to make a great variety of pâtés, terrines, and galantines. It can also be changed according to any of the variations listed by using different meats. Once the basic technique is understood, any kind of pâté can be produced.

The recipe should be viewed as a basic procedure that can be varied in ways other than those indicated following the recipe, just as sausage meat can be varied. The varieties and quantities of spices can be changed. In addition, the fineness of the grind can be varied to make pâtés of varying textures.

The proportion of fat can be increased or reduced, but remember that making the forcemeat too lean will reduce its eating quality. Although at first glance the recipe looks as if it calls for 50 percent fat, this is not the case, as the liver should be included as part of the meat. The proportion of fat is 44 percent. Taking the first column of ingredient quantities as an example, using 1 lb lean pork, 12 oz fat, and 4 oz liver lowers the proportion of fat to 38 percent (not counting, of course, the smaller amount of fat within the meats). Using 12 oz lean pork, 1 lb fat, and 4 oz liver raises the fat proportion to 50 percent.

Basic Pork Forcemeat

Yield: 2 lb (900 g)

U.S.	Metric	Ingredients	PROCEDURE
14 oz	400 g	Lean pork	1. Before beginning, make sure that all equipment and all ingredients are well chilled. Forcemeats must be kept cold at all times to prevent the fat from softening or melting.
14 oz	400 g	Pork fat	
		Marinade:	2. Cut the fat and meat into small dice.
1½ oz	45 g	Shallots, minced	3. Sweat the minced shallots in the butter until soft. Add half of the white wine and reduce by half. Cool completely.
½ oz	15 g	Butter	4. Combine the meat and fat with the shallots, the rest of the wine, the bay leaves, brandy, salt, spice mixture, and pepper. Toss to mix well. Cover and refrigerate overnight.
2 oz	60 mL	White wine	
2	2	Bay leaves	
1 oz	30 mL	Brandy	5. Remove the bay leaves. Grind the meat and fat twice through the fine blade of a meat grinder.
2½ tsp	12 mL	Salt	
½ tsp	2 mL	Pâté spice or quatre épices (see note)	
¼ tsp	1 mL	White pepper	
4 oz	100 g	Chicken livers, soaked, cleaned, and puréed (see p. 674)	6. Combine the ground meats and liver purée.
			7. Beat the eggs lightly and mix in thoroughly. (Note: The eggs are optional and are omitted in many pâtés.)
2	2	Eggs (see step 7)	8. Make a quenelle (a small ball of forcemeat) and poach in simmering water. Cool. Taste and correct the seasonings in the forcemeat.

Per 1 ounce:
Calories, 150; Protein, 3 g; Fat, 14 g (89% cal.); Cholesterol, 54 mg; Carbohydrates, 0 g; Fiber, 0 g; Sodium, 200 mg.

9. Keep the forcemeat chilled until ready for use.

Note: Pâté spice may be purchased in various blends, or you may make your own blend to taste. Pâté spice usually contains black and white pepper, cloves, nutmeg, ginger, cayenne, bay leaf, thyme, and marjoram. Grind very fine and sift through a sieve. For quatre épices, see page 657.

VARIATIONS

Omit the pork, fat, livers, and eggs in the basic recipe. Substitute the following ingredients and quantities. Vary seasonings to taste.

Veal Forcemeat

9 oz	250 g	Lean pork
9 oz	250 g	Lean veal
14 oz	400 g	Fresh pork fat
3	3	Eggs

Chicken Forcemeat I

9 oz	250 g	Lean pork
9 oz	250 g	Chicken meat
14 oz	400 g	Fresh pork fat
3	3	Eggs

Chicken Forcemeat II

1 lb 2 oz	500 g	Chicken meat
14 oz	400 g	Fresh pork fat
3	3	Eggs

Duck, Pheasant, or Game Forcemeat

7 oz	200 g	Lean pork, or a mixture of pork and veal
7 oz	200 g	Duck, pheasant, or game meat
14 oz	400 g	Fresh pork fat
4 oz	100 g	Livers, soaked, cleaned, and puréed
1	1	Eggs

TERRINES AND PÂTÉS

Terrines and pâtés are baked forcemeats, often but not always containing one or more types of garnish. Strictly speaking, the difference between the two lies in how they are baked. By definition, a terrine is baked in an earthenware dish. The dish itself is also called a *terrine*, a word derived from the French *terre*, meaning "earth." Today other materials besides earthenware, such as glass or metal, may be used for terrines. Terrines may be presented in their baking dish, or they may be unmolded.

A pâté is, by definition, baked in a crust. The word *pâté* (with an accent on the *e*) is derived from the word *pâte* (without the accent), meaning "pastry." Today, however, the word pâté is often used for various terrines baked without a pastry crust. To avoid confusion, the term *pâté en croûte* is used to specify a pâté with a crust. In this book, the terms *terrine* and *pâté* are used in their traditional, literal senses.

It should be noted that many kinds of products are called *terrines* because they are prepared in terrine molds. The terrines discussed in this section are based on the straight forcemeats we have just considered. Other kinds of terrines are discussed in a later section.

Preparing Pâtés

The essential difference between a pâté and a terrine is the crust. Although a heavy pastry crust may not be suitable for all kinds of terrine mixtures, the typical baked forcemeat-type terrine under consideration here can usually be made with or without a crust.

This section concentrates on the specific procedures for making the pastry and finishing the assembled pâté. Making the meat filling is the same as for terrines and is not repeated here. To make a pâté en croûte, apply the following procedure to the Veal and Ham Terrine and to any of the variations following the basic recipe (see p. 680).

Pastries used to enclose pâtés are of various types, but the most commonly used are similar to pie pastries, but sturdier. A recipe for this type of *pâte à pâté*, or pâté pastry, is included here. Its advantage over many other types of pâté pastry is that it is relatively good to eat. Some authorities argue about whether the dough around a pâté is meant to be eaten. But because customers are not necessarily aware of this argument, it is best to use a pastry that is reasonably pleasant to eat.

Traditional English pâtés, or raised meat pies, use a hot water pastry that can be modeled like clay and that is very sturdy when baked. Pastries used for display—that is, for show platters not intended to be eaten—are also made to be sturdy and easy to handle. These pastries are not considered here.

The procedure for assembling a pâté follows the pastry recipe (Figure 23.3 and p. 678).

Pâté Pastry (Pâte à Pâté)

Yield: 1 lb 12 oz (900 g)

U.S.	Metric	Ingredients	PROCEDURE
1 lb	500 g	Flour	1. Place the flour in a large mixing bowl. Add the butter and lard. Rub them in until no lumps of fat remain.
4 oz	125 g	Butter	
3½ oz	110 g	Lard	
1	1	Eggs	2. Beat the egg with the water and salt until the salt is dissolved.
3 oz	110 mL	Cold water	3. Add the liquid to the flour mixture. Mix gently until it is completely absorbed.
1¼ tsp	7 mL	Salt	
			4. Gather the dough into a ball. On a work surface, knead the dough for a few minutes until it is smooth.
			5. Place the dough in a pan and cover with plastic film. Refrigerate until needed, or at least 4 hours.

Per 1 ounce:
Calories, 120; Protein, 2 g; Fat, 7 g (53% cal.); Cholesterol, 20 mg; Carbohydrates, 20 g; Fiber, 0 g; Sodium, 140 mg.

Figure 23.3 Making a pâté en croûte.

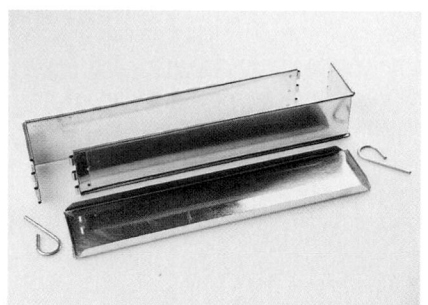

(a) Collapsible molds are used to make pâtés en croûte because they can be removed from the mold without damaging it. Assemble the mold and grease the inside well.

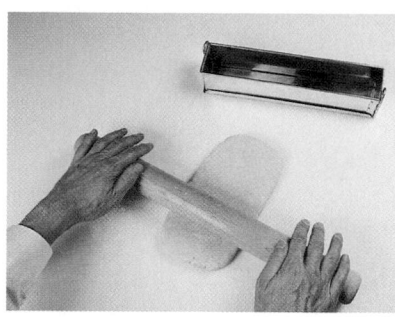

(b) Lightly roll the pastry into a rectangle, keeping it thick.

(c) Work the dough into a boat shape. Dust heavily with flour and fold the dough lengthwise to make a pocket.

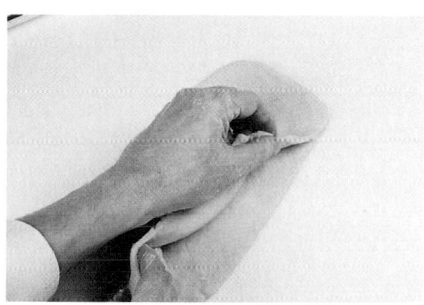

(d) Roll the double thickness of dough into a rectangle the size of the mold. Open the pocket.

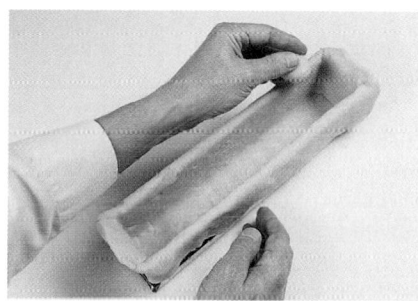

(e) Fit the dough into the mold. Carefully work it to fit snugly. A ball of dough dipped in flour helps to fit the dough into the corners without tearing it.

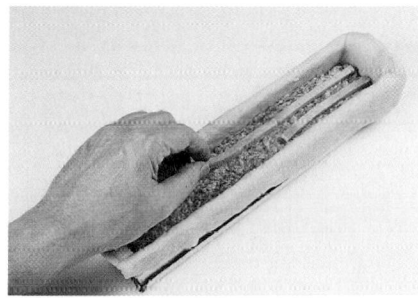

(f) Partially fill the mold with forcemeat and arrange the garnish according to the instructions in the specific recipe.

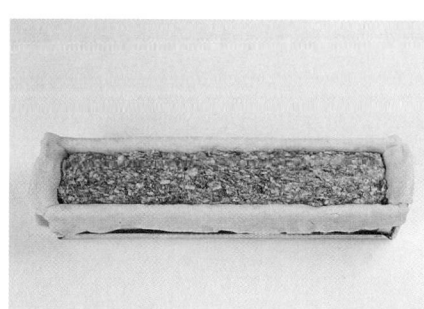

(g) Finish filling the mold, mounding the forcemeat slightly.

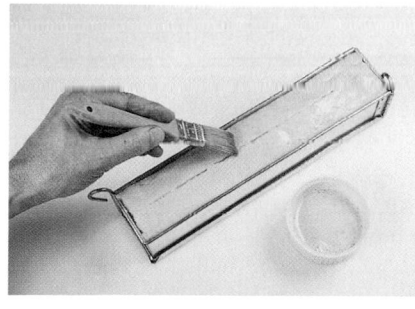

(h) Fold the ends and then sides of the dough over the top of the forcemeat, trimming the dough so that it meets in the middle. Eggwash the dough.

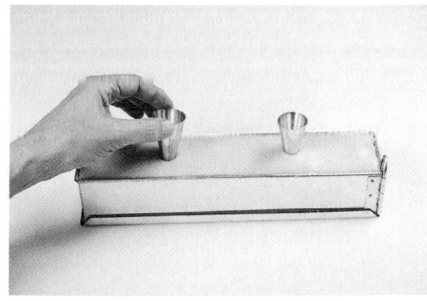

(i) Roll out and cut the top pastry and fit it in place, making sure it is sealed well to the dough below it. Eggwash. Make holes in the top and fit pastry tubes in them or serve as chimneys to allow the escape of steam and to prevent melted fat from bubbling over the top crust as the pâté bakes.

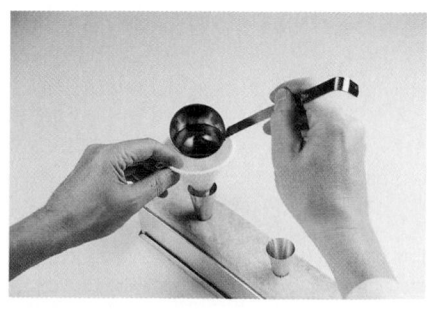

(j) After the pâté has baked and cooled, pour liquid aspic through the chimneys to fill the spaces left when the forcemeat shrank during baking.

1. Prepare the pastry in advance so that it has plenty of time to rest. Remove it from refrigeration long enough ahead of time to allow it to warm up slightly.

2. Prepare the molds by greasing them well on the inside. The directions here pertain to standard rectangular pâté molds. These usually are hinged and collapsible so that it is easy to remove the pâté without damaging it. If you are using bottomless molds, then also grease the sheet pans on which they are to set. For molds of other shapes, modify the pastry-molding procedure as necessary to fit the shape.

3. For best results, mold the pastry so that it is of even thickness, has no seams, and fits the mold perfectly. First, work the pastry with the hands for a few seconds to make it pliable. Then shape it into a rectangle and roll it slightly with a rolling pin to flatten it, keeping it quite thick.

4. Make an indentation down the center of the dough with the fingers. Gradually make the dough into a sort of boat shape. Dust the inside of the dough shape well with flour (to keep the two layers of dough from sticking together) and fold the dough along the indentation to make a pocket.

5. Gently roll out the dough to make a rectangle the size of the mold. Be careful not to roll the dough too thin, which would make it fragile. Open up the pocket.

6. Fit the opened pocket into the mold. Carefully mold the pastry to the shape of the mold by pushing the dough with your fingers. Make sure that there are no air bubbles between the dough and mold. A ball of dough dipped in flour is useful for pushing the dough into the corners of the mold without tearing it.

7. If the pâté is to be made without a top crust, leave a rim of dough about ¼ inch (5 mm) above the top of the mold. Crimp this rim to make a decorative border. If there is to be a top crust, leave a rim of half the width of the mold and let it hang over the sides. (For an alternative method, see step 10.)

8. The mold is now ready to fill. For display pieces, it is common practice to line the inside of the dough with thin sheets of fatback. For pâtés to be eaten, however, it is more appetizing to omit the fat lining. Fill the mold with the desired forcemeat and garnish as for terrines (see p. 679). Mound the filling slightly so that the top crust, if used, will have an attractive domed shape. The dough should hold this shape even as the forcemeat shrinks and settles during baking.

   If the pâté is not to have a top crust, it is now ready for baking. Skip to step 12. Baking without a top crust is easier and allows you to make an attractive aspic glaze with decorations for the top.

9. Fold the rim of the dough from the sides of the mold over the top of the filling. If using a top crust:
   - Roll out a sheet of dough.
   - Lay the sheet of dough on top of the mold, trim it to size, and remove it.
   - Brush the edges of dough from the sides of the mold with egg wash.
   - Return the pastry top to the mold and fit it in place, gently sealing it to the egg-washed dough.

10. As an alternative method for fitting the top crust:
    - Leave a ¼-inch (5-mm) rim of dough, as in step 7.
    - Brush the inside of this rim with egg wash.
    - Roll out and cut a top crust slightly larger than the top of the mold. Place it on top of the filled mold.
    - Crimp or pinch the two layers of pastry together with the fingers to seal.

11. Decorate the top crust with pastry cutouts, if desired. Seal the cutouts to the crust with egg wash. Make one or two vent holes in the top crust to allow the steam to escape. Fit pastry tubes into these holes to form chimneys in order to keep juices from running over the top crust and spoiling its appearance.

12. To bake:
    - Preheat an oven to 400°F (200°C). Place the pâté on a sheet pan (if you are using a bottomless mold, it will, of course, already be on a sheet pan) and put it in the oven.
    - After 10 minutes, reduce the heat to 350°F (175°C). The higher initial temperature helps to brown the pastry. Bake at this lower temperature until the internal temperature reaches 160° to 165°F (72°C).
    - For an average rectangular mold, the baking time will be about 1 to 2 hours. Small molds that make 1 to 4 portions will take 45 minutes or less. For very large molds, use a baking temperature of 325°F (160°C) so that they cook evenly. Extend the baking time accordingly.

13. Remove the pâté from the oven. Let the pâté cool to room temperature in its mold. For a pâté made without a top crust, first let it cool until it is warm. Then let it finish cooling with a weight on top in order to give the pâté a firmer texture. The weight should be large enough to cover the meat but small enough so that it doesn't touch the pastry rim. This can be accomplished by cutting a board to the proper size, laying it in place on the pâté, and placing the weights on the board. (Obviously, this cannot be done if there is a top crust.)

14. When the pâté is cool, prepare an aspic jelly. Melt the aspic and flavor it, if desired, with a little sherry, port, or Madeira wine. Cool it according to the procedure on page 670. Fill the pâté with the aspic.
    - If the pâté has a pastry top, pour the aspic through the vent hole or holes, using a funnel, until the pâté is completely full.
    - If the pâté has no top crust, fill it with enough aspic to completely cover the top of the meat. Refrigerate until the aspic is set.

15. Remove the pâté carefully from the mold.

16. Pâtés without a top crust may now be decorated and reglazed with aspic if desired. Decorate as desired (using the materials suggested on page 671) by dipping the decorations in liquid aspic and setting them in place. Chill briefly, then apply a little more aspic to glaze the top.

17. For storage, handling, and presentation, see page 666.

Preparing Forcemeat Terrines

Terrines, like pâtés, may be baked in molds of various shapes and sizes. Traditional oval molds, for example, have long been popular. For ease of portion control, however, rectangular molds are the most appropriate.

A terrine may be lined with thin sheets of fatback, although this is optional. The layer of fat does not contribute significantly, as is widely believed, to keeping the meat moist during baking; after all, the terrine mold itself is more moistureproof than the layer of fat. Although such a fat lining is traditional, today's diners are more likely to find a rim of fat unappetizing. Of course, the fat layer can be removed before serving. Alternatively, a sheet of caul fat, which is much thinner than a sheet of fatback, can be used to line the mold.

Procedure for Preparing Forcemeat Terrines

1. Prepare the desired forcemeat (see p. 675).

2. Prepare the selected garnish. Meat garnishes are usually cut into strips, which are laid lengthwise in the mold.

3. Marinate the garnish as desired. This step is optional but adds to the flavor.

4. Prepare the mold. Do not use a hinged or collapsible mold, which cannot be placed in a water bath. If desired, line the mold with thin sheets of fatback (sliced on a slicing machine) or with a sheet of caul fat, letting the excess hang over the sides. Make the sheets of fat sufficiently large so that the amount of fat hanging over the sides can be folded over to cover the top completely. If the mold is not lined with fat, grease it well.

5. Place a layer of forcemeat in the bottom of the mold. If no garnish is used, simply fill the mold. Spread the forcemeat evenly and rap the mold sharply on the workbench to dislodge any air bubbles.

6. Arrange a layer of garnish on top of the forcemeat.

7. Continue adding forcemeat and garnish until they are all used. End with a layer of forcemeat on top. Two or three layers of garnish are usually sufficient.

8. If a fat lining has been used, fold the excess fat over the top of the forcemeat to cover it.

9. Cover the top with a sheet of aluminum foil. Cut a few holes in the foil to allow steam to escape.

10. Place the mold in a water bath for baking. Make sure the bath is deep enough to allow the hot water to come halfway up the sides of the mold. Bake at 350°F (175°C) until the internal temperature registers 165°F (74°C).

11. Remove the terrine from the water bath and place it on a rack to cool. When it has cooled somewhat but is still warm, finish cooling the pâté with a weight, as explained in the procedure for making pâtés. It should not be weighted when it is still hot because it is too fragile when hot and may split or fracture, and the weight may force out too much juice. If a looser texture is desired, cool the terrine without weighting it.

12. When the terrine is completely cool, cover and refrigerate it.

13. The terrine may be sealed with a layer of fat or aspic. These protect the terrine from air and help preserve it.

   • To add a layer of fat, melt lard (or rendered duck fat or other fat appropriate to the terrine), then let stand until cool but still liquid. The terrine should be cool, about 50°F (10°C). Pour in enough fat to cover the meat completely. Let stand until the fat has congealed, then cover and refrigerate. The purpose of this fat is only to extend the keeping qualities of the terrine. It should be removed before serving.

   • Add aspic to a terrine in the same way as adding a layer of fat; see also the procedure for adding aspic to a pâté, page 678. Unlike melted fat, aspic extends the storage life of a terrine only a few days because the aspic itself dries out. On the other hand, aspic contributes to both flavor and appearance. If desired, apply decorations to the top of the terrine and add another layer of aspic to glaze.

Veal and Ham Terrine

Yield (approximate): 2 lb (1 kg)

U.S.	Metric	Ingredients	PROCEDURE
2 lb	1 kg	Veal Forcemeat (p. 675) Garnish:	1. Prepare the forcemeat according to the recipe on p. 675. Refrigerate it until it is very cold.
4 oz	125 g	Veal, lean, trimmed	2. Cut the veal, ham, and fatback for the garnish into strips about ¼ inch (6 mm) thick. Mix with the brandy and marinate in the refrigerator 1 hour or longer.
4 oz	125 g	Smoked ham	
1 oz	30 g	Fresh pork fatback	
2 oz	60 mL	Brandy	
as needed	as needed	Fresh pork fatback or caul fat for lining molds (optional)	3. Have ready a 2-qt (2-L) rectangular terrine mold. 4. If using fatback to line the mold, have the fat very cold. Cut it on a slicer into broad, thin slices less than ⅛ inch (3 mm) thick. Line the mold with the slices, overlapping them by about ¼ inch (6 mm). Let the tops of the slices hang over the edges. If using caul fat, line the mold with a large sheet of caul, letting the edges hang over the edge of the mold. If not using caul or fat, grease the mold well. 5. Fill the terrine with alternating layers of forcemeat and garnish, beginning and ending with forcemeat and laying the strips of garnish lengthwise in the terrine. Press the meat firmly into the terrine so that there are no air bubbles. 6. If using sheets of fat to line the mold, fold the overhanging fat over the top of the forcemeat to cover. 7. Cover with foil. 8. Set the terrine in a hot water bath. Bake at 350°F (175°C) until the internal temperature is 165°F (74°C). 9. Remove from the oven and cool until just warm. Weight and continue to cool, following the basic procedure on page 679. Finish, if desired, with a layer of melted fat or aspic, as described in the basic procedure.

Per 1 ounce:
Calories, 170; Protein, 5 g; Fat, 15 g (83% cal.); Cholesterol, 50 mg;
Carbohydrates, 0 g; Fiber, 0 g; Sodium, 250 mg.

VARIATIONS

Veal and Ham Terrine with Foie Gras

Prepare as in the basic recipe, but place a layer of sliced, cooked foie gras down the center of the terrine. Use slices of foie gras terrine (p. 693) or canned foie gras pâté. A row of sliced truffles may be placed on top of the foie gras layer.

Veal and Tongue Terrine

Use cooked, cured beef tongue in place of the ham.

Rabbit Terrine

Bone out a rabbit, keeping the loin meat in 2 long strips. Make a rabbit forcemeat by following the veal forcemeat recipe but substituting meat from the rabbit legs for all or part of the veal. Soak, clean, and liquefy the rabbit liver according to the procedure on page 674. Add it to the forcemeat. Omit the garnish from the basic recipe, instead using the rabbit loins marinated in the brandy. Fold the thin end of each loin back on itself so that it is of uniform thickness. When filling the terrine, put half the forcemeat into the mold, lay the loins end to end down the center of the terrine, then fill with the remaining forcemeat.

    Optional step: Make a stock with the rabbit bones. Reduce the stock to a glaze, cool, and mix with the forcemeat.
    Optional step: Add a small quantity of nuts, such as skinned pistachios, to the forcemeat.

Game Terrine

Prepare as in the basic recipe, using Game Forcemeat (p. 675) and using strips of game meat instead of the veal and ham for garnish. Optional: Add a small quantity of green peppercorns, rinsed and drained, to the forcemeat.

Duck Terrine

Bone out a duck. Use the leg meat, any trimmings, and the liver for making Duck Forcemeat (p. 675). Flavor the forcemeat lightly with grated orange zest, using the zest of half an orange for each 2 lb (1 kg) forcemeat. If desired, flavor the forcemeat with duck stock reduced to a glaze and cooled. Use the breast meat for garnish, omitting the veal and ham from the basic recipe but keeping the fatback. Cut the breast meat into strips and marinate in the brandy with the fatback strips.

Country Terrine

Use pork forcemeat, keeping the grind rather coarse. Chop the garnish coarsely and mix with the forcemeat.

GALANTINES

A *galantine* is a ground meat mixture—that is, a forcemeat—that is wrapped in the skin of the product it is made from, such as chicken or duck. A galantine is almost always poached although, in some instances, it is roasted.

A galantine is made by rolling up a forcemeat in a large piece of skin, giving it a cylindrical or sausage shape that yields round slices. Consequently, the name galantine is also given to forcemeats or other mixtures (such as mousselines) that are rolled into a sausage shape in a piece of parchment, plastic film, or other material.

A finished galantine is often displayed whole, decorated and glazed with aspic, with a few slices removed to show a cut cross section. For à la carte service, slices of galantine are served the same way as slices of pâté and terrine.

The following is a representative galantine recipe. The procedure is illustrated in Figure 23.4.

Chicken Galantine

Yield: 3 lb (1.25 kg)

U.S.	Metric	Ingredients	PROCEDURE
1	1	Roasting chicken, about 5 lb (2.25 kg)	1. One day in advance, prepare the chicken. Cut off the wings at the second joint. Slit the skin of the chicken along the backbone and carefully remove the skin in one piece. Remove the breasts, keeping them whole. Remove the meat from the legs and wings and reserve it for making the forcemeat.
to taste	to taste	Salt	
to taste	to taste	White pepper	2. Lay the skin flat, inside up, and trim it into a neat rectangle. Remove all fat and connective tissue. Place a piece of cheesecloth on a sheet pan and lay the skin in the center of it.
4 oz	125 mL	Brandy	
			3. Butterfly the breast meat and pound it flat so that the two breasts together make a rectangle. Place the flattened breast meat on the center of the skin. There should be at least 1–2 inches (2–5 cm) of skin showing around all sides of the breast meat rectangle. Sprinkle with salt, white pepper, and half of the brandy. Cover with plastic film and refrigerate overnight.
			4. Trim all fat and connective tissue from the leg and wing meat and measure 9 oz (250 g) for making the forcemeat. Measure another 8 oz (225 g) leg meat for the garnish and mix it with the remaining brandy. Reserve any remaining meat for another use.
			5. Use the carcass and giblets for making stock.
1 lb	450 g	Chicken Forcemeat I, p. 675, made with part of the leg meat (see step 3)	6. Prepare the forcemeat, grinding it very fine by using a food processor or by passing it 3 times through the fine blade of a grinder. Keep it cold at all times.
1	1	Liver from the chicken	7. Soak, clean, and liquefy the livers according to the procedure on page 674. Mix the liver purée with the forcemeat.
		Garnish:	8. Cut the chicken leg meat, ham, tongue, pimiento, and truffle into small dice.
8 oz	225 g	Leg meat from the chicken (from step 4)	9. Mix the diced garnish and the pistachios into the forcemeat until well combined.
2 oz	60 g	Smoked ham	10. Drain the brandy from the chicken skin and pat dry with a clean towel.
2 oz	60 g	Cured beef tongue, cooked	11. Form the forcemeat into a cylinder the length of the breast meat rectangle. Place the forcemeat on the breast meat and roll it up into the skin with the aid of the cheesecloth.
1 oz	30 g	Pimientos, rinsed and dried	12. Roll the galantine in the cheesecloth and tie the ends. Then roll the galantine in a sheet of parchment, working to get the roll as smooth as possible. Tie the roll loosely at 2-inch (5-cm) intervals. (This method is used when the galantine must be completely smooth, with no tie marks. For a simpler method, tie the cheesecloth roll in 3 or 4 places and at the ends.)
1 oz	30 g	Truffles (optional)	
2 oz	60 g	Pistachios, blanched and skinned	
as needed	as needed	Chicken stock	13. Poach the galantine slowly in chicken stock until the internal temperature is 160°F (71°C). This will take about 45–60 minutes. Retie the galantine, which will have shrunk, then let it cool completely in the stock.
			14. Remove from the stock, unwrap, and decorate as desired.

Per 1 ounce:
Calories, 90; Protein, 5 g; Fat, 7 g (70% cal.); Cholesterol, 30 mg; Carbohydrates, 0 g; Fiber, 0 g; Sodium, 100 mg.

Figure 23.4 Making a chicken galantine.

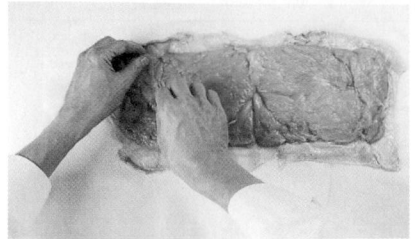

(a) Place the flattened breast meat on the center of the skin so that there is an inch or two (3–5 cm) of skin showing around all sides.

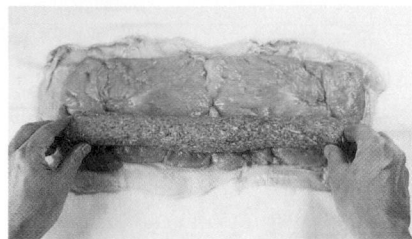

(b) Shape the forcemeat into a cylinder and place it along one edge of the rectangle of chicken as shown.

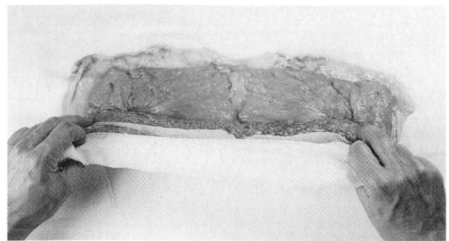

(c) With the aid of the cheesecloth, roll up the forcemeat in the chicken skin. Do not roll the cheesecloth into the chicken.

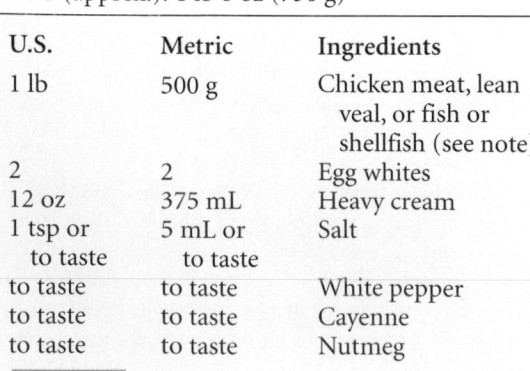

(d) Tie the ends of the cheesecloth securely. Proceed as indicated in the recipe on p. 681.

Terrines Based on Mousselines

The body of most fish terrines, as well as some vegetable terrines and other specialty items, consists of a mousseline forcemeat. They are made like traditional terrines, except that a mousseline forcemeat takes the place of the straight forcemeat.

A mousseline forcemeat consists of raw, puréed fish, poultry, or meat combined with heavy cream and, usually but not always, eggs or egg whites. Because they contain no starch or binder, and because of the large quantity of cream they contain, mousselines are the most delicate of forcemeats. The procedure for making a mousseline forcemeat is detailed in the basic recipe below.

Ingredient proportions in mousseline forcemeat depend on the qualities of the meat or fish being used. The albumin content of the egg white makes the mousseline firm when it is cooked. If the meat or fish you are using has a high albumin content, however, you may be able to reduce the quantity of egg white or, in some cases, you may not need any egg. Similarly, the amount of cream depends on the firmness of the fish and on the intended use of the forcemeat. If it is to be the base of a terrine that will be sliced, too much cream will make it too delicate. On the other hand, for small timbale molds and similar items that don't need to be as firm, the quantity of cream can be increased beyond the amount indicated in the recipe below.

As for straight forcemeats, it is important to keep the ingredients cold at all times.

The procedure for assembling and cooking a mousseline terrine is the same as for making a regular forcemeat terrine (see p. 679), except that the internal temperature, when done, is slightly lower, about 158° to 160°F (70°C).

Cooked vegetables, fish fillets, and other appropriate items are used as garnish. Two or more mousselines can be layered in the mold to make multicolored terrines. Alternatively, a mousseline forcemeat can be spread on the bottom and sides of the mold, which is then filled with a different mousseline plus garnish and topped with a layer of the first mousseline.

Basic Mousseline Forcemeat

Yield (approx.): 1 lb 8 oz (750 g)

U.S.	Metric	Ingredients	PROCEDURE
1 lb	500 g	Chicken meat, lean veal, or fish or shellfish (see note)	1. Dice the meat and place in the container of a food processor. Process until puréed.
2	2	Egg whites	2. Add the egg whites and process until well blended.
12 oz	375 mL	Heavy cream	3. Force the purée through a sieve to remove sinews and other connective tissue.
1 tsp or to taste	5 mL or to taste	Salt	4. Put the purée into a stainless-steel bowl that is nested in another bowl of crushed ice. Chill until the purée is very cold.
to taste	to taste	White pepper	5. Gradually blend in the cream by hand.
to taste	to taste	Cayenne	6. Season with salt, white pepper, cayenne, and a dash of nutmeg.
to taste	to taste	Nutmeg	7. Test the seasoning and consistency by poaching, cooling, and tasting a small quenelle. Adjust as necessary.

Per 1 ounce:

Calories, 70; Protein, 5 g; Fat, 6 g (73% cal.); Cholesterol, 35 mg; Carbohydrates, 0 g; Fiber, 0 g; Sodium, 120 mg.

Note: Use lean, skinless chicken meat, lean veal, fillets from lean, white fish, or shellfish such as scallops, shrimp, or lobster.

Terrine of Vegetables with Chicken Mousseline

Yield: 2 lb (1 kg)

U.S.	Metric	Ingredients	PROCEDURE
1 lb 8 oz	750 g	Chicken Mousseline Forcemeat (p. 682)	1. Mix the chicken mousseline with the chopped herbs and the glace de volaille, if used.
2 tbsp	7 g	Chopped parsley	
1 tsp	1 g	Fresh tarragon, chopped	
½ oz	15 g	Glace de volaille, melted (optional)	
2 oz	60 g	Zucchini, small, trimmed	2. Cut the zucchini into strips about ¼–½ inch (1 cm) wide. Blanch 2 minutes in salted water, drain, and chill.
2 oz	60 g	Red bell pepper, cored and seeded	3. Char and peel the red pepper (see p. 443). Cut it into strips.
2 oz	60 g	Carrots, trimmed and peeled	4. Cut the carrots into strips like the zucchini. Blanch 3 minutes, drain, and chill.
2 oz	60 g	Green beans, trimmed	5. Blanch the green beans for 1–2 minutes, depending on their tenderness.
2 oz	60 g	Shiitake mushroom caps	6. Cut the mushroom caps in half. Blanch for 30 seconds, drain, cool, and pat dry to remove extra moisture.

7. Butter well the bottom and sides of a 1½-qt (1.5-L) terrine mold.
8. Spread one-third of the mousseline on the bottom of the mold, being sure to eliminate air bubbles.
9. Arrange the carrot strips and beans lengthwise in the mold, pushing them partway into the mousseline. Keep the vegetables at least ½ inch (5 mm) from the sides of the mold (see Figure 23.5).
10. Spread a thin layer of mousseline over the vegetables. Arrange the mushroom caps down the center of the mold, then cover with another thin layer of mousseline. About one-third of the mousseline should be left.
11. Arrange the pepper and zucchini strips lengthwise in the mold, adding a little more mousseline as necessary.
12. Top with the remaining mousseline, again spreading it carefully to avoid air bubbles. Rap the terrine sharply on the workbench to eliminate any remaining air bubbles. Smooth the top of the mousseline with a spatula.
13. Cover tightly with foil. Set in a hot water bath and bake in an oven heated to 325°F (165°C) until set firm, about 1 hour and 15 minutes.
14. Cool thoroughly, then chill well in the refrigerator.
15. Unmold. Slice carefully with a knife dipped in hot water. Serve garnished with a few salad greens and an appropriate cold sauce.

Per 1 ounce:
Calories, 60; Protein, 4 g; Fat, 5 g (67% cal.); Cholesterol, 25 mg; Carbohydrates, 1 g; Fiber, 0 g; Sodium, 90 mg.

VARIATIONS

Instead of the vegetables indicated, select your choice of seasonal vegetables.

For a more luxurious terrine, include thin slices of truffle with the garnish, or omit the parsley and add minced truffle to the mousseline.

Seafood Terrine with Vegetables

Use a fish or shellfish mousseline instead of the chicken mousseline. Reduce the number and quantity of vegetables. Add to the garnish some strips of smoked salmon.

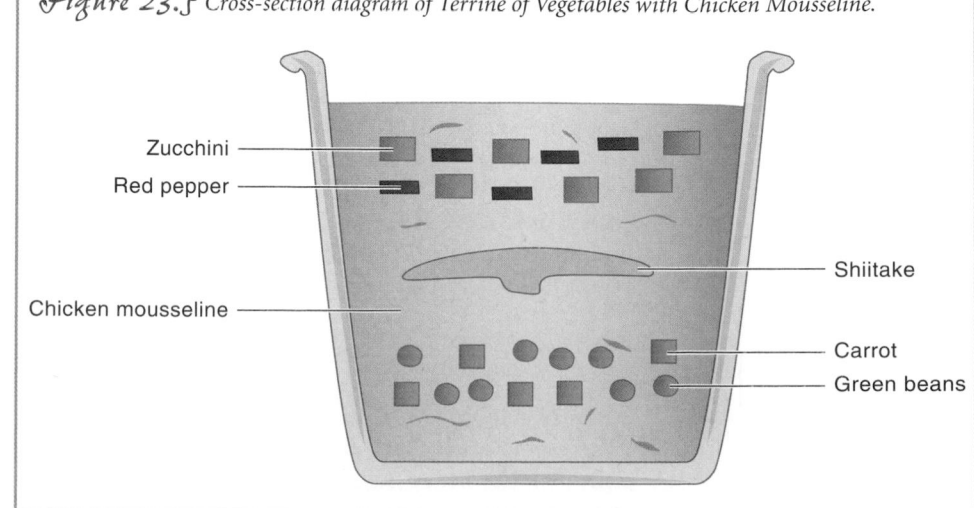

Figure 23.5 Cross-section diagram of Terrine of Vegetables with Chicken Mousseline.

Zucchini
Red pepper
Chicken mousseline
Shiitake
Carrot
Green beans

Terrines and Other Molds with Gelatin

All the terrines we have discussed so far are traditional cooked terrines—that is, the raw force-meat is cooked in the mold. There are many kinds of uncooked terrines as well. These are not cooked after assembly but are chilled until set. Any ingredients that require cooking are cooked before assembly. The terrines we discuss in this section rely on gelatin for their structure.

Preparing these items in terrine molds allows them to be cut into slices for serving, just as traditional forcemeat terrines are. They can also be made in molds of any other shape, including portion-size molds, which can simply be unmolded and garnished for serving. Cooked terrines, on the other hand, are best made in regularly shaped, symmetrical molds so that they cook uniformly.

Most molds bound with gelatin fall into two general categories: those based on aspics and those based on mousses.

ASPIC MOLDS

Aspic-based terrines are simply glorified gelatin molds. That is, they consist of various solid ingredients held together by gelatin in the form of aspic jelly.

The proportion of aspic to solids can vary greatly. At one extreme, there may be just enough aspic to hold the solid ingredients together, so that the aspic jelly itself is almost not evident. On the other hand, the aspic may predominate, with various solid ingredients suspended in it at intervals. For this latter type to succeed, the aspic jelly must be of excellent quality, with good flavor, not too firm a texture, and sparkling clarity.

The majority of aspic terrines fall somewhere between these extremes.

The following procedure is applicable to the production of most aspic terrines and other aspic molds:

1. Either line the mold with aspic, following the procedure on page 672, or pour a layer of aspic into the bottom of the mold. Chill until firm.
2. Arrange a layer of garnish in the mold.
3. Add just enough aspic jelly to cover the solid garnish. Chill until firm.
4. Repeat steps 2 and 3 until the mold is full.
5. For best storage, leave the aspic in the mold, covered tightly with plastic film, until service time.

Terrines made by this method depend on a crystal-clear aspic jelly for their appearance and are often very elegant. Another approach is simply to combine the jelly with a mixture of ingredients and fill the terrine with this mixture. A clarified aspic may not be necessary for this method. Terrines made this way range from coarse, peasant-style dishes to more elaborate constructions such as the Lentil and Leek Terrine on page 687.

Headcheese and a number of other commercially made luncheon-meat loaves are examples of this type of terrine. Tripes à la Môde de Caen (p. 280), when properly made, can also be chilled until solid and unmolded because it contains enough natural gelatin from the calves' feet and other ingredients. Jambon Persillé or Parslied Ham (p. 688) is another example of a country-style aspic-based terrine made with unclarified jelly.

MOUSSES

A savory cold *mousse*, as used for the base of a terrine, is a preparation of puréed meat, poultry, fish, vegetable, or other food, bound with gelatin and usually lightened with the addition of partially whipped heavy cream. (It is true that the terms *mousse* and *mousseline* are often used more or less interchangeably, but we use them here in two distinct senses in order to avoid confusion.)

The gelatin used to bind or set the mousse may be added in the form of an aspic jelly or as powdered gelatin softened and dissolved in another liquid ingredient.

Because mousses, like aspics, are not cooked after assembly but merely chilled, they are often prepared not only in terrines but in various decorative, irregularly shaped molds. The production of mousses is relatively simple. The procedure consists of four main steps:

1. Purée the main ingredient.
2. Add the aspic jelly or dissolved gelatin.
3. Fold in the lightly whipped cream and season to taste.
4. Pour into the prepared mold.

Molds are usually lined with aspic jelly and decorated according to the procedures on page 672. As with other kinds of terrines, garnish, if any, is either mixed with the mousse or arranged in the mold as the mousse is added.

Although this method is really little more than mixing together the ingredients in a given order, two precautions must be taken:

1. **Carry out the entire procedure, including the pouring of the mixture into the mold, quickly and in one continuous process.**
   If you stop partway through the procedure, the gelatin is likely to set, and you will have a lumpy, poorly mixed product.

2. **Do not overwhip the cream.**
   Whip it only until it forms soft mounds. When cream is overwhipped, it breaks and becomes grainy. This same effect can be caused by the extra beating the cream gets when it is being folded into the mousse mixture. A mousse made with overwhipped cream tastes dry and grainy, not smooth and creamy.

Mousses can also be made without gelatin or other binders. A soft mousse is simply a puréed or ground food with the addition of lightly whipped cream. Although these soft mousses are too soft to be used in terrines, they can be spooned into neat, oval quenelle shapes onto salad plates, garnished attractively, and served as elegant first courses.

Terrine of Vegetables and Chicken in Aspic

Yield: approximately 2 lb 8 oz (1.1 kg)

U.S.	Metric	Ingredients	PROCEDURE
6 oz	175 g	Cooked chicken breast, boneless and skinless	1. If the chicken pieces are large, cut them in half lengthwise. They should be no more than about 2–2½ inches (5–6 cm) wide. Arrange them on a rack with the best side up. Coat them with a thin layer of chaud-froid. Chill until set.
2–4 oz	100 g	Mayonnaise chaud-froid (p. 670)	
		Vegetable garnish AP:	2. Trim and peel the carrots. Cut into long batonnet shapes. Cook the carrots until tender but still firm. Chill.
4 oz	115 g	Carrots	3. Trim the artichokes down to the bases, rubbing with cut lemon to keep them from darkening. Cook in water with a little lemon juice until tender. Drain and chill. Cut crosswise into strips about ¼ inch (6 mm) thick.
2	2	Artichokes, medium	
1	1	Lemon	4. Trim the stems from the spinach and rinse in several changes of water. Blanch, drain, rinse in cold water, and squeeze firmly to remove excess moisture. Chop coarsely.
8 oz	225 g	Spinach	
4 oz	115 g	Tomatoes, whole, fresh	5. Peel the tomatoes, cut them in half horizontally, and remove seeds and juice. Place them on a cutting board cut side down and slice vertically into slices about ¼ inch (6 mm) thick. Salt the slices lightly and let drain. Dry lightly on clean toweling.
3 oz	90 g	Green beans	6. Trim the green beans and cook until tender but still firm. Chill.
6 oz	175 g	Asparagus	7. Remove the woody bottoms from the asparagus spears. Peel the lower ends of the spears. Cook until tender but still firm. Chill.
1 pt (approximately)	500 mL (approximately)	Aspic jelly	8. Melt and cool the aspic jelly according to the procedure on page 670.
			9. Line a 1½-qt (1.4-L) terrine mold with a layer of aspic according to the procedure on page 672 or ladle a ¼-inch (6-mm) layer of aspic onto the bottom of the mold. Chill until set.
			10. Arrange the carrots and then the spinach in the mold. Add just enough aspic to cover. (See Figure 23.6. Note that this diagram shows only the relative positions of the ingredients. The actual proportion of vegetables is greater than shown.) Chill until set.
			11. Arrange half of the chicken pieces down the center of the mold, chaud-froid side down. Place the artichokes and beans alongside the chicken. Add just enough aspic to cover. Chill until set.
			12. Arrange the rest of the chicken, the tomato, and the asparagus in the mold. Add just enough aspic to cover. Chill overnight, until set firm.
			13. For service, unmold and slice carefully with a sharp knife dipped in hot water. Serve with a vinaigrette.

Per 1 ounce:
Calories, 20; Protein, 2 g; Fat, 1 g (36% cal.); Cholesterol, 5 mg; Carbohydrates, 2 g; Fiber, 1 g; Sodium, 20 mg.

VARIATIONS

Substitute other appropriate vegetables in season. Other items, such as turkey, rabbit, fresh or smoked fish, and seafood, can be substituted for the chicken, or omit the protein item entirely and increase the quantity of vegetables.

Terrine of Vegetables with Foie Gras in Aspic

Substitute slices of foie gras terrine (p. 693) for the chicken. Omit the chaud-froid.

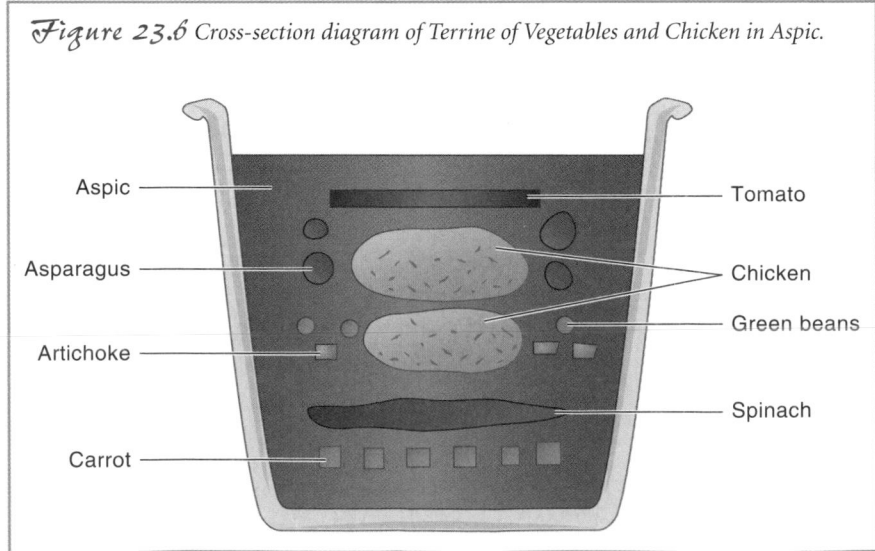

Figure 23.6 Cross-section diagram of Terrine of Vegetables and Chicken in Aspic.

Aspic — Tomato
Asparagus — Chicken
— Green beans
Artichoke — Spinach
Carrot

Lentil and Leek Terrine with Smoked Turkey and Prosciutto

Yield: approximately 2 lb (1 kg)

U.S.	Metric	Ingredients	PROCEDURE
5 oz	150 g	Lentils, preferably green Le Puy variety (see note)	1. Soak the lentils several hours or overnight. Drain, combine with the carrots, the onion stuck with the cloves, and the bay leaf in a heavy pot. Add enough water to cover by several inches (more than 5 cm). Simmer until tender but still firm and whole. For presoaked green lentils, this takes less than 10 minutes. Drain in a fine strainer. Discard the onion, cloves, and bay leaf. Cool the lentils.
2 oz	60 g	Carrots, cut brunoise	
1 medium	1 medium	Onion, whole, peeled	
2	2	Cloves	
1	1	Bay leaf	
2 lb	1 kg	Leeks, small (see note)	2. Trim the root ends and the coarse leaves from the leeks, leaving the lighter green parts attached so that the leeks will be as long as possible. Wash carefully. Simmer or steam until tender. Chill.
6 oz	185 g	Smoked turkey	3. Cut the turkey into long strips about ½ inch (12 mm) wide. Wrap each strip in a slice of prosciutto.
2 oz	60 g	Prosciutto, sliced tissue-thin	
5 oz	150 mL	Chicken stock	4. Soften the gelatin in the stock, then heat to dissolve it. Cool the aspic slightly. Because this is a very strong aspic, it should be kept slightly warm or it will solidify too quickly when mixed with the lentils.
½ oz	15 g	Gelatin powder	
to taste	to taste	Salt	

5. Mix the aspic with the lentils. Add salt to taste. From this point, the terrine must be assembled quickly so that it is finished before the aspic sets.

6. Line a 1¼-qt (1.25-L) terrine with plastic film to make unmolding easier. Cover the bottom of the terrine with a layer of leeks arranged lengthwise and end to end. Arrange them tightly against each other so that there are no gaps (see Figure 23.7). If using large leeks, cut them in half lengthwise and arrange in the mold cut side up.

7. Fill the terrine with the lentils, alternating with the turkey strips. Arrange the strips lengthwise and at intervals so that they are distributed evenly in the lentils.

8. Top with another layer of leeks, pressing them down firmly and leveling the top. If using large leeks, cut in half lengthwise and place them cut side down in the terrine.

9. Cover and chill overnight, until set firm.

10. Unmold and slice with a sharp knife dipped in hot water. Plate and garnish with a few salad greens. Serve with a vinaigrette, preferably made with walnut or hazelnut oil.

Per 1 ounce:
Calories, 40; Protein, 4 g; Fat, 1 g (11% cal.); Cholesterol, 5 mg; Carbohydrates, 5 g; Fiber, 1 g; Sodium, 60 mg.

Note: Green Le Puy lentils give the best results, as they retain their shape well and have the best appearance. The amount of leeks needed depends on the trimming yield, which can vary greatly. You will need enough trimmed, cooked leeks to cover the top and bottom of the terrine mold. Very small leeks are best because they cover the top and bottom of the terrine without filling it too much. Larger leeks can be cut in half lengthwise.

VARIATIONS

Various items can be used instead of the turkey and prosciutto, such as ham, duck breast cooked rare, or loin of rabbit.

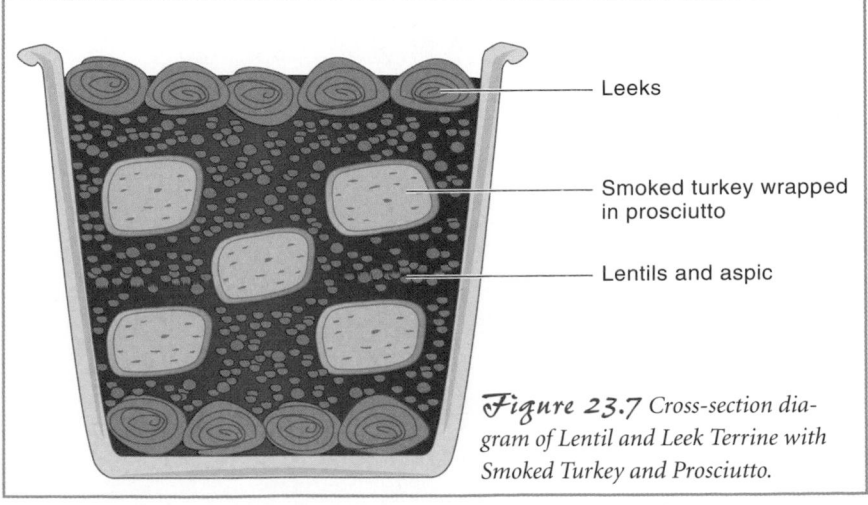

Leeks

Smoked turkey wrapped in prosciutto

Lentils and aspic

Figure 23.7 Cross-section diagram of Lentil and Leek Terrine with Smoked Turkey and Prosciutto.

Jambon Persillé (Parslied Ham in Aspic)

Yield: approximately 2 lb (1 kg)

U.S.	Metric	Ingredients
2	2	Pig feet, split
1	1	Onion, stuck with 1 clove
		Sachet:
1	1	Garlic clove
1	1	Bay leaf
½ tsp	2 mL	Thyme
½ tsp	2 mL	Tarragon
12 oz	350 mL	White wine
as needed	as needed	White stock
1 lb 8 oz	750 g	Mild-cured ham, in 1 or more large pieces

PROCEDURE

1. Put the pig feet, onion, sachet, and wine in a heavy pot. Add enough white stock to cover. Simmer 2 hours, adding more stock or water as needed.

2. Add the ham to the pot. Add more stock as needed. Simmer until the ham is tender. Cooking time will vary greatly, depending on the ham.

3. Remove the ham. Trim off any fat and skin. Cut the ham into large dice. Remove any meat from the pig feet, chop it, and add it to the ham. (Skin from the feet may also be added, if desired.) Chill the meat.

4. Skim and strain the cooking liquid. The stock may be clarified if desired, but this is not necessary if a traditional rustic look is desired. The pig feet should have yielded sufficient gelatin, but test to make sure and add more gelatin if needed to make a strong aspic; see the procedure on page 668.

U.S.	Metric	Ingredients
½ cup	30 g	Chopped parsley
½ oz	15 mL	Wine vinegar
if needed	if needed	Salt
if needed	if needed	Pepper

5. Melt the aspic (if it has congealed), and add the vinegar and parsley. Taste and add salt and pepper if necessary.

6. Select the desired molds; large salad bowls are traditional. Line the bottom of the mold with a thin layer of the parsley aspic. Chill until firm.

7. Combine the ham and aspic and pour into the mold. Chill until set.

8. To serve, unmold and slice. Serve unadorned or plated with salad greens and vinaigrette.

Per 1 ounce:
Calories, 96; Protein, 10 g; Fat, 6 g (49% cal.); Cholesterol, 34 mg; Carbohydrates, 1 g; Fiber, 0 g; Sodium, 385 mg.

Tricolor Vegetable Terrine

Yield: approximately 1 lb 12 oz (800 g)

U.S.	Metric	Ingredients	PROCEDURE
1 lb	450 g	Spinach	1. Have ready a 1-qt (1-L) terrine mold. For ease of unmolding, line with plastic film.
¼ oz	7 g	Shallot, minced	
¼ oz	7 g	Butter	2. Trim the stems from the spinach and wash it well in several changes of water. Cook in boiling, salted water until done, about 2 minutes, and drain. Rinse under cold water to cool. Drain. Squeeze dry.
1 tsp	5 mL	Gelatin powder	
1 oz	30 mL	Chicken stock, vegetable stock, or water, cold	
to taste	to taste	Salt	3. Chop the spinach into fine pieces by hand or in a food processor.
2 oz	60 mL	Heavy cream	4. Sweat the shallots in butter until soft. Add the spinach and cook slowly until quite dry. Cool thoroughly but do not chill.
			5. Soften the gelatin in the stock, then heat until it is dissolved. Cool and stir into the spinach. Add salt to taste.
			6. Quickly whip the cream until it forms soft peaks. Immediately fold it into the spinach mixture. Pour it into the mold and smooth with a spatula. Chill until set.
5 oz	150 g	Cauliflower, trimmed	7. Steam the cauliflower and turnips until they are tender. Purée in a food processor. For the smoothest texture, force the purée through a sieve. Mix the vegetables together. Heat slowly in a large sauté pan to dry out the purée slightly. Cool thoroughly but do not chill.
2 oz	60 g	White turnips, peeled	
1 tsp	5 mL	Gelatin powder	
1 oz	30 mL	Chicken stock, vegetable stock, or water, cold	
to taste	to taste	Salt	8. Repeat steps 5 and 6 to make the white mousse. Pour it into the mold on top of the green mousse. Chill.
2 oz	60 mL	Heavy cream	
7 oz	200 g	Carrots, trimmed and peeled	9. Trim, cook, and purée the carrots in the same way, and dry the purée as above. Repeat steps 5 and 6 to make the orange mousse, and add it to the terrine (see Figure 23.8). Chill until set firm.
1 tsp	5 mL	Gelatin powder	
1 oz	30 mL	Chicken stock, vegetable stock, or water, cold	10. Unmold the terrine and slice to serve. Garnish as desired and serve with an appropriate cold sauce.
to taste	to taste	Salt	
2 oz	60 mL	Heavy cream	

Per 1 ounce:
Calories, 30; Protein, 1 g; Fat, 3 g (65% cal.); Cholesterol, 10 mg;
Carbohydrates, 2 g; Fiber, 1 g; Sodium, 20 mg.

VARIATIONS

Other vegetable purées may be substituted for those in the basic recipe.

For a low-fat version, omit the gelatin powder, stock, and heavy cream. In place of the stock and cream, use an equal quantity of a strong aspic. Mix the aspic with the vegetable purées.

Figure 23.8 Cross-section diagram of Tricolor Vegetable Terrine.

Carrot mousse

Cauliflower mousse

Spinach mousse

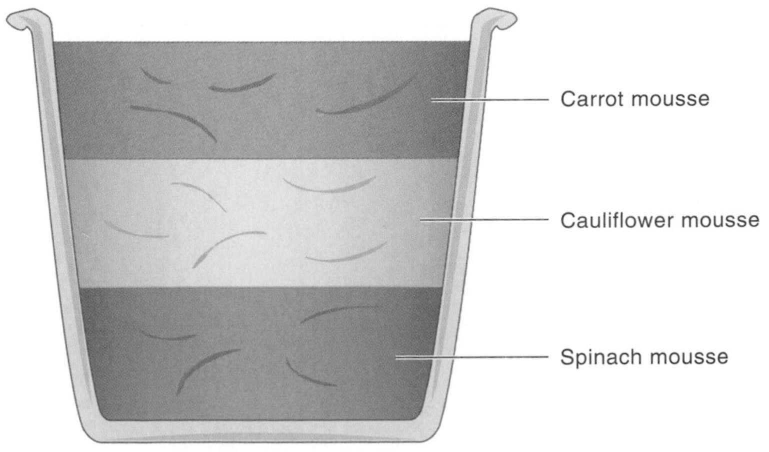

Ham Mousse

Yield: 2 lb (1 kg)

U.S.	Metric	Ingredients	PROCEDURE
1 lb	500 g	Cooked, lean smoked ham	1. Select a mold or molds totaling about 1 qt (1 L) in capacity. If desired, line the molds with aspic and decorate them according to the procedure on page 672. Keep chilled until needed.
5 oz	150 mL	Chicken velouté	
1 tbsp	15 mL	Madeira wine	2. Grind the ham until it is very fine.
to taste	to taste	White pepper	3. Mix the velouté with the puréed ham. Add the Madeira and season to taste with white pepper, dry mustard, and salt. No salt may be needed if the ham is very salty.
to taste	to taste	Dry mustard	
to taste	to taste	Salt	
¼ oz	7 g	Gelatin powder	4. Soften the gelatin in the stock. Heat the stock until the gelatin dissolves, then cool the liquid aspic, but do not let it set.
4 oz	125 mL	Chicken stock, cold	
8 oz	250 mL	Heavy cream	5. Whip the cream until it forms soft peaks.
			6. Add the aspic jelly to the ham mixture and stir until well combined.
			7. Quickly and thoroughly fold the cream into the ham mixture. Taste and adjust seasonings if necessary.
			8. Fill the prepared molds. Chill several hours or overnight until set firm. Unmold just before serving.

Per 1 ounce:
Calories, 50; Protein, 3 g; Fat, 4 g (69% cal.); Cholesterol, 20 mg; Carbohydrates, 1 g; Fiber, 0 g; Sodium, 190 mg.

VARIATIONS

For a denser but less rich mousse, reduce the quantity of cream as desired.

Substitute prosciutto for one-eighth to one-fourth of the cooked ham.

Instead of velouté, substitute mayonnaise thinned with cream to the thickness of velouté.

Mousses of other meats, poultry, and fish may be prepared according to the same procedure, substituting an appropriate stock (such as fish stock for fish mousse) and using appropriate seasonings in place of the mustard and Madeira (for example, salmon mousse flavored with dill, cayenne, and white wine).

Mousse of Foie Gras

Yield: 1 lb (500 g)

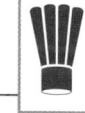

U.S.	Metric	Ingredients	PROCEDURE
8 oz	250 g	Foie gras (see note)	1. Force the foie gras through a sieve to purée it.
4 oz	125 mL	Aspic jelly	2. Melt and cool the aspic according to the procedure on page 670. Add it to the foie gras, mixing it in thoroughly.
4 oz	125 mL	Heavy cream	
to taste	to taste	Salt	3. Whip the cream until it forms soft peaks. Quickly and thoroughly fold it into the foie gras.
to taste	to taste	White pepper	
			4. While folding in the cream, taste and adjust the seasonings with salt and white pepper. It is best to do this while folding in the cream so that there is no delay that would allow the gelatin to set too early and excess mixing, which may overwhip the cream.
			5. Pour at once into a terrine or other mold. Cover tightly and chill at least 1 day.
			6. This dish is very rich and should be served in small quantities, about 2 oz (60 g) per portion. Serve by dipping a spoon into hot water and drawing it across the surface of the terrine, as though scooping ice cream. Place the spoonful in the center of a plate and serve with melba toasts and raw vegetable garnish or salad greens.

Per 1 ounce:
Calories, 50; Protein, 3 g; Fat, 4 g (66% cal.); Cholesterol, 95 mg; Carbohydrates, 1 g; Fiber, 0 g; Sodium, 85 mg.

Note: See page 691 for a discussion of foie gras. Cooked, not raw foie gras is called for in this recipe. Terrine of Foie Gras (p. 693) may be used. If fresh foie gras products are not available, canned foie gras may be used.

Foie Gras, Liver Terrines, and Rillettes

The chapter concludes with three traditional terrines that require somewhat different techniques from those already discussed. It should be noted that, although these items are especially high in fat and cholesterol, they are as popular as they have ever been, even in these times of diet consciousness.

FOIE GRAS TERRINES

The most prized and, perhaps, the most famous ingredient for pâtés and terrines in classical cuisine is *foie gras* (fwah grah). This French term means "fat liver." Foie gras is the fatted liver of specially fed varieties of ducks and geese. Until recently, only canned or processed foie gras products were available in North America. Now, however, the breed of duck that is raised to produce foie gras (called the *mullard*, a cross between the muscovy and white pekin ducks) is grown domestically. Consequently, fresh, raw duck foie gras is now sold in this country. Its availability has created a great deal of enthusiasm among cooks in spite of its high price.

The special feeding of the ducks makes the livers very large, more than 1 lb (500 g) as a rule, with a high fat content. A good-quality fresh foie gras is a pale yellowish-tan color with a smooth, velvety texture, almost the feel of butter. The liver has two lobes, one large and one small.

It is important to be aware that foie gras consists mostly of fat. Indeed, the rich flavor of the fat is the whole reason that foie gras is so highly prized. Any fat that cooks out during preparation is carefully saved and used for another purpose. Those who must avoid fats, especially animal fats, should probably steer clear of this delicacy. For the rest of us, the high price of foie gras helps to protect our health by making overindulgence unlikely.

There are usually two grades of domestic duck foie gras. The A grade is larger, usually 1¼ lb (600 g) or more, with relatively few blemishes and blood spots. The B grade is smaller and has more blood spots and veins.

Preparing Foie Gras for Cooking

No matter how a raw foie gras is to be prepared, it should first be rinsed in cold water and examined closely for green spots. These are caused by bile; they must be cut or scraped away because the bile has a strong, bitter taste. Also, if there are any bits of external fat, remove them.

Next, the liver should be soaked. (This step is not required, but it does improve the product.) Place it in lightly salted ice-cold water or milk to cover. Let stand for up to 2 hours, no longer. Remove from the salted liquid and rinse in fresh, cold water.

For cold preparations such as terrines and mousses, the liver should first be deveined. To devein the foie gras, first let it come to room temperature. Its fat content makes a cold liver too brittle to devein without excessive breakage, which would result in more cooking loss. When the liver is at room temperature, even the heat of the hands melts the fat, so it is important to handle the liver lightly and to work quickly.

Begin by separating the two lobes and laying them, smooth side down, on a clean work surface. Carefully trim off any bloody spots. Grasping a lobe with your thumbs at the sides and fingers underneath in the center, very lightly bend the lobe lengthwise. The top, rough surface should open up slightly, revealing a heavy vein that runs lengthwise through the liver. (If it does not open up, help it along with a shallow incision with the point of a paring knife.) Carefully pull out this vein, along with any other heavy veins that are attached, all the while being careful to keep the liver as intact as possible. Repeat with the other lobe. The foie gras is now ready to be made into a terrine.

No matter how a foie gras is cooked, it is essential to avoid even the slightest overcooking. The liver is delicate, and the fat cooks out very quickly. Even a few seconds too long in a sauté pan can reduce a slice of foie gras to a few specks of connective tissue floating in a puddle of very expensive grease.

LIVER TERRINES

Liver terrines, often called *liver pâtés*, are popular, inexpensive appetizers—except, of course, for those made with foie gras. The classic liver terrine is a mixture of liquefied livers—that is, cleaned, soaked, blended, and strained according to the procedure on page 674—with eggs and seasonings, baked in a terrine until set. An example of this type of recipe can be found on page 694.

This kind of liver terrine generally contains flour as a stabilizer. Because the liver forcemeat is liquid, the flour improves the texture of the cooked product by helping to bind the moisture. Heavy cream is also included in most recipes as a source of fat. Other sources of fat sometimes used in addition to or in place of the cream are ground pork fat, ground bacon, marrow, and rendered foie gras fat left over from making terrines.

Another type of liver terrine consists of a basic pork forcemeat with a liver content high enough so that the flavor of the liver predominates. To make this type of terrine, make the forcemeat on page 675 but use 6 times the quantity of liver. The forcemeat will be quite soft. Follow the basic procedure for making forcemeat terrines (see p. 679), using whole, trimmed chicken livers marinated in brandy as the garnish.

A quick and simple substitute for these more elaborate terrines might be considered a type of rillettes (see the next section), as it consists of a seasoned mixture of cooked meat (liver, in this case) and fat. This is the type of chicken liver pâté found on delicatessen and coffee-shop menus. To make this type of pâté, sauté some chicken livers, mash or purée them, and mix the purée with about one-eighth its weight in rendered chicken fat, pork fat, soft butter, or other fat, or else with one-fourth its weight in cream cheese. Season as desired, with salt, pepper, herbs, brandy or sherry, and/or sautéed minced onion.

RILLETTES

In France's Loire valley, the first thing that customers are likely to be served in a typical neighborhood restaurant, whether they order it or not, is a crock of rillettes and some country bread to spread it on. Variations on this unpretentious dish have become widely popular and are served even in elegant restaurants.

Rillettes (ree yet) is a dish made of pork cooked slowly until it is very tender, then shredded, mixed with its own fat, seasoned, and packed into crocks or terrines.

Variations of the classic dish can be made by using other meats in addition to or instead of pork. Items rich in fat, such as duck and goose, are especially appropriate. Rillettes of lean meats, such as chicken, turkey, and rabbit, can be made, but some pork fat or other fat must be added to them when they are cooking.

Some chefs even serve rillettes made from fish, such as salmon or cod. The basic procedure is the same, except that the cooking time is, of course, much shorter. The cooked fish is shredded, mixed with just enough butter or other fat to give it a pleasant texture, and seasoned well.

A typical recipe for classic pork rillettes is on page 694. Follow the same basic procedure to make duck rillettes and other variations. A recipe for rillettes made with fish is on page 695.

Terrine of Foie Gras

Yield: variable, depending on size of liver

U.S.	Metric	Ingredients
1	1	Fresh, A-grade duck foie gras, about 1½ lb (700 g)
1 tsp	5 mL	Salt
¼ tsp	1 mL	White pepper
½–1 oz	15–30 mL	Choice of wine or liquor: port, Madeira, Sauternes, cognac, or armagnac

PROCEDURE

1. Soak, rinse, and devein the foie gras as described on page 691.

2. Place the liver in a bowl and season with salt and white pepper. Add the selected wine or liquor, using the smaller quantity for cognac or armagnac; if using a sweet wine, use up to but not more than the larger quantity indicated. Turn the liver gently so that all sides are moistened.

3. Cover and refrigerate. Marinate for 24 hours.

4. Remove the livers from refrigeration about 1–2 hours before cooking time and let them come to room temperature. This is essential for the proper cooking of the terrine.

5. Pack the large lobe (or the pieces of the large lobe, if it broke up during deveining) into the selected terrine, smooth side down. Top with the small lobe, smooth side up. Press the liver in firmly to eliminate air spaces. Cover with foil.

6. Place several folded kitchen towels on the bottom of a roasting pan or other pan used as a hot water bath. (This helps to insulate the terrine from strong bottom heat.) Place the terrine in the pan and add warm, not hot, water to come halfway up the sides of the terrine.

7. Place the terrine in an oven preheated to 200°–215°F (100°C). Bake until the proper doneness, as determined by an instant-read thermometer (see the following paragraph). This will take from 45 minutes to a little over 1 hour.

   The terrine is done when the thermometer reads from 113°–130°F (45°–54°C). At the lower end of this range, the cooled terrine will be rather pink in the center, with a soft, creamy texture. At the higher end, the terrine will be firmer and less pink, but more fat will have cooked out, resulting in a lower yield. The right degree of doneness is a matter of personal preference.

8. Remove the terrine from the hot water bath and set on a rack to cool. After about 10 minutes, weight it with a board that just fits inside the top of the terrine, or with another terrine, and several pounds of weights. When the terrine is almost cool but the fat is still liquid, pour off all the melted fat and juices. Separate and discard the juices. Reserve the fat. Put the weights back on the terrine and continue to cool.

9. When the terrine is cold, unmold it and remove and discard any bits of blood or juice on the bottom of the foie gras. Clean out the mold and put the foie gras back in it. Heat the reserved fat just until melted and pour it over the terrine. Refrigerate until cold, then cover tightly and refrigerate for 3–5 days so that the flavors can develop.

10. To unmold, dip the terrine in warm water for a few seconds, then invert on a platter or cutting board. Slice with a sharp knife dipped in hot water before each slice. Serve with a little chopped aspic and toasted brioche, or with salad greens and a mild vinaigrette made with walnut oil.

Per serving:
Calories, 50; Protein, 6 g; Fat, 2 g (32% cal.); Cholesterol, 165 mg; Carbohydrates, 1 g; Fiber, 0 g; Sodium, 160 mg.

Chicken Liver Terrine

Yield: 2 lb (1 kg)

U.S.	Metric	Ingredients	PROCEDURE
1 lb	500 g	Chicken livers	
8 oz	250 mL	Heavy cream	
5	5	Eggs, lightly beaten	
2 oz	60 g	Flour	
2 tsp	10 mL	Salt	
½ tsp	2 mL	White pepper	
1½ oz	50 mL	Brandy	
as needed	as needed	Caul fat or thin slices of pork fatback for lining the mold (optional)	

1. Soak, rinse, liquefy, and strain the livers, following the procedure on page 674.
2. Mix in the remaining ingredients until smooth. If necessary, strain to eliminate lumps.
3. If possible, cover and refrigerate this mixture overnight. This helps eliminate air bubbles that may have gotten in and allows the flour to absorb moisture.
4. Line a terrine mold with caul or fatback, or grease it very generously with butter or lard.
5. Cover with foil. Bake in a water bath at 300°F (150°C) until set. The water in the water bath should come up to the same level as the liver mixture. Cooking time will depend on the size and shape of the terrine; approximate time is about 2 hours. Check it periodically after about 1½ hours so that it does not overbake.
6. Remove from the water bath and cool on a rack. Refrigerate overnight or longer. Unmold and slice, or serve directly from the terrine.

Per 1 ounce:
Calories, 60; Protein, 4 g; Fat, 4 g (57% cal.); Cholesterol, 105 mg; Carbohydrates, 2 g; Fiber, 0 g; Sodium, 170 mg.

VARIATIONS

Substitute calf liver or pork liver for the chicken liver.

Rillettes of Pork

Yield: approximately 1 lb (500 g)

U.S.	Metric	Ingredients	PROCEDURE
2 lb	1 kg	Pork butt or shoulder, with fat but without skin and bones	
2	2	Bay leaves	
pinch	pinch	Thyme	
1	1	Onion, small, studded with 2 cloves	
2 oz	60 mL	Water	
1½ tsp	2 mL	Salt	

1. Cut the meat, with all the fat, into large dice.
2. Cut off 1–2 ounces (30–60 g) of the fat and render it slowly in a large, heavy pot. Add the meat and brown it lightly and gently over moderate heat.
3. Add the remaining ingredients. Cover and cook slowly in a low oven or on the range over very low heat, until the meat is very tender. This will take several hours. Check periodically to see if the meat has become dry. If it has, add 1–2 ounces (30–60 mL) water.
4. Remove the bay leaves, onions, and cloves. Place the contents of the pot in a colander set over a large bowl. Press firmly on the meat and collect the fat and drippings in the bowl. Separate the fat and juices and reserve them separately.
5. Pound the meat with a large pestle or mallet, then shred it with two forks until the meat is a mass of fibers and no lumps. Alternatively, place the meat in the bowl of a mixer and mix with the paddle attachment at lowest speed until the meat is thoroughly shredded.
6. Add as much of the rendered fat as desired and mix it with the shredded meat. Taste and adjust the seasonings. It should be well seasoned because it is to be served cold. If the mixture seems dry, add some of the reserved juices to achieve the desired consistency. The mixture should be thick but spreadable, neither too dry nor too soft.
7. Pack into crocks or terrines and smooth the top. If the rillettes are to be kept for more than 1–2 days, seal the surface from the air by covering with a layer of melted fat. Refrigerate overnight or longer. Remove the layer of fat before serving.
8. Serve with crusty bread and sour pickles.

Per 1 ounce:
Calories, 110; Protein, 9 g; Fat, 8 g (67% cal.); Cholesterol, 35 mg; Carbohydrates, 2 g; Fiber, 0 g; Sodium, 240 mg.

VARIATIONS

Rillettes of Duck, Goose, Rabbit, Turkey, or Chicken

Substitute any of the above meats for all or part of the pork. Lean meats should be cooked with additional pork fat to supply enough rendered fat to blend with the shredded meat.

Rillettes of Salmon, Haddock, or Finnan Haddie

Yield: 1 lb 4 oz (600 g)

U.S	Metric	Ingredients	PROCEDURE
1 lb	500 g	Salmon, haddock, or finnan haddie, skinless and boneless	1. Combine the fish and wine in a saucepan or sauté pan. Poach the fish gently just until it is done. Because there is not enough wine to cover the fish, turn the fish over occasionally during cooking so that it cooks evenly.
8 oz	250 mL	White wine	2. Drain the fish and cool completely.
4 oz	125 g	Butter, unsalted	3. Break the fish into small pieces, then mash with a fork until there are no lumps.
2 tsp	10 mL	Lemon juice	4. Soften the butter, then mix it with the fish until uniformly blended. Season to taste with lemon juice, salt, white pepper, and hot pepper sauce.
to taste	to taste	Salt	
to taste	to taste	White pepper	5. Pack the mixture into small ramekins or crocks for individual service. Chill.
to taste	to taste	Hot pepper sauce	
as desired	as desired	Caviar, for garnish	6. Top each portion with a small spoonful of caviar just before serving. Use salmon caviar for salmon rillettes, or any desired caviar for haddock or finnan haddie rillettes.
			7. For service, place the ramekin on a small plate lined with a folded napkin or a doily. Arrange slices of toast or bread on the underliner around the ramekin, or serve the toast on the side.

Per 1 ounce:
Calories, 70; Protein, 59 g; Fat, 6 g (72% cal.); Cholesterol, 25 mg; Carbohydrates, 0 g; Fiber, 0 g; Sodium, 55 mg.

Terms for Review

garde manger
aspic jelly
aspic powder
chaud-froid sauce
mayonnaise chaud-froid

forcemeat
garnish (pâté)
pâté
terrine

pâté de campagne
pâté en croûte
pâte à pâté
galantine

mousseline forcemeat
mousse
foie gras
rillettes

Questions for Discussion

1. Explain how to slice a meat terrine.
2. Why are mustards and vinaigrettes often served with pâtés and terrines?
3. What are three purposes of using aspic as a coating or glaze for cold foods?
4. Describe how to make mayonnaise chaud-froid.
5. Describe how to melt and cool aspic jelly.
6. What are the basic ingredients in a typical pork forcemeat?
7. How are raw livers prepared for use in forcemeats?
8. What is the purpose of pouring a layer of melted fat over a terrine after baking?
9. What is the difference between the terms mousseline and mousse, as used in this chapter?
10. What are the four basic steps in the production of a molded mousse? Why is it important to perform these steps quickly?
11. Why is it important not to overcook foie gras?

chapter 24

696

Food Presentation and Garnish

The setting is a dining room in an elegant restaurant or hotel. The tables are set with the finest crystal, china, and linen. On cue, the waiters appear with gleaming, ornate silver platters bearing, perhaps, a roast saddle of lamb or a loin of veal, juicy, brown, and aromatic, surrounded by a colorful array of vegetables, carefully cut and arranged. After an opening like that, the food could taste like nearly anything and everyone would still be happy.

That's an exaggeration, of course. We still want food that tastes good. But the example emphasizes the importance of the appearance of food. Throughout this book, we stress making food look good as well as taste good. We talk about accurate, neat cutting of vegetables and fruits, about proper trimming of meats, poultry, and fish, about grill-marking steaks, about maintaining color in cooked vegetables, and about attractive plating of salads.

In this chapter, we continue the discussion of making food attractive. With your instructor's guidance, you will learn effective ways to present food beyond simply adding that same old sprig of parsley.

Hot Food Presentation

The Importance of Appearance

We eat for enjoyment as well as for nutrition and sustenance. Cooking is not just a trade but an art that appeals to our sense of taste, smell, and sight.

"The eye eats first" is a well-known saying. Our first impressions of a plate of food set our expectations. The sight of food stimulates our appetites, starts our digestive juices flowing, and makes us eager to dig in. Our meal becomes exciting and stimulating.

On the other hand, if the food looks carelessly served, tossed onto the plate in a sloppy manner, we assume it was cooked with the same lack of care. If the colors are pale and washed out, with no color accent, we expect the flavors to be bland and monotonous. If the size of the plate makes the steak *look* small (even if it's not), we go away unsatisfied.

Your job as a cook and a chef, then, is to get your customers interested in your food or, better yet, excited about it. You can't afford to turn them off before they even taste it. Your success depends on making your customers happy.

Making food look good requires, first of all, that you use proper cooking techniques. If a fish is overcooked and dry or a green vegetable is drab and mushy, it won't look good no matter what you do with it.

Second, serving attractive food is largely a matter of being neat and careful and using common sense. This is an aspect of the professionalism we discussed in Chapter 1. Professionals take pride in their work and in the food they serve. They don't put up a plate with sauce accidentally dribbled across the rim and maybe a thumbprint or two for extra effect—not because their supervisors told them not to or because a rule in a textbook says so, but because it's not professional.

Third, beyond just being neat, effective food presentation depends on developing an understanding of techniques involving balance, arrangement, and garniture. These are the subjects of our next sections.

Fundamentals of Plating

We've said before that a plate of food is like a picture, and the rim of the plate is the frame. This does not mean that you have to spend as much time arranging the plate as Rembrandt did painting a portrait, but it does mean that you should think a little like an artist and strive for a pleasing arrangement.

One caution: Don't get carried away. A plate that's too elaborate can be as bad as one that's too careless. Besides, you want that hot dinner to be still hot when it reaches the customer, and you don't have time to get too fancy.

BALANCE

Balance is a term we used when talking about menu planning in Chapter 6. The rules of good menu balance also apply to plating. Select foods and garnishes that offer variety and contrast while avoiding combinations that are awkward or jarring.

Colors

Two or three colors on a plate are usually more interesting than just one. Visualize this combination: poached chicken breast with suprême sauce, mashed potatoes, and steamed cauliflower. Appetizing? Or how about fried chicken, French fries, and corn? Not quite as bad, but still a little monotonous.

Many hot foods, especially meats, poultry, and fish, have little color other than shades of brown, gold, or white. It helps to select vegetables or accompaniments that add color interest—one reason why green vegetables are so popular.

Garnish is often unnecessary, especially if the accompaniments have color, but it is very important, in some cases. The classic combination of broiled steak (brown) and baked potato (brown and white) looks a little livelier with even the simple addition of a healthy sprig of watercress or parsley.

Shapes

Plan for variety of shapes and forms as well as of colors. For example, you probably do not want to serve brussels sprouts with meatballs and new potatoes. Your customers might get up a game of marbles. Green beans and whipped potatoes might be better choices for accompaniment.

Cutting vegetables into different shapes gives you great flexibility. Carrots, for example, which can be cut into dice, rounds, or sticks (batonnet, julienne, etc.), can be adapted to nearly any plate.

Textures

Textures are not strictly visual considerations, but they are important in plating as in menu planning (Chapter 6). Good balance requires a variety of textures on the plate. Perhaps the most common error is serving too many soft or puréed foods, such as baked salmon loaf with whipped potatoes and puréed squash.

Flavors

You can't see flavors, either, but this is one more factor you must consider when balancing colors, shapes, and textures on the plate. Consult the menu planning guidelines in Chapter 6.

PORTION SIZE

Portion sizes are important for presentation as well as for costing.

Match Portion Sizes and Plates

Too small a plate makes an overcrowded, jumbled, messy appearance. Too large a plate may make the portions look skimpy.

Balance the Portion Sizes of the Various Items on the Plate

One item, generally a meat, poultry, or fish preparation, is usually considered the main item on the plate. It is the center of attention and is larger than the accompaniments. Don't let the main item get lost amid excessive garnish and huge portions of vegetable and starch items.

Where there is no main item, as in some vegetable plates, strive for a logical balance of portions.

ARRANGEMENT ON THE PLATE

Until recent years, plated main courses followed a standard pattern: meat or fish item at the front of the plate (closest to the diner), vegetable and starch items at the rear.

This arrangement is still the most commonly used because it is one of the simplest and most convenient. Nevertheless, many creative chefs are eager to display their creativity with imaginative plating presentations.

A style popular with today's chefs is to stack everything on one multilayered tower in the center of the plate. When used with restraint, this can make an effective and impressive plating. Often, however, it is carried to extremes, and customers are faced with the job of carefully deconstructing a towering pile of food and rearranging the items on the plate so that it is possible to begin eating. Some chefs like this style so much that they use it for nearly everything on the menu. Perhaps it works best for small dishes, such as some appetizers and the small portions of a tasting menu. It is important to keep the convenience and comfort of the diner in mind when plating.

The following patterns are examples of today's plating styles. For illustrations, refer to the photographs accompanying the recipes.

- The classic arrangement: main item in front, vegetables, starch items, and garnish at the rear.

- The main item alone in the center of the plate, sometimes with a sauce or simple garnish.
- The main item in the center, with vegetables distributed randomly around it, sometimes with a sauce underneath.
- The main item in the center, with neat piles of vegetables carefully arranged around it in a pattern.
- A starch or vegetable item heaped in the center; the main item sliced and leaning up against it; additional vegetables, garnish, and/or sauce on the plate around the center items.
- Main item, vegetable and starch accompaniments, and other garnish stacked neatly one atop the other in the center of the plate. Sauces or additional garnish may be placed around the outside.
- Vegetable in center of plate, sometimes with sauce; main item (in slices, medallions, small pieces, etc.) arranged around it toward the outside of the plate
- Slices of the main item shingled on a bed of vegetables or a purée of vegetables or starch, with, perhaps, additional garnish to one side or around.
- Various asymmetrical or random-looking arrangements that don't seem to follow any pattern. These often create the impression that the food was rushed to the dining room the instant it was cooked, without thought to the design. Of course, to be effective, these arrangements are carefully thought out in advance.

The following guidelines will help you plate attractive, appealing food, no matter what plating style you are using.

1. **Keep food off the rim of the plate.**
   This guideline means, in part, selecting a plate large enough to hold the food without it hanging off the edge. In general, the rim should be thought of as the frame for the food presentation. Some chefs like to decorate this frame with a sprinkling of spice or chopped herbs or dots of a sauce. When tastefully done, this can enhance the appeal of the plate but, if overdone, it can make the plate look unattractive.

2. **Arrange the items for the convenience of the customer.**
   Put the best side of the meat forward. The customer should not have to turn the item around to start on it. The bony or fatty edge of the steak, the back side of the half duckling, the boniest parts of the chicken pieces, and so on, should face away from the customer. Tall, precarious towers of food are difficult to eat, and the customer may have to rearrange the food before eating.

3. **Keep space between items, unless, of course, they are stacked on one another.**
   Don't pile everything together in a jumbled heap. Each item should have its own identity. This is, of course, related also to selecting the right plate size.
   Even when items are stacked, this should be done neatly so that each item is identifiable.

4. **Maintain unity.**
   Basically, there is unity when the plate looks like one meal that happens to be made up of several items rather than like several unrelated items that just happen to be on the same plate.
   Create a center of attention and relate everything to it. The meat is generally the center of attention and is often placed front and center. Other items are placed around and behind it so as to balance it and keep the customer's eyes centered rather than pulled off the edge of the plate.

5. **Make the garnish count.**
   Garnishes are added not just for color. Sometimes they are needed to balance a plate by providing an additional element. Two items on a plate often look unbalanced, but adding a garnish completes the picture.
   On the other hand, don't add unnecessary garnishes. In many or even most cases, the food is attractive and colorful without garnish, and adding it clutters the plate and increases your food cost as well.

6. **Don't drown every plate in sauce or gravy.**

   Sometimes ladling sauce all over an item hides colors and shapes. If the item is attractive by itself, let the customer see it. Ladle the sauce around or under it, or possibly covering only part of it, as with a band of sauce across the center.

7. **Keep it simple.**

   As you have heard before, simplicity is more attractive than overworked, contrived arrangements and complicated designs. Unusual patterns are occasionally effective, but avoid making the food look too cute or too elaborate.

   One of the simplest plating styles can also be one of the most attractive if it is carefully done—that is, placing only the meat or fish item and its sauce, if any, in the center of the plate, and serving vegetable accompaniments in separate dishes. This method is widely used in restaurants to simplify service in the kitchen. However, it is usually best to use this method for only some of the menu items in order to avoid monotony.

TEMPERATURE

Serve hot foods hot, on hot plates.
Serve cold foods cold, on cold plates.

Your arrangement of beautiful food will not make much of a final impression if you forget this rule.

Garnish

WHAT IS GARNISH?

The word *garnish* is derived from a French word meaning "to adorn" or "to furnish." In English, we use the word to mean to decorate or embellish a food item by the addition of other items. The word is used also for the decorative items themselves.

This definition, at first, seems vague because it could include just about anything. But, in fact, the term has been used for a great variety of preparations and techniques in the history of classical and modern cuisines. Let's look at some of these styles of garnish and what they mean to today's cooks and chefs.

CLASSICAL GARNISH

In classical cooking, the terms *garnish* and *garniture* have been used the way we use the term *accompaniments*. In other words, garnishes are any items placed on the platter or plate or in the soup bowl in addition to the main item. It happens that these accompaniments also make the food look more attractive, but that is not the emphasis.

The classical French chef had a tremendous repertoire of simple and elaborate garnishes, and they all had specific names. A trained chef, or a well-informed diner, for that matter, knew that the word *Rachel* on the menu meant that the dish was served with artichoke bottoms filled with poached marrow and that *Portugaise* meant a garnish of stuffed tomatoes.

There were so many of these names, however, that no one could remember them all. So they were cataloged in handbooks to be used by chefs. *Le Répertoire de la Cuisine*, one of these handbooks, has 209 listings in the garnish section alone, not to mention nearly 7000 other preparations, all with their own names. The garnishes may be as simple as the one called *Concorde* or as complex as the one called *Tortue*, quoted here to give you an idea of the complexity and elaborateness of classical garnish.

Concorde (*for large joints*)—Peas, glazed carrots, mashed potatoes.

Tortue (*for Entrées*)—Quenelles, mushroom heads, gherkins, garlic, collops of tongue and calves' brains, small fried eggs, heart-shaped croutons, crayfish, slices of truffles. Tortue sauce.

Classical Terms in the Modern Kitchen

Many of the classical names for garnishes are still used in modern kitchens, although they have lost the precise meanings they once had. You will encounter these terms frequently, so it is worthwhile learning them.

Remember that the following definitions are not the classical ones but simply the garnish or accompaniment generally indicated by the terms in today's kitchens.

Bouquetière: "bouquet" of vegetables
Jardinière: "garden" vegetables
Printanière: spring vegetables
Primeurs: first spring vegetables

These four terms refer to assortments of fresh vegetables, including carrots, turnips, peas, pearl onions, green beans, cauliflower, sometimes asparagus, and artichokes.

Clamart: peas
Crécy: carrots
Doria: cucumbers (cooked in butter)
Dubarry: cauliflower
Fermière: carrots, turnips, onions, and celery, cut into uniform slices
Florentine: spinach
Forestière: mushrooms
Judic: braised lettuce
Lyonnaise: onions
Niçoise: tomatoes concassé cooked with garlic
Parmentier: potatoes
Princesse: asparagus
Provençale: tomatoes with garlic, parsley, and, sometimes, mushrooms and/or olives
Vichy: carrots (especially Carrots Vichy, p. 465)

MODERN HOT PLATTER GARNISH

In classical cuisine, food was nearly always brought to the dining room on large platters and then served, rather than being plated in the kitchen, as is most often done today.

This practice has decreased in popularity but is still often used for banquets, and nothing stimulates appetites as much as a succulent roast on a silver platter, sumptuously adorned with a colorful variety of vegetable garnishes.

The classical garnitures most often adapted to modern platter presentation are those called bouquetière, jardinière, and printanière. At one time, these were specific vegetable assortments cut in prescribed ways. Today they are taken in a more general way, meaning colorful assortments of various fresh vegetables.

Platter garnish need not be elaborate or difficult to prepare. A simple assortment of colorful vegetables, carefully cut and properly cooked to retain color and texture, is appropriate to the most elegant presentation. Stuffed vegetables, such as tomato halves filled with peas, are a little fancier, but still easy to prepare. Borders of duchesse potatoes are also popular (see p. 492).

Many of the rules of proper plating apply to platter arrangement as well—for example, those that call for neatness, balance of color and shape, unity, and preserving the individuality of the items. Following are a few other guidelines that apply to hot platter presentation and garnish.

1. **Vegetables should be in easily served units.**
   In other words, don't heap green peas or mashed potatoes on one corner of the platter. More suitable are vegetables such as cauliflower, broccoli, boiled tomatoes, asparagus spears, whole green beans, mushroom caps, or anything that comes in large or easy-to-handle pieces. Small vegetables such as peas can be easily served if they are used to fill artichoke bottoms, tomato halves, or tartlet shells.

2. **Have the correct number of portions of each item.**
   Vegetables like brussels sprouts and tournéed carrots are easily portioned in the dining room if they are arranged in little portion-size piles.

3. **Arrange the garnishes around the platter to get the best effect from the different colors and shapes.**

   The meat, poultry, or fish is usually placed in the center of the platter, or in a row or rows, and the garnishes are arranged around it.

4. **Avoid being too elaborate.**

   While it is sometimes desirable to make ornate platters, simplicity is usually preferable to an overworked appearance. Let the attractiveness of the food speak for itself. The garnish should never dominate or hide the meat, which is the center of attention.

5. **Serve extra sauce or gravy in a sauceboat.**

   If it is appropriate, dress or nap the meat or fish items with some of the sauce, but don't drown the entire platter with it.

6. **Serve hot foods hot, on a hot platter.**

   Don't spend so much time arranging the food that it's cold by the time it reaches the dining room.

SIMPLE PLATE GARNISH

To many people, the word "garnish" means a sprig of parsley. What this implies is that garnish is often nothing more than an afterthought, a meaningless scrap of something routinely planted on the plate without regard to its function or appropriateness.

Just as bad is the practice in some restaurants of adopting a single garnish, such as a cinnamon apple ring on a leaf of lettuce, and using it routinely on every plate, from prime rib to batter-fried shrimp. No one garnish is appropriate for every plate. In the case of the apple ring, it is appropriate for very few.

The only solution to this problem is to learn a wide variety of garnishes and to give more thought and imagination to garniture.

Let's consider two approaches to plating from the point of view of garnish.

1. **No garnish.**

   Many or even most plates need no added garnish. If the accompanying vegetables and starches provide an attractive balance and color combination, the garnish may just clutter the plate. Leave it off.

   Actually, this is much the same as classical garniture, as discussed above. The accompaniments become the garnish because they do the job of balancing the plate for an attractive presentation.

2. **Simple decorative garnish.**

   Sometimes it is necessary to serve the accompanying vegetables in side dishes, as when they do not add much contrast to the plate, such as a baked potato served with a steak or French fries served with fried chicken or fish. A simple garnish may then be helpful to provide a color accent or balance to the plate.

   A simple, decorative garnish should be edible, appropriate to the food, and planned into the plate layout, not just stuck on haphazardly.

   Although modern plating styles have made simple garnishes less frequently used than in years past, they sometimes play a useful role.

Simple Decorative Techniques

The following procedures are a useful selection of techniques for adding decorative touches to food presentations. Most of these are vegetable-cutting techniques, but several other procedures are explained and illustrated as well.

Fried Parsley

1. Separate sprigs and remove coarse stems.

2. Wash. Dry *thoroughly*.

3. Deep-fry for just a few seconds, until crisp but still green.

4. Drain on absorbent paper. Serve immediatoly.

Cucumbers

1. For decorative slices, score unpeeled cucumber with a fork or flute with a channel knife before slicing (see Figure 24.1).

2. For twists, cut slices three-fourths of the way across, twist open, and stand on plate.

3. For cups, cut fluted cucumber in 1-inch (2.5 cm) sections, hollow out slightly with a melon ball cutter or spoon, and fill with an appropriate condiment or sauce.

Figure 24.1 Cucumber garnishes can be made more decorative by scoring the cucumber before slicing or cutting.

(a) Scoring with a fork.

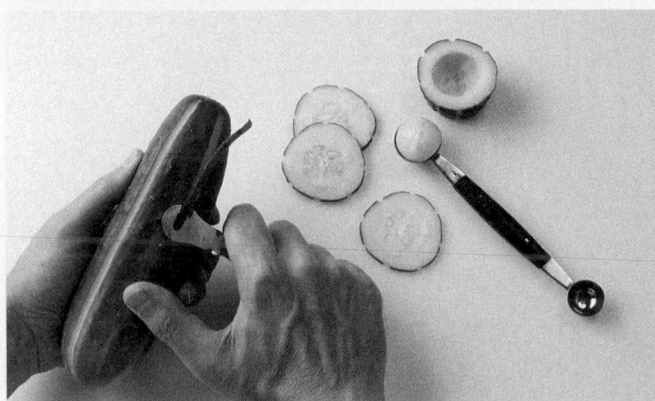

(b) Scoring with a channel knife.

Mushroom Caps

1. Fluting mushrooms is a technique that takes a great deal of practice. Follow the steps in Figure 24.2, or watch your instructor demonstrate. Then, whenever you have to slice mushrooms, practice fluting a few. Eventually you'll get it.

2. To keep mushrooms white, simmer 2 to 3 minutes in salted water with a little butter and lemon juice.

Figure 24.2 *Basic methods for fluting mushrooms.*

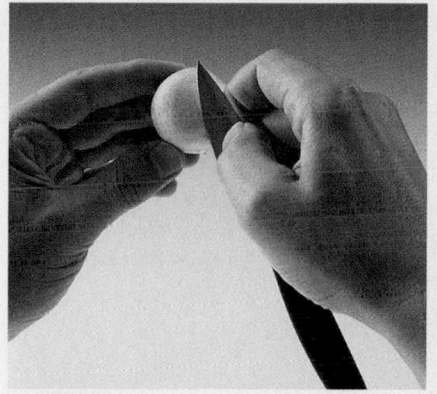

(a) **Method 1:** *Grasping the blade of a paring knife, hold the edge against the center of the mushroom cap at a sharp angle.*

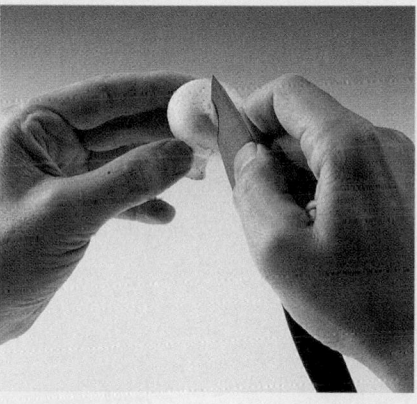

(b) *Begin to rotate the blade toward the edge of the cap so that it cuts a shallow groove in the mushroom.*

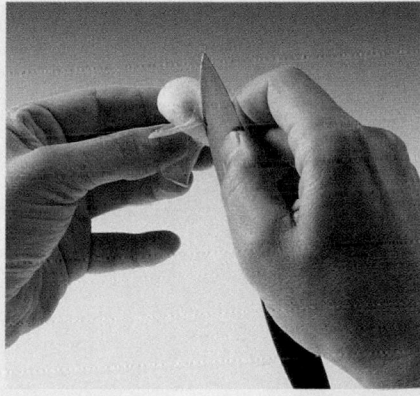

(c) *The first cut is completed.*

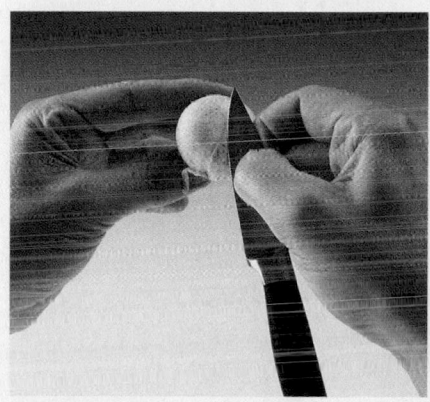

(d) *Rotate the mushroom a few degrees and cut a second groove next to the first.*

(e) *Continue making cuts all around the mushroom.*

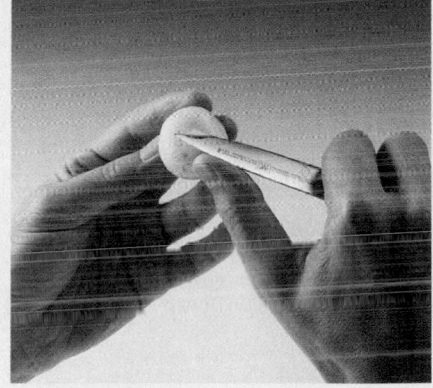

(f) **Method 2:** *Similar to Method 1, except that you hold the edge of the blade away from you. Rest the thumb of your knife hand on the mushroom and brace the back of the blade. Rotate the knife, using your thumb as the pivot point.*

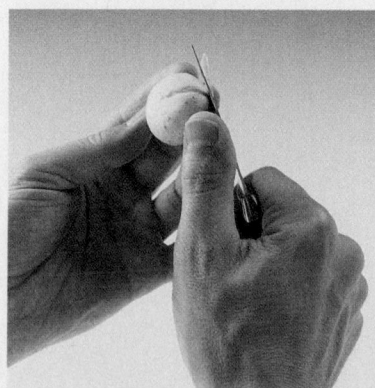

(g) *Turn the knife until the groove extends to the edge of the mushroom cap.*

(h) *Continue cutting grooves as in Method 1.*

(i) *The fluted mushroom cap.*

(j) *To decorate the center of the cap, press the point of the knife into the mushroom to form a star.*

Radishes

1. Radishes can be cut in many ways to make decorative garnishes, as illustrated in Figure 24.3.

2. After cutting, soak the radishes in ice water until they open up.

Figure 24.3 Radishes can be cut into many decorative forms, including those shown here.

Scallion Brushes

1. Cut off the root ends of the scallions, including the little hard core. Cut the white part into 2-inch (5-cm) sections.

2. With a thin-bladed knife, split both ends of the scallion pieces with cuts ½ inch (15 mm) deep. Make enough cuts to separate the ends into fine shreds, as shown in Figure 24.4.

3. Soak in cold water until the ends curl up.

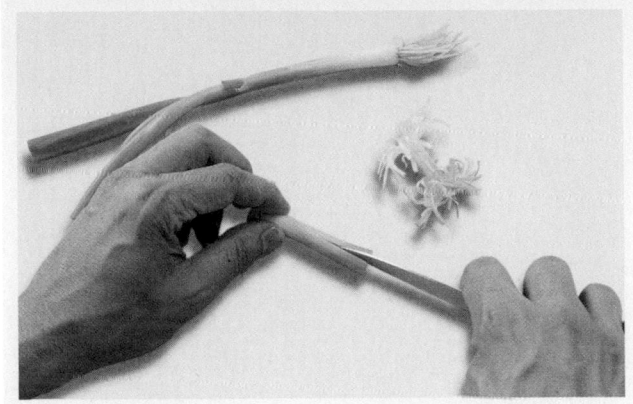

Figure 24.4 Scallions being cut for garnish.

Pickle Fans

1. With the stem end of the pickle away from you, make a series of thin vertical slices the length of the pickle, but do not cut through the stem end (Figure 24.5).

2. Spread the pickle into a fan shape as shown.

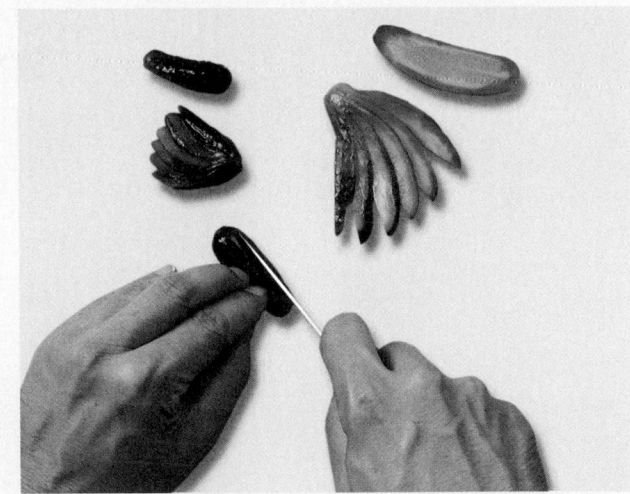

Figure 24.5 Pickle fans may be cut from tiny gherkins or from slices of larger dill pickles.

Lemons

Figure 24.6 Lemon garnishes.

(a) Decorate lemon slices and wedges with paprika or chopped parsley. You may also use peeled lemon slices.

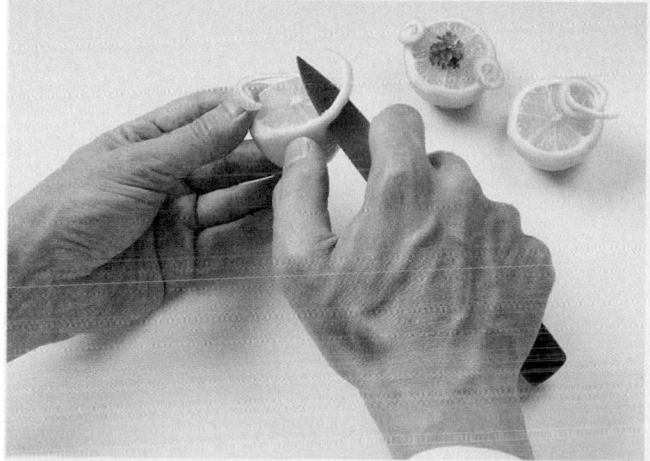

(b) Make simple lemon halves more decorative by cutting as shown.

1. Fluted lemon slices and twisted slices are cut the same way as cucumbers. Slices placed directly on fish or meat are cut from *peeled* lemons.

2. Dip half the slice in paprika or finely chopped parsley for a colorful effect, as shown in Figure 24.6a. For just a line of paprika down the center, bend the slice between the fingers, as shown in the illustration, and dip lightly in paprika.

3. Wedges are often more attractive if the ends of the lemons are cut off first. For added color, dip the edge of the wedge in paprika as shown (Figure 24.6a).

4. For lemon halves, first cut a thin slice from each end of the lemon so the halves stand straight. Cut a long strip from the outer edge of the lemon half as shown in Figure 24.6b, but do not detach it. Tie a knot in the strip, being careful not to break it. Alternatively, cut two strips, one from either side, and make two knots. Decorate with parsley.

5. For a sawtooth edge, cut the pattern as shown in Figure 24.6c, piercing all the way to the center of the lemon with the knife. Separate the halves. Decorate with parsley, or dip the points of the teeth in paprika.

(c) This illustration shows another way of presenting lemon halves as garnish. After cutting, decorate the halves with paprika or parsley.

Frosted Grapes

1. Separate the grapes into small bunches. Brush with lightly beaten egg white and sprinkle with granulated sugar.

2. Let dry before serving.

Toast Points

1. Cut slices of pullman bread in half diagonally. Trim off the crusts and cut each piece into a heart shape as shown (Figure 24.7). Save the trimmings for bread crumbs.

2. Sauté the pieces in butter and oil until golden on both sides.

3. Dip the tips into the sauce being served with the dish the toast points are to garnish, then into chopped parsley.

Figure 24.7 To prepare toast points, cut bread slices into triangles or heart shapes as shown. Fry the bread shapes in butter and dip the tips in sauce and then in parsley.

Shaping Quenelles

1. This technique is used for making neat shapes of puréed or finely chopped foods. Select two spoons whose bowls are the same length as the quenelle you want to make. Scoop a portion of the mixture to be shaped in one spoon (see Figure 24.8).

2. With the second spoon, carefully pick up the mixture from the first spoon. This forces the food into an oval shape.

3. Continue once or twice more, as necessary, to make a neat shape.

4. Carefully place the quenelle on the plate.

Figure 24.8 Shaping quenelles with two spoons.

(a) Pick up a portion of the mixture in one spoon. Position a second spoon as shown.

(b) Scoop the mixture with the second spoon. If the mixture is stiff, press the two spoons together lightly while scooping to help shape the quenelle.

(c) Again scoop the mixture with the first spoon to complete the shape.

(d) Deposit the quenelle on the plate.

Shaping Foods with a Ring Mold

1. Place a ring mold of the desired size on a plate in the position in which you want the food.

2. Fill the mold with the food item. Use a spatula or palette knife to level the top, if desired (see Figure 24.9).

3. Carefully lift off the mold, leaving the shaped food in place.

Figure 24.9 Shaping food with a ring mold.

(a) Position a ring mold on the plate. Fill with the food and level the top with a palette knife or spatula.

(b) Carefully lift off the mold.

Cold Food Presentation and Buffet Service

The buffet is a popular and profitable form of food presentation found in nearly every kind of food service operation. There are at least three reasons for this popularity:

1. **Visual appeal.**

   An attractive presentation of foods has the effect of lavishness and ample quantity, and careful arrangement and garnish suggest quality as well.

2. **Efficiency.**

   The buffet allows the restaurant to serve a large number of people in a short time with relatively few service personnel.

3. **Adaptability.**

   Buffet service is adaptable to nearly every kind of food (except items that must be cooked to order, like broiled and deep-fried foods) and to all price ranges, occasions, restaurant styles, and local food customs.

Buffet Arrangement and Appearance

The buffet's visual appeal is, perhaps, its greatest attraction for the customer. Eye appeal of food is always important, but perhaps nowhere more important than on a buffet, because the appearance sells the food. A buffet is not just food service—it is food display.

LAVISHNESS AND ABUNDANCE

Above all else, a buffet should look lavish and plentiful. The appearance of an abundance of food beautifully laid out is exciting and stimulating to the appetite. There are many ways to create this look.

1. **Color.**

   A variety of colors is as vital on a buffet as it is on a single plate. Plan menus and garnish so that you have enough color on the table.

2. **Height.**

   Flat foods on flat trays on flat tables are uninteresting to the eye.

   A centerpiece is an important feature, giving height and focus to the buffet. Ice carvings, tallow sculptures, and floral or fruit displays are some possibilities. These should be placed on a separate table behind the food table.

   Centerpieces on individual platters also add height. Large food items such as large cheeses and whole roasts being carved at the table are also effective. Multilevel tables, when available, are used to good effect.

3. **Full platters and bowls.**

   Replenish items as they become depleted. A nearly empty bowl isn't as appetizing as a full one.

   Arrange platters so that they still have interest even when portions have been removed (more on this later).

4. **Proper spacing.**

   While you shouldn't crowd the items, don't spread them so far apart that the table looks half empty.

SIMPLICITY

This sounds like a contradiction to the lavishness principle, but it's not. You need to strike a good balance between the two. Lavishness is not the same as clutter.

1. **Overdesigned, overdecorated food scares people away from eating it.**
   How many times have you heard someone say, "Oh, it's so pretty I don't want to touch it"? Even if they don't say it, they'll think it.
   Too much design detracts from the food. Sometimes food is so overdecorated that it no longer looks like food. This completely defeats the purpose. The customer should at least be able to identify the food for what it is.

2. **Excessive garnish is quickly destroyed as customers take portions.**

ORDERLINESS

A buffet should look like it was planned, not like it just happened. Customers prefer food presentations that look carefully done, not just thrown together.

1. Simple arrangements are much easier to keep neat and orderly than are complicated designs.

2. Colors and shapes should look lively and varied, but make sure they go together and do not clash.

3. Keep the style consistent. If it's formal, then everything should be formal. If it's casual or rustic, then every part of the presentation should be casual or rustic. If it's a Mexican fiesta, don't include German sauerbraten just because your specialty happens to be sauerbraten.
   This is true not only of the food but of the dishes and serving pieces, too. Don't use ornate silver serving pieces for a country theme, for example.

MENU AND SERVING SEQUENCE

Practical reasons as well as visual appeal determine the order in which foods are arranged on the buffet. As far as possible, it is good to have items in the proper menu order (for example, appetizers first, main course afterward, desserts last) if only to avoid confusing the customers, who might otherwise wonder what the food is and how much they should take. But there are many reasons for changing the order. The following should be taken into account when arranging a buffet.

1. Hot foods are best served last. If served first, hot foods get cool while the guests make other selections from the cold foods. Also, it is more effective, visually, to place the decorative cold platters first and the less attractive chafing dishes last.

2. The more expensive foods are usually placed after the less expensive items. This gives you some control of food cost, as the guests' plates will be nearly full of other attractive foods by the time they get to the costly items.

3. Sauces and dressings should be placed next to the items with which they are to be served. Otherwise, the customer might not match them with the right foods.

4. A separate dessert table is often a good idea. This approach allows guests to make a separate trip for dessert without interfering with the main serving line. It is also possible, if the menu is large, to have a separate appetizer table.

5. Plates, of course, must be the first items on the table. Silverware, napkins, and other items not needed until the guest sits down to eat should be at the end of the buffet table or set in place on the dining tables.

The Cocktail Buffet—An Exception

One kind of buffet doesn't conform to this menu order pattern. The cocktail buffet displays appetizers intended to accompany drinks and other refreshments at receptions, cocktail parties, and cocktail hours preceding banquets and dinners. There is no serving line—or, looking at it a different way, there is a separate line for each item.

1. Only appetizer-type foods are served: tasty, well-seasoned foods in small portions.

2. Stacks of small plates are placed beside each item rather than at the beginning of the table.

3. The table or tables must be easy to get to from all parts of the room and must not block traffic. Do not place them next to the entry because guests gather around them, blocking movement into and out of the room.

Cold Platter Presentation

The cold platter is the mainstay of the buffet and offers the most opportunity for visual artistry. It also can be one of the most demanding forms of food presentation, particularly in the case of show platters, which require great precision, patience, and artistic sense.

Cold platters can range from a simple tray of cold cuts to elaborate constructions of pâtés, meats, poultry, or fish decorated with aspic, truffles, and vegetable flowers. In this chapter, we have space only for a discussion of general guidelines that you can apply both to formal buffet platters and to simple cold food arrangements. To learn more detailed, complex techniques, you will have to depend on your instructors, more advanced courses, and on-the-job experience. But this section should help you take the foods available in whatever kitchen you find yourself working and produce an attractive, appetizing buffet.

BASIC PRINCIPLES OF PLATTER PRESENTATION

1. The three elements of a buffet platter:
   - Centerpiece or *grosse pièce* (gross pyess). This may be an uncut portion of the main food item, such as a pâté or a cold roast, decorated and displayed whole. It may be a separate but related item, such as a molded salmon mousse on a platter of poached slices of salmon in aspic. It may be something as simple as a bowl or *ravier* (rahv yay; an oval relish dish) of sauce or condiment. Or it may be strictly for decoration, such as a butter sculpture or a squash vase filled with vegetable flowers. Whether or not the grosse pièce is intended to be eaten, it should be made of edible materials.
   - The slices or serving portions of the main food item, arranged artistically.
   - The garnish, arranged artistically, in proportion to the cut slices.

2. The food should be easy to handle and serve, so that one portion can be removed without ruining the arrangement.

3. A simple design is best. Simple arrangements are easier to serve, more appetizing than overworked food, and more likely to be still attractive when they are half demolished by the guests.

   Simple arrangements may be the hardest to produce. Everything has to be perfect because less decoration is available to divide the attention.

4. Attractive platter presentations may be made on silver or other metals, mirrors, china, plastic, wood, or many other materials, as long as they are presentable and suitable for use with food. Metal platters that might cause discoloration or metallic flavors are often covered with a thin layer of aspic before the food is placed on them.

5. Once a piece of food has touched the tray, do not remove it. Shiny silver or mirror trays are easily smudged, and you'll have to wash the tray and start over again. This shows the importance of good planning.

   Following this rule also helps eliminate overhandling of food, which is a bad sanitary practice.

6. Think of the platter as part of the whole buffet. It must look attractive and appropriate not only by itself but among the other presentations on the table. The arrangement should always be planned from the same angle from which it will be seen on the buffet.

DESIGNING THE PLATTER

1. **Plan ahead.**
   Making a sketch is a good idea. Otherwise, you might have half the food on the platter and suddenly realize you have to start over because everything doesn't fit the way you had hoped. The result is wasted time and excessive handling of food.

   One way to start a sketch is to divide the platter into six or eight equal parts, as in Figure 24.10. This helps you avoid lopsided or crooked arrangements by giving you equally spaced markers to guide you. It is relatively easy, then, to sketch in a balanced, symmetrical layout, as the examples show.

2. **Plan for movement in your design.**
   This doesn't mean that you should mount the food on little wheels. It means that a good design makes the eye move across the platter following the lines you have set up.

   Most food for platters consists of single small portions arranged in rows or lines. The trick is to put movement into those lines by curving or angling them, as shown in Figure 24.11. In general, curves and angles are said to have movement. Square corners do not.

3. **Give the design a focal point.**
   This is the function of the centerpiece, which emphasizes and strengthens the design by giving it direction and height. This may be done directly, by having the lines point directly to it, or more subtly, by having the lines angle toward it or sweep around it in graceful curves. Again, see Figures 24.10 and 24.11.

   Note that the centerpiece isn't always in the center, in spite of its name. Because of its height, it should be at the back or toward the side so it doesn't hide the food. Remember, you are designing the platter from the customer's point of view.

   It's not necessary for every platter on the buffet to have a centerpiece. Some of them should, however, or the buffet will lack height and be less interesting to the eye.

4. **Keep items in proportion.**
   The main items on the platter—the slices of meat, pâté, or whatever—should *look* like the main items. The centerpiece should not be so large or so tall that it totally dominates the platter. The garnish should enhance, not overwhelm, the main item in size, height, or quantity. The number of portions of garnish should be in proportion to the amount of the main item.

   The size of the platter should be in proportion to the amount of food. Don't select one that is so small as to become crowded or so large as to look almost empty even before the first guest has arrived.

   Keep enough space between items or between rows so that the platter doesn't look jumbled or confused.

   Figure 24.10 indicates placement of garnish as well as of the main item. Note how the arrangement of garnish reflects or accents the pattern established by the sliced foods.

5. **Let the guest see the best side of everything.**
   Angle overlapping slices and wedge-shaped pieces toward the customer. Make sure that the best side of each slice is face up.

CHEESE PLATTERS

Cheese trays are popular on both luncheon buffets as a main course item and on dinner buffets as a dessert item. Cheeses are presented much differently than the other cold buffet foods we have been talking about.

First, whole cheeses or cheeses in large pieces are generally more attractive than an arrangement of slices. This also helps the guest identify the varieties. Be sure to supply several knives so guests can cut their own portions.

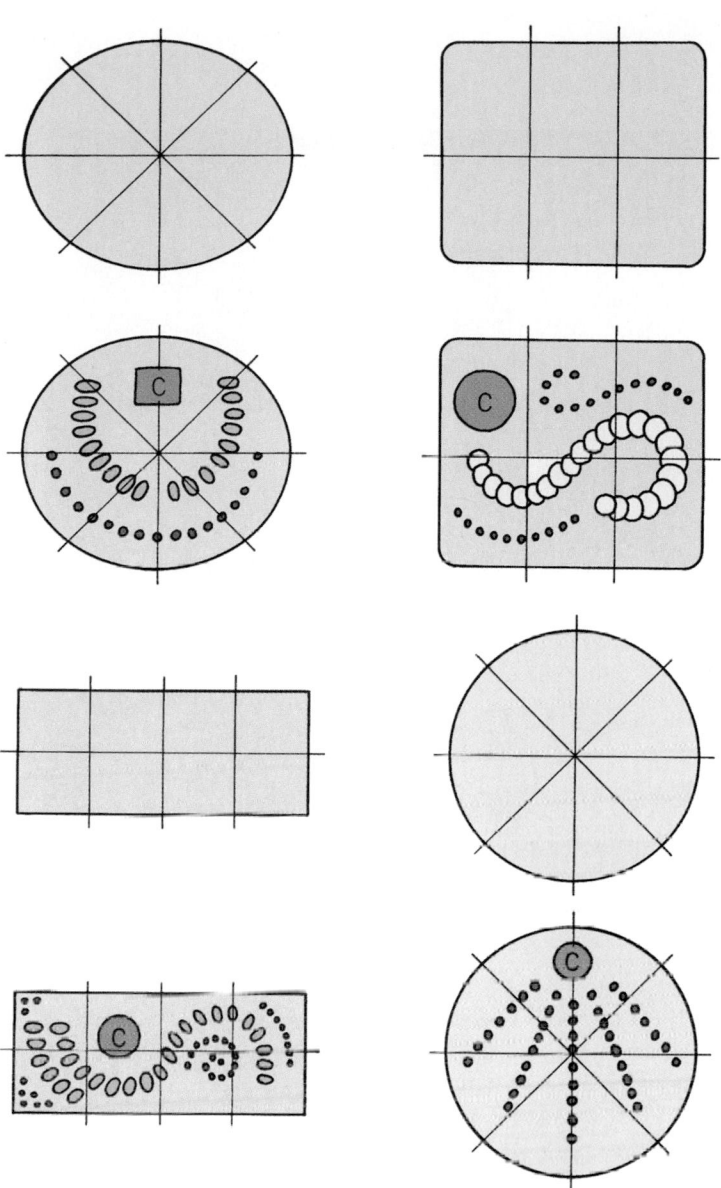

Figure 24.10 Begin your planning sketch of a buffet platter by dividing the tray into six or eight sections. This helps you lay out a balanced, symmetrical design. The examples shown here indicate the placement of the main items (usually slices of foods), the centerpiece (labeled c), and the garnish (shown as tiny circles).

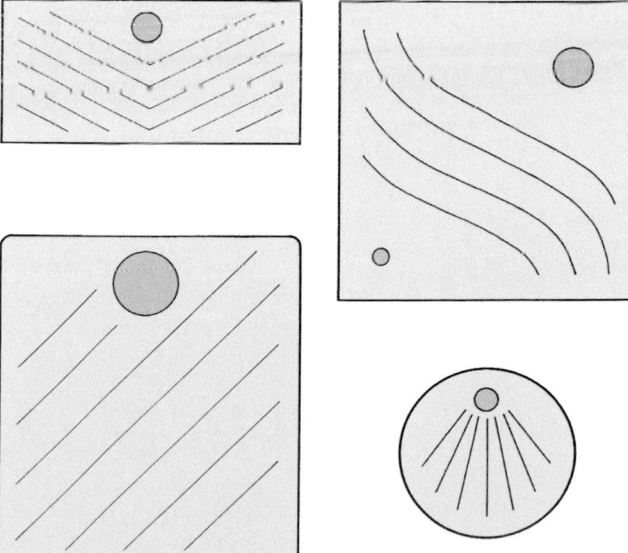

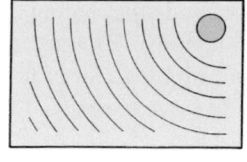

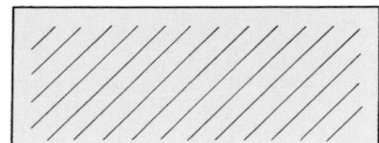

Figure 24.11 Arranging rows of foods in curves or angled lines gives movement to the design.

One type of cheese and fruit presentation for buffet service.

Second, an assortment of fresh fruit is often included on a cheese tray. This adds a great deal to the appearance of a cheese presentation, and the flavors go well with cheese. The photograph shows an example of a cheese and fruit presentation.

A NOTE ON SANITATION

Cold food for buffets presents a special sanitation problem. This is because the food spends a great deal of time out of refrigeration while it is being assembled and decorated and again while it sits on the buffet. For this reason, it is particularly important to follow all the rules of safe food handling. Keep foods refrigerated whenever they are not being worked on. Also, keep them chilled until the last minute before they are brought out for service.

For a buffet service that lasts a long time, it is a good idea to make each course or item on a number of small platters rather than on one big one. The replacements can then be kept refrigerated until needed.

Hot Foods for Buffets

Everything we have learned about the preparation and holding of hot foods in quantity applies to hot foods for buffets. Hot items are nearly always served from chafing dishes, which may be ornate silver affairs or simple steam table pans kept warm over hot water. These foods cannot be elaborately decorated and garnished the way cold foods can. On the other hand, the bright, fresh, juicy appearance and good aroma of properly cooked hot food is generally sufficient to arouse appetites.

Hot foods for chafing dishes should be easily portioned (such as vegetables served with a kitchen spoon) or already portioned in the pan (braised pork chops, sliced baked ham, and poached fish fillets, for example). Items less suitable for buffets are those that must be cooked to order and served immediately, such as most broiled and deep-fried foods.

Whole roasts are popular items at buffets, carved to order by a member of the kitchen staff. Especially attractive are large roasts such as hams, turkeys, and large cuts of beef such as steamship round.

As we have said, hot foods are best placed at the end of the buffet so that they do not cool on the guests' plates before they are seated and so that the decorated cold foods can steal the show.

Terms for Review

unity of arrangement	Bouquetière	Dubarry	Lyonnaise
garnish	Jardinière	Fermière	Parmentier
garniture	Printanière	Florentine	grosse pièce
classical garnish	Clamart	Forestière	ravier

Questions for Discussion

1. Discuss the idea of professionalism and how it applies to the presentation of food.

2. Following are several popular food combinations. Describe what plating problems they present, if any, and how you might efficiently and economically solve them.

   Fish and chips (deep-fried fillets and French fries)
   Prime rib of beef and baked potato
   Meat loaf, mashed potatoes, and gravy
   Open-faced hot turkey sandwich
   Beef stroganoff and egg noodles
   Chicken à la king in a patty shell

3. What is meant by plating food for the convenience of the customer, and how does this affect other rules of plating?

4. When is it a good idea not to add a garnish to a plate?

5. What is the difference between a cocktail buffet and a luncheon or dinner buffet?

6. Customers like to see a lot of food on a buffet. Is it correct to say, then, that the best way to please customers is to put out as much food as possible? Explain your answer.

7. When you are preparing a cold buffet platter, why is it a good idea to plan ahead by making a sketch? What would you include in the sketch? What do the terms movement and focal point mean in platter design?

chapter 25

Recipes from International Cuisines

The popularity of ethnic and international cuisines is booming. While there is a surge of interest in North American regional cuisine, there are also more ethnic restaurants than ever before. Japanese, Chinese, and Mexican restaurants, among others, are springing up not just in big cities but in suburbs and small towns as well.

Many of the most creative chefs have been inspired by these cuisines and have borrowed some of their techniques. For example, many North American and French chefs, looking for ways to make their own cooking lighter and more elegant, have found ideas in the cuisine of Japan. In the southwestern United States, a number of chefs have transformed Mexican influences into an elegant and original cooking style of their own.

Foreign influences are not new, of course. Classical cuisine is full of terms that reveal foreign inspiration, like *Espagnole, Hongroise,* and *Japonaise.* It is important to remember, however, that a dish inspired by a foreign cuisine may not be the same as an authentic dish from that cuisine. For example, we fill a French omelet with a type of tomato sauce and call it Spanish. But in Spain, the classic omelet is a thick, flat mixture of eggs, potatoes, and onions.

This chapter can present only a small selection of typical recipes from some of these influential cuisines. After having had experience with this small sampling, students are encouraged to continue their own research. The bibliography at the end of the book lists titles that can help.

At the end of the chapter, a short glossary of foreign words and phrases used in this chapter appears instead of the usual Terms for Review.

After reading this chapter, you should be able to prepare some typical recipes from Japan, China, Mexico, and from Italy and other European countries.

Japanese

The appearance of the food in Japan is very important. In most cases, each dish is presented carefully and attractively in a separate bowl or dish. Portions are generally small, and a formal dinner consists of a sequence of many small dishes.

Most Japanese foods are delicately seasoned, unlike the more highly spiced foods of other Asian regions, such as Thailand and parts of China. Simmering, steaming, and grilling are perhaps the most important cooking methods, in contrast to the stir-frying that is so important in China. The single most important food in the Japanese diet is plain steamed or boiled rice. The word for boiled rice, *gohan*, also means "meal."

Fish dominates the cuisine of this island country. Dishes like sashimi (sliced raw fish), sushi, and simple grilled fish are frequently encountered. The basic stock, called *dashi*, is made from dried, shaved bonito (a type of fish) and a kind of seaweed. It is used in soups, simmered dishes, and sauces.

Sushi has become especially popular in Western countries, but there is much confusion about it. Sushi is often equated with raw fish but, in fact, the term refers to cooked rice lightly flavored with seasoned vinegar. The rice is served with various garnishes, which include not only raw fish (no doubt the most popular garnish for sushi rice) but also cooked seafood and many kinds of vegetables and pickles. Incidentally, in Japanese, an initial *s*, as in the word *sushi*, may change to a *z* when it is in the middle of a compound word, as in *nigirizushi* (p. 720).

 ## Dashi

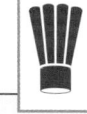

Yield: 2 qt (2 L)

U.S.	Metric	Ingredients	PROCEDURE
4½ pt	2.25 L	Water, cold	1. Put the water in a pot and add the kombu. Bring to a boil over moderately high heat.
2 oz	60 g	Kombu (giant kelp for stock)	2. Just as the water comes to a boil, remove the kombu.
1½ oz	50 g	Katsuobushi (dried bonito flakes)	3. Remove from the heat and immediately add the bonito flakes. Let the flakes settle to the bottom. This will take 1–2 minutes.
			4. Strain through a china cap lined with cheesecloth. Use the dashi within 1 day.

Per 1 ounce:
Calories, 2; Protein, 0 g; Fat, 0 g (0% cal.); Cholesterol, 0 mg;
Carbohydrates, 0 g; Fiber, 0 g; Sodium, 3 mg.

VARIATIONS

Instant dashi is also available. Its quality is good enough for simmered dishes and miso soup, but not for good clear soup. Follow label instructions.

Vegetarian Dashi

Omit the bonito flakes and use only the kombu.

Clear Soup with Shrimp

Portions: 10   Portion size: 6 oz (200 mL)

U.S.	Metric	Ingredients	PROCEDURE
2 qt	2 L	Dashi	1. Bring the dashi to a simmer. Carefully add salt to taste.
to taste	to taste	Salt	2. Add soy sauce. (The soup should be crystal clear.)
1 tbsp	15 mL	Japanese soy sauce	
		Garnish:	3. Cut lemon zest into very fine julienne.
1–2 strips	1–2 strips	Lemon zest	4. Trim and wash the snow peas. Cut them crosswise at an angle, making diamond shapes. Blanch them 1 minute in boiling water. Drain and cool.
15	15	Snow peas	
10	10	Medium shrimp	5. Peel and devein the shrimp. Blanch them in boiling water just until cooked, no more than 1 minute. Drain.
			6. Rinse soup cups or bowls in hot water to warm them. In each bowl put 1 shrimp, a few pieces of snow peas, and a few threads of lemon zest.
			7. Make sure that the soup is very hot—almost at the boiling point—and ladle 6 oz (200 mL) into each bowl. Serve at once.

Per serving:
Calories, 15; Protein, 2 g; Fat, 0 g (0% cal.); Cholesterol, 10 mg; Carbohydrates, 1 g; Fiber, 0 g; Sodium, 115 mg.

VARIATIONS

Garnish: Clear soup garnish can be varied considerably. Always use just a few carefully chosen items. Don't clutter the bowl. The effect should be like an elegant little still-life painting seen through the perfectly clear soup. All cutting should be done carefully and neatly. Garnish items include:

Tofu, cut in small cubes
Cooked pork loin or chicken breast, cut in small dice, batonnet, or julienne
Lobster tail, in thin slices
Cooked fish, separated into flakes (use a type that separates into large, firm flakes, such as snapper or cod)
Small clams, steamed and removed from shell (the broth can be clarified, diluted, and used for soup base instead of dashi)
Carrots, cut julienne
Fresh white mushrooms, sliced thin
Dried shiitake mushrooms, soaked, simmered, and cut into julienne
Wakame (a type of seaweed); soak until soft, cut into small pieces and discard the hard ribs, and simmer in the soup 2 minutes
Chinese cabbage, shredded.
Watercress leaves
Fresh ginger root, cut into fine shreds (use only a few shreds per serving)
Bamboo shoots, sliced thin
White radish, sliced thin or shredded

Miso Soup

Miso soup is made simply by dissolving *miso* (fermented paste made of soybeans, barley, and/or rice) in dashi. The two main categories of miso are *white miso*, which is actually light yellowish in color and has a sweet, mild taste, and *red* or *dark miso*, which comes in varying shades of reddish brown and is stronger and saltier in taste. General proportions for soup are 4 tbsp (60 mL) red miso or 6 tbsp (90 mL) white miso per quart (liter) of dashi. Put the miso in a small bowl and carefully stir in a ladleful of hot dashi. Stir until completely lump-free. Add enough dashi so that the miso is thin and pourable. (Do not add miso directly to soup or it will not mix in properly.) Carefully stir the dissolved miso into the remaining hot dashi. Season to taste and, if desired, add 1–2 teaspoons (5–10 mL) soy sauce. Add desired garnish as for clear soup, except that the garnish can be added directly to the soup kettle. Because this is a heartier soup, it is more often garnished with tofu and vegetables rather than more delicate seafood. Stir before serving, as the miso settles out.

Sushi Rice

Yield: about 2½ lb (1.1 kg)

U.S.	Metric	Ingredients	PROCEDURE
3 cups	750 mL	Japanese short-grain rice (see note)	1. Wash the rice in several changes of cold water. Drain well.
3½ cups	900 mL	Water, cold	2. Put the drained rice in a heavy saucepan and add the measured water. Cover tightly and let stand at least 30 minutes.
			3. With the cover in place, set the pan over high heat and bring to a boil. When boiling, reduce the heat to medium and let cook until all the water is absorbed. Do not remove the cover to check, but listen to the sounds. The bubbling will stop, and there will be a faint hissing sound.
			4. Reduce the heat to very low and cook another 5 minutes. Then remove from heat and let stand at least 15 minutes before removing the cover. You now have the basic white rice that is eaten with Japanese meals.
3–4 oz	100–125 mL	Sushi vinegar (see note)	5. In Japan, mixing in the vinegar is done in a special wooden tub that is used only for this purpose (to avoid off flavors). The advantage of wood is that it absorbs excess moisture. If you use a nonabsorbent mixing bowl, transfer the rice to a clean bowl whenever the mixing bowl becomes coated with moisture. Using a wooden paddle or plastic spatula, break up the hot rice to get rid of all lumps. At the same time, fan the rice to cool it.
			6. When the rice is slightly warm to the touch, begin adding the sushi vinegar. Add a little at a time while mixing gently. The rice is ready when it has a glossy appearance and a very mild taste of the vinegar. The vinegared rice is best if used within 2–3 hours, and it must not be refrigerated.

Per 1 ounce:
Calories, 40; Protein, 1 g; Fat, 0 g (0% cal.); Cholesterol, 0 mg; Carbohydrates, 9 g; Fiber, 0 g; Sodium, 105 mg.

Note: Do not confuse Japanese short-grain rice with glutinous rice, which is an entirely different product. Sushi vinegar is commercially available, but it can also be made in the kitchen. Combine 1 pint (500 mL) Japanese rice vinegar, 8 oz (250 g) sugar, and 4 oz (125 g) salt. Heat and stir until the sugar and salt are dissolved, then cool.

VARIATIONS

Nigirizushi (Finger Sushi)

1. Prepare *wasabi* (green horseradish) by mixing wasabi powder with a little water to form a thick paste. Let stand, covered, a few minutes to allow flavor to develop.
2. Prepare sushi toppings by cutting very fresh fish fillets (use saltwater fish or smoked salmon) into slices about 1½ × 2½ inches (4 × 6 cm). Tuna, the most popular fish for sushi, is tender and is usually cut about ¼ inch (6 mm) thick. Other fish are cut thinner.
3. Wet your hands with cold water to keep the rice from sticking to them, then pick up about 2 tbsp (30 mL) sushi rice. Shape it into firm oval about 1½ inches (4 cm) long (see Figure 25.1). Pick up a slice of fish in one hand. Dip a finger of the other hand in the wasabi and spread a very small amount on the underside of the fish slice. Drape the fish over the oval of rice, with the wasabi underneath next to the rice, and press it gently but firmly in place. Serve with soy sauce for dipping.

Kappa-maki (Cucumber Roll)

To make rolled sushi, you will need a special bamboo mat called a *sudare* (see Figure 25.1). You could also use a sheet of parchment, but the roll will be harder to make.

1. Peel a cucumber. Cut it in half and scrape out the seeds. Cut lengthwise into julienne.
2. Cut a sheet of *nori* (a type of seaweed for rolled sushi) in half crosswise. Toast it by passing it briefly above a burner flame, being careful not to burn it.
3. Put the bamboo mat on the table in front of you with the bamboo strips horizontal. Put the half sheet of nori on the mat, smooth side down.
4. Cover the two-thirds of the nori closest to you with a layer of sushi rice about ¼ inch (6 mm) thick.
5. Spread a light streak of wasabi from right to left across the middle of the rice.
6. Lay strips of cucumber evenly on top of the strip of wasabi.
7. Lift the edge of the mat closest to you and roll up firmly. This is best done by lifting the mat with the thumbs while holding the cucumber in place with the fingers. Press the roll in the mat gently but firmly to make it tight.
8. Wipe the blade of a very sharp knife, then cut the roll in half crosswise. Do not saw the roll but cut it cleanly with a single stroke. Wiping the blade on a damp cloth after every cut, cut each half roll into 4 pieces.

Tekka-maki (Tuna Roll)

Make *Kappa-maki*, but instead of cucumber, use raw tuna cut into batonnet strips.

Chirashizushi (Scatter Sushi)

Fill a serving bowl half full of sushi rice. Carefully and attractively arrange an assortment of raw fish, cooked shrimp, crab meat, and neatly cut vegetables such as snow peas, cucumber, carrots, mushrooms, and pickled ginger on top of the rice.

Figure 25.1 Making sushi.

(a) For nigirizushi, wet your hands with cold water to keep the rice from sticking to them. Form a bit of rice into a small oval in one hand.

(b) In the other hand, pick up a slice of fish and smear a dab of wasabi on the bottom of it.

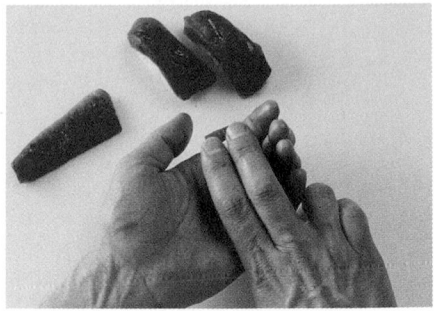

(c) Top the rice with the fish, wasabi side against the rice, and press in place in the palm of one hand with two fingers of the other.

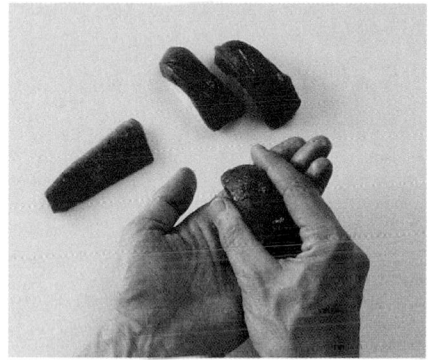

(d) Turn it over and press the same way. Then press the sides with the thumb and forefinger to finish shaping it.

(e) For rolled sushi, put a half piece of nori on the sudare (bamboo mat). Wetting your hands with cold water to keep the rice from sticking to them, spread a layer of sushi rice over the bottom two-thirds of the nori.

(f) Lay strips of the filling across the middle of the rice.

(g) Holding the filling in place with the fingers, lift the corner of the mat with the thumbs and roll up.

(h) Press the mat firmly and evenly to make a tight roll.

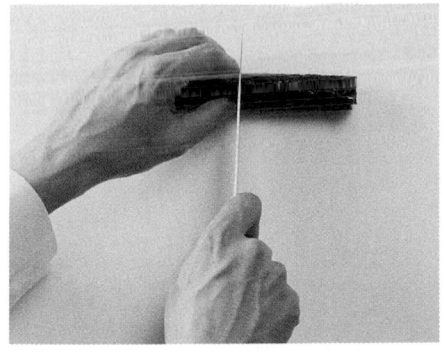

(i) Cut the roll in half with a single forward stroke, using a dampened knife.

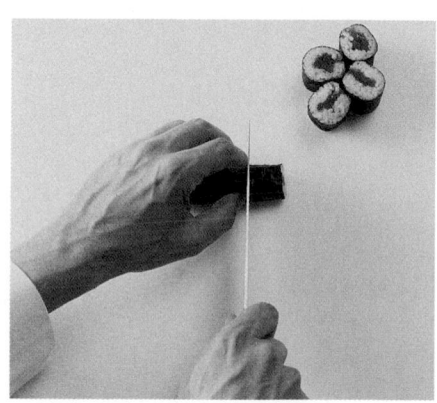

(j) Wipe the blade between cuts, and cut each half-roll into three or four pieces.

Shrimp and Vegetable Tempura

Portions: 16   **Portion size:** 3 shrimp, plus vegetables

U.S.	Metric	Ingredients	PROCEDURE
48	48	Large shrimp	1. Peel the shrimp, leaving the tails attached. Devein and butterfly them.
4	4	Green peppers	
1 lb 4 oz	600 g	Sweet potatoes	2. Core and seed the peppers. Cut each one lengthwise into 8 wedges or strips.
32	32	Small mushrooms (or halves or quarters of large mushrooms)	3. Peel the sweet potatoes. Cut into slices about ¹⁄₆ inch (4 mm) thick.
			4. Clean the mushrooms and trim the bottoms of the stems.
1½ lb	750 g	Cake flour or other low-gluten flour	5. Sift the flour into a mixing bowl.
			6. Mix together the water and egg yolks.
1½ pt	750 mL	Water, ice-cold	7. Mix the liquid into the flour until just combined. Do not worry about a few lumps. The batter should be somewhat thinner than pancake batter.
6	6	Egg yolks	
1½ pt	750 mL	Dashi	8. Make a dipping sauce by combining the dashi, soy sauce, and mirin.
5 oz	150 mL	Soy sauce	
3 oz	100 mL	Mirin (sweet rice wine)	
as needed	as needed	Flour for dredging	9. Divide the shrimp and vegetables equally among the 16 portions. Fry the vegetables first, then the shrimp, by dredging with flour, shaking off the excess, then dipping in the batter and dropping into clean frying fat at 350°F (175°C). Fry just until lightly golden.
8 oz	250 g	Grated daikon (large white Japanese radish)	
3 tbsp	45 mL	Grated fresh ginger root	10. Drain and serve at once. Tempura is traditionally served on a bamboo tray covered with a clean piece of absorbent paper. Accompany with about 2 oz (60 mL) dipping sauce in a shallow bowl. Put a small mound each of grated daikon and grated ginger on each serving tray. The diner mixes these to taste into the dipping sauce.

Per serving:
Calories, 380; Protein, 11 g; Fat, 12 g (28% cal.); Cholesterol, 115 mg; Carbohydrates, 56 g; Fiber, 3 g; Sodium, 560 mg.

Oyako Donburi

Portions: 16   **Portion size:** see procedure

U.S.	Metric	Ingredients	PROCEDURE
2 qt	2 L	Dashi	1. Combine the dashi, soy sauce, sugar, and sake in a saucepan. Bring to a simmer to dissolve the sugar. Remove from heat and reserve.
5 oz	150 mL	Soy sauce	
5 oz	150 g	Sugar	
2 oz	60 mL	Sake (optional)	
3 qt	3 L	Raw Japanese short-grain rice	2. Cook the rice by following steps 1–4 in the recipe for sushi rice, page 720. Keep it hot.
1½ lb	725 g	Boneless, skinless chicken meat	3. Cut the chicken into strips 1 inch (2½ cm) wide, then slice diagonally ¼ inch (6 mm) thick.
16	16	Scallions	4. Trim the roots and the coarser greens from the scallions, leaving the tender green parts intact. Cut diagonally into ½-inch (1-cm) pieces.
16	16	Eggs	5. For each portion, put 1½ oz (45 g) chicken, 1 sliced scallion, and 4½ oz (125 mL) dashi mixture in a small sauté pan. Simmer until the chicken is nearly done.
			6. Break 1 egg into a bowl. Mix lightly but do not beat.
			7. Pour the egg in a stream around the chicken in the skillet. Continue to simmer until the egg is half set.
			8. Put 1½ cups (375 mL) hot rice in a large, deep soup bowl.
			9. When the egg is nearly set, give the egg and chicken mixture a light stir and pour the contents of the skillet over the rice.

Per serving:
Calories, 570; Protein, 23 g; Fat, 8 g (13% cal.); Cholesterol, 240 mg; Carbohydrates, 98 g; Fiber, 4 g; Sodium, 600 mg.

Note: The name of this dish, *oyako*, means "parent and child," referring to the chicken and egg. A *donburi* is a type of serving bowl, and the word also refers to foods served in this type of bowl, generally rice with toppings and sauce.

VARIATION

Tendon

Omit the chicken, scallions, and egg in the recipe above. Reduce the dashi to 1 qt (1 L) and double the amount of sake. Top each bowl of rice with 1 piece of shrimp tempura and 2 pieces of vegetable tempura. Pour about 2½ oz (75 mL) hot dashi mixture over the rice and serve. (The name of this dish comes from the first syllables of "tempura" and "donburi.")

Japanese Specialties.
Front, left to right: Chicken Teriyaki garnished with a pickled ginger shoot and shiso, a Japanese herb; assorted Sushi; Green Beans with Sesame Dressing. Back, left to right: Chawan Mushi; Clear Soup with Shrimp.

Chawan Mushi (Japanese Steamed Custard)

Portions: 16   Portion size: 7 oz (200 g)

U.S.	Metric	Ingredients	PROCEDURE
12 oz	375 g	Boneless, skinless chicken breast meat	1. Cut the chicken breast into ½-inch (1-cm) dice. Mix with the soy sauce and sake and marinate for 15 minutes. Drain.
1 tbsp	15 mL	Soy sauce	2. Divide the chicken, shrimp, scallions, and water chestnuts equally among 16 custard cups or other 8-oz (250-mL) heatproof cups.
1 tbsp	15 mL	Sake (optional)	
16	16	Small shrimp, peeled and deveined	
6	6	Scallions, sliced thin	
4 oz	125 g	Water chestnuts, sliced	
12	12	Large eggs	3. Beat the eggs lightly in a bowl.
2 qt	2 L	Dashi or chicken stock	4. Mix in the dashi or stock, soy sauce, and mirin. Season to taste with a little salt.
1 tbsp	15 mL	Soy sauce	5. Carefully remove any foam from the egg mixture. Ladle about 5½ oz (160 mL) of the egg mixture into each cup. There should be no bubbles or foam on the surface.
2 tbsp	30 mL	Mirin (sweet rice wine)	
to taste	to taste	Salt	6. Cover each cup tightly with foil and place in a steamer. Steam for about 15 minutes or until the custard is set.
			7. Serve hot or cold. This savory custard is eaten with a spoon and with chopsticks for the solid pieces.

Per serving:
Calories, 100; Protein, 11 g; Fat, 4.5 g (41% cal.); Cholesterol, 180 mg;
Carbohydrates, 3 g; Fiber, 0 g; Sodium, 210 mg.

Green Beans with Sesame Dressing

Portions: 16   Portion size: 2 oz (60 g)

U.S.	Metric	Ingredients	PROCEDURE
1 cup	250 mL	White sesame seeds	1. Toast the sesame seeds in a dry skillet, stirring and tossing regularly, until light golden.
1½ oz	50 mL	Soy sauce	2. Using a spice grinder or mortar and pestle, grind the sesame seeds to a paste.
2 tbsp	30 g	Sugar	3. Mix in the soy sauce and sugar. Thin with dashi or water. Set aside.
2 oz	60 mL	Dashi or water	
2 lb	1 kg	Green beans	4. Wash the green beans and trim the ends. Cut into 1-inch (2½-cm) lengths.
			5. Cook the beans in boiling, salted water until crisp-tender. Drain, cool under cold, running water, and drain again.
			6. Mix the beans with the dressing.

Per serving:
Calories, 80; Protein, 3 g; Fat, 4.5 g (48% cal.); Cholesterol, 0 mg;
Carbohydrates, 8 g; Fiber, 3 g; Sodium, 150 mg.

VARIATIONS

Other mild green vegetables, such as spinach and asparagus, can be served the same way.

Sesame Miso Dressing

Reduce the sesame seeds to ½ cup (125 mL). Omit the soy sauce and sugar, and add 4 oz (125 g) white or red miso. Use mirin (sweet rice wine) instead of dashi or water to thin the dressing. Use as a dressing for vegetables, in the same manner as sesame dressing.

Chicken Teriyaki

Portions: 16   **Portion size:** 1 chicken breast or thigh

U.S.	Metric	Ingredients	PROCEDURE
		Teriyaki sauce:	1. Combine the sake, soy sauce, mirin, and sugar. Heat to a simmer to dissolve the sugar. Cool.
3 oz	75 mL	Sake	
7 oz	175 mL	Soy sauce	
6 oz	150 mL	Mirin (sweet rice wine)	
2 tbsp	25 mL	Sugar	
16	16	Boneless chicken breasts or thighs, skin on or off as desired	2. Heat a thin film of oil in a skillet. Put in the chicken pieces, skin side down. Cook until browned and half done. Turn and cook the other side.
as needed	as needed	Vegetable oil	3. Remove the chicken and degrease the pan.
			4. Deglaze the pan with the teriyaki sauce and bring the sauce to a boil.
			5. Return the chicken to the pan. Turn it in the pan until it is lightly glazed.
			6. Remove the chicken from the pan and reserve the sauce. Cut each piece of chicken crosswise, on the diagonal, into strips ½ inch (1 cm) wide.
			7. Plate the chicken, keeping each piece assembled in its original form. Spoon a little of the sauce on top.

Per serving:
Calories, 280; Protein, 31 g; Fat, 11 g (38% cal.); Cholesterol, 85 mg;
Carbohydrates, 6 g; Fiber, 0 g; Sodium, 780 mg.

VARIATIONS

Other items, such as small beefsteaks, fish fillets, and scallops, can be cooked this way. In the case of fish fillets, keep the skin on if possible, and use the skin side as the presentation side.

Chinese

China is a vast country, and the climate and food resources vary greatly from region to region. Consequently, there is no single Chinese cooking style but rather an array of regional styles. The styles of Beijing in the north, Canton in the southeast, and Sichuan in the western interior, to name three of the most famous, are perhaps as different as the styles of Germany, France, and Italy.

Nevertheless, we can make some generalizations about Chinese cooking that may help clarify it. In the first place, meat does not play the central role it does in North American and European cooking. Vegetables and grains are more important and supply the bulk of the diet. Rice is the most important grain, while noodles and other wheat products are also eaten frequently, especially in the north.

A typical meal has no main dish. Rather, cooked dishes are generally considered accompaniments for rice, which is the most important item in the meal. Portions of these side dishes are usually small, and a meal may consist of a large assortment of such dishes. Serving dishes are placed in the center of the table, and each diner takes a small quantity of each, as desired, to eat between bites of rice.

Although some foods are stewed or simmered for a long time, in most cases, cooking times are short, while preparation times are long. A great deal of trimming, cutting, and slicing is required, but once this is done, many dishes are cooked and sent to the table in a matter of minutes.

Many of the cooking techniques we are familiar with, including deep-frying, steaming, and simmering, have a place in Chinese cooking. From our point of view, perhaps the most important and typically Chinese cooking technique is stir-frying. The basic procedure is explained on page 728, and recipes are included that use this technique.

Egg Rolls or Spring Rolls

Yield: 16 pieces

U.S.	Metric	Ingredients	PROCEDURE
1 oz	30 mL	Oil	1. Heat the oil in a wok or sauté pan. Stir-fry the meat, cabbage, scallions, bean sprouts, black mushrooms, bamboo shoots, and shrimp.
6 oz	175 g	Cooked meat or poultry, cut fine julienne	
6 oz	175 g	Chinese cabbage, shredded	2. Add the soy sauce, sherry, and stock. Continue to stir and cook for another 1–2 minutes.
3	3	Scallions, shredded	3. Mix the cornstarch with the cold water. Stir into the vegetable mixture and cook until reduced and thickened.
6 oz	175 g	Bean sprouts	
5	5	Dried black mushrooms (stems discarded), soaked in boiling water, cut julienne	4. Remove from the heat and adjust the seasonings. Cool thoroughly.
2 oz	60 g	Bamboo shoots, cut julienne	
1½ oz	45 g	Raw shrimp, chopped	
2 tsp	10 mL	Soy sauce	
1 tsp	5 mL	Sherry or shaoxing wine	
3 oz	100 mL	Chicken stock	
1½ tsp	7 mL	Cornstarch	
1 tbsp	15 mL	Cold water	

U.S.	Metric	Ingredients	PROCEDURE
16	16	Egg roll skins or spring roll skins	5. Lay an egg roll skin on the worktable with one of the corners toward you. Spoon about 1½ oz (45 g) filling onto the lower half of the skin in a sort of sausage shape. (See Figure 25.2.)
as needed	as needed	Egg, beaten	6. Fold the lower corner of the skin (the corner pointing at you) over the filling so that it is covered. Then start to roll it up like a cylinder, giving it just a half turn.
			7. Brush the left and right corners with a little beaten egg. Fold one corner over the filling, then the other, pressing down to seal. At this point, it should look like an open envelope.
			8. Brush the top corner with beaten egg. Roll into a firm, compact cylinder. Seal the top corner well.
			9. Repeat with the remaining skins and filling.
			10. Deep-fry the egg rolls until the skins are crisp and brown. (*Note:* Egg roll skins are heavier than spring roll skins. They must be thoroughly fried or they will be doughy.) Drain and serve at once, with a little hot mustard or bottled duck sauce for dipping.

Per 1 roll:
Calories, 180; Protein, 8 g; Fat, 8 g (38% cal.); Cholesterol, 25 mg; Carbohydrates, 21 g; Fiber, 1 g; Sodium, 240 mg.

Figure 25.2 Rolling egg rolls.

(a) Lay an egg roll skin on the bench with one corner toward you. Place the filling as shown.

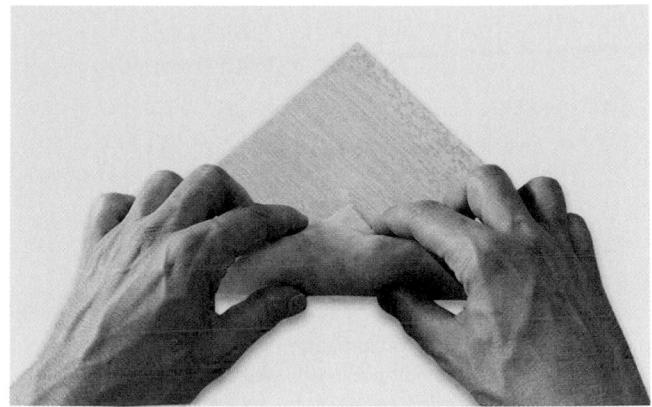

(b) Fold the lower corner of the skin over the filling and roll it up about one-third of the way.

(c) Brush the left and right corners of the skin with beaten eggs.

(d) Fold the corners over the filling so that the skin resembles an open envelope.

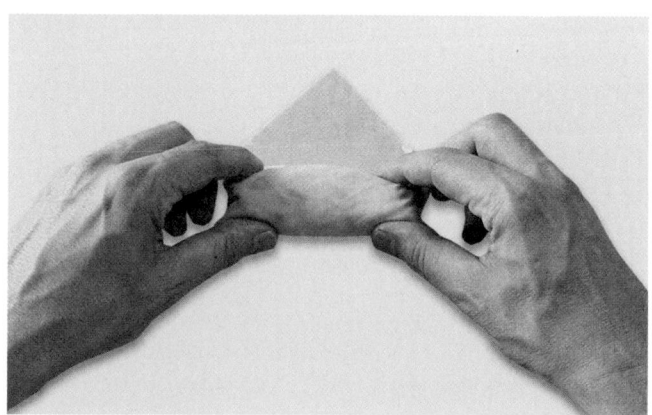

(e) Brush the top edge with egg and roll up tightly.

(f) When completely rolled, egg rolls are ready to be cooked.

Basic Procedure for Stir-Frying

1. Heat a wok or sauté pan over high heat until very hot.

2. Add a small quantity of oil and let it heat.

3. Add seasonings for flavoring the oil, one or more of the following: salt, garlic, ginger root, scallions.

4. If meat, poultry, or seafood items are part of the dish, add them now. As when sautéing, do not overload the pan. Leave it untouched for a few moments so the food pieces begin to brown properly. Then stir and toss them with a spatula so that they sear and cook evenly.

5. If any liquid seasoning for the meat is used, such as soy sauce, add it now, but only in small quantities, so that the meat continues to fry and does not start to simmer or stew.

6. Remove the meat from the pan or leave it in, depending on the recipe. If a small quantity of quick-cooking vegetables is used, the meat can sometimes be left in the pan and the vegetables cooked with it. Otherwise, remove the meat when it is almost done and keep it on the side while cooking the vegetables.

7. Repeat steps 2 and 3 if necessary.

8. Add the vegetables to the pan and stir-fry. If more than one vegetable is used, add the longer-cooking one first and the shorter-cooking ones last.

9. Some dishes are dry-fried, meaning prepared without liquid or sauce. In this case, simply return the meat item, if any, to the pan to reheat with the vegetables, then serve. Otherwise, proceed to the next step.

10. Add liquid ingredients, such as stock or water, and continue to cook and stir until the vegetables are almost cooked.

11. Add the meat item, which was removed in step 6, to the pan to reheat.

12. Optional but widely used step: Add a mixture of cornstarch and water to the pan and cook until lightly thickened.

13. Serve at once.

Stir-Fried Beef with Green Peppers

Portions: 16   **Portion size:** 4 oz (125 g)

U.S.	Metric	Ingredients	PROCEDURE
2½ lb	1.2 kg	Flank steak	1. Cut the flank steak lengthwise (with the grain) into strips 2 inches (5 cm) wide. Then cut the strips crosswise into very thin slices. (This is easier if the meat is partially frozen.)
4 oz	125 mL	Soy sauce	
1 oz	30 mL	Sherry or shaoxing wine	
5 tsp	25 mL	Cornstarch	2. Toss the meat with the soy sauce, sherry, and cornstarch. Let marinate 30 minutes or longer.
6	6	Green peppers	3. Core and seed the peppers. Cut them into large dice.
4 slices	4 slices	Ginger root	4. Have the ginger, garlic, and scallions ready in separate containers.
1–2	1–2	Garlic cloves, sliced	
2 oz	60 g	Scallions, sliced	
3–4 oz	90–125 mL	Oil	5. Stir-fry the beef in 3 or more batches, depending on the size of the pan or wok. Use a little of the oil for each batch, as needed.
½ tsp	2 mL	Salt	
2 oz	60 mL	Chicken stock	6. As each batch of the beef is cooked, remove it from the pan and set it aside.
			7. Heat additional oil in the pan and add the salt, ginger, garlic, and scallions. Stir-fry for a few seconds to develop flavor.
			8. Add the peppers and stir-fry until lightly cooked but still crisp.
			9. Add the broth and toss the vegetables a few times.
			10. Return the meat to the pan. Toss the meat with the vegetables until it is hot and evenly combined with the peppers. Serve at once.

Per serving:
Calories, 180; Protein, 16 g; Fat, 11 g (54% cal.); Cholesterol, 35 mg; Carbohydrates, 5 g; Fiber, 1 g; Sodium, 525 mg.

VARIATIONS

Other vegetables may be used instead of the peppers, such as celery, broccoli, snow peas, green beans, asparagus, mushrooms, and bok choy. Or use 2 or 3 fresh vegetables, plus water chestnuts and/or bamboo shoots.

Chicken or pork may be used instead of beef. If chicken is used, cut it into medium dice or batonnet. Also, reduce the quantity of soy sauce to avoid discoloring the light meat of the chicken.

Stir-Fried Mixed Vegetables

Portions: 16   Portion size: 4 oz (125 g)

U.S.	Metric	Ingredients
1½ lb	750 g	Chinese cabbage
16	16	Dried black mushrooms
6 oz	175 g	Bamboo shoots, drained
4 oz	125 g	Celery
4 oz	125 g	Carrots
15-oz can	425-g can	Baby corn
4	4	Scallions

PROCEDURE

1. Cut off the root end of the cabbage and separate the leaves. Cut out the thick center ribs, then cut them crosswise into 2-inch (5-cm) chunks. Cut the thin, leafy parts into shreds.
2. Soak the mushrooms in boiling water to cover. When soft, drain and squeeze dry, reserving the liquid. Discard the stems and cut the caps into julienne.
3. Cut the bamboo shoots into thin slices.
4. Cut the celery on the diagonal into thin slices.
5. Cut the carrot into julienne.
6. Drain the baby corn.
7. Slice the scallions at a sharp angle into shreds.

U.S.	Metric	Ingredients
2–3 oz	60–90 mL	Oil
1 clove	1 clove	Garlic, crushed (optional)
5 slices	5 slices	Ginger root
1 tsp	5 mL	Salt
12 oz	350 mL	Water or chicken stock
1 oz	30 mL	Soy sauce (optional)
¼ cup	25 g (60 mL)	Cornstarch
3 oz	100 mL	Water, cold
1 tsp	5 mL	Sesame oil (optional)

8. Heat the oil in a wok or large sauté pan.
9. Add the garlic and cook about 15 seconds to flavor the oil, then remove and discard the garlic.
10. Add the ginger and salt and let cook about 15 seconds.
11. Add the cabbage ribs and stir-fry for 1–2 minutes.
12. Add the remaining vegetables, except for the shredded cabbage leaves. Continue to stir-fry for another 1–2 minutes. Add the shredded cabbage.
13. Add the stock and soy sauce and continue to stir and cook until the vegetables are cooked but still crisp.
14. Mix the cornstarch with the cold water, then stir it, a little at a time, into the vegetables to thicken the sauce. Do not add it all at once because you may not need it all. The sauce should not be too thick, about the consistency of a light velouté sauce.
15. Stir in the sesame oil and serve at once.

Per serving:
Calories, 90; Protein, 2 g; Fat, 4 g (36% cal.); Cholesterol, 0 mg; Carbohydrates, 14 g; Fiber, 3 g; Sodium, 165 mg.

VARIATIONS

This is a basic procedure for stir-fried vegetables. One or two vegetables, or any harmonious assortment, can be cooked using the same recipe, merely substituting different vegetable ingredients.

Basic Fried Rice

Portions: 16   Portion size: 6 oz (175 g)

U.S.	Metric	Ingredients	PROCEDURE
4 lb	1.8 kg	Cooked rice, cold	1. Break up the rice to remove all lumps.
4–6 oz	125–175 mL	Oil	2. Divide the rice and other ingredients into two or more batches, depending on the size of the pan or wok. Do no more than 1–2 lb (½–1 kg) rice at one time. If you fry too much at once, it will not fry properly.
1 lb	450 g	Cooked meat (cut into shreds) or seafood (flaked or sliced)	
3 oz	90 g	Scallions, sliced thin	3. Heat a small amount of oil in the wok. Add the meat and stir-fry for 1–2 minutes.
1 lb	450 g	Vegetables (see variations), shredded or small dice	4. Add the scallions and stir-fry for 1 minute.
			5. Add any raw vegetables and stir-fry until almost done.
4–6 oz	125–175 mL	Soy sauce (optional)	6. Add the rice and stir-fry until it is hot and lightly coated with oil.
to taste	to taste	Salt	7. Add any cooked vegetables and mix in.
4–8	4–8	Eggs, beaten	8. Add soy sauce, if used, and salt.
			9. Add beaten egg and mix in. Stir-fry lightly to cook the egg, then serve.

Per serving:
Calories, 280; Protein, 11 g; Fat, 10 g (33% cal.); Cholesterol, 70 mg;
Carbohydrates, 35 g; Fiber, 2 g; Sodium, 35 mg.

VARIATIONS

The quantities given in the basic recipe are only guidelines, but rice should be the predominant ingredient. You can omit the meat or fish items. For plain rice, you can omit the vegetables too.

Eggs can be omitted, or they can be added to fried rice in several other ways:

1. Remove the meat and vegetables from the pan when they are cooked. Add the egg to the pan and scramble. Add the rice, return the meat and vegetables to the pan, and continue with the recipe.
2. In step 9, push the rice to the sides of the pan. Add the egg to the well in the middle. When it starts to set, gradually mix in the rice.
3. Scramble the eggs separately and add to the rice at the end.
4. Mix the raw beaten egg with the cold cooked rice before cooking.

Suggested Ingredients

Meats: cooked pork, beef, chicken, duck, ham, bacon, Chinese sausage
Seafood: shrimp (diced or whole), crab, lobster
Vegetables: bamboo shoots, bean sprouts, celery, peas, mushrooms, onions, peppers, water chestnuts

Pearl Balls

Yield: about 40 pieces

U.S.	Metric	Ingredients	PROCEDURE
2 cups	500 mL	Glutinous rice	1. Wash the rice in several changes of cold water. Drain. Add enough fresh water to cover by 1 inch (2½ cm). Let soak for at least 30 minutes.
3 tbsp	45 mL	Cornstarch	2. Mix together the cornstarch and water.
1 oz	30 mL	Water, cold	3. Combine all ingredients except the glutinous rice and mix together.
2 lb	900 g	Ground pork	
4	4	Scallions, minced	4. Form the meat mixture into small meatballs, about 1 oz (30 g) each.
8	8	Water chestnuts, minced	
2 tsp	10 mL	Fresh ginger root, minced	5. Drain the rice. Roll the balls in the rice so that they are well coated.
2	2	Eggs, beaten	
1 oz	30 mL	Soy sauce	6. Line a rack or perforated steamer pan with cheesecloth. Arrange the meatballs in the pan, allowing about ½ inch (1–2 cm) between them.
1 oz	30 mL	Sherry or shaoxing wine	
2 tsp	10 mL	Sugar	7. Steam for 30–45 minutes, until the rice is translucent and the pork is done.
1½ tsp	7 mL	Salt	

Per 1 piece:
Calories, 70; Protein, 5 g; Fat, 3.5 g (49% cal.); Cholesterol, 25 mg;
Carbohydrates, 3 g; Fiber, 0 g; Sodium, 145 mg.

VARIATIONS

Fried Pork Balls

Omit the rice coating and cook the meatballs by deep-frying them.

Wontons

The pork mixture can be used for wonton filling. Put a small spoonful of meat in the center of a wonton skin. Moisten the edges with beaten egg, then fold the skin in half to make a triangle (or, if you are using round wonton skins, a semicircle) enclosing the filling. Moisten one of the two corners (on the folded edge) with egg, then twist the wonton to bring the two corners together. Press the corners together to seal. Makes 60 or more wontons, depending on size. Wontons can be cooked by simmering, steaming, or deep-frying. They are often served in chicken broth as wonton soup.

Eggplant, Sichuan Style

Portions: 16   Portion size: 2–2½ oz (60–75 g)

U.S.	Metric	Ingredients	PROCEDURE
2 oz	60 mL	Chili paste with garlic (Sichuan paste)	1. Mix together the chili paste, soy sauce, wine, vinegar, sugar, and stock or water.
1 oz	30 mL	Soy sauce	
2 oz	60 mL	Sherry or shaoxing wine	
1 oz	30 mL	Red wine vinegar	
1 tsp	5 mL	Sugar	
2 oz	60 mL	Chicken stock or water	
2½ lb	1.1 kg	Eggplant	2. Peel the eggplant if the skin is tough. Otherwise, leave it on. Cut the eggplant into 1-inch (2½-cm) dice.
4 cloves	4 cloves	Garlic	
1 tsp	5 mL	Ginger root	3. Mince the garlic, ginger, and scallions.
6	6	Scallions	4. Heat the oil in a sauté pan and sauté the eggplant until lightly browned.
2–3 oz	60–90 mL	Oil	
1 tbsp	15 mL	Sesame oil	5. Add the garlic, ginger, and scallions and sauté another minute.
			6. Add the chili paste mixture and stir in. Cover and cook over low heat until the eggplant is tender, about 15–20 minutes.
			7. Uncover. The sauce should be quite thick so, if necessary, cook uncovered for a few minutes to reduce the liquid.
			8. Add the sesame oil and serve.

Per serving:
Calories, 70; Protein, 1 g; Fat, 4.5 g (57% cal.); Cholesterol, 0 mg;
Carbohydrates, 6 g; Fiber, 2 g; Sodium, 250 mg.

Red-Cooked Chicken

Portions: 16   Portion size: ⅛ chicken

U.S.	Metric	Ingredients	PROCEDURE
2	2	Chickens, about 4 lb (1.8 kg) each	1. Cut each chicken into eighths.
2 cloves	2 cloves	Star anise	2. Tie the star anise, ginger root, and Sichuan peppercorns in a cheesecloth bag.
3 slices	3 slices	Ginger root	3. Combine the soy sauce and water or stock in a pot and add the spice bag, sugar, scallions, and sherry. Bring to a boil.
1 tbsp	15 mL	Sichuan peppercorns	
½ pt	250 mL	Soy sauce	4. Add the chicken. Simmer until tender.
2 pt	1 L	Water or chicken stock	5. Serve the chicken hot or cold. If it is to be served cold, cool it and store it in the cooking liquid. The liquid may be reused for another batch.
1 oz	30 g	Sugar	
2	2	Scallions	
2 oz	60 mL	Sherry or shaoxing wine	

Per serving:
Calories, 260; Protein, 29 g; Fat, 14 g (49% cal.); Cholesterol, 90 mg;
Carbohydrates, 3 g; Fiber, 0 g; Sodium, 990 mg.

VARIATIONS

The star anise and Sichuan peppercorns may be omitted for a simpler version of this dish.

Other meats (using cuts appropriate for simmering) may be cooked this way, including pork, beef, tripe, and duck.

Tea-Smoked Duck

Yield: 1 duck

U.S.	Metric	Ingredients	PROCEDURE
3 tbsp	45 mL	Coarse salt	1. Toast the salt and Sichuan peppercorns in a dry skillet over moderate heat, until the peppercorns are fragrant.
1 tbsp	15 mL	Sichuan peppercorns	2. Cool the mixture, then crush with a rolling pin.
1	1	Duck, about 5 lb (2.3 kg)	3. Clean the duck well, removing excess fat. Flatten the duck slightly by pressing down on the breastbone to break it.
			4. Rub the duck inside and out with the salt and peppercorn mixture.
			5. Put the duck in a hotel pan, weight it down, and refrigerate it for 1–2 days.
6	6	Scallions, trimmed	6. Rinse the duck.
4 slices	4 slices	Ginger root	7. Put the scallions and ginger slices in the cavity.
			8. Steam the duck for 1–1½ hours, until tender.
3 oz	90 g	Raw rice	9. Line a large wok or other heavy pan with aluminum foil.
½ cup	125 mL	Brown or black tea leaves	10. Mix together the rice, tea leaves, and sugar. Put the mixture in the bottom of the wok.
2 oz	60 g	Sugar	11. Put the duck on a rack over the tea mixture and cover the pan tightly.
			12. Set the pan over high heat for 5 minutes, then over moderate heat for 20 minutes. Turn the heat off and let stand another 20 minutes without uncovering.
			13. Cool the duck. Chop it into pieces measuring 1–2 inches (3–5 cm), bones and all. Alternatively, bone it out and cut the meat into strips 1 inch (2.5 cm) wide. This dish is normally served at room temperature.

Per ⅙ of recipe:
Calories, 520; Protein, 30 g; Fat, 43 g (75% cal.); Cholesterol, 130 mg;
Carbohydrates, 2 g; Fiber, 1 g; Sodium, 2969 mg.

VARIATIONS

For spicier duck, add 1 tsp (5 mL) five-spice powder to the dry marinade after toasting.

Crispy Duck

This variation may be made with smoked duck or with steamed but unsmoked duck (step 8). When the duck is cool, cut it into quarters. You may bone it if desired, but try to keep it in its original shape. Deep-fry until the skin is crisp. Drain, cut up, and serve at once. (*Optional step:* Rub cornstarch into the skin before deep-frying.)

Mexican

Much of what we think of as Mexican cuisine does not really represent the great range of dishes in that country. The land and climate vary so much within Mexico's large area that the cooking of Sonora and Chihuahua in the north have little in common with the cooking of Oaxaca and Yucatan in the south. The style of the dishes familiar to diners in the United States and Canada—the well-known tacos and enchiladas, for example—is based primarily on northern Mexican influences. These influences combine with the culinary traditions of the southwestern United States to form a cuisine sometimes called Tex-Mex, as well as related styles in New Mexico and other regions of the southwestern United States.

The recipes in this section go beyond the usual Tex-Mex dishes but, in such a short space, it is impossible even to begin to give an idea of the richness of Mexican cooking. This chapter restricts itself to a sampling of the better-known dishes. (Another Mexican classic, Guacamole, is found in Chapter 20.)

One of the most familiar dishes, the *enchilada,* can be defined as a tortilla moistened with a sauce made with chiles and filled with meat or cheese. Because enchiladas are made in hundreds of varieties, they can perhaps be better explained by means of a procedure rather than a recipe.

The recipes for Ancho Sauce, Salsa Verde Cocida, Salsa Roja, Carnitas, and Picadillo can be used for enchilada ingredients. Unless Mexican cheeses are available, the most appropriate cheeses to use in Mexican cooking are Monterey jack, American munster, and mild cheddar or colby.

General Procedures for Making Enchiladas

Method 1

1. Fry tortillas quickly to soften them (do not fry until crisp). Keep them warm and moist between towels.

2. Dip the tortillas in sauce.

3. Fill with desired meat or cheese filling and roll up. Arrange in baking dish.

4. Ladle a little sauce over the enchiladas.

5. Top with grated cheese.

6. Bake at 350°F (175°C) until hot, about 15 to 20 minutes.

Method 2

1. Dip tortillas in sauce to coat lightly.

2. Fry quickly in shallow oil.

3. Fill and roll up.

4. Serve immediately. Alternatively, bake with a sauce and topping as in Method 1.

Salsa Cruda

Yield: 1 qt (1 L)

U.S.	Metric	Ingredients	PROCEDURE
1 lb 4 oz	600 g	Fresh tomatoes	1. Chop the tomatoes fine. (You may peel them, but it is not necessary.)
6 oz	175 g	Fresh green chiles, such as jalapeño or serrano	2. Remove the stem end of the chiles. Chop the chiles fine.
6 oz	175 g	Onion	3. Mince the onion.
½–1 oz	15–30 g	Fresh cilantro leaves, chopped	4. Mix together the tomato, chiles, onion, cilantro, and lime juice or vinegar. Dilute with water or tomato juice to make thick, chunky sauce.
1 tbsp	15 mL	Lime juice or vinegar	5. Add salt to taste.
2–4 oz	60–125 mL	Water or tomato juice, cold	6. This sauce is used as a table condiment with many dishes, including eggs, broiled meats, tacos, tortillas, and beans. It is best if used within a few hours.
1½ tsp	7 mL	Salt	

Per 1 ounce:
Calories, 10; Protein, 0 g; Fat, 0 g (0% cal.); Cholesterol, 0 mg;
Carbohydrates, 2 g; Fiber, 0 g; Sodium, 110 mg.

Salsa Verde Cocida

Yield: 1 qt (1 L)

U.S.	Metric	Ingredients	PROCEDURE
4	4	13-oz (368-g) cans whole tomatillos (Mexican green tomatoes)	1. Drain the tomatillos.
2 oz	60 g	Onion, chopped	2. Combine the tomatillos, onion, garlic, chiles, and coriander in a blender. Blend to a smooth purée.
4 cloves	4 cloves	Garlic, chopped	
2–4 oz	60–125 g	Green chiles, such as jalapeño or serrano, canned or fresh	
1 oz	30 g	Fresh coriander leaves (optional)	
1 oz	30 mL	Oil	3. Heat the oil in a large saucepan. Add the purée and cook 4–5 minutes, until slightly thickened.
to taste	to taste	Salt	4. Season to taste with salt.

Per 1 ounce:
Calories, 25; Protein, 2 g; Fat, 1 g (27% cal.); Cholesterol, 0 mg;
Carbohydrates, 4 g; Fiber, 1 g; Sodium, 55 mg.

VARIATIONS

Salsa Roja

Substitute 2 lb (1 kg) red, ripe tomatoes, peeled, or canned red tomatoes for the tomatillos. The onion may be included or omitted to create slightly different flavors.

Tomato Broth for Chiles Rellenos

Prepare as for Salsa Roja, using the onion but omitting the chiles and coriander. After step 3, add 3 pt (1.5 L) pork stock (including the cooking liquid from making picadillo (p. 735) for the filling for the chiles) and/or chicken stock. Also, add a sachet containing 6 whole cloves, 10 peppercorns, 2 bay leaves, and 1 small cinnamon stick. Simmer until slightly thickened to the consistency of a thick broth or thin sauce.

Ancho Sauce

Yield: about 1½ pt (750 mL)

U.S.	Metric	Ingredients	PROCEDURE
8	8	Dried ancho chiles	1. Toast the chiles lightly in a dry skillet, until softened. Split them open. Remove and discard the seeds and core.
			2. Soak the chiles for about 30 minutes in enough hot water to cover. Drain.
2 oz	60 g	Onion, chopped	3. Combine the chiles, onion, garlic, and water or stock in a blender. Blend to a smooth purée.
3 cloves	3 cloves	Garlic, chopped	
1 pt	500 mL	Water or chicken stock	
1 oz	30 mL	Oil	4. Heat the oil in a saucepan and add the chile purée. Simmer 2–3 minutes.
to taste	to taste	Salt	5. Season to taste with salt.

Per 1 ounce:
Calories, 30; Protein, 1 g; Fat, 1.5 g (46% cal.); Cholesterol, 0 mg;
Carbohydrates, 3 g; Fiber, 1 g; Sodium, 5 mg.

VARIATION

Blend 8 oz (250 g) chopped tomato with the chiles in step 3.

Shredded Pork (Carnitas)

Yield: about 3½ lb (1.6 kg)

U.S.	Metric	Ingredients
6 lb	2.8 kg	Pork butt or shoulder, boned
1	1	Medium onion, cut in half
1 clove	1 clove	Garlic, chopped
1 tbsp	15 mL	Salt
¼ tsp	1 mL	Pepper
1 tsp	5 mL	Oregano
1 tsp	5 mL	Cumin seeds

PROCEDURE

1. Remove most of the large chunks of fat from the pork, leaving a little of it on. Cut the meat into strips measuring 1 × 2 inches (2.5 × 5 cm).
2. Put the pork in a large pot with the rest of the ingredients. Add water to barely cover the meat.
3. Bring to a boil, reduce heat, and simmer slowly, uncovered, until all the liquid has evaporated. By this time, the meat should be tender. If it is not, add more water and continue to cook until it is.
4. Remove the onion and discard it.
5. Lower the heat and let the meat cook in the rendered fat, stirring from time to time, until the meat is browned and very tender. Shred the meat slightly.
6. Serve as a snack, an appetizer, or a filling for tortillas, either as it is or moistened with any of the sauces in this section or with guacamole.

Per 4 ounces:
Calories, 390; Protein, 31 g; Fat, 28 g (67% cal.); Cholesterol, 120 mg; Carbohydrates, 0 g; Fiber, 0 g; Sodium, 590 mg.

VARIATIONS

Picadillo

Add a little extra water to the basic recipe so that some liquid will be left when the meat is tender. Drain and degrease the liquid and use it to make Tomato Broth for Chiles Rellenos (p. 734). Heat 3 oz (90 g) oil or lard and sauté 6 oz (175 g) onion, medium dice, and 4 cloves garlic, chopped. Add the meat, plus a sachet containing 10 peppercorns, 1 small cinnamon stick, and 6 cloves, and brown slowly. Add 4 oz (125 g) raisins, 4 oz (125 g) slivered almonds, and 2 lb (900 g) peeled, seeded, chopped tomatoes. Cook slowly until almost dry. Serve as is or as a stuffing for Chiles Rellenos (p. 737).

Shortcut Picadillo

Instead of preparing Shredded Pork, use 5 lb (2.3 kg) raw ground pork. Sauté it with the onion and garlic in the Picadillo recipe, then proceed as directed with the rest of the recipe.

Mole Poblano de Pollo *or* de Guajolote

Portions: 16   Portion size: 3 oz (90 mL) sauce
chicken or turkey quantity variable

U.S.	Metric	Ingredients	PROCEDURE
15	15	Mulato chiles (see note)	1. Remove and discard the seeds and stem ends of the chiles. Grind the chiles to a powder.
1½ oz	45 g	Sesame seeds	
4 oz	125 g	Almonds	2. Grind the sesame seeds in a spice grinder or with a mortar and pestle. Set them aside and grind the almonds in the same way.
3	3	Tortillas	
6 oz	175 g	Lard, or rendered chicken fat, turkey fat, or pork fat	3. Fry the tortillas in the fat for about 30 seconds. Drain and reserve the fat for step 6. Break the tortillas into pieces.
¼ tsp	1 mL	Ground cloves	4. Put the ground sesame, ground almonds, tortillas, cloves, cinnamon, pepper, and coriander into the container of a blender.
½ tsp	2 mL	Cinnamon	
½ tsp	2 mL	Black pepper	
¼ tsp	1 mL	Ground coriander	5. Peel the tomatoes if they are fresh. Add the tomatoes and the garlic to the blender. Blend to a smooth purée. If the mixture is too thick to blend, add a little chicken or turkey broth or water.
8 oz	225 g	Tomatoes, canned or fresh	
4 cloves	4 cloves	Garlic, chopped	6. Heat the reserved fat from step 3 in a saucepot over moderate heat. Add the powdered chiles and cook for about 30 seconds. Be careful not to let it burn.
1 oz	30 g	Bitter (unsweetened) chocolate, grated or broken into pieces	7. Add the purée from the blender. Cook 5 minutes, stirring constantly. The mixture will be very thick.
			8. Add the chocolate. Stir constantly until the chocolate is completely blended in. *The sauce may be prepared to this point 1–2 days ahead of time and held in the refrigerator.*
10–14 lb	4.5–6.5 kg	Chicken (pollo) or turkey (guajolote), disjointed	9. Put the poultry, onion, carrot, garlic, peppercorns, and salt in a large pot. Add enough water to cover.
			10. Simmer until the poultry is tender.
6 oz	175 g	Onion, chopped	11. Remove the poultry from the broth and set aside to keep warm.
2 oz	60 g	Carrot, chopped	
1 clove	1 clove	Garlic	12. Strain the broth. Measure 3 pt (1.5 L) broth and stir it into the chile sauce base. Simmer slowly for 30–45 minutes, until the flavors have blended and the mixture has the consistency of a light sauce. (Reserve the remaining broth for another use.)
8	8	Peppercorns	
4 tsp	20 mL	Salt	
as needed	as needed	Water	
as needed	as needed	Lard	13. Heat the lard in a sauté pan and brown the cooked poultry pieces lightly. (This step is optional.)
to taste	to taste	Salt	14. Add the poultry to the sauce and simmer a few minutes until quite hot.
			15. Adjust the seasoning with salt, if necessary, and serve.

Per serving:
Calories, 510; Protein, 38 g; Fat, 36 g (63% cal.); Cholesterol, 120 mg;
Carbohydrates, 9 g; Fiber, 4 g; Sodium, 420 mg.

Note: Instead of mulato chile peppers, you may use ancho or pasilla chiles or a mixture of different kinds. If none of these is available, you may substitute about 1 cup (125 g) chili powder.

Chiles Rellenos

Portions: 16   Portion size: 1 pepper

U.S.	Metric	Ingredients	PROCEDURE
16	16	Chiles poblanos (see note)	1. Char the chiles over a gas flame until the skin is blackened. Rub off the blackened skin under running water.
3 lb (approximately)	1.4 kg (approximately)	Picadillo (see note)	2. Slit one side of each pepper and remove the seeds, but be careful to keep the peppers intact. 3. Stuff the peppers with the picadillo.
12	12	Egg yolks	4. Beat the egg yolks and water slightly, then mix in the flour and salt.
1 oz	30 mL	Water	5. Whip the whites until they form soft peaks. Fold them into the yolk mixture.
1 oz	30 g	Flour, sifted	
½ tsp	2 mL	Salt	6. Carefully dust the filled peppers with flour, then dip in the egg batter. Deep-fry at 350°F (175°C) until lightly browned. (Hint: Carefully lower each pepper into the fat with the slit side up. If the slit tends to open, spoon a little of the batter over the slit. This helps keep the opening sealed and the filling in the pepper.)
12	12	Egg whites	
as needed	as needed	Flour for dredging	
3–4 pt	1.5–2 L	Tomato Broth for Chiles Rellenos (p. 734)	7. For each portion, ladle 3–4 oz (90–125 mL) broth into a broad serving bowl or soup plate. Place 1 chile in the center of the bowl and serve at once.

Per serving:
Calories, 430; Protein, 24 g; Fat, 30 g (62% cal.); Cholesterol, 210 mg;
Carbohydrates, 17 g; Fiber, 2 g; Sodium, 460 mg.

Note: Anaheim peppers or frying peppers may be used if poblanos are not available, but the results will not be as flavorful. The exact amount of filling needed depends on the size of the peppers.

VARIATIONS

For cheese-filled chiles, use chunks of American munster or Monterey jack cheese instead of the picadillo.

For baked chiles rellenos, omit the egg batter and simply bake the stuffed chiles in a casserole until they are heated through. Serve with the tomato broth as in the basic recipe.

Frijoles

Portions: 16–20   Portion size: 4 oz (125 g)

U.S.	Metric	Ingredients	PROCEDURE
1½ lb	750 g	Dried pinto beans or pink beans	1. Combine the beans, water, onion, garlic, and chile in a pot. Bring to a boil, reduce heat, and simmer, covered, for 1½ hours. Check the pot from time to time and add more water, if needed, to keep the beans covered.
3 qt	3 L	Water, cold (see note)	
6 oz	175 g	Onion, sliced thin	
1–2 cloves	1–2 cloves	Garlic, chopped	
1	1	Jalapeño or other green chile, chopped (optional)	2. Add the lard and salt. Continue to simmer until the beans are tender. Do not let the beans go dry. There should always be some broth. Add hot water if necessary.
2 oz	60 g	Lard or rendered pork fat	
2 tsp	10 mL	Salt	3. The beans will hold refrigerated for several days.

Per serving:
Calories, 170; Protein, 8 g; Fat, 4 g (20% cal.); Cholesterol, 5 mg;
Carbohydrates, 27 g; Fiber, 9 g; Sodium, 290 mg.

Note: The beans may be soaked overnight, if desired (although many Mexican cooking authorities feel that the results are not as good). If they are soaked, reduce the water for cooking to 1½ pt (750 mL).

VARIATION

Frijoles Refritos

For the quantity of beans in the basic recipe, make in at least 3 batches. Mash the beans coarsely. Heat 2 oz (60 g) lard in a large sauté pan. Add 2 oz (60 g) chopped onion and fry until soft, but do not brown. Add one-third of the cooked, mashed beans (about 1½ lb or 750 g, including broth) to the pan. Stir and mash the beans over heat until the beans start to dry out and pull away from the sides of the pan. Roll the mass out of the pan like an omelet. Sprinkle with grated cheese (mild cheddar or Monterey jack) and serve with tortilla chips.

Arroz a la Mexicana

Portions: 16   Portion size: 4½ oz (125 g)

U.S.	Metric	Ingredients	PROCEDURE
1½ lb	700 g	Long-grain rice	1. Rinse the rice well to remove excess starch. Soak in cold water for at least 30 minutes. Drain well.
3 oz	90 mL	Oil	
12 oz	350 g	Tomato purée	2. Heat the oil in a pot and add the rice. Stir over moderate heat until it begins to brown lightly.
3 oz	90 g	Onion, chopped fine	
2 cloves	2 cloves	Garlic, mashed to a paste	3. Add the tomato purée, onion, and garlic. Cook until the mixture is dry. Be careful not to let it burn.
3½ pt	1.75 L	Chicken stock	
1 tbsp	15 mL	Salt	4. Add the chicken stock and stir. Simmer, uncovered, over medium heat until most of the liquid has been absorbed.

5. Cover, turn the heat to very low, and cook for 5–10 minutes, until the rice is tender.

6. Remove from the heat and let it stand, without removing the cover, for 15–30 minutes before serving.

Per serving:
Calories, 230; Protein, 4 g; Fat, 6 g (24% cal.); Cholesterol, 5 mg;
Carbohydrates, 39 g; Fiber, 1 g; Sodium, 440 mg.

VARIATION

Arroz Verde

Omit the tomato purée. Purée in a blender the onion and garlic along with the following: 6 oz (175 mL) water, 3 tbsp (45 mL) chopped fresh cilantro leaves, ¾ cup (45 g or 200 mL) chopped parsley, and 3 oz (90 g) green chiles (or part green chiles and part green bell peppers). Use this purée in place of the tomato purée. Reduce the quantity of stock to 3 pt (1.5 mL). You may use water instead of stock.

Elote con Queso

Portions: 16   Portion size: 3½ oz (100 g)

U.S.	Metric	Ingredients	PROCEDURE
6	6	Anaheim chiles (see note)	1. Char the chiles over an open flame or under a broiler until the skin is black. Rub off the blackened skin under running water.
4 oz	125 g	Onion	
2 oz	60 g	Butter	
2½ lb	1.2 kg	Whole kernel corn (frozen or fresh)	2. Remove and discard the seeds and stem ends from the chiles. Cut the chiles into medium dice.
to taste	to taste	Salt	3. Cut the onion into small dice. Cook it slowly in the butter until it is soft. Do not brown.
10 oz	300 g	Mild cheddar cheese, grated	4. Add the diced chile and cook 5 minutes.

5. Add the corn and cook over moderate heat until it is thawed (if using frozen corn) or no longer raw (if using fresh corn).

6. Add salt to taste.

7. Put the corn in a shallow baking pan or in individual gratin dishes and bake at 350°F (175°C), covered, for 10 minutes.

8. Uncover and top with the grated cheese. Bake until very hot and the cheese is melted and bubbling.

Per serving:
Calories, 160; Protein, 7 g; Fat, 9 g (48% cal.); Cholesterol, 25 mg;
Carbohydrates, 15 g; Fiber, 2 g; Sodium, 150 mg.

Note: Canned, diced chiles (10–12 oz/300–350 g, drained) may be used in place of the fresh Anaheims. Omit steps 1 and 2 in the procedure.

VARIATIONS

If you wish, this may be cooked entirely on top of the range. Simply mix in the grated cheese before serving.

Fresh zucchini, cut into small dice, may be substituted for one-third to one-half of the corn. Add to the onion at the same time as the chiles.

Italian

Italian foods have long enjoyed great popularity outside Italy. The style of cooking most familiar in North America was developed in the kitchens of Italian immigrants, most of whom came from the southern part of Italy. Many of these dishes are excellent in their own right, but they are not really typical of Italian cooking as a whole.

It is nearly impossible to generalize about Italian cooking because it varies so much from region to region. It is often said that the cooking of southern Italy is based on olive oil and tomatoes, while that of the north is based on butter and cream, but that is too simplistic to be completely accurate.

We can make a few generalizations about Italian cooking, but keep in mind that there are many exceptions. In the first place, it is true that tomatoes are important in Italian cooking, but most Italian dishes are made without tomato sauce. There are even many pasta dishes made without tomatoes.

Second, sauces and other dishes simmered for hours, or heavy casseroles loaded with sauce and cheese, are not wholly typical of Italian cooking. They do exist, of course, but there are just as many, if not more, simple grilled, boiled, and fried dishes, quickly prepared and enhanced with just a few seasonings to highlight the natural flavor of the basic ingredients.

The recipes in this section are intended to give you a little idea of the range of Italian dishes. Most of them, by the way, are made without tomato sauce. In addition, a number of Italian dishes appear elsewhere in this book. Look especially for the pasta and risotto recipes in Chapter 18.

Zuppa di Ceci e Riso

Portions: 16   **Portion size:** 6 oz (175 mL)

U.S.	Metric	Ingredients	PROCEDURE
3 oz	90 mL	Olive oil	1. Heat the oil over moderate heat. Add the garlic and rosemary. Cook for a few seconds.
1 clove	1 clove	Garlic, chopped	
1½ tsp	7 mL	Rosemary, chopped fine	2. Add the tomatoes. Bring to a boil, then simmer until most of the juice has evaporated.
1 lb	450 g	Canned plum tomatoes, crushed or chopped	3. Add the stock and the rice. Simmer for 15 minutes.
5 pt	2.5 L	White stock (chicken, veal, or pork)	4. Add the chickpeas and continue to simmer until the rice is tender and the flavors are well blended.
6 oz	175 g	Rice (raw)	5. Season to taste with salt and pepper.
1½ lb	700 g	Cooked chickpeas, drained	6. Sprinkle each portion with a little chopped parsley.
to taste	to taste	Salt	
to taste	to taste	Pepper	
3 tbsp	45 mL	Chopped parsley	

Per serving:
Calories, 170; Protein, 6 g; Fat, 7 g (36% cal.); Cholesterol, 5 mg;
Carbohydrates, 22 g; Fiber, 4 g; Sodium, 55 mg.

Polenta

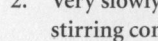

Yield: about 5 lb (2.5 kg)

U.S.	Metric	Ingredients	PROCEDURE
5 pt	2.5 L	Water	
1 tbsp	15 mL	Salt	
1 lb	500 g	Polenta (Italian coarse-grained yellow cornmeal)	

1. Bring the water and salt to a boil in a saucepot.
2. Very slowly sprinkle the cornmeal into the boiling water, stirring constantly. This must be done slowly and carefully to avoid lumps. (See Figure 25.3.)
3. Cook over low heat, stirring almost constantly. The polenta will become thicker as it cooks and will eventually start to pull away from the sides of the pot. This will take about 20–30 minutes.
4. Lightly moisten a large flat surface, such as a wooden board or a platter.
5. Pour the polenta onto this board or platter. Serve immediately, hot, or let cool and use in any of a number of ways, including the variations below.

Per 1 ounce:
Calories, 20; Protein, 0 g; Fat, 0 g (0% cal.); Cholesterol, 0 mg; Carbohydrates, 4 g; Fiber, 0 g; Sodium, 90 mg.

VARIATIONS

Freshly made hot polenta is good with many kinds of stews and other braised dishes that provide plenty of flavorful juices for the polenta to soak up. It is also served with grilled dishes.

Polenta con Sugo di Pomodoro

Serve hot polenta with tomato sauce or Meat Sauce (p. 516).

Polenta con Salsicce

Serve hot polenta with pork sausages cooked with tomatoes or tomato sauce.

Polento al Burro e Formaggio

Stir 6 oz (175 g) fresh butter and 2–3 oz (60–90 g) grated parmesan cheese into hot polenta as soon as it is cooked.

Polenta Fritta or Grigliata

Let polenta cool and cut it into slices ½ inch (1 cm) thick. Pan-fry in oil until a thin crust forms. Alternatively, heat slices on a grill or broiler until hot and lightly grill-marked.

Polenta Grassa

This can be prepared in two ways.

1. Pour a layer of hot polenta into a buttered baking dish. Cover with sliced fontina cheese and dot with butter. Cover with another layer of polenta, then another layer of cheese and butter. Bake until very hot.
2. Prepare as in the first method, but instead of the hot, freshly made polenta, use cold polenta cut into thin slices.

Polenta Pasticciata

Prepare Meat Sauce (p. 516), using pork sausage in addition to the beef. Also, add sautéed sliced mushrooms to the sauce. Cut cold polenta into thin slices. Fill a baking pan with alternating layers of polenta slices, meat sauce, and parmesan cheese. Bake until hot.

Polenta Pasticciata

Figure 25.3 Making polenta.

(a) Slowly sprinkle the polenta into the simmering water, stirring constantly to avoid lumps.

(b) Simmer while stirring until the polenta reaches the desired texture. Serve at once or proceed to the next step.

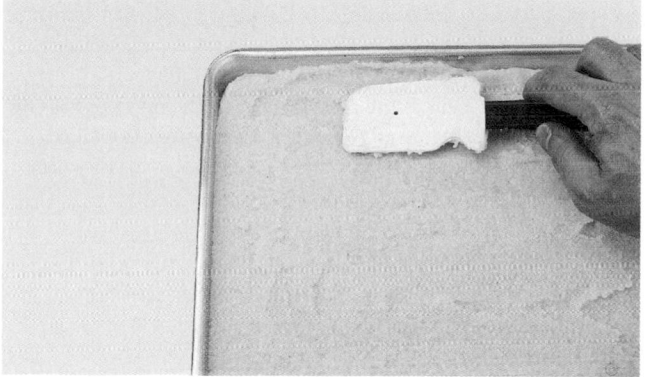

(c) Pour the polenta into a sheet pan and cool.

(d) Cut into desired shapes.

Mozzarella in Carozza

Portions: 16

U.S.	Metric	Ingredients	PROCEDURE
1 lb	450 g	Mozzarella cheese (see note)	1. Cut the mozzarella into slices. Make 16 sandwiches with the bread.
32 slices	32 slices	White bread	2. Beat the eggs with a large pinch of salt.
8–10	8–10	Eggs	3. Dip the sandwiches in the eggs to coat both sides.
pinch	pinch	Salt	4. Pan-fry (or deep-fry) until both sides are golden brown and the cheese is melted. Serve at once.
as needed	as needed	Oil for pan-frying	

Per serving:
Calories, 350; Protein, 15 g; Fat, 17 g (44% cal.); Cholesterol, 130 mg;
Carbohydrates, 34 g; Fiber, 1 g; Sodium, 550 mg.

Note: If possible, use freshly made mozzarella cheese or mozzarella di bufala (p. 631). Commercial low-moisture mozzarella, formulated for pizzas, does not have the same fresh milk flavor.

VARIATIONS

This appetizer is sometimes served with a sauce made by heating butter and a little olive oil with mashed anchovies. Because this sauce is almost all fat, however, it is not really appropriate to a fried dish. It is more appropriate to the following:

Spiedini alla Romana

Cut fresh mozzarella, preferably mozzarella di bufala, into slices ½ inch (1 cm) thick. Also, cut a loaf of thin Italian bread into slices 1½ inches (4 cm) thick. Alternate 4 slices of bread with 3 slices of mozzarella on skewers, beginning and ending with bread. Heat very carefully in a broiler or on a grill to toast the bread and lightly heat the cheese. Serve with the anchovy sauce described above.

Pesce con Salsa Verde

Portions: 16   **Portion size:** 1 piece of fish, plus 1½ oz (45 mL) sauce

U.S.	Metric	Ingredients	PROCEDURE
		Court bouillon:	1. Combine the court bouillon ingredients in a pot. Simmer for 15 minutes.
4 oz	125 g	Onion, sliced	
1 oz	30 g	Celery, chopped	
6–8	6–8	Parsley stems	
1	1	Bay leaf	
¼ tsp	1 mL	Fennel seeds	
1½ tsp	7 mL	Salt	
1 pt	500 mL	White wine	
3 qt	3 L	Water	
		Salsa verde:	2. Soak the bread in the vinegar for 15 minutes, then squeeze it out.
3 slices	3 slices	White bread, crusts removed	3. Combine the parsley, garlic, capers, and anchovies on a cutting board and chop them very well.
4 oz	125 mL	Wine vinegar	
1½ oz	50 g	Parsley, leaves only	4. Mash the egg yolks and the bread pulp together in a bowl, then add the chopped parsley mixture and mix together until well combined.
1 clove	1 clove	Garlic	
3 tbsp	45 mL	Capers, drained	5. Very slowly beat in the olive oil as though you were making mayonnaise. When all the oil has been added, the sauce should have a creamy texture, not as thick as mayonnaise.
4	4	Anchovy fillets	
3	3	Hard-cooked egg yolks	
1 pt	500 mL	Olive oil	
to taste	to taste	Salt	6. Season to taste with salt and pepper.
to taste	to taste	Pepper	
16	16	Fish steaks, fillets, or small whole fish	7. Poach the fish in the court bouillon.
			8. Drain well. Top each portion with 1½ oz (45 mL) sauce and serve immediately.

Per serving:
Calories, 510; Protein, 20 g; Fat, 46 g (81% cal.); Cholesterol, 100 mg;
Carbohydrates, 4 g; Fiber, 0 g; Sodium, 340 mg.

Note: Some of the fish that can be used for this recipe are halibut, sea bass, striped bass, red snapper, bluefish, and porgy.

Zuppa di Vongole

Portions: 16

U.S.	Metric	Ingredients	PROCEDURE
15 lb	7 kg	Small clams, such as littlenecks	1. Scrub the clams under cold water to remove sand and grit from the shells.
1 pt	500 mL	Water	2. Put the clams and water in a heavy covered pot and heat gently, just until the clams open. Set the clams aside. Strain and reserve the liquid.
			3. Depending on how you wish to serve them, you can leave the clams in the shell or shell all but 4–6 of them per portion to use as garnish.
6 oz	175 mL	Olive oil	4. Heat the olive oil in a large pot. Sauté the onion until soft but not brown.
5 oz	150 g	Onion, small dice	5. Add the garlic and cook another minute.
3–5 cloves	3–5 cloves	Garlic, chopped	6. Add the parsley and the wine and boil for 1 minute.
6 tbsp	90 mL	Chopped parsley	7. Add the tomatoes and the reserved clam juice. Simmer 5 minutes.
12 oz	350 mL	White wine	8. Taste for seasonings and adjust if necessary.
1½ lb	700 g	Canned plum tomatoes, with juice, coarsely chopped	9. Add the clams and reheat them gently. Do not overcook, or the clams will be tough.
			10. Serve with plenty of crusty bread for dipping in the broth.

Per serving:
Calories, 660; Protein, 93 g; Fat, 18 g (25% cal.); Cholesterol, 240 mg; Carbohydrates, 22 g; Fiber, 1 g; Sodium, 470 mg.

VARIATIONS

Zuppa di Cozze

Substitute mussels for the clams.

Zuppa di Frutti di Mare

Use a mixture of clams, mussels, squid (cut up), and shrimp (shelled). Keep all the items separate. Cook the clams and mussels as in the basic recipe. Add the squid at the same time as the tomatoes and broth. Simmer slowly, covered, until tender. Add the shrimp and cook just 1 minute before adding the clams and mussels.

Zuppa di Pesce

Use a mixture of shellfish and fin fish, as desired. Add each type of fish just long enough before the end of cooking so that it cooks through without overcooking.

Costolette di Vitello Ripiene alla Valdostana

Portions: 16   **Portion size:** 1 chop

U.S.	Metric	Ingredients	PROCEDURE
16	16	Veal rib chops	1. Remove the chine and feather bones so that only the rib bone is attached to each chop. 2. Cut a pocket in each, as shown in Figure 11.5. 3. Flatten the chops lightly with a cutlet pounder to increase the diameter of the eye. Be careful not to tear a hole in the meat.
12 oz	350 g	Fontina cheese	4. Cut the cheese into thin slices.
to taste	to taste	Salt	5. Stuff the chops with the cheese, making sure all of the cheese is inside the pockets, with none hanging out. Press the edges of the pockets together and pound lightly to seal. If this is done carefully, you don't need to skewer them shut.
to taste	to taste	White pepper	
		Standard Breading Procedure:	
as needed	as needed	Flour	6. Season the chops with salt and pepper.
as needed	as needed	Egg wash	7. Set up a breading station. Crumble the rosemary and mix it with the bread crumbs.
as needed	as needed	Bread crumbs	
1½ tsp	7 mL	Rosemary	8. Bread the chops.
as needed	as needed	Butter	9. Sauté the chops in butter and serve immediately.

Per serving:
Calories, 500; Protein, 35 g; Fat, 30 g (56% cal.); Cholesterol, 185 mg; Carbohydrates, 19 g; Fiber, 1 g; Sodium, 530 mg.

VARIATION

Costolette alla Milanese

Omit the cheese stuffing and the rosemary. Do not cut pockets in the meat. Flatten the chops with a cutlet pounder until they are half their original thickness. Bread and sauté them as in the basic recipe.

Saltimbocca alla Romana

Portions: 16   **Portion size:** 2 pieces

U.S.	Metric	Ingredients	PROCEDURE
32	32	Veal scaloppine, about 1½–2 oz (45–60 g) each	1. Pound the scaloppine with a cutlet pounder. Season with salt and white pepper. Put 1 slice of prosciutto and 1 sage leaf on top of each and fasten with a toothpick.
to taste	to taste	Salt	
to taste	to taste	White pepper	2. Sauté briefly in butter on both sides.
32	32	Thin slices of prosciutto, about the same diameter as the scaloppine	3. Add the wine and continue to cook until the meat is done and the wine is partly reduced, no more than 5 minutes. 4. Remove the meat from the pan and serve, ham side up, with a spoonful of the pan juices over each.
32	32	Sage leaves	
4 oz	125 g	Butter	
12 oz	350 mL	White wine	

Per serving:
Calories, 320; Protein, 28 g; Fat, 21 g (60% cal.); Cholesterol, 115 mg; Carbohydrates, 0 g; Fiber, 0 g; Sodium, 800 mg.

Lombatine di Maiale alla Napoletana

Portions: 16   Portion size: 1 chop, 3–4 oz (90–125 g) vegetables

U.S.	Metric	Ingredients	PROCEDURE
6	6	Italian peppers or bell peppers; red or green	1. Char the peppers over a gas flame until the skin is black. Rub off the blackened skin under cold running water. Remove and discard the seeds and core and cut the peppers into batonnet (see note).
1 lb 8 oz	700 g	Mushrooms	
3 lb	1.4 kg	Tomatoes	2. Slice the mushrooms.
			3. Peel, seed, and chop the tomatoes.
6 oz	175 mL	Olive oil	4. Heat the olive oil in a large sauté pan or brazier. Add the garlic cloves. Sauté them until they are light brown, then remove and discard them.
2 cloves	2 cloves	Garlic, crushed	
16	16	Pork loin chops	
to taste	to taste	Salt	5. Season the chops with salt and pepper. Brown them in the olive oil. When they are well browned, remove and set them aside.
to taste	to taste	Pepper	

6. Add the pepper and mushrooms and sauté briefly, until wilted.

7. Add the tomatoes and return the chops to the pan. Cover and cook on the range or in a low oven until the pork is done. The vegetables should give off enough moisture to braise the chops, but check the pan from time to time to make sure it is not dry.

8. When the chops are done, remove them from the pan and keep them hot. If there is a lot of liquid in the pan, reduce it over high heat until there is just enough to form a little sauce for the vegetables.

9. Adjust the seasoning. Serve the chops topped with the vegetables.

Per serving:
Calories, 430; Protein, 45 g; Fat, 23 g (49% cal.); Cholesterol, 125 mg;
Carbohydrates, 9 g; Fiber, 2 g; Sodium, 100 mg.

Note: Charring and peeling the peppers is optional, but it improves the flavor and removes the peel, which would otherwise come off during cooking and make the vegetable mixture less attractive.

VARIATION

Pollo con Peperoni all'Abruzzese

Double the quantities of peppers. Increase the tomatoes to 4½ lb (2 kg). Omit the mushrooms and garlic. Add 1 lb (450 g) sliced onions and sauté them with the peppers. Instead of pork, use 8–10 lb (3.6–4.5 kg) chicken parts. Season with a little basil. If desired, reduce the quantity of chicken in the above recipe and add some Italian pork sausages.

Italian Specialties.
Left: Spiedini alla Romana; right: Lombatine de Maiale alla Napoletana.

Spinaci alla Romana

Portions: 16   Portion size: 3 oz (90 g)

U.S.	Metric	Ingredients	PROCEDURE
6 lb	2.7 kg	Spinach	1. Trim and wash the spinach. Cook in a small quantity of boiling water until wilted. Drain, cool under running water, and drain again. Press excess water out of the spinach, but do not squeeze too dry.
1½ oz	45 mL	Olive oil	
1½ oz	45 g	Fat from prosciutto or pork, small dice	2. Heat the oil in a pan. Add the fat and render it. Remove and discard the cracklings (solid pieces remaining from the fat).
1½ oz	45 g	Pine nuts	3. Add the spinach, pine nuts, and raisins. Sauté until hot.
1½ oz	45 g	Raisins	
to taste	to taste	Salt	4. Season with salt and pepper.
to taste	to taste	Pepper	

Per serving:
Calories, 100; Protein, 5 g; Fat, 7 g (57% cal.); Cholesterol, 5 mg;
Carbohydrates, 7 g; Fiber, 3 g; Sodium, 90 mg.

VARIATIONS

Chopped garlic may be sautéed in the fat before the spinach is added.

Lean prosciutto, sliced thin, then diced, may be added.

Spinaci alla Piemontese

Omit the oil, fat, nuts, and raisins. Heat 8 chopped anchovy fillets and 2 chopped garlic cloves in 4 oz (125 g) butter, then add the boiled, drained spinach and sauté.

Cipolline in Agrodolce

Portions: 16   Portion size: 3½ oz (100 g)

U.S.	Metric	Ingredients	PROCEDURE
4½ lb	2 kg	Pearl onions	1. Blanch the onions for 1 minute. Drain and peel.
1 pt	500 mL	Water	2. Put the onions in a sauté pan in a single layer. Add the water and cook slowly, uncovered, for about 20 minutes, until fairly tender. Add a little water if necessary during cooking so that the pan does not become dry. Stir gently from time to time.
2 oz	60 g	Butter	
3 oz	90 mL	Wine vinegar	3. Add the vinegar, sugar, and salt. Cover lightly. Cook over low heat until the onions are very tender and the liquid is syrupy, about 30 minutes. If necessary, remove the cover toward the end of the cooking time to let the liquid reduce. The onions should be lightly browned by the time they are done.
1½ oz	45 g	Sugar	
1½ tsp	7 mL	Salt	

Per serving:
Calories, 120; Protein, 2 g; Fat, 3 g (23% cal.); Cholesterol, 10 mg;
Carbohydrates, 21 g; Fiber, 1 g; Sodium, 270 mg.

European Classics

This last section is a collection of recipes from many parts of Europe. Its main purpose is simply to give you additional experience with a variety of international dishes.

It is often impossible to draw the line between local and international recipes because countries and cuisines borrow so much from each other. Canada and the United States, in particular, inherited their culinary traditions largely from Europe. Many familiar, everyday dishes in America, for example, originated in Europe but have been completely absorbed into the local cuisine. Even names from other languages, like pizza, have become so familiar that English-speaking people no longer think of them as foreign.

Throughout this book, you can find recipes from many European countries, such as Borscht and Sirniki from Russia; Scotch Broth and Welsh Rabbit from the British Isles; Coq au Vin, Ratatouille, and Choucroute Garni from various regions of France; Sauerbraten from Germany; Avgolemono from Greece; Romesco from Spain; and Swedish Meatballs (called *Köttbullar* in Swedish) from Scandinavia. The recipes that follow are in addition to this list.

Brandade de Morue (France)

Yield: about 2½ lb (1.25 kg)

U.S.	Metric	Ingredients	PROCEDURE
2 lb	1 kg	Salt cod	1. Soak the salt cod in cold water for 24 hours, changing the water several times. 2. Put the cod in a pot with enough water to cover. Bring to a boil, reduce heat, and simmer 5–10 minutes, just until the cod is cooked and flakes. Do not overcook, or it will not absorb liquids well in the next steps. Remove the fish from the water, flake it, and remove the skin and bones.
1–2 cloves	1–2 cloves	Garlic, crushed to a paste	3. Work the fish, while it is still hot, and the garlic into a smooth, lump-free paste. This can be done by hand with a bowl and wooden spoon or with a mixer with the paddle attachment. (A food processor may also be used, but be careful not to process the fish until it is totally puréed.)
8 oz	250 mL	Olive oil	
8 oz	250 mL	Milk, cream, or half-and-half	
to taste	to taste	White pepper	4. Warm the oil and milk or cream in separate pans.
to taste	to taste	Salt	5. Gradually beat the oil into the cod paste alternately with the milk, adding just a little at a time, until the mixture is the consistency of mashed potatoes.
as needed	as needed	Toast points fried in olive oil (see p. 707)	6. Add white pepper to taste. Salt may not be necessary because the dried cod is salty. 7. Serve warm as a dip, with toast points for dipping.

Per 1 ounce:
Calories, 80; Protein, 6 g; Fat, 6 g (69% cal.); Cholesterol, 20 mg;
Carbohydrates, 0 g; Fiber, 0 g; Sodium, 175 mg.

VARIATIONS

Brandade can be reheated slowly over low heat, stirring frequently.

Brandade can be mixed with mashed potatoes in varying proportions.

If you add too much oil or cream in step 5, or if you add it too quickly, the brandade can break or curdle. It can usually be rescued by beating it vigorously. If this doesn't work, add a little mashed potatoes.

Rohkostsalatteller (Germany)

Portions: 16   **Portion size:** see procedure

U.S.	Metric	Ingredients	PROCEDURE
6 oz	175 mL	White wine vinegar	1. Make a dressing by mixing together the vinegar, sour cream, salt, sugar, and chives. Set aside.
1 pt	500 mL	Sour cream	
2 tsp	10 mL	Salt	
½ tsp	2 mL	Sugar	
2 tbsp	30 mL	Chopped chives	
1 lb	450 g	Carrots	2. Peel the carrots. Shred them on a coarse grater.
2 tbsp	30 mL	Horseradish, well drained	3. Mix the carrots with the horseradish, then with 6 oz (175 mL) sour cream dressing or just enough to bind. Season to taste with salt.
to taste	to taste	Salt	
1 lb 6 oz	625 g	Cucumbers	4. Peel the cucumbers. Cut them into thin slices. Toss with the coarse salt and let stand for 1–2 hours.
1 tbsp	15 mL	Coarse salt	5. Press the juices out of the cucumbers. Rinse off excess salt and drain.
2 oz	60 mL	White wine vinegar	
3 oz	90 mL	Water	6. Mix together the vinegar, water, sugar, dill, and white pepper.
1 tbsp	15 mL	Sugar	7. Mix this dressing with the cucumbers. If necessary, add salt to taste.
2 tsp	10 mL	Fresh dill weed, chopped	
pinch	pinch	White pepper	
1 lb 4 oz	575 g	Celery root	8. Peel the celery root. Grate it on a coarse grater. Immediately mix with the lemon juice.
1½ oz	50 mL	Lemon juice	
5 oz	150 mL	Heavy cream	9. Mix in the cream. Season with salt and white pepper.
to taste	to taste	Salt	
to taste	to taste	White pepper	
2 lb	900 g	Bibb or Boston lettuce greens	10. If necessary, thin the remaining sour cream dressing with a little water until it is the consistency of heavy cream.
16	16	Tomato wedges	11. Toss the greens with the dressing. Plate in the center of large salad plates.
			12. Around the outside edge of each plate, arrange 1 tomato wedge and about 1 oz (30 g) each of the carrot, cucumber, and celery salads.

Per serving:
Calories, 140; Protein, 3 g; Fat, 10 g (58% cal.); Cholesterol, 25 mg;
Carbohydrates, 13 g; Fiber, 3 g; Sodium, 730 mg.

Caldo Verde (Portugal)

Portions: 16   Portion size: 10 oz (300 mL)

U.S.	Metric	Ingredients	PROCEDURE
2 oz	60 mL	Olive oil	1. Heat the oil in a soup pot. Add the onion and garlic. Cook slowly until soft, but do not brown.
12 oz	350 g	Onion, chopped fine	
1 clove	1 clove	Garlic, chopped fine	2. Add the potatoes and water. Simmer until the potatoes are very tender.
4 lb	1.8 kg	Potatoes, peeled and sliced	
4 qt	4 L	Water	3. Purée the soup or, for a coarser texture, simply mash it in the pot.
1 lb	450 g	Hard, spicy garlic sausage (see note)	4. Cut the sausage into thin slices. Heat it slowly in a sauté pan to cook off some of the fat. Drain.
to taste	to taste	Salt	5. Add the sausage to the soup. Simmer 5 minutes. Season to taste.
to taste	to taste	Pepper	
2 lb	900 g	Kale	6. Remove the hard center ribs from the kale. Shred as fine as possible, about as thin as threads.
			7. Add to the soup. Simmer 5 minutes. Check the seasoning.
			8. This soup should be accompanied by chunks of coarse peasant bread.

Per serving:
Calories, 270; Protein, 10 g; Fat, 15 g (48% cal.); Cholesterol, 25 mg;
Carbohydrates, 26 g; Fiber, 3 g; Sodium, 370 mg.

Note: Because authentic Portuguese *chouriço* sausage is not widely available, you may substitute Spanish *chorizo* or Italian pepperoni.

Carbonnade à la Flammande (Belgium)

Portions: 16   Portion size: 6–7 oz (175–200 g)

U.S.	Metric	Ingredients	PROCEDURE
3 lb	1.4 kg	Onions	1. Peel the onions. Cut them into small dice.
as needed	as needed	Beef fat or vegetable oil	2. Cook over moderate heat in a little fat until golden. Remove from the heat and set aside.
6 oz	175 g	Flour	3. Season the flour with salt and pepper. Dredge the meat in the flour. Shake off the excess flour.
2 tsp	10 mL	Salt	
1 tsp	5 mL	Pepper	4. Brown the meat well in a sauté pan. Do a little at a time to avoid overcrowding the pan. As each batch is browned, add it to the pot with the onions.
5 lb	2.3 kg	Beef chuck, 1-inch (2.5-cm) dice	
2½ pt	1.25 L	Dark beer	5. Deglaze the sauté pan with the beer and add it to the pot. Add the stock, sachet, and sugar.
2½ pt	1.25 L	Brown stock	
		Sachet:	6. Bring to a boil, cover, and transfer to the oven. Cook at 325°F (160°C) until very tender, about 2–3 hours.
2	2	Bay leaves	
1 tsp	5 mL	Thyme	7. Degrease. Adjust the consistency of the sauce. If it is too thin, reduce over moderately high heat. If it is too thick, dilute with brown stock.
8	8	Parsley stems	
8	8	Peppercorns	
1 tbsp	15 mL	Sugar	8. Taste and adjust the seasonings. Serve with plain boiled potatoes.

Per serving:
Calories, 450; Protein, 30 g; Fat, 26 g (52% cal.); Cholesterol, 100 mg;
Carbohydrates, 19 g; Fiber, 1 g; Sodium, 290 mg.

Dillkött (Sweden)

Portions: 16   **Portion size:** 6 oz (175 g)

U.S.	Metric	Ingredients	PROCEDURE
7 lb	3.2 kg	Boneless, trimmed veal shoulder, breast, or shank	1. Cut the veal into 1-inch (2.5-cm) dice.
1	1	Medium onion stuck with 2 cloves	2. Put the meat in a pot with the onion, sachet, water, and salt. Bring to a boil and skim well.
		Sachet:	3. Reduce the heat and add the dill. Simmer slowly until the meat is very tender, about 1½–2 hours.
1	1	Bay leaf	4. Strain off the broth into another pan. Discard the onion and the sachet.
5–6	5–6	Parsley stems	
6	6	Peppercorns	
2 qt	2 L	Water	
1 tbsp	15 mL	Salt	
2 tbsp	30 mL	Fresh dill weed, chopped (see note)	
		Roux:	5. Reduce the broth over high heat to 1 qt (1 L).
2 oz	60 g	Butter	6. Make a blond roux with the flour and butter. Thicken the broth with it.
2 oz	60 g	Flour	7. Add the lemon juice, brown sugar, dill, and capers. Adjust the seasonings.
1 oz	30 mL	Lemon juice or wine vinegar	
1½ tsp	7 mL	Brown sugar	
2 tbsp	30 mL	Fresh dill weed, chopped	
2 tbsp	30 mL	Capers, drained	

Per serving:
Calories, 280; Protein, 36 g; Fat, 12 g (41% cal.); Cholesterol, 165 mg;
Carbohydrates, 3 g; Fiber, 0 g; Sodium, 640 mg.

Note: If fresh dill is not available, substitute one-third its quantity of dried dill.

VARIATION

Dillkött på Lamm
Substitute lamb shoulder or shank for the veal.

Paella (Spain)

Portions: 16   **Portion size:** see procedure

U.S.	Metric	Ingredients	PROCEDURE
2	2	Chickens, 2½–3 lb (1.1–1.4 kg) each	1. Cut each chicken into 8 pieces.
as needed	as needed	Olive oil	2. In a large sauté pan, brown the chicken in olive oil. Remove and set aside.
8 oz	225 g	Chorizo sausage (see note)	3. Using additional oil as needed, briefly sauté the sausage, pork, shrimp, squid, and peppers. Do each ingredient separately, then remove to separate containers.
2 lb	900 g	Lean pork, cut into large dice	
16	16	Large shrimp, peeled and deveined	
2 lb	900 g	Squid, cleaned (p. 376), cut into rings	
2	2	Red bell peppers, large dice	
2	2	Green bell peppers, large dice	
16	16	Small clams	4. Combine the clams and mussels with the water in a covered pot. Steam them just until they open.
16	16	Mussels	5. Remove the shellfish and set them aside. Strain the liquid, then add enough chicken stock to measure 2 qt (2 L).
8 oz	250 mL	Water	
as needed	as needed	Chicken stock	6. Add the saffron to the stock mixture.
1 tsp	5 mL	Saffron	
12 oz	350 g	Onion, small dice	7. In the skillet used for browning the meats, sauté the onion and garlic until soft. Use additional olive oil if necessary.
6 cloves	6 cloves	Garlic, minced	
2 lb	900 g	Tomatoes, chopped	8. Add the tomatoes and rosemary. Cook until most of the liquid has evaporated and the tomatoes form a rather dry paste.
2 tsp	10 mL	Rosemary	
2 lb	900 g	Short-grain rice, such as Italian arborio	9. Add the rice and stir. Add the chicken, sausage, pork, squid, and peppers.
2 tsp	10 mL	Salt	10. Bring the stock mixture to a boil in a separate pot, then add to the rice and stir. Add salt and pepper to taste.
to taste	to taste	Pepper	11. Bring to a simmer, cover, and put in an oven heated to 350°F (175°C) for 20 minutes. (This dish is traditionally made uncovered on top of the stove, but making it in the oven is more practical for restaurants because it requires less attention.)
4 oz	125 g	Cooked green peas	12. Remove the pan from the oven. Check the moisture level and add more stock if necessary. It should be quite moist but not soupy.
16	16	Lemon wedges	13. Sprinkle the peas over the rice. Then arrange the shrimp, clams, and mussels on top. Cover loosely and let stand 10 minutes to heat the shellfish.

Per serving:
Calories, 630; Protein, 52 g; Fat, 22 g (32% cal.); Cholesterol, 260 mg; Carbohydrates, 52 g; Fiber, 5 g; Sodium, 630 mg.

14. For each portion, allow 8 oz (225 g) rice and vegetables, 1 shrimp, 1 clam, 1 mussel, 1 piece of chicken, and at least 1 piece each of pork, sausage, and squid. Garnish each portion with 1 lemon wedge.

Note: If chorizo sausage is not available, use pepperoni sausage or other hard, spicy sausage. You may cut the sausage into ½-ounce (15-g) chunks before sautéing or cut them up just before serving.

Paella

Lecsó (Hungary)

Portions: 16   Portion size: 4 oz (125 g)

U.S.	Metric	Ingredients	PROCEDURE
1 lb 8 oz	750 g	Onions	1. Peel the onion and cut into fine dice.
3 lb	1.5 kg	Green peppers or Hungarian or Italian frying peppers	2. Core and seed the peppers. Cut into thin slices.
3 lb	1.5 kg	Tomatoes, as ripe as possible	3. Peel, seed, and chop the tomatoes. 4. Heat the lard over low heat. Add the onion and cook slowly for 5–10 minutes, until it is quite soft.
3 oz	100 g	Lard	5. Add the peppers and cook for another 5–10 minutes.
3 tbsp	20 g	Hungarian paprika	6. Add the tomatoes and paprika. Cover and simmer for 15–20 minutes, until vegetables are tender.
to taste	to taste	Salt	7. Season to taste with salt. Add 1–2 pinches of sugar if desired.
pinch	pinch	Sugar	

Per serving:
Calories, 110; Protein, 2 g; Fat, 6 g (46% cal.); Cholesterol, 5 mg;
Carbohydrates, 14 g; Fiber, 3 g; Sodium, 10 mg.

VARIATIONS

This dish may be used as a vegetable or an appetizer or served with rice or boiled noodles. Smoked sausages are often added to it as a luncheon dish, or it may be served with eggs prepared in a variety of ways. The portion size indicated is rather large because this dish is often served as part of a main course. For a side dish portion, you may want to reduce the portion size to 2½–3 oz (75–100 g).

Colcannon (Ireland)

Portions: 16   Portion size: 5 oz (150 g)

U.S.	Metric	Ingredients	PROCEDURE
4 lb	1.8 kg	Potatoes	1. Peel and eye the potatoes. Cut them into uniform sizes. Simmer in salted water until tender.
2 lb	900 g	Cabbage	2. While the potatoes are cooking, trim the cabbage and cut it into wedges. Steam until tender.
6 oz	175 g	Leeks or scallions	3. Cook the leeks or scallions very slowly in a little of the butter until tender.
4 oz	125 g	Butter	
6 oz	175 mL	Milk or cream, hot	4. Mash the potatoes and add the leeks or scallions and the rest of the butter. Mix in the milk or cream and the parsley.
2 tbsp	30 mL	Chopped parsley (optional)	5. Chop the cabbage fine and stir it into the potatoes until well mixed. Season with salt and white pepper.
to taste	to taste	Salt	
to taste	to taste	White pepper	6. If the mixture seems dry, mix in additional milk or cream to bring to a smooth, moist consistency.
as needed	as needed	Additional hot milk or cream	

Per serving:
Calories, 160; Protein, 3 g; Fat, 6 g (33% cal.); Cholesterol, 15 mg;
Carbohydrates, 24 g; Fiber, 3 g; Sodium, 75 mg.

Moussaka (Greece)

Portions: 16   **Portion size:** 9 oz (250 g)

U.S.	Metric	Ingredients	PROCEDURE
1 lb	450 g	Onion, small dice	1. Sauté the onion and garlic in the olive oil until soft. Remove with a slotted spoon.
3 cloves	3 cloves	Garlic, chopped	
2 oz	60 mL	Olive oil	2. Add the meat to the pan and brown lightly.
3½ lb	1.6 kg	Ground lamb or beef	3. Return the onion and garlic to the pot and add the tomato, wine, parsley, oregano, and cinnamon. Simmer, uncovered, until the liquid has reduced and the mixture is thick.
2 lb 4 oz	1 kg	Tomatoes, canned or fresh, peeled and chopped, with juice	
4 oz	100 mL	Red wine	4. Season to taste with salt and pepper.
2 tbsp	30 mL	Chopped parsley	
1½ tsp	7 mL	Oregano	
¼ tsp	1 mL	Cinnamon	
to taste	to taste	Salt	
to taste	to taste	Pepper	
4 lb	1.8 kg	Eggplant	5. Peel the eggplant if the skin is tough. Cut into ½-inch (1-cm) slices.
as needed	as needed	Olive oil	
to taste	to taste	Salt	6. Fry the eggplant slices in olive oil until tender. Set aside and season with salt.
1 qt	1 L	Béchamel, cold	7. Season the béchamel (which should be quite thick when cold) with a little salt, white pepper, and nutmeg.
to taste	to taste	Salt	
to taste	to taste	White pepper	8. Beat the eggs and mix into the béchamel.
to taste	to taste	Nutmeg	
4	4	Eggs	
as needed	as needed	Olive oil	9. Oil the bottom of a hotel pan or other pan measuring 12 × 20 inches (30 × 50 cm) with olive oil. Sprinkle lightly with bread crumbs.
as needed	as needed	Bread crumbs	
2 oz	60 g	Romano or parmesan cheese, grated	10. Arrange the eggplant slices in the pan so that they completely cover the bottom. Push them together as necessary.
			11. Put the meat mixture on the eggplant in a smooth layer.
			12. Pour the béchamel over the top and sprinkle with the grated cheese.
			13. Bake at 350°F (175°C) until hot and the top is golden, about 45–60 minutes.
			14. Cut into squares to serve.

Per serving:
Calories, 470; Protein, 24 g; Fat, 33 g (62% cal.); Cholesterol, 140 mg; Carbohydrates, 20 g; Fiber, 4 g; Sodium, 580 mg.

Foreign Terms Used in This Chapter

Following are brief explanations of the foreign-language terms for food items and cooked dishes in this chapter. The language that the term comes from is indicated in parentheses. Please note that this may not correspond to the country that the food comes from. For example, many of the foods whose names are in Spanish are not from Spain but from Mexico.

The following abbreviations are used: J. = Japanese; Ch. = Chinese; Sp. = Spanish; It. = Italian; Fr. = French. The first six entries, by the way, all refer to place names in Italy.

all'Abruzzese (It.): in the style of Abruzzo.
alla Milanese (It.): in the style of Milan.
alla Napoletana (It.): in the style of Naples.
alla Piemontese (It.): in the style of Piedmont.
alla Romana (It.): in the style of Rome.
alla Valdostana (It.): in the style of the Val d'Aosta.
ancho chile (Sp.): see chile.
arroz (Sp.): rice.
arroz verde (Sp.): green rice; rice cooked with herbs.
brandade de morue (Fr.): purée of salt cod.
burro (It.): butter.
caldo verde (Portuguese): a Portuguese soup made with potatoes, kale, and sausages.
carbonnade à la Flammande (Fr.): Flemish-style beef braised in beer.
carnitas (Sp.): "little meats"; browned pieces of pork.
ceci (It.): chickpeas.
chawan mushi (J.): savory steamed custard.
chile (Sp.): any of a variety of hot capsicum peppers, which may be fresh and green (such as poblano, jalapeño, and serrano) or red-ripe and dried (such as ancho, pasilla, and mulato).
chiles rellenos (Sp.): stuffed chiles.
chirashizushi (J.): scatter sushi; various fish and other garnish arranged on a bed of sushi rice.
cipolline in agrodolce (It.): sweet-and-sour pearl onions.
colcannon (Irish/English): a mixture of mashed potatoes and cabbage.
costellete di vitello ripiene (It.): stuffed veal chop.
cozze (It.): mussels.
daikon (J.): giant white radish.
dashi (J.): Japanese soup stock.
dillkött (Swedish): meat stew flavored with dill.
elote con queso (Sp.): corn with cheese.
enchilada (Sp.): a tortilla moistened with a sauce made with chiles and filled with meat or cheese.
formaggio (It.): cheese.
frijoles (Sp.): beans.
frijoles refritos (Sp.): "well-fried beans"; often called "refried beans."
fritta (It.): fried.
frutti di mare (It.): "fruits of the sea"; shellfish.
grassa (It.): fat.
grigliata (It.): grilled.
guajolote (Sp.): turkey.
kappa-maki (J.): rolled sushi filled with cucumber.
lecsó (Hungarian): a cooked mixture of peppers, tomatoes, and onions.
lombatine di maiale (It.): pork loin chop.
mirin (J.): sweet rice wine.
miso (J.): a fermented paste made of soybeans, barley, or rice.
mole poblano (Sp.): a spicy chile sauce, generally seasoned with bitter chocolate, or a dish (most often turkey or chicken) made with this sauce.
moussaka (Greek): a layered casserole made with eggplant and spicy ground lamb or other meat.

mozzarella in carrozza (It.): "mozzarella in a carriage"; a fried mozzarella sandwich.

mulato chile (Sp.): see chile.

nigirizushi (J.): finger sushi, or small ovals of sushi rice with topping.

nori (J.): a type of seaweed made into thin sheets, often used for sushi.

oyako donburi (J.): "parent-and-child bowl"; rice topped with chicken and egg in a thin sauce or broth.

paella (Sp.): an elaborate rice casserole containing a variety of meats, seafood, and vegetables.

pasilla chile (Sp.): see chile.

pasticciata (It.): made like a pie or pastry.

pesce (It.): fish.

picadillo (Sp.): a spiced ground or shredded meat, often used as a stuffing or filling.

poblano chile (Sp.): see chile.

polenta (It.): Italian cornmeal.

pollo (It., Sp.): chicken.

pollo con peperoni (It.): chicken with peppers.

riso (It.): rice.

rohkostsalatteller (German): raw vegetable salad plate.

saké (J.): rice wine.

salsa cruda (Sp.): uncooked sauce.

salsa roja (Sp.): red sauce.

salsa verde (Sp., It.): green sauce.

salsa verde cocida (Sp.): cooked green sauce.

salsicce (It.): sausages.

saltimbocca (It.): "jump in the mouth"; a dish of veal cutlets with ham and sage.

sashimi (J.): sliced raw fish.

serrano chile (Sp.): see chile.

shaoxing (Ch.): a Chinese wine similar to sherry.

Sichuan (Ch.) peppercorn: a dried bud used as a spice.

spiedini (It.): skewers.

spinaci (It.): spinach.

sudare (J.): a bamboo mat used for rolling sushi.

sugo di pomodoro (It.): tomato sauce.

sushi (J.): vinegared rice garnished with raw fish or other foods.

tekka-maki (J.): rolled sushi filled with raw tuna.

tempura (J.): Japanese-style batter-fried foods.

tendon (J.): rice topped with tempura and a seasoned broth.

teriyaki (J.): broiled, grilled, or griddled foods with a soy sauce glaze.

tomatillo (Sp.): a Mexican vegetable resembling a small green tomato.

vongole (It.): clams.

wakame (J.): a type of seaweed.

wasabi (J.): Japanese green horseradish.

wonton (Ch.): meat-filled dumpling.

zuppa (It.): soup.

Questions for Discussion

1. Explain the basic procedure for making dashi.
2. Explain how to make miso soup.
3. Describe the composition of sushi rice.
4. Describe a basic procedure for stir-frying.
5. Give one basic procedure for assembling an enchilada.
6. True or false: Most Italian dishes are served with tomato sauce. Discuss.

Bakeshop Production: Basic Principles and Ingredients

At one time, it was common for food service establishments to produce all their own breads, desserts, and other baked goods. Today, most operations find it more economical to buy these products from commercial bakeries. However, many owners and chefs have discovered that offering fresh, "home-baked" breads, cakes, and pastries attracts customers and increases profits. With little more than an oven and a mixer, many cooks turn out attractive baked items that set their operations apart from competitors.

For this reason, it is important for you to learn the fundamentals of baking, even if you intend to become a cook rather than a baker. These chapters will not make a professional baker out of you. A baker requires far more technical and specialized information than can be presented in this short space. But you will learn the basic methods for producing a wide variety of breads, desserts, and pastries with only the simplest of resources.

In this chapter, we introduce bakeshop production with a discussion of the basic processes and ingredients common to nearly all baked goods. This will give you the understanding necessary to proceed to actual production in the succeeding chapters.

Basic Principles of Baking

After reading this chapter,
you should be able to

1. Explain why it is important to weigh baking
   ingredients.

2. Use a baker's balance
   scale.

3. Calculate formulas
   based on baker's per-
   centages.

4. Explain the factors that
   control the develop-
   ment of gluten in baked
   products.

5. Explain the changes
   that take place in a
   dough or batter as it
   bakes.

6. Prevent or retard the
   staling of baked items.

7. Describe the major
   ingredients of baked
   goods and their func-
   tions and characteristics.

If you consider that most bakery products are made of the same few ingredients—flour, short-ening, sugar, eggs, water or milk, and leavening—you should have no difficulty understanding the importance of accuracy in the bakeshop, where slight differences in proportions or proce-dures can mean great differences in the final product.

If you have begun your food service studies in a kitchen production laboratory, you have surely been told many times of the importance of measurement, not only for portion control and cost control but also for consistency in the quality of the final product. However, you have, no doubt, also learned that there is a great deal of margin for error and that it is possible (if not desirable) to cook many foods without measuring anything. Coming into the bakeshop, where measurement is absolutely essential, may be a bit of a shock to you after your kitchen experi-ences, but it should reinforce the habits of accuracy that you may have let slip.

If, on the other hand, you are beginning your practical studies in the bakeshop, then you will do well to pay particular attention to the principles of measurement presented here. They will be valuable to you throughout your career.

Formulas and Measurement

Bakers generally talk about "formulas" rather than "recipes." If this sounds more to you like the chemistry lab than the kitchen, it is with good reason. The bakeshop is much like a chemistry laboratory both in the scientific accuracy of all the procedures and in the complex reactions that take place during mixing and baking.

MEASUREMENT

All ingredients must be weighed. Accuracy of measurement, as we have already said many times, is critical in the bakeshop. Measurement is by weight rather than by volume measure because weight is much more accurate. Unlike in recipes for the home baker, you will not see a profes-sional baker's formula calling for 6 cups of flour.

To demonstrate to yourself the importance of weighing rather than measuring by volume, measure 1 cup flour in two ways. (1) Sift some flour and lightly spoon it into a dry measure. Level the top and weigh the flour. (2) Scoop some unsifted flour into the same measure and pack it lightly. Level the top and weigh the flour. Note the difference. No wonder home recipes can be so inconsistent!

The baker's term for weighing out ingredients is *scaling.*

The following ingredients may be measured by *volume* because they weigh *1 pound per pint* or *1 kilogram per liter:*

Water   Milk   Eggs

Thus, if a formula calls for 2 pounds eggs, you may measure 2 pints (1 quart). (Liquid flavoring ingredients, such as vanilla extract, normally measured in very small quantities, may also be measured by volume; 1 tablespoon equals ½ ounce.) In the metric system, 1 milliliter water weighs 1 gram; 1 liter weighs 1 kilogram. All other liquid ingredients (such as corn syrup and molasses) and all dry ingredients are normally weighed.

Procedure for Using a Baker's Scale

The principle of using a baker's scale is simple: The scale must balance before setting the weights, and it must balance again after scaling. The example cited illustrates using a scale with U.S. units. The same procedure is used for metric scales.

1. Set the scale scoop or other container on the *left* side of the scale.

2. Balance the scale by placing counterweights on the *right* side and/or adjusting the ounce weight on the horizontal bar.

3. Set the scale for the desired weight by placing weights on the *right* side and/or by moving the ounce weight. For example, to set the scale for 1 pound 8 ounces, place a 1-pound weight on the *right* side and move the ounce weight to the right 8 ounces. If the ounce weight is already over 8 ounces, so that you cannot move it another 8, add 2 pounds to the *right* side of the scale and subtract 8 ounces by moving the ounce weight 8 places to the *left*. The result is still 1 pound 8 ounces.

4. Add the ingredient being scaled to the left side until the scale balances.

A baker's balance scale.

BAKER'S PERCENTAGES

Bakers use a simple but versatile system of percentages for expressing their formulas. Bakers' percentages express the amount of each ingredient used as a percentage of the amount of flour used.

To put it differently, the percentage of each ingredient is its total weight divided by the weight of the flour and multiplied by 100 percent, or

$$\frac{\text{weight of ingredient}}{\text{weight of flour}} \times 100\% = \% \text{ of ingredient}$$

Thus, flour is always 100 percent. (If two kinds of flour are used, their total is 100 percent.) Any ingredient that weighs the same as the flour is also given as 100 percent. The following ingredients from a cake formula illustrate how these percentages are used. Both U.S. and metric examples are given. (Note that numbers may be rounded off for practical measuring.) Check the figures with the above equation to make sure you understand them.

Ingredient	Weight	Percentage
Cake flour	5 lb	100%
Sugar	5 lb	100%
Baking powder	4 oz	5%
Salt	2 oz	2.5%
Emulsified shortening	2 lb 8 oz	50%
Skim milk	3 lb	60%
Egg whites	3 lb	60%
	18 lb 14 oz	377.5%

Ingredient	Weight	Percentage
Cake flour	2500 g	100%
Sugar	2500 g	100%
Baking powder	125 g	5%
Salt	60 g	2.5%
Emulsified shortening	1250 g	50%
Skim milk	1500 g	60%
Egg whites	1500 g	60%
	9435 g	377.5%

The advantage of using *baker's percentages* is that the formula is easily adapted for any yield, and single ingredients may be varied without changing the whole formulation. Please remember that these numbers do not refer to the percentage of the total yield. They are simply a way of expressing *ingredient proportions*. The total of these percentage numbers will always be greater than 100 percent.

Procedure for Calculating the Weight of an Ingredient If the Weight of Flour Is Known

1. Change the ingredient percentage to decimal form by moving the decimal point two places to the left.

2. Multiply the weight of the flour by this decimal to get the weight of the ingredient.

   Example: A formula calls for 20 percent sugar and you are using 10 pounds flour. How much sugar do you need?

   20% = 0.20

   10 lb × 0.20 = 2 lb sugar

   Note: In the U.S. system, weights must normally be expressed all in one unit, either ounces or pounds, in order for the calculation to work, as explained in Chapter 5.

   Example (Metric): A formula calls for 20 percent sugar and you are using 5000 grams (5 kg) flour. How much sugar do you need?

   20% = 0.20

   5000 g × 0.20 = 1000 g sugar

Procedure for Converting a Formula to a New Yield

1. Change the total percentage to decimal form by moving the decimal point two places to the left.

2. Divide the desired yield by this decimal figure to get the weight of flour.

3. If necessary, round off this number to the next highest figure. This will allow for losses in mixing, makeup, and panning, and it will make calculations easier.

4. Use the weight of flour and remaining ingredient percentages to calculate the weights of the other ingredients, as in the previous procedure.

   Example: In the previous sample cake formula, how much flour is needed if you require 6 pounds (or 3000 grams) of cake batter?

   6 lb = 96 oz

   377.5% = 3.775

   96 oz ÷ 3.775 = 25.43 oz

   or, rounded off, 26 oz (1 lb 10 oz)

   3000 g ÷ 3.775 = 794.7 g

   or, rounded off, 800 g

Clearly, the percentage system we have been discussing is used only when flour is a major ingredient, as in breads, cakes, and cookies. For these formulas, we use a written format different from our regular recipe format in this book.

In these formulas, the indicated yield is the total weight of the ingredients. This figure indicates the weight of the batter or dough. It is the figure that we need to know for the purpose of scaling the dough or batter into loaves or pans. The finished weight of the baked goods will be less because moisture is lost during baking.

Also, please note that all yields, including percentage totals, are rounded off to the next lower whole number. This eliminates unimportant fractions and makes reading and calculating easier.

SELECTION OF INGREDIENTS

In addition to measuring, there is another basic rule of accuracy in the bakeshop: *Use the exact ingredients specified.*

As you will learn in this chapter, different flours, shortenings, and other ingredients do not function alike. Bakers' formulas are balanced for specific ingredients. Do not substitute bread flour for pastry flour or regular shortening for emulsified shortening, for example. They won't work the same way.

Occasionally, a substitution may be made, such as active dry yeast for compressed yeast (see p. 769), but not without adjusting the quantities or rebalancing the formula.

Mixing and Gluten Development

WHAT IS GLUTEN?

Gluten is a substance made up of proteins present in wheat flour; it gives structure and strength to baked goods.

In order for gluten to be developed, the proteins must first absorb water. Then, as the dough or batter is mixed or kneaded, the gluten forms long, elastic strands. As the dough or batter is leavened, these strands capture the gases in tiny pockets or cells, and we say the product "rises." When the product is baked, the gluten, like all proteins (see p. 52), coagulates or solidifies and gives structure to the product.

HOW DOES THE BAKER CONTROL GLUTEN?

Flour is mostly starch, but its protein or gluten content, not its starch, concerns the baker most. Without gluten proteins to give structure, baked goods would not hold together.

The baker must be able to control the gluten, however. For example, we want French bread to be firm and chewy, which requires much gluten. On the other hand, we want cakes to be tender, which means we want very little gluten development.

Ingredient proportions and mixing methods are determined, in part, by how they affect the development of gluten. The baker has several methods for adjusting gluten development.

1. **Selection of flours.**
   Wheat flours are classified as *strong* or *weak*, depending on their protein content.

   Strong flours come from *hard wheat* and have a high protein content.
   Weak flours come from *soft wheat* and have a low protein content.

   Thus, we use strong flours for breads and weak flours for cakes.
   Only wheat flour develops gluten. To make bread from rye and other grains, the formula must be balanced with some high-gluten flour, or the bread will be heavy.

2. **Shortening.**
   Any fat used in baking is called a *shortening* because it shortens gluten strands. It does this by surrounding the particles and lubricating them so they do not stick together. Thus, *fats are tenderizers*. A cookie or pastry that is very crumbly, due to high fat content, is said to be "short."
   You can see why French bread has little or no fat, while cakes contain a great deal.

3. **Liquid.**
   Because gluten proteins must absorb water before they can be developed, the amount of water in a formula can affect toughness or tenderness. Pie crusts and crisp cookies are made with very little liquid to keep them tender.

4. **Mixing methods.**
   In general, the more a dough or batter is mixed, the more the gluten develops. Thus, bread doughs are mixed or kneaded for a long time to develop the gluten. Cakes, pie crusts, muffins, and other products that must be tender are mixed for a short time.
   It is possible to overmix bread dough, however. Gluten strands stretch only so far. They break if the dough is overmixed.

The Baking Process

The changes undergone by a dough or batter as it bakes are basically the same for all baked products, from breads to cookies and cakes. You should know what these changes are so you can learn how to control them.

The stages in the baking process take place as follows.

1. **Formation and expansion of gases.**
   Some gases are already present in the dough, as in proofed bread dough and in sponge cake batters. As they are heated, the gases expand and leaven the product.

   Some gases are not formed until heat is applied. Yeast and baking powder form gases rapidly when first placed in the oven. Steam is also formed as the moisture of the dough is heated.

   Leavening and leavening agents are discussed in more detail beginning on page 768.

2. **Trapping of the gases in air cells.**
   As the gases form and expand, they are trapped in a stretchable network formed by the proteins in the dough. These proteins are primarily gluten and, sometimes, egg protein.

   Without gluten or egg protein, the gases would escape, and the product would not be leavened. Breads without enough gluten are heavy.

3. **Coagulation of proteins.**
   Like all proteins, gluten and egg proteins coagulate or solidify when they reach high enough temperatures. This is the process that gives structure to baked goods.

   Correct baking temperature is important. If the temperature is too high, coagulation will start too soon, before the expansion of gases has reached its peak. The product will have poor volume or a split crust. If the temperature is too low, the proteins will not coagulate soon enough, and the product may collapse.

4. **Gelatinization of starches.**
   The starches absorb moisture, expand, and become firmer.

5. **Evaporation of some of the water.**
   This takes place throughout the baking process.

6. **Melting of shortenings.**
   Different shortenings melt—and release trapped gases—at different temperatures, so the proper shortening should be selected for each product.

   As the fats melt, they surround the air cells and make the product more tender.

7. **Browning of the surface and crust formation.**
   Browning occurs when sugars caramelize and starches and proteins undergo certain changes. This contributes to flavor. Milk, sugar, and egg increase browning.

   A crust is formed as water evaporates from the surface and leaves it dry.

Staling

Staling is the change in texture and aroma of baked goods due to the change in structure and the loss of moisture by the starch granules. Stale baked goods have lost their fresh-baked aroma and are firmer, drier, and more crumbly than fresh products.

Prevention of staling is a major concern of the baker because most baked goods lose quality rapidly.

Staling can be slowed by these techniques.

1. **Protecting the product from air.**
   Wrapping bread in plastic and covering cakes with icing are two examples.

   Unfortunately, hard-crusted breads, which stale rapidly, should not be wrapped, or the crusts will become soft. These bread products should always be served fresh.

2. **Adding moisture retainers to the formula.**
   Fats and sugars are good moisture retainers, and products high in these ingredients keep best.

   Some of the best French bread has no fat at all, and if it is not served within hours of baking, it will begin to stale. For longer keeping, bakers often add a very small amount of fat and/or sugar to the formula.

3. **Freezing.**

Baked goods frozen *before* they become stale maintain quality for longer periods. They should be served very soon after thawing. Frozen breads may be reheated with excellent results if they are to be served immediately.

Refrigerating actually seems to speed staling rather than slowing it. Only baked goods that could develop health hazards, such as those with cream fillings, are refrigerated.

Loss of crispness is caused by absorption of moisture, so it is, in a sense, the opposite of staling. This is a problem with low-moisture products such as cookies and pie crusts. The problem is usually solved by proper storage in airtight wraps or containers to protect the products from moisture in the air. Prebaked pie shells should be filled as close to service time as possible.

Ingredients

The following introduction to baking ingredients is necessarily simplified. If you decide to pursue a career as a baker, you will need to learn a great deal of technical information. However, the basic information presented here is enough to enable you to produce a full range of baked items in a small bakeshop or restaurant kitchen.

Flours, Meals, and Starches

WHITE WHEAT FLOUR

White wheat flour is milled from wheat kernels after the outer covering, called *bran*, and the germ are removed. Wheat flour contains about 63 to 73 percent starch and 7 to 15 percent protein. The rest is moisture, fat, sugar, and minerals.

Wheat flour is the source of the protein called *gluten*, which you remember is one of the essential elements in baking. Bakers select flour on the basis of its gluten content. Flours high in protein are called *strong*, and those low in protein are called *weak*.

For our purposes, in the small bakeshop, we need to know about three kinds of wheat flour.

1. *Bread flour* is a strong flour that is used for making breads, hard rolls, and any product that requires high gluten. The best bread flours are called *patents*. *Straight* flours are also strong flours.

2. *Cake flour* is a weak or low-gluten flour made from soft wheat. It has a soft, smooth texture and a pure white color. Cake flour is used for cakes and other delicate baked goods that require low gluten content.

3. *Pastry flour* is lower in gluten than bread flour but higher than cake flour. It has the same creamy white color as bread flour, not the pure white of cake flour. Pastry flour is used for cookies, pie pastry, some sweet yeast doughs, biscuits, and muffins.

Being able to identify these three flours by sight and touch is an important skill because, sooner or later, someone will dump a bag of flour into the wrong bin, and you will need to recognize the problem.

Bread flour feels slightly coarse when rubbed between the fingers. If squeezed into a lump, it falls apart as soon as the hand is opened. Its color is creamy white.
Cake flour feels smooth and fine. It stays in a lump when squeezed in the palm of the hand. Its color is pure white.
Pastry flour feels like cake flour but has the creamy color of bread flour.

All-purpose flour, seen in retail markets, is not often found in bakeshops. This flour is formulated to be slightly weaker than bread flour so that it can be used for pastries as well. A professional baker, however, prefers to use flours that are formulated for specific purposes because these give the best results.

WHOLE WHEAT FLOUR

Whole wheat flour is made by grinding the entire wheat kernel, including the bran and germ. The germ, which is the embryo of a new wheat plant, is high in fat, which can become rancid. This is why whole wheat flour does not keep as well as white flour.

Because it is made from wheat, whole wheat flour contains gluten, so it can be used alone in bread making. However, a bread made with 100 percent whole wheat will be heavy because the gluten strands are cut by the sharp edges of the bran flakes. Also, the fat from the wheat germ contributes slightly to the shortening action. This is why most whole wheat breads are strengthened with white bread flour.

Bran flour is flour to which bran flakes have been added. The bran may be coarse or fine, depending on specifications.

RYE FLOUR

Next to white and whole wheat, rye is the most popular flour in bread making. Because rye flour does not develop gluten, breads made with it are heavy unless some hard wheat flour is added.

Rye flour is available in three shades, *light, medium,* and *dark*. *Rye meal* or *pumpernickel* is a coarse meal made from the whole rye grain. It looks something like oatmeal.

Rye blend is a mixture of rye flour and hard wheat flour.

OTHER FLOURS

Products milled from other grains are occasionally used to add variety to baked goods. These include cornmeal, buckwheat flour, soy flour, potato flour, oat flour, and barley flour. The term *meal* is used for products that are not as finely ground as flour.

All these products must normally be used in combination with wheat flour because they do not form gluten.

STARCHES

In addition to flours, other starch products are also used in the bakeshop. Unlike flour, they are used primarily to thicken puddings, pie fillings, and similar products. The principles of thickening with starches are covered in Chapter 8.

The most important starches in dessert production are as follows:

1. *Cornstarch* has a special property that makes it valuable for certain purposes. Products thickened with cornstarch set up almost like gelatin when cooled. For this reason, it is used to thicken cream pies and other products that must hold their shape.

2. *Waxy maize* and other *modified starches* also have valuable properties. They do not break down when frozen, so are used for products that are to be frozen. Also, they are clear when cooked, and give a brilliant, clear appearance to fruit pie fillings.

   Waxy maize does not set up firm like cornstarch but makes a soft paste, which has the same consistency hot and cold. Thus, it is not suitable for cream pie fillings.

3. *Instant starches* are precooked or pregelatinized, so they thicken cold liquids without further cooking. They are useful when heat will damage the flavor of the product, as in fresh fruit glazes (such as strawberry).

Fats

We have said that one of the main functions of fats in baking is to shorten gluten strands and tenderize the product. We can summarize the reasons for using fats in baked items as follows:

- To tenderize the product and soften the texture.
- To add moistness and richness.
- To increase keeping quality.

- To add flavor.
- To assist in leavening when used as creaming agents or when used to give flakiness to puff pastry, pie dough, and similar products.

SHORTENINGS

Any fat acts as a shortening in baking because it shortens gluten strands and tenderizes the product. However, we usually use the word *shortening* to mean any of a group of solid fats, usually white and tasteless, that are especially formulated for baking.

Because shortenings are used for many purposes, manufacturers have formulated different kinds of fats with different properties. Following are the three main types of shortening.

Regular Shortenings

These shortenings have a tough, waxy texture, and small particles of the fat tend to hold their shape in a dough or batter. This type of shortening does not melt until a high temperature is reached.

Regular shortening has good creaming ability. This means that a large quantity of air can be mixed into it to give a batter lightness and leavening power. Therefore, it is used in products mixed by the creaming method, such as certain cookies.

Because of its texture, this type of shortening is used for flaky products such as pie crusts and biscuits. It is also used in breads and many pastries. Unless another shortening is specified, regular shortening is generally used.

Emulsified Shortenings

These are soft shortenings that spread easily throughout a batter and quickly coat the particles of sugar and flour. Because of their easy spreading, they give a smoother and finer texture to cakes and make them moister.

Emulsified shortening is often used whenever the weight of sugar in a cake batter is greater than the weight of flour. Because this shortening spreads so well, a simpler mixing method can be used, as explained in Chapter 29. Such cakes are referred to as *high-ratio cakes*, so emulsified shortening is sometimes called *high-ratio shortening*.

In addition, emulsified shortening is used in certain icings because it can hold more sugar and liquid without curdling.

Puff Pastry Shortenings

Puff pastry shortenings are firm like regular shortening. They are especially formulated for puff pastry and other doughs that form layers, such as Danish pastry.

BUTTER AND MARGARINE

Shortenings are manufactured to have certain textures and hardness. Butter, on the other hand, is a natural product that doesn't have these advantages. It is hard and brittle when cold and soft at room temperature, and it melts easily. Consequently, doughs made with butter are hard to handle. Margarine is a little easier to handle, but it has many of the same disadvantages.

On the other hand, butter and margarine have two major advantages.

1. **Flavor.**
   Shortenings are intentionally flavorless, but butter has a highly desirable flavor.

2. **Melting qualities.**
   Butter melts in the mouth. Shortenings do not. After eating pastries or icings made with shortening, one can be left with an unpleasant film of shortening coating the mouth.

For these reasons, many bakers and pastry chefs feel that the advantages of butter outweigh its disadvantages for some purposes.

OILS

Oils are liquid fats. They are not often used as shortening in baking because they spread through a batter or dough too thoroughly and shorten too much. Their usefulness in the bakeshop is limited primarily to greasing pans and proofing bowls, to deep-frying doughnuts, and to serving as a wash for some kinds of rolls. A few quick breads and cakes use oil as a shortening.

LARD

Lard is the rendered fat of hogs. Because of its plastic quality, it was once highly valued for making flaky pie crusts. Since the development of modern shortenings, it is not often used in the bakeshop.

Sugars

Sugars or sweetening agents are used for the following purposes in baking:

- To add sweetness and flavor.
- To create tenderness and fineness of texture by weakening the gluten structure.
- To give crust color.
- To increase keeping qualities by retaining moisture.
- To act as creaming agents with fats.

We customarily use the term *sugar* for regular refined sugars derived from sugar cane or beets. The chemical name for these sugars is *sucrose*. However, other sugars of different chemical structure are also used in the bakeshop. The following are the more important sugars.

REGULAR REFINED SUGARS, OR SUCROSE

Refined sugars are classified by the size of grains.

1. Granulated sugar.
    Regular granulated, also called *fine granulated* or *table sugar*, is the most familiar and the most commonly used.
    Very fine and *ultrafine sugars* are finer than regular granulated. They are prized for making cakes and cookies because they make a more uniform batter and can support higher quantities of fat.
    Sanding sugars are coarser and are used for coating doughnuts, cakes, and other products.
2. Confectioners' or powdered sugars.
    These sugars are ground to a fine powder and mixed with a small amount of starch to prevent caking. They are classified by coarseness or fineness.
    10X is the finest sugar. It gives the smoothest textures in icings.
    6X is the standard confectioners' sugar. It is used in icings, toppings, and cream fillings.
    Coarser types (*4X* and *XX*) are used for dusting or for any purposes for which 6X and 10X are too fine.

MOLASSES AND BROWN SUGAR

Molasses is concentrated sugar cane juice. *Sulfured molasses* is a byproduct of sugar refining. It is the product that remains after most of the sugar has been extracted from cane juice. *Unsulfured molasses* is not a byproduct but a specially manufactured sugar product. Its taste is less bitter than that of sulfured molasses.

Molasses contains large amounts of sucrose, plus other sugars, acids, and impurities.

Brown sugar is mostly sucrose, but it also contains varying amounts of molasses and other impurities. The darker grades contain more molasses.

Because molasses and brown sugar contain acids, they can be used with baking soda to provide leavening (see p. 769).

Molasses retains moisture in baked goods and so prolongs freshness. However, crisp cookies made with molasses quickly become soft for the same reason.

CORN SYRUP

Corn syrup is a liquid sweetener consisting mainly of a sugar called glucose. It is made by converting cornstarch into simpler sugar compounds by the use of enzymes.

Corn syrup aids in retaining moisture and is used in some icings and in candy making.

GLUCOSE SYRUP

While corn syrup contains other sugars in addition to glucose, pure glucose syrup is also available. It resembles corn syrup but is colorless and nearly tasteless. If a recipe calls for glucose syrup and none is available, substitute light corn syrup.

HONEY

Honey is a natural sugar syrup consisting largely of glucose and fructose, plus other compounds that give it flavor. Honeys vary considerably in flavor and color, depending on their source. Flavor is the major reason for using honey, especially because it can be expensive.

Honey contains *invert sugar*, which means that it stays smooth and resists crystallizing. Like molasses, it contains *acid*, which enables it to be used with baking soda as a leavening.

MALT SYRUP

Malt syrup is used primarily in yeast breads. It serves as food for the yeast and adds flavor and crust color to the breads.

Liquids

Gluten cannot be developed without moisture, so liquids are essential to the baking process.

Pie crusts provide a good illustration of how liquids function in baking. If too much water is incorporated in a pie dough, a lot of gluten develops and the crust is tough. If no water at all is used, no gluten develops and the crust does not hold together.

Some of the moisture in doughs and batters changes to steam during baking. This contributes to leavening.

WATER

Water is the basic liquid in baking, especially in breads.

Tap water is normally suitable for most baking purposes. However, in some localities, the water may be *hard*, meaning that it contains many dissolved minerals. These minerals interfere with proper gluten development. In these areas, the water may have to be treated for use in baking.

MILK AND CREAM

Milk products, as described in Chapter 21, are important in baking. These products include liquid whole and skim milk, buttermilk, and dry milk solids.

Milk contributes to the texture, flavor, nutritional value, keeping quality, and crust color of baked goods.

1. Whole milk contains fat, which must be calculated as part of the shortening in a dough. For this reason, whole and skim milk are not interchangeable in a formula unless adjustments are made for the fat.

2. Buttermilk, which is slightly acid, is often used in conjunction with baking soda as a leavening agent in quick breads.

3. Cream is not often used as a liquid in doughs and batters, except in a few specialty products. In these instances, it is used as a shortening as well as a liquid because of its fat content.
   Cream is more important in the production of fillings and toppings.

4. Dry milk is often used because of its convenience and low cost. In some formulas, it is not necessary to reconstitute it. The milk powder is included with the dry ingredients, and water is used as the liquid.

OTHER SOURCES OF LIQUIDS

Eggs, honey, molasses, and even butter (about 15 percent water) contribute moisture to a dough or batter. In many cookies, for example, eggs are the only liquid in the formula.

Eggs

FORMS

As we discussed in Chapter 21, eggs are purchased in the following forms:

1. Whole shell eggs.
2. Frozen: whites, yolks, whole, and whole with extra yolks.
3. Dried: whole, whites, yolks.

FUNCTIONS

Eggs perform the following functions in baking.

1. **Structure.**
    Like gluten protein, egg protein coagulates to give structure to baked products. This is especially important in high-ratio cakes, where the high sugar and fat content weakens the gluten.
    If used in large quantities, eggs make baked products tough or chewy unless balanced by high fat and sugar, which are tenderizers.

2. **Emulsification of fats.**
    Egg yolks contain natural emulsifiers, which help produce smooth batters. This contributes to volume and to texture.

3. **Leavening.**
    Beaten eggs incorporate air in tiny cells or bubbles. In a batter, this trapped air expands when heated and aids in leavening.

4. **Shortening action.**
    The fat in egg yolks acts as a shortening. This is an important function in products that are low in other fats.

5. **Moisture.**
    Whole eggs are about 70 percent water, egg whites about 86 percent water, and egg yolks about 49 percent water. This moisture must be calculated as part of the total liquid in a formula.

6. **Flavor.**

7. **Nutritional value.**

8. **Color.**
    Yolks impart a yellow color to doughs and batters. Also, eggs brown easily and contribute to crust color.

Leavening Agents

Leavening is the production or incorporation of gases in a baked product to increase volume and to produce shape and texture. These gases must be retained in the product until the structure is set enough (by the coagulation of gluten and egg protein) to hold its shape.

Exact measurement of leavening agents is important because small changes can produce major defects in baked products.

YEAST

Fermentation is the process by which yeast acts on carbohydrates and changes them into carbon dioxide gas and alcohol. This release of gas produces the leavening action in yeast products. The alcohol evaporates completely during and immediately after baking.

Yeast is a microscopic plant. As a living organism, it is sensitive to temperatures.

45°F (7°C)	Inactive; storage temperature
60° to 70°F (15° to 20°C)	Slow action
70° to 90°F (20° to 32°C)	Best growth; proofing temperature for bread doughs
Above 100°F (38°C)	Reaction slows
140°F (60°C)	Yeast is killed

Yeast is available in two forms: compressed and active dry. Most bread formulas call for compressed yeast. *To convert to active dry yeast, use only 40 percent of the weight of compressed yeast specified.* In other words, in place of 1 pound compressed, use 6.5 ounces dry yeast (0.40 × 16 ounces), or in place of 500 grams compressed yeast, use 200 grams dry (0.40 × 500 grams). Dry yeast must be dissolved in 4 times its weight of warm water (about 110°F/43°C) before use.

Yeast contributes flavor in addition to leavening action.

CHEMICAL LEAVENERS

Chemical leaveners are those that release gases produced by chemical reactions.

Baking Soda

Baking soda is the chemical sodium bicarbonate. If *moisture* and an *acid* are present, soda releases carbon dioxide gas, which leavens the product.

Heat is not necessary for the reaction (although the gas is released faster at higher temperatures). For this reason, products leavened with soda must be baked at once or the gases will escape and leavening power will be lost.

Acids that react with soda in a batter include honey, molasses, buttermilk, fruits, cocoa, and chocolate. Sometimes cream of tartar is used for the acid. The amount of soda used in a formula is generally the amount needed to balance the acid. If more leavening power is needed, baking powder, not more soda, is used.

Baking Powder

Baking powders are mixtures of baking soda plus an acid to react with it.

Because baking powders do not depend on acid ingredients for their leavening power in a formula, they are more versatile.

Single-acting baking powders require only moisture to be able to release gas. Like baking soda, they can be used only if the product is to be baked immediately after mixing.

Double-acting baking powders release some gas when cold, but they require heat for complete reaction. Thus, cake batters made with these can incorporate the leavening agent early in the mixing period and can stand for some time before being baked.

Do not include more baking powder than necessary in a formula because undesirable flavors may be created.

Baking Ammonia

Baking ammonia is the chemical ammonium carbonate. It decomposes during baking to form carbon dioxide gas and ammonia gas. Only heat and moisture are necessary for it to work. No acids are needed.

Because it decomposes completely, it leaves no residue that can affect flavor. However, it can be used only in small products, like cookies, which allow the ammonia gas to be completely driven off.

Baking ammonia releases gases quickly, so it is sometimes used in products like cream puffs where rapid leavening is desired.

AIR

Air is incorporated into a batter primarily by two methods, creaming and foaming. This air expands during baking and leavens the product.

1. *Creaming* is the process of beating fat and sugar together to incorporate air. It is an important technique in cake and cookie making. Some pound cakes and cookies are leavened almost entirely by this method.

2. *Foaming* is the process of beating eggs, with or without sugar, to incorporate air. Foams made with whole eggs are used to leaven sponge cakes, while angel food cakes, meringues, and soufflés are leavened with egg white foams.

STEAM

When water turns to steam, it expands to 1600 times its original volume. Because all baked products contain some moisture, steam is an important leavening agent.

Puff pastry, cream puffs, popovers, and pie crusts use steam as their major or only leavening agent.

If the starting baking temperature for these products is high, steam is produced rapidly and leavening is greatest.

Salt, Flavorings, and Spices

SALT

Salt plays an important role in baking. It is more than just a seasoning or flavor enhancer. It also has these functions:

1. Salt strengthens gluten structure and makes it more stretchable. Thus, it improves the texture of breads.
2. Salt inhibits yeast growth. It is, therefore, important for controlling fermentation in bread doughs and in preventing the growth of undesirable wild yeasts.

For these reasons, the quantity of salt in a formula must be carefully controlled.

CHOCOLATE AND COCOA

Chocolate and cocoa are derived from cocoa or cacao beans. When the beans are roasted and ground, the resulting product is called *chocolate liquor*, which contains a white or yellowish fat called *cocoa butter*.

Cocoa is the dry powder that remains after part of the cocoa butter is removed from chocolate liquor.

Dutch process cocoa is processed with an alkali. It is slightly darker, smoother in flavor, and more easily dissolved in liquids than regular cocoa.

Bitter or *unsweetened chocolate* is straight chocolate liquor. In some less expensive brands, some of the cocoa butter may be replaced by another fat.

Sweet chocolate is bitter chocolate with the addition of sugar in varying amounts. If the percentage of sugar is low, it is sometimes called *semisweet* or *bittersweet*.

Milk chocolate is sweet chocolate with the addition of milk solids. It is used primarily in candy making. (None of the recipes in this book call for milk chocolate.)

Cocoa and chocolate are high in starch. When cocoa is added to a cake formula, it is sometimes considered part of the flour proportion for this reason.

SPICES

Spices are discussed in detail in Chapter 4. The most important spices in the bakeshop are cinnamon, nutmeg, mace, cloves, ginger, caraway, cardamom, allspice, anise, and poppy seed.

Because spices are used in small quantities, it is not much more expensive to use the best quality, and the results are superior.

Spices should be measured by weight unless the quantity is so small that measuring spoons are necessary.

EXTRACTS AND EMULSIONS

Extracts are flavorful oils and other substances dissolved in alcohol. These include vanilla, lemon, and bitter almond.

Emulsions are flavorful oils mixed with water with the aid of emulsifiers such as vegetable gums. Lemon and orange are the most frequently used emulsions.

The flavorings of extracts and emulsions may be natural or artificial. Natural flavorings give the best results, but they are often expensive. Artificial flavorings must be used in moderation to avoid creating strong or undesirable flavors in baked items.

Terms for Review

gluten	pastry flour	sucrose	creaming
strong flour	whole wheat flour	confectioners' sugar	foaming
weak flour	rye blend	leavening	extract
shortening	pumpernickel	fermentation	emulsion
staling	regular shortening	chemical leavener	
bread flour	emulsified	single- and double-	
cake flour	shortening	acting baking	
		powders	

Questions for Discussion

1. Below are ingredients for a white cake. The weight of the flour is given, and the proportions of other ingredients are indicated by percentages. Calculate the weights required for each.

Cake flour	3 lb or 1500 g (100%)
Baking powder	4%
Shortening	50%
Sugar	100%
Salt	1%
Milk	75%
Egg whites	33%
Vanilla	2%

2. Discuss four factors that affect the development of gluten in doughs and batters.

3. Why do some cakes fall if they are removed from the oven too soon?

4. Which kind of cake would you expect to have better keeping qualities—a sponge cake, which is low in fat, or a high-ratio cake?

5. Why is white wheat flour used in rye breads? in whole wheat breads? Some bakeries in Europe produce a kind of pumpernickel bread with 100 percent rye flour. What would you expect its texture to be like?

6. Describe how to distinguish among bread, pastry, and cake flours by touch and sight.

7. What is the difference between regular and emulsified shortenings?

8. Shortbread is a type of cookie made with flour, butter, and sugar, but no liquid. What would you expect its texture to be like? Why?

chapter 27

Yeast Products

*I*n its simplest form, bread is nothing more than a dough of flour and water, leavened by yeast and baked. In fact, some hard-crusted French breads contain only these ingredients, plus salt. Other kinds of bread contain additional ingredients, including sugar, shortening, milk, eggs, and flavorings. But flour, water, and yeast are still the basic building blocks of all breads.

Yet for something that seems so simple, bread can be one of the most exacting and complex products to make. Success in bread making depends largely on your understanding two basic principles: gluten development, which we discussed in the previous chapter, and yeast fermentation, which we have touched on and which we study in greater detail here.

This chapter focuses on the production of many kinds of yeast products, including breads, dinner rolls, sweet rolls, Danish pastry, and croissants.

Understanding Yeast Products

Yeast Product Types

Although all yeast doughs are made according to essentially the same basic principles, it is useful to divide yeast products into categories such as the following.

After reading this chapter, you should be able to

1. Prepare breads and dinner rolls.

2. Prepare sweet dough products.

3. Prepare Danish pastry and croissants.

REGULAR YEAST DOUGH PRODUCTS

Lean Dough Products

A lean dough is one that is low in fat and sugar.

- Hard-crusted breads and rolls, including French and Italian breads, kaiser rolls and other hard rolls, and pizza. These are the leanest of all bread products.
- Other white breads and dinner rolls. These have a higher fat and sugar content and, sometimes, also contain eggs and milk solids. Because they are slightly richer, they generally have soft crusts.
- Whole grain breads. Whole wheat and rye breads are the most common. Many varieties of rye bread are produced with light or dark flours or with pumpernickel flour and with various flavorings, especially molasses and caraway seeds.

Rich Dough Products

There is no exact dividing line between rich and lean doughs but, in general, rich doughs contain higher proportions of fat, sugar, and, sometimes, eggs.

- Nonsweet breads and rolls, including rich dinner rolls and brioche. These have a high fat content but low enough sugar so that they can be served as dinner breads. Brioche dough is especially rich, made with a high proportion of butter and eggs.
- Sweet rolls, including coffee cakes and many breakfast and tea rolls. These have high fat and sugar and, often, eggs. They are usually made with a sweet filling or topping.

ROLLED-IN YEAST DOUGH PRODUCTS

Rolled-in doughs are those in which a fat is incorporated into the dough in many layers by means of a rolling and folding procedure. The alternating layers of fat and dough give the baked product a flaky texture.

- Nonsweet rolled-in doughs: croissants.
- Sweet rolled-in doughs: Danish pastry.

Mixing Methods

Mixing yeast doughs has three main purposes:

1. To combine all ingredients into a uniform, smooth dough.
2. To distribute the yeast evenly throughout the dough.
3. To develop gluten.

Two principal mixing methods are used for yeast doughs: the straight dough method and the sponge method.

STRAIGHT DOUGH METHOD

There is only one step in this method, as practiced by many bakers.

Procedure: Straight Dough Mixing Method

Combine all ingredients in the mixing bowl and mix.

Some bakers dissolve the compressed yeast in some of the water before adding the remaining ingredients. Others omit this step. Active dry yeast, on the other hand, must be rehydrated before mixing.

The advantage of softening the yeast in water is that it helps to ensure that the yeast is evenly distributed in the dough.

MODIFIED STRAIGHT DOUGH METHOD FOR RICH DOUGHS

For rich sweet doughs, the method is modified to ensure even distribution of the fat and sugar.

Procedure: Modified Straight Dough Method

1. Soften the yeast in part of the water.
2. Combine the fat, sugar, salt, milk solids, and flavorings and mix until well combined, but do not whip until light.
3. Add the eggs gradually, as fast as they are absorbed.
4. Add the liquid and mix briefly.
5. Add the flour and yeast. Mix into a smooth dough.

SPONGE METHOD

Sponge doughs are prepared in two stages.

Procedure: Sponge Method

1. Combine the liquid (or part of the liquid), the yeast, and part of the flour (and, sometimes, part of the sugar). Mix into a thick batter or soft dough. Let ferment until double in bulk.
2. Punch down and add the rest of the flour and remaining ingredients. Mix to a uniform, smooth dough.

Steps in Yeast Dough Production

The production of yeast breads involves 12 basic steps. These steps are applied to yeast products in general, with variations depending on the particular product.

1. Scaling ingredients
2. Mixing
3. Fermentation
4. Punching
5. Scaling
6. Rounding
7. Benching
8. Makeup and panning
9. Proofing
10. Baking
11. Cooling
12. Storing

As you can see, mixing of ingredients into a dough is only one part of a complex procedure.

SCALING INGREDIENTS

All ingredients must be weighed accurately. The only items that may be measured by volume are water, milk, and eggs, which may be scaled at 1 pint per pound (or 1 liter per kilogram).

MIXING

Use the *dough arm* attachment when using a vertical mixer. Mix for the specified time.

The first two purposes of mixing—combining the ingredients into a dough and distributing the yeast—are accomplished during the first part of mixing. The remaining time is necessary to develop the gluten. Overmixed and undermixed doughs have poor volume and texture. (Review "Gluten Development," p. 761.)

It is necessary for you to learn to tell by sight and feel when a dough is thoroughly mixed. This can be done only through experience and with the guidance of your instructor. A properly developed dough feels smooth and elastic. A lean dough should not be sticky.

Sometimes it is necessary to add a little more flour if the dough hasn't lost its stickiness after most of the mixing time has passed.

Rich doughs are generally undermixed slightly because a greater tenderness is desired for these products.

Note: Mixing times given in bread formulas in this book are guidelines only. Small mixers might be damaged if they are run at too high a speed with a stiff dough. In such cases, use a lower speed and extend the mixing time as necessary. Depending on the mixer, developing a dough at first or slow speed requires about twice as much mixing time as at second speed. Follow the manufacturer's recommendations.

FERMENTATION

Fermentation is the process by which yeast acts on the sugars and starches in the dough to produce carbon dioxide gas and alcohol.

Procedure for Fermenting Yeast Doughs

1. Place the dough in a lightly oiled container and oil the surface to prevent a crust from forming. (This may not be necessary if humidity is high—about 75 percent.)

2. Cover the container lightly and let the dough rise at a temperature of about 80°F (27°C).

3. Fermentation is complete when dough has doubled in volume. If fermentation is complete, a dent will remain after the hand is pressed into the top of the dough.

Gluten becomes smoother and more elastic during fermentation. An underfermented dough does not develop proper volume, and the texture will be coarse. A dough that ferments too long or at too high a temperature becomes sticky, hard to work, and slightly sour.

An underfermented dough is called a *young dough.* An overfermented dough is called an *old dough.*

Doughs with weak gluten, such as rye doughs and rich doughs, are usually underfermented or "taken to the bench young."

PUNCHING

Punching is *not* hitting the dough with your fist. It is a method of deflating the dough that *expels carbon dioxide, redistributes the yeast* for further growth, *relaxes the gluten,* and *equalizes the temperature* throughout the dough.

Procedure for Punching Yeast Doughs

Pull up the dough on all sides, fold over the center, and press down. Then turn the dough upside down in the bowl.

A second fermentation and punching may or may not take place, depending on the product.

SCALING

Using a baker's scale, divide the dough into pieces of uniform weight, according to the product being made.

During scaling, allowance is made for weight loss due to evaporation of moisture in the oven. This weight loss is approximately 10 to 13 percent of the weight of the dough. Allow an extra 1½ to 2 ounces of dough for each 1 pound of baked bread, or 50 to 65 grams per 500 grams.

ROUNDING

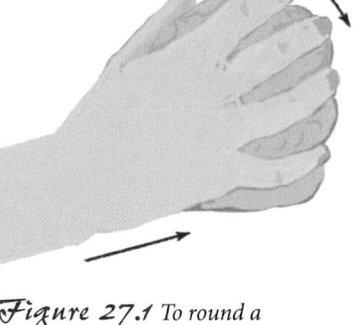

After scaling, the pieces of dough are shaped into smooth, round balls. This procedure forms a kind of skin by stretching the gluten on the outside of the dough into a smooth layer. Rounding simplifies later shaping of the dough and also helps retain gases produced by the yeast.

Your instructor will demonstrate rounding techniques. Machines are also available that divide and round portions of dough automatically. Figure 27.1 illustrates a piece of dough being rounded by hand.

Figure 27.1 To round a piece of dough, roll the dough on the bench with the palm of your hand. As you rotate the dough, use the edge of your hand to pinch the dough against the bench. This movement stretches the surface of the dough so that it is completely smooth except for a seam at the bottom where it was pinched together.

BENCHING

Rounded portions of dough are allowed to rest on the bench for 10 to 15 minutes. This relaxes the gluten to make shaping the dough easier. Also, *fermentation* continues during this time.

MAKEUP AND PANNING

The dough is shaped into loaves or rolls and placed in pans or on baking sheets. For all loaves and rolls, the seam must be centered on the bottom to avoid splitting during baking.

Breads and rolls take a great many forms. A variety of shapes and techniques is presented in the next section.

PROOFING

Proofing is a continuation of the process of yeast *fermentation*, which increases the volume of the shaped dough. Bakers use different terms so they can distinguish between fermentation of the mixed dough and proofing of the made-up product before baking. Proofing temperatures are generally higher than fermentation temperatures.

Procedure for Proofing Yeast Dough Products

Place the panned products in a proof box at 80° to 85°F (27° to 30°C) and about 70 to 80 percent humidity, as indicated in the formula. Proof until double in bulk.

If a proof box is not available, come as close to these conditions as you can by covering the products to retain moisture and setting them in a warm place.

Underproofing results in poor volume and dense texture. Overproofing results in coarse texture and some loss of flavor.

Rich doughs are slightly underproofed because their weaker gluten structure will not withstand much stretching.

BAKING

As you recall from the previous chapter, many changes take place in the dough during baking. The most important changes are these:

1. *Oven spring,* which is the rapid rising in the oven due to production and expansion of trapped gases as a result of the oven heat. The yeast is very active at first but is killed when the temperature inside the dough reaches 140°F (60°C).

2. Coagulation of proteins and gelatinization of starches. In other words, the product becomes firm and holds its shape.

3. Formation and browning of the crust.

Load the ovens carefully, as proofed doughs are fragile until they become set by baking.

Oven temperatures must be adjusted for the product being baked. Rolls spaced apart are baked at a higher temperature than large loaves so they become browned in the short time it takes to bake them. In general, lean breads such as those popular in North America are baked at 400°F to 425°F (200°C to 220°C), while some French breads and rolls are baked at 425° to 475°F (220° to 245°C). Rich doughs and sweet doughs are baked at a lower temperature, 350° to 400°F (175° to 200°C) because their fat, sugar, and milk content makes the crust brown faster.

Hard-crusted breads are baked with steam injected into the oven during the first part of the baking period. This aids the formation of a thin, crisp crust.

Rye breads also benefit from baking with steam for the first ten minutes.

A break on the side of the loaf is caused by continued rising after the crust is formed. To allow for this final expansion, hard-crusted breads are cut or *scored* before baking by making shallow slashes on the top of the loaf with a sharp knife or razor.

Small rolls bake completely without a break, so they are usually not scored.

Baking times vary considerably, depending on the product. A golden-brown crust color is the normal indication of doneness. Loaves sound hollow when thumped if they are done.

COOLING

After baking, bread must be removed from pans and cooled rapidly on racks to allow the escape of excess moisture and alcohol created during fermentation.

Rolls baked apart from each other on sheets may be left on them because they will get adequate air circulation.

If soft crusts are desired, breads may be brushed with melted shortening before cooling.

Do not cool in a draft, or crusts may crack.

STORING

Breads to be served within 8 hours may be left on racks. For longer storage, wrap cooled breads in moistureproof bags to retard staling. Bread must be thoroughly cool before wrapping, or moisture will collect inside the bags.

Wrapping and freezing maintains quality for longer periods. Refrigeration, on the other hand, increases staling.

Hard-crusted breads should not be wrapped (unless frozen), or the crusts will soften.

Because of the complexity of bread production, many things can go wrong. To remedy common bread faults, check Table 27.1 for possible causes and correct your procedures.

TABLE 27.1

Bread Faults and Their Causes

Fault	Causes
Shape	
Poor volume	Too much salt
	Too little yeast
	Weak flour
	Under- or overmixing
	Improper fermentation or proofing
	Oven too hot
Too much volume	Too little salt
	Too much yeast
	Too much dough scaled
	Overproofing
Poor shape	Too much liquid
	Improper molding or makeup
	Improper proofing
	Too much steam in oven
Split or burst crust	Overmixing
	Underfermentation
	Improper molding—seam not on bottom
	Oven too hot
	Not enough steam in oven
Texture and crumb	
Too dense or close grained	Too little yeast
	Underproofing
	Too much salt
	Too little liquid
Too coarse or open	Too much yeast
	Too much liquid
	Incorrect mixing time
	Improper fermentation
	Overproofing
	Pan too large
Streaked crumb	Improper mixing procedure
	Poor molding or makeup techniques
	Too much flour used for dusting
Poor texture or crumbly	Fermentation time too long or too short
	Overproofing
	Baking temperature too low
	Flour too weak
	Too little salt
Gray crumb	Fermentation time too long or temperature too high
Crust	
Too dark	Too much sugar or milk
	Underfermentation (young dough)
	Oven temperature too high
	Baking time too long
	Insufficient steam at beginning of baking
Too pale	Too little sugar or milk
	Overfermentation (old dough)
	Overproofing
	Oven temperature too low
	Baking time too short
	Too much steam in oven
Too thick	Too little sugar or fat
	Overfermentation (old dough)
	Baked too long and/or at too low a temperature
	Too little steam
Blisters on crust	Too much liquid
	Improper fermentation
	Improper shaping of loaves
Flavor	
Flat taste	Too little salt
Poor flavor	Inferior, spoiled, or rancid ingredients
	Poor bakeshop sanitation
	Under- or overfermentation

Dough Formulas and Techniques
Bread and Roll Formulas

The basic yeast dough mixing and baking methods discussed earlier in this chapter apply to the following formulas. Therefore, the methods are not repeated in detail for each formula. The basic procedures are indicated, and you should refer to the first part of this chapter if you need to refresh your memory for details.

Makeup techniques for loaves, rolls, and other items are described and illustrated after this recipe section.

 ## Hard Rolls

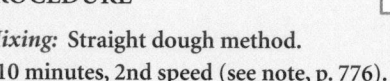

Ingredients	U.S.		Metric	Percentage
Water	1 lb	8 oz	700 g	55%
Yeast, fresh		1.5 oz	45 g	3.5%
Bread flour	2 lb	12 oz	1250 g	100%
Salt		1 oz	30 g	2.25%
Sugar		1 oz	30 g	2.25%
Shortening		1 oz	30 g	2.25%
Egg whites		1 oz	30 g	2.25%
Yield:	4 lb	9 oz	2115 g	167%

Per 1 roll:
Calories, 90; Protein, 3 g; Fat, 1 g (10% cal.); Cholesterol, 0 mg;
Carbohydrates, 17 g; Fiber, 1 g; Sodium, 200 mg.

PROCEDURE

Mixing: Straight dough method.
 10 minutes, 2nd speed (see note, p. 776).

Fermentation: About 1 hour at 80°F (27°C).

Scaling and makeup:
 Rolls—1 lb (500 g) per dozen.
 French-type loaf—18 oz (550 g) per loaf.
 See makeup techniques after recipe section.
 Dock after proofing. Brush with water.

Baking: 425°F (220°C). Steam for first 10 minutes.

 ## Soft Rolls

Ingredients	U.S.		Metric	Percentage
Water	1 lb	4 oz	600 g	45%
Yeast, fresh		2 oz	60 g	4.5%
Bread flour	2 lb	12 oz	1300 g	100%
Salt		1 oz	30 g	2.25%
Sugar		4 oz	125 g	9%
Nonfat milk powder		2 oz	60 g	4.5%
Shortening		2 oz	60 g	4.5%
Butter or margarine		2 oz	60 g	4.5%
Eggs		4 oz	125 g	9%
Yield:	5 lb	1 oz	2420 g	183%

Per 1 roll:
Calories, 100; Protein, 3 g; Fat, 2.5 g (21% cal.); Cholesterol, 10 mg;
Carbohydrates, 18 g; Fiber, 1 g; Sodium, 200 mg.

PROCEDURE

Mixing: Straight dough method.
 10–12 minutes at 2nd speed (see note, p. 776).

Fermentation: 1½ hours at 80°F (27°C).

Scaling and makeup:
 16–20 oz (450–600 g) per dozen rolls.
 See makeup techniques after recipe section.

Baking: 400°F (200°C).

French Bread

Ingredients	U.S.		Metric	Percentage
Water	1 lb	12 oz	875 g	58%
Yeast, fresh		1.5 oz	45 g	3%
Bread flour	3 lb		1500 g	100%
Salt		1 oz	30 g	2%
Yield:	4 lb	14 oz	2450 g	163%

PROCEDURE

Mixing: Straight dough method. Dissolve yeast in water before adding flour and salt.
3 minutes at 2nd speed; rest 2 minutes; 3 minutes more at 2nd speed (see note, p. 776).

Fermentation: 1½ hours at 80°F (27°C).
Punch down.
1 hour at 80°F (27°C).

Scaling and makeup: French loaves—12 oz (350 g).
Round loaves—18 oz (550 g).
Rolls—16–20 oz (450–600 g) per dozen.
See makeup techniques after recipe section.

Baking: 400°F (200°C). Steam for first 10 minutes.

Per 1 ounce:
Calories, 60; Protein, 2 g; Fat, .5 g (7% cal.); Cholesterol, 0 mg;
Carbohydrates, 13 g; Fiber, 0 g; Sodium, 140 mg.

 ## White Pan Bread

Ingredients	U.S.		Metric	Percentage
Water	1 lb	8 oz	750 g	60%
Yeast, fresh		1.5 oz	45 g	3.75%
Bread flour	2 lb	8 oz	1250 g	100%
Salt		1 oz	30 g	2.5%
Sugar		1.5 oz	45 g	3.75%
Nonfat milk powder		2 oz	60 g	5%
Shortening		1.5 oz	45 g	3.75%
Yield:	4 lb	7 oz	2225 g	178%

PROCEDURE

Mixing: Straight dough method.
10 minutes at 2nd speed (see note, p. 776).

Fermentation:
1 hour at 80°F (27°C).

Makeup: Pan loaves. See makeup techniques after recipe section.

Baking: 400°F (200°C).

Per 1 ounce:
Calories, 70; Protein, 2 g; Fat, 1 g (13% cal.); Cholesterol, 0 mg;
Carbohydrates, 13 g; Fiber, 0 g; Sodium, 160 mg.

VARIATION

Whole Wheat Bread

Prepare basic White Pan Bread using

Bread flour	1 lb		500 g	40%
Whole wheat flour	1 lb	8 oz	750 g	60%

 ## Rye Bread and Rolls

Ingredients	U.S.		Metric	Percentage
Water	1 lb	8 oz	750 g	60%
Yeast, fresh		1.5 oz	45 g	3.75%
Rye flour	1 lb		500 g	40%
Bread flour	1 lb	8 oz	750 g	60%
Salt		1 oz	30 g	2.5%
Shortening		1 oz	30 g	2.5%
Molasses		1 oz	30 g	2.5%
Caraway seeds		0.5 oz	15 g	1.25%
Yield:	4 lb	4 oz	2150 g	172%

PROCEDURE

Mixing: Straight dough method.
5–6 minutes at 2nd speed (see note, p. 776).

Fermentation:
1 hour at 80°F (27°C).

Scaling and makeup:
1 lb (500 g) per pan loaf.
1 lb (500 g) per dozen rolls.
See makeup techniques after recipe section.

Baking:
400°F (200°C). Steam for first 10 minutes.

Per 1 ounce:
Calories, 60; Protein, 2 g; Fat, 1 g (14% cal.); Cholesterol, 0 mg;
Carbohydrates, 12 g; Fiber, 2 g; Sodium, 160 mg.

Focaccia

Ingredients	U.S.		Metric	Percentage
Water	1 lb	8 oz	750 g	60%
Yeast, fresh		1 oz	35 g	2.75%
Bread flour	2 lb	8 oz	1250 g	100%
Salt		0.7 oz (3½ tsp)	20 g	1.75%
Sugar		0.2 oz (1¼ tsp)	6 g	0.5%
Olive oil		2 oz	60 g	5%
Yield:	4 lb	3 oz	2121 g	170%

Per 1 ounce:
Calories, 70; Protein, 2 g; Fat, 1 g (13% cal.); Cholesterol, 0 mg;
Carbohydrates, 12 g; Fiber, 1 g; Sodium, 115 mg.

PROCEDURE

Mixing: Straight dough method.
  8 minutes at first speed (see note, p. 776).

Fermentation: 1½ hours at 80°F (27°C) or 2 hours at 75°F
  (24°C).

Makeup: Oil sheet pans with olive oil. Roll out dough to about
  ¾ inch (2 cm) thick and place in pans (see Figure 27.2).
  Brush tops generously with olive oil. After proofing, press
  dimples into the dough at approximately 3-inch (8-cm)
  intervals.

Baking: 425°F (220°C). Steam for first 10 minutes.

VARIATIONS

Rosemary Focaccia

After pressing in the dimples, sprinkle the top with rosemary (preferably fresh) and coarse salt.

Olive Focaccia

Mix 30% (12 oz/375 g) chopped oil-cured black olives into the dough.

Figure 27.2 Focaccia.

(a) Roll and stretch the dough into a rectangle large enough to fill the pan.

(b) Place the dough in the pan. Top with olive oil. With the fingertips, poke holes heavily at regular intervals.

(c) Top with the desired topping, such as fresh herbs and coarse salt.

Brioche

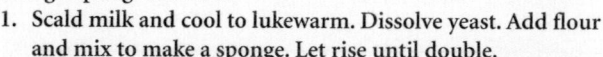

Ingredients	U.S.		Metric	Percentage
Milk		8 oz	250 g	20%
Yeast, fresh		2 oz	60 g	5%
Bread flour		8 oz	250 g	20%
Eggs	1 lb	4 oz	625 g	50%
Bread flour	2 lb		1000 g	80%
Sugar		2 oz	60 g	5%
Salt		0.5 oz	15 g	1.25%
Butter, softened	1 lb	8 oz	750 g	60%
Yield:	6 lb		3010 g	241%

Per 1 roll:
Calories, 160; Protein, 4 g; Fat, 10 g (56% cal.); Cholesterol, 60 mg;
Carbohydrates, 14 g; Fiber, 0 g; Sodium, 190 mg.

PROCEDURE

Mixing: Sponge method:
1. Scald milk and cool to lukewarm. Dissolve yeast. Add flour
   and mix to make a sponge. Let rise until double.
2. Gradually mix in eggs and then dry ingredients (using the
   paddle attachment) to make a soft dough.
3. Beat in butter, a little at a time, until completely absorbed
   and dough is smooth. Dough will be very soft and sticky.

Fermentation: Cover with plastic film and place in retarder
  overnight.

Makeup: 1½ oz (50 g) per roll.
  See makeup techniques after recipe section. Dough is very
  soft and is easiest to make up when chilled.
  Egg wash after proofing.

Baking: 400°F (200°C).

VARIATION

To make the dough less sticky and less difficult to handle, reduce the butter to 35–50% (14–20 oz/450–625 g). This adjustment also reduces cost. However, the brioche will not be as rich and delicate.

Sweet Roll Dough

Ingredients	U.S.		Metric	Percentage
Milk	1 lb		500 g	40%
Yeast, fresh		3 oz	100 g	7.5%
Butter/margarine/ shortening (see note)		8 oz	250 g	20%
Sugar		8 oz	250 g	20%
Salt		0.5 oz	15 g	1.25%
Eggs		6 oz	175 g	15%
Bread flour	1 lb 12 oz		875 g	70%
Pastry flour		12 oz	375 g	30%
Yield:	5 lb 1 oz		2540 g	203%

Per 1 ounce:
Calories, 90; Protein, 2 g; Fat, 3 g (30% cal.); Cholesterol, 15 mg;
Carbohydrates, 14 g; Fiber, 1 g; Sodium, 95 mg.

PROCEDURE

Mixing: Modified straight dough method:
1. Scald milk. Cool to lukewarm. Dissolve yeast in milk.
2. Mix fat, sugar, and salt until smooth, using paddle. Beat in eggs.
3. Add liquid and flour. With dough arm, mix 4 minutes at 2nd speed.

Fermentation: 1½ hours at 80°F (27°C).

Makeup: See makeup techniques after recipe section.

Baking: 375°F (190°C).

Note: Any of the fats listed may be used either alone or in combination.

VARIATION

Raised Doughnuts

Prepare basic sweet roll dough but reduce the fat and sugar by half. Mace, nutmeg, or other spices may be added.

Scaling: 1½ oz (50 g) each.
Give full proof.
Frying: 360°F (182°C).
Drain. Roll in cinnamon sugar or 6X sugar when cool.

Rolled-In Doughs: Danish Pastry and Croissants

Rolled-in doughs contain many layers of fat sandwiched between layers of dough. These layers create the flakiness that you are familiar with in Danish pastry.

Two basic kinds of rolled-in yeast doughs are made in the bakeshop:

- sweet: Danish pastry
- nonsweet: croissants

Rolled-in doughs are mixed only slightly because the rolling-in procedure continues to develop the gluten.

Butter is the preferred fat for flavor and the melt-in-the-mouth quality of rolled-in doughs. Specially formulated shortenings are available when lower cost and greater ease of handling are more important considerations.

Danish Pastry

Ingredients	U.S.		Metric	Percentage
Milk	1 lb		400 g	40%
Yeast, fresh		2.5 oz	65 g	6.25%
Butter		5 oz	125 g	12.5%
Sugar		6 oz	150 g	15%
Salt		0.5 oz	12 g	1.25%
Cardamom		1 tsp	2 g (5 mL)	0.2%
Eggs		8 oz	200 g	20%
Egg yolks		2 oz	50 g	5%
Bread flour	2 lb		800 g	80%
Cake flour		8 oz	200 g	20%
Butter	1 lb	4 oz	500 g	50%
Yield:	6 lb	4 oz	2499 g	250%

Per 1 ounce:
Calories, 110, Protein, 2 g; Fat, 6 g (53% cal.); Cholesterol, 35 mg;
Carbohydrates, 10 g; Fiber, 0 g; Sodium, 120 mg.

PROCEDURE

Mixing: Modified straight dough method:
1. Scald milk. Cool to lukewarm. Dissolve yeast in milk.
2. Mix butter, sugar, salt, and spice until smooth, using paddle. Beat in eggs.
3. Add liquid (from step 1) and flour. With dough arm, mix 3–4 minutes on 2nd speed.
4. Rest in retarder 20–30 minutes.
5. Roll in remaining butter and give 3 three-folds, as shown in Figure 27.3.

Makeup: See makeup techniques after recipe section.

Proofing: 90°F (32°C) with little steam. Egg wash after proofing.

Baking: 375°F (190°C).

Figure 27.3 Rolling-in procedure for Danish and croissant dough.

(a) Roll the dough into a rectangle about 3 times as long as it is wide and ½ to ¾ inch (1 to 2 cm) thick. Smear the butter over two-thirds of the length of the dough, leaving a margin at the edges.

(b) Fold the unbuttered third over the center third.

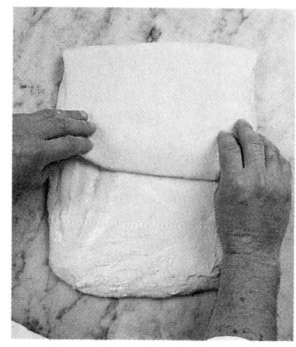

(c) Fold the remaining third on top. Rest the dough in the retarder (under refrigeration) for 20 to 30 minutes to allow the gluten to relax.

(d) Place the dough on the bench at right angles to its position in step (c). Take this step before each rolling-out of the dough so that the gluten is stretched in all directions, not just lengthwise. Roll the dough into a rectangle.

(e) Fold again into thirds by first folding the top third over the center. Be sure to brush off excess dusting flour from between the folds.

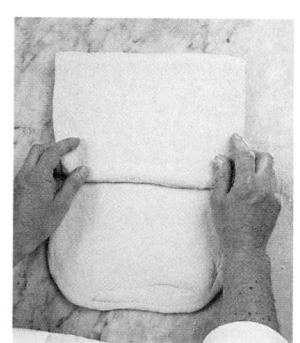

(f) Fold over the remaining third. You have now completed the first turn or fold—incorporating the butter doesn't count as a turn. Press one finger in the dough near the end to make one indentation. This indicates "1 turn" to anyone who may have to take up where you left off, or to you if you have several batches going. Refrigerate the dough for 20 to 30 minutes to relax the gluten. Repeat the above rolling and folding procedures for a second and third turn, resting the dough between turns. Mark the number of turns in the dough with two or three fingers. After the third turn, rest the dough in the retarder for several hours or overnight. Cover it with plastic film to prevent crusting. The dough is then ready for makeup.

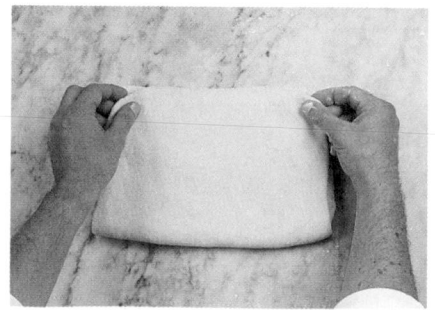

Croissants

Ingredients	U.S.		Metric	Percentage
Milk	1 lb		450 g	57%
Yeast, fresh		1 oz	30 g	4%
Sugar		1 oz	30 g	4%
Salt		0.5 oz	15 g	2%
Butter, soft		3 oz	80 g	10%
Bread flour	1 lb	12 oz	800 g	100%
Butter	1 lb		450 g	57%
Yield:	4 lb	1 oz	1855 g	234%

Per 1 ounce:
Calories, 110; Protein, 2 g; Fat, 7 g (57% cal.); Cholesterol, 20 mg;
Carbohydrates, 10 g; Fiber, 0 g; Sodium, 160 mg.

PROCEDURE

Mixing: Straight dough method.
Scald milk, cool to lukewarm, and dissolve yeast. Add remaining ingredients except last 1 lb (450 g) butter. Mix into a smooth dough. Do not overmix.

Fermentation: 1 hour at 80°F (27°C).
Punch down, spread out on flat pan, and rest in retarder 30 minutes.
Roll in last amount of butter and give 3 three-folds (see Figure 27.3). Rest in retarder overnight.

Makeup: See Figure 27.20 on page 793.

Proofing: 80°F (27°C).
Egg wash after proofing.

Baking: 400°F (200°C).

Rolling-In Procedure for Danish and Croissant Dough

The rolling-in procedure has two parts.

1. Enclosing the fat in the dough.
In the method illustrated in Figure 27.3, the fat is spotted on two-thirds of the dough and the dough is folded in thirds like a business letter. This results in five layers: three layers of dough and two layers of fat.

2. Rolling out and folding the dough to increase the number of layers.
In these doughs, we use a *simple fold*, or *three-fold*, which means that we fold the dough in thirds. Each complete rolling and folding step is called a *turn*. We give the dough three turns, creating over 100 layers of dough and fat.

In Chapter 31, you will learn an even more complex rolling-in procedure used for puff pastry, which is leavened only by steam, not by yeast. This procedure produces over 1000 layers!

FILLINGS AND TOPPINGS FOR SWEET DOUGH PRODUCTS AND DANISH

Cinnamon Sugar

Yield: about 1 lb (500 g)

U.S.	Metric	Ingredients	PROCEDURE
1 lb	500 g	Sugar	Stir together thoroughly.
0.5 oz	15 g	Cinnamon	

Per 1 ounce:
Calories, 110; Protein, 0 g; Fat, 0 g (0% cal.); Cholesterol, 0 mg;
Carbohydrates, 0 g; Fiber, 0 g; Sodium, 0 mg.

Streusel or Crumb Topping

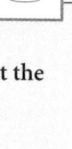

Yield: 2 lb (1 kg)

U.S.	Metric	Ingredients	PROCEDURE
8 oz	250 g	Butter and/or shortening	Rub all ingredients together until crumbly.
5 oz	150 g	Granulated sugar	
4 oz	120 g	Brown sugar	
½–1 tsp	2–5 mL	Cinnamon or mace	
½ tsp	2 mL	Salt	
1 lb	500 g	Pastry flour	

Per 1 ounce:
Calories, 130; Protein, 1 g; Fat, 6 g (40% cal.); Cholesterol, 15 mg;
Carbohydrates, 19 g; Fiber, 2 g; Sodium, 85 mg.

VARIATION

Nut Streusel

Add 4 oz (125 g) finely chopped nuts to basic mixture.

 ## Clear Glaze for Coffee Cakes and Danish

Yield: 2 lb (1 kg)

U.S.	Metric	Ingredients	PROCEDURE
1 cup	250 mL	Water	1. Mix together and bring to a boil. Stir to ensure that the sugar is completely dissolved.
1 lb	500 g	Light corn syrup	
8 oz	250 g	Granulated sugar	2. Brush on while hot.

Per 1 ounce:
Calories, 70; Protein, 0 g; Fat, 0 g (0% cal.); Cholesterol, 0 mg;
Carbohydrates, 18 g; Fiber, 0 g; Sodium, 15 mg.

 ## Date, Prune, or Apricot Filling

Yield: 3 lb (1.5 kg)

U.S.	Metric	Ingredients	PROCEDURE
2 lb	1 kg	Dates, prunes (pitted), or dried apricots	1. Chop dried fruit very fine or pass through a grinder.
6 oz	200 g	Sugar	2. Combine all ingredients in a saucepan. Bring to a boil. Simmer and stir until thick and smooth, about 10 minutes.
1 pt	500 mL	Water	3. Cool before using.

Per 1 ounce:
Calories, 65; Protein, 0 g; Fat, 0 g (0% cal.); Cholesterol, 0 mg;
Carbohydrates, 17 g; Fiber, 1 g; Sodium, 0 mg.

Almond Filling

Yield: 3 lb (1500 g)

U.S.	Metric	Ingredients	PROCEDURE
1 lb	500 g	Almond paste	1. With paddle attachment, mix almond paste and sugar at low speed until evenly mixed.
1 lb	500 g	Sugar	
8 oz	250 g	Butter and/or shortening	2. Mix in fat and flour until smooth.
4 oz	125 g	Pastry or cake flour	3. Beat in eggs, a little at a time, until smooth.
4 oz	125 g	Eggs	

Per 1 ounce:
Calories, 130; Protein, 1 g; Fat, 7 g (48% cal.); Cholesterol, 20 mg;
Carbohydrates, 16 g; Fiber, 1 g; Sodium, 45 mg.

Cheese Filling

Yield: 4½ lb (2250 g)

U.S.	Metric	Ingredients	PROCEDURE
2 lb	1 kg	Baker's cheese	1. Using the paddle attachment, cream the cheese, sugar, and salt until smooth.
10 oz	300 g	Sugar	
0.25 oz	6 mL	Salt	
6 oz	200 g	Eggs	2. Add the eggs, butter, vanilla. Blend in.
6 oz	200 g	Butter and/or shortening, soft	
1 tbsp	15 mL	Vanilla	
3 oz	100 g	Cake flour	3. Add the cake flour. Blend until just absorbed.
6 oz or more	200 g or more	Milk	4. Add the milk, a little at a time, adding just enough to bring the mixture to a smooth, spreadable consistency.
8 oz	250 g	Raisins (optional)	5. Stir in the raisins, if desired.

Per 1 ounce:
Calories, 60; Protein, 3 g; Fat, 3.5 g (50% cal.); Cholesterol, 20 mg;
Carbohydrates, 5 g; Fiber, 0 g; Sodium, 110 mg.

Makeup Techniques

The object of yeast dough makeup techniques is to shape the dough into rolls or loaves that bake properly and have an attractive appearance. When you shape a roll or loaf correctly, you stretch the gluten strands on the surface into a kind of smooth skin. This tight gluten surface holds the item in shape. This is especially important for loaves and rolls that are baked freestanding, not in pans.

Units that are not made up correctly develop irregular shapes and splits and may flatten out on the pan.

Following are a few of the many makeup techniques for yeast doughs.

HARD ROLLS AND BREADS

Round Rolls

1. Scale the dough as indicated in the recipes, usually 1 pound (450 g) per dozen.
2. Round each unit as shown in Figure 27.4.
3. Place rolls 2 inches (5 cm) apart on sheet pans sprinkled with cornmeal.

Figure 27.4 Rounding small rolls.

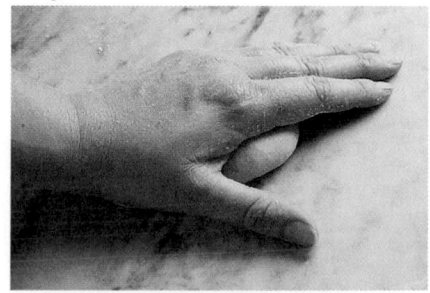

(a) Holding the palm of the hand fairly flat, roll the dough in a tight circle on the workbench. Do not use too much flour for dusting, as the dough must stick to the bench a little for the technique to work.

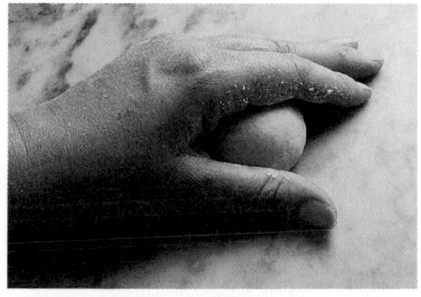

(b) As the ball of dough takes on a round shape, gradually cup your hand.

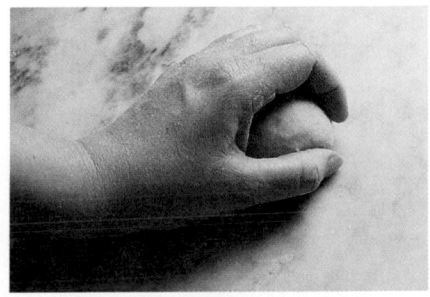

(c) The finished ball of dough should have a smooth surface, except for a slight pucker on the bottom.

Round Loaves

1. Flatten the rounded, benched dough into a circle. Fold the four sides over the center, then round again.
2. Place on sheet pans sprinkled with cornmeal.

Club Rolls

1. Make up as shown in Figure 27.5.
2. Place 2 inches (5 cm) apart on sheet pans sprinkled with cornmeal.

Crescent Rolls

1. Scale dough into 20-ounce (600-g) units.
2. After rounding and benching, flatten the dough and roll it out into a circle 12 inches (30 cm) across.
3. With a pastry wheel, cut the dough circle into 12 equal wedges or triangles. (Alternative method: For large quantities of dough, roll it out into a rectangle and cut like croissant dough. See Figure 27.20 on p. 793.)
4. Roll the triangles into crescents using the same technique as for croissants (see Figure 27.20 on p. 793).
   Note: If using soft roll dough, brush the dough with butter before cutting it into triangles. Do not use any fat with hard roll doughs.

French-type Loaves

1. Scale the dough into units weighing 12 to 18 ounces (350 to 500 g).
2. Make up as shown in Figure 27.6.

Figure 27.5 Making club rolls.

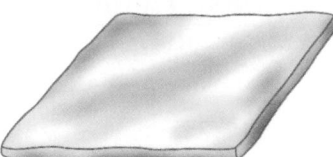

(a) Flatten the piece of dough roughly into a rectangle.

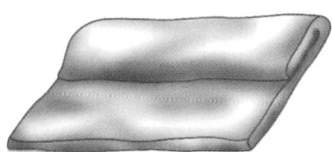

(b) Begin to roll the dough by folding over the back edge of the rectangle. Press the seam firmly with your fingertips.

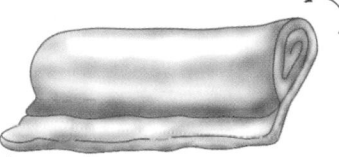

(c) Continue to roll the dough, always pressing the seam firmly after each turn. As you roll the dough, the front edge will appear to shrink. Stretch the front corners as shown by the arrows to keep the width uniform.

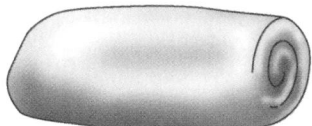

(d) When the roll is finished, seal the seam well so that you have a tight roll.

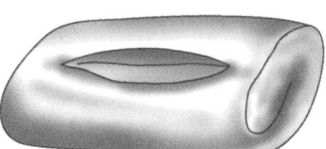

(e) Dock the proofed roll with a single slash to give the baked roll this appearance.

Figure 27.6 Making French-type loaves.

(a) Flatten the rounded, relaxed dough with your hands or with a rolling pin. Then stretch the oval with the hands to lengthen it.

(b) Roll the dough tightly.

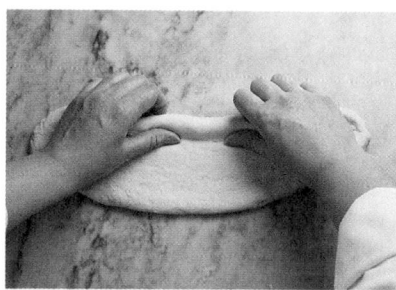

(c) Seal the seam well. If a longer, thinner loaf is required, relax the rolled units again for a few minutes. Flatten them with your palms and stretch the dough lightly to increase its length. Once again, roll tightly and seal the seam. Roll the loaf on the bench under your palms to make it even and to stretch it to the desired shape and length.

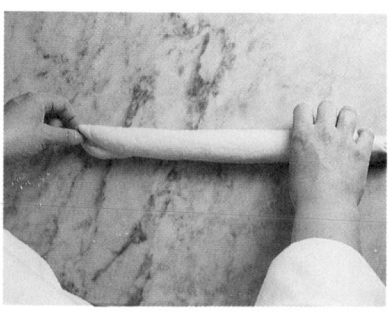

(d) Place the dough seam-side down on pans dusted with cornmeal. Proofing the loaves on special trough-shaped pans maintains their shape. Proof. Wash with water. Slash with diagonal cuts or with one lengthwise cut; this can be done before or after proofing.

SOFT ROLL DOUGHS

Tied or Knotted Rolls

1. Scale dough to 16 to 20 ounces (450 to 600 g) per dozen.

2. With the palm of the hand, roll each unit on the workbench into a strip or rope of dough.

3. Tie rolls as shown:

   Single-knot rolls: Figure 27.7
   Double-knot rolls: Figure 27.8
   Braided rolls: Figure 27.9
   Figure eight rolls: Figure 27.10

4. Place 2 inches (5 cm) apart on greased baking sheets.

5. Egg wash after proofing.

Pan Rolls

1. Scale dough to 16 to 20 ounces (450 to 600 g) per dozen.

2. Make up as for round hard rolls.

3. Place on greased pans ½ inch (1 cm) apart.

Parker House Rolls

1. Scale dough to 16 to 20 ounces (450 to 600 g) per dozen.

2. Make up as shown in Figure 27.11.

3. Place on greased baking sheet ½ inch (1 cm) apart.

Cloverleaf Rolls

1. Scale dough to 16 to 20 ounces (450 to 600 g) per dozen.

2. Make up and pan as shown in Figure 27.12.

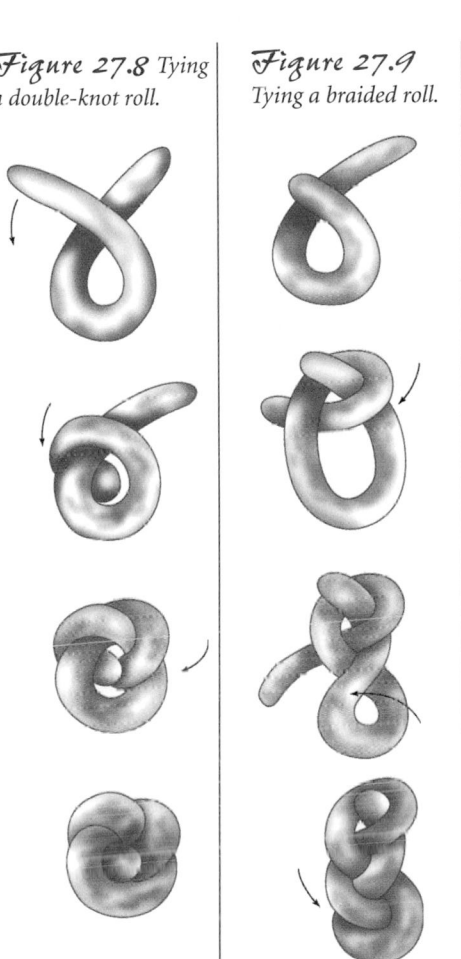

Figure 27.7 Tying a single-knot roll.

Figure 27.8 Tying a double-knot roll.

Figure 27.9 Tying a braided roll.

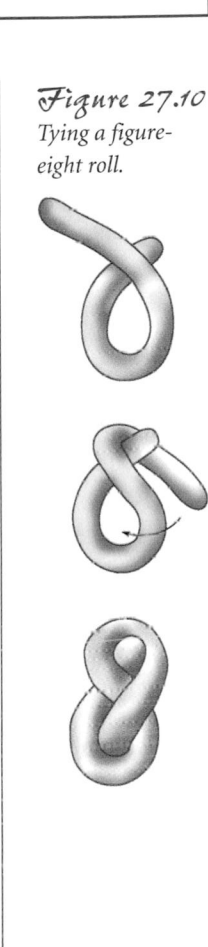

Figure 27.10 Tying a figure-eight roll.

Figure 27.11 Parker House rolls.

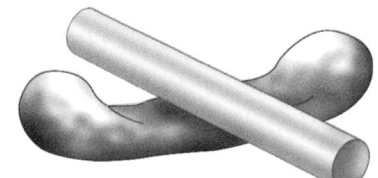

(a) Round the scaled piece of dough.

(b) Flatten the center of the dough with a thin rolling pin as shown.

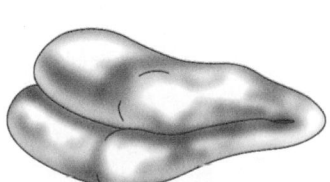

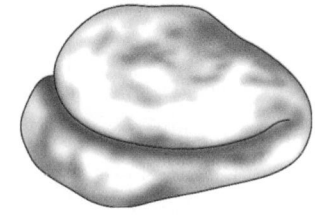

(c) Fold the dough over and press down on the folded edge to make a crease.

(d) The baked roll has this shape.

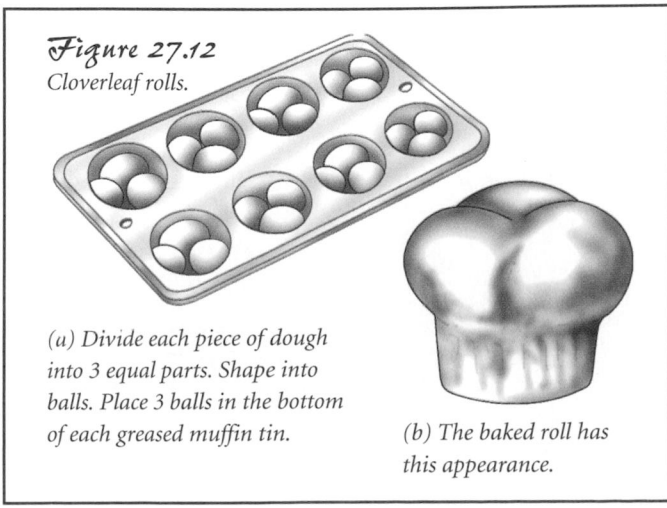

Figure 27.12 Cloverleaf rolls.

(a) Divide each piece of dough into 3 equal parts. Shape into balls. Place 3 balls in the bottom of each greased muffin tin.

(b) The baked roll has this appearance.

Figure 27.13 Butterflake rolls.

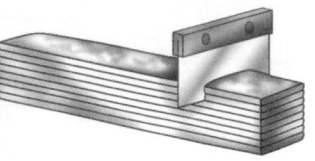

(b) Stack 6 strips. Cut into pieces 1½ inches (3.5 cm) long.

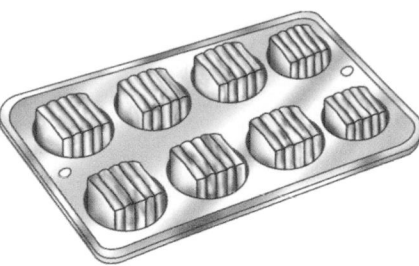

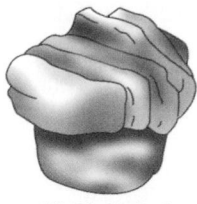

(a) Roll the dough into a thin rectangle. Brush with melted butter. Cut into strips 1 inch (2.5 cm) wide.

(c) Place the pieces on end in greased muffin tins. Proof.

(d) The baked rolls have this appearance.

Figure 27.14 Pan loaves.

(a) Start with the rounded, benched dough. Flatten it with the palms of the hands.

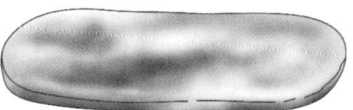

(b) Stretch it into a long rectangle.

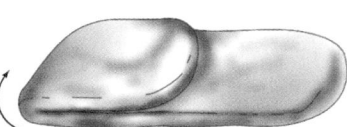

(c, d) Fold into thirds.

(e) Roll the dough into a tight roll of the same length as the pan it is to be baked in. Seal the seam well and place the dough seam side down in the greased pan.

Butterflake Rolls

Make up as shown in Figure 27.13.

PAN LOAVES

Shaping dough into loaves to be baked in loaf pans is illustrated in Figure 27.14.

BRIOCHE

Brioche dough may be made into many shapes, but the traditional shape is shown in Figure 27.15.

SWEET DOUGH PRODUCTS

Note: Many sweet dough products may be glazed with Clear Glaze (p. 786) and/or iced with Flat Icing (p. 819) after baking. Flat icing is drizzled over the cooled products, so that it doesn't cover them completely.

Cinnamon Rolls

1. Scale dough into 20-ounce (600-g) units. On a floured board, roll each piece of dough into a rectangle measuring 9 × 12 inches and about ¼ inch thick (23 × 30 × 6 mm).
2. Brush with butter and sprinkle with 2 ounces (60 g) cinnamon sugar.
3. Roll up like a jelly roll 12 inches (30 cm) long, as shown in Figure 27.16.
4. Cut into 1-inch (2.5-cm) rolls.
5. Place cut side down in greased muffin tins or on greased sheet pans. One full-size pan, 18 × 26 inches (46 × 66 cm), holds 48 rolls placed 6 by 8.

For variations on the basic cinnamon roll shape, see Figure 27.16.

Cinnamon Raisin Rolls

Prepare like cinnamon rolls, but add 2 ounces (60 g) raisins to the filling.

Figure 27.15 Making brioche.

(a) For a small brioche, roll the dough into a round piece.

(b) Using the edge of your hand, pinch off about one-fourth of the dough without detaching it. Roll the dough on the bench so that both parts are round.

(c) Place the dough in the tin, large end first. With your fingertips, press the small ball into the larger one as shown.

(d) For large brioche, separate the two parts of the dough. Place the large ball in the tin and make a hole in the center. Form the smaller ball into a pear shape and fit it into the hole.

(e) A baked large brioche.

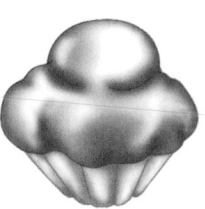

Figure 27.16 The filled dough roll is the starting point for a variety of sweet dough and Danish products.

(a) Roll the dough into a rectangle. Brush with butter and sprinkle with cinnamon sugar, or spread with desired filling.

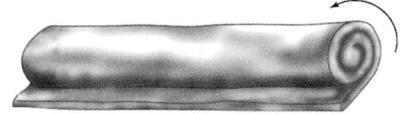

(b) Roll up like a jelly roll.

(c) For cinnamon rolls and similar products, cut off pieces 1 inch (2.5 cm) in length.

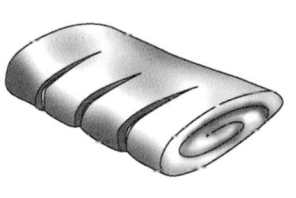

(d) For combs or bear claws, make the roll thinner and cut it into longer pieces. Flatten slightly and cut partway through each piece in 3 to 6 places as shown. Leave straight or bend into a curve to open the cuts.

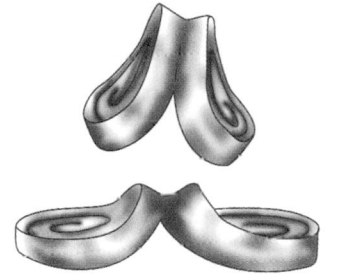

(e) For figure-eight cinnamon rolls, cut the rolls almost through as shown. Open them and lay them flat on the baking sheet.

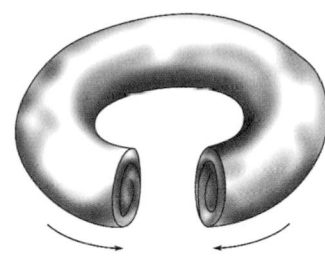

(f) To make a wreath-shaped coffee cake, join the ends of the dough roll to make a circle.

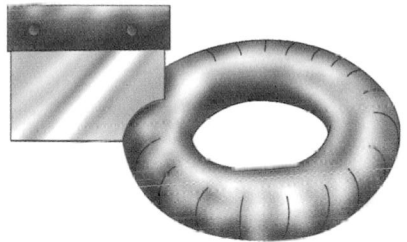

(g) Cut partway through the dough at 1-inch (2.5-cm) intervals as shown.

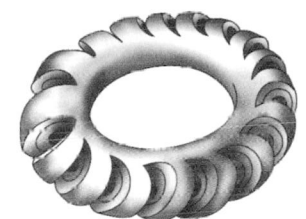

(h) Twist each segment outward to open the cuts.

Caramel Rolls

1. Prepare like cinnamon rolls.
2. Before panning, spread the bottoms of the pans or muffin tins with the following mixture. Use about 1 ounce (30 g) of the mixture per roll.

    2 lb (1 kg) brown sugar
    8 oz (250 g) corn syrup
    10 oz (300 g) butter
    4 oz (125 mL) water

    Cream the sugar, corn syrup, and butter. Beat in the water.

    Quantities given are enough for 1 sheet pan of 48 rolls.

Caramel Nut Rolls or Pecan Rolls

Prepare like caramel rolls, but sprinkle the sugar-butter mixture in the pans with chopped nuts or pecan halves before placing the rolls in the pans.

Wreath Coffee Cake

1. Make a filled dough roll as for cinnamon rolls, but do not cut it into separate pieces. Other fillings, such as prune or date, may be used instead of butter and cinnamon sugar.
2. Shape the roll into a circle as shown in Figure 27.16f–h. Place on a greased baking sheet. Cut and shape as shown in the illustration.
3. Egg wash after proofing.

Figure 27.17 Braided coffee cake.

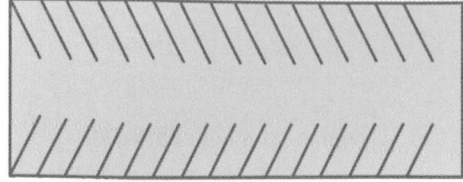

(a) Roll the dough into a rectangle 8 inches (20 cm) wide, 12 to 18 inches (30 to 46 cm) long, and less than ¼ inch (6 mm) thick. Make diagonal cuts from the outer edges 1 inch (2.5 cm) apart and 3 inches (7.5 cm) long, as shown.

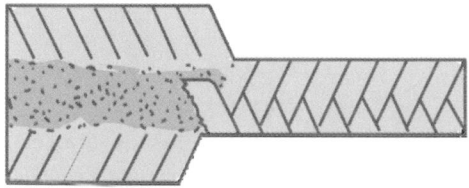

(b) Spread the filling down the center and fold alternate strips of dough over the filling.

Filled Coffee Cake

1. Scale dough into 12-oz (350-g) units.
2. Roll each unit into a rectangle measuring 9 × 18 inches (23 × 46 cm).
3. Spread half of each rectangle with desired filling, using about 6 ounces (175 g) filling.
4. Fold the unspread half over the spread half to make a 9-inch (23-cm) square.
5. Place in greased 9-inch (23-cm) square pan.
6. Sprinkle with Streusel Topping (p. 786), about 4 ounces (125 g) per pan.
7. Proof and bake.

Braided Coffee Cake

Make up as shown in Figure 27.17. Egg wash after proofing.

ROLLED-IN DOUGH PRODUCTS

Danish Rolls and Coffee Cakes

Most of the techniques given in the previous section for sweet dough products may be used for Danish pastry.

Two additional methods are illustrated in Figures 27.18 and 27.19.

Baked Danish dough products are frequently glazed with Clear Glaze (p. 786) and/or iced with Flat Icing (p. 819).

Croissants

The method for making up croissants is illustrated in Figure 27.20.

Figure 27.18 Spiral Danish rolls.

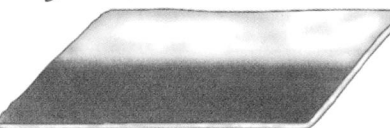

(a) Roll the dough into a rectangle 16 inches (40 cm) wide and less than ¼ inch (6 mm) thick. (The length of the rectangle depends on the quantity of dough.) Brush the dough with melted butter. Sprinkle half of it with cinnamon sugar as shown.

(b) Fold the unsugared half over the sugared half. You now have a rectangle 8 inches (20 cm) wide. Roll the dough gently with a rolling pin to press the layers together.

(c) Cut the dough into strips ½ inch (1 cm) wide.

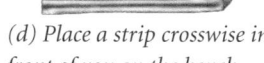

(d) Place a strip crosswise in front of you on the bench.

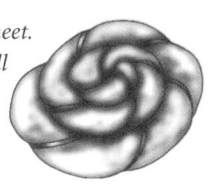

(e) With the palms of your hands on the ends of the strip, roll one end toward you and the other away from you so that the strip twists. Stretch the strip slightly as you twist it.

(f) Curl the strip into a spiral shape on the baking sheet. Tuck the end underneath and pinch it against the roll to seal it in place. If desired, press a hollow in the center of the roll and place a spoonful of filling (such as a fruit filling) in the center.

Figure 27.19 Danish pockets.

(a) Roll the dough to less than ¼ inch (6 mm) thick and cut into 5-inch (13-cm) squares. Place desired filling on the center of each square. Brush the corners lightly with water—this helps them seal when pressed together.

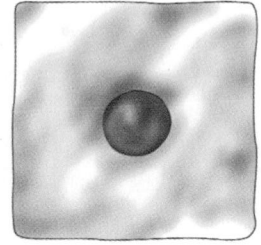

(b) Fold two opposite corners over the center. Press down firmly to seal them. (If desired, rolls may be left in this shape.)

(c) Fold the other two corners over the center and again press them firmly together.

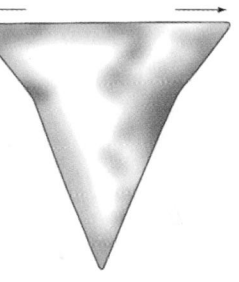

Figure 27.20 Making croissants.

(a) Roll the dough into a rectangle 10 inches (26 cm) wide and about ⅛ inch (3 mm) thick. (The length depends on the amount of dough used.)

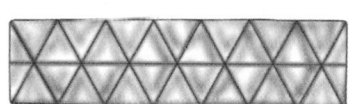

(b) Cut into triangles as shown. Special roller cutters are available that do this quickly.

(c) Place a triangle on the bench in front of you. Stretch the back corners outward slightly, as shown by the arrows.

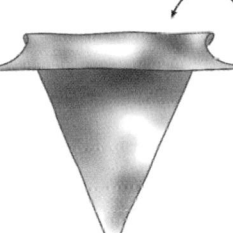

(d) Begin to roll the dough toward the point.

(e) Stretch the point of the triangle slightly as you roll it.

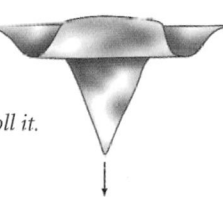

(f) Finish rolling the dough.

(g) Bend the roll into a crescent shape. The point of the triangle must be toward the inside of the crescent and tucked under the roll so that it won't pop up during baking.

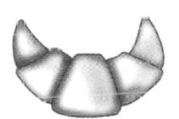

Terms for Review

lean dough	sponge method	punching
rolled-in dough	fermentation	proofing
straight dough method	young and old doughs	oven spring

Questions for Discussion

1. What are the three major purposes of mixing yeast doughs?

2. Explain the difference in procedure between the straight dough method and the sponge method. How is the straight dough method sometimes modified for sweet doughs, and why is this necessary?

3. What are the 12 steps in the production of yeast products? Explain each briefly.

4. Judging from what you know about fermentation of doughs, do you think it might be necessary for bakers to modify procedures from winter to summer? How?

5. As you know, butter is very hard when cold and melts easily at warm temperatures. What precautions do you think are necessary when using butter as the rolling-in fat for Danish pastry

chapter 28

Quick Breads

uick breads are the perfect solution for those operations that want to offer their patrons fresh, homemade bread products but can't justify the labor cost of making yeast breads. Also, quick breads have the advantage of being easily made in almost unlimited varieties, using such ingredients as whole wheat flour, rye flour, cornmeal, bran, oatmeal, and many kinds of fruits, nuts, and spices.

As their name implies, quick breads are quick to make. Because they are leavened by chemical leaveners and steam, not by yeast, no fermentation time is necessary. And because they are usually tender products with little gluten development, mixing them takes just a few minutes.

Although prepared biscuit and muffin mixes are available, the only extra work that making these products from scratch requires is the time to scale a few extra ingredients. With a careful and imaginative selection of ingredients and an understanding of basic mixing methods, you can create superior products.

You may already have studied two kinds of quick breads in the breakfast chapter: pancakes and waffles. In this chapter, we present two basic mixing methods and apply them to biscuits, muffins, quick loaf breads and coffee cakes, and corn breads. In addition, we discuss popovers, which are leavened by steam only.

After reading this chapter, you should be able to

1. Prepare baking powder biscuits and variations.

2. Prepare muffins, loaf breads, coffee cakes, and corn breads.

3. Prepare popovers.

TYPES OF DOUGH

Dough mixtures for quick breads are generally of two types:

1. *Soft doughs* are used for biscuits. These products are rolled out and cut into desired shapes. They are mixed by the biscuit method.

2. *Batters* may be either *pour batters*, which are liquid enough to pour, or *drop batters*, which are thicker and drop from a spoon in lumps.

Most quick-bread batters are mixed by the muffin method, except for drop biscuits, which are mixed by the biscuit method, and some rich cakelike muffins and coffee cakes, which are mixed by a cake-mixing method called the *creaming method*. The biscuit and muffin methods are presented in this chapter. The creaming method is presented in Chapter 29, along with other cake methods.

The muffins and loaf breads in this chapter should be thought of as breads rather than as tea cakes. They are lower in fat and sugar than some of the rich, cakelike muffins sometimes seen.

GLUTEN DEVELOPMENT IN QUICK BREADS

Only slight gluten development is desired in most quick breads. Tenderness is the desired quality, in contrast to the chewy quality of yeast breads.

In addition, chemical leavening agents do not create the same kind of textures that yeast does and are not strong enough to create a light, tender product if the gluten is too strong.

1. Muffin, loaf bread, and pancake batters are mixed as little as possible, just until the dry ingredients are moistened. This, plus the presence of fat and sugar, keeps gluten development low.

   Overmixing muffins produces not only toughness but also irregular shapes and large, elongated holes inside the product. This latter condition is called *tunneling*.

2. Biscuit dough is often lightly kneaded, enough to develop some flakiness but not enough to toughen the product.

3. Popovers are the exception among quick breads. They are made with a thin batter and leavened by steam only. Large holes develop inside the product during baking, and the structure must be strong enough to hold without collapsing. Thus, bread flour is used, and the batter is mixed well to develop the gluten. The high percentage of egg in popovers also helps build structure.

THE BISCUIT METHOD

Procedure: Biscuit Method

1. Scale all ingredients accurately.

2. Sift the dry ingredients together into a mixing bowl.

3. Cut in the shortening, using the paddle attachment or the pastry knife attachment. If preferred, you may also cut in the fat by hand, using a pastry blender or your fingers. Continue until the mixture resembles coarse cornmeal.

4. Combine the liquid ingredients. Biscuits may be prepared in advance up to this point. Portions of each mixture may then be scaled and combined just before baking.

5. Combine the liquid ingredients.

6. Add the liquid to the dry ingredients. Mix just until the ingredients are combined and a soft dough is formed. Do not overmix.

7. Bring the dough to the bench and knead it lightly by pressing it out and folding it in half. Rotate the dough 90 degrees after each fold.

8. Repeat this procedure about 10 to 20 times, or for about 30 seconds. The dough should be soft and slightly elastic but not sticky. Overkneading toughens the biscuits. The dough is now ready for makeup.

Variations on the basic procedure produce different characteristics in the finished product.

1. Using slightly more shortening and cutting it in less—until the pieces are the size of peas—produces a flakier biscuit.

2. Omitting the kneading step produces a tender, crustier biscuit, but with less volume.

MAKEUP OF BISCUITS

1. Roll the biscuit dough into a sheet about ½ inch (1 cm) thick, being careful to roll it evenly and to a uniform thickness.

   Biscuits approximately double in height during baking.

2. Cut into desired shapes.

   When using round hand cutters, cutting straight down produces the best shape after baking. Do not twist the cutter. Space the cuts closely to minimize scraps.

   Cutting into squares or triangles with a pastry cutter or knife eliminates scraps that would have to be rerolled. Roller cutters also eliminate or reduce scraps. Reworked scraps are tougher.

3. Place the biscuits ½ inch (1 cm) apart on baking sheet for crisp-crusted biscuits, or touching each other for softer biscuits. Bake as soon as possible.

   If desired, the tops may be brushed with egg wash or milk before baking to aid browning.

THE MUFFIN METHOD

This mixing method is used not only for muffins but also for pancakes, waffles, quick loaf breads, and coffee cakes. Loaf breads and coffee cakes are sometimes higher in fat and sugar than muffins, so they can withstand more mixing without toughening.

Procedure: Muffin Method

1. Sift together the dry ingredients (see Figure 28.1).

2. Combine all liquid ingredients, including melted fat or oil.

3. Add the liquids to the dry ingredients and mix just until all the flour is moistened. The batter will look lumpy. Do not overmix.

4. Pan and bake immediately. The dry and liquid mixtures may be prepared in advance. Once they are combined, the batter should be baked without delay, or loss of volume may result. When portioning batter into muffin tins, be careful not to stir the mix and toughen it. Scoop the batter from the outside edge for best results.

Figure 28.1 The muffin method.

(a) Sift together the dry ingredients.

(b) Add the combined liquid ingredients to the dry ingredients and mix just until the flour is moistened.

(c) Pan and bake immediately. Scoop the batter from the outside edge to minimize additional mixing.

SUMMARY: BISCUIT AND MUFFIN METHODS

Biscuit Method	*Muffin Method*
1. Combine dry ingredients and cut in fat.	1. Combine dry ingredients.
2. Combine liquid ingredients.	2. Combine liquid ingredients, including melted fat.
3. Add liquid and dry ingredients and mix just until combined.	3. Add liquid to dry ingredients and mix just until combined.
4. If required, knead very lightly.	

Formulas

Biscuits

Ingredients	U.S.		Metric	Percentage
Bread flour	1 lb	4 oz	600 g	50%
Pastry flour	1 lb	4 oz	600 g	50%
Salt		0.75 oz	25 g	2%
Sugar		2 oz	60 g	5%
Baking powder		2.5 oz	75 g	6%
Shortening (regular) and/or butter		14 oz	425 g	35%
Milk	1 lb	10 oz	775 g	65%
Yield:	5 lb	5 oz	2560 g	213%

PROCEDURE

Mixing and makeup: Biscuit method.

Scaling: Approximately 1 lb (500 g) per dozen 2-inch (5-cm) biscuits.

Baking: 425°F (220°C), about 15 minutes.

Per 1 biscuit:
Calories, 130; Protein, 2 g; Fat, 7 g (48% cal.); Cholesterol, 0 mg; Carbohydrates, 15 g; Fiber, 1 g; Sodium, 260 mg.

VARIATIONS

Buttermilk Biscuits
Use buttermilk instead of regular milk.

Cheese Biscuits
Add 30% (12 oz/360 g) grated cheddar cheese to dry ingredients.

Currant Biscuits
Add 15% (6 oz/180 g) dried currants to dry ingredients. Increase sugar to 10% (4 oz/125 g). Sprinkle tops with cinnamon sugar before baking.

Herb Biscuits
Add 5% (2 oz/60 g) fresh chopped parsley to the dry ingredients.

Plain Muffins

Ingredients	U.S.		Metric	Percentage
Pastry flour	2 lb	8 oz	1250 g	100%
Sugar		12 oz	375 g	30%
Baking powder		2.5 oz	75 g	6%
Salt		0.5 oz	15 g	1.25%
Eggs, beaten		8 oz	250 g	20%
Milk	2 lb		1000 g	80%
Melted butter or shortening		12 oz	375 g	30%
Yield:	6 lb	11 oz	3340 g	267%

Per 1 muffin:
Calories, 160; Protein, 3 g; Fat, 7 g (37% cal.); Cholesterol, 35 mg; Carbohydrates, 24 g; Fiber, 3 g; Sodium, 310 mg.

PROCEDURE

Mixing: Muffin method.

Scaling and panning: Grease and flour muffin tins or use paper liners. Scale batter with No. 16 scoop, 2 oz (60 g) per unit.

Baking: 400°F (200°C), about 20 minutes.

VARIATIONS

Raisin Spice Muffins

Add 20% raisins (8 oz/250 g), 2 tsp (10 mL) cinnamon, and ½ tsp (2 mL) nutmeg to the dry ingredients.

Date Nut Muffins

Add 15% (6 oz/185 g) each chopped dates and chopped walnuts to the dry ingredients.

Blueberry Muffins

Gently fold 40% (1 lb/500 g) well-drained blueberries into the finished batter.

Whole Wheat Muffins

Use 70% (1 lb 12 oz/875 g) pastry flour and 30% (12 oz/375 g) whole wheat flour. Reduce baking powder to 4% (1½ oz/50 g) and add 0.75% (2 tsp/10 mL) baking soda. Add 10% (4 oz/125 g) molasses to the liquid ingredients.

Corn Muffins

Use 75% (1 lb 14 oz/950 g) pastry flour and 25% (10 oz/300 g) yellow cornmeal. (See also Corn Bread formula.)

Bran Muffins

Use 30% (12 oz/375 g) bran, 40% (1 lb/500 g) bread flour, and 30% (12 oz/375 g) pastry flour. Add 15% (6 oz/185 g) raisins to the dry ingredients. Add 15% (6 oz/185 g) molasses to the liquid ingredients. Increase eggs to 30% (12 oz/375 g).

Crumb Coffee Cake

Increase sugar and fat to 50% (1 lb 4 oz/625 g) each. Pour into greased, paper-lined sheet pan and spread smooth. Top with 80% (2 lb/1 kg) Streusel Topping (p. 786). Bake at 360°F (180°C), about 30 minutes.

Muffins, clockwise from top: blueberry, corn, bran

Banana Bread

Ingredients	U.S.		Metric	Percentage
Pastry flour	1 lb	8 oz	700 g	100%
Sugar		10 oz	275 g	40%
Baking powder		1.25 oz	35 g	5%
Baking soda		1 tsp	3.5 g (5 mL)	0.5%
Salt		2 tsp	9 g (10 mL)	1.25%
Chopped walnuts		6 oz	175 g	25%
Eggs		10 oz	275 g	40%
Ripe banana pulp, puréed	1 lb	8 oz	700 g	100%
Oil, melted shortening, or butter		8 oz	225 g	33%
Yield:	5 lb	4 oz	2397 g	344%

Per 1 ounce:
Calories, 90; Protein, 2 g; Fat, 4.5 g (41% cal.); Cholesterol, 15 mg;
Carbohydrates, 12 g; Fiber, 1 g; Sodium, 120 mg.

PROCEDURE

Mixing: Muffin method.

Scaling: 1 lb 10 oz (750 g) per loaf pan measuring 8½ × 4½ inches (22 × 11 cm).

Baking: 375°F (190°C), about 50 minutes.

Corn Bread, Muffins, or Sticks

Ingredients	U.S.		Metric	Percentage
Pastry flour	1 lb	4 oz	600 g	50%
Cornmeal	1 lb	4 oz	600 g	50%
Sugar		6 oz	175 g	15%
Baking powder		2.5 oz	75 g	6%
Salt		0.75 oz	25 g	2%
Eggs, beaten		8 oz	250 g	20%
Milk	2 lb	2 oz	1000 g (1 L)	85%
Melted butter or shortening		12 oz	350 g	30%
Yield:	6 lb	7 oz	3075 g	258%

Per 1 muffin:
Calories, 160; Protein, 3 g; Fat, 7 g (39% cal.); Cholesterol, 35 mg;
Carbohydrates, 22 g; Fiber, 2 g; Sodium, 380 mg.

PROCEDURE

Mixing: Muffin method.

Scaling: 60 oz (1700 g) per half-size sheet pan (13 × 18 inches/33 × 46 cm).
24 oz (725 g) per 9-inch (23 cm) square pan or per dozen muffins.
10 oz (300 g) per dozen corn sticks.
Grease and flour pans well.

Baking: 400°F (200°C) for corn bread, 25–30 minutes.
425°F (220°C) for muffins or sticks, 15–20 minutes.

Orange Nut Bread

Ingredients	U.S.		Metric	Percentage
Sugar		12 oz	350 g	50%
Grated orange zest		1 oz	30 g	4%
Pastry flour	1 lb	8 oz	700 g	100%
Nonfat dry milk		2 oz	60 g	8%
Baking powder		1 oz	30 g	4%
Baking soda		2 tsp	10 g	1.4%
Salt		2 tsp	10 g (10 mL)	1.4%
Chopped walnuts		12 oz	350 g	50%
Eggs		5 oz	150 g	20%
Orange juice		6 oz	175 g	25%
Water		15 oz	450 g	65%
Oil, melted butter, or shortening		2.5 oz	75 g	10%
Yield:	4 lb	7 oz	2390 g	329%

PROCEDURE

Mixing: Muffin method.
  Blend the sugar and orange zest thoroughly before adding remaining dry ingredients to ensure even distribution.

Scaling: 1 lb 10 oz (750 g) per loaf pan measuring 8½ × 4½ inches (22 × 11 cm).

Baking: 375°F (190°C), about 50 minutes.

Per 1 ounce:
Calories, 80; Protein, 2 g; Fat, 4 g (39% cal.); Cholesterol, 5 mg; Carbohydrates, 12 g; Fiber, 1 g; Sodium, 130 mg.

Popovers

Ingredients	U.S.		Metric	Percentage
Eggs	1 lb	4 oz	625 g	125%
Milk	2 lb		1000 g (1 L)	200%
Salt		0.25 oz (1¼ tsp)	8 g (6 mL)	1.5%
Melted butter or shortening		2 oz	60 g	12.5%
Bread flour	1 lb		500 g	100%
Yield:	4 lb	6 oz	2193 g	439%

PROCEDURE

Mixing: 1. Beat eggs, milk, and salt together with whip attachment, until well blended. Add melted fat.
  2. Replace whip with paddle. Mix in flour until completely smooth.

Scaling and panning: Grease every other cup of muffin pans—popovers need room for expansion. Fill cups about two-thirds full, about 1½ oz (50 g) batter per unit.

Baking: 450°F (230°C) for 10 minutes. Reduce heat to 375°F (190°C) for 20–30 minutes. Before removing them from oven, be sure popovers are dry and firm enough to avoid collapsing. Remove from pans immediately.

Per 1 popover:
Calories, 70; Protein, 3 g; Fat, 3 g (38% cal); Cholesterol, 60 mg; Carbohydrates, 8 g; Fiber, 0 g; Sodium, 95 mg.

Terms for Review

pour batter	tunneling	muffin method
drop batter	biscuit method	

Questions for Discussion

1. If you made a batch of muffins that came out of the oven with strange, knobby shapes, what would you expect was the reason?

2. What is the most important difference between the biscuit method and the muffin method?

3. Why do popovers require more mixing than other quick breads?

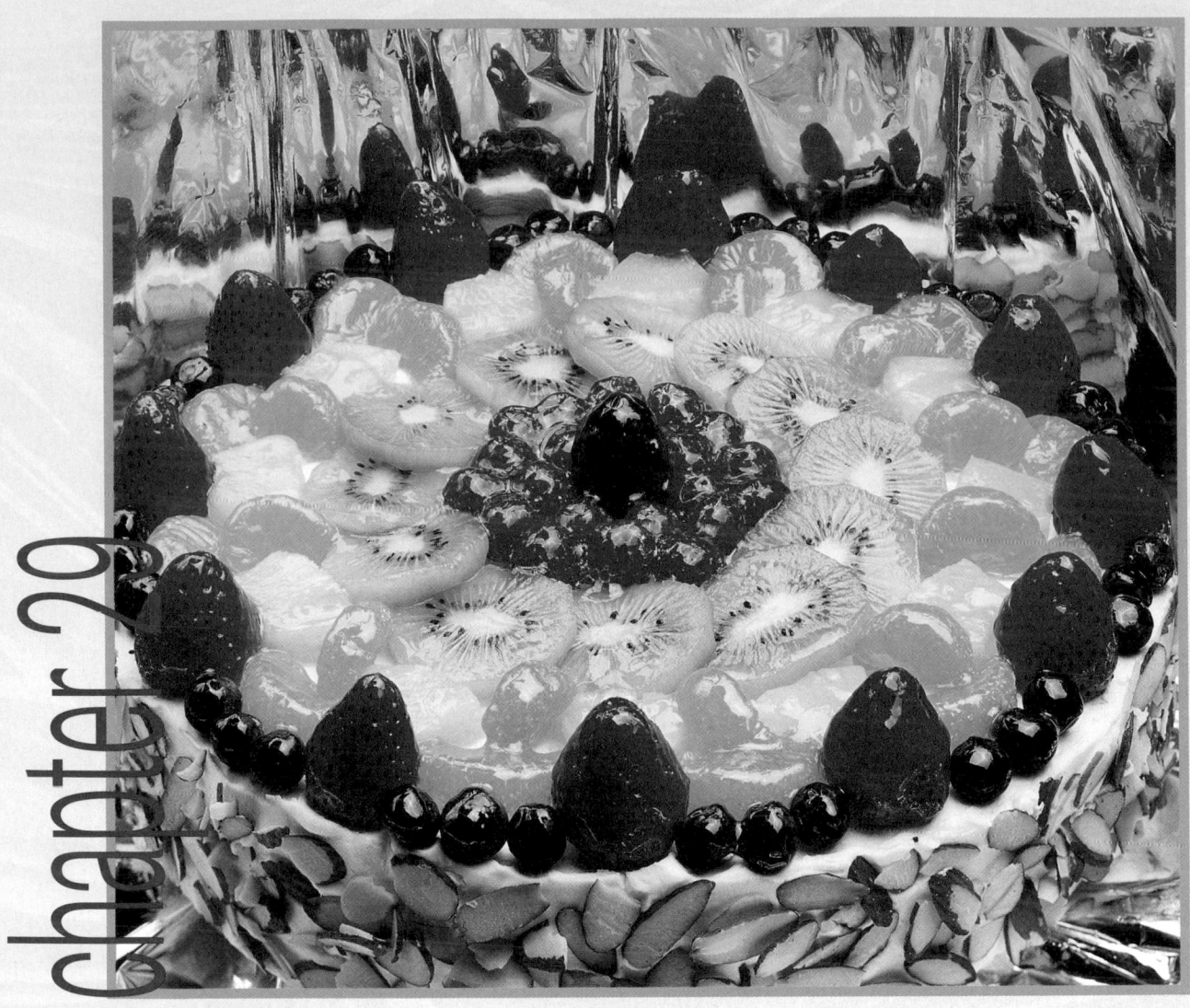

chapter 29

Cakes and Icings

Cakes are the richest and sweetest of all the baked products we have studied so far. From the baker's point of view, producing cakes requires as much precision as producing breads, but for completely opposite reasons. Breads are lean products that require strong gluten development and careful control of yeast action during the long fermentation and proofing periods. Cakes, on the other hand, are high in both fat and sugar. The baker's job is to create a structure that will support these ingredients and yet keep it as light and delicate as possible. Fortunately, producing cakes in quantity is relatively easy if the baker has good, well-balanced formulas, scales ingredients accurately, and understands basic mixing methods well.

Cakes owe their popularity to their richness and sweetness but also to their versatility. They can be presented in many forms, from simple sheet cakes in cafeterias to elaborately decorated works of art for weddings and other important occasions. With only a few basic formulas and a variety of icings, the chef or baker can construct the perfect dessert for any occasion or purpose.

After reading this chapter,
you should be able to

1. Demonstrate the five
   basic cake mixing
   methods.

2. Describe the characteristics of high-fat cakes
   and low-fat cakes.

3. Prepare high-fat, or
   shortened, cakes and
   low-fat, or foam-type,
   cakes.

4. Prepare the six basic
   types of icings.

5. Assemble and ice layer
   cakes, small cakes, and
   sheet cakes.

Understanding Cake Making

Basic Mixing Methods

The mixing methods presented in this chapter are basic for most types of cakes prepared in the modern bakeshop. Each of these methods is used for particular types of formula.

High-fat or shortened cakes
    Creaming method
    Two-stage or blending
      method

Low-fat or foam-type cakes
    Foaming or sponge method
    Angel food method
    Chiffon method

We discuss these cake types in detail after you have had a chance to study the actual procedures.

CREAMING METHOD

This method, also called the *conventional method*, was, for a long time, the standard method for mixing butter cakes. Recently, the development of emulsified or high-ratio shortenings has led to the development of simpler mixing methods for shortened cakes. But the creaming method is still used for many types of butter cakes.

Procedure: Creaming Method

1. Scale ingredients accurately. Have all ingredients at room temperature.

2. Place the butter or shortening in the mixing bowl. With the paddle attachment, beat slowly until the fat is smooth and creamy.

3. Add the sugar. Cream the mixture at moderate speed until the mixture is light and fluffy.
   Some bakers prefer to add the salt and flavorings with the sugar to ensure uniform distribution. If melted chocolate is used, it is added during creaming.

4. Add the eggs, a little at a time. After each addition, beat until the eggs are absorbed before adding more. The mixture should be light and fluffy after the eggs are beaten in.

5. Scrape down the sides of the bowl to ensure even mixing.

6. Add the sifted dry ingredients (including the spices, if they were not added in step 3), alternating with the liquids. This is done as follows:

   • Add one-fourth of the dry ingredients. Mix just until blended in.

   • Add one-third of the liquid. Mix just until blended in.

   • Repeat until all ingredients are used. Scrape down the sides of the bowl occasionally for even mixing.

   The reason for adding dry and liquids alternately is that the batter may not absorb all the liquid unless some of the flour is present to aid in absorption.
   Cocoa, if used, is included with the flour.

TWO-STAGE METHOD

This method, also called the *blending method*, was developed for use with modern high-ratio shortenings (see Chapter 26). Although it is simpler than the creaming method, it produces a very smooth batter that bakes up into a fine-grained, moist cake. It is called two-stage because the liquids are added in two stages.

Procedure: Two-Stage Method

1. Scale ingredients accurately. Have all ingredients at room temperature.

2. Sift the flour, baking powder, soda, and salt into the mixing bowl and add the shortening. With the paddle attachment, mix at low speed for 2 minutes. Stop the machine, scrape down the bowl and beater, and mix again for 2 minutes.
   If melted chocolate is used, blend it in during this step.
   If cocoa is used, sift it with the flour in this step or with the sugar in step 3.

3. Sift the remaining dry ingredients into the bowl and add part of the water or milk. Blend at low speed for 3 to 5 minutes. Scrape down the sides of the bowl and the beater several times to ensure even mixing.

4. Combine the remaining liquids and lightly beaten eggs. With the mixer running, add this mixture to the batter in three parts. After each part, turn off the machine and scrape down the bowl.
   Continue mixing for a total of 5 minutes in this stage.
   The finished batter is normally quite liquid.

Variation

This variation combines steps 2 and 3 into one step.

1. Scale ingredients as in the basic method.

2. Sift all dry ingredients into the mixing bowl. Add the shortening and part of the liquid. Mix on low speed for 7 to 8 minutes. Scrape down the sides of the bowl and the beater several times.

3. Continue with step 4 in the basic procedure.

FOAMING OR SPONGE METHOD

All egg-foam cakes are similar in that they contain little or no shortening and depend for most or all of their leavening on the air trapped in beaten eggs.

One mixing method is usually presented as the basic method for all foam cakes. However, because whole-egg foams and egg-yolk foams are handled differently than egg-white foams, we discuss two separate, although similar, methods. A third method, for chiffon cakes, is somewhat unusual. It combines an egg-white foam with a high-fat batter made with oil.

First, the method for sponge cakes:

Procedure: Foaming or Sponge Method

1. Scale ingredients accurately. Have all ingredients at room temperature.
   If butter is included, it must be melted.
   If liquid and butter are included, heat them together, just until the butter is melted.

2. Combine the eggs and sugar and warm to about 110°F (43°C). This may be done in one of two ways.
   • Stir the egg-sugar mixture over a hot water bath.
   • Warm the sugar on a sheet pan in the oven (do not get it too hot) and gradually beat it into the eggs. The reason for this step is that the foam attains greater volume if warm.

3. With the whip attachment, beat the eggs at high speed until light and thick. This may take 10 to 15 minutes.
   This step is important. One of the most frequent causes of failure in the sponge method is not whipping the eggs and sugar enough. The foam must be very thick. When the beater is lifted from the bowl, the foam should fall slowly from it and make a ribbon that slowly sinks into the batter in the bowl. (See Figure 29.1.)

4. Fold in the sifted flour, being careful not to deflate the foam. Many bakers do this by hand.
   If other dry ingredients are used, such as cornstarch or baking powder, they are first sifted with the flour.

5. If melted butter or a butter-liquid mixture is being used, fold it in at this point. Be careful not to overmix, or the cake will be tough (because of developed gluten).

6. Immediately pan and bake the batter. Delays cause loss of volume.

Variations

Some formulas contain water or some other liquid, but no butter (so you cannot heat the liquid and butter together, as in the basic procedure). In this case, the liquid is usually added after step 3 and before folding in the flour. Either whip it in a steady stream or stir it in, as indicated in the recipe.

In some formulas, the egg yolks and whites are separated. Use the yolks and part of the sugar to make the foam in steps 2 and 3. Use the remaining sugar to whip with the whites. Fold the egg-white foam into the batter after step 5.

Figure 29.1

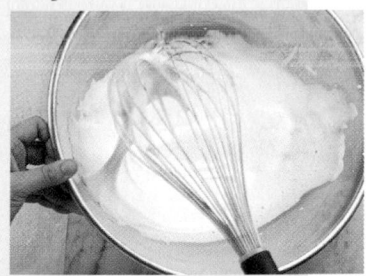

(a) With a wire whip or the whip attachment of a mixer, beat the eggs until they are very thick and light.

(b) Fold in the sifted flour in three or four stages, until all the flour is blended in.

ANGEL FOOD METHOD

Angel food cakes are based on egg-white foams and contain no fat. For success in beating egg whites, review the principles of egg foams in Chapter 21.

Procedure: Angel Food Method

1. Scale ingredients accurately. Have all ingredients at room temperature. You may warm the egg whites slightly for better volume.

2. Sift the flour with half the sugar. This step helps the flour mix more evenly with the foam.

3. Beat the egg whites, using the whip attachment, until they form soft peaks.
   Add salt and cream of tartar near the beginning of the beating process.

4. Gradually beat in the sugar that was not mixed with the flour. Continue to beat until the egg whites form soft, glossy peaks. Do not overbeat.

5. Fold in the flour-sugar mixture just until it is thoroughly absorbed, but no longer.

6. Pan and bake immediately.

CHIFFON METHOD

Chiffon cakes and angel food cakes are both based on egg-white foams. But here the similarities in the mixing methods end. In angel food cakes, a dry flour-sugar mixture is folded into the egg whites. In chiffon cakes, a batter containing flour, egg yolks, vegetable oil, and water is folded into the whites.

Whip egg whites for chiffon cakes until they are a little firmer than those for angel food cakes, but not until they are dry. Chiffon cakes contain baking powder, so they do not depend on the egg foam for all their leavening.

Procedure: Chiffon Method

1. Scale all ingredients accurately. Have all ingredients at room temperature. Use a good-quality, flavorless vegetable oil.

2. Sift the dry ingredients, including part of the sugar, into the mixing bowl.

3. Mixing with the paddle attachment at second speed, gradually add the oil, then the egg yolks, water, and liquid flavorings, all in a slow, steady stream. While adding the liquids, stop the machine several times and scrape down the bowl and the beater. Mix until smooth, but do not overmix.

4. Whip the egg whites until they form soft peaks. Add the cream of tartar and sugar in a stream and whip to firm, moist peaks.

5. Fold the whipped egg whites into the flour-liquid mixture.

6. Immediately deposit batter in ungreased tube pans (like angel food cakes) or in layer pans that have had the bottoms greased and dusted, but not the sides (like sponge layers).

PREPARED MIXES

Many mixes are available that contain all ingredients except water and, sometimes, egg. These products also contain emulsifiers to ensure even blending of ingredients. To use them, follow the package instructions exactly.

Most mixes produce cakes with excellent volume, texture, and tenderness. Whether or not they also taste good is a matter of opinion. On the other hand, cakes made from scratch are not necessarily better. They are better only if they are carefully mixed and baked and are prepared using good, tested formulas and high-quality ingredients.

Cake Formula Types

The proper mixing method for a particular formula depends on the balance of ingredients. A baker can look at the ingredients in a formula and know immediately which mixing method to use.

If *fat is high*, use the creaming method or the two-stage method.

The two-stage method may be used if the percentage of sugar is over 100 percent and if the fat is emulsified shortening.

In other cases, the creaming method is used.

If f*at is low* and *eggs and sugar are high*, use an egg-foam method.

HIGH-FAT CAKES

The creaming method's major disadvantage is the labor it requires. The two-stage method is quicker, but because the flour is mixed for a long time, two conditions are necessary to prevent the gluten from developing toughness:

1. Increased percentage of sugar (sugar is a tenderizer).
2. Emulsified shortening, which blends thoroughly to prevent toughness.

Cakes made by the two-stage method have good volume and lightness, a fine, velvety texture, and great tenderness. Butter cakes made by the creaming method are usually graded lower because the texture is coarser and the tenderness is generally somewhat less.

One factor seems to be neglected when cakes are rated, however—flavor. Shortening contributes no flavor to cakes, only texture. Butter, on the other hand, is highly prized for its flavor. It also influences texture because it melts in the mouth, while shortening does not. Thus, butter cakes are and always will be in demand. Therefore, the creaming method is important for you to know.

LOW-FAT CAKES

High-fat cakes depend on air incorporated by the creaming action of the fat and sugar for some of their leavening and much of their texture. Low-fat or no-fat cakes obviously cannot. They must depend on the foaming action of eggs.

Sponge cakes have a springy texture and are tougher than shortened cakes. This makes them valuable for many kinds of desserts that require much handling to assemble. For example, many European-style cakes or tortes are made by cutting sponge cake layers horizontally into thin layers and stacking them with a variety of rich fillings, creams, icings, and fruits.

Even if a high-ratio cake survived all this without breaking into crumbs, it would probably disintegrate when it absorbed moisture from the fillings. In addition, sponge layers in this kind of cake are usually moistened with a flavored sugar syrup to compensate for their lack of moisture.

The *fruit torte* (illustrated in the photograph) is an example of this type of cake. Genoise layers are split, moistened with dessert syrup (p. 870), layered and iced with whipped cream, and topped with attractively arranged fruit pieces. The fruit is then coated with glaze (p. 821) to protect it and enhance its appearance.

Sponge sheets for jelly rolls and other rolled cakes are made without shortening, so they do not crack when rolled.

Flour for sponge cakes must be weak to avoid making the cake tough. Cornstarch is often added to cake flour for sponge cakes to weaken the flour further.

Fruit Torte

Scaling and Panning

PAN PREPARATION

Prepare pans before mixing cake batters so that cakes can be baked without delay as soon as they are mixed.

1. For high-fat cakes, the bottoms of layer pans must be greased, preferably with a commercial pan greasing preparation. If this is not available, dust the greased pan with flour and tap out the excess.
2. For sheet cakes, line the pan with greased parchment.

3. For angel food cakes, do not grease the pan. The batter must be able to cling to the sides in order to rise.

4. For sponge cake layers with a small percentage of fat, grease the bottoms but not the sides.

Procedure for Scaling Creaming-Method Batters

These batters are thick and do not pour easily. Scale cakes as follows:

1. Place the prepared cake pan on the left side of a balance scale. Balance the scale by placing another pan on the right side.
2. Set the scale for the desired weight.
3. Add batter to the left pan until the scale balances.
4. Remove the pan from the scale and spread the batter smooth with a spatula.
5. Repeat with remaining pans.
6. Give the pans several sharp raps on the bench to free large trapped air bubbles. Bake immediately.

Procedure for Scaling Two-Stage Batters

These batters are more liquid than creamed batters. They may be scaled like creamed batters or, for greater speed, they may be scaled as follows:

1. Place an empty volume measure on the left side of a balance scale. Balance the scale to zero.
2. Set the scale for the desired weight.
3. Pour batter into the measure until the scale balances.
4. Note the volume of batter in the measure.
5. Pour the measured batter into a prepared pan, quickly scraping out the measure to get all the batter.
6. Scale the remaining cakes with the volume measure, using the volume noted in step 4.
7. Give the pans several sharp raps on the bench to free large trapped air bubbles. Bake immediately.

Procedure for Scaling Foam Cakes

Foam cake batters should be handled as little as possible and baked immediately in order to avoid deflating the beaten eggs. Although they may be scaled like creamed batters, many bakers prefer to eyeball them in order to minimize handling.

1. Have all prepared pans lined up on the bench.
2. Scale the first pan as for creamed batters.
3. Quickly fill remaining pans to the same level as the first pan, judging the level by eye.
4. Spread the batter smooth and bake immediately.

See Table 29.1 for average scaling weights as well as baking temperatures and times.

Baking and Cooling

BAKING

Cake structure is fragile, so proper baking conditions are essential for high-quality products. The following guidelines will help you avoid cake failures.

1. Preheat the ovens. (But to conserve expensive energy, don't preheat longer than necessary.)
2. Make sure ovens and shelves are level.
3. Do not let pans touch each other in oven. If pans touch, air circulation is inhibited and the cakes rise unevenly.

4. Bake at the correct temperature.

   Too hot an oven causes the cake to set unevenly or to set before it has fully risen. Crusts will be too dark.

   Too slow an oven causes poor volume and texture because the cake doesn't set fast enough and may fall.

5. Do not open the ovens or disturb the cakes until they have finished rising and are partially browned. Disturbing the cakes before they are set may cause them to fall.

6. If steam in the oven is available, use it for creamed and two-stage batters. These cakes bake with a flatter top if baked with steam because the steam delays the formation of the top crust.

7. Tests for doneness:
   * Shortened cakes shrink away from sides of pan slightly.
   * Cakes are springy. The center of the tops springs back when pressed slightly.
   * A cake tester or pick inserted in the center of the cake comes out clean.

TABLE 29.1

Average Cake Scaling Weights, Baking Temperatures, and Times

Pan Type and Size	Scaling Weight		Baking Temperature		Approximate Baking Time in Minutes
	U.S.	Metric	U.S.	Metric	
High-fat cakes					
Round layers					
6 in. (15 cm)	8–10 oz	230–285 g	375°F	190°C	18
8 in. (20 cm)	14–18 oz	400–510 g	375°F	190°C	25
10 in. (25 cm)	24–28 oz	680–800 g	360°F	180°C	35
12 in. (30 cm)	32–40 oz	900–1100 g	360°F	180°C	35
Sheets and square pans					
18 × 26 in. (46 × 66 cm)	7–8 lb	3.2–3.6 kg	360°F	180°C	35
18 × 13 in. (46 × 33 cm)	3½–4 lb	1.6–1.8 kg	360°F	180°C	35
9 × 9 in. (23 × 23 cm)	24 oz	680 g	360°F	180°C	30–35
Loaf (pound cake)					
2¼ × 3½ × 8 in. (6 × 9 × 20 cm)	16–18 oz	450–500 g	350°F	175°C	50–60
2¾ × 4½ × 8½ in. (7 × 11 × 22 cm)	24–27 oz	680–765 g	350°F	175°C	55–65
Cupcakes					
per dozen	18 oz	510 g	385°F	195°C	18–20
Foam-type cakes					
Round layers					
6 in. (15 cm)	5–6 oz	140–170 g	375°F	190°C	20
8 in. (20 cm)	10 oz	280 g	375°F	190°C	20
10 in. (25 cm)	16 oz	450 g	360°F	180°C	25–30
12 in. (30 cm)	24 oz	700 g	360°F	180°C	25–30
Sheets (for jelly roll or sponge roll)					
18 × 26 in., ½ in. thick (46 × 66 cm, 12 mm thick)	2½ lb	1.2 kg	375°F	190°C	15–20
18 × 26 in., ¼ in. thick (46 × 66 cm, 6 cm thick)	28 oz	800 g	400°F	200°C	7–10
Tube (angel food and chiffon)					
8 in. (20 cm)	12–14 oz	340–400 g	360°F	180°C	30
10 in. (25 cm)	24–32 oz	700–900 g	350°F	175°C	50
Cupcakes					
per dozen	10 oz	280 g	375°F	190°C	18–20

Note: The weights given are averages. Weights may be increased by 25% if thicker layers are desired. Baking times may then need to be increased slightly.

T A B L E 29.2

Common Cake Faults and Their Causes

Fault	Causes
Volume and shape	
Poor volume	Too little flour
	Too much liquid
	Too little leavening
	Oven too hot
Uneven shape	Improper mixing
	Batter spread unevenly
	Uneven oven heat
	Oven racks not level
	Cake pans warped
Crust	
Too dark	Too much sugar
	Oven too hot
Too light	Too little sugar
	Oven not hot enough
Burst or cracked	Too much flour or flour too strong
	Too little liquid
	Improper mixing
	Oven too hot
Soggy	Underbaked
	Cooling in pans or with not enough ventilation
	Wrapping before cool
Texture	
Dense or heavy	Too little leavening
	Too much liquid
	Too much sugar
	Too much shortening
	Oven not hot enough
Coarse or irregular	Too much leavening
	Too little egg
	Improper mixing
Crumbly	Too much leavening
	Too much shortening
	Too much sugar
	Wrong kind of flour
	Improper mixing
Tough	Flour too strong
	Too much flour
	Too little sugar or shortening
	Overmixing
Poor flavor	
	Poor-quality ingredients
	Poor storage or sanitation
	Unbalanced formula

COOLING AND REMOVING FROM PANS

1. Cool layer cakes and sheet cakes 15 minutes in pans and turn out while slightly warm. They are too fragile to turn out when hot, and they may break.
2. Turn out layer cakes onto racks to finish cooling.
3. To turn out sheet cakes:
   - Sprinkle top lightly with granulated sugar.
   - Set an empty sheet pan on top, bottom side down.
   - Invert both pans.
   - Remove top pan.
   - Peel parchment off cake.
4. Cool angel food cakes upside down in pans. Support the edges of the pan so that the top of the cake is off the bench. When cool, loosen the cake from the sides of the pan with a knife or spatula and pull out carefully.

COMMON CAKE FAULTS AND THEIR CAUSES

Errors in mixing, scaling, baking, and cooling cakes cause many kinds of defects and failures. For easy reference, these defects and their possible causes are summarized in the troubleshooting guide in Table 29.2.

Altitude Adjustments

At high altitudes, atmospheric pressure is much lower than at sea level. This factor must be taken into account in cake baking. Formulas must be adjusted to suit different baking conditions over 2000 or 3000 feet (600 or 900 meters) above sea level.

Although general guidelines can be given, the exact adjustments required vary for different kinds of cake. Many manufacturers of flour, shortening, and other bakery ingredients supply detailed information and adjusted formulas for any given locality.

In general, the following adjustments must be made above elevations of 2000 or 3000 feet (600 or 900 meters). See Table 29.3 for more specific adjustments.

Leavening
Leavening gases expand more when air pressure is lower, so baking powder and baking soda must be *decreased*.

Creaming and foaming procedures should also be reduced so that less air is incorporated.

Tougheners: Flour and Eggs
Cakes require firmer structure at high altitudes. Both eggs and flour must be increased to supply proteins for structure.

Tenderizers: Shortening and Sugar
Shortening and sugar must be *decreased* so that the structure of the cake is firmer.

TABLE 29.3

Approximate Formula Adjustment in Shortened Cakes at High Altitudes

Ingredient	Increase or Decrease	Percentage Adjustment		
		2500 Feet (750 m)	5000 Feet (1500 m)	7500 Feet (2300 m)
Baking powder	Decrease	20%	40%	60%
Flour	Increase	—	4%	9%
Eggs	Increase	2½ %	9%	15%
Sugar	Decrease	3%	6%	9%
Fat	Decrease	—	—	9%
Liquid	Increase	9%	15%	22%

To make adjustments, multiply the percentage indicated by the amount of ingredient and add or subtract as indicated.

Example: To adjust 1 lb (16 oz) eggs for 7500 feet:

$$0.15 \times 16 \text{ oz} = 2.4 \text{ oz}$$
$$16 \text{ oz} + 2.4 \text{ oz} = 18.4 \text{ oz}$$

Liquids

At high altitudes, water boils at a lower temperature and evaporates more easily. Liquids must be *increased* to prevent excess drying both during and after baking. This also helps compensate for the decrease in moisturizers (sugar and fat) and the increase in flour, which absorbs moisture.

Baking Temperatures

Increase baking temperatures about 25°F (14°C) above 3500 feet.

Pan Greasing

High-fat cakes tend to stick at high altitudes. Grease pans more heavily. Remove baked cakes from pans as soon as possible.

Storing

Wrap or ice cakes as soon as they are cool to prevent drying.

Cake Formulas

Creaming Method

Yellow Butter Cake

Ingredients	U.S.		Metric	Percentage	PROCEDURE
Butter	1 lb	2 oz	550 g	60%	*Mixing:* Creaming method.
Sugar	1 lb	8 oz	725 g	80%	*Scaling and baking:* See Table 29.1.
Salt		0.25 oz (1¼ tsp)	9 g (6 mL)	1%	
Eggs		14 oz	400 g	45%	
Cake flour	1 lb	14 oz	900 g	100%	
Baking powder		1.5 oz	45 g	5%	
Milk	1 lb	4 oz	600 g	67%	
Vanilla		0.5 oz	15 mL	1.5%	
Yield:	6 lb	12 oz	3244 g	359%	

Per 1 ounce:
Calories, 100; Protein, 1 g; Fat, 4.5 g (42% cal.); Cholesterol, 25 mg;
Carbohydrates, 13 g; Fiber, 0 g; Sodium, 115 mg.

Brown Sugar Spice Cake

Ingredients	U.S.		Metric	Percentage
Butter and/or shortening	1 lb	2 oz	600 g	60%
Brown sugar	1 lb	14 oz	1100 g	100%
Salt		0.5 oz	15 g	1.5%
Eggs	1 lb	2 oz	600 g	60%
Cake flour	1 lb	14 oz	1000 g	100%
Baking powder		1.5 oz	30 g	3%
Baking soda		1 tsp	3 g (3 mL)	0.3%
Cinnamon		1 tbsp	5 g (15 mL)	0.5%
Ground cloves		1½ tsp	3 g (7 mL)	0.3%
Nutmeg		1 tsp	2 g (3 mL)	0.2%
Milk	1 lb	8 oz	800 g	80%
Yield:	7 lb	9 oz	4058 g	405%

PROCEDURE

Mixing: Creaming method.

Scaling and baking: See Table 29.1.

Per 1 ounce:
Calories, 90; Protein, 1 g; Fat, 4 g (39% cal.); Cholesterol, 30 mg;
Carbohydrates, 13 g; Fiber, 0 g; Sodium, 135 mg.

VARIATION

Carrot Nut Cake

Reduce the milk to 70% (1 lb 5 oz/700 g). Add 40% (12 oz/400 g) grated fresh carrots, 20% (6 oz/200 g) finely chopped walnuts, and 0.5% (2 tsp/6 g or 10 mL) grated orange zest after eggs are beaten in. Omit cloves.

Chocolate Butter Cake

Ingredients	U.S.		Metric	Percentage
Butter or part butter and part shortening	1 lb		500 g	67%
Sugar	1 lb	12 oz	875 g	116%
Salt		0.33 oz	10 g	1.5%
Unsweetened chocolate, melted		8 oz	250 g	33%
Eggs		12 oz	375 g	50%
Cake flour	1 lb	8 oz	750 g	100%
Baking powder		1 oz	30 g	4%
Milk		12 oz	375 g	50%
Vanilla		2 tsp	10 mL	1.5%
Yield:	6 lb	5 oz	3175 g	423%

PROCEDURE

Mixing: Creaming method. Blend in the melted chocolate after the fat and sugar are well creamed.

Scaling and baking: See Table 29.1.

Per 1 ounce:
Calories, 110; Protein, 1 g; Fat, 5 g (43% cal.); Cholesterol, 25 mg;
Carbohydrates, 14 g; Fiber, 0 g; Sodium, 110 mg.

Old-Fashioned Pound Cake

Ingredients	U.S.		Metric	Percentage
Butter or butter and shortening combined (see note)	1 lb		500 g	100%
Sugar	1 lb		500 g	100%
Vanilla		2 tsp	10 mL	2%
Eggs	1 lb		500 g	100%
Cake flour	1 lb		500 g	100%
Yield:	4 lb		2000 g	402%

Per 1 ounce:
Calories, 110; Protein, 2 g; Fat, 7 g (51% cal.); Cholesterol, 45 mg;
Carbohydrates, 13 g; Fiber, 0 g; Sodium, 70 mg.

PROCEDURE

Mixing: Creaming method. Add the eggs and the cake flour alternately to avoid curdling the mixture.

Scaling and baking: See Table 29.1.

Note: If you are using unsalted butter or shortening, add 1.5% (¼ oz/1¼ tsp or 6 mL) salt during the first stage of mixing.

VARIATIONS
Mace or grated lemon or orange zest may also be used to flavor pound cake.

Raisin Pound Cake
Add 25% (4 oz/125 g) raisins or dried currants that were soaked in boiling water and drained well.

Chocolate Pound Cake
Add 25% (4 oz/125 g) unsweetened chocolate to the butter and sugar after the creaming stage.

Marble Pound Cake
Fill pans one-third full of the basic yellow batter. Add a layer of Chocolate Pound Cake batter, then finish with the yellow batter. Run a spatula blade through the layers to marble them.

Two-Stage Method

White Cake

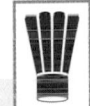

Ingredients	U.S.		Metric	Percentage
Cake flour	1 lb	8 oz	700 g	100%
Baking powder		1.5 oz	45 g	6.25%
Salt		0.5 oz	15 g	2%
Emulsified shortening		12 oz	350 g	50%
Sugar	1 lb	14 oz	875 g	125%
Skim milk		12 oz	350 g	50%
Vanilla		2 tsp	10 mL	1.5%
Almond extract		1 tsp	5 mL	0.75%
Skim milk		12 oz	350 g	50%
Egg whites	1 lb		475 g	67%
Yield:	6 lb	12 oz	3175 g	452%

Per 1 ounce:
Calories, 90; Protein, 1 g; Fat, 3 g (33% cal.); Cholesterol, 0 mg;
Carbohydrates, 13 g; Fiber, 0 g; Sodium, 105 mg.

PROCEDURE

Mixing: Two-stage method.

Scaling and baking: See Table 29.1.

VARIATIONS
Use water instead of milk and add 10% (2½ oz/70 g) nonfat dry milk powder to the dry ingredients.

Flavor with lemon extract or emulsion instead of vanilla and almond.

Yellow Cake
Reduce shortening to 45% (11 oz/325 g). Substitute whole eggs for egg whites, using the same total weight (67%). Use 2% vanilla (½ oz/15 g) and omit almond extract.

Devil's Food Cake

Ingredients	U.S.		Metric	Percentage
Cake flour	1 lb	8 oz	700 g	100%
Cocoa		4 oz	125 g	17%
Salt		0.5 oz	15 g	2%
Baking powder		0.75 oz	20 g	3%
Baking soda		0.5 oz	15 g	2%
Emulsified shortening		14 oz	400 g	58%
Sugar	2 lb		925 g	133%
Skim milk	1 lb		475 g	67%
Vanilla		2 tsp	10 mL	1.5%
Skim milk		12 oz	350 g	50%
Eggs	1 lb		475 g	67%
Yield:	7 lb	8 oz	3500 g	500%

PROCEDURE

Mixing: Sponge method.

Scaling and baking: See Table 29.1.

Per 1 ounce:
Calories, 90; Protein, 1 g; Fat, 4 g (39% cal.); Cholesterol, 15 mg; Carbohydrates, 13 g; Fiber, 1 g; Sodium, 105 mg.

Foaming Methods

Sponge Cake (Genoise)

Ingredients	U.S.		Metric	Percentage
Eggs	2 lb	4 oz	1050 g	150%
Sugar	1 lb	8 oz	700 g	100%
Cake flour	1 lb	8 oz	700 g	100%
Butter, melted		8 oz	225 g	33%
Vanilla (or lemon flavor)		0.5 oz	15 mL	2%
Yield:	5 lb	12 oz	2690 g	385%

PROCEDURE

Mixing: Foaming method.

Scaling and baking: See Table 29.1.

Per 1 ounce:
Calories, 90; Protein, 2 g; Fat, 3 g (31% cal.); Cholesterol, 55 mg; Carbohydrates, 13 g; Fiber, 0 g; Sodium, 35 mg.

VARIATIONS

Chocolate Genoise

Substitute 4 oz (125 g) cocoa powder for 4 oz (125 g) flour.

Sponge Roll or Jelly Roll

Prepare basic formula, but omit butter. Add the vanilla to the beaten eggs just before folding in the flour. Spread *evenly* in parchment-lined pans. When baked and cooled, trim the edges. Cut in half or into quarters. Spread each rectangle with desired filling (jelly, buttercream, etc.) and roll up so that the long side of the rectangle becomes the length of the roll. Ice or sprinkle with 6X sugar.

Milk and Butter Sponge

Ingredients	U.S.		Metric	Percentage
Sugar	1 lb	4 oz	625 g	125%
Eggs, whole		12 oz	375 g	75%
Egg yolks		4 oz	125 g	25%
Salt		0.25 oz (1¼ tsp)	7 g (6 mL)	1.5%
Cake flour	1 lb		500 g	100%
Baking powder		0.5 oz	15 g	3%
Skim milk		8 oz	250 g	50%
Butter		4 oz	125 g	25%
Vanilla		1 tbsp	15 mL	3%
Yield:	4 lb		2037 g	407%

PROCEDURE

Mixing: Sponge method. Heat the milk and butter until the butter is melted; fold into batter (step 5 in basic procedure).

Scaling and baking: Cake layers; see Table 29.1.

Per 1 ounce:
Calories, 90; Protein, 2 g; Fat, 2.5 g (25% cal.); Cholesterol, 50 mg; Carbohydrates, 15 g; Fiber, 0 g; Sodium, 90 mg.

Jelly Roll Sponge

Ingredients	U.S.		Metric	Percentage
Sugar		11 oz	325 g	100%
Eggs, whole		10 oz	300 g	90%
Egg yolks		2 oz	65 g	20%
Salt		0.25 oz (1¼ tsp)	7 g (7 mL)	2%
Corn syrup		1.5 oz	45 g	14%
Water		1 oz	30 g	10%
Vanilla		1 tsp	5 mL	1.5%
Hot water		4 oz	125 g	36%
Cake flour		11 oz	325 g	100%
Baking powder		1 tsp	5 g (5 mL)	1.5%
Yield:	2 lb	8 oz	1232 g	375%

PROCEDURE

Mixing: Sponge method. Add the syrup, the first quantity of water, and the vanilla to the sugar and eggs in the first mixing stage. When the foam is completely whipped, stir in the second quantity of water.

Scaling and baking: See Table 29.1. One recipe makes 1 sheet pan. Line the pans with greased paper. Immediately after baking, turn out of pan onto a sheet of parchment and remove the paper from the bottom of the cake. Spread with jelly and roll up tightly. When cool, dust with confectioners' sugar.

Per 1 ounce:
Calories, 80; Protein, 2 g; Fat, 1 g (12% cal.); Cholesterol, 50 mg; Carbohydrates, 15 g; Fiber, 0 g; Sodium, 40 mg

Yellow Chiffon Cake

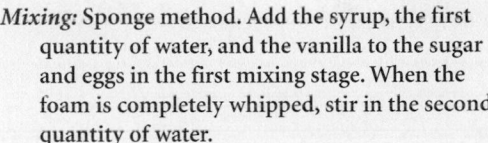

Ingredients	U.S.		Metric	Percentage
Cake flour	1 lb	4 oz	500 g	100%
Sugar	1 lb		400 g	80%
Salt		0.5 oz	12 g	2.5%
Baking powder		1 oz	25 g	5%
Vegetable oil		10 oz	250 g	50%
Egg yolks		10 oz	250 g	50%
Water		15 oz	375 g	75%
Vanilla		0.5 oz	12 mL	2.5%
Egg whites	1 lb	4 oz	500 g	100%
Sugar		10 oz	250 g	50%
Cream of tartar		1¼ tsp	2.5 g (5 mL)	0.5%
Yield:	6 lb	7 oz	2576 g	515%

PROCEDURE

Mixing: Chiffon method.

Scaling and baking: See Table 29.1.

Per 1 ounce:
Calories, 90; Protein, 1 g; Fat, 3.5 g (38% cal.); Cholesterol, 35 mg; Carbohydrates, 12 g; Fiber, 0 g; Sodium, 95 mg.

VARIATION

Chocolate Chiffon Cake

Add 20% cocoa (4 oz/100 g); sift it with the flour. Increase the egg yolks to 60% (12 oz/300 g). Increase the water to 90% (1 lb 2 oz/450 g).

Angel Food Cake

Ingredients	U.S.		Metric	Percentage
Egg whites	2 lb		1000 g	267%
Cream of tartar		0.25 oz (1 tbsp)	8 g (15 mL)	2%
Salt		1 tsp	5 g (5 mL)	1.5%
Sugar	1 lb		500 g	133%
Vanilla		2 tsp	10 mL	2.5%
Almond extract		1 tsp	5 mL	1.25%
Sugar	1 lb		500 g	133%
Cake flour		12 oz	375 g	100%
Yield:	4 lb 12 oz		2403 g	640%

PROCEDURE

Mixing: Angel food method.

Scaling and baking: See Table 29.1.

Per 1 ounce:
Calories, 70; Protein, 2 g; Fat, 0 g (0% cal.); Cholesterol, 0 mg;
Carbohydrates, 16 g; Fiber, 0 g; Sodium, 50 mg.

VARIATION

Chocolate Angel Food Cake
Substitute 3 oz (90 g) cocoa for 3 oz (90 g) flour.

Icings: Production and Application

Producing and Handling Basic Types

Icings or frostings (the two terms mean the same thing) are sweet coatings for cakes and other baked goods. Icings have three main functions:

1. They improve the keeping qualities of the cake by forming a protective coating around it.
2. They contribute flavor and richness.
3. They improve appearance.

There are six basic kinds of icings:

Fondant	Fudge-type icing
Buttercream	Flat-type icing
Foam-type icing	Royal or decorator's icing

In addition, we consider two other preparations for cakes:

Glazes	Fillings

Use top-quality flavorings for icings so that they enhance the cake rather than detract from it. Use moderation when adding flavorings and colors. Flavors should be light and delicate. Colors should be delicate, pastel shades—except chocolate, of course.

FONDANT

Fondant is a sugar syrup that is crystallized to a smooth, creamy white mass. It is familiar as the icing for napoleons, éclairs, petits fours, and some cakes. When applied, it sets up into a shiny, nonsticky coating.

Because it is difficult to make in the bakeshop, fondant is almost always purchased already prepared, either in ready-to-use moist form or in a dry form that requires only the addition of water.

Guidelines for Using Fondant

1. Heat fondant over a warm water bath, stirring constantly, to thin the icing and make it pourable. *Do not heat over 100°F (38°C),* or it will lose its shine.

2. If the fondant is still too thick, thin it with a little simple sugar syrup or water (simple syrup blends in more easily).

3. Add flavorings and colorings as desired.

4. To make *chocolate fondant,* stir melted bitter chocolate into warm fondant until the desired color and flavor are reached. Chocolate thickens the fondant, so the icing may require more thinning with sugar syrup.

5. Apply fondant by pouring it over the item or by dipping items into it.

BUTTERCREAM

Buttercream icings are light, smooth mixtures of fat and confectioners' sugar. They may also contain eggs to increase their smoothness or lightness. These popular icings are used for many kinds of cake. They are easily flavored and colored to suit a variety of purposes.

We consider three basic kinds of buttercream:

1. *Simple buttercreams* are made by creaming together fat and sugar to the desired consistency and lightness. A small quantity of egg whites may be whipped in.

   Decorator's buttercream is a simple buttercream used for making flowers and other cake decorations. It is creamed only a little because if too much air is beaten in, it would not be able to hold delicate shapes.

2. *Meringue-type buttercreams* are prepared by first beating egg whites and adding a boiling syrup or just sugar. Soft butter is then mixed into the meringue. This is a very light, smooth icing.

3. *French buttercreams* are similar to the meringue type, but the foam is made with egg yolks (and, sometimes, whole eggs) and boiling syrup. This is a very rich, light icing.

   Butter, especially sweet, unsalted butter, is the preferred fat for buttercreams because of its flavor and melt-in-the-mouth quality. Icings made with shortening only can be unpleasant because the fat congeals and coats the inside of the mouth and does not melt. However, butter makes a less stable icing because it melts so easily. There are two ways around this problem:

1. Use buttercreams in cool weather only.

2. Blend a small quantity of emulsified shortening with the butter to stabilize it.

Simple Buttercream

Yield: 3 lb 10 oz (1850 g)

U.S.	Metric	Ingredients	PROCEDURE
1 lb	500 g	Butter	1. Cream together the butter, shortening, and sugar until well blended, using the paddle attachment.
8 oz	250 g	Shortening	
2 lb	1 kg	Confectioners' sugar (10X)	2. Add the egg whites, lemon juice, and vanilla. Blend in at medium speed. Then mix at high speed until light and fluffy.
2.5 oz	75 g	Egg whites	
2 tsp	10 mL	Lemon juice	
1 tbsp	15 mL	Vanilla	

Per 1 ounce:
Calories, 150; Protein, 0 g; Fat, 10 g (58% cal.); Cholesterol, 15 mg;
Carbohydrates, 16 g; Fiber, 0 g; Sodium, 65 mg.

VARIATIONS

Decorator's Buttercream

Use 1 lb 8 oz (750 g) regular shortening, no butter. Omit lemon juice and vanilla. Reduce egg whites to 2 oz (60 g). Blend at low speed until smooth; do not whip.

Cream Cheese Icing

Substitute cream cheese for the butter and shortening. Omit egg whites. If necessary, thin the icing with cream or milk. If desired, flavor with grated lemon or orange zest instead of vanilla.

Meringue-Type Buttercream

Yield: 5 lb 12 oz (2900 g)

U.S.	Metric	Ingredients	PROCEDURE
2 lb 8 oz	1 kg 250 mL	Sugar Water	1. Combine the sugar and water in a saucepan. Bring to a boil, stirring to dissolve the sugar. 2. Continue to boil until the syrup reaches a temperature of 240°F (115°C).
1 lb	500 g	Egg whites	3. While the syrup is boiling, beat the egg whites in a clean, grease-free bowl, using the whip attachment, until they form firm, moist peaks. Do not overbeat. 4. As soon as the syrup reaches 240°F (115°C), pour it very slowly into the egg whites while the mixer is running at medium speed. 5. Continue to beat until the meringue is cool and forms stiff peaks. (You have now made an Italian meringue. For more information, see Chapter 31.)
2 lb 8 oz 2 tsp 1 tbsp	1 kg 250 g 10 mL 15 mL	Butter, soft Emulsified shortening Lemon juice Vanilla	6. With the mixer still running at medium speed, begin adding the butter, a little at a time. Add it just as fast as it can be absorbed by the meringue. 7. When all the butter is beaten in, add the shortening in the same way. 8. Beat in the lemon juice and vanilla.

Per 1 ounce:
Calories, 130; Protein, 1 g; Fat, 10 g (67% cal.); Cholesterol, 20 mg;
Carbohydrates, 10 g; Fiber, 0 g; Sodium, 90 mg.

French Buttercream

Yield: 5 lb 8 oz (2750 g)

U.S.	Metric	Ingredients	PROCEDURE
2 lb 8 oz	1 kg 250 mL	Sugar Water	1. Combine the sugar and water in a saucepan. Bring to a boil, stirring to dissolve the sugar. 2. Continue to boil until the syrup reaches a temperature of 240°F (115°C).
12 oz	375 g	Egg yolks	3. While the syrup is boiling, beat the yolks with the whip attachment until they are thick and light. 4. As soon as the syrup reaches 240°F (115°C), pour it very slowly into the beaten yolks while the mixer is running at second speed. 5. Continue to beat until the mixture is cool and the yolks are very light and thick.
2 lb 8 oz 1 tbsp	1.25 kg 15 mL	Butter, soft Vanilla	6. With the mixer still running, add the butter, a little at a time. Add it just as fast as it can be absorbed by the mixture. 7. Beat in the vanilla. If the icing is too soft, refrigerate until it is firm enough to spread.

Per 1 ounce:
Calories, 150; Protein, 1 g; Fat, 12 g (71% cal.); Cholesterol, 80 mg;
Carbohydrates, 10 g; Fiber, 0 g; Sodium, 110 mg.

VARIATIONS

Flavored buttercreams are made by adding the desired flavoring to any of the basic buttercream recipes. In addition to the two variations given below, extracts and emulsions such as lemon, orange, and almond may be used.

Chocolate Buttercream

Add 4–5 oz (125–150 g) sweet chocolate, melted and cooled, to each 1 pound (500 g) buttercream.

Coffee Buttercream

For each 1 pound (500 g) buttercream, add 1½ tbsp (22 mL) instant coffee dissolved in 2 tsp (10 mL) hot water.

FOAM-TYPE ICING

Foam icings, sometimes called *boiled icings,* are simply meringues made with a boiling syrup. Some also contain stabilizing ingredients like gelatin.

Foam-type icings should be applied thickly to cakes and left in peaks and swirls.

These icings are not stable. They should be used the day they are prepared. *Italian meringue,* discussed in Chapter 31, is the simplest foam-type icing. Follow the recipe on page 862 but add 8 ounces (250 g) corn syrup to the sugar and water for the boiled syrup. The meringue is usually flavored with vanilla.

FLAT ICING

Flat icings, also called *water icings,* are simply mixtures of 10X sugar, water, and, sometimes, corn syrup and flavoring. They are used mostly for coffee cakes, Danish pastry, and sweet rolls. Flat icings are warmed to 100°F (38°C) for application and are handled like fondant.

FUDGE-TYPE ICING

Fudge-type icings are rich cooked icings. Many are made somewhat like candy. Fudge icings are heavy and thick, and they may be flavored with a variety of ingredients. They are used on cupcakes, layer cakes, loaf cakes, and sheet cakes.

Fudge icings are stable and hold up well on cakes and in storage. Stored icings must be covered tightly to prevent drying and crusting.

To use stored fudge icing, warm it in a double boiler until soft enough to spread.

Fudge-type icings do not necessarily contain chocolate. Plain white fudge icings may be flavored with vanilla, almond, maple, coffee, or other desired flavoring.

 ## Flat Icing

Yield: 2 lb 8 oz (1250 g)

U.S.	Metric	Ingredients	PROCEDURE
2 lb	1 kg	Confectioners' sugar (10X or 6X)	1. Mix all ingredients together until smooth.
6 oz	180 g	Water, hot	2. To use, place desired amount in a double boiler. Warm to 100°F (38°C) and apply to the product to be iced.
2 oz	60 g	Corn syrup	
1½ tsp	8 mL	Vanilla	

Per 1 ounce:
Calories, 90; Protein, 0 g; Fat, 0 g (0% cal.); Cholesterol, 0 mg; Carbohydrates, 24 g; Fiber, 0 g; Sodium, 0 mg.

Caramel Fudge Icing

Yield: 4 lb (2 kg)

U.S.	Metric	Ingredients	PROCEDURE
3 lb	1500 g	Brown sugar	1. Combine the sugar and milk in a saucepan. Bring to a boil, stirring to dissolve the sugar. Using a brush dipped in water, wash down the sides of the saucepan to prevent sugar crystals from forming. (See "Sugar Cooking," Chapter 32.)
1½ pt	750 mL	Milk	
12 oz	375 g	Butter or shortening	2. Boil the mixture slowly, without stirring, until it reaches 240°F (115°C).
¼ tsp	1 mL	Salt	3. Pour the mixture into the bowl of a mixer. Add the butter and salt. Mix in with the paddle attachment.
1 tbsp	15 mL	Vanilla	4. Turn off the machine. Let the mixture cool to 110°F (43°C).
			5. Add the vanilla and turn the machine on low speed. Beat the icing until it is smooth and creamy in texture. If it is too thick, thin it with a little cream or milk.
			6. Spread on cooled cake while the icing is warm, or rewarm it in a double boiler.

Per 1 ounce:
Calories, 130; Protein, 0 g; Fat, 4.5 g (33% cal.); Cholesterol, 15 mg; Carbohydrates, 21 g; Fiber, 0 g; Sodium, 65 mg.

Quick White Fudge Icing

Yield: 5 lb 3 oz (2600 g)

U.S.	Metric	Ingredients	PROCEDURE
8 oz	250 mL	Water	1. Place the water, butter, shortening, syrup, and salt in a saucepan. Bring to a boil.
4 oz	125 g	Butter	
4 oz	125 g	Emulsified shortening	
3 oz	90 g	Corn syrup	
½ tsp	2 mL	Salt	
4 lb	2 kg	Confectioners' sugar (10X or 6X)	2. Sift the sugar into the bowl of a mixer.
			3. Using the paddle attachment and with the machine running on low speed, add the boiling water mixture. Blend until smooth. Icing will become lighter the more it is mixed.
1 tbsp	15 mL	Vanilla	4. Blend in the vanilla.
			5. Use while still warm, or rewarm in a double boiler. If necessary, thin with hot water.

Per 1 ounce:
Calories, 110; Protein, 0 g; Fat, 2.5 g (20% cal.); Cholesterol, 5 mg;
Carbohydrates, 23 g; Fiber, 0 g; Sodium, 25 mg.

VARIATION

Quick Chocolate Fudge Icing

Omit the butter in the basic recipe. Beat in 12 oz (375 g) melted unsweetened chocolate after the boiling water has been added. Thin with more hot water as needed.

Cocoa Fudge Icing

Yield: 4 lb 12 oz (2375 g)

U.S.	Metric	Ingredients	PROCEDURE
2 lb	1 kg	Granulated sugar	1. Combine the sugar, syrup, water, and salt in a saucepan. Bring to a boil, stirring to dissolve the sugar. Boil the mixture until it reaches 240°F (115°C). (See "Sugar Cooking," Chapter 32.)
10 oz	300 g	Corn syrup	
8 oz	250 mL	Water	
1 tsp	5 mL	Salt	
8 oz	250 g	Butter or part butter and part emulsified shortening	2. While the sugar is cooking, mix the fat, sugar, and cocoa until evenly combined, using the paddle attachment of the mixer.
1 lb	500 g	Confectioners' sugar (10X or 6X)	3. With the machine running at low speed, very slowly pour in the hot syrup.
6 oz	175 g	Cocoa	4. Mix in the vanilla. Continue to beat until the icing is smooth, creamy, and spreadable. If necessary, thin with a little hot water.
to taste	to taste	Vanilla	
as needed	as needed	Hot water	5. Use while still warm, or rewarm in a double boiler.

Per 1 ounce:
Calories, 110; Protein, 0 g; Fat, 2.5 g (20% cal.); Cholesterol, 5 mg;
Carbohydrates, 22 g; Fiber, 1 g; Sodium, 60 mg.

VARIATION

Vanilla Fudge Icing

Use evaporated milk or light cream instead of water for the syrup. Omit cocoa. Adjust consistency with additional confectioners' sugar (to thicken) or water (to thin). Other flavorings may be used in place of vanilla, such as almond, maple, peppermint, or coffee.

ROYAL ICING

Royal icing, also called *decorating* or *decorator's icing*, is similar to flat icings except that it is much thicker and is made with egg whites, which make it hard and brittle when dry. It is used almost exclusively for decorative work.

To prepare royal icing:

1. Place the desired amount of 10X sugar in a mixing bowl. Add a small quantity of cream of tartar (for whiteness)—about ⅛ teaspoon per pound of sugar (1 g per kilogram).

2. Beat in egg white, a little at a time, until the sugar forms a smooth paste. You will need 2 to 3 ounces egg whites per pound of sugar (125 g per kilogram).

3. Keep unused icing covered with a damp cloth at all times to prevent hardening.

GLAZES

Glazes are thin, glossy, transparent coatings that give shine to baked products and help prevent drying.

The simplest glaze is a sugar syrup or diluted corn syrup brushed onto coffee cakes or Danish while the glaze is hot. See Chapter 27 for recipe. Syrup glazes may contain gelatin or waxy maize starch. Fruit glazes, the most popular being apricot, are available commercially prepared. They are melted, thinned with a little water, and brushed on while hot.

Fruit glazes may also be made by melting apricot or other preserves and forcing them through a strainer.

One of the most common uses of glazes in cake making is to coat the fruit arranged on the top of fruit tortes (see p. 807).

FILLINGS

Fillings are sometimes used instead of icings between cake layers. Fillings are also used in such products as jelly rolls, Danish, and other pastries.

1. **Fruit fillings.**
   Fruit fillings may be cooked or uncooked.

   Cooked fruit fillings are chopped or puréed fruits or fruit juices thickened with starch or eggs. They are prepared somewhat like pie fillings (see Chapter 31).

   Uncooked fruit fillings include jellies and preserves and dried fruits that have been ground and flavored (see recipes in Chapter 27). Fresh fruits, such as the strawberries in strawberry shortcake, are also used.

   Many ready-to-use fruit fillings are on the market.

2. **Cream fillings.**
   Cream fillings include pastry cream (recipes in Chapter 32) and various pudding-type preparations.

   Desserts with cream fillings should be assembled as close to service time as possible and kept refrigerated to avoid health hazards.

3. **Whipped cream.**
   Whipped cream is used as a dessert topping, filling, and frosting. See page 629 for instructions on whipping and handling heavy cream.

   Artificial whipped toppings resemble whipped cream in appearance. They should be used only if your customers actually like them.

Assembling and Icing Cakes

SELECTION OF ICING

The flavor, texture, and color of the icing must be compatible with the cake.

1. **In general, use heavy frostings with heavy cakes and light frostings with light cakes.**
    For example, ice angel food cakes with a simple flat icing, fondant, or a light, fluffy boiled icing.
    High-ratio cakes go well with buttercreams and fudge-type icings.
    Shortened sponge layer cakes (genoise) are often combined with fruits or fruit fillings, light French or meringue-type buttercream, whipped cream, or flavored fondant.

2. **Use the best-quality flavorings, and use them sparingly. The flavor of the frosting should not be stronger than the cake.**
    Fudge-type icings may be flavored more strongly, as long as the flavor is of good quality.

3. **Use coloring sparingly. Light, pastel shades are more appetizing than loud colors.**
    Paste colors give the best results. Mix a little color with a small portion of the icing, then use this icing to color the rest.

Procedure for Assembling Layer Cakes

1. Cool cake layers completely before assembling and icing.

2. Trim layers, if necessary.
    - Remove any ragged edges.
    - Slightly rounded tops are easily covered by icing, but excessively large bumps may have to be cut off.
    - If desired, layers may be split in half horizontally. This makes the cake higher and increases the proportion of filling to cake. See Figure 29.2.

3. Brush all crumbs from cakes. Loose crumbs make the icing process difficult.

4. Place the bottom layer *upside down* (to give a flat surface for the filling) on a cardboard cake circle of the same diameter. Place the cake in the center of a cake turntable.
    If a cake circle or turntable is not available, place the cake on a serving plate and slip sheets of waxed paper or parchment under the edges of the cake to keep the plate clean.

5. Spread filling on the bottom layer out to the edges. If the filling is different from the icing for the outside of the cake, be careful not to spread the filling over the edges.
    Use the proper amount of filling. If applied too heavily, it will ooze out when the top layer is set in place.

6. Place the top layer on the bottom layer, right side up.

7. Ice the cake:
    - If a thin or light icing is used, pour or spread the icing onto the center of the cake. Then spread it to the edges and down the sides with a spatula.
    - If a heavy icing is used, it may be necessary to spread the sides first, then place a good quantity of icing in the center of the top and push it to the edges with the spatula.

    Pushing the icing rather than pulling or dragging it with the spatula prevents pulling up crumbs and getting them mixed with the icing.
    Use enough icing to cover the entire cake generously, but not excessively, with an even layer.
    Smooth the icing with the spatula or leave it textured or swirled, as desired.
    The finished, iced cake should have a perfectly level top and perfectly straight, even sides.

Figure 29.2 Cake layers may be split in half horizontally, using a long-bladed, serrated knife.

SMALL CAKES

1. Cupcakes are iced by dipping the tops in a soft icing. Twist the cakes slightly and pull them out quickly in one smooth motion.

   Cupcakes may also be iced by spreading icing on with a spatula. Practice is necessary to develop speed and efficiency.

2. Petits fours are tiny cakes cut from sheet cakes. Select a cake that doesn't crumble easily. Carefully cut it into desired shapes. Remove all crumbs and place the cakes on a rack over a sheet pan. Ice by pouring fondant or flat icing over them to cover completely.

SHEET CAKES

Sheet cakes are ideal for volume service because they require little labor to bake, ice, and decorate, and they keep well as long as they are uncut.

For special occasions, sheet cakes are sometimes decorated as a single unit with a design or picture in colored icing, a "Happy Special Occasion" message, and so on. It is more common, however, to ice them for individual service, as in the following procedure.

Procedure for Icing Sheet Cakes

1. Turn out the cake onto the bottom of another sheet pan or tray, as described on page 810. Cool the cake thoroughly.

2. Trim the edges evenly with a serrated knife.

3. Brush all crumbs from the cake.

4. Place a quantity of icing in the center of the cake. With a spatula, push the icing to the edges. Smooth the top with the spatula, giving the entire cake an even layer of icing.

5. With a long knife or spatula, mark the entire cake off into portions, as in Figure 29.3, by pressing the back of the knife lightly into the icing. Do not cut the cake.

6. Using a paper cone or pastry bag fitted with a star tube, pipe a rosette or swirl of icing onto the center of each marked-off portion, or select another decoration, as desired. Whatever decorations you use, keep them simple, and make them the same for every portion. The finished sheet cake will resemble that in Figure 29.4.

7. Hold for service. Cut as close as possible to service time to keep the cake from drying.

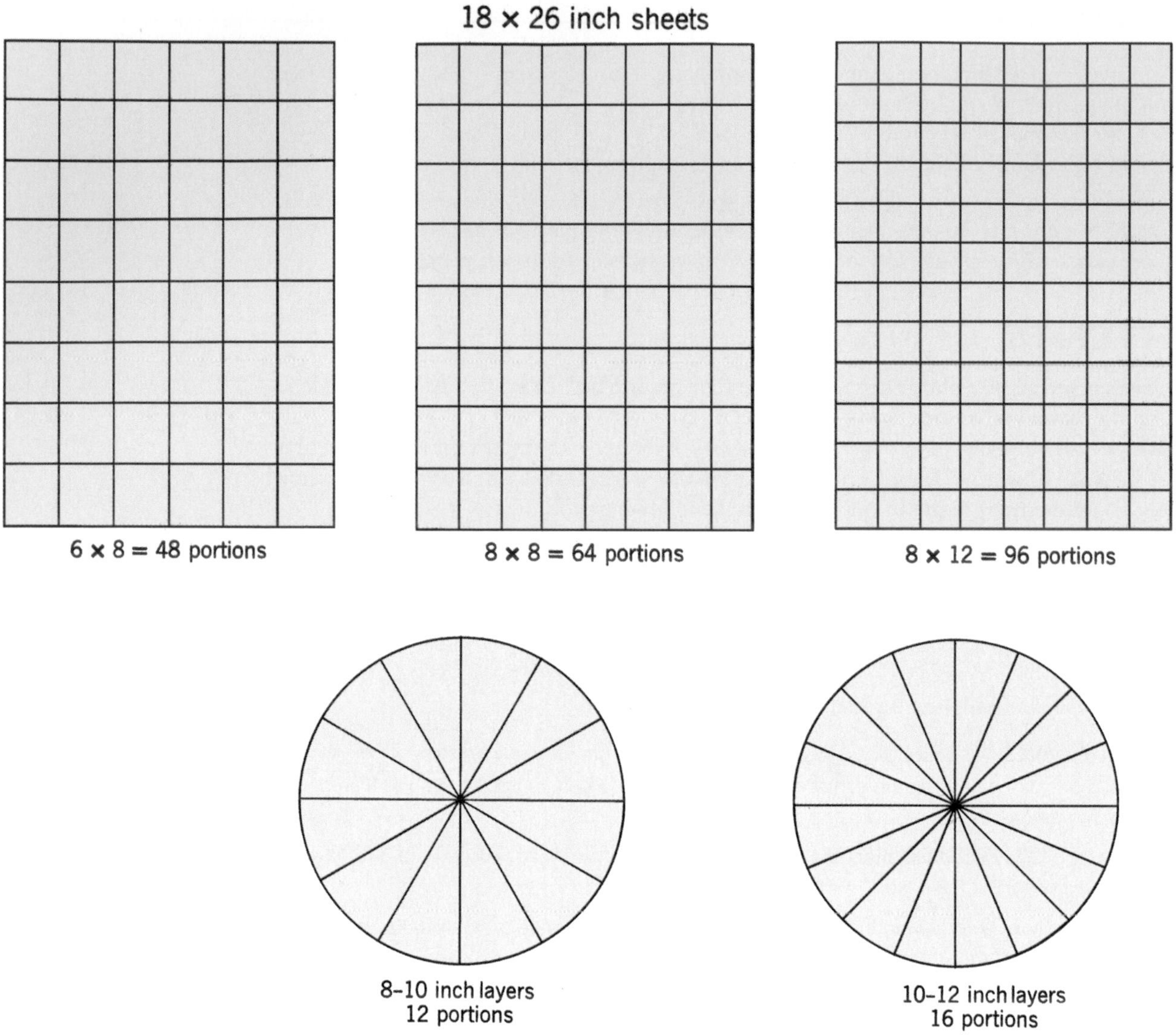

18 × 26 inch sheets

6 × 8 = 48 portions   8 × 8 = 64 portions   8 × 12 = 96 portions

8–10 inch layers
12 portions

10–12 inch layers
16 portions

Figure 29.3 Cake-cutting guides for sheet cakes and round layer cakes. For sheets measuring 13 × 18 inches (33 × 46 cm), simply divide the above diagrams for full-sized sheet cakes in half.

Figure 29.4 A finished sheet cake marked off into portions and decorated so that each portion is identical.

Terms for Review

creaming method	angel food method	fondant	flat icing
two-stage method	chiffon method	buttercream	fudge icing
blending method	high-fat cakes	foam icing	royal icing
foaming method	low-fat cakes		glaze

Questions for Discussion

1. Briefly list the steps in each of the four basic cake-mixing methods presented in this chapter.

2. What are the reasons, in the creaming method, for creaming the butter and sugar until the mixture is light and fluffy?

3. In both the creaming method and the two-stage method, scraping down the sides of the bowl is emphasized. Why is this necessary?

4. What might the finished product be like if you tried to mix a low-fat cake by the two-stage method? Explain.

5. Examine the following cake formulas and indicate which mixing method you would use for each.

CAKE 1

2 lb	Cake flour	1 kg
1 lb 2 oz	Emulsified shortening	525 g
1 oz	Salt	30 g
1.5 oz	Baking powder	45 g
2 lb 8 oz	Fine granulated sugar	1250 g
1 lb	Skim milk	500 g
1 lb 5 oz	Whole eggs	650 g
10 oz	Skim milk	300 g

CAKE 2

3 lb	Whole eggs	1.5 kg
1 lb	Egg yolks	500 g
2 lb 4 oz	Sugar	1125 g
2 lb	Cake flour	1 kg
6 oz	Cornstarch	175 g
6 oz	Melted butter	175 g

CAKE 3

1 lb	Butter	500 g
8 oz	Shortening	250 g
4 lb	Sugar	2 kg
1 oz	Vanilla	30 g
1 lb 4 oz	Whole eggs	625 g
3 lb 8 oz	Cake flour	1750 g
10 oz	Cocoa powder	300 g
1.5 oz	Baking soda	45 g
3 lb	Buttermilk	1.5 kg
1 lb 8 oz	Water	750 g

6. What is the most important rule to consider when using fondant?

7. Compare the keeping qualities of simple buttercreams and meringue-type buttercreams.

8. List the steps in assembling and icing a three-layer cake.

chapter 30

Cookies

The word cookie means "small cake," and that's exactly what a cookie is. In fact, some cookies are made from cake batter. For some products, such as certain kinds of brownies, it's difficult to know whether to classify them as cakes or cookies.

Most cookie formulas, however, call for less liquid than cake formulas do. Cookie doughs range from soft to very stiff, unlike the thinner batters for cakes. This difference in moisture content means some differences in mixing methods, although the basic procedures are much like those for cakes.

The most apparent differences between cakes and cookies are in the makeup. Because most cookies are individually formed or shaped, a great deal of hand labor is involved. Learning correct methods and practicing diligently are essential for efficiency.

Cookie Characteristics and Their Causes

Cookies come in an infinite variety of shapes, sizes, flavors, and textures. Characteristics that are desirable in some are not desirable in others. For example, we want some cookies to be crisp and others to be soft. We want some to hold their shape and others to spread during baking. In order to produce the characteristics we want and to correct faults, it is useful to know what causes these characteristics.

After reading this chapter, you should be able to

1. List the factors responsible for crispness, softness, chewiness, and spread in cookies.

2. Demonstrate the three basic cookie mixing methods.

3. Prepare the seven basic cookie types: dropped, bagged, rolled, molded, icebox, bar, and sheet.

4. Prepare pans for, bake, and cool cookies.

CRISPNESS

Cookies are crisp if they are very low in moisture. The following factors contribute to crispness:

1. Low proportion of liquid in the mix. Most crisp cookies are made from a stiff dough.
2. High sugar and fat content.
3. Evaporation of moisture during baking due to high temperatures and/or long baking.
4. Small size or thin shape, so the cookies dry quickly during baking.
5. Proper storage. Crisp cookies can become soft if they absorb moisture.

SOFTNESS

Softness is the opposite of crispness, so it has the opposite causes, as follows:

1. High proportion of liquid in mix.
2. Low sugar and fat.
3. Honey, molasses, or corn syrup included in formulas. These sugars are *hygroscopic*, which means they readily absorb moisture from the air or from their surroundings.
4. Underbaking.
5. Large size or thick shape. The cookies retain moisture.
6. Proper storage. Soft cookies can become stale and dry if not tightly covered or wrapped.

CHEWINESS

Moisture is necessary for chewiness, but other factors are also required. In other words, all chewy cookies are soft, but not all soft cookies are chewy.

1. High sugar and liquid content, but low fat content.
2. High proportion of eggs.
3. Strong flour, or gluten developed during mixing.

SPREAD

Spread is desirable in some cookies, while others must hold their shape. Several factors contribute to spread or lack of spread.

1. Sugar.
   High sugar content increases spread. Coarse granulated sugar increases spread, whereas fine sugar or confectioners' sugar reduces spread.

2. Leavening.
   High baking soda or baking ammonia content encourages spread. So does long creaming, which incorporates air.

3. Temperature.
   Low oven temperature increases spread. High temperature decreases spread because the cookie sets up before it has a chance to spread too much.

4. **Liquid.**
   A slack batter—that is, one with a high liquid content—spreads more than a stiff dough.

5. **Flour.**
   Strong flour or activation of gluten decreases spread.

6. **Pan grease.**
   Cookies spread more if baked on a heavily greased pan.

Mixing Methods

Cookie-mixing methods are much like cake-mixing methods. The major difference is that less liquid is usually incorporated, so mixing is somewhat easier.

Less liquid means that gluten is less developed by the mixing. Also, a smooth, uniform mix is easier to obtain.

There are three basic cookie mixing methods:

1. One-stage
2. Creaming
3. Sponge

These methods are subject to many variations due to differences in formulas. The general procedures are as follows, but always be sure to follow the exact instructions when a formula indicates a variation in the procedure.

ONE-STAGE METHOD

This method is the counterpart of the blending or two-stage cake-mixing method, discussed in the previous chapter. Cake batters have more liquid, so it must be added in two or more stages in order to blend uniformly. Low-moisture cookies, on the other hand, can be mixed all in one stage.

Procedure for One-Stage Method

1. Scale ingredients accurately. Have all ingredients at room temperature.
2. Place all ingredients in mixer. With the paddle attachment, mix at low speed until uniformly blended. Scrape down the sides of the bowl as necessary.

CREAMING METHOD

This is nearly identical to the creaming method for cakes. Because cookies require less liquid, it is not necessary to add the liquid alternately with the flour. It can be added all at once.

Procedure for Creaming Method

1. Scale ingredients accurately. Have all ingredients at room temperature.
2. Place the fat, sugar, salt, and spices in the mixing bowl. With the paddle attachment, cream these ingredients at low speed.
   For light cookies, cream until the mix is light and fluffy, incorporating more air for leavening.
   For a dense, chewy cookie, cream only slightly.
3. Add the eggs and liquid, if any, and blend in at low speed.
4. Sift in the flour and leavening. Mix until just combined.

SPONGE METHOD

This method is essentially the same as the egg-foam methods for cakes. The procedure varies considerably, depending on the ingredients. Batches should be kept small because the batter is delicate.

Procedure for Sponge Method

1. Scale all ingredients accurately. Have all ingredients at room temperature, or warm the eggs slightly for greater volume, as for sponge cakes.

2. Following the procedure given in the formula used, whip the eggs (whole, yolks, or whites) and the sugar to the proper stage: soft peaks for whites, thick and light for whole eggs or yolks.

3. Fold in the remaining ingredients as specified in the recipe. Be careful not to overmix or to deflate the eggs.

Types and Makeup Methods

We can classify cookie types by makeup method as well as by mixing method. Grouping by the makeup method is perhaps more useful from the point of view of production because mixing methods are relatively simple, whereas makeup procedures vary considerably.

In this section, we present basic procedures for producing seven cookie types:

1. Dropped   5. Icebox
2. Bagged   6. Bar
3. Rolled   7. Sheet
4. Molded

No matter what makeup method you use, follow one important rule: *Make all cookies of uniform size and thickness.* This is essential for even baking. Because baking times are so short, small cookies may burn before large ones are done.

DROPPED COOKIES

Dropped cookies are made from a soft dough or batter. They are fast and easy to make up. Many sponge or foam-type batters are made up as dropped cookies.

1. Select the proper size scoop for accurate portioning.

    A No. 30 scoop makes a large cookie, about 1 oz (30 g).
    A No. 40 scoop makes a medium cookie.
    Nos. 50, 60, or small scoops make small cookies.

2. Drop the cookies onto the prepared baking sheets. Allow enough space between cookies for spreading.

3. Rich cookies spread by themselves. However, if the formula requires it, flatten the mounds of batter slightly with a weight dipped in sugar.

BAGGED COOKIES

Bagged or pressed cookies are also made from soft doughs. The dough must be soft enough to be forced through a pastry bag, but stiff enough to hold its shape.

1. Fit a pastry bag with a tip of the desired size and shape. Fill the bag with the cookie dough. Review Figure 18.3 for tips on use of the pastry bag.

2. Press out cookies of desired shape and size directly onto prepared cookie sheets.

ROLLED COOKIES

Cookies rolled and cut from a stiff dough are not often made in commercial food service because they require excessive labor. Also, scraps are always left over after cutting. When rerolled, these scraps make inferior, tough cookies.

1. Chill dough thoroughly.

2. Roll dough to ⅛ inch (3 mm) thick on a floured canvas or floured workbench. Use as little flour as possible for dusting because the flour can toughen the cookies.

3. Cut out cookies with cookie cutters and place on prepared baking sheets. Cut as close together as possible to reduce the quantity of scraps.

MOLDED COOKIES

The first part of this procedure (steps 1 and 2) is simply a fast and fairly accurate way of dividing the dough into equal portions. Each piece is then molded into the desired shape. This usually consists of simply flattening the pieces out with a weight. For some traditional cookies, special molds are used to flatten the dough and, at the same time, stamp it with a design.

The pieces may also be shaped by hand into crescents, fingers, or other shapes.

1. Roll the dough into long cylinders about 1 inch (2½ cm) thick, or whatever size is required. (Refrigerate the dough if it is too soft to handle.)

2. With a knife or bench scraper, cut the roll into 1-ounce (30-g) pieces, or whatever size is required.

3. Place the pieces on prepared baking sheets, leaving 2 inches (5 cm) of space between each.

4. Flatten cookies with a weight (such as a can) dipped in granulated sugar after pressing each cookie.

   A fork is sometimes used for flattening the dough, as for peanut butter cookies.

5. Alternative method: After step 2, shape the dough by hand into desired shapes.

ICEBOX COOKIES

The icebox or refrigerator method is ideal for operations that wish to have freshly baked cookies on hand at all times. The rolls of dough may be made up in advance and stored. Cookies can easily be cut and baked as needed.

1. Scale dough into pieces of uniform size, from 1½ pounds (700 g), if you are making small cookies, to 3 pounds (1400 g), for large cookies.

2. Form the dough into cylinders from 1 to 2 inches (2½ to 5 cm) in diameter, depending on the size cookie desired.

   For accurate portioning, it is important to make all the cylinders of dough the same thickness and length.

3. Wrap the cylinders in parchment or waxed paper, place them on sheet pans, and refrigerate overnight.

4. Unwrap the dough and cut into slices of *uniform thickness*. The exact thickness required depends on the size of the cookie and how much the dough spreads during baking. The usual range is from ⅛ to ½ inch (3 to 12 mm).

   A slicing machine is recommended for ensuring even thickness. Doughs containing nuts or fruits should be sliced by hand with a knife.

5. Place the slices on prepared baking sheets, allowing 2 inches (5 cm) of space between cookies.

BAR COOKIES

Bar cookies are so called because the dough is shaped into long bars, which are baked and then cut. After cutting, they may be baked again, as in the case of biscotti, which means "twice baked." Do not confuse bar cookies with sheet cookies (see below), which are often called "bars" by consumers.

1. Scale the dough into 1¾-pound (800-g) units (1-pound units, or 500-g units, may be used for smaller cookies).

2. Shape the pieces of dough into cylinders the length of the sheet pans. Place three strips on each greased pan, spacing them well apart.

3. Flatten the dough with the fingers into strips about 3 to 4 inches wide and about ¼ inch thick (8 to 10 cm wide, 6 mm thick).

4. If required, brush with egg wash.

5. Bake as directed in the formula.

6. After baking, while cookies are still warm, cut each strip into bars about 1¾ inches (4½ cm) wide.

SHEET COOKIES

Sheet cookies vary so much that it is nearly impossible to give a single procedure for all of them. Some of them are almost like sheet cakes, only denser and richer. They may even be iced like sheet cakes. Others consist of two or three layers added and baked in separate stages. The following procedure is a general guideline only.

1. Spread the cookie mixture into prepared sheet pans. Make sure the thickness is even.

2. If required, add topping or brush with an egg wash.

3. Bake as directed. Cool.

4. Apply icing or topping, if any.

5. Cut into individual squares or rectangles.

Panning, Baking, and Cooling

PREPARING THE PANS

1. Use clean, unwarped pans.

2. Lining the sheets with parchment or silicone paper is fast, and it eliminates the necessity of greasing the pans.

3. A heavily greased pan increases the spread of the cookie. A greased and floured pan decreases spread.

4. Some high-fat cookies can be baked on ungreased pans.

BAKING

1. Most cookies are baked at a relatively high temperature for a short time.

2. Too low a temperature increases spreading and may produce hard, dry, pale cookies.

3. Too high a temperature decreases spreading and may burn the edges or bottoms.

4. Even one minute of overbaking can burn cookies, so watch them closely. Also, the heat of the pan continues to bake the cookies even after they are removed from the oven.

5. Doneness is indicated by color. The edges and bottoms should just be turning a light golden color.

6. With some rich doughs, burnt bottoms may be a problem. In this case, *double-pan* the cookies by placing the sheet pan on a second pan of the same size.

COOLING

1. Remove the cookies from the pans while they are still warm, or they may stick.

2. If the cookies are very soft, do not remove them from the pans until they are cool enough and firm enough to handle. Cookies may be soft when hot but become crisp when cool.

3. Do not cool cookies too rapidly or in cold drafts, or they may crack.

4. Cool completely before storing.

Chocolate Chip Cookies

Ingredients	U.S.		Metric	Percentage
Butter and/or shortening	12 oz		350 g	60%
Granulated sugar	10 oz		300 g	50%
Brown sugar	10 oz		300 g	50%
Salt	0.25 oz (1½ tsp)		8 g (7 mL)	1.25%
Eggs	6 oz		175 g	30%
Vanilla	2 tsp		10 mL	1.5%
Water	2 oz		60 g	10%
Pastry flour	1 lb	4 oz	600 g	100%
Baking soda	0.25 oz (1½ tsp)		8 g (7 mL)	1.25%
Chocolate chips	1 lb	4 oz	600 g	100%
Chopped walnuts or pecans	8 oz		250 g	40%
Yield:	5 lb	8 oz	2661 g	444%

PROCEDURE

Mixing: Creaming method. Blend in chocolate chips and nuts last.

Makeup: Drop method. Use greased or parchment-lined baking sheets.

Baking: 375°F (190°C), 8–12 minutes, depending on size.

Per 1 ounce:
Calories, 120; Protein, 2 g; Fat, 7 g (47% cal.); Cholesterol, 15 mg;
Carbohydrates, 16 g; Fiber, 1 g; Sodium, 90 mg.

VARIATION

Brown Sugar Nut Cookies

Omit granulated sugar and use 100% (1 lb 4 oz/600 g) brown sugar. Omit chocolate chips and increase nuts to 100% (1 lb 4 oz/600 g).

Oatmeal Raisin Cookies

Ingredients	U.S.		Metric	Percentage
Butter and/or shortening	8 oz		250 g	67%
Brown sugar	1 lb		500 g	133%
Salt	1 tsp		5 g (5 mL)	1.5%
Eggs	4 oz		125 g	33%
Vanilla	2 tsp		10 mL	3%
Milk	1 oz		30 g	8%
Pastry flour	12 oz		375 g	100%
Baking powder	0.5 oz (1 tbsp)		15 g	4%
Baking soda	0.25 oz (1½ tsp)		8 g	2%
Rolled oats (quick cooking)	10 oz		300 g	83%
Raisins (see note)	8 oz		250 g	67%
Yield:	3 lb	11 oz	1858 g	500%

PROCEDURE

Mixing: Creaming method. Combine oats with other dry ingredients after they are sifted. Mix raisins into dough last.

Makeup: Drop method. Use greased or parchment-lined baking sheets.

Baking: 375°F (190°C), 10–12 minutes, depending on size.

Per 1 ounce:
Calories, 110; Protein, 2 g; Fat, 4 g (31% cal.); Cholesterol, 15 mg;
Carbohydrates, 18 g; Fiber, 1 g; Sodium, 135 mg.

Note: If raisins are hard and dry, soak them in hot water 30 minutes, drain, and dry well before adding to cookie dough.

Tea Cookies

Ingredients	U.S.		Metric	Percentage
Butter or half butter and half shortening	1 lb		500 g	67%
Granulated sugar		8 oz	250 g	33%
Confectioners' sugar		4 oz	125 g	17%
Eggs		6 oz	175 g	25%
Vanilla (or almond extract)		1½ tsp	8 mL	1%
Cake flour	1 lb	8 oz	750 g	100%
Yield:	3 lb	10 oz	1823 g	243%

PROCEDURE

Mixing: Creaming method.

Makeup: Bagged method. Make small cookies, about 1 inch (2.5 cm) in diameter, using a star tube or plain tube. Bag out onto ungreased or parchment-lined baking sheets.

Baking: 375°F (190°C), about 10 minutes.

Per 1 ounce:
Calories, 130; Protein, 1 g; Fat, 7 g (50% cal.); Cholesterol, 30 mg; Carbohydrates, 15 g; Fiber, 0 g; Sodium, 70 mg.

VARIATIONS

Almond Tea Cookies

Add 17% (4 oz/125 g) almond paste. Blend it thoroughly with the sugar before adding the butter.

Sandwich-Type Cookies

Select cookies with the same size and shape. Turn half of them over and dot the centers of the flat sides with a small amount of jam or fudge icing. Sandwich with the remaining cookies.

Chocolate Tea Cookies

Substitute 6 oz (175 g) cocoa for 6 oz (175 g) flour.

Ladyfingers

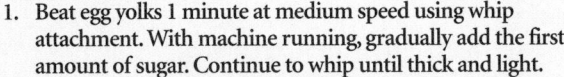

Ingredients	U.S.	Metric	Percentage
Egg yolks	6 oz	180 g	60%
Sugar	3 oz	90 g	30%
Egg whites	9 oz	270 g	90%
Sugar	5 oz	150 g	50%
Lemon juice	½ tsp	1 mL	0.4%
Pastry flour	10 oz	300 g	100%
Yield:	2 lb 1 oz (enough for about 6 dozen ladyfingers)	990 g	340%

PROCEDURE

Mixing: Sponge method.

1. Beat egg yolks 1 minute at medium speed using whip attachment. With machine running, gradually add the first amount of sugar. Continue to whip until thick and light.
2. Whip the egg whites until they form soft peaks. Add the sugar and lemon juice and beat until stiff but still moist.
3. Sift the flour and fold into the yolks.
4. Fold the whites into the batter.

Makeup: Bagged method. Use plain tube. Bag out strips measuring 3 inches × ¾ inch (7½ × 2 cm) onto pans that have been lined with parchment or greased and floured.

Baking: 375°F (190°C), about 10 minutes.

Per ladyfinger:
Calories, 35; Protein, 1 g; Fat, 1 g (24% cal.); Cholesterol, 30 mg; Carbohydrates, 6 g; Fiber, 1 g; Sodium, 5 mg.

Coconut Macaroons (Meringue Type)

Ingredients	U.S.		Metric
Egg whites		8 oz	250 g
Cream of tartar		1 tsp	2 g (5 mL)
Sugar	1 lb	4 oz	625 g
Vanilla (or rum flavor)		0.5 oz	15 mL
Macaroon coconut	1 lb		500 g
Yield:	2 lb 12 oz		1392 g

PROCEDURE

Mixing: Sponge method.

1. Beat the egg whites and cream of tartar until they form soft peaks. Gradually beat in the sugar. Continue to beat until stiff and glossy.
2. Fold in the coconut.

Makeup: Bagged method. Bag out with a star tube onto parchment-lined baking sheets.

Baking: 300°F (150°C), about 30 minutes.

Per 1 ounce:
Calories, 120; Protein, 1 g; Fat, 7 g (48% cal.); Cholesterol, 0 mg; Carbohydrates, 16 g; Fiber, 2 g; Sodium, 15 mg.

Sugar Cookies

Ingredients	U.S.		Metric	Percentage
Butter and/or shortening	1 lb		500 g	40%
Sugar	1 lb	4 oz	625 g	50%
Salt		2 tsp	10 g (10 mL)	0.9%
Eggs		4 oz	125 g	10%
Milk		4 oz	125 g	10%
Vanilla		½ oz	15 mL	1.25%
Cake flour	2 lb	8 oz	1250 g	100%
Baking powder		1¼ oz	35 g	3%
Yield:	5 lb	5 oz	2685 g	215%

PROCEDURE

Mixing: Creaming method.

Makeup: Rolled method. Before cutting the rolled-out dough, wash with milk and sprinkle with sugar. Use greased or parchment-lined baking sheets.

Baking: 375°F (190°C), 8–10 minutes.

Per 1 ounce:
Calories, 120; Protein, 1 g; Fat, 4.5 g (36% cal.); Cholesterol, 15 mg;
Carbohydrates, 17 g; Fiber, 0 g; Sodium, 150 mg.

VARIATIONS

Lemon rind, extract, or emulsion may be used in place of vanilla.

Rolled Brown Sugar Cookies

Increase butter to 50% (1 lb 4 oz/625 g). Omit granulated sugar and use 60% (1 lb 8 oz/750 g) brown sugar.

Rolled Chocolate Cookies

Substitute 4 oz (125 g) cocoa for 4 oz (125 g) flour.

Shortbread Cookies

Ingredients	U.S.		Metric	Percentage
Butter	1 lb	8 oz	750 g	75%
Sugar	1 lb		500 g	50%
Salt		0.25 oz (1½ tsp)	8 g (7 mL)	0.75%
Egg yolks (see note)		8 oz	250 g	25%
Flavoring (optional; see note)				
Pastry flour	2 lb		1000 g	100%
Yield:	5 lb		2508 g	250%

PROCEDURE

Mixing: Creaming method.

Makeup: Rolled method. Roll dough ¼ inch (½ cm) thick (this is thicker than most rolled cookies). Use greased or parchment-lined baking sheets.

Baking: 350°F (175°C), about 15 minutes.

Per 1 ounce:
Calories, 130; Protein, 2 g; Fat, 8 g (53% cal.); Cholesterol, 55 mg;
Carbohydrates, 14 g; Fiber, 2 g; Sodium, 105 mg.

Note: Traditional Scottish shortbread is made with butter, flour, and sugar—no eggs, flavoring, or liquid. Because the dough is crumbly, it is not rolled out but rather pressed into pans or molds and baked. For the recipe given here, you may make the cookies without added flavoring or flavor to taste with vanilla, almond, or lemon.

Cinnamon Cookies

Ingredients	U.S.	Metric	Percentage
Butter and/or shortening	1 lb	500 g	80%
Granulated sugar	8 oz	250 g	40%
Brown sugar	8 oz	250 g	40%
Salt	1 tsp	5 g (5 mL)	0.9%
Cinnamon	0.33 oz (1½ tbsp)	10 g	1.7%
Eggs	3 oz	90 g	15%
Milk	1 oz	30 g	5%
Pastry flour	1 lb 4 oz	625 g	100%
Yield:	3 lb 8 oz	1760 g	282%

PROCEDURE

Mixing: Creaming method.

Makeup: Molded method. Roll cut pieces in cinnamon sugar before placing on greased baking sheets and pressing flat.

Baking: 375°F (190°C), about 10 minutes.

Per 1 ounce:
Calories, 130; Protein, 1 g; Fat, 7 g (48% cal.); Cholesterol, 25 mg; Carbohydrates, 16 g; Fiber, 1 g; Sodium, 110 mg.

VARIATION

Chocolate Cinnamon Cookies
Substitute 4 oz (125 g) cocoa for 4 oz (125 g) flour.

Raisin Spice Bars

Ingredients	U.S.	Metric	Percentage
Sugar	1 lb 8 oz	700 g	100%
Butter and/or shortening	8 oz	225 g	33%
Eggs	8 oz	225 g	33%
Molasses	4 oz	125 g	17%
Pastry flour	1 lb 8 oz	700 g	100%
Cinnamon	2 tsp	4 g (10 mL)	0.6%
Ground cloves	½ tsp	1 g (2 mL)	0.16%
Ground ginger	1 tsp	2 g (5 mL)	0.3%
Baking soda	¾ tsp	3 g (3 mL)	0.5%
Salt	1 tsp	5 g (5 mL)	0.75%
Raisins (see note)	1 lb	475 g	67%
Yield:	5 lb 4 oz	2465 g	350%

PROCEDURE

Mixing: One-stage method.

Makeup: Bar method. Egg wash with whole eggs or egg whites.

Baking: 350°F (175°C), about 15 minutes.

Per 1 ounce:
Calories, 100; Protein, 1 g; Fat, 2.5 g (21% cal.); Cholesterol, 15 mg; Carbohydrates, 20 g; Fiber, 1 g; Sodium, 65 mg.

Note: If raisins are hard and dry, soak them in hot water 30 minutes, drain, and dry well before adding to the mix.

Peanut Butter Cookies

Ingredients	U.S.	Metric	Percentage
Butter and/or shortening	12 oz	375 g	75%
Brown sugar	8 oz	250 g	50%
Granulated sugar	8 oz	250 g	50%
Salt	1 tsp	5 g (5 mL)	1%
Peanut butter	12 oz	375 g	75%
Eggs	4 oz	125 g	25%
Pastry flour	1 lb	500 g	100%
Baking soda	1 tsp	5 g (5 mL)	1%
Yield:	3 lb 12 oz	1885 g	377%

Per 1 ounce:
Calories, 130; Protein, 2 g; Fat, 8 g (53% cal.); Cholesterol, 20 mg;
Carbohydrates, 14 g; Fiber, 1 g; Sodium, 135 mg.

PROCEDURE

Mixing: Creaming method. Cream peanut butter with the fat and sugar.

Makeup: Molded method. Use a fork instead of a weight to flatten the cookies. Use greased or parchment-lined baking sheets.

Baking: 375°F (190°C), 8–12 minutes, depending on size.

Icebox Cookies

Ingredients	U.S.	Metric	Percentage
Butter and/or shortening	2 lb	1000 g	67%
Granulated sugar	1 lb	500 g	33%
Confectioners' sugar	1 lb	500 g	33%
Salt	0.5 oz	15 g	1%
Eggs	8 oz	250 g	17%
Vanilla	0.5 oz	15 mL	1%
Pastry flour	3 lb	1500 g	100%
Yield:	7 lb 9 oz	3780 g	252%

Per 1 ounce:
Calories, 120; Protein, 1 g; Fat, 6 g (44% cal.); Cholesterol, 25 mg;
Carbohydrates, 16 g; Fiber, 1 g; Sodium, 110 mg.

PROCEDURE

Mixing: Creaming method.

Makeup: Icebox method. Scale dough strips to 1½ lb (750 g) each. Slice cookies ¼ inch (½ cm) thick. Bake on ungreased pans.

Baking: 375°F (190°C), about 12 minutes.

VARIATIONS

To reduce spread, use all confectioners' sugar.

Butterscotch Icebox Cookies

In place of sugars in basic recipe, use 67% (2 lb/1 kg) brown sugar and use only butter. Increase eggs to 25% (12 oz/375 g). Add 1 tsp (5 g or 5 mL) baking soda to the flour.

Chocolate Icebox Cookies

Add 17% (8 oz/250 g) melted unsweetened chocolate to the creamed butter and sugar.

Nut Icebox Cookies

Add 25% (12 oz/375 g) finely chopped nuts to the sifted flour in the basic recipe or the Butterscotch or Chocolate Cookie recipes.

Brownies

Ingredients	U.S.		Metric	Percentage
Unsweetened chocolate	1 lb		450 g	100%
Butter	1 lb 8 oz		675 g	150%
Eggs	1 lb 8 oz		675 g	150%
Sugar	3 lb		1350 g	300%
Salt		0.25 oz (1½ tsp)	7 g (7 mL)	1.5%
Vanilla		1 oz	30 mL	6%
Cake flour	1 lb		450 g	100%
Chopped walnuts or pecans	1 lb		450 g	100%
Yield:	9 lb 1 oz		4087 g	907%

PROCEDURE

Mixing: Sponge method.
1. Melt chocolate and butter together in a double boiler. Stir so that the mixture is smooth. Let it cool to room temperature.
2. Blend the eggs, sugar, and salt until well mixed, but do not whip. Add the vanilla.
3. Blend in the chocolate mixture.
4. Sift the flour and fold it in.
5. Fold in the nuts.

Makeup: Sheet method. Grease and flour the pans or line them with parchment. Quantity of basic recipe is enough for 1 full sheet pan, 18 × 26 inches (46 × 66 cm), 2 half-size sheet pans, 4 pans measuring 9 × 13 inches (23 × 33 cm), or 6 square pans measuring 9 inches (23 cm) per side.

If desired, batter may be sprinkled with an additional 50% (8 oz/225 g) chopped nuts after panning.

Baking: 325°F (165°C), about 60 minutes. For 2-inch (5-cm) square brownies, cut sheet pan 8 × 12 to yield 96 pieces.

Per 1 brownie:
Calories, 190; Protein, 3 g; Fat, 12 g (54% cal.); Cholesterol, 45 mg; Carbohydrates, 20 g; Fiber, 1 g; Sodium, 95 mg.

VARIATION

Butterscotch Brownies or Blondies

Omit chocolate. Use brown sugar instead of granulated sugar. Increase flour to 1 lb 6 oz (600 g).

Almond Biscotti

Ingredients	U.S.		Metric	Percentage
Eggs		10 oz	300 g	35%
Sugar	1 lb	2 oz	550 g	65%
Salt		0.4 oz (2 tsp)	12 g (10 mL)	2%
Vanilla		0.3 oz (2 tsp)	8 mL	1%
Grated orange zest		0.1 oz (1¼ tsp)	3 g	0.5%
Pastry flour	1 lb	12 oz	850 g	100%
Baking powder		0.7 oz	20 g	2.5%
Blanched whole almonds		10 oz	300 g	35%
Yield:	4 lb	3 oz	2047 g	241%

PROCEDURE

Mixing: Sponge method.
1. Combine the eggs, sugar, and salt. Stir over hot water to warm the mixture. Whip until thick and light.
2. Fold in the vanilla and orange zest.
3. Sift together the flour and baking powder. Fold in the egg mixture.
4. Mix in the almonds.

Makeup: Bar method. Shape into logs about 2–2½ inches (6 cm) thick. Dust your hands and the workbench with flour. The dough will be soft, sticky, and difficult to handle, but the logs do not have to be perfectly shaped. Egg wash.

Baking: 325°F (160°C) about 30–40 minutes, until light golden.

Finishing: Let cool slightly. Slice diagonally about ½ inch (12 mm) thick. Place cut side down on sheet pans. Bake at 275°F (135°C) until toasted and golden brown, about 30 minutes.

Per 1 ounce:
Calories, 110; Protein, 3 g; Fat, 4.5 g (36% cal.); Cholesterol, 15 mg; Carbohydrates, 15 g; Fiber, 2 g; Sodium, 110 mg.

Terms for Review

spread	sponge method	rolled cookies	bar cookies
one-stage method	dropped cookies	molded cookies	sheet cookies
creaming method	bagged cookies	icebox cookies	

Questions for Discussion

1. What makes cookies crisp, and how can you keep them crisp after they are baked?

2. If you baked some cookies that were unintentionally chewy, how would you correct them in the next batch?

3. Describe briefly the difference between the creaming method and the one-stage method.

4. Besides cost control, why is accurate scaling and uniform sizing important when making up cookies?

chapter 31

Pies and Pastries

On the North American frontier, it was not uncommon for the pioneer housewife to bake 21 pies a week—one for every meal. Pies were so important to the settlers that in winter, when fruits were unavailable, cooks would bake pies for dessert out of whatever materials were available, such as potatoes, vinegar, and soda crackers.

Few of us today eat pie at every meal. Nevertheless, pies are still a favorite dessert. Most customers will order and pay a higher price for a piece of chocolate cream pie than for chocolate pudding, even if the pie filling is the same as the pudding and even if they leave the crust uneaten.

In this chapter, we present the preparation of pie crusts and fillings. In addition, we discuss how to make puff pastry, éclair paste, meringues, and fruit desserts.

After reading this chapter,
you should be able to

1. Prepare flaky pie dough
   and mealy pie dough.

2. Prepare crumb crusts
   and short, or cookie,
   crusts.

3. Assemble and bake
   pies.

4. Prepare the following
   pie fillings: fruit fillings
   using the cooked juice
   method, the cooked
   fruit method, and the
   old-fashioned method;
   custard or soft fillings;
   cream pie fillings; and
   chiffon fillings.

5. Prepare puff pastry
   dough and puff dough
   products.

6. Prepare éclair paste
   and éclair paste prod-
   ucts.

7. Prepare standard
   meringues and
   meringue products.

8. Prepare fruit desserts.

Pies

Pie Doughs

Before you begin studying this section, it would be a good idea for you to review the section on gluten development in Chapter 26. Pie pastry is a simple product in terms of its ingredients: flour, shortening, water, and salt. Yet success or failure depends on how the shortening and flour are mixed and how the gluten is developed. The key to making pie dough is proper technique, and you will remember the techniques better if you understand why they work.

INGREDIENTS

Flour

Pastry flour is the best choice for pie doughs. It has enough gluten to produce the desired structure and flakiness, yet is low enough in gluten to yield a tender product, if handled properly.

If stronger flours are used, the percentage of shortening should be increased to provide more tenderness.

Fat

Regular hydrogenated shortening is the most popular fat for pie crusts because it has the right plastic consistency to produce a flaky crust. It is firm and moldable enough to make a dough that is easily worked. Emulsified shortening should not be used because it blends too quickly with the flour, making a flaky pastry difficult to achieve.

Butter contributes excellent flavor to pie pastry, but it is not frequently used in volume production for two reasons: it is expensive, and it melts very easily, making the dough difficult to work.

It is desirable, if costs permit, to blend a quantity of butter into the shortening used for pie crusts to improve flavor. The quantity of pie crust that is dumped in the garbage after customers have eaten out the filling is evidence that many people are not satisfied with the taste of pie crusts made with shortening.

If all butter is used in place of shortening, the percentage of fat in the formula should be increased by about one-fourth. (If 1 pound shortening is called for, use 1 pound 4 ounces butter. If 500 grams shortening are called for, use 625 grams butter.) The liquid should be reduced slightly, as butter contains moisture.

Lard is an excellent shortening for pies because it is firm and plastic. Some people dislike its flavor, however, so it is not widely used in food service.

Liquid

Water is necessary to develop some gluten in the flour and to give structure and flakiness to the dough. If too much water is used, the crust will become tough because of too much gluten development. If not enough water is used, the crust will fall apart.

Milk makes a richer dough that browns more quickly. However, the crust is less crisp and the production cost is higher.

Whether water or milk is used, it must be added cold (40°F/4°C or colder) to maintain proper dough temperature.

Salt

Salt has some tenderizing and conditioning effect on the gluten. However, its main contribution is to flavor.

Salt must be dissolved in the liquid before being added to the mix to ensure even distribution.

TEMPERATURE

Pie dough should be kept cool, about 60°F (15°C), during mixing and makeup for two reasons:

1. Shortening has the best consistency when cool. If it is warm, it blends too quickly with the flour. If it is very cold, it is too firm to be easily workable.

2. Gluten develops more slowly at cool temperatures than at warm temperatures.

PIE DOUGH TYPES

There are two basic types of pie dough: flaky and mealy.

The difference between the two is how the fat is blended with the flour. Complete mixing procedures are given later. First, it is important to understand the basic distinction between the two types.

Flaky Pie Dough

For flaky dough, the fat is cut or rubbed into the flour until the particles of shortening are about the size of peas or hazelnuts. That is, the flour is not completely blended with the fat, and the fat is left in pieces. (Many bakers distinguish between this crust, which they call *short-flake*, and *long-flake* crusts, in which the fat is left in pieces the size of walnuts and the flour is even less coated with shortening.)

When water is added, the flour absorbs water and develops some gluten. When the dough is rolled out, the lumps of fat and moistened flour are flattened and become flakes of dough separated by layers of fat.

Mealy Pie Dough

For mealy dough, the fat is blended into the flour more thoroughly, until the mixture looks like coarse cornmeal. Because the flour is more completely coated with fat:

- The crust is very short and tender because less gluten can develop.
- Less water is needed in the mix because the flour won't absorb as much as in flaky dough.
- The baked dough is less likely to absorb moisture from the filling and become soggy.

Mealy dough is used for bottom crusts in baked fruit pies and soft or custard-type pies because it resists sogginess. Flaky doughs are used for top crusts and for prebaked pie shells.

Trimmings

Reworked scraps or trimmings will be tougher than freshly made dough. They may be combined with mealy dough and used for bottom crusts only.

MIXING PIE DOUGHS

Hand mixing is best for small quantities of dough, especially flaky dough, because it gives more control over the mixing. Quantities up to 10 pounds (or 5 kilograms) can be mixed almost as quickly by hand as by machine.

For machine mixing, use a pastry knife or paddle attachment and blend at low speed.

Procedures for rolling pie doughs and lining pie pans are discussed in the next section, "Assembly and Baking."

Flaky Pie Dough
Mealy Pie Dough

Ingredients	Flaky			Mealy		
	U.S.	Metric	Percentage	U.S.	Metric	Percentage
Pastry flour	2 lb 8 oz	1000 g	100%	2 lb 8 oz	1000 g	100%
Shortening	1 lb 12 oz	700 g	70%	1 lb 10 oz	700 g	65%
Salt	0.75 oz (4 tsp)	20 g	2%	0.75 oz (4 tsp)	20 g	2%
Water	12 oz	300 g	30%	10 oz	300 g	25%
Yield:	5 lb	2020 g	202%	4 lb 12 oz	1920 g	192%

PROCEDURE

Mixing:

1. Collect all equipment.
2. Collect and scale ingredients.
3. Dissolve salt in water. Set aside.
4. Place flour and shortening in mixing bowl.
5. Rub or cut shortening into flour to the proper degree:

   For mealy dough—until it resembles coarse cornmeal.

   For flaky dough—until fat particles are the size of peas or hazelnuts.
6. Add salt and water. Mix very gently, just until water is absorbed. Do not overwork the dough.
7. Place the dough in pans, cover with plastic film, and place in refrigerator or retarder for several hours.

Per 1 ounce:
Calories, 130; Protein, 1 g; Fat, 10 g (65% cal.); Cholesterol, 0 mg;
Carbohydrates, 11 g; Fiber, 20 g; Sodium, 105 mg.

OTHER PIE CRUSTS

Crumb Crusts

Graham cracker crusts are popular because they have an appealing flavor and are much easier to make than pastry crusts. For variations, vanilla or chocolate wafer crumbs or gingersnap crumbs may be used instead of graham cracker crumbs. Ground nuts may be added for special desserts.

Crumb crusts are used only for unbaked pies, such as cream pies and chiffon pies. Be sure that the flavor of the crust is compatible with the filling. A lime chiffon pie with a chocolate crumb crust is not an appealing combination. Some cream fillings are so delicate that they would be overwhelmed by a crust that is too flavorful.

Baking the crust makes a firmer, less crumbly crust and increases flavor.

Short-Dough Crusts

Short pastry is actually a kind of cookie dough. It is richer than regular pie pastry and contains butter, sugar, and eggs. Because it is difficult to handle, it is used primarily for small fruit tarts.

Graham Cracker Crust

Yield: 2 lb (900 g) **Crusts for:** 4 pies, 9 inches (23 cm) in diameter
5 pies, 8 inches (20 cm) in diameter

U.S.	Metric	Ingredients	PROCEDURE
1 lb	450 g	Graham cracker crumbs	1. Mix crumbs and sugar in mixing bowl.
8 oz	225 g	Sugar	2. Add butter and mix until evenly blended and crumbs are all moistened by the melted butter.
8 oz	225 g	Butter, melted	3. Scale the mixture into pie pans: 8 oz (225 g) for 9-inch (23-cm) pans; 6 oz (175 g) for 8-inch (20-cm) pans.
			4. Spread mixture evenly on bottom and sides of pan. Press another pan on top to pack crumbs evenly.
			5. Bake at 350°F (175°C) for 10 minutes.
			6. Cool thoroughly before filling.

Per 1 ounce:
Calories, 140; Protein, 1 g; Fat, 7 g (45% cal.); Cholesterol, 15 mg;
Carbohydrates, 18 g; Fiber, 0 g; Sodium, 140 mg.

VARIATIONS

Substitute chocolate or vanilla wafer crumbs or gingersnap crumbs for the cracker crumbs.

Short Dough

Yield: 6 lb 5 oz (3.1 kg)

U.S.	Metric	Ingredients	PROCEDURE
2 lb	1 kg	Butter or part butter and part shortening	1. Using the paddle attachment, mix the butter, sugar, and salt at low speed until smooth and evenly blended.
12 oz	375 g	Sugar	
1 tsp	5 mL	Salt	
9 oz	275 g	Eggs	2. Add the eggs and mix until just absorbed.
3 lb	1.5 kg	Pastry flour, sifted	3. Add the flour. Mix just until evenly blended.
			4. Chill several hours before using.

Per 1 ounce:
Calories, 130; Protein, 2 g; Fat, 8 g (53% cal.); Cholesterol, 30 mg;
Carbohydrates, 14 g; Fiber, 2 g; Sodium, 100 mg

Procedure for Making Small Fruit Tarts

1. Roll out chilled short dough on a floured surface until it is slightly less than ¼ inch (5 mm) thick.

2. With a round cutter about ½ inch (1 cm) larger than the top diameter of your individual tart shells, cut the dough into circles.

3. For each shell, fit a circle of dough into a tin and press it well against the bottom and sides. If you are using fluted tins, make sure the dough is thick enough on the sides so that it won't break apart at the ridges.

4. Fit paper liners inside the shells and fill with dried beans to keep the dough from blistering or puffing while baking.

5. Bake at 400°F (200°C) for about 15 minutes or until the shells are fully baked. Remove the paper liners and the beans.

6. Cool the shells completely and remove them from the tins.

7. Fill the shells half full of vanilla pastry cream (see Chapter 32).

8. Arrange well-drained fresh, cooked, or canned fruits over the pastry cream.

9. Brush the top with apricot glaze, melted currant jelly, or other desired glaze (see Chapter 29).

10. Keep refrigerated until service.

Assembly and Baking

TYPES OF PIES

Pies may be classified into two groups based on method of assembling and baking.

1. **Baked pies.**
   Raw pie shells are filled and then baked. *Fruit pies* contain fruit fillings and usually have a top crust. *Soft pies* are those with custard-type fillings or, in other words, liquid fillings that become firm when their egg content coagulates. They are usually baked as single-crust pies.

2. **Unbaked pies.**
   Baked pie shells are filled with a prepared filling, chilled, and served when the filling is firm enough to slice. *Cream pies* are made with pudding or boiled custard-type fillings. *Chiffon pies* are made with fillings that are lightened by the addition of beaten egg whites and, sometimes, whipped cream. Gelatin or starch gives them a firm consistency.

Procedure for Rolling Pie Dough and Lining Pans

1. Scale the dough.

8 ounces (225 g) for 9-inch (23-cm) bottom crusts

6 ounces (175 g) for 9-inch (23-cm) top crusts

6 ounces (175 g) for 8-inch (20-cm) bottom crusts

5 ounces (150 g) for 8-inch (20-cm) top crusts

Experienced bakers are able to roll crusts using less dough because less needs to be trimmed when the dough is rolled to a perfect circle of the exact size needed.

2. Dust the bench and rolling pin lightly with flour.

Too much dusting flour toughens the dough. Use no more than needed to prevent sticking.

3. Roll out the dough.

Flatten the dough lightly and roll it out to a uniform ⅛-inch (3-mm) thickness. Use even strokes and roll from the center outward in all directions. Lift the dough frequently to make sure it is not sticking. The finished dough should form a perfect circle.

4. Place the dough in a pan.

To lift the dough without breaking it, roll it lightly around the rolling pin. Allow the dough to drop into the pans and press it into the corners without stretching it. Stretched dough shrinks during baking. There should be no air bubbles between the dough and the pan.

5. For single-crust pies, flute the edges, if desired, and trim off excess dough.

Some bakers feel that fluted edges add to the appearance of the product. Others feel that fluting takes too much time and only produces a rim of heavy dough that customers leave on their plates.

6. For two-crust pies:

Fill with cold filling, place the second crust on top, and seal the top and bottom crusts together at edges. Flute, if desired, and trim excess dough. Apply desired wash or glaze to top.

7. Bake as directed in the recipe.

Procedure for Preparing Baked Pies

Note: For pies without a top crust, omit steps 3 through 7.

1. Line the pie pan with the pie dough as in the basic procedure (Figure 31.1).

2. Fill with *cooled* filling. See Table 31.1 for scaling instructions. Do not drop filling on the rim of the pie shell; this makes it hard to seal the rim to the top crust. To avoid spilling custard filling, place the empty shell on the rack in the oven, then pour in the filling.

3. Roll out dough for the top crust.

4. Perforate the top crust to allow steam to escape during baking.

5. Moisten the rim of the bottom crust to help seal it to the top crust.

6. Fit the top crust in place. Seal the edges together firmly and trim excess dough. An easy way to do this is to press the rim with the tines of a fork. Alternatively, the rim may be fluted. An efficient way to trim excess dough is to rotate the pie tin while pressing on the edges with the palms of the hands.

7. Brush the top with the desired wash: milk, cream, eggs and milk, or water. Sprinkle with granulated sugar if desired.

8. Place the pie on the lower level of an oven preheated to 425° to 450°F (220° to 230°C). The high initial heat helps set the bottom crust to avoid soaking. Fruit pies are usually baked at this high heat until done. For custard pies, reduce the heat to 325° to 350°F (165° to 175°C) after 10 minutes to avoid overcooking and curdling the custard. Custard pies include all those containing large quantities of egg, such as pumpkin pie and pecan pie.

TABLE 31.1

Scaling Instructions for Baked Pies

Pie Size		Weight of Filling	
U.S.	Metric	U.S.	Metric
8 inches	20 cm	26–30 oz	750–850 g
9 inches	23 cm	32–40 oz	900–1150 g
10 inches	25 cm	40–50 oz	1150–1400 g

Note: Weights are guidelines only. Exact weights may vary, depending on the filling and the depth of the pans.

Figure 31.1 Preparing baked pies.

(a) Line the pie pans with the pie dough.

(b) Fill with cooled fillings.

(c) Fit the top crusts in place.

(d) Seal the top crust to the rim and trim the dough from the edges.

THE SOGGY BOTTOM

A common pie fault is an underbaked bottom crust or a crust that soaks up moisture from the filling. Soggy bottoms can be avoided in several ways.

1. Use mealy dough for bottom crusts. Mealy dough absorbs less liquid than flaky dough.

2. Use high bottom heat, at least at the beginning of baking, to set the crust quickly. Bake the pies at the bottom of the oven.

3. Do not add hot fillings to unbaked crusts.

4. Use dark metal pie tins, which absorb heat. (If you use disposable aluminum pans, choose pans with the bottoms colored black.)

Procedure for Preparing Unbaked Pies

1. Line a pie pan with pie dough as in basic procedure.

2. Dock the crust well with a fork to prevent blistering.

3. Place another pan inside the first one so that the dough is between two pans. This is called *double-panning*.

4. Place the pans upside down in an oven preheated at 450°F (230°C). Baking upside down helps keep the dough from shrinking down into the pan.
   Some bakers like to chill the crusts before baking to relax the gluten and help reduce shrinkage.

5. Bake at 450°F (230°C) for 10 to 15 minutes. The top pan may be removed during the last part of baking so that the crust can brown.

6. Cool the baked crust completely.

7. Fill with cream or chiffon filling. Fill as close as possible to service time to prevent soaking the crust.

8. Chill the pie until it is set enough to slice.

Fillings

STARCHES FOR FILLINGS

Many kinds of pie filling, especially fruit fillings and cream fillings, depend on starch for their thick texture.

Types

Cornstarch is used for cream pies because it sets up into a firm gel that holds its shape when sliced. Cornstarch may also be used for fruit pies.

Waxy maize and other *modified starches* are best for fruit pies because they are clear when set and make a soft paste rather than a firm gel. Waxy maize should be used for pies that are to be frozen because it is not broken down by freezing.

Flour, tapioca, and other starches are used less frequently. Flour has less thickening power than other starches and makes the product cloudy.

Instant or *pregelatinized starch* needs no cooking because it has already been cooked. When used with certain fruit fillings, it eliminates the need to cook the filling before making up the pie. It has no advantage, however, if the filling must be cooked because it contains such ingredients as raw fruit or eggs.

Starches differ in thickening power, so follow the formulas exactly.

Cooking Starches

To avoid lumping, starches must be mixed with a cold liquid or sugar before being added to a hot liquid.

Sugar and *strong acids* reduce the thickening power of starch. When possible, all or part of the sugar and strong acids like lemon juice should be added *after the starch has thickened*.

FRUIT FILLINGS

Fruit pie fillings consist of fruits and fruit juices, sugar, spices, and a starch thickener.

Fruits for Pie Fillings

Fresh fruits make excellent pies if they are at their seasonal peak. Fresh apples are used extensively for high-quality pies. But the quality of fresh fruits can vary considerably, and they require a lot of labor.

Frozen fruits are widely used for pies because they are consistent in quality and readily available.

Canned fruits can also be of high quality. Solid pack (with little juice) gives a higher yield of fruit per can than syrup or water pack.

Dried fruits must be rehydrated by soaking and, usually, simmering before they are made into pie fillings.

Fruits must have sufficient acid (tartness) to make flavorful fillings. If they lack natural acid, you may need to add lemon, orange, or pineapple juice to supply the acid.

Cooked Juice Method

The advantage of this method is that only the juice is cooked. The fruit retains better shape and flavor because it is subjected to less heat and handling. This method is used when the fruit requires little or no cooking before filling the pie. Examples: cherry, peach, most frozen or canned fruits. Fresh berries can also be prepared by this method. Some of the berries are cooked or puréed to provide juice. The remaining berries are mixed with the finished gel.

Procedure: Cooked Juice Method

1. Drain the juice from the fruit.
2. Measure the juice and, if necessary, add water or other fruit juice to bring it to the desired volume.
3. Bring the juice to a boil.
4. Dissolve the starch in cold water and stir it into the boiling juice. Return the juice to the boil and cook until it is clear and thickened.
5. Add sugar, salt, and flavorings and stir until dissolved.
6. Pour the thickened juice over the drained fruit and mix gently. Be careful not to break or mash the fruit.
7. Cool.

Cooked Fruit Method

This method is used when the fruit requires cooking or there is not enough liquid for the cooked juice method. Examples: fresh apple, raisin, rhubarb.

Procedure: Cooked Fruit Method

1. Bring the fruit and its juice or water to a boil. Some sugar may be added to the fruit to draw out juices.
2. Dissolve the starch in cold water and stir it into the fruit. Return the fruit mixture to a boil and cook until it is clear and thickened. Stir while cooking.
3. Add sugar, salt, flavorings, and other ingredients and stir until dissolved.
4. Cool as quickly as possible.

Variation

Some fruits, such as fresh apples, may be cooked in butter rather than boiled in water for better flavor.

Old-fashioned Method

This method is best suited to pies made with fresh apples or peaches. It is not as widely used in food service as the other methods because it is more difficult to control the thickening of the juices.

Procedure: Old-Fashioned Method

1. Mix the starch and spices with the sugar until uniformly blended.

2. Mix the fruit with the sugar mixture.

3. Fill the unbaked pie shell with the fruit.

4. Place lumps of butter on top of the filling.

5. Cover with a top crust or with Streusel (p. 786) and bake.

COOKED JUICE METHOD

Apple Pie Filling (Canned Fruit)

Yield: about 9½ lb (4.5 kg)
　　　　 five 8-inch (20-cm) pies
　　　　 four 9-inch (23-cm) pies
　　　　 three 10-inch (25-cm) pies

U.S.	Metric	Ingredients	PROCEDURE
6 lb 8 oz	3 kg	Canned apples (1 No. 10 can)	1. Drain the apples and save the juice.
as needed	as needed	Water	2. Add enough water to the juice to measure 1½ pt (750 mL).
8 oz	250 mL	Water, cold	3. Mix the cold water and starch.
3 oz	90 g	Cornstarch or modified starch	4. Bring the juice mixture to a boil.
			5. Stir in the starch mixture and return to a boil.
1 lb 4 oz	575 g	Sugar	6. Add the remaining ingredients (except the drained apples). Simmer until the sugar is dissolved.
¼ oz (1¼ tsp)	7 g (6 mL)	Salt	7. Pour the syrup over the apples and mix gently. Cool completely.
¼ oz (4¼ tsp)	7 g (21 mL)	Cinnamon	8. Fill pie shells. Bake at 425°F (220°C) for about 30–40 minutes.
1 tsp	2 g (5 mL)	Nutmeg	
3 oz	90 g	Butter	

Per 1 ounce:
Calories, 30; Protein, 0 g; Fat, .5 g (14% cal); Cholesterol, 0 mg;
Carbohydrates, 7 g; Fiber, 0 g; Sodium, 25 mg.

VARIATIONS

Dutch Apple Pie Filling

Simmer 8 oz (250 g) raisins in water. Drain and add to Apple Pie Filling.

Cherry Pie Filling

Use 1 No. 10 can sour cherries instead of apples. Increase starch to 4 oz (125 g). Add 1½ oz (45 mL) lemon juice in step 6. Increase the sugar to 1 lb 12 oz (800 g). Omit cinnamon and nutmeg. Add almond extract to taste (optional). If desired, color with 2–3 drops red coloring.

Peach Pie Filling

Use 1 No. 10 can sliced peaches, preferably solid or heavy pack, instead of apples. Omit cinnamon and nutmeg.

Pineapple Pie Filling

Use 1 No. 10 can crushed pineapple instead of apples. Increase liquid in step 1 to 1 qt (1 L). Increase starch to 4 oz (125 g). Use 1 lb 8 oz (700 g) sugar and 8 oz (250 g) corn syrup. Omit cinnamon and nutmeg.

Apple Pie with Streusel Topping

Blueberry Pie Filling (Frozen Fruit)

Yield: about 10 lb (4.3 kg)
      five 8-inch (20-cm) pies
      four 9-inch (23-cm) pies
      three 10-inch (25-cm) pies

U.S.	Metric	Ingredients	PROCEDURE
7 lb	3.2 kg	Frozen unsweetened blueberries	1. Thaw blueberries in original container without opening.
as needed	as needed	Water	2. Drain the berries. Add enough water to the juice to measure 1 pt (500 mL). Stir in the sugar.
8 oz	250 g	Sugar	
8 oz	250 mL	Water, cold	3. Mix the cornstarch and cold water.
4 oz	125 g	Cornstarch or modified starch	4. Bring the juice mixture to a boil. Stir in the starch. Return to a boil to thicken.
1 lb 2 oz	500 g	Sugar	5. Stir in the sugar, salt, cinnamon, and lemon juice. Stir over heat until the sugar is dissolved.
¼ oz (1¼ tsp)	7 g (6 mL)	Salt	6. Pour the syrup over the drained blueberries. Mix gently. Cool completely.
¼ oz (4¼ tsp)	7 g (21 mL)	Cinnamon	7. Fill pie shells. Bake at 425°F (220°C) for about 30 minutes.
2 oz	60 mL	Lemon juice	

Per 1 ounce:
Calories, 30; Protein, 0 g; Fat, 0 g (0% cal.); Cholesterol, 0 mg;
Carbohydrates, 8 g; Fiber, 1 g; Sodium, 20 mg.

VARIATIONS

Apple Pie Filling

Use 7 lb (3.2 kg) frozen apples instead of blueberries. Reduce second quantity of sugar to 12 oz (350 g). Reduce starch to 3 oz (90 g). Add 1 tsp (5 mL) nutmeg and 4 oz (125 g) butter in step 5.

Cherry Pie Filling

Use 7 lb (3.2 kg) frozen cherries instead of blueberries. Increase liquid in step 2 to 1½ pt (750 mL). Decrease starch to 3½ oz (100 g). Reduce second quantity of sugar to 14 oz (400 g). Omit cinnamon and reduce lemon juice to 1 oz (30 mL).

Fresh Strawberry Pie Filling

Yield: about 12 lb (5.5 kg)
      six 8-inch (20-cm) pies
      five 9-inch (23-cm) pies
      four 10-inch (25-cm) pies

U.S.	Metric	Ingredients	PROCEDURE
9 lb	4.1 kg	Fresh whole strawberries	1. Hull, wash, and drain the berries. Set aside 7 lb (3.2 kg) berries. These may be left whole if small or cut in halves or quarters if large.
1 pt	500 mL	Water, cold	2. Mash or purée the remaining 2 lb (900 g) berries. Mix with the water. (If a clear filling is desired, this mixture may be strained.)
1 lb 12 oz	800 g	Sugar	3. Mix together the sugar, starch, and salt. Stir into the cold juice and water mixture until no lumps remain.
4 oz	125 g	Cornstarch or modified starch	4. Bring to a boil, stirring constantly. Cook until thickened.
1 tsp	5 mL	Salt	5. Remove from heat and stir in the lemon juice.
2 oz	60 mL	Lemon juice	6. Cool to room temperature but do not chill.
			7. Stir to eliminate lumps. Fold in the reserved berries.
			8. Fill baked pie shells and chill (do not bake).

Per 1 ounce:
Calories, 25; Protein, 0 g; Fat, 0 g (0% cal.); Cholesterol, 0 mg;
Carbohydrates, 6 g; Fiber, 0 g; Sodium, 10 mg.

COOKED FRUIT METHOD

Rhubarb Pie Filling

Yield: about 11 lb (5 kg)
six 8-inch (20-cm) pies
five 9-inch (23-cm) pies
four 10-inch (25-cm) pies

U.S.	Metric	Ingredients	PROCEDURE
7 lb	3.2 kg	Fresh rhubarb	1. Cut the rhubarb into 1-inch (2½-cm) pieces.
1 pt	500 mL	Water	2. Combine the rhubarb, water, and sugar in a saucepan.
1 lb	450 g	Sugar	Bring to a boil and simmer 2 minutes.
8 oz	250 mL	Water	3. Mix the water and starch. Stir into the rhubarb and boil
5 oz	150 g	Cornstarch	until thick and clear.
1 lb	450 g	Sugar	4. Add the remaining ingredients. Stir gently until the sugar is
2 tsp	10 mL	Salt	dissolved and the butter is melted.
2 oz	60 g	Butter	5. Cool completely.
			6. Fill pie shells. Bake at 425°F (220°C), about 30–40 minutes.

Per 1 ounce:
Calories, 30; Protein, 0 g; Fat, .5 g (14% cal.); Cholesterol, 0 mg;
Carbohydrates, 7 g; Fiber, 0 g; Sodium, 30 mg.

VARIATION

Fresh Apple Pie Filling

Use 10 lb (4.5 kg) fresh peeled and sliced apples instead of rhubarb. Flavor with 1 tbsp (15 mL) cinnamon, 1 tsp (5 mL)
nutmeg, and 1–2 oz (30–60 mL) lemon juice during step 4.

Raisin Pie Filling

Yield: about 10½ lb (4.8 kg)
six 8-inch (20-cm) pies
five 9-inch (23-cm) pies
four 10-inch (25-cm) pies

U.S.	Metric	Ingredients	PROCEDURE
4 lb	1.8 kg	Raisins	1. Combine the raisins and water in a saucepan. Simmer 5
2 qt	2 L	Water	minutes.
8 oz	250 mL	Water, cold	2. Mix the water and starch. Stir into the raisins and simmer
2½ oz	75 g	Cornstarch or modified	until thickened.
		starch	
1 lb 4 oz	575 g	Sugar	3. Add the remaining ingredients. Stir until sugar is dissolved
2 tsp	10 mL	Salt	and mixture is uniform.
3 oz	90 mL	Lemon juice	4. Cool thoroughly.
1 tbsp	15 mL	Grated lemon zest	5. Fill pie shells. Bake at 425°F (220°C) for about 30–40 minutes.
1 tsp	5 mL	Cinnamon	
3 oz	90 g	Butter	

Per 1 ounce:
Calories, 50; Protein, 0 g; Fat, 0 g (0% cal.); Cholesterol, 0 mg;
Carbohydrates, 12 g; Fiber, .5 g; Sodium, 35 mg.

OLD-FASHIONED METHOD

 Old-Fashioned Apple Pie Filling

Yield: about 11 lb (5 kg)
six 8-inch (20-cm) pies
five 9-inch (23-cm) pies
four 10-inch (25-cm) pies

U.S.	Metric	Ingredients	PROCEDURE
9 lb EP	4.1 kg EP	Fresh peeled, sliced apples	1. Select firm, tart apples.
2 oz	60 mL	Lemon juice	2. Combine apple slices and lemon juice in a large mixing bowl and toss to coat apples with the juice.
2 lb	900 g	Sugar	3. Mix together the sugar, starch, salt, and spices.
3 oz	90 g	Cornstarch	4. Add to the apples and toss gently until well mixed.
¼ oz (1¼ tsp)	7 g (6 mL)	Salt	
¼ oz (4¼ tsp)	7 g (21 mL)	Cinnamon	
1 tsp	5 mL	Nutmeg	
3 oz	90 g	Butter	5. Fill pie shells. Dot the filling with butter before setting the top crusts in place. Bake at 400°F (200°C) for about 45 minutes.

Per 1 ounce:
Calories, 40; Protein, 0 g; Fat, 5 g (11% cal.); Cholesterol, 0 mg;
Carbohydrates, 9 g; Fiber, 0 g; Sodium, 20 mg.

CUSTARD OR SOFT FILLINGS

Custard, pumpkin, pecan, and similar pies are made with an uncooked liquid filling containing eggs. The eggs coagulate when the pie is baked, setting the filling.

The greatest difficulty in cooking soft pies is cooking the crust completely yet not overcooking the filling. Start the pie at the bottom of a hot oven (425° to 450°F/220° to 230°C) for first 10 minutes to set the crust. Then reduce heat to 325° to 350°F (165° to 175°C) to cook the filling slowly.

To test for doneness:

1. Shake the pie very gently. If it is no longer liquid, it is done. The center will still be slightly soft but will continue cooking in its own heat after it is removed from oven.

2. Insert a thin knife 1 inch (2.5 cm) from the center. It will come out clean if the pie is done.

 **Custard Pie Filling**

Yield: 8 lb (3.6 kg)
five 8-inch (20-cm) pies
four 9-inch (23-cm) pies
three 10-inch (25-cm) pies

U.S.	Metric	Ingredients	PROCEDURE
2 lb	900 kg	Eggs	1. Beat the eggs lightly. Add sugar, salt, and vanilla. Blend until smooth. Do not whip air into the mixture.
1 lb	450 g	Sugar	
1 tsp	5 mL	Salt	
1 oz	30 mL	Vanilla	
2½ qt	2.5 L	Milk (see note)	2. Stir in the milk. Skim off any foam.
1–1½ tsp	5–7 mL	Nutmeg	3. Pour into the unbaked pie shells.
			4. Sprinkle tops with nutmeg.
			5. Bake at 450°F (230°C) for 15 minutes. Reduce heat to 325°F (165°C) and bake until set, about 20–30 minutes more.

Per 1 ounce:
Calories, 35; Protein, 2 g; Fat, 1.5 g (33% cal.); Cholesterol, 35 mg;
Carbohydrates, 5 g; Fiber, 0 g; Sodium, 35 mg.

Note: For a richer custard, use part milk and part cream.

VARIATION

Coconut Custard Pie Filling

Use 10 oz (275 g) unsweetened, flaked coconut. Sprinkle coconut into pie shells before adding custard mixture. Coconut may be toasted lightly in oven before adding to pies, if desired. Omit nutmeg.

Pumpkin Pie Filling

Yield: about 8½ lb (4 kg)
five 8-inch (20-cm) pies
four 9-inch (23-cm) pies
three 10-inch (25-cm) pies

U.S.	Metric	Ingredients	PROCEDURE
3 lb 6 oz	1.5 kg	Pumpkin purée, 2 No. 2½ cans, or ½ No. 10 can	1. Place pumpkin purée in the bowl of a mixer fitted with a whip attachment.
2 oz	60 g	Pastry flour	2. Sift together the flour, spices, and salt.
4 tsp	20 mL	Cinnamon	3. Add the flour mixture and sugar to the pumpkin. Mix at second speed until smooth and well blended.
½ tsp	2 mL	Nutmeg	
½ tsp	2 mL	Ground ginger	
¼ tsp	1 mL	Ground cloves	
2 tsp	10 mL	Salt	
1 lb 4 oz	575 g	Brown sugar	
12 oz	350 g	Eggs	4. Add the eggs and mix in. Scrape down the sides of the bowl.
4 oz	125 g	Corn syrup or half corn syrup and half molasses	5. Turn the machine to low speed. Gradually pour in the syrup-molasses mixture, then the milk. Mix until evenly blended.
1½ qt	1.5 L	Milk	6. Fill the pie shells. Bake at 450°F (230°C) for 15 minutes. Lower heat to 350°F (175°C) and bake until set, about 30–40 minutes more.

Per 1 ounce:
Calories, 30; Protein, 1 g; Fat, 0.5 g (14% cal.); Cholesterol, 10 mg; Carbohydrates, 6 g; Fiber, 0 g; Sodium, 45 mg.

VARIATIONS

Sweet Potato Pie Filling
Substitute canned sweet potatoes, drained and puréed, for the pumpkin.

Squash Pie Filling
Substitute puréed squash for the pumpkin.

Pecan Pie Filling

Yield: 8 lb (3.6 kg) filling plus 1 lb 4 oz (575 g) pecans
five 8-inch (20-cm) pies
four 9-inch (23-cm) pies
three 10-inch (25-cm) pies

U.S.	Metric	Ingredients	PROCEDURE
2 lb	900 g	Sugar (see note)	1. Using the paddle attachment at low speed, blend the sugar, butter, and salt until evenly blended.
8 oz	225 g	Butter	
1½ tsp	7 mL	Salt	
2 lb	900 g	Eggs	2. With the machine running, add the eggs, a little at a time, until they are all absorbed.
3 lb 8 oz (about ½ pt)	1.6 kg	Dark corn syrup	3. Add the syrup and vanilla. Mix until well blended.
1 oz	30 mL	Vanilla	
1 lb 4 oz	575 g	Pecans	4. To assemble pies, distribute pecans evenly in pie shells. Fill with syrup mixture.
			5. Bake at 450°F (230°C) for 10 minutes. Reduce heat to 325°F (165°C). Bake about 40 minutes more, until set.

Per 1 ounce:
Calories, 120; Protein, 1 g; Fat, 5 g (38% cal.); Cholesterol, 35 mg; Carbohydrates, 17 g; Fiber, 0 g; Sodium, 70 mg.

Note: Brown sugar may be used if darker color and stronger flavor are desired.

CREAM PIE FILLINGS

Cream pie fillings are the same as puddings, which, in turn, are the same as a basic pastry cream with added flavorings such as vanilla, chocolate, coconut. Lemon filling is made by the same method, using water and lemon juice instead of milk.

The one difference between puddings and pie fillings that you should note is that *cream pie fillings are made with cornstarch* so that slices hold their shape when cut. Puddings may be made with flour, cornstarch, or other starches.

Techniques and recipes for these fillings are included in Chapter 32, along with other basic creams and puddings.

CHIFFON PIES

Chiffon fillings are made by adding gelatin to a cream filling or to a thickened fruit and juice mixture; egg whites and/or whipped cream are then folded in. The mixture is then poured into baked pie shells and allowed to set.

These preparations are the same as chiffon desserts, bavarians, and some mousses and cold soufflés. To avoid unnecessary repetition, techniques and recipes for these products are included in Chapter 32 with other puddings and creams.

Pastries, Meringues, and Fruit Desserts

In addition to pie dough, two other pastries have great importance in bakeshops and kitchens: *puff pastry*, used for such products as napoleons and turnovers, and *éclair* or *choux paste*, used for éclairs and cream puffs. These products are also used in the hot food kitchen and the pantry in the preparation of a number of hors d'oeuvres, entrées, and side dishes.

Meringues and fruit desserts are also covered in this section. Meringues are not only important as pie toppings but also can be formed, baked until crisp, and used in many of the same ways as pastry shells for desserts.

Puff Pastry

Puff pastry is one of the most remarkable products of the bakeshop. Although it includes no added leavening agent, it can rise to 8 times its original thickness when baked.

Puff pastry is a rolled-in dough, like Danish and croissant dough. This means that it is made up of many layers of fat sandwiched in between layers of dough. Unlike Danish dough, however, puff pastry contains no yeast. Steam, created when the moisture in the dough layers is heated, is responsible for the spectacular rising power of puff pastry.

Puff pastry or puff dough is one of the most difficult of all bakery products to prepare. Because it consists of over 1000 layers, many more than in Danish dough, the rolling-in procedure requires a great deal of time and care.

Like so many other products, there are nearly as many versions of puff pastry as there are bakers. Both formulas and rolling-in techniques vary. The formula provided here contains no eggs, for example, although some bakers add them.

The folding-in technique used here differs somewhat from that used by European pastry chefs, although it is widely used by American bakers. (See Figure 31.2.)

Butter is the preferred fat for rolling in because of its flavor and melt-in-the-mouth quality. Special puff pastry shortening is also available. This shortening is much easier to work with than butter because it is not as hard when refrigerated and doesn't soften and melt as easily as butter at warm temperatures. It is also less expensive than butter. However, puff pastry shortening can be unpleasant to eat because it tends to congeal and coat the inside of the mouth.

Skill at producing puff pastry requires careful attention to your instructor and diligent practice. Take special note of any alternative methods your instructor may present.

Puff Pastry

Ingredients	U.S.		Metric	Percentage
Bread flour	3 lb		1500 g	75%
Cake flour	1 lb		500 g	25%
Butter, soft		8 oz	250 g	12.5%
Salt		1 oz	30 g	1.5%
Water, cold	2 lb	4 oz	1125 g	56%
Butter	4 lb		2000 g	100%
Bread flour (see note)		8 oz	250 g	12.5%
Yield:	11 lb	5 oz	5655 g	282%

Per 1 ounce:
Calories, 120; Protein, 1 g; Fat, 9 g (69% cal.); Cholesterol, 25 mg;
Carbohydrates, 8 g; Fiber, 0 g; Sodium, 150 mg.

PROCEDURE

Mixing:

1. Place the first quantities of flour and butter in a mixing bowl. With a paddle attachment, mix at low speed until well blended.
2. Dissolve the salt in the cold water.
3. Add the salted water to the flour and mix at low speed until a soft dough is formed. Do not overmix.
4. Remove the dough from the mixer and let rest in the refrigerator for 20 minutes.
5. Cream the last quantities of butter and flour at low speed in the mixer until the mixture is about the same consistency as the dough, neither too hard nor too soft.
6. Roll the butter into the dough following the procedure shown in Figure 31.2. Give the dough 4 four-folds or 5 three-folds.

Note: The purpose of the 8 oz (250 g) bread flour is to absorb some of the moisture of the butter. Omit if puff paste shortening is used instead of butter.

Figure 31.2 Rolling-in procedure for puff pastry.

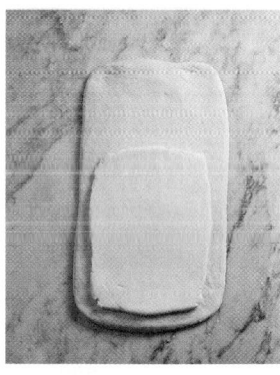   

(a) Dust the bench lightly with flour. Roll dough to a rectangle about 3 times as long as it is wide and about ½ inch (1–1½ cm) thick. Make the corners as square as possible. Form the butter into a rectangle two-thirds the size of the dough, leaving room around the edges, and place on the dough as shown.

(b) Fold the third without fat over the center third.

(c) Fold the remaining third on top. Fold all ends and corners evenly and squarely. This procedure, enclosing the butter in the dough, does not count as one of the folds. The folding procedure starts with the next step.

(d) Turn the dough 90 degrees on the bench so that the length becomes the width. This step must be taken before each rolling-out so that the gluten is stretched in all directions, not just lengthwise. Failure to do this results in products that deform or shrink unevenly when they bake. Before rolling, beat the dough lightly as shown so that the butter is evenly distributed. Roll the dough into a rectangle. Make sure the corners are square. Roll smoothly and evenly. Do not press down when rolling, or the layers may stick together and the product not rise properly.

(Continued)

Figure 31.2
(Continued)

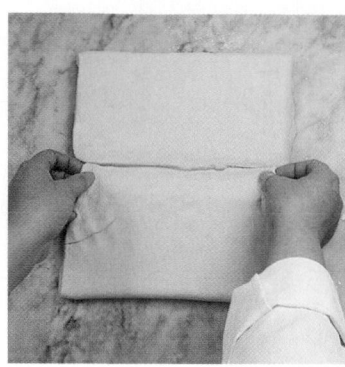

(e) Brush excess flour from the top of the dough.

(f) Fold the top edge of the dough to the center. Make sure the corners are square and even. Again brush off excess flour.

(g) Fold the bottom edge to the center.

(h and i) Fold the dough in half like closing a book. You have now given the dough one four-fold. Refrigerate the dough for 15 to 20 minutes to relax the gluten. Do not refrigerate it too long, or the butter will become too hard. (If it does, let it soften a few minutes at room temperature before proceeding.) Give the dough another 3 four-folds, as in steps f to h. After another rest, the dough is ready to be rolled out and made up into the desired products. (Alternative method: Instead of giving the dough 4 four-folds, you may give it 5 three-folds.) See Figure 27.3 for the three-fold method.

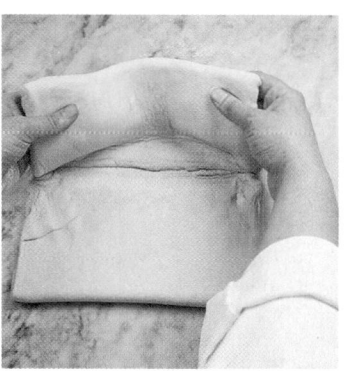

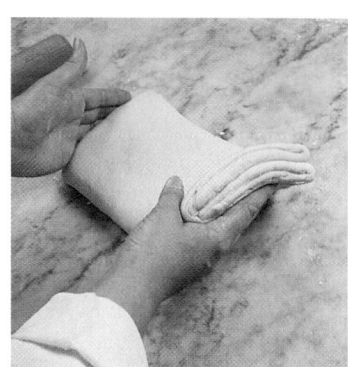

BLITZ PUFF PASTRY

This product is much easier and quicker to make than classic puff dough. (*Blitz* is the German word for "lightning.") It does not rise nearly as high as true puff pastry, so it is not suitable for patty shells and other products where a high, light pastry is desirable. However, it bakes up crisp and flaky and is perfectly suitable for napoleons and similar desserts that are layered with cream fillings.

Blitz puff paste, as you will see, is actually a flaky pie dough that is rolled and folded like regular puff dough.

Blitz Puff Pastry

Ingredients	U.S.	Metric	Percentage
Bread flour	1 lb	500 g	50%
Pastry flour	1 lb	500 g	50%
Butter, slightly softened	2 lb	1000 g	100%
Salt	0.5 oz	15 g	1.5%
Water, cold	1 lb	500 g	50%
Yield:	5 lb	2515 g	250%

PROCEDURE

Mixing:
1. Sift the two flours together into a mixing bowl.
2. Cut the butter into the flour as for pie dough, but leave the fat in very large lumps, 1 inch (2½ cm) across.
3. Dissolve the salt in the water.
4. Add the water to the flour-butter mixture. Mix until the water is absorbed.
5. Let the dough rest for 15 minutes. Refrigerate if the bakeshop is warm.
6. Dust the bench with flour and roll out the dough into a rectangle. Give the dough three 4-folds.

Per 1 ounce:
Calories, 120; Protein, 1 g; Fat, 9 g (69% cal.); Cholesterol, 25 mg; Carbohydrates, 8 g; Fiber, 1 g; Sodium, 160 mg.

VARIATION
Reduce the butter to 75% (1 lb 8 oz/750 g).

General Guidelines for Makeup of Puff Dough Products

1. The dough should be cool and firm when it is rolled and cut. If it is too soft, the layers may stick together at the cuts, preventing proper rising.

2. Cut with straight, firm, even cuts. Use a sharp cutting tool.

3. Avoid touching the cut edges with your fingers, or the layers may stick together.

4. For best rising, place units upside down on baking sheets. Even sharp cutting tools may press the top layers of dough together. Baking upside down puts the stuck-together layers at the bottom.

5. Avoid letting egg wash run down the edges. Egg wash can cause the layers to stick together at the edges.

6. Rest made-up products for 30 minutes in a cool place or in the refrigerator before baking. This relaxes the gluten and reduces shrinkage.

7. Press trimmings together, keeping the layers in the same direction. After being rolled out and given another three-fold, they may be used again, although they will not rise as high.

8. Baking temperatures of 400° to 425°F (200° to 220°C) are best for most puff dough products. Cooler temperatures do not create enough steam in the products to leaven them well. Higher temperatures set the crust too quickly.

Procedure for Making Turnovers

1. Roll out puff pastry dough to ⅛ inch (3 mm) thick.

2. Cut the dough into 4-inch (10-cm) squares (Figure 31.3). Wash the edges of each with water.

3. Portion the desired filling into the center of each square.

4. Fold diagonally and press the edges together.

5. Puncture the tops with a knife in two or three places to allow steam to escape. Rest 30 minutes.

6. Brush the tops with egg wash, if desired, or brush with milk or water and sprinkle with sugar.

7. Bake at 400°F (200°C) until crisp and brown.

Figure 31.3 *Makeup of turnovers.*

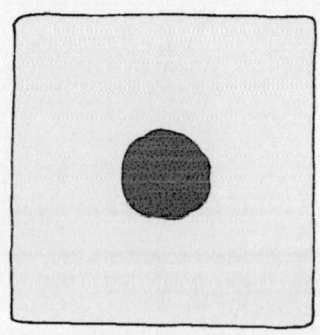

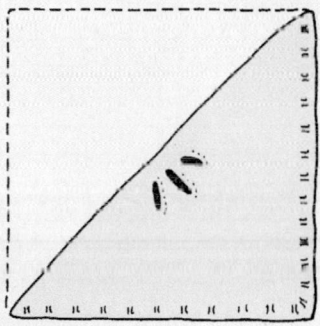

(a) Cut the dough into 4-inch (10-cm) squares. Wash the edges with water and place filling in the center of each square.

(b) Fold over diagonally and press the edges together. Puncture two or three steam holes in top.

Procedure for Making Pinwheels

Figure 31.4 *Makeup of pinwheels.*

(a) Cut the dough into 5-inch (12-cm) squares. Wash the centers with water. Cut diagonally from the corners to 1 inch (2.5 cm) from center.

1. Roll out puff dough to ⅛ inch (3 mm) thick.
2. Cut the dough into 5-inch (12-cm) squares (Figure 31.4).
3. Wash the centers with water.
4. Cut diagonally from the corners to about 1 inch (2½ cm) from the centers.
5. Fold every other corner into the centers and press in place.
6. Bake at 400°F (200°C).
7. Let cool. Spoon desired fruit filling into the centers. Dust lightly with confectioners' sugar. (Pinwheels may also be filled before baking if the filling is thick and not likely to burn.)

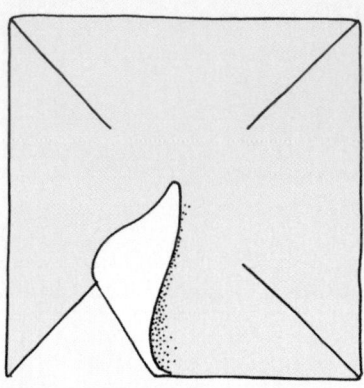 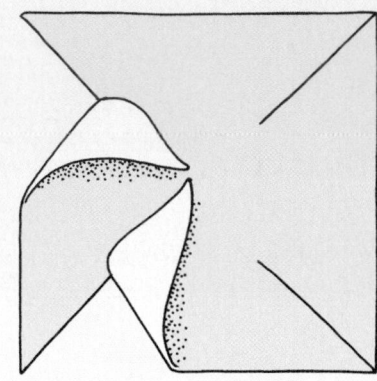 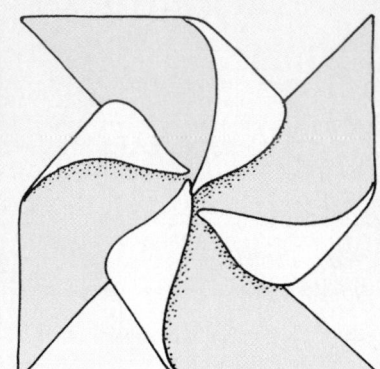

(b, c, d) Fold every other corner to the center and press down. Fill the center with fruit filling before or after baking.

Procedure for Making Patty Shells

1. Roll out puff dough to ⅛ inch (3 mm) thick.
2. Roll a second piece of dough to ¼ inch (6 mm) thick.
3. Cut out the same number of circles from each piece of dough with a round 3-inch (7½-cm) cutter (Figure 31.5).
4. With a 2-inch (5-cm) cutter, cut out the centers of the *thick* circles.
5. Wash the thin circles with water or egg wash and place a ring on top of each. Wash the top carefully with egg wash (do not drip wash down the edges). Rest 30 minutes.
6. Place a sheet of greased parchment over the tops of the shells to prevent their toppling over while baking.
7. Bake at 400°F (200°C) until brown and crisp.

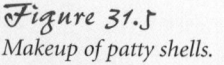

Figure 31.5
Makeup of patty shells.

 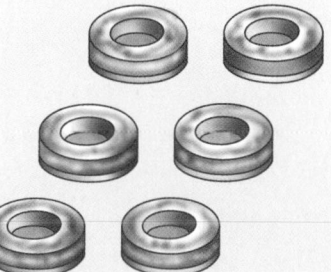

(a) Roll 1 sheet of puff dough ⅛ inch (3 mm) thick and another sheet ¼ inch (6 mm) thick. Cut an equal number of 3-inch (7.5-cm) circles from each. Cut out the centers of the thick circles with a 2-inch (5-cm) cutter.

(b) Wash the thin circles with water or egg wash and place the thick circles on top.

Procedure for Making Cream Horns

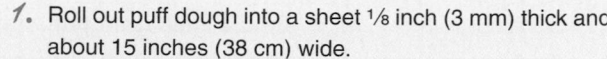

Figure 31.6
Makeup of cream horns.

(a) Roll puff dough to ⅛ inch (3 mm) thick and cut it into strips 1¼ inches (3 cm) wide and 15 inches (38 cm) long. Wash the strips with water and press one end (washed side out) onto one end of a cream horn tube as shown.

(b) Roll the dough strip in a spiral by turning the tube. Overlap the edges by about ⅜ inch (1 cm). Do not stretch the dough.

(c) Roll completely and press the end in place to seal.

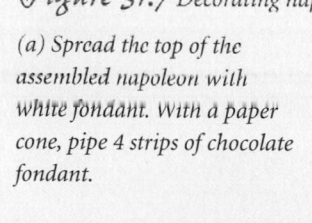

1. Roll out puff dough into a sheet ⅛ inch (3 mm) thick and about 15 inches (38 cm) wide.

2. Cut out strips 1¼ inches (3 cm) wide by 15 inches (38 cm) long.

3. Wash the strips with water.

4. With the washed side out, roll the strips diagonally onto cream horn tubes, making a spiral (Figure 31.6). Overlap the edges by about ⅜ inch (1 cm). If you are using conical tubes, start at the small end.

5. Roll in granulated sugar and lay on baking sheets. The end of the dough strip should be on the bottom so that it does not pop up during baking. Rest 30 minutes.

6. Bake at 400°F (200°C) until brown and crisp.

7. Slip out the tubes while still warm.

8. Just before service, fill the horns from both ends with whipped cream or pastry cream, using a pastry bag with a star tip. Dust with confectioners' sugar.

Procedure for Making Napoleons

1. Roll puff dough into a very thin sheet about the size of a sheet pan. Blitz puff paste or rerolled trimmings may be used.

2. Place on sheet pan and let rest 30 minutes.

3. Dock with a fork to prevent blistering.

4. Bake at 400°F (200°C) until brown and crisp.

5. Trim the edges of the pastry sheet and cut with a serrated knife into equal strips 4 inches (10 cm) wide. Set the best one aside for the top layer. (If one of the strips breaks, don't be upset. It can be used as the middle layer.)

6. Spread one rectangle with Vanilla Pastry Cream (p. 873) or with a mixture of pastry cream and whipped cream.

7. Top with a second sheet of pastry.

8. Spread with another layer of pastry cream.

9. Place a third pastry rectangle on top, flattest side up.

10. Ice top with fondant (p. 816).

11. To decorate, pipe 4 strips of chocolate fondant lengthwise on the white fondant. Draw a spatula or the back of a knife across the top in opposite directions, 1 inch (2½ cm) apart, as shown in Figure 31.7.

12. Cut into strips 2 inches (5 cm) wide.

Figure 31.7 *Decorating napoleons.*

(a) Spread the top of the assembled napoleon with white fondant. With a paper cone, pipe 4 strips of chocolate fondant.

(b) Draw a spatula or the back of a knife across the icing at 2-inch (5-cm) intervals.

(c) Draw the spatula in the opposite direction in the center of these 2-inch (5-cm) intervals as shown.

(d) Cut the napoleon into strips 2 inches (5 cm) wide.

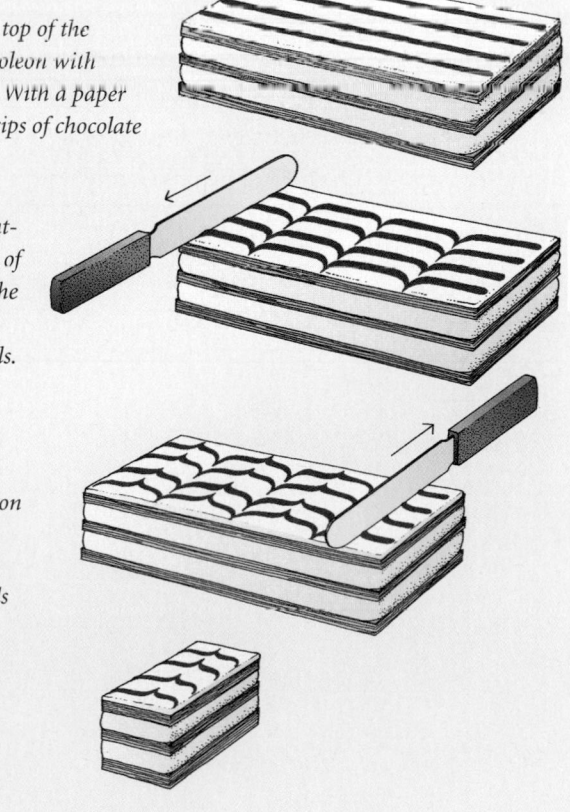

Éclair Paste

Éclairs and cream puffs are made from a dough called *éclair paste* or *choux paste*. The French name *pâte à choux* (pot a shoo) means "cabbage paste," referring to the fact that cream puffs look like little cabbages.

Unlike puff pastry, éclair paste is extremely easy to make. The dough itself can be prepared in just a few minutes. This is fortunate because for best baking results, the dough should not be prepared ahead of time.

In principle, éclair paste is similar to popover batter, even though one is a thick dough and the other a thin batter. Both products are leavened by steam, which expands the product rapidly and forms large holes in the center. The heat of the oven then coagulates the gluten and egg proteins to set the structure and make a firm product. A strong flour is necessary for sufficient structure.

Éclair paste must be firm enough to hold its shape when piped from a pastry bag. Occasionally, you may find a formula that produces too slack a dough. Correct such a formula by reducing the water or milk slightly.

Proper baking temperatures are important. Start at a high temperature (425° to 475°F/215° to 245°C) for the first 10 minutes to develop steam. Then reduce the heat to 375° to 425°F (190° to 215°C) to finish baking and set the structure. The products must be firm and dry before being removed from the oven. If they are removed too soon or cooled too quickly, they may collapse. Some bakers like to leave them in a turned-off oven with the door ajar. However, if the oven must be heated again for other products, this may not be the best idea, especially in these times of high energy costs. It may be better to bake the products thoroughly, remove them carefully from the oven, and let them cool slowly in a warm place.

Éclair Paste

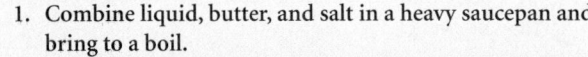

Ingredients	U.S.		Metric	Percentage
Water, milk, or half water and half milk	1 lb	4 oz	500 g	167%
Butter or regular shortening		8 oz	200 g	67%
Sugar		2 tsp	10 g (10 mL)	3%
Salt		1 tsp	5 g (5 mL)	1.5%
Bread flour		12 oz	300 g	100%
Eggs		12 oz	300 g	100%
Yield:	3 lb	4 oz	1315 g	438%

Per 1 ounce:
Calories, 70; Protein, 2 g; Fat, 4 g (56% cal.); Cholesterol, 35 mg; Carbohydrates, 5 g; Fiber, 0 g; Sodium, 90 mg.

PROCEDURE

Mixing:
1. Combine liquid, butter, and salt in a heavy saucepan and bring to a boil.
2. Remove pan from heat and add the flour all at once. Stir quickly.
3. Return the pan to moderate heat and stir vigorously until the dough forms a ball and pulls away from the sides of the pan.
4. Transfer the dough to the bowl of a mixer. If you wish to mix by hand, leave it in the saucepan.
5. With the paddle attachment, mix at low speed until the dough has cooled slightly. It should be about 140°F (60°C)—still very warm, but not too hot to touch.
6. At medium speed, beat in the eggs, a little at a time. Add no more than one-fourth of the eggs at once, and wait until they are completely absorbed before adding the remainder. When all the eggs are absorbed, the paste is ready to use.

Procedure for Making Cream Puffs

1. Line sheet pans with silicone paper or butter them lightly.

2. Fit a large pastry bag with a plain tube. Fill the bag with the choux paste.

3. Pipe round mounds of dough about 1½ inches (4 cm) in diameter onto the lined baking sheets. If preferred, you may drop the dough from a spoon (see Figure 31.8).

4. Bake at 425°F (215°C) for 10 minutes. Lower heat to 375°F (190°C) until well browned and very crisp.

5. Remove from oven and cool slowly in a warm place.

6. When cool, cut a slice from the top of each puff. Fill with whipped cream, Vanilla Pastry Cream (p. 873), or desired filling, using a pastry bag with a star tube.

7. Replace the tops and dust with confectioners' sugar.

8. Fill the puffs as close to service as possible. If cream-filled puffs must be held, keep them refrigerated.

9. Unfilled and uncut puffs, if they are thoroughly dry, may be held in plastic bags in the refrigerator for 1 week. Recrisp in oven for a few minutes before use.

Figure 31.8 For cream puffs or profiteroles, pipe choux paste into the bulbs of desired size, paste onto greased sheet pans, or onto pans that have been lined with parchment.

Procedure for Making Éclairs

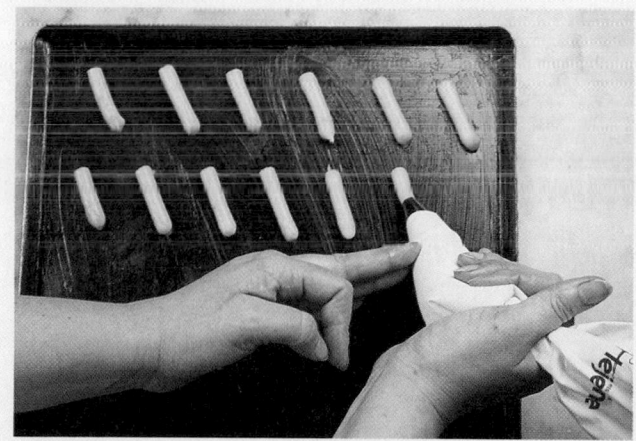

Figure 31.9 For éclairs, pipe choux paste into fingers of desired size onto greased sheet pans, or onto pans that have been lined with parchment.

1. Proceed as for cream puffs, except pipe the dough into strips about ¾ inch (2 cm) wide and 3 to 4 inches (8 to 10 cm) long (see Figure 31.9). Bake as for cream puffs.

2. Fill baked, cooled éclair shells with pastry cream. Two methods may be used:
   - Make a small hole in one end of the shell and fill using a pastry bag or a doughnut-filling pump.
   - Cut a slice lengthwise from the top and fill using a pastry bag.

3. Dip the tops of the éclairs in chocolate fondant (p. 817).

4. For service and holding, see cream puffs.

Variation: Frozen Éclairs or Profiteroles

1. Fill éclairs or small cream puffs (profiteroles) with ice cream. Keep frozen until service.

2. At service time, top with chocolate syrup.

Procedure for Making French Crullers or French Doughnuts

1. Cut sheets of parchment paper to the same width as your deep fryer.

2. Using a pastry bag with a star tube, pipe choux paste onto the parchment in circles (doughnut shapes) about 2 inches (5 cm) across.

3. Slide the paper with the paste into a deep fryer heated to 375°F (190°C). Remove the paper as the doughnuts release and float free.

4. Fry the doughnuts on both sides until golden brown. French doughnuts must be completely fried, or they may collapse when cooling. Remove and drain on absorbent paper.

5. When cooled, drizzle fondant icing over the tops.

Meringues

Meringues are beaten egg whites sweetened with sugar. Their most frequent use in North America is for pie toppings and cake icings (known as boiled icing). They are also used to give volume and lightness to buttercream icings and to such preparations as dessert soufflés.

Another excellent use for meringues is to bake them in a slow oven until crisp. In this form, they can be used in place of cake layers or pastry shells to make light, elegant desserts. Chopped nuts may be folded into meringue before forming and baking to make these desserts more flavorful.

Basic rules for beating egg whites are discussed in Chapter 21, pages 614–615. Please review this section before attempting to make any of the following preparations. We repeat one rule here because it is so important:

Make sure that all equipment is free of any trace of fat or grease, and that the egg whites have no trace of yolk in them. Even a small trace of fat will prevent the whites from foaming properly.

Soft meringues, used for pie topping, may be made with as little as 1 pound of sugar per pound of egg whites. *Hard meringues,* baked until crisp, are made with up to twice as much sugar as egg whites.

BASIC MERINGUES

The stiffness to which meringues are beaten may vary, as long as they are not beaten until they are too stiff and dry. For most purposes, they are beaten until they form stiff, or nearly stiff, moist peaks.

1. *Common meringue* is made from egg whites at room temperature, beaten with sugar. It is the easiest to make, and it is reasonably stable due to the high percentage of sugar.

2. *Swiss meringue* is made from egg whites and sugar that are warmed over a double boiler while beating. Warming gives this meringue better volume and stability.

3. *Italian meringue* is made by beating a hot sugar syrup into the egg whites. This meringue is the most stable of the three because the egg whites are actually cooked by the heat of the syrup. When flavored with vanilla, this meringue is also known as *boiled icing.* It is also used in meringue-type buttercream icings.

Meringue

Ingredients	Common Meringue	Swiss Meringue	Italian Meringue
Egg whites	1 lb/500 g	1 lb/500 g	1 lb/500 g
Sugar	2 lb/1 kg	2 lb/1 kg	2 lb/1 kg
Water	—	—	8 oz/250 mL

Per 1 ounce of Common or Swiss:
Calories, 80; Protein, 1 g; Fat, 0 g (0% cal.); Cholesterol, 0 mg;
Carbohydrates, 19 g; Fiber, 0 g; Sodium, 15 mg.

Note: For soft meringues to top pies, use half the amount of sugar.

Procedure for Making Common Meringue

1. With the whip attachment, beat the egg whites at high speed until they form soft peaks.
2. Gradually add the sugar with the machine running.
3. Continue to beat until the meringue forms stiff but moist peaks.

Procedure for Making Swiss Meringue

1. Place the egg whites and sugar in a stainless-steel bowl or the top of a double boiler. Beat with a wire whip over hot water until the mixture is warm (about 120°F/50°C).
2. Transfer the mixture to the bowl of a mixing machine and whip at high speed until stiff peaks form.

Procedure for Making Italian Meringue

1. Heat the sugar and water in a saucepan until the sugar dissolves and the mixture boils. Boil until a candy thermometer placed in the mixture registers 240°F (115°C).
2. While the syrup is cooking, beat the egg whites in a mixing machine until they form soft peaks.
3. With the machine running, very slowly beat in the hot syrup.
4. Continue beating until the meringue forms firm peaks.

MERINGUE DESSERTS

Procedure for Making Pie Topping

1. Make common meringue or Swiss meringue using equal parts sugar and egg whites. Beat until just stiff.
2. Spread a generous amount (2 to 3 cups/500 to 700 mL) of meringue on still-warm pies. Mound it slightly and be sure to attach it to the edge of the crust all around. If this is not done, the meringue may slide around on the finished pie. Leave the meringue in ripples or peaks.
3. Bake at 400°F (200°C) until the surface is attractively browned.
4. Remove from oven and cool.

Procedure for Making Baked Meringue Shells

1. Beat common or Swiss meringue until stiff.
2. Using a pastry bag or a spoon, form the meringue into small nest shapes on a parchment-lined baking sheet.
3. Bake at 200° to 225°F (about 100°C) until crisp but not browned. This will take 1 to 3 hours.
4. Cool the shells and remove from the parchment. Be careful, as they may be fragile.
5. Use in place of pastry shells for fruit tarts, fill with whipped cream and fresh strawberries or raspberries, or fill with a scoop of ice cream and garnish with chocolate or raspberry sauce. Crisp meringues with ice cream make a dessert called *meringue glacée* (glah say).

Procedure for Making Japonaise Meringues

Japonaise (zhah po nez) meringues are used like cake layers. They may be filled and iced with light buttercream, chocolate mousse, whipped cream, or similar light icings and creams.

1. Prepare 1 recipe (1 pound or 500 g egg whites plus 2 pounds or 1 kg sugar) Swiss meringue.

2. Quickly but carefully fold in 1 pound (500 g) finely chopped hazelnuts.

3. With a pastry bag, form circles of the desired diameter and about ½ inch (1½ cm) thick on parchment-lined sheet pans, as shown in Figure 31.10.

4. Bake as for meringue shells.

Figure 31.10 *To make meringue layers, mark a circle on a sheet of parchment and pipe the meringue in a spiral to fill the circle.*

Procedure for Making Baked Alaska

1. Pack softened ice cream into a dome-shaped mold of the desired size. Freeze solid.

2. Prepare a layer of sponge cake the same size as the flat side of the mold and about ½ inch (1½ cm) thick.

3. Unmold the frozen ice cream onto the cake layer so that the cake forms a base for the ice cream.

4. With a spatula, cover the entire dessert with a thick layer of meringue. If desired, decorate with more meringue forced from a pastry bag.

5. Bake at 450°F (230°C) until the meringue is golden brown.

6. Serve immediately.

Fruit Desserts

Fruit desserts are included here because many are similar to pies or pie fillings. Special favorites include cobblers, which are much like fruit pies made in large baking pans without a bottom crust; crisps, which are like cobblers, but with brown-sugar streusel topping instead of a pastry crust; and bettys, which have alternate layers of rich cake crumbs and fruit. Also, don't overlook fresh fruits for dessert, served plain, lightly sweetened, or with cream.

Fruit Cobbler

Yield: 1 pan, 12 × 20 inches (30 × 50 cm) **Portions:** 48 **Portion size:** about 5 oz (150 g)

U.S.	Metric	Ingredients	PROCEDURE
12–15 lb	5.5–7 kg	Fruit pie filling (apple, cherry, blueberry, peach, etc.)	1. Place fruit filling in a baking pan measuring 12 × 20 inches (30 × 50 cm) (see note).
2 lb	1 kg	Flaky pic pastry	2. Roll out the pastry in a rectangle to fit the top of the baking pan. Place the pastry on the filling and seal the edges to the side of the pan. Pierce small holes in the pastry to allow steam to escape.
			3. Bake at 425°F (220°C) for about 30 minutes, until the top is browned.
			4. Cut the dessert 6 × 8 to make 48 portions. Serve warm or cold.

Per serving:
Calories, 200; Protein, 1 g; Fat, 7 g (29% cal.); Cholesterol, 0 mg; Carbohydrates, 37 g; Fiber, 2 g; Sodium, 115 mg.

Note: If possible, use stainless-steel pans instead of aluminum pans. The acid of the fruit will react with aluminum and create an undesirable flavor.

Apple Betty

Yield: 1 pan, 12 × 20 inches   **Portions:** 48   **Portion size:** 4 oz (125 g)
(30 × 50 cm)

U.S.	Metric	Ingredients	PROCEDURE
8 lb EP	4 kg EP	Apples, peeled and sliced	1. Combine the apples, sugar, salt, nutmeg, lemon zest, and lemon juice in a bowl. Toss gently until well mixed.
1 lb 8 oz	750 g	Sugar	
1½ tsp	7 mL	Salt	
1 tsp	5 mL	Nutmeg	
1 tbsp	15 mL	Grated lemon zest	
2 oz	60 mL	Lemon juice	
2 lb	1 kg	Yellow or white cake crumbs	2. Place one-third of the apple mixture in an even layer in a well-buttered baking pan measuring 12 × 20 inches (30 × 50 cm).
8 oz	250 g	Melted butter	3. Top with one-third of the cake crumbs.
			4. Continue until all the apples and crumbs have been used. You will have 3 layers of fruit and 3 layers of crumbs.
			5. Pour the melted butter evenly over the top.
			6. Bake at 350°F (175°C) for about 1 hour, until fruit is tender.

Per serving:
Calories, 200; Protein, 1 g; Fat, 7 g (30% cal.); Cholesterol, 20 mg;
Carbohydrates, 36 g; Fiber, 2 g; Sodium, 180 mg.

Apple Crisp

Yield: 1 pan, 12 × 20 inches (30 × 50 cm)   **Portions:** 48   **Portion size:** 4 oz (125 g)

U.S.	Metric	Ingredients	PROCEDURE
8 lb EP	4 kg EP	Apples, peeled and sliced	1. Toss the sliced apples gently with the granulated sugar and lemon juice.
4 oz	125 g	Granulated sugar	
2 oz	60 mL	Lemon juice	2. Spread the apples evenly in a baking pan measuring 12 × 20 inches (30 × 50 cm) (see note).
1 lb	500 g	Butter	3. Rub the butter, brown sugar, cinnamon, and flour together until well blended and crumbly.
1 lb 8 oz	750 g	Brown sugar	
2 tsp	10 mL	Cinnamon	4. Sprinkle evenly over the apples.
1 lb 8 oz	750 g	Pastry flour	5. Bake at 350°F (175°C) for about 45 minutes, until the top is browned and the apples are tender.

Per serving:
Calories, 180; Protein, 2 g; Fat, 8 g (37% cal.); Cholesterol, 20 mg;
Carbohydrates, 28 g; Fiber, 2 g; Sodium, 85 mg.

Note: If possible, use stainless-steel pans instead of aluminum pans. The acid of the fruit will react with aluminum and create an undesirable flavor.

VARIATION

Peach, Cherry, or Rhubarb Crisp
Substitute the indicated fruit for the apples. If rhubarb is used, increase the sugar in step 1 to 12 oz (350 g).

Poached Pears

Portions: 24   Portion size: 2 pear halves

U.S.	Metric	Ingredients	PROCEDURE
2 qt	2 L	Water	1. Combine the water and sugar in a trunnion kettle or large saucepot. Bring to a boil, stirring until the sugar is dissolved.
3 lb	1.5 kg	Sugar	
4 tsp	20 mL	Vanilla	2. Remove from heat and add the vanilla.
24	24	Pears	3. Peel the pears. Cut them in half and remove the cores with a melon ball cutter.
			4. Add the pears to the syrup and simmer very slowly until just tender.
			5. Let the pears cool in the syrup. When cool, refrigerate in the syrup until needed for service.

Per serving:
Calories, 320; Protein, 1 g; Fat, .5 g (1% cal.); Cholesterol, 0 mg;
Carbohydrates, 82 g; Fiber, 4 g; Sodium, 5 mg.

VARIATIONS

Pears in Wine

Substitute red or white table wine for the water. Omit vanilla. Add 1 sliced lemon to the syrup. Peel the pears but leave them whole.

Poached Peaches

Substitute peaches for pears in basic recipe.

Peaches in Wine

Substitute peaches for pears in recipe for Pears in Wine.

Raspberry or Cherry Gratin

Portions: 1

U.S.	Metric	Ingredients	PROCEDURE
1	1	Genoise layer (see step 2)	1. Select a shallow gratin dish or other heatproof dish large enough to hold the fruit in a shallow layer.
3 oz	90 g	Raspberries or sweet, pitted cherries	2. Cut a thin slice of genoise, about ⅜ inch (1 cm) thick, to cover the bottom of the dish.
			3. Arrange the fruit on top of the genoise.
2 oz	60 g	Pastry cream	4. Combine the pastry cream, whipped cream, and flavoring. Spread the mixture over the fruit to cover completely.
1 oz	30 g	Whipped cream	
to taste	to taste	Optional flavoring: kirsch, orange liqueur, or raspberry or cherry brandy	
¼ oz	7 g	Sliced almonds	5. Mix the almonds and butter and sprinkle over the pastry cream. Dredge the top heavily with confectioners' sugar.
¼ oz	7 g	Melted butter	
as needed	as needed	Confectioners' sugar	6. Place under a broiler or in the top of a hot oven for a few minutes to brown the top. Serve hot.

Per serving:
Calories, 480; Protein, 7 g; Fat, 27 g (50% cal.); Cholesterol, 165 mg;
Carbohydrates, 53 g; Fiber, 7 g; Sodium, 145 mg.

Terms for Review

flaky pie dough	cream pie	four-fold	soft meringue
mealy pie dough	chiffon pie	blitz puff pastry	hard meringue
crumb crust	instant starch	napoleon	common meringue
short dough	cooked juice method	éclair paste	Swiss meringue
fruit pie	cooked fruit method	pâte à choux	Italian meringue
soft pie	puff pastry	profiterole	meringue glacée
			Baked Alaska

Questions for Discussion

1. Discuss the factors that affect tenderness, toughness, and flakiness in pie dough. Why should emulsified shortening not be used for pie dough?

2. What kind of crust or crusts would you use for a pumpkin pie? an apple pie? a banana cream pie?

3. What would happen to a flaky pie dough if you mixed it too long before adding the water? after adding the water?

4. How can you prevent shrinkage when baking pie shells?

5. What are the remedies for soggy or undercooked bottom pie crusts?

6. What starch would you use to thicken apple pie filling? chocolate pie filling? lemon pie filling? peach pie filling?

7. Why is lemon juice added to lemon pie filling after the starch has thickened the water? Wouldn't this thin the filling?

8. Why is it important to bake cream puffs and éclairs thoroughly and to cool them slowly?

9. Briefly describe the difference between common, Swiss, and Italian meringues.

chapter 32

Creams, Custards, Puddings, Frozen Desserts, and Sauces

A quick glance at this last chapter may give you the impression that you will be overwhelmed with a great many recipes and techniques within a few pages. Among the subjects covered are custard sauces, pastry cream, puddings, custards, mousses, bavarians, soufflés, ice cream, and dessert sauces.

It's all much simpler than it seems. Once you have learned three basic preparations—vanilla custard sauce, pastry cream, and baked custard—you will have learned most of the rest. Vanilla custard sauce, also called crème anglaise (krem awng glezz) or English cream, is the basis for bavarians, ice cream, and some dessert sauces. Pastry cream, with a variety of flavorings, is also used for pie fillings and puddings and is the basis for some soufflés. Many baked puddings are baked custard with added starch or fruit ingredients.

There seems little point in giving you recipes for cream pie fillings in the pie section, a recipe for pastry cream filling for napoleons in the puff pastry section, and recipes for boiled puddings in the pudding section, and never tell you that they are all basically the same preparation. You are not just learning a collection of unrelated recipes; you are learning to cook and to understand what you are cooking.

Sugar Cooking

Understanding sugar cooking is important in the preparation of desserts and confections because sugar syrups of various strengths are often required (see, for example, Italian Meringue, p. 862).

After reading this chapter, you should be able to

1. Cook sugar syrups to the seven stages of hardness.

2. Prepare crème anglaise, pastry cream, and baked custard.

3. Prepare starch-thickened puddings and baked puddings.

4. Prepare bavarians, chiffons, mousses, and dessert soufflés.

5. Assemble frozen desserts.

6. Prepare dessert sauces.

BASIC PRINCIPLES

The principle of sugar cooking is fairly simple. A solution of syrup of sugar and water is boiled to evaporate part of the water. As the water is boiled off, the temperature of the syrup gradually rises. When all the water has evaporated, what you have left is melted sugar. The sugar then begins to *caramelize* or turn brown and change flavor. If heating continues, the sugar continues to darken and then burn.

A syrup cooked to a high temperature is harder when it is cooled than a syrup cooked to a lower temperature. For example, a syrup cooked to 240°F (115°C) forms a soft ball when cooled. A syrup cooked to 300°F (150°C) is hard and brittle when cooled.

One part water (by weight) is enough to dissolve and cook 3 to 4 parts sugar. There is no point in adding more water than is necessary because you just have to boil it off.

SIMPLE SYRUP

Simple syrup is a solution of equal weights of sugar and water. For example, combine equal weights of water and granulated sugar in a saucepan, stir, and bring to a boil to dissolve the sugar. Cool the syrup.

Dessert syrup is a flavored simple syrup used to moisten and flavor some cakes (see p. 807). (Many chefs use 2 or 3 parts water to 1 part sugar for a less sweet syrup.) Flavorings may be extracts, such as vanilla, or liquors, such as rum or kirsch. Add flavorings after the syrup has cooled because flavor may be lost if they are added to hot syrup. Syrups may also be flavored by boiling them with lemon or orange rind.

CRYSTALLIZATION

Graininess is a common fault in many candies and desserts. Graininess results when cooked sugar crystallizes or turns to tiny sugar crystals rather than staying dissolved in the syrup. If even one sugar crystal comes in contact with a cooked syrup, it can start a chain reaction that turns the whole thing into a mass of sugar crystals.

To avoid crystallization during the first stages of boiling, use one of the following techniques:

1. Wash down the sides of the saucepan with a brush dipped in water. This removes crystals that may seed the whole batch.

2. When first bringing the syrup to a boil, cover the pan and boil for several minutes. Condensed steam will wash down the sides of the pan. Uncover and finish cooking without stirring.

Sometimes, an acid such as cream of tartar is added to a syrup before cooking. Acids change some of the sugar to *invert sugar*, which resists crystallizing. Corn syrup is sometimes added for the same reason.

STAGES OF SUGAR COOKING

Testing the temperature with a candy thermometer is the most accurate way to determine the desired doneness of a syrup.

In the old days, syrups were tested by dropping a little bit into a bowl of cold water and checking the hardness of the cooled sugar. The stages of doneness were given names that described their hardness. Table 32.1 lists these stages of sugar cooking.

Basic Custards and Creams

The three preparations presented in this section are among the most basic and useful preparations in the bakeshop. All three can be classified as custards because they consist of a liquid thickened by the coagulation of eggs.

Crème anglaise, or vanilla custard sauce, is a stirred custard. It consists of milk, sugar, and egg yolks (and vanilla) stirred over very low heat until lightly thickened.

Pastry cream contains starch thickeners as well as eggs, resulting in a much thicker and more stable product. It is used as a cake and pastry filling, as a filling for cream pies, and as a pudding. With additional liquid, it is used as a custard sauce.

Baked custard, like vanilla custard sauce, also consists of milk, sugar, eggs, and flavoring (usually whole eggs are used for greater thickening power). But, unlike the sauce, it is baked rather than stirred over heat so that it sets and becomes firm. Baked custard is used as a pie filling, as a dessert by itself, and as a basis for many baked puddings.

All of these preparations are subject to a wide range of variations. Because they are based on eggs, it would be helpful for you to review the basic egg cooking principles discussed in Chapter 21.

TABLE 32.1

Stages of Doneness in Sugar Cooking

Stage	Temperature	
	°F	°C
Thread	230	110
Soft ball	240	115
Firm ball	245	118
Hard ball	250–260	122–127
Small crack	265–270	130–132
Crack	275–280	135–138
Hard crack	290–310	143–155
Caramel	320–340	160–170

CRÈME ANGLAISE

The following recipe gives the method for preparing vanilla custard sauce, or crème anglaise. Special care is necessary in preparing this sauce because the eggs can curdle easily if overcooked. The following guidelines will help you be successful.

1. Use clean, sanitized equipment and follow strict sanitation procedures. Egg mixtures can be contaminated easily by bacteria that cause food poisoning.

2. Heat the milk to scalding (just below simmering) in a double boiler before combining with the egg yolks. This makes the final cooking much shorter.

3. *Slowly* beat the hot milk into the beaten eggs and sugar. This raises the temperature of the eggs gradually and helps prevent curdling. (The same principle is used in tempering a cream–egg yolk liaison in sauce making.)

4. Heat the mixture slowly in a double boiler, stirring constantly to prevent curdling.

5. To test for doneness, two methods are available. Keep in mind that this is a very light sauce, so you can't expect a lot of thickening.

    • Check the temperature with a thermometer. When it reaches 185°F (85°C), the sauce is cooked. Never let the temperature go above 190°F (87°C).

    • When the mixture lightly coats the back of a spoon instead of running off like milk, the sauce is cooked.

6. *Immediately* cool the sauce by setting the pan or bowl in ice water. Stir occasionally to cool it evenly.

7. If the sauce curdles, it is sometimes possible to save it. Immediately stir in 1 to 2 ounces (30–60 mL) cold milk, transfer the sauce to a blender, and blend at high speed.

Crème Anglaise (Vanilla Custard Sauce)

Yield: about 2½ pt (1.25 L)

U.S.	Metric	Ingredients	PROCEDURE
12	12	Egg yolks	1. Review the guidelines for preparing vanilla custard sauce preceding this recipe.
8 oz	250 g	Sugar	2. Combine the egg yolks and sugar in the bowl of a mixer. Beat with the whip attachment until thick and light.
1 qt	1 L	Milk	3. Scald the milk in a double boiler.
			4. With the mixer running at low speed, very gradually pour the scalded milk into the egg yolk mixture.
			5. Pour the mixture back into the double boiler. Heat it slowly, stirring constantly, until it thickens enough to coat the back of a spoon (or until it reaches 185°F/85°C).
1 tbsp	15 mL	Vanilla	6. Immediately remove the top part of the double boiler from the heat and set it in a pan of cool water. Stir in the vanilla. Stir the sauce occasionally as it cools.

Per 1 ounce:
Calories, 60; Protein, 2 g; Fat, 2.5 g (38% cal.); Cholesterol, 65 mg; Carbohydrates, 7 g; Fiber, 0 g; Sodium, 15 mg.

VARIATION

Chocolate Crème Anglaise

Melt 6 oz (175 g) sweetened chocolate. Stir into the Crème Anglaise while it is still warm (not hot).

PASTRY CREAM

Although it requires more ingredients and steps, pastry cream is easier to make than custard because it is less likely to curdle. Pastry cream contains a starch thickening agent that stabilizes the eggs. It can actually be boiled without curdling. In fact, it must be brought to a boil, or the starch will not cook completely and the cream will have a raw, starchy taste.

Strict observance of all sanitation rules is essential when preparing pastry cream because of the danger of bacterial contamination. Use clean, sanitized equipment. Do not put your fingers in the cream, and do not taste it except with a clean spoon. Chill the finished cream rapidly in shallow pans. Keep the cream and all cream-filled products refrigerated at all times.

The procedure for preparing pastry cream is given in the following recipe. Note that the basic steps are similar to those for custard sauce. In this case, however, a starch is mixed with the eggs and half the sugar to make a smooth paste. (In some recipes with lower egg content, it is necessary to add a little cold milk to provide enough liquid to make a paste.) Meanwhile, the milk is scalded with the other half of the sugar (the sugar helps protect the milk from scorching on the bottom of the pan).

The egg mixture is then tempered with some of the hot milk, returned to the kettle, and brought to a boil. Some chefs prefer to add the cold paste gradually to the hot milk, but the tempering procedure given here seems to give better protection against lumping and curdling.

Pastry Cream Variations

Cream pie fillings and puddings are actually pastry cream flavored with various ingredients.

Cornstarch should be used as the thickening agent when the cream is to be used as a pie filling so that the cut slices hold their shape. For other uses, either cornstarch or flour may be used. Remember that twice as much flour as cornstarch is required for the same thickening power. Other variations are possible, as you will see in the recipes. Sometimes whipped cream is folded into cold pastry cream to lighten it and make it creamier.

Lemon pie filling is also a variation of pastry cream. It is made with water instead of milk, and it is flavored with lemon juice and grated lemon rind.

Vanilla Pastry Cream

Yield: about 2¼ qt (2.25 L)

U.S.	Metric	Ingredients	PROCEDURE
8 oz	250 g	Sugar	1. In a heavy saucepan or trunnion kettle, dissolve the sugar in the milk and
2 qt	2 L	Milk	bring just to a boil.
8	8	Egg yolks	2. With a whip, beat the egg yolks and whole eggs in a stainless-steel bowl.
4	4	Whole eggs	3. Sift the starch and sugar into the egg. Beat with the whip until perfectly
5 oz	150 g	Cornstarch	smooth.
8 oz	250 g	Sugar	4. Temper the egg mixture by slowly beating in the hot milk in a thin
			stream.
			5. Return the mixture to the heat and bring to a boil, stirring constantly.
4 oz	125 g	Butter	6. When the mixture comes to a boil and thickens, remove from the heat.
1 oz	30 mL	Vanilla	7. Stir in the butter and vanilla. Mix until the butter is melted and completely blended in.
			8. Pour into a clean, sanitized hotel pan or other shallow pan. Dust lightly with sugar and cover with waxed paper to keep a crust from forming. Cool and chill as quickly as possible.
			9. For filling pastries such as éclairs and napoleons, whip the chilled pastry cream until smooth before using.

Per 1 ounce:
Calories, 70; Protein, 2 g; Fat, 3 g (38% cal.); Cholesterol, 45 mg; Carbohydrates, 9 g; Fiber, 0 g; Sodium, 30 mg.

VARIATIONS

For a lighter pastry cream filling, fold whipped heavy cream into the chilled pastry cream. Quantities may be varied to taste. For every 2 qt (2 L) pastry cream, whip 1–2 cups (250–500 mL) heavy cream.

Chocolate Pastry Cream
Melt together 4 oz (125 g) sweetened chocolate and 4 oz (125 g) unsweetened chocolate. Stir into the hot pastry cream.

Coffee Pastry Cream
Add 4 tbsp (60 mL) instant coffee powder to the milk in step 1.

CREAM PIE FILLINGS
Quantities for four 8-inch (20-cm) pies

Vanilla Cream Pie Filling
This is the same as Vanilla Pastry Cream. Fill prebaked pie shells with cooled but not chilled filling.

Coconut Cream Pie Filling
Add 8 oz (250 g) toasted unsweetened coconut to Vanilla Pastry Cream.

Banana Cream Pie Filling
Using Vanilla Cream Pie Filling, pour half of the filling into the pie shells, cover with sliced bananas, and fill with remaining filling. (Bananas may be dipped in lemon juice to help prevent browning.)

Chocolate Cream Pie Filling I
This is the same as Chocolate Pastry Cream, above.

Chocolate Cream Pie Filling II
In step 1, use only 3½ pt (1.75 L) milk. Add 3 oz (90 g) cocoa to dry ingredients (sugar and cornstarch) in basic Vanilla Pastry Cream recipe. Add 8 oz (250 mL) cold milk to the eggs.

Butterscotch Cream Pie Filling
Combine 2 lb (900 g) brown sugar and 10 oz (300 g) butter in a saucepan over low heat. Heat and stir until butter is melted and ingredients are blended. Omit all the sugar from the basic Vanilla Pastry Cream recipe (steps 1 and 3). Increase the starch to 6 oz (175 g). As the mixture is nearing a boil in step 5, gradually stir in the brown sugar mixture. Finish as in basic recipe.

Lemon Pie Filling
Follow the procedure for Vanilla Pastry Cream, but make the following ingredient adjustments:
1. Use water instead of milk.
2. Increase sugar in step 1 to 1 lb (450 g).
3. Increase the cornstarch to 6 oz (175 g).
4. Add the grated zest of 2 lemons to the egg mixture.
5. Add 8 oz (250 mL) lemon juice to the finished, hot cream instead of the vanilla.

CREAM PUDDINGS

Vanilla Pudding
Coconut Pudding
Banana Cream Pudding
Chocolate Pudding I and II
Butterscotch Pudding

For each of these puddings, prepare the corresponding pie filling but use only *half* the cornstarch.

BAKED CUSTARD

Baked custard is a mixture of eggs, milk, sugar, and flavorings that is baked until the eggs coagulate and the custard is set. A good custard holds a clean, sharp edge when cut.

The following recipe gives the procedure for making baked custard. Note these points in particular:

1. Scald the milk before beating it slowly into the eggs. This reduces cooking time and helps the product cook more evenly.

2. Remove any foam, which would mar the appearance of the finished product.

3. Bake at 325°F (165°C). High temperatures increase the risk of overcooking and curdling.

4. Bake in a water bath so that the outside edges are not overcooked before the inside is set.

5. To test for doneness, insert a thin-bladed knife about 1 to 2 inches (3–5 cm) from the center. If it comes out clean, the custard is done. The center may not be completely set, but the custard will continue to cook in its own heat after removal from the oven.

Baked Custard

Portions: 24   **Portion size:** 5 oz (150 g)

U.S.	Metric	Ingredients	PROCEDURE
2 lb	1 kg	Eggs	1. Combine the eggs, sugar, salt, and vanilla in a mixing bowl. Mix until thoroughly blended, but do not whip.
1 lb	500 g	Sugar	
1 tsp	5 mL	Salt	
1 oz	30 mL	Vanilla	
2½ qt	2.5 L	Milk	2. Scald the milk in a double boiler or in a saucepan over low heat.
			3. Gradually pour the milk into the egg mixture, stirring constantly.
			4. Skim off all foam from the surface of the liquid.
			5. Arrange custard cups in a shallow baking pan. (Butter the insides of the cups if the custards are to be unmolded.)
			6. Carefully pour the custard mixture into the cups. If any bubbles form during this step, skim them off.
			7. Set the baking pan on the oven shelf. Pour enough hot water into the pan around the cups so that the level of the water is about as high as the level of the custard mixture.

Per serving:
Calories, 190; Protein, 8 g; Fat, 7 g (33% cal.); Cholesterol, 175 mg; Carbohydrates, 24 g; Fiber, 0 g; Sodium, 190 mg.

8. Bake at 325°F (165°C) until set, about 45 minutes.
9. Carefully remove from the oven and cool. Store, covered, in refrigerator.

VARIATION

Crème Caramel

Cook 1½ lb (750 g) sugar and 4 oz (125 g) water until it caramelizes (see the section on sugar cooking at the beginning of this chapter). Line the bottoms of the custard cups with the hot caramel. (Be sure the cups are clean and dry.) Fill with custard and bake as in basic recipe.

Puddings

It is difficult to give a definition of pudding that includes everything by that name. The term is used for such different dishes as chocolate pudding, blood sausages (blood puddings), and steak-and-kidney pudding. In this chapter, however, we consider only the more popular dessert puddings.

Two kinds of puddings, starch-thickened and baked, are the most frequently prepared in food service kitchens. These are the types we discuss here. A third type, steamed pudding, is less often served, and then mainly in cold weather, because steamed puddings are usually rather heavy and filling.

STARCH-THICKENED PUDDINGS

These are also called *boiled puddings* because they are boiled in order to cook the starch that thickens them.

1. **Cornstarch pudding or blancmange.**
   Cornstarch pudding consists of milk, sugar, and flavorings and is thickened with cornstarch (or, sometimes, another starch). If enough cornstarch is used, the hot mixture may be poured into molds, chilled, and unmolded for service.

2. **Cream puddings.**
   Cream puddings, as you learned in the previous section, are the same as pastry cream. Puddings are usually made with less starch, however, and may contain any of several flavoring ingredients, such as coconut or chocolate. Butterscotch pudding is given its flavor by using brown sugar instead of white sugar.

   If you look again at the recipe for Vanilla Pastry Cream (p. 873), you will see that the only difference between cornstarch puddings and cream puddings is that the latter contain eggs. In fact, cream puddings may be made by stirring hot cornstarch pudding into beaten eggs, then heating the entire mixture to just below the simmer. Care must be taken to avoid curdling the eggs if this method is used.

   A basic recipe for cornstarch pudding follows. Recipes for cream puddings are included among the variations following the recipe for Vanilla Pastry Cream.

Blancmange, English Style

Portions: 24   Portion size: 4 oz (125 g)

U.S.	Metric	Ingredients	PROCEDURE
2 qt	2 L	Milk	1. Combine the milk, sugar, and salt in a heavy saucepan and bring to a simmer.
12 oz	375 g	Sugar	
½ tsp	2 mL	Salt	
8 oz	250 g	Cornstarch	2. Mix the cornstarch and cold milk until perfectly smooth.
1 pt	500 mL	Milk, cold	3. Pouring in a thin stream, add about 1 cup (250 mL) hot milk to the cornstarch mixture.
			4. Stir this mixture back into the hot milk.
			5. Stir over low heat until the mixture thickens and comes to a boil.
1 tbsp	15 mL	Almond or vanilla extract	6. Remove from heat and add desired flavoring.
			7. Pour into ½-cup (125-mL) molds. Cool, then chill. Unmold for service.

Per serving:
Calories, 150; Protein, 3 g; Fat, 3.5 g (20% cal.); Cholesterol, 15 mg; Carbohydrates, 28 g; Fiber, 0 g; Sodium, 100 mg.

Note: French blancmange is very different from English. The French style is made with almond milk and gelatin.

VARIATIONS

Blancmange or cornstarch pudding may be flavored in any way that cream puddings are. See the variations following the Vanilla Pastry Cream recipe.

BAKED PUDDINGS

Baked puddings are custards that contain additional ingredients, usually in large quantities. Bread pudding, for example, is made by pouring a custard mixture over pieces of bread in a pan and baking it in the oven. Rice pudding is another popular item, made of cooked rice and custard.

The procedure for making baked puddings is the same as for making baked custard. A water bath may not be necessary if the starch content of the pudding is high.

Soft pie fillings, such as pumpkin, could also be considered baked puddings.

Rice Pudding

Portions: 25   Portion size: 5 oz (150 g)

U.S.	Metric	Ingredients	PROCEDURE
1 lb	450 g	Rice (medium or long grain)	1. Wash the rice well. Drain.
3 qt	3 L	Milk	2. Combine the rice, milk, vanilla, and salt in a heavy saucepan. Cover and simmer over very low heat until the rice is tender, about 30 minutes. Stir occasionally to be sure the mixture doesn't scorch on the bottom. Remove from heat when cooked.
2 tsp	20 mL	Vanilla	
½ tsp	2 mL	Salt	
2	2	Whole eggs	3. Combine the eggs, yolks, sugar, and cream in a mixing bowl. Mix until evenly combined.
4	4	Egg yolks	4. Ladle some of the hot milk from the cooked rice into this mixture and mix well. Then very slowly stir the egg mixture back into the hot rice.
1 lb	450 g	Sugar	
1 pt	500 mL	Light cream	
as needed	as needed	Cinnamon	5. Pour into a buttered baking pan, 12 × 20 inches (30 × 50 cm). Sprinkle the top with cinnamon.

Per serving:
Calories, 270; Protein, 7 g; Fat, 9 g (30% cal.); Cholesterol, 80 mg;
Carbohydrates, 40 g; Fiber, 0 g; Sodium, 120 mg.

6. Bake in a water bath at 350°F (175°C) for 30–40 minutes, until set. Serve warm or chilled.

VARIATION

Raisin Rice Pudding
Add 8 oz (250 g) raisins to the cooked rice and milk mixture.

Bread and Butter Pudding

Portions: 25   Portion size: 6½ oz (200 g)

U.S.	Metric	Ingredients	PROCEDURE
2 lb	1 kg	White bread, in thin slices	1. Cut each slice of bread in half. Brush both sides of each piece with melted butter.
8 oz	250 g	Melted butter	2. Arrange the bread overlapping in a buttered baking pan, 12 × 20 inches (30 × 50 cm).
2 lb	1 kg	Eggs	3. Mix together the eggs, sugar, salt, and vanilla until thoroughly combined.
1 lb	500 g	Sugar	4. Gradually stir in the milk.
1 tsp	5 mL	Salt	
1 oz	30 mL	Vanilla	
2½ qt	2.5 L	Milk	
as needed	as needed	Cinnamon	5. Pour the custard mixture over the bread slices in the pan. Let stand, refrigerated, for 1 hour or longer, so that the bread absorbs the custard mixture.
as needed	as needed	Nutmeg	6. Sprinkle the top lightly with cinnamon and nutmeg.
			7. Set the pan in a larger pan containing about 1 inch (3 cm) hot water.
			8. Place in an oven preheated to 350°F (175°C). Bake about 1 hour, until set.

Per serving:
Calories, 350; Protein, 11 g; Fat, 16 g (41% cal.); Cholesterol, 190 mg;
Carbohydrates, 41 g; Fiber, 1 g; Sodium, 440 mg.

9. Serve warm or cold with whipped cream or light custard sauce, or dusted with confectioners' sugar.

VARIATION

Cabinet Pudding
Prepare in individual custard cups instead of a baking pan. Substitute diced sponge cake for the bread and omit the melted butter. Add about 1 tbsp (15 mL) raisins to each cup before pouring in the custard mix.

Bavarians, Chiffons, Mousses, and Soufflés

All the preparations in this section have one thing in common: They all have a light, fluffy, or puffed texture that is created by the addition of whipped cream, beaten egg whites, or both.

Although these particular products may be new to you, you should have little trouble learning to prepare them if you have already studied the previous chapter and the first part of this chapter. Once you have learned to prepare crème anglaise, pastry cream, starch-thickened fruit fillings, meringues, and whipped cream and have learned to work with gelatin (read p. 566 if you have not yet studied gelatin), all you have to do is combine these products in different ways to make bavarians, chiffons, mousses, and soufflés.

Let's look at these four items separately to see what they are made of. Afterward, we examine the procedures for assembling them.

BAVARIANS

A bavarian, also known as bavarian cream or bavaroise, is made of three basic elements: crème anglaise (flavored as desired), gelatin, and whipped cream.

That's all there is to it. Gelatin is softened in cold liquid, stirred into the hot crème anglaise until dissolved, and chilled until almost set. Whipped cream is then folded in, and the mixture is poured into a mold until set. It is unmolded for service.

Accurate measuring of the gelatin is important. If not enough gelatin is used, the dessert will be too soft to hold its shape. If too much is used, it will be too firm and rubbery.

CHIFFONS

Chiffons are most popular as fillings for chiffon pies, but they may also be served more simply as puddings and chilled desserts.

The major difference between chiffons and bavarians is the use of beaten egg whites in place of or in addition to whipped cream. In other words, chiffons are made of a base plus gelatin plus beaten egg whites. (Some chiffons also contain whipped cream in addition to the egg whites.)

Bases for chiffons include the following three main types.

1. **Thickened with starch.**
   The procedure is the same as for fruit pie fillings made by the cooked juice or cooked fruit method, except that the fruit is finely chopped or puréed. Most fruit chiffons are made this way.

2. **Thickened with egg.**
   The procedure is the same as for custard sauce or crème anglaise. Many chocolate chiffons are made this way, as is pumpkin chiffon.

3. **Thickened with egg and starch.**
   The procedure is the same as for pastry cream. Lemon chiffon is usually made this way.

MOUSSES

There are so many varieties of mousse that it is impossible to give a rule for all of them. In general, we define a mousse as any soft or creamy dessert that is made light and fluffy by the addition of whipped cream, beaten egg whites, or both. Note that bavarians and chiffons both fit this description. In fact, they are often served as mousses, but with the gelatin reduced or left out so that the mousse is softer.

Many kinds of base are used for mousses. The bases may be nothing more than melted chocolate or puréed fresh fruit, or they may be more complex, like the bases for chiffons.

Some mousses contain both beaten egg whites and whipped cream. When this is the case, most chefs prefer to fold in the egg whites first, even though they may lose some volume. The reason is that if the cream is added first, there is more danger that it will be overbeaten and turn to butter during the folding and mixing procedure.

If egg whites are folded into a *hot* base, they will cook or coagulate, and the mousse will be firmer and more stable. Whipped cream should never be folded into hot mixtures, or it will melt and deflate.

DESSERT SOUFFLÉS

Soufflés are lightened with beaten egg whites, then baked. Baking causes the soufflé to rise like a cake because the air in the egg foam expands when heated.

To understand the structure of dessert soufflés, we can divide their preparation into four stages:

1. Base.
   Many kinds are used for dessert soufflés. Most are heavy, starch-thickened preparations, such as pastry cream or sweetened white sauce.

2. Egg yolks.
   When used, these are added to the base.

3. Egg whites.
   Whenever possible, egg whites should be whipped with some of the sugar. This makes dessert soufflés more stable than entrée soufflés.

4. Baking.
   Review the section on entrée soufflés (p. 621) so that you understand the general principles of baking soufflés.

SUMMARY AND COMPARISON

1. Bavarian.
   Base: custard sauce
   Gelatin
   Whipped cream

2. Chiffon.
   Base: Starch thickened (fruit filling type)
         Egg thickened (custard type)
         Egg and starch thickened (pastry cream type)
   Gelatin
   Egg whites
   (Optional whipped cream)

3. Mousse.
   Base: many varieties
   Little or no gelatin
   Egg whites and/or whipped cream

4. Soufflé.
   Base: many varieties, usually containing egg yolk
   Egg whites
   Baked

General Procedure

The following is a general procedure only. It is not a detailed method for one specific dessert but will give you a basic understanding that will help you tackle many recipes. These basic steps apply to most bavarians, chiffons, mousses, and soufflés.

1. Prepare the base.

2. If gelatin is used, soften it in cold liquid and stir it into the hot base until dissolved. Chill until almost set.

3. Fold in the beaten egg whites and/or whipped cream.

4. Chill (for bavarians, chiffons, and mousses) or bake (for soufflés).

Bavarian Cream

Portions: 24   **Portion size:** 3 oz (90 g)

U.S.	Metric	Ingredients	PROCEDURE
1½ oz	45 g	Gelatin (unflavored)	1. Soak the gelatin in cold water.
10 oz	300 mL	Cold water	
		Crème anglaise:	2. Prepare the crème anglaise: Whip the egg yolks and sugar until thick and light. Scald the milk and slowly stir it into the egg yolk mixture, beating constantly. Cook over a hot water bath, stirring constantly, until it just thickens slightly. (Review p. 871 for details on making crème anglaise.)
12	12	Egg yolks	
8 oz	250 g	Sugar	
1 qt	1 L	Milk	
1 tbsp	15 mL	Vanilla	
			3. When the sauce is still hot, add the softened gelatin. Stir until the gelatin is dissolved.
			4. Cool in the refrigerator or over crushed ice, stirring occasionally to keep the mixture smooth.
1 qt	1 L	Heavy cream	5. While the custard sauce is cooling, whip the cream until it forms soft, not stiff, peaks. Do not overwhip.
			6. When the custard sauce is very thick but not yet set, fold in the whipped cream.
			7. Pour into molds or into serving dishes.
			8. Chill until completely set. If prepared in molds, unmold for service.

Per serving:
Calories, 240; Protein, 5 g; Fat, 19 g (70% cal.); Cholesterol, 165 mg; Carbohydrates, 13 g; Fiber, 0 g; Sodium, 45 mg.

VARIATIONS

Chocolate Bavarian Cream

Add 12 oz (350 g) sweetened chocolate, chopped or grated, to the hot crème anglaise. Stir until completely melted and blended in.

Coffee Bavarian Cream

Add 3 tbsp (45 mL) instant coffee powder to the hot crème anglaise.

Strawberry Bavarian Cream

Reduce the milk to 1 pt (500 mL) and the sugar to 6 oz (175 g) when making the crème anglaise. Mash 1 lb (500 g) strawberries with 6 oz (175 g) sugar, or use 1½ lb (700 g) frozen, sweetened strawberries. Stir this purée into the custard sauce before adding the whipped cream.

Raspberry Bavarian Cream

Prepare like Strawberry Bavarian Cream, using raspberries.

Strawberry Chiffon Dessert or Pie Filling

Yield: 6 lb 8 oz (3 kg)
       six 8-inch (20-cm) pies
       five 9-inch (23-cm) pies
       four 10-inch (25-cm) pies

U.S.	Metric	Ingredients	PROCEDURE
4 lb	1800 g	Frozen sweetened strawberries (see note)	1. Thaw and drain the strawberries, reserving the juice. Chop the strawberries coarsely.
1 tsp	5 mL	Salt	2. Place the reserved juice and salt in a saucepan. Bring to a boil.
1 oz	30 g	Cornstarch	
4 oz	125 mL	Water	3. Dissolve the cornstarch in the water and stir into the strawberry juice. Cook until thick. Remove from heat.
1 oz	30 g	Gelatin	4. Soften the gelatin in the water. Add to the hot, thickened fruit juice and stir until completely dissolved.
8 oz	250 mL	Water, cold	
1 oz	30 mL	Lemon juice	5. Stir in the lemon juice and the drained strawberries.
			6. Chill the mixture until thickened but not set.
1 lb	450 g	Egg whites	7. Beat the egg whites until they form soft peaks.
12 oz	350 g	Sugar	8. Gradually add the sugar and continue to beat until a thick, glossy meringue is formed.
			9. Fold the meringue into the fruit mixture.
			10. Portion into individual serving dishes or fill baked pie shells.
			11. Chill until set.

Per 1 ounce:
Calories, 40; Protein, 1 g; Fat, 0 g (0% cal.); Cholesterol, 0 mg;
Carbohydrates, 9 g; Fiber, 0 g; Sodium, 30 mg.

Note: To use fresh strawberries, slice or dice 3 lb (1.4 kg) fresh, hulled strawberries and mix with 1 lb (450 g) sugar. Let stand 2 hours in refrigerator. Drain and reserve juice. Proceed as in basic recipe.

VARIATIONS

For a creamier chiffon, reduce egg whites to 12 oz (350 g). Whip 1 pt (500 mL) heavy cream and fold it in after the meringue.

Raspberry Chiffon Dessert or Pie Filling

Substitute raspberries for strawberries in basic recipe.

Pineapple Chiffon Dessert or Pie Filling

Use 3 lb (1.4 kg) crushed pineapple. Mix the drained juice with an additional 1 pt (500 mL) pineapple juice and add 8 oz (225 g) sugar.

Frozen Strawberry or Raspberry Mousse

Omit gelatin and second quantity of water from basic recipe or from raspberry variation. Reduce egg whites to 8 oz (225 g). Whip 1½ pt (750 mL) heavy cream and fold it in after the meringue. Pour into molds or other containers and freeze.

Chocolate Chiffon Dessert or Pie Filling

Yield: 7 lb (3.2 kg)
  six 8-inch (20-cm) pies
  five 9-inch (23-cm) pies
  four 10-inch (25-cm) pies

U.S.	Metric	Ingredients	PROCEDURE
10 oz	300 g	Unsweetened chocolate	1. Combine the chocolate and water in a heavy saucepan. Bring to a simmer, stirring constantly until smooth.
1½ pt	750 mL	Water	
1 lb	450 g	Egg yolks	2. Beat the egg yolks and sugar together with the whip attachment until thick and light.
1 lb	450 g	Sugar	3. With the mixer running, gradually pour in the chocolate mixture.
			4. Return the mixture to the saucepan and stir over very low heat until thickened. Remove from heat.
1 oz	30 g	Gelatin	5. Soften the gelatin in the water. Add to the hot chocolate mixture and stir until the gelatin is completely dissolved.
8 oz	250 mL	Water, cold	6. Chill until thick but not set.
1 lb 4 oz	575 g	Egg whites	7. Beat the egg whites until they form soft peaks.
1 lb 8 oz	700 g	Sugar	8. Gradually beat in the sugar. Continue beating until a firm, glossy meringue is formed.
			9. Fold into the chocolate mixture.
			10. Pour into serving dishes or into baked pie shells. Chill until set.

Per 1 ounce:
Calories, 70; Protein, 2 g; Fat, 2.5 g (30% cal.); Cholesterol, 50 mg; Carbohydrates, 11 g; Fiber, 0 g; Sodium, 10 mg.

VARIATION

Chocolate Cream Chiffon Pie Filling

For a creamier chiffon, reduce the egg whites to 1 lb (450 g). Whip 1 pt (500 mL) heavy cream and fold it in after the meringue.

Lemon Chiffon Dessert or Pie Filling

Yield: 7 lb (3.2 kg)

six 8-inch (20-cm) pies

five 9-inch (23-cm) pies

four 10-inch (25-cm) pies

U.S.	Metric	Ingredients	PROCEDURE
1½ pt	750 mL	Water	1. Dissolve the sugar in the water and bring to a boil.
8 oz	250 g	Sugar	
12 oz	375 g	Egg yolks	2. Beat together the egg yolks, water, cornstarch, sugar, and lemon zest until smooth.
4 oz	125 mL	Water, cold	3. Gradually beat in the boiling water in a thin stream.
3 oz	90 g	Cornstarch	4. Return the mixture to the heat and bring to a boil, beating constantly with a whip.
8 oz	250 g	Sugar	
		Grated zest of 4 lemons	5. As soon as the mixture thickens and boils, remove it from the heat.
1 oz	30 g	Gelatin	6. Soften the gelatin in the cold water.
8 oz	250 mL	Water, cold	7. Add the gelatin to the hot lemon mixture. Stir until it is dissolved.
12 oz	350 mL	Lemon juice	8. Stir in the lemon juice.
			9. Chill until thick but not set.
1 lb	450 g	Egg whites	10. Beat the egg whites until they form soft peaks.
1 lb	450 g	Sugar	11. Gradually add the sugar and continue to beat until a thick, glossy meringue is formed.

Per 1 ounce:

Calories, 50; Protein, 1 g; Fat, 1 g (18% cal.); Cholesterol, 40 mg;
Carbohydrates, 9 g; Fiber, 0 g; Sodium, 10 mg.

12. Fold the meringue into the lemon mixture.

13. Pour into individual serving dishes or fill baked pie shells.

14. Chill until set.

VARIATIONS

Lime Chiffon Dessert or Pie Filling

Substitute lime juice and zest for the lemon.

Orange Chiffon Dessert or Pie Filling

Use orange juice instead of water in step 1 and omit the first 8 oz (250 g) sugar. Substitute orange zest for the lemon zest. Reduce the lemon juice to 4 oz (125 mL).

Frozen Lemon Mousse

Omit the gelatin and the water used to dissolve it. Decrease egg whites to 12 oz (350 g). Whip 1 qt (1 L) heavy cream and fold it in after meringue. Pour into molds or other containers and freeze.

Pumpkin Chiffon Dessert or Pie Filling

Yield: 7 lb 12 oz (3.4 kg)
        six 8-inch (20-cm) pies
        five 9-inch (23-cm) pies
        four 10-inch (25-cm) pies

U.S.	Metric	Ingredients	PROCEDURE
2½ lb	1.2 kg	Pumpkin purée	1. Combine the pumpkin, brown sugar, milk, egg yolks, salt, and spices. Mix until smooth and uniform.
1 lb 4 oz	600 g	Brown sugar	
12 oz	350 g	Milk	2. Place in a double boiler. Cook, stirring frequently, until thickened or until the temperature of the mixture reaches 185°F (85°C). Remove from heat.
12 oz	350 g	Egg yolks, beaten	
1 tsp	5 mL	Salt	
4 tsp	20 mL	Cinnamon	
2 tsp	10 mL	Nutmeg	
1 tsp	5 mL	Ground ginger	
1 oz	30 g	Gelatin	3. Soften the gelatin in the water.
8 oz	250 mL	Water, cold	4. Add it to the hot pumpkin mixture and stir until dissolved.
			5. Chill until very thick but not set.
1 lb	450 g	Egg whites	6. Beat egg whites until they form soft peaks.
1 lb	450 g	Granulated sugar	7. Gradually add the granulated sugar and continue to beat until a thick meringue is formed.
			8. Fold the meringue into the pumpkin mixture.
			9. Portion into individual serving dishes or fill baked pie shells. Chill until set.

Per 1 ounce:
Calories, 50; Protein, 1 g; Fat, 1 g (18% cal.); Cholesterol, 35 mg; Carbohydrates, 9 g; Fiber, 0 g; Sodium, 30 mg.

VARIATION

Pumpkin Cream Chiffon

Reduce the egg whites to 12 oz (350 g). Whip 1 pt (500 mL) heavy cream and fold it in after the meringue.

Vanilla Soufflé

Portions: 10   Portion size: 4½ oz (125 g)

U.S.	Metric	Ingredients	PROCEDURE
3 oz 3 oz	90 g 90 g	Flour Butter	1. Work the flour and butter together to form a smooth paste.
1 pt 4 oz	500 mL 125 g	Milk Sugar	2. Dissolve the sugar in the milk and bring to a boil. Remove from the heat. 3. With a wire whip, beat in the flour paste. Beat vigorously to make sure there are no lumps. 4. Return the mixture to the heat and bring to a boil, beating constantly. Simmer for several minutes, until the mixture is very thick and no starchy taste remains. 5. Transfer the mixture to a mixing bowl. Cover and let cool for 5–10 minutes.
as needed as needed	as needed as needed	Butter Sugar	6. While the mixture is cooling, butter the soufflé dishes well and coat with sugar. For 1 recipe, use 1 dish, 10 inches (25 cm) in diameter; 2 dishes, 7 inches (18 cm) in diameter; or 10 single-portion dishes.
8 2 tsp	8 10 mL	Egg yolks Vanilla	7. Quickly beat the egg yolks and vanilla into the milk mixture.
8–10 2 oz	8–10 60 g	Egg whites Sugar	8. Beat the egg whites until they form soft peaks. Add the sugar and beat until the mixture forms firm, moist peaks. 9. Fold the egg whites into the soufflé base. 10. Pour the mixture into the prepared baking dishes and smooth the tops. 11. Bake at 375°F (190°C). Approximate baking times are 45–50 minutes for a 10-inch (25-cm) dish, 30–40 minutes for a 7-inch (18-cm) dish, and 15 minutes for single-portion dishes.

Per serving:
Calories, 270; Protein, 8 g; Fat, 13 g (44% cal.); Cholesterol, 195 mg;
Carbohydrates, 29 g; Fiber, 0 g; Sodium, 150 mg.

VARIATIONS

Chocolate Soufflé

Add 3 oz (90 g) melted unsweetened chocolate and 1 oz (30 g) melted sweet chocolate to the base after step 5.

Lemon Soufflé

Instead of vanilla, use the grated zest of 2 lemons for flavoring.

Liqueur Soufflé

Flavor with 2–3 oz (60–90 mL) liqueur, such as kirsch or Grand Marnier, added after step 5.

Coffee Soufflé

Flavor with 2 tbsp (30 mL) instant coffee powder, added to the milk in step 2.

Chocolate Mousse

Yield: about 5½ lb (2.5 kg) or 4 qt (4 L)　　**Portions:** 25　　**Portion size:** 5 fl oz (150 mL)

U.S.	Metric	Ingredients	PROCEDURE
2 lb	900 g	Semisweet chocolate	1. Melt the chocolate over hot water.
8 oz	225 g	Butter	2. Remove from the heat and add the butter. Stir until the butter is melted and completely mixed in.
12 oz	350 g	Egg yolks	3. Add the egg yolks, one at a time. Mix in each yolk completely before adding the next.
1 lb	450 g	Egg whites	4. Beat the egg whites until they form soft peaks. Add the sugar and beat until the egg whites form stiff but moist peaks. Do not overbeat.
5 oz	150 g	Sugar	5. Fold the egg whites into the chocolate.
1 pt	500 mL	Heavy cream	6. Whip the heavy cream until it forms soft peaks. Fold it into the chocolate mixture.
			7. Spoon the mousse into serving dishes or use a pastry bag fitted with a star tube.
			8. Chill the mousse well before serving.

Per serving:
Calories, 380; Protein, 6 g; Fat, 29 g (64% cal.); Cholesterol, 220 mg;
Carbohydrates, 30 g; Fiber, 2 g; Sodium, 120 mg.

Note: This mixture may also be used as a filling for cakes, pastries, and baked meringues. For another, very different chocolate mousse recipe, see the variation following the recipe for Chocolate Chiffon earlier in this chapter.

Frozen Desserts

The popularity of ice cream needs no explanation. Whether served as a plain scoop of vanilla ice cream in a dish or as an elaborate assemblage of fruits, syrups, toppings, and numerous flavors of ice cream and sherbet, frozen desserts appeal to just about everyone.

CLASSIFICATION

1. **Ice cream.**
   Ice cream is a smooth, frozen mixture of milk, cream, sugar, flavorings, and, sometimes, eggs. *Philadelphia-style* ice cream contains no eggs, while *French-style* ice cream contains egg yolks. The eggs add richness and help make a smoother product because of the emulsifying properties of the yolks.
   Ice milk is like ice cream, but with a lower butterfat content.
   Frozen yogurt contains yogurt in addition to the normal ingredients for ice cream or ice milk.

2. **Sherbet.**
   Sherbets and *ices* are made from fruit juices, water, and sugar. American sherbets usually contain milk or cream and, sometimes, egg whites. The egg whites increase smoothness and volume. Ices, also called *water ices*, contain only fruit juice, water, sugar, and, sometimes, egg whites. They do not contain milk products. The French word *sorbet* (sor bay) is sometimes used for these products. *Granité* (grah nee tay) is a coarse, crystalline ice made without egg white.

3. **Still-frozen dessert.**
   Ice cream and sherbet are churn-frozen, meaning that they are mixed constantly while being frozen. If they were not churned, they would freeze into solid blocks of ice. The churning keeps the ice crystals small and incorporates air into the ice cream.
   Frozen soufflés and *frozen mousses* are made like chilled mousses and bavarians. That is, whipped cream, beaten egg whites, or both are folded in to give them lightness. This allows them to be still-frozen in an ordinary freezer.

PRODUCTION AND QUALITY

Until recently, few establishments made their own ice cream because of the labor involved, the equipment required, and the convenience of commercially made products. Also, in some areas, strict health codes made it difficult for all but large producers to make ice cream. Today, more and more restaurants are making their own ice creams and sorbets.

A basic ice cream mix is simply a crème anglaise or custard sauce mixed with 1 or 2 parts heavy cream for every 4 parts milk used in the sauce. This base is flavored as desired with vanilla, melted chocolate, instant coffee, crushed strawberries, and so on. It is then chilled thoroughly, then frozen according to the instructions for the particular equipment being used.

When the mix has frozen, it is transferred to containers and placed in a deep-freeze at below 0°F (−18°C) to harden. (Soft-frozen or soft-serve ice creams are served directly as they come from the churn freezer without being hardened.)

Whether you make ice cream or buy it, you should be aware of the following quality factors:

1. *Smoothness* is related to the size of the ice crystals in the product. Ice cream should be frozen rapidly and churned well during freezing so that large crystals don't have a chance to form.

    Rapid hardening helps keep crystals small. So do eggs and emulsifiers or stabilizers added to the mix.

    Large crystals may form if ice cream is not stored at a low enough temperature (below 0°F/−18°C).

2. *Overrun* is the increase in volume due to the incorporation of air when freezing ice cream. It is expressed as a percentage of the original volume of the mix. For example, if the ice cream doubles in volume, the amount of increase is equal to the original volume and the overrun is 100 percent.

    Some overrun is necessary to give a smooth, light texture. Ice cream with too much overrun is airy and foamy and lacks flavor. It was once thought that ice cream should have from 80 to 100 percent overrun and that less would make it heavy and pasty. This may be true for ice creams containing gums and other stabilizers. However, some high-quality manufacturers produce rich (and expensive) ice cream with as little as 20 percent overrun.

3. *Mouth feel* or *body* depends, in part, on smoothness and overrun as well as on other qualities. Good ice cream melts in the mouth to a smooth, not too heavy liquid. Some ice creams have so many stabilizers that they never melt to a liquid. Unfortunately, many people have become so accustomed to these products that an ice cream that actually does melt strikes them as not rich enough.

STORAGE AND SERVICE

1. Store ice creams and sherbets at 0°F (−18°C) or lower. This low temperature helps prevent the formation of large ice crystals.

2. For service, temper frozen desserts at 8° to 15°F (−13° to −9°C) for 24 hours so that they are soft enough to serve.

3. When serving, avoid packing the ice cream. The best method is to draw the scoop across the surface of the product so that the product rolls into a ball in the scoop.

4. Use standard scoops for portioning ice cream. Normal portions for popular desserts are as follows:

Parfait	3 No. 30 scoops
Banana split	3 No. 30 scoops
À la mode topping for pie or cake	1 No. 20 scoop
Sundae	2 No. 20 scoops
Plain dish of ice cream	1 No. 10, 12, or 16 scoop

5. Measure syrups, toppings, and garnishes for portion control. For syrups, use pumps that dispense measured quantities, or use standard ladles.

POPULAR ICE CREAM DESSERTS

1. *Parfaits* are made by alternating layers of ice cream and fruit or syrup in a tall, narrow glass. They are usually named after the syrup or topping. For example: a *chocolate parfait* comprises three scoops of vanilla or chocolate ice cream alternating with layers of chocolate syrup and topped with whipped cream and shaved chocolate.

2. *Sundaes* or *coupes* consist of one or two scoops of ice cream or sherbet in a dish or glass, topped with any of a number of syrups, fruits, toppings, and garnishes. They are quick to prepare, unlimited in variety, and as simple or as elegant as you could wish—served in an ordinary soda fountain glass, a silver cup, or a crystal champagne glass.

    Two sundaes have become classics:

    Peach Melba. Vanilla ice cream topped with a fresh, poached, or canned peach half, napped with sweetened raspberry purée (Melba sauce), and garnished with slivered almonds.

    Pear Belle Hélène. Vanilla ice cream topped with a poached or canned pear half, napped with chocolate sauce, and garnished with toasted sliced almonds.

3. *Bombes* are ice cream molds made by lining a chilled mold with softened ice cream, freezing it hard, then filling the center with another flavor of ice cream or sherbet and freezing it again. (More than two flavors may be used.) The dessert is unmolded onto a cold platter for service and decorated as desired with whipped cream, fruits, and/or confections.

    Although bombes are usually made in decorative round molds, layered frozen desserts are also made in other molds, such as cake pans and loaf pans. A *cassata* is an Italian style layered ice cream dessert often made in a loaf pan or other rectangular pan.

4. *Meringue glacée.* See discussion of meringues, page 863.

5. *Baked Alaska.* See discussion of meringues, page 864.

6. *Frozen éclairs* and *profiteroles.* See discussion of éclair pastries, page 860.

Dessert Sauces

Most dessert sauces fall into three categories.

1. **Custard sauces.**
    Vanilla custard sauce or crème anglaise is presented early in this chapter. It is among the most basic preparations in dessert cookery. Chocolate or other flavors may be added to create other varieties. See recipe on page 872.

2. **Fruit purées.**
    These are simply purées of fresh or cooked fruits, sweetened with sugar. Other flavorings and spices are sometimes added. Some fruit sauces are thickened with cornstarch or other starch.

    Raspberry sauce and *strawberry sauce*, two popular items, can be made by simply puréeing frozen sweetened berries or by puréeing fresh berries and adding sugar to taste. See also the recipe for Applesauce, page 163.

3. **Syrups.**
    This is a broad category that includes such products as chocolate sauce and caramel sauce. An understanding of sugar cooking is necessary to produce many of these sauces.

    The following recipes are popular examples of this category of sauce.

Chocolate Sauce

Yield: 2 qt (2 L)

U.S.	Metric	Ingredients	PROCEDURE
1 qt	1 L	Water	1. Combine the water, sugar, and syrup and bring to a boil, stirring to dissolve the sugar.
4 lb	2 kg	Sugar	
12 oz	375 g	Corn syrup	2. Boil 1 minute and remove from heat. Let cool 1–2 minutes.
1 lb	500 g	Unsweetened chocolate, melted	3. Melt the chocolate and butter together over low heat. Stir until smooth.
4 oz	125 g	Butter	4. Very slowly stir the hot syrup into the chocolate.
			5. Place over moderate heat and bring to a boil. Boil for 4 minutes.
			6. Remove from heat and cool.

Per 1 ounce:
Calories, 170; Protein, 1 g; Fat, 5 g (24% cal.); Cholesterol, 5 mg;
Carbohydrates, 34 g; Fiber, 1 g; Sodium, 25 mg.

Caramel Sauce

Yield: 1½ qt (1.5 L)

U.S.	Metric	Ingredients	PROCEDURE
2 lb	1 kg	Sugar	1. Combine the sugar, water, and lemon juice in a heavy saucepan. Bring to a boil, stirring to dissolve the sugar.
8 oz	250 g	Water	
1 tbsp	15 mL	Lemon juice	2. When the sugar is dissolved, cover the pan and boil for 2 minutes.
			3. Uncover and cook to the caramel stage (see pages 870–871). Toward the end of the cooking time, turn the heat very low to avoid burning the sugar or getting it too dark. It should be a golden color.
			4. Remove from heat and cool 5 minutes.
3 cups	750 mL	Heavy cream	5. Bring the heavy cream to a boil. Add a few ounces (50–100 mL) of the heavy cream to the caramel.
			6. Stir and continue to add the cream slowly.
			7. Return to the heat and stir until all the caramel is dissolved.
			8. Let cool completely.
1 pt	500 mL	Milk	9. Stir the milk into the cooled caramel to thin it.

Per 1 ounce:
Calories, 130; Protein, 1 g; Fat, 6 g (39% cal.); Cholesterol, 20 mg;
Carbohydrates, 20 g; Fiber, 0 g; Sodium, 10 mg.

VARIATIONS

Hot Caramel Sauce

Prepare as directed through step 7. Omit the milk.

Clear Caramel Sauce

Substitute 10–12 oz (300–350 mL) water for the heavy cream and omit the milk. If the sauce is too thick when cool, add more water.

Terms for Review

simple syrup	cream pudding	Philadelphia-style ice cream	still-frozen
dessert syrup	baked pudding	French-style ice cream	overrun
crystallize	bavarian	ice milk	parfait
crème anglaise	chiffon	sherbet	coupe
pastry cream	mousse	ice	Peach Melba
blancmange	ice cream	granité	bombe

Questions for Discussion

1. How can you avoid unwanted crystallization when cooking sugar syrups?

2. Light custard sauce and pastry cream both contain eggs. Why is it possible to boil pastry cream but not custard sauce?

3. Explain the importance of sanitation in the production of pastry cream. What specific steps should you take to ensure a safe product?

4. Light custard sauce, pastry cream, and baked custard are made with basic techniques that are also used for the following preparations. Identify which of the three techniques is used for each.

Coconut cream pie	French vanilla ice cream
Baked rice pudding	Pumpkin pie
Butterscotch pudding	Custard pie
Chocolate bavarian	Lemon meringue pie

5. Briefly describe the differences among bavarians, chiffons, mousses, and soufflés.

6. When making dessert soufflés, what is the advantage of beating the egg whites with part of the sugar?

7. What difficulty would you encounter, when making a bavarian or chiffon, if you chilled the gelatin mixture too long before folding in the whipped cream or egg whites?

Appendix 1

METRIC CONVERSION FACTORS

Weight
    1 ounce equals 28.35 grams
    1 gram equals 0.035 ounce
    1 pound equals 454 grams
    1 kilogram equals 2.2 pounds

Volume
    1 fluid ounce equals 29.57 milliliters
    1 milliliter equals 0.034 ounce
    1 cup equals 237 milliliters
    1 quart equals 946 milliliters
    1 liter equals 33.8 fluid ounces

Length
    1 inch equals 25.4 millimeters
    1 centimeter equals 0.39 inch
    1 meter equals 39.4 inches

Temperature
To convert Fahrenheit to Celsius:
    Subtract 32. Then multiply by $5/9$.

    Example: Convert 140°F to Celsius.
$$140 - 32 = 108$$
$$108 \times 5/9 = 60°C$$

To convert Celsius to Fahrenheit:
    Multiply by $9/5$. Then add 32.

    Example: Convert 150°C to Fahrenheit.
$$150 \times 9/5 = 270$$
$$270 + 32 = 302°F$$

Note: The metric equivalents in the recipes in this book are rounded off. See page 78 for complete explanation.

Appendix 2

STANDARD CAN SIZES

| Can Name | Volume | | Approximate Weight[a] | |
	U.S.	Metric	U.S.	Metric
6 oz	5.75 fl. oz	170 mL	6 oz	170 g
8 oz	8.3 fl. oz	245 mL	8 oz	227 g
No. 1 picnic	10.5 fl. oz	311 mL	10½ oz	298 g
No. 211 cylinder	12 fl. oz	355 mL	12 oz	340 g
No. 300	13.5 fl. oz	399 mL	14 oz	397 g
No. 303	15.6 fl. oz	461 mL	16–17 oz	454–482 g
No. 2	20 fl. oz	591 mL	1 lb 4 oz	567 g
No. 2½	28.5 fl. oz	843 mL	1 lb 13 oz	822 g
No. 3 cylinder	46 fl. oz	1360 mL	3 lb	1360 g
No. 5	56 fl. oz	1656 mL	3 lb 8 oz	1588 g
No. 10	103.7 fl. oz	3067 mL	6½–7 lb	2722–2948 g

[a]Because the density of foods varies, so does the net weight for any given size can.

Appendix 3

APPROXIMATE WEIGHT–VOLUME EQUIVALENTS OF DRY FOODS

The following equivalents are rough averages only. Actual weight per volume varies considerably. For accurate measurement, all ingredients should be weighed.

Bread flour, sifted
1 lb = 4 cups
1 cup = 4 oz

Bread flour, unsifted
1 lb = 3⅓ cups
1 cup = 4.75 oz

Cake flour, sifted
1 lb = 4¼ cups
1 cup = 3.75 oz

Cake flour, unsifted
1 lb = 3½ cups
1 cup = 4.5 oz

Granulated sugar
1 lb = 2¼ cups
1 cup = 7 oz

Confectioners' sugar, sifted
1 lb = 4 cups
1 cup = 4 oz

Confectioners' sugar, unsifted
1 lb = 3½ cups
1 cup = 4.5 oz

Cornstarch, sifted
1 lb = 4 cups
1 cup = 4 oz
1 oz = 4 tbsp = ¼ cup
1 tbsp = 0.25 oz

Cornstarch, unsifted
1 lb = 3½ cups
1 cup = 4.5 oz
1 oz = 3½ tbsp
1 tbsp = 0.29 oz

Cocoa, unsifted
1 lb = 5 cups
1 cup = 3.2 oz
1 oz = 5 tbsp
1 tbsp = 0.2 oz

Gelatin, unflavored
1 oz = 3 tbsp
¼ oz = 2¼ tsp
1 tbsp = 0.33 oz
1 tsp = 0.11 oz

Baking soda
Baking powder (phosphate type and sodium aluminum sulfate type)
1 oz = 2 tbsp
¼ oz = 1½ tsp
1 tbsp = 0.5 oz
1 tsp = 0.17 oz

Cream of tartar
1 oz = 4 tbsp
¼ oz = 1 tbsp
1 tsp = 0.08 oz

Salt
1 oz = 5 tsp
¼ oz = 1¼ tsp
1 tsp = 0.2 oz

Cinnamon
1 oz = 17 tsp
¼ oz = 4¼ tsp
1 tsp = 0.06 oz

Ground spices (except cinnamon)
1 oz = 14 tsp
¼ oz = 3½ tsp
1 tsp = 0.07 oz

Grated lemon zest
1 oz = 4 tbsp
1 tsp = 0.08 oz

Dried beans
1 cup = 6.5 oz
1 lb = 2½ cups
(yields 6 cups cooked)

Rice, long grain
1 cup = 7 oz
1 lb = 2¼ cups
(yields 8 cups cooked)

Appendix 4

KITCHEN MATH EXERCISES—METRIC VERSIONS

This appendix includes metric sample calculations corresponding to the calculations in the text that use U.S. measures. Refer to the appropriate pages in the text for explanations.

Recipe Conversion, Pages 80-81

Beef tenderloin tips
and mushrooms à la crème

    Portions: 8
    Portion size: 250 g

Butter	60 g
Onions	125 g
Flour	15 mL
Mushrooms	250 g
Beef tenderloin	1250 g
White wine	125 mL
Prepared mustard	10 mL
Brown sauce	750 mL
Heavy cream	250 mL
Salt	to taste
Pepper	to taste

To determine quantities for 18 portions, divide new yield by old yield to find conversion factor:

$$\frac{\text{new yield}}{\text{old yield}} = \frac{18}{8} = 2.25$$

EXAMPLE 1

Ingredient	Quantity	Times	Conversion Factor	Equals	New Quantity (rounded off)
Butter	60 g	×	2.25	=	135 g
Onions	125 g	×	2.25	=	275 g
Flour	15 mL	×	2.25	=	35 mL
Mushrooms	250 g	×	2.25	=	575 g
Beef tenderloin	1250 g	×	2.25	=	2800 g
White wine	125 mL	×	2.25	=	275 mL
Prepared mustard	10 mL	×	2.25	=	23 mL
Brown sauce	750 mL	×	2.25	=	1700 mL
Heavy cream	250 mL	×	2.25	=	575 mL

To determine quantities for 40 portions at 175 grams each, first find the total yield of the old recipe. Multiply the portions by the portion size:

$$8 \text{ (portions)} \times 250 \text{ g} = 2000 \text{ g}$$

Do the same calculation for the desired yield:

$$40 \text{ (portions)} \times 175 \text{ g} = 7000 \text{ g}$$

Divide the desired yield by the old yield to find the conversion factor:

$$7000 \div 7000 = 3.5$$

EXAMPLE 2

Ingredient	Quantity	Times	Conversion Factor	Equals	New Quantity (rounded off)
Butter	60 g	×	3.5	=	200 g
Onions	125 g	×	3.5	=	450 g
Flour	15 mL	×	3.5	=	50 mL
Mushrooms	250 g	×	3.5	=	875 g
Beef tenderloin	1250 g	×	3.5	=	4375 g
White wine	125 mL	×	3.5	=	450 mL
Prepared mustard	10 mL	×	3.5	=	35 mL
Brown sauce	750 mL	×	3.5	=	2625 mL
Heavy cream	250 mL	×	3.5	=	875 mL

COMPLETED RAW YIELD TEST FORM (METRIC)—P. 86

Item	veal leg to scaloppine	Test number	3	Date	6/5/2002
Purveyor	ABC Meats	Price per pound	$11.00	Total cost	$148.50
AP weight (1)	13.5 kg	Lb price (2)	$11.00	Total cost (3)	$148.50

Trim, salvage, and waste:

	Item	Weight	Value/lb	Total Value (lb × value)
(4)	fat	1.14 kg	$ .25	$ .29
(5)	bone	1.5 kg	$ .88	$1.32
(6)	ground veal	0.95 kg	$9.75	$9.26
(7)	stew meat	1.4 kg	$10.95	$15.33
(8)	unusable trim	0.4 kg	0	0
(9)	cutting loss	0.09 kg	0	0
(10)				
	Total Weight (4 through 10) (11)	5.48 kg	Total Value (4 through 10) (12)	$26.20

Total yield of item (13)	8.02 kg
Net cost (3 minus 12) (14)	$122.30
Cost per lb (14 divided by 13) (15)	$15.25
Percentage of increase (15 divided by 2) (16)	1.39 (139%)

COMPLETED COOKED YIELD TEST FORM (METRIC)—P. 87

Item	roast fresh ham	Test number	2	Date 6/5/2002

AP price per kg $7.75

Cooking temperature   165°C

Net raw weight (1) 5.5 kg	Net cost per kg (2)	$8.73
	Total net cost (3)	$48.02

Weight as served (4)   3.75 kg

Cooked cost per kg (3 divided by 4) (5) $12.81

Shrinkage (1 minus 4) (6)   1.75 kg

Percentage of shrinkage (6 divided by 1) (7)   32%

Total percentage of cost increase (5 divided by AP price per kg) (8)   165%

METRIC EXAMPLE: COSTING A RECIPE—P. 88
ITEM: BAKED RICE

Ingredient	Recipe Quantity	AP Quantity	Price	Total Amount
Rice, long grain	2 kg	2 kg	$1.59/kg	$3.18
Butter	375 g	0.375 kg	4.25/kg	1.59
Onions	500 g	0.5 kg	0.79/kg	0.40
Chicken stock	4 L	4 L	0.30/L	1.20
Salt	30 g	0.03 kg	0.35/kg	0.01
			Total cost	$6.38
			Number of portions	50
			Cost per portion	$0.13

Appendix 5

EGGS AND SAFETY

The following guidelines are reprinted from Joan K. Loken, *The HACCP Food Safety Manual.* New York: John Wiley & Sons, 1995, pp. 122–123.

EGGS AND EGG-BASED PRODUCTS

Outbreaks of salmonellosis have been traced to clean, whole, uncracked-shell eggs contaminated with *Salmonella enteritidis.* Whole-shell eggs are now classified as potentially hazardous foods by the [U.S.] FDA.

The following guidelines, which treat eggs as potentially hazardous foods during storage, handling, preparation, and service, must be followed to prevent the possibility of foodborne illness:

- Store eggs at refrigerated temperatures of 40°F [4°C] or lower.
- When using eggs for menu service, it is best to keep them refrigerated and pull as needed. If this is not feasible, pull one layer at a time if used quickly, or ice eggs in a pan.
- Cooked eggs must be held at 140°F [60°C] or higher.
- Cook eggs thoroughly until both the yolk and white are firm, not runny.

Scrambled – 1 minute on cooking surface of 250°F [121°C]

Poached – 5 minutes in boiling water

Soft-boiled – 7 minutes in boiling water

Sunnyside – 7 minutes on cooking surface of 250°F [121°C], or covered 4 minutes at 250°F [121°C]

Fried, over easy – 3 minutes at 250°F [121°C], then turn and fry another 2 minutes on the other side.

- Avoid pooling raw eggs for holding. Eggs may be pooled in small quantities for immediate cooking and serving.
- For lightly cooked egg items, such as custards, French toast, mousse, and meringues, pasteurized eggs should be used.
- Avoid raw egg menu items. Review menus, recipes, and preparation procedures using raw eggs. Pasteurized eggs may be substituted for Caesar salad, hollandaise and béarnaise sauces, eggnog, ice cream, and egg-fortified beverages.
- Pasteurized eggs require the same time and temperature handling as other potentially hazardous foods.
- Wash hands with hot, soapy water before and after handling eggs and egg products.
- Wash and sanitize utensils, equipment, and the work area after handling eggs and egg products.
- Do not reuse a container that has held a raw egg mixture. Use a clean, sanitized container for each batch.

Bibliography

A

Amendola, Joseph. *The Baker's Manual for Quantity Baking and Pastry Making*, 5th ed. New York: John Wiley & Sons, 2002.

Anderson, Jean. *The Food of Portugal*. New York: Morrow, 1986.

Anderson, Jean, and Hedy Wurz. *The New German Cookbook*. New York: HarperCollins, 1993.

Andoh, Elizabeth. *At Home with Japanese Cooking*. New York: Knopf, 1980.

B

Bayless, Rick. *Authentic Mexican*. New York: Morrow, 1987.

Bertolli, Paul, and Alice Waters. *Chez Panisse Cooking*. New York: Random House, 1988.

Bickel, Walter, ed. *Hering's Dictionary of Classical and Modern Cookery*. London: Virtue, 1991.

Bissel, Frances. *The Book of Food*. New York: Henry Holt, 1994.

Bocuse, Paul. *Paul Bocuse's French Cooking*. New York: Pantheon, 1977.

Boni, Ada. *Italian Regional Cooking*. New York: Bonanza, 1969.

Bugialli, Giuliano. *Classic Techniques of Italian Cooking*. New York: Simon & Schuster, 1982.

Bugialli, Giuliano. *The Fine Art of Italian Cooking*. New York: Times Books, 1977.

C

Casas, Penelope. *The Foods and Wines of Spain*. New York: Knopf, 1987.

Claiborne, Craig, and Virginia Lee. *The Chinese Cookbook*. Philadelphia: Lippincott, 1972.

Cordon Bleu, Le. *Kitchen Essentials*. New York: John Wiley & Sons, 2001.

Cox, Beverly. *Cooking Techniques*. Boston: Little, Brown, 1981.

Culinary Institute of America. *Garde Manger: The Art and Craft of the Cold Kitchen*. New York: John Wiley & Sons, 2000.

Culinary Institute of America. *The Professional Chef*, 7th ed. New York: John Wiley & Sons, 2002.

Culinary Institute of America. *The Professional Chef's Knife Kit*. New York: John Wiley & Sons, 2000.

Culinary Institute of America. *Techniques of Healthy Cooking*, 2nd ed. New York: John Wiley & Sons, 2000.

D

David, Elizabeth. *French Provincial Cooking*. Harmondsworth, England: Penguin, 1960.

David, Elizabeth. *Italian Food*. Harmondsworth, England: Penguin, 1954.

Davidson, Alan. *The Oxford Companion to Food*. Oxford: Oxford University Press, 1999.

D'Ermo, Dominique. *The Modern Pastry Chef's Guide to Professional Baking*. New York: Harper & Row, 1962.

E

Egan, Maureen, and Susan Davis Allen. *Healthful Quantity Baking*. New York: John Wiley & Sons, 1992.

Escoffier, A. *The Escoffier Cook Book*. New York: Crown, 1969.

F

Feinstein, Andrew Hale, and John M. Stefanelli. *Purchasing: Selection and Procurement for the Hospitality Industry*, 5th ed. New York: John Wiley & Sons, 2002.

Friberg, Bo. *The Professional Pastry Chef*, 4th ed. New York: John Wiley & Sons, 2002.

G

Gisslen, Wayne. *Advanced Professional Cooking*. New York: John Wiley & Sons, 1992.

Gisslen, Wayne. *Professional Baking*, 3rd ed. New York: John Wiley & Sons, 2001.

Grausman, Richard. *At Home with the French Classics*. New York: Workman, 1988.

H

Hazan, Marcella. *The Classic Italian Cookbook*. New York: Knopf, 1976.

Hazan, Marcella. *More Classic Italian Cooking*. New York: Knopf, 1978.

Hom, Ken. *Chinese Technique*. New York: Simon & Schuster, 1981.

K

Kapoor, Sandy. *Professional Healthy Cooking*. New York: Wiley, 1995.

Katsigris, Costas, and Chris Thomas. *Design and Equipment for Restaurants and Foodservice*. New York: John Wiley & Sons, 1999.

Kennedy, Diana. *The Cuisines of Mexico*, 2nd ed. New York: Harper & Row, 1986.

Kennedy, Diana. *Mexican Regional Cooking*. New York: Harper & Row, 1978.

Kinsella, John, and David T. Harvey. *Professional Charcuterie.* New York: John Wiley & Sons, 1996.

Knight, John B., and Lendel H. Kotschevar. *Quantity Food Production, Planning, and Management,* 3rd ed. New York: John Wiley & Sons, 2000.

L

Lang, George. *The Cuisine of Hungary.* New York: Bonanza, 1971.

Larousse, David Paul. *The Professional Garde Manger.* New York: John Wiley & Sons, 1996.

Larousse, David Paul. *The Sauce Bible.* New York: John Wiley & Sons, 1993.

Librairie Larousse. *Larousse Gastronomique.* New York: Clarkson Potter, 2001.

Loken, Joan K. *The HACCP Food Safety Manual.* New York: John Wiley & Sons, 1995.

M

McClane, A.J. *The Encyclopedia of Fish.* New York: Holt, Rinehart & Winston, 1977.

McGee, Harold. *The Curious Cook.* San Francisco: North Point Press, 1990.

McGee, Harold. *On Food and Cooking.* New York: Scribners, 1984.

Miller, Gloria Bley. *The Thousand Recipe Chinese Cookbook.* New York: Grosset & Dunlap, 1970.

Mizer, David A., Mary Porter, Beth Sonnier, and Karen Eich Drummond. *Food Preparation for the Professional,* 3rd ed. New York: Wiley, 2000.

N

National Association of Meat Purveyors. *Meat Buyers Guide.* Reston, Virginia, 1997.

National Restaurant Association Educational Foundation. *ServSafe Coursebook,* 2nd ed. Chicago, 2002.

P

Pauli, Eugen. *Classical Cooking the Modern Way: Recipes,* 3rd ed. Arno Schmidt, trans. and Margaret Schmidt, ed. New York: John Wiley & Sons, 1997.

Pauli, Eugen. *Classical Cooking the Modern Way: Methods and Techniques,* 3rd ed. Arno Schmidt, trans. and Margaret Schmidt, ed. New York: John Wiley & Sons, 1999.

Pepin, Jacques. *The Art of Cooking.* New York: Knopf, 1987.

Pepin, Jacques. *La Technique: The Fundamental Techniques of Cooking: An Illustrated Guide.* New York: Quadrangle/Times Books, 1976.

Peterson, James. *Fish and Shellfish.* New York: Morrow, 1996.

Peterson, James. *Sauces,* 2nd ed. New York: John Wiley & Sons, 1997.

Peterson, James. *Splendid Soups: Recipes and Master Techniques for Making the World's Best Soups.* New York: John Wiley & Sons, 2001.

S

Saulnier, L. *La Répertoire de la Cuisine.* Woodbury, N.Y.: Barron's, 1976.

Schmidt, Arno, and Inja Nam. *The Book of Hors d'Oeuvres and Canapés.* New York: John Wiley & Sons, 1996.

Schneider, Elizabeth. *Uncommon Fruits and Vegetables: A Common-sense Guide.* New York: Harper & Row, 1986.

Sheraton, Mimi. *The German Cookbook.* New York: Random House, 1965.

Shugart, Grace, and Mary K. Molt. *Food for Fifty,* 9th ed. New York: Macmillan, 1992.

Somerville, Annie. *Field of Greens.* New York: Bantam, 1993.

Sonnenschmidt, Frederic H., and Jean F. Nicolas. *The Professional Chef's Art of Garde Manger,* 5th ed. New York: John Wiley & Sons, 1993.

Sultan, William J. *Practical Baking,* 5th ed. New York: John Wiley & Sons, 1990.

T

Torres, Marimar. *The Spanish Table.* Garden City, N.Y.: Doubleday, 1986.

Tsuji, Shizuo. *Japanese Cooking: A Simple Art.* Tokyo: Kodansha, 1980.

W

Waters, Alice. *Chez Panisse Vegetables.* New York: HarperCollins, 1996.

Willan, Anne. *La Varenne Pratique.* New York: Crown, 1989.

Glossary

Note: Phonetic guides are included for difficult French words, giving the approximate pronunciation using English sounds. Exact rendering is impossible in many cases because French has a number of sounds that don't exist in English. For foreign terms used in Chapter 25, see glossary at the end of that chapter, pages 754–755.

A

Adductor Muscle The muscle with which a mollusk closes its shell. In the case of American and Canadian scallops, this is usually the only part that is eaten.

Aging Holding meats in coolers under controlled conditions to allow natural tenderizing to take place.

À la Carte (1) Referring to a menu on which each individual item is listed with a separate price. (2) Referring to cooking to order, as opposed to cooking ahead in large batches.

Al Dente Firm, not soft or mushy, to the bite. Said of vegetables and pasta.

Allemande (1) German style. (2) A sauce made of velouté (usually veal), a liaison, and lemon juice.

Allumette Cut into matchstick shapes; usually refers to potatoes.

Anthocyanins Red or purple pigments in vegetables and fruits.

Antipasto Italian hors d'oeuvre.

AP Weight As purchased; the weight of an item before trimming.

Arborio Rice A variety of short-grain rice from Italy.

Argenteuil (ar zhawn toy) Garnished with asparagus.

Aspic Jelly A clarified stock that contains enough gelatin so that it solidifies when cold.

Aspic Powder Unflavored gelatin mixed with a powdered stock base.

AS Weight As served; the weight of an item as sold or served, after processing and/or cooking.

Au Gratin (oh gra tan) Having a browned or crusted top, often made by topping with bread crumbs, cheese, and/or a rich sauce and passing under the broiler or salamander.

Au Jus (oh zhoo) Served with its natural juices, usually unthickened pan drippings.

Au Sec (oh seck) Until dry.

Avgolemono Greek soup made of chicken stock, egg, and lemon juice.

B

Bacteria Microscopic organisms, some of which can cause disease, including food-borne disease.

Bain-Marie A container of hot water used for keeping foods hot.

Bake To cook foods by surrounding them with hot, dry air. Similar to roast, but the term bake usually applies to breads, pastries, vegetables, and fish.

Baked Alaska A dessert consisting of ice cream on a sponge-cake base, covered with meringue and browned in the oven.

Barbecue To cook with dry heat created by the burning of hardwood or by the hot coals of this wood.

Bard To tie thin slices of fat, such as pork fatback, over meats with no natural fat cover to protect them while roasting.

Basic Grind Referring to sausages made simply by grinding meats to various stages of coarseness or fineness.

Basmati Rice A variety of long-grain rice from India.

Batonnet Cut into sticks, about ¼ × ¼ × 2½–3 inches (6 mm × 6 mm × 6–7.5 cm).

Batter Semiliquid mixture containing flour or other starch, used for the production of such products as cakes and breads and for coating products to be deep-fried.

Bavarian Cream A dessert made of custard sauce, gelatin, and whipped cream.

Béarnaise (bare nez) A sauce made of butter and egg yolks and flavored with a reduction of vinegar, shallots, tarragon, and peppercorns.

Béchamel A sauce made by thickening milk with a roux.

Beignet Fritter.

Beurre Manié (burr mahn yay) A mixture of equal parts raw butter and flour mixed together into a smooth paste.

Beurre Noir (burr nwahr) Butter heated until it is dark brown, then flavored with vinegar.

Beurre Noisette (burr nwah zett) Whole butter heated until it is light brown.

Bisque A cream soup made from shellfish.

Bivalve A mollusk with a pair of hinged shells, such as clam and oyster.

Blanch To cook an item partially and briefly in boiling water or in hot fat. Usually a pre-preparation technique, as to loosen peels from vegetables, fruits, and nuts, to partially cook French fries or other foods before service, to prepare for freezing, or to remove undesirable flavors.

Blancmange (1) An English pudding thickened with cornstarch. (2) A French almond-flavored pudding containing gelatin and milk.

Blanquette A white stew made of white meat or poultry simmered without preliminary browning and served with a white sauce.

Boar Wild pig, or the meat from this animal.

Boeuf à la Môde A classic French dish of braised beef.

Boil To cook in water or other liquid that is bubbling rapidly, about 212°F (100°C) at sea level and at normal pressure.

Bombe A molded ice cream or sherbet dessert.

Bordelaise A brown sauce flavored with a reduction of red wine, shallots, pepper, and herbs and garnished with marrow.

Botulism A deadly food-borne intoxication usually associated with improperly canned foods.

Bouquet Garni A combination of fresh herbs tied together, used for flavoring.

Bouquetière (book tyair) Garnished with an assortment or bouquet of fresh vegetables, such as artichokes, carrots, turnips, green beans, peas, cauliflower, and potatoes.

Braise (1) To cook covered in a small amount of liquid, usually after preliminary browning. (2) To cook (certain vegetables) slowly in a small amount of liquid without preliminary browning.

Brine Cure A curing method in which the food is immersed in a solution (brine) made of the curing ingredients dissolved in water.

Brioche Rich yeast dough containing large amounts of eggs and butter, or the product made from this dough.

Broil To cook with radiant heat from above.

Broth A flavorful liquid obtained from the simmering of meats and/or vegetables.

Brunoise (broon wahz) (1) Cut into very small (⅛ inch/3 mm) dice. (2) Garnished with vegetables cut in this manner.

Bulgur A type of cracked wheat that has been partially cooked.

Buttercream An icing made of butter and/or shortening blended with confectioners' sugar or sugar syrup and, sometimes, other ingredients.

Butterflied Cut partially through and spread open to increase the surface area.

C

Calamari Italian for "squid" (plural).

Calorie The amount of heat needed to raise the temperature of 1 kg water by 1°C. Used as a measure of food energy.

Canapé (can ah pay) Tiny open-faced sandwich, served as an hors d'oeuvre.

Capon A castrated male chicken.

Cappuccino Mixture of equal parts espresso and frothy, steamed milk.

Caramelization The browning of sugars caused by heat.

Carbohydrates Any of a group of compounds, including starches and sugars, that supply energy to the body.

Carême, Marie-Antoine Famous nineteenth-century French chef, often considered the founder of classical cuisine.

Carotenoids Yellow or orange pigments in vegetables and fruits.

Carpaccio Very thin slices of meat or fish, served raw.

Carry-over Cooking The rise in temperature inside roast meat after it is removed from the oven.

Caul A fatty membrane that covers the stomach of a pig; used for wrapping meats for cooking and for lining terrines.

Celsius Scale The metric system of temperature measurement, with 0°C set at the freezing point of water and 100°C set at the boiling point of water.

Centi- Prefix in the metric system meaning "one-hundredth."

Cephalopod A member of the class of mollusks that includes octopus and squid.

Certified Pork Pork that is guaranteed or certified to be free of trichinosis.

Charcuterie (shar koo tree) The art of preparing fresh and cured pork products, including sausages and pâtés.

Charcutier (shar koo tyay) One who prepares and sells pork products, including sausages and pâtés.

Chasseur (sha sur) "Hunter style," usually referring to items served with a brown sauce containing mushrooms, tomato, and white wine.

Chaud-Froid An opaque sauce containing gelatin, used to coat certain cold foods.

Chef The person in charge of a kitchen or of a department of a kitchen.

Chèvre A cheese made from goat's milk.

Chiffon (1) A light, fluffy dessert or pie filling containing gelatin and beaten egg whites. (2) A type of cake made with an egg-white foam and with oil as a shortening.

Chiffonade Cut into fine shreds; usually said of leafy vegetables and herbs.

China Cap A cone-shaped strainer.

Chitterlings Pork intestines.

Chlorophyll Green pigment in vegetables and fruits.

Cholesterol A fatty substance found in foods derived from animal products and in the human body; it has been linked to heart disease.

Chop To cut into irregularly shaped pieces.

Choucroute (shoo kroot) Sauerkraut.

Choucroute Garni Sauerkraut cooked with sausage, pork, and, sometimes, poultry products. A specialty of Alsace, France.

Chowder A hearty American soup made from fish, shellfish, and/or vegetables, usually containing milk and potatoes.

Cilantro The fresh coriander plant, used as an herb.

Clamart Garnished with or containing peas.

Clarified Butter Purified butterfat, with water and milk solids removed.

Clearmeat A mixture of ground meat, egg whites, and flavoring ingredients, used to clarify consommés.

Club Sandwich A sandwich consisting of three slices of toast and filled with such ingredients as sliced chicken or turkey, lettuce, tomato, and bacon.

Coagulation The process by which proteins become firm, usually when heated.

Cocktail A type of appetizer generally made of seafood or fruit and often served with a tart or tangy sauce.

Cold Smoking A smoking method in which the foods are smoked at a low temperature, usually at or below 85°F (30°C), so that the food is not cooked during the smoking.

Collagen A type of connective tissue in meats that dissolves when cooked with moisture.

Collagen Casing An edible artificial sausage casing molded from animal materials.

Combi (Combination) Oven An oven that can operate in conventional, convection, and steamer modes.

Complementary Protein Protein supplied by foods that, if eaten together, supply all the amino acids necessary in the human diet.

Complete Protein A protein that supplies all the amino acids necessary in the human diet.

Compound Butter A mixture of raw butter and various flavoring ingredients.

Concasser To chop coarsely.

Conduction The transfer of heat from one item to something touching it or a cooler part of the first item.

Consommé A rich, flavorful seasoned stock or broth that has been clarified to make it perfectly clear and transparent.

Convection The transfer of heat by the movement of a liquid or gas.

Convection Oven An oven in which hot air is circulated by a fan.

Convenience Food Any food product that has been partially or completely prepared or processed by the manufacturer.

Coq au Vin (coke oh van) A French dish of chicken braised in wine.

Coral The roe or eggs of certain shellfish.

Coulis A vegetable or fruit purée, used as a sauce.

Coupe A dessert consisting of one or two scoops of ice cream or sherbet in a dish or glass, topped with syrups, fruits, toppings, and/or garnishes; a sundae.

Course A food or group of foods served at one time or intended to be eaten at the same time.

Court Bouillon (koor bwee yohn) Water containing seasonings, herbs, and, usually, an acid; used for cooking fish.

Couscous A type of granular pasta from North Africa, cooked like a grain.

Cream Soup A soup thickened with roux or another thickening agent and containing milk and/or cream.

Crécy (kray see) Garnished with or containing carrots.

Crème Anglaise (krem awng lezz) A light vanilla-flavored custard sauce made of milk, sugar, and egg yolks.

Crème Fraîche A thick, slightly aged heavy cream.

Crépinette A sausage patty wrapped in caul.

Critical Control Point (CCP) An action that can be taken to eliminate or minimize a food safety hazard.

Croissant A crescent-shaped roll made from a rich, rolled-in yeast dough.

Croquette (crow kett) Food that has been puréed or bound with a thick sauce, made into small shapes, breaded, and fried.

Cross-Contamination The transfer of bacteria to food from another food or from equipment or work surfaces.

Crudité (croo dee tay) A raw vegetable served as a relish.

Crustacean A sea animal with a segmented shell and jointed legs, such as lobster and shrimp.

Curing Salt See Prague Powder #1.

Custard A liquid that is thickened or set firm by the coagulation of egg protein.

Cuttlefish A cephalopod similar to squid but with a chalky interior bone and a squatter body shape.

Cycle Menu A menu that changes every day for a certain period, then repeats the same daily items in the same order.

D

Danish A rich, sweet, flaky yeast dough containing layers of rolled-in fat.

Deci- Prefix in the metric system meaning "one-tenth."

Deep-fry To cook submerged in hot fat.

Deglaze To swirl a liquid in a sauté pan or other pan to dissolve cooked particles or food remaining on the bottom.

Demiglaze A rich brown sauce that has been reduced by half.

Demitasse Literally, "half cup." Strong, black coffee served in small cups after dinner.

Doria Garnished with cucumbers cooked in butter.

Drawn With entrails removed.

Dressed (1) Poultry market form: killed, bled, and plucked. (2) Fish market form: viscera, scales, head, tail, and fins removed.

Drop Batter A batter that is too thick to pour but that drops from a spoon in lumps.

Dry Cure A curing method in which the curing ingredients are packed or rubbed over the food.

Dry-Heat Cooking Method A method in which heat is conducted to foods without the use of moisture.

Dubarry Garnished with or containing cauliflower.

Duchesse Potatoes (doo shess) Potato purée mixed with butter and egg yolks.

Dumpling Any of a variety of small starch products made from soft dough or batter and cooked by simmering or steaming.

Duxelles A coarse paste or hash made of finely chopped mushrooms sautéed with shallots.

E

Elastin A type of connective tissue in meats that does not dissolve when cooked.

Emincer (em an say) To cut into very thin slices.

Emulsified Grind Referring to sausages made by processing the meat and fat to a purée, usually with the addition of water or another liquid.

Emulsion A uniform mixture of two unmixable liquids.

Entremetier (awn truh met yay) The cook who prepares vegetables, starches, soups, and eggs.

Epazote (ep ah so tay) A pungent herb, used in Mexican cooking.

EP Weight Edible portion; the weight of an item after all trimming and preparation is done.

Escoffier, Georges Auguste Great chef of the early twentieth century and the father of modern cookery.

Espagnole A sauce made of brown stock and flavoring ingredients and thickened with a brown roux.

Espresso, Expresso Strong, dark coffee made from beans roasted until almost black, ground very fine, and brewed under steam pressure.

Étuver (ay too vay) To cook or steam an item in its own juices; to sweat.

Executive Chef The manager of a large kitchen or food production department.

Extended Meal Service Service of a meal at which customers eat at different times.

F

Farro A grain that is the ancestor of modern wheat.

Fermentation The process by which yeast acts on carbohydrates to change them into carbon dioxide gas and alcohol.

Fermière (fair myair) Garnished with carrots, turnips, onions, and celery cut into uniform slices.

Fettuccine Flat egg noodles.

Fiber A group of indigestible carbohydrates found in grains, fruits, and vegetables.

Fillet, Filet (1) Meat: Boneless tenderloin. (2) Fish: Boneless side of fish.

Flavones White pigments in vegetables and fruits.

Florentine Garnished with or containing spinach.

Flow of Food The path that food travels in a food service operation from receiving to serving.

Foie Gras (fwah grah) Liver of specially fattened geese and ducks.

Fondant A smooth, creamy white icing or candy consisting of very finely crystallized sugar syrup.

Fond Lié A sauce made by thickening brown stock with cornstarch or a similar starch.

Fondue, Swiss A dish consisting of melted Gruyère and Emmenthaler cheeses and white wine into which cubes of bread are dipped and eaten. From the French word meaning "melted."

Food Danger Zone The temperature range of 41° to 140°F (5° to 60°C), in which bacteria grow rapidly.

Forcemeat A seasoned mixture of ground meats and other foods, used as a filling or stuffing or as a base for terrines and pâtés.

Forestière Garnished with mushrooms.

Free-Range Referring to animals, usually poultry, that are allowed to move relatively freely outdoors as they are raised for market.

French Dressing Salad dressing made of oil, vinegar, and seasonings.

French-style Ice Cream Ice cream containing egg yolks.

Fricassée A white stew in which the meat is cooked in fat without browning before liquid is added.

Frisée A variety of curly endive or chicory that is more tender and lighter in color than curly endive.

Frittata A flat, unfolded omelet.

Fry To cook in hot fat.

Fumet (foo may) A flavorful stock, usually fish stock.

G

Galantine A forcemeat wrapped in the skin of the animal from which it is made, such as a chicken or duck, or rolled into a cylinder without the skin.

Game Meat from animals and birds normally found in the wild; many game animals are now farm-raised.

Garde Manger (gard mawn zhay) (1) The cook in charge of cold food production, including salads and buffet items. (2) The department of a kitchen in which these foods are prepared.

Garni Garnished. Having had garnish added to it.

Garnish (1) Decorative edible item used to ornament or enhance the eye appeal of another food item. (2) To add such a decorative item to food.

Garniture (1) Garnish. (2) The act or process of garnishing.

Gastrique A mixture of caramelized sugar and vinegar, used to flavor sauces.

Gazpacho A cold Spanish soup made of puréed raw vegetables.

Gelatinization The process by which starch granules absorb water and swell in size.

Gelée Aspic jelly.

Genoise (zhen wahz) A French sponge cake.

Glace de Viande (glahss duh vee awnd) Meat glaze; a reduction of brown stock.

Glaze (1) A stock that is reduced until it coats the back of a spoon. (2) A shiny coating, such as a syrup, applied to a food. (3) To make a food shiny or glossy by coating it with a glaze or by browning it under a broiler or in a hot oven.

Gluten A substance, made of proteins present in wheat flour, that gives structure and strength to baked goods.

Glutinous Rice A type of short-grain rice that becomes sticky and chewy when cooked.

Goulash A Hungarian stew flavored with paprika.

Gram The basic unit of weight in the metric system; equal to about one-thirtieth of an ounce.

Granité (grah nee tay) A coarse, crystalline frozen dessert made of water, sugar, and fruit juice or other flavoring.

Gras Double (grah doo bl') A type of beef tripe that is smooth rather than honeycombed.

Green Meat Meat that has not had enough time after slaughter to develop tenderness and flavor.

Griddle To cook on a flat, solid cooking surface called a griddle.

Grill To cook on an open grid over a heat source.

Grillardin (gree ar dan) Broiler cook.

Gross Pièce (gross pyess) Centerpiece of a buffet platter.

Guinea A domestically raised relative of the pheasant.

H

HACCP Hazard Analysis Critical Control Point; a food safety system of self-inspection, designed to highlight hazardous foods and to control food handling to avoid hazards.

Hare A game animal similar to rabbit, with dark red, lean meat.

Hash (1) To chop. (2) A dish made of chopped foods.

Hazard A potentially dangerous food condition due to contamination, growth of pathogens, survival of pathogens, or presence of toxins.

Herbs The leaves of certain plants, used in flavoring.

Hollandaise A sauce made of butter, egg yolks, and flavorings (especially lemon juice).

Hominy Corn that has been treated with lye.

Homogenized Milk Milk that has been processed so that the cream doesn't separate out.

Hongroise (ong grwahz) Hungarian style.

Hot Smoking A smoking method in which the foods are smoked at a temperature high enough to cook or partially cook them.

Hygroscopic Readily absorbing moisture.

I

Induction Cooktop A type of cooktop that works by using magnetic energy to make pots hot without getting hot itself.

Infection Disease, including much food-borne disease, caused by bacteria in the body.

Intoxication Disease caused by poisons that bacteria produce while they are growing in food.

J

Jardinière (zhar din yair) Garnished with fresh "garden" vegetables, such as carrots, turnips, green beans, peas, and cauliflower.

Jasmine Rice A type of aromatic rice from Southeast Asia.

Judic Garnished with braised lettuce.

Julienne (1) Cut into small, thin strips, about ⅛ × ⅛ × 2½ inches (3 mm × 3 mm × 6½ cm). (2) Garnished with foods cut in this manner.

Jus (zhoo) Unthickened juices from a roast.

Jus Lié Thickened juices from a roast.

K

Kasha Whole buckwheat groats.

Kilo- Prefix in the metric system meaning "one thousand."

L

Lacto-ovo-vegetarian Referring to a vegetarian diet that includes dairy products and eggs.

Lacto-vegetarian Referring to a vegetarian diet that includes milk and other dairy products.

Lard (1) The rendered fat of hogs. (2) To insert strips of fat into meats low in marbling.

Lasagne Broad, flat egg noodles, or a baked, layered casserole made with these noodles.

Leading Sauce A basic sauce used in the production of other sauces. The five leading hot sauces are béchamel, velouté, espagnole, tomato, and hollandaise. Mayonnaise and vinaigrette are often considered leading cold sauces.

Leavening The production or incorporation of gases in a baked product to increase volume and to produce shape and texture.

Lemongrass A tropical grass with the aroma of lemon, used for flavoring.

Liaison A binding agent, usually made of cream and egg yolks, used to thicken sauces and soups.

Liter The basic unit of volume in the metric system; equal to slightly more than 1 quart.

London Broil Flank steak or other cut of beef broiled rare and cut in thin slices.

Lyonnaise (lee oh nez) Containing or garnished with onions.

M

Macaroni Noodle product made of flour and water and dried.

Mâche A small, tender leafy green with a delicate taste.

Magret The boneless breast of the moulard duck.

Maître d'Hôtel Butter (may truh doh tell) Compound butter containing parsley and lemon juice.

Marbling The fat deposited within muscle tissue.

Marinate To soak a food in a seasoned liquid.

Marsala A flavorful sweet to semidry wine from Sicily.

Mayonnaise A semisolid cold sauce or dressing consisting of oil and vinegar emulsified with egg yolks.

Mayonnaise Chaud-Froid A mixture of aspic jelly and mayonnaise, used like regular chaud-froid.

Meringue A foam made of beaten egg whites and sugar.

Meringue Glacée Baked meringue shells served with ice cream.

Mesclun A mixture of tender baby lettuces.

Meter The basic unit of length in the metric system: slightly longer than 1 yard.

Meunière Referring to fish prepared by dredging in flour and sautéing, served with brown butter, lemon juice, and parsley.

Microwave Radiation generated in special ovens and used to cook or heat foods.

Milli- Prefix in the metric system meaning "one-thousandth."

Mince To chop into very fine pieces.

Minestrone Italian vegetable soup.

Mirepoix (meer pwah) A mixture of rough-cut or diced vegetables, herbs, and spices, used for flavoring.

Mise en Place (meez on plahss) French term meaning "everything in place." The setup for food production. All the preparations and organization that must be made before actual production can begin.

Moist-Heat Cooking Methods Methods in which heat is conducted to foods by water or other liquid or by steam.

Mollusk A soft-bodied sea animal, usually inside a pair of hinged shells, such as clam and oyster.

Monter au Beurre (mohn tay oh burr) To finish a sauce or soup by swirling in raw butter until it is melted.

Mornay A sauce made of béchamel and Gruyère cheese.

Moulard A breed of duck with a thick, meaty breast, raised for its large, fatty liver.

Mousse A soft, creamy food, either sweet or savory, made light by the addition of whipped cream, beaten egg whites, or both.

Mousseline Forcemeat A forcemeat made of puréed fish, poultry, or meat, heavy cream, and, usually, egg whites.

Mozzarella A mild unripened cheese, used in pizzas and many other Italian-style dishes.

N

Natural Casing A sausage casing made from the intestines of meat animals.

Navarin A brown lamb stew.

New England Boiled Dinner A dish consisting of simmered corned beef and simmered vegetables, served together.

Niçoise (nee swahz) (1) Prepared in the style of Nice, France. (2) Garnished with or containing tomato concassé cooked with garlic.

Nitrosamine A cancer-causing compound formed when meats containing sodium nitrate are subjected to high heat.

Nouvelle Cuisine A modern style of cooking that emphasizes lightness of sauces and seasonings, shortened cooking times, and new and sometimes startling combinations of foods.

O

Offal Variety meats.

Oolong A greenish-brown, partially fermented tea.

Organic Grown or raised without chemical growth enhancers or medications or, for plants, without artificial fertilizers or pesticides.

Oven Spring The rapid rise of yeast goods in the oven due to production and expansion of trapped gases as a result of the oven heat.

Overrun The increase in volume of ice cream or frozen desserts due to the incorporation of air while freezing.

P

Pan Gravy A type of sauce made with the pan drippings of the meat or poultry it is served with.

Pan-Broil To cook uncovered in a sauté pan or skillet without fat.

Pan-Fry To cook in a moderate amount of fat in an uncovered pan.

(en) Papillote (on poppy yote) Wrapped in paper or foil for cooking so that the food is steamed in its own moisture.

Parboil To cook partially in a boiling or simmering liquid.

Parcook To partially cook by any method.

Parfait A dessert consisting of alternating layers of ice cream and fruit or syrup in a tall, narrow glass.

Parmentier (par mawn tyay) Garnished with or containing potatoes.

Pasta General term for any shape of macaroni product or egg noodles.

Pasteurized Heat-treated to kill bacteria that might cause disease or spoilage.

Pastry Cream A thick custard sauce containing eggs and starch.

Pâté A dish made of a baked forcemeat, usually in a crust.

Pâte à Choux (pot a shoo) A soft dough used for making éclairs and cream puffs. Also called éclair paste.

Pâte à Pâté Dough or pastry used to make a crust for pâtés.

Pâté de Campagne A pâté or terrine characterized by a coarse texture.

Pâté en Croute A pâté in a pastry crust.

Pathogen A bacteria that causes disease.

Pâtissier (pa tees syay) Pastry cook.

Peach Melba A sundae consisting of vanilla ice cream, a peach half, and Melba (raspberry) sauce.

Persillade (pear see yahd) A mixture of bread crumbs, parsley, and garlic, used to coat roast meat items, usually lamb.

Pesco-vegetarian Referring to a vegetarian diet that includes fish.

Philadelphia-style Ice Cream Ice cream containing no eggs.

Pigment Any substance that gives color to an item.

Pilaf Rice or other grain product that is first cooked in fat, then simmered in a stock or other liquid, usually with onions, seasonings, or other ingredients.

Poach To cook gently in water or another liquid that is hot but not actually bubbling, about 160° to 180°F (71° to 82°C).

Poissonier (pwah so nyay) Fish cook.

Polenta Italian-style cornmeal.

Portion Control The measurement of portions to ensure that the correct amount of an item is served.

Potentially Hazardous Food A food that provides a good environment for the growth of hazardous bacteria.

Pot Roast A large cut of meat cooked by braising.

Poulette Allemande sauce flavored with mushrooms, parsley, and lemon juice.

Pour Batter A batter that is liquid enough to pour.

Poussin A young chicken weighing 1 pound (500 g) or less.

Pozole Whole-grain hominy.

Prague Powder #1 A blend of 6 percent sodium nitrite and 94 percent sodium chloride (table salt), used to cure meats; also called curing salt and tinted curing mix.

Prague Powder #2 A curing mixture similar to Prague Powder #1 but containing sodium nitrate in addition to sodium nitrate.

Primal Cut One of the primary divisions of meat quarters, foresaddles, hindsaddles, and carcasses as they are broken down into smaller cuts.

Primeur (pree mur) Garnished with fresh spring vegetables such as carrots, turnips, green beans, peas, cauliflower, and small potatoes.

Princesse Garnished with asparagus.

Printaniere (pran tawn yair) Garnished with fresh spring vegetables such as carrots, turnips, pearl onions, peas, green beans, and asparagus.

Prix Fixe (pree fix) French term meaning "fixed price"; referring to a menu offering a complete meal, with a choice of courses, for one given price.

Process Cheese A product made by grinding and melting one or more cheeses, blending them with other ingredients, and pouring the mixture into molds to solidify.

Profiterole A tiny round pastry made from éclair paste; filled with savory fillings and served as an hors d'oeuvre, or filled with ice cream and served as a dessert.

Provençale (pro vawn sal) Garnished with or containing tomatoes, garlic, parsley, and, sometimes, mushrooms and olives.

Puff Pastry A light, flaky pastry made from a rolled-in dough and leavened by steam.

Pullman Loaf A long, rectangular loaf of bread.

Pumpernickel (1) Coarsely ground rye flour. (2) Bread made with this flour.

Purée (1) A food product that has been mashed or strained to a smooth pulp. (2) To make such a pulp by mashing or straining a food.

Q

Quail A small game bird, now domestically raised, usually weighing 6 ounces (175 g) or less.

Quatre Épices A spice mixture commonly used to season sausages and forcemeats; French for "four spices."

Quiche A savory tart or pie consisting of a custard baked in a pastry shell.

Quick Bread A bread leavened by chemical leaveners or steam rather than yeast.

R

Radiation The transfer of energy by waves, such as infrared or light waves.

Raft The coagulated clearmeat that forms when stock is clarified.

Ratatouille (ra ta twee) A Southern French vegetable stew of onions, tomatoes, zucchini, eggplant, and green peppers.

Ravier (rahv yay) Oval relish dish.

Ravioli Dumplings consisting of filled egg noodles.

Recipe A set of instructions for producing a certain dish.

Reduce To cook by simmering or boiling until quantity is decreased; often done to concentrate flavors.

Reduction (1) A liquid concentrated by cooking it to evaporate part of the water. (2) The process of making such a liquid.

Relish A type of appetizer consisting of raw or pickled vegetables.

Ricotta An Italian-style cheese similar to cottage cheese but smoother, moister, and sweeter in flavor.

Rillettes (ree yet) A seasoned mixture of meat, such as pork, and fat, mashed to a paste; served as an appetizer.

Risotto A moist Italian dish of rice cooked in butter and stock.

Rissolé (riss oh lay) Browned. Often referring to potatoes cut in small shapes, parboiled, and browned in hot fat.

Roast To cook foods by surrounding them with hot, dry air, in an oven or on a spit over an open fire.

Roe Fish eggs.

Roesti Potatoes Boiled potatoes that are grated, formed into small cakes, and pan-fried until crisp.

Rolled-in Dough Dough in which a fat is incorporated into the dough in many layers by means of a rolling and folding procedure.

Roquefort A blue-veined cheese made in Roquefort, France, from sheep's milk.

Rotisserie An item of cooking equipment that slowly rotates meat or other foods in front of a heating element.

Rotisseur (ro tee sur) Cook who prepares roasted, braised, and broiled meats.

Rough Prep The preliminary processing of ingredients to the point at which they can be used in cooking.

Roux A cooked mixture of equal parts flour and fat.

Royal Icing An icing made of confectioners' sugar and egg whites, used for decorating.

Russet Starchy potato often used for baking and deep-frying.

Rye Blend A mixture of rye flour and hard wheat flour.

S

Sachet (sa shay) A mixture of herbs and spices tied in a cheesecloth bag.

Salamander Small broiler used primarily for browning or glazing the tops of certain items.

Salmonella A widespread food-borne disease, spread by improper food handling and inadequate sanitation.

Sanitize To kill disease-causing bacteria, usually by heat or by chemical disinfectants.

Saturated Fat A fat that is normally solid at room temperature.

Sauce A flavorful liquid, usually thickened, that is used to season, flavor, and enhance other foods.

Saucier (so see ay) Sauce cook; prepares sauces and stews and sautés foods to order.

Sauerbraten A German dish consisting of beef marinated and then cooked with vinegar and other ingredients.

Sausage   A mixture of ground meat, usually pork, and seasonings, usually stuffed into casings.

Sausage, Cured   A sausage that contains nitrites or nitrates.

Sausage, Fresh   A sausage that contains no nitrites or nitrates.

Sauté   To cook quickly in a small amount of fat.

Scampi   A kind of shellfish similar to large shrimp. In the United States, the term is often used for large shrimp, especially if broiled with garlic butter.

Sear   To brown the surface of a food quickly at high temperature.

Semolina   A hard, high-protein flour often used for the best-quality macaroni products.

Set Meal Service   Service of a meal at which all the customers eat at one time.

Shirred Egg   Egg baked in a shallow, buttered dish.

Short   Having a high fat content, which makes the product (such as a cookie or pastry) crumbly and tender.

Shortening   (1) Any fat used in baking to tenderize the product by shortening gluten strands. (2) A white, tasteless, solid fat formulated for baking or deep frying.

Shred   To cut into thin but irregular strips, either with the coarse blade of a grater or with a knife.

Sieve Size   Size of individual pieces, usually of canned vegetables.

Simmer   To cook in water or other liquid that is bubbling gently, about 185° to 200°F (85° to 93°C).

Sirniki   Russian pan-fried cheesecakes.

Slurry   A mixture of raw starch and cold liquid, used for thickening.

Small Sauce   A sauce made by adding one or more ingredients to a leading sauce.

Smoke-Roast   To cook with dry heat in the presence of wood smoke.

Sodium Nitrate   A compound, $NaNO_3$, used to cure meats.

Sodium Nitrite   A compound, $NaNO_2$, used to cure certain meats, especially air-dried meats.

Soft-Shell Crab   A just-molted crab whose new shell has not yet hardened.

Solanine   A poisonous substance found in potatoes that have turned green.

Sorbet   (sor bay)   Sherbet, usually made without milk products.

Soufflé   A light, fluffy baked egg dish consisting of a base (such as a heavy white sauce) mixed with egg yolks and flavoring ingredients into which beaten egg whites are folded just before baking. May be sweet or savory.

Sous Chef   (soo shef)   Cook who supervises food production and who reports to the executive chef.

Spaetzle   Small dumplings or noodles made from a thin egg and flour batter.

Spelt   A type of wheat grain similar to farro.

Spice   Any part of a plant, other than the leaves, used in flavoring foods.

Squab   Young, domestically raised pigeon.

Staling   The change in texture and aroma of baked goods due to the loss of moisture by the starch granules.

Standard Breading Procedure   The procedure for coating a food product with bread crumbs (or other crumbs or meal) by passing it through flour, then egg wash, then crumbs.

Standardized Recipe   A set of instructions describing the way a particular establishment prepares a particular dish.

Staphylococcus, Staph   A bacterium that causes food-borne disease by producing a toxin or poison in improperly stored foods.

Static Menu   A menu that offers the same dishes every day.

Station Chef   Cook in charge of a particular department in a kitchen or food production facility.

Steam   To cook by direct contact with steam.

Stew   (1) To simmer a food or foods in a small amount of liquid that is usually served with the food as a sauce. (2) A dish cooked by stewing, usually one in which the main ingredients are cut in small pieces.

Stock   A clear, thin (that is, unthickened) liquid flavored with soluble substances extracted from meat, poultry, and fish, and their bones, and from vegetables and seasonings.

Streusel   (stroy zel)   A crumbly topping for baked goods, consisting of fat, sugar, and flour rubbed together.

Strong Flour   Flour with a high protein or gluten content.

Suprême Sauce   A sauce made of chicken velouté and heavy cream.

Surimi   A processed seafood product manufactured to resemble shellfish such as crab.

Sweat   To cook in a small amount of fat over low heat, sometimes covered.

Sweetbreads   The thymus gland of calves and young animals, used as food.

Swiss Steak   Beef round steaks braised in brown sauce.

T

Table d'Hote   (tobble dote)   (1) Referring to a fixed price menu with no choices. (2) Referring to a menu on which prices are listed for complete meals rather than for each separate item.

Tang   The portion of a metal knife blade that is inside the handle.

Tasting Menu   A type of fixed price menu designed to showcase the chef's art by presenting a series of small courses.

Tatsoi   A leafy vegetable or salad green related to mustard and watercress.

Temper   To raise the temperature of a cold liquid gradually by slowly stirring in a hot liquid.

Tinted Curing Mix   See Prague Powder #1.

Tomalley   The liver of lobsters and some other shellfish.

Tournant   (toor nawn)   Cook who replaces other station cooks; relief cook or swing cook.

Tournedos   (toor nuh doe)   A small beef steak cut from the tenderloin.

Treviso   A red-leafed relative of radicchio and Belgian endive with elongated leaves.

Trichinosis A food-borne disease caused by a parasite, sometimes found in undercooked pork.

Tripe The muscular stomach lining of beef or other meat animals.

Truit au Bleu Poached trout that was alive until cooking time and that turns blue when cooked in court bouillon.

Trunnion Kettle A steam-jacketed kettle that can be tilted for emptying.

Truss To tie poultry into a compact shape for cooking.

Tunneling A condition of muffin products characterized by large, elongated holes; caused by overmixing.

U

Univalve A mollusk with a single shell, such as abalone.

Unsaturated Fat A fat that is normally liquid at room temperature.

V

Variety Meats Various organs, glands, and other meats that don't form a part of the dressed carcass.

Vegan Referring to a vegetarian diet that omits all animal products, including dairy products and eggs.

Velouté A sauce made by thickening white stock with a roux.

Venison The meat of wild or farm-raised deer.

Vent To allow circulation or escape of a liquid or gas, such as by setting a pot of hot stock on blocks in a cold water bath so that the cold water can circulate around the pot.

Viande (vee awnd) French for "meat."

Vichyssoise (vee she swahz) Cold purée of leek and potato soup with cream.

Vin Wine.

Vin Blanc White wine.

Vin Rouge Red wine.

Vinaigrette Dressing or sauce made of oil, vinegar, and flavoring ingredients.

Vitamin Any of a group of compounds that are present in foods in very small quantities and that are necessary for regulating body functions.

Volatile Evaporating quickly when heated.

W

Wash (1) To brush or coat a food item with a liquid such as egg wash or milk. (2) The liquid used in this procedure.

Waxy Potato A young potato high in sugar and low in starch.

Weak Flour Flour with a low protein or gluten content.

Welsh Rabbit A dish made of melted cheddar cheese and, usually, ale or beer. Sometimes called *Welsh rarebit*.

White Pekin The most common breed of domestic duck in the United States.

Whitewash A thin mixture or slurry of flour and cold water.

Winterized Oil Vegetable oil that stays clear and liquid when refrigerated.

Wrap A sandwich in which the filling is wrapped, like a Mexican burrito, in a large flour tortilla or similar flatbread.

Z

Zest The colored part of the peel of citrus fruits.

U.S.-U.K. Cooking Vocabulary

A

Aging (meat) Hanging.
All-Purpose Flour Plain flour.
Arugula Rocket.
Atholl Brose Scottish combination of oatmeal, honey, and whisky. Eaten for breakfast or used as a pastry filling.

B

Bake Includes oven cooking with steam.
Beef Tenderloin Fillet of beef.
Belgian Endive Chicory.
Beurre Manié Kneaded butter.
Boston Lettuce Round or cabbage lettuce.
Braid Plait.
Brassicas Vegetables of the cabbage family (includes broccoli and cauliflower).
Brine A preserving solution of water, salt, saltpeter, and aromatics, used for soaking meats such as tongue and brisket.
Broil Grill.
Brown Sugar (soft) Muscovado sugar.
Brown Sugar (unrefined) Demerara sugar.

C

Canning Jars Kilner jars.
Casserole Earthenware or cast-iron dish with one or two handles and a lid.
Celery Root Celeriac.
Channel Knife Canelle knife.
Cheesecloth Muslin.
Chicken Breasts (boneless, skinless) Suprêmes: boneless, skinless, chicken breasts.
Chickpea Flour Gram flour.
Cilantro Coriander.
Clarification Refers to the process of clearing stocks or to the mixture (raft).
Clotted Cream The resulting thick layer formed by heating heavy cream and then leaving it to cool.
Confectioners' or Powdered Sugar Icing sugar.
Cookies Biscuits.
Cornstarch Cornflour.
Croutes Small slice of bread; may be toasted.

D

Daikon Radish Mooli.
Dessert Pudding.
Doneness Degree of cooking.

E

Eggplant Aubergine.

F

Filet Mignon Fillet steak.
Fish Poacher Fish kettle.
Food Mill Mouli.

H

Hard Flour (high gluten) Strong flour.
Hard Fruits Apples, pears.
Heavy Cream Double cream.
Hotel Rack Best end of neck of lamb.

I

Italian Parsley Flat-leaf or continental parsley.

J

Jelly Roll Pan Swiss roll tin.
Joint (1) A piece of meat used for roasting, with or without the bone. (2) To cut up (as in poultry or meat).
Jus, Simple Gravy Roast gravy.

L

Legumes (dried) Pulses.
Liaison Thickener; mixture to thicken sauces.
Light Cream Single cream.

M

Malt Syrup Maltose, malt.
Meat Grinder Mincer.
Molasses Black treacle.

O

Offset Spatula Angled spatula; step palette knife.

P

Pastry Dough Paste.
Peanut Oil Groundnut oil.
Pit To stone.
Porcini Ceps.
Prosciutto Ham Parma ham.
Puff Pastry Puff.

R

Romaine Lettuce Cos lettuce.
Rutabaga Swede.

S

Salmon Roe Keta.
Sanding Sugar Nibbed sugar.
Scallion Green onion.
Season (condition a pan) Prove.
Sheet Pan Swiss roll tin.

Snow Peas Mangetout.
Strainer Sieve.

T

Tomato Paste Tomato purée.

V

Van Dyking English technique for serving fish whole, the cutting of the tail in the form of a V.
Very Fine Granulated Sugar Castor sugar.

W

Weak flour Soft flour.
Whole Wheat Flour Whole meal flour.

Z

Zucchini (large) Marrow.
Zucchini Courgette.

French-English Cooking Vocabulary

A

Abaisser (ah bay say) To roll a dough to the desired thickness with the aid of a rolling pin.

Abats (ah bah) Offal; internal organs of butchered animals sold mainly by stores called triperies that specialize in this. White offal are sweetbreads, feet, brains. Red offal are heart, lungs, liver.

Abattis (ah bah tee) The feet, neck, head, wingtips, liver, gizzard, and heart of poultry.

Accommoder (ah koh mo day) To prepare and season a dish for cooking.

Acidifier (ah si di fee ay) To add lemon juice or vinegar to fruits, vegetables, and fish to prevent oxidation.

Aciduler (ah see dyoo lay) To make a preparation slightly acidic, tart, or tangy by adding a little lemon juice or vinegar.

Affuter (ah foo tay) To sharpen the cutting edge of a knife by using a steel or sharpening stone.

Aiguillette (ay gee yet) A long, narrow slice of meat cut from the breast of poultry (especially duck) and game birds.

Aiguiser (ay gee zay) See Affuter.

Allumettes (al loo met) (1) A type of savory petits fours (long rectangle of puff pastry) covered with cheese or filled with anchovies. (2) Very thin French fries; pommes allumettes.

Anglaise (on glez) (1) A mixture of whole eggs, oil, water, salt, and pepper, used to help coat food with flour and bread crumbs. (2) A dish cooked in boiling water (e.g., potatoes).

Aplatir (ah pla teer) To flatten a piece of meat or fish in order to make it more tender and to facilitate cooking.

Appareil (ah pa ray) A mixture of the principal elements of a final recipe (usually egg based).

Aromate (ah row mat) A condiment or vegetable with a characteristic smell or taste (spices and herbs). Often used in reference to a combination of flavoring vegetables, such as carrot, onion, leek, and celery.

Arroser (ah row zay) To baste; the wetting of meat or fish with a liquid or fat during or after cooking.

Aspic (a spik) A dish composed of meat, vegetables, and/or fish that is cooked, chilled, and molded in gelatin.

Assaisonner (ah say zo nay) To season; the addition of a preparation of certain ingredients that bring out the flavor of the food.

Attendrir (ah ton drear) (1) To allow a piece of meat to age under refrigeration for a few days to make it more tender. (2) To become stale.

Au Jus (oh zhu) Served with natural cooking juices.

B

Bain-marie (ban marie) A hot water bath; a way of cooking or warming food by placing a container in a pot of very hot water. Used for preparations that must not cook over direct heat, for keeping delicate sauces hot, and for melting chocolate.

Ballotine (ball oh teen) A large piece of meat or a whole bird that is boned and stuffed.

Barder (bar day) To cover or wrap a piece of meat, poultry, and, occasionally, pastry with a very thin piece of pork fat for protection and basting during cooking. This prevents drying out.

Barquette (bar ket) A small, long oval pastry mold.

Basquaise (bas kez) In the Basque style; usually indicates the presence of red peppers in the dish.

Bâtonnet (ba tow nay) Small stick; refers to a type of vegetable cut.

Batterie (bat tric) Set; complete set of kitchen utensils.

Bavarois (ba var wha) Bavarian cream; a cold dessert made from crème anglaise, set with gelatin and whipped cream.

Béchamel (beh sha mel) White sauce made from milk and white roux.

Beignet (ben yay) Food dipped in a thin batter and deep-fried.

Bercy (bear see) A classic sauce with a white wine base, used for fish.

Beurre (burr) Butter.

Beurre Blanc (burr blahn) Butter-based sauce made from a reduction of dry white wine, vinegar, and shallots. Mainly served with poached or grilled fish.

Beurre Clarifié (burr cla ri fee ay) Clarified butter; butter that is gently melted in order to remove the impurities that float to the top and the whey that sinks to the bottom.

Beurre Composé (burr com po zay) Butter that is mixed with one or more ingredients, such as anchovy butter (butter and crushed anchovies).

Beurre ½ Sel (burr demi cell) Lightly salted butter containing up to 5 percent salt.

Beurre Fermier (burr fair miay) Farm-fresh butter.

Beurre Laitier (burr lay tee ay) Dairy-made butter.

Beurre Manié (burr man yay) Butter mixed with an equal amount of flour; used to thicken sauces.

Beurre Noisette (burr nwa set) Brown butter; butter that is cooked until colored a light brown (see Noisette).

Beurre Pasteurisé (burr pass ter ee zay) Factory-produced and -pasteurized butter.

Beurre en Pommade (burr on poh mahd) Softened (not melted) butter.

Beurrer (burr ray) (1) To lightly coat a container with butter in order to prevent sticking. (2) To add butter to a sauce or dough.

Beurre Salé (burr sa lay) Salted butter containing up to 10 percent salt.

Beurre Sec (burr sek) Dry butter; butter with a minimum water content. The percentage of water can vary from 5 to 8 percent, depending on the quality of butter.

Biscuit (beace quee) (1) A small cake or cookie. (2) A specific type of sponge cake, similar to genoise.

Bisque (bisk) Type of soup usually made from a shellfish base and thickened.

Blanc (blahn) (1) White. (2) A mixture of flour and cold water that is added to acidulated water (usually lemon juice) to prevent certain foods from discoloring during cooking.

Blanchir (blon sheer) To blanch. (1) To place vegetables or meats in cold water and then bring to a boil (or to plunge in boiling water) in order to precook, soften, or remove an excess of flavor (acidity, saltiness, or bitterness). (2) To whip sugar and eggs together until light in color. (3) To soak meat in cold water in order to remove excess blood, salt, and/or impurities.

Blondir (blon deer) To cook in fat in order to color lightly.

Bouchée (boo shay) A small round of puff pastry that can be filled with different mixtures.

Bouillir (boo year) To boil; to bring a liquid to the boiling point.

Boulangère (boo lawn zhare) Cooked with veal stock, onions, and potatoes; a style of meat preparation.

Bouquet Garni (boo kay gar nee) A mixture of herbs enclosed in the green portion of a leek used to flavor dishes during their cooking.

Braiser (bray zay) To braise; to cook a meat in a covered dish in or over gentle heat with a little liquid and, usually, on a bed of finely diced vegetables.

Brider (bree day) To truss; to tie a bird so that it keeps its shape during cooking.

Brochette (broe shet) (1) A skewer made of wood or bamboo. (2) Small pieces of food stuck on a long piece of metal or wood and grilled.

Broyer (broy yay) To crush or grind finely.

Brunoise (broon waz) Vegetables cut into very small regular cubes.

C

Cacao (ka ka oh) Cocoa.

Calvados (cal vaw dose) An alcoholic beverage distilled from cider, made exclusively in the Normandy region.

Canapé (can ah pay) Bite-sized slice of sandwich or other type of bread, toasted or not toasted, which is spread or garnished with various ingredients.

Canard (can arr) Duck or drake.

Caneton (can e tone) Male duckling.

Canette (can net) Female duckling.

Canneler (can nel lay) To channel, to flute, to groove.

Capre (capr) Caper.

Caraméliser (care a mel lee zay) To caramelize; to coat a mold with cooked sugar; to cook sugar until dark for use in other preparations (to coat or to make a sauce).

Cêpe (sepp) Bolete or porcini mushroom.

Champignon (shamp pin yon) Mushroom.

Champvallon (shamp val lawn) Preparation of lamb chops cooked in the oven with potatoes and onions.

Chantilly (shawn tee yee) Whipped cream to which sugar and vanilla have been added.

Chapelure (shap a lure) Dried bread crumbs made from both the crust and center of dried bread. Used for breading.

Charlotte (shar lott) (1) A dessert made in a special mold. (2) A savory preparation made in this mold.

Chaud-Froid (show fwah) A dish prepared hot but served cold and covered with a specific sauce (sauce chaud-froid, made from ⅓ velouté, ⅓ gelatin, and ⅓ cream).

Chemiser (shem ee zay) To line the interior of a mold before filling.

Chèvre (shevr) Goat.

Chiffonade (shi foe nod) Leafy herbs and greens that are finely shredded.

Chinois (shee nwah) China cap sieve; a fine conical strainer.

Chiqueter (sheek ah tay) To lightly score the cut edges of puff pastry to help ensure that it rises straight and evenly.

Cidre (seedr) Hard cider.

Ciseler (see ze lay) (1) To score; to make incisions in certain fish in order to facilitate cooking. (2) To finely mince; a manner of finely cutting onions, shallots, and garlic.

Citronner (see trone nay) (1) To rub foods with lemon to prevent them from discoloring. (2) To add lemon juice.

Clarifier (clare re fee ay) (1) To clarify; to clear a cloudy liquid by straining, heating, and gently simmering with egg whites. (2) Process of separating milk solids from butter.

Clouter (cloo tay) To stud; to pierce cured tongue with strips of truffle; to pierce an onion with a whole clove.

Coller (cole lay) To thicken or set using gelatin, as in making jelly or fruit mousse.

Concasser (cone cas say) To break up coarsely with a knife or mortar.

Concassé (de tomates) (cone cas say duh to maht) Peeled, seeded, and diced tomatoes.

Confit (cone fee) A food that is saturated with one of the following: vinegar (for vegetables); sugar (for fruits); alcohol (for fruits); fat (for poultry).

Consommé (cone so may) Clear bouillon made from meat, fish, or vegetables; served hot or cold.

Contiser (cone tee zay) To loosen the skin of fowl, game, and some fish in order to insert a thin slice of truffle.

Coquille (coe key) Shell.

Cordée (core day) Referring to a dough or potato purée that becomes elastic from overworking.

Coriandre (core ree andr) Cilantro (fresh), coriander.

Corne (corn) Plastic tool used for scraping the contents out of containers.

Corser (core say) To give strength or body to the flavor of a preparation.

Coucher (koo shay) (1) To lay; to place a rolled piece of dough on a baking sheet. (2) To spread; to spread a layer of cream or other garnish. (3) To pipe; to cover with a layer, using a piping bag.

Coulis (koo lee) A smooth purée of fruits or vegetables; used as a sauce.

Coupe (koop) Cup.

Couper (koo pay) To cut.

Court Bouillon (core bwee yone) A cooking liquid, composed of water, aromatic vegetables, and, sometimes, white wine vinegar, in which fish and certain meats are cooked.

Crécy (kreh see) Refers to dishes containing carrots. The name of an area known for its carrot production.

Crème Anglaise (krem on glez) A sweet sauce made from eggs, sugar, and milk that is cooked to 85°C (185°F).

Crème Fouettée (krem foo eh tay) Whipped cream; cream that has been whisked in order to incorporate air.

Crème Fraîche (krem fresh) A type of heavy cream.

Crème Pâtissière (krem pa tis see air) Pastry cream; milk thickened with flour or flan powder, used for pastry making.

Crémer (krem may) (1) To cream together sugar and butter. (2) To add cream.

Crème Renversée (krem ron vare say) Caramel flan; a mixture of sugar, milk, and eggs poured into a mold, usually lined with caramel, then gently cooked in the oven in a hot water bath.

Crème de Riz (krem de ree) Cream of rice; a powder made from finely ground rice, used in pastry or to thicken sauces.

Crêpe (krep) Very thin pancake.

Crépine (kreh peen) Pork caul.

Crever (kreh vay) To blanch rice by placing it in cold water, then bringing to a boil for a few minutes. It is usually the first step in making rice desserts.

Croquette (kroh kett) A breaded, fried item consisting of a mixture of fruit, fish, or vegetables. Can be savory or sweet and in any shape.

Croustade (krew stod) (1) A crisp crust that is fried. (2) An empty pastry case.

Croûte (kroot) Crust; the brown outer covering of bread. A meat or fish en croûte is one that is wrapped in a crust.

Croûton (kroo tohn) A slice or piece of toasted bread.

Crudité (kroo dee tay) Raw vegetable, sliced or cut, served with a vinaigrette or mayonnaise as a first course.

Cuisson (kwees sohn) The cooking; the action and manner of cooking a food.

D

Dariole (dahr ree ole) A small thimble-shaped mold.

Darne (darn) Thick slice, containing the central bone, cut from round fish.

Daube (dobe) Stew of meat braised in red wine.

Décanter (day kahn tay) (1) To allow the impurities in a liquid to sink to the bottom so that the liquid can be gently poured off, leaving the residue. (2) To separate meat from its cooking liquid in order to finish the sauce.

Décortiquer (day kor tee kay) To shell; to remove the outer covering from shellfish and crustaceans.

Découper (day koo pay) To cut; to cut using scissors, a knife, or pastry cutter.

Déglacer (day gla say) To deglaze; to dissolve with liquid the substance attached to the bottom of a pan.

Dégorger (day gor zhay) To degorge; to soak an ingredient in cold water in order to remove blood, salt, or impurities; to lightly salt vegetables in order to extract the maximum amount of water.

Dégraisser (day gray say) To degrease; to remove excess fat from the surface of a food or sauce.

Délayer (day lay yay) (1) To thin with water. (2) To dissolve in liquid.

Demi-glace (de mee glass) Meat, fish, or chicken stock, reduced to a concentrated form.

Démouler (day moo lay) To unmold; to carefully remove a preparation from the container in which it was placed to give it a specific form.

Dénerver (day nair vay) To remove the tendons from meat and fowl.

Dénoyauter (day noy oh tay) To pit; to remove the seed or pit of stone fruits and olives with a knife or pitter.

Dépouiller (day pwee yay) (1) To remove the skin that forms on the top of a sauce or soup. (2) To skin; to remove the skin of a small animals, fish, etc.

Dés (day) Cubes; small regular squares.

Désosser (day zohs say) To debone; to remove the bones from meat and fowl.

Dessécher (day se shay) To dry out; to remove moisture through heat.

Détailler (day tie yay) To cut up; to cut into pieces.

Détendre (day ton dr) To loosen (in consistency); to add a liquid to a preparation, such as a sauce.

Détrempe (day trompe) Dough made of flour and water, used for puff pastry.

Détremper (day trompe pay) To moisten with a liquid.

Dorer (doe ray) To brush with beaten egg or egg yolk in order to give a deep color and shine.

Dorure (doe ruhr) Egg wash; beaten egg or egg yolk, with water and/or salt added, used to color doughs just before cooking.

Douille (doo yeey) Pastry tip; a conical piece made of metal or plastic, used in decorating with a pastry bag.

Dresser (dres say) To dress; to arrange the prepared food on a plate or platter before serving.

Duchesse (dew shess) Mashed potatoes with the addition of egg yolks.

Dugléré (dew glay ray) A classic preparation for fish incorporating white wine and tomato; named for a nineteenth-century chef.

Duroc (dew rock) Classic preparation of small pieces of meat served with pan-fried potatoes, tomato sauce, and chasseur sauce. Named after the nineteenth-century chef Marshall Duroc.

Duxelles (duke sell) Finely chopped mushrooms cooked in butter with minced shallots; used as a garnish or filling.

E

Ébarber (eh bar bay) To debeard; to remove the fins and bones of fish; to remove the filaments from poached eggs.

Ébouillanter (eh boo yawn tay) To dip in boiling water; to scald.

Ébullition (eh boo lee see own) Boiling point; the appearance of bubbles in a hot liquid (98° to 100°C/208° to 212°F).

Écailler (eh kie yay) To scale; to remove the scales from fish.

Écailles (eh kie) Scales (of fish, snakes, etc.).

Écaler (eh kah lay) To shell (eggs); to remove the shell from soft- and hard-boiled eggs.

Écumer (eh kue may) To skim; to remove the foam from the surface of a boiling liquid.

Effiler (eh fee lay) To slice very thinly (e.g., almonds).

Égoutter (eh goo tay) To strain; to remove the cooking liquid by pouring into a strainer.

Émietter (eh myet tay) To crumble; to break into small pieces.

Émincer (eh man say) To cut into thin slices.

Émonder (eh moan day) To skin; to remove the skin from fruits and vegetables by heating.

En Croûte (on kroot) Wrapped in pastry.

En Robe (on robe) Coated or covered.

Enrober (on robe bay) To coat; to completely cover with various ingredients, such as chocolate or dough.

Entremet (on tre may) Literally, "between courses"; originally a course served between the roast and the dessert. Today it is a mousse-based cake.

Éplucher (eh ploo shay) To peel; to remove the skin or inedible part of fruits and vegetables.

Éponger (eh pone jay) To sponge; to remove excess liquid or fat by absorbing with a kitchen or paper towel.

Escaloper (eh scal oh pay) To cut scallops; to cut meat or fish on a bias.

Essence (ess sahns) Essence; concentrated extract, used as a flavoring (e.g., coffee essence).

Étuver (eh too vay) To stew, to cook slowly; to cook gently while covered with fat and a little water without changing the color of the ingredients.

Évider (eh vee day) To hollow, to gut; to hollow the center of an ingredient (poultry, fruit, vegetables).

F

Farce (farce) Forcemeat stuffing; a mixture of various ground ingredients (meat, herbs, vegetables), used to fill poultry, fish, vegetables, etc.

Farcir (far seer) To stuff; to fill poultry, fish, or meat with a forcemeat stuffing.

Fariner (far ee nay) To flour, to dredge; to sprinkle flour on fish or meat or to sprinkle a mold and tap out the excess.

Fermière (fair mee yare) Farm-made or farm-raised.

Ficeler (fee se lay) To tie with string.

Filet (fee lay) Fillet.

Fines Herbes (feen zairb) Mix of edible aromatic plants used as seasoning (parsley, tarragon, chives).

Flamber (flom bay) Flambé. (1) To use a flame in order to remove the down from poultry. (2) To light alcohol in a preparation (e.g., crêpes suzette).

Flan (flahn) (1) Open pastry case or shell. (2) A custard tart.

Fleuron (flur rohn) Piece of puff pastry cut into crescent shapes, served as decoration with fish dishes.

Foie Gras (fwah grah) Fattened duck or goose liver.

Foncer (fone say) To line the bottom and sides of a mold or pan with dough.

Fond (fohn) Stock.

Fondant (fawn daunt) (1) A sugar icing used for glazing pastries. (2) Referring to something that melts in the mouth (literally, "melting").

Fondre (fone dr) (1) To melt; to turn a solid into liquid by heating (e.g., butter). (2) To cook, covered, certain vegetables in water and butter (e.g., mushrooms) until the liquid has completely evaporated, without changing the color of the ingredients.

Fondu (fone dew) Melted.

Fontaine (fone ten) A well; a deep impression made in flour in order to add other ingredients for making a dough.

Fraiser (fray zay) To mix a dough evenly by smearing it with the fleshy part of the palm of the hand.

Frémir (fray meer) To simmer; to bring a liquid just to the boiling point, the bubbles being barely perceptible.

Fricassée (free kah say) (1) A way of cutting a chicken into eight pieces. (2) A preparation in which meat or poultry is cut into pieces before being braised.

Frire (freer) To deep-fry.

Friture (free tur) (1) Deep fryer. (2) Deep-fried foods.

Fumet (few may) (1) Cooking aroma. (2) Sauce made from cooking juices. (3) Basic stock made from fish and used to make sauces.

Fusil (few zee) Sharpening steel; long, rounded metal tool, used to keep the cutting edge of a knife sharp.

G

Galantine (ga lawn teen) Cold poached meat that has been stuffed and larded, served with gelatin made from the poaching liquid.

Garniture (gar nee tur) Garnish; served as an accompaniment to a dish (usually vegetables).

Gastrique (ga streek) A caramel delazed with vinegar used as a base for a sweet and sour sauce (as with duck à l'orange).

Gaufrette (go frett) Waffle.

Gelée (jel lay) Gelatin, aspic; meat or fish stock that has been clarified, then set with gelatin. Used in various preparations en gelée to give shine to foods as well as to protect them from drying out.

Genoise (zhen wahz) Genoese sponge cake.

Glaçage (glah sahj) Glaze; mixture of ingredients with a syrupy consistency, sweet or savory, used to coat pastries, candies, and certain savory foods.

Glace (glahss) (1) Ice cream. (2) Glaze; stock reduced until thick and syrupy.

Glacé (glah say) (1) Glazed (usually refers to vegetables). (2) Frozen. (3) Served with ice cream (e.g., meringue glacé).

Glacer (glah say) To glaze; to cover or coat pastries with a glaze.

Goujonnettes (goo zhone nett) Strips of fish, breaded and deep-fried.

Graisser (gray say) To grease; to coat or cover with fat before baking or roasting in the oven.

Grandmère (grahn mare) A classic garniture made from bacon, sautéed button mushrooms, and glazed pearl onions.

Gratiner (gra tee nay) (1) To brown under the grill or salamander. (2) To glaze.

(a la) Grecque (ah la grek) Refers to a preparation of vegetables cooked in white wine.

Griller (gree yay) To grill; to cook on a grill.

H

Habiller (ah bee yay) To dress; to prepare an item, such as fish or meat, for cooking.

Hacher (ah shay) To chop; to reduce to small pieces with a knife.

Hareng (a rehng) Herring.

Haricot (are ree co) Bean.

Haricot Blanc (are ree co blahn) White bean.

Haricot Vert (are ree co vare) Green bean.

Historié (ee stow ree ay) Decorated.

Hollandaise (awl lawn daze) Hot emulsion sauce made from egg yolks and clarified butter and flavored with lemon juice.

Homard (oh mahr) Lobster.

Huile (weel) Oil.

Huile d'Olive (weel doe leave) Olive oil.

Huile d'Arachide (weel da rah sheed) Peanut oil.

Huile de Noix (weel de nwah) Walnut oil.

I

Imbiber (am bee bay) To imbibe; to wet or soak an element with stock or syrup.

Inciser (an see zay) To incise; to make small, shallow cuts in order to speed cooking.

Incorporer (an core po ray) To incorporate; to gradually mix ingredients together by gently mixing.

Infuser (an few zay) To place an element into simmering water and let sit so that the element flavors the water (e.g., tea).

J

Jambon (zhom bohn) Ham.

Jambonnette (zhom bo nett) Stuffed chicken leg made to resemble a small ham.

Jardinière (zhar dee nyair) Literally, "pertaining to a garden"; a mixture of carrots, turnips cut into sticks, green beans, and green peas. Cooked separately, then served together as an accompaniment.

Jarret (zhah ray) Knuckle or shank of meat.

Jet (zhett) A dash of liquid, a squirt.

Joue (zhoo) Cheek (beef or pork).

Julienne (zhoo lee yen) Cut into very fine strips.

Jus (zhoo) Juice; liquid made from pressing a fruit or vegetable or from the cooking of a meat.

L

Lait (lay) Milk.

Langoustine (lawn goo steen) Dublin Bay prawn.

Lard (lahr) Solid fat from pork. Lard gras contains fat only, while lard maigre (bacon) contains meat as well.

Larder (lahr day) To lard; to insert strips of pork fat into lean meats, using a larding needle, in order to prevent the meat from drying out during cooking.

Lardon (lahr doan) A small piece or strip of slab bacon.

Légume (leh gyoom) Vegetable.

Lentille (lawn teey) Lentil.

Levain (le vanh) Starter dough; a dough made from live yeast and flour, used to make breads.

Lever (le vay) To rise; to leave a dough to rise (as with brioche, bread, croissants).

Lever les Filets (le vay lay fee lay) To fillet; to remove the fillets of a fish using a knife.

Levure (le vure) Yeast.

Levure Chimique (le vure she meek) Baking powder; odorless and flavorless rising agent made from bicarbonate of soda and cream of tartar.

Liaison (lee ay zonh) Thickener; element or mixture used to thicken a liquid or sauce.

Lier (lee ay) To thicken; to change the consistency of a liquid by adding a roux, starch, egg, flour, or beurre manié.

Lotte (lot) Monkfish.

M

Macédoine (mass e dwan) A mixture of vegetables or fruit, cut into small cubes.

Macérer (mass e ray) To macerate; to soak an element in alcohol in order to flavor it (usually done for pastry).

Magret (mah gray) The breast meat of a fattened duck.

Manchonner (mahn show nay) To remove the meat that covers the end of a bone, such as a chicken leg or a rack of meat, in order to achieve a clean presentation.

Mandoline (man do leen) A slicer with several blades, allowing various cuts and thicknesses of fruits and vegetables.

Mange Tout (manj too) Chinese pea pods or snow peas.

Manier (man yay) To knead.

Mariner (mar ee nay) To marinate; to soak a piece of meat or fish in a liquid and aromatics in order to tenderize, flavor, and preserve. Can also be used to tame the flavor of strong-flavored game.

Médaillon (may die yohn) Medallion; round slice of meat, fowl, fish, or crustacean, served hot or cold.

Meringue (me rang) Mixture of beaten egg whites and sugar.

Meringue Glacée (me rang gla say) Vacherin.

Mie de Pain (mee de pan) Fresh bread crumbs.

Mijoter (mee joo tay) To simmer; to cook over gentle heat.

Mirepoix (meer pwah) (1) Vegetables cut into cubes, the size depending on the length of cooking. (2) A certain blend of aromatic vegetables (onions, carrots, and celery).

Monder (moan day) To skin; to remove the skin of certain fruits or vegetables (e.g., peaches, tomatoes) by plunging into boiling water.

Monter (moan tay) (1) To mount; to whisk (egg whites, cream) in order to incorporate air and increase the volume. (2) To add butter to a sauce in small pieces.

Morille (mow reey) Morel mushroom.

Mouiller (moo yay) To wet; to add a liquid to a preparation before cooking.

Mouler (moo lay) To mold; to fill a mold before or after cooking.

Moulu (moo loo) Milled; ground.

N

Napper (nap pay) To coat; to cover a food, savory, or sweet with a light layer of sauce, aspic, or jelly.

Navarin (na va rahn) Brown lamb stew containing tomato.

Nem (nem) Vietnamese-style spring roll.

Noircir (nwahr seer) To blacken; to darken when exposed to air (said of certain fruits and vegetables).

Noisette (nwah set) A hazelnut. See also Beurre Noisette.

O

Œuf (euf) Egg.

Oie (wah) Goose.

Graisse d'Oie (gress dwah) Goose fat.

Os (ohss) Bone.

Ôter (oh tay) To remove.

Ouvrir (oov rear) To open.

P

Paner (pan ay) To coat a food with fresh or dry bread crumbs after dipping in an anglaise (see Anglaise) and then cook.

Panier (pan yay) Basket. (1) A frying basket, used with a deep fryer in order to easily plunge foods into and remove them from the hot oil. (2) A steam basket, used for placing foods to be steamed. (3) Nestling baskets; a frying tool in the form of two ladle-shaped baskets, one slightly smaller than the other, used to form nests of shredded potatoes with which to decorate certain platters.

Papillote (pa pee yote) (1) Buttered or oiled paper, used to wrap fruits, meats, fish, etc. for cooking. (2) Paper frill used to decorate the ends of bones of certain poultry and meats.

Parer (pah ray) To trim; to remove the nerves or excess fat from meat or fish, or to remove the damaged or inedible portions of fruit and vegetables before cooking or serving.

Parfait (par fay) A frozen dessert made of a sweet egg-yolk foam and whipped cream.

Parfumer (par few may) To flavor.

Passer (pas say) To strain, generally using a strainer or china cap sieve.

Pâte (pat) Dough or batter.

Pâté (pat tay) Chopped meat, poultry, fish, etc., cooked in a dough. Today considered almost synonymous with terrine.

Pâtissier (pat tee see ay) Pastry chef.

Pâton (pat tohn) Large square piece of dough (puff pastry, bread) before cooking.

Paupiette (po pee yet) Thin piece of meat or fish that is stuffed, rolled, tied, and cooked.

Pavé (pa vay) Thick cross-section slices of fish fillets.

Paysanne (pay yee zahn) Vegetables cut into small, thin triangles or squares.

Persillade (pear see yahd) A mixture of parsley and chopped garlic.

Pétrir (pe trear) To knead; to work a dough.

Piler (pee lay) To grind (e.g., with a mortar and pestle); to make a powder by crushing with a mortar and pestle.

Pilon (pee lohn) (1) A pestle; a tool used for crushing and grinding. (2) The drumstick of a chicken leg.

Piment (pee mon) Chile pepper.

Pincée (pan say) A pinch; small quantity of a dry ingredient measured by pinching with the thumb and index finger.

Pincer (pan say) To pinch; to use a pastry crimper to crimp the edges of dough before cooking.

Pintade (pan todd) Guinea fowl.

Piquer (pee kay) (1) To pick; to lard a piece of meat, using a larding needle, in order to keep the meat from drying out during cooking. (2) To make small holes in dough, using a fork, to prevent it from rising too much.

Pluche (ploosh) Sprig; small leaves picked off the stems (e.g., sprig of chervil).

Pocher (po shay) To poach; to cook in barely simmering water.

Poêler (po e lay) To pan-fry; to cook an element in a frying pan over high heat with minimal oil.

Pointe (pwahnt) Point (of a knife). (1) A small quantity measured using the point of a knife (e.g., point of ground vanilla). (2) The tip of something (e.g., tip of asparagus).

Poivron (pwahv rohn) Sweet bell pepper.

Poulet (poo lay) Chicken.

Pousser (poos say) To rise; (literally, "to push"). (1) To leave a yeast dough to increase in volume. (2) To feed meat into a meat grinder.

Poussin (poos san) Cornish game hen.

Praliné (prah leen) Caramelized sugar with almonds or hazelnuts, ground to a smooth paste, used to flavor and decorate pastries.

Primeur (pree mer) Early vegetable or fruit.

Profiterole (pro feet er role) Choux ball filled with sweet or savory filling. The best known is a dessert filled with vanilla ice cream and served with chocolate sauce.

Provençale (pro von sal) Provence style; refers to dishes containing one or all of the following: olive oil, tomatoes, garlic, peppers, and olives.

Q

Quadriller (ca dree yay) (1) To mark squares or diamonds on meat, using a grill. (2) To mark squares using a knife.

Quatre épices (catr eh peace) Four spices; a mixture of ground pepper, cinnamon, nutmeg, and cloves. Often used to flavor meat stuffings.

Quenelle (kuh nel) (1) Dumpling made of meat, poultry, or fish purée, mixed with egg white and cream. Usually molded with two spoons into an egg shape. (2) Oval three-sided shape made using two large spoons.

Quiche (keesh) Savory tart with a creamy egg base (e.g., quiche Lorraine: bacon and cheese custard tart).

R

Rafraîchir (rah fray sheer) To refresh, to cool, to chill; to quickly cool in cold water a food that has been blanched.

Raidir (ray deer) To seize or sear (esp. in boiling fat); to pre-cook without coloring.

Râper (ra pay) To grate; to reduce to thin slices or powder using a grating tool (e.g., with cheese).

Rassis (ras see) Stale, not fresh.

Ratatouille (ra tah too yee) Dish made from red peppers, onions, tomatoes, zucchini, eggplant, and, often, olives.

Rectifier (reck tee fee yay) To rectify; to correct the seasoning of a dish.

Réduire (ray dweer) To reduce; to heat a liquid or to reduce it in volume by boiling.

Relever (re le vay) To reinforce flavor through the use of spices.

Remonter (re moan tay) To remount; to repair a sauce or a cream that has separated in order to return it to its proper appearance and texture.

Revenir (faire) (re ve near fehr) To quickly color a food in hot fat or oil.

Rissoler (rees so lay) To cook a food in hot fat or oil until well colored.

Rondelle (ron dell) Small, round slice.

Roux (roo) A cooked mixture of equal amounts of flour and fat (usually butter). The three types of roux—white, blond, and brown, vary in color depending on how long they cook.

S

Sabayon (sa ba yohn) A thick, frothy sauce, either sweet or savory, that is made from whisking egg yolks and liquid over low heat. Similar to the Italian zabaglione.

Saisir (say zeer) To seize; to quickly color over very high heat at the start of cooking.

Salamandre (sal ah mandr) A salamander or broiler; the upper heating element in an oven or a professional appliance, used to brown foods.

Saupoudrer (so poo dray) To sprinkle; to evenly distribute a powder over the surface of a dish or dessert.

Sauter (so tay) To sauté (literally, "to jump"); to cook over high heat, stirring constantly to prevent sticking.

Singer (san jay) To sprinkle with flour at the start of cooking in order to eventually give a certain consistency to the sauce.

Siroper (seer oh pay) To add syrup to a pastry. (See Imbiber.)

Sorbet (soar bay) Flavored water ice; frozen confection made from fruit juice or pulp and sugar syrup.

Sous Chef (soo shef) Second to the chef.

Suer (soo ay) To sweat; to gently cook vegetables in a little fat, without coloring them, in order to bring out their flavor.

Suprême (soo prem) (1) The breast part of the fowl. (2) A fillet of fish.

Suprême Sauce (soo prem sauce) Classic sauce made from a velouté enriched with cream.

T

Tailler (tie yay) To cut in a precise fashion.

Tamis (ta mee) Drum sieve.

Tamiser (ta mee zay) To sift; to press through a fine drum sieve.

Tapenade (ta peh nahd) Purée of black olives, anchovies, and olive oil.

Terrine (tare reen) (1) A deep rectangular mold traditionally made of white porcelain, used to cook seasoned ground meats, fish, or poultry. (2) The food cooked in such a mold.

Timbale (tam ball) (1) A mold in the shape of a large thimble. (2) Type of dough shaped as a container, baked, and filled with various foods.

Tourer (tour ray) To turn; to roll and fold butter into a dough (e.g., for puff pastry, croissants).

Tourner (tour nay) To turn. (1) To give certain vegetables a regular long shape, using a knife. (2) To mix ingredients together by mixing in a circular motion.

Travailler (tra vie yay) To work; to knead, mix, soften.

Tremper (trom pay) To soak; to dip; to wet.

Truffer (troo fay) To add chopped truffles to a dish, stuffing, or foie gras. To slide a thin slice of truffle under the skin of poultry.

Turban (toor bahn) (1) A type of ring mold. (2) Food prepared in such a mold.

V

Vallée d'Auge (val lay dozh) In the style of a region of Normandy; indicates a dish prepared with cider, apples, and cream.

Vanner (van nay) To mix a cream or sauce as it cools in order to prevent lumps or the formation of a skin on the surface.

Vapeur (va purr) Steam.

Velouté (ve loo tay) A thickened sauce made from a white stock and a roux.

Vinaigre (vee negre) Vinegar.

Vinaigrette (vee ne gret) A sauce made of vinegar, oil, and seasonings.

Volaille (voe lye) Poultry.

Blanc de Volaille (blahn duh voe lye) Chicken breast.

Cuisse de Volaille (kweese duh voe lye) Chicken leg.

Z

Zester (zes tay) To zest; to remove the colored part of the skin of a citrus fruit (e.g., orange, lemon).

Subject Index

Note: Titles are indexed by categories, such as beef recipes, veal recipes, chicken recipes, and so on. Thus, to find the recipe for London Broil, for example, look under the heading Beef recipes. See also the separate recipe index on page 941.

A

Acid:
  and bacterial growth, 15
  in clarification, 173
  and connective tissue, 211
  and curdling of milk, 629
  in consommé production, 173
  effects of on foods, 52
  and egg foams, 615
  in marinades, 119
  and starch, 847
  in stocks, 127
  and vegetable cooking, 430, 433
Aging, of meat, 213
Altitude:
  effect of on cakes, 810-811
  effect of on cooking, 56
Ammonia, baking, 769
Antelope, 234
Antipasto, 599
AP (as purchased) measurement, 84
Arrowroot, 138
Aspic, 667-668, 670-672

B

Bacteria, 14-18
  diseases caused by, 16-18
  growth of, 15-16, 25
  protection against, 16
Baked Alaska, 864
Baking ammonia, 769
Baking, 57-58, 62
  bread, 777-778
  cake, 808-809
  cookies, 832
  potatoes, 493
  poultry, 312-322
  vegetables, 472-478
Baking powder, 769
Baking soda, 769
  and vegetable cooking, 430, 433
  effect of on fiber, 53
Barbecue, 57-58, 62

Barding, 225, 241
Barley, 505, 509, 512
Base (stock), 133-134
Basting, 241, 323
Batonnet, 115
Batter, for frying, 122, 480-482
Bavarian cream, 877, 878, 879
Beans, dried, 449-450
Béarnaise, *see* Sauce; Sauce recipes
Béchamel sauce, *see* Sauce; Sauce recipes
Beef:
  cooking methods, 224, 225
  cuts, 216-217, 221
  tenderloin, preparing, 270
  See also Meat
Beef recipes:
  "Boiled," 278
  Barbecued Beef Sandwich, 591
  Boeuf à la Mode, 286
  Boeuf Bourgignon, 285
  Broiled Strip Loin Steak Maître d'Hôtel, 258
  California Burger, 589
  Carbonnade à la Flammande, 749
  Charbroiled Minute Steak with Blue Cheese Butter, 259
  Chile con Carne, 287
  Chopped "Steaks" with Marjoram, Grilled, 260
  Entrecôte Sauté Bordelaise, 268
  Hamburger variations, 589
  Hungarian Goulash, 290
  Jardinière, Braised, 283
  London Broil, 259
  Meatballs, Baked, 254
  Meatballs, Swedish, 293
  Meat Loaf, Home-Style, 254
  Meat Loaf, Italian-Style, 254
  Medallions with Two Peppers, 271
  Moussaka, 753
  New England Boiled Dinner, 278
  Oriental Salad with Beef, 552
  Oxtails, Braised, 284
  Pot Pie, 285

Ladyfingers, 834
Macaroons, Coconut (Meringue-Type), 834
Oatmeal Raisin, 833
Peanut Butter, 837
Raisin Spice Bars, 836
Rolled Brown Sugar, 835
Rolled Chocolate, 835
Sandwich-Type, 834
Shortbread, 835
Sugar, 835
Tea, 834
Cooking methods, *See also* Baking; Boiling;
    Braising; Broiling; Deep-frying;
    Griddling; Pan-broiling; Poaching;
    Roasting; Simmering; Steaming
dry-heat, 57-60
moist-heat, 55-57
Corn syrup, 766
Cornstarch, 138, 764
Court bouillon, 411, 413
Couscous, 505
Crab, 383-384
Crab recipes:
    Cakes, with Roasted Pepper Rémoulade, 405
    Cornmeal-Crusted Soft-Shell, with
        Cornmeal Pancakes and Roasted
        Tomatoes, 406
    Crab and Asparagus Charlotte, 564
    Crab Beignets, 607
    Crab Louis, 556
    Crab Salad, 556
    Soft-Shell, Sautéed, 402
    Seafood Quiche, 623
Crayfish, 384
Cream, 628
    in baking, 767
    in sauces, 141
    in soup, 183
    whipping, 629
Creaming, and leavening, 769
Crème anglaise, 871-872
Crème patissière, 860-862
Critical Control Point, 24, 25, 73
Croissant, 774, 785, 793
Cross-contamination, 22, 25
Crudités, 596
Cryovac, 213
Cured foods, 644-646
Curing salt, 645
Custard, 622-623, 852-853, 871-876
    Japanese, 724
Cutting techniques, basic, 114-118
Cuttlefish, 376

D

Dairy products, 627-637; *see also* Butter;
    Cheese; Cream; Milk
Deep fryers, 37

Deep-frying, 60, 62
    fish, 408-410
    potatoes, 500-503
    poultry, 328, 330, 335
    preparation for, 120-122
    vegetables, 480-482
Deglazing, 140, 264
Demiglaze, 143, 149
Dessert, frozen, 885-887
Dessert, fruit, 864-866
Dessert recipes, frozen:
    Baked Alaska, 864
    Lemon Mousse, 882
    Meringue Glacé, 863
    Profiteroles, 861
    Strawberry or Raspberry Mousse, 880
Dessert recipes, fruit:
    Apple Betty, 865
    Apple Crisp, 865
    Cobbler, 864
    Date, Prune, or Apricot Filling for Sweet
        Rolls, 696
    Fritters, 482
    Peach, Cherry, or Rhubarb Crisp, 865
    Peaches, Poached, 866
    Pears, Poached, 866
    Raspberry or Cherry Gratin, 866
Dice, 115
Dips, 596-598
Dressing, *see* Salad dressing; Stuffing and dressing
Dry rub, 120
Duck, 300, 301
    wild, 302, 353
Duck recipes:
    with Cabbage, Braised, 346
    Confit, 355
    Crispy, 732
    Forcemeat, 675
    in Paprika, Roast, 320
    Rillettes, 694
    Roast, with Caramelized Apples, 319
    with Sauerkraut, Braised, 346
    Sausage, 660
    Smoked, 649
    Tea-Smoked, 732
    Terrine, 680
Dumplings, 527-529
    Potato Dumplings, 527
    Potato Gnocchi with Tomato Sauce, 528
    Spaetzle, 528

E

Éclair paste, 860-862
Egg, 612-623, 768, 897
    in breading, 121
    composition and grading, 612-613
    in consommé production, 173
    cooking, 615-623

Recipe Index

Brandade de Morue, 747
Bratwurst, Fresh, 659
Bread and Butter Pudding, 876
Breaded Pork Cutlets, 265
Breaded Veal Cutlets, 265
Breast of Chicken en Croûte, 321
Breast of Guinea Fowl en Croûte with Madeira
    Sauce, 321
Brioche, 782
Brisket, Simmered Fresh Beef ("Boiled Beef"),
    280
Broccoli Mornay, 459
Broccoli with Cheddar Cheese Sauce, 459
Broiled Fish Fillets or Steaks with Garlic Butter,
    398
Broiled Fish Steaks Maître d'Hôtel, 395
Broiled Lamb Chops, 260
Broiled Lamb Kidneys with Bacon, 262
Broiled Lobster, 397
Broiled Mako Shark Steaks with Browned
    Garlic Vinaigrette, 396
Broiled Poussin or Cornish Hens with Mustard
    Crust, 325
Broiled Rock Cornish Game Hen, 324
Broiled Rock Lobster Tail, 392
Broiled Scallops, 398
Broiled Shrimp, Scampi Style, 398
Broiled Smoked Pork Chop with Flageolet
    Beans and Wilted Arugula, 260
Broiled Strip Loin Steak Maître d'Hôtel, 258
Broiled Tarragon Chicken, 324
Broiled Tomato Slices, 479
Brown Lamb Stew (Navarin of Lamb), 285
Brown Rice with Pecans and Poblanos, 512
Brown Sauce, 148
Brown Stock, Basic, 132
Brown Sugar Nut Cookies, 833
Brown Sugar Spice Cake, 812
Brown Veal Stew with White Wine, 285
Brown Veal Stew, 285
Brownies, 838
Brunswick Soup, 181
Brussels Sprouts Paysanne, 462
Bulgur Pilaf with Lemon, 511
Butter Sauce, Herbed, 154
Butter Sauce, Red (Beurre Rouge), 154
Butter Sauce, Red Wine, for Fish, 155
Butter:
    Anchovy, 154
    Curry, 155
    Escargot (Snail), 154
    Garlic, 154
    Herb, 154
    Maître d'Hôtel, 154
    Mustard, 154
    Scallion, 154
    Shallot, 154
    Shrimp, 154

Buttercream, Simple, 817
Buttered Vegetables, 458
Buttermilk Batter, 481
Buttermilk Biscuits, 798
Butternut Squash Soup with Caramelized
    Apples, 191
Butterscotch Brownies, 838
Butterscotch Cream Pie Filling, 873
Butterscotch Icebox Cookies, 837
Butterscotch Pudding, 873

C

Cabinet Pudding, 876
Caesar Salad, 543
Cajun-Style Sausage, 663
Caldo Verde, 749
Calf's Liver Lyonnaise, 274
California Burger, 589
California Cheeseburger Deluxe, 589
California Cheeseburger, 589
Capons, Roast, 317
Caramel Fudge Icing, 819
Caramel Sauce, 888
Caramel Sauce, Clear, 888
Caramel Sauce, Hot, 888
Carbonnade à la Flamande, 749
Carrot Celery Salad, 581
Carrot Coleslaw, 547
Carrot Nut Cake, 812
Carrot Pineapple Salad, 551
Carrot Raisin Salad, 551
Carrot Salad, 551
Carrots with Orange and Cumin, 471
Cauliflower au Gratin, 460
Celery Consommé, Essence of, 175
Celery Leaf Fritters, 482
Celery Salad, 551
Chantilly Dressing, 576
Charbroiled Minute Steak with Blue Cheese
    Butter, 259
Charcutière Sauce, 149
Chasseur Sauce, 149
Château Potatoes, 499
Chaud-Froid, Classical, 669
Chaud-Froid, Mayonnaise, 670
Chawan Mushi (Japanese Steamed Custard),
    724
Cheddar Cheese Dip, 597
Cheddar Cheese Sauce, 145
Cheese and Chili Dip, 597
Cheese Biscuits, 798
Cheese Filling, 787
Cheese Sauce, Cheddar, 145
Cheese Soufflé, 622
Cheese Straws, 636
Cheese Wafers, 636
Cheeseburger (plain), 589
Cheeseburger with Bacon, 589